SATELLIT 700

No matter where you go, the Grundig Satellit 700 is there for you. The Satellit 700 is the world's most advanced shortwave portable radio. This is the portable for serious listening to international broadcasts and long distance shortwave two-way communications.

Covers all shortwave bands, plus FM-stereo, AM and LW. Single sideband (SSB) circuitry allows for reception of two-way shortwave amateur, shortwave maritime and shortwave aeronautical communications.

"The best portable introduced this year is Grundig's Satellit 700."

PWBR, 1993

GRUNDIG

Call for information: U.S. 1-800-872-2228 or 415-361-1611
Canada 800-637-1648 • Fax: 415-361-1724

1997 PASSPORT TO WORLD BAND RADIO

WHEN AND WHERE
WorldScan®

MAKING CONTACT

1997 PASSPORT TO WORLD BAND RADIO

ISSN 0897-0157

International Broadcasting Services, Ltd.

Our reader is the most important person in the world!

Editorial

Editor-in-Chief	Lawrence Magne
Editor	Tony Jones
Contributing Editors	Jock Elliott (U.S.), Craig Tyson (Australia)
Consulting Editors	John Campbell (England), Don Jensen (U.S.)
WorldScan® Contributors	James Conrad (U.S.), Alok Dasgupta (India), Manosij Guha (India), Anatoly Klepov (Russia), Marie Lamb (U.S.), *Número Uno*/Jerry Berg (U.S.), Toshimichi Ohtake (Japan), *Radio Nuevo Mundo* (Japan), Henrik Klemetz (Colombia), Takayuki Inoue Nozaki (Japan), Nikolai Rudnev (Russia), Don Swampo (Uruguay), Vladimir Titarev (Ukraine), David Walcutt (U.S.), Juichi Yamada (Japan)
WorldScan® Software	Richard Mayell
Laboratory	Sherwood Engineering Inc.
Cover Artwork	Gahan Wilson
Sketch Art	Leigh Ann Smith
Graphic Arts	Bad Cat Design
Printing	Rand McNally

Administration

Publisher	Lawrence Magne
Associate Publisher	Jane Brinker
Advertising & Distribution	Mary Kroszner, MWK
Offices	IBS North America, Box 300, Penn's Park PA 18943, USA; World Wide Web: http://www.passport.com *Advertising & Distribution:* Phone +1 (215) 794-3410; Fax +1 (215) 794 3396; E-mail mwk@passport.com *Editorial:* Fax +1 (215) 598 3794 *Orders (24 hours):* Phone +1 (215) 794-8252; Fax +1 (215) 794 3396; E-mail mwk@passport.com
Media Communications	Jock Elliott, Pickering Lane, Troy NY 12180, USA; Fax +1 (518) 271 6131; E-mail lightkeepe@aol.com

Bureaus

IBS Latin America	Tony Jones, Casilla 1844, Asunción, Paraguay; Fax +595 (21) 390 675; E-mail schedules@passport.com
IBS Australia	Craig Tyson, Box 2145, Malaga WA 6062; Fax +61 (9) 342 9158; E-mail addresses@passport.com
IBS Japan	Toshimichi Ohtake, 5-31-6 Tamanawa, Kamakura 247; Fax +81 (467) 43 2167; E-mail ibsjapan@passport.com

Library of Congress Cataloging-in-Publication Data
Passport to World Band Radio.
1. Radio Stations, Shortwave—Directories. I. Magne, Lawrence
    TK9956.P27   1996   384.54'5   96-22739
    ISBN 0-914941-39-9

PASSPORT, PASSPORT TO WORLD BAND RADIO, *WorldScan, Radio Database International, RDI White Papers* and *White Papers* are registered trademarks of International Broadcasting Services, Ltd., in the United States, Canada, United Kingdom and various other parts of the world.

Copyright © 1996 International Broadcasting Services, Ltd.

SONY

Vacation companion

- Digital Dial Scale
- 1kHz Step Tuning
- 20 Memory Presets
- Dual Standby Function
- Rotary Encoder

WORLD BAND RECEIVER

SW40

FM Stereo/SW/MW/LW **ICF-SW40**

Business assistant

Back side
(Stereo Cassette Recorder)

- Compact Cassette Recorder
- Stereo Recording & Playback
- 2-Timer Recording
- 32 Memory Presets
- Synchronous Detector & SSB

WORLD BAND RECEIVER

SW1000T

FM Stereo / SW / MW / LW PLL Synthesized
Receiver with Built-in Stereo Cassette Recorder
ICF-SW1000T

SONY WORLD BAND RECEIVER

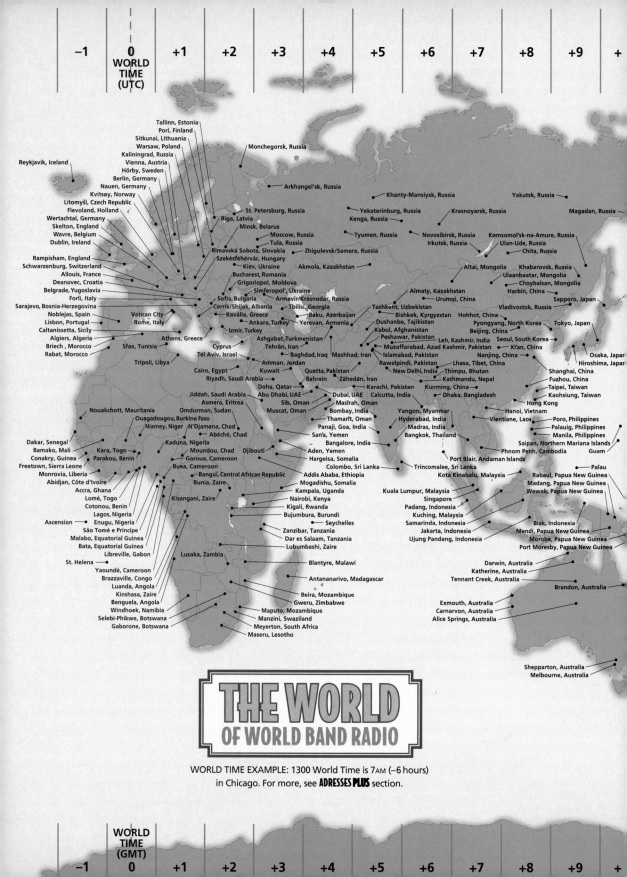

THE WORLD OF WORLD BAND RADIO

WORLD TIME EXAMPLE: 1300 World Time is 7AM (–6 hours) in Chicago. For more, see ADRESSES PLUS section.

11 +12 −11 −10 −9 −8 −7 −6 −5 −4 −3 −2

Anchor Point, Alaska, USA

Palana, Russia

Petropavlovsk-Kamchatskiy, Russia

Calgary AB, Canada

Vancouver BC, Canada

Toronto ON, Canada
Montréal PQ, Canada
Scotts Corners ME, USA
Sackville NB, Canada
St. John's NF, Canada

Halifax NS, Canada
Noblesville IN, USA
Bethel PA, USA
Red Lion PA, USA
Upton KY, USA
Nashville TN, USA
Greenville NC, USA
Cypress Creek SC, USA
McCaysville GA, USA
Birmingham AL, USA
New Orleans LA, USA
Okeechobee FL, USA
Miami FL, USA
Havana, Cuba

Salt Lake City UT, USA
Boulder CO, USA
Delano CA, USA
Rancho Simi CA, USA
Dallas TX, USA
Mesquite NM, USA

Hermosillo, Mexico

ekaha, Kauai Island, Hawai'i, USA

Naalehu, "Big Island," Hawai'i, USA

Linares, Mexico
Mérida, Mexico
México City, Mexico
Veracruz, Mexico
Puerto Cabezas, Nicaragua
Guatemala City, Guatemala
Tegucigalpa, Honduras
San José, Costa Rica
Santa Fé de Bogotá, Colombia
Villavicencio, Colombia
Florencia, Colombia
Quito, Ecuador
Tena, Ecuador
Loja, Ecuador
Iquitos, Perú
Cajamarca, Perú
Pucallpa, Perú
Guayaramerín, Bolivia
Cobija, Bolivia
Lima, Perú
Cusco, Perú
Arequipa, Perú
La Paz, Bolivia
Santa Cruz, Bolivia
Sucre, Bolivia
Asunción, Paraguay
Encarnación, Paraguay

Santo Domingo, Dominican Republic
Anguilla
Antigua
Bonaire, Netherlands Antilles
Caracas, Venezuela
Puerto Ayacucho, Venezuela
Georgetown, Guyana
Paramaribo, Surinam
Montsinéry, French Guiana

Cayenne, French Guiana

Belem, Brazil
Manaus, Brazil

Porto Velho, Brazil
Salvador, Brazil
Cuiabá, Brazil
Brasília, Brazil
Goiânia, Brazil

Belo Horizonte, Brazil
Rio de Janeiro, Brazil
São Paulo, Brazil
Curitiba, Brazil
Foz do Iguaçu, Brazil
Florianópolis, Brazil
Porto Alegre, Brazil
Artigas, Uruguay
Montevideo, Uruguay
Buenos Aires, Argentina

Tarawa, Kiribati

Honiara, Solomon Islands

Port-Vila, Vanuatu

Tahiti, French Polynesia

Mendoza, Argentina
Santiago, Chile
Malargüe, Argentina

Temuco, Chile

Rangitaiki, New Zealand

Levin, New Zealand

Coyhaique, Chile

Base Esperanza, Antarctica (−3)

11 +12 −11 −10 −9 −8 −7 −6 −5 −4 −3 −2

Ten of the Best: 1997's Top Shows

*M*ost media outlets are ratings-driven and pre-dictable—30 channels sound like five. However, this isn't true with world band, especially with "the best of world band" offerings for 1997.

But these are just the tip of the teepee. The rest, hundreds of shows you won't hear anywhere else, are in What's On Tonight in this PASSPORT. That "TV Guide" type section leads you through the full range of choices of what's being aired in English around the clock.

As always, all times given are World Time.

"A Good Life"
Radio Netherlands

Forget the title! This show doesn't give spiritual guidance or tell you how to make the most of your retirement. Instead, it reveals how people around the globe, rich and poor, try to improve their lot—no mean task in a world of over-stretched budgets and constricted labor markets.

Subjects vary from the down-to-earth—starting a small business or cleaning up the local water supply—to such offbeat themes as street children in Zimbabwe or Chinese economic migrants in Tibet.

"A Good Life" is a good catch—just the kind of show that Radio Netherlands does best. Eastern North America, "The Good Life" is aired 2354 Monday and 0054 Saturday (Friday evening in North America) on 6020 and 6165 kHz, with 9845 kHz also available in summer.

Bush House, international broadcasting's Rock of Gibraltar, is the legendary home of the BBC World Service. From here emanate three shows that are among this year's best. BBC

9

RNW

Widely traveled Ginger da Silva hosts "A Good Life," Radio Netherlands' global development program. It spotlights the ingenious ways people throughout the world try to better their lives.

West Coast, shoot for 0454 Saturday (Friday evening, local date) on 5995 (or 9590) and 6165 kHz. *Europe* is served winter at 1254 Monday and 1154 Friday on 6045 and 7190 kHz, replaced summer by 1054 Monday and 1154 Friday on 6045 and 9650 kHz.

For the *Middle East*, it's year-round at 1354 Friday on 13700 kHz. If you're in *East and Southeast Asia*, try 1054 Monday and 0954 Friday, winters on 7260 and 9810 kHz, summers on 12065 and 13705 kHz. Prime

time for *Southern Africa* is 1754 Friday on 6020 kHz.

Best for *Australasia* is 0854 Monday on 9720 kHz (also on 13700 kHz, November-March) and 0754 Friday on 9720 and 11895 (or 9700) kHz. Or try the broadcasts for East and Southeast Asia, above.

"Europe Today" BBC World Service

Five days each week—six if it's evening—listeners from Madrid to Moscow have their ears glued to "their" program. Winner of a 1996 Sony gold award, the BBC's "Europe Today" provides an up-to-the-minute melange of news, comment and analysis from, about and for Europe. For Europhiles, it's "must" listening.

The show's breadth of coverage is matched by the BBC's outstanding professionalism. Politics, sports, finance and press reviews all fit smartly into the mix, along with human-interest stories you're unlikely to find anywhere else.

In *Europe*, the "breakfast" edition can be heard Monday through Friday winters at 0430 and 0630 on 3955, 6180 and 6195 kHz; summers at 0330 and 0430 on 6180, 6195, 9410 and 12095 kHz. The evening broadcast goes out Sunday through Friday winters at 1700 on 3955, 6180, 6195, 9410 and 12095 kHz; summers at 1600 on 9410, 12095 and 15070 kHz.

Some of these frequencies can also be heard in parts of *Eastern North America*, especially the "evening" edition. "Europe Today" is also available for listeners in the *Middle East*—mornings on 9410 and 12095 kHz, evenings on 9410, 12095 and 15070 kHz.

BBC

"Europe Today" covers events and trends from Moscow to Dublin. It originates from the finest news facilites on earth, those of the BBC World Service at Bush House in London.

"Kilimandjaro" Afrique Numéro Un

If English is all you're listening to, you're missing some juicy stuff. Music is the

ENHANCE YOUR ADVENTURE!

ALPHA DELTA MODEL VRC

Announcing the ALPHA DELTA Model VRC Variable Response Console. Finally, an advanced audio processing speaker system that offers studio level audio quality for music, voice, and CW/data for the communications enthusiast. The Model VRC enhances the reception capabilities of *ANY* receiver, transceiver or scanner— even the expensive ones using DSP! Our exclusive ducted port bass reflex speaker system offers state-of-the-art performance at an extemely reasonable price. Custom Designed for the Model VRC.

- Low distortion, low harmonic push-pull audio amplifier. Outperforms the typical single-ended types

- Adjustable 12 dB bass boost/cut circuitry enhances both voice and music. LED reads out in dB

- Adjustable sharp cut-off "Sampled Data Switched Capacitor Audio Filter" can be set for optimum interference reduction for any mode and any band condition. AM, FM, SSB, CW or data. LED light bar readout shows cut-off frequency and is calibrated in kHz

- Peaking circuitry (20 dB) allows CW/data signals to "pop" out of the background

- Continuously adjustable 40 dB deep notch circuitry effectively takes out interfering heterodynes

---

- At your Alpha Delta dealer. For direct U.S. orders add $7.00 shipping and handling. Exports quoted.
- Alpha Delta Model VRC Variable Response Console...$249.95 ea
- Alpha Delta Model VRC-2 Ducted Port Bass Reflex Speaker-same as above but no amplifier/filter
  (a pair of these are great for your stereo or PC!)..$ 99.95 ea

---

ALPHA DELTA COMMUNICATIONS, INC.

P.O. Box 620, Manchester, KY 40962 • 606-598-2029 • FAX 606-598-4413

Alpha Blondy is but one of many top African singers heard weekdays on "Kilimandjaro," the highly rated program aired over Gabon's Afrique Numéro Un.

ultimate universal tongue, with a gumbo of offerings on world band. Although much is aimed at audiences outside the English-speaking world, these programs can be heard irrespective of boundaries.

In the Fifties, young Americans found themselves intrigued by music on low-powered rhythm-and-blues stations tucked away at the top end of the AM dial. That same sense of "roots evolving into tomorrow" can be found today on "Kilimandjaro," a down-home showcase of Africa's liveliest rhythms from the Gabonese commercial station, Afrique Numéro Un. If you want to explore Africa through its music, "Kilimandjaro"—that's how it's spelled in French—is the way to

go. It's mostly music, so the small amount of spoken French doesn't intrude.

Although targeting its programs at Francophone Africa, the station is widely heard elsewhere, including parts of *Europe* and *Eastern North America*. Weekdays at 1713-1830, dial up 15475 or 9580 kHz—as a bonus for music buffs, news at 1800-1811 is sometimes skipped. Saturdays, this time slot is devoted to African rap music, which you can also hear weekdays at 1603-1700, just before "Kilimandjaro." Okay, it's "just" rap, but it's some of the best rap around. Sundays, there's an in-depth program about African music with interesting interviews, but *en français*.

An Advanced Receiver, for a Very Affordable Price

ICOM's taken its advanced Next Generation technology and studiously applied it to the world of receivers. The result: ICOM's all new IC-R8500. Sharing the performance level of it's award-winning IC-R9000 big brother, ICOM's newest receiver is available for a fraction of the price.

Extra-Wide Coverage and All Modes!

Cover frequencies from 100 kHz to 1,999.99 MHz* using 10 Hz tuning steps. You'll receive SSB (USB, LSB), AM (normal/narrow/wide), FM (normal/narrow), WFM, and CW modes!

Built-In ICOM Computer Hardware

The new IC-R8500 is designed to grow along with your communication needs. Built right in is the famous, ICOM-developed CI-V computer control interface. Also built-in is an industry standard RS-232C port. When using the IC-R8500 with a PC, advanced software control and the programming of up to 800 memory channels (20 banks of 40 channels) are just keystrokes away!

IF-Shift and APF!

Signals come in loud and clear with ICOM's IC-R8500! An IF-Shift function rejects nearby interfering signals in

SSB modes. An APF (Audio Peak Filter) provides tone control when in FM mode and boosts specific frequencies in CW mode. And an AFC (Auto Frequency Control) compensates for FM, FM-N or WFM station frequency drift, keeping the IC-R8500 right on frequency!

Other IC-R8500 Features:

- High Stability (<30 MHz: ±100 Hz, VHF/UHF: ±3 ppm)
- 1000 Memory Channels: 20 Banks of 40 (total of 800 "normal"), 100 Skip Scan, and 100 Auto Write Memory Scan
- New DDS (Digital Direct Synthesis)
- New PLL (Phase-Locked Loop)
- Selectable AGC Time Constant
- S-Meter Squelch
- Noise Blanker (SSB/AM)
- 3 Antenna Connectors
- Operates on AC or DC

IC-R8500
ICOM's Next Generation World Receiver

Call ICOM's brochure hotline: (206) 450-6088. Or contact ICOM Technical Support in the HamNet forum on CompuServe® @75540,525 (Internet: 75540.525 @ compuserve.com.) © 1996 ICOM America, Inc., 2380-116th Ave. N.E., Bellevue, WA 98004. The ICOM logo is a registered trademark of ICOM, Inc. *Specifications are guaranteed 0.1 to 1000 MHz and 1240 to 1300 MHz. As of June 1996 this device has not been approved by the Federal Communications Commission. This device is not, and may not be, offered for sale or lease, or sold or leased until the approval of the FCC has been obtained. All stated specifications are subject to change without notice or obligation. All ICOM radios significantly exceed FCC regulations limiting spurious emissions. CompuServe is a registered trademark of CompuServe, Incorporated, an H&R Block Company. R8500PWBR696Y

ICOM

THE NEXT GENERATION

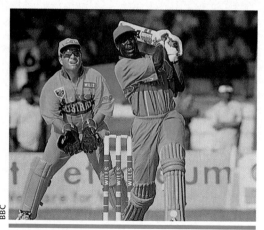

BBC

The BBC World Service's "Sports Roundup" knows no boundaries—it's "must" listening for serious sports aficionados from Atlanta to Adelaide. Here, the BBC covers the 1996 Cricket World Cup game between Australia and Kenya. (Australia won.)

"Sports Roundup"
BBC World Service

TV, cable and satellite channels provide us with an apparently endless choice of sports programming, both live and recorded. But are we really given the choice we are led to believe we're being offered?

And what about keeping up with what is happening in the rest of the sporting world? Television certainly shows us the action, but falls woefully short in providing a comprehensive picture of all that is going on. It's *déjà la même chose* all over again.

One surefire way of keeping on the ball is to tune to the BBC World Service's daily "Sports Roundup," a program with a track record like no other. Its closely-packed 15 minutes of news, results and previews cover everything from baseball to billiards, football to chess. An added bonus is that it is regularly updated, day and night, to keep up to the minute with sporting events around the globe.

If, as sometimes happens, "the Beeb" is foolish enough to reschedule or drop one of the program's slots, listener reaction is both swift and vocal—even from

media-rich countries like the United States. This show is a sporting "must."

"Sports Roundup" is beamed to *North America* at 0315 on 5975, 6175, 7325 (winter) and 9590/9895 kHz. It's on again at 1245 Sunday through Friday on 5965/9515 and 15220 kHz; also, 1505 Monday through Thursday on 9515, 11865 (summer), 15220 (summer), 15260 (winter) and 17840 kHz. The last two slots are at 1745 on 17840 kHz; and at 2245 on 5975, 6175, 7325 (winter) and 9590 kHz.

The first airing for *Europe* is at 0315— winters on 3955 and 6195 kHz, summers on 6180, 6195 and 9410 kHz. At 0945 and (Sunday through Friday) 1505, choose from 9410, 12095, 15070 and 17640 kHz. At 1745 winters, shoot for 3955, 6180, 6195 and 9410 kHz; summers, it's on 6195, 9410, 12095 and 15070 kHz. Winters, there is another opportunity at 2245 Sunday through Friday on 3955 and 6195 kHz.

For the *Middle East* the opener is at 0315 on 9410 and either or both of 11760 and 12095 kHz; 0945 on 9410 (or 15070), 15575 and 17640 kHz; 1505 (Sunday through Friday) on 9410 (winter), 12095 and 15070 kHz; and 1745 on 7160, 9410, 12095 and 15070 kHz. Listeners in *Southern Africa* can tune at 0315 on 3255, 6005, 6190 and 9600 kHz; 0615 (Monday through Friday) on 6190, 9600 and 11940 kHz; 0945 on 15400 kHz; 1245 (Sunday through Friday) on 6190 and 11940 kHz; and 1745 on 3255, 6190 and 15400 kHz.

In *East Asia*, go for 0135 on 6195 and 15360 kHz; 0315 on 15360 kHz; 0945 on 6195, 9740 and 17830 kHz; 1245 (Monday through Friday) on 6195, 9740, 11955 and 15280 kHz; 1505 (Sunday) on 5990, 6195 and 9740 kHz; and 2245 on 7110 and 11955 kHz (5905 kHz may also be available in winter). For *Australasia*, it's 0945 on 15280 kHz; 1245 (Monday through Friday) and 1505 (Sunday) on 9740 kHz; and 2245 on 11695 and 11955 kHz. At certain times of the year, 6195 kHz may also be available for all these slots.

NRD-535D

"Best Communications Receiver"
World Radio TV Handbook 1992

"Unsurpassed DX Performance"
Passport to World Band Radio 1992

Setting the industry standard once again for shortwave receivers, the NRD-535D is the most advanced HF communications receiver ever designed for the serious DXer and shortwave listener. Its unparalleled performance in all modes makes it the ultimate receiver for diversified monitoring applications.

Designed for DXers by DXers! The NRD-535D (shown above with optional NVA-319 speaker) strikes the perfect balance between form and function with its professional-grade design and critically acclaimed ergonomics. The NRD-535D is the recipient of the prestigious World Radio TV Handbook Industry Award for "Best Communications Receiver."

- Phase-lock ECSS system for selectable-sideband AM reception.
- Maximum IF bandwidth flexibility! The Variable Bandwidth Control (BWC) adjusts the wide and intermediate IF filter bandwidths from 5.5 to 2.0 kHz and 2.0 to 0.5 kHz—continuously.
- Stock fixed-width IF filters include a 5.5 kHz (wide), a 2.0 kHz (intermediate), and a 1.0 kHz (narrow). Optional JRC filters include 2.4 kHz, 300 Hz, and 500 Hz crystal type.
- All mode 100 kHz – 30 MHz coverage. Tuning accuracy to 1 Hz, using JRC's advanced Direct Digital Synthesis (DDS) PLL system and a high-precision magnetic rotary encoder. The tuning is so smooth you will swear it's analog! An optional high-stability crystal oscillator kit is also available for ±0.5 ppm stability.
- A superior front-end variable double tuning circuit is continuously controlled by the CPU to vary with the receive frequency automatically. The result: Outstanding 106 dB Dynamic Range and +20 dBm Third-Order Intercept Point.
- Memory capacity of 200 channels, each storing frequency, mode, filter, AGC and ATT settings. Scan and sweep functions built in. All memory channels are tunable, making "MEM to VFO" switching unnecessary.
- A state-of-the-art RS-232C computer interface is built into every NRD-535D receiver.
- Fully modular design, featuring plug-in circuit boards and high-quality surface-mount components. No other manufacturer can offer such professional-quality design and construction at so affordable a price.

JRC *Japan Radio Co., Ltd.*

Japan Radio Company, Ltd., New York Branch Office – 430 Park Avenue (2nd Floor), New York, NY 10022, USA Fax: (212) 319-5227

Japan Radio Company, Ltd. – Akasaka Twin Tower (Main), 17-22, Akasaka 2-chome, Minato-ku, Tokyo 107, JAPAN Fax: (03) 3584-8878

"Our Treasure Chest"
Voice of Russia

An old adage says, "it's an ill wind that blows no good," and Russian winds are like anybody else's. When the financial axe fell at the Voice of Russia and staff left for greener pastures, resources had to be rationalized. So what better way than to resurrect gems from the station's vast archives?

Judging from the Voice of Russia's official schedule, the original idea was to run a series about Russian history under the title, "Our Treasure Chest." Somewhere along the line, though, there was an apparent change of mind, so the slot wound up being allocated to all sorts of programs. Not that the Voice of Russia broadcasts offer any clue as to what is actually going on—they merely go straight into the show without any introduction whatsoever. Nor is there any enlightening announcement at the end.

What we do have, though, are some exceptional shows, be they documentaries or recordings of classical music. The latter can feature little-known works by Russian and other CIS composers, or Russian performances of music by Western composers.

An added attraction is that when an opera is featured that's based on a literary work, the musical performances sometimes alternate with readings from the original text, especially if it is a poem. This works to particularly good effect with dramatic operas like Anton Rubinstein's "The Demon." Since there is no predetermined schedule for this slot, the surprise factor is considerably greater than with most other programs.

Europe and Eastern North America: 2030 winter on 5940, 5995, 6055, 6130, 7180 and 7205 kHz; and 1930 summer on 7240, 7350, 9880, 11630 and 11675 kHz. *Western North America*: 0430 winter on 5920, 7175, 7270 and 7330 kHz; and 0330 summer on 12010, 12050, 13645, 13665, 15180 and 15880 kHz. *Southern Africa*: 2030 winter 7325 and 9470 kHz; and 1930 summer on 11765 kHz. There are no available channels for Asia, Australasia and the Middle East.

"Weekend"
(Various Stations)

While multinational joint productions for television are not unusual, it is less common to come across similar ventures in international radio. Full marks, then, to four of Europe's leading stations for producing a lively and interesting weekly look at how different European cultures view the world.

Although "Weekend" is put together through the collective effort of stations in only four countries—Britain's BBC World Service, Holland's Radio Netherlands, Germany's Deutsche Welle and Radio France Internationale—it mirrors views and prejudices from all over Europe. It's truly eclectic, peering into everything from Javanese restaurants to Joan of Arc, from soccer fanaticism to sexual services for women. Some editions include "Eurovictim of The Week," which exposes legal and consumer woes.

Although a joint production by four stations, "Weekend" is aired only by Radio Netherlands and the BBC World Service. Stranger still, the BBC only beams it to listeners in Europe and the Middle East.

For *Europe*, keep a Saturday appointment with Radio Netherlands at 1154 on 6045 and 7190/9650 kHz, or the BBC at 1701 on 3955 (winter), 6195, 9410, 12095 and 15070 kHz. Same day in the *Middle East*, choose between 1354 (RN) on 13700 kHz, and 1701 (BBC) on 9410, 12095 and 15075 kHz. The airing for *Southern Africa* is four hours later, at 1754 on 6020 kHz.

In *East and Southeast Asia*, try 0954 Saturday on 9720, 12065 and 13705 kHz.

QUALITY COMMUNICATIONS EQUIPMENT SINCE 1942

The same applies for *Australasia*, but two hours earlier, at 0754 on 9720 and 11895/9700 kHz.

Listeners in *Eastern North America* can try the BBC at 1701 Saturday on 9410, 12095 or 15070 kHz, depending on their location. Otherwise, it's 0054 Sunday (Saturday evening, North American date) on 6020, 6165 and 9845 kHz. Farther west, try the repeat broadcast four hours later, at 0454, on 6165 and 5995/9590 kHz.

"Music USA-Jazz"/"Music USA-Standards"
Voice of America

Friday, May 17, 1996, marked the end of an era. Long-time VOA broadcaster and jazz authority Willis Conover finally succumbed to the illness he had battled for years. For millions of listeners worldwide, it was like losing an old friend.

For many, the name of Willis Conover was synonymous not only with the VOA, but with America itself. Over the years, he received rapturous receptions in places as far away and politically diverse as

Willis Conover, the high priest of jazz authorities, died in 1996. Yet, his show lives on through replays heard worldwide over the Voice of America. Here, exactly 21 months before his death, an open-shirted Conover meets with musician, composer and educator Dr. Billy Taylor.

tropical Brazil and communist Eastern Europe, where flowers were strewn in his path by adoring multitudes. He was an ambassador *extraordinaire* not only for jazz, but also for his country. In the 1989 edition of PASSPORT, he was cited as having the best music program on the air.

Willis actually had two shows on the VOA, "Music USA-Jazz" and "Music USA-Standards," the latter featuring great American vocalists and big bands. Before he died, he expressed a desire that the shows continue after his death—not a difficult wish to fulfill, considering the vast archives he left behind.

As of now, the VOA program schedule is undergoing considerable reorganization. While nothing is certain, music from the Conover archives is likely to be heard at the following times:

If you live in *North America and the Caribbean*, try the 1130 Saturday airing of great standards on 6165, 7405 and 9590 kHz. In the *Middle East* and parts of *Europe* and *North Africa*, try 1410 and 2010 Saturday for jazz, then 1930 Sunday for the standards. At 1410 winter, tune to 15205 kHz; in summer, it's 15255 kHz. For the 1930 and 2010 slots, go for 9760 and, in summer, 9770 kHz.

East and Southeast Asia get just one opportunity—1410 Saturday, jazz, on 6160/6110, 9760, 15160 (summer) and 15425 kHz. This slot is also available for *Australasia* on 15425 kHz. Alas, no space has been found in the VOA's African service for either show, a regrettable omission.

"John Peel"
BBC World Service

The BBC program guide calls it "alternative pop music," but many would query whether it is at all popular, or indeed music. What nobody can doubt is that it sounds different.

Groups like Blonde Redhead, The Mad Professor and International Strike Force

ANYPLACE.
ANYWHERE.
ANYTIME.

Travel the airwaves with Grundig's portable digital Yacht Boy 400.
Listening has never been easier... the BBC commentary from London, the news from Berlin, Beijing, the Balkans and more. Imagine!

Only Grundig with its reputation for world class electronics could offer a radio so advanced and compact: AM/FM Stereo/Shortwave, digital tuning, auto scan and 40-memories, clock alarm and timer. Also includes *Grundig Shortwave Listening Guide*, batteries, external antenna, earphones and carrying case.

Rated best in its class!

YACHT BOY 400

Features:

- Shortwave/AM/FM and Longwave
- Continuous shortwave from 1.6–30 MHz
- Clock, alarm and timer
- 40 randomly programmable memories
- Multifunction liquid crystal display
- Phase-lock-loop tuning
- Size: 7-3/4"L x 4-5/8"H x 1-1/4"W
- Weight: 1 lb. 5 oz.

GRUNDIG

Call for information: U.S. 1-800-872-2228 or 415-361-1611
Canada 800-637-1648 • Fax: 415-361-1724

may not have large international followings, but the weekly John Peel show, which features them and their like, certainly does. Otherwise, the BBC would have taken it off the air years ago.

Much of the attraction is John Peel himself. Self-portrayed as a writer of record-sleeve notes and a fanatical supporter of the Liverpool Football Club, he is the antithesis of the popular image of a disc jockey. Yet, he is admired by public and professionals alike. His offbeat humor and casual style belie the fact he is a seasoned professional who learned his trade in small American stations and with the European pirate stations back in the Sixties.

If alternative pop music is your cup of tea, this show is tailor-made. If not, you can do the same as many others—savor Peel's opening gems, then tune elsewhere. Be forewarned, though, that the timings for this show were changed quite a bit during 1996, and there may be more unwelcome surprises for 1997.

"John Peel" can be heard in *North America* winters at 1830 Sunday on 17840 kHz. For year-round opportunities, try 1215 Tuesday on 5965/9515, 6195 and 15220 kHz; and 0615 Wednesday on 5975

and 6175 kHz (9640 kHz may also be available in winter).

First shot for *Europe* is at 1430 Monday on 9410, 12095, 15070 and 17640 kHz. It's repeated at 2030 Thursday on 3955 (winter), 6180, 6195, 7325, 9410 and (summer) 12095 kHz.

In the *Middle East*, choose from 1430 Monday on 12095, 15070, 15575 and 17640 kHz; 0330 Tuesday on 11760 kHz—winters also on 9410 kHz. At 2030 Thursday it's on 9410 and (summer) 12095 and 15070 kHz. If you are in *Southern Africa*, try 2130 Sunday on 3255, 6005 and 6190 kHz; and 1500 Monday on 6190, 11940 and 21470/21660 kHz.

For *East and Southeast Asia* there's 0825 Thursday on 9740, 11955 and 15280 kHz; with a repeat 12 hours later, at 2030, on 11955 kHz. These same time slots are also available to *Australasia* at 0825 on 11955 kHz, and at 2030 on 9740 and 11955 kHz.

"Moscow Yesterday and Today" Voice of Russia

In these heady days of high technology and the Internet, anything from a prior era tends to be given short shrift. But fortunately for those who hanker after yesteryear, it is still possible to find an occasional reminder of how it used to be—when chips were for eating, and drives were things you took on Sunday.

Such is "Moscow Yesterday and Today," a program which recreates, through words and music, images from the near and distant past.

Excerpts from centuries-old diaries, readings from wormy books, accounts of ages-old customs, sonorous Russian bells, early religious music, murder plots, revolutions and spellbinding choral music—these are just some of the ingredients which make up this 25-minute journey into Slavic history.

Voice of Russia

The Voice of Russia's "Moscow Yesterday and Today" recreates, through words and music, memories from Russia's Soviet and Czarist past.

As changing world events bring us all closer, it's exciting to get the news direct from a foreign station. So tune in and listen – even when you're 12 time zones away. The drama of survival efforts. Crisis monitoring when conventional communications break down. The uncertainty of economic trends. And colorful cultural activities.

Don't wait for someone else to tell you what's happening. The FRG-100 Worldwide Desktop Communications Receiver puts you in the action now! The FRG-100 is a winner, too. It won the prestigious WRTH award for "Best Communications Receiver" in December 1992. No surprise with exclusive features like adjustable SSB carrier offset and selectable tuning steps in 10, 100 and 1000 Hz.

But you're the real winner! Priced lower than receivers with fewer features costing much more, the FRG-100 delivers extraordinary, affordable performance. For news and entertainment from far away places – a little closer than before – listen to the FRG-100 at your Yaesu dealer today.

YAESU
Performance without compromise.^{SM}

FRG-100
Worldwide Desktop Communications Receiver

- Covers all short-wave bands including 50 kHz-30 MHz
- 50 Memory Channels
- Twin 12/24 Hour Clocks
- Programmable On/Off Timers
- Selectable Tuning Steps (10, 100, 1000 Hz)
- Built-in Selectable Filters 2.4, 4, 6 kHz (250 or 500 Hz options)
- Dual Antenna Connections (Coax and Long Wire)
- Bright LCD Display
- Operates on AC or DC
- Compact Desktop Size
- Memory or Group Scanning
- 16 Preprogrammed Broadcast Bands

Yaesu helps bring the world a little closer.

"Moscow Yesterday and Today" is aired at 0130 Wednesday and Friday; 0530 Sunday; 0630 Tuesday, Thursday and Saturday; 0730 Wednesday and Friday; 1030 Tuesday, Thursday and Saturday; 1330 Wednesday and Friday; 1630 Tuesday, Thursday, Saturday and Sunday; and 1930 Monday, Wednesday, Friday and Sunday. All transmissions are one hour earlier in summer.

Best winter bets for *Europe* are 1630 on 6130, 7115, 7180 and 7330 kHz; and 1930 on 5940, 5995, 6055, 6130, 7180 and 7205 kHz. In summer, try 1530 on 9880 kHz; and 1830 on 7240, 7350, 9880, 11630 and 11675 kHz.

Reception in *Eastern North America* is usually best on some of the European frequencies during the local afternoon. If you can't listen then, try 0130 winter on 7105 and 7125 kHz, or 0030 summer on 7125, 7250, 9620 and 9665 kHz.

Western North America gets a much better deal. For winter, the 0530, 0630 and 0730 slots are all audible on 5905, 5920, 5930, 7175, 7270 and 7330 kHz; in summer they are one hour earlier on 12010, 12040 (0530 and 0630 only), 12050, 13645, 13665, 15180 and 15880 kHz.

Winter in the *Middle East*, go for 1630 on 4740, 4940, 4975, 6175, 7210, 7275, 9470, 9635 and 11945 kHz; and 1930 on 7210 and 9585 kHz. Best summer slots are 1530 on 4740, 4940, 4975, 9365, 9595, 11775, 11835, 15320, 15350 and 15540 kHz; and 1830 on 9365, 11765, 11775 and 11960 kHz.

For *Southern Africa*, best winter (local summer) choices are 1630 on 7275, 7325, 9470, 9505 and 11865 kHz; and 1930 on 7200, 7255, 7325, 9470 and 9505 kHz. Midyear, your local winter, try 1530 on 9975, 11775, 12025, 15350, 15560 and 17750 kHz; and 1830 on 9975, 11765, 11775 and 11960 kHz.

There's practically nothing for *East Asia*, except for 0930 summer on 7150 kHz. However, some of the channels for *Southeast Asia* may be worth checking: winter,

at 0630 and 0730 on 15160 and 17560 kHz; and 1030 on 9685, 13785, 15490, 17755 and 17860 kHz. In summer, shoot for 0530 and 0630 on 15470 and 17580 kHz; and 0930 on 12025 and 15580 kHz.

Winter (local summer) slots for *Australasia* are 0630 and 0730 on 12025, 15470, 17570 and 21790 kHz; and 1030 on 9450, 12005, 12025 and 17860 kHz. For midyear, your local winter, try 0530 on 15470 and 17580 kHz; 0630 on 15470, 15490, 15560 and 17580 kHz; and 0930 on 9835 and 11800 kHz.

"Britain Today" BBC World Service

One of the major strengths of world band radio is that most stations are public broadcasters who are not subject to popularity polls or pressures from commercial sponsors. Yet, that strength can also be a weakness, as government broadcasters struggle to present their nations' perspectives to the outside world.

What could and should be a series of interesting cameos can become little more than a boring string of facts and figures, or accounts of the recent activities of local political figures.

Not so with the BBC World Service's "Britain Today," a quarter-hour slot which bears little resemblance to the five-minute "News about Britain" from which it evolved.

Rather than recite a string of news items about events in the United Kingdom, the program concentrates on short background reports and human-interest stories. These often are local reflections of much larger issues, some of which are common to all cultures. Aircraft safety, law and order, child abuse, capital punishment, consumer affairs and public health are just some of the subjects which come under scrutiny. In most cases, they are topics to which all of us can relate.

Sometimes, though, the stories cover subjects so outlandish, that it is difficult to believe that such things can still exist in a developed Western democracy. Few are aware, for example, that in at least one part of the British Isles, a woman can still be sentenced to life imprisonment for having an abortion.

Unlike some other BBC programs, "Britain Today" is easily heard in all target areas. Broadcasts are daily, unless otherwise indicated.

For *North America* there is a daily broadcast at 0045 on 5975, 7125, 7325 (winter) and 9590 kHz; and another at 1645 Sunday through Friday on 9515 (winter) and 17840 kHz. In *Europe*, tune in at 1215 on 9410, 12095, 15075 and 17640 kHz. Again at 1645, Monday through Friday only, on 6195 (winter), 9410, 12095 and 15070 kHz; and 2115 on 3955 (winter), 6180, 6195, 7325, 9410 and (summer) 12095 kHz.

Timings for the *Middle East* are the same as for Europe: 1215 on 11760, 15070, 15575 and 17640 kHz; 1645 Monday through Friday on 9410, 12095 and 15070 kHz; and 2115 on 9410 and (summer) 12095 and 15070 kHz. In *Southern Africa*, it's 1215 Monday through Saturday on 6190, 11940 and 21660 kHz; and 2115 on 3255, 6005 and 6190 kHz.

For *East and Southeast Asia*, try at 0045 on 6195 and 15360 kHz; 1215 Monday through Friday on 6195, 9740, 11955 and 15280 kHz; and 1645 on 3915, 7135 (winter) and 7180 kHz. Listeners in *Australasia* get a bit of a raw deal, but can shoot for 1215 Monday through Friday on 9740 kHz—6195 kHz may also be available for part of the year. Another option is at 0045 on 6195 kHz, but this tends to be limited to local winter months.

_____

Prepared by the staff of PASSPORT TO WORLD BAND RADIO.

Compleat Idiot's Guide to Getting Started

Welcome to World Band Radio!

World band radio is information and entertainment, on the spot—your unfiltered connection to what's going on all over. But it's not as easy to receive as conventional radio, so here's the right way to go about tuning it in.

"Must" #1: Set Clock for World Time

Research has shown that world band listeners who try to wing it without PASSPORT have about a 50–50 chance of dropping out within their first year of listening. Yet, less than one person in 20 who uses PASSPORT gives up. That's mainly because PASSPORT takes away the "hit-and-miss" of radio purchases and tuning in.

But to make this work, world band schedules use the *World Time* standard. After all, world band radio is global, with nations broadcasting around-the-clock from virtually every time zone.

Imagine the chaos if each broadcaster used its own local time for scheduling. In England, 9 PM is different from nine in the evening in Japan or Canada. How would anybody know when to tune in?

To eliminate confusion, international broadcasters use World Time, or UTC, as a standard reference. Formerly and in some circles still known as Greenwich Mean Time (GMT), it is keyed to the Greenwich meridian in England and is announced in 24-hour format, like military time. So 2 PM, say, is 1400 ("fourteen hundred") hours.

There are four easy ways to know World Time. First, you can tune to one of the standard time stations, such as WWV in Colorado and WWVH in Hawaii in the United States, or CHU in Ottawa, Canada. WWV and WWVH are on 5000, 10000 and 15000 kHz around-the-clock, with WWV also on 2500 and 20000 kHz; CHU is on 3330, 7335 and 14670 kHz. There, you will hear time

Compact portables fit easily into carry-on luggage, yet are large enough to offer pleasant sound. Sony's popular ICF-SW7600G excels in reducing fading and interference.   SONY "pips" every second, followed just before the beginning of each minute by an announcement of the exact World Time. Boring, yes, but very handy when you need it.

Second, you can tune to one of the major international broadcasters, such as London's BBC World Service or Washington's Voice of America. Most announce World Time at the top of the hour.

Third, you can access the Internet Web site http://www.greenwich2000.com/time.htm, but you'll need to have your slow-loading graphics switched on to see the clock display. This site also provides gobs of information about all aspects of UTC.

Fourth, here are some quick calculations.

If you live on the East Coast of the United States, *add* five hours winter (four hours summer) to your local time to get World Time. So, if it is 8 PM EST (the 20th hour of the day) in New York, it is 0100 hours World Time.

On the U.S. West Coast, add eight hours winter (seven hours summer).

In Britain, it's easy—World Time (oops, Greenwich Mean Time) is the same as local winter time. However, you'll have to subtract one hour from local summer time to get World Time.

Elsewhere in Western Europe, subtract one hour winter (two hours summer) from local time.

Live elsewhere? Flip through the next pages until you come to "How to Set Your World Time Clock."

Once you know the correct World Time, set your radio's clock so you'll have it handy whenever you want to listen. No 24-hour clock? Pick up the phone and order one (world band specialty firms sell them for as little as $10, see box). Unless you enjoy doing weird computations in your head (it's 6:00 PM here, so add five hours to make it 11:00 PM, which on a 24-hour clock converts to 23:00 World Time—but, whoops, I forgot that it's summer and I should have added four hours instead of five . . .), it'll be the best ten bucks you ever spent.

"Must" #2: Understand World Day

There's a trick to World Time that can occasionally catch even the most experienced listener—even some radio stations.

Bargains in World Time Clocks

Each of the following simple clocks contains identical "mechanisms"...

★ ★ ★ **MFJ-24-107B**, $9.95. Despite its paucity of features, this "Volksclock" does the trick.

★ ★ ★ **NI8F LCD**, $14.95. Same as the MFJ, above, but with a handsome walnut frame instead of aluminum. It is less likely than MFJ models to scratch surfaces. From Universal Radio.

★ ★ ★ **MFJ-108**, $19.95. For those who also want local time. Two LCD clocks—24-hour format for World Time, separate 12-hour display for local time—side-by-side.

MFJ-24 HOUR LCD CLOCK
MODEL MFJ-107B

Unless your radio already has a built-in clock, World Time doesn't come any cheaper than one of these MFJ or Universal clocks.

What happens at midnight? A new *World Day* arrives as well.

Remember: Midnight World Time means a new day, too. So if it is 9 PM EST Wednesday in New York, it is 0200 hours World Time *Thursday*. Don't forget to "wind your calendar"!

"Must" #3: Know How to Find Stations

You can find world band stations by looking them up in PASSPORT's by-country or "What's On Tonight" sections. Or you can flip through PASSPORT's vast Blue Pages to surf within the several *segments*, or "bands"—neighborhoods within the shortwave spectrum where stations are found.

Most stations are found in nine main "neighborhoods."

Incidentally, frequencies may be given in kilohertz, kHz, or Megahertz, MHz. The only difference is three decimal places, so 6175 kHz is the same as 6.175 MHz. But forget all the technobabble. All you need to know is that 6175, with or without decimals, refers to a certain spot on your radio's dial.

Here are the main "neighborhoods" where you'll find world band stations and when they're most active. Except for the 4750-5075 kHz segment, which has mainly low-powered Latin American and African stations, you'll discover a huge variety of stations.

4750-5075 kHz	Night and twilight, mainly during winter
5730-6205 kHz	Night and twilight; sometimes day, too
7100-7595 kHz	Night, early morning and late afternoon
9350-10000 kHz	Night (except winter), early morning and late afternoon
11550-12160 kHz	Night (except winter) and day, especially dusk
13570-13870 kHz	Day and, to some degree, night
15000-15710 kHz	Day and, to some degree, night
17500-17900 kHz	Day and, rarely, night
21450-21850 kHz	Day only

First Taste: PASSPORT's Five-Minute Start

In a hurry? Here's how to get to first base pronto:

1. Wait until evening. If you live in a concrete-and-steel building, put the radio by a window.

2. Make sure your radio is plugged in or has fresh batteries. Extend the telescopic antenna fully and vertically. Set the DX/local switch (if there is one) to "DX," but otherwise leave the controls the way they came from the factory.

3. Turn on your radio. Set it to 5900 kHz and begin tuning slowly toward 6200 kHz. You will now begin to encounter a number of stations from around the world. Adjust the volume to a level that is comfortable for you. *Voilà!* You are now an initiate of world band radio.

Other times? Read this article. It tells you how to tune by day or night. Too, refer to the handy "Best Times and Frequencies for 1997" box at the end of this chapter.

ANYPLACE. ANYWHERE. ANYTIME.

No matter where you go, the Grundig Satellit 700 is there for you. The Satellit 700 is the world's most advanced shortwave portable radio. This is the portable for serious listening to international broadcasts and long distance shortwave two-way communications.

Covers all shortwave bands, plus FM-stereo, AM and LW. Single sideband (SSB) circuitry allows for reception of two-way shortwave amateur, shortwave maritime and shortwave aeronautical communications.

"The best portable introduced this year is Grundig's Satellit 700."
PWBR, 1993

SATELLIT 700

Features:

Unprecedented memory capacity. 512 user-programmable positions, plus 120 preprogrammed frequencies.

Advanced synchronous detector minimizes broadcast interference.

Excellent sensitivity. Even weak signals come in more clearly.

Superior sideband performance. Helps eliminate unwanted noises providing clear, natural voice quality.

Multi-function liquid crystal display. Including frequency, band, mode, TIME I and II, battery strength, antenna and more.

Size: 12-1/4"L x 7-1/4"H x 3"

Weight: 4 lbs

GRUNDIG

Call for information: U.S. 1-800-872-2228 or 415-361-1611
Canada 800-637-1648 • Fax: 415-361-1724

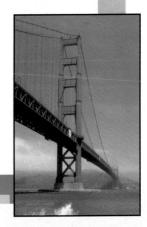

London's BBC World Service Shop is a favorite haunt of world band and Beeb devotees. Surrounding a stack of PASSPORT books are sales assistant Rafa Estfania, in T-shirt, along with World Service Press Office clerical assistant Graham Lovatt and manager Bernard Mahon.

If you're a newbie to world band radio, you'll be used to hearing local stations at the same place on the dial day and night. Things are a lot different when you roam the international airwaves.

> Savor the sound of foreign tongues sprinkled alongside English shows.

World band radio is like a global bazaar where merchants come and go at different times. Similarly, stations enter and leave a given spot on the dial throughout the day and night. Where you once tuned in, say, a French station, hours later you might find a Russian or Chinese broadcaster roosting on that same spot—or on a nearby perch. If you suddenly hear interference from a station on an adjacent channel, it doesn't mean something is wrong with your radio; it means another station has begun broadcasting on a nearby frequency. There are more stations on the air than there is space for them, so sometimes they try to outshout each other.

To cope with this, purchase a radio with superior adjacent-channel rejection, also known as selectivity. PASSPORT REPORTS, a major section of this book, tells you how successfully the various radios leap this hurdle.

One of the most pleasant things about world band radio is cruising up and down the airwaves. Daytime, you'll find most stations above 11500 kHz; night, below 10000 kHz.

OUT OF THIN AIR AND INTO THE THICK OF THINGS.

THE DRAKE R8A

The Drake R8A World Band Communications Receiver. Turn it on, tune it in, and as easy as that, you're hearing world events as they happen… uncensored and complete. And with the R8A's astounding clarity, it's almost as if you're there. In fact, no other communications receiver puts you closer to the action in even the most distant parts of the world.

If you're a hobbyist, you'll marvel at the R8A's simplicity of operation. If you're an expert, you'll admire the high-powered features. The Drake R8A offers superior performance in a complete package that includes built-in filters and other unique features that have made Drake the foremost name in world band communications. The R8A from Drake…you've got to hear it to believe it.

DRAKE, FOR A WORLD OF DIFFERENCE.

DRAKE

R.L. Drake Company, P.O. Box 3006, Miamisburg, Ohio 45343, U.S.A. ■ Sales Office: 513.866.2421 ■ Fax: 513.866.0806 ■ Service and Parts: 513.746.6990 ■ In Canada: 705.742.3122
© 1995 The R.L. Drake Company   *DRAKE* is a registered trademark of The R.L. Drake Company.

Setting Your World Time Clock

PASSPORT's "Addresses PLUS" lets you arrive at the local time in another country by adding or subtracting from World Time. Use that section to determine the time within a country you are listening to.

This box, however, gives it from the other direction; that is, what to **add or subtract from your local time** to determine *World Time* from certain parts of the world. Use this box to set your World Time clock.

Where You Are	*To Determine World Time*
Europe	
United Kingdom and Ireland London, Dublin	Same time as World Time winter, subtract 1 hour summer
Continental Western Europe; parts of Central and Eastern Continental Europe Berlin, Stockholm, Prague	Subtract 1 hour winter, 2 hours summer
Elsewhere in Continental Europe Belarus, Bulgaria, Cyprus, Estonia, Finland, Greece, Latvia, Lithuania, Moldova, Romania, Russia (Kaliningradskaya Oblast), Turkey and Ukraine	Subtract 2 hours winter, 3 hours summer
North America	
Newfoundland St. John's NF, St. Anthony NF	Add 3½ hours winter, 2½ hours summer
Atlantic St. John NB, Battle Harbour NF	Add 4 hours winter, 3 hours summer
Eastern New York, Atlanta, Toronto	Add 5 hours winter, 4 hours summer
Central Chicago, Nashville, Winnipeg	Add 6 hours winter, 5 hours summer
Mountain Denver, Salt Lake City, Calgary	Add 7 hours winter, 6 hours summer
Pacific San Francisco, Vancouver	Add 8 hours winter, 7 hours summer
Alaska Anchorage, Fairbanks	Add 9 hours winter, 8 hours summer
Hawaii Honolulu, Hilo	Add 10 hours year round

Tune slowly, savor the sound of foreign tongues sprinkled alongside English shows. Enjoy the music, weigh the opinions of other peoples.

> Stations can sometimes be heard far beyond where they are beamed.

If a station disappears, there is probably nothing wrong with your radio. The atmosphere's *ionosphere* reflects world band signals, and it changes constantly. The result is that broadcasters operate in different parts of the world band spectrum, depending upon the time of day and season of the year. PASSPORT's schedules show you where to tune and retune. On advanced radios, you can store these favorite channels on presets for immediate call-up, day-after-day.

That same changeability can also work in your favor, especially if you like to eavesdrop on signals not intended to be heard by you. Sometimes stations from exotic locales—places you would not ordinarily hear—arrive at your radio, thanks to the shifting characteristics of the ionosphere. Unlike other media, world band radio sometimes allows sta-

...Continued

Where You Are	To Determine World Time
Mideast & Southern Africa	
Egypt, Israel, Lebanon and Syria	Subtract 2 hours winter, 3 hours summer
South Africa, Zambia and Zimbabwe	Subtract 2 hours year round
East Asia & Australasia	
China, including Hong Kong and Taiwan	Subtract 8 hours year round
Japan	Subtract 9 hours year round
Australia: Victoria, New South Wales, Tasmania	Subtract 11 hours local summer, 10 local winter (midyear)
Australia: South Australia	Subtract 10½ hours local summer, 9½ hours local winter (midyear)
Australia: Queensland	Subtract 10 hours year round
Australia: Northern Territory	Subtract 9½ hours year round
Australia: Western Australia	Subtract 8 hours year round
New Zealand	Subtract 13 hours local summer, 12 hours local winter (midyear)

GRUNDIG
made for you

German shortwave technology in its most advanced form. For serious listening to international broadcasts and long distance two-way communications. More flexibility than any other shortwave portable.

Digital/Alphanumeric display with PLL tuning, general coverage shortwave receiver, with SSB and advanced synchronous detector. Dual clocks and turn on/off timers. Sleep timer. Eight character memory page labeling. 512 memories standard; 2048 possible with optional memofiles. Multivoltage adapter. Built-in Ni-cad charger.

Continuous shortwave tuning from 1.6 to 30 megahertz covers all shortwave bands, plus FM-stereo, AM and LW. Single sideband (SSB) circuitry allows for reception of two-way amateur, military and commercial communications, including maritime and aeronautical.
120 factory pre-programmed frequencies for world-wide reception. Dual conversion superheterodyne receiver design.

SATELLIT 700

WORLD'S MOST ADVANCED SHORTWAVE PORTABLE

Multifunction Liquid Crystal Display: The LCD shows time, frequency band, alphanumeric memory labels, automatic turn on/off, sleep timer, bandwidth select position, synchronous detector status and USB/LSB status.

Tuning Made Simple With both a tuning dial, and direct entry keypad, tuning into your favorite broadcast is both quick and easy.

Synchronous Detector is but one of the many functions available with the Satellit 700. The synchronous detector helps to eliminate interference so that what you hear is as ear pleasing as possible.

YACHT BOY 400

THE ULTIMATE IN DIGITAL TECHNOLOGY

Noted for its exacting controls, including fine tuning, volume and high/low tone controls.

Multi-Function Liquid Crystal Display: The LCD shows simultaneous displays of time, frequency, band, alarm function and sleep timer.

The Digital Key Pad: The key pad itself is a marvel of performance with 40 pre-set stations. It's intelligently designed and easy to use.

GRUNDIG
made for you

Grundig's Yacht Boy 400 has received rave reviews from the shortwave press for combining a wealth of sophisticated features in one compact, portable package that doesn't cost a fortune. It incorporates features found on stationary shortwave systems that cost thousands, such as outstanding audio quality, precise 0.1 kHz increment tuning, up/down slewing, frequency scanning, signal strength indication, and single-sideband signal demodulation.

But the Yacht Boy advantage mentioned most often in reviews was its ease of use for the novice listener. Following the included shortwave guide, in moments you can be listening to foreign broadcasts beamed to North America.

Soon, you will be scanning the airwaves to tune in exotic music programs and sports events from faraway locales. Yacht Boy even picks up shortwave amateur (ham radio) broadcasts and shortwave aviation/military frequencies (cockpit-to-tower communications). The possibilities for family fun, education, and enjoyment are boundless.

For travel or home use, Grundig adds in a dual-time travel clock with snooze and sleep timer. FM band is stereophonic with your headphones. The lighted LCD panel is easy to read in the dark. Comes with a form-fitting pouch, integral telescoping antenna and advanced external antenna on a compact reel, carry-strap, batteries, and complete instructions.

Best Times and Frequencies for 1997

With world band, if you dial around randomly, you're almost as likely to get dead air as you are a favorite program. For one thing, a number of world band segments are alive and kicking by day, while others are nocturnal. Too, some fare better at specific times of the year.

"Neighborhoods" Where to Tune

Official "neighborhoods," or segments, of the shortwave spectrum are set aside for world band radio by the International Telecommunication Union. However, the ITU countenances some broadcasting outside these parameters, so the "real world" situation is actually more generous. This is what's shown below.

This guide is most accurate if you're listening from north of Africa or South America. Even then, what you'll actually hear will vary—depending upon such variables as your precise location, where the station transmits from, the time of year and your radio (e.g., see Propagation in the glossary). Although world band is active 24 hours a day, signals are usually best from around just before sunset until sometime after midnight. Too, try a couple of hours on either side of dawn.

Here, then, are the most attractive times and frequencies for world band listening, based on reception conditions forecast for the coming year. Unless otherwise indicated, frequency ranges are occupied mainly by international broadcasters, but also include some domestic stations or overseas relays of domestic stations. In the Americas, 3900-4000 kHz and 7100-7300 kHz are reserved for use by amateur radio ("hams"), even though world band transmissions from other parts of the world manage to be heard there.

Rare Reception

2 MHz (120 meters) **2300-2500 kHz** (virtually all domestic stations)

Limited Reception Winter Nights

3 MHz (90 meters) **3200-3400 kHz** (mostly domestic stations)

Good-to-Fair during Winter Nights in Europe and Asia

4 MHz (75 meters) **3900-4080 kHz** (international and domestic stations, primarily not in or beamed to the Americas—3900-3950 mainly Asian and Pacific transmitters; 3950-4000 also includes European and African transmitters)

Some Reception during Nights

5 MHz (60 meters) **4700-5100 kHz** (mostly domestic stations)

Excellent during Nights
Regional Reception Daytime

6 MHz (49 meters) **5730-6250 kHz**

tions to be heard thousands of miles beyond where they are beamed.

"Must" #4: Obtain A Radio That Can Hack It

If you haven't yet purchased a world band radio, here's some good news: Although cheap radios should be avoided—they suffer from one or more major defects— you don't need an expensive set to enjoy exploring the world's airwaves. With one of the better-rated portables, about the price of a VCR, you'll be able to hear much of what world band has to offer.

You won't need an outside antenna, either, unless you're using a tabletop model. All portables, and to some extent portatops, are designed to work off the built-in telescopic antenna. Try, though, to purchase a radio with digital frequency display. Its accuracy will make tuning around the bands far easier than with outmoded slide-rule tuning.

... Continued

**Good during Nights except Mid-Winter
Variable during Mid-Winter Nights
Regional Reception Daytime**

7 MHz (41 meters) **7100-7600 kHz** (below 7300 kHz, no American-based transmitters and few transmissions targeted to the Americas)

**Good during Summer Nights
Some Reception Daytime and Winter Nights
Good Asian and Pacific Reception Mornings in America**

9 MHz (31 meters) **9020-9080 kHz/9250-10000 kHz**
11 MHz (25 meters) **11500-12160 kHz**

**Good during Daytime
Generally Good during Summer Nights**

13 MHz (22 meters) **13570-13870 kHz**
15 MHz (19 meters) **15000-15800 kHz**

**Good during Daytime
Variable, Limited Reception Summer Nights**

17 MHz (16 meters) **17480-17900 kHz**
19 MHz (15 meters) **18900-19020 kHz** (virtually no stations for now)
21 MHz (13 meters) **21450-21850 kHz**

Rare Reception Daytime

25 MHz (11 meters) **25670-26100 kHz** (virtually no stations for now)

N. Carleton

Shortwave is a great way to teach youngsters history and current events, as PBS' "Where in The World Is Carmen Sandiego?" has shown. Teacher Neil Carleton poses with members of the Shortwave Listening Club at the G.L. Comba Public School in Almonte, Ontario, Canada. Carleton is expected to start another such club, his third, at the new school he'll be teaching at in 1997.

Does that mean you should avoid a tabletop or portatop model? Hardly, especially if you listen during the day, when signals are weaker, or to hard-to-hear stations. The best-rated tabletop, and even portatop, models can bring faint and difficult signals to life—especially when they're connected to a good external antenna. But if you just want to hear the big stations, you'll do fine with a moderately priced portable. PASSPORT REPORTS rates virtually all available models.

Radio in hand, read your owner's manual. You'll find that, despite a few unfamiliar controls, your new world band receiver isn't all that much different from radios you have used all your life. Experiment with the controls so you'll become comfortable with them. After all, you can't harm your radio by twiddling switches and knobs.

"Must" #5: Refer to PASSPORT

All right, you already know this. But it gives us an excuse to share with you a thought from one of our readers in Texas. He says that "PASSPORT is like a good barbecue pit. The more you use it, the better it gets."

Couldn't have put it better ourselves, except barbecue tastes better.

Prepared by Jock Elliott, Tony Jones and Lawrence Magne.

WiNRADiO
DIGITAL COVERAGE RADIO!

WiNRADiO, the ultimate computer controlled radio package. Covers 500kHz to 1.3GHz using internal receiver card and user friendly software. Controls at the click of a mouse or using a keyboard.

- Scan for exotic stations from faraway places.
- Eavesdrop on aircraft and maritime communications.
- Intercept clandestine stations.
- Monitor emergency services.
- Receive satellite and Space Shuttle signals.
- Witness combat transmissions making history.
- Unblocked versions are available for authorized users.

Your Window to the World!!!

WATSON

Power Supplies

Accurate RF meter with manual calibrations for measuring Forward Power, Reflected Power, and VSWR.

Scanning Antennas

Seeking to extend your receiver's range? These antennas are designed to bring you the best reception possible. High quality engineering and ergonomic design.

DAIWA

CN400 Series Power meters

CS201 Coaxial Switch

PS50TM Power Supply

Daiwa's Rugged, Reliable and Professional products: cavity switches, regulated power supplies, cross-needle meters, VHF/UHF amplifiers and more. Call for a catalog

LA2190HK Linear Amp

CN101 SWR Meter

Contact your favorite dealer today!!!

EDCO

**325 Mill Street
Vienna, VA. 22180
703.938.8105
FAX: 703.938.4525
http://www.elecdist.com**

First Tries:
Easy Catches

Here they are: ten different types of stations you can listen to right away in English. They're easy to tune, whatever your location, and provide a good sampling of what world band has to offer. All times are World Time.

EUROPE
France

Large and expanding, **Radio France Internationale** exists mainly to spread French language and culture throughout the world. Still, it has a scattering of English-language shows that cover matters ignored by most other media. They're not always audible at the most convenient times, but informative programs and polished presentation make this station worth flushing out.

North America: 1200-1255, year-round, on 13625 kHz; additionally, try 11615, 15325, 15530 or 17575 kHz. The 1600 broadcast to Africa is also sometimes audible in eastern North America; *see* below for details.

Europe: 1200-1255 on 9805, 15155 and 15195 kHz. The 1600 African Service is also on 6175 kHz for European listeners.

Middle East: 1400-1455 on 17560 kHz; 1600-1655 on 9485 or 11615 kHz, and 1600-1730 (targeted at East Africa) on 9485 or 15460 kHz.

Asia: 1200-1255 on 11600 kHz, and 1400-1455 on 7110 and 12030 (or 15405) kHz.

Africa: RFI's broadcasts for Africa are one of the best sources of news about that continent, and can often be heard well outside the intended target area. Audible at 1600-1655 on 6175, 11615, 11700, 12015 and 15530 kHz; and at 1600-1730 on one or more of: 11615, 15210 and 15460 kHz.

The BBC World Service's Outlook, an award-winning news and human-interest show, celebrates its 31st year on the air in 1997. John Tidmarsh has been soldiering with it from the outset. BBC

Filipino journalist Socorro Salcedo can be heard on Deutsche Well's Asia-Pacific Report, at least until sometime in 1996. "Soccy," who is a German-Asian exchange staffer, recently obtained her master's degree in journalism from Northwestern University in the United States.

Germany

Germany's mighty **Deutsche Welle** is respected as a thoroughly professional source of credible news and analysis. Particularly strong on European affairs, Deutsche Welle also offers insightful coverage of African and Asian events—a welcome change from the geographical myopia of many other news sources. Technical excellence combined with German professionalism make this "German Wave" a welcome player on the world band scene.

North and Central America: 0100-0150 winters on 5960, 6040, 6085, 6145, 9555, 9670 and 9700 kHz; summers on 6040, 6085, 6145, 9640 and 11740 kHz. The next edition is at 0300-0350: winters on 6045, 6085, 6120, 9530 and 9650 kHz; summers on 6085, 6185, 9535, 9615 and 9640 kHz. The third and final airing goes out at 0500-0550, winters on 5960, 6045, 6120 and 6185 kHz; and summers on 5960, 6045, 6185 and 9515 kHz. This last slot is best for western North America.

Europe: 2000-2050, winters on 5960 and 7285 kHz, and summers on 7170 and 9615 kHz.

Middle East: 0400-0450 on (winter) 6065 or (summer) 7150 kHz, 1600-1700 on 9735

kHz (intended for Africa), and 1900-1950 on (summer) 13690 or (winter) 13790 kHz.

Southern Africa: 0400-0450 winters on 6015, 6065, 7225, 7265 and 9565 kHz; summers on 5990, 6015, 7150, 7225, 9565 and 11765 kHz. The second slot is at 0900-0950 on 9565 (summer), 11725 (winter), 15145 (winter), 15225 (summer), 15410 and 21600 kHz; and the third and final broadcast goes out at 1600-1700 on 7185, 9735, 11965 and 17800 kHz.

Asia and the Pacific: 0900-0950 winters on 6160, 7380, 11715, 17780, 17820 and 21680 kHz; summers on 6160, 11730, 12055, 17715 and 21680 kHz. A second broadcast goes out at 2100-2150 on 7115 (summer), 9670, 9765 and 11785 kHz. There's also an additional transmission for South and Southeast Asia at 2300-2350, winters on 6000, 6160, 7150 and 7235 kHz; summers on 5980, 7235, 9690 and 12045 kHz.

Holland

Like modern Holland itself, **Radio Nederland**, or **Radio Netherlands**, earns high marks for its willingness to take risks by innovating. Programs are diced, sliced and tossed like salad, and there's also first-rate analysis of events in Europe and beyond. Thanks to several relay transmitters, you can hear this station from just about anywhere in the world.

North America: Easily heard throughout much of North America at 2330-0125 on 6020, 6165 and (summer) 9845 kHz. For western parts, try 0430-0525 on 5995 (or 9590) and 6165 kHz. Too, the broadcasts for Africa at 1830-2025 on 15315 and 17605 kHz are often well heard in parts of North America.

Europe: 1130-1325 winters on 6045 and 7190 kHz; 1030-1225 summers on 6045 and 9650 kHz.

Middle East: 1330-1425 on 13700 kHz.
Southern Africa: 1730-1925 on 6020 kHz.

High Dynamic Range Short Wave Receiver.
Designed & Built in the UK

✓ Wide frequency coverage 0-32MHz with DDS
✓ All mode reception; USB, LSB, CW, AM,
  Synchronous AM, NFM, DATA
✓ Advanced IP3 greater than +30dBm (+35dBm typical)
✓ High dynamic range >100dB (typical 104dB 20/40kHz)
✓ TCXO frequency standard fitted
✓ Variable bandwidth synchronous detector with
  selection of USB, LSB, DSB or anything in between
✓ Passband tuning approx ± 4.2kHz
✓ Re-configurable receiver, switch between several favourite setups
✓ Clock & timer facility
✓ Supplied with full function infrared hand control, PSU & manual

AOR LTD, 2-6-4 Misuji, Taito-Ku, Tokyo 111, Japan
AOR MANUFACTURING LTD, AOR (UK) LTD, 4E East Mill, Bridgefoot, Belper, Derbyshire DE56 2UA. England
Fax: +44 1773 880780   Tel: +44 1773 880788   info@aor.uk   http://www.demon.co.uk/aor

AOR®

Radio Netherlands' Anne Blair Gould hosts The Research File every Monday and Thursday. Before she joined the station, she taught biology at a private boy's school in England.

East Asia: 0930-1125 winters on 7260 and 9810 kHz, and summers on 12065 and 13705 kHz.

Australia and the Pacific: 0730-0825 on any two of the three channels 9700, 9720 and 11895 kHz; and 0830-0925 (extended to 1025 from April to September) on 9720 kHz. Too, the 0930-1125 broadcasts for East Asia are often heard in Australasia.

Russia

The **Voice of Russia** is today's reincarnation of the old Radio Moscow. But unlike its predecessor, it offers credible news and frank observations ("crime is so bad, they're even stealing the light bulbs"), as well as world-class music and entertainment. Incredibly, you can still hear the familiar booming voice of Joe Adamov, known to generations worldwide ever since he covered the siege of Moscow during World War II. Now, though, he tells not only the good, but also the bad and the ugly.

The station's staff and budget have shrunk since the end of the Cold War. Yet,

the Voice of Russia still manages to provide a listenable signal to most parts of the world—although in eastern North America it can be iffy.

Eastern North America: Reception quality varies, but best is usually late afternoon and early evening. Winter, try the following frequencies: 5940 (2230-2400 and 0300-0400), 7105 (2300-0600), 7125 (2300-0200), 7180 (1600-0100 and 0400-0600) and 7400 (2130-2300). Best summer channels are 7125 (2230-0100), 7230 (0300-0500), 7240 (2100-0300), 7250 (2100-2300 and 0000-0100), 9620 (0030-0500), 9665 (2030-0100) and 11750 (2100-2400). In addition, try the frequencies, given below, beamed to Europe—a number of them often make it to eastern North America. If you don't find anything on these channels, dial around nearby. The Voice of Russia is not renowned for sticking to its frequencies, but it tends to stay within the same segments of the world band spectrum.

Western North America: 0200-0800 (one hour earlier in summer). Reception is more reliable than out east, and channel usage is more predictable. Not all frequencies are in use for the entire period, but several of them are. In winter, choose from 5905, 5920, 5930, 7175, 7270, 7330, 7345, 9580, 12030 and 13640 kHz; for summer reception, try 12010, 12040, 12050, 13645, 13665, 15180 and 15580 kHz.

Europe: Nominally 1700-2300, but opens earlier on some channels. One hour earlier in summer. Best winter choices are in the 6, 7 and 9 MHz segments. Try 5940, 5995, 6055, 6130, 7180, 7205 and 9890 kHz. For summer, dial around the 7, 9, 11 and 15 MHz ranges; worth a look are 7240, 7250, 7350, 9480, 9665, 9880, 11630, 11675 and 15400 kHz. Times vary for each channel.

Middle East: 1400-2000 (one hour earlier in summer). Winter, try 6175, 7130, 7165, 7275, 9635, 11765 and 12065 kHz between 1400 and 1700; and 7210, 7255,

The ultimate veteran of international broadcasting is "Jolly Joe" Adamov, center, shown with Katherine Lawson and her husband. Ms. Lawson, who owns a store in Maine featuring Russian art and handicrafts, recently sponsored a trip bringing Adamov to a Monitoring Times convention in Atlanta. Adamov has been an English-language announcer at Radio Moscow, now the Voice of Russia, since the Germans attacked Russia in World War II.

9505 and 9585 kHz thereafter. Best summer bets can be found among 7225, 9595, 9830, 11775, 11835, 11945, 11960, 11985, 15320, 15350 and 15540 kHz. Times vary for each channel, and some frequencies carry languages other than English for part of the time.

Southern Africa: 1500-2100, although start time may be earlier in some cases. One hour earlier in summer. Channels can vary, but for winter try 7255, 7325, 9470 and 9505 kHz; in summer, go for 9975, 11765 and 11775 KHz. If these are unsatisfactory, dial around nearby. Too, some frequencies targeted at the Middle East are also audible in southern Africa.

East Asia: Alas, not much, because of few available transmitters in the Russian Far East. Try at 1000-1200 winter in the 5940-6060 kHz range, and 0900-1200 summer on 7150 kHz.

Australasia: 0600-1200. Winter on 9450, 12005, 12025, 15160, 15470, 17860, 17880 and 21790 kHz. Summer on 9835, 11800, 15490, 15560, 17570 and 17870 kHz. Not all frequencies are available for the full period.

Switzerland

Swiss Radio International offers solid, authoritative news, especially during the week. And because it is close to international agencies like the Red Cross, SRI covers topics conventional news media miss or gloss over, such as Third World and humanitarian issues. But if all this is

a bit heavy to digest after a day's work, try weekends, when the shows are lighter.

North America: 0100-0130 on 6135, 9885 and 9905 kHz; 0400-0430 on 6135 and 9885 kHz; and 0400-0500 on 9905 kHz.

Europe: (everything one hour earlier in summer) 0600-0615 and 0715-0730 on 6165 and 7410 (or 9535) kHz, 1100-1130 and 1300-1400 on 6165 and 9535 kHz; 1800-1830 on 7510 (or 9905) kHz, and 2000-2030 on 6165 kHz.

Middle East: 1700-1730 on 5850 (12075 in summer), 9885 and 13635 kHz.

Southern Africa: 0600-0630 on 11860 (or 12070) and 13635 kHz, and 2000-2030 on 9770 (or 9870), 9885, 9905 and 11640 kHz.

East and Southeast Asia: 1100-1130 on 9885 (winter), 11640 (winter), 13635 and (summer) 15415 and 17515 kHz; and 1300-1330 on 7230, 7480, 11640 (15480 in summer) and 13635 kHz.

Australasia: 0900-0930 on 9885, 11640 (17515 in summer) and 13685 kHz.

United Kingdom

Jewel in the crown? That's what people used to call the **BBC World Service**, but today some wonder whether a new management regime is bent on making the jewel into a zircon.

Few would dispute "the Beeb's" continuing status as the world's leading international broadcaster. For one thing, it is the organization most responsible for today's worldwide acceptance of Western political values and the English language.

Yet, in recent years the BBC World Service has had to endure a thankless series of Major budget cuts, the latest of which may result in a number of shows no longer even being produced by the World Service. Additionally, the station has stuck to an earlier decision to introduce "streaming"—different programs to different areas—despite howls from frustrated listeners.

But in this changed environment, technically savvy listeners are finding an unexpected bonus: BBC broadcasts targeted at other parts of the world sometimes provide better reception and different programming than those beamed to their area. This means you might be able to hear two or more different "streams" at the same time.

North America: Winter mornings, easterners can listen at 1100-1300 on 5965 kHz; 1300-1400 on 5965 and 9515 kHz; 1400-1600 on 9515 and 15260 kHz; and 1600-1715 on 9515 kHz. The summer schedule is 1000-1200 on 5965 kHz; 1200-1300 on 9515 kHz; 1300-1400 on 9515 and 11865 kHz; and 1400-1600 on 9515 (to 1615), 11865 and 15220 kHz. Listeners in or near the Caribbean area can tune in at 1000-1100 on 6195 kHz; 1200-1400 on 6195 and 15220 kHz; and 1400-1800 (1900 in winter) on 17840 kHz.

For winter reception in western North America, try 1300-1400 on 9740 and 15220 kHz; 1400-1600 on 15260 and 17840 kHz; and 1600-1900 on 17840 kHz. In summer, it's 1215-1300 on 15220 kHz; 1300-1600 on 9515, 11865, 15220 and (from 1400) 17840 kHz; and 1600-1800 on 17840 kHz.

Want to keep in touch with what's happening in the Islands? In eastern North America, go for 5975 kHz, or even 15390 or 17715 kHz, at 2100-2200. This slot contains the informative Caribbean Report, a one-of-a-kind show aired at 2115-2130 Monday through Friday.

Throughout the evening, most North Americans can listen in at 2200-0700 (0800 in winter) on a number of frequencies. Best bets are 5975, 6175, 7325 (2230-0330 winter), 9590 (to 0230 summer, 0330 winter) and 9640 kHz (0500-0800 winter). For the West Coast, 9640 kHz is also available at 0500-0815.

Europe: A slam-bang powerhouse 0300-2330 (one hour earlier in summer) on 3955 (winter), 6180, 6195, 7325, 9410,

Can't get enough Shortwave?

The one and only
Car World Band Receiver!

$549*

Detachable Security Face Plate

Becker Mexico 2340

Features:

AM, FM, LW, SW, 5.9 – 15.7 MHZ
Multicolor Display
Cassette Dolby B&C
CD Ready with Optional Becker 2630 or 2660
1 MHZ Tuning Shortwave
Presets: AM10, FM40, LW10, SW10

IT DOESN'T GET BETTER THAN THIS!

BECKER
AUTOMOTIVE SYSTEMS

*Plus Shipping and Handling

RJS Almost Direct
434 Ridgedale Ave. Suite 295
East Hanover, NJ 07936
email: RJSDRCT@aol.com

Questions: **201-428-2911**
Order: **800-RJS-DRCT**
(757-3728)

NHK

Radio Japan has superior coverage of Asian affairs. Here, Radio Japan journalists Eiji Miyagi (wearing glasses), Yoko Satake, Rika Kuwahara and Akemi Yoda cover a conference in Beijing, China.

12095 and 15070 kHz (times vary for each channel).

Middle East: 0300-2230 year-round. Key frequencies (times vary according to whether it is winter or summer) are 9410, 11760, 12095, 15070, 15575 and 17640 kHz.

Southern Africa: 0300-2200 on (among others) 3255, 6005, 6190, 9600, 11940, 15400, 21470 and 21660 kHz (times vary for each channel).

East Asia: 0000-0330 on 15360 kHz; 0330-0500 on 11955 and 15280 kHz; 0500-0900 on 9740, 11955, 15280 and (till 0800) 15360 kHz; 0900-1000 on 9740 and 17830 kHz; 1000-1100 on 6195, 9740 and 15360 kHz; 1100-1300 on 6195, 9740, 11955 and 15280 kHz; 1300-1615 on 6195 and 9740 kHz; and then on 3915 and 7180 kHz till 1745. Mornings, try 2000-2100 on 11955 kHz; 2100-2200 on 3915, 5990, 11945 and 11955 kHz; 2200-2300 on 6195, 7110 and 11955 kHz; and 2300-0030 on 6195, 9580, 11945 and 11955 kHz.

Australia and New Zealand: 0500-0600 on 11955 and 15360 kHz; 0600-0800 on 7145, 11955 and 15360 kHz; 0800-0900 on 11955 kHz; 0930-1030 (October to March) on 15280 kHz; 1100-1130 on 6100 or 9700 kHz; 1130-1615 on 9740 kHz; 1830-2000

on 9740 kHz; 2000-2200 on 9740 and 11955 kHz; and 2200-2400 on 11955 kHz. At 2200-2300, 9660 and 12080 kHz are also available for some parts of the region. From April to September, 6195 kHz is also in use at 0945-1615 and 2100-0200.

ASIA
Japan

With relay facilities on five continents, **Radio Japan** is no technological slouch. Yet, its shows have a strong Japanese flavor and, like the local food, are best digested in relatively small portions. Although best known as a source of up-to-the-minute Asian news, the station also offers a kaleidoscopic view of Japanese life and culture. Most transmissions last for an hour.

Eastern North America: 1100 on 6120 kHz, and again at 0300 (0100 summer) on 5960 kHz.

Western North America: 0100 and 0300 on 9605 (or 11790) and 11885 kHz; 0500 on 6110 kHz (may also be available winters on 9605 and 11885 kHz); 1400 on 9535 and 11705 kHz; and 1500, 1700 and 1900 on 9535 kHz. There is also a 30-minute broadcast to Hawaii, western North America and Central America at 0500-0530 on 11885, 11895 and 11960 (or 15230) kHz.

Europe: 0500 winter on 5975 or 6150 kHz, replaced summer by 7230 kHz; 0700 on 7230 kHz; and 2300 on 5965, 6055 or 6155 kHz.

Middle East: 0700 on 15165 kHz, and 1700 on 11930 kHz.

Southern Africa: 1500 on 15355 kHz.

Asia: 0100 on 11840, 11860, 11890 (or 11900), 11910, 17810 and 17845 kHz; 0300 on 11840 and 17810 kHz; 0500 on 11725, 11740 and 17810 kHz; 0600 on 11725 and 17810 kHz; 0700 on 11725, 11740, 17810 and 21610 kHz; 0900 on 6090 (or 9610) and 15190 kHz; 1100 on 6090 (or 9610)

RCSS™ REMOTE

RCSS™ Remote pictured with optional wideband receiver internally installed.

Simultaneous High Speed Data and Full Duplex Audio Over a Single Phone Line.

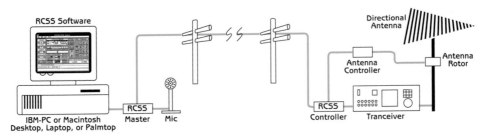

RCSS™ Remote provides a unique solution to remote systems control. It enables high speed data and full duplex wideband audio over any standard or cellular phone line. Audio and data are transferred simultaneously, not time sliced, providing true real time control.

Remote operation can be fully automated with RCSS™ software. A simple point and click graphical user interface via Microsoft Win-

dows™ provides quick learning and easy operation. RCSS™ software is also available separately to provide automated control of AOR and ICOM receivers, among others.

The RCSS™ master unit can be used with any serial terminal including desktops, laptops, and the new palmtops. RCSS™ Remote is housed in a rugged aluminum case for military style dependability. It is constructed using several processors and the latest DSP technology

available. All RCSS™ components are fully shielded from RF leakage. Power is supplied from either AC or DC sources for portability.

The RCSS™ modular design allows the configuration to be modified as user needs expand. Special user developed programs can be uploaded for custom applications.

For more information call, write, fax, or e-mail today. Or, via computer, visit our web page at http://www.sasiltd.com/sasi

SYSTEMS & SOFTWARE
INTERNATIONAL·LTD

Systems & Software International is in its 10th year, and manufactures all equipment in the USA. Please contact us at:
4639 Timber Ridge Drive, Dumfries, Virginia, 22026-1059, USA; **(703) 680-3559**; Fax (703) 878-1460; E-mail 74065.1140@compuserve.com

and 15350 kHz; 1400 on 6090 (or 9610), 11895 and 9695 (or 11915) kHz; 1500 on 7240 (or 11930) and 9695 (or 11915) kHz; 1700 on 6035 (or 6150), 7280 (or 11880) and 9580 kHz; 1900 on 6035 (or 6150) and 9580 kHz; 2100 on 6035, 7125 (or 9535) and 7140 (or 9560) kHz; and 2300 on 7125 (or 9535) and 7140 (or 9560) kHz. Transmissions to Asia are often heard in other parts of the world, as well.

Australasia: 0500 on 11920 kHz; 0600 on 11850 kHz; 0700 on 11850 and 11920 kHz; 0900 on 11850 kHz; 1900 on any two channels from 6035, 7140 and 11850 kHz; and 2100 and 2300 on 11850 kHz.

NORTH AMERICA
Canada

Despite one heart-stopping crisis after another, **Radio Canada International** continues to survive, much to the relief of its many faithful listeners. Although offering some of its own productions, crafted for an international audience, a razor-thin budget forces it to grab free domestic-service shows from its parent organization, the Canadian Broadcasting Corporation. While predominantly of interest to compatriots abroad, much of the output still appeals to non-Canadians.

North America: Morning reception is better in eastern North America than farther west, but evening broadcasts are easily audible in virtually the whole United States. Winters, the first daytime slot is at 1300-1400 on 9635 and 11955 kHz. This is followed Monday through Friday by 60 minutes of *The Best of Morningside*, and Sunday by the three-hour *Sunday Morning*, both on 9640 and 11955 kHz. In summer the same broadcasts go out one hour earlier on 9640 (except for 1300-1600 Sunday), 11855 and 13650 kHz. During winter, evening broadcasts air at 2300-0100 on 5960 and 9755 kHz; 0200-0300 on 5905, 6010 and 9755

kHz; and 0300-0400 on 6010 and 9755 kHz. The summer schedule is 2200-2400 on 5960, 9755 and 13670 kHz; 0100-0200 on 6120, 9755 and 13670 kHz; and 0200-0300 on 6120 (Sunday and Monday only), 9755 and 13670 kHz.

A 30-minute program for Canadian peacekeepers in Haiti goes out weeknights at 0300-0330 winter on 6010 and 9755 kHz; summer, it's one hour earlier on 6120, 9535 and 11715 kHz.

The evening transmission for Africa is also audible in parts of North America; winters at 2100-2230 on 13690, 15140 and 17820 kHz; and summers one hour earlier on 13670, 15150 and 17820 kHz.

Europe: Winters at 1430-1500 on 9555, 11915, 11935 and 15325 kHz; 1745-1800 (Monday through Friday only) on 5995, 9555, 11935, 15325 and 17820 kHz; 2100-2200 on 5925, 5995, 7260, 9805, 11945 and 13650 kHz; and 2200-2230 on 5995, 7260 and 9805 kHz. Summer broadcasts are one hour earlier: 1330-1400 Monday through Saturday on 17820 kHz, and daily on 11935, 15325 and 21455 kHz; 1645-1700 (Monday through Friday) on 9555, 11935, 15325 and 17820 kHz; and 2000-2130 on 5995, 7235, 11690, 13650 and 15325 kHz.

Europe, Middle East and Africa: There is a special program for Canadian peacekeeping forces which is broadcast winter weekdays at 0600-0630 on 6050, 6150, 9740, 9760 and 11905 kHz. Summers, it goes out one hour earlier on 6050, 7295, 15430 and 17840 kHz.

Middle East: Winters, at 0400-0430 on 6150, 9505 and 9645 kHz; 1430-1500 on 9555, 11935 and 15325 kHz; and 1745-1800 (Monday through Friday only) on 5995 and 9555 kHz. In summer, try 0400-0430 on 11835, 11905 and 15275 kHz; 1330-1400 on 15325 and 21455 kHz; 1645-1700 (weekdays only) on 9555 and 11935 kHz; and 2000-2130 on 5995 kHz.

Southern Africa: 2100-2230 winter (summer in Southern Hemisphere) on

The Voice of America covers African affairs far better than most. Here, Nigerian Nobel Laureate Wole Soyinka prepares for an interview to be aired worldwide. Soyinka, who fled Nigeria in 1994, also has appeared over the disestablishmentarian "Radio Democratic International Nigeria."

13690 and (to 2200) 15150 and 17820 kHz; and 2000-2130 summer on 13670, 15150 and 17820 kHz.

Asia: To East Asia at 1200-1230, winter on 6150 and 11730 kHz, and summer on 9660 and 15195 kHz; 1330-1400 on 6150 (summers on 11795) and 9535 kHz; to South Asia at 1630-1700 on 7150 and 9550 kHz; and to Southeast Asia at 2200-2230 on 11705 kHz.

United States

At one point after the end of the Cold War, the United States government turned inward so strongly that it almost extinguished the great **Voice of America**. But wiser voices finally prevailed, so gone is the specter of a Void of America.

Aside from its mainstream programming, "The Voice" offers popular regional variations like *Daybreak Africa* and the excellent *Report to the Americas.* Although targeted at Africa, Latin America, the Caribbean and the Pacific, these shows are widely heard elsewhere, including within the United States.

North America: The two best times to listen are when the VOA broadcasts to South America and the Caribbean: at 0000-0200 on 5995, 6130, 7405, 9455, 9775 and 13740 kHz (with 11695 at 0000-0100); and 1000-1200 on 6165, 7405 and 9590 kHz. The African Service can also be heard in much of North America. Best bets are 1600-1800 on 15410 and 15445 kHz, and 1800-2200 (Saturdays to 2130) on 15410 and 15580 kHz.

Europe lost its VOA channels to the financial axe in 1995, and was left to rely on broadcasts beamed to other areas. Try 0400-0700 on 7170 kHz, and 1700-2200 (summer only) on 9760 kHz. Other options include frequencies targeted at listeners in the Middle East—see below.

Middle East: 0400 (0500 in winter)-0600 on 15205 kHz; 1400-1500 (winter) on 15205 kHz; 1500-1800 on 9700 and 15205 kHz; 1700-1900 (winter) on 6040 kHz; 1900-2100 (winter) on 9585 kHz; and 1800-2100 (summer) on 9760 and 9770 kHz.

Southern Africa: 0300-0500 on 6080, 7280 and (to 0430) 7340 kHz; 0500-0630 (to 0700 weekends) on 6035 and 9630 kHz; 1600-2200 (to 2130 Saturday) on 7415, 11880 (or 11890), 11965 (or 11975), 13710, 15410, 15445, 15580 and 17895 kHz (not all available throughout the full broadcast).

Australasia: 1000-1200 on 5985, 11720 and 15425 kHz; 1200-1330 on 11715 and 15425 kHz, 1330-1500 on 15425 kHz; 1900-2000 on 9525, 11870 and 15180 kHz; 2100-2200 on 11870, 15185 and 17735 kHz; 2200-2400 on 15185, 15305 and 17735 kHz; and 0000-0100 on 15185 and 17735 kHz.

East Asia: 1100-1200 on 9760, 11720 and 15160 kHz; 1200-1330 on 9760, 11715 and 15160 kHz; 1330-1500 on 9760 and 15160 kHz; 2200-2400 on 15290, 15305, 17735 and 17820 kHz; and 0000-0100 on 15290, 17735 and 17820 kHz.

Where else but in America would one of the country's best international newscasters be a religious station? Yet, **Monitor Radio International** is just that, at least

Hear The Difference
Dual DSPs Make...

NIR-12 Dual DSP Noise Reduction Unit

NIR-12 Dual DSP Noise Reduction Unit

The NIR-12 is the most advanced DSP noise reduction unit available. Unparalleled performance, super-selective FIR filters, fully adjustable center frequency and bandwidth, **both Dynamic Peaking and Spectral Subtraction Noise Reduction**, spectral multi-tone NOTCH filter. All NIR-12 modes are usable simultaneously. Use on all operating modes including AMTOR and PACTOR. Installed between the receiver audio and external speaker. **$349.95**

Eliminate power line noise
before it enters the receiver

ANC-4 Antenna Noise Canceller

ANC-4 Antenna Noise Canceller

Eliminates power line noise before it enters the receiver to let you hear signals you did not know were there. Reduces any locally-generated noise typically 50dB. Useable between 100kHz and 80MHz. Noisewhip and wire antenna supplied with each unit. Auto xmit switchover up to 200W. Installed between the antenna and receiver. **$175.00**

 *JPS Communications Inc.*

P.O. Box 97757 ◆ Raleigh NC 27624-7757 ◆ USA
Tech Line: 919.790.1048 ◆ **Fax:** 919.790.1456 ◆ **Email:** jps@nando.net

ORDER LINE: 800.533.3819

http://emporium.turnpike.net/J/JPS/jps.html.

Adventist World Radio recently moved its office in Germany to historic Newbold College in England, shown here after a recent snowfall.

on weekdays. This station's international news fare, unembellished by audience-grabbing gimmicks, gives the much larger Voice of America a very good run for its money. Weekends, unfortunately for news hounds, the station airs mostly religious programming, from and about the Christian Science church.

Saturday through Monday, except for Australasia, some channels carry programs in languages other than English.

North America: In eastern North America, try 0000 on 7535 kHz; 1000, 1100 and 1200 on 6095 kHz; and 2100 on 9355, 11550 or 13770 kHz (depending on the time of year). Farther west, you can listen at 0100 on 7535 kHz, 0200 and 0300 on 5850 kHz, and at 1300 on 6095 kHz. Although beamed elsewhere, 9430 kHz also provides good reception in parts of North America at 0000-0300.

Europe: 0400, 0500, 0600, 0700, 0800 and 0900 on 7535 kHz (with 15665 kHz also available at 0800); 1800 and 1900 on

any two frequencies from 9355, 9370, 13770 and 15665 kHz; 2000 and 2100 on any two of 7510, 9355, 11550, 13770 and 15665 kHz; and 2200 and 2300 on 7510 or 13770 kHz.

Middle East: 1800 and 1900 on (winters) 9355 or (summers) 13770 kHz.

Southern Africa: 0300 on 7535 kHz (beamed to East Africa); 0400 on 9840 kHz; and 1600, 1700 and 1800 on 17510 or 18930 (or 21640) kHz. 9355 kHz is also available at 1600 and 1700.

East Asia: 0900 and 1000 on 9430 kHz; 1100, 1400 and 1500 on 9355 kHz; 2200 and 2300 on (winter) 9430 or (summer) 15405 or 15665 kHz. The 2200 broadcast is also available year-round on 13840 kHz.

Australasia: 0800 on 9425 or 13615 kHz; 0900 on 13615 kHz; 1000 on 13625 or 13840 kHz; 1100 and 1200 on 9425 or 9430 kHz; 1800 winter (summer in the Southern Hemisphere) on 9355 kHz; 2000 summer on 9570 or 11550 kHz; 2100 on 13840 kHz; and 2300 on 13625 kHz.

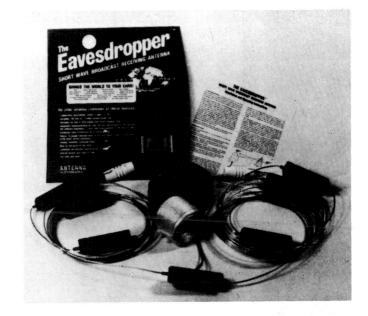

Sports commmentators Jim "The Huge One" Rome and Lee "Hacksaw" Hamilton are top rated in the San Diego, California, market over XTRA AM-690, transmitting from Mexico. They can now be heard around the world weekdays over Internet RealAudio, URL http://www.audionet.com.

Fat Lady's Arm Bowls with Chickens

The impact on programming is already beginning to be felt. On a recent talk show over Salt Lake City's KCNR, the host spoke approvingly of the "Fat Lady's Arm" pub in New Zealand providing frozen chickens to clients for use as bowling balls.

Why? Because, he indicated, the station knows it has a significant Web radio audience in New Zealand from all the e-mail it gets, and the use of chickens as bowling balls has outraged some animal-rights activists in that country.

RealAudio A Snap to Use

Web radio derived from the thinking of Philadelphia's Howard Morgan and others who envisioned using advanced compression techniques to shoehorn audio through the Internet. What was originally envisioned was an Internet telephone service as an alternative to long-distance providers.

But while the phone idea became mired down in technical and legal issues, Progressive Networks in Seattle created RealAudio, a freebie software package to carry low-fidelity audio through the Internet. Originally operating at no more than 14.4 kilobaud, like many new computer applications it tended to disappoint once the novelty wore thin. Even ordinary talk could be difficult to understand, and music was hopeless.

But now it's also operating at 28.8 kilobaud, the rate used by today's modems, with results improved to the point where the future is clear. Before long, bandwidth, or throughput, will be increased to where compression can be less severe. Then, audio via the Internet will be a serious competitor for the ears of millions.

RealAudio's listening quality at 14.4 kb

is comparable to a mediocre world band signal, whereas at 28.8 kb this becomes fair-to-good by world band standards. Because of the extreme compression used, signals at either rate tend to sound "wavery," like a shortwave signal suffering from heavy flutter fading. This means that talk over 28.8 kb is almost completely intelligible, whereas music is, well, tolerable.

RealAudio's high cards are simplicity and reliability. Once you get to a station's Web site (see accompanying listing), all you do is click onto the RealAudio or other obvious icon, and in seconds the

Must Haves

To get started in style, go for:

• A suitable operating system, with Windows 95 and Windows NT being excellent choices. If your computer will handle these, it will also handle the requirements of Web radio. Most PCs now come with Windows 95 installed.

• Sound Blaster or other audio board, along with suitable drivers/software. PCs typically come bundled with these. Separate, figure $90–300 for the board, plus an hour of tech time for installation if you don't do it yourself.

• Amplified computer speakers or headphones. Around $60.

• A 28.8 kb modem. A 14.4 kb modem will allow you to receive some of Web radio's offerings, but the result will probably disappoint. Many computers come bundled with internal 28.8 kb modems; otherwise, figure $100–300.

• An Internet provider that operates fully at 28.8 kb or better. Our tests show that some providers are better than others, with certain of the major providers, such as CompuServe, being unable to handle Web radio properly. Remember, if you're going to listen for hours on end, local phone-line charges can add up, so having a flat-fee line for unlimited calling to your provider may make good sense.

• Microsoft Explorer (http://www.microsoft.com/ie) or Netscape Navigator (http://www.netscape.com) software. Versions 3.x of both of these were in beta stages when we tested, and both work fine, as does Netscape 2.0. Microsoft Explorer, which has sprung to life in its v3.0 incarnation, already comes free with Windows 95 and NT, and is easy to upgrade online. Early versions of Netscape Navigator are also downloadable for free, but best if you prefer Netscape is to cough up for the latest version—under $50.

• RealAudio software. The latest version, currently 2.0, as well as the old v1.0 can be downloaded for free from Web radio sites, or by going to http://www.realaudio.com.

• StreamWorks software is also downloaded free from its clients' Web radio sites, or by going to http://www.xingtech.com or http://streamworks.com.

• Zip/unzip software to download audio material on file. This software can be downloaded automatically for free, when needed, from Web radio sites, if you don't already have it.

• Anti-virus software, such as the excellent Norton AntiVirus (http://www.symantec.com), under $80. Downloading files from the Internet can introduce catastrophic viruses into your computer, so this is a "must." Even downloading zip/unzip shareware has been known to introduce viruses, so get this first!

station is booming away and stays locked in. A handy volume control appears on the screen, too, and with Windows can be brought back up at any time just by clicking the RealAudio button on the taskbar at the bottom of the screen.

StreamWorks: Superior Sound, Intricate Operation

A second major Web radio player is StreamWorks, created by Xing Technology of Arroyo Grande, California, which is also venturing into video offerings. It operates audio from 14.4 to 112 kb, with the highest rate being for dual-channel ISDN connections. Its audio fidelity, baud-for-baud, is much better than RealAudio's—anywhere from poor-to-good at 14.4 kb, fair-to-very good at 28.8 kb.

But at the default settings, there are more dropouts—brief interruptions of silence. These are reduced, but not eliminated completely, if you click on the "Advanced" button in the Setup menu, then raise the MPEG Audio Buffer by a healthy amount.

However, it is far less user friendly than RealAudio, and disconnects are much more common. To make matters worse, twice after StreamWorks disconnected, using Windows 95 and the beta version 2 of Microsoft Explorer 3.0, on one configuration—but not others—we encountered system crashes. However, version 2.0 is just now being released and may resolve these difficulties. Perhaps for these reasons, StreamWorks hasn't caught on as well as RealAudio.

Both RealAudio and StreamWorks suffer from audible harmonic distortion. However, this diminishes with bandwidth.

Who Listens and Who Pays?

Right now, Web radio is about where wireless radio was back in the 1920s and early Thirties. It's new, it's exciting, and starting to catch on beyond the *cognoscenti*. But like early radio, Web radio hasn't quite yet found its economic moorings.

One plus for existing broadcasters is that out-of-pocket costs to relay over the Internet are minimal. But those whose programming is custom-made for the Internet are stuck having to cover every dollar from income generated over the 'Net.

For Web radio distributors, however, things are tougher. Take AudioNet, currently the big enchilada in the field. Right now, it takes in zero income, but still the bills have to be paid. Their envisaged solution is eventually to take in "banner" and other ads, like various firms already do on their Web pages. Whether this will be economically viable remains to be seen, but from this may emerge diverse forms of revenue generation: fees from stations or listeners, software and other sales to listeners, or air time leased to non-broadcasting organizations. If the economic creativity in this field can approach its technological prowess, viable answers will be found.

Audience characteristics point to some possible solutions. Where Web radio excels is not so much in reaching established listeners. Rather, it shines by carrying existing, altered or entirely original programming to new niche audiences.

Take the typical American family, for example. It moves, on the average, once every five years. Much of this is from town-to-town, so over time they form affinities with cities and regions often not otherwise audible except over the Web.

For starters, young adults from the American Midwest have long moved away in droves to find greater economic opportunity out on the coasts. Yet, their hearts remain in Kansas, Minnesota or the Texas Panhandle. It's precisely this group which accounted for the unexpected success of public radio's "Prairie Home Companion."

Ditto Filipinos, Greeks, Palestinians and others who migrate to various parts of the globe in search of economic opportunity or political freedom.

While most local advertisers couldn't care less about these "expats," there are economic interests—gift vendors, sports teams, charities, universities with diaspora alumni—which stand to profit from reaching Web radio audiences.

Winners and Losers: A Non-Zero-Sum Game

Will Web radio replace world band for over-the-air broadcasting?

Given the history of similar situations, it's hardly likely, at least anytime soon. When direct satellite radio became feasible, predictions immediately sprung up that this would replace world band, probably before the end of the Nineties. That was several years ago, but direct satellite simply hasn't caught on as a mass delivery medium for radio. However, it has brought high-quality audio to serve niche audiences, and in the process hasn't diminished listenership to world band, which continues to grow.

Similarly, after the end of the Cold War, program placement, or relaying international broadcasts over local AM/FM stations or cable systems, was seen as the "new wave." Placement has indeed been more successful in reaching audiences than direct satellite delivery. But far from diminishing world band listening, by making international programs more visible it has actually served to bring new listeners to world band.

For obvious reasons, this has been true in those target areas where the "plug might be pulled" on controversial broadcasts, which are often the very ones that form the raison d'être for official international broadcasting. But this has also been true in North America, where censorship is virtually unknown.

With local placement and Web radio, bandscanning—channel surfing—is extremely difficult. While the proportion of international listening done by bandscanning is lower than that done by those tuning directly to stations they want, it is a more popular means of tuning than many realize. World band is ideal for this.

Web Radio = Wired Radio

Web radio also stands out because it is wired radio—plugged into a fixed site, like a tabletop radio. But the vast majority of radio listening is done on portables or car radios. Indeed, in the Nineties nearly all growth in world band radio sales has been in portables, whereas sales of tabletop receivers—never big sellers even in the best of times—have declined both in market share and in absolute numbers. Mediumwave AM/FM radio sales have followed a similar trajectory.

Web radio is wired radio, which in simpler forms is nothing new. Historically, in communities where both wired and wireless radio have carried comparable material, people who can afford wireless radio have sprung for it nearly every time.

But Web radio is here, and can be used to full advantage with the growing installed base of personal computers. Because, unlike over-the-air radio, it can carry an almost unlimited number of stations, it can tap the vast market of homesick folks and others afar who wish to keep in touch with news, chat and sports in faraway local communities. And while its offerings today are limited, and audio quality often worse than world band, Web radio appears to be poised for solid growth in the years to come.

Prepared by the staff of PASSPORT TO WORLD BAND RADIO. Our thanks to AudioNet, Buckingham Computers, Comcat, Inc., and David Walcutt.

 **RADioNet**

BETA TEST VERSION 0.95

ABC RADIO NEWS ON THE HOUR

LOCAL NEWS SUMMARY
(CHOOSE CITY)

 **NEWSFLASH!**

Troops in Saudi Arabia may be relocated

SAN FRANCISCO   CHICAGO   NEW YORK

LOS ANGELES

ABCNEWS
WORLD NEWS TONIGHT

THIS WEEK WITH DAVID BRINKLEY

PETER JENNINGS' JOURNAL

HUGH DOWNS' PERSPECTIVE

The Best of Hugh Downs' "Perspective"

 THE BUZZ
COOL CLIPS

Need a laugh?
tHe buZz is the place!

 SOUNDBOX

Entertainment & computer news

 VIEWPOINT

Opinions and commentary

 INSIDE WASHINGTON

Capital news, and Whitewater & Filegate Updates

NATIONAL SPORTS NEWS
The latest headlines & commentary

NATIONAL WEATHER FORECAST
Temperatures & Conditions

 **BusinessWeek RadioNet**

 **MONEYTALK**

Questions? Comments? Send email to ABC RadioNet
(c)1996 ABC Radio Networks, Inc.

Web Radio II:
Where to Listen

*H*ere's where to tune in Web radio—wherever you live—using an ordinary telephone line and a modem.

Wherever possible, we show several Web sites, or URLs, to increase the odds your server will digest at least one. If not, the server may be unable to make a direct connection, or the URL details may have been altered. Use Excite, Alta Vista or another search engine, or shorten the URL by a segment or two. Otherwise, attempt again later, as the station may be off the air or encountering technical difficulties, which are most common weekends.

Most Web radio stations operate live, some offer only archival audio, and a few helpful stations offer both. Some university stations are inactive during school holidays, and a few stations aren't daily. NetRadio Network (USA) and Station "i" (Japan) are also included as examples of non-broadcasters "broadcasting" on the Web.

Where a city is given, that's a local station. Information on selected Web radio stations—languages, home pages, e-mail, postal addresses, fax numbers, phone lines, personnel, giveaways and more—are in PASSPORT's "Addresses PLUS" section, icons ▣ and ▣.

Feedback and updates? Your thoughts on Web radio? They're always welcomed at e-mail mwk@passport.com or fax +1 (215) 598 3794. Enjoy!

Prepared by the staff of PASSPORT TO WORLD BAND RADIO.

Where do you go for great country music, blues and rock? Why, Australia, of course! Sydney's KICK pulses away 24 hours a day, allowing it to be heard on Web radio anytime, anywhere.

AUSTRALIA
Fox-FM, Melbourne—http://www.fox.com.au/
KICK-AM, Sydney—http://www.kick-am.com.au/
Radio Australia—http://www.wrn.org/stations/abc.html
3ZZZ-FM, Melbourne—http://www.sustance.com/catalan/index.html

AUSTRIA
Österreichischer Rundfunk-Blue Danube Radio—http://www.wrn.org/stations/danube.html
Radio Austria International—http://www.wrn.org/stations/orf.html

BELGIUM
Radio Vlaanderen Internationaal—http://www.wrn.org/stations/rvi.html

France's Europe 2 has a highly rated Web site, and includes such on-air personalities as Géraldine Carre (right), heard each weekday afternoon, Paris time.

BRAZIL
Radio Jornal UFPE, Recife—(unconfirmed, site under construction) http://www.df.ufpe.br or http://www.radio-jornal.df.ufpe.br

CANADA
CBC—(general) http://www.cbc.ca/; ("Quirks and Quarks") http://www.radio.cbc.ca/radio/programs/current/quirks/
CBC Stereo—http://www.cbcstereo.com/RealTime/soundz/realaudio/ra_menu.html
CFRA, Ottawa ON (news/talk)—http://www.cfra.com/
CFTR, Toronto (news)—http://www.canoe.ca/680News/streamworks.html
CHMB, Vancouver BC (Chinese)—http://www.am1320.com/live/index.htm
CHOG-Talk 640, Toronto (news/talk)—http://www.audionet.com/ or http://207.113.204.163/pub/talk640/talk640.htm
CHOZ, St. John's NF (rock)—http://www.ozfm.newcomm.net/
CHUM, Toronto ON (rock)—http://www.1050chum.com/1050-7/1050-7b.html
CILQ-Q107, Toronto ON (rock)—http://www.q107.com/, http://207.113.204.163/pub/q107/q107.htm or http://www.audionet.com/
CKNW, Vancouver BC (sports)—http://www.cknw.com/onair/index.htm
CKUA, Calgary AB (rock)—http://www.cadvision.com/ckua/
Radio Canada International-CBC—http://www.wrn.org/stations/rci.html

CHINA
FM Select—http://www.metroradio.com.hk or http://www.asiaonline.net/metro
Hong Kong Commercial Radio—http://www.asiaonline.net/comradio/lt881.htm
Radio Television Hong Kong—http://www.wrn.org/stations/rthk.html

CHINA (TAIWAN)
International Community Radio—http://www.icrt.com.tw/FFen_live.html

CZECH REPUBLIC
Kiss 88.3 FM Hády, Brno (?)—http://www.cz./cgi-bin/cz?asc=/ra/default.html
Radio Prague—http://www.radio.cz or http://www.wrn.org/stations/prague.html

FINLAND
KissFM, Helsinki—http://www.kiss.fi/welcome.shtml
Radio Moro, Tampere—http://www.alexpress.fi/moro/

FRANCE
Europe 2 (for now, audio clips only)—http://www.europe2.fr/radioclip/index.html
France 3 (TV audio)—http://www.sv.vtcom.fr/ftv/
Radio France (France info, etc.)—(browser must support Java) http://www.radio-France.fr/

Italy's national broadcaster, RAI, is now on Web radio in Italian, at http://www.rai.it/grr/. English is expected to follow shortly.

Radio France Internationale—http://www.wrn.org/stations/rfi.html
Wit-FM, Gironde (Bordeaux-Médoc)—http://www.quaternet.fr:8081/live/ecoute1.html

GERMANY
Bayerischer Rundfunk-Bayern 5—http://mats.gmd.de/BR5/.bin/br5mail
Deutsche Welle—http://www.dmc.net/dw/dw.html; http://mainnet.dmc.net/dw/dw.html; or http://www.wrn.org/stations/dw.html

HOLLAND (THE NETHERLANDS)
May reactivate RealAudio service:
Radio Netherlands--http://www.rnw.nl/rnw

HUNGARY
Radio Budapest— http://www.wrn.org/stations/hungary.html

IRELAND
Radio Telefís Eireann—http://www.wrn.org/stations/rte.html

ISRAEL
Kol Israel—http://www.artificia.com/html.news.cgi

ITALY
Radiolina, Sardinia—http://www.vol.it/RADIOLINA/index.htm
Radiopadova, Padova—http://intercity.shiny.it/radiopd/rpdlive.html
Radio Stereo 5, Cuneo—http://www.cuneo.alpcom.it/azi/stereo5.html
Radio X, Cagliari—http://www.vol.it/UK/EN/SPETTACOLI/RADIOX/
RTV Italiana-RAI—http://www.rai.it/grr/

JAPAN
JOAV— "J-WAVE", Tokyo—http://www.infojapan.com/JWAVE/
JOER—"RCC RADIO", Hiroshima (during baseball games only)—http://www.rcc-hiroshima.co.jp/
JOFV, Osaka—http://www.fm802.co.jp/textindex.html
Station "i", Kyoto (Web-only radio)—http://www.age.or.jp/station-i/

KOREA (REPUBLIC)
Radio Korea International—http://www.wrn.org/stations/kbs.html
YTN (TV audio)—http://www.ytn.co.kr/ytn10.htm

MALAYSIA
RTM-Radio Malaysia, Kuala Lumpur—http://www.asiaconnect.com.my/rtm-net/live/
Time Highway Radio, Kuala Lumpur—http://thr.time.com.my/

NORWAY
Radio Hele Norge-P4—(audio unconfirmed) http://www.p4.no/
RaDIO TaNGO, Oslo—http://www.riksnett.no/radiotango/

PARAGUAY
Stations that could activate Web radio in 1997 (use search engine or e-mail):
Radio Cardinal AM, ZP7
Radio Libre
Radio Ñandutí, ZP14
Radio Ñandutí FM Concert, ZPV14

POLAND
Polish Radio Warsaw—http://www.wrn.org/stations/poland.html

PORTUGAL
Rádio Comercial, Lisbon—http://www.radiocomercial.pt/audio/audio.html
Televisão Independente-TVi (TV audio)—http://cibertribe.pt/tvi/versao2x/mainframe.html

ROMANIA
Radio România International—http://www.wrn.org/stations/romania.html

RUSSIA
Voice of Russia—http://www.wrn.org/stations/vor

London's The Phoenix is owned by none other than Virgin Records. It's one of the best Web radio sites around for hearing what's up-and-coming in today's music.

Here's one you *gotta* hear! California's KPIG offers an ingenious mix of rock, folk and country to a self-described audience of piggies and piglets. Now heard worldwide on Web radio, "107 oink 5" has some of the best music and presentations on the air anywhere. It's CyberSwine Web radio site is no slouch, either—PASSPORT staffers rate it *número uno.*

SOUTH AFRICA
Channel Africa—http://www.wrn.org/stations/
africa.html
SPAIN
Catalunya Ràdio, Barcelona—http://
www.catradio.es/cr/cr-ecr00.html
SWEDEN
Bandit 105.5, Stockholm—http://www.bandit.se/
Power 106, Stockholm—http://
www.power106.telegate.se/live.html
Radio Rix, Stockholm—http://www.everyday.se/
radiorix/
Radio Sweden—http://www.wrn.org/stations/rs.html
or http://www.sr.se/rs/index.htm
SWITZERLAND
Radio Zürisee, Rapperswil—http://www.world.ch/
radio/online/
UNITED KINGDOM
BBC World Service—for now, only a brief and
probably temporary audio clip from the "Neil Show"
at http://www.bbc.co.uk/andrewneil/, but site worth
an occasional perusal for increased activity

Satellite Media Services—http://www.sms.co.uk/
real.html
Virgin Radio, London—http://
www.virginradio.co.uk/home.html
World Radio Network (major hyperlink)—http://
www.wrn.org or http://town.hall.org/radio
UNITED NATIONS
United Nations Radio—http://www.nexus.org/IRN/
index.html or http://www.wrn.org/stations/un.html
USA
LOCAL STATIONS
Alabama
WZZK, Birmingham (country)—http://
www.bhm.tis.net/wzzk/audio/audio.htm
Arkansas
KXRJ, Russellville (college sports, jazz, classical,
alternative)—http://broadcast.atu.edu/index.htm
California
KAVL, Lancaster (metro Los Angeles; sports)—http:/
/www.audionet.com or http://207.113.204.163/pub/
kavl/kavl.htm

KBLA, Los Angeles (Korean)—http://radiokorea.com/homepage/radioko.htm, http://207.113.204.163/pub/kbla/kbla.htm or http://www.audionet.com/

KCR, San Diego (rock)—http://www.kcr.sdsu.edu/kcr/ or http://www.kcrw.org/

KFMB, San Diego (rock)—http://www.histar.com/home_af.html

KHJJ—"KHJ", Lancaster (metro Los Angeles; news/talk)—(possibly to activate shortly) http://www.audionet.com/

KKLA, Los Angeles (religious)—http://www.kkla.com

KNBR, San Francisco (sports/talk/personality)—(possibly to activate shortly) http://www.audionet.com/

KOME, San Jose (rock)—(possibly to activate shortly) http://www.audionet.com/

KPIG, Freedom (metro San Jose/Santa Cruz; rock/folk)—http://www.kpig.com/welcome.htm or http://kpig.com/live1.htm

KRSI—"Radio Sedaye Iran", Santa Monica (Persian)—(possibly to activate shortly) http://www.krsi.com/

KUSF, San Francisco (alternative, community)—http://www.audionet.com/pub/kusf/kusf.htm; http://138.202.168.1/busstop/; http://web.usfca.edu/kusf/

KWBR, Arroyo Grande (rock)—http://www.xingtech.com/streams/index.html

KWNK, West Hills (metro Los Angeles; sports)—http://207.113.204.163/pub/kwnk/kwnk.htm or http://www.audionet.com/

KZAP, Chico (rock)—http://www.kzap.com/live.html

XHRM—"The Flash", San Diego/Mexico (rock)—http://www.theflash.com/

XTRA, San Diego/Mexico (sports)—http://www.xtrasports.com/, http://207.113.204.163/pub/xtra/xtra.htm or http://www.audionet.com/

XTRA—XETRA "91X", San Diego/Mexico (rock)—http://www.91x.com/

Connecticut
WKSS, Meriden-Hartford (rock)—http://www.kiss957.com/

WGCH, Greenwich (community)—(active as of presstime) http://www.internetwork.com/

District of Columbia
(Also, see Maryland)
WMET (news/talk)—http://www.audionet.com/ or http://207.113.204.163/pub/wmet.htm

Florida
WAVQ, Inglis FL (easy listening)—http://www.relax.com/

WFLA, Tampa (news/talk)—(possibly to activate shortly) http://www.audionet.com/

WPSL, Port St. Lucie (news/talk)—http://www.wpsl.com/ or http://www.audionet.com/pub/wpsl/wpsl.htm

WQAM, Hollywood (metro Miami; sports)—http://www.audionet.com/pub/wqam/wqam.htm or http://204.58.152.70/pub/WQAM/WQAM.htm

Illinois
WEBX, Champaign-Urbana (post-modern rock)—http://www.webxfm.com/webaudio.html

WMVP, Chicago (sports)—http://www.audionet.com/ or http://207.113.204.163/pub/wmvp/wmvp.htm

WVVX/WKTA, Highland Park-Evanston (metro Chicago; Rebel Radio-heavy metal rock)—http://www.rebelradio.com/

Indiana
WIBC, Indianapolis (news/talk)—http://www.audionet.com/ or http://207.113.204.163/pub/wibc/wibc.htm

WUEV, Evansville (jazz and blues, university sports, international broadcasts via World Radio Network)—http://www.evansville.edu/~wuevweb/

Kansas
KCTV, Kansas City (TV audio)— http://www.kctv.com/

KJHK, Lawrence (KU sports, Kansas news)—(hopes to offer RealAudio or StreamWorks before long; currently audible via arcane audio systems; e-mail comments via Web site) http://www.cc.ukans.edu/~kjhknet/tune-in.html

Louisiana
KLSU, Baton Rouge (alternative rock, LSU sports)—http://www.cyberview.net/klsu/ or http://www.audionet.com/pub/lsu/lsu.htm

WWOZ, Metairie (metro New Orleans; jazz and blues)—http://nt.accesscom.net/wwoz/ or http://www.audionet.com/

Maryland
WBAL, Baltimore (news/talk)—http://wbal.com/, http://www.wbal.com/, http://207.113.204.163/pub/wbal/wbal.htm or http://www.audionet.com/

WTEM, Bethesda (metro Washington DC; sports)—http://www.wtem.com/, http://207.113.204.163/pub/wtem/wtem.htm or http://www.audionet.com/

Michigan
WKFR, Battle Creek-Kalamazoo (post-modern rock; sound clips, mainly for potential advertisers, with occasional live audio)—http://www.wkfr.com/

WKZO, Kalamazoo (business-farm-financial-sports news, Chamber of Commerce, talk)—http://www.kazoobiz.com/enterp/kzo.htm

WRKR, Kalamazoo (rock; sound clips only)—http://www.wrkr.com/

Mississippi
WHJT, Clinton-Jackson (religious)—http://www.mc.edu/~alive935/live.html

University of Kansas Jayhawk sports, along with Kansas news, can be heard over KJHK, Lawrence. Right now, you need special equipment, but they're hoping to add RealAudio or StreamWorks soon so more PC owners can tune in.

New Orleans is *the* home for jazz and blues, and WWOZ brings it to the world live on the Web. There's a menu of pre-recorded music, as well.

Missouri
KCTV, Kansas City (TV audio)— http://www.kctv.com/
KXOK, St. Louis (urban/soul)—http://www.kxok.com/ or http://www.audionet.com/

Nevada
KOOL, Las Vegas (rock)—http://www.vegasradio.com/kool.html

New Jersey
WJUX, Dumont-Fort Lee (big band, '40s and '50s pop)—(possibly to activate shortly) http://www.audionet.com/
WKXW/WBBS, Trenton-Millville-Atlantic City (New Jersey news, traffic and weather; personal talk; classic rock)—http://www.nj1015.com/

New York
(Also, see New Jersey)
WAMC, Albany (news/talk)—http://www.audionet.com/pub/wamc/wamc.htm
WBBR, New York (news/talk)—http://www.bloomberg.com/wbbr/
WFAS, White Plains (rock)—(active as of presstime) http://www.internetwork.com/
WGR, Buffalo (sports)—http://ns1.moran.com/htmld/ wgr55/, http://207.113.204.163/pub/wgr/wgr.htm or http://www.audionet.com/
WOR, New York (news/talk)—http://www.audionet.com/ or http://207.113.204.163/pub/wor/wor.htm

North Carolina
WRAL, Raleigh (easy listening)—http://www.wralfm.com/, http://207.113.204.163/pub/wral/wral.htm or http://www.audionet.com/
WXYC, Chapel Hill (eclectic rock, talk in university environment)—http://sunsite.unc.edu/wxyc/index.html

Ohio
WCLT, Newark-Columbus (country)—http://www.wclt.com/realaudio.htm
WKSU, Kent (classical, National Public Radio news and analysis)—http://www.wksu.kent.edu/
WLVQ, Columbus (rock)—http://www.qfm96.com/home.html
WTUE, Dayton (rock; ABC news headlines and musical clips only)—http://arsdayton.com/wtue.html
WZOO, Ashtabula (light rock)—http://www.knownet.net/wzoo.htm

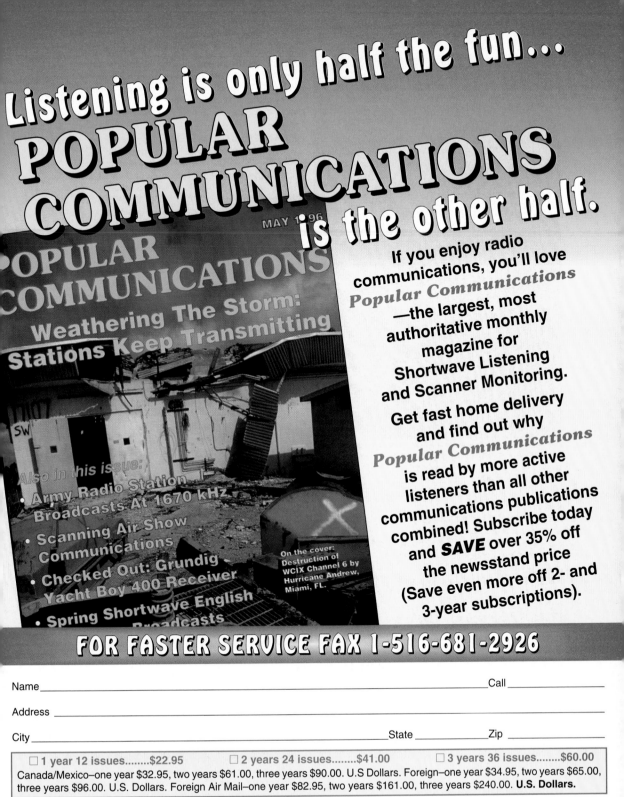

Stacey West brings country music and Texas kick to the world each weekday over Dallas' popular KPLX, now on Web radio.

Oklahoma
KTRT, Tulsa (news/talk)—http://www.ktrt.com/home.html, http://207.113.204.163/pub/ktrt/ktrt.htm or http://www.audionet.com/

Oregon
KBNP, Portland (business news)—http://www.teleport.com/~kbnp, http://207.113.204.163/pub/kbnp/kbnp.htm or http://www.audionet.com/
KFXX, Portland (sports)—http://www.kfxx.com/, http://207.113.204.163/pub/kfxx/kfxx.htm or http://www.audionet.com/
KGON, Portland (oldies)—http://www.kgon.com/, http://207.113.204.163/pub/kgon/kgon.htm or http://www.audionet.com/
KNRK, Portland (alternative rock)—http://www.knrk.com/, http://207.113.204.163/pub/knrk/knrk.htm or http://www.audionet.com/

Pennsylvania
WRRK, Pittsburgh (oldies)—http://www.rrk.com/live.htm, http://207.113.204/163/pub/wrrk/wrrk.htm or http://www.audionet.com

Tennessee
WHBQ, Memphis (sports)—http://www.audionet.com/ or http://207.113.204.163/pub/whbq/whbq.htm

WRLT, Nashville (rock)—http://wrlt.com/, http://www.wrlt.com/ or http://www.audionet.com/
WRVR, Memphis (adult contemporary)—http://www.audionet.com/ or http://207/113/204/163/pub/wrvr/wrvr.htm

Texas
KAAM, Plano (metro Dallas; easy listening)—http://www.audionet.com/pub/kaam/kaam.htm
KALK—"KLAKE", Winfield-Mt. Pleasant (easy listening)—http://www.1starnet.com/clients/klake/klake, http://206.103.100.4/clients/klake/livefeed.html, http://207.113.204.163/pub/klake/klake.htm or http://www.audionet.com/
KDGE, Dallas (alternative rock)—http://www.kdge.com/kdge/, http://207.113.204.163/pub/edge/edge.htm or http://www.audionet.com/
KGSR, Austin (adult alternative)—(possibly to activate shortly) http://www.audionet.com/
KHCB, Houston (religious)—http://www.khcb.org/
KKDA—"K104", Grand Prairie (metro Dallas; urban/soul)—http://www2.k104.com/k104.html or http://www.audionet.com/
KKMY, Beaumont (adult contemporary)—(possibly to activate shortly) http://www.audionet.com/
KLIF, Dallas (news/talk/sports)—http://www.klif.com/ or http://www.audionet.com/pub/klif/kliflive.htm
KLLL, Lubbock (country)—http://www.klll.com/
KLVI, Beaumont (news/talk)—(possibly to activate shortly) http://www.audionet.com/
KOYN, Paris (country)—http://www.1starnet.com/clients/koyn/koyn, http://207.113.204.163/pub/koyn/koyn.htm or http://www.audionet.com/
KPLX, Dallas (country, NASCAR reports)—http://www.kplx.com/ or http://www.audionet.com/pub/kplx/kplx.com

KPRC, Houston (news/talk)—http://www.audionet.com/ or http://207.113.204.163/pub/supertalk/supertalk.htm
KROX, Austin (alternative rock)—http://www.audionet.com/pub/krox/krox.htm
KSJL, San Antonio (urban contemporary)—(possibly to activate shortly) http://www.audionet.com/
KSKY, Dallas (religious)—http://www.ksky.com/, http://207.113.204.163/pub/ksky/ksky.htm or http://www.audionet.com/

Classical music used to be scarce-to-nil on radio or TV, but no more. Seattle's KING now airs recorded classics, as well as broadcasts from the Seattle Opera, to Web radio listeners.

KTBZ, Houston (alternative rock)—http://www.thebuzz.com/, http://207.113.204.163/pub/ktbz/ktbz.htm or http://www.audionet.com/
KTCK, Dallas (sports)—http://www.audionet.com/ or http://207.113.204.163/pub/ktck/ktck.htm
KYKR, Beaumont (country)—(possibly to activate shortly) http://www.audionet.com/
KZPS, Dallas (oldies)—http://kzps.com/kzps/, http://207.113.204.163/pub/kzps/kzps.htm or http://www.audionet.com
WOAI, San Antonio (news/talk)—http://www.woai.com/, http://207.113.204.163/pub/woai/woai.htm or http://www.audionet.com/

Utah
KCNR, Salt Lake City (news/talk)—http://www.kdcol.com/~kcnr/, http://207.113.204.163/pub/kcnr/kcnr.htm or http://www.audionet.com/

Vermont
WGDR, Plainfield (college variety)—http://sun.goddard.edu/students/wgdr/index.html

Washington State
KING, Seattle (classical)—http://www.king.org/
TVW (TV audio)—http://www.tvw.org/newra.htm

INTERNATIONAL ORGANIZATIONS
ABC RadioNet—http://www.abcradionet.com/
Air Force Radio News—http://brooks.af.mil/realaudio/newsbyte.html
American Independent Network (TV audio)—http://www.audionet.com/ or http://207.113.204.163/pub/ain/ain.htm
AudioNet (major hyperlink)—http://www.audionet.com/, http://207.113.204.163/ or http://207.113.204.163/pub/
Bloomberg Information News—http://www.bloomberg.com/wbbr/
College Radio Network—http://www.internetwork.com/crn/crn.htm
C-Span—http://www.c-span.org/realaudio.html
Internet Multicasting Service—http://town.hall.org/radio/
National Public Radio—(general) http://www.npr.org/index.html or http://www.wrn.org/stations/npr.html; ("Car Talk") http://cartalk.com

TODD HERMAN   MARTIN DAVIES   RICK TAYLOR
PHOTOILLUSTRATION BY STEVE & HEIHER DAVIS
Check out the trip to Las Vegas!
LAS VEGAS

It's no gamble when you click onto KCNR. It's Salt Lake City's home for Supertalk radio.

THE Broadcast Network on the Internet!

NEW TODAY · SPORTS · RADIO STATIONS · PROGRAM GUIDE · MUSIC · BOOKS · LIVE!
HELP   MAIL   LINKS   ABOUT
CD JUKEBOX · FREE SOFTWARE

With dozens of North American stations under its wing, AudioNet is Web radio's Big Enchilada. It gives listeners "one-stop shopping," along with a calendar of upcoming special programs.

NetRadio Network (Web-only radio)—http://www.netradio.net/index.html or http://www.audionet.com/netradio
Prime Sports Radio Network—http://libertysports.com/radio.htm, http://207.113.204.163/pub/psr/psr.htm or http://www.audionet.com
RealAudio (major hyperlink)—http://www.realaudio.com or http://www.prognet.com
RFE-RL—http://www.rferl.org/
StreamWorks—http://www.streamworks.com or http://www.xingtech.com
SW Network—http://www.swnetworks.com/cgi-bin/Webdriver?Mlval=realaudio.htm
Talk America Radio Network—http://www.talkamerica.com/
Trinity Broadcasting Network (TV audio)—http://www.tbn.org
United Broadcasting Network—http://www.audionet.com/ or http://207.113.204.163/pub/ubn/ubn.htm
Voice of America—http://www.voa.gov/programs/audio/realaudio or http://www.wrn.org/stations/voa.html

VATICAN CITY STATE
Vatican Radio—http://wrn.org/stations/vatican.html

BRITAIN'S BEST SELLING RADIO MAGAZINES

ARE NOW AVAILABLE WORLDWIDE

TO SUBSCRIBE TO
PRACTICAL WIRELESS OR
SHORT WAVE MAGAZINE JUST
COMPLETE THE FORM BELOW AND
MAIL OR FAX IT THROUGH – OR
CALL US WITH YOUR CREDIT CARD
NUMBER AND WE'LL START YOUR
SUBSCRIPTION IMMEDIATELY.

Practical Wireless

Subscribe to *PW* now and you'll find out why we're
Britain's best selling amateur radio magazine.
We regularly feature:

★ News & reviews of the latest
   equipment
★ Antenna Workshop
★ Bits & Bytes – the computer in
   your shack
★ Novice Natter
★ Focal Point – the world of ATV
★ Valve & Vintage
★ Equipment construction

and much, much more. *PW*
has something for radio
enthusiasts everywhere.

1 YEAR SUBSCRIPTION RATES

❏ PRACTICAL WIRELESS
❏ £25.00 (UK)
❏ £30.00 (Europe)
❏ £32.00 (Rest of World)
❏ $50 (USA)

❏ SHORT WAVE MAGAZINE
❏ £25.00 (UK)
❏ £30.00 (Europe)
❏ £32.00 (Rest of World)
❏ $50 (USA)

SPECIAL JOINT SUBSCRIPTION
(BOTH MAGAZINES – 1 YEAR)

❏ £45.00 (UK)
❏ £54.00 (Europe)
❏ £58.00 (Rest of World)
❏ $90 (USA)

(All credit card orders are charged in pounds sterling – all cheques
must be in US dollars or British pounds please.)

Name...

Address..

....

....

Post/Zip code ....

Telephone No ....
❏ I enclose cheque/PO (Payable to PW Publishing Ltd £($) ....
❏ Please charge to my Visa/Mastercard the amount of £($) ....

Card No...

Expiry Date..

Please start my subscription with the ....issue

Signature ....

Short Wave Magazine

For everyone, from the newcomer to the
experienced radio monitor, *SWM* is the
listeners magazine with
articles and features written
specifically to help the
listener find out what to buy
and where and how to listen.
Regular features include:

★ News & reviews of the latest
   equipment
★ Utility receiving & decoding
★ Broadcast Stations
★ Bandscan
★ Airband
★ Info in Orbit
★ Scanning

CREDIT CARD ORDERS
(+44) 1202 659930
FAX ORDERS
(+44) 1202 +659950
INTERNET
orders@pwpub.demon.co.uk

PW Publishing Ltd.,
Arrowsmith Court,
Station Approach,
Broadstone,
Dorset BH18 8PW, UK

Some of the most enthusiastic world band listeners live in frosty Finland. Here, Pirkko Soininen loads up sleds with essential gear, including a Grundig Satellit radio, as she prepares to mush north.

1997 PASSPORT REPORTS

How To Choose a World Band Radio

Some electronic goodies, like VCRs, have evolved into commodity products. With a little common sense you can pretty much get what you want without fuss or bother.

Not so world band receivers, which vary greatly from model to model. As usual, money talks—but even that's a fickle barometer. Some models use old technology, or misapply new technology, so they're unhandy or function poorly. But others can perform nicely, indeed.

Crammed with Stations

World band radio is a jungle: *1,100 channels*, with stations scrunched cheek-by-jowl. This crowding is much greater than on FM or mediumwave AM. To make matters worse, the international voyage often causes signals to be weak and quivery. To cope, a radio has to perform some exceptional electronic gymnastics. Some succeed, others don't.

This is why PASSPORT REPORTS was created. Since 1977 we've tested hundreds of world band products—the good, the bad and the ugly. These evaluations include rigorous hands-on use by veteran listeners and newcomers alike, plus specialized lab tests we've developed over the years. These form the basis of this PASSPORT REPORTS, and for premium models are detailed to the nth degree in our acclaimed series of Radio Database International White Papers®.

Taiwanese workers assemble Sangean world band portables. Sangean now also produces in China.   Robert C. Crane

Five Things to Check for

Before you pore over which radio does what, here's a basic checklist to get oriented.

What to spend? Don't be fooled by the word "radio"—able world band radios are sophisticated devices. Yet, for all they do, they cost only about as much as a VCR.

If you're just starting out, figure the equivalent of what sells in the United States for $100–200, and which sells for £60–130 in the United Kingdom, in a model with two-and-a-half stars or more. If you're looking for top performance, shoot for a portable with three-and-a-half stars—at least $350 or £360—or look into one of the sophisticated portatop or tabletop models that cost at least twice as much.

If price isn't a reliable guide, why not go for the cheapest? Research shows that once the novelty wears thin, most people quit using cheap radios, especially those under $80 or £60. On most stations they sound terrible, and they're clumsy to tune.

How Many Radios Are Sold?

Worldwide, there are probably something like half a billion radios with world band coverage of some sort. Most are inexpensive analog portables used by listeners in Africa and Asia, especially in those countries where domestic news sources are considered to be less-than-credible, or which lack adequate coverage of international or regional affairs.

Within North America and Europe, where media choices abound, listening is driven more by want than need. In the United States listenership has been rising over the last ten years, even while sales of world band receivers have fluctuated. In the past couple of years, for example, "Internet mania" and the trough of the 11-year sunspot cycle have resulted in a drop in overall world band radio sales. Yet, world band listenership has continued to rise.

How's that? For one thing, the boatloads of cheap shortwave radios being hawked just a few years ago have all but disappeared from the market. Also, sales of pricey tabletop "supersets" have dropped off from around three percent of the total market to under two percent.

But in the great midrange between those two extremes, sales of nicely per-forming portables have held relatively constant. Very roughly 400,000 such units appear to be sold each year in the United States, largely by Grundig, Sony and Radio Shack. In particular, sales of "value" digital portables in the $100–200 range have been rising, with the number of world band radios of all types in actual use appearing to be around four-to-six million.

This is our own latest estimate. Industry statistics and leaks run the gamut from under 200,000 to nearly a million units per year. The lowball figure is almost certainly missing data from one or more key manufacturers, whereas the higher number appears to reflect wishful thinking.

Research has shown that people quickly tire of the dismal performance of cheap models, whereas better models tend to be listened to regularly. And as the sunspot cycle begins its anticipated upward movement in a year or so, and the Internet is accepted for what it is rather than as a novelty, it is the sales of worthy world band radios—not cheap clunkers—that is expected to show a healthy uptick.

What kind of stations do you want to hear? Just the biggies? Or do you also hanker for soft voices from exotic lands? Figure that out, then choose a model that surpasses it by a good notch or so. This helps ensure against disappointment without wasting money. After all, you don't need a Ferrari to go to the mall, but you also don't want a golf cart for the autobahn.

> Once the novelty wears thin, most people quit using cheap radios.

Keep in mind that most portables don't do brilliantly with tough signals—those that are weak, or hemmed in by interference from other stations. If it's important to you to ferret out as much as possible, think four stars—perhaps five—in a porta-top or tabletop. The rub is that these cost much more, usually $700 or £400 and up.

Radio Budapest

When popular announcer Enikő Zsuffa is not entertaining listeners over Radio Budapest's English service, she heads to Hungary's rally race tracks to demonstate her competitive driving talents. Lately, she's also been preparing a series introducing listeners to Hungary's historic wine regions.

Where are you located? Signals are strongest in and around Europe, second-best in eastern North America. If you live

Passport Standards

Our reviewers, and no one else, have written everything in PASSPORT REPORTS. These include our laboratory findings, all of which are done independently for us by a specialized contract laboratory that is recognized as the world's leader in this field. (For more on this, please see the Radio Database International White Paper, *How to Interpret Receiver Lab Tests and Measurements*.)

Our review process is completely separate from any advertising, and our review team members may not accept review fees from manufacturers or "permanently borrow" radios. Neither International Broadcasting Services nor any of its editors owns any stake in, or is employed by, firms which manufacture, sell or distribute world band radios, antennas or related hardware.

PASSPORT recognizes superior products regardless of when they first happen to appear on the market. So we don't bestow annual awards, which recognize only models released during a given year. Some years, many worthy models are introduced, whereas in other years virtually none appear. Thus, a "best" receiver for one year may be markedly inferior to a "non-best" receiver from another year.

Instead, we designate each exceptional model, regardless of its year of introduction, as *Passport's Choice.*

1997 marks the 20th year we've been adhering to these standards. We hope to be doing more of the same for years to come.

Better portables are almost always serviced or replaced within warranty. If you can possibly swing it, insist upon a replacement. Repairs to portables, even from major manufacturers, can be a nightmare.

After warranty expiration, nearly all factory-authorized service departments for portables tend to fall woefully short, sometimes making radios worse instead of better. Grundig worldwide—and, in the United States, Radio Shack and Sangean—spring to mind as exceptions, mainly because they have been shown to be unusually willing to replace faulty products from dissatisfied customers. However, note that Sangean offices service only Sangean-brand products, not those made by Sangean for other firms and sold under other names.

On the other hand, for tabletop models factory-authorized service is usually avail-

Outdoor Antennas: Who Needs Them?

If you're wondering what accessory antenna you'll need for your new radio, the answer for portables and portatops is usually simple: none, or almost none, as all come with built-in telescopic antennas. Indeed, for evening use in Europe or eastern North America nearly all portables perform *less* well with sophisticated outboard antennas than with their built-in ones.

But if you listen during the day, or live in such places as the North American Midwest or West, your portable may need more oomph. The best solution in the United States is also the cheapest: ten bucks or so for Radio Shack's 75-foot (23-meter) "SW Antenna Kit," which comes with insulators and other goodies, plus $2 for a claw clip. The antenna itself may be a bit too long for your circumstances, but you can always trim it.

Alternatively, many electronics and world band specialty firms sell the necessary parts and wire for you to make your own. An appendix in the recently revised Radio Database International White Paper® *Evaluation of Popular Outdoor Antennas* gives minutely detailed step-by-step instructions for making and erecting such an antenna.

Basically, you attach the claw clip onto your radio's rod antenna (this is usually better than the set's external antenna input socket, which may have a desensitizing circuit), then run it out of your window, as high as is safe and practical, to something like a tree. Unless you want to become Crispy the Cadaver, *keep your antenna clear of any hazardous wiring—the electrical service to your house, in particular—and respect heights.* If you live in an apartment, run it to your balcony or window—as close to the fresh outdoors as possible.

This "volksantenna"—best disconnected when you're not listening, and especially when thunder, snow or sand storms are nearby—will probably help with most signals. But if it occasionally makes a station sound worse, just disconnect the claw clip and use your radio's telescopic antenna.

It's a different story with tabletop receivers. They require an external antenna, either passive or electrically amplified ("active"). Although portatop models don't require an outboard antenna, they invariably work better with one.

able to keep them purring for many years to come. Drake and Watkins-Johnson are legendary in this regard within North America, as is Lowe in Europe. Although it's too early to be certain, AOR's new facility in the United Kingdom will probably also be a superior service center for the new AOR AR7030, which is engineered and manufactured in England.

Service can also be first-rate at a number of other firms, such as Japan Radio, Kenwood and Yaesu. Yet, Drake, Lowe and Watkins-Johnson stand apart because they also tend to maintain a healthy parts inventory, even for older models.

Of course, nothing quite equals service at the factory itself. So if repair is especially important to you, bend a little toward the home team: Drake and Watkins-Johnson in the United States, Grundig in Germany, Lowe in the United Kingdom, Japan Radio in Japan, AOR in the United Kingdom and Japan, and so on.

... Continued

Amplified antennas use short wire or rod elements, but beef up incoming signals with electronic circuitry. For apartment dwellers and some others, they can be a godsend—provided they work right. Choosing a suitable amplified antenna for your tabletop or portatop receiver takes some care, as some are pretty awful. Yet, certain models—notably, Britain's Datong AD 370—work relatively well.

If you have space outdoors, a passive outdoor wire antenna is much better, especially when it's designed for world band frequencies. Besides not needing problematic electronic circuits, a good passive antenna also tends to reduce interference from the likes of fluorescent lights and electric shavers—noises which amplified antennas boost, right along with the signal. As the cognoscenti put it, the "signal-to-noise ratio" tends to be better with passive antennas.

With any outdoor antenna, especially if it is high out in the open, disconnect it and affix it to something like an outdoor ground rod if there is lightning nearby. Handier, and nearly as effective except for a direct strike, is a modestly priced lightning protector, such as is made by Alpha Delta. Or, if you have deep pockets, the $295 Ten-Tec Model 100 protector, which automatically shuts out your antenna and power cord when lightning appears nearby. Otherwise, sooner or later, you may be facing a costly repair bill.

A surge protector on the radio's power cord is good insurance, too. These are available at any computer store, and cheap MOV-based ones are usually good enough. But you can also go for the whole hog, as we do, with the innovative $150 Zero Surge ZS 900 (U.S. phone 800/996-6696; elsewhere +1 908/996-7700).

Many firms—some large, some tiny—manufacture world band antennas. Among the best passive models—all under $100 or £60—are those made by Antenna Supermarket and Alpha Delta Communications, available from world band stores. A detailed report on these is available as the same Radio Database International White Paper® mentioned above, *Evaluation of Popular Outdoor Antennas*.

Portables for 1997

*I*nterested in hearing major world band stations? If so, a good portable provides real value. Unless you live in a high-rise, the best digitally tuned portables will almost certainly meet your needs—especially evenings, when signals are strongest.

That's singularly true in Europe and the Near East, or even along the east coast of North America. Signals tend to come in well in these places, where virtually any well-rated portable should be all you need.

Weak Signals?

But signals are weaker in places like central and western North America, Australasia, and the Caribbean or Pacific islands. There, focus on models PASSPORT has found to be unusually sensitive to weak signals (see next page).

Yet, even in Europe and eastern North America, daytime signals tend to be weaker than at night. If you listen then—some stations and programs are heard in North America only during the day, and they sure beat daytime TV—weak-signal performance should be a priority.

Longwave Useful for Some

The longwave band is still used for some domestic broadcasts in Europe, North Africa and Russia. If you live in or travel to these parts of the world, longwave coverage is a slight plus for daytime listening to regional radio stations, especially in the hinterland. Otherwise, forget it.

Keep in mind, though, that when a low-cost model is available with longwave, that band may be included at the expense of some world band coverage.

Grundig's excellent Satellit 700, shown above, is made in Portugal. However, the Satellit 900, which will eventually replace it, will probably be manufactured in Asia, as is the analog Grundig Traveller II shown below.

Pulling In Weak Stations

Many portables are designed to work well in Europe, where mighty signals can overwhelm radio innards. To get around this, engineers limit signal sensitivity to make a radio "hear" all stations as though they weaker than they really are. Problem is, if you are listening from western or central North America, New Zealand or other region where signals tend to be weak, something else is needed. Something sensitive to weak signals.

Best Radios

Best is to purchase a radio designed to work well where signals are weak. Here are PASSPORT's choices, listed in order of their ability to flush out anemic signals. While this ability centers around sensitivity to weak signals, there are other factors taken into account, such as the ability to produce intelligible audio at low signal levels. Keep in mind that sample-to-sample variations can affect weak-signal sensitivity and that, as our detailed ratings show (see Advantages), several other models are close runners-up.

- Sony ICF-2010
- Grundig Satellit 700
- Grundig Yacht Boy 305

Not good enough? If mobility isn't crucial, go for one of the better portatop or tabletop models with a worthy external antenna designed for non-portable receivers, such as those made under the "Eavesdropper" and "Alpha Delta" labels.

Make Your Radio "Hear" Better

Regardless of which portable you own, you can give it at least some additional sensitivity on the cheap.

How cheap? Nothing, for starters.

Find Your Room's "Sweet Spots"

Just wander around the room looking for "sweet spots." Stations may come in stronger if the radio is placed in one of these endowed locations than if you simply plop it down. Try near windows, appliances, telephones and the like; although at times these locations make things worse by introducing electrical noise. Just keep trying.

If your portable has an AC adaptor, try that, then batteries; usually the AC adaptor does a better job. Best is the adaptor designed for your radio by the manufacturer and certified by the appropriate safety authorities, such as Underwriters Laboratories. If you travel abroad, look for a multivoltage version—standard on a few models.

Outdoor Antenna Best

An outdoor antenna can help. With portable antennas, simplest is best. Use an alligator or claw clip to connect several meters or yards of insulated wire, elevated outdoors above the ground, to your set's telescopic antenna. It's fast and cheap, yet effective.

Fine Print: Under the right conditions, outdoor wire antennas can feed static electricity, along with signals you want, right into your radio. You'd expect this with thunderstorms and lightning pounding away. But what you might not anticipate is that you can also get this snap, crackle and pop during breezy snowstorms or sand storms.

Static electricity fries semiconductors faster than you can say "Colonel Sanders," so use outdoor antennas only when needed, disconnecting them during stormy conditions and when the radio is off. And try to avoid touching the antenna during dry weather, as you may discharge static electricity from your body right into the radio.

More Fine Print: Outboard antennas can sometimes cause "overloading," usually at certain times of the day on one or more frequency segments with lots of strong signals. You'll know this is happening when you tune up and down, and most of what you hear sounds like murmuring in a TV courtroom scene. Remedy: Disconnect the wire antenna and revert to the telescopic rod.

Fancy outdoor wire antennas? These are designed for tabletop and portatop models. For portables, a length of ordinary insulated wire works better and costs less.

If you live in a weak-signal part of the world, such as the North American Midwest or West, and want something with more oomph, best is to erect an inverted-L (so-called "longwire") antenna. This is available as a kit through Radio Shack and some other radio specialty outlets, or may be easily constructed from detailed instructions found in the recently revised RDI White Paper, *Popular Outdoor Antennas.*

Indoor Solutions, Too

Antennas, like football players, almost always do best outdoors. But if your supplementary antenna simply must be indoors, it can work to best advantage if you place it along the middle of a window with Velcro or tape. Another solution, if you're listening in a reinforced-concrete building which absorbs radio signals, is to use the longest telescopic car antenna you can find. Affix it outdoors, almost horizontally, onto a windowsill or balcony rail.

Amplified, or "active," antennas often do more harm than good with portables. Yet, those made by Sony have consistently tested out to be relatively problem-free, even if they do little to actually boost signal strength. Their high card is that they have long cords which allow you to place the antenna near the outdoors, where reception tends to be best, but to leave the radio where you listen.

Inexpensive electronic signal-booster devices usually fare much more poorly than Sony's offerings, although anecdotal evidence suggests that some can help in given listening situations. Purchase these on a money-back basis so you can experiment with little risk.

Good things come in small packages, and world band pocket radios don't get any smaller or better than the accessory-laden Sony ICF-SW100S. In some countries, it's also sold bareback as the ICF-SW100E.

★ ★ ★   *Passport's Choice*

Sony ICF-SW100S

Price: $399.95 in the United States. CAN$599.00 in Canada. £179.95 in the United Kingdom.

Advantages: Extremely small. Superior overall world band performance for size. Excellent synchronous detection with selectable sideband. Good audio when earpieces (supplied) are used. FM stereo through earpieces. Exceptional number of helpful tuning features, including "page" storage with presets. Tunes in precise 100 Hz increments. Worthy ergonomics for size and features. Illuminated display. Clock for many world cities, which can be made to work as a *de facto* World Time clock. Timer/snooze features. Travel power lock. Receives longwave and Japanese FM bands. Amplified outboard antenna (supplied), in addition to usual built-in antenna, enhances weak-signal reception. High-quality travel case for radio. *Except for North America:* Self-regulating AC adaptor, with American

and European plugs, adjusts automatically to all local voltages worldwide.

Disadvantages: Tiny speaker, although an innovative design, has mediocre sound and limited loudness. Weak-signal sensitivity could be better, although outboard active antenna (supplied) helps. Expensive. No tuning knob. Clock not readable when station frequency displayed. As "London Time" is used by the clock for World Time, the summertime clock adjustment cannot be used if World Time is to be displayed accurately. Rejection of certain spurious signals ("images"), and 10 kHz "repeats" when synchronous selectable sideband off, could be better. In some urban locations, FM signals (from 87.5 to 108 MHz) can break through into world band segments with distorted sound, e.g. between 3200 and 3300 kHz. Synchronous selectable sideband tends to lose lock if batteries not fresh, or if NiCd cells are used. Batteries run down faster than usual when radio off. "Signal-seek" scanner sometimes stops 5 kHz before a strong "real" signal. No meaningful signal-strength indicator. Mediumwave AM reception only fair. Mediumwave AM channel spacing adjusts peculiarly. Flimsy battery cover. Cable connecting two halves of clamshell reportedly tends to lose continuity with extended or rough use. *North America:* AC adaptor 120 Volts only.

Note: With any pocket or compact Sony portable having synchronous selectable sideband, it's a good idea to check in the store, or immediately after purchase, to ensure it was aligned properly at the factory: 1) put fresh batteries into the radio, 2) tune in a local mediumwave AM station, and 3) adjust the "sync" function back and forth between LSB and USB. If all is well, the audio will sound similar in both cases—*similar*, not identical, as there will always be at least some difference. However, if one choice sounds significantly muddier and bassier than the other, the unit is probably out of alignment and you should select another sample.

Bottom Line: An engineering *tour de force*. Speaker and, to a lesser extent, weak-signal sensitivity keep it from being all it could have been. Yet, it still is the handiest pocket portable around, and one of the niftiest gift ideas in years.

★ ★ ★   *Passport's Choice*

Sony ICF-SW100E

Price: £179.95 in the United Kingdom. AUS$649.00 in Australia. Currently not distributed by Sony within North America.
Bottom Line: This version, available in Europe but not North America, nominally includes a case, tape-reel-type passive antenna and earbuds. Otherwise, it is identical to the Sony ICF-SW100S, above.

★ ★ ★   *Passport's Choice*

Sangean ATS 606p
Sangean ATS 606
Siemens RK 659

Price: *ATS 606p:* $189.95, in the United States. CAN$279.00 in Canada. Around $250 within European Community. *ATS 606:* $169.95 in the United States. CAN$239.00 in Canada. Around $230 within European Community. AUS$249.00 in Australia.
Advantages: Exceptional simplicity of operation for technology class. Speaker audio quality superior for size class, improves with (usually supplied) earpieces. Various helpful tuning features. Keypad has exceptional feel and tactile response. Longwave. World Time clock, displayed separately from frequency, and local clock. Alarm/snooze features. Travel power lock. Clear warning when batteries weak. Stereo FM via earpieces. Superior FM reception. Superior quality of construction. *ATS 606p:* Reel-in passive wire

The Sangean ATS 606, offered with accessories as the ATS 606p, is the sensible choice among better pocket portables. Nice performance, fairly priced.

antenna. Self-regulating AC adaptor, with American and European plugs, adjusts automatically to most local voltages worldwide.
Disadvantages: No tuning knob. Tunes only in coarse 5 kHz increments. World Time clock readable only when radio is switched off. Display not illuminated. Keypad not in telephone format. No meaningful signal-strength indicator. No carrying strap or handle. *ATS 606:* AC adaptor extra.
Bottom Line: A sensible choice, thanks to superior sound through the speaker. If the regular "606" Sangean version seems Spartan, there's the "606p" version, complete with handy goodies. It's well worth the small extra price.

New for 1997

★ ★   ¢

Grundig Traveller II Digital
Grundig TR II Digital
Grundig Yacht Boy 320

Price: $109.95 in the United States. CAN$129.95 in Canada. £59.95 in the United Kingdom.

Electronic goodies have a way of getting "lost" in luggage and hotels. A good hedge is the Grundig Yacht Boy 320, also sold as the Grundig Traveller II Digital and TR II Digital. It's an okay radio that's cheaper than most other pocket portables.

Advantages: Price. Superior audio quality for pocket size. 24-hour clock with alarm feature and clock-radio capability. Up/down slew tuning with "signal-seek" scanning. Illuminated LCD. Travel power lock (see Disadvantages). FM in stereo through earpieces, not included.

Disadvantages: Poor rejection of certain spurious signals ("images"). Doesn't cover 7400-9400 kHz world band range, although it can be tricked into receiving the lower part of this range at reduced strength by tuning the 6505-6700 kHz "image" frequencies. Lacks keypad and tuning knob. Few presets (e.g., only five for 2300-7400 kHz range). Tunes world band only in coarse 5 kHz steps. Even-numbered frequencies displayed with final zero omitted; e.g., 5.73 rather than conventional 5.730 or 5730. Poor spurious-signal ("image") rejection. So-so adjacent-channel rejection (selectivity). World Time clock not displayed independent of frequency. Nigh-useless signal-strength indicator. LCD illumination not disabled when travel power lock activated. No carrying strap or handle. AC adaptor extra. No longwave.

Bottom Line: Warts and all, a decent offering at an attractive price, with audio quality superior to that of most pocket models. Grundig's slightly larger, but better, Yacht Boy 305 is worth considering as a comparably priced alternative.

Evaluation of New Model: This latest model from Grundig, at 0.41 kg with batteries, just squeaks into pocket status at under one pound. It's small, to be sure, yet nowhere as tiny as Sony's innovative and costly ICF-SW100S. But the Grundig's size allows it to have a relatively large speaker, so it sounds much more pleasant.

This value-priced new model covers FM in stereo through earpieces (not included), mediumwave AM 520-1710 kHz, and world band 2300-7400 kHz and 9400-26100 kHz in five kilohertz chunks.

There is an unhandy and archaic "SW1/SW2" switch, and between the SW1 and SW2 tuning ranges is that "hole" between 7400-9400 kHz where it won't pick up any stations. However, because the TR II is single conversion, you can "trick" it into receiving powerful world band stations between 7405-7600 kHz by tuning the "image repeats" 900 kHz lower; that is, between 6505-6700 kHz. Thus, say, 7465 kHz appears at lower strength on 6565 kHz.

Like Grundig's compact Yacht Boy 305, this model is made in China. And like some other Chinese models, it displays "even" shortwave frequencies as "XX.XX MHz," so 12050 kHz shows up as 12.05 MHz, and so on. It also omits the leading "tens" zero from the 24-hour clock display, so 02:27 shows as 2:27.

The clock displays when the radio is off, and also by pressing a button when the radio is on. The clock circuitry includes an alarm feature and clock-radio capability.

There is neither a keypad nor a tuning knob—major omissions—and the radio won't demodulate single-sideband signals used by hams and utility stations. However, it does have a travel power lock and a pushbutton light for the LCD. That light stays on so long as you hold down a button, unfortunately even when the travel power lock is activated. There's a handy elevation panel, too, and the telescopic antenna swivels and rotates; but there's no carrying handle or strap.

To compensate partially for no keypad or tuning knob, the radio has a meter button which carousels the radio up the world band spectrum segment-by-segment. Along with the slew/signal-seek scanning, this allows for reasonably quick tuning. Aiding that to a limited extent are five presets for FM, five for mediumwave AM, five for SW1 (2300-7400 kHz) and five for SW2 (9400-26100 kHz).

By and large, performance is okay, with weak-signal sensitivity and dynamic range being a bit better than you might expect in this price class. Selectivity is decent, but adjacent-channel rejection is still not what it should be. Rejection of spurious images, from signals 900 kHz higher, is dreadful. Yet, overall, reception quality is more pleasant than virtually anything else in its price and size class, at least for hearing major broadcasters from afar.

The Grundig Traveler II/Yacht Boy 320 is attractively priced. Although low-frequency audio is thin, the radio has superior audio quality for a pocket model—a strong point, considering how bad small radios can sound. But it's still not in the same league as pricier pocket radios, or even the compact Grundig Yacht Boy 305 that sells for very little more.

Tips for Globetrotting

Airport security and customs personnel are used to world band portables, which have become a staple among world travelers. Yet, a few simple practices will help in avoiding hassles:

- Take along a pocket or compact model, nothing larger. Portable radios are a favorite of terrorists for stashing explosives, but for their misdeeds to succeed they need a radio of reasonable proportions.
- Models with built-in recorders (see next chapter), especially if they're not small, may attract unfavorable attention. So at the very least, give yourself a few extra minutes to clear security.
- Stow your radio in a carry-on bag, not in checked luggage or on your person.
- Take along fresh batteries so you can demonstrate that the radio actually works, as gutted radios can be used to carry illegal material. To ensure batteries haven't run down by accident in your carry-on, be sure to activate your radio's power lock, if it has one.
- If asked what the radio is for, state that it is for your personal use.
- If traveling in zones of war or civil unrest, or off the beaten path in parts of Africa, take along a radio you can afford to lose.
- If traveling to Bahrain, avoid taking a radio which has the word "receiver" on its case. If this is impractical, use creative, but not amateurish or obvious, means to disguise or eliminate the offending term.

Theft? Remember that radios, cameras, binoculars, laptop computers and the like are almost always stolen to be resold. The more used the item looks—affixing worn stickers helps—the less likely it is to be confiscated by corrupt inspectors or stolen by thieves.

Sangean's ATS-202 is a passable performer at an affordable price.

★ ★

Sangean ATS-202

Price: $99.95 in the United States. CAN$119.95 in Canada.

Advantages: Weak-signal sensitivity a bit better than most. World Time clock. Travel power lock. Alarm and snooze features. Illuminated display. Tunes using ten presets, signal-seek scanning and up/down slewing. Superior quality of construction.

Disadvantages: Doesn't tune important 7300-7600 kHz and 9020-9495 kHz ranges. Adjacent-channel rejection (selectivity) mediocre. Spurious-signal ("image") rejection poor. Lacks keypad and tuning knob. Sometimes requires adjusting band switch when changing world band frequencies. Tunes only in coarse 5 kHz increments. World Time clock readable only when radio is off. Audio, although otherwise reasonable, somewhat tinny. Batteries can run down more quickly than usual with radio off.

Bottom Line: Lackluster performance and limited frequency coverage, but attractive price.

COMPACT PORTABLES

Good for Travel, Fair for Home

Compacts tip in at one to two pounds, under a kilogram, and are typically sized 8 × 5 × 1.5", or 20 × 13 × 4 cm. Like pocket models, they feed off "AA" (UM-3 penlite) batteries—but, usually, more of them. They travel almost as well as smaller models, but sound better and usually receive better, too. For some travelers, they also suffice as home sets—something pocket units can't really do. However, if you don't travel abroad often, you may find better value and performance in a lap portable.

Which stand out? Three, in particular, provide an unusually favorable intersection of price and performance. Grundig's Yacht Boy 400 has superior audio quality and two bandwidths, and it's straightforward to operate. For hearing signals hemmed in by interference, the Sony ICF-SW7600G brings real affordability to synchronous selectable sideband. Both are outstanding buys, especially if you don't live where signals are relatively weak.

If you are in a weak-signal area, consider the Grundig Yacht Boy 305, a relative bargain. Otherwise, step up to the larger Sony ICF-2010, or even a portatop or tabletop model. But between the similarly priced YB 400 and ICF-SW7600G, the latter has a slight edge in such weak-signal parts of the world as central and western North America.

Goodies? Among three-star models, the Sony ICF-SW55 and the new Sangean ATS 909 are laden with features and accessories that come standard. Of course, they cost more, too.

For superior quality of construction, look to Panasonic or Sangean. For simplicity of operation, there are the various Grundig Yacht Boy compacts, especially the 305, as well as Sony's new ICF-SW40, among others.

We have only a handful of favorite radios at PASSPORT, and this is one of them—Grundig's sensibly priced Yacht Boy 400. Pleasant sound is just one of its advantages.

Grundig Yacht Boy 400

Price: $199.95 in the United States. CAN$249.95 in Canada. £119.95 in the United Kingdom. £119.95 in the United Kingdom. AUS$399.00 in Australia.

Advantages: Unusually good value. Audio quality clearly tops in size category. Two bandwidths, both well-chosen. Easy to operate and ergonomically superior for advanced-technology radio. A number of helpful tuning features, including keypad, up/down slewing, 40 station presets, "signal seek" frequency scanning and scanning of station presets. Signal-strength indicator. World Time clock with second time zone, any one of which is shown at all times; however, clock displays seconds only when radio is off. Illuminated display. Alarm/snooze features. Demodulates single-sideband signals, used by hams and utility stations, with unusual precision for a portable. Fishing-reel-type outboard passive antenna to supplement telescopic antenna. Generally superior FM performance. FM in stereo through headphones. Longwave.

Disadvantages: Circuit noise ("hiss") can be slightly intrusive with weak signals. AC adaptor not standard or offered; in North America, Grundig recommends the Radio Shack adaptor #273-1455. No tuning knob. At some locations, there can be breakthrough of powerful AM or FM stations. Keypad not in telephone format. No LSB/USB switch.

Bottom Line: This model is preferred over other compacts by our panelists in Eastern North America and Europe for listening to major world band stations. The Grundig Yacht Boy's audio quality is tops within its size class, even though circuit noise with weak signals could be lower. (It helps if you clip on several yards or meters of strung-out doorbell wire to the built-in antenna).

Sony ICF-SW7600G

Price: $199.95 in the United States. CAN$299.00 in Canada. £159.99 in the United Kingdom. AUS$499.00 in Australia. ¥2,700 (about $325) in China.

Advantages: Unusually good value. Far and away the least-costly model available with high-tech synchronous detection

Sony's innovative ICF-SW7600G is the least costly radio with ear-pleasing synchronous selectable sideband.

coupled to selectable sideband; this generally performs very well, reducing adjacent-channel interference and fading distortion on world band, longwave and mediumwave AM signals (see Disadvantages). Single bandwidth, especially when the synchronous-detection feature is used, exceptionally effective at adjacent-channel rejection. Numerous helpful tuning features, including keypad, two-speed up/down slewing, 20 presets (ten for world band) and "signal-seek" scanning. Demodulates single-sideband signals, used by hams and utility stations, with unusual precision for a portable. World Time clock, easy to set. Tape-reel-type outboard passive antenna accessory comes standard. Snooze/timer features. Illuminated display. Travel power lock. FM stereo through earpieces or headphones. Receives longwave and Japanese FM bands. Dead-battery indicator. Comes standard with vinyl carrying case.

Disadvantages: Certain controls, notably for synchronous selectable sideband, located unhandily at the side of the cabi-

Important Things to Look For

- **Helpful tuning features.** Digitally tuned models are by now so superior and cost-effective that they are virtual "musts." Most such models come with such useful tuning aids as direct-frequency access via keypad, presets (programmable channel memories), up-down tuning via tuning knob and/or slew keys, band/segment selection, and signal-seek or other scanning. In general, the more such features a radio has, the easier it is to tune—no small point, given that a hundred or more channels may be audible at any one time. However, there is the occasional model, identified in PASSPORT REPORTS under "Disadvantages," with tuning features that are so sophisticated that they can make tuning excessively complicated for some users.

- **Worthy audio quality.** Few models, especially among portables, have rich, full audio, but some are distinctly better than others. If you listen regularly and have either exacting ears or difficulty in hearing, focus on those models with superior audio quality—and try to buy on a money-back or exchange basis.

- **Effective adjacent-channel rejection ("selectivity").** World band stations are packed together about twice as closely as ordinary mediumwave AM stations, so they tend to interfere with each other. Radios with superior selectivity are better at rejecting this. However, better selectivity also means less high-end ("treble") audio response, so having more than one "bandwidth" allows you to choose between superior selectivity ("narrow bandwidth") when it is warranted, and more realistic audio ("wide bandwidth") when it is not.

- **Synchronous selectable sideband.** This advanced feature further improves audio quality and selectivity. First, it virtually eliminates distortion resulting from fading. Second, because each world band signal consists of two identical "halves," in a number of situations it can simultaneously reduce adjacent-channel interference by selecting the "better half." *Tip:* On portables with this feature that have only one bandwidth, you can usually increase high-end ("treble") audio response by detuning the radio one or two kilohertz with the synchronous selectable sideband feature activated. (Of course, you can do this on *any* radio, but if it doesn't have this feature distortion will tend to increase the more you detune.)

net. No tuning knob. Clock not readable when radio is switched on. No meaningful signal-strength indicator. No AC adaptor comes standard, and polarity difference disallows use of customary Sony adaptors. No earphones/earpieces come standard.

Note: With any compact or pocket Sony portable having synchronous selectable sideband, it's a good idea to check in the store, or immediately after purchase, to ensure it was aligned properly at the factory: 1) put fresh batteries into the radio, 2) tune in a local mediumwave AM station, and 3) adjust the "sync" function back and forth between LSB and USB. If all is well, the audio will sound similar in both cases—*similar*, not identical, as there will always be at least some difference. However, if one choice sounds significantly muddier and bassier than the other, the unit is probably out of alignment and you should select another sample.

Bottom Line: The best compact model available for rejecting adjacent-channel interference and selective fading distortion—a major plus—but audio quality otherwise is *ordinaire*. A worthy value, mainly because it comes with synchronous selectable sideband. Quality control, after hiccups in early production, now seems to be quite good.

...Continued

- **Sensitivity to weak signals.** How a radio sounds doesn't mean much if the radio can't cough up the station in the first place. Most models have adequate sensitivity for listening to major stations if you're in such parts of the world as Europe, North Africa or the Near East. However, in places like North America west of the east coast, or Australia, received signals tend to be weak, and thus sensitivity becomes important. If you're in western North America, this is a crucial factor.

- **Superior ergonomics or ease of use.** Certain radios are easier to use than others. In some cases, that's because they don't have features which complicate operation. For example, a radio without single-sideband reception (for hearing hams and other non-world-band signals) is inherently more foolproof to use for world band than one with this feature. However, even models with complex features can be designed to operate relatively intuitively.

- **World Time clock.** Unless you listen to nothing more than the same one or two stations, a World Time clock (24-hour format) borders on a "must." You can buy these separately for as little as $10, but many radios come with them built in. Best among the built-ins is one that always displays World Time; worst is a radio that has to be switched off for the clock to display, or which has a 12-hour-format clock. As a compromise, some models have a button that allows you to display the time briefly.

- **AC adaptor.** Back when portables were larger, they sometimes could be plugged right into the wall, as well as run off batteries. Now, an AC adaptor is needed. An AC adaptor that comes standard with the radio is best, as it is designed to work with the radio, and a multivoltage adaptor is ideal if you spend a lot of time traveling abroad. It's a sad commentary that $60 telephone answering machines and the like come standard with an AC adaptor, but not most world band portables costing far more.

If you like to hear the same roster of stations, consider the Sony ICF-SW55. Its presets display actual station names, along with other helpful information.

★ ★ ★

Sony ICF-SW55

Price: $349.95 in the United States. CAN$599.00 in Canada. £249.95 in the United Kingdom. AUS$819.00 in Australia.

Advantages: Although sound emerges through a small port, rather than the usual speaker grille, audio quality is better than most in its size class. Dual bandwidths. Tunes in precise 0.1 kHz increments (displays only in 1 kHz increments). Controls neatly and logically laid out. Innovative tuning system, including factory pre-stored station presets and displayed alphabetic identifiers for groups ("pages") of stations. Weak-signal sensitivity a bit better than most. Good single-sideband reception, although reader reports continue to complain of some BFO "pulling" or "wobbling" (not found in our unit). Comes complete with carrying case containing reel-in wire antenna, AC adaptor, DC power cord and in-the-ear earpieces. Signal/battery strength indicator. Local and World Time clocks, either (but not both) of which is displayed separately from frequency.

Summer time adjustment for local time clock. Snooze/alarm features. Five-event (daily only) timer nominally can automatically turn on/off certain cassette recorders—a plus for VCR-type multiple-event recording. Illuminated display. Receives longwave and Japanese FM bands.

Disadvantages: "Page" tuning system difficult for some to grasp. Operation sometimes unnecessarily complicated by any yardstick, but especially for listeners in the Americas. Spurious-signal rejection, notably in higher world band segments, not fully commensurate with price class. Wide bandwidth somewhat broad for world band reception. Display illumination dim and uneven. Costly to operate from batteries. Cabinet keeps antenna from tilting fully, a slight disadvantage for reception of some FM signals.

Bottom Line: If the ICF-SW55's operating scheme meets with your approval—for example, if you are comfortable utilizing the more sophisticated features of a typical VCR or computer—and you're looking for a small portable with good audio, this radio is a superior performer in its size class. It can also tape like a VCR, provided you have a suitable recorder to connect to it.

New for 1997
★ ★ ★

Sangean ATS 909
Siemens RK 777

Price: *Sangean:* $299.95 in the United States. CAN$449.00 in Canada.

Advantages: Exceptionally wide range of tuning facilities and hundreds of presets, including one which works with a single touch. Alphanumeric station descriptors. Two voice bandwidths, well-chosen. Tunes single sideband in unusually precise 0.04 kHz increments. Sensitivity to weak signals slightly above average. Superb multivoltage AC adaptor with North American and European plugs. Travel power lock. 24-hour clock shows at all times, and can display local time in various cities of the world. 1-10 digital signal-strength indicator. Clock radio function offers three "on" times for three discrete frequencies. Snooze feature. FM performs well overall, has RDS feature, and is in stereo through earpieces, included. Superior quality of construction.

Disadvantages: Lacks synchronous selectable sideband. Tuning knob tends to mute stations during bandscanning; remediable by modification via at least one American dealer (C. Crane). Large for a compact. Signal-seek scanner tends to stop on few active shortwave signals. Although scanner can operate out-of-band, reverts to default (in-band) parameters after one pass. Two-second wait between when preset is keyed and station becomes audible. Under certain conditions, alphanumeric station descriptor stays on full time, regardless of when designated station is active, and can even repeat the same single station ID throughout all channels in the world band spectrum; solution, commanding the set to revert to page 29 every time this happens, adds to tuning complexity. "Page" tuning system difficult for some to grasp, preceding aside. No carrying handle or strap. 24-hour clock set up to display home time, not World Time, although this is easily overcome by not using world-cities-time feature. Clock does not compensate for daylight (summer) time in each displayed city. RDS, which can automatically display FM-station IDs and update clock, requires strong signal to activate. AC adaptor lacks UL approval.

Bottom Line: The best offering from Sangean in years, though software is not the best. Especially appropriate for those seeking a wide range of operating fea-

tures or superior tuning of single-sideband signals.

Evaluation of New Model: Relatively hefty for a compact, the feature-laden Sangean ATS 909—generally similar to the Sony ICF-SW55, preceding—appeared only weeks before we went to press.

For travelers, there's a power lock to keep batteries from running down in transit, plus an indicator to let you know when the batteries get low. There's also a soft carrying pouch, although there's no carrying handle or strap whatsoever—a peculiar omission in a portable of this size. Another plus for travelers is that it comes standard with a multivoltage AC adaptor which automatically adjusts to the local current. In some parts of the world—possibly all—an international converter plug is also thrown in.

The '909 covers FM in stereo through earpieces, included, and receives the full radio spectrum from longwave through shortwave. A 24-hour clock displays at all times, and there is a system that shows local times in 42 cities of the world—more on this later. There is also something of a "triple-banger" clock-radio function which allows three on-times and frequencies to

Sangean's new ATS 909 is similar to the Sony ICF-SW55, but its software is strange at times.

Want a digital radio in analog drag? Try the new Sony ICF-SW40, foolproof to operate.

New for 1997

★ ★ ½   ¢

Sony ICF-SW40

Price: $149.95 in the United States
Advantages: Relatively affordable. Technologically unintimidating, using advanced digital circuitry in a radio disguised as slide-rule, or analog, tuned. 24-hour clock. Double-conversion circuitry, unusual in price class, reduces likelihood of reception of spurious "image" signals. Two "on" timers and snooze facility. Travel power lock. Illuminated LCD. Covers Japanese FM band.
Disadvantages: Single bandwidth is relatively wide, reducing adjacent-channel rejection. No keypad. Lacks coverage of 1625-1705 kHz portion of North American mediumwave AM band. No single-sideband or synchronous selectable sideband.
Bottom Line: Just the radio for Andy Rooney! If you're turned off by the 1990's cultural infatuation with things digital and complex, Sony's ICF-SW40 will feel like an old friend in your hands. Otherwise, look elsewhere.
Evaluation of New Model: Sony's new ICF-SW40 stands out in the pack by having digital frequency readout that's cleverly disguised to look like old-fashioned analog readout. Yes, it looks just like ye

olde slide-rule-tuned radio, right down to a fake moving "needle"!

Why, you ask, would anybody want to make a calculator that looks like a slide rule? According to Sony, it's to make available an attractive option for traditionalists comfortable with slide-rule-type dials—but who nonetheless want some of the benefits, such as presets, of today's digital technology. Such people tend to be overlooked in the general rush to a technological Shangri-La, often because they're busy and have better things to do than wrestle with high-tech puzzles.

The SW40 covers longwave, mediumwave AM, FM and shortwave continuously from 3850-26100 kHz. FM is in stereo with headphones, but mono through the speaker, and it covers both the Japanese and traditional FM bands. But there's a rub if you're in North America: Mediumwave AM-band coverage goes no higher than 1620 kHz, so it misses most of the extended North American AM band, which goes to 1705 kHz.

The SW40 may look like an analog radio, but for the most part it tunes like it's digital. As you'd expect, there's the traditional tuning knob, but that's true on many purely digital models, as well. That knob has manually selectable tuning rates, which helps with bandscanning. Shortwave, for example, tunes in either 1 kHz or 5 kHz increments.

The radio also has 20 presets, or memories, which you select by pushing a button, then spinning the tuning knob—an eminently sensible arrangement, as you can see the offerings simply and quickly. And you can carousel upwards from one world band segment to another just by pressing the "SW" button. These advanced tuning features are intuitive and very easy to use, even if the tuning knob doesn't turn very smoothly.

But there's a price to be paid for having a digital radio in drag. There's no such thing as a genuine analog radio with a keypad, so there's none on the SW40. That's a distinct drawback that arguably carries the "analog" ruse too far. There's no single-sideband, either— much less synchronous selectable sideband—but both these features, worthy though they are, tend to complicate operation unnecessarily for many listeners.

There's also a 24-hour clock, as well as two "on" timers which automatically switch off after 60 minutes, making it something of a "double-banger" clock radio. But unlike that arrangement on the new Sangean ATS 909, when the timer switches on, the SW40 plays only the last-selected frequency. There's also a snooze timer that shuts off the radio after 15, 30 or 60 minutes.

For travelers, there's a power lock to keep the radio from switching on accidentally. And there's a light for the LCD, as well as a low-battery indicator.

The SW40 is just about the cheapest radio available with double conversion, so it's disinclined to produce image, or "ghost," signals. Dynamic range is good, too, and its audio quality and sensitivity are okay. The single bandwidth has obviously been chosen to give good fidelity to reasonably powerful, clean signals, but it's too wide for listening under congested conditions.

The Sony ICF-SW40, sans keypad or single sideband, and with a single and relatively wide bandwidth, is definitely not a radio for enthusiasts. Yet, it works nicely for program listeners who want something handy and uncomplicated to operate, with good reception of the major stations and even some less-powerful broadcasters.

★ ★½   ¢

Radio Shack/Realistic DX-375

Price: $99.99 in the United States. Not available in Australia.

Advantages: Excellent value. Several handy tuning features. Weak-signal sensitivity a bit above average. Relatively easy to use for digital portable in its price class. Stereo FM through headphones, not supplied. Travel power lock. Timer. 30-day money-back trial period in the United States.

Disadvantages: Mediocre spurious-signal ("image") rejection. Unusually long pause of silence when tuning from channel to channel. Antenna swivel sometimes needs tightening. AC adaptor plug easy to insert accidentally into headphone socket. Build quality, although adequate, appears to be slightly below average. Static discharges sometimes disable microprocessor (usually remediable if batteries are removed for a time, then replaced). No World Time clock. AC adaptor extra. No longwave.

Bottom Line: No Volvo, but if you absolutely, positively don't want to spend more than $100, this is still a sensible choice.

In some countries, Radio Shack and Tandy stores are as ubiquitous as hamburger outlets. This makes their compact DX-375 a popular choice, even if by now other models offer slightly more for the money.

The Tesonic R-3000 has appeared under various brand names. Attractive price, but mediocre quality control.

★ ★   ¢

Tesonic R-3000

Price: *R-3000:* ¥620 (about US$71) in China.

Advantages: Relatively inexpensive for a model with digital frequency display, keypad and station presets (18 for world band, 18 for FM and mediumwave AM). Up/down slew tuning with "signal-seek" scanning. Slightly better adjacent-channel rejection (selectivity) than usual for price category. World Time and local clocks (see Disadvantages). Alarm/snooze timer. Illuminated display. FM stereo via optional headphones.

Disadvantages: Mediocre build quality, with one sample having poor sensitivity, another having skewed bandwidth filtering. Inferior dynamic range and spurious-signal rejection. Does not tune 5800-5815, 9300-9495, 11500-11575, 13570-13870, 15000-15095, 18900-19020 kHz and some other useful portions of the world band spectrum. No tuning knob. Tunes world band only in coarse 5 kHz steps. No longwave. No signal-strength indicator. No travel power lock (lock provided serves another function), but power switch not easy to turn on accidentally. No AC adaptor. Clocks do not display

independent of frequency. Static discharges occasionally disable microprocessor in high-static environments (usually remediable if batteries are removed for a time, then replaced).

Bottom Line: Made by the Disheng Electronic Cooperative, Ltd., in Guangzhou, China, this bargain-priced model has excellent features, with much-improved performance over our original test in 1992. However, lacks complete frequency coverage and appears to have unusually high sample-to-sample variations in performance.

★ ★

Sangean ATS 800A
Roberts R801
Siemens RP 647G4

Price: *Sangean:* $89.95 in the United States. CAN$129.95 in Canada. Not available in Australia. CAN$14.95 in Canada. ADP-808 120 VAC adaptor extra. *Roberts:* £79.99 in the United Kingdom. *Siemens:* The equivalent of about US$90 in the European Union.

Advantages: Already-pleasant speaker audio improves with headphones. Five station preset buttons retrieve up to ten world band and ten AM/FM stations. Reasonable adjacent-channel rejection (selectivity) for price class. Weak-signal sensitivity a bit better than most. Simple to operate for radio at this technology level. World Time clock. Timer/snooze/alarm features. Travel power lock. Low-battery indicator. Stereo FM via earpieces, supplied in Sangean version. Superior quality of construction.

Disadvantages: Mediocre spurious-signal ("image") rejection. Inferior dynamic range, especially a drawback for listeners in Europe, North Africa and the Near East. Does not tune such important world band ranges as 7305-7600, 9300-9495 and 21755-21850 kHz. Tunes world

Sangean's ATS 800A has little but price to commend it, but is well constructed.

Illuminated display. Alarm/snooze features. FM stereo (see Disadvantages) via earbuds, included.

Disadvantages: Requires patience to get a station, as it tunes world band only via 10 station presets and multi-speed up/down slewing/scanning. Tunes world band only in coarse 5 kHz steps. Even-numbered frequencies displayed with final zero omitted; e.g., 5.75 rather than conventional 5.750 or 5750. Poor spurious-signal ("image") rejection. So-so adjacent-channel rejection (selectivity). World Time clock not displayed independent of frequency. Does not receive relatively unimportant 6200-7100 kHz portion of world band spectrum. Does not receive 1615-1705 kHz portion of expanded AM band in the Americas. No signal-strength indicator. No travel power lock. Mediumwave AM tuning increments not switchable, which may make for inexact tuning in some parts of the world other than where the radio was purchased. FM selectivity and capture ratio mediocre. FM stereo did not trigger on our unit.

Bottom Line: Made by a joint venture between Xin Hui Electronics and Shang-hai Huaxin Electronic Instruments. No prize, but as good you'll find among the truly cheap, which probably accounts for its being the #1 seller among digital world band radios in China.

band only in coarse 5 kHz steps. No tuning knob; tunes only via multi-speed up/down slewing buttons. No longwave. Signal-strength indicator nigh useless. No display illumination. Clock not displayed separately from frequency. No carrying strap or handle. AC adaptor extra. *Sangean:* FM tuning steps do not conform to channel spacing in much of the world outside the Americas. *Sangean and Siemens:* Do not receive 1635-1705 kHz portion of expanded AM band in Americas.

Comment: Strong signals within the 7305-7595 kHz range can be tuned, at reduced strength, via the "image" signal 900 kHz down; e.g., 7425 kHz may be heard on 6525 kHz.

Bottom Line: Not competitive within its price class.

★ ★

Bolong HS-490

Price: ¥360 (about US$41) in China.
Advantages: Inexpensive for a model with digital frequency display, ten world band station presets, and ten station presets for mediumwave AM and FM. World Time clock (see Disadvantages). Tape-reel-type outboard passive antenna accessory comes standard. AC adaptor.

The so-so Bolong HS-490 is the #1 seller in China.

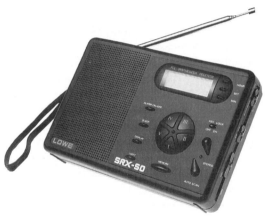

Sold under many names, the Amsonic AS-908 offers little but low price.

★ ★

Price: *Lowe:* £39.95 in the United Kingdom. *Galaxis:* About the equivalent of US$33 in the European Union. *Morphy Richards:* £37.00 in the United Kingdom. *Yorx:* CAN$56 in Canada.

Advantages: Inexpensive for a model with digital frequency display, five world band station presets (ten on the Yorx), plus ten station presets for mediumwave AM and FM. Relatively simple to operate for technology class. Illuminated display. Alarm/snooze features. FM stereo via headphones. *Except Yorx:* World Time clock. Longwave. *Yorx:* Ten, rather than five, world band station presets. AC adaptor and stereo earpieces come standard. *Galaxis and Lowe:* Headphones included.

Disadvantages: Substandard build quality. No tuning knob; tunes only via station presets and multi-speed up/down slewing/scanning. Tunes world band only in coarse 5 kHz steps. Even-numbered frequencies displayed with final zero omitted; e.g., 5.75 rather than conven-

tional 5.750 or 5750. Poor spurious-signal ("image") rejection. Mediocre selectivity. Does not receive 1605-1705 kHz portion of expanded AM band in the Americas. No signal-strength indicator. No travel power lock. Clock not displayed independent of frequency display. Mediumwave AM tuning increments not switchable, which may make for inexact tuning in some parts of the world other than where the radio was purchased. Power switch has no position labeled "off," although "auto radio" power-switch position performs a comparable role. *Except Yorx:* Does not tune important 5800-5895, 17500-17900 and 21750-21850 kHz segments; 15505-15695 kHz tunable only to limited extent (see Comment). No AC adaptor. *Yorx:* Does not receive 7300-9499 and 21750-21850 kHz portions of the world band spectrum. Clock in 12-hour format.

Comment: Strong signals within the 15505-15800 kHz range can be tuned via the "image" signal 900 kHz down; e.g., 15685 kHz may be heard on 14785 kHz.

Bottom Line: Outclassed by newer models.

★ ★

Price: $49.95 plus $4 shipping by mail order in the United States. About the equivalent of US$50 in China.

Advantages: One of the least costly portables with digital frequency display and presets (ten for world band, ten for AM/FM) and "signal-seek" scan tuning. Slightly more selective than usual for price category. Relatively simple to operate for technology class. World Time clock. Alarm/snooze features. Illuminated display. FM stereo via optional headphones.

Disadvantages: Mediocre build quality. Relatively lacking in weak-signal sensitivity. No tuning knob; tunes only via presets and multi-speed up/down slewing.

Tunes world band only in coarse 5 kHz steps. Mediumwave AM tuning steps do not conform to channel spacing in much of the world outside the Americas. Frequency display in confusing XX.XX/XX.XX5 MHz format. Poor spurious-signal ("image") rejection. Mediocre dynamic range. Does not tune relatively unimportant 6200-7100 and 25600-26100 kHz world band segments. Does not receive longwave band or 1615-1705 kHz portion of expanded AM band in the Americas. No signal-strength indicator. No travel power lock switch. No AC adaptor. Antenna swivels, but does not rotate; swivel breaks relatively easily. Limited dealer network.

Bottom Line: Audi cockpit, moped engine.

★ ★

Rodelsonic Digital World Band
Rodelvox Digital World Band
Amsonic AS-138
Dick Smith Digitor A-4336
Scotcade 65B 119 UCY Digital
Shimasu PLL Digital
World Wide 4 Band Digital Receiver

Price: *Rodelvox and Rodelsonic:* $99.95 plus $6.95 shipping in United States. *Amsonic:* ¥265 (about US$31) in China. *Dick Smith Digitor:* AUS$79.95. *Scotcade:* £29.99 plus shipping in the United Kingdom.

Advantages: Relatively inexpensive for a model with digital frequency display and 20 station presets (ten for world band, ten for mediumwave AM and FM). Relatively simple to operate for technology class. Alarm/snooze features with World Time clock. Illuminated display. FM stereo via optional headphones.

Disadvantages: Poor build quality. Modest weak-signal sensitivity. No tuning knob; tuned only by station presets and multi-speed up/down slewing/scanning. Tunes world band only in coarse 5 kHz steps. Even-numbered frequencies dis-

played with final zero omitted; e.g., 5.75 rather than conventional 5.750. Poor spurious-signal ("image") rejection. Mediocre dynamic range. Does not receive 1635-1705 kHz portion of expanded AM band in the Americas. No signal-strength indicator. Clock in 12-hour format, not displayed independent of frequency. No travel power lock. No AC adaptor. Quality of construction appears to be below average. Mediumwave AM tuning increments not switchable, which may make for inexact tuning in some parts of the world other than where the radio was purchased. *Except Scotcade:* Does not tune important 7305-9495 and 21755-21850 kHz segments. No longwave.

Note: The Amsonic is available in at least five versions: AS-138 for China, AS-138-0 for Europe, AS-138-3 for USA/Canada, AS-138-4 for Japan, and AS-138-6 for other countries and Europe. Each version has FM and mediumwave AM ranges and channel spacing appropriate to the market region, plus the Japanese version replaces coverage of the 21 MHz band with TV audio.

Comment: Strong signals within the 7305-7595 kHz range can be tuned via the "image" signal 900 kHz down; e.g., 7435 kHz may be heard on 6535 kHz.

Bottom Line: Poorly made, no bargain.

★ ★

Jäger PL-440
Omega

Price: *Jäger:* $79.95 plus $6.00 shipping in the United States. *Omega:* 1,500 francs in Belgium.

Advantages: Relatively inexpensive for a model with digital frequency display. Tuning aids include up/down slewing buttons with "signal-seek" scanning, and 20 station presets (five each for world band, FM, longwave and mediumwave AM). Relatively simple to operate for tech-

The Jäger PL-440 is still occasionally found under the Omega label. It just squeaks into two-star status.

nology class. World Time clock. Snooze/ timer features. Longwave. Antenna rotates and tilts, unusual in price class. Travel power lock.

Disadvantages: Mediocre build quality. Limited coverage of world band spectrum omits important 5800-5945, 15605-15695, 17500-17900 and 21450-21850 kHz ranges, among others. No tuning knob; tunes only via station presets and multi-speed up/down slewing/scanning. Tunes world band only in coarse 5 kHz steps. Tortoise-slow band-to-band tuning, remediable by using station presets as band selectors. Slow one-channel-at-a-time slewing is the only means for bandscanning between world band segments. Slightly insensitive to weak signals. Poor adjacent-channel rejection (selectivity). Even-numbered frequencies displayed with final zero omitted; e.g., 5.75 rather than conventional 5.750 or 5750. No signal-strength indicator. Clock not displayed independent of frequency display. Display not illuminated. Not offered with AC adaptor. Does not receive 1605-1705 kHz portion of expanded AM band in the Americas. Lacks selector for 9/10 kHz mediumwave AM steps.

Bottom Line: An Omega not to watch out for.

★½ **Aroma SEG SED-ECL88C** and **Giros R918**. Avoid.

LAP PORTABLES

Good for Home, Fair for Travel

If you're looking for a home set, yet one that also can be taken out in the back-yard and on the occasional trip, a lap portable is probably your best bet. These are large enough to perform well and can sound pretty good, yet are compact enough to tote in your suitcase now and then. Most take 3-4 "D" (UM-1) cells, plus a couple of "AA" (UM-3) cells for their fancy computer circuits.

How large? Typically just under a foot wide—that's 30 cm—and weighing in around 3-4 pounds, or 1.3-1.8 kg. For air travel, that's okay if you are a dedicated listener, but a bit much otherwise. Too, larger sets with snazzy controls occasion-ally attract unwanted attention from suspicious customs and airport-security personnel in some parts of the world.

Two stand out for most listeners: the high-tech Sony ICF-2010, formerly also sold as the ICF-2001D; and Grundig's sleek Satellit 700, soon to be replaced by the Satellit 900. The mid-priced Sony is the obvious choice for radio enthusiasts, whereas the Grundig should appeal to the larger body of regular listeners to world band, FM and mediumwave AM stations.

The revised Sony ICF-SW77, like opera, is not for everybody. With this high-tech wonder, it's either love or hate—little between.

★ ★ ★½ *Passport's Choice*

Sony ICF-2010

Price: $379.95 in the United States. CAN$599.00 in Canada. ¥4,500 (about $540) in China. No longer distributed at retail in several parts of the world, but is available worldwide by mail order from North American world band specialty firms.

Advantages: High-tech synchronous detection with selectable sideband; on the '2010, this feature performs very well, indeed, reducing adjacent-channel interference and fading distortion on world band, longwave and mediumwave AM signals. This is further aided by two bandwidths which offer superior tradeoff between audio fidelity and adjacent-channel rejection (selectivity). Use of 32 separate station preset buttons in rows and columns is ergonomically the best to be found on any model, portable or tabletop, at any price—simply pushing one button one time brings in your station, a major convenience. Numerous other helpful tuning features. Weak-signal sensitivity better than most. Tunes and displays in precise 0.1 kHz increments. Separately displayed World Time clock. Alarm/snooze features, with four-event timer. Illuminated LCD. Travel power lock. Signal-strength indicator. Covers longwave and the Japanese FM band. FM unusually sensitive to weak signals, making it appropriate for fringe reception in some areas (see Disadvantages). Some passable reception of air band signals (most versions). AC adaptor.

Disadvantages: Audio quality only average, with mediocre tone control. Controls and high-tech features, although exceptionally handy once you get the hang of them, initially may intimidate or confuse. Station presets and clock/timer features immediately erase whenever computer batteries are replaced, and also sometimes when set is jostled (changing to a different brand of battery sometimes helps); this erasing also sometimes happens irregularly with no apparent cause on aging units. Wide bandwidth tends to be broad for world band reception, but narrower aftermarket (non-Sony) replacement filters reportedly cause sound to be muffled. "Signal-seek" scanning works poorly. Telescopic antenna swivel gets slack with use, requiring periodic adjust-

The Mother of All Portables is Sony's ICF-2010. Great performance, and tunes with only one push of a button.

ment of tension screw. Synchronous selectable sideband subject to imperfect alignment, both from factory and from seeming drift after purchase, causing synchronous selectable sideband reception to be more muffled in one sideband than the other, particularly with the narrow bandwidth. Synchronous selectable sideband does not switch off during tuning. Lacks up/down slewing. Keypad not in telephone format. LCD clearly readable only when radio viewed from below. Chugs slightly when tuned. 100 Hz tuning resolution means that non-synchronous single-sideband reception can be mistuned by up to 50 Hz. In urban areas, FM band can overload badly, causing false "repeat" signals to appear (see Advantages). Air band insensitive to weak signals.

Bottom Line: Our panelists, like opinionated Supreme Court justices, usually issue split decisions, but not with this model. Since its introduction, it has always been, and very much still is, our unanimous favorite among portables. It is among the best portables for rejection of one of world band's major bugaboos, adjacent-channel interference, and yet it is able to retain a relatively wide audio bandwidth for listening pleasure. Alone among sophisticated portables, it allows dozens of stations to be brought up literally at the single touch of a button. Except for everyday audio quality and urban FM, Sony's high-tech offering is, for many, the best performing portable—regardless of where you live.

 An *RDI WHITE PAPER* is available for this model.

★ ★ ★½   *Passport's Choice*

Grundig Satellit 700

Price: $499.95 in the United States. CAN$649.95 in Canada. £369.95 in the United Kingdom. AUS$1,190.00 in Australia.

Advantages: Superior audio quality, aided by separate continuous bass and treble controls. High-tech synchronous detector circuit with selectable sideband reduces adjacent-channel interference and fading distortion on world band, longwave and mediumwave AM signals (see Disadvantages); it also provides superior reception of reduced-carrier single-sideband signals. Two bandwidths offer superior tradeoff between audio fidelity and adjacent-channel rejection (selectivity). Weak-signal sensitivity better than most; to aid in hearing weak-signals, if an external antenna is connected to the radio's antenna socket, leave the antenna switch set to "INT," switching over to the "EXT" position only if and when you encounter overloading. 512 station presets standard; up to 2048 station presets optionally available. Schedules for 22 stations stored by factory in memory. Stored station names appear on LCD. Numerous other helpful tuning features. Tunes and displays in precise 0.1 kHz increments in synchronous and single-sideband modes; this, along with a fine-tuning clarifier, produce the best tuning configuration for single sideband in a conventional travel-weight portable. Separately displayed World Time clock. Alarm/snooze features with superior timer that, in principle, can also control a recorder. Superior FM reception. Stereo FM through headphones. Illuminated LCD, which is clearly visible from a variety of angles. Travel power lock. Heavy-duty telescopic antenna. Screw mounts for mobile or maritime operation. Runs off AC power worldwide. Comes with built-in NiCd battery charger. RDS circuitry for FM. Excellent operator's manuals.

Disadvantages: Chugs when tuned slowly by knob; worse, mutes completely when tuned quickly, making bandscanning unnecessarily difficult. Using station presets relatively complex. Synchronous selectable sideband feature produces minor background rumble and has relatively little sideband separation. Some overall distortion except in AM mode. Wide bandwidth a touch broad for most world band reception. Keypad lacks feel and is not in telephone format. Antenna keels over in certain settings. Location of tuning controls and volume control on separate sides of case tend to make listening a two-handed affair.

Note: This model may be replaced in early 1997 by the Satellit 900.

Bottom Line: An excellent offering, the favorite model of a broad swathe of regular world band program listeners. Withal, notably for bandscanning, not quite all it should be.

The Grundig Satellit 900 is scheduled to replace the Satellit 700, shown on page 88.

Retested for 1977

★ ★ ★½

Top of Sony's line is the ICF-SW77, but for many it is too complicated to operate. Still, those who like it, love it.

Sony ICF-SW77
Sony ICF-SW77E

Price: $499.95 in the United States. CAN$699.00 in Canada. £349.95 in the United Kingdom. AUS$1,249.00 in Australia. ¥8,000 (about $960) in China.

Advantages: A rich variety of tuning features, including innovative computer-type graphical interface not found on other world band models. Synchronous selectable sideband, which in most samples performs as it should, is exceptionally handy to operate; it significantly reduces fading distortion and adjacent-channel interference on world band, longwave and mediumwave AM signals. Two well-chosen bandwidths provide superior adjacent-channel rejection. Tunes in exacting 50 Hz increments; displays in precise 100 Hz increments. Two illuminated multi-function liquid crystal displays. Pre-set world band segments. Keypad tuning. Tuning "knob" with two speeds. 162 station presets, including 96 frequencies stored by country or station name. "Signal-seek" scanning. Separately displayed World Time and local time clocks. Station name appears on LCD when station presets used. Signal-strength indicator. Flip-up chart for calculating time differences. VCR-type five-event timer controls radio and optional outboard recorder alike. Continuous bass and treble tone controls. Superior FM audio quality. Stereo FM through headphones. Receives longwave and Japanese FM. AC adaptor.

Disadvantages: Excruciatingly complex for many, but by no means all, to operate. Station presets can't be accessed simply, as they can on most models. Synthesizer chugging, as bad as we've encountered in our tests, degrades the quality of tuning by knob. Dynamic range only fair.

Synchronous selectable sideband subject to imperfect alignment, both from factory and from seeming drift after purchase, causing synchronous selectable sideband reception to be more muffled in one sideband than the other, particularly with the narrow bandwidth. Flimsy telescopic antenna. Display illumination does not stay on with AC power. On mediumwave AM band, relatively insensitive, sometimes with spurious sounds during single-sideband reception; this doesn't apply to world band reception, however. Mundane reception of difficult FM signals. Signal-strength indicator over-reads.

Bottom Line: Our retest of the Sony ICF-SW77 for 1997 produced no surprises, except for sample-to-sample variability—seemingly a problem with all Sony models having synchronous selectable sideband. The '77, a generally superior performer since it was improved a few years back, uses innovative high technology in an attempt to make listening easier. Results, however, are a mixed bag: What is gained in convenience in some areas is lost in others. The upshot is that whether using the '77 is enjoyable or a hair-pulling exercise comes down to personal taste. In our survey some relish it, most don't. Best bet: If you're interested, try it out first.

Sangean's ATS-818 is a big seller, especially under the Radio Shack and Roberts labels. It's a predictable performer except for bandscanning.

★ ★½

Sangean ATS-818
Radio Shack/Realistic DX-390
Roberts R817

Price: *Sangean:* $199.95 in the United States. CAN$289.00 in Canada. £169.95 in the United Kingdom. AUS$349.00 in Australia. *Radio Shack/Realistic:* $219.99 (as low as $169.99 during special sales) plus optional #273-1655 AC adaptor at Radio Shack stores in the United States. CAN$299.95 plus #273-1454 AC adaptor in Canada. No longer available in Australia. *Roberts:* £169.95 in the United Kingdom.

Advantages: Superior overall world band performance. Numerous tuning features, including 18 world band station presets. Two bandwidths for good fidelity/interference tradeoff. Superior spurious-signal ("image") rejection. Illuminated display. Signal-strength indicator. Two 24-hour clocks, one for World Time, with either displayed separately from frequency. Alarm/snooze/timer features.

Travel power lock. FM stereo through headphones. Longwave. Superior quality of construction. *Sangean:* AC adaptor. *Radio Shack/Realistic:* 30-day money-back trial period in United States.

Disadvantages: Mutes when tuning knob turned quickly, making bandscanning difficult (*see Note, below*). Wide bandwidth a bit broad for world band reception. Keypad not in telephone format. For single-sideband reception, relies on a touchy variable control instead of separate LSB/USB switch positions. Does not come with tape-recorder jack. *Radio Shack/Realistic:* AC adaptor, which some readers complain causes hum and buzz, is extra.

Note: Tuning-knob muting reportedly can be eliminated, albeit with some side effects, by disabling or removing diode D29, according to reader Steven Johnson. We can't vouch for this or any other homebrew modification, but if you are comfortable working with electronic circuitry and wish to take the plunge, you can get further information by writing him at P.O. Box 80042, Fort Wayne IN 46898 USA. He tells us he will be glad to reply, but please enclose a self-addressed stamped envelope, or outside the United States a self-addressed envelope with 3 IRCs or $1, to cover return postage.

Bottom Line: A decent, predictable radio—performance and features, alike—but mediocre for bandscanning.

The PASSPORT *portable-radio review team includes regulars Lawrence Magne, Jock Elliott and Tony Jones, with laboratory measurements performed independently by Sherwood Engineering. Additional research this year by John Campbell (U.K.), Lamar Johnson (U.S.), Lars Rydén (China), Harlan Seyfer (China) and Craig Tyson (Australia), with a tip of the hat to Paul Donegan and Hugh Waters (Singapore).*

Oldies, Some Goodies

The following digital models reportedly have been discontinued, yet may still be available new at a limited number of retail outlets. Cited are typical recent sale prices in the United States ($) and United Kingdom (£). Prices elsewhere may differ.

Sangean ATS-803A
Siemens RK 651
Supertech SR-16H

★ ★ ★   *Passport's Choice* ¢

The best radio Sangean ever manufactured, and a pity that it was discontinued in 1995. This lap model is occasionally still found for under the equivalent of $140.

Panasonic RF-B65
Panasonic RF-B65D
Panasonic RF-B65L
National B65

★ ★ ★

A slightly fancier version of the current Panasonic RF-B45, this model is well-constructed and easy-to-use. A good choice for Europe or eastern North America, where world band signals are relatively strong. Still widely available in some countries. Under $270 or £170.

Sony ICF-SW7600

★ ★ ★·

Worthy and proven all-around performer. Similar to the current Sony ICF-SW7600G (see), but without synchronous selectable sideband. Under $200 or £180.

Sony ICF-SW1S   *Passport's Choice*

★ ★ ★

Although pricey with mediocre speaker sound, the itsy Sony ICF-SW1S, a generally superior performer, is about as close as you'll get to a "world band Walkman" this side of the current Sony ICF-SW100. Under $300 or £230.

Sony ICF-SW1E   *Passport's Choice*

★ ★ ★

Identical to Sony ICF-SW1S, above, except lacks a carrying case and most accessories. Never available in North America. Under $300 or £180.

Sony ICF-SW33

★ ★½

A good performer, but inconvenient to tune—something of a fancier version of the current Sony ICF-SW30. Nominally not in the product line, but still widely available, so who knows. Under $180, CAN$300 or £90.

Sony's ICF-SW33 is still widely available.

Analog Portables

With digitally tuned portables now commonplace and affordable, there's little reason to purchase an analog, or slide-rule-tuned, model. They lack every tuning aid except a knob, and their coarse indicators make it almost impossible to tell the frequency.

Yet, for the money—nearly all sell for under the equivalent of US$100 or £70—these models sometimes have better weak-signal sensitivity than some of their digital counterparts. However, if you're located where signals are weak, such as western North America, and watching your budget, you'll be far better off with the digitally tuned Grundig Yacht Boy 305, which costs little more.

Listed in order of overall performance.

Pocket Analog Portables

★ ★ **Sony ICF-SW22.** Tiny, with superior spurious signal ("image") rejection, but tinny sound and limited frequency coverage.

★½ **Grundig Yacht Boy 207, Grundig Yacht Boy 217, Panasonic RF-B11, Sangean MS-103, Sangean MS-103L, Sangean MS-101, Aiwa WR-A100, Radio Shack/Realistic DX-351, Roberts R101, Sangean SG-789A** and **Sangean SG-789L.**

Compact Analog Portables

★½ **Sangean SG-700L, Radio Shack/Realistic DX-350, Panasonic RF-B20L, Panasonic RF-B20, National B20, Grundig Yacht Boy 230, Amsonic AS-912, Panopus Yacht Boy 230, Sangean SG 621, Sangean SG 631, Siemens RK 710, Sony ICF-SW10, Roberts R621, Elektro AC 100, International AC 100, SoundTronic Multi- band Receiver, Pomtrex 120-00300, TEC 235TR, MCE-7760, Pace, SEG Precision World SED 110, Kchibo KK-210B** and **Kchibo KK-168.**

★ **Windsor 2138, Apex 2138, Garrard Shortwave Radio 217, Silver International MT-798, Panashiba FX-928, Shiba Elec- tronics FX-928, Cougar H-88, Cougar RC210, Precision World SED 901, Opal OP-35, Grundig Traveller II (analog ver- sion)** and **Siemens RK 702.**

Although the Grundig Traveller II analog portable is Grundig's worst-performing model, it reportedly sells well. The new Grundig Traveller II Digital is far superior.

Full-Sized Analog Portable

★ **Venturer Multiband, Alconic Series 2959, Dick Smith D-2832, Rhapsody Multiband, Shimasu Multiband, Steepletone MBR-7, Steepletone MBR-8, Radio Shack/Realistic SW-100, Electro Brand SW-2000** and **Electro Brand 2971.**

Recording Shows While You're Away!

Millians do it daily: record television programs on VCRs so they can be enjoyed at a more convenient time. You'd think that with world band radio sales rising for several years now, there would be any number of world band cassette recorders, or WCRs, from which to choose. But until recently, there were none other than glorified boom boxes with Stone Age shortwave bands.

This drought was relieved in 1992 when Sangean introduced their value-priced WCR, the ATS-818CS, which has gone on to became a major seller. Now, Sony has bowed in with its own offering—the ICF-SW1000T.

There's no question which is better: the Sony. It's lots smaller, too, so it's less likely to raise eyebrows among airport security personnel. But its price difference over the Sangean—a nice, serviceable model—is considerable.

Wrestle with your conscience, then decide.

> No question which is better: the Sony. But the Sangean is nice, and much cheaper.

That's it? Not quite. The Aiwa HS-TS5000 is a world band radio with a built-in cassette. As it sells for under $100, it might seem like the perfect solution . . . except that it can't do any off-air recording!

Keep in mind that a few ordinary portables can be programmed to switch not only themselves on and off, but also a cassette recorder. Less handy, but it can be cheaper.

Sony is the Master of Shoehorning, and its new ICF-SW1000T worldband cassette recorder is no exception. Even including its stereo recorder, it's no larger than most ordinary compact models. Easy on batteries, too.

New for 1997
★ ★ ★

Passport's Choice

Sony ICF-SW1000T

Price: $549.95 in the United States. CAN$779.00 in Canada. £429.99 in the United Kingdom.

Advantages: Relatively small, important for airport security. Synchronous selectable sideband reduces adjacent-channel interference and fading distortion on world band, longwave and mediumwave AM signals (see Disadvantages). Single bandwidth, especially when the sync feature is used, exceptionally effective at adjacent-channel rejection. Numerous helpful tuning features, including keypad, two-speed up/down slewing, 32 presets and "signal-seek" scanning. Effectively demodulates single-sideband signals, used by hams and utility stations. World Time clock, easy to set. Snooze/timer features. Illuminated display. Travel power lock. FM stereo through earpieces (supplied). Receives longwave and Japanese FM bands. Tape-reel-type outboard passive antenna accessory included.

Dead-battery indicator. Comes standard with lapel mic and vinyl carrying case.

Disadvantages: Expensive. Incredibly at this price, only one bandwidth, and no AC adaptor comes standard. Synchronous selectable sideband feature, at least on our unit, needed fairly fresh batteries to maintain lock needed for proper performance. No tuning knob. Clock not readable when radio switched on except for ten-seconds when button is pushed. No meaningful signal-strength indicator. No recording-level indicator. Lacks built-in mic and stereo mic facility. Lacks flip-out elevation panel; uses less-handy plug-in elevation tab, instead. FM sometimes overloads. Telescopic antenna exits from the side, which limits tilting choices for FM.

Note: With any compact or mini Sony portable having synchronous selectable sideband, it's a good idea to check in the store, or immediately after purchase, to ensure it was aligned properly at the factory: 1) put fresh batteries into the radio, 2) tune in a local mediumwave AM station, and 3) adjust the "sync" function back and forth between LSB and USB. If all is well, the audio will sound similar in both cases—*similar*, not identical, as there will always be at least some difference. However, if one choice sounds significantly muddier and bassier than the other, the unit is probably out of alignment and you should select another sample.

Bottom Line: An innovative, neat little package—but pricey.

Evaluation of New Model: Smaller than most compact portables sans recorders, Sony's new ICF-SW1000T—the latest Sony model to sound like a carburetor part number—is best described as an improved Sony ICF-SW7600G compact portable, but with a built-in cassette recorder and a page-based system of 32 presets. It's a great radio, but relatively pricey.

For all that money, you get a radio that does things none other quite does. To begin with, Sony's engineers have shoehorned all manner of gear into a surprisingly small box. In part, this has been done by using a small speaker and only three little "AA" batteries, one of which is used for the recorder. And thanks to some technological gymnastics, this trio of batteries lasts a surprisingly long time.

When you think of VCRs—especially Sony VCRs—what springs to mind is a Frankenstein monster to operate. But the '1000T WCR is a relief from all that. Its "page" system of presets, for example, is handy and nigh foolproof, as is operation of the synchronous selectable sideband.

Indeed, the radio is surprisingly intuitive to operate, with a silly exception: One of the two radio batteries has to be installed backwards, with the positive end scrunched against a coiled-spring contact that would normally be negative. Otherwise, the radio won't work.

Performance is at least as good as on the '7600G, or even the pricier ICF-SW100S. Sensitivity to weak signals is reasonable—best below 16 MHz—and although there's no second bandwidth—surprising at this price—the lone bandwidth works nicely. Audio quality through the speaker is okay, nothing more.

The 1000T's built-in recorder has two user-programmable on/off events, like a VCR. This is a big improvement over the Sangean offering's single event with only the "on" setting being programmable, like an ordinary clock radio.

The ICF-SW1000T's recorder uses full-sized cassettes, loaded from the back of the radio and controlled from the top.

Except to some extent with reverse-direction recording, operation is straightforward, with good results in both mono and stereo. However, it's easy to activate the recorder by accident if you grasp the radio, as the buttons are at the top, where hands usually land when a radio is grabbed on the fly. True, you can use the lock switch to deactivate those buttons, but that also knocks out the radio controls. Too, rewind time is slow.

All recorders have bias circuits which can cause radio interference, so the '1000T has a three-position "ISS" switch to allow you to change that bias slightly if you encounter internally generated interference while taping. Of course, to put this to use, you have to do a dry run on the frequency to be taped before setting the timer, unless you're going to be around to monitor the taped broadcast.

Unlike most cassette recorders, the '1000T comes with no built-in mic. However, a plug-in lapel mic is included. The recorder automatically detects and adjusts for the type of magnetic media (regular or CrO_2) in use. Yet, peculiarly, the owner's manual twice indicates CrO_2 cassettes are not to be used!

In all, Sony's ICF-SW1000T does just about everything it should, and has only limited drawbacks. It's clearly a better recording device, and overall a better radio receiver, than Sangean's ATS-818CS offering. The Sony's size is much handier, too, although the Sangean has better, if also not inspiring, audio quality.

The value choice among worldband cassette recorders is the Sangean ATS-818CS, also offered by Radio Shack, Roberts and Siemens. Although it has limited features and is relatively large, its quality of construction is superior.

★ ★   ¢

Radio Shack/Realistic DX-392
Roberts RC818
Sangean ATS-818CS
Siemens RK 670

Price: *Radio Shack:* $259.99 in the United States. *Roberts:* £199.99 in the United Kingdom. *Sangean:* $224.95 in the United States; CAN$359.00 in Canada; AUS$399.95 in Australia.

Advantages: Price relative to competition. Superior overall world band performance. Numerous tuning features, including 18 world band station presets. Two bandwidths for good fidelity/interference tradeoff. Superior spurious-signal ("image") rejection. Illuminated display. Signal-strength indicator. Two 24-hour clocks, one for World Time, with either displayed separately from frequency. Alarm/snooze/timer features. Travel power lock. FM stereo through headphones. Longwave. Built-in condenser mic. Superior quality of construction, including tape deck. *Sangean:* Supplied with AC adaptor. *Radio Shack/Realistic:*

30-day money-back trial period (in United States).

Disadvantages: No multiple recording events, just one "on" time only (quits when tape runs out). Mutes when tuning knob turned quickly, making bandscanning difficult (see Note under review of regular Sangean ATS-818 portable). Wide bandwidth a bit broad for world band reception. Keypad not in telephone format. For single-sideband reception, relies on a touchy variable control instead of separate LSB/USB switch positions. Recorder has no level indicator, no stereo and no counter. Fast-forward and rewind controls installed facing backwards. *Radio Shack/Realistic:* AC adaptor, which some readers complain causes hum and buzz, is extra.

Bottom Line: Good value, but only single-event.

The PASSPORT *worldband cassette recorder review team: Lawrence Magne and Tony Jones.*

World Band in Your Car!

*L*ocal radio can wear down even the most patient driver, given station after station that drones on with formula programming. No wonder, then, that CD and cassette players are popular as an alternative.

But what about world band? Although shortwave sparkles evenings, it's also alive and well during the afternoon rush hour—to some extent mornings, as well. And it's heard from city to city, with no searches for new stations as the asphalt slips by. So, why aren't world band car radios more common? After all, Philips once made the DC-777, an excellent car stereo with world band, but that's long gone (see PASSPORT '93).

Becker to The Rescue

Nobody really knows. But the result is that for some time, world band in cars has largely been limited to portables on the seat or dash. But portables don't have outdoor antennas—a "must" inside a metal cage—and their audio output is usually too puny to overcome traffic noises.

Now, Becker, the German firm which provides gilt-edged radios for Mercedes-Benz, has come to the rescue with the Mexico 2340, $549.95 in the United States. It's available throughout much of Europe and North America, and comes with the usual stereo features, including an inboard cassette drive and optional outboard CD changer. And, no, you don't have to buy a Mercedes to own one—they're sold aftermarket. In fact, the 2340 doesn't even come with Mercedes cars unless ordered specially from the factory.

We first encountered Becker world band in the early

127

Sixties. Even then, international stations sounded better on a Becker than anything else. With Becker, now as then, you also get quality of construction long associated with that name and Mercedes-Benz. Good as the old Philips radio was, it wasn't made to hold up to the rigors of daily use.

Noise Inherent with Car Radio

Unlike most world band radios, those in cars have to overcome electrical noise from ignitions, microprocessor chips, wiper motors and the like. Diesels generate no ignition noise, but even they are a poor substitute for the relative quiet of a home environment.

> Car radios have to overcome ignition noise, but it's generally not serious.

There's not much you can do about electrical noise, but it's generally not serious enough to dampen listening to major world band stations. The Becker is sensitive enough for this and more, and you can improve weak-signal sensitivity by replacing your car's telescopic antenna with one that's longer. (Avoid amplified antennas, though. They tend to cause more problems than they solve.)

Buying a longer telescopic antenna is a nice idea in any event, but it becomes a virtual necessity if your car has a wire antenna embedded in the windshield or roof. Too, the Becker's microprocessor circuitry puts out its own small share of electrical noise that might whine in the background if an outboard telescopic antenna isn't used.

Ergonomics Essential

When you're driving along crowded roads, you can't devote much attention to the nuances of tuning stations. Ergonomics thus are not a luxury, but an important safety issue, just as with cellular car phones.

Fortunately, the Becker has reasonable ergonomics, albeit with a learning curve, weird keypad and no tuning knob. There are ten one-push buttons to call up presets—ten presets for world band, 30 for FM—as well as for direct-frequency entry. An even bigger plus is that its "signal-seek" scan circuit works well—essential for safe tuning while you're barreling down the highway surrounded by eighteen-

You usually find Becker car radios in Mercedes-Benz luxury cars.
But their model 2340 stereo system, which includes world band,
is now available for installation in any type of automobile.

Michael Pilla Photography

wheelers. Tuning is precise, too—1 kHz increments throughout the longwave, mediumwave AM and world band ranges.

There's only one bandwidth, an ergonomic virtue even if normally two bandwidths would be better. It's well chosen, being narrow enough to keep most interference at bay, yet wide enough to let through surprisingly pleasant audio.

Superb Audio Quality

The Becker is designed for quality audio reproduction, and sounds like it. Even allowing for the vagaries of world band reception, hearing this radio makes you wonder why world band portables and tabletops can't do as well.

The only slight hiccup is with fading. Fading is a fact of life with world band, and the Philips model had a superb automatic-gain-control (AGC) circuit which zapped nearly every trace of it. Here, the Becker fares less well, but still passes muster.

> This Becker radio sounds simply magnificent.

The end result is that the Becker sounds simply magnificent for listening to world band programs, better than virtually any regular tabletop or portable model. If your ears crave rich, full audio, then the 2340 may have you looking forward to driving just to hear how pleasant world band can really sound. And not just world band—FM and mediumwave AM also perform commendably, and the FM comes with an RDS system for automatic identification of stations.

Surely, then, this must be The Perfect Radio. Well, not quite . . .

Limited Frequency Coverage

Heading the no-no list is limited frequency coverage: Becker's pride and joy

only covers between 5900 and 15700 kHz. Daytime, that means you miss the 17, 19, 21 and 26 MHz segments, although of these only the first and third really count.

Evenings, you can't tune in the growing roster of stations between 5730-5895 kHz, much less the Latin American and other stations found between 4750-5100 kHz and even lower. It's not a life-or-death situation, but coverage from at least 4.7-22 MHz would have been much better.

Ditto the mediumwave AM band, which covers only 531-1600 kHz. That's a hundred kilohertz—ten channels—lower than the upper limit of AM in North America, and one silly kilohertz higher than the 530 kHz occupied by a couple of Canadian stations.

Birdies, Images, Chugging and Pauses

There are spurious "images" from signals 900 kHz higher, as well as a few silent-carrier "birdies," including one covering time stations on 10000 kHz. These cause no more of a problem than they do on some worthy small portables, such as the Grundig Yacht Boy 305. But they are there, and on a radio in this price class they shouldn't be.

Tuning can annoy, too. There's chugging during bandscanning, and the radio has to stop to "think" in silence for a second or two when coming onto a new station.

"World on Wheels" Works Well

Fortunately—after all, it's the only act in town—the great-sounding Becker Mexico 2340 generally checks out well. And, unlike most other car radios that seem to be made like Dixie cups, it's made to perform dependably over the passage of time.

Prepared by George Zeller and Lawrence Magne.

Choosing a Premium Receiver?

Get premium advice before you buy!

If you could, you'd spend weeks with each receiver, learning its charms and foibles. Seeing for yourself how it handles—*before* you spend.

Now, you can do the next best thing—better, some folks insist. Radio Database International White Papers®, from the PASSPORT® TO WORLD BAND RADIO library of in-depth test reports, put the facts right into your hands.

We test run each receiver for you. Put it through comprehensive laboratory and bench tests to find out where it shines. And where it doesn't.

Then our panel takes over: DXers, professional monitors, program listeners—experts all. They're mean, grumpy, hypercritical . . . and take lots of notes. They spend weeks with each receiver, checking ergonomics and long-run listening quality with all kinds of stations. Living with it day and night.

With PASSPORT's RDI White Papers®, these findings—the good, the bad and the ugly—are yours, along with valuable tips on how to operate your radio to best advantage. Each receiver report covers one model in depth, and is $6.95 postpaid in the United States; US$6.95 or CAN$9.45 in Canada; US$8.95 airmail in the European Union, Scandinavia, Australia, New Zealand and Japan; US$13.95

registered air elsewhere. Separate reports are available for each of the following premium radios:

AOR AR3030
Drake R8A
Drake SW8
Icom IC-R71A/D/E (while supplies last)
Icom IC-R9000
Japan Radio NRD-535/NRD-535D
Kenwood R-5000
Lowe HF-150
Lowe HF-225 (while supplies last)
Sony ICF-2010/ICF-2001D
Yaesu FRG-100

Reports for other models will be added throughout 1997. Ask for our latest info sheet, or visit our Web site at http://www.passport.com.

Other PASSPORT RDI White Papers available:

How to Interpret Receiver Specifications and Lab Tests
Popular Outdoor Antennas (new edition)

Available from world band radio dealers or direct. For VISA/Master Card orders, call our 24-hour automated order line: +1 (215) 794-8252, or fax +1 (215) 794 3396. Or send your check or money order (Pennsylvania add 42¢ per report), specifying which report or reports you want, to:

U.S.: EEB, Grove, Universal
Canada: Sheldon Harvey (Radio Books)
Japan: IBS Japan
Latin America: IBS Latin America

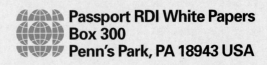 **Passport RDI White Papers**
Box 300
Penn's Park, PA 18943 USA

"We strongly recommend the PASSPORT RDI White Papers before purchasing any receiver over $100. The *Consumer Reports* of shortwave radio." —What's New, *Monitoring Times*

Accessory Speakers for Pleasant Audio

Almost any world band receiver sounds better with a worthy outboard speaker. Amplified PC speakers can provide pleasant results, but you usually have to buy two when you need only one. Manufacturers of tabletop receivers also offer accessory speakers, but they rarely help much.

So two world band specialty firms, Alpha Delta Communications and Grove Enterprises, have taken world band speakers a useful step further. Both now offer serious devices having enhanced sound quality, plus the ability to manipulate audio in various ways.

Alpha Delta Offers Superior Bass

Alpha Delta's Variable Response Console, $249.95, comes with a cast-aluminum housing measuring 8¼" W × 8¼" H × 6" D, or 210 × 210 × 152 mm. It looks as if it were designed to withstand blows from Arnold Schwarzenegger.

Controls include a power button, a knob for adding or subtracting bass, a high frequency cutoff control, and a knob for adjusting input audio from the receiver. Overall volume, however, continues to be controlled through the receiver's volume control.

In addition to a headphone jack, there are pushbuttons for selecting normal, peak, and notch functions, as well as a pair of knobs—bandwidth and frequency—that work in concert with those peak and notch functions. Taken together, these controls can boost a selected range of frequencies by using the peak function, or attenuate them by selecting the notch function.

The bass control boosts or diminishes bass, as you prefer. But there is no control, as such, for boosting treble. Instead, the treble control only allows a level to be set at which high frequencies are cut off. Aiding this is a handy set of LEDs with a graphic display of how the bass and treble controls have been adjusted.

Grove Has Multiple Features

The Grove SP-200A Sound Enhancer, at $199.95, attempts to do even more. With an attractive solid-oak cabinet suitable for a living room, the SP-200A measures 10⅞" W × 7¼" H × 6⅝" D, or 277 × 184 × 168 mm.

The '200A is loaded with features. There is a combination power and volume control that includes a bypass position, so you can use the SP-200A's speaker or headphone jack to skirt its audio-shaping circuitry. There are bass and treble knobs; a switch for selecting normal, notch, or peak functions; and frequency and bandwidth knobs that operate in concert with these other controls.

In addition, the SP-200A offers an audio squelch, a noise limiter, automatic tape recorder activation—a useful feature for some—and an LED to indicate that audio input is sufficient for the SP-200A to operate properly.

Side-by-Side: How They Perform

With such enhanced-fidelity models as the Lowe Europa, the Alpha Delta and Grove units perform similarly. Yet the Alpha Delta, which includes bass-reflex speaker design, offers better bass response, which makes it an obvious choice for shortwave program listeners looking for rich, full audio.

Additionally, the Alpha-Delta's ability to select a high-frequency cutoff level is a distinct advantage with receivers that offer only one bandwidth.

Grove's model is notable not only for its wide range of useful features, but also for having a slight edge in treble response. The Grove and Alpha Delta models both allow given audio frequencies to be boosted or notched out, and the notches are singularly effective against offending heterodynes. But those notches are fussy to adjust.

As to the related peaking function, both models works well; each improves the readability of signals that are "down in the mud." The SP-200A's noise limiter also improves, to a limited extent, the listenability of scratchy AM signals in the mediumwave broadcast band.

Which?

So which is the better outboard speaker?

For those who already own a superior world band receiver with a squelch control, the Alpha Delta VRC offers a welcome improvement in aural performance. In particular, those seeking fuller low-end audio will be especially pleased with it. If you want to add squelch and noise-limiter functions, the Grove SP-200A offers these features and more, and for less money.

These speakers aren't cure-alls. Yet, their additional audio-processing controls help in a number of ways to make listening more pleasurable, and both offer a significant improvement over speakers found in many world band receivers.

For quality receivers with superior audio but pedestrian speakers—especially those made by Drake, Lowe and Watkins-Johnson—worthy outboard speakers allow them to operate to full advantage. Because one person's idea of good sound is not necessarily that of somebody else, both Alpha Delta and Grove allow their speaker accessories to be returned for a full refund within 30 days.

—————————

Prepared by Jock Elliott, with Lawrence Magne.

Portatop Receivers for 1997

Superior Performance at Affordable Prices

Most of us buy a world band radio to function not in just one room, but all over the house—maybe outdoors, too. That's why portables sell so well. Yet, even the very best portables don't sound as good as some tabletop models. Nor can they cut the mustard with really tough signals.

Solution: Combine the most desirable characteristics of portables and tabletops into one single receiver, a portatop. For years, now, manufacturers have been nibbling at the edges of this idea. Finally, they're getting it right.

Revised Drake SW8 a Winner

Since the spring of 1994, the American firm of R.L. Drake has been offering the SW8, a "serious" portatop that is completely self-contained. But from the outset, it was a radio with a good case of "It was okay, but . . ."

No more. Well, sort of, because no radio is all things to all people, but the SW8 now comes close. Read our review to see why.

"Letterman's Radio" Offers Best Audio

Lowe Electronics, squirreled away in the English Midlands, offers its own portatop, the HF-150. It also came on the market with a good dose of the okaybuts . . . but, unlike its Drake counterpart, the HF-150 has stayed pretty much the same as it was when it came out in 1992. Which is to say this is still one whale of a receiver, which is why the hypercritical CBS entertainer Dave Letterman swears by his '150.

Our equally hypercritical panelists agree: It's the best-sounding world band radio of any type, except for the Becker world band car radio reviewed elsewhere in this section.

Okay, but . . . it's awkward to carry around as a portable, and usually requires a separate outboard preselector if used near mediumwave AM or longwave transmitters. No FM, either.

Both portatops are outstanding buys, especially with the Lowe now selling in some countries for less than in the past. Note, though, that while the Drake comes ready to roar, with the Lowe you pay extra for such features as a keypad. Both models, but especially the Drake, work best when connected to an external antenna, betraying their origins as reworked tabletop supersets. But that same genealogy is why, unlike with most portables, top-notch repairs will be available for portatops for years to come.

What Passport's Ratings Mean

(Good Fine Print)

Star ratings: ★ ★ ★ ★ ★ is best. We award stars solely for overall performance and meaningful features; price, appearance and the like are not taken into account. To facilitate comparison, the same rating system that is used for portatop models is also used for portable and tabletop models, reviewed elsewhere in this PASSPORT. Whether a radio is portable, a portatop or a tabletop model, a given rating—three stars, say—means largely the same thing. With portatop models, there is roughly equal emphasis on the ability to flush out tough, hard-to-hear signals, and program-listening quality with stronger broadcasts.

Passport's Choice portatop models are our test team's personal picks of the litter—what we would buy for ourselves.

: denotes a price-for-performance value. A designated model may or may not be low-priced for its class, but it *will* provide exceptional performance for the money spent.

Prices: As of this year, only observed approximate selling, or "street," prices (including VAT, where applicable) are cited in PASSPORT. Prices vary plus or minus, so take them as the general guide they are meant to be.

Improved for 1997   ¢

★ ★ ★ ★½   *Passport's Choice*

Drake SW8

Price: $699.00 in the United States. CAN$999.95 in Canada. £649.00 in the United Kingdom. AUS$1,599.00 in Australia.

Advantages: Attractive price for level of performance and features that come standard. Portatop design approaches tabletop performance with many of the conveniences of a portable; portability made easier by optional carrying case. Above-average audio quality with internal speaker or headphones. High-tech synchronous selectable sideband feature reduces adjacent-channel interference and fading distortion on world band, longwave and mediumwave AM signals; sync now locks acceptably. Three bandwidths provide worthy adjacent-channel rejection. Continuous tone control. Numerous helpful tuning aids, including 70 presets. Helpful signal-strength indicator, digital. Single-sideband reception well above the portable norm. Weak-signal sensitivity excellent with external antenna. Superior blocking performance aids usable sensitivity. Two timers and 24-hour clocks (*see* Disadvantages). Display illuminated. FM, in mono through speaker but stereo through headphones, performs well. Covers longwave down to 100 kHz and VHF aeronautical band. Superior factory service. 15-day money-back trial period if ordered from the factory or certain dealers.

Disadvantages: Still sounds "hissy" when used with built-in antenna, although it is better in this regard than it used to be; clipping on an extra length of wire to the built-in antenna helps greatly. Bereft of certain features—among them notch filter, adjustable noise blanker and passband tuning—found on premium-priced tabletop models. Ergonomics mediocre, including pushbuttons that rock on their centers. Key pushes must each be done within three seconds, lest receiver wind up being mistuned or placed into an unwanted operating mode. Wide bandwidth—nominally 6 kHz, actually 7.8 kHz—broader than it should be. Drake's 120 VAC power supply, via a separate outboard adaptor. Telescopic antenna doesn't swivel fully for best FM reception. Clocks don't display when frequency is shown. Carrying/elevation handle clunky to adjust, with adjustment stops that can break if handle forced. Optional MS8 outboard speaker not equal to receiver's

fidelity potential (see review of accessory speakers elsewhere in this section).

Improvements for 1997: According to Drake, their exercise in upgrading the SW8 is now complete, and what a worthy effort it has been. Synchronous selectable sideband, lacking in years past, is now included—a major step forward—and it works well, too. Thanks to coping with a ground loop, hum is now greatly reduced. FM selectivity is tighter. Europeans and others will also appreciate longwave coverage, down to 100 kHz, added for 1997.

Bottom Line: The Drake SW8 is now just what a top-notch radio should be: performance only a skootch below that of the fanciest tabletop supersets, yet at a price that's much lower. Think of it as an "SW8A," because it has been so improved over time that it really qualifies as a new model. Now, it is a superior all-around receiver for use both indoors and out, as well as temptingly priced.

 An *RDI WHITE PAPER* is available for this model.

Nicely improved and now offering an optional carrying case, the Drake SW8 is the Prince of Portatops. Less costly than a tabletop model, too.

Now priced to move, the rugged Low HF-150 portatop features top-notch audio fidelity. Lacks front-end selectivity, though.

★ ★ ★ ★   *Passport's Choice* ¢

Lowe HF-150

Price, without keypad or other options: $589.95 in the United States (add about $140 for HF-150M marine version, not tested). CAN$979.00 in Canada. £419.95 in the United Kingdom (add about £20 for HF-150M marine version, not tested). AUS$1,150.00 in Australia.

Advantages: Attractive price for level of performance, but the keypad, a virtual necessity, and some other features cost extra. Top-notch world band and medium-wave AM audio quality—a treat for the ears—provided a good external speaker or simple headphones are used (see review of accessory speakers elsewhere in this section). High-tech synchronous detection reduces fading distortion on world band, longwave and mediumwave AM signals. Synchronous detection circuit, which holds lock unusually well, also allows for either selectable-sideband or double-sideband reception. Synchronous detector switches out automatically during tuning, which aids in bandscanning. Exceptionally rugged cast-aluminum housing of a class normally associated with professional-grade equipment. Mouse keypad, virtually foolproof and a *de rigeur* option, performs superbly for tuning and presets. 60 presets store frequency and mode. Tunes, but does not display, in exacting 8 Hz increments, the most precise found in any model with portable characteristics. Single-sideband reception well above the portable norm. Small footprint saves space and adds to portability. Optional accessory kit, necessary for real portability, provides telescopic antenna, rechargeable nickel-cadmium batteries (four hours per charge) and shoulder strap with built-in antenna. High weak-signal sensitivity with accessory antenna helps make for exceptional portable performance and obviates the need for a large outdoor antenna. Excellent operating manual. Available with IF-150 optional computer interface. Superior factory service.

Disadvantages: Grossly inferior front-end selectivity can result in creation of spurious signals if the radio is connected to a significant external antenna or used near mediumwave AM transmitters; depending upon several variables, this may be a couple of kilometers or miles, or it may be several. (Lowe's excellent optional PR-150 preselector eliminates this disadvantage, albeit at a hefty cost in treasure, bulk and simplicity of operation. Also, Kiwa Electronics's BCB Rejection Filter accomplishes much the same thing more simply and at lower cost. However, neither solution is practical during portable operation.) Requires AK-150 option to be a true portatop. Lacks FM broadcast reception, normally found on portables. Built-in speaker produces only okay audio quality as compared to simple earphones or a good external speaker. No tone control. Frequency displays no finer than 1 kHz resolution. Lacks lock indicator or similar aid (e.g., finer frequency-display resolution) for proper use of synchronous detector, which can result in less-than-optimum detector performance. Bereft of certain features—among them notch filter, adjustable noise blanker and passband tuning—found on premium-priced tabletop models. Lacks signal-strength indicator. Operation of some front-panel button functions tends to be confusing until you get the hang of it. Light weight allows radio to slide on table during operation more than do heavier models. Lacks much-needed elevation feet. Erratic contact on outboard-speaker socket. Display not illuminated. AC power supply via a separate outboard adaptor, rather than inboard. *Portable operation:* Telescopic antenna tilts properly, but is clumsy to rotate. Comes with no convenient way to attach keypad to cabinet (remediable by affixing sticky-backed Velcro). This—plus the use of an outboard AC adaptor, the need for an external speaker or headphones for proper fidelity, and no dial illumination—all conspire to make this model less handy to tote around than a conventional portable.

Bottom Line: This tough little radio, with outstanding synchronous selectable sideband, provides superb fidelity on world band, longwave and mediumwave AM— *if* you don't live near any longwave or mediumwave AM transmitters. If audio quality is your passion, with other factors being secondary, this is the portatop model to get—indeed, for audiophiles this is arguably the *tabletop* model to get! But beware the possible need at your location for an outboard preselector or high-pass filter, as the front end on this radio is as bad as we've ever encountered.

 An *RDI WHITE PAPER* is available for this model.

The PASSPORT *portatop review team includes Jock Elliott, along with Lawrence Magne, Tony Jones and Craig Tyson, with helpful observations by Marie Lamb. Laboratory measurements by Robert Sherwood.*

One Fine Oldie!

The following model has been discontinued for some time, yet might still be available new. Cited are typical recent sale prices in the United States ($) and United Kingdom (£). Prices elsewhere may differ.

For pleasant listening on world band or FM, the D2999 is hard to beat.

★ ★ ★

Magnavox D2999
Philips D2999

Passport's Choice

Every time we think this model has disappeared completely, a reader writes that one has been found gathering dust on some dealer's shelf. A fine-sounding receiver—a classic, really, that continues to be used by one of our editors who is awash in radios. A delightful portatop with superior audio quality, FM and world band performance, among other virtues. If you can find one, grab it! Under $400 or £300.

Tabletop Receivers for 1997

More Stations, Better Fidelity

*T*abletop receivers excel at flushing out tough game— faint stations, often swamped by competing signals. That's why they are prized by serious radio aficionados known as "DXers," a term derived from telegraph code meaning long distance.

But tabletop models aren't for everybody. If all you want to hear are the major stations and a portable can't quite hack it, you can get excellent results for less money with the Lowe HF-150 or Drake SW8, reviewed in portatop section.

Big Guns for American West–Aussies, too

Tabletop models, like portatops, are the heavy metal needed where signals are weak, but folks are strong. Places like the North American Midwest and West, or Australia and New Zealand. Even elsewhere there can be a problem when world band signals have to follow paths over or near the geomagnetic North Pole. To check, place a string on a globe—a map won't do—between you and where signals come from. If the string passes near or above latitude 60° N, beware.

Hear More Daytime Signals

With the end of the Cold War, some stations have compressed their hours of transmission. The result is that some excellent English-language programs are heard only during the day.

Daytime signals are weaker, especially when they're not beamed to your part of

Engineer John Thorpe designs the AOR AR7030. Thorpe has almost singlehandedly put Britain into the top ranks of tabletop manufacturers.   Richard Hillier, AOR

the world. However, thanks to the scattering properties of shortwave, you can still eavesdrop on many of these "off-beam" signals. But it's harder, and that's where a tabletop's longer reach comes in.

Good High-Rise Listening, but No FM

In high-rise buildings—especially in urban areas—portables can disappoint. Reinforced buildings soak up signals from afar, and local broadcast and cellular transmitters can interfere.

Here, your best bet for bringing in tough stations is to connect a tabletop or portatop model to an insulated-wire antenna that runs along, or protrudes just outside, a window or balcony. Also try an ordinary telescopic car antenna sticking out from a window or balcony ledge, flagpole-style. If your radio has a built-in preamplifier, all the better. With portatop models, the built-in preamplifier can be accessed by connecting your antenna to the receiver's whip-antenna input.

You can also try amplified ("active") antennas that have reception elements and amplifiers in separate modules, not together as part of the same cabinet. Properly made active antennas are found only at world band specialty outlets, but even these sometimes produce false signals—although Datong models are superior in this regard. The quality of performance of active antennas is very location-specific, so try to purchase these on a returnable basis.

Tabletop receivers are pricier than portables. For that extra money you tend to get not only better performance, but also a better-made device. However, what you rarely find in a tabletop is reception of the everyday 87.5-108 MHz FM band.

External Antenna a "Must"

Most tabletop models also require an outboard world band antenna. Even those that have a built-in antenna should have an outboard antenna to perform to full advantage.

Tabletop performance is greatly determined by antenna quality and placement. A first-rate world band outdoor wire antenna, such as those made by Antenna Supermarket and Alpha Delta, usually sells for under $100—a bargain, given all they do. If you don't live in an apartment, this is the way to go. Check with the newly revised Radio Database International White Paper, *PASSPORT Evaluation of Popular Outdoor Antennas*, for the full story.

Virtually Every Model Tested

Every receiver evaluated, regardless of its introduction year, has been put through stringent testing hurdles we have honed since 1977, when we first started reviewing world band equipment.

First, receivers are thoroughly tested in the laboratory, using techniques we developed specially for the strenuous requirements of world band reception. Each receiver then undergoes extensive hands-on evaluation, usually for months, before we begin preparing our detailed internal report. That report, in turn, forms the basis for this PASSPORT REPORTS.

Unabridged Reports Available

These unabridged laboratory and hands-on test results are too exhaustive to reproduce here. However, for many tabletop models they are available as PASSPORT's Radio Database International White Papers—details on availability are elsewhere in this book.

Tips for Using this Section

Receivers are listed in order of suitability for listening to difficult-to-hear world band stations. Important secondary consideration is given to audio fidelity and ergonomics. We cite street prices, which are as of when we go to press. Of course, street prices vary plus or minus, so take them as the general guide they are meant to be.

Unless otherwise stated, all tabletop models have:

- Digital frequency synthesis and display.
- Full coverage of at least the 155-29999 kHz longwave, mediumwave AM and shortwave spectra—including all world band segments—but no coverage of the FM broadcast band (87.5-108 MHz).
- A wide variety of helpful tuning features.
- Synchronous selectable sideband, which reduces interference and fading distortion.
- Proper demodulation of non-world-band shortwave signals. These include single-sideband and CW (Morse code); also, with suitable ancillary devices, radio teletype and radio fax.
- Meaningful signal-strength indication.
- Illuminated display.

What Passport's Rating Symbols Mean

Star ratings: ★ ★ ★ ★ ★ is best. We award stars solely for overall performance and meaningful features; price, appearance and marginal features are not taken into account. To facilitate comparison, the same rating system is also used for portable and portatop models, reviewed elsewhere in this PASSPORT. Whether a radio is portable, a portatop or a tabletop model, a given rating—three stars, say—means largely the same thing. However, with tabletop models there is a slightly greater emphasis on the ability to flush out tough, hard-to-hear signals, as this is one of the main reasons these sets are chosen.

Passport's Choice tabletop models are our test team's personal picks of the

litter—serious radios that, funds allowing, we would buy ourselves.

¢: No, this doesn't mean cheap. *None* of these models is cheap! Rather, it denotes a model that costs appreciably less than usual for the level of performance provided.

PROFESSIONAL-GRADE MONITOR RECEIVERS

Get what you pay for? Not necessarily.

Costly professional-grade monitor receivers are designed and made for military, commercial and surveillance applications. These activities have only some things in common with the needs of world band listeners, unless you're bouncing around mountain trails in a Hummer. Result: They usually provide little or no improvement in performance over regular tabletop models costing a fraction as much.

But there is one exception, the Watkins-Johnson HF-1000, especially when equipped with the fidelity-enhancing Sherwood SE-3 accessory. But be prepared not only for sticker shock, but also to be exacting in selecting and erecting a suitable antenna if you want it to work properly.

★ ★ ★ ★ ★   *Passport's Choice*

Watkins-Johnson HF-1000

Price: $3,799.00 in the United States. CAN$5,400 in Canada. £4,495.00 in the United Kingdom. Not available in Australia.

Advantages: Generally superior audio quality (see Disadvantages), especially when used with the Sherwood SE-3 fidelity-enhancing accessory and a worthy external speaker. Unparalleled bandwidth

If money is no object, the Watkins-Johnson HF-1000 is the *ne plus ultra* in world band receivers. Virtually identical to a receiver designed for the world's most prestigious surveillance agency, it calls for operating skill and patience, as well as an exceptional antenna.

flexibility, with no less than 58 outstandingly high-quality bandwidths. Digital signal processing (DSP). Tunes and displays in extremely precise .001 kHz increments. Extraordinary operational flexibility—virtually every receiver parameter is adjustable. 100 station presets. Synchronous detection reduces distortion with world band, mediumwave AM and longwave signals (see Disadvantages). Built-in preamplifier. Tunable notch filter. Highly adjustable scanning of both frequency ranges and channel presets. Easy-to-read displays. Large tuning knob. Can be fully and effectively computer and remotely controlled. Passband offset (see Disadvantages). Built-in test equipment (BITE) diagnostics. Superior factory service.

Disadvantages: Very expensive. Static and modulation splash sound harsher than with most other models. Complex to operate to full advantage. Synchronous detection not sideband-selectable, so it doesn't aid in reduction of adjacent-channel interference; however, manufacturer states that they hope to remedy this in due course. Requires coaxial antenna feedline to avoid receiver-generated digital noise. Passband offset operates only in CW mode. Jekyll-and-Hyde ergonomics: sometimes wonderful, sometimes awful. Large rack-oriented footprint suboptimal

for tabletop use. No traditional cabinet, and front-panel rack "ears" protrude. In principle, mediocre front-end selectivity; however, problems were not apparent during listening tests; and, if needed (say, if you live very close to a mediumwave AM station), a sub-octave preselector option can be added or installed at factory. Cumbersome operating manual.

Note: Within the Americas and many other parts of the world, the optional preselector offered by Watkins-Johnson is rarely necessary. However, within Europe and other strong-signal parts of the world, the preselector may improve spurious-signal rejection.

Bottom line: The Watkins-Johnson HF-1000 is a true "superset," both for program listening and DXing. With a final solution to the digital hash problem, and the addition of a tone control, passband tuning, and synchronous selectable sideband, the '1000 would have been even better. Fortunately, the Sherwood SE-3 accessory remedies all but the hash issue, and improves audio fidelity, to boot. And one of the antennas (Alpha-Delta "DX-Ultra") that we tested with the '1000 eliminates nearly all the hash problem. Thus, the HF-1000 now is exceptionally well-suited to demanding aficionados with suitable financial wherewithal—provided they want a high degree of manual receiver control.

★ ★ ★ ★

Icom IC-R9000

Price: $6,199.00 in the United States. CAN$9,000.00 in Canada. £4,080.00 in the United Kingdom. AUS$8,200.00 in Australia.

Advantages: Exceptional tough-signal performance (see Note, below). Flexible, above-average audio for a tabletop model when used with suitable outboard speaker. Three AM-mode bandwidths (see Note, below). Tunes and displays frequency in precise 0.01 kHz increments. Video display of radio spectrum occupancy, a rarely found feature. Sophisticated scanner/timer. Extraordinarily broad coverage of radio spectrum. Exceptional assortment of flexible operating controls and sockets. Good ergonomics. Superb reception of utility and ham signals. Two 24-hour clocks.

Disadvantages: Dreadfully expensive. No synchronous selectable sideband. Power supply runs hot. Both AM-mode bandwidths too broad for most world band applications. Both single-sideband bandwidths almost identical. Dynamic range merely adequate. Reliability, especially when roughly handled, may be

wanting. Front-panel controls of only average construction quality.

Note: The above star rating can be viewed as conservative *if*, at a minimum, the barn-wide 11.3 kHz AM-mode bandwidth filter is changed to something in the vicinity of 4.5-5.5 kHz.

Bottom Line: The Icom IC-R9000, with at least one changed AM-mode bandwidth filter—available from some world band specialty firms—is pretty much right up there with the best-performing models for DX reception of faint, tough signals. This is especially true if you have the fingers of a safecracker and don't mind using the set's SSB circuitry to manually tune AM-mode signals (so-called manual ECSS reception). Where it shines is if you want a visual indication of spectrum occupancy and certain other characteristics of stations within a designated segment of the radio spectrum. Nevertheless, this model has been around for several years, and other models now offer virtually the same level, or even better, construction quality and performance, plus synchronous selectable sideband—sadly lacking on the 'R9000—for far less money.

 An *RDI WHITE PAPER* is available for this model.

Icom's big-ticket IC-R9000 is of interest mainly for its video display, which shows radio-spectrum activity.

TABLETOP RECEIVERS

If you want a top performer to unearth tough signals, read on. Five-star tabletop models should satisfy even the fussiest, and four-star models are no slouches, either.

The best tabletop models are the Ferraris and Mercedes of the radio world. As with their automotive counterparts, like-ranked receivers may come out of the curve at the same speed, though how they do it can differ greatly from model to model. So if you're thinking of choosing from the top end, study each contender in detail.

The hot new model for 1997 is the AOR AR7030, but it's definitely not for everyone. Because it's so unusual, in our review we've stemwound so you'll know what's what. For something similarly outstanding, but with relatively familiar operation, the Drake R8A, upgraded only a year ago, is hard to beat.

Too much money? Look into portatop models, which offer more value than the two low-cost tabletop models introduced this year.

★ ★ ★ ★ ★   *Passport's Choice*

Drake R8A

Price: $1,099.00 in the United States. CAN$1,559.00 in Canada. £1,295 in the United Kingdom.
Advantages: Superior all-round performance for sophisticated listening to world band programs. Above-average audio quality, especially with suitable outboard

For many, the popular Drake R8A provides the best intersection of performance, price and ease of operation.

speaker. High-tech synchronous selectable sideband generally pserforms well for reduced fading and easier rejection of interference (see Disadvantages). Five bandwidths, four suitable for world band—among the best configurations of any model tested. Highly flexible performance controls, including variable (albeit AF) notch filter and excellent passband offset. Superior reception of utility, ham and mediumwave AM signals. Tunes in precise 0.01 kHz increments. Displays frequency in precise 0.01 kHz increments. Superior blocking performance. Slow/fast/off AGC. Sophisticated scan functions. Can access all station presets quickly via tuning knob and slew buttons. Built-in preamplifier. Accepts two antennas. Two 24-hour clocks, with seconds displayed numerically, and timer features. Superior factory service. 15-day money-back trial period if ordered from the factory or certain dealers.

Disadvantages: Notch filter so fussy to adjust that panelists generally ignored it. Notch depth not as deep as manufacturer's specifications would suggest, although this may vary from sample-to-sample. Synchronous detector only fair at holding lock when the passband offset is tuned well away from the carrier frequency. Most pushbuttons rock on their centers. Ergonomics okay, but not all they could have been. Matching optional MS8 outboard speaker not equal to receiver's fidelity potential.

Bottom Line: A top performer in or near its price class, with much-improved ergonomics over the R8 model sold until early 1995. However, the synchronous detector doesn't lock in as consistently as it should, and is actually worse than on the original R8. A good speaker is a "must" for the R8A to really shine—but don't bother with Drake's mediocre MS8 offering.

 An *RDI WHITE PAPER* is available for this model.

New for 1997

AOR AR7030

Price: $1,149.95 in the United States. £799.00 in the United Kingdom. ¥129,800 in Japan.

Advantages: In terms of sheer performance for program listening, as good a radio as we've ever tested. Except for sensitivity to weak signals (see Disadvantages), easily overcome, the same comment applies to DX reception. Exceptionally quiet circuitry. Superior audio quality. Synchronous selectable sideband performs quite well for reduced fading and easier rejection of interference. Synchronous detection circuit allows for either selectable-sideband or double-sideband reception. Best dynamic range of any consumer-grade radio we've ever tested. Nearly all other lab measurements are top-drawer. Four voice bandwidths (2.3, 7.0, 8.2 and 10.3 kHz), with cascaded ceramic filters, come standard; up to six, either ceramic or mechanical, upon request (see Disadvantages). Superior audio quality, so it's well suited to listening to programs hour after hour. Advanced tuning and operating features aplenty, including passband tuning, although promised tunable AF notch option still not available as of press time. Built-in preamplifier (see Disadvantages). Automatically self-aligns all bandwidths for optimum performance, then displays the measured bandwidth of each. Remote keypad (see Disadvantages). Accepts two antennas. IF output. World Time clock, which displays seconds, and timer/snooze features. Superior mediumwave AM performance. Superior factory service.

Disadvantages: Most unusual ergonomics of any radio we've ever tested; some panelists feel they are totally unacceptable ("the operating system from Hell," as one put it), whereas others feel that operation is fine once you get used to it after studying the helpful owner's manual. Remote control unit, which has to be aimed carefully at the receiver, is required if you want to use certain features, such as direct frequency entry; not all panelists were enthusiastic about this arrangement, wishing that a mouse-type umbilical cable had been used instead. Although remote keypad can operate from across a room, the LCD characters are too small and lack sufficient intensity to be seen from such a distance. LCD omits certain important information, such as signal strength indication, when radio in various status modes. Sensitivity to weak signals good, as are related noise-floor measurements, but could be a bit better; a first-rate antenna should overcome this. Because of peculiar built-in preamplifier/attenuator design in which the two are linked, receiver noise rises slightly when preamplifier used in +10 dB position, or attenuator used in –10 dB setting. When six bandwidths used (four standard ceramics, two optional mechanicals), ultimate rejection, although superb with widest three bandwidths, cannot be measured beyond –80/–85 dB on narrowest three bandwidths because of phase noise; still, ultimate rejection is excellent even with these three narrow bandwidths. Lacks, and would profit from, a bandwidth of around 4 to 5 kHz; a Collins mechanical bandwidth filter of 3.5 kHz (nominal at –3 dB, measures 4.17 kHz at –6 dB) is an option. Such Collins filters, in the two optional-bandwidth slots, measure as having poorer shape factors (1:1.8 to 1:2) than the standard-slot MuRata ceramic filters (1:1.5 to 1:1.6). LCD emits some digital electrical noise, potentially a problem if an amplified (active) antenna is used with its pickup element (e.g., telescopic rod) placed near the receiver. Minor microphonics (audio feedback), typically when internal speaker is used, noted in laboratory; in actual listening, however, this

Simple on the outside, but a gorilla within, the new AOR AR7030 is downright eccentric to operate. To reach full DX capability, it needs an accessory filter, plus a high-gain antenna such as described in PASSPORT's RDI White Paper on antennas.

proved not to be a problem. Uses AC adaptor instead of built-in power supply. No tunable notch filter or noise blanker, but these may be available as options in the near future.

Bottom Line: A sterling performer, especially with the shakedown cruise now behind it, but operation is especially peculiar and cumbersome—give it five stars for performance, with a big question mark for ergonomics. Were it not for these ergonomics and slightly limited sensitivity to weak signals, the '7030 would be the best receiver available at any price. This is a radio you'll really need to get your mitts on for a few days before you'll know whether it's love or hate—or something in between. As one of our panelists put it, "inside this box there is an exceptional receiver struggling to get out."

The AOR AR7030 gets five stars for performance, with a big question mark for ergonomics.

Evaluation of New Model: Here's a new wrinkle. An established Japanese electronics company sets up a small branch in England, and within a short time that facility goes on to make a product that's not only more advanced and better than those of the parent company, but just

about any other company. So much for ethnic stereotypes!

This is, in fact, exactly what happened with the AR7030, engineered and manufactured in Britain by a spanking-new subsidiary of the Japanese AOR company. We've tested a number of '7030s throughout 1996, and watched bit by bit as the factory has made one small improvement after another. Now, it's to the point where it is an outstanding device for program listening, and nearly as good for DXing—not only on world band, but also on the mediumwave AM band.

Features Aplenty

The '7030 has a roster of advanced features to warm the heart of the true aficionado. These include synchronous selectable sideband; synchronous double sideband; four standard voice bandwidths that with optional filters can be raised to six; clock and timer facilities; passband tuning; a six-level attenuator/preamplifier; squelch; rear connectors for coaxial and wire antennas; a switch for choosing between antennas, including a whip; and a tilt bail to angle the receiver. Interestingly for a receiver in this price range, there is also an IF output, which can be used for such things as the Sherwood SE-3 fidelity-enhancing accessory or various professional ancillary devices.

A tunable audio notch filter is on the griddle, we're told. Of course, we haven't tested it as yet, so we can't say how deep the notch will be, or whether it will require the fingers of a safecracker to operate.

The '7030 comes with a wireless infra-red remote control capable of manipulating most receiver functions: volume, tuning, tone, bandwidth selection, mode, VFO selection, passband tuning, frequency entry and memory. Some liked it, others didn't and would have preferred a cable interface instead of wireless. The remote can operate the receiver all the way across the room, if you want, but at a certain point you won't be able to see the digits on the LCD—they're just not prominent enough.

Exceptional Performance

The '7030 excels in nearly all aspects of performance. The standard bandwidths offer superior ultimate rejection and shape factors, thanks in part to their being cascaded so the filters work together rather than separately. Image rejection is superb, too, as is first IF rejection.

Interestingly, the receiver includes a useful software routine for self-aligning all bandwidths—standard or optional—for optimum performance. This scheme also automatically detects and measures each bandwidth filter, then displays the measured bandwidth. This feature, normally found only on such professional supersets as the Racal RA6790/GM, is much more than a gimmick—it actually helps ensure proper alignment as components age over time. As a bonus, the '7030 accepts not only MuRata ceramic filters, but also Collins mechanical filters.

Dynamic range is breathtaking at spacings of 5 kHz and 20 kHz, with respective third-order intercept points being +1 dB and +30 dB. Indeed, it is so outstanding that our laboratory manager had to visit with Hewlett-Packard's signal-generator maven and upgrade certain of our testing gear in order for us to be able to accurately measure performance of this caliber. Had we not done this, we would have wound up "measuring the measuring equipment," as unfortunately some testing laboratories have done, rather than the receiver proper.

What these measurements showed is that the '7030's dynamic range and third-order intercept points are at levels normally associated only with the finest in professional hardware. Yet, the '7030 does this at a fraction of the price.

One anomaly we discovered was that powerful mediumwave AM signals at the upper end of the band could penetrate well into the shortwave spectrum. Within days of our report, the factory found the cause and changed the design to correct it, and should now be incorporating the improved circuit in their regular production. AOR has been commendably swift in upgrading other reported shortcomings, as well, which suggests that the '7030 will get even better over time.

> The '7030's dynamic range is at a level normally associated only with the finest professional receivers.

The '7030 is exceptionally quiet and pleasant to listen to for extended periods, in part because the synchronous detector tends to work very well when it is used to full advantage. Also helping is that overall distortion is good-to-excellent in the AM mode, and excellent-to-superb when the synchronous detector is in use. Blocking, a variable affecting sensitivity when strong signals are present on nearby frequencies, is also excellent.

Bandwidth and Sensitivity Anomalies

Okay, but . . . For real flexibility, this receiver needs a bandwidth in the 4 to 5 kHz range, such as the Collins 3.5 kHz (nominal at –3 dB), which measures 4.2 kHz at the usual –6 dB. AOR or its dealers can custom-install such a filter, or you can install it yourself in one of the two optional positions. This is made especially straightforward by the receiver's self-aligning feature.

One of our test units was ordered with the nominal 2.3 kHz and 3.5 kHz Collins filters installed in the optional-bandwidth filter slots. Thanks to cascading, even the simple MuRata filters work nicely, and so, too, do the Collins offerings. Although the mechanical filters give off a different type of sound than ceramics do, the real difference is that the standard MuRata ceramic filters have better shape factors than the much-ballyhooed Collins mechanicals. This replicates our findings in this regard with other models of receivers.

Although cascading improves overall filter performance, unless the cascaded filters have similar bandwidths, the benefits are not felt equally throughout the filter slope. For example, cascading might greatly improve ultimate selectivity—say, to –90 dB—but do less to improve performance at –30 dB, which is the sort of region where listeners and even DXers need selectivity much more often than at –90 dB. Again, how much benefit at what point of the filter slope depends on the specifics of the filters being cascaded.

We couldn't measure the '7030's ultimate selectivity beyond –80/–85 dB with the three narrowest filters of the six because of noise limitation; the wider filters measured cleanly down to –90 dB. Even then, ultimate rejection is clearly superior.

Some receivers are as sensitive to weak signals as a bat is to the sound of mosquitos' wings. The discontinued Sony ICF-6800W (White) is one of the best in this regard, as are some samples of the old R-390 American military receiver. But the '7030, with its primary emphasis on strong-signal-handling capability—and also because of a peculiar design in which the inboard preamplifier and attenuator are linked—is not quite in this league, even with the preamplifier on. However, with a first-rate outdoor antenna, and/or a worthy outboard preamplifier or amplified preselector, this can be overcome, especially as the receiver's circuitry is exceptionally quiet.

The '7030 is powered by an AC adaptor, rather than an inboard power supply. Such adaptors are fine and well for portables and cordless drills, but on a premium receiver an inboard power supply should be considered de rigueur.

The adaptor puts out a relatively unusual 15 VDC that can't be equaled by 12-Volt car and boat batteries. However, the radio will function off 12 Volts, albeit with reduced performance.

Unusual Ergonomics

But the real hangup many will have, and many of our panel had, is with how the set operates. Most of our test panel felt its ergonomics were awful, although a vocal minority insisted they were fine once you got the hang of things.

You'd never realize this just by looking at the receiver. Its front panel is the very model of modern simplicity, with only three knobs and nine buttons. There is, for example, no keypad for direct frequency entry on the face of the radio (although there is such a keypad, in standard telephone format, on the remote control).

AOR, while trying to simplify operation, actually made the receiver more complicated and confusing than it should be.

Yet, looks are deceptive. To the left of the main display is a button turning the receiver on and off, while below it is another, easily confused with the first, labeled "MENU." Underneath the main display are one knob and four buttons, the functions of which are controlled by the menu button. The labels above the knob and four buttons change according to which menu is activated, and there are even branching trees of menus that come into play as different buttons are pushed or the knob is turned.

AOR, while trying to simplify operation, actually made the receiver more complicated and confusing to operate than it should be. It helps if you operate it mostly from the remote control, like a TV or VCR, and use the front panel buttons and knobs only when necessary. Trouble is, that keypad has to be aimed carefully at the receiver if it is to work properly. Some panelists were not amused by this arrangement, and would have preferred a mouse-type umbilical cable, as on the Lowe HF-150, to the present keypad's wireless interface.

> There's no way to predict how any given person will react. Some hated it, others loved it.

The emphasis on front-panel simplification has also resulted in an LCD that is not only too small, but also ceases to display essential information at times. For example, if you operate the radio in a certain way, such information as signal strength vanishes so other information can be shown. The LCD also emits some digital electrical noise, which might commingle to disturb received signals if you are using an active antenna with its pickup element—telescopic rod, loop, or what-haveyou—near the receiver. The solution, of course, is to move the antenna pickup element farther away from the radio.

The bottom line is that there's no way to predict how any given person will react to the '7030's *modus operandi*. We anticipated that those with strong computer backgrounds would lean more towards it than traditionalists, but reality turned out to be as complicated as the receiver's operating system. Some "gearheads" hated it, others loved it. Some traditionalists embraced it, others didn't.

Take these examples. The Sony ICF-SW77 is probably the closest portable analogue to the '7030 when it comes to complexity of operation. One of our panelists is ecstatic about the '77, but couldn't wait to get rid of the '7030. Yet, an octogenarian non-panelist colleague, whose heart glows when he lays hands on a traditional receiver having lots of dedicated knobs, found the '7030 to be a delight after a couple of days of practice and studying the owner's manual.

Great Receiver, but Could Be Better

From a consumer's perspective, where should the '7030 go? In a perfect world, it could evolve into two receivers. One might be similar to the present version, but with vastly improved software and a couple of extra controls, including one to allow for simplification of the menu operation. Another would retain the '7030's hardware, but with a larger front panel supplementing the menu system with a number of dedicated controls for various functions. Both versions would have a much larger LCD that displays vital information at all times.

Still, today's AOR AR7030 is clearly a winner . . . *if* you can live with its weird operating scheme. It offers performance that is top-drawer and—ergonomics aside—is as superb a receiver as we've ever tested. But if there has ever been a receiver that needs to be purchased on a returnable basis, this is it.

★ ★ ★ ★ ★   *Passport's Choice*

Japan Radio NRD-535D

Price: $1,699.00 in the United States. CAN$2,949.00 in Canada. £2,499.00 in the United Kingdom. AUS$4099.95 in Australia.
Evaluation: See below.

The best Japanese receiver tested is the Japan Radio NRD-535D, often used by serious DXers for snaring hard-to-hear signals.

★ ★ ★ ★½

Japan Radio NRD-535

Price: $1,429.00 in the United States. CAN$1,749.00 in Canada. £1,195.00 in the United Kingdom. AUS$3,299.95 in Australia.

Advantages: One of the best and quietest DX receivers ever tested. Top-notch ergonomics, including non-fatiguing display. Construction quality slightly above average. Computer-type modular plug-in circuit boards ease repair. Highly flexible operating controls, including 200 superb station presets, tunable notch filter and passband offset. Superior reception of utility and ham signals. One of the few receivers tested that tunes frequency in exacting 0.001 kHz increments. Displays frequency in precise 0.01 kHz increments. Slow/fast/off AGC. Superior front-end selectivity. Sophisticated scan functions. World Time clock with timer features; displays seconds, albeit only if a wire inside the receiver is cut. Excellent optional NVA-319 outboard speaker. *NRD-535D:* Synchronous selectable sideband for reduced fading and easier rejection of interference. Continuously variable bandwidth in single-sideband (narrow bandwidth) and AM (wide bandwidth) modes.

Disadvantages: Audio quality, although improved over some earlier Japan Radio offerings, still somewhat muddy. Dynamic range and blocking performance adequate, but not fully equal to price class. Excessive beats, birdies and radiated digital noise. AGC sometimes causes "pop" sounds. Clock shares readout with frequency display. Clock not visible when receiver off. Front feet do not tilt receiver upwards. *NRD-535:* No synchronous selectable sideband. *NRD-535D:* Synchronous detection circuit locking performance suboptimal, notably with passband offset in use. Variable bandwidth comes at the expense of deep-skirt selectivity.

Note: Also available in a specially upgraded "NRD-535SE" version for $1,995 from Sherwood Engineering in the United States. More complicated to operate than the regular NRD-535D, but performance, especially fidelity, is exemplary. Informally rated ★ ★ ★ ★ for ergonomics, ★ ★ ★ ★ ★ for performance, in 1994 PASSPORT.

Bottom Line: An exceptional receiver for snaring tough DX signals, notably in the "D" version, with the best ergonomics we've come across in a tabletop model. However, its lack of full-fidelity audio makes it far from the ideal receiver for listening to the more easily-heard world band programs over periods of time. Superior quality of construction.

 An *RDI WHITE PAPER* is available that covers both factory versions of this model.

The Lowe HF-225 Europa, engineered by John Thorpe (page 138), is beloved by a small but diehard following of exacting radio enthusiasts. Because it will be replaced by the forthcoming HF-250 Europa, there is only a small remaining window of opportunity to purchase the '225.

Newly Tested for 1997
★ ★ ★ ★¼

Lowe HF-225 Europa

Price, including keypad and DSB synchronous detector: $1,099.95 in the United States. CAN$1,499.00 in Canada. £599.00 in the United Kingdom.

Advantages: Well suited for serious DXing, and for the most part also for pleasant listening to world band programs hour after hour. Exceptional audio with outboard speaker or headphones. Straightforward to operate. Generally excellent ergonomics, especially keypad. Four excellent bandwidths, nicely spaced and usually with tight and deep selectivity for optimum world band reception under varying conditions. Tunes in precise 8 Hz increments. Physically rugged. Synchronous detector reduces distortion (see Disadvantages). Optional field-portable configuration, tested. Small footprint.

Disadvantages: Synchronous detector works only in double sideband, not selectable sideband, so it doesn't aid in reduction of adjacent-channel interference. Frequency displays in relatively coarse 1 kHz increments. Front-end selectivity only fair. Limited operational flexibility, including AGC. No tunable notch filter. No passband tuning. Optional portable configuration relatively insensitive to weak signals. Uses AC adaptor instead of built-in power supply.

Note: The original HF-225, a reduced-performance, lower-priced version of the Europa, continues to be offered for sale from various dealers. An RDI White Paper exists for this model, and will be available while existing supplies last.

Bottom Line: A hardy, easy-to-operate set with superior audio quality and DX performance. A replacement, the HF-250 Europa, is to be introduced by early 1997. However, given the performance of the relatively new Lowe HF-250, there is no guarantee that a new Europa will necessarily be better than the existing version.

★ ★ ★ ★

Kenwood R-5000

Price: $1,069.95 in the United States. CAN$1,499.00 in Canada. £999.95 in the United Kingdom. AUS$1,625.00 in Australia.

Once a top choice among tabletop offerings, the Kenwood R-5000 has failed to keep up with advances in technology. Still, it performs well, and is available in some parts of the world where higher-rated receivers aren't sold.

Advantages: Good audio, provided a suitable outboard speaker is used. Exceptionally flexible operating controls, including tunable notch filter and passband offset. Tunes and displays frequency in precise 0.01 kHz increments. Excellent reception of utility and ham signals. Superior frequency-of-repair record. In some parts of the world, easier to find than other tabletop models.

Disadvantages: No synchronous selectable sideband. Ergonomics only fair—especially keypad, which uses an offbeat horizontal format. Mediocre wide bandwidth filter supplied with set; replacement with high-quality YK-88A-1 substitute adds to cost. Audio significantly distorted at tape-recording output.

Note: Some R-5000 units have been found to develop significant hum after long-term use. The manufacturer advises that this is caused by deterioration of the IF board's ground connection to the chassis. The remedy is to clean the IF board foil under the mounting screws, then re-affix those screws snugly.

Bottom Line: The Kenwood R-5000's combination of superior tough-signal performance and good audio quality once made it a top choice for tough-signal DXing, as well as listening to world band programs. Now, it's fast becoming a technological also-ran.

 An *RDI WHITE PAPER* is available for this model.

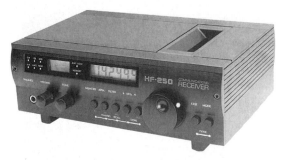

The HF-250 is the first radio from Lowe Electronics that's designed by their new engineering staff. It's shortly to be followed by the HF-250 Europa—and possibly more new offerings, as well.

★ ★ ★ ★

Lowe HF-250

Price: $1,299.00 in the United States. CAN$1,899.00 in Canada. £799.00 in the United Kingdom. AUS$2,500.00 in Australia.

Advantages: Top-notch world band and mediumwave AM audio quality, aided by effective tone control, so it's well suited to listening to world band programs hour after hour. Clean, simple panel keeps operating controls to a minimum. Synchronous detection circuit allows for either selectable-sideband for reduced fading and easier rejection of interference, or double-sideband reception for reduced fading (see Disadvantages). Four voice bandwidths. Exceptionally rugged cast-aluminum housing of a class normally associated with professional-grade equipment. Relatively small footprint. Four voice bandwidth filters. Digital display unusually easy to read. World Time clock shows seconds numerically (see Disadvantages). Superior factory service.

Disadvantages: Expensive for what it is. Synchronous detector only okay in holding lock with signals suffering from flutter fading. Operation of some front-panel button functions tends to be confusing until you get the hang of it. Nonstandard keypad layout. Bereft of certain features—among them notch filter, adjustable AGC

and passband tuning—found on some premium-priced models. Occasional minor hum from AC adaptor unless antenna uses coaxial-cable feedline. Signal-strength indicator has small numbers, hard to read. Clock not displayed when frequency is showing. Minor "braap" chugging within some frequency ranges.

Bottom Line: Think of the Lowe HF-250 as a cleaned-up HF-150 that while generally moving forward, also took a couple of steps backward with the offbeat keypad and "on-during-bandscanning" synchronous detector that could be better at holding lock. It's a hardy, advanced-fidelity receiver for the dedicated listener to world band programs.

 An *RDI WHITE PAPER* is available for this model.

★ ★ ★ ★

AOR AR3030

Price: $699.95 in the United States. CAN$1,499.00 or less in Canada. £699.00 in the United Kingdom. AUS$1,599.00 in Australia.

Advantages: Good-to-excellent in most laboratory measurements of receiver performance. Relatively low price. Two well-chosen bandwidths. Tunes in very precise 0.005 kHz increments, displays in precise 0.01 Hz increments. Various scanning schemes. Easy-to-use, well-laid-out controls are largely intuitive and easy to operate. Very low audio distortion in single-sideband mode. Synchronous detector reduces distortion with world band, mediumwave AM and longwave signals (see Disadvantages). Superior weak-signal sensitivity within certain world band segments, such as 9 MHz (see Disadvantages). Small. Light. Can be run off batteries for short periods. Easy-to-read display. Can be computer controlled.

Disadvantages: Dynamic range, only fair at 5 kHz spacing, can cause overloading in and around 9 MHz segment. Weak-signal sensitivity only fair within tropical segments. Synchronous detector is not sideband-selectable, so it doesn't aid in reduction of adjacent-channel interference. Synchronous detector must be exactly center-tuned; otherwise, it may distort with a powerful station. Lacks some of the exotic controls that DXers can use, such as a notch filter and passband tuning. Needs an external speaker or headphones to take full advantage of its otherwise-good audio. Tilt bail does not latch properly. Small tuning knob. Non-standard layout for numeric keypad. Runs off external AC adaptor, rather than internal power supply—albeit one that is approved by Underwriters Laboratories. Increasingly hard to find.

Bottom Line: A decent little receiver at an attractive price that offers generally pleasant results for program listening.

 An *RDI WHITE PAPER* is available for this model.

★ ★ ★ ★

Icom IC-R71A
Icom IC-R71E
Icom IC-R71D

Price: *IC-R71A:* $1,299.00 in the United States. CAN$1,899.00 in Canada. No longer available in Australia. *IC-R71E:* £875.00 in the United Kingdom. *IC-R71E and IC-R71D:* $1,000-1,800 in continental Europe.

Advantages: Variable bandwidth. Superb reception of weak, hard-to-hear signals. Reception of faint signals alongside powerful competing ones aided by superb ultimate selectivity, as well as excellent dynamic range. Flexible operating controls, including tunable notch filter. Excellent reception of utility and ham signals.

Recent price reduction has made the AOR AR3030 a bargain. Unlike its new AR7030 sibling, it is made in Japan.

Tunes in precise 0.01 kHz increments, even though it displays in 0.1 kHz increments.

Disadvantages: Mediocre audio. No synchronous selectable sideband. Diminutive controls, and otherwise generally substandard ergonomics. Should backup battery die, operating system software erases, requiring reprogramming by Icom service center (expected battery life is in excess of 10 years).

Bottom Line: The Icom IC-R71 was once a favorite among those chasing faint, hard-to-hear signals. Now, it is no longer competitive for either program listening or chasing faint DX signals. Nominally discontinued but still widely sold, so who knows.

 An *RDI WHITE PAPER* is available for this model, while supplies last.

Icom's IC-R71A is nominally discontinued in many markets, but is still easy to find. In its heyday, it was good enough that a major government surveillance agency used it to eavesdrop from ships.

Yaesu has long excelled in making affordable tabletop receivers. Its "Frog-100" is no exception, although it works best when equipped with an accessory keypad.

★ ★ ★ ★   ¢

Yaesu FRG-100

Price: $669.00 in the United States. CAN$899.00 in Canada. £549.00 in the United Kingdom. AUS$1,199.00 in Australia.

Advantages: Excellent performance in many respects. Relatively low price. Covers 50 Hz to 30 MHz in the LSB, USB, AM and CW modes. Includes three bandwidths, a noise blanker, selectable AGC, two attenuators, the ability to select 16 pre-programmed world band segments, two clocks, on-off timers, 52 tunable station presets that store frequency and mode data, a variety of scanning schemes and an all-mode squelch. A communications-FM module, 500 Hz CW bandwidth and high-stability crystal are optional.

Disadvantages: No keypad for direct frequency entry (remediable, see Note, below). No synchronous selectable sideband. Lacks features found in "top-gun" receivers: passband offset, notch filter, adjustable RF gain. Simple controls and display, combined with complex functions, can make certain operations confusing. Dynamic range only fair. Uses AC adaptor instead of built-in power supply.

Note: An outboard accessory keypad is virtually a "must" for the FRG-100, and is a no-brainer to attach. Brodier E.E.I. (3 Place de la Fontaine, F-57420 Curvy, France) makes the best keypad, sold

direct and through Universal Radio in the United States, Martin Lynch in England and Charly Hardt in Remscheid, Germany. Reasonably similar is the costlier QSYer— SWL Version, available from Stone Mountain Engineering Company in Stone Mountain GA 30086 USA. These we've tested, but another, the KPAD100, has since appeared from Lowe Electronics in the United Kingdom.

Bottom Line: While sparse on features, in many respects the Yaesu FRG-100 succeeds in delivering worthy performance within its price class. Its lack of a keypad for direct frequency entry is now easily remediable (see Note, above).

 An *RDI WHITE PAPER* is available for this model.

Reintroduced for 1997

★ ★ ★½

Icom IC-R72
Icom IC-R72A
Icom IC-R72E

Price (approximate): $1,019.00 in the United States. CAN$1,499.00 in Canada. £799.95 in United Kingdom. AUS$1,299.00 in Australia.

Advantages: Pleasant audio with outboard speaker or headphones. Generally superior ergonomics. Tunes and displays frequencies in precise 0.01 kHz increments. World clock/timer. Operates for about one hour off built-in rechargeable battery—useful during power failure. Novel center-tuning LED for world band and certain other signals. Superb image and IF rejection. Small footprint. Smoothly operating tuning knob. Preamplifier.

Disadvantages: Much too expensive for what it is. No synchronous selectable sideband. Wide bandwidth too broad. Dreadful audio from built-in speaker. Noisy synthesizer. Noise blanker reduces

Icom's IC-R72 provides a level of overall performance similar to that found with some portables. Yet, it's priced right up there with well-rated tabletop models.

dynamic range. Relatively few features, compared to better models. In our unit, poor low-frequency audio reproduction in upper-sideband.

Bottom Line: This model has come and gone, then nominally been resurrected—most recently within the United States—although finding it on sale before we went to press was another matter. It's nice, but nothing special, and based on the last known prices was excessively costly. Any number of other models offer far better value.

New for 1997

★ ★½   ¢

Radio Shack/Realistic DX-394

Price: $299.99 in the United States. CAN$399.99 in Canada. £349.99 in the United Kingdom.

Advantages: Low price. Advanced tuning features include 160 tunable presets (see Disadvantages). Tunes and displays in precise 0.01 kHz. Modest size, light weight and built-in telescopic antenna provide some portable capability. Bandwidths have superior shape factors and ultimate rejection. Two 24-hour clocks, one of which shows independent of frequency display. Five programmable timers. 30/60 minute snooze feature. Noise blanker. 30-day money-back trial period in the United States.

Disadvantages: What appear to be four bandwidths turn out to be virtually one bandwidth, and it is too wide for optimum reception of many signals. Bandwidths, such as they are, not selectable independent of mode. No synchronous selectable sideband. Presets cumbersome to use. Poor dynamic range for a tabletop, a potential problem in Europe and other strong-signal parts of the world if an external antenna is used. Overall distortion, although acceptable, higher than desirable.

Bottom Line: This is Radio Shack's first foray into the tabletop market in years. The result is a radio of modest dimensions and equally modest performance, but in North America it is sensibly priced for what it does.

Evaluation of New Model: The Radio Shack DX-394, which resembles a scanner, is the first world band tabletop from Radio Shack since a couple of earnest, but flawed, tries several years back.

The '394, made in Japan, is surprisingly diminutive. It covers the usual 0.15-30 MHz portions of the longwave, mediumwave

---

Looking Ahead . . .

Icom is introducing a new world band tabletop receiver, the under-$2,000 model IC-R8500, by early 1997. This is certainly good news, even if it's long overdue. In recent years, most Icom models have been seriously overpriced for what they do, and not the performers they should be. Yet, theirs is an organization with considerable technological skill, so their new model is worth looking forward to.

The Shack is back! For the first time in years, Radio Shack is offering a tabletop model—a modest performer, but priced to move.

AM and world band spectra. However, as is the unfortunate custom with tabletop models, it omits FM.

It comes complete with the usual roster of advanced tuning features, including a variable-rate tuning knob and "signal-seek" scanning; an illuminated LCD that reads out the frequency precisely to the nearest 10 Hz; a 30/60 minute snooze function; two 24-hour clocks, one of which can be seen when the frequency is displayed; five programmable timers; a digital signal-strength indicator that looks like it's analog; a noise blanker; and a receiver lock. There's a built-in telescopic antenna to give it a touch of portatop status, plus feet which can be flipped down to angle the receiver for comfortable operation.

There are 160 tunable memory presets: ten each for longwave, mediumwave AM and world band—plus 130 more, divided among 13 world band segments. However, to call up a preset requires choosing the meter band of the station, then pushing one of the ten presets available for that band. Ergonomically, this is an awkward arrangement, and it's not helped by a keypad that's not in the standard telephone configuration.

In many respects, the '394 performs well. Sensitivity to weak signals and the related variable of blocking are both above average, and image rejection is excellent. There appear to be four bandwidths, too: one for the AM mode, including world band; one for single sideband, a mode commonly used by hams and utility stations; and two for CW, or Morse code. All bandwidths have excellent ultimate rejection and shape factors, two variables that are important in keeping adjacent-channel interference at bay.

But there's a rub, and it's a doozy: The four apparent bandwidths on the '394 are so similar that they are virtually identical. The widest bandwidth, for AM/world band, measures 7.2 kHz. This would be fine if there were a second and narrower choice. However, the next bandwidth, for single sideband, is 6 kHz, which is much too wide for this mode—2 to 3 kHz would have been more appropriate. To top it off, both CW bandwidths are an identical 5.7 kHz; that's about *ten times* too wide for that mode!

In addition, bandwidths can't be selected independently of mode. Of course, that hardly matters, as all bandwidths are essentially the same. What the '394 clearly needs is a second voice bandwidth of perhaps 4 kHz, with a third around 2.5 kHz, each selectable independent of mode. Even two bandwidths—say, 6 kHz and 3 kHz—would suffice for AM/world band and single-sideband.

The '394 has poor dynamic range by tabletop standards. In North America, the set does not overload badly. However, in Europe and other strong-signal parts of the world this may be a problem, depending on the specifics of your listening situation.

Audio is plagued by distortion—as high as 12-30% at lower audio frequencies, and there's no synchronous selectable sideband to help out. While the radio sounds acceptable at first, distortion like this tends to produce mental fatigue over time.

Obviously, this is no Drake R8A. But at the '394's rock-bottom price, its competition isn't so much from tabletop models as it is from portables. Looked at this way, the '394's less-than-sterling performance characteristics come off relatively well, in part because portables have to compromise performance in order to keep battery consumption down.

Overall, the Radio Shack/Realistic DX-394 is a decent receiver for relatively little money. But it's no barn burner.

New for 1997
★ ★½

Drake SW1

Price: $299.95 in the United States.
Advantages: Low price, especially for high level of construction quality. Dynamic range, sensitivity to weak signals and certain other performance variables above average for price class. Pleasant audio. Large, bright digital display using LEDs much easier to read indoors than most. Easiest and simplest to use of any tabletop tested, with quality ergonomics. Superior factory service. 15-day money-back trial period if ordered from the factory or certain dealers.
Disadvantages: Mediocre adjacent-channel rejection (selectivity) from the single bandwidth. No features—*nada*, not even a signal-strength indicator—except for tuning. No single sideband. No synchronous selectable sideband. Increments for tuning and frequency display are relatively coarse. Annoying chugging during bandscanning. Uses AC adaptor.
Bottom Line: Okay as far as it goes, but where's the radio? And why such mediocre selectivity and loud chugging? Still, in many respects, such as quality of con-

struction and service, Drake's SW1 offers real value at an exceptionally low price. A somewhat similar model, also manufactured by Drake, has been offered by the United Broadcasting Network (*see* Addresses PLUS, under "USA"). As UBN programs tend to be heard on relatively clear channels, that version makes sense for their listeners. In either case, because of build quality and service, no other model of world band radio of any type under $500 comes as close to being a "friend for life."

Evaluation of New Model: Looking for features aplenty? Read no further.

Take the front panel. It has only up/down slewing keys, which tune in single-channel (5 kHz) increments; a tuning knob that dials in 1 kHz increments; a volume knob; an RF gain control; and several large, bright LEDs that are exceptionally easy to read indoors.

There's also a keypad with 32 presets. With it, direct frequency entry becomes as simple as the receiver itself. If you want to hear, say, the BBC World Service on 5975, all you do is press 5, 9, 7, 5, ENTER.

This dearth of controls leaves front-panel acreage aplenty for a quality speaker—a big improvement over models with top-firing speakers. Except for the virtually pointless RF gain control, there's not a nonessential item to be found. Elsewhere on the cabinet, there's a headphone jack, a coaxial antenna connector,

Drake's robust new SW1 is the essence of simplicity at low cost, with an easy-to-read display and top-notch factory service.

a pair of clips for wire antennas, and a socket for the AC adaptor.

There is only one 5.5 kHz bandwidth, and no signal-strength indicator or tone control. Single-sideband capability or synchronous selectable sideband? Forget it!

No flip-down feet or bail to angle the receiver, either, which takes the basics concept to extremes. The only option is a plastic carrying handle—odd, inasmuch as the SW1 is clearly not a portatop. And, of course, with this kind of bare-bones approach, there are none of the exotic controls found on kilobuck supersets.

What you do get is superior quality of construction, along with Drake's legendary service that's available even years after a model has been discontinued. The SW1 is made to last, but if it hiccups along the way, it can be serviced properly—something virtually unheard of with plastic portables.

Sensitivity to weak signals is quite good. Also, unlike plastic portables, the SW1 has enough dynamic range so you can usually connect it to a high-performance antenna without encountering overloading. And sound from the front-firing speaker is pleasant, indeed.

Okay, but . . . While the single bandwidth offers nice fidelity with stations in the clear, it is otherwise too wide, with skirt selectivity that's not up to snuff. This means that you often hear adjacent-channel heterodyne interference—a thoroughly annoying 5,000 Hz whistle that's one of the banes of mediocre shortwave radios. Why Drake, of all manufacturers, fell into this trap, who knows. But it should an easy fix by Drake, should they eventually choose to do so, or even aftermarket by shortwave specialty firms.

Another glitch is loud chugging when the receiver is tuned by knob. Turn it fast, such as when bandscanning, and all you hear is a series of pops which obscure stations that otherwise would be audible. Again, it's puzzling why Drake would design a receiver with this type of shortcoming.

Withal, the Drake SW1 is a decent offering at an attractive price, especially if you're looking for a receiver that's affordable, uncomplicated and robust, with service to match. But it would profit from a good going-over to clear up a couple of annoying shortcomings, as well as to add certain key features consumers have come to expect in this price category.

The PASSPORT *tabletop-model review team consists of Jock Elliott and Lawrence Magne, including John Campbell and Tony Jones, with Avery Comarow, George Heidelman and David Walcutt. Laboratory measurements by Robert Sherwood.*

Innovative Device Reduces Noise

*T*he scene: an ancient slave galley, somewhere in the Mediterranean. The coxswain, who controls the speed of the boat through the beat of his drum, addresses the slaves chained to their rowing benches.

"I've got good news and bad news," he says. "The good news is that you'll get extra rations at dinner." There is wild cheering in the ranks. "The bad news," he goes on, "is that after dinner, the captain wants to go water skiing."

Reduces Noise Before It Gets to Radio

Similarly, the $175 ANC-4 Antenna Noise Canceller from the American firm of JPS Communications brings with it both good news and bad news. The good news is that the ANC-4 can be highly effective in reducing local electrical noise—from power lines, computers, dimmers, TVs and such—*before* it gets into your receiver. The bad news is that the ANC-4 has a fairly steep learning curve, is fussy to operate and, when all is said and done, may not solve your particular noise problem.

More Effective Than a Noise Blanker

The ANC-4 is clearly not just another noise blanker. Conventional noise blankers work only when the noise level is stronger than the level of the received signal. This makes them pretty marginal, as most electrical noise disrupts world band signals even when the noise is weaker than the signal. Instead, the ANC-4 uses phase-cancellation circuitry and a separate "noise antenna" to reduce electrical noise—even though it's weaker than the received signal.

Electric-noise pollution is world band's dirty little secret. Now, there's an off-the-shelf solution that really works, the JPS ANC-4 Antenna Noise Canceller.

Easy to Set Up ...

The ANC-4 is small enough to perch on its rubber feet atop almost any world band tabletop or portatop receiver. Festooned on the front panel are pushbuttons for power, phase range and frequency range, as well as knobs for adjusting noise phase and noise gain. On the back panel is a connector for the noise antenna, with another such connector atop the cabinet. There are also a grounding attachment, PL-259 connectors for the main antenna and receiver, and a plug for the AC adaptor which comes standard. The entire assembly is wrapped in a bulldog-tough metal case that has become a hallmark of JPS gear.

The technical manual for the ANC-4 is well-written and covers the ground thoroughly. From the "Quick Operation" guide at the beginning to the "Troubleshooting" section at the back, it is clear, informative, and acquits itself well. As we'll see in a moment, however, actual operation is not pushbutton-easy.

However, setting up the ANC-4 is no problem. All you do is connect the AC adaptor and one of the two noise antennas supplied. Then affix the ANC-4 to your outside antenna, connect the unit to your receiver, attach the ANC-4 to your station ground, and turn on the power. This done, you're now ready to start up the slope of a learning curve, like with new computer software.

... But Requires Skill to Operate

To begin with, there is no way to know which antenna is going to work better for canceling the noise problem you have without first trying one antenna, then the other. In principle, you should resist the urge to connect the ANC-4 to a noise antenna other than the whip or short wire that are supplied. That's because a powerful or efficient antenna, such as an outdoor inverted-L, may overload the ANC-4 and render it ineffective. However, in practice this approach may work, anyway, so try it out and see what works best.

In addition, even though the manual says to choose one noise antenna or the other, there are rare occasions when using *both* antennas is optimum.

> Actual operation is not pushbutton-easy, but a "lazy-boy" approach often works.

Ah, but there is good news. Judging from our test findings, you may well find that the short wire antenna works best nearly all the time. We can't guarantee it—results differ markedly from location-to-location—but the odds are that you can get away with this "lazy boy" approach.

Thereafter, operating the ANC-4 is definitely more art than science. To quote from the manual: "Turn the NOISE GAIN control slowly clockwise while observing the receiver 'S' meter. Note when the noise level changes, whether increase or decrease. Now adjust the NOISE PHASE until you see the 'S' meter dip. If you do not see a dip or rise in the 'S' meter reading, trying changing the PHASE RANGE pushbutton to the OUT position and re-adjust the NOISE PHASE control. One of the settings of the PHASE RANGE switch will provide the proper phase so that a good null can be attained. If not, try the HI range of the FREQ RANGE switch."

If all that doesn't work, you can try the other noise antenna and start the process over again. But once you get the ANC-4 adjusted, you can't just set it and leave it. For example, if the noise environment changes as you shift among world band segments, you have to redo the trial-and-error adjustment process.

Results Vary According to Conditions

How well the ANC-4 works depends not only upon your skills, but also upon the specific characteristics of your location. For example, at one of PASSPORT's relatively quiet listening posts in an upstate New York suburb, the ANC-4 slightly reduced "fried egg" noises on 11 meters. Yet, the overall effect was hardly worth the hassle.

Yet, at an urban location in Ohio, where local electrical noises were much worse, the ANC-4 was able to reduce the strength of local noises sufficiently to copy a number of otherwise-unreadable signals. In this sort of hostile setting, the ANC-4 clearly has the potential of being a godsend.

Even then, the ANC-4 is not magic. It won't reduce all noise sources to zero. But it can decrease noise to the point where the desired signal can be heard. JPS claims a 40 dB noise reduction, but we found it ranges from as little as 10-20 dB to as great as 60-70 dB. The difficulty is that there is no way to know if the ANC-4 will solve *your* local noise problems without your trying it. As a result, you should purchase the ANC-4 on a refundable basis.

The ANC-4 causes a 6 dB insertion loss during operation, which means that signal strength to the receiver is slightly lower than it otherwise would be. Yet, this wasn't found to be a problem, as when there is noise present the improvement is usually far greater than the minor signal attenuation. Of course, when there is no noise the ANC-4 need not be used, and thus there is no insertion loss.

Bottom Line

If you're into instant gratification—push button, noise begone!—the ANC-4 is not for you. But if you are a dedicated DXer or exacting program listener with a local noise problem, and you're willing to put in time to learn the art of operating the ANC-4, this innovative noise canceling unit has real potential for turning listening frustration into listening pleasure.

Prepared by Jock Elliott and George Zeller.

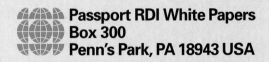

Where to Find It:

Index to Radios for 1997

PASSPORT TO WORLD BAND RADIO *tests nearly every model on the market. Here's your guide to the exact page where each of these reviews can be found. Digital models in **bold** are new or upgraded for 1997.*

For premium receivers and antennas, there are also comprehensive PASSPORT® Radio Database International White Papers®. These usually run 15-30 pages in length, with one report thoroughly covering a single model or topic. Each RDI White Paper®—$5.95 in North America, $7.95 airmail in most other regions—contains virtually all our panel's findings and comments during hands-on testing, as well as laboratory measurements and what these mean to you.

They're available from key world band dealers; or, if you prefer, you can contact our 24-hour automated VISA/MC order lines (voice +1 215/794-8252; fax +1 215/794 3396), write us at PASSPORT RDI White Papers, Box 300, Penn's Park, PA 18943 USA, or click onto our Web site at http://www.passport.com.

Radio Database International White Paper® available.

M. Kroszner

Although virtual travel gets the spotlight, physical travel also brings people closer together. The English Channel tunnel, a dream of emperors and kings past, now carries sleek Eurostar trains between the Continent and England.

WORLDSCAN®

What's On Tonight?

*I*nternational broadcasting is a global bazaar, heard over everything from local stations to Web radio. Yet, the technology of world band radio is the preferred choice of millions, and no wonder. It's affordable, easy to use, and offers a vast range of programs at the touch of a button.

And what programs! The best news, and the greatest variety of music and entertainment. With world band radio, the whole world is at your fingertips.

There's almost too much to choose from, so here is a selection of the better shows from all over—and where and when to hear them. To help you separate the thoroughbreds from the merely good, here are some handy symbols:

- ■ Station with programs that are almost always superior
- ● First-class program

To be as helpful as possible throughout the year, PASSPORT's schedules consist not just of observed activity, but also that which we have creatively opined will take place during the forthcoming year. This latter material is original from us, and may be not as exact as factual information.

Key frequencies are given for North America, Europe, East Asia and Australasia, plus general coverage of the Mideast, Southern Africa and Southeast Asia. Information on secondary and seasonal channels, as well as channels for other parts of the world, are in Worldwide Broadcasts in English and the Blue Pages.

Times are given in World Time, days as World Day, both explained in the Glossary and Compleat Idiot's Guide to Getting Started. Many stations announce World Time at the beginning of each broadcast or on the hour.

"Summer" and "winter"? These refer to seasons in the Northern Hemisphere. Many stations supplement their programs with newsletters, tourist brochures, magazines, books and other goodies—often free. See Addresses PLUS for how you can get them.

The sounds and traditions of Taiwan are brought to the world daily over the Voice of Free China.   R. Crane

0000-0559

North America—Evening Prime Time
Europe & Mideast—Early Morning
Australasia & East Asia—Midday and Afternoon

00:00

■BBC World Service for the Americas. It may be under siege from funders and planners, but the BBC World Service is still well out in front when it comes to world band programs. With much of the "Beeb" in a state of flux, it is difficult to predict what the 1997 program lineup is going to be. In the meantime, though, this is what you get. The first half-hour consists of the comprehensive ●*Newsdesk*, which is then followed by a 15-minute feature and ●*Britain Today*. Pick of the litter are Tuesday's ●*Global Concerns* (Monday evening, local American date), Wednesday's ●*Folk Routes* and Sunday's ●*Letter from America*. On other days you can hear the likes of *Development 97* (Monday), *From Our Own Correspondent* (Thursday), *Good Books* (Friday) and Saturday's *Seven Days*. Audible on 5975, 6175, 7325 (winter), 9590 and 9915 kHz.

■BBC World Service for Asia. Identical to the service for the Americas, except for some of the features at 0030. Audible in East and Southeast Asia (till 0030) on 7110, 9580, 11945 and 15280 kHz; and a full hour on 6195 and 15360 kHz.

Monitor Radio International, USA. North America's number one station for news and in-depth analysis. A one-hour show updated throughout the day and broadcast to different parts of the globe. *News*, then ●*Monitor Radio*—news analysis and news-related features with emphasis on international developments. The final 10 minutes consist of a listener-response program and a religious article from the *Christian Science Monitor* newspaper. To Eastern North America and the Caribbean Tuesday through Friday (Monday through Thursday, local American day) on 7535 kHz, and heard throughout much of the United States on 9430 kHz although targeted to Central and South America. On other days, the broadcasts feature Herald of Christian Science and Christian Science Sentinel religious programming (all of it not necessarily in English) or transmissions of the Sunday Service from the Mother Church in Boston. Also available to Southeast Asia on 15665 kHz.

Radio Bulgaria. Winters only at this time. *News*, then Tuesday through Friday there's 15 minutes of current events in *Today*, replaced Saturday by *Weekly Spotlight*. The remainder of the broadcast is given over to features dealing with Bulgarian life and culture, and includes some lively Balkan folk music. Sixty minutes to Eastern North America and Central America on 7480 and 9700 kHz. One hour earlier in summer.

Radio Exterior de España ("Spanish National Radio"). *News*, then Tuesday through Saturday (local weekday evenings in the Americas) it's *Panorama*, which features a recording of popular Spanish music, a commentary or a report, a review of the Spanish press, and weather. The remainder of the program is a mixture of literature, science, music and general programming. Tuesday (Monday evening in North America), there's *Sports Spotlight* and *Cultural Encounters*; Wednesday features *People of Today* and *Entertainment in Spain*; Thursday brings *As Others See Us* and, biweekly, *The Natural World* or *Science Desk*; Friday has *Economic Report* and *Cultural Clippings*; and

Saturday offers *Window on Spain* and *Review of the Arts*. The final slot is give over to a language course, *Spanish by Radio*. On the remaining days, you can listen to Sunday's *Hall of Fame*, *Distance Unknown* (for radio enthusiasts) and *Gallery of Spanish Voices*; and Monday's *Visitors' Book*, *Great Figures in Flamenco* and *Radio Club*. Sixty minutes to Eastern North America on 9540 kHz.

Radio Canada International. Winters only at this time. Tuesday through Saturday (weekday evenings in North America), it's the final hour of the CBC domestic service *news* program ●*As It Happens*, which features international stories, Canadian news and general human interest features. Sundays feature ●*Quirks and Quarks* (science), replaced Monday by the cultural *Tapestry*, both from the CBC's domestic output. To North America on 5960 and 9755 kHz. One hour earlier in summer.

Voice of Russia World Service. Beamed to Eastern North America at this hour. Winters, *news* and opinion take up the first 30 minutes, followed by some excellent musical fare during the second half-hour. Monday and Saturday (Sunday and Friday evenings local American days), there's the incomparable ●*Folk Box*; Thursday brings ●*Music at Your Request*; and Wednesday and Friday feature jazz. Summers, it's *News*, followed Tuesday through Saturday by *Focus on Asia and the Pacific* and either ●*Moscow Yesterday and Today* (Wednesday and Friday) or *This is Russia*. On the remaining days there's a listener-response program, then ●*Audio Book Club* (Sunday) or *Russian by Radio* (Monday). Not the easy catch it used to be, so you have to dial around a bit. Winters, the pickings are slim, indeed; try 7105, 7125 and 7180 kHz. Failing these, try other frequencies in the 7 MHz segment, or the bottom end of the 6 MHz range (5900-5940 kHz). Best summer options are 7125, 7250, 9530, 9620 and 9665 kHz.

Radio Yugoslavia. Monday through Saturday (Sunday through Friday, local American evenings) and summers only at this time. *News* and information with a strong regional slant, and worth a listen if you are interested in the area. Thirty minutes to Eastern and Central North America on 9580 and 11870 kHz. One hour later in winter.

Radio Pyongyang, North Korea. Strictly of curiosity value only, this station continues to occupy the basement of world band programming. Epithets like "Great Leader" and "Beloved Comrade" continue to abound, as do choral praises of the two Kims. The last of the old-style communist stations, and unlikely to change, at least for the time being. Fifty boring minutes to the Americas on 11335, 13760 and 15130 kHz.

Radio Ukraine International. Summers only at this time. An hour's ample coverage of just about everything Ukrainian, including news, sports, politics and culture. Well worth a listen is ●*Music from Ukraine*, which fills most of the Monday (Sunday evening in the Americas) broadcast. Sixty minutes to Eastern North America on 7150 and 9550 kHz. One hour later in winter.

Radio Australia. Part of a 24-hour service to Asia and the Pacific, but which can also be heard at this time throughout much of North America. Begins with world *news*, then Monday through Friday there's *Network Asia*, replaced Saturday by *Feedback* (a listener-response program) and *Indian Pacific*, and Sunday by *Charting Australia* and *Correspondents' Report*. Targeted at Asia and the Pacific on about ten channels, and heard in North America (from 0030, and best during summer) on 13755, 17795 and 17860 kHz. In East Asia, try 13605 and 17715 kHz; for southeastern parts, choose from 11640, 15240, 15415, 15510 and 17750 kHz. Be forewarned, several of these channels are only available from 0030 onwards.

Douglas Garlinger, Director of Engineering for WHRI in Indiana and KWHR in Hawaii, visits Tian'anmen Square in the heart of Beijing.

Radio Prague, Czech Republic. *News,* then Tuesday through Saturday (weekday evenings in the Americas), there's *Current Affairs.* These are followed by one or more features. Tuesday has *Magazine '96;* Wednesday, it's *Talking Point* and *What's Up?;* Thursday has *From the Archives* and *The Arts;* Friday brings *Economic Report* and *I'd Like You to Meet...;* and Saturday there's *Between You and Us.* Sunday's offerings include a musical feature, replaced Monday by *The Week in Politics, From the Weeklies* and *What's Up?* Thirty minutes to North America on 5930 and 7345 kHz.

Voice of America. First hour of the VOA's two-hour broadcasts to the Caribbean and Latin America. *News,* followed by split programming Tuesday through Saturday (Monday through Friday eve-

nings in the Americas). Listeners in the Caribbean can tune in to ●*Report to the Caribbean,* followed by *Music USA.* For Latin America there is ●*VOA Business Report* (replaced Saturday be *Newsline*) and Special English news and features. On Sunday, both services carry *Agriculture Today,* followed by *Communications World* (Caribbean) or the Special English feature ●*American Stories* (Latin America). Monday's programming consists of ●*VOA Business Report* (Caribbean) or ●*Encounter* (Latin America), with the second half-hour's ●*Spotlight* being common to both services. An excellent way to keep in touch with events in the Western Hemisphere. The service to the Caribbean is on 6130, 9455 and 11695 kHz; and the one to the Americas is on 5995, 7405, 9775 and 13740 kHz. The final hour of a separate service to East and Southeast Asia and Australasia (see 2200) can be heard on 7215, 9770, 11760, 15185, 15290, 17735 and 17820 kHz.

Croatian Radio. Eight minutes of *news* from Croatian Radio's Zagreb studio. Best heard in Europe and Eastern North America, but also heard elsewhere. Channel usage varies, but try 5895, 7165, 7370 and 13830 kHz.

Radio Thailand. *Newshour.* Not the exotic fare you'd expect from a country like Thailand. This station now has considerable transmitter capacity, but its programs still leave a lot of room for improvement. Thirty minutes for East African insomniacs on 9680 (or 9690) kHz, and a full hour to Asia on 9655 and 11905 kHz.

China Radio International. *News* and commentary, followed Wednesday through Saturday (Tuesday through Friday evenings in the Americas) by *Current Affairs.* These are followed by various feature programs, such as *Cultural Spectrum* (Friday); *Listeners' Letterbox* (Monday and Wednesday); *China Scrapbook, Cooking Show, Travel Talk* and ●*Music from China* (Sunday); *Sports Beat* and *Music Album* (Monday); *Learn to Speak Chinese* (Tuesday and Thursday); and Saturday's *In the Third World.* Mondays, there is also a biweekly *Business Show* which alternates with *China's Open Windows.* One hour to Eastern North America on 9710 and 11695 (or 11715) kHz.

All India Radio. The final 45 minutes of a much larger block of programming targeted at Southeast Asia, and heard well beyond. On 7150, 9705, 9950 and 11620 kHz.

Radio Cairo, Egypt. The final half-hour of a 90-minute broadcast to Eastern North America on 9900 kHz. See 2300 for specifics.

Radio New Zealand International. A friendly package of *news* and features sometimes replaced by live sports commentary. Part of a much longer broadcast

for the South Pacific, but also heard in parts of North America (especially during summer) on 15115 kHz.

FEBC Radio International, Philippines. *Good Morning from Manila,* a potpourri of secular and religious programming targeted at South and Southeast Asia, but heard well beyond. The first 60 minutes of a two-hour broadcast on 15450 kHz.

WWCR, Nashville, Tennessee. Carries a variety of disestablishmentarian programs at this hour, depending on the day of the week. Winters on 5065 kHz, there's "The Voice of Liberty" and "The Hour of Courage"; in summer it's "Protecting your Wealth", "World of Prophecy" and "Full Disclosure Live." On 7435 kHz, look for yet more of the same.

WJCR, Upton, Kentucky. Twenty-four hours of gospel music targeted at North America on 7490 and (at this hour) 13595 kHz. Also heard elsewhere, mainly during darkness hours. For more religious broadcasting at this hour, try **WYFR-Family Radio** on 6085 kHz, and **KTBN** on (winters) 7510 or (summers) 15590 kHz. For something a little more controversial, tune to Dr. Gene Scott's University Network, via **WWCR** on 13845 kHz or **KAIJ** on 13815 kHz. Traditional Catholic programming can be heard via **WEWN** on 7425 kHz.

00:30

Radio Nederland. *News,* then Tuesday through Sunday (Monday through Saturday evenings in North America) there's ●*Newsline,* a current affairs program. These are followed by a different feature each day, including the well-produced ●*Research File* (science, Tuesday); *Mirror Images* (arts in Holland, Wednesday); a feature documentary (Thursday); *Media Network* (Friday); ●*A Good Life* (Saturday); and Sunday's ●*Weekend.*

MFJ's high performance *tuned* active antenn rivals long wires hundreds of feet long!

MFJ-1020B

$79⁹⁵

Receive strong clear signals from all over the world with this indoor *tuned* active antenna that rivals the reception of long wires hundreds of feet long!

"World Radio TV Handbook" says MFJ-1020 is a "fine value . . . fair price . . . performs very well indeed!"

Set it on your desktop and listen to the world!

No need to hassle with putting up an outside antenn and then have to disconnect it during storms.

Covers 300 kHz to 30 MHz so you can pick up all of your favorite stations. And discover new ones you couldn't get before. Tuned circuitry minimizes intermodulation, improves selectivity and reduces nois from phantom signals, images and out-of-band signals

Adjustable telescoping whip gives you maximum signal with minimum noise. Full set of controls for tun ing, band selection, gain and On-Off/Bypass. 5x2x6 ir

Doubles as preselector for external antenna. Use 9 volt battery or 110 VAC with MFJ-1312, $12.9⁵

MFJ tunable DSP filter

MFJ-784B
$249⁹⁵

Super filter uses state-of-the-art *Digital Signal Processing* technology!

It *automatically* searches for and eliminates *multiple* heterodynes.

Tunable, pre-set and programmable "brick wall" filters with *60 dB attenuation just 75 Hz away from cutoff frequency* literally knocks out interference signals.

Adaptive *noise reduction* reduces random background noise up to 20 dB.

Works with all signals including all voice, CW and data signals. Plugs between radio and speaker or phones.

Dual Tunable Audio Filter

MFJ-752C
$99⁹⁵

Two separately tunable filters let you peak desired signals and notch out interference at the same time. You can peak, notch, low or high pass signals to eliminate hetero-dynes and interference. Plugs between radio and speaker or phones. 10x2x6 in.

Super Active Antenna

"World Radio TV Handbook" says MFJ-1024 is a "first rate easy-to-operate active antenna . . . quiet . . . excellent dynamic range . . . good gain . . . low noise . . . broad frequency coverage."

Mount it outdoors away from elec-trical noise for maximum signal, minim-um noise. Covers 50 KHz to 30 MHz.

Receives strong, clear signals from all over the world. 20dB attenuator, gain control, ON LED. Switch two receivers and aux. or active antenna. 6x3x5 in. remote has 54 inch whip, 50 ft. coax. 3x2x4 in. 12 VDC or 110 VAC with MFJ-1312, **MFJ-1024 $129⁹⁵** $12.95.

DXers' World Map Clock

Shows time of any DX throughout the world on world map! Displays day/ week/ month/date/year and hour /minute/second in 12 or 24 hour format. Has daylight-savings-time feature.

MFJ-112 $24⁹⁵

Push-buttons let you move a flashing time zone east and west on the map to a major city in every time zone. 4¹/₂x3³/₈x2¹/₄ in.

MFJ Antenna Matcher

MFJ-959B $99⁹⁵

Matches your antenna to your receiver so you get maximum signal and minimum loss.

Preamp with gain control boosts weak stations 10 times. 20 dB attenuator prevents overload. Pushbuttons let you select 2 antennas and 2 receivers. Covers 1.6-30 MHz. 9x2x6 inches.

SWL's Guide for Apartments

World renowned SWL expert Ed Noll's newest book gives you the key to hearing news as it happens, concerts from Vienna and soccer games from Germany!

MFJ-36 $9⁹⁵

He tells you what shortwave bands to listen to, the best times to tune in, how to DX and QSL, how to send for schedules and construct *indoor* antennas plus many band by band DX tips.

High-Q Passive Preselector

MFJ-956 $39⁹⁵

High-Q passive LC preselector that lets you boost your favorite stations while rejecting images, intermod and other phantom signals. 1.5-30 MHz. Has bypass and receiver grounded position.

High-Gain Preselector

MFJ-1045C $69⁹⁵

High-gain, high-Q receiver preselector covers 1.8-54 MHz. Boost weak signals 10 times with low noise dual gate MOSFET. Reject out-of-band signals and images with high-Q tuned circuits. Pushbuttons let you select 2 antennas and 2 receivers. Dual coax and phono connectors. Use 9-18 VDC or 110 VAC with MFJ-1312, $129.95.

MFJ-1278B Multimode

MFJ-1278B $299⁹⁵

Discover a whole new world of communications you never knew existed with this MFJ-1278B, your receiver and computer.

You'll have fun listening to world-wide *packet* networks and watching hams exchange *color SSTV* pictures with their buddies around the world.

You'll marvel at *full color FAX* news photos as they come to life on your screen. You'll see weather changes on highly detailed *weather maps*.

You'll eavesdrop on late breaking news as it happens on *RTTY*. Wanna copy some *CW*? Just watch your screen

Requires MFJ-1289, $59.95, MultiCom™, software and cables.

Tap into *secret* Shortwave Signals

Turn mysterious signals into exciting text messages with this new MFJ MultiReader™

MFJ-462B

$169⁹⁵

Plug this *MFJ MultiReader*™ into your shortwave receiver's earphone jack.

Then *watch* mysterious chirps, whistles and buzzing sounds RTTY, ASCII, AMTOR and CW turn into exciting text messages as they scroll across your easy-to-read LCD display.

You'll *read* fascinating commerical, military, diplomatic, weather, aeronautical, maritime and amateur traffic from all over the world . . . traffic your friends can't read -- unless they have a decoder.

Eavesdrop on the World

Eavesdrop on the world's press agencies transmitting *edited* late breaking news in English -- China News in Taiwan, Tanjug Press in Serbia, Iraqui News in Iraq.

Printer monitors 24 hours a day

MFJ's exclusive *TelePrinterPort*™ lets you monitor any station 24 hours a day by printing their transmissions on your Epson compatible printer. Printer cable, **MFJ-5412**, $9.95.

MFJ *MessageSaver*™

You can save several pages of text in 8K of memory for re-reading or later review using MFJ's exclusive *MessageSaver*™.

Easy to use, tune and read

It's easy to use -- just push a button to select modes and features from a menu.

It's easy to tune -- a precision tuning indicator makes tuning your receiver fast and easy for best copy.

It's easy to read -- the 2 line 16 character LCD display is mounted on a sloped front panel for easy reading.

Copies most standard shifts and speeds. Has *MFJ AutoTrak*™ Morse code speed tracking.

Use 12 VDC or use 110 VAC with MFJ-1312B AC adapter, $12.95. 5¼x2½x5¼ inches.

Easy-Up Antennas Book

How to build and set up inexpensive, easy tested wire antennas using readily available parts that'll bring signals in like you've never heard before. Covers antennas from 100 KHz to 1000 MHz.

MFJ-38 $16⁹⁵

Compact Active Antenna

Plug this new *compact* MFJ all band active antenna to your general coverage receiver and you'll hear strong clear signals from all over the world from 300 KHz to 200 MHz.

MFJ-1022 $39⁹⁵

Detachable 20 inch telescoping antenna. 9 volt battery or 110 VAC with MFJ-1312B, $12.95. 3⅛x1¼x4 in.

MFJ Antenna Switches

MFJ-1704 $9⁹⁵   **MFJ-1702B $21⁹⁵**

MFJ-1704 heavy duty antenna switch lets you select 4 antennas or ground them for static and lightning protection. Unused antennas automatically grounded. Replaceable lightning surge protection device. Good to over 500 MHz. 60 db isolation at 30 MHz. **MFJ-1702B**, $21.95, for 2 antennas.

Super Hi-Q Loop™ Antenna

The *MFJ Super Loop*™ is a professional quality remotely tuned 10 to 30 MHz high-Q loop antenna. It's very quiet and has a very narrow bandwidth that reduces receiver overloading and out-of-band interference.

MFJ-1782 $269⁹⁵

MFJ 12/24 Hour Clocks

MFJ-107B $9⁹⁵   **MFJ-105B $19⁹⁵**
MFJ-108B $19⁹⁵

MFJ-108B, *dual* clock displays 24 UTC and 12 hour local time.

MFJ-107B, single clock shows you 24 hour UTC time. *3 star rated* by *Passport to World Band Radio!*

MFJ-105B, accurate 24 hour UTC quartz *wall clock* with huge 10 inch face.

World Band Radio Kit

MFJ-8100K $59⁹⁵ *kit*
MFJ-8100W $79⁹⁵ *wired*

Build this *regenerative* shortwave receiver *kit* and listen to shortwave signals from all over the world. With just a 10 foot wire antenna.

Has RF stage, vernier reduction drive, smooth regeneration, five bands.

Code Practice Oscillator

MFJ-557 $24⁹⁵

Have fun learning Morse code with this MFJ-557 Deluxe Code Practice Oscillator. It's mounted with Morse key and speaker on a heavy steel base so it stays put on your table. Earphone jack, tone, volume controls, adjustable key.

Enjoy World Bands in your car

Add *World Band* shortwave reception to your AM car radio and hear late breaking news as it happens from all over the world! Covers 19, 25, 31, 49 Meters. Plugs between radio and antenna.

MFJ-306 $79⁹⁵

Personal Morse Code Tutor™

Learn Morse code anywhere with this pocket size battery operated *MFJ Personal Morse Code Tutor*™!

MFJ-411 $79⁹⁵

This pocket size tutor takes you from zero code speed with a beginner's course to Extra Class with customized code practice.

Select letters, numbers, punctuations or prosigns or any combination or words or QSOs with normal or Farnsworth spacing. Use earphones or built-in speaker.

Receive FAX, WeFAX, RTTY, ASCII, Morse Code

Use your PC computer and radio to receive and display brilliant *full color* FAX news photos and incredible 16 gray level WeFAX weather maps. Also receives RTTY, ASCII and Morse code.

MFJ-1214PC $149⁹⁵

Animate weather maps. Display 10 global pictures *simultaneously*. Zoom any part of picture or map. Frequency manager lists over 900 FAX stations. Automatic picture capture and save.

Includes interface, software, cables, power supply, manual, Jump-Start™ guide.

Monday's features are a listener-response program and *Sounds Interesting*. Fifty-five minutes to North America on 6020, 6165 and (summers) 9845 kHz; and a full hour to South Asia (also widely heard in other parts of the continent, as well as Australasia), winters on 5905 and 7305 kHz, and summers on 9860 and 11655 kHz.

Radio Vlaanderen Internationaal, Belgium. Winters only at this time; Tuesday through Saturday (weekday evenings in North America), there's *News*, *Press Review* and *Belgium Today*, followed by features like *Focus on Europe* (Tuesday), *Living in Belgium* and *Green Society* (Wednesday), *The Arts* and *Around Town* (Thursday), *Economics* and *International Report* (Friday), and *The Arts* and *Tourism* (Saturday). Weekend features include *Music from Flanders* (Sunday) and Monday's *P.O. Box 26* and *Radio World*. Thirty minutes to Eastern North America on 5900 (or 6030) kHz; also audible on 9925 kHz, though beamed elsewhere. One hour earlier in summer.

Radio Sweden. Tuesday through Saturday (weekday evenings in the Americas), it's *news* and features in *Sixty Degrees North*, concentrating heavily on Scandinavian topics. Tuesday's accent is on sports; Wednesday has electronic media news; Thursday brings *Money Matters*; Friday features ecology or science and technology; and Saturday offers a review of the week's news. Sunday, there's *Spectrum* (arts) or *Sweden Today* (current events), while Monday's offering is *In Touch with Stockholm* (a listener-response program) or the musical *Sounds Nordic*. Thirty minutes to South America, also audible in Eastern North America on 6065 and (winter) 9850 kHz.

Radio Vilnius, Lithuania. A half hour that's heavily geared to *news* and background reports about events in Lithuania. Of broader appeal is *Mailbag*, aired every other Sunday (Saturday evenings local American date). For a little Lithuanian music, try the next evening, following the news. To Eastern North America winters on 5910 kHz, and summers on 6120 or 9560 kHz.

Voice of the Islamic Republic of Iran. One hour of *news*, commentary and features with a strong Islamic slant. Targeted at North and Central America. Try 6015, 6150, 6175, 7180, 9022 and 9670 kHz. Apart from 9022 kHz, channel usage tends to be variable.

Radio Thailand. *Newshour*. Thirty minutes to North America winters on 11905 kHz, and summers on 15370 kHz. Also available year-round to Asia on 9655 and 11905 kHz.

HCJB—Voice of the Andes, Ecuador. Tuesday through Saturday (weekday evenings in North America), there's the popular *Focus on the Family*, hosted by James Dobson. This is replaced weekends by Sunday's *Musical Mailbag* and Monday's *Mountain Meditations*. To Eastern North America on 9745 kHz.

00:50

Radio Roma, Italy. *News* and some uninspiring Italian music make up this 20-minute broadcast to North America. Better than what it used to be, but still has a long way to go. On 6005, 9645 (or 9675) and 11800 kHz.

01:00

■**BBC World Service for the Americas.** ●*Newsdesk*, followed Tuesday through Saturday (weekday evenings in the Americas) by the interesting ●*Outlook* (30 years, and still going strong). The religious *Words of Faith* rounds off the hour. Weekends, these are replaced by Sunday's ●*People and Politics* and Monday's ●*Short Story* (or *Seeing Stars*) and *On the Move*. Audible in North America on 5975, 6175, 7325 (winter), 9590 and 9915 kHz.

■**BBC World Service for Asia.** Thirty minutes of ●*Newsdesk*, five more of *World News*, and ten of ●*Sports Roundup*. The final quarter-hour is given over to features: ●*Letter from America* (Sunday), *The Farming World* (Monday), *Development 97* (Tuesday), ●*Health Matters* (Wednesday), *From Our Own Correspondent* (Thursday), ●*The Learning World* (Friday) and last but not least, ●*Global Concerns* (Saturday). Audible in East Asia on 15360 kHz, and Southeast Asia on 6195 kHz.

Monitor Radio International, USA. See 0000 for program details. Tuesday through Saturday (Monday through Friday, local American date) on 7535 kHz, and heard throughout much of the United States on 9430 kHz although targeted at Central and South America. On other days, the broadcasts feature Herald of Christian Science and Christian Science Sentinel religious programming (all of it not necessarily in English) or transmissions of the Sunday Service from the Mother Church in Boston.

Radio Canada International. Summers only. *News*, followed Tuesday through Saturday (weeknights local American date) by *Spectrum* (topics in the news), which in turn is replaced Sunday by *Innovation Canada* (science) and ●*Earth Watch*. On Monday (Sunday evening in North America) there's *Arts in Canada* and a listener-response program. Sixty minutes to North America on 6120 and 9755 kHz. You can also try 9535, 11715 and 13670 kHz, but they are only available for the first 30 minutes, except for weekends. One hour later in winter.

■**Deutsche Welle,** Germany. *News*, followed Tuesday through Saturday (weekday evenings in the Americas) by the comprehensive ●*European Journal*—

commentary, interviews, background reports and analysis. This is followed by *German Tribune* (Tuesday and Thursday), *Come to Germany* (Wednesday), *Arts on the Air* (Friday), or Saturday's *Through German Eyes*. Sunday is given over to *Inside Europe* and *Religion and Society*; Monday brings *Living in Germany* and *German by Radio*. Fifty minutes of very good reception in North America and the Caribbean, winters on 5960, 6040, 6085, 6145, 9555 and 9670 kHz; and summers on 6040, 6085, 6145, 9640 and 11740 kHz.

Radio Slovakia International. *Slovakia Today*, a 30-minute window on Slovakian life and culture. Tuesday (Monday evening in the Americas), there's a potpourri of short features; Wednesday puts the accent on tourism and Slovak personalities; Wednesday has a historical feature; Thursday's slot is devoted to business and economy; and Friday brings a mix of politics, education and science. Saturday has a strong cultural content; Sunday features the "Best of" series; and Monday brings *Listeners' Tribune* and some enjoyable Slovak music. To Eastern North America and Central America on 5930 and 7300 kHz, and to South America on 9440 kHz.

Radio Norway International. Mondays (Sunday evenings, local American date) only. *Norway Now*. Thirty minutes of *news* and chat from and about Norway. To North and Central America winters on 7465 kHz, and summers on 9560 kHz.

Radio Budapest, Hungary. Summers only at this time. *News* and features, some of which are broadcast on a regular basis. These include Monday's *Bookshelf* (local Sunday evening in North America), a press review (Tuesday, Wednesday, Friday and Saturday), *Profiles* (Wednesday), and *Focus on Business* (Thursday). Thirty minutes to North America on 9840 and 11870 kHz. One hour later in winter.

Radio Prague, Czech Republic. Repeat of the 0000 broadcast. Thirty minutes to North America on 6200 and 7345 kHz.

Swiss Radio International. *Newsnet.* A workmanlike compilation of news and background reports on world and Swiss events. Somewhat lighter fare on Sunday (Saturday evening in North America), when the biweekly *Capital Letters* (a listener-response program) alternates with *Name Game* and *Sounds Good.* A half hour to North America and the Caribbean on 6135, 9885 and 9905 kHz.

Radio Japan. *News*, then Tuesday through Saturday (weekday evenings local American date) there's 10 minutes of *Asian Top News* followed by a half-hour feature. Take your pick from *Profile* (Tuesday), *Enjoy Japanese* (Wednesday and Friday), *Town and Around* (Thursday) and Saturday's *Music and Book Beat.* On the remaining days, look for *Asia Weekly* (Sunday) or Monday's *Let's Learn Japanese, Media Roundup* and *Viewpoint.* The broadcasts end with the daily *Tokyo Pop-in.* One hour to Eastern North America summers only on 5960 kHz via the powerful relay facilities of Radio Canada International in Sackville, New Brunswick. Also year-round to Western North America on 11885, 9605 (winter) and (summer) 11790 kHz. Also available to Asia on 11840, 11860, 11890/11900, 11910, 17810 and 17845 kHz.

Radio Exterior de España ("Spanish National Radio"). Repeat of the 0000 transmission. To Eastern North America on 9540 kHz.

Radio For Peace International, Costa Rica. One of the few remaining places where you can still find the peace and "peoplehood" ideals of the Sixties. This hour is the start of English programming—the initial hour being in Spanish.

FIRE (Feminist International Radio Endeavour) is one of the better offerings from the mélange of programs that make up RFPI's eight-hour cyclical blocks of predominantly counterculture programming. Sixty minutes of variable reception in Europe and the Americas on 6205 and 7385 kHz. Some transmissions are in the single-sideband mode, which can be properly processed only on certain radios.

Voice of Vietnam. A relay via the facilities of the Voice of Russia, Begins with *news*, then there's *Commentary* or *Weekly Review*, followed by short features and some pleasant Vietnamese music (especially at weekends). Repeated at 0130, 0200 and 0230 on the same channel. To Eastern North America winter on 5940 kHz, and summer on 7250 kHz.

Voice of Russia World Service. Continuous programming to North America at this hour. *News*, features and music. Tuesday through Saturday, winters, it's *Focus on Asia and the Pacific*, replaced summers by ●*Commonwealth Update* (Tuesday through Saturday only). The second half-hour contains some interesting fare. In summer, look for Tuesday's ●*Folk Box* (Monday evening local American date), ●*Music at Your Request* (Wednesday and Friday), Russian jazz (Thursday and Saturday), and ●*Music and Musicians* (from 0111, Sunday and Monday). Pick of the winter fare is ●*Moscow Yesterday and Today* (Wednesday and Friday) and Sunday's ●*Audio Book Club.* Where to tune? In Eastern North America winters, shoot for 7105 and 7125 kHz. Best bets in summer are likely to be 9530 and 9620 kHz (7240 kHz is another possibility). If these don't hack it, dial around nearby—the Voice of Russia tends to change its frequencies more often than most other stations. Western

> The Voice of Vietnam brings news of a country emerging from generations of war and devastation. Plaintive Vietnamese music, too.

Find Your Place in the World with Grundig

Grundig's Yacht Boy 400 –

Powerful enough to hear the world, yet small enough to fit in your hand. This award-winning radio features 40 presets for quick recall plus selectable wide/narrow bandwidth filter, and built-in clock with dual alarms and sleep timer. Cover AM/FM/LW and continuous short wave bands from 1.6 to 30 MHZ. Complete with travel case and carrying strap.

Grundig's Yacht Boy 305 –

This new world band radio features circuitry superior to comparable analog (dial tune) radios. Its digital technology allows you to precisely "fine tune" distant signals for crystal clear reception and rock-solid frequency stability. To catch the news, weather or even music from around the world, simply autoscan through AM, FM or the shortwave spectrum.

Grundig's Compact World Traveller II Digital –

The Grundig digital, portable AM/FM/SW radio is big on features, yet small enough to fit into a pocket or handbag. Keep track of time and events at home or away with…
• Dual quartz controlled alarm clocks • sleep timer
• 20 station memory • auto search and manual tuning
• protective travel pouch, *Grundig Shortwave Listening Guide.*

North America, it's summers only. Try 12010, 12050, 13665, 15180, 15425 and 15580 kHz.

Radio Habana Cuba. The start of four hours of continuous programming to Eastern North America, and made up of *news* and features such as *Latin America Newsline, DXers Unlimited, The Mailbag Show* and ●*The Jazz Place*, interspersed with some good Cuban music. To Eastern North America on 6000 and 9820 kHz. Also available on 9830 kHz upper sideband, though not all radios, unfortunately, can process such signals.

Radio Australia. *World News*, followed Monday through Friday by *Australian News*, a sports bulletin and *Network Asia*. Weekends, there's *Oz Sounds* and *Australia Today* (Saturday), and *Book Reading* and *The Europeans* (Sunday). Continuous programming to Asia and the Pacific on about ten channels, and heard in North America (best during summer) on 13755, 15240 and 17795 kHz. Best bets for East Asia are 13605 and 17715 kHz; in southeastern parts, tune to 11640, 15415, 15510 and 17750 kHz. In Europe, try 15510 kHz. Some channels carry a separate sports service on winter Saturdays.

Radio Yugoslavia. Monday through Saturday (Sunday through Friday, local American evenings) and winters only at this time. *News* and short reports, dealing almost exclusively with local and regional topics. Worth a listen. Thirty minutes to Eastern and Central North America on 6195 and 7115 kHz. One hour earlier in summer.

HCJB—Voice of the Andes, Ecuador. Tuesday through Saturday (weekday evenings in North America) it's *Studio 9*, featuring nine minutes of world and Latin American *news*, followed by 20 minutes of in-depth reporting on Latin America. The final portion of *Studio 9* is given over to one of a variety of 30-minute features— including *You Should Know* (issues and ethics, Tuesday), *El Mundo Futuro* (science,

Wednesday), *Ham Radio Today* (Thursday), *Woman to Woman* (Friday), and the unique and enjoyable ●*Música del Ecuador* (Saturday). On Sunday (Saturday evening in the Americas), the news is followed by *DX Partyline*, which in turn is replaced Monday by *Saludos Amigos*— HCJB's international friendship program. Continuous programming to Eastern North America on 9745 kHz.

Voice of America. *News*, followed Tuesday through Saturday (Monday through Friday evenings in the target area) by the outstanding ●*Report to the Americas*, a series of news features about the United States and other countries in the Western Hemisphere. This is replaced Sunday by *On the Line* and ●*Press Conference USA*, and Monday by the science program ●*New Horizons* and ●*Issues in the News*. To the Americas on 5995, 6130, 7405, 9455, 9775 and 13740 kHz.

Croatian Radio. Eight minutes of *news* from Croatian Radio's Zagreb studio. Best heard in Europe and Eastern North America, but also heard elsewhere. Channel usage varies, but try 5895, 7165, 7370 and 13830 kHz.

WRMI-Radio Miami International, Miami, Florida. Tuesday through Saturday only (local weekday evenings in the Americas). Part of a much longer multilingual transmission to the Caribbean. Thirty minutes of *Viva Miami!*—a potpourri of information, music and entertainment. Also includes regular weather updates during the hurricane season (June-November). Heard in much of the Americas on 9955 kHz. Repeated one hour later during winter.

Radio Ukraine International. Winters only at this time; see 0000 for program details. Sixty minutes of informative programming targeted at Eastern North America and European night owls. Try 5915, 6010, 6055 and 9620 kHz. One hour earlier in summer.

Radio New Zealand International. A

package of *news* and features sometimes replaced by live sports commentary. Part of a much longer broadcast for the South Pacific, but also heard in parts of North America (especially during summer) on 15115 kHz.

Radio Tashkent, Uzbekistan. *News* and features with a strong Uzbek flavor; some exotic music, too. A half hour to West and South Asia and the Mideast, occasionally heard in North America; winters on 5955, 5975, and 7285 kHz; summers on 7190 and 9715 kHz.

FEBC Radio International, Philippines. The final 30 minutes of *Good Morning from Manila* (see 0000 for specifics), followed by a half hour of religious fare. Targeted at South and Southeast Asia on 15450 kHz, but heard well beyond.

"American Dissident Voices", **WRNO.** This time summers only. Neo-Nazi anti-Israel program, hosted by Kevin Alfred Strom. Only of interest to those with similar beliefs. Thirty minutes Sunday (Saturday evening local American date) on 7355 kHz; try four hours later on 7395 kHz if preempted by live sports. Targeted at North America, but reaches beyond. Is followed by "Herald of Truth", another disestablishmentarian program of a similar vein.

WWCR, Nashville, Tennessee. Carries a variety of disestablishmentarian programs at this hour, depending on the day of the week. Winters, there's "Protecting your Wealth", "World of Prophecy" and "Full Disclosure Live" on 5065 kHz; while 7435 kHz carries a similar bunch of programs.

WJCR, Upton, Kentucky. Continues with country gospel music for North American listeners on 7490 and 13595 kHz. Also with religious programs to North America at this hour are **WYFR-Family Radio** on 6065 and 9505 kHz, **WWCR** on 13845 kHz and **KTBN** on 7510 kHz. For traditional Catholic programming, tune to **WEWN** on 7425 kHz.

01:30

Radio Austria International. ●*Report from Austria,* which includes a brief bulletin of *news,* followed by a series of current events and human interest stories. Ample coverage of national and regional issues, and an excellent source for news of Central and Eastern Europe. Thirty minutes to North America on 9655 kHz.

Radio Sweden. *News* and features of mainly Scandinavian content; see 0030 for specifics. Thirty minutes to Asia and Australasia on one or more frequencies. Try 7120 and 7290 kHz.

Radio Nederland. *News,* followed Tuesday through Saturday by ●*Newsline,* a current affairs program. Then there's a different feature each day, including ●*A Good Life* (Tuesday); *Sounds Interesting* (Thursday); ●*Research File* (science, Friday) and a documentary (Saturday). One hour to South Asia (also widely heard in other parts of the continent, as well as Australasia); winters on 5905, 7305, 9860 and 11655 kHz; and summers on 9860, 9890 and 11655 kHz.

Voice of Greece. Preceded and followed by programming in Greek. Approximately 10 minutes of English *news,* then Greek music, a short feature about the country, and more music. Resumes programming in Greek at 0200. To North America on any three frequencies from 6260, 7448, 9420, 9935 and 11645 kHz.

01:45

Radio Tirana, Albania. Approximately 10 minutes of *news* and commentary from one of Europe's least known countries. To North America on 6140 and 7160 kHz.

02:00

■**BBC World Service for the Americas.** Thirty minutes of ●*Newsday,* followed by

Meridian (Tuesday through Thursday, Saturday), *Thirty-Minute Drama* (Friday) and classical music (Sunday). Audible in North America on 5975, 6175, 7325 (winter) and 9590 kHz.

■BBC World Service for Asia. ●*Newsday* and a 30-minute feature. Pick of the pack are ●*Discovery* (Tuesday), ●*Assignment* (Thursday), ●*Thirty-Minute Drama* (Friday) and Saturday's ●*People and Politics*. Continuous to East and Southeast Asia on 15360 kHz.

Monitor Radio International, USA. See 0000 for program details. To Western North America Tuesday through Friday (Monday through Thursday, local American days) on 5850 kHz. Also audible throughout much of North America on 9430 kHz, although not necessarily beamed there. Programming on the remaining days relates to the teachings and experiences of the Christian Science Church.

Radio Cairo, Egypt. Repeat of the 2300 broadcast, and the first hour of a 90-minute potpourri of *news* and features about Egypt and the Arab world. Fair reception and mediocre audio quality to North America on 9475 kHz.

Radio Argentina al Exterior—R.A.E. Tuesday through Saturday only. *News* and short features dealing with aspects of life in Argentina, interspersed with samples of the country's various musical styles, from tango to zamba. Fifty-five minutes to North America on 11710 kHz.

Radio Budapest, Hungary. This time winters only; see 0100 for specifics. Thirty minutes to North America on 6190, 9850 and 11870 kHz. One hour earlier in summer.

Radio Canada International. Starts off with *News*, then Tuesday through Saturday winter (weeknights local American date) it's *Spectrum*. Sunday, there's *Innovation Canada* and the environmental ●*Earth Watch*, replaced Monday by *The Arts in Canada* and *Mailbag*. Summers,

News is followed by features taken from the Canadian Broadcasting Corporation's domestic output. Tuesday through Saturday, there's *The Best of Morningside*; Sunday features *Double Exposure* and *Canadian Air Farce*; and Monday has *The Inside Track* (sports) and *Now the Details*, a current affairs feature. One hour winters to North America on 5905, 6010 and 9755 kHz; and summers on 6120 (Sunday and Monday), 9755 and 13670. Tuesday through Saturday, 6120 kHz carries a special broadcast for Canadian peacekeepers in the Caribbean, 30 minutes of which is in French.

Radio Yugoslavia. Winters only at this time. *News* and reports with a strong regional slant. An informative half hour to Western North America on 6100 and 7115 kHz.

■Deutsche Welle, Germany. *News*, followed Monday through Friday by the highly informative package of ●*Asia-Pacific Report* and ●*European Journal*—commentary, interviews, background reports and analysis. These are replaced Saturday by *Commentary*, *The Week in Germany* and *Economic Notebook*. Sunday programming features *Commentary* (or *Sports Report*) and *Mailbag Asia*. Fifty minutes nominally targeted at South Asia, but widely heard elsewhere. Winters on 6035, 6130, 7265, 7285, 7355, 9515, 9615 and 9690 kHz; and summers on 7285, 9615, 9640, 9690, 11945, 11965 and 12045 kHz.

HCJB—Voice of the Andes, Ecuador. A mixed bag of religious and secular programming, depending on the day of the week. Tuesday (Monday evening in North America) is given over to *Master Control* and *Classical Favorites*; Wednesday airs *Unshackled* and *SHOUT!*; and Thursday brings *The Latest Catch* (a feature for radio enthusiasts), *The Book Nook* and *Sounds of Joy*. On Friday, you can hear the Australian-produced *Pacific*

Grundig World Class Receivers

Rated Best in its Class

YACHT BOY 400

Travel the airwaves with Grundig's portable digital **Yacht Boy 400**. Listening has never been easier, the BBC commentary from London, the news from Berlin, Beijing, the Balkans and more. Imagine!

Only Grundig with its reputation for world class electronics could offer a radio so advanced and compact. AM/FM/ Shortwave digital tuning, auto scan, and 40-memory presets, clock alarm and timer. Also includes **Grundig Shortwave Listening Guide**, 4AA batteries, external antenna, earphones and carrying case.

Currents and *Inspirational Classics*; Saturday has the Europe-oriented *On-Line* followed by *On Track* (contemporary Christian music); Sunday features *Sounds of Joy* and *Solstice* (a youth program); and Monday is devoted to *Radio Reading Room* and *Dr. Francis Schaeffer.* Continuous to North America on 9745 kHz.

Voice of Free China, Taiwan. *News,* followed by features. The last is *Let's Learn Chinese*, which has a series of segments for beginning, intermediate and advanced learners. Other features include *Jade Bells and Bamboo Pipes* (Monday), *Kaleidoscope* and *Main Roads and Byways* (Tuesday), *Music Box* (Wednesday), *Perspectives* and *Journey into Chinese Culture* (Thursday), *Confrontation* and *New Record Time* (Friday), *Reflections* (Saturday) and *Adventures of Mahlon and Jeanie* and *Mailbag Time* (Sunday). One hour to North and Central America on 5950, 9680 and 11740 kHz; to East Asia on 7130 and 15345 kHz; and to Southeast Asia on 11825 kHz.

Voice of Russia World Service. Continuous to North America at this hour. *News,* features and music to suit all tastes. Winter fare includes ●*Commonwealth Update* (Tuesday through Saturday), ●*Music and Musicians* (Sunday and Monday), and after 0230, ●*Folk Box* (Tuesday), ●*Music at Your Request* (Wednesday and Friday) and jazz on Thursday and Saturday. Best in summer is ●*Audio Book Club* at 0231 Thursday and Saturday; though some listeners may prefer *Science and Engineering* (0211 Wednesday) or the business-oriented *Newmarket* (0211 Tuesday). A listener-response program is aired at the same time Thursday through Monday. Note that these days are World Time; locally in

North America it will be the previous evening. Winters in Eastern North America, try 7105 kHz; in summer there's 9530 and 9620 kHz. Failing these, dial around nearby—the Voice of Russia tends to change its frequencies more often than most other stations. Western North America is better served. Winters, choose from 5920, 7270, 7345, 9580, 12030 and 13640 kHz; summers from 12010, 12050, 13645, 13665, 15180 and 15580 kHz.

Radio Habana Cuba. See 0100 for program details. Continues to Eastern North America on 6000 and 9820 kHz. Also available on 9830 kHz upper sideband.

Radio Australia. Continuous programming to Asia and the Pacific, but well heard in much of North America. Begins with *World News*, then Monday through Friday there's a summary of the latest sports news followed by *Network Asia*. At 0210 Saturday, there's *Beat of the Pacific* (indigenous music and musicians) and *Indian Pacific*. These are replaced Sunday by *Charting Australia* and *Correspondents' Report.* Targeted at Asia and the Pacific on about ten channels, and heard in North America (best during summer) on 13755, 15240 and 17795 kHz. For East and Southeast Asia, choose from 11640, 13605, 15415, 15510, 17715 and 17750 kHz. European night owls can try 15510 kHz. Some of these channels carry a separate sports service on summer weekends and winter Saturdays.

Radio For Peace International, Costa Rica. Part of an eight-hour cyclical block of social-conscience and counter-culture programming audible in Europe and the Americas on 6205 and 7385 kHz. One of international broadcasting's more unusual features, *The Far Right Radio*

> Who can resist the romantic strains of Pacific Island music? Listen to the "Bali Ha'i of the airwaves"—Radio Australia's *Beat of the Pacific*, beamed throughout the Pacific Islands and the world each Saturday.

Review, can be heard at 0200 Wednesday (Tuesday evening in the Americas). As we go to press, there's a communications feature, *World of Radio*, at the same time Sunday, but the timing of this program tends to change. Some transmissions are in the single-sideband mode, which can be properly processed only on some radios.

Croatian Radio. Eight minutes of *news* from Croatian Radio's Zagreb studio. Best heard in Europe and Eastern North America, but also heard elsewhere. Channel usage varies, but try 5895, 7165, 7370 and 13830 kHz.

Voice of Vietnam. A relay to Eastern North America via the facilities of the Voice of Russia. See 0100 for further details.

Radio Korea International, South Korea. Opens with *news* and commentary, followed Tuesday through Thursday (Monday through Wednesday evenings in the Americas) by *Seoul Calling*. Weekly features include *Echoes of Korean Music* and *Shortwave Feedback* (Monday), *Tales from Korea's Past* (Tuesday), *Korean Cultural Trails* (Wednesday), *Pulse of Korea* (Thursday), *From Us to You* (a listener-response program) and *Let's Learn Korean* (Friday), *Let's Sing Together* and *Korea Through Foreigners' Eyes* (Saturday), and Sunday's *Discovering Korea*, *Korean Literary Corner* and *Weekly News*. Sixty minutes to the Americas on 11725, 11810 and 15575 kHz; and to East Asia on 7275 kHz.

Radio Romania International. *News*, commentary, press review and features on Romania. Regular spots include Wednesday's *Youth Club* (Tuesday evening, local American date), Thursday's *Romanian Musicians*, and Friday's *Listeners' Letterbox* and ●*Skylark* (Romanian folk music). Fifty-five minutes to North America on 5990, 6155, 9510, 9570 and 11940 kHz.

"American Dissident Voices", **WRNO.** Winter Sundays only (Saturday evenings, local American date) at this time. See 0100 for program details. Thirty minutes to North America and beyond on 7355 kHz; try four hours later on 7395 kHz if preempted by live sports.

WWCR, Nashville, Tennessee. Carries a variety of disestablishmentarian programs at this hour, depending on the day of the week, and whether it is summer or winter. These include "Protecting Your Wealth", "World of Prophecy" and "Radio Free America"; choose between 5065 and 2390 (or 7435) kHz.

WJCR, Upton, Kentucky. Continues with country gospel music for North American listeners on 7490 kHz. Also with religious broadcasts to North America at this hour are **WYFR-Family Radio** on 6065 and 9505 kHz, **WWCR** on 5935 kHz, **KAIJ on** 5810 kHz, and **KTBN** on 7510 kHz. Traditional Catholic programming can be heard via **WEWN** on 7425 kHz.

02:30

Radio Austria International. Repeat of the 0130 broadcast. A half hour to the Americas on 9655, 9870 and 13730 kHz.

Radio Sweden. *News* and features concentrating heavily on Scandinavia. See 0030 for program details. Thirty minutes to North America on one or more channels from 6090, 7115, 7120 and 7290 kHz.

Radyo Pilipinas, Philippines. Monday through Saturday, the broadcast opens with *Voice of Democracy* and closes with *World News*. These are separated by a daily feature: *Save the Earth* (Monday), *The Philippines Today* (Tuesday), *Changing World* (Wednesday), *Business Updates* (Thursday), *Brotherhood of Men* (Friday), and Saturday's *Listeners and Friends*. Sunday fare consists of *Asean Connection*, *Sports Focus* and *News Roundup*. Approximately one hour to South and East Asia on 17760, 17865 and 21580 kHz.

Radio Budapest, Hungary. Summers only at this time. *News* and features, some of which are broadcast on a regular basis. These include Tuesday's *Musica Hungarica* (local Monday evening in North America), *Focus on Business* and *The Weeklies* (Thursday), *Letter Home* (Friday) and *Profiles* (Sunday). Thirty minutes to North America on 9840 and 11870 kHz. One hour later in winter.

Radio Nederland. Repeat of the 0030 transmission. Fifty-five minutes to South Asia, but heard well beyond, on 9860, 9890 (summers) and 11655 kHz.

Radio Tirana, Albania. Currently being run on a shoestring budget. Programs mainly consist of *news* about the country plus some lively Albanian music. Twenty-five minutes to North America on 6140 and 7160 kHz.

02:50

Vatican Radio. Concentrates heavily, but not exclusively, on issues affecting Catholics around the world. Twenty minutes to Eastern North America, winters on 6095 and 7305 kHz, and summers on 7305 and 9605 kHz.

03:00

■BBC World Service for the Americas. Five minutes of world *news*, followed by 10 minutes of the best business and financial reporting to be found on the international airwaves. The next quarter-hour is devoted to the highly informative ●*Sports Roundup.* These are followed Tuesday through Saturday (weekday evenings in the Americas) by ●*The World Today* (analysis of current events) and ●*Off the Shelf* (book readings). Other offerings at this hour include *From Our Own Correspondent* and *Write On* (Sunday), and ●*Brain of Britain* or its substitute (0330 Monday). Audible in North America on 5975, 6175, 7325 (till 0330, winters only) and 9590/9895 kHz.

■BBC World Service for Europe (and the Mideast). Begins with *World News* and ●*Sports Roundup,* then Monday through Friday summers it's ●*Europe Today.* Winters (and for the Mideast, year-round), there are a number of features: ●*Jazz for the Asking* (Monday), ●*John Peel* (Tuesday), ●*Discovery* (Wednesday), *New Ideas* (Thursday) and Friday's secular and well-produced ●*Focus on Faith.* Saturday brings *The Vintage Chart Show,* replaced Sunday by short features. To Eastern Europe on 6180 (summers), 6195 and (summers) 9410 kHz, and to the Mideast on 9410, 11760 and (summer) 12095 kHz. In summer, the first frequency carries *Europe Today,* and the remainder the alternative features.

■BBC World Service for Africa. Identical to the service for Europe until 0330, then there's a daily bulletin of African *news,* followed Monday through Friday by *Network Africa,* a fast-moving breakfast show. On Saturday it's *African Quiz* or *This Week And Africa,* replaced Sunday by *Postmark Africa.* If you are interested in what's happening in the continent, tune to 3255, 6005, 6190 and 9600 kHz.

■BBC World Service for Asia. *World News* and ●*Sports Roundup,* followed on the half-hour by the weekday ●*Off the Shelf* (readings from world literature). The final 15 minutes are taken up by a feature, the best of which is undoubtedly Thursday's ●*Folk Routes.* The Saturday slot is given over to *The Vintage Chart Show,* and Sunday's offerings are *From Our Own Correspondent* and *Write On.* Continuous to East and Southeast Asia till 0330 on 15360 kHz, and thereafter only to East Asia on 11955 and 15280 kHz.

Monitor Radio International, USA. See 0000 for program details. To Western North America, Tuesday through Friday (Monday through Thursday, local Ameri-

Terry Waite, former hostage and author, speaks on the VOA's "Talk to America." During events such as the Iran hostage crisis, the VOA's world band signals have been able to get through even when all other channels of credible information have been cut off.

can days) on 5850 kHz. Also to East Africa (and heard well beyond) on 7535 kHz. Programs on other days are religious in nature.

Radio Canada International. Winters only at this time. Starts off with *News*, then Tuesday through Saturday (week-nights local American date) there's a program for Canadian peacekeepers in the Caribbean. Weekends, there's a full hour of programs from the domestic ser-vice of RCI's parent organization, the Canadian Broadcasting Corporation: *Double Exposure* and *Royal Canadian Air Farce* (Sunday), replaced Monday by *The Inside Track* and *Now the Details*. To Eastern North America and the Caribbean on 6010 and 9755 kHz. One hour earlier in summer.

Voice of Free China, Taiwan. Similar to the 0200 transmission, but with the same programs broadcast one day later. To North and Central America on 5950 and 9680 kHz; to East Asia on 11745 and

15345 kHz; and to Southeast Asia on 11825 kHz.

China Radio International. Repeat of the 0000 transmission. One hour to North America on 9690, 9710 and 11695 (or 11715) kHz.

■**Deutsche Welle,** Germany. *News*, then Tuesday through Saturday (week-day evenings in North America) it's ●*European Journal*—a comprehensive package of commentary, interviews, background reports and analysis. This is followed by *Economic Notebook* (Tues-day), ●*Insight* (Wednesday), *German by Radio* (Thursday), *Science and Technology* (Friday), and *Through German Eyes* (Saturday). Sunday and Monday, there's a repeat of the 0100 broadcast. Fifty min-utes to North America and the Caribbean, winters on 6045, 6085, 6120, 9530 and 9650 kHz; and summers on 6085, 6185, 9535, 9615 and 9640 kHz.

Voice of America. Three and a half hours (four at weekends) of continuous programming aimed at an African audi-ence. Monday through Friday, there's the informative and entertaining ●*Daybreak Africa*, followed by 30 minutes of *State-side* (America and the Americans). Week-end programming consists of *News* and *VOA Saturday/VOA Sunday*, a mixed bag of sports, science, business and other features. Although beamed to Africa, this service is widely heard elsewhere, includ-ing parts of the United States. Try 4750/ 4950, 5980 (summer), 6035 (winter), 6080, 6115 (summer), 6125 (winter), 7105, 7280 (summer), 7290, 7340, 7405 (winter), 7415 (winter), 9575 (winter) and (summer) 15300 kHz.

Voice of Russia World Service. Continues to North America. *News*, then winters it's a listener-response program (Thursday through Monday), the business-oriented *Newmarket* (Tuesday), or *Science and Engineering* (Wednesday). At 0331, there's ●*Audio Book Club* (Thursday and Saturday), *Kaleidoscope* (Tuesday),

Carmelo Ciancio/VOA

Russian by Radio (Wednesday and Friday), and music on Sunday and Monday. Note that these days are World Time, so locally in North America it will be the previous evening. In summer, look for *News and Views* followed by ●*Our Treasure Chest* (sometimes preempted by mind-numbing religious paid programming). For Eastern North America winters, it's either 5940 or 7105 kHz; summers, try 7230 and 9620 kHz. Failing these, try dialing around nearby—the Voice of Russia is not renowned for sticking to its frequencies. Western North America gets a better deal. Good winter bets are 5920, 7270, 7345 and 9580 kHz; in summer, go for 12010, 12050, 13645, 13665, 15180 and 15580 kHz.

Radio Australia. *World News*, followed Monday through Friday by a sports bulletin and *Network Asia*. These are replaced weekends by Saturday's *Ockham's Razor* (science) and *Soundabout* (pop and rock), and Sunday's *Book Reading* and *At Your Request*. Continuous to Asia and the Pacific on about ten channels, and heard in North America (best during summer) on 13755, 15240 and 17795 kHz. In East and Southeast Asia, pick from 11640, 13605, 15415, 15510, 17715 and 17750 kHz. If you're in Europe, and not still asleep, try 15510 kHz. Some of these channels carry a separate sports service at weekends. A popular choice with many listeners.

Radio Habana Cuba. Continuous programming to Eastern North America on 6000 and 9820 kHz, and also available on 9830 kHz upper sideband.

Radio Norway International. Winter Mondays (Sunday evenings, local American date) only. *Norway Now*. *News* and features from one of the friendliest stations on the international airwaves. Thirty minutes to Western North America on 7465 kHz.

Radio Thailand. *Newshour*. Thirty minutes to Western North America winters on 11890 kHz, and summers on 15370

kHz. Also available to Asia on 9655 and 11905 kHz.

Radio Ukraine International. Summers only at this time. Repeat of the 0000 broadcast (see there for specifics). One hour to Eastern North America on 7150 and 9550 kHz. One hour later in winter.

HCJB—Voice of the Andes, Ecuador. Predominantly religious programming at this hour. Try *Joy International*, a selection of Christian music favorites, at 0330 Monday (local Sunday in North America). Continuous to the United States and Canada on 9745 kHz.

Radio Prague, Czech Republic. Repeat of the 0000 broadcast. A half hour to North America on 5930 and 7345 kHz.

Radio Cairo, Egypt. The final half-hour of a 90-minute broadcast to North America on 9475 kHz.

Radio Japan. *News*, followed by the weekday *Radio Japan Magazine Hour*. This consists of *News Commentary*, *Japan Diary*, *Close Up*, a feature (two on Tuesday) and a final news bulletin. Monday (Sunday evening in North America), you can hear *Sports Column*, Tuesday features *Japanese Culture* and *Today*, Wednesday has *Asian Report*, Thursday brings *Crosscurrents*, and Friday's offering is *Business Focus*. Weekend fare is made up of Saturday's *This Week* and Sunday's *Hello from Tokyo*. Sixty minutes to Western North America winters on 9605 and 11960 kHz, and summers on 11790 and 15230 kHz. Available to East and Southeast Asia on 11840 and 17810 kHz. Winters only, can also be heard in Eastern North America on 5960 kHz.

Croatian Radio. Eight minutes of *news* from Croatian Radio's Zagreb studio. Best heard in Europe and Eastern North America, but also heard elsewhere. Channel usage varies, but try 5895, 7165, 7370 and 13830 kHz.

Channel Africa, South Africa. Monday through Friday, it's 60 minutes of *News* and *Dateline Africa*. Saturday, the first half-hour is made up of *News* and *Sport*, then comes *News in Brief* and ●*Sounds of Soweto*. The Sunday lineup is *Religions of the World*, *Crossroads*, *South African News* and *Prominent People*. The first part of a two-hour broadcast to East, Central and Southern Africa on 3220 (summer), 5955 and (winter) 9585 kHz. These seasons apply to the Northern Hemisphere, and will be reversed for listeners south of the Equator. Sometimes audible in Europe and Eastern North America.

Radio New Zealand International. A friendly broadcasting package targeted at a regional audience. Part of a much longer transmission for the South Pacific, but also heard in parts of North America (especially during summer) on 15115 kHz. Often carries commentaries of local sporting events.

Voice of Turkey. Summers only at this time. *News*, followed by *Review of the Turkish Press* and features (some of them arcane) with a strong local flavor. Selections of Turkish popular and classical music complete the program. Fifty minutes to Eastern North America on 9655 kHz, to the Mideast on 9685 kHz, and to Southeast Asia and Australasia on 17705 kHz. One hour later during winter.

WJCR, Upton, Kentucky. Continues with country gospel music for North American listeners on 7490 kHz. Also with religious programs to North America at this hour are **WYFR-Family Radio** on 6065 and 9505 kHz, **WWCR** on 5935 kHz, **KAIJ** on 5810 kHz and **KTBN** on 7510 kHz. For traditional Catholic fare, try **WEWN** on 7425 kHz.

"For the People," WHRI, Noblesville, Indiana. A two-hour edited repeat of the 1900 (1800 in summer) broadcast. Promotes classic populism—an American political tradition going back to 1891. Suspicious of concentrated wealth and power, *For the People* promotes economic nationalism ("buying foreign amounts to treason"), little-reported health concepts

and a sharply progressive income tax, while opposing the "New World Order" and international banking. This two-hour talk show, hosted by former deejay Chuck Harder, can be heard Tuesday-Saturday (Monday through Friday local days) on 5745 kHz. Targeted at North America, but heard beyond.

Radio For Peace International, Costa Rica. Continues with a variety of counterculture and social-conscience features. There is also a listener-response program at 0330 Wednesday (Tuesday evening in the Americas). Audible in Europe and the Americas on 6205 and 7385 kHz. Some transmissions are in the single-sideband mode, which can be properly processed only on some radios.

WWCR, Nashville, Tennessee. "Radio Free America", a populist show hosted by Tom Valentine for two hours Tuesday through Saturday (Monday through Friday evenings, local American date). Winters, starts at this time; summers, it is already at its halfway point. Well heard in North America on 5065 kHz.

03:30

United Arab Emirates Radio, Dubai. *News*, then a feature devoted to Arab and Islamic history or culture. Twenty-five minutes to North America on 11945, 13675, 15400 and 21485 kHz; heard best during the warm-weather months.

Radio Sweden. Repeat of the 0230 transmission. See 0030 for program details. Thirty minutes to North America on 7115 or 7120 kHz.

Radio Prague, Czech Republic. Repeat of the 0000 broadcast. A half hour to the Mideast and beyond. Winters on 6200 kHz, and summers on 9480 kHz.

Radio Budapest, Hungary. This time winters only; see 0230 for specifics. Thirty minutes to North America on 5965, 9850 and 11870 kHz. One hour earlier in summer.

TUNING INTO THE WORLD WITH GRUNDIG

Satellit 700
- Unprecedented memory capacity
- Advanced synchronous detector
- Excellent sensitivity
- Superior sideband performance
- Eight charter alphanumeric labeling capacity
- Multi-function liquid crystal display
- RDS capacity for FM stations

Yacht Boy 400
- Shortwave/AM/FM/and Longwave
- Continuous shortwave from 1.6 - 30 MHz
- Clock, alarm, and timer
- 40 randomly programmable memories
- Multifunction liquid crystal display
- Phase-lock-loop timing

Yacht Boy 305
- Shortwave/AM/FM
- Continuous shortwave from 2.3 - 21.85 MHz
- 30 memory presets allow you to customize your favorite stations for simple recall
- DX/Local switch allows optimization of receiver for incoming signals
- Digital PLL tuning for absolute accuracy and rock-solid frequency stability

LENTINI COMMUNICATIONS, INC.

21 Garfield Street, Newington, CT 06111
New Equipment Pricing and Orders:
1-800-666-0908
Hours M-F 10-6, Sat 10-4

Out of State, Technical, Used Gear & Info:
1-203-666-6227
24 Hr Fax **1-203-667-3561**
C.O.D.'s OK, Same Day Shipping

RDP International—Radio Portugal.
News, which usually takes up at least
half the broadcast, followed by features:
Visitor's Notebook (Tuesday), *Musical
Kaleidoscope* (Wednesday), *Challenge of
the 90's* (Thursday), *Spotlight on Portugal*
(Friday), and either *Listeners' Mailbag* or
DX Program and *Collector's Corner* (Saturday). There are no broadcasts on Sunday or Monday (Saturday and Sunday
evenings local North American days).
Only fair reception in Eastern North
America—worse to the west—on 6130 (or
6095) and 9570 kHz. May be one hour
later in winter.

Voice of Greece. Actual start time
subject to slight variation. Ten to fifteen
minutes of English *news*, preceded by
long periods of Greek music and programming. To North America on any
three frequencies from 6260, 7448, 9420,
9935 and 11645 kHz.

04:00

■BBC World Service for the Americas.
Starts with the half-hour ●*Newsdesk*,
followed Tuesday through Saturday (local
weekday evenings in the Americas) by
the eclectic and entertaining ●*Outlook*.
The hour is rounded off by *Press Review*.
These are replaced Sunday by ●*Science
in Action*, and Monday by ●*The Learning
World* and ●*Health Matters*. A full hour of
top-notch programming to North America
on 5975 and 6175 kHz.

**■BBC World Service for Europe
(and the Mideast).** The half-hour
●*Newsdesk*, followed Monday through
Friday by ●*Europe Today* or features:
●*Off the Shelf* is at 0430 daily, followed
by *Country Style* (Monday), ●*Health
Matters* (Tuesday), *The Farming World*
(Wednesday), *From Our Own Correspon-
dent* (Thursday) and ●*Folk Routes* (Friday).
Saturday, there's *Jazz Now and Then* and
Seven Days, replaced Sunday by

●*Weekend* (or ●*Short Story/Seeing Stars*)
and *On the Move*. Continuous to Europe
on 6180 and 6195 kHz (also on 9410 and
12095 kHz during summer), and to the
Mideast on 9410, 11760, 12095 (summer)
and 15575 KHz. The channels of 9410 and
12095 kHz carry mainstream European
programming, the remainder the alternative programs.

■BBC World Service for Africa.
●*Newsdesk*, followed at 0430 by *African
News*. Monday through Friday, this is
followed by *Network Africa*, Saturday by
a repeat of the 0330 feature, and Sunday
by *The Arts House*. Targeted at African
listeners, but also heard elsewhere, on
3255, 6005, 6190, 7160 and 9600 kHz.

■BBC World Service for Asia. First
it's ●*Newsdesk*, then one or more features. The Tuesday and Thursday slots
are given over to *Multitrack* (pop music);
Monday features the *Composer of the
Month* (classical); and Friday has the
interesting and informative ●*Focus on
Faith*. Best of the weekend offerings is
●*Short Story* at 0430 Sunday. Continuous
to East Asia on 11955 and 15280 kHz.

Monitor Radio International, USA.
See 0000 for program details. Tuesday
through Friday to Eastern Europe on 7535
kHz, and to central and southern Africa on
9840 kHz. Programming on the remaining
days relates to the beliefs and teachings
of the Christian Science Church.

Radio Habana Cuba. Continuous
programming to Eastern North America
and the Caribbean on 6000, 6180 and
9820 kHz. Also available on 9830 kHz
upper sideband.

Swiss Radio International. Repeat of
the 0100 broadcast to North America on
6135, 9885 and 9905 kHz. Look for an
additional 30-minute feature on 9905 kHz
which is a simulcast of SRI's satellite
programming.

HCJB—Voice of the Andes, Ecuador.
Sixty minutes of religious programming.
Songs in the Night (0400 Monday), *After-*

glow (0430 Sunday and Monday) and *Nightsounds* (0430 Tuesday through Saturday) probably offer the most appeal. Continuous to Eastern North America on 9745 kHz.

Radio Australia. *World News*, then Monday through Friday it's a short summary of the latest sports news followed by *Pacific Beat* and ●*International Report*. These are replaced Saturday by *Book Reading* and *Health Report*, and Sunday by *Feedback* and *Media Report*. Continuous to Asia and the Pacific on about ten channels, and heard in North America (best during summer) on 13755, 15240 and 17795 kHz. For East and Southeast Asia, choose from 11640 (weekends only), 13605, 15415, 15510, 17715 and 17750 kHz (15510 and 17715 kHz are only available from 0430 on weekdays). Some channels carry separate sports programming at weekends.

■Deutsche Welle, Germany. *News*, followed Monday through Friday by ●*Africa Report* (*Africa Highlight* on Mondays) and the informative and in-depth ●*European Journal*. Saturday features *Commentary*, *Africa This Week* and ●*Man and Environment*; substituted Sunday by *Sports Report* (or *Commentary*), *International Talking Point* and *People and Places*. A 50-minute broadcast aimed primarily at East and Southern Africa, but also heard in parts of the Mideast and Eastern North America. Winters on 6015, 6045, 6065, 7225, 7265 and 9565 kHz; and summers on 5990, 6015, 6185, 7150, 7225, 9565 and 11765 kHz.

Radio Canada International. *News*, then Tuesday through Saturday it's the topical *Spectrum*. This is replaced Sunday by the science feature *Innovation Canada*, and Monday by a listener-response program. Thirty minutes to the Mideast, winters on 6150, 9505 and 9645 kHz; summers on 11835, 11905 and 15275 kHz.

China Radio International. Repeat of the 0000 transmission. One hour to North America on 9730 and (summer) 9560 kHz.

Radio Norway International. Summer Mondays (Sunday evenings in the target area) only. *Norway Now*. A half hour of *news* and human-interest stories targeted at Western North America on 7465 (or 7520) kHz.

Radio Bulgaria. Summers only at this time. Starts with 15 minutes of *news*, followed Tuesday through Friday by *Today* (current events), and Saturday by *Weekly Spotlight*, a summary of the major political events of the week. At other times, there are features dealing with multiple aspects of Bulgarian life and culture, including some lively Balkan folk music. To Eastern North America and Central America on 9700 and 11720 kHz. One hour later in winter.

Voice of America. Directed to Africa and the Mideast, but widely heard elsewhere. *News*, followed Monday through Friday by ●*VOA Business Report*. On the half-hour, the African service continues with ●*Daybreak Africa*, replaced to other areas by *Stateside*—a look at issues and personalities in all walks of American life. Weekends, the *news* is followed by 50 minutes of *VOA Saturday/VOA Sunday*. To North Africa and the Mideast on 7170 (North Africa only), and (summer) 11965 and 15205 kHz. The mainstream African service is available on 4750/4950, 6035 (winter), 6080, 6125 (winter), 7180 (winter), 7265 and 7280 (summer), 7405 and 7415 (winter), 9575 and 9775 (winter), 12080 and (summer) 15300 kHz. Reception of some of these channels is also good in North America.

Channel Africa, South Africa. *News*, then a variety of features. These include *Call Back to the Past* (daily, but different time on Tuesday), *South African News* (Saturday through Monday), ●*Sounds of Soweto* (Monday), *English for Africa* and *New Releases* (Tuesday), *Earthrise Africa* (Wednesday and Friday), *Short Story*

(Wednesday), *Travel Africa* and *Artist of the Week* (Thursday), *Prominent People* (Friday), and *Technology for Us* and *SA Top Ten* on Saturday. The list is rounded off by *Sunday Magazine*. The second and final part of a two-hour broadcast to East, Central and Southern Africa on 3220 (summer), 5955 and (winter) 9585 kHz. These seasons apply to the Northern Hemisphere, and will be reversed for listeners south of the Equator. Sometimes audible in Europe and Eastern North America.

Radio Romania International. Similar to the 0200 transmission (see there for specifics). Fifty-five minutes to North America on 5990, 6155, 9510, 9570 and 11940 kHz.

Radio Ukraine International. Winters only at this time. Repeat of the 0100 broadcast (see 0000 for specifics). Sixty minutes to North America on 5915, 6010 and 7205 kHz. One hour earlier in summer.

Voice of Turkey. Winters only at this time. See 0300 for specifics. Fifty minutes to Eastern North America on 9655 kHz, to the Mideast on 9685 kHz, and to Southeast Asia and Australasia on 9560 kHz. One hour earlier in summer.

WJCR, Upton, Kentucky. Continues with country gospel music for North American listeners on 7490 kHz. Also with religious programs to North America at this hour are **WYFR-Family Radio** on 6065 and 9505 kHz, **WWCR** on 5935 kHz, **KAIJ** on 5810 kHz and **KTBN** on 7510 kHz. Traditional Catholic programming is available via **WEWN** on 7425 kHz

Kol Israel. Summers only at this time. *News* for 15 minutes from Israel Radio's domestic network. To Europe and Eastern North America on 7465 and 9435 kHz, and to Australasia on 17545 kHz. One hour later in winter.

Radio New Zealand International. Continues with regional programming for the South Pacific. Part of a much longer broadcast, which is also heard in parts of North America (especially during summer) on 15115 kHz. Sometimes carries commentaries of local sporting events.

Radio For Peace International, Costa Rica. Part of an eight-hour cyclical block of predominantly social-conscience and counterculture programming. Some of the offerings at this hour include a women's news-gathering service, *WINGS,* (0430 Friday); a listener-response program (same time Saturday); and *The Far Right Radio Review* (0400 Sunday). Audible in Europe and the Americas on 6205 and 7385 kHz. Some transmissions are in the single-sideband mode, which can be properly processed only on some radios.

> Where have all the flowers gone? To Costa Rica, where Sixties' political counterculture has evolved into Radio for Peace International, heard daily.

Voice of Russia World Service. Continuous to North America at this hour. Winters, it's *News and Views,* replaced Tuesday through Saturday summers by the timely ●*Commonwealth Update.* The final half-hour contains some interesting fare. Summer pickings include *Jazz Show* (Monday), ●*Music at Your Request* (Wednesday), ●*Folk Box* (Thursday), *Kaleidoscope* (Friday) and Sunday's retrospective ●*Moscow Yesterday and Today.* The winter slot is filled by ●*Our Treasure Chest* (except when preempted by paid religious programming). In Eastern North America, try 7105 and 7180 kHz for winter, and 7230 and 9620 kHz for summer. Farther west, best winter bets are 5920, 7175, 7270 and (from 0430) 7330 kHz; in summer, try 12010, 12050, 13645, 13665, 15180 and 15580 kHz.

"For the People," WHRI, Noblesville, Indiana. See 0300 for specifics. The second half of a two-hour broadcast tar-

Gilfer First in Shortwave

GRUNDIG

Yacht Boy 400

Wherever and whenever news is happening, Grundig will be there. With digital technology that stretches to the farthest corners of the globe, bringing back the news with striking clarity, before the ink has dried on the newsprint.

Rated the best! "In all, the Grundig Yacht Boy 400 is the best compact shortwave portable we have tested." -Passport to World Band Radio

Advanced Features:

- PLL-synthesized tuning.
- Continuous SW coverage (1.6 - 30 MHz), plus LW, MW and FM stereo.
- SSB capable.
- 40-memory channels.
- Clock, timer and alarm functions.

The YB-400 delivers amazing audio for a radio of this size!

geted weeknights to North America on 5745 kHz.

Croatian Radio. Eight minutes of *news* from Croatian Radio's Zagreb studio. Best heard in Europe and Eastern North America, but also heard elsewhere. Channel usage varies, but try 5895, 7165, 7370 and 13830 kHz.

Radio Pyongyang, North Korea. Fifty soporific minutes of old-fashioned communist propaganda. To Southeast Asia on 15180, 15230 and 17765 kHz.

WWCR, Nashville, Tennessee. Carries a variety of disestablishmentarian programs at this hour, depending on the day of the week, and whether it is summer or winter. These include "America First Radio", "Hour of the Time", "Duncan Long Show" and "Radio Free America"; choose between 5065 and 2390 (or 7435) kHz.

04:30

Radio Yugoslavia. Summers only at this time. *News* and short background reports heavily geared to local issues. Worth a listen if you are interested in the region. Thirty minutes to Western North America on 9580 and 11870 kHz.

Radio Nederland. Repeat of the 0030 transmission. Fifty-five minutes to Western North America on 5995 (winter), 6165 and (summer) 9590 kHz.

05:00

■**BBC World Service for the Americas.** Thirty minutes of ●*Newsday*, followed by some of the BBC's best output. Take your choice from ●*Anything Goes* (Monday), ●*Omnibus* (Tuesday), *Composer of the Month* (classical music, Wednesday), ●*Assignment* (Thursday), ●*Focus on Faith* (Friday), *Music Review* (Saturday) and Sunday's ●*Play of the Week*. Audible in North America (better to the west) on 5975 and 6175 kHz (9640 kHz may also be available in winter).

■**BBC World Service for Europe (and the Mideast).** ●*Newsday*, followed weekdays on the half-hour by ●*Europe Today* or one or more features, depending on which channel you're listening to. Monday's feature is *Composer of the Month*; Tuesday (at 0545) there's ●*The Learning World*; Wednesday's offering is ●*Omnibus*; Thursday brings ●*Assignment*; and Friday serves up a variety of short features. At the same time weekends, it's ●*Science in Action* (Saturday) or Sunday's *In Praise of God*. Continuous to Europe on 3955 (winter), 6180, 6195, 9410 and (summer) 12095 kHz; and to the Mideast on 9410, 11760, 12095 and 15575 kHz.

■**BBC World Service for Africa.** Thirty minutes of ●*Newsday*, then weekdays it's a continuation of *Network Africa*. This is replaced Saturday by *Talkabout Africa* and Sunday by *Postmark Africa*. Continuous programming on 3255, 6005, 6190, 7160, 9600, 15420 and 17885 kHz.

■**BBC World Service for Asia and the Pacific.** ●*Newsday* and a variety of features. These include ●*Anything Goes* (Sunday), ●*Omnibus* (Tuesday), ●*Brain of Britain* or its substitute (Wednesday), ●*Network UK* (Friday) and Saturday's classical *Music Review*. Continuous to East and Southeast Asia on 9740, 11955, 15280 and 15360 kHz; and to Australasia on 11955 and 15360 kHz.

Monitor Radio International, USA. See 0000 for program details. Tuesday through Friday to Europe on 7535 kHz. On other days, programs are of a religious nature.

■**Deutsche Welle,** Germany. Repeat of the 50-minute 0100 transmission to North America, winters on 5960, 6045, 6120 and 6185 kHz; and summers on 5960, 6045, 6185 and 9515 kHz. This slot is by far the best for Western North America.

Radio Exterior de España ("Spanish National Radio"). Repeat of the 0000 and 0100 transmissions to North America, on 9540 kHz.

Radio Canada International. Summer weekdays only. See 0600 for program details. To Europe, Africa and the Mideast on 6050, 7295, 15430 and 17840 kHz. One hour later during winter.

Vatican Radio. Summers only at this time. Twenty minutes of programming oriented to Catholics. To Europe on 5880 and 7250 kHz. Frequencies may vary slightly. One hour later in winter.

Channel Africa, South Africa. Monday through Friday, it's *News* and *Dateline Africa*. Weekends, opens and closes with *News*, much of it dealing with South African issues. The rest of the broadcast is given over to features: *Mailbag, Farming for Africa* and *Channel Africa Sport* (Saturday) and *Checkpoint* and *Women Today* Sunday. Fifty-five minutes to West Africa winters on 11900 kHz, and summers on 9590 or 9675 kHz; also to Southern Africa on 5955 or 7185 kHz. Sometimes audible in Europe and Eastern North America.

> With guns nearly silent, the Balkans are regaining their ancient charm. Local perspective is captured for a worthwhile half hour each day over Radio Yugoslavia.

China Radio International. This time winters only. Repeat of the 0000 broadcast; one hour to North America on 9560 kHz.

HCJB—Voice of the Andes, Ecuador. Repeat of the 0100 transmission. To Western North America on 9745 kHz.

Voice of America. Continues with the morning broadcast to Africa and the Mideast. Starts with *News*, followed weekdays by *VOA Today*—a conglomeration of business, sports, science, entertainment and virtually anything else that may be newsworthy. On weekends, the news is followed by an extended version of *VOA Saturday/VOA Sunday*. To the Mideast and North Africa on 6140 (summer), 7170, 9700 (winter), 11805 and 11965 (summer) and 15205 kHz; and to the rest of Africa on 4750/4950, 5970 (summer), 5990 (win-

ter), 6035, 6080, 7195 (summer), 7295 (winter), 9530(summer) and 12080 kHz. Some of these channels provide reasonable reception in parts of North America.

Radio Bulgaria. Winters only at this time; see 0400 for specifics. A distinctly Bulgarian potpourri of news, commentary, interviews and features, plus a fair amount of music. Sixty minutes to Eastern North America and Central America on 7480 and 9700 kHz. One hour earlier in summer.

Radio Habana Cuba. Repeat of the 0100 transmission. To Western North America winter on 6000 (or 9505) kHz, and summer on 9820 kHz. Also available to Europe on 9830 kHz upper sideband.

Voice of Nigeria. Targeted at West Africa, but also audible in parts of Europe and North America, especially during winter. Monday through Friday, opens with the lively *Wave Train* followed by *VON Scope*, a half hour of *news* and press comment. Pick of the weekend programs is ●*African Safari*, a musical journey around the African continent, which can be heard Saturdays at 0500. This is replaced Sunday by five minutes of *Reflections* and 25 minutes of music in *VON Link-Up*, with the second half-hour taken up by *News*. The first 60 minutes of a daily two-hour broadcast on 7255 kHz. Has been very irregular in recent times.

Radio New Zealand International. Continues with regional programming for the South Pacific. Part of a much longer broadcast, which is also heard in parts of North America (especially during summer) on 9570 or 11900 kHz.

Radio Australia. *World News*, then Monday through Friday there's *Australian News*, a sports bulletin and a feature for listeners in the Pacific. Weekends, look for Saturday's *Oz Sounds* and One

World, or Sunday's *Beat of the Pacific* and *Australian Music Show.* Continuous to Asia and the Pacific on about ten channels, and heard in North America (best during summer) on 11880, 15240 and 17795 kHz. For East and Southeast Asia, choose from 11640 (weekends only), 13605, 15415 and 17715 kHz. Some channels carry alternative sports programming at weekends.

Voice of Russia World Service. Continues winters to Eastern North America, and year-round to Western North America. Tuesday through Saturday, winters, the first half-hour features *News* and ●*Commonwealth Update,* the latter replaced summers by *Focus on Asia and the Pacific.* At 0531 winters, look for some interesting musical shows, including ●*Music at Your Request* (Wednesday), ●*Folk Box* (Thursday), and Monday's jazz feature. Summers, this slot is given over to either ●*Moscow Yesterday and Today* (Tuesday, Thursday and Saturday) or *This is Russia.* Winters to Eastern North America on 7105 and 7180 kHz, and to western parts on 5905 (from 0530), 5920, 5930, 7175, 7270 and 7330 kHz. Summers in Western North America, shoot for 12010, 12040 (from 0530), 12050, 13645, 13665 and 15580 kHz. Also available summers for East and Southeast Asia and Australasia on 15470 and 17580 kHz.

Radio For Peace International, Costa Rica. Continues at this hour with a potpourri of United Nations, counterculture and other programs. These include *WINGS* (news for and of women, 0530 Wednesday) and *Vietnam Veterans Radio Network* (0530 Thursday). Audible in Europe and the Americas on 6205 and 7385 kHz. Some transmissions are in the single-sideband mode, which can be properly processed only on some radios.

Kol Israel. Winters only at this time. *News* for 15 minutes from Israel Radio's domestic network. To Europe and Eastern North America on 7465 and 13755 kHz, and to Australasia on 17545 kHz. One hour earlier in summer.

Radio Japan. Repeat of the 0300 broadcast, except that Sunday's *Hello from Tokyo* is replaced by *Let's Learn Japanese, Media Roundup* and *Viewpoint;* and the daily end-of-broadcast news gives way to *Tokyo Pop-in.* Sixty minutes to Europe winters on 5975 and 6150 kHz, and summers on 7230 kHz; to East and Southeast Asia on 11725, 11740 and 17810 kHz; to Australasia on 11920 kHz; and to Western North America on 6110 kHz. There is also a 30-minute broadcast to West North America and Central America on 11885, 11895, 11960 (winter) and (summer) 15230 kHz.

> Israel Radio's morning newscast in English is listened to by nearly every international journalist in the Middle East. On world band, you can hear it live–mornings in Europe, evenings in North America.

Croatian Radio. Winters only at this time. Eight minutes of *news* from Croatian Radio's Zagreb studio. Best heard in Europe and Eastern North America, but also heard elsewhere. Channel usage varies, but try 5895, 7165, 7370 and 13830 kHz. One hour earlier in summer.

WWCR, Nashville, Tennessee. Carries a variety of disestablishmentarian programs at this hour, depending on the day of the week, and whether it is summer or winter. These include winter's "America First Radio", "Hour of the Time" and "Duncan Long Show"; and summer's "Herald of Truth", "The Hour of Courage" and "Seventieth Week Magazine." On 5065 and 2390 (or 7435) kHz.

WJCR, Upton, Kentucky. Continues

with country gospel music for North American listeners on 7490 kHz. Also with religious programs to North America at this hour are **WYFR-Family Radio** on 5985 kHz, **WWCR** on 5935 kHz, **KAIJ** on 5810 kHz and **KTBN** on 7510 kHz. For traditional Catholic programming (some of which may be in Spanish), tune to **WEWN** on 7425 kHz.

05:15

Swiss Radio International. Summers only at this time. Fifteen minutes of *news* to Europe on 6165 and 9535 kHz. One hour later in winter.

05:30

Radio Austria International. ●*Report from Austria;* see 0130 for more details. Year-round to North America on 6015 kHz, and winters only to Europe and the Mideast on 6155, 13730, 15410 and 17870 kHz.

United Arab Emirates Radio, Dubai. See 0330 for program details. To East Asia and Australasia on 15435, 17830 and 21700 kHz.

Radio Thailand. A new transmission, introduced during summer of 1996. Thirty minutes to Europe on 15115 kHz.

Radio Romania International. *News,* commentary, a press review, and one or more short features. Thirty minutes to southern Africa (and heard elsewhere) on 11810 (or 11740), 11940, 15250 (or 15270), 15340 (or 15365), 17745 (winter) and 17790 kHz.

Radio Almaty, Kazakhstan. Summers only at this time. See 0630 for further details. Thirty minutes to Asia on 4820, 5970, 5985, 6060, 6075, 7115, 7235, 7280, 9505, 9550, 9690 and 9705 kHz; and to Europe (via relay facilities in Ukraine) on 11705 kHz. One hour later during winter.

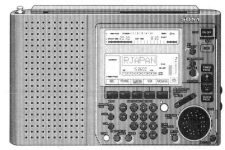

06:00

■BBC World Service for the Americas.
Monday through Saturday, there's 15
minutes of *World News* followed by one or
more features. These include ●*The
Greenfield Collection* (classical music,
Tuesday), ●*John Peel* and *Development
97* (Wednesday), *Jazz Now and Then* and
Sports International (Thursday) and
●*Short Story* (0615 Friday). Sunday, it's a
continuation of ●*Play of the Week*, which
can run to either 0630 or 0700. If it's the
former, you also get 30 minutes of ●*Jazz
for the Asking*. Continuous to North
America (better to the west) on 5975 and
6175 kHz (9640 kHz may also be available
in winter).

**■BBC World Service for Europe
(and the Mideast).** Winters, it's
●*Newsday*, followed weekdays on the
half-hour by ●*Europe Today* or one or
more features, depending on which channel you're listening to. Summers, it's
World News followed Tuesday through
Saturday by ●*The World Today* and features. At 0630 summers and on some
winter channels, pick from the following:
●*Andy Kershaw's World of Music*
(Monday), ●*Anything Goes* (Tuesday),
●*Megamix* (Wednesday), *Sports International* (Thursday), ●*Global Concerns*
(0645 Saturday) and Sunday's ●*Jazz for
the Asking*. Continuous to Europe on 3955
(winter), 6180, 6195, 9410, 11780 (winter)
12095 and (summer) 15575 kHz; and to
the Mideast on 9410 (winter), 11760,
12095 (winter) and 15575 kHz.

■BBC World Service for Africa.
Opens with 15 minutes of *World News*,
then Monday through Friday it's ●*Sports
Roundup* and the breakfast show *Network
Africa*. Saturday has a quarter-hour feature followed by a repeat of the 0330 show,
and Sunday airs *Development 1997* and
African Perspective. Continuous to most
parts of the continent on 6005, 6190, 7160,
9600, 11940 and 15400 kHz.

**■BBC World Service for Asia and
the Pacific.** *World News*, followed Tuesday through Saturday by ●*The World
Today*, and replaced Sunday by ●*Letter
from America* and Monday by ●*The
Learning World*. Offerings on the half-
hour include the arts show *Meridian*
(Sunday, Tuesday, Wednesday and Saturday), ●*Jazz for the Asking* (Monday)
and Thursday's gripping ●*Thirty Minute
Drama*. Continuous to East and Southeast
Asia on 9740, 11955, 15280 and 15360 kHz;
and to Australasia on 7145, 11955 and
15360 kHz.

Monitor Radio International, USA.
See 0000 for program details. Tuesday
through Friday to Western Europe on 7535
kHz. Weekend programs deal with various
aspects of the Christian Science faith.

Radio Habana Cuba. Repeat of the
0200 transmission. To Western North
America winter on 6000 (or 9505) kHz,
and summer on 9820 kHz. Also available
to Europe on 9830 kHz upper sideband.

Croatian Radio. Monday through
Saturday, summers only at this time;
actually starts at 0603. Ten minutes of on-
the-spot *news* from one of Europe's most
troubled areas. Intended mainly for
Europe and Australasia at this hour, but
also heard elsewhere. Frequencies vary,
but try 5895, 5920, 7165, 7370, 9830 and
13830 kHz. Although not available at this
time Sunday, there is a short summary of

news at 0703 for those who have an interest in the region. One hour later during winter.

Radio Norway International. Summer Sundays only. *Norway Now*. Thirty minutes of *news* and human-interest stories. To Europe on 7180 kHz, and to Australasia on 7295 and 9590 kHz.

Swiss Radio International. *Newsnet*. A workmanlike compilation of news and background reports on world and Swiss events. Look for some lighter fare on Saturdays, when the biweekly *Capital Letters* (a listener-response program) alternates with *Name Game* and *Sounds Good*. A half hour to West and Southern Africa on 9885, 11860 (or 12070) and 13635 kHz.

Radio Canada International. Winter weekdays only. Thirty minutes targeted at Canadian peacekeepers overseas. To Europe, Africa and the Mideast on 6050, 6150, 9740, 9760 and 11905 kHz. One hour earlier in summer.

Voice of America. Final segment of the transmission to Africa and the Mideast. Monday through Friday, the mainstream African service carries just 30 minutes of ●*Daybreak Africa*, with other channels carrying a full hour of *news* and *VOA Today*—a mixed bag of popular music, interviews, human interest stories, science digest and sports news. Weekend programming is the same to all areas—a bulletin of *news* followed by 50 minutes of *VOA Saturday/VOA Sunday*. To North Africa and the Mideast on 6140 (summer), 7170, 11805, 11825 (winter), 11965 (summer) and 15205 kHz; and to mainstream Africa on 4750/4950, 5970 (summer), 5990 (winter), 6035, 6080, 7195 (summer), 7285 (winter), 9530 (summer), 11950, 12080 and (winter) 15600 kHz. Several of these channels provide good reception in North America.

> Radio New Zealand International often relays its national network programs to a worldwide audience. This provides an interesting peek inside the day-to-day life of a distant and lovely land.

Radio Australia. *World News*, then Monday through Friday it's the latest sports headlines, *Pacific Beat* and a regional weather report for the South Pacific. These are followed on the half-hour by ●*International Report*. Weekends, there's *Book Reading* and *Indian Pacific* (Saturday), replaced Sunday by *Feedback* (a listener-response program) and *Correspondents' Report*. Continuous to Asia and the Pacific on about ten channels, and heard in North America (best during summer) on 9860, 11880 and 15240 kHz. Listeners in East and Southeast Asia can choose from 11640 (weekends only), 13605, 15415 and 17715 kHz. Some channels carry an alternative sports program until 0630 at weekends (0730 in summer).

Voice of Nigeria. The second (and final) hour of a daily broadcast intended for listeners in West Africa, but also heard in parts of Europe and North America (especially during winter). Features vary from day to day, but are predominantly concerned with Nigerian and West African affairs. There is a listener-response program at 0600 Friday and 0615 Sunday, and other slots include *Across the Ages* and *Nigeria and Politics* (Monday), *Southern Connection* and *Nigerian Scene* (Tuesday), *West African Scene* (0600 Thursday) and *Images of Nigeria* (0615 Friday). There is a weekday 25-minute program of *news* and commentary on the half-hour, replaced weekends by the more in-depth *Weekly Analysis*. To 0657 on 7255 kHz. Has been very irregular in recent times.

Radio New Zealand International. Continues with regional programming for the South Pacific. Part of a much longer broadcast, which is also heard in parts of North America (especially during summer) on 9570 or 11900 kHz.

Voice of Russia World Service.
News, then winters it's *Focus on Asia and the Pacific* (Tuesday through Saturday), *Science and Engineering* (Sunday), and *Mailbag* (Monday). In summer, the news is followed by *Science and Engineering* (Monday, Friday and Saturday), the business-oriented *Newmarket* (Tuesday and Thursday), and a listener-response program on Tuesday and Sunday. The second half-hour is given over to ●*Moscow Yesterday and Today* (Tuesday, Thursday and Saturday in winter; Wednesday and Friday for summer); *Russian by Radio* (Sunday and Monday, summer); and *This is Russia* on the remaining days. Continuous to Western North America winters on 5905, 5920, 5930, 7175, 7270 and 7330 kHz; and summers on 12010, 12040, 12050, 13645, 13665 and 15580 kHz. Also heard in Southeast Asia and Australasia at this time. For winter (local summer in Australia), try 12025, 15160, 15470, 17560, 17570 and 21790 kHz; in summer, go for 15470, 15490, 15560, 17570 and 17580 kHz.

Radio For Peace International,
Costa Rica. Continues with counterculture and social-conscience programs—try Monday's *The Far Right Radio Review*. Audible in Europe and the Americas on 6205 and 7385 kHz. Some transmissions are in the single-sideband mode, which can be properly processed only on some radios.

Radio Pyongyang, North Korea. See 1100 for specifics. Fifty minutes to Southeast Asia on 15180 and 15230 kHz.

Vatican Radio. Winters only at this time. Twenty minutes with a heavy Catholic slant. To Europe on 4005 and 5882 kHz. One hour earlier in summer. Frequencies may vary slightly.

WJCR, Upton, Kentucky. Continues with country gospel music to North America on 7490 kHz. Also with religious programs for North American listeners at this hour are **WYFR-Family Radio** on 5985 kHz, **WWCR** on 5935 kHz, **KAIJ** on 5810 kHz,

KTBN on 7510 kHz, and **WHRI-World Harvest Radio** on 5760 and 7315 kHz. Traditional Catholic fare (some of it may be in Spanish) is available on 7425 kHz.

Voice of Malaysia. Actually starts at 0555 with opening announcements and program summary, followed by *News*. Then comes *This is the Voice of Malaysia*, a potpourri of news, interviews, reports and music. The hour is rounded off with *Personality Column*. Part of a 150-minute broadcast to Southeast Asia and Australia on 6175, 9750 and 15295 kHz.

Radio Japan. Repeat of the 0300 transmission, except that the end-of-broadcast news is replaced by *Tokyo Pop-in*. Sixty minutes to East and Southeast Asia on 11725, 11860 and 17810 kHz; and to Australasia on 11850 kHz.

HCJB—Voice of the Andes, Ecuador. Tuesday through Saturday, a repeat of the 0200 broadcast. Pick of the remaining fare is *Musical Mailbag* (0630 Sunday) and *Radio Reading Room* (0600 Monday). One hour of predominantly religious programming. To Western North America on 9745 kHz.

06:15

Swiss Radio International. Fifteen minutes of *news* to Europe on 6165, (winter) 7410 and (summer) 9535 kHz.

06:30

Radio Austria International. ●*Report from Austria* (see 0130). A half hour via the Canadian relay, aimed primarily at Western North America on 6015 kHz.

Radio Vlaanderen Internationaal, Belgium. Summers only at this time. *News*, then *Press Review* (except Sunday), followed Monday through Friday by *Belgium Today* (various topics) and features like *The Arts* (Monday and Thursday, *Tourism* (Monday), *Focus on Europe* (Tuesday),

Living in Belgium and *Green Society* (Wednesday), *Around Town* (Thursday), and *Economics* and *International Report* (Friday). Weekend features consist of Saturday's *Music from Flanders* and Sunday's *P.O. Box 26* (a listener-response program) and *Radio World*. Thirty minutes to Europe on 5985 and 9925 kHz; and to Australasia on 9925 kHz. One hour later in winter.

Radio Romania International. Actually starts at 0631. A nine-minute news broadcast to Europe winters on 7105, 9510, 9570, 9665 and 11745 kHz; and summers on 9550, 9665 and 11810 kHz.

Radio Almaty, Kazakhstan. Winters only at this time. Due to financial constraints, news and features have largely been replaced by exotic Kazakh music. Thirty minutes to Asia on 4820, 5970, 5985, 6060, 6075, 7115, 7235, 7280, 9505, 9550, 9690 and 9705 kHz; and to Europe (via relay facilities in Ukraine) on 9560 kHz. One hour earlier in summer.

06:45

Radio Romania International. *News*, commentary, a press review and short features, with interludes of lively Romanian folk music. Fifty-five minutes to East Asia and Australasia on 11740, 11840, 15250, 15270, 15405, 17720 and 17805 kHz, some of which are seasonal.

07:00

■**BBC World Service for the Americas.** Winters only at this time. Fifteen minutes of *World News*, then it's a mixed bag. Best of the pack are *A Jolly Good Show* (Monday), ●*The Greenfield Collection* (classical music, Tuesday), ●*Megamix* (a youth magazine, 0730 Wednesday), *From Our Own Correspondent* (0715 Thursday) and Friday's inimitable ●*Andy Kershaw's World of Music* (well worth staying up for).

Continuous to North America (and better to the west) on 5975 and 6175 kHz (9640 kHz may also be available in winter).

■**BBC World Service for Europe (and the Mideast).** *World News* followed by features, some of which are amongst the BBC's best. Try ●*Off the Shelf* (0715 weekdays), then at 0730, *The Vintage Chart Show* (Monday) *New Ideas* (Tuesday), ●*Discovery* (Wednesday) and Thursday's ●*Network UK*. Weekends, look for Saturday's *From the Weeklies* and ●*People and Politics*, replaced Sunday by ●*Short Story* (or *Seeing Stars*), *From Our Own Correspondent* and *Write On*. Continuous to Europe on 3955 (winter), 6195, 7325 (winter), 9410, 12095 and 15485 kHz; and to the Mideast on 9410 (winter), 11760, 15575 and 17640 kHz.

■**BBC World Service for Asia and the Pacific.** *World News*, then Monday through Fridays there's ●*Off the Shelf* (readings from world literature). Best of the remaining offerings are ●*Folk Routes* and *From Our Own Correspondent* (Sunday), ●*Andy Kershaw's World of Music* (Wednesday), *Sports International* (Thursday) and Saturday's ●*People and Politics*. For a younger audience, *Multitrack* (0730 Tuesday and Friday) should fit the bill. Continuous to East and Southeast Asia on 9740, 11955, 15280 and 15360 kHz; and to Australasia on 7145, 11955 and 15360 kHz.

Monitor Radio International, USA. See 0000 for program details. Monday through Friday to Western Europe on 7535 kHz. Weekends are given over to non-secular programming, mainly of interest to members of, and others interested in, the Christian Science Church.

Voice of Malaysia. First, there is a daily feature with a Malaysian theme (except for Thursday, when *Talk on Islam* is aired), then comes a half hour of *This is the Voice of Malaysia* (see 0600), followed by 15 minutes of *Beautiful Malaysia*. Not much doubt about where the broadcast originates! Continuous to Southeast Asia and Australia on 6175, 9750 and 15295 kHz.

Radio Prague, Czech Republic. Summers only at this time. See 0800 for specifics. Thirty minutes to Europe on 7345 and 9530 kHz. One hour later in winter.

Radio Australia. *World News*, then Monday through Friday it's news and features for listeners in the Pacific. Saturday, look for *Oz Sounds* and the environmental *One World*, and Sunday there's a different edition of *Oz Sounds* followed by *At Your Request*. Continuous to Asia and the Pacific on about ten channels, and heard in North America (best during summer) on 9580 (from 0730), 9860, 11880 and 15240 kHz. In East and Southeast Asia, take your pick from 9710 (from 0730), 15415, 15530 and 17715 kHz.

Radio For Peace International, Costa Rica. The final 60 minutes of an eight-hour cyclical block of United Nations, counterculture and social-conscience programming. Audible in Europe and the Americas on 6205 and 7385 kHz. Some transmissions are in the single-sideband mode, which can be properly processed only on some radios.

Voice of Russia World Service. *News*, followed Tuesday through Saturday summers by the informative ●*Commonwealth Update*. The second half-hour consists of various styles of music. At 0711 Sunday and Monday, it's time to enjoy the excellent ●*Music and Musicians*. Winter's offerings are a mixed bag, with *Science and Engineering* (0711 Monday, Friday and Saturday) alternating with *Mailbag* and the business-oriented *Newmarket*. The final 25 minutes or so is divided between *This is Russia* (Tuesday, Thursday and Saturday), ●*Moscow Yesterday and Today* (Wednesday and Friday), and *Russian by Radio* on the remaining days. To Western North America (winters only)

on 5905, 5920, 5930, 7175, 7270 and 7330 kHz. Also year-round to Southeast Asia and Australasia, winters on 12025, 15160, 15470, 17560, 17570 and 21790 kHz; and summers on 15470, 15560, 17570 and 17580 kHz.

WJCR, Upton, Kentucky. Continues with country gospel music for North American listeners on 7490 kHz. Also with religious programs to North America at this hour are **WWCR** on 5935 kHz, **KAIJ** on 5810 kHz, **KTBN** on 7510 kHz, and **WHRI-World Harvest Radio** on 5745 and 9495 kHz. For traditional Catholic programming, tune **WEWN** on 7425 kHz.

Radio Pyongyang, North Korea. See 1100 for specifics. Fifty minutes from the last of the old-time communist stations. To Southeast Asia on 15340 and 17765 kHz.

Radio Norway International. Winter Sundays only. *Norway Now*. A half hour of *news* and human-interest stories targeted at Australasia on 7180 kHz.

Croatian Radio. Monday through Saturday, winters only at this time; actually starts at 0703 (Sunday, there is a brief summary at 0803). Ten minutes of English *news* from one of Croatian Radio's domestic networks. In times of crisis, one of the few sources of up-to-date news on what is actually happening in the region. Frequency usage varies, but try 5985, 5920, 7165, 7370, 9830 and 13830 kHz. One hour earlier in summer.

Radio New Zealand International. Continues with regional programming for the South Pacific. Part of a much longer broadcast, which is also heard in parts of North America (especially during summer) on 6100, 9570 or 9700 kHz.

Voice of Free China, Taiwan. Repeat of the 0200 transmission. Best heard in southern and western parts of the United States on 5950 kHz.

Radio Japan. Monday through Friday,

> If PASSPORT in print isn't enough for you, try us on the last Sunday of the month over Radio Japan's *Media Roundup*.

it's *Radio Japan News Round* followed by *Radio Japan Magazine Hour*, which consists of *Close Up* and a feature (two on Tuesday). On Monday you can hear *Sports Column*, Tuesday has *Japanese Culture* and *Today*, Wednesday features *Asian Report*, Thursday brings *Crosscurrents*, and Friday's offering is *Business Focus*. Weekend fare is made up of a bulletin of *news*, followed by Saturday's *This Week* or Sunday's *Let's Learn Japanese*, *Media Roundup* and *Viewpoint*. The broadcast ends with a daily *news* summary. Sixty minutes to Europe on 5975 (winter), 7230 and 15165 kHz; to the Mideast on 15165 kHz; to Africa on 15165 and 17815 kHz; to East and Southeast Asia on 11725, 11740, 17810 and 21610 kHz; and to Australasia on 11850 and 11920 kHz.

HCJB—Voice of the Andes, Ecuador. Opens with 30 minutes of syndicated religious programming—except for *The Latest Catch* and *The Book Nook* (Wednesday), *On Line* (Friday) and *Musical Mailbag* (Saturday). Then comes the weekday *Studio 9* (see 0030 for more details, except that all features are one day earlier), replaced Saturday by *DX Partyline*, and Sunday by *Saludos Amigos*—the HCJB international friendship program. To Europe winters on 6050 kHz, and summers on 11615 kHz. A separate block of religious programming is broadcast to Australasia on 5900 or 9445 kHz.

07:15

Swiss Radio International. Winters only at this time. Fifteen minutes of *news* to Europe on 6165 and 7410 kHz. One hour earlier in summer.

07:30

Radio Nederland. *News*, then Monday through Saturday it's ●*Newsline* followed by a feature. Pick of the pack are

●*Research File* (science, Monday); ●*A Good Life* (Friday); and the Saturday ●*Weekend*. Other offerings include *Mirror Images* (Tuesday), a documentary (Wednesday), and Thursday's *Media Network*. Sunday, there's a listener-response program and *Sounds Interesting*. To Australasia on 9720 and 9700 or 11895 kHz. Well worth a listen.

Radio Austria International. Summers only at this time. ●*Report from Austria*, which includes a short bulletin of *news* followed by a series of current events and human interest stories. Ample coverage of national and regional issues, and a valuable source of news about Central and Eastern Europe. Thirty minutes to Europe on 6155 and 13730 kHz, and to the Mideast on 15410 and 17870 kHz.

Radio Vlaanderen Internationaal, Belgium. Winters only at this time. See 0630 for program details. Thirty minutes to Europe on 5985 (or 5910) and 9920 (or 9925) kHz, with the latter channel also available for Australasia. One hour earlier in summer.

07:45

Voice of Greece. Actual start time varies slightly. Ten minutes of English news from and about Greece. Part of a longer broadcast of predominantly Greek programming. To Europe and Australasia on two or more channels from 7450, 9425 and 11645 kHz.

08:00

■**BBC World Service for Europe (and the Mideast).** *News*, then the religious *Words of Faith*, followed by a wide variety of programming, depending on the day of the week. Choice programs include ●*The Greenfield Collection* (Sunday), ●*Thirty-Minute Drama* (Tuesday), ●*Concert Hall* (alternating periodically with ●*International Recital* or ●*From the Proms*) (Wednesday), *Composer of the Month* and ●*Health Matters* (Thursday), *Music Review* (Friday) and *A Jolly Good Show* (Saturday). Continuous to Europe on 6195 (winter), 7325 (winter), 9410, 12095, 15485 and 17640 kHz; and to the Mideast on 9410 (winter), 11760, and 17640 kHz.

■BBC World Service for Asia and the Pacific. Begins with *World News*, and unlike the service for Europe, ends with *Words of Faith*. Between the two extremes there is classical music on Sunday, Monday and Tuesday; the youth-oriented ●*Megamix* (Wednesday), *Good Books* and ●*John Peel* (Thursday), and *A Jolly Good Show* (Saturday). Continuous to East and Southeast Asia on 9740, 11955 and 15280 kHz, and to Australasia on 11955 kHz.

R. Crane

Chinese sandalwood carver continues an ancient tradition, using new tools.

Monitor Radio International, USA. See 0000 for program details. Tuesday through Friday to Europe on 7535 or 15665 kHz, and to Australasia on 9845 (or 13840) and 11550 kHz. Weekend programs are devoted to the teachings and beliefs of the Christian Science Church.

HCJB—Voice of the Andes, Ecuador. Continuous programming to Europe and Australasia. For Europe there's the final 30 minutes of *Studio 9* (or weekend variations), while Australasia gets a full hour's serving of predominantly religious fare. To Europe winters on 6050 kHz, and summers on 11615 kHz; and to Australasia on 5900 or 9445 kHz.

Voice of Malaysia. *News* and commentary, followed Monday through Friday by *Instrumentalia*, which is replaced weekends by *This is the Voice of Malaysia* (see 0600). The final 25 minutes of a much longer transmission targeted at Southeast Asia and Australia on 6175, 9750 and 15295 kHz.

Croatian Radio. Monday through Saturday, summers only at this time; actually starts at 0803. Ten minutes of English *news* from one of the domestic networks (replaced Sunday by a brief summary at 0903). A good way to keep abreast of events in one of Europe's most unstable regions. Frequency usage varies, but try 5895, 5920, 7165, 7370, 9830 and 13830 kHz. One hour later in winter.

Radio Norway International. Summer Sundays only. *Norway Now*. A pleasant half hour of *news* and human-interest stories from and about Norway. To Australasia on 17860 kHz.

Radio Prague, Czech Republic. Winters only at this time. *News*, then Monday through Friday there's *Current Affairs*. These are followed by one or more features. Monday has *Magazine '96*; Tuesday, it's *Talking Point* and *What's Up?*; Wednesday has *From the Archives* and *The Arts*; Thursday brings *Economic Report* and *I'd Like You to Meet...*; and

Friday there's *Between You and Us*. Saturday's offerings include a musical feature, replaced Sunday by *The Week in Politics*, *From the Weeklies* and *What's Up?* Thirty minutes to Europe on 5930 and 7345 kHz. One hour earlier in summer.

Radio Pakistan. Opens with a brief bulletin of *news* followed by recitations from the Koran (with English translation). This in turn is followed by a press review and a ten-minute interlude of Pakistani music. On the half-hour there's a feature on Pakistan or Islam, which then gives way to extracts from Pakistani concert recordings. Fifty minutes to Europe on 15470/15475 and 17895/17900 kHz.

Radio Australia. Part of a 24-hour service to Asia and the Pacific, but which can also be heard at this time throughout much of North America. Begins with *World News* and a sports bulletin, then Monday through Friday there's ●*International Report* and *Stock Exchange Report*. Weekends on the half-hour, it's Saturday's *Indian Pacific* and Sunday's *Correspondents' Report*. To Asia and the Pacific on a variety of channels, and audible in North America on 9580 and 9860 kHz. Best bets for East and Southeast Asia are 9510, 9710 and 13605 kHz. Listeners in Europe and the Mideast can try 21725 kHz.

Radio Austria International airs everything from Viennese waltzes to an avalanche of Alpine news.

WJCR, Upton, Kentucky. Continues with country gospel music to North America on 7490 kHz. Other U.S. religious broadcasters operating at this hour include **WWCR** on 5935 kHz, **KAIJ** on 5810 kHz, **KTBN** on 7510 kHz, and **WHRI-World Harvest Radio** on 5745 and 9495 kHz. Traditional Catholic programming can be heard via **WEWN** on 7425 kHz.

Radio Pyongyang, North Korea. See 1100 for specifics. Fifty minutes of mediocrity to Southeast Asia on 15180 and 15230 kHz.

Voice of Russia World Service. *News*, then Tuesday through Saturday winters, it's ●*Commonwealth Update* followed by a half hour of music. On the remaining days, you can hear the enjoyable ●*Music and Musicians*. In summer, the *news* is followed Tuesday through Saturday by *Focus on Asia and the Pacific*. This in turn gives way, on the half-hour, to some entertaining musical fare—●*Folk Box* (Wednesday and Saturday), *Yours for the Asking* (Monday), ●*Music at Your Request* (Tuesday), and Friday's *Jazz Show*. Continuous to East and Southeast Asia, winters on 9685, 17560 and 17860 kHz; and summers on 15470, 15560 and 15580 kHz. Also available to Australasia winters on 12025, 15160, 17860 and 17880 kHz; and summers on 9835, 11800, 11985, 12025, 15470 and 15560 kHz.

KTWR-Trans World Radio, Guam. Actually starts at 0755. Eighty minutes of evangelical programming targeted at East Asia on 15200 kHz.

Radio New Zealand International. *News* and features, music or special programs for the South Sea Islands, all with a distinctly Pacific flavor. Sometimes includes relays from the domestic National Radio. Part of a much longer broadcast for the South Pacific, but well heard in North America winters on 9700, and summers on 6100 kHz.

Radio Korea International, South Korea. Opens with *news* and commentary, followed Monday through Wednesday by *Seoul Calling*. Weekly features include *Echoes of Korean Music* and *Shortwave Feedback* (Sunday), *Tales from Korea's Past* (Monday), *Korean Cultural Trails* (Tuesday), *Pulse of Korea* (Wednesday), *From Us to You* (a listener-response program) and *Let's Learn Korean* (Thursday), *Let's Sing Together* and *Korea Through Foreigners' Eyes* (Friday), and Saturday's

Discovering Korea, Korean Literary Corner and *Weekly News Focus*. Sixty minutes to Europe on 7550 and 13670 kHz.

08:30

Radio Austria International. Winters only at this time. The comprehensive ●*Report from Austria*; see 0130 for more details. A half hour to Europe on 6155 and 13730 kHz, and to Australia and the Pacific on 17870 kHz.

Radio Slovakia International. *Slovakia Today*—30 minutes of *news*, reports and features, all with a distinct Slovak flavor. Tuesday, there's a potpourri of short features; Wednesday puts the accent on tourism and Slovak personalities; Wednesday has a historical feature; Thursday's slot is devoted to business and economy; and Friday brings a mix of politics, education and science. Saturday has a strong cultural content; Sunday features the "Best of" series; and Monday brings *Listeners' Tribune* and some enjoyable Slovak music. To Australasia on 11990, 15460 (or 21705) and 17485 (or 17550) kHz.

Radio Nederland. The second of three hours aimed at Australasia. *News*, followed Monday through Saturday by ●*Newsline*, then a feature program. Choice pickings include ●*A Good Life* (Monday), ●*Research File* (Thursday) and Friday's documentary. Monday through Friday, there is also a daily *Press Review*. On 9720 and, during winter in the Northern Hemisphere, 13700 kHz.

Radio Vilnius, Lithuania. Summers only at this time; see 0930 for program specifics. Thirty minutes to Europe on 9710 kHz. One hour later in winter.

Voice of Armenia. Summer Sundays only. Mainly of interest to Armenians abroad. Thirty minutes of Armenian *news* and culture. To Europe on 15270 (or 15170) kHz. One hour later in winter.

09:00

■**BBC World Service for Europe (and the Mideast).** Starts with *News* and ●*World Business Report/Review*, and ends with *Sports Roundup*. The remaining time is taken up by a series of 30-minute features, the pick of which are ●*Anything Goes* (Monday), ●*Brain of Britain* or its substitute (Tuesday), ●*Andy Kershaw's World of Music* (Wednesday), *Sports International* (Thursday) and ●*Focus on Faith* (Friday). Continuous to Europe on 9410, 12095, 15485 and 17640 kHz; and to the Mideast on 9410 (winter), 11760, 15575 and 17640 kHz.

■**BBC World Service for Asia and the Pacific.** Starts and ends like the service for Europe, but the features are different. Interesting offerings include ●*Science in Action* (0915 Sunday), ●*Health Matters* (0930 Monday), *Country Style* (0915 Tuesday), *Composer of the Month* (0915 Wednesday), *From Our Own Correspondent* and *The Farming World* (Thursday), ●*On the Move* (0930 Friday) and ●*Development 97* (0930 Saturday). Continuous to East and Southeast Asia on 9740 and 17830 kHz.

Monitor Radio International, USA. See 0000 for program details. Tuesday through Friday (Monday through Friday in summer), to Europe on 7535 kHz, to East Asia on 9430 kHz, and to Australasia on 13840 kHz. Also audible in parts of North America on 7395 kHz, though targeted farther south. Weekend programs are of a religious nature and are mainly of interest to members of, and others interested in, the Christian Science faith.

■**Deutsche Welle,** Germany. *News*, followed Monday through Friday by ●*Newsline Cologne*, *Hallo Africa* and *African News*. Weekend fare consists of Saturday's *Germany This Week*, *Mailbag Africa* and *Saturday Special*; and Sunday's *Arts on the Air* and *German by Radio*. Fifty minutes to East and

Southern Africa on 9565, 11725 and 15145 (winter), 15225 (summer), 15410, 17800 and 21600 kHz.

■**Deutsche Welle,** Germany. *News,* followed Monday through Friday by ●*Newsline Cologne* and a feature: *Science and Technology* (Monday), ●*Man and Environment* (Tuesday), ●*Insight* (Wednesday), *Living in Germany* (Thursday) and *Spotlight on Sport* (Friday). These are replaced Saturday by *International Talking Point, Development Forum* and *Religion and Society;* and Sunday by *Arts on the Air* and *German by Radio.* Fifty minutes to Asia and Australasia winters on 6160, 7380, 11715, 17780, 17820 and 21680 kHz; and summers on 6160, 11730, 12055, 17715 and 21680 kHz.

Radio New Zealand International. Continuous programming for the islands of the South Pacific, where the broadcasts are targeted. Summers on 6100 kHz, and winters on 9700 kHz. Audible in much of North America.

Radio Vlaanderen Internationaal, Belgium. Monday through Saturday, summers only at this time. *News* and *Press Review,* followed Monday through Friday by *Belgium Today* (various topics) and features like *Tourism* (Monday), *Focus on Europe* (Tuesday), *Living in Belgium* and *Green Society* (Wednesday), *The Arts* (Monday and Thursday), *Around Town* (Thursday), and *Economics and International Report*(Friday). Saturday features *Music from Flanders.* Thirty minutes to Europe on 6035 kHz, and to Africa on 15545 and 17595 kHz. One hour later in winter.

Croatian Radio. Monday through Saturday, winters only at this time; actually starts at 0903 (Sunday, there is only a brief summary at 1003). Ten minutes of on-the-spot *news* from the Balkans. Frequencies vary, but try 5895, 5920, 7165, 7370, 9830 and 13830 kHz. One hour earlier during summer.

HCJB—Voice of the Andes, Ecuador.

Monday through Friday it's *Studio 9*, featuring nine minutes of world and Latin American *news*, followed by 20 minutes of in-depth reporting on Latin America. The final portion of *Studio 9* is given over to one of a variety of 30-minute features—including *You Should Know* (issues and ethics, Monday), *El Mundo Futuro* (science, Tuesday), *Ham Radio Today* (Wednesday), *What's Cooking in the Andes* (Thursday) and Friday's thoroughly enjoyable ●*Música del Ecuador*. On Saturday, the news is followed by *DX Partyline*, which in turn is replaced Sunday by *Saludos Amigos*—HCJB's international friendship program. Continuous to Australasia on 5900 or 9445 kHz.

China Radio International. *News* and commentary, followed Tuesday through Friday by *Current Affairs*. These are followed by various feature programs, such as *Cultural Spectrum* (Thursday); *Listeners' Letterbox* (Sunday and Tuesday); *China Scrapbook, Cooking Show, Travel Talk* and ●*Music from China* (Saturday); *Sports Beat* and *Music Album* (Sunday); *Learn to Speak Chinese* (Monday and Wednesday); and Friday's *In the Third World*. Sundays, there is also a biweekly *Business Show* which alternates with *China's Open Windows*. One hour to Australasia on 11755 and 15440 kHz.

Voice of Russia World Service. Tuesday through Saturday, winters, *News* is followed by *Focus on Asia and the Pacific*. This is replaced summers by a variety of features—Wednesday and Sunday offer the business-oriented *Newmarket*, Thursday features *Science and Engineering*, and there's a listener-response program on Monday, Tuesday and Friday. In winter, the second half-hour concentrates mainly on music, with the main attractions being ●*Folk Box* (Wednesday and Saturday),

> With luck, location and a powerful radio, you might be able to eavesdrop on Radio Ulaanbaatar in Mongolia. Its talks touch on anything from ethnic customs to much-needed thermal underwear.

●*Music at Your Request* (Tuesday), and Friday's *Jazz Show*. For summer, there's *This is Russia* (Wednesday and Friday), *Timelines* (Sunday), ●*Audio Book Club* (Monday), and ●*Moscow Yesterday and Today* on the remaining days. Sixty minutes of continuous programming beamed to Asia and the Pacific. For East and Southeast Asia winters, try 9685 and 17860 kHz; and summers on 12025 and 15580 kHz. Best winter bets for Australasia are 9450, 12005, 12025, 17860 and 17880 kHz; in summer, go for 9835 and 11800 kHz.

Swiss Radio International. Thirty minutes of *news* and background reports on world and Swiss events. Look for some lighter fare on Saturdays, when *Capital Letters* (a biweekly listener-response program) alternates with *Name Game* and *Sounds Good*. To Australasia on 9885, 11640 (winter), 13685 and (summer) 17515 kHz.

Radio Prague, Czech Republic. This time summers only. Repeat of the 0700 broadcast (see 0800 for program specifics). Thirty minutes to East Africa and the Mideast on 17485 kHz; also to West Africa and beyond on 15640 kHz.

Radio Australia. *World News*, followed Monday through Friday by *Australian News* and *Australia Today*. These are replaced weekends by Saturday's 50-minute *Science Show* and Sunday's *Oz Sounds* and *Soundabout*. Continuous to Asia and the Pacific on a number of channels, and heard in North America on 9580 and 9860 kHz. In Europe and the Mideast, try 21725 kHz, while listeners in East and Southeast Asia can choose from 9510 and 13605 kHz.

Radio For Peace International, Costa Rica. *FIRE* (Feminist International Radio Endeavour). Repeat of the 0100 broadcast. To the Americas on 6205 and 7385 kHz.

KTWR-Trans World Radio, Guam. Actually starts at 0855. Evangelical programming to Australasia on 11830 kHz.

WJCR, Upton, Kentucky. Continues with country gospel music to North America on 7490 kHz. Other U.S. religious broadcasters operating at this hour include **WWCR** on 5935, **KAIJ** on 5810, **KTBN** on 7510 kHz, and **WHRI-World Harvest Radio** on 5745 and 9495 kHz. Traditional Catholic programming is aired via **WEWN** on 7425 kHz.

Radio Japan. Repeat of the 0300 broadcast; see there for specifics. Up-to-the-minute news from and about the Far East. Sixty minutes to East and Southeast Asia on 6090 (winter), 9610 (summer) and 15190 kHz; and to Australasia on 11850 kHz.

anything from ethnic customs to thermal underwear. The entire Sunday broadcast is given over to exotic Mongolian music. Thirty minutes to East Asia and Australasia on 9960 (or 11850) and 12085 kHz. Frequencies may vary a little.

FEBC Radio International, Philippines. Opens with *World News Update*, then it's mostly religious features. For something with a more general appeal, try Thursday's *Mailbag* or Sunday's *DX Dial* (a show for radio enthusiasts). The first half-hour of a 90-minute predominantly religious broadcast targeted at East and Southeast Asia on 11635 kHz.

Voice of Armenia. Winter Sundays only. Mainly of interest to Armenians abroad. Thirty minutes of Armenian *news* and culture. To Europe on 15270 kHz. One hour earlier in summer.

09:30

Radio Austria International. ●*Report from Austria* (see 0730). Monday through Saturday, summers only at this time. To Europe on 6155 and 13730 kHz, and to East Asia and Australasia on 15450 and 17870 kHz.

Radio Nederland. Repeat of the 0730 broadcast. Fifty-five minutes to Australasia on 9720 kHz; and a full hour to East and Southeast Asia winters on 7260 and 9810 kHz, and summers on 12065 and 13705 kHz. Recommended listening.

Radio Vilnius, Lithuania. Winters only at this time. A half hour that's mostly *news* and background reports about events in Lithuania. Of broader appeal is *Mailbag*, aired every other Sunday. For a little Lithuanian music, try the second half of Monday's broadcast. To Europe on 9710 kHz. One hour earlier in summer.

Radio Ulaanbaatar, Mongolia. Most days, it's *news*, reports and short features, all with a Mongolian slant. Some of the topics tend to be unusual, and can feature

---

10:00

■**BBC World Service for the Americas.** ●*Newsdesk*, followed on the half-hour by a mixed bag of features. These include *Composer of the Month* (classical music, Monday), ●*Brain of Britain* or its substitute (Tuesday), ●*Jazz for the Asking* (Wednesday), *Meridian on Screen* (cinema, Thursday), the excellent ●*Andy Kershaw's World of Music* (Friday) and *From the Weeklies* and ●*Letter from America* (Saturday). To North America and the Caribbean on 5965 (winter) and 6195 kHz.

■**BBC World Service for Europe (and the Mideast).** ●*Newsdesk*, followed on the half-hour by 15 minutes of programming for students of English (alternative features are carried on some channels for the Mideast). At 1045 Monday through Friday, you can enjoy ●*Off the Shelf*, serialized readings of world literature. This is replaced weekends by Alistair Cooke's ●*Letter from America* (Saturday), and Sunday's ●*Short Story* (or *Seeing Stars*). Continuous to Europe on 9410, 12095, 15485 and 17640 kHz; and to the Mideast on 11760, 15575 and 17640 kHz.

■BBC World Service for Asia and the Pacific. Thirty minutes of ●*Newsdesk*, then features. Try ●*Anything Goes* (Monday), Thursday's ●*Brain of Britain* (or replacement quiz), and Friday's *The Vintage Chart Show*. Continuous to East and Southeast Asia on 6195, 9740, 15280 and 15360 kHz; and to Australasia on 6195, 15280 or 15360 kHz (varies on a seasonal basis). Some of these channels close at 1030, but others are available for the full hour.

Monitor Radio International, USA. See 0000 for program details. Monday through Friday to Eastern North America and the Caribbean on 6095 kHz, and to South America (and audible in parts of North America) on 7395 kHz. Weekend programming is non-secular, and is devoted to the teachings and beliefs of the Christian Science Church.

Radio Australia. *World News*, then weekdays it's *Asia Focus*, ●*International Report* and *Stock Exchange Report*. Saturday brings *Ockham's Razor* (science) and *Background Report*, replaced Sunday by *Charting Australia* and *Report from Asia*. Continuous to Asia and the Pacific, and heard in North America on 9580 and 9860 kHz. In Europe and the Mideast, try 21725 kHz. Listeners in East and Southeast Asia can choose between 9510 and 13605 kHz.

Swiss Radio International. Summers only at this time. *Newsnet*—news and background reports on world and Swiss events. Look for some lighter fare on Saturdays, when the biweekly *Capital Letters* (a listener-response program) alternates with *Name Game* and *Sounds Good*. Thirty minutes to Europe on 6165 and 9535 kHz. One hour later in winter.

Radio Prague, Czech Republic. This time winters only. Repeat of the 0800 broadcast (see there for specifics). Thirty minutes to the Mideast and beyond on 15640 kHz.

Radio New Zealand International. A mixed bag of Pacific regional *news*, features, and relays of the domestic National Radio network. Continuous to the Pacific; summers on 6100 kHz, and winters on 9700 kHz. Easily audible in much of North America.

Voice of Vietnam. Begins with *news*, then there's *Commentary* or *Weekly Review*, followed by short features and some pleasant Vietnamese music (especially at weekends). Heard extensively on 9840 and (winters) 12020 or (summers) 15010 kHz. Targeted to Asia at this hour.

Radio Vlaanderen Internationaal, Belgium. Monday through Saturday, winters only at this time. See 0900 for program details. Thirty minutes to Europe on 6035 kHz, and to Africa on 15510 and 17595 kHz. One hour earlier in summer.

Voice of America. The start of VOA's daily broadcasts to the Caribbean. *News*, followed Monday through Friday by *VOA Today*—a compendium of news, sports, science, business and other features. Replaced weekends by *VOA Saturday/VOA Sunday*, which have less accent on news, and more on features. On 6165, 7405 and 9590 kHz. For a separate service to Australasia, see the next item.

Voice of America. *News*, followed Monday through Friday by *Stateside*, a look at issues and personalities in different walks of American life. This is replaced Saturday by ●*Encounter* and *Communications World*, and Sunday by *Critic's Choice* and a feature in slow-speed English. To Australasia on 5985, 11720, and 15425 kHz.

Radio For Peace International, Costa Rica. Another hour of counterculture and social-conscience programs. Offerings at this hour include *The Far Right Radio Review* (1000 Wednesday) and *My Green Earth* (a nature program for children, 1030 Monday). Continuous to North and Central America on 6205 and 7385 kHz. Some transmissions are in the single-sideband mode, which can be properly processed only on some radios.

China Radio International. Repeat of the 0900 broadcast. One hour to Australasia on 11755 and 15440 kHz.

FEBC Radio International, Philippines. The final hour of a 90-minute mix of religious and secular programming for East and Southeast Asia. Monday through Friday, it's *Focus on the Family*, then a 15-minute religious feature, *Asian News Update* (on the half-hour) and *In Touch*. All weekend offerings are religious in nature. On 11635 kHz.

All India Radio. *News*, then a composite program of commentary, press review and features, interspersed with ample servings of enjoyable Indian music.

To East Asia on 11585, 15050 and 17890/ 13700 kHz; and to Australasia on 13700, 15050 and 17387/17890 kHz.

WJCR, Upton, Kentucky. Continues with country gospel music to North America on 7490 kHz. Other U.S. religious broadcasters operating at this hour include **WWCR** on 5935 kHz, **KTBN** on 7510 kHz, **WYFR-Family Radio** on 5950 kHz, and **WHRI-World Harvest Radio** on 6040 and 9495 kHz. For traditional Catholic programming, try **WEWN** on 7425 kHz.

Voice of Russia World Service. *News*, followed winters by a variety of features. Sunday and Wednesday it's business in *Newmarket*, Thursday features *Science and Engineering*, and there's a listener-response program on Monday, Tuesday and Friday. The second

half-hour's brings ●*Audio Book Club* (Monday), ●*Moscow Yesterday and Today* (Tuesday, Thursday and Saturday), *Timelines* (Sunday) and *This is Russia* on the remaining days. In summer, the news is followed Tuesday through Saturday by the timely ●*Commonwealth Update*, replaced Sunday and Monday by *Science and Engineering*. These, in turn, are followed by ●*Audio Book Club* (Wednesday and Friday), *Timelines* (Saturday), *Russian by Radio* (Tuesday and Thursday), and the aptly-named *Kaleidoscope* on Sunday and Monday. Continuous to Asia and the Pacific. For Southeast Asia, try the winter channels of 7305, 9685, 13785, 15490, 17755 and 17860 kHz; and summer, choose from 12025, 15170, 17610 and 17775 kHz. Winters (local summers) in Australasia, go for 9450, 12005, 12025, 17860 and 17880 kHz; midyear, choose from 9835, 11800 and 17560 kHz.

HCJB—Voice of the Andes, Ecuador. Sixty minutes of religious and secular programming to Australasia. See 0200 for program specifics, except that features are one day earlier, and not necessarily in the same order. On 5900 or 9445 kHz.

ics). A half hour to Europe on 7345 and 9505 kHz. One hour later during winter.

Radio Nederland. Repeat of the 0830 broadcast without the press review (except for Europe). Fifty-five minutes to East and Southeast Asia winters on 7260 and 9810 kHz, and summers on 12065 and 13705 kHz (also audible in Australasia). A full hour summers to Western Europe on 6045 and 9650 kHz.

Radio Austria International. ●*Report from Austria* (see 0730). A half hour to Europe Monday through Saturday winters on 6155 and 13730 kHz, and to Australasia on 17870 kHz. Daily in summer, to East Asia on 15450 kHz, and to Australia and the Pacific on 17870 kHz.

YLE Radio Finland. Summers only at this time; see 1130 for specifics. Thirty minutes to Southeast Asia and Australasia on 13645 and 15235 kHz. One hour later in winter.

United Arab Emirates Radio, Dubai. *News,* then a feature dealing with one or more aspects of Arab life and culture. Weekends, there are replies to listeners' letters. To Europe on 13675, 15395, 17825 (or 17630) and 21605 kHz.

10:30

Radio Korea International, South Korea. Summers only at this time. Starts off with *News,* followed Monday through Wednesday by *Economic News Briefs.* The remainder of the 30-minute broadcast is taken up by a feature: *Shortwave Feedback* (Sunday), *Seoul Calling* (Monday and Tuesday), *Pulse of Korea* (Wednesday), *From Us to You* (Thursday), *Let's Sing Together* (Friday) and *Weekly News Focus* (Saturday). On 11715 kHz via their Canadian relay, so this is the best chance for North Americans to hear the station. One hour later in winter.

Radio Prague, Czech Republic. This time summers only. Repeat of the 0700 broadcast (see 0800 for program specif-

---

11:00

■**BBC World Service for the Americas.** ●*Newsdesk,* followed on the half-hour by a variety of features, depending on the day of the week. Try *Jazz Now and Then* (1130 Tuesday), ●*Thirty-Minute Drama* (Wednesday), *From Our Own Correspondent* and ●*The Learning World* (Thursday), ●*Focus on Faith* (Friday) and Saturday's ●*People and Politics.* To Eastern North America and the Caribbean on 5965, 6195 and 15220 kHz. Weekdays, for the first half-hour, 6195 and 15220 kHz carry alternative programming for the Caribbean.

■**BBC World Service for Europe (and the Mideast).** Thirty minutes of the comprehensive ●*Newsdesk,* then a feature. Tuesday, Thursday, Friday and Saturday bring *Meridian* (the arts), while Monday has ●*Omnibus* and Wednesday airs the excellent ●*Thirty-Minute Drama*. Continuous to Europe on 9410, 12095, 15485 and 17640 kHz; and to the Mideast on 11760, 15575 and 17640 kHz.

■**BBC World Service for Asia and the Pacific.** Similar to the service for Europe, except for Sunday (first part of ●*Play of the Week*), Monday (light entertainment) and Friday's classical *Music Review*. Continuous to East and Southeast Asia on 6195, 9740, 11955 and 15280 kHz. The first half-hour is available to Australasia via Radio New Zealand International on 9700 (or 6100) kHz, but then the service is resumed via the BBC's own facilities on 9740 kHz.

Monitor Radio International, USA. See 0000 for program details. Audible Monday through Friday in Eastern North America and the Caribbean on 6095 kHz, and in Central and South America on 7395 kHz. Weekends are given over to programming of a religious nature, not all of it necessarily in English.

Voice of Asia, Taiwan. One of the few stations to open with a feature: *Asian Culture* (Monday), *Touring Asia* (Tuesday), *World of Science* (Wednesday), *World Economy* (Thursday), and music on the remaining days. There is also a listener-response program on Saturday. After the feature there's a bulletin of news, and no matter what comes next, the broadcast always ends with *Let's Learn Chinese*. One hour to Southeast Asia on 7445 kHz.

Radio Australia. The first half-hour consists of world and Australian *news* followed by a sports bulletin. Then comes a feature. Choose from *Innovations* (Monday), *Arts Australia* (Tuesday), ●*Science File* (Wednesday), *Book Talk* (Thursday), *Talking Politics* (Friday), *Business Weekly* (Saturday) and *Australia Today* (Sunday). Continuous to Asia and the Pacific on several channels, and easily heard in most of North America on 9580 and 9860

Yuquis tribesman from the Amboró National Park near Radio Televisión Colonia in southern Bolivia. The fierce Yuquis recently almost killed a Roman Catholic priest who came out to evangelize among them.

Yrey Fausto Montaño Ustárez

kHz. Beamed to East and Southeast Asia on 9510 and 13605 kHz till 1130, and 9560, 9615 and 11660 kHz from then onwards. Audible in Europe and the Mideast on 21725 kHz.

HCJB—Voice of the Andes, Ecuador. Thirty minutes of religious programming to Australasia. Sunday through Friday it's *Songs in the Night*, replaced Saturday by *Afterglow*. On 5900 or 9445 kHz. For a separate service to the Americas, see the next item.

HCJB—Voice of the Andes, Ecuador. First 60 minutes of a four-hour block of religious programming to the Americas on 12005 and (from 1130) 15115 kHz.

Voice of America. The second, and final, hour of the morning broadcast to the Caribbean. *News*, followed Monday through Friday by *Stateside*, a look at issues and personalities in the United

States. Weekend fare consists of *Agriculture Today* and ●*Music USA-Standards* (Saturday), and *Critic's Choice* and *Studio One* (Sunday). On 6165, 7405 and 9590 kHz. For a separate service to Asia and Australasia, see the next item.

Voice of America. These programs are, in the main, different from those to the Caribbean. *News*, then Saturday it's *Agriculture Today* and ●*Press Conference USA*; Sunday there's ●*New Horizons* and ●*Issues in the News*; and weekdays have *Music USA*. To East Asia on 6110 (or 6160), 9760 and 15160 kHz, and to Australasia on 5985, 9645, 11720 and 15425 kHz.

Radio Jordan. Summers only at this time. A 60-minute partial relay of the station's domestic broadcasts, beamed to Europe and Eastern North America on 11970 kHz. One hour later in winter.

Voice of Russia World Service. Continuous programming to Asia and the Pacific. Starts with *News*, then Tuesday through Saturday winters, it's the informative ●*Commonwealth Update*, replaced Sunday and Monday by *Science and Engineering*. Summers at this time, there's *News and Views*, with the second half-hour mostly given over to a variety of musical styles, including the top-rated ●*Folk Box* (Tuesday and Wednesday) and ●*Music at Your Request* (Monday and Saturday). Winters at 1131, it's the literary ●*Audio Book Club* (Wednesday and Friday), the eclectic *Kaleidoscope* (Sunday and Monday), *Russian by Radio* (Tuesday and Thursday) or the musical *Timelines*. Winters to Southeast Asia on 12055, 13785, 15490, 17860 and 17890 kHz; summers on 15170, 15460, 15560, 17610, 17755 and 17860 kHz. Winter reception is also possible in parts of Australasia on 9450, 12005, 17860 and 17880 kHz; mid-year, try 9920 and 17560.

Voice of Vietnam. Repeat of the 1000

broadcast. A half hour to Asia on 7285 and 9730 kHz. Both frequencies vary somewhat.

Radio Singapore International. A three-hour package for Southeast Asia, and widely heard elsewhere. Starts with a summary of *news* and weather conditions in Asia and the Pacific, followed by a wide variety of short features, depending on the day of the week. These include Monday's eclectic *Frontiers*, Tuesday's *Kaleidoscope*, the literary *Bookmark* (Friday), and *Dateline RSI* (a listener-participation program, Sunday). At 1120 Monday through Friday, it's the *Business and Market Report*. There's *news* on the half-hour, then weekdays there's a brief press review, music, and either *Newsline* (1145 Monday, Wednesday and Friday) or *Business World* (same time, Tuesday and Thursday). Weekends, it's *The Week Ahead* (1133 Saturday and Sunday), *Regional Press Review* and *Newsline* (Saturday) or *The Sunday Interview*. On 6015 and 6155 kHz.

CBC North-Québec, Canada. Summers only at this time; see 1200 for specifics. Intended for a domestic audience, but also heard in the northeastern United States on 9625 kHz.

Swiss Radio International. Thirty minutes of *news* and background reports on world and Swiss events. Look for some lighter fare on Saturdays, when *Capital Letters* (a biweekly listener-response program) alternates with *Name Game* and *Sounds Good*. To Europe winters on 6165 and 9535 kHz, and year-round to East Asia and Australasia on 9885 and 11640 (winter), 13635 (all-year) and (summer) 15415 and 17515 kHz.

Radio Japan. On weekdays, opens with *Radio Japan News Round*, with news oriented to Japanese and Asian affairs. This is followed by *Radio Japan Magazine*

> World band covers just about any topic imaginable, but how about a program each Saturday in Latin? From Finland?

Hour, which includes features like *Sports Column* (Monday), *Japanese Culture* and *Today* (Tuesday), *Asian Report* (Wednesday), *Crosscurrents* (Thursday) and *Business Focus* (Friday). *Commentary* and *News* round off the hour. These are replaced Saturday by *This Week*, and Sunday by *Hello from Tokyo*. One hour to North America on 6120 kHz, and to East and Southeast Asia on 6090 (winter), 9610 (summer) and 15350 kHz.

Radio For Peace International, Costa Rica. Continues with a variety of counterculture and social-conscience features. There is also a listener-response program at 1130 Wednesday. To North and Central America on 6205 and 7385 kHz. Some transmissions are in the single-sideband mode, which can be properly processed only on some radios.

Radio Pyongyang, North Korea. One of the last of the old-time communist stations, with quaint terms like "Great Leader" and "Unrivaled Great Man" being the order of the day. Starts with "news", with much of the remainder of the broadcast devoted to revering the late Kim Il Sung. Abominably bad programs, but worth the occasional listen just to hear how awful they are. Fifty minutes to North America on 6575, 9975 and 11335 kHz.

WJCR, Upton, Kentucky. Continues with country gospel music to North America on 7490 kHz. Other U.S. religious broadcasters operating at this hour include **WWCR** on 5935 (or 15685) kHz, **KTBN** on 7510 kHz, **WYFR-Family Radio** on 5950 and 7355 (or 11830) kHz, and **WHRI-World Harvest Radio** on 6040 and 9495 kHz. Traditional Catholic programming (some of which may be in Spanish) can be found on **WEWN** on 7425 kHz.

11:30

YLE Radio Finland. *News*, followed by a melange of Finnish and other Scandi-navian general interest stories interspersed with Finnish music. Saturdays at 1053, look for a world band curiosity, *Nuntii Latini* (news in Latin). A half hour summers to North America on 11900 and 15400 kHz, and winters to Australasia on 15240 and 17825 kHz.

Radio Korea International, South Korea. Winters only at this time. See 1030 for program details. A half hour on 9650 kHz via their Canadian relay, so a good chance for North Americans to hear the station. One hour earlier in summer.

Radio Nederland. Repeat of the 0730 broadcast; see there for specifics. One hour to Western Europe on 6045 and (winter) 7130 or (summer) 9650 kHz.

Radio Austria International. Summers only at this time. ●*Report from Austria* (see 0730 for further details). Thirty minutes to Western Europe and Eastern North America on 13730 kHz.

Radio Prague, Czech Republic. Winters only at this time. Repeat of the 0700 transmission (see 0800 for specifics). A half hour to Europe on 7345 and 9505 kHz. One hour earlier in summer.

Radio Sweden. Summers only at this time; see 1230 for program details. To North America on 11650 and 15240 kHz.

Radio Bulgaria. Summers only at this time. *News*, then Monday through Thursday there's 15 minutes of current events in *Today*. This is replaced Friday by *Weekly Spotlight*, a summary of the week's major political events. The remainder of the broadcast is given over to features dealing with Bulgaria and its people, plus some lively folk music. Sixty minutes to East Asia on 13790 kHz. One hour later during winter.

Voice of the Islamic Republic of Iran. Sixty minutes of *news*, commentary and features, much of it reflecting the Islamic point of view. Targeted at the Mideast and South and Southeast Asia on 11745, 11790, 11875 (summer), 11930, 15260 and 11930 kHz.

12:00

■BBC World Service for the Americas.
World News, then it's 10 minutes of specialized business and financial reporting. Next come one or more features, the best of which are ●*John Peel* (1215 Tuesday), *The Vintage Chart Show* (same time Wednesday), ●*Assignment* (1215 Thursday) and Sunday's ●*Anything Goes.* ●*Sports Roundup* follows at 45 minutes past the hour, except for Saturday, when it is replaced by the final quarter-hour of the popular *A Jolly Good Show.* Continuous to North America and the Caribbean on 5965 (winter), 6195, 9515 (summer) and 15220 kHz. Weekdays, for the first 15 minutes, 6195 and 15220 kHz carry alternative programming for the Caribbean.

■BBC World Service for Europe (and the Mideast). *World News*, ●*World Business Report/Review/Brief* (easily the best program of its kind) and ●*Britain Today.* On the half-hour, look for ●*Andy Kershaw's World of Music* (Monday), light entertainment (Tuesday), *Composer of the Month* (Wednesday), ●*Assignment* (Thursday), ●*Science in Action* (Friday), ●*Brain of Britain* or its substitute (Saturday) and Sunday's ●*Anything Goes.* Topnotch programming to Europe on 9410, 12095, 15485 and 17640 kHz; and to the Mideast on 11760, 15575 and 17640 kHz.

■BBC World Service for Asia and the Pacific. Monday through Saturday, opens with *World News* and ●*World Business Report/Review.* Weekdays, these are followed by ●*Britain Today* ●*Off the Shelf* (readings of world literature) and ●*Sports Roundup*, replaced Saturday by ●*Science in Action* and Alistair Cooke's ●*Letter from America.* Sunday is given over to the second half of ●*Play of the Week* (followed by ●*Andy Kershaw's World of Music* if it ends by 1230). Continuous to East and Southeast Asia on 6195, 9740, 11955 and 15280 kHz; and to Australasia on 9740 kHz.

Monitor Radio International, USA. See 0000 for program details. Monday through Friday to Eastern North America on 6095 kHz, to Central and South America on 9455 kHz, to East Asia on 9355 kHz, and to Australasia on 9430 kHz. Weekends, the news-oriented fare gives way to religious programming.

Radio Canada International. Summer weekdays only. Tuesday through Saturday, it's a shortened version of the Canadian Broadcasting Corporation's domestic *news* program ●*As It Happens*, which is replaced Sunday by ●*Quirks and Quarks*, and Monday by *Double Exposure* and *Royal Canadian Air Farce*. Sixty minutes to North America and the Caribbean on 9640, 11855 and 13650 kHz. One hour later in winter.

Radio Tashkent, Uzbekistan. *News* and commentary, followed by features such as *Life in the Village* (Wednesday), a listeners' request program (Monday), and local music (Thursday). Heard better in Asia, Australasia and Europe than in North America. Thirty minutes winters on 5060, 5975, 6025 and 9715 kHz; and summers on 7285, 9715 and 15295 kHz.

■Radio France Internationale. The first 30 minutes consist of *news* and correspondents' reports, with a review of the French press rounding off the half-hour. The next 25 minutes are given over to a series of short features, including

Sunday's *Paris Promenade* and *Club 9516* (a listener-response program); the weekday *RFI Europe*; sports (Monday and Thursday); *Arts in France*, *Books* and *Science Probe* (Tuesday); *Bottom Line* (business and finance) and *Land of France* (Wednesday); the biweekly *North/ South* (or *Planet Earth*) and *The Americas* (Thursday); *Film Reel* and *Made in France* (Friday); and Saturday's *Focus on France*, *Spotlight on Africa* and *Counterpoint* (human rights) or *Echoes from Africa*. A fast-moving information-packed 55 minutes to Europe on 9805, 15155 and 15195 kHz; and to North America on 11615 (15530 in summer) and 13625 kHz. In Eastern North America, you can also try 15325 kHz, targeted at West Africa.

Polish Radio Warsaw, Poland. This time summers only. Fifty-five minutes of news, commentary, features and music—all with a Polish accent. Monday through Friday, it's *News from Poland*—a potpourri of news, reports and interviews. This is followed by *Jazz, Folk, Rock and Pop from Poland* (Monday), *Request Concert* and *A Day in the Life of...* (Tuesday), classical music and the historical *Flashback* (Wednesday), a communications feature and *Letter from Poland* (Thursday), and a Friday feature followed by *Business Week*. The Saturday broadcast begins with a bulletin of *news*, then there's *Weekend Papers* (a press review), *What We Said* (a summary of the station's output during the previous week) and an arts magazine, *Focus*. Sundays, you can hear *Weekend Commentary*, *Panorama* (a window on day-to-day life in Poland) and *Postbag*, a listener-response program. To Europe on 6095, 7145, 7270, 9525 and 11815 kHz. This last frequency can be heard weekends in the northeastern United States and southeastern Canada, when the broadcast is not subject to co-channel interference from the Radio Exterior de España relay in Costa Rica. One hour later in winter.

Radio Australia. *World News*, then a feature. These include the scientific *Ockham's Razor* (Saturday) and *Charting Australia* (Sunday and Wednesday). Weekdays on the half-hour, it's ●*International Report*, which is replaced Saturday by *Background Report*, and Sunday by *Report on Asia*. Not the most original of titles, but not much doubt about the content. Continuous to Asia and the Pacific, and well heard in North America on 5995 and 11800 kHz. In Southeast Asia, tune to 9560, 9615 and 11660 kHz.

Radio Jordan. Winters only at this time. A 60-minute partial relay of the station's domestic broadcasts, beamed to Europe and Eastern North America on 11970 (or 11940) kHz. One hour earlier in summer.

Croatian Radio. Summers only at this time; actually starts at 1203. Ten minutes of English *news* from one of the domestic networks. A valuable source of up-to-the-minute information from the region. Heard best in Europe at this hour, but also audible in Eastern North America. Channel usage varies, but try 5895, 5920, 7165, 7370, 9830 and 13830 kHz. One hour later in winter.

Swiss Radio International. Summers only at this time. Sixty minutes of *news*, background reports and features, and a simulcast of SRI's satellite programming. To Europe on 6165 and 9535 kHz. One hour later in winter.

Radio Korea International, South Korea. Opens with *news* and commentary, followed Monday through Wednesday by *Seoul Calling*. Weekly features include *Echoes of Korean Music* and *Shortwave Feedback* (Sunday), *Tales from Korea's Past* (Monday), *Korean Cultural Trails* (Tuesday), *Pulse of Korea* (Wednesday), *From Us to You* (a listener-response program) and *Let's Learn Korean* (Thursday), *Let's Sing Together* and *Korea Through Foreigners' Eyes* (Friday), and Saturday's *Discovering Korea, Korean Literary Corner*

VOA senior producer Brian Cislak moderates a panel discussion on international AIDS prevention. World band as a vehicle to educate Africans about AIDS was the spark behind the new BayGen Freeplay windup radio (p. 106).

Carmelo Ciancio/VOA

and *Weekly News Focus*. Sixty minutes to East Asia on 7285 kHz.

CBC North-Québec, Canada. Part of an 18-hour multilingual broadcast for a domestic audience, but which is also heard in the northeastern United States. Weekend programming at this hour is in English, and features *news* followed by the enjoyably eclectic ●*Good Morning Québec* (Saturday) or *Fresh Air* (Sunday). Starts at this time winters, but summers it is already into the second hour. On 9625 kHz.

HCJB—Voice of the Andes, Ecuador. Continuous religious programming to North America on 12005 and 15115 kHz. Monday through Friday, there's the live— and lively—*Morning in the Mountains*.

Radio Norway International. Summer Sundays only. *Norway Now*, a friendly 30-minute package of *news* and features aimed at Europe on 9590 kHz, and East Asia on 13800 and 15305 kHz.

Radio Singapore International. Continuous programming to Southeast Asia

and beyond. Starts with a brief summary of *news*, then the musical *E-Z Beat*. This is followed weekdays by the *Business and Market Report*, *news* on the half-hour, and then a feature. Monday, it's *Bookmark*, replaced Tuesday by *Reflections*, and Wednesday by *Frontiers*. Thursday brings *Snapshots*, and Friday has a listener-participation program, *Dateline RSI*. These are replaced Saturday by *Snapshots*, *Asean Notes* and *Arts Arena*, and Sunday by *Frontiers* and *Kaleidoscope*. On 6015 and 6155 kHz.

Voice of Free China, Taiwan. *News*, followed by features. The last is *Let's Learn Chinese*, which has a series of segments for beginning, intermediate and advanced learners. Other features include *Jade Bells and Bamboo Pipes* (Monday), *Kaleidoscope* and *Main Roads and Byways* (Tuesday), *Music Box* (Wednesday), *Perspectives* and *Journey into Chinese Culture* (Thursday), *Confrontation* and *New Record Time* (Friday), *Reflections* (Saturday) and *Adventures of*

Mahlon and Jeanie and *Mailbag Time* (Sunday). One hour to East Asia on 7130 kHz, and to Australasia on 9610 kHz.

Voice of America. *News*, followed Monday through Friday by *Stateside*. End-of-week programming consists of Saturday's *On the Line* and *Communications World*, and Sunday's ●*Encounter* and *Studio One*. To East Asia on 6110 (or 6160), 9760, 11715 and 15160 kHz; and to Australasia on 9645, 11715 and 15425 kHz.

China Radio International. *News* and a variety of features—see 0900 for specifics. One hour to Southeast Asia on 7410 (or 9565), 9715 and 11660 kHz; and to Australasia on 7385 and 11795 kHz.

Radio Nacional do Brasil (Radiobras), Brazil. Monday through Saturday, you can hear *Life in Brazil* or *Brazilian Panorama*, a potpourri of news, facts and figures about this fascinating land, interspersed with examples of the country's various unique musical styles. The *Sunday Special*, on the other hand, is devoted to one particular theme, and often contains lots of exotic Brazilian music. Eighty minutes to North America on 15445 kHz.

Voice of Russia World Service. Continuous programming to Asia at this hour. Winters, it's *News and Views*, then twenty-five minutes of entertainment. ●*Music at Your Request* (Monday and Saturday) and ●*Folk Box* (Tuesday and Wednesday) are undoubtedly the choice offerings. On the remaining days, look for *This is Russia* (Sunday), *Yours for the Asking* (Friday) and Thursday' *Jazz Show*. Tuesday through Saturday, summers, there's *Focus on Asia and the Pacific*, then ●*Moscow Yesterday and Today* (Wednesday and Friday), *This is Russia* (Tuesday and Thursday) or music. Pick of the weekend's programs is ●*Music and Musicians* at 1311 Sunday. Winters in Southeast Asia, try 13785, 17755 and 17860 kHz; best in summer are 15170, 15510, 17610, 17755 and 17775 kHz. There's not much for East

Asia during winter, but try 9800 kHz for summer.

WJCR, Upton, Kentucky. Continues with country gospel music to North America on 7490 kHz. Other U.S. religious broadcasters operating at this hour include **WWCR** on 5935 (or 13845) and 15685 kHz, **KTBN** on 7510 kHz, **WYFR-Family Radio** on 5950, 6015 (or 7355), 11830 and 11970 (or 17750) kHz, and **WHRI-World Harvest Radio** on 6040 and 9495 kHz. For traditional Catholic programming, tune **WEWN** on 7425 kHz.

12:15

Radio Cairo, Egypt. The start of a 75-minute package of news, religion, culture and entertainment, much of it devoted to Arab and Islamic themes. The initial quarter-hour consists of virtually anything, from quizzes to Islamic religious talks, then there's *news* and commentary, which in turn give way to political and cultural items. To Asia on 17595 kHz.

12:30

Radio Bangladesh. *News*, followed by Islamic and general interest features and pleasant Bengali music. Thirty minutes to Southeast Asia, also heard in Europe, on 7185 and 9548 kHz. Frequencies may be slightly variable.

Radio Canada International. *News*, followed Monday through Friday by *Spectrum* (topical events). Saturday features the environmental *Earth Watch*, and *The Mailbag* occupies the Sunday slot. Thirty minutes to East and Southeast Asia, winters on 6150 and 11730 kHz, and summers on 9660 and 15195 kHz.

Radio Nederland. Repeat of the 0830 broadcast (see there for specifics), except for the press review. Fifty-five minutes to Europe winters on 6045 and 7130 kHz.

YLE Radio Finland. See 1130 for

program specifics. Daily to North America winters on 11735 and 15400 kHz, and Monday through Saturday summers on 11900 and 15400 kHz.

Voice of Vietnam. Repeat of the 1000 transmission. A half hour to Asia on 9840 and 12020 (or 15010) kHz. Frequencies may vary slightly.

Radio Thailand. A new transmission, introduced during summer of 1996. Thirty minutes to Southeast Asia and Australasia on 9885 kHz.

Radio Ulaanbaatar, Mongolia. Repeat of the 0930 broadcast (see there for specifics). Thirty minutes to Australasia on 7530 (or 9745) and 12085 kHz. Frequencies may vary slightly. Occasionally heard in Eastern North America.

Voice of Turkey. This time summers only. Fifty minutes of *news*, features and Turkish music beamed to Europe on 9445 kHz, and to the Mideast and Southwest Asia on 9630 kHz. One hour later in winter.

Radio Sweden. Monday through Friday, it's *news* and features in *Sixty Degrees North*, concentrating heavily on Scandinavian topics. Monday's accent is on sports; Tuesday has electronic media news; Wednesday brings *Money Matters*; Thursday features ecology or science and technology; and Friday offers a review of the week's news. Saturday's slot is filled by *Spectrum* (arts) or *Sweden Today*, and Sunday fare consists of *In Touch with Stockholm* (a listener-response program) or the musical *Sounds Nordic*. A half hour to Asia and Australasia on 9830/9835 (winter), 13740 and 15240 kHz.

Radio Vlaanderen Internationaal, Belgium. Summer Sundays only at this time. *News, P.O. Box 26* (a listener-response program) and *Radio World*. Thirty minutes to Eastern North America on 13610 kHz, and to Southeast Asia on 15540 kHz. One hour earlier in summer.

Radio Bulgaria. See 1230 for specifics. Sixty minutes, winters only, to the Far East on 9445 or 9810 kHz (one hour earlier in

summer); and year-round to South and East Asia on (winter) 11605 or (summer) 15620 kHz.

Radio Korea International, South Korea. Starts off with *news*, followed Monday through Wednesday by *Economic News Briefs*. The remainder of the broadcast is taken up by a feature: *Shortwave Feedback* (Sunday), *Seoul Calling* (Monday and Tuesday), *Pulse of Korea* (Wednesday), *From Us to You* (Thursday), *Let's Sing Together* (Friday) and *Weekly News Focus* (Saturday). Thirty minutes to East and Southeast Asia on 9570, 9640 and 13670 kHz.

Voice of Greece. Summers only at this time, and actually starts around 1235. Several minutes of English news surrounded by a lengthy period of Greek music and programming. To North America on 15175 and 15650 kHz. One hour later during winter.

13:00

■**BBC World Service for the Americas.** ●*Newshour*—the *crème de la crème* of all news shows. Sixty minutes to North America and the Caribbean on 6195, 9515, 9590 (winter), 11865 (summer) and 15220 kHz.

■**BBC World Service for Europe (and the Mideast).** Same as for the Americas. Sixty minutes of quality news reporting to Europe on 9410, 12095, 15485 and 17640 KHz; and to the Mideast on 11760, 15575 and 17640 kHz.

■**BBC World Service for Asia and the Pacific.** Same as for Europe and the Americas. Broadcast worldwide at this hour, it's too good to miss. Continuous to East Asia on 6195, 9740, 11955 and 15280 kHz; and to Australasia on 9740 kHz.

Monitor Radio International, USA. See 0000 for program details. Monday through Friday to North America on 6095 and 9455 kHz, to South Asia on 9355 kHz, and to East Asia on 9385 kHz. Weekends are given over to religious offerings from and about the Christian Science Church.

Radio Canada International. Tuesday through Friday winters, it's a shortened version of the Canadian Broadcasting Corporation's domestic *news* program ●*As It Happens*. This is replaced Sunday by ●*Quirks and Quarks*, and Monday by *Double Exposure* and *The Mailbag*. For summer, it's the weekdays-only *Best of Morningside*. Sixty minutes to North America and the Caribbean on 9640, 11855 and (summer) 13650 kHz. For an additional service, see the next item.

Radio Canada International. Summers only at this time; see 1400 for program details. Sunday only to North America and the Caribbean on 11855 and 13650 kHz.

Radio Pyongyang, North Korea. Repeat of the 1100 transmission. Fifty minutes to Europe on 9345 and 11740 kHz, to North America on 13760 and 15230 kHz, and to South and Southeast Asia on 9640 and 15230 kHz.

> BBC's *Newshour* is the *crème de la crème* of news programs—on radio or television. This one show alone justifies the cost of a world band radio. Daily, except when preempted occasionally on Saturdays for live sports.

Swiss Radio International. Repeat of the 1100 broadcast. *Newsnet*—a workmanlike compilation of news and background reports on world and Swiss events. Somewhat lighter fare on Saturday, when the biweekly *Capital Letters* (a listener-response program) alternates with *Name Game* and *Sounds Good*. Look for an additional 30-minute feature to Europe, which is a simulcast of SRI's satellite programming. A full hour winters to Europe on 6165 and 9535 kHz, and 30 minutes year-round to East and Southeast Asia on 7230, 7480, 11640 (winter), 13635 and (summer) 15480 kHz.

Radio Norway International. Sundays only. *Norway Now*. A friendly half hour of *news* and human-interest stories,

winters to Europe on 9590 kHz, to East Asia on 7315 (or 11850) kHz, and to Southeast Asia and Western Australia on 15605 kHz; in summer, the broadcast is aimed at Eastern North America on 15340 kHz, and at Southeast Asia and Western Australia on 13800 kHz.

Radio Nacional do Brasil (Radiobras), Brazil. The final 20 minutes of the broadcast beamed to North America on 15445 kHz.

Radio Vlaanderen Internationaal, Belgium. Monday through Saturday, summers only at this time. Repeat of the 0900 broadcast; see there for program details. Thirty minutes to Eastern North America on 13610 kHz, and to Southeast Asia on 15540 kHz. One hour later in winter.

China Radio International. See 0900 for specifics. One hour to Western North America summers on 7405 kHz; and year-round to Southeast Asia on 7410 (or 9565), 9715 and 11660 kHz; and to Australasia on 7385 kHz.

Polish Radio Warsaw, Poland. This time winters only. *News*, commentary, music and a variety of features. See 1200 for specifics. Fifty-five minutes to Europe on 6095, 7145, 7270, 9525 and 11815 kHz. Listeners in southeastern Canada and the northeastern United States can also try 11815 kHz, especially weekends, when co-channel Radio Exterior de España is off the air. One hour earlier during summer.

Radio Prague, Czech Republic. Summers only at this time. *News*, then Monday through Friday there's *Current Affairs*. These are followed by one or more features. Monday has *Magazine '96*; Tuesday, it's *Talking Point* and *What's Up?*; Wednesday has *From the Archives* and *The Arts*; Thursday brings *Economic Report* and *I'd Like You to Meet...*; and Friday there's *Between You and Us*.

Saturday's offerings include a musical feature, replaced Sunday by *The Week in Politics*, *From the Weeklies* and *What's Up?* Thirty minutes to Western Europe (also audible in easternmost parts of North America) on 11660 kHz, and to East Africa and beyond on 17485 kHz. One hour later in winter.

Radio Cairo, Egypt. The final half-hour of the 1215 broadcast, consisting of listener participation programs, Arabic language lessons and a summary of the latest news. To Asia on 17595 kHz.

CBC North-Québec, Canada. Continues with multilingual programming for a domestic audience. *News*, then winter Saturdays it's the second hour of ●*Good Morning Québec*, replaced Sunday by *Fresh Air*. In summer, the news is followed by *The House* (Canadian politics, Saturday) or the highly professional ●*Sunday Morning*. Weekday programs are mainly in languages other than English. Audible in the northeastern United States on 9625 kHz.

Radio Romania International. First afternoon broadcast for European listeners. *News*, commentary, press review, and features about Romanian life and culture, interspersed with some lively Romanian folk music. Fifty-five minutes winters on 11940, 15390 and 17745 kHz; summers on 9690, 11940, 15365 and 17720 kHz.

Croatian Radio. Winters only at this time; actually starts at 1303. Ten minutes of on-the-spot *news* from Croatian Radio's Zagreb studio. Best heard in Europe at this hour, but also audible in Eastern North America. Frequency usage varies, but try 5895, 5920, 7165, 7370, 9830, 11635 and 13830 kHz. One hour earlier during summer.

Radio Australia. *World News*, then Monday through Friday it's *Asia Focus*, replaced Saturday by *Business Weekly*, and Sunday by *Oz Sounds*. On the half-hour, choose from *The Europeans* (Sunday), *The Australian Music Show* (Monday), *Jazz Notes* (Tuesday), ●*Blacktracker* (Wednesday), *Australian Country Style* (Thursday), and Friday's ●*Music Deli*. Continuous to Asia and the Pacific on a number of frequencies, and tends to be easily audible in much of North America on 5995, 9580 and 11800 kHz. Available to Southeast Asia on 9560 and 9615 kHz.

Radio Singapore International. The third and final hour of a daily broadcasting package to Southeast Asia and beyond. Starts with a summary of the latest *news*, then it's pop music. On the half-hour, there's a 10-minute *news* bulletin (replaced by a short summary at weekends), followed by *Newsline* (Monday, Wednesday and Friday), *Business World* (Tuesday and Thursday), *Regional Press Review* (Saturday), or *The Sunday Interview*. On 6015 and 6155 kHz.

> *Audio Book Club* combines literary readings with dramatic interludes and creative sound effects. The result is a show H.G. Wells might have done had he been Russian. Monday and Saturday over the Voice of Russia.

WJCR, Upton, Kentucky. Continues with country gospel music to North America on 7490 kHz. Other U.S. religious broadcasters operating at this hour include **WWCR** on 5935 (or 13845) and 15685 kHz, **KTBN** 7510 kHz, **WYFR-Family Radio** on 5950, 6015 (or 9705), 11830 and 11970 (or 17750) kHz, and **WHRI-World Harvest Radio** on 6040 and 15105 kHz. Traditional Catholic programming is available via **WEWN** on 7425 kHz.

Voice of Russia World Service. Continues to much of southern Asia. *News*, then very much a mixed bag depending on the day and season. Winter programming includes *Focus on Asia and the Pacific* (Tuesday through Saturday) and Sunday's ●*Music and Musicians*, both of which start at 1311. During the second half-hour, look for the retrospective ●*Moscow Yesterday and Today* (Wednesday and Friday), *This is Russia* (Tuesday and Thursday), and *Russian by Radio* on Monday. At the same time summer, there's the business feature *Newmarket* (Tuesday), *Science and Engineering* (Sunday), and a listener-response program on most of the other days. ●*Audio Book Club* (Monday and Saturday) is the obvious choice from 1330 onwards, and alternates with *Kaleidoscope* (Tuesday and Thursday), *Russian by Radio* (Wednesday and Friday) or a music program. Winters in Southeast Asia, try 12055 and 15470 kHz; best for summer are 15460, 15560, 17610 and 17755 kHz.

HCJB—Voice of the Andes, Ecuador. Sixty minutes of religious broadcasting. Look for the live *Morning in the Mountains* at 1330 weekends. Continuous to the Americas on 12005 and 15115 kHz.

FEBC Radio International, Philippines. The first 60 minutes of a three-hour (mostly religious) package to South and Southeast Asia. Weekdays, starts with *Good Evening Asia*, which includes *News Insight* and a number of five-minute features (worldband enthusiasts should look for Wednesday's *DX Dial*). Other offerings include *World News Update* (1330 Monday through Saturday) and *News from the Philippines* (1335 weekdays). Most of the remaining features are religious in nature. On 11995 kHz.

Voice of America. *News,* followed most days by features for students of English. One notable exception is *Critic's Choice* at 1310 Sunday. To East Asia on 6110 (or 6160), 9760 and 15160 kHz; and to Australasia on 9645 and 15425 kHz. Both areas are also served by 11715 kHz until 1330.

13:30

United Arab Emirates Radio, Dubai. *News,* then a feature devoted to Arab and Islamic history and culture. Twenty-five minutes to Europe (also audible in Eastern North America) on 13675, 15395, 17825 (or 17630) and 21605 kHz.

Radio Austria International. Summers only at this time. ●*Report from Austria* (see 0730 for more details). A half hour to Europe on 6155 and 13730 kHz.

Radio Vlaanderen Internationaal, Belgium. Winter Sundays only at this time. *News, P.O. Box 26* (a listener-response program) and *Radio World*. Thirty minutes to Eastern North America on 13670 kHz. One hour later in winter. May also be available to Southeast Asia—try 15540 kHz or nearby.

Voice of Turkey. This time winters only. *News,* followed by *Review of the Turkish Press* and features (some of them arcane) with a strong local flavor. Selections of Turkish popular and classical music complete the program. Fifty minutes to Europe on 9445 kHz, and to the Mideast and Southwest Asia on 9630 kHz. One hour earlier in summer.

YLE Radio Finland. Winters only at this time. Repeat of the 1230 broadcast; see 1130 for program specifics. A half hour Monday through Saturday to North America on 11735 and 15400 kHz. One hour earlier in summer.

Radio Canada International. *News,* followed Monday through Friday by *Spectrum* (topical events), Saturday by *Innovation Canada*, and Sunday by a listener-response program. To East Asia on 6150 (winter), 11795 (summer) and 9535 kHz. Also to Europe, the Mideast and Africa, summers only, on 11935, 15325, 17820 and 21455 kHz. The frequency of 17820 kHz is not available on Sundays.

RDP International—Radio Portugal. Monday through Friday, summers only, at this time. See 1900 for program details. Thirty minutes to the Mideast and South Asia on 21515 kHz. One hour later during winter.

●*Discovery* (science, 1530 Tuesday) and *The Farming World* and the youth-oriented ●*Megamix* (Thursday). Other options include Friday's *Write On* and ●*Concert Hall* (or its substitute), Saturday's *Sportsworld* and Sunday's *From Our Own Correspondent*. Continuous to North America on 9515, 9590 (winter), 11865 (summer), 15220 (or 15260) and 17840 kHz.

■**BBC World Service for Europe (and the Mideast).** Sunday through Friday, the first half-hour consists of *World News* and ●*Sports Roundup* followed by a feature for students of English. The next 30 minutes feature some good BBC output, including *From Our Own Correspondent* (Sunday), ●*Omnibus* (Monday), ●*The Learning World* (Tuesday) and ●*Network UK* (Thursday). Saturday airs five minutes of *news* followed by *Sportsworld*. Continuous to Europe on 6195 (winter), 9410, 12095 and 15485 kHz; and to the Mideast on 9410 (winter) and 12095 kHz.

■**BBC World Service for South Asia.** *World News*, then weekdays it's ●*Sports Roundup*. A mixed bag of features follow on the quarter-hour. Weekends, there's Saturday's live *Sportsworld*, and Sunday's excellent ●*Play of the Week*. On 5975 and 11750 kHz. Part of an 18-hour continuous block of programming, and a valid alternative for parts of Western North America on 11750 kHz.

■**BBC World Service for Asia and the Pacific.** Monday through Friday, it's a quarter-hour of *East Asia Today* followed by 45 minutes of programming for students of English. Weekends, there's Saturday's *Sportsworld*, replaced Sunday by ●*Sports Roundup* and the best of classical music in ●*Concert Hall* or its substitute. Be warned—the music is sometimes preempted by live sports. Continuous to East and Southeast Asia on 6195 and 9740

> If you have an enhanced-fidelity receiver, tune in Sundays to the BBC's *Concert Hall* for some of the best in classical music.

kHz; and to Australasia on 9740 kHz. Also audible in Western North America on 9740 kHz.

Monitor Radio International, USA. See 0000 for program details. Monday through Friday to East Asia on 9355 kHz, and Southeast Asia on 12160 kHz. Weekends are devoted to the beliefs and teachings of the Christian Science Church.

China Radio International. See 0900 for program details. One hour to Western North America winters on 7405 kHz. One hour earlier during summer.

Radio Australia. *World News*, followed Monday through Friday by *Asia Focus*, and weekends by *Oz Sounds*. On the half-hour, except Sunday (when *Fine Music Australia* is aired), there is a repeat of the 1130 features (see 1100 for specifics). Continuous to Asia and the Pacific, and also audible in Western North America on 5995, 6060, 9580, 11800 and 12080 kHz. To Southeast Asia on 11660 kHz and (from 1530) 6090/7260 and 9615 kHz. For East Asia, try 6080 kHz at 1530-1630. Also audible in Europe on 11660 kHz.

Radio Pyongyang, North Korea. See 1100 for program details. Fifty minutes to Europe, the Mideast and beyond on 9325, 9640, 9975 and 13785 kHz.

Voice of America. Continues with programming to the Mideast. *News*, then Monday through Friday there's *Newsline*. Best of the weekend offerings is the Sunday science program ●*New Horizons*. On the half-hour, it's *Music USA* (weekdays), *Press Conference USA* (Saturday) and *Studio One* (Sunday). Winters on 9575 and 15205 kHz, and summers on 9700, 15205 and 15255 kHz. Also heard in much of Europe.

Kol Israel. Winters only at this time. A 30-minute relay from Israel Radio's domestic network. To Europe and Eastern

North America on 9390 and 11685 kHz. One hour earlier in summer.

Radio Norway International. Winter Sundays only. *Norway Now.* News and features from and about Norway. A pleasant thirty minutes to the Mideast on 9520 and 11730 kHz.

Channel Africa, South Africa. *News,* then features. These include *Yours and Mine* (Monday, Tuesday, Thursday and Friday), *Actuality* (Tuesday), *Face to Face* (Wednesday), *SA This Week* (Thursday), *Network Africa* (Friday) and Saturday's *Yours for the Asking.* The Sunday lineup consists of *Religions of the World, All That Jazz* and *Miscellany.* The first of three hours to East, Central and Southern Africa on 3220 (or 9530) and 7155 kHz.

Radio Canada International. Continuation of the CBC domestic program ●*Sunday Morning.* Sunday only to North America and the Caribbean on 9640 (winter), 11855 and (summer) 13650 kHz.

Radio Japan. *News,* then weekdays there's 10 minutes of *Asian Top News* followed by a half-hour feature. Take your pick from *Profile* (Monday), *Enjoy Japanese* (Tuesday, repeated Thursday), *Town and Around* (Wednesday) and Friday's *Music and Book Beat.* Weekends, look for *Asia Weekly* (Saturday) or Sunday's *Hello from Tokyo.* The broadcasts end with the daily *Pop-in* (Sunday excepted) and a summary of *news.* To Western North America on 9535 kHz; to Southern Africa on 15355 kHz; and to South and Southeast Asia winters on 7240 and 9695 kHz, and summers on 11880/11930 and 11915 kHz.

Voice of Russia World Service. Predominantly news-related fare for the first half-hour, then a mixed bag, depending on the day and season. At 1531 winter, look for ●*Folk Box* (Monday), *Jazz Show* (Wednesday), *Yours for the Asking* (Tuesday and Thursday), ●*Music at Your Request* (Friday) and the eclectic *Kaleidoscope* (Sunday). Summers at this time,

This is Russia (Monday, Wednesday and Friday) alternates with the interesting ●*Moscow Yesterday and Today.* Continuous to the Mideast winters on 4740, 4940, 4975, 7130, 7165, 9635, 11765, 11945 and 12065 kHz; and summers on 4740, 4940, 4975, 9675, 11835, 11910, 11945, 12035, 15320, 15350, 15540, 15560 and 17750 kHz. In East and Southern Africa, best winter bets are 7325, 9470 and 11945 kHz; for summer, choose from 9365, 9975, 11775, 11945, 12025 and 15560 kHz. Also audible in Northern Europe at this hour. Try 7115 kHz in winter, and 9880 kHz in summer.

Radio Ulaanbaatar, Mongolia. *News,* reports and short features, with Sunday featuring lots of exotic local music. Jazz enthusiasts might recognize *Seven Steppes to Dzavhan,* though the modern version is miles away from the original. Thirty minutes to South and Southeast Asia on 7530 (winter), 9740 (summer) and 12085 kHz. Frequencies may vary slightly.

FEBC Radio International, Philippines. The final 60 minutes of a three-hour (mostly religious) broadcast to South and Southeast Asia. For secular programming, try the five-minute *World News Update* at 1530 Monday through Saturday, and a listener-response feature at 1540 Saturday. On 11995 kHz, and often heard outside the target area.

WJCR, Upton, Kentucky. Continues with country gospel music to North America on 7490 and 13595 kHz. Other U.S. religious broadcasters operating at this hour include **WWCR** on 13845 and 15685 kHz, **KTBN** on 7510 (or 15590) kHz, and **WYFR-Family Radio** on 11830 and (winter) 15215 kHz. Traditional Catholic programming is available from **WEWN** on 7425 kHz.

Radio Jordan. A partial relay of the station's domestic broadcasts, beamed to Europe on 11970 kHz. Continuous till 1730, and one hour earlier in summer.

CFRX-CFRB, Toronto, Canada. See 1400.

Radio Nederland. A repeat of the 1330 broadcast; see 0730 for program specifics. Fifty-five minutes to South Asia and beyond on 9890/9895 and 15150 kHz.

Radio Austria International. Winters only at this time. ●*Report from Austria*, a half hour of news and human interest stories. Ample coverage of national and regional issues, and a valuable source of news about Central and Eastern Europe. To South and Southeast Asia on 11780 kHz.

Voice of the Islamic Republic of Iran. Sixty minutes of *news*, commentary and features, most of it reflecting the Islamic point of view. To South and Southeast Asia (and also heard elsewhere) on 9575 (winter), 11790 (winter), 11875 (summer), 15260 and 17750 kHz.

■BBC World Service for the Americas. *World News*, then it's predominantly arts or sports. *Meridian* (an arts magazine) is aired Monday, Tuesday, Wednesday and Friday. Sports fans come into their own on Saturday (*Sportsworld*) and Thursday (*Sports International*). On Sunday, it's a documentary or general feature. The hour is rounded off with the 15-minute ●*Britain Today*. Continuous to North America on 9515 and 17840 kHz.

■BBC World Service for Europe (and the Mideast). Sunday through Friday summer, it's ●*Europe Today*, replaced winter by *World News* and ●*The World Today* (except Sunday). Weekdays on the half-hour, there's ●*World Business Report*, which is followed 15 minutes later by ●*Britain Today*. Saturday brings the action-packed *Sportsworld*, while summer Sundays are given over to the first part of ●*Play of the Week*. Continuous to Europe on 6195 (winter), 9410, 12095 and 15485 kHz; and to the Mideast on 9410 and 12095 kHz.

■BBC World Service for Asia and the Pacific. *World News*, then weekdays it's mostly a series of shows (mainly rock or popular music) geared to a youthful audience. *Multitrack* airs on Monday, Wednesday and Friday, ●*Megamix* on Tuesday, and *Sports International* on Thursday. Weekend fare consists of Saturday's *Sportsworld* and Sunday's *In Praise of God* and ●*Short Story* (replaced once a month by *Seeing Stars*). Continuous to East and Southeast Asia on 3915, 6195, 7180 and 9740 kHz; and to Australasia (till 1615) on 9740 kHz.

Monitor Radio International, USA. A one-hour show updated throughout the day and broadcast to different parts of the globe. *News*, then ●*Monitor Radio*—news analysis and news-related features with emphasis on international developments. The final 10 minutes consist of a listener-response program and a religious article from the *Christian Science Monitor* newspaper. Available Monday through Friday to Africa and beyond on 9355 and 18930 (or 17510) kHz. Weekends, this news programming is replaced by religious offerings from and about the Christian Science Church, not necessarily all in English.

■Radio France Internationale. *News*, press reviews and correspondents' reports, with particular attention paid to events in Africa. These are followed by two or more short features (basically a repeat of the 1200 broadcast, except for weekends when there is more emphasis on African themes). A fast-moving fifty-five minutes to Africa on 11615, 11700, 12015, 15460 and 15530 kHz. Also heard on 9485 and 15210 kHz on a seasonal basis. Available in Europe on 6175 kHz, and in parts of the Mideast on 11615 and 15460 kHz (9485 kHz may replace either or both of these channels in winter). Some of these frequencies are also audible, to a varying degree, in Eastern North America. Best bet is 11700 kHz.

United Arab Emirates Radio, Dubai. Starts with a feature on Arab history or culture, then music, and a bulletin of *news* at 1630. Answers listeners' letters at weekends. Forty minutes to Europe (also heard in Eastern North America) on 13675, 15395, 17630 (or 17825) and 21605 kHz.

■**Deutsche Welle,** Germany. *News,* followed Monday through Friday by ●*Newsline Cologne* and a feature: *Science and Technology* (Monday), ●*Man and Environment* (Tuesday), ●*Insight* (Wednesday), *Living in Germany* (Thursday) and *Spotlight on Sport* (Friday). Weekends, the Saturday news is followed by *Africa in the German Press, Focus on Development* (or *Women on the Move*), *Economic Notebook* and *Jazz;* and Sunday

it's *Germany This Week, Religion and Society, Through German Eyes* and *Hits in Germany.* Sixty minutes aimed primarily at Africa, but also audible in the Mideast. Winters on 7195, 9735, 11965, 13610 and 15145 kHz; and summers on 6170, 7225, 9875 and 13690 kHz.

Radio Korea International, South Korea. Opens with *news* and commentary, followed Monday through Wednesday by *Seoul Calling.* Weekly features include *Echoes of Korean Music* and *Shortwave Feedback* (Sunday), *Tales from Korea's Past* (Monday), *Korean Cultural Trails* (Tuesday), *Pulse of Korea* (Wednesday), *From Us to You* (a listener-response program) and *Let's Learn Korean* (Thursday), *Let's Sing Together* and *Korea Through Foreigners' Eyes* (Friday), and Saturday's *Discovering Korea, Korean Literary Corner*

WVHA, transmitting from Olamon, Maine, has gone to some length to counter a 1995 newspaper article which suggested it had been stockpiling for security purposes. Rather, say WVHA officials, the station lays aside food for distribution to over 100 nearby needy families. Shown: (left, standing) Patricia Edwards, Treasurer; Kathleen Greenfield, Chairman; Alan Scott, Director; Dianne Osbourne, President; and, seated, Pastor John Osbourne. *[Prophecy Countdown]*

and *Weekly News Focus*. One hour to East Asia on 5975 kHz, and to the Mideast and much of Africa on 9515 and 9870 kHz.

Radio Norway International. Summer Sundays only. *Norway Now.* A half hour of *news* and human-interest stories targeted at Western North America on 11840 kHz, East Africa on 13805 kHz, and South Asia and beyond on 11860 kHz.

Radio Pakistan. Fifteen minutes of *news* from the Pakistan Broadcasting Corporation's domestic service, followed by a similar period at dictation speed. Intended for the Mideast and Africa, but heard well beyond on several channels. Choose from 9485, 9515, 9785, 11570, 11745, 11935, 13590 and 15555 kHz.

Radio Prague, Czech Republic. Summers only at this time. *News*, reports and features with a distinctly Czech slant, including *Magazine '96* (Monday), *Talking Point* (Tuesday), *From the Archives* and *The Arts* (Wednesday), *Economic Report* and *I'd Like You to Meet...* (Thursday), *Between You and Us* (Friday), and a musical feature on Saturday. A half hour to Europe on 5930 kHz, and to East Africa and the Mideast on 17485 kHz. One hour later in winter.

Channel Africa, South Africa. *News*, then features. Try *Newswatch* (Monday through Wednesday); *Today's Dreams Tomorrow*, *Realities* and *Profile* (Saturday); and *Short Story*, *Africa Live* and *Health Forum* on Sunday. Continuous programming to East, Central and Southern Africa on 3220 (or 9530) and 7155 kHz; and 55 minutes to West Africa winters on 15240 kHz, and summers on 9530 kHz. Sometimes audible in parts of Europe and Eastern North America.

Voice of Vietnam. Repeat of the 1000 transmission. A half hour to Africa (and heard well beyond) on 9840 and 12020 (or 15010) kHz.

Radio Australia. *World News*, then Monday through Friday it's *Australia Today*, replaced Saturday by *Asia Focus*, and Sunday by *Business Weekly*. Weekdays on the half-hour there's ●*International Report*, replaced weekends by *Background Report* (Saturday), and *Report from Asia* (Sunday). Continuous to Asia and the Pacific on a number of frequencies, and also audible in Western North America on 5995, 6060, 9580, 11800 and 12080 kHz. In Southeast Asia, tune to 9615 and 11660 kHz. This last frequency is also audible in Europe.

Radio Ethiopia. An hour-long broadcast divided into two parts by the 1630 *news* bulletin. Regular weekday features include *Kaleidoscope* and *Women's Forum* (Monday), *Press Review* and *Africa in Focus* (Tuesday), *Guest of the Week* and *Ethiopia Today* (Wednesday), *Ethiopian Music* and *Spotlight* (Thursday) and *Press Review* and *Introducing Ethiopia* on Friday. For weekend listening, try *Contact* and *Ethiopia This Week* (Saturday), or Sunday's *Listeners' Choice* and *Commentary*. Best heard in parts of Africa and the Mideast, but sometimes audible in Europe. On 7165, 9560 and 11800 kHz.

Radio Jordan. A partial relay of the station's domestic broadcasts, beamed to Europe on 11970 kHz. Continuous till 1730 (1630 during winter).

Voice of Russia World Service. *News*, then very much a mixed bag, depending on the day and season. Winters, there's *Focus on Asia and the Pacific* (Tuesday through Saturday) and *Mailbag* (Monday), followed on the half-hour by *This is Russia* (Monday, Wednesday and Friday) or ●*Moscow Yesterday and Today* on the remaining days. Pick of the summer programming is ●*Music and Musicians* (1611 Saturday). Other options (all at 1611) include *Science and Engineering* (Tuesday and Wednesday), *Mailbag* (Thursday and Sunday) and the business-oriented *Newmarket* (Monday and Friday). Continuous to the Mideast winters on 4740, 4940, 4975, 6175, 7210, 7275, 9635 and 11945 kHz; and summers on 9635,

9675, 11945 and 15350 kHz. For East and Southern Africa, try 7210, 7275, 7325, 9470, 9505 and 11865 kHz in winter; and 9365, 9675, 9975, 11775, 11945, 12025 and 15350 kHz in summer. Also available to Europe, winters on 7115, 7180 and 7330 kHz; and summers on 7240, 7290, 7350, 9880, 11630 and 11675 kHz.

Radio Canada International. Winters only. Final hour of CBC's ●*Sunday Morning.* Sunday only to North America and the Caribbean on 9640 and 11855 kHz.

"Rush Limbaugh Show," WRNO, New Orleans, Louisiana. Summer weekdays only at this time. The first sixty minutes of a three-hour live package. Arguably of little interest to most listeners outside North America, but popular and controversial within the United States. To North America and Caribbean on 7355 (or 15420) kHz.

China Radio International. *News* and commentary, followed Tuesday through Friday by *Current Affairs.* These are followed by various feature programs, such as *Cultural Spectrum* (Thursday); *Listeners' Letterbox* (Sunday and Tuesday); *China Scrapbook, Cooking Show, Travel Talk* and ●*Music from China* (Saturday); *Sports Beat* and *Music Album* (Sunday); *Learn to Speak Chinese* (Monday and Wednesday); and Friday's *In the Third World.* Sundays, there is also a biweekly *Business Show* which alternates with *China's Open Windows.* One hour to East and Southern Africa on 11575, 15110 and 15130 kHz.

Voice of America. Several hours of continuous programming aimed at an African audience. Monday through Friday, starts with *news* and features for listeners who use English as a second language. Followed on the half-hour by *Africa World Tonight.* Weekends, it's a full hour of *Nightline Africa*—special news and features on African affairs. Heard well beyond the target area—including North America—on a number of frequencies.

Try 6035, 11880, 13710, 15225, 15225, 15410, 15445 and 17895 kHz, some of which are seasonal. For a separate service to the Mideast, see the next item.

Voice of America. *News,* followed most days by features in "Special" (slow-speed) English. Mainstream VOA programming is heard at 1610 weekends, in Saturday's *On the Line* and Sunday's ●*Encounter.* To the Mideast winters on 9575 and 15205 kHz, and summers on 9700, 15205 and 15255 kHz. Also heard in much of Europe.

WJCR, Upton, Kentucky. Continues with country gospel music to North America on 7490 and 13595 kHz. Other U.S. religious broadcasters operating at this hour include **WWCR** on 13845 and 15685 kHz, **KTBN** on 15590 kHz, and **WYFR-Family Radio** on 11705 (or 15215) and 11830 kHz. Traditional Catholic programming can be heard via **WEWN** on 7425 kHz.

CFRX-CFRB, Toronto, Canada. See 1400.

16:15

Radio Tirana, Albania. Summers only at this time. Approximately 10 minutes of *news* and commentary from and about Albania. To Europe on 7155 and 9740 kHz. One hour later during winter.

16:30

Radio Slovakia International. Summers only at this time; see 1830 for specifics. Thirty minutes of friendly programming to Western Europe on 5915, 6055 and 7345 kHz. One hour later in winter.

Radio Canada International. *News,* then Monday through Friday it's *Spectrum* (current events). *Innovation Canada* airs on Saturday, and a listener-response program occupies Sunday's slot. A half hour to Asia on 7150 and 9550 kHz.

Radio Austria International. Winters only at this time; an informative half-hour of ●*Report from Austria*. To South and Southeast Asia on 11780 kHz.

Radio Cairo, Egypt. The first 30 minutes of a two-hour package of Arab music and features reflecting Egyptian life and culture, with *news* and commentary about events in Egypt and the Arab world. There are also quizzes, mailbag shows, and answers to listeners' questions. Mediocre audio quality often spoils what otherwise could be an interesting broadcast. To southern Africa on 15255 kHz.

Radio Almaty, Kazakhstan. Summers only at this time. See 1730 for further details. Thirty minutes to Asia on 4820, 5970 and 9505 kHz. One hour later during winter.

17:00

■**BBC World Service for the Americas.** *World News*, followed by ten informative minutes of specialized business and financial reporting. Then there's a variety of features, depending on the day of the week. Fans of classical music can try Sunday's *Record News* or Monday's *Composer of the Month*. Best of the remainder are Wednesday's ●*Brain of Britain* (or its substitute), Thursday's secular and wide-ranging ●*Focus on Faith*, Friday's *The Vintage Chart Show*, and Saturday's swinger, ●*Jazz for the Asking*. To North America on 17840 kHz.

■**BBC World Service for Europe (and the Mideast).** Sunday through Friday winter, it's ●*Europe Today*, replaced summer by *World News* and ●*The World Today* (except Sunday). Weekdays on the half-hour, look for one or more short features—best are Wednesday's ●*Health Matters* and Thursday's *From Our Own Correspondent*. Most days, the hour is rounded off with the informative ●*Sports Roundup*. Also worth a listen is ●*Weekend*, at 1701 Saturday. Continuous to Europe on 3955 (winters), 6180, 6195, 9410, 12095

and 15485 kHz; and to the Mideast on 9410 and 12095 kHz. Some of these channels are also heard in Eastern North America.

■**BBC World Service for Africa.** *World News*, *Focus on Africa*, *African News* and ●*Sports Roundup*. Part of a 20-hour daily service to the African continent on a variety of channels, including 6190, 15400 and 17830 kHz. The last two channels are widely heard outside Africa, including parts of North America.

Monitor Radio International, USA. See 1600 for program details. Available Monday through Friday to Africa and beyond on 9355 and 18930 (or 17510) kHz. Weekend programming at this and other times is of a religious nature, and may be in languages other than English.

Radio Pakistan. Opens with 15 minutes of *news* and commentary. The remainder of the broadcast is taken up by a repeat of the features from the 0800 transmission (see there for specifics). Fifty minutes to Europe on 5825 and 11570 kHz.

Radio Prague, Czech Republic. See 1600 for specifics. A half hour of *news* and features beamed to Europe, winters on 5930 kHz and summers on 5835 kHz; also winters to the Mideast on 9430 kHz, and summers to central and southern Africa on 15640 kHz.

Radio Australia. Begins with world and Australian *news*, followed by a sports bulletin. On the half-hour, choose from *Australia Today* (Sunday), *The Australian Music Show* (Monday), *Jazz Notes* (Tuesday), ●*Blacktracker* (aboriginal music, Wednesday), *Australian Country Style* (Thursday), ●*Music Deli* (Friday), and Saturday's environmental *One World*. Continuous to southern Asia and the Pacific on a number of channels, and heard in Western North America on 6060, 9580, 9860 and 12080 kHz. Also audible in Europe on 11660 kHz.

Swiss Radio International. World and Swiss *news* and background reports.

Information at the expense of entertainment, though Saturday's programming has a lighter touch to it. Thirty minutes to the Mideast and East Africa on 5850 (winter), 9885, 12075 (summer) and 13635 kHz. May also be available to northern Europe on 7510 or 9905 kHz.

Polish Radio Warsaw, Poland. This time summers only. Monday through Friday, it's *News from Poland*—a compendium of news, reports and interviews. This is followed by *Request Concert* and *A Day in the Life of...* (Monday), classical music and the historical *Flashback* (Tuesday), a communications feature and *Letter from Poland* (Wednesday), a feature and a talk or special report (Thursday), and Friday's *Focus* (the arts in Poland) followed by *Business Week*. The Saturday broadcast begins with a bulletin of *news*, then there's *Weekend Papers* (a press review), *Panorama* (a window on day-to-day life in Poland) and a listener-response program, *Postbag*. Sundays, you can hear *What We Said* (a summary of the station's output during the previous week) and *Jazz, Folk, Rock and Pop from Poland*. Fifty-five minutes to Europe on 6095, 7270 and 7285 kHz. One hour later during winter.

Radio Jordan. Winters only at this time. The last 30 minutes of a partial relay of the station's domestic broadcasts, beamed to Europe on 11970 kHz.

Voice of Russia World Service. The initial half-hour is taken up winters by *News* and features (see 1600 summer programs), with the choice plum being Saturday's ●*Music and Musicians*. On the half-hour, it's science, business or a listener-response show, depending on the day of the week. Summers, there's the daily *News and Views* followed by a variety of features. Best of the final 30 minutes are ●*Music at Your Request*

The world's people sound off to Washington by phone and e-mail each weekday on the VOA's *Talk to America*.

(Thursday), ●*Folk Box* (Friday), *Kaleidoscope* (Sunday) and Tuesday's *Jazz Show*. Continuous to Europe winters on 5940, 5995, 6055, 7115, 7180, 7205 and 9890 kHz; and summers on 7440, 9480, 9880 and 11630 kHz. Also to the Mideast winters on 4740 and 7210 kHz, and summers on 9365 and 9675 kHz. In East and Southern Africa, try 7210, 7255, 7325, 9470 and 9505 kHz in winter (summer in the Southern Hemisphere); and 9365, 9675, 9975 and 11775 kHz in summer.

Radio For Peace International, Costa Rica. The first daily edition of *FIRE* (Feminist International Radio Endeavour), and the start of the English portion of an eight-hour cyclical block of predominantly social-conscience and counterculture programming. Audible in North America and elsewhere on 6200 and 15050 kHz. Some transmissions are in the single-sideband mode, which can be properly processed only on some radios.

Radio Japan. Repeat of the 1500 broadcast, except that Sunday's *Hello from Tokyo* is replaced by *Let's Learn Japanese*, *Media Roundup* and *Viewpoint*. One hour to the Mideast on 11930 kHz; to Western North America on 9535 kHz; and to Asia on 6035/6150 (East), 7280/11880 (South) and (Southeast) 9580 kHz.

Channel Africa, South Africa. *News*, then features: *Africa Alive*, *Travel Africa* and *Sport* (Monday); *Spotlight* and *All That Jazz* (Tuesday); *Farming for Africa*, *Nations of the World* and *Health Forum* (Wednesday); *Checkpoint*, *English for Africa* and *Technology for Us* (Thursday); *African Tapestry* (Friday); and *International Top Ten* on Saturday. The Sunday slot is occupied by *Evergreens* and *Reggae and Rap*. The broadcasts end with a daily bulletin of South African news. The final 55 minutes of a three-hour block of programming to East, Central and Southern Africa on 3220 (or 9530) and 7155 kHz.

Radio Pyongyang, North Korea. Repeat of the 1100 transmission. Fifty minutes to Europe, the Mideast and beyond on 9325, 9640, 9975 and 13785 kHz.

China Radio International. Repeat of the 1600 transmission. One hour to East and Southern Africa on 7405, 9570 and 11910 kHz.

Voice of America. Continuous programming to the Mideast and North Africa. *News,* then Monday through Friday it's the interactive *Talk to America.* Weekend offerings include Saturday's *Communications World* and Sunday's *Critic's Choice* and ●*Issues in the News.* Winters on 6040, 9760 and 15205 kHz; and summers on 9700, 9760 and 15255 kHz. Also heard in much of Europe. For a separate service to Africa, see the next item.

Voice of America. Programs for Africa. Monday through Saturday, identical to the service for Europe and the Mideast (see previous item). On Sunday, opens with *News,* then it's *Voices of Africa* and ●*Music Time in Africa.* Audible well beyond where it is targeted. On 6035, 7415, 11920, 11975, 12040, 13710, 15410, 15445 and 17895 kHz, some of which are seasonal. For yet another service (to East Asia and the Pacific), see the next item.

Voice of America. Monday through Friday only. *News,* followed by the interactive *Talk to America.* Sixty minutes to Asia on 5990, 6045, 6110/6160, 7125, 7215, 9525, 9645, 9670, 9770, 11945, 12005 and 15255 kHz, some of which are seasonal. For Australasia, try 9525 and 15255 kHz in winter, and 7150 and 7170 kHz in summer.

■**Radio France Internationale.** An additional half-hour (see 1600) of predominantly African fare. To East Africa on any two frequencies from 9485, 11615, 15210 and 15460 kHz. Also audible in parts of the Mideast, and occasionally heard in Eastern North America.

Radio Cairo, Egypt. See 1630 for specifics. Continues with a broadcast to southern Africa on 15255 kHz.

"Rush Limbaugh Show," WRNO, New Orleans, Louisiana. Monday through Friday only; see 1600 for specifics. Starts at this time winters; summers, it's already into the second hour. Continuous to North America and the Caribbean on 7355 (or 15420) kHz.

WJCR, Upton, Kentucky. Continues with country gospel music to North America on 7490 and 13595 kHz. Other U.S. religious broadcasters operating at this hour include **WWCR** on 13845 and 15685 kHz, **KTBN** on 15590 kHz, and **WHRI-World Harvest Radio** on 13760 and 15105 kHz.

CFRX-CFRB, Toronto, Canada. See 1400.

17:15

Radio Tirana, Albania. Winters only at this time. Approximately 10 minutes of *news* and commentary from and about Albania. To Europe on 7155 and 9740 kHz. One hour earlier during summer.

17:30

Radio Nederland. Targeted at Africa, but heard well beyond. *News,* followed Monday through Saturday by *Newsline* and a feature. Choice pickings include ●*Research File* (Monday), ●*A Good Life* (Friday), and Saturday's ●*Weekend.* For other interesting offerings, try *Mirror Images* (Tuesday) or Wednesday's documentaries, some of which are excellent. Other programs include Thursday's *Media Network* and Sunday's *Sounds Interesting.* Monday through Friday there is also a *Press Review.* One hour on 6020, 7120 (summer), 9605 (winter) and 11655 kHz.

Radio Austria International. Summers only at this time; the informative ●*Report from Austria.* A half hour to Europe on 6155 and 13730 kHz, to the Mideast on 9665 kHz, and to South and Southeast Asia on 11780 kHz.

Radio Slovakia International. This time winters only; see 1830 for program specifics. Thirty pleasant minutes to Western Europe on 5915, 6055 and 7345 kHz. One hour earlier in summer.

Radio Romania International. *News,* commentary, a press review, and one or more short features. Thirty minutes to East and Southern Africa (also audible in parts of the Mideast). Winters on 9750, 11740 and 11940 kHz; and summers on 9550, 9750, 11830 and 11940 kHz.

Radio Almaty, Kazakhstan. Winters only at this time. Due to financial constraints, news and features have largely been replaced by recordings of exotic Kazakh music. If you like world music, this is definitely a station to try for. Heard in Asia on 4820, 5970 and 9505 kHz, and in Europe (via relay facilities in Ukraine) on 5940 kHz. One hour earlier in summer.

17:45

All India Radio. The first 15 minutes of a two-hour broadcast to Europe, Africa and the Mideast, consisting of regional and international *news*, commentary, a variety of talks and features, press review and enjoyably exotic Indian music. Continuous till 1945. To Europe on 7410, 9950 and 11620 kHz; to the Mideast on 13700 kHz; and to Africa on 9650, 11935 and 15075 kHz.

Voice of Armenia. Monday through Friday, summers only at this time. Mainly of interest to Armenians abroad. Fifteen minutes of *news* from and about Armenia. To Eastern Europe and the Mideast on 4810, 4990 and 7480 kHz. One hour later in winter.

1800-2359
Europe & Mideast—Evening Prime Time
East Asia—Early Morning
Australasia—Morning
Eastern North America—Afternoon
Western North America—Midday

18:00

■BBC World Service for the Americas.
Winters only at this time. ●*Newsdesk*, then
most days it's music. Monday, Thursday
and Saturday feature *Multitrack* (sounds
and issues from the world of pop music);
Sunday brings the unique and inimitable
●*John Peel* ("action for all the family");
Tuesday has an entertainment feature;
Thursday, it's the ever-popular ●*Anything
Goes*; and Friday gives us ●*Andy
Kershaw's World of Music*, a class act by
any yardstick. To North America on
17840 kHz.

**■BBC World Service for Europe
(and the Mideast).** Thirty minutes of
●*Newsdesk*, with the next half-hour containing some varied and interesting fare.
Sunday, there's ●*Global Concerns*, replaced Monday by ●*Brain of Britain* (or
its substitute), and Tuesday by light entertainment (often humorous). Then it's
●*Discovery* (Wednesday). ●*Assignment*
(Thursday), ●*Focus on Faith* (Friday) and
Science in Action Saturday). Continuous
to Europe on 3955 (winter), 6180, 6195,
9410, 12095 (summer) and 15485 kHz;
and to the Mideast on 9410 and (summer)
12095 kHz. Some of these channels provide fair to good reception in Eastern
North America.

■BBC World Service for Africa.
●*Newsdesk*, then Monday through Friday
it's *Focus on Africa*. This is replaced Saturday by *Music Review* (classical), and
Sunday by *A Jolly Good Show*. Continuous
programming to the African continent

(and heard well beyond) on 3255, 6005
(from 1830), 6190, 9630 (from 1830), 15400
and 17830 kHz. The last two channels are
audible in parts of North America.

■BBC World Service for the Pacific.
Identical to the service for Europe at this
hour, but only available from 1830 onwards. To Australasia on 9740 kHz.

Monitor Radio International, USA.
See 1600 for program details. Monday
through Friday to Europe on 9355, 11550,
13770 and 15665 kHz (some of which are
seasonal); and to South Africa on 9385
and 17510 (or 18930) kHz.

Radio Kuwait. The start of a three-
hour package of *news*, Islamic-oriented
features and western popular music.
Some interesting features, even if you
don't particularly like the music. There is
a full program summary at the beginning
of each transmission, to enable you to
pick and choose. To Europe and Eastern
North America on 11990 kHz.

Voice of Vietnam. Repeat of the 1000
transmission. A half hour to Europe on
9840 and 12020 (or 15010) kHz.

Radio For Peace International,
Costa Rica. Part of a continuous eight-
hour cyclical block of predominantly
social-conscience and counterculture
programming. One of international
broadcasting's more unusual features,
The Far Right Radio Review, can be heard
at 1800 Tuesday. To North America and
beyond on 6200 and 15050 kHz. Some
transmissions are in the single-sideband
mode, which can be properly processed
only on some radios.

Radio Vlaanderen Internationaal, Belgium. Summers only at this time. See 1900 for program details. Thirty minutes to Europe on 5910 kHz, and to Africa on 13645 kHz. One hour later in winter.

All India Radio. Continuation of the transmission to Europe, Africa and the Mideast (see 1745). *News* and commentary, followed by programming of a more general nature. To Europe on 7410, 9950 and 11620 kHz; to the Mideast on 13700 kHz; and to Africa on 9650, 11935 and 15075 kHz.

Radio Prague, Czech Republic. Winters only at this time. Repeat of the 1700 broadcast (see 1600 for program details). A half hour to Europe on 5835 kHz, and to Australasia on 9430 kHz.

Radio Norway International. Summer Sundays only. *Norway Now.* Repeat of the 1200 transmission. Thirty minutes of friendly programming from and about Norway. To Europe on 7485 kHz, to the Mideast on 9590 kHz, and to Africa on 13805 and 15220 kHz.

Radio Australia. *World News,* followed Monday through Friday by *Asia Focus* and ●*International Report.* Saturday, it's *Pacific Religion* and *Background Report,* replaced Sunday by *Letters to the Editor* and *Report from Asia.* Continuous to Asia and the Pacific on a number of channels, and also audible in Western North America on 9580, 9860 and 12080 kHz. In Southeast Asia, tune to 7330 kHz. This channel should also be audible in Europe, interference permitting.

Radio Nacional do Brasil (Radiobras), Brazil. Monday through Saturday, you can hear *Life in Brazil* or *Brazilian Panorama,* a potpourri of news, facts and figures about this fascinating land, interspersed with examples of the country's various unique musical styles.

> Russia is really many "little Russias," embracing a polyglot of peoples under one tent. This ethnic diversity, from Cossacks to Mongolians, bursts into song each Monday in *Folk Box.*

The *Sunday Special,* on the other hand, is devoted to one particular theme, and often contains lots of exotic Brazilian music. Eighty minutes to Europe on 15265 kHz.

Polish Radio Warsaw, Poland. This time winters only. See 1700 for program specifics. *News,* music and features, covering multiple aspects of Polish life and culture. Fifty-five minutes to Europe on 6095, 7270 and 7285 kHz. One hour earlier in summer.

Voice of Russia World Service. Predominantly news-related fare during the initial half-hour, with *News and Views* the daily winter offering. In summer, it's ●*Commonwealth Update* Monday through Friday, and the business-oriented *Newmarket* on Saturday. At 1830, winter features include Tuesday's *Jazz Show,* Wednesday's *Yours for the Asking,* Thursday's ●*Music at Your Request* and Friday's exotic ●*Folk Box.* In summer, *This is Russia* (Tuesday, Thursday and Saturday) alternates with ●*Moscow Yesterday and Today.* Continuous to Europe winters on 5940, 7180, 7205 and 9890 kHz; and summers on 7240, 7290, 7350, 9480, 9880, 11630 and 11675 kHz. Some of these channels can be heard in parts of Eastern North America. Also to the Mideast winters on 7210 kHz, and summers on 9365, 9675 and 11945 kHz. For East and Southern Africa, try 7210 and 7255 kHz in winter, and 9365, 9675, 9975 and 11945 kHz in summer (local winter south of the Equator).

Voice of America. Continuous programming to the Mideast and North Africa. Repeat of the 1600 broadcast except at 1810 weekends, when you can hear *Agriculture Today* (Saturday) or ●*Encounter* (Sunday). On 6040 (winter) and 9760 kHz. For a separate service to Africa, see the next item.

Voice of America. Monday through Friday, it's 60 minutes of *Africa World Tonight*. Weekends, there's Saturday's *Agriculture Today* or Sunday's ●*Encounter*, followed on the half-hour by *news* and features in "Special" (slow-speed) English. To Africa, but heard well beyond, on 4875 (Monday through Friday), 7275, 11920, 11975, 12040, 13710, 15410, 15580 and 17895 kHz, some of which are seasonal.

Radio Algiers, Algeria. *News*, then rock and popular music, with an occasional brief feature also thrown in. One hour of so-so reception in Europe, and occasionally heard in Eastern North America. Try 11715, 15160 or 15205 kHz. Sometimes heard irregularly on 17745 kHz.

Radio Cairo, Egypt. See 1630 for specifics. The final 30 minutes of a two-hour broadcast to southern Africa on 15255 kHz.

Radio Omdurman, Sudan. A one-hour package of *news* and features (often from a pro-government viewpoint), plus a little ethnic Sudanese music. Better heard in Europe than in North America, but occasionally audible in the eastern United States. On 9024 kHz.

"Rush Limbaugh Show," WRNO, New Orleans, Louisiana. Monday through Friday only; see 1600 for specifics. Continuous to North America and the Caribbean on 7355 (or 15420) kHz.

"For the People," WHRI, Noblesville, Indiana. Summers only at this time; see 0300 for specifics. Three hours of live populist programming targeted at North America on 9495 kHz. One hour later in winter.

WJCR, Upton, Kentucky. Continues with country gospel music to North America on 7490 and 13595 kHz. Other U.S. religious broadcasters operating at this time include **WWCR** on 13845 and 15685 kHz, **KTBN** on 15590 kHz, and **WHRI-World Harvest Radio** on 13760 and 15105 kHz. For traditional Catholic programming, tune **WEWN** on 7425 kHz.

CFRX-CFRB, Toronto, Canada. See 1400.

18:15

Radio Bangladesh. *News*, followed by Islamic and general interest features; some nice Bengali music, too. Thirty minutes to Europe on 7190 and 9568 kHz, and irregularly to the Mideast on 15520 kHz. Frequencies may be slightly variable.

18:30

Radio Nederland. Well heard in parts of North America, despite being targeted at Africa. *News*, followed Monday through Saturday by *Newsline* and a feature. These include ●*A Good Life* (Monday), *Sounds Interesting* (Wednesday), ●*Research File* (Thursday) and Friday's documentary. Weekends feature programs which tend to rotate on a seasonal basis. Sixty minutes on 4945 and 6015 (winter), 6020, 7120 (summer), 7300 and 9605 (winter), 9860, 9895, 11655 and 13700 (summer), 15315 and 17605 kHz. The last two frequencies, via the relay in the Netherlands Antilles, are best for North American listeners.

Radio Slovakia International. Summers only at this time, and a repeat of the 1630 broadcast. Thirty minutes of *news* and features with a strong Slovak flavor. Monday, there's a variety of short features; Tuesday spotlights tourism and Slovak personalities; Wednesday's slot is devoted to business and economy; Thursday brings a mix of politics, education and science. and Friday has a strong cultural content. Saturday features the "Best of" series; and Sunday brings *Listeners' Tribune* and some enjoyable Slovak music. To Western Europe on 5915, 6055 and 7345 kHz. One hour later in winter.

Voice of Turkey. This time summers only. *News*, followed by *Review of the*

Turkish Press, then features on Turkish history, culture and international relations, interspersed with enjoyable selections of the country's popular and classical music. Fifty minutes to Western Europe on 9445 and 9535 kHz. One hour later in winter.

Radio Sweden. Monday through Friday, it's *news* and features in *Sixty Degrees North*, concentrating heavily on Scandinavian topics. Monday's accent is on sports; Tuesday has electronic media news; Wednesday brings *Money Matters*; Thursday features ecology or science and technology; and Friday offers a review of the week's news. Saturday's slot is filled by *Spectrum* (arts) or *Sweden Today*, and Sunday fare consists of *In Touch with Stockholm* (a listener-response program)

or the musical *Sounds Nordic*. Thirty minutes to Europe, the Mideast and Africa on 6065, 7240 (or 11615) and 9655 kHz.

Radio Korea International, South Korea. Starts off with *news*, followed Monday through Wednesday by *Economic News Briefs*. The remainder of the broadcast is taken up by a feature: *Shortwave Feedback* (Sunday), *Seoul Calling* (Monday and Tuesday), *Pulse of Korea* (Wednesday), *From Us to You* (Thursday), *Let's Sing Together* (Friday) and *Weekly News Focus* (Saturday). Thirty minutes to Europe summers on 3955 kHz. This station reorganized its schedule for summer 1996, so the former winter timing of 2000 is almost certainly subject to change. Try 1830 or 1930 on 3970 kHz.

If you see the Star of David in a Lebanese shop, as shown here, almost certainly you've stumbled across a faithful listener to the Voice of Hope. Located near the Israeli border, this Christian station—not affiliated with Adventist stations of the same name—has endured rocket attacks and gunfire from Lebanese *fedayeen*.

Radio Tirana, Albania. Summers only at this time. *News,* with much of the remainder of the broadcast being devoted to lively Albanian music. Thirty minutes to Europe on 7270 and 9740 kHz. One hour later during winter.

Radio Yugoslavia. Summers only at this time. *News* and background reports with a strong regional slant. Thirty minutes to Europe on 6100 kHz, and to Southern Africa on 9720 kHz. One hour later during winter.

18:45

Voice of Armenia. Monday through Friday, winters only at this time. Mainly of interest to Armenians abroad. Fifteen minutes of *news* from and about Armenia. To Eastern Europe and the Mideast on 4810, 4990 and 7480 kHz. One hour earlier in summer.

19:00

■**BBC World Service for Europe (and the Mideast).** ●*Newshour,* the standard for all in-depth news shows from international broadcasters. Sixty fully packed minutes to Europe on 3955 (winters), 6180, 6195, 9410 and (summers) 12095 and 15485 kHz; and to the Mideast on 5975, 9410 and (summer) 12095 kHz. Some of these channels are also easily heard in Eastern North America.

■**BBC World Service for the Pacific.** ●*Newshour.* The best. To Australasia on 9740 and 11955 kHz.

■**BBC World Service for Africa.** A series of features aimed at the African continent, but worth a listen even if you live farther afield. The list includes *Fast Track* and ●*Thirty Minute Drama* (Monday), *Money Focus* and *Meridian* (Tuesday), *Talkabout Africa* and ●*Assignment* (Wednesday), *The Art House* and *Meridian* (Thursday), *African Quiz* or *African Perspective* (Friday), the pulsating ●*Jive Zone* and the arts show *Meridian* (Saturday) and *Postmark Africa* (1905 Sunday). Continuous programming to the African continent (and heard well beyond) on 6005, 6190, 9630, 15400 and 17830 kHz. The last two channels are audible in parts of North America.

Monitor Radio International, USA. See 1600 for program details. Monday through Friday to Europe and the Mideast on 9355 or 11550 kHz, to Eastern Europe on 11550 or 13770 kHz, to West Africa on 17510 kHz, and to Southern Africa on 9385 kHz. This news-oriented programming is replaced weekends by non-secular offerings from and about Christian Scientists.

Radio Nacional do Brasil (Radiobras), Brazil. Final 20 minutes of the 1800 broadcast to Europe on 15265 kHz.

Radio Vlaanderen Internationaal, Belgium. Winters only at this time. Weekdays, there's *News, Press Review* and *Belgium Today,* followed by features like

Focus on Europe (Monday), *Living in Belgium* and *Green Society* (Tuesday), *The Arts* (Wednesday and Friday), *Around Town* (Wednesday), *Economics* and *International Report* (Thursday), and *Tourism* (Friday). Weekend features include *Music from Flanders* (Saturday) and Sunday's *P.O. Box 26* (a listener-response program) and *Radio World*. Twenty-five minutes to Europe on 5910 kHz; also to Africa (and heard elsewhere) on 9925 kHz. One hour earlier in summer.

Radio Australia. Begins with *World News*, *Pacific News* (Monday through Friday) and *Sports Report*. These are followed, on the half-hour, by a feature. Choose from *Innovations* (Monday), *Arts Australia* (Tuesday), ●*Science File* (Wednesday), *Book Talk* (Thursday), *Talking Politics* (Friday), *One World* (the environment, Saturday) and *Business Weekly* (Sunday). Continuous to Asia and the Pacific on a number of channels, and also audible in Western North America on 9580, 9860 and 12080 kHz. In Southeast Asia, try 7330 kHz. This channel should also be audible in Europe, interference permitting.

Radio Norway International. Winter Sundays only. *Norway Now*. News and features from and about Norway. Thirty minutes to Europe on 5960 kHz, to Australasia on 7115 kHz; and to Africa on 7485 and 9590 kHz.

Radio Kuwait. See 1800; continuous to Europe and Eastern North America on 11990 kHz.

Kol Israel. Summers only at this time. ●*Israel News Magazine*. Thirty minutes of even-handed and comprehensive news reporting from and about Israel. To Europe and North America on 7465, 11605 and 15615 kHz; to Central and South America on 9435 kHz, and to Africa and South

America on 15640 kHz. One hour later in winter.

All India Radio. The final 45 minutes of a two-hour broadcast to Europe, Africa and the Mideast (see 1745). Starts off with *news*, then continues with a mixed bag of features and Indian music. To Europe on 7410, 9950 and 11620 kHz; to the Mideast on 13700 kHz; and to Africa on 9650, 11935 and 15075 kHz.

Radio Bulgaria. Summers only at this time. *News*, then Monday through Thursday there's 15 minutes of current events in *Today*, replaced Friday by *Weekly Spotlight*, a summary of the week's major political stories. The remainder of the broadcast is given over to features dealing with Bulgaria and Bulgarians, and includes some lively ethnic music. To Europe, also audible in Eastern North America, on 9700 and 11720 kHz. One hour later during winter.

> If you're lucky enough to already be familiar with Andean music, you'll need no prodding to hear the delightful *Música del Ecuador*. On Saturday from HCJB in Quito.

HCJB—Voice of the Andes, Ecuador. The first of three hours of religious and secular programming targeted at Europe. Monday through Friday it's *Studio 9*, featuring nine minutes of world and Latin American *news*, followed by 20 minutes of in-depth reporting on Latin America. The final portion is given over to one of a variety of 30-minute features—including *You Should Know* (issues and ethics, Monday), *El Mundo Futuro* (science, Tuesday), *Ham Radio Today* (Wednesday), *Woman to Woman* (Thursday) and Friday's exotic and enjoyable ●*Música del Ecuador*. On Saturday, the news is followed by *DX Partyline*, which in turn is replaced Sunday by *Saludos Amigos*—HCJB's international friendship program. Winter on 11960 kHz, and summer on 15540 kHz.

Radio Budapest, Hungary. Summers only at this time. *News* and features, some of which are broadcast on a regular basis.

These include Sunday's *Bookshelf*, a press review (Monday, Tuesday, Thursday and Friday), *Profiles* (Tuesday), and *Focus on Business* (Wednesday). Thirty minutes to Europe on 3955, 6140, 7130 and 9835 kHz. One hour later in winter.

■**Deutsche Welle,** Germany. A shortened version of the 1600 broadcast, and without Saturday's jazz feature and Sunday's *Germany This Week*. Fifty minutes to Africa and the Mideast, and heard well beyond. Winters, try 9670, 9765, 11785, 11810, 11865, 13790, 15145 and 15425 kHz; in summer, go for 7170, 9670, 9735, 11740, 11785, 13690 and 13790 kHz.

Radio Romania International. *News*, commentary, press review and features. Regular spots include *Youth Club* (Tuesday), *Romanian Musicians* (Wednesday), and Thursday's *Listeners' Letterbox* and ●*Skylark* (Romanian folk music). Fifty-five minutes to Europe; winters on 6105, 7105, 7195 and 9510 kHz; and summers on 9550, 9690, 11810 and 11940 kHz. Also audible in Eastern North America.

Radio Japan. Repeat of the 1500 transmission; see there for specifics. One hour to East and Southeast Asia on 6035/6150 and 9580 kHz; to Australasia on 6035, 7140 and 11850 kHz; and to Western North America on 9535 kHz.

Voice of Russia World Service. *News*, followed winter weekdays by ●*Commonwealth Update*, and Saturday by *Newmarket*. Summers, choose from *Science and Engineering* (Thursday), *Newmarket* (Wednesday and Sunday) and *Mailbag* most other days. On the half-hour, the winter offerings are *This is Russia* (Tuesday, Thursday and Saturday) and ●*Moscow Yesterday and Today* on the remaining days. In summer it's ●*Our Treasure Chest*, chock-full of broadcasting jewels. To Europe winters on 5940, 5995, 6055, 7180, 7205 and 9890 kHz; and summers on 7240, 7290, 7350, 7440, 9480, 9880, 11630 and 11675 kHz. Some of these channels are audible in parts of

Eastern North America. Also available winters to the Mideast on 9585 kHz, and summers on 11765 and 11945 kHz. In Southern Africa, go for 7210, 7255, 9470 and 9505 kHz in winter (your local summer); midyear, try 11765 and 11945 kHz.

Voice of Greece. Winters only at this time, and actually starts about three minutes into the broadcast, following some Greek announcements. Approximately ten minutes of *news* from and about Greece. To Europe on 9375 or 9380 kHz.

RDP International—Radio Portugal. Monday through Friday, summers only, at this time. *News*, then features: *Visitor's Notebook* (Monday), *Musical Kaleidoscope* (Tuesday), *Challenge of the 90's* (Wednesday), *Spotlight on Portugal* (Thursday), and either *Listeners' Mailbag* or *DX Program* and *Collector's Corner* (Friday). Thirty minutes to Europe on 6130, 9780 and 9815 kHz, and to Africa on 15515 kHz. One hour later in winter.

Radio Thailand. A 60-minute package of *news*, features and (if you're lucky) enjoyable Thai music. To Northern Europe winters on 7295 kHz, and summers on 7210 kHz. Also available to Asia on 9655 and 11905 kHz.

Radio For Peace International, Costa Rica. Continues with a variety of counterculture and social-conscience features. There is also a listener-response program at 1930 Tuesday. Audible in Europe and North America on 6200 and 15050 kHz. Some transmissions are in the single-sideband mode, which can be properly processed only on some radios.

Swiss Radio International. This time summers only. World and Swiss *news* and background reports, with some lighter and more general features on Saturdays. Thirty minutes on 6165 kHz. One hour later during winter.

Voice of Vietnam. Repeat of the 1800 transmission (see 1000 for program specifics). A half hour to Europe on 9840 and 12020 (or 15010) kHz.

Voice of America. Continuous programming to the Mideast and North Africa. *News*, followed weekdays by *Europe Edition* and *Dateline Bosnia*. Weekend offerings include *Press Conference USA* (Saturday) and *Newsline* and ●*Music USA-Standards* on Sunday. On 9760 and (summer) 9770 kHz. Also heard in Europe. For a separate service to Africa, see the next item.

Voice of America. *News*, then Monday through Friday it's *Europe Edition*, an editorial and *World of Music*. Weekends, choose from Saturday's *Voices of Africa* and *Press Conference USA*, and Sunday's *Newsline* and ●*Music Time in Africa*. Continuous to most of Africa on 4875, 6035, 7375, 7415, 11920, 11975, 12040, 15410, 15445 and 15580 kHz, some of which are seasonal. For yet another service, to Australasia, see the following item.

Voice of America. Weekday programs are the same as for the Mideast (see above). On weekends, look for *Press Conference USA* (1930 Saturday) and Sunday's *Newsline* and ●*Music USA-Standards*. One hour to Australasia on 9525, 11870 and 15180 kHz.

"Rush Limbaugh Show," WRNO, New Orleans, Louisiana. See 1600 for specifics. Winters only at this time. The final sixty minutes of a three-hour presentation. Popular and controversial within the United States, but of little interest to most other listeners. To North America and the Caribbean on 7355 (or 15420) kHz.

Radio Korea International, South Korea. Repeat of the 1600 broadcast. Sixty minutes to East Asia on 5975 and 7275 kHz.

Radio Argentina al Exterior—R.A.E. Monday through Friday only. *News* and short features dealing with Argentinian life and culture, interspersed with fine examples of the country's various musical styles, from chamamé to zamba. Fifty-five minutes to Europe on 15345 kHz.

"For the People," WHRI, Noblesville,

Indiana. See 0300 for specifics. Monday through Friday only. A three-hour populist package broadcast live to North America on 9495 kHz.

WJCR, Upton, Kentucky. Continues with country gospel music to North America on 7490 and 13595 kHz. Other U.S. religious broadcasters operating at this time include **WWCR** on 13845 and 15685 kHz, **KTBN** on 15590 kHz, and **WHRI-World Harvest Radio** on 13760 kHz. For traditional Catholic programming, try **WEWN** on 7425 kHz.

CFRX-CFRB, Toronto, Canada. See 1400.

19:30

Polish Radio Warsaw, Poland. Summers only at this time. Weekdays, it's *News from Poland*— news, reports and interviews on the latest events in the country. This is followed by classical music and the his-

U.S. Attorney General Janet Reno guests on "Press Conference USA" over the Voice of America.

torical *Flashback* (Monday), *DX-Club* and *Letter from Poland* (Tuesday), a feature and a talk or special report (Wednesday), *Focus* (the arts in Poland) and *A Day in the Life of...* (Thursday), and *Postbag* (a listener-response program) followed by *Business Week* (Friday). The Saturday transmission begins with a bulletin of *news*, then there's *Weekend Papers* (a press review) and, later in the broadcast, *Jazz, Folk, Rock and Pop from Poland*. Sundays, you can hear *Panorama* (a window on day-to-day life in Poland) and *Request Concert*. Fifty-five minutes to Europe on 6035, 6095 and 7285 kHz. One hour later during winter.

Radio Slovakia International. Winters only at this time, and a repeat of the 1730 broadcast. *News* and features with a strong Slovak accent. See 1930 for program specifics. Thirty minutes to Western Europe on 5915, 6055 and 7345 kHz. One hour earlier in summer.

Voice of Turkey. Winters only at this time. See 1830 for program details. Some rather unusual programming and friendly presentation make this station worth a listen. Fifty minutes to Europe on 9445 kHz. One hour earlier in summer.

Radio Ulaanbaatar, Mongolia. *News*, reports and short features with the accent on local topics. Some exotic Mongolian music, too, especially on Sundays. Thirty minutes to Europe winters on 4080 and 7530 kHz, and summers on 9745 and 12085 kHz. Frequencies may vary slightly.

Voice of the Islamic Republic of Iran. Sixty minutes of *news*, commentary and features with a strong Islamic slant. Not the lightest of programming fare, but reflects a point of view not often heard in western countries. To Europe on 7260 and 9022 kHz.

Radio Yugoslavia. Winters only at this time; see 1830 for specifics. Thirty minutes to Europe on 6100 kHz, and to Southern Africa on 9720 kHz. One hour earlier in summer.

Radio Austria International. News and human-interest stories in ●*Report from Austria*. A half hour winters to Europe on 5945 and 6155 kHz, but year-round to the Mideast on 9665 kHz, and to Africa on 13730 kHz.

Radio Tirana, Albania. Winters only at this time. Currently being run on a shoestring budget, so broadcasts are often limited to *news* and pleasant Albanian music. Thirty minutes to Europe on 7270 and 9740 kHz. One hour earlier during summer.

Radio Nederland. Repeat of the 1730 transmission; see there for specifics. Fifty-five minutes to Africa on 4945, 6020 (winter), 7120 and 7205 (summer), 7300 and 9605 (winter), 9860 and 9895 (summer), 11655, 15315 and 17605 kHz. The last two frequencies are heard well in many parts of North America.

Radio Roma, Italy. Actually starts at 1935. Approximately 12 minutes of *news*, then music. Twenty uninspiring minutes to Western Europe winters on 6030 and 7235 kHz, and summers on 7235, 9670 and 11905 kHz.

19:50

Vatican Radio. Summers only at this time. Twenty minutes of programming oriented to Catholics. To Europe on 4005, 5880 and 7250 kHz. One hour later in winter.

20:00

■**BBC World Service for Europe (and the Mideast).** Starts with a brief summary of the latest *news*, then Monday through Friday it's the popular and long-running ●*Outlook*, followed by five minutes of the religious *Words of Faith*. On the half-hour, the programs are geared to younger listeners: *Multitrack* (Monday, Wednesday and Friday), ●*Megamix* (Tuesday) and

●*John Peel* (Thursday). Much of the weekend fare consists of classical music:●*The Greenfield Collection* (2001 Saturday) and ●*Concert Hall* (alternating periodically with ●*International Recital* or ●*From the Proms*) at the same time Sunday. Continuous to Europe on 3955 (winter), 6180, 6195, 7325, 9410 and (summer) 12095 and 15485 kHz; and to the Mideast on 9410 and (summer) 12095 kHz. Some of these channels are also audible in Eastern North America.

■**BBC World Service for Asia and the Pacific.** Identical to the service for Europe at this hour. To East and Southeast Asia on 11955 kHz, and to Australasia on 9740 and 11955 kHz.

■**BBC World Service for Africa.** The incomparable ●*Newshour.* Continuous programming to the African continent (and heard well beyond) on 6005, 6190, 9630, 15400 and 17830 kHz. The last two channels are audible in parts of North America.

Monitor Radio International, USA. See 1600 for program details. Monday through Friday to Europe on any two frequencies from 5850, 7510, 11550 and 13770 kHz; and to Australasia on 13840 kHz. Replaced weekends by programs devoted to the beliefs and teachings of the Christian Science Church.

■**Deutsche Welle,** Germany. *News,* followed Monday through Friday by the in-depth ●*European Journal, View Point* and a feature on Germany. Take your pick from *Come to Germany)* (Tuesday), *German Tribune* (Wednesday), *Living in Germany* (Thursday) or Friday's *Through German Eyes.* The Monday slot is devoted to a language lesson, *German by Radio.* On the remaining days, look for Saturday's *Sports Report, Germany This Week* and ●*Weekend;* replaced the next day by *Arts on the Air* and *Sunday Concert.* Fifty minutes to Europe winters on 5960 and 7285 kHz, and summers on 7170 and 9615 kHz.

Radio Canada International. Summers only at this time. The first hour of a 90-minute broadcast to Europe and beyond. *News,* followed Monday through Friday by *Spectrum* (current events), which is replaced Saturday by *Innovation Canada* and ●*Earth Watch,* and Sunday by *Arts in Canada* and *The Inside Track.* To Europe and Africa on 5995 (also available in the Mideast), 7235, 11690, 13650, 13670, 15150, 15325, 17820 and 17870 kHz. Some of these are audible in parts of North America. One hour later during winter.

Radio Damascus, Syria. Actually starts at 2005. *News,* a daily press review, and different features for each day of the week. These can be heard at approximately 2030 and 2045, and include *Arab Profile* and *Palestine Talk* (Monday), *Syria and the World* and *Listeners Overseas* (Tuesday), *Around the World* and *Selected Readings* (Wednesday), *From the World Press* and *Reflections* (Thursday), *Arab Newsweek* and *Cultural Magazine* (Friday), *Welcome to Syria* and *Arab Civilization* (Saturday), and *From Our Literature* and *Music from the Orient* (Sunday). Most of the transmission, however, is given over to Syrian and some western popular music. One hour to Europe, often audible in Eastern North America, on 12085 and 13610 (or 15095) kHz.

Radio Norway International. Summer Sundays only. *Norway Now.* Thirty friendly minutes to Australasia on 9590 kHz.

Swiss Radio International. Thirty minutes of *Newsnet*—news and background reports on world and Swiss events. Somewhat lighter fare on Saturday, when the biweekly *Capital Letters* (a listener-response program) alternates with *Name Game* and *Sounds Good.* To Europe winters on 6165 kHz (one hour earlier in summer), and year-round to Africa (also audible in Eastern North

America) on 9770 or (9870), 9885, 9905 and 11640 kHz.

Radio Australia. Starts with world *news*, then Monday through Friday it's *Australia Today*, replaced Saturday by *Pacific Religion* and Sunday by *Letters to the Editor*. Weekdays on the half-hour, look for ●*International Report*; Saturday, it's *Media Report*; and Sunday features *The Sports Factor*. Continuous to Asia and the Pacific on several channels, and audible in Western North America on 9580, 9860 and 12080 kHz. In Southeast Asia, try 7330 kHz. This channel should also be audible in Europe, interference permitting.

Voice of Russia World Service. *News*, then summers it's more of the same in *News and Views*, replaced winters by a series of features. These include *Science and Engineering* (Thursday), the business-oriented *Newmarket* (Wednesday and Sunday) and *Mailbag* most other days. Winters on the half-hour, it's time for

> Because Bulgarians don't get around the world the way some people do, their beguiling folk songs have been a well-kept secret. No longer. Thanks to Radio Bulgaria's broadcasts in English, this captivating music is now heard worldwide.

●*Our Treasure Chest*, replaced summers by a number of features. Choose from *Jazz Show* (Friday), *Yours for the Asking* (Tuesday), ●*Music at Your Request* (Wednesday), ●*Folk Box* (Thursday) and Saturday's *Kaleidoscope*. Continuous to Europe winters on 5940, 5995, 6055, 7180, 7205, 9795 and 9890 kHz; and summers on 7350, 9480, 9795, 9880, 11630 and 11675 kHz. Some of these channels are audible in Eastern North America. Also winters only to Southern Africa (your local summer) on 7325 and 9470 kHz.

Radio Kuwait. The final sixty minutes of a three-hour broadcast to Europe and Eastern North America (see 1800). Regular features at this time include *Theater in Kuwait* (2000), *Saheeh Muslim* (2030) and *News in Brief* at 2057. On 11990 kHz.

Radio Bulgaria. This time winters only; see 1900 for specifics. Sixty minutes of *news* and entertainment, including lively Bulgarian folk rhythms. To Europe, also heard in Eastern North America, on 7335 and 9700 kHz. One hour earlier during summer.

Voice of Greece. Summers only at this time and actually starts about three minutes into the broadcast, after a little bit of Greek. Approximately ten minutes of *news* from and about Greece. To Europe on 7430 or 9420 kHz.

Radio Budapest, Hungary. Winters only at this time; see 2100 for specifics. Thirty minutes to Europe on 3975, 5970, 7250 and 9835 kHz. One hour earlier in summer.

China Radio International. *News* and commentary, followed Tuesday through Friday by *Current Affairs*. These are followed by various feature programs, such as *Cultural Spectrum* (Thursday); *Listeners' Letterbox* (Sunday and Tuesday); *China Scrapbook*, *Cooking Show*, *Travel Talk* and ●*Music from China* (Saturday); *Sports Beat* and *Music Album* (Sunday); *Learn to Speak Chinese* (Monday and Wednesday); and Friday's *In the Third World*. Sundays, there is also a biweekly *Business Show* which alternates with *China's Open Windows*. One hour to Europe on 6950 and 9920 kHz, and to East and Southern Africa on 9440, 11715 and 15110 kHz.

Radio Nacional de Angola ("Angolan National Radio"). The first 30 minutes or so consist of a mix of music and short features, then there's *news* near the half-hour. The remainder of the broadcast is given over to some thoroughly enjoyable Angolan music. Sixty minutes to Southern Africa on 3354 and 9535 kHz, with the second frequency also audible in parts of Europe and Eastern North America, especially during winter.

Radio Pyongyang, North Korea. Repeat of the 1100 broadcast. To Europe, the Mideast and beyond on 6575, 9345, 9640 and 9975 kHz.

RDP International—Radio Portugal. Winter weekdays only. *News,* followed by a feature about Portugal; see 1900 for more details. Thirty minutes to Europe on 6130, 9780 and 9815 kHz, and to Africa on 15515 kHz. One hour earlier in summer.

"For the People," WHRI, Noblesville, Indiana. Monday through Friday only; see 0300 for specifics. Part of a three-hour populist package broadcast live to North America on 9495 kHz.

Kol Israel. Winters only at this time. Thirty minutes of *news* and in-depth reporting from and about Israel. To Europe and North America on 7418, 7465 and 9435 kHz; to Central and South America on 9845 kHz; and to Africa and South America on 13750 kHz. One hour earlier in summer.

YLE Radio Finland. Summers only at this time; see 2130 for specifics. A half hour to Europe and West Africa on 9855 and 15440 kHz. One hour later in winter.

HCJB—Voice of the Andes, Ecuador. Continues with a three-hour block of religious and secular programming to Europe. Monday through Friday it's the same features as 0200 (see there for specifics), but one day earlier. Weekends, look for *Solstice* and *Sports Spectrum* on Saturday, replaced Sunday by *Radio Reading Room* and *Joy International.* Winter on 11960 kHz, and summer on 15540 kHz.

Voice of America. *News.* Listeners in the Mideast can then hear ●*Music U.S.A. (Jazz)*—replaced Sunday by *The Concert Hall*—on 9760, (summer) 9770 and (winter) 15205 kHz. For African listeners there's the weekday *Africa World Tonight,* replaced weekends by *Nightline Africa,* on 6035, 7275, 7375, 7415, 11715, 11855, 15410,

15445, 15580, 17725 and 17755 kHz, some of which are seasonal. Both transmissions are heard well beyond their target areas, including parts of North America.

Radio For Peace International, Costa Rica. Part of an eight-hour cyclical block of predominantly social-conscience and counterculture programming. Some of the offerings at this hour include a women's news-gathering service, *WINGS,* (2030 Thursday) and a listener-response program (same time Friday). Audible in Europe and North America on 6200 and 15050 kHz. Some transmissions are in the single-sideband mode, which can be properly processed only on some radios.

WJCR, Upton, Kentucky. Continues with country gospel music to North America on 7490 and 13595 kHz. Other U.S. religious broadcasters which operate at this time include **WWCR** on 13845 and 15685 kHz, **KTBN** on 15590 kHz, and **WHRI-World Harvest Radio** on 13760 kHz. For traditional Catholic programming, tune **WEWN** on 7425 kHz.

Radio Prague, Czech Republic. Summers only at this time. *News,* then Monday through Friday there's *Current Affairs.* These are followed by one or more features. Monday has *Magazine '96;* Tuesday, it's *Talking Point* and *What's Up?;* Wednesday has *From the Archives* and *The Arts;* Thursday brings *Economic Report* and *I'd Like You to Meet...;* and Friday there's *Between You and Us.* Saturday's offerings include a musical feature, replaced Sunday by *The Week in Politics, From the Weeklies* and *What's Up?* Thirty minutes to Europe on 5930 kHz, and to Southeast Asia and the Pacific on 11640 kHz.

CFRX-CFRB, Toronto, Canada. See 1400.

20:30

Radio Sweden. Summer weekends only at this time. Saturday, there's *Spectrum*

(arts) or *Sweden Today* (current events). Sunday fare consists of *In Touch with Stockholm* (a listener response program) or the musical *Sounds Nordic*. Thirty minutes to Europe, Africa and the Mideast on 6065, 9430 and 9655 kHz.

Voice of Vietnam. Repeat of the 1800 transmission (see 1000 for program specifics). A half hour to Europe on 9840 and 12020 (or 15010) kHz.

Radio Yugoslavia. Summers only at this time. *News* and information with a strong regional flavor. Thirty minutes to Australasia on 7230 kHz.

Radio Thailand. Fifteen minutes of *news* targeted at Europe. Winters on 11805 kHz, and summers on 9555 kHz. Also available to Asia on 9655 and 11905 kHz.

Radio Dniester International, Moldova. Monday, Wednesday and Thursday, summers only at this time. A 30-minute broadcast from the Russian separatists in the Pridnestrovye region of the country. See 2130 for specifics. To Europe (and audible in Eastern North America) on 11750 kHz. One hour later in winter. Operates irregularly due to financial constraints and electricity supply problems.

Polish Radio Warsaw, Poland. Winters only at this time. See 1930 for program specifics. Fifty-five minutes of *news*, music and features spotlighting Poland past and present. To Europe on 6035, 6095 and 7285 kHz. One hour earlier during summer.

Voice of Armenia. Summers only at this time. Mainly of interest to Armenians abroad. Thirty minutes of Armenian *news* and culture. To Europe on 9965 and 11615 kHz. Sometimes audible in Eastern North America. One hour later in winter.

Radio Nederland. Repeat of the 1830 broadcast. Fifty-five minutes to Africa (and heard well beyond), winters on 4945 and 7300 kHz, and summers on 9860, 9895 and 11655 kHz.

Radio Roma, Italy. Actually starts at 2025. Twenty minutes of *news* and music targeted at the Mideast on 6035 and 7235 (or 7290) kHz. Not as bad as it used to be, but could be a lot better.

All India Radio. The first 15 minutes of a much longer broadcast, consisting of a press review, Indian music, regional and international *news*, commentary, and a variety of talks and features of general interest. Continuous till 2230. To Western Europe on 7410, 9950 and 11620 kHz; to Southeast Asia on 9910 kHz; and to Australasia on 7150 and 11715 kHz.

Vatican Radio. Winters only at this time, and actually starts at 2050. Twenty minutes of predominantly Catholic fare. To Europe on 4015 and 5882 kHz. Frequencies may vary slightly. One hour earlier in summer.

■**BBC World Service for the Americas.** *World News*, then ten minutes of specialized business and financial reports. Monday through Friday, these are followed by ●*The World Today* or ●*Caribbean Report* (see 2115 for specifics). On the half-hour, choose from ●*Health Matters* and *Development 97* (Monday), ●*Discovery* (science, Tuesday), ●*Assignment* (Wednesday), *Sports International* (Thursday), ●*Network UK* (Friday), ●*Global Concerns* and ●*Letter from America* (Saturday) and a couple of short features on Sunday. To Eastern North America and the Caribbean on 5975 kHz. If you prefer *The World Today* to the Caribbean alternative, try 11750 kHz, targeted at South America.

■**BBC World Service for Europe (and the Mideast).** Opens with the same 15 minutes as on the Americas service (see above), and then it's ●*Britain Today*. On the half-hour, look for the arts show

Meridian (Tuesday, Wednesday, Thursday and Saturday), replaced Friday by ●*People and Politics*. Sunday swings to ●*Jazz for the Asking*. Continuous to Europe on 3955 (winters), 6180, 6195, 7325, 9410 and (summers) 12095 kHz; and to the Mideast on 9410 and (summer) 12095 kHz. Also audible in Eastern North America.

BBC World Service for Asia and the Pacific. *World News*, a business report and a wide variety of features. Pick of the litter are ●*Omnibus* (2115 Monday), ●*Discovery* and ●*The Learning World* (Wednesday) and ●*Network UK* and *From Our Own Correspondent* (Thursday). Continuous to East and Southeast Asia on 3915, 5990, 6195, 11945 and 11955 kHz; and to Australasia on 9740 and 11955 kHz.

Monitor Radio International, USA. See 1600 for program details. Monday through Friday to Europe (also audible in Eastern North America) on any two frequencies from 5850, 7510, 11550 and 13770 kHz; and to Australasia on 13840 kHz. Weekend programming is non-secular, and mainly of interest to Christian Scientists.

Radio Exterior de España ("Spanish National Radio"). *News*, followed Monday through Friday by *Panorama* (Spanish popular music, commentary, press review and weather), then a couple of features: *Sports Spotlight* and *Cultural Encounters* (Monday); *People of Today* and *Entertainment in Spain* (Tuesday); *As Others See Us* and, biweekly, *The Natural World* or *Science Desk* (Wednesday); *Economic Report* and *Cultural Clippings* (Thursday); and *Window on Spain* and *Review of the Arts* (Friday). The broadcast ends with a language course, *Spanish by Radio*. On weekends, there's Saturday's *Hall of Fame*, *Distance Unknown* (for radio enthusiasts) and *Gallery of Spanish Voices*; replaced Sunday by *Visitors' Book*, *Great Figures in Flamenco* and *Radio Club*. One hour to Europe on 6125 kHz, and to Africa on 11775 kHz.

Radio Ukraine International. Summers only at this time. *News*, commentary, reports and interviews, covering multiple aspects of Ukrainian life. Saturdays feature a listener-response program, and most of Sunday's broadcast is a showpiece for Ukrainian music. Sixty minutes to Europe on 5905, 6010, 6020 and 9560 kHz; to Southern Africa on 9875 kHz; and to Australasia on 7375 kHz. Also audible in parts of Eastern North America. One hour later in winter.

Radio Canada International. Winters, the first hour of a 90-minute broadcast; summers, the last half-hour of the same. Winters, there's *News*, followed Monday through Friday by *Spectrum* (current events), which is replaced Saturday by *Innovation Canada* and ●*Earth Watch*, and Sunday by *Arts in Canada* and a

With the breakup of the former Czechoslovakia, Radio Prague is now free to concentrate its reporting on the affairs of the Czech Republic. Yet another major world band station, RFE-RL, is now headquartered in dynamic Prague. An international broadcasters' conference was recently hosted by them in Prague, shown reposing under a blanket of snow.

Don Swampo

listener-response program. Summer weekdays, it's the CBC domestic service's ●*The World at Six*, with weekend fare consisting of *Royal Canadian Air Farce* (Saturday) and Sunday's *The Mailbag*. To Europe and Africa winters on 5925, 5995, 7235, 9805, 11945, 13670, 13690, 15150 and 17820 kHz; and summers on 5995 (also for the Mideast), 7235, 11690, 13650, 13670, 15150, 15325 and 17820 kHz. Some of these are also audible in parts of North America.

Radio Vlaanderen Internationaal, Belgium. Summers only at this time. Repeat of the 1800 transmission (see 1900 for program details). Thirty minutes daily to Europe on 5910 kHz. One hour later in winter.

Radio Prague, Czech Republic. Winters only at this time; see 2000 for program details. *News* and features dealing with Czech life and culture. A half hour to Eastern North America on 5930 kHz, and to West Africa on 7345 kHz.

Radio Bulgaria. This time summers only; see 1900 for specifics. *News*, features and some entertaining folk music. To Europe and Eastern North America on 9700 and 11720 kHz. One hour later during winter.

China Radio International. Repeat of the 2000 transmission. One hour to Europe on 6950 and 9920 kHz. A 30-minute shortened version is also available summers (2100-2130) on 6165 kHz.

Voice of Russia World Service. The

first 30 minutes have the accent heavily on *news*, the only exceptions being summer weekends—●*Music and Musicians* (2111 Saturday) and *Science and Engineering* (same time Sunday). Winters on the half-hour, look for a choice of features: *Yours for the Asking* (Tuesday), *Jazz Show* (Monday and Friday), ●*Music at Your Request* (Wednesday), ●*Folk Box* (Thursday) and *Kaleidoscope* (Saturday). Summers, these are replaced by *Science and Engineering* (Monday and Friday), *Newmarket* (Tuesday) and a listener-response program most other days. Continuous to Europe winters on 5940, 5995, 6055, 7170 (from 2130), 7180, 7205, 7400 and 9890 kHz; and summers on 7350, 9480, 9580, 9665, 9710, 9880 and 11630 kHz. Several of these channels are also audible in Eastern North America.

Radio Budapest, Hungary. Summers only at this time. *News* and features, some of which are broadcast on a regular basis. These include Monday's *Musica Hungarica*, *Focus on Business* and *The Weeklies* (Wednesday), *Letter Home* (Thursday) and *Profiles* (Saturday). Thirty minutes to Europe on 3955, 5935, 7250 and 9835 kHz. One hour later in winter.

> Some clear Sunday evening, take your portable outdoors. There, under the stars where flamenco was originally danced, tune in *Great Figures in Flamenco* to transport your mind back to a time of raw passion and courage. From Spanish National Radio in Madrid.

Radio Australia. *World news*, then Monday through Friday it's discussion in *Australia Talks Back*. Saturday's offering is *Hindsight*, and *The Science Show* airs on Sunday. Continuous to Asia and the Pacific on a number of frequencies. To East Asia on 9850, 11695 and 13605 kHz; to Southeast Asia on 11855 kHz; and audible in Western North America on 9860 kHz (replaced by 17860 kHz at 2130).

■**Deutsche Welle,** Germany. *News*, followed Sunday through Thursday by ●*European Journal* and ●*Asia-Pacific Report*. The remaining days' programs include *Germany This Week* and *Economic Notebook* (Friday), and Saturday's *Mailbag Asia*. Fifty minutes to Asia and Australasia on 7115 (summer), 9670, 9765 and 11785 kHz.

Radio Japan. Repeat of the 1700 transmission; see there for specifics. One hour to East and Southeast Asia winters on 6035, 7125 and 7140 kHz; and summers on 6035, 9535 and 9560 kHz. Also to Australasia on 11850 kHz. There is also a separate 10-minute *news* broadcast to Southeast Asia on 7190 or 11685 kHz.

Radio Yugoslavia. *News* and short background reports, mostly about local issues. An informative half-hour summers to Europe on 6100 and 6185 kHz, and winters to Australasia on 9595 kHz.

Radio Romania International. *News*, commentary and features (see 1900), interspersed with some thoroughly enjoyable Romanian folk music. One hour to Europe winters on 5955, 5990, 7105 and 7195 kHz; summers on 5990, 7105, 7195 and 9690 kHz. Also audible in Eastern North America.

Radio Habana Cuba. A 60-minute package of *news* (predominantly about Cuba and Latin America), features about the island and its people, and some thoroughly enjoyable Cuban music. To Europe on (winter) 9550 kHz and (summer) 11705 or 13715 kHz.

Radio Korea International, South Korea. Repeat of the 1900 broadcast; see 1600 for program details. Sixty minutes to Europe on 6480 and 15575 kHz.

Radio For Peace International, Costa Rica. Continues at this hour with a potpourri of United Nations, counterculture and other programs. These include *WINGS* (news for and of women, 2130 Tuesday) and *Vietnam Veterans Radio*

Network (same time Wednesday). Audible in Europe and North America on 6200 and 15050 kHz. Some transmissions are in the single-sideband mode, which can be properly processed only on some radios.

HCJB—Voice of the Andes, Ecuador. The final sixty minutes of a three-hour block of predominantly religious programming to Europe, winter on 11960 kHz, and summer on 15540 kHz.

Voice of America. Monday through Friday, it's one hour of *World Report*. Weekends, there's *News* and a variety of features, depending on the area served. Pick of the litter is the science program ●*New Horizons* (Africa, and the Mideast at 2110 Sunday). Other offerings include *VOA Pacific* (Australasia, same time Sunday), ●*Issues in the News* (Africa, 2130 Sunday; Australasia, 2130 Saturday), *Studio One* (Europe and Mideast, 2130 Sun) and *On the Line* (Europe, Africa and the Mideast at 2110 Saturday). To the Mideast and North Africa winters on 6070, 9595, 9760 and 15205 kHz; and summers on 6040, 9535 and 9760 kHz; to Africa on 6035, 7375, 7415, 11715, 11975, 13710, 15410, 15445, 15580 and 17725 kHz (some of which are seasonal); and to Southeast Asia and the Pacific on 11870, 15185 and 17735 kHz.

All India Radio. Continues to Western Europe on 7410, 9950 and 11620 kHz; to Southeast Asia on 9910 kHz; and to Australasia on 7150 and 11715 kHz. Look for some authentic Indian music from 2115 onwards. The European frequencies are also audible in parts of Eastern North America.

"For the People," WHRI, Noblesville, Indiana. winters only at this time. Monday through Friday only; see 0300 for specifics. The final hour of a three-hour populist package broadcast live to North America on 9495 kHz. One hour earlier in summer.

CFRX-CFRB, Toronto, Canada. See 1400. Summers at this time, you can hear ●*The World Today*, 90 minutes of news,

interviews, sports and commentary. On 6070 kHz.

21:15

Radio Damascus, Syria. Actually starts at 2110. *News*, a daily press review, and a variety of features (depending on the day of the week) at approximately 2130 and 2145. These include *Arab Profile* and *Economic Affairs* (Sunday), *Camera and Masks* and *Selected Readings* (Monday), *Reflections* and *Back on the Stage* (Tuesday), *Listeners Overseas* and *Palestine Talking* (Wednesday), *From the World Press* and *Arab Women in Focus* (Thursday), *Arab Newsweek* and *From Our Literature* (Friday), and *Human Rights* and *Syria and the World* (Saturday). The transmission also contains Syrian and some western popular music. Sixty minutes to North America and Australasia on 12085 and 13610 (or 15095) kHz.

■**BBC World Service for the Caribbean.** ●*Caribbean Report*, although intended for listeners in the area, can also be clearly heard throughout much of Eastern North America. This brief, 15-minute program provides comprehensive coverage of Caribbean economic and political affairs, both within and outside the region. Monday through Friday only, on 6110, 15390 and 17715 kHz.

Radio Cairo, Egypt. The start of a 90-minute broadcast devoted to Arab and Egyptian life and culture. The initial quarter-hour of general programming is followed by *news*, commentary and political items. This in turn is followed by a cultural program until 2215, when the station again reverts to more general fare. A Middle Eastern melange, including exotic Arab music, beamed to Europe on 9900 kHz.

WJCR, Upton, Kentucky. Continuous gospel music to North America on 7490 and 13595 kHz. Other U.S. religious broadcasters operating at this hour include **WWCR** on 13845 and 15685 and kHz, **KTBN** on 15590 kHz, and **WHRI-World Harvest Radio** on 13760 kHz. Traditional Catholic programming is available from **WEWN** on 7425 kHz.

21:30

BBC World Service for the Falkland Islands. *Calling the Falklands* is one of the curiosities of international broadcasting, and consists of news and features for this small community in the South Atlantic. Topics can be extremely varied, from trans-polar expeditions to Argentinian politics. Fifteen minutes Tuesdays and Fridays on 11680 kHz—easily heard in Eastern North America.

YLE Radio Finland. Winters only at this time. *News*, followed by a mix of Finnish and other Scandinavian general interest stories; some Finnish music, too. Saturdays at 2053, look for a world band curiosity, *Nuntii Latini* (news in Latin). Thirty minutes to Europe on 6120 kHz. One hour earlier in summer.

Radio Dniester International, Moldova. Monday, Wednesday and Thursday, winters only at this time. A 30-minute broadcast from the Russian-separatists in the Pridnestrovye region of the country. Starts with *News Magazine*, then there is a translated interview or speech on a local topic. Moldovan music and a press review usually make up the rest of the broadcast. To Europe (also audible in Eastern North America) on 6205 kHz. One hour earlier in summer. Irregular operation due to electricity supply problems and financial constraints.

Voice of the Islamic Republic of Iran. A recently-introduced service to Australasia. Sixty minutes of *news*, commentary and features with a strong Islamic slant. On 6175 and 9670 kHz, but may be subject to change.

Voice of Armenia. Winters only at this time. Mainly of interest to Armenians

abroad. Thirty minutes of Armenian *news* and culture. To Europe on 7480 and 9965 kHz, and sometimes audible in Eastern North America. One hour earlier in summer.

Radio Sweden. Thirty minutes of predominantly Scandinavian fare (see 1830 for specifics). Year-round to Europe on 6065 kHz, and summer to Africa and the Mideast on 6065, 9430 and 9655 kHz. May be weekends only during winter.

22:00

■**BBC World Service for the Americas.** Thirty minutes of the comprehensive ●*Newsdesk*, then weekdays there's 15 minutes of specialized business and financial reports (replaced Sunday by *The Farming World*). Monday through Saturday, the final quarter-hour is given over to ●*Sports Roundup*. The Saturday slot is devoted to the first part of ●*Play of the Week*, a *tour de force* of world theater. Audible in North America and the Caribbean on 5975, 6175, 9590 and 9915 kHz.

■**BBC World Service for Europe (and the Mideast).** Thirty minutes of ●*Newsdesk*, and that is it for summer. Winter weekday evenings, continues with ●*The World Today* and ●*Sports Roundup*, with the choice weekend show being ●*Letter from America* (2230 Sunday). To Europe on 3955 (winter), 6195, 9410 and (summer) 12095 kHz; and to the Mideast on 9410 and (summer) 12095 kHz. Also audible in Eastern North America.

■**BBC World Service for Asia and the Pacific.** Starts with 30 minutes of ●*Newsdesk*, and ends with a quarter-hour of ●*Sports Roundup*. In-between, it's the weekday ●*World Business Report* (Tuesday through Saturday local Asian days), Saturday's *Jazz Now and Then*, or Sunday's *Country Style*. Continuous to East and Southeast Asia on 6195, 7110 and 11955 kHz; and to Australasia on 9660, 11955 and 12080 kHz.

Some American religious stations have taken to airing the audio portion of television broadcasts over world band. Here, WVHA's Scott des Islets directs the satellite feed from the Florida studio for downlink to their shortwave transmission facility in Maine.

Monitor Radio International, USA. See 1600 for program details. Monday through Friday to Western Europe (and audible in Eastern North America) on 7510 kHz, to South America on 13770 kHz, and to East Asia on 9430 (or 15405) and 13840 kHz. Weekend programming concentrates on Christian Science beliefs and teachings.

Radio Bulgaria. Winters only at this time; see 1900 for specifics. Sixty minutes of *news* and features from and about Bulgaria, interspersed with lively Bulgarian folk music. To Europe and Eastern North America on 7105 and 9700 kHz. One hour earlier in summer.

Radio Cairo, Egypt. The second half of a 90-minute broadcast to Europe on 9900 kHz; see 2115 for program details.

Voice of America. The beginning of a three-hour block of programs to East and Southeast Asia and the Pacific. *News,* followed Sunday through Thursday (Monday through Friday in the target areas) by *VOA Today.* On the remaining days, it's *VOA Saturday* or *VOA Sunday.* Not very original, but at least you know which station you're hearing. To East and Southeast Asia on 7215, 9705, 9770, 11760, 15185, 15290, 15305, 17735 and 17820 kHz; and to Australasia on 15185, 15305 and 17735 kHz. There is a separate 30-minute weeknight service to Africa which features *Music USA* on 7340, 7375 and 7415 kHz.

Radio Australia. *World News,* then Sunday through Thursday it's *Network Asia.* Friday's offerings are *Feedback* (a listener-response program) and *Fine Music Australia,* and Saturday's presentation is the call-in extravaganza, *Australia All Over*—dial +61 (2) 333-1020 if you would like to take part. Continuous to Asia and the Pacific on several frequencies. To East Asia on 11695 kHz, and to Southeast Asia on 11855 kHz. Also audible in Western North America on 17795 and 17860 kHz.

Voice of Russia World Service. *News*, then Monday through Friday winters, it's *Focus on Asia and the Pacific* followed by a feature (see 2100 summer programs). Saturday's spot is given over to the excellent ●*Music and Musicians*, and Sunday airs *Science and Engineering*. Summers, there's the weekday ●*Commonwealth Update*, replaced weekends by unscheduled features and music. On the half-hour, ●*Audio Book Club* (Tuesday and Sunday) alternates with *Russian by Radio* or a music program. Winters to Europe on 5995, 6055, 7140, 7205, 7360, 7400 and 9890 kHz (some of which are audible in Eastern North America); and summers to Eastern North America on 7250, 7360 (or 9530), 9665 and (if reactivated) 11750 kHz.

Voice of Free China, Taiwan. *News*, then features. The last is *Let's Learn Chinese*, which has a series of segments for beginning, intermediate and advanced learners. Other features include *Jade Bells and Bamboo Pipes* (Monday), *Kaleido-scope* and *Main Roads and Byways* (Tuesday), *Music Box* (Wednesday), *Perspectives* and *Journey into Chinese Culture* (Thursday), *Confrontation* and *New Record Time* (Friday), *Reflections* (Saturday) and *Adventures of Mahlon and Jeanie* and *Mailbag Time* (Sunday). Sixty minutes to Western Europe, winters on 5810 and 9985 kHz, and summers on 15600 and 17750 kHz.

Croatian Radio. Summers only at this time. Eight minutes of on-the-spot *news* from what continues to be one of Europe's most volatile regions. Best heard in Europe and Eastern North America at this hour, but also heard elsewhere. Channel usage varies, but try 5895, 7165, 7370, 9830, 11635 and 13830 kHz. One hour later during winter.

Radio Habana Cuba. Sixty minutes of *news* (mainly about Cuba and Latin America), features about the island and its inhabitants, and some thoroughly enjoyable Cuban music. To the Caribbean and southern United States on 6180 kHz, and to Eastern North America and Europe on (winter) 9505 and (summer) 13715 kHz upper sideband.

Radio Budapest, Hungary. Winters only at this time; see 2100 for specifics. Thirty minutes to Europe on 3955, 5935, 7250 and 9835 kHz. One hour earlier in summer.

Voice of Turkey. Summers only at this time. *News*, followed by *Review of the Turkish Press* and features with a strong local flavor. Selections of Turkish popular and classical music complete the program. Fifty minutes to Europe on 7280 and 9655 kHz, to Eastern North America on 9655 kHz, and to much of Asia and Australasia on 9560 kHz. One hour later during winter.

Radio Yugoslavia. Winters only at this time. Repeat of the 1930 broadcast. Thirty minutes to Europe on 6100 and 6185 kHz. One hour earlier in summer.

China Radio International. Repeat of the 2000 broadcast. One hour to Europe winters on 7170 kHz, summers on 9880 kHz. A shortened version is also available winters at 2200-2230 on 3985 kHz.

Radio Vlaanderen Internationaal, Belgium. Winters only at this time. Repeat of the 1900 broadcast; see there for program details. Thirty minutes to Europe on 5910 kHz, also audible in parts of Eastern North America. One hour earlier in summer.

Radio Canada International. This time winters only. The final half-hour of a 90-minute broadcast. Monday through Friday, it's the CBC domestic service's ●*The World at Six*, with weekend fare consisting of Saturday's *Innovation Canada* and Sunday's *The Mailbag*. To Europe and Africa on 5995, 7235, 9805, 11945, 13690 and 15150 kHz. For a separate summer service, see the following item.

Radio Canada International. Summers only; a relay of CBC domestic programming, except for the final 30 minutes weekends. Monday through Friday, there's ● *The World at Six*; Saturday and Sunday, *The World This Weekend*. On the half-hour, the weekday ●*As It Happens* is replaced Saturday by *The Mystery Project* and Sunday by *Now the Details*. Sixty minutes to North America on 5960, 9755 and 13670 kHz. One hour later in winter. For a separate year-round service to Asia, see the next item.

Radio Canada International. Monday through Friday, it's ●*The World At Six*; Saturday and Sunday summer, *The World This Weekend*. Winter weekends, look for Saturday's *Royal Canadian Air Farce* and Sunday's *The Inside Track*. Thirty minutes to Southeast Asia on 11705 kHz.

Radio Norway International. Sundays only. *Norway Now*. Thirty minutes of *news* and human-interest stories from and about Norway. Winters to East Asia on 7115 kHz, and to Eastern North America on 6200 kHz; in summer, to Australasia on 9485 kHz.

Radio Roma, Italy. Approximately ten minutes of *news* followed by a quarter-hour feature (usually music). An uninspiring 25 minutes to East Asia on 5990 (or 5975), 9710 and 11815 kHz.

Radio Ukraine International. Winters only at this time. A potpourri of all things Ukrainian, with the Sunday broadcast often featuring some excellent music. Sixty minutes to Europe, Africa, the Mideast and beyond on 4795, 4820, 5905, 5940, 6010, 6020, 6055, 6080, 6130, 7135, 7205, 7240 and 9620 kHz. Also audible in parts of Eastern North America. One hour earlier in summer.

> That's funny, but your name doesn't sound funny. True, but the *Royal Canadian Air Farce* is one of the most side-splitting comedy series of all time. Loud and clear Saturdays over Radio Canada International.

United Arab Emirates Radio, Abu Dhabi. Begins with *Readings from the Holy Koran*, in which verses are chanted in Arabic, then translated into English. This is followed by an Arab cultural feature. The second half-hour is a relay of Capital Radio in Abu Dhabi, complete with pop music and local contests. To North America on 9605, 9695 and 9770 kHz (with possible alternatives being 7215, 11885 and 13605 kHz).

Radio For Peace International, Costa Rica. Continues with counterculture and social-conscience programs—try *The Far Right Radio Review* at 2200 Sunday. Audible in Europe and North America on 6200, 7385 and 15050 kHz. Some transmissions are in the single-sideband mode, which can be properly processed only on some radios.

All India Radio. The final half-hour of a transmission to Europe, Southeast Asia and Australasia, consisting mainly of news-related fare. To Europe on 7410, 9950 and 11620 kHz; to Southeast Asia on 9910 kHz; and to Australasia on 7150 and 11715 kHz. Frequencies for Europe are also heard in parts of Eastern North America.

WJCR, Upton, Kentucky. Continues with country gospel music to North America on 7490 and 13595 kHz. Other U.S. religious broadcasters heard at this hour include **WWCR** on 13845 kHz, **KAIJ** on 13815 kHz, **KTBN** on 15590 kHz, and **WHRI-World Harvest Radio** on 5745 (or 13760) kHz. For traditional Catholic programming, try **WEWN** on 7425 kHz.

CFRX-CFRB, Toronto, Canada. If you live in the northeastern United States or southeastern Canada, try this pleasant little local station, usually audible for hundreds of miles/kilometers during daylight hours on 6070 kHz. At this time, you can hear ●*The World Today* (summers, starts at 2100)—90 minutes of news, sport and interviews.

22:30

Radio Sweden. Winters only at this time. Repeat of the 2130 broadcast (see 1830 for program details). Thirty minutes of *news* and features, with the accent heavily on Scandinavian topics. To Europe on 6065 kHz.

Radio Austria International. The informative and well-presented ●*Report from Austria.* A half hour to Europe on 5945 and 6155 kHz.

Radio Prague, Czech Republic. *News*, reports and features from and about the Czech Republic. These include *Magazine '96* and *What's Up?* (Monday), *Talking Point* (Tuesday), *From the Archives* and *The Arts* (Wednesday), *Economic Report* and *I'd Like You to Meet...* (Thursday), *Between You and Us* (Friday), and a musical feature on Saturday. A half hour to Eastern North America on 5930 (winter), 7345 and (summer) 11600 kHz.

Voice of Greece. Actually starts around 2235. Fifteen minutes of English news from and about Greece. Part of a much longer, predominantly Greek, broadcast. To Australasia on 9425 kHz.

22:45

All India Radio. The first 15 minutes of a much longer broadcast, consisting of Indian music, regional and international *news*, commentary, and a variety of talks and features of general interest. Continuous till 0045. To Southeast Asia (and beyond) on 7150, 9705, 9950 and 11620 kHz.

Vatican Radio. Twenty minutes of religious and secular programming to East and Southeast Asia and Australasia on 6065, 7305, 9600 and 11830 kHz, some of them seasonal.

BBC

When it comes to a straight newscast—television or radio—nothing on earth equals the BBC World Service's "Newshour," here presented by Robin Lustig. It's heard at prime time in various parts of the world, but Americans can hear it only in the morning.

23:00

■**BBC World Service for the Americas.** Sunday through Friday, opens with *World News*, with the rest of the hour being taken up by a wide variety of features, depending on the day of the week. There's something to suit all tastes, but relatively little to please everyone. Fans of classical music can listen at 2310 Sunday and 2315 Monday, while those who like pop music can tune to *Multitrack* at 2330 Monday, Wednesday and Friday. If you don't like either kind, try *Country Style* at 2315 Wednesday. Younger listeners can go for ●*Megamix*, a well put together youth show at 2330 Tuesday. Of more general

0200-0230	**S** 6120 (E North Am & C America), 9535 & **S** 11715 (C America & S America)
0200-0300 ⬅	9755 (E North Am & C America)
0200-0300	**W** 5905 (W North Am), **W** 6010 & **S** 9755 (E North Am & C America), **W** 11725 & **S** 13670 (S America)
0230-0300	**S** Su/M 6120 (E North Am & C America), **S** Su/M 9535, **W** 9535 & **S** Su/M 11715 (C America & S America)
0300-0330	**W** 6010 (E North Am & C America), **W** 9755 (C America)
0330-0400	**W** Su/M 6010 (E North Am & C America), **W** Su/M 9755 (C America)
0400-0430	**W** 6150, **W** 9505, **W** 9645, **S** 11835, **S** 11905 & **S** 15275 (Mideast)
0500-0530	**S** M-F 7295 (W Europe & N Africa), **S** M-F 15430 (Africa), **S** M-F 17840 (Africa & Mideast)
0600-0630 ⬅	M-F 6050 (Europe)
0600-0630	**W** M-F 6150 (Europe), **W** M-F 9740 (Africa), **W** M-F 9760 (Europe & N Africa), **W** M-F 11905 (Mideast)
1200-1300	**S** 13650 (E North Am & C America)
1230-1300	**W** 6150 & **S** 9660 (E Asia), **W** 11730 & **S** 15195 (SE Asia)
1300-1400 ⬅	9640 (E North Am), 11855 (E North Am & C America)
1300-1400	**S** M-F 13650 (E North Am & C America)
1300-1600	**S** Su 13650 (E North Am & C America)
1330-1357	9535 (E Asia)
1330-1400	**W** 6150 & **S** 11795 (E Asia), **S** 15325 & **S** M-Sa 17820 (Europe), **S** 21455 (E Europe & Mideast)
1400-1500 ⬅	M-F 9640 (E North Am), Su-F 11855 (E North Am & C America)
1400-1700	**W** Su 9640 (E North Am)
1430-1500 ⬅	11935 (Europe)
1430-1500	**W** 9555 (Europe & Mideast), **W** 11915 & **W** 15325 (Europe)
1500-1700 ⬅	Su 11855 (E North Am & C America)
1630-1657	7150 & 9550 (S Asia)
1630-1700	6550 (E Asia)
2000-2100	**S** 17820 (Africa), **S** 17870 (Europe)
2000-2130	**S** 5995 (Europe & Mideast), **S** 11690 & **S** 13650 (Europe), **S** 13670 (Africa), **S** 15325 (Europe)
2100-2130	17820 (Africa)
2100-2200	**W** 5925 & **W** 13650 (Europe)
2100-2230 ⬅	7235 (S Europe & N Africa), 15150 (Africa)
2100-2230	**W** 5995 (Europe & N Africa), **W** 9805 (W Europe & N Africa), **W** 11945 (Europe), **W** 13690 (Africa)
2130-2200	**W** 17820 (Africa)
2200-2230	11705 (SE Asia), **S** 15305 (C America & S America)
2200-2300	**S** 5960 (E North Am), **S** 13740 (C America)
2200-2400	**S** 13670 (C America & S America)
2300-2330	**W** 9535, 11940 & **S** 15305 (C America & S America)
2300-2400 ⬅	9755 (E North Am)
2300-2400	5960 (E North Am)
2330-2400	**W** Sa/Su 6040 (C America), **W** Sa/Su 9535, Sa/Su 11940 & **S** Sa/Su 15305 (C America & S America)

CHINA
CHINA RADIO INTERNATIONAL

0000-0100	9710 & 11695/11715 (N America)
0300-0400	9690 (N America & C America), 9710 & 11695/11715 (N America)
0400-0500	9730 (W North Am)
0500-0600 ⬅	9560 (N America)
0900-1100	**W** 8260 & 8450 (E Asia), 11755, 15440 & 17710 (Australasia)
1140-1155	8660 (E Asia), 11445 & 15135 (SE Asia)
1200-1300	8425 (E Asia), 11795 (Australasia)
1200-1400	9715 & 11660 (SE Asia), 15440 (Australasia)
1210-1225	8660 (E Asia), 11445, 12110 & 15135 (SE Asia)
1400-1600 ⬅	7405 (W North Am)
1400-1600	9785 & 11815 (S Asia)
1440-1455	8660 (E Asia), 11445 & 15135 (SE Asia)
1600-1700	15110 (C Africa & S Africa), 15130 (S Africa)
1600-1800	11575 (E Africa & S Africa)
1700-1800	5220 (E Asia), **W** 7150 (E Africa & S Africa), 7405 (Africa), 9570 (E Africa & S Africa)
1900-2000	**W** 6955 (N Africa & W Africa), **S** 11515 (Mideast & N Africa)
1900-2100	9440 (N Africa & W Africa)
2000-2130	11715 (S Africa), 15110 (C Africa & S Africa)
2000-2200	5220 (E Asia), 6950 & 9920 (Europe)
2100-2130	11790 (C Africa & E Africa)
2100-2200	**S** 6010
2200-2230 ⬅	3985 (Europe)
2200-2300	**W** 7170 & **S** 9880 (Europe)

CHINA (TAIWAN)
VOICE OF FREE CHINA

0200-0300	5950 (E North Am), 7130 (E Asia), 11740 (C America)
0200-0400	9680 (W North Am), 11825 (SE Asia), 15345 (E Asia)
0300-0400	5950 (E North Am & C America), 11745 (E Asia)
0700-0800	5950 (C America)
1200-1300	7130 (E Asia), 9610 (Australasia)
2200-2300	**W** 5810, **W** 9985, **S** 15600 & **S** 17750 (Europe)

VOICE OF ASIA—(SE Asia)

| 1100-1200 | 7445 |

CLANDESTINE (AFRICA)
"RADIO DEMOCRAT INTL"—(W Africa)

| 2100-2200 | 6205/7195 |

COSTA RICA
ADVENTIST WORLD RADIO

0500-0600	5030 & 6150 (C America), 7375 (C America & S America), 9725 (C America)
1100-1300	5030 & 6150 (C America), 7375 (C America & S America), 9725 & 13750 (C America)
1600-1700	Sa/Su 9725 & Sa/Su 13750 (C America)
2300-2400	5030, 6150, 9725 & 13750 (C America)

Carmelo Ciancio/VOA

The Dalai Lama, Tibetan spiritual leader, visits with the VOA's Tibetan Service. Although Chinese authorities, in defiance of a signed agreement, continue to jam the VOA, skillful station engineers have managed to get much of Washington's message through, anyway.

RADIO FOR PEACE INTERNATIONAL

0100-1200	6205 USB (N America), 7385 (C America & N America)
1700-2400	6200 (C America), 15050 USB (N America)
2200-2400	7385 (C America & N America)

CROATIA
CROATIAN RADIO

0000-0008	W 5895 (Europe), S 7165 & W 7370 (E North Am)
0100-0108	W 5895 & S 7165 (Europe), W 7370 (E North Am)
0200-0208 ←	5895 (Europe & N America)
0200-0208	S 7165 (Europe)
0300-0308 ←	5895 (Europe & N America)
0300-0308	S 7165 (Europe)
0400-0408 ←	5895 (Europe & N America)
0400-0408	S 7165 (Europe)
0500-0508 ←	5895 (Europe & N America)
1800-1808	S 7165 (Europe)
1900-1908 ←	13830 (E North Am)
1900-1908	W 5895 & W 7370 (Europe)
2100-2108	S 7165 (Europe), S 11635 (N America)
2200-2208	W 5895 (Europe), S 7165 (E North Am)
2300-2308	W 5895 (Europe), S 7165 & W 7370 (E North Am)

CUBA
RADIO HABANA

0100-0500	6000 (E North Am), 9820 (N America), 9830 USB (E North Am)
0400-0500	6180 (C America)
0500-0700	W 6000/9505 & S 9820 (W North Am), 9830 USB (Europe)
2100-2200	W 9550, S 11705/13715 & S 13725 USB (Europe & E North Am)
2200-2300	6180 (C America), W 9505 USB (Europe & E North Am)

CZECH REPUBLIC
RADIO PRAGUE

0000-0030	5930 & 7345 (E North Am)
0100-0130	6200 & 7345 (E North Am)
0300-0330	5930 & 7345 (E North Am)
0330-0400	W 6200 & S 9480 (Mideast & S Asia)
0700-0730	S 9530 (W Europe)
0800-0830 ←	7345 (W Europe)
0800-0830	W 5930 (W Europe)
0900-0930	S 15640 (W Africa), S 17485 (E Africa & Mideast)
1000-1030	W 15640 (S Asia), W 17485 (W Africa)
1130-1200 ←	7345 (N Europe), 9505 (W Europe)
1300-1330	S 11660 (W Europe)

1400-1430 ◨	17485 (E Africa)
1400-1430	**W** 13580 (E North Am)
1600-1630	**S** 17485 (E Africa)
1700-1730 ◨	5930 (W Europe)
1700-1730	**W** 9430 (Mideast & E Africa), **S** 15640 (C Africa)
1800-1830 ◨	5835 (W Europe)
1800-1830	**W** 9430 (Australasia)
2000-2030	**S** 5930 (W Europe), **S** 11640 (S Asia & Australasia)
2100-2130	**W** 5930 (E North Am), **W** 7345 (W Africa)
2230-2300	**W** 5930 & 7345 (E North Am), **S** 9430 (W Africa), **S** 11600 (E North Am)

DENMARK
RADIO ABC—(Europe)

0900-1300 ◨	Su 7570/9990

ECUADOR
HCJB-VOICE OF THE ANDES

0030-0500	9745 (E North Am)
0030-1130	21455 USB (Europe & Australasia)
0500-0700	9745 (W North Am)
0700-0830	**W** 6050 & **S** 11615 (Europe)
0700-1130	5900/9445 (Australasia)
1100-1500	12005 (C America)
1130-1430	15115 (N America & S America)
1200-1600	21455 USB (Europe & Australasia)
1430-1600	15115 (S America)
1700-2000	21455 USB (Europe & Australasia)
1900-2200	**W** 11960 & **S** 15540 (Europe)

EGYPT
RADIO CAIRO

0000-0030	9900 (E North Am)
0200-0330	9475 (N America)
1215-1330	17595 (S Asia)
1630-1830	15255 (C Africa & S Africa)
2030-2200	15375 (W Africa)
2115-2245	9900 (Europe)
2300-2400	9900 (E North Am)

FINLAND
YLE RADIO FINLAND

1030-1100	**S** 13645 & **S** 15235 (SE Asia & Australasia)
1130-1200	**S** 11900 (N America), **W** 15240 (E Asia & SE Asia), **W** 17825 (SE Asia & Australasia)
1230-1300 ◨	15400 (N America)
1230-1300	**W** 11735 & **S** M-Sa 11900 (N America)
1330-1400 ◨	M-Sa 15400 (N America)
1330-1400	**W** M-Sa 11735 (N America)
2030-2100	**S** 9855 & **S** 15440 (Europe & W Africa)
2130-2200	**W** 6120 (Europe & W Africa)

FRANCE
RADIO FRANCE INTERNATIONALE

1200-1300	9805 (E Europe), 11600 (SE Asia), **W** 11615 (E North Am), 13625 (N America & C America), 15155 & 15195 (E Europe), 15325 (W Africa), 15530 (C America), **W** 17575 (Irr) (N America)
1400-1455	5220/4130 (E Asia)
1400-1500	7110 (S Asia), **W** 12030 & **S** 15405 (S Asia & SE Asia), 17560 (Mideast)

1600-1700	6175 (Europe & N Africa), 11615 (N Africa), **S** 11615 (Mideast), 11700 (W Africa), 12015 & 15530 (S Africa)
1600-1730	**W** 9485 (Mideast & E Africa), **S** 15210 & **S** 15460 (E Africa)

GERMANY
DEUTSCHE WELLE

0100-0150	6040 & 6085 (N America), 6145, **S** 9640, **W** 9670 & **S** 11740 (N America & C America)
0200-0250	**W** 6035, **W** 7265, 7285, **W** 7355, **W** 9515 & 9615 (S Asia), **S** 9640 (N America & C America), 9690, **S** 11945, **S** 11965 & **S** 12045 (S Asia)
0300-0350	**W** 6045 (N America), 6085, **S** 6185, 9535 & **S** 9615 (N America & C America), **S** 9640 & **W** 9650 (N America)
0400-0450	**S** 5990 (S Africa), **S** 6015 & **W** 6065 (Africa), **S** 6185 (N America), **S** 7150 (Mideast & Africa), 7225 & **W** 7265 (Africa), **S** 9565 & **W** 9565 (S Africa), **S** 11765 (Africa)
0500-0550	**S** 5960 (N America), **S** 6045 (N America & C America), **W** 6120 (N America), **W** 6145 (N America & C America), 6185 (W North Am), **S** 9515 & **W** 9650 (N America)
0600-0650	**W** 7225, **W** 9565, **W** 11765, **S** 11915, 13790, **S** 15185 & **S** 15225 (W Africa), 17820 (E Asia), **S** 17875 (Africa), **S** 21680 & **W** 21705 (Mideast)
0900-0950	6160 & **W** 7380 (Australasia), **W** 11715 & **S** 11730 (SE Asia & Australasia), **S** 12055 (E Asia), **S** 17715 & **W** 17820 (SE Asia & Australasia), **S** 21680 (Australasia)
0900-1000	9565 (Africa), **W** 15145 (E Africa), 15410 (S Africa), 17800 (W Africa), 21600 (Africa)
1100-1200	15370 (C Africa & W Africa), **S** 15410 (W Africa), **W** 15410 (S Africa), **S** 17715 & **S** 17765 (W Africa), **W** 17780 (Africa), 17800 & **S** 17860 (W Africa), **S** 21600 (Africa)
1600-1650	6170 (S Asia), **W** 7195 (S Africa), 7225, **W** 7305, **W** 9585, **S** 9875 & **S** 13690 (S Asia)
1600-1700	**S** 7185 (S Africa), 9735 (Africa), 11965 (S Africa), 13610 (Africa), **W** 15145 (E Africa & S Africa), **S** 17800 (Africa)
1900-1950	**S** 7170, **W** 9640 & **S** 9670 (Africa), **S** 9735, **W** 9765 & **S** 11740 (W Africa), **W** 11785 (Africa), **S** 11785 & **W** 11810 (W Africa), **S** 13690 (Mideast), **W** 13690 (E Africa), **S** 13790, **W** 15135 & **W** 15425 (W Africa)
2000-2050	**W** 5960, **S** 7170, **W** 7285 & **S** 9615 (Europe)
2100-2150	**S** 7115 (Australasia), **W** 9615 (W Africa), 9670 (SE Asia & Australasia), **S** 9735 (W Africa), 9765 (SE Asia & Australasia), **S** 11765 (W Africa), 11785 (SE Asia & Australasia), **W** 11865 (W Africa), **W** 15275 (W Africa & Americas)

2300-2350	**S** *5980* (S Asia & SE Asia), **W** 6000 (SE Asia), **W** *6160* (S Asia & E Asia), **S** 7235 (E Asia), **W** 7235 (SE Asia), **S** 9690 (E Asia), **S** *12045* (S Asia & SE Asia)

GHANA
GHANA BROADCASTING CORPORATION
0000-0100 &	
0350-0910	4915
0500-0905	3366
0910-1115	M-F 4915 (Irr)
0910-1225	Sa/Su 4915
1225-1705	M-F 6130
1225-2400	4915
1700-2400	3366

GREECE
FONI TIS HELLADAS
0130-0200	**W** 7448, **W** 9420 & 9935/6260 (N America)
0330-0345	**W** 7448 & **W** 9420 (N America)
0745-0755	7450, **S** 9425 & 11645 (Europe & Australasia)
1235-1245	**S** 15175 (Europe & N America)
1335-1345 ⬅	15650 (Europe & N America)
1335-1345	**W** 9420 (Europe & N America)
1840-1855	11645 & 15150 (Africa)
1900-1910	**W** 9375/9380 (Europe)
2000-2010	**S** 7430/9420 (Europe)
2235-2245	9425 (Australasia)
2335-2350	**S** 9395 (C America & S America), **S** 9425 (C America & Australasia), **W** 9425 (C America), 11595 & **W** 11640 (S America)

GUAM
KSDA-ADVENTIST WORLD RADIO
1000-1100	9370 (E Asia)
1030-1100	9530 (E Asia)
1330-1400	9650 (E Asia)
1600-1700	**S** 7395 & **W** 7400 (S Asia)
1730-1800	9370 (W Asia)
2130-2200	**W** 9495 & **S** 15310 (E Asia)
2300-2400	**S** 11775 & **W** 11980 (SE Asia)

KTWR-TRANS WORLD RADIO
0755-0915	15200 (SE Asia)
0855-1000	11830 (Australasia)
1500-1630	11580 (S Asia & SE Asia)

GUYANA
VOICE OF GUYANA
0900-2100	5950
2100-0900	3290

HOLLAND
RADIO NETHERLANDS
0000-0125	6020 (E North Am), *6165* (N America), **S** *9845* (E North Am)
0030-0130	**S** *9860* (S Asia)
0030-0225	**W** *5905*, **W** *7305* & 11655 (S Asia)
0130-0325	9860 & **S** *9890* (S Asia)
0230-0325	*11655* (S Asia)
0430-0525	**W** *5995*, *6165* & **S** *9590* (W North Am)
0730-0825	**S** *9700* & **W** *11895* (Australasia)
0730-1025	*9720* (Australasia)
0830-0925	**W** *13700* (Australasia)

0930-1125	**W** *7260* (E Asia), **W** *9810* (SE Asia), **S** *12065* & **S** *13705* (E Asia & Australasia)
1030-1225	**S** *9650* (W Europe)
1130-1325 ⬅	*6045* (W Europe)
1130-1325	**W** *7190* (W Europe)
1330-1425	13700 (Mideast & S Asia)
1330-1625	**S** *9890* & **W** *9895* (S Asia), *15150* (S Asia & E Asia)
1430-1525	**W** *13700* (S Asia)
1730-1925	*6020* (S Africa), **W** 9860 & **S** 11655 (W Africa)
1730-2025	**S** *7120* & **W** *9605* (E Africa)
1830-1925	**W** 6015 (S Europe & W Africa), **S** *13700* (W Africa)
1830-1930	**W** *4945* (Mideast & N Africa), 9895 (W Africa)
1830-2025	*15315* & *17605* (W Africa)
1830-2125	**W** 7300 (W Africa), **S** 9860 (E Africa)
1930-2025	*4945* (Mideast & N Africa), **W** 6020 (N Africa & W Africa), **S** *7205* (C Africa & W Africa), **W** *11655* (W Africa & C Africa)
1930-2125	**S** 9895 & **S** 11655 (W Africa)
2030-2125	**W** *4945* (Mideast & N Africa)
2330-2400	6020 (E North Am), *6165* (N America), **S** *9845* (E North Am)

HUNGARY
RADIO BUDAPEST
0100-0130	**S** 9840 (N America)
0200-0230 ⬅	11870 (N America)
0200-0230	**W** 6190 & **W** 9850 (N America)
0230-0300	**S** 9840 (N America)
0330-0400 ⬅	11870 (N America)
0330-0400	**W** 5965 & **W** 9850 (N America)
1900-1930	**S** 6140 (N Europe), **S** 7130 (W Europe)
2000-2030 ⬅	3975 (Europe), 9835 (W Europe)
2000-2030	**W** 5970 (N Europe), **W** 7250 (W Europe)
2200-2230 ⬅	3975 (Europe), 5935 (N Europe), 7250 & 9835 (W Europe)

INDIA
ALL INDIA RADIO
0000-0045	7150 & 9705 (SE Asia), 9950 (E Asia), 11620 (E Asia & SE Asia)
1000-1100	11585 (E Asia), 13700 (Australasia), 15050 (E Asia & Australasia), 17387/ 17890 (Australasia)
1330-1500	7410, 11620 & 13750 (SE Asia)
1745-1945	7410 (N Europe), 9650 (N Africa & W Africa), 9950 (W Europe), 11935 (E Africa), 13700 (Mideast & W Asia), 15075/15050 (E Africa)
2045-2230	7150 (Australasia), 7410 (W Europe), 9910 (SE Asia), 9950 & 11620 (W Europe), 11715 (Australasia)
2245-2400	7150 & 9705 (SE Asia), 9950 (E Asia), 11620 (E Asia & SE Asia)

INDONESIA
VOICE OF INDONESIA
0100-0200 &	
0800-0900	9525 (Asia & Pacific)
2000-2100	9525 (Europe)

IRAN
VOICE OF THE ISLAMIC REPUBLIC
0030-0130	ⓦ 6150/6015 (Europe & C America), ⓢ 6175 (C America), ⓦ 7100 (N America), ⓢ 7180 (C America), ⓢ 7260 (E North Am), 9022 (N America), ⓦ 9670 (E North Am)
1130-1230	11745 (Mideast), ⓢ 11790 (W Asia), ⓦ 11790 (S Asia & SE Asia), ⓢ 11875 (S Asia), 11930 (Mideast), 15260 & 17750 (S Asia & SE Asia)
1530-1630	ⓦ 9575 (S Asia), ⓦ 11790 (S Asia & SE Asia), ⓢ 11875 (S Asia), 15260 & 17750 (S Asia & SE Asia)
1930-2030	7260 & 9022 (Europe)
2130-2230	ⓢ 6175 & ⓢ 9670 (Australasia)

IRELAND
RADIO TELEFIS EIREANN—(North America)
1000-1030 🏳	M-F 5065
1100-1130 🏳	Sa/Su 5065
1930-2000 🏳	M-F 12160
2000-2030 🏳	Sa 12160
2100-2130 🏳	Su 12160

ISRAEL
KOL ISRAEL
0400-0415	ⓢ 9435 (Europe)
0500-0515 🏳	7465 (W Europe & E North Am), 17545 (Australasia)
0500-0515	ⓦ 5885 (Europe)
1400-1430	ⓢ 12077 & ⓢ 15615 (W Europe & E North Am)
1500-1530	ⓦ 9435 & ⓦ 11605 (W Europe & E North Am)
1900-1930	ⓢ 11605 (W Europe & E North Am), ⓢ 15615 (W Africa & S America), ⓢ 15640 (E Europe)
2000-2030 🏳	7465 & 9435 (W Europe & E North Am), 15640 (S America)
2000-2030	ⓦ 7418 (E Europe), ⓦ 9845 (W Africa & S America), ⓦ 13750 (S America)

ITALY
IRRS-SHORTWAVE—(Europe)
0600-0630 🏳	M-F 3985
0630-0830 🏳	3985
0830-1030 🏳	M-F 3985
0830-1430 🏳	7125
1430-2100 🏳	3985
2100-2300 🏳	F-Su 3980/3950

RADIO ROMA-RAI INTERNATIONAL
0050-0100	6005 (E North Am)
0050-0110	9645/9675 (E North Am & C America), 11800 (N America & C America)
0425-0440	5990/5975 (S Europe), 7275 (S Europe & N Africa)
1935-1955	ⓦ 6030, 7235, ⓢ 9670 & ⓢ 11905 (N Europe)
2025-2045	ⓦ 5990, 7110, 9710 & ⓢ 11840 (Mideast)
2200-2225	5990/5975, 9710 & 11815 (E Asia)

JAPAN
RADIO JAPAN/NHK
0100-0200	ⓢ 5960 (E North Am), ⓦ 9605 & ⓢ 11790 (W North Am), 11840 (E Asia), 11860 (SE Asia), 11885 (W North Am),

11890/11900 (S Asia), 11910 (E Asia), 17810 (SE Asia), 17845 (S Asia)
0300-0400	ⓦ 5960 (E North Am), ⓦ 9605 & ⓢ 11790 (W North Am), 11840 (E Asia), ⓦ 11960 & ⓢ 15230 (W North Am), 17810 (SE Asia)
0500-0530	11885 (W North Am), 11895 (C America), ⓦ 11960 & ⓢ 15230 (W North Am)
0500-0600	ⓦ 5975 (Europe), 6110 (W North Am & C America), ⓦ 6150 & ⓢ 7230 (Europe), 11740 (SE Asia), 11920 (Australasia)
0500-0800	11725 (E Asia), 17810 (SE Asia)
0600-0700	11860 (E Asia)
0600-0800	11850 (Australasia)
0700-0800	ⓦ 5975 & 7230 (Europe), 11740 (SE Asia), 11920 (Australasia), 15165 (Europe, N Africa & Mideast), 17815 (C Africa), 21610 (SE Asia)
0900-1000	ⓦ 6090 & ⓢ 9610 (E Asia), 11850 (Australasia), 15190 (SE Asia)
1100-1200	ⓦ 6090 (E Asia), 6120 (E North Am), ⓢ 9610 (E Asia), 15350 (SE Asia)
1400-1500	ⓦ 6090 & ⓢ 9610 (E Asia), 11705 (W North Am), 11895 (S Asia)
1400-1600	9535 (W North Am), ⓦ 9695 & ⓢ 11915 (SE Asia)
1500-1600	ⓦ 7240 & ⓢ 11880/11930 (S Asia), 15355 (S Africa)
1700-1800	6150/6035 (E Asia), ⓦ 7280 (S Asia), 9535 (W North Am), 9580 (SE Asia), ⓢ 11880 (S Asia), 11930 (Mideast & N Africa)
1900-2000	6035 (Australasia), 6150/6035 (E Asia), 7140 (Australasia), 9535 (W North Am), 9580 (SE Asia), 11850 (Australasia)
2100-2110	ⓦ 7190, ⓢ 9570 & 11685 (SE Asia)
2100-2200	6035 & ⓦ 7125 (SE Asia), ⓦ 7140 (E Asia), ⓢ 9535 (SE Asia), ⓢ 9560 (E Asia), 11850 (Australasia)
2300-2400	ⓢ 5965, ⓦ 6055 & ⓦ 6155 (Europe), ⓦ 7125 (SE Asia), ⓦ 7140 (E Asia), ⓢ 9535 (SE Asia), ⓢ 9560 (E Asia), 11850 (Australasia)

JORDAN
RADIO JORDAN—(W Europe & E North Am)
1200-1300 &	
1500-1730 🏳	11970

KAZAKHSTAN
RADIO ALMATY/R KAZAKHSTAN
0530-0600	ⓢ 11705 (W Europe)
1700-1730	ⓦ 5940 (S Europe & N Africa)

KENYA
KENYA BROADCASTING CORPORATION
0200-2100	4885 & 4935

KOREA (DPR)
RADIO PYONGYANG
0000-0050	11335, 13760 & 15130 (Americas)
0400-0450	15180, 15230 & 17765 (SE Asia)
0600-0650	15180 & 15230 (SE Asia)
0700-0750	15340 (E Asia & S Asia), 17765 (SE Asia)
0800-0850	15180 & 15230 (SE Asia)
1100-1150	6575, 9975 & 11335 (Americas)
1300-1350	9345 (Europe), 9640 (S Asia), 11740

(Europe), 13760 (Americas), 15230
(SE Asia & N America)

1500-1550 &	
1700-1750	9325 (Europe), 9640 (Mideast & Africa), 9975 (Africa), 13785 (Europe)
2000-2050	6575 & 9345 (Europe), 9640 (Mideast & Africa), 9975 (Africa)
2300-2350	[W] 11700 (C America), 13650 (Americas)

KOREA (REPUBLIC)
RADIO KOREA INTERNATIONAL
0200-0300	7275 (E Asia), 11725 & 11810 (S America), 15575 (N America)
0800-0900	7550 & 13670 (Europe)
1030-1100	[S] 11715 (E North Am)
1130-1200	[W] 9650 (E North Am)
1200-1300	7285 (E Asia)
1230-1300	9570 (SE Asia), 9640 (E Asia), 13670 (SE Asia)
1600-1700	5975 (E Asia), 9515 & 9870 (Mideast & Africa)
1830-1900	[S] 3955 (W Europe)
1900-2000	5975 & 7275 (E Asia)
1930-2000	[W] 3970 (W Europe)
2100-2200	6480 & 15575 (Europe)

KUWAIT
RADIO KUWAIT—(Europe & E North Am)
| 1800-2100 | 11990 |

LEBANON
VOICE OF LEBANON
0900-0915,	
1315-1330 &	
1800-1815 [◄]	6550

LIBERIA
LIBERIAN COMMUNICATIONS NETWORK
| 0500-1800 | 6110/6100 |
| 1800-0200 | 5100 |

LITHUANIA
RADIO VILNIUS
0030-0100	[S] 9560/6120 (E North Am)
0030-0100	[W] 5910
0930-1000 [◄]	9710 (Europe)

MALAWI
MALAWI BROADCASTING CORP
0255-0710	3380, 5995
0710-1400	5995
1400-2210	3380, 5995

MALAYSIA
RADIO MALAYSIA KOTA KINABALU
| 0800-1600 & | |
| 2300-0200 | 5980 |
RADIO MALAYSIA SARAWAK
0000-0100,	
0500-0800,	
1030-1200,	
1400-1600 &	
2330-2400	7160
RADIO MALAYSIA
| 24 Hr | 7295 |
VOICE OF MALAYSIA—SE Asia & Australasia
| 0555-0825 | 6175, 9750, 15295 |

MOLDOVA
RADIO DNIESTER INTERNATIONAL—(W Europe & E North Am) (Temporarily Inactive)
| 2030-2100 | [S] M/W/Th 11750 |
| 2130-2200 | [W] M/W/Th 6205 |
RADIO MOLDOVA INTERNATIONAL
0330-0400 &	
0430-0500	[W] 7500 & [S] 7520 (E North Am)
2200-2230 &	
300-2330	[S] 7520 (Europe)

MONACO
TRANS WORLD RADIO—(W Europe)
0740-0905 [◄]	7115/7110
0905-0920 [◄]	Su-F 7115/7110
1230-1255 [◄]	Sa/Su 7115/7110

MONGOLIA
RADIO ULAANBAATAR
0930-1000	[W] 9960 & 12085 (Australasia)
1230-1300	[W] 9950 & 12085 (Australasia)
1500-1530	[W] 7530 & [W] 9950 (S Asia & SE Asia)
1930-2000	[W] 4081 & 7530 (Europe)

NAMIBIA
NAMIBIAN BROADCASTING CORPORATION
0000-0600 [→]	3290
0400-0600 [→]	3270
0600-1600 [→]	4930, 4965
1600-1910 [→]	3270
1600-2400 [→]	3290

NEW ZEALAND
RADIO NEW ZEALAND INTERNATIONAL—(Pacific)
0000-0458	15115
0459-0716	[S] 9570/9795
0500-0715	[W] 11900
0715-0758	[W] Sa/Su 11900
0716-0758	[S] Sa/Su 9570/9795
0717-0758	[W] Sa/Su 9700
0717-0759	[S] M-F 6100
0758-1130	[W] 9700
0759-1130	[S] 6100
1130-1206	[S] Th-Tu 6100 & [W] Th-Tu 9700
1207-1649	[S] 6100 (Irr)
1207-1650	[W] 9875 (Irr)
1650-1850	[W] M-F 9875
1650-1853	[S] M-F 6145
1850-1950	[S] 11735
1850-1953	[W] M-F 9875
1950-2215	11735
2217-2400	15115
RADIO READING SERVICE
| 24 Hr | 3935 |
| 1900-0500 [→] | 5960, 7290 |

NIGERIA
RADIO NIGERIA
0400-2308	6090, 7275
0430-1000	3326
0430-1030	3970
0430-2300	4770, 9570
0430-2308	4990, 6025, 6050
1000-1700	7285
1445-2030	3970
1700-2308	3326
VOICE OF NIGERIA—(Africa)
| 0455-0700, | |

1000-1100,	
1500-1700 &	
1900-2100	7255 (Irr)

NORWAY
RADIO NORWAY INTERNATIONAL

0100-0130	[W] M 7465 (E North Am & C America), [S] M 9560 (N America)
0300-0330	[W] M 7465 (W North Am)
0400-0430	[S] M 7520 (W North Am)
0600-0630	[S] Su 7295 (Australasia), [S] Su 9590 (W Africa & Australasia)
0700-0730	[W] Su 7180 (W Europe & Australasia)
0800-0830	[S] Su 17855 (Australasia)
1200-1230	[S] Su 9590 (Europe), [S] Su 13800 & [S] Su 15305 (E Asia)
1300-1330	[W] Su 9590 (Europe), [W] Su 9795 (E Asia), [S] Su 13800 (SE Asia & Australasia), [S] Su 15340 (N America), [W] Su 15605 (SE Asia & Australasia)
1400-1430	[W] Su 11840 (N America)
1500-1530	[W] Su 9520 & [W] Su 11730 (Mideast)
1600-1630	[S] Su 11860 (S Asia), [S] Su 13805 (E Africa)
1800-1830	[S] Su 7485 (Europe), [S] Su 9590 (Mideast), [S] Su 13805 (W Africa), [S] Su 15220 (C Africa)
1900-1930	[W] Su 5930 (Australasia), [W] Su 5960 (Europe), [W] Su 7485 (W Africa), [W] Su 9590 (C Africa)
2000-2030	[S] Su 9590 (Australasia)
2200-2230	[W] Su 6200 (E North Am), [W] Su 7115 (E Asia), [S] Su 9485 (Australasia)

PAKISTAN
RADIO PAKISTAN

0230-0245	7290 (S Asia), 15190/15120 (S Asia & SE Asia), 17705 (SE Asia), 17725 (E Africa), 21730/15485 (S Asia & SE Asia)
0800-0850 &	
1105-1120	[W] 15470 & 17900/17895 (Europe)
1600-1630	7230 (S Asia), 9485, 9515/9785 & 11570 (Mideast), 11745/11935 (E Africa & S Africa), 13590 (Mideast), 15555 (E Africa & S Africa)
1700-1750	5825 & [S] 11570 (Europe)

PAPUA NEW GUINEA
NBC

0000-0700	9675
0700-0800	9675/4890
0800-1200 &	
1930-2208	4890
2210-2400	9675

PHILIPPINES
FEBC RADIO INTERNATIONAL

0000-0200	15450 (S Asia & SE Asia)
0930-1100	11635 (E Asia & Australasia)
1300-1600	11995 (S Asia & SE Asia)

RADIO VERITAS ASIA—(Mideast)

1515-1525	11715
1525-1555	W/Sa/Su 11715

RADYO PILIPINAS

0230-0330	17760 & 17865/17840 (S Asia), 21580 (E Asia)
0330-0400	13770 (SE Asia), 15330 (E Asia), 17730 (W North Am)

POLAND
POLISH RADIO

1300-1355 [▣]	6095, 7145, 7270 & 9525 (W Europe), 11815 (W Europe & E North Am)
1800-1855 [▣]	6095, 7270 & 7285 (W Europe)
2030-2125 [▣]	6035, 6095 & 7285 (W Europe)

PORTUGAL
RDP INTERNATIONAL (RADIO PORTUGAL)

0330-0400	Tu-Sa 6095/6130 & Tu-Sa 9570 (E North Am)
1530-1600 [▣]	M-F 21515 (Mideast & S Asia)
2100-2130 [▣]	M-F 6130, M-F 9780 & M-F 9815 (Europe), M-F 15515 (Irr) (E Africa & S Africa)

ROMANIA
RADIO ROMANIA INTERNATIONAL

0200-0300 &	
0400-0500	5990 (E North Am), 6155, 9510, 9570 & 11940 (N America)
0530-0600	[S] 11810, [W] 11940, 15250, [S] 15340 & [W] 15380 (C Africa & S Africa), [W] 17720 (Africa), 17745 & 17790 (C Africa & S Africa)
0632-0641	[W] 7105, [W] 7175, [S] 7225, [S] 9550, 9665, [W] 11775 & [S] 11810 (Europe)
0645-0715	Su 11775 & Su 15335 (Australasia)
0645-0745	M-Sa 15250, M-Sa 17720 & M-Sa 17805 (Australasia)
1300-1400	[W] 9690, [W] 11790 & 11940 (Europe), [S] 15365 & [S] 17720 (W Europe)
1430-1530	[W] 11740 & [S] 11775 (S Asia), [W] 11810 & 15335 (Mideast & S Asia), 17720 (S Asia & SE Asia)
1730-1800	[W] 9510 (Africa), [W] 9750 & [W] 11740 (S Africa), [W] 11940 & [S] 15340 (N Africa & C Africa), 15365 (C Africa & S Africa), [S] 17805 (E Africa)
1900-2000	[W] 5955, [W] 5995, [W] 6105, [W] 6190, [W] 7195, [S] 9550, [S] 9690, [S] 11810 & [S] 11940 (Europe)
2100-2200	[W] 5990, [W] 6105, [W] 6190, [W] 7105, 7195, [S] 9550, [S] 9690 & [S] 11940 (Europe)

RUSSIA
VOICE OF RUSSIA

0000-0100	[S] 7125 (W Europe & E North Am), [W] *7180* (N Europe, E North Am & C America), [S] 7250 (E North Am), [S] *9665* (E North Am & C America)
0000-0200	[W] *7125* (N Europe, W Europe & E North Am)
0000-0500	[S] 9620 (E North Am & C America)
0000-0600	[W] 7105 (Europe & E North Am)
0100-0500	[S] 15180 (W North Am)
0100-0700	[S] 12010, [S] 12050, [S] 13665 & [S] 15580 (W North Am)
0200-0300	[W] 12030 & [W] 13640 (W North Am)
0200-0400	Tu-Sa 7345 (W North Am)
0200-0700	[S] 13645 (W North Am)
0200-0800	[W] 5920 & [W] 7270 (W North Am)
0300-0400	[W] 5940 (E North Am)
0300-0500	[S] *7230* (C America)
0400-0600	[W] *7180* (N Europe, E North Am & C America)
0400-0800	[W] 7175 (W North Am)

0430-0800	**W** 7330 (W North Am)
0500-0800	**W** 5930 (W North Am), **S** 17580 (SE Asia)
0500-0900	**S** 15470 (E Asia & Australasia)
0530-0700	**S** 12040 (W North Am)
0530-0800	**W** 5905 (W North Am)
0600-0700	**S** 15490 (SE Asia & Australasia)
0600-0800	**W** 15470, 17570 & **W** 21790 (Australasia)
0600-0900	**W** 15160 (Australasia), **S** 15560 (SE Asia & Australasia), **W** 17560 (SE Asia)
0600-1100	**W** 12025 (Australasia)
0800-1000	**S** 15580 (E Asia & SE Asia)
0800-1100	**W** 9685 (SE Asia)
0800-1300	**W** 17860 (S Asia, SE Asia & Australasia), **W** 17880 (Australasia)
0830-1100	**S** 9835 (Australasia), **S** 11800 (S Pacific), **S** 12025 (SE Asia)
0830-1200	**W** 12005 (Australasia)
0930-1100	**W** 7305 (SE Asia)
0930-1200	**W** 9450 (Australasia)
1000-1100	**W** *17755* (S Asia & SE Asia)
1000-1200	**S** 7150 (E Asia), **W** 15490 (S Asia & SE Asia), **W** 15560 (S Asia), **S** 17560 (Australasia)
1000-1300	**S** 11880 (S Asia), **W** *13785* & **S** *15170* (S Asia & SE Asia), **S** 15490 (S Asia), **S** *17775* (S Asia & SE Asia)
1000-1400	**S** 17610 (S Asia & SE Asia)
1030-1300	**S** 11655 (S Asia)
1100-1200	**W** 12055, **S** 15460, **S** 15560 & **W** 17890 (SE Asia)
1100-1300	**S** 9920 (Australasia), **W** *15120* (S Asia), *17755* (S Asia & SE Asia)
1200-1300	**W** 9725 (W Asia & S Asia), **S** 11785 & **S** 15110 (S Asia), **S** 15230 (W Asia & S Asia), **S** 15510 (S Asia & SE Asia)
1200-1400 ⬅	*4740* (W Asia & S Asia)
1200-1400	**S** 9800 (E Asia)
1230-1300	**W** 9875 (S Asia & SE Asia), **S** 15435 (S Asia)
1300-1400 ⬅	*4975* (W Asia & S Asia)
1300-1400	**W** 12055, **S** 15460, **W** 15470 & **S** 15560 (SE Asia), **S** *17755* (S Asia & SE Asia)
1300-1500	**S** *15340* (W Africa & S America)
1400-1500	**S** 11985 (Mideast & W Asia)
1400-1600	**W** 7130 & **W** 7165 (Mideast & W Asia), **S** *11835* & **W** 12065 (Mideast), **S** *15320* (Mideast & W Asia), **S** 15540 (Mideast), **S** 15560 (Mideast & E Africa)
1400-1700	**S** *11945* & **S** 15350 (Mideast & E Africa), **S** 17525
1400-1800	**W** 9470 (C Africa & S Africa)
1430-1600	**S** 9595 (W Asia & S Asia)
1500-1600	**W** *11765* (Mideast & W Asia), **S** 12035 (Mideast & E Africa), **S** *17750* (Mideast)
1500-1700 ⬅	*4740, 4940* & *4975* (W Asia & S Asia)
1500-1700	**W** 9635 (Mideast), **W** *9905* (W Asia & S Asia), **W** *11945* (Mideast & C Africa), **S** 12025 (E Africa)
1500-1800	**W** 7115 (N Europe), **W** 7325 (C Africa & S Africa)
1500-1900	**S** *9365* (Mideast & E Africa), **S** 9675 (Mideast & S Africa), **S** *9975* (S Africa), **S** 11775 (N Africa & E Africa)
1500-2000	**S** *15400* (N Europe & E North Am)
1500-2200	**S** 9880 (Europe)
1530-1600	**W** 6005 (Mideast & W Asia)
1600-1700	**W** 5925 (N Africa), **W** Su-F 6005 (Mideast & W Asia), **W** 6175 (Mideast & N Africa), **S** 7240 (N Europe), **W** 7275 (Mideast & E Africa), **S** 7290 (N Europe), **W** 7330 (Europe), **S** 7350 (N Europe), **W** 9865 (W Africa), **S** 11675 (N Europe), **W** *11865* (C Africa)
1600-2000	**W** 7210 (Mideast & E Africa), **W** *9505* (S Africa)
1600-2100	**W** 9490 (W Africa)
1600-2200	**S** 9480 (N Europe), **S** 11630 (W Europe)
1600-2400	**W** *7180* (N Europe, E North Am & C America)
1630-1800	**S** 7440 (Europe & W Africa)
1630-1900	**W** 7175 & **W** *13670* (W Africa)
1700-1800	**W** *4740* (W Asia & S Asia), **W** M/W/F/Sa 5935 (Mideast & W Asia), **W** 5995 & **W** 6055 (N Europe), *6590* (E Asia), **S** *17875* (W Africa)
1700-2000	**W** 7255 (E Africa & S Africa)
1700-2200	**W** 5940 (N Europe)
1700-2300	**W** 7205 (N Europe & W Europe), **W** 9890 (N Europe)
1730-1800	**W** 7130 (Mideast & W Asia), **W** *9585* (Mideast & N Africa), **S** 12065 (Mideast & W Asia)
1800-2000	**S** 7240 & **S** 7290 (N Europe), **S** *11945* (Mideast & E Africa)
1800-2100	**S** 11675 (N Europe)
1800-2200	**S** 7350 (N Europe)
1830-2000	**S** 11765 (Mideast & E Africa)
1900-2000	**S** 7440 (Europe & W Africa), **S** *17875* (W Africa)
1900-2100	**W** 7325 & **W** 9470 (C Africa & S Africa), **W** *9585* (Mideast & N Africa)
1900-2300	**W** 5995 & **W** 6055 (N Europe)
1930-2000	**W** 7200 (E Africa & S Africa)
2000-2100	**W** 7175 (W Africa), **W** 9795 (S Europe), **W** *13670* (W Africa)
2030-2300	**S** 11890 (S America)
2030-2400	**S** 9665 (E North Am & C America)
2100-2200	**S** 9580 (Europe), **S** 9710 (Europe & W Africa)
2100-2400	**S** *11750* (E North Am)
2120-2300	**W** 7400 (W Europe & C America)
2130-2200	**W** 7170 (Europe)
2130-2300	**S** 7250 (E North Am)
2200-2300	**W** 7140 & **W** 7360 (Europe), **S** 11860 (W Europe & S America)
2220-2400	**W** 5940 (E North Am)
2230-2300	**S** *11840* (S America)
2230-2400	**S** 7125 (W Europe & E North Am)
2300-2400	**W** 7105 (Europe & E North Am), **W** *7125* (N Europe, W Europe & E North Am), **W** 7170 (Europe), **W** 7205 & **W** *9550* (C America), **W** 9795 (S America)

SEYCHELLES
FEBA RADIO

0500-0545	F 15555 (E Africa & Mideast)
1500-1530	12090/11870 (S Asia)
1500-1600	M-Sa 9810 (W Asia & S Asia)
1530-1545	Sa-M 12090/11870 (S Asia)

SINGAPORE
RADIO SINGAPORE INTERNATIONAL—(SE Asia)
1100-1400   6015 & 6155
RADIO CORPORATION OF SINGAPORE
1400-1700 &
2300-1100   6155

SLOVAKIA
RADIO SLOVAKIA INTERNATIONAL
0100-0130   5930 & 7300 (E North Am & C America),
              9440 (S America)
0830-0900   11990, **S** 15460, 17485/17550 &
              W 21705 (Australasia)
1730-1800 &
1930-2000 ▆▆▆ 5915, 6055 & 7345 (W Europe)

SOLOMON ISLANDS
SOLOMON ISLANDS BROADCASTING
0000-0030   M-F 5020, M-F 9545
0000-0230   Sa 5020, Sa 9545
0030-0230   Su 5020, Su 9545
0100-0800   M-F 5020, M-F 9545
0500-0800   Sa 5020, Su 5020, Sa 9545, Su 9545
0815-1130   Su 5020, Su 9545
0830-0900   M-F 5020, M-F 9545
0845-1100   Sa 9545
0845-1130   Sa 5020
0915-0930 &
0945-1130   M-F 5020, M-F 9545
1900-1930   Sa 5020
1900-2030   M-F 5020
1945-2400   Sa 5020
2000-2015 &
2030-2330   Su 5020
2045-2400   M-F 5020
2100-2330   Su 9545
2100-2400   M-F 9545, Sa 9545

SOUTH AFRICA
CHANNEL AFRICA
0300-0455   **S** 3220 (S Africa), 5955 & **W** 9585
              (E Africa & C Africa)
0500-0555   **S** 5955 & **W** 7185 (S Africa), **W** 11900
              (W Africa)
0500-0600   **S** 9590/9675 (W Africa)
1500-1755   **S** 3220 (S Africa), **S** 7155 (E Africa &
              C Africa), **W** 7155 (S Africa), **W** 9530
              (E Africa & C Africa)
1600-1655   **W** 15240 (W Africa)
1600-1700   **S** 9530 (W Africa)
SOUTH AFRICAN BROADCASTING CORP
0000-0300   3320 (S Africa)
0000-0435   3230
0435-0550   **S** 3230
0440-0555   **W** 5965 (S Africa)
0555-0650   5965 (S Africa)
0650-1525   **S** 5965 (S Africa)
0655-1650   **W** 7270 (S Africa)
1530-1655   **S** 3230
1655-2400   3230
2300-2400   3320 (S Africa)
TRANS WORLD RADIO—(W Africa)
0600-0657   11730

SPAIN
RADIO EXTERIOR DE ESPANA
0000-0200 &

0500-0600   9540 (N America & C America)
1200-1400   *5220/4130* (E Asia)
2100-2200   6125 (Europe), 11775 (Africa)

SRI LANKA
SRI LANKA BROADCASTING CORPORATION
0030-0430   9720 & 15425 (S Asia)
1030-1130   11835 (SE Asia & Australasia), 17850
              (SE Asia)
1230-1730   6075, 9720 & 15425 (S Asia)
2000-2130   9720 (E Asia)

SUDAN
RADIO OMDURMAN—(Europe, Mideast & Africa)
1800-1900   9024

SWAZILAND
TRANS WORLD RADIO
0430-0600   3200 (S Africa)
0430-0805   5055 & 6070 (S Africa)
0505-0805   9500 (S Africa)
0605-0805   9650 (S Africa)
0805-0835   M-F 5055, M-F 6070, M-F 9500 & M-F
              9650 (S Africa)
1600-1830   9500 (E Africa)
1745-1800   M-F 3200 (S Africa)
1800-2015   **S** 3200 (S Africa)
2015-2045   Su 3200 (S Africa)

SWEDEN
RADIO SWEDEN
0030-0100   6065 & **S** 9810 (S America)
0130-0200   9695/9895 (SE Asia & Australasia),
              W 11695 (S Asia)
0230-0300 ▆▆▆ 7120/7115 (N America)
0230-0300   **S** 9850 (N America)
0330-0400 ▆▆▆ 7120/7115 (N America)
0330-0400   **S** 9850 (N America)
1130-1200   **S** 13740 & **S** 15120 (E Asia &
              Australasia), **S** 15240 (S Asia)
1230-1300   **W** 13775 & **W** 15120 (E Asia &
              Australasia), **S** 15240 (E North Am),
              W 15240 (S Asia)
1330-1400 ▆▆▆ 11650 (N America)
1330-1400   15240 (E North Am)
1430-1500 ▆▆▆ 11650 (N America)
1430-1500   **W** 15240 (E North Am)
1715-1745 ▆▆▆ 6065 (Europe)
1730-1800   **S** 15600 (Europe & Africa)
1830-1900 ▆▆▆ 6065 (Europe & Mideast), 13690/13605
              (Mideast)
1830-1900   **W** 9655 (Europe & N Africa)
2130-2200 ▆▆▆ 6065 (Europe & Mideast), 9655 (Europe
              & Africa)
2230-2300 ▆▆▆ 6065 (Europe)

SWITZERLAND
SWISS RADIO INTERNATIONAL
0100-0130   6135 (E North Am), 9885 (E North Am &
              C America), *9905* (N America & C
              America)
0400-0430   6135 (W North Am), 9885 (N America)
0400-0500   *9905* (N America & C America)
0515-0530   **S** 9535 (S Europe & E Europe)
0600-0630   9885 & **S** 11860 (W Africa), **W** 12070 &
              S 13635 (S Africa), **W** 13635 (W Africa)
0615-0630 ▆▆▆ 6165 (Europe & N Africa)

0615-0630 [W] 7410 (E Europe), [S] 9535 (S Europe & E Europe)
0715-0730 ⬛ 6165 (Europe & N Africa)
0715-0730 [W] 7410 (E Europe)
0900-0930 9885, [W] 11640, 13685 & [S] 17515 (Australasia)
1100-1130 ⬛ 6165 (Europe & N Africa), 9535 (S Europe & W Europe)
1100-1130 [W] 9885, [W] 11640, 13635, [S] 15415 & [S] 17515 (E Asia)
1300-1330 7230 (SE Asia), 7480 (E Asia), [W] 11640, 13635 & [S] 15480 (SE Asia)
1300-1400 ⬛ 6165 (Europe & N Africa), 9535 (S Europe & W Europe)
1500-1530 [W] 9885 & 12075 (C Asia & S Asia), 13635 & [S] 15530 (W Asia & S Asia)
1700-1730 [W] 5850 (Mideast), [W] 7510 (N Europe), 9885 (Mideast), [S] 9905 (N Europe), [S] 12075 (Mideast), 13635 (E Africa)
2000-2030 ⬛ 6165 (Europe & N Africa)
2000-2030 [W] 9770 (S Africa), [S] 9870 (Africa), 9885 (S Africa), 9905 & [S] 11640 (Africa), [W] 11640 (S Africa)

SYRIA
RADIO DAMASCUS
2005-2105 13610/15095 (Europe)
2110-2210 12085 (N America), 13610/15095 (Australasia)

TANZANIA
RADIO TANZANIA—(E Africa)
0330-0430 &
0900-1030 5050
1030-1530 Sa/Su 5050
1530-1915 5050

THAILAND
RADIO THAILAND
0000-0030 [W] 9680 & [S] 9690 (S Asia & E Africa)
0000-0100 9655 & 11905 (Asia)
0030-0100 [W] 11905 & [S] 15370 (N America)
0300-0330 9655 (Asia), [W] 11890 (W North Am), 11905 (Asia), [S] 15370 (W North Am)
0530-0600 15115 (Europe)
1230-1300 9885 (SE Asia & Australasia)
1400-1430 9830 (SE Asia & Australasia)
1900-2000 [S] 7210 & [W] 7295 (N Europe), 9655 & 11905 (Asia)
2030-2045 [S] 9555 (Europe), 9655 (Asia), [W] 11805 (Europe), 11905 (Asia)

TURKEY
VOICE OF TURKEY
0300-0350 [S] 17705 (S Asia, SE Asia & Australasia)
0400-0450 ⬛ 9655 (Europe & E North Am), 9685 (Mideast & W Asia)
0400-0450 [W] 9560 (W Asia, S Asia & Australasia)
1330-1420 ⬛ 9445 (Europe), 9630 (W Asia & S Asia)
1830-1850 [S] 9535 (Europe)
1930-2020 ⬛ 9445 (Europe)
2300-2350 ⬛ 7280 (Europe), 9560 (W Asia, S Asia & Australasia), 9655 (Europe & E North Am)

UKRAINE
RADIO UKRAINE
0000-0100 [S] 7150 & [S] 9550 (E North Am)
0100-0200 [W] 6010 (W Europe & C America), [W] 6055 (W North Am), [W] 9620 (W Africa & S America)
0130-0200 [W] 5915 (W Europe & E North Am)
0300-0400 [S] 7150 & [S] 9550 (E North Am)
0400-0500 [W] 5915 (W Europe & E North Am), [W] 6010 (W Europe & C America), [W] 7205 (W Europe, W Africa & S America)
2100-2200 [S] 6010 (S Europe & N Africa), [S] 6020 (E Europe), [S] 7375 (Australasia), [S] 9560 (S Europe & N Africa), [S] 9875 (S Africa)
2200-2300 ⬛ 5905 (S Europe & N Africa), 6080 (W Asia)
2200-2300 [W] 4795 & [W] 4820 (Europe), [W] 5940 (S Europe & N Africa), [W] 6010 (N Europe, W Europe & C America), [W] 6020 (N Europe & E North Am), [W] 6055 (Mideast & E Africa), [W] 6130 (W Europe, N Africa & E North Am), [W] 7135 (W Asia), [W] 7205 (W Europe, W Africa & S America), [W] 7240 (W Europe), [W] 9620 (W Africa & S America)

UNITED ARAB EMIRATES
UAE RADIO FROM ABU DHABI
2200-2400 9605 & 9695 (E North Am), 9770 (W North Am)
UAE RADIO IN DUBAI
0330-0400 11945, 13675, 15400 & 21485 (E North Am & C America)
0530-0600 15435 (Australasia), 17830 (E Asia), 21700 (Australasia)
1030-1110,
1330-1400 &
1600-1640 13675 & 15395 (Europe), 17825/17630 (N Africa), 21605 (Europe)

UNITED KINGDOM
BBC WORLD SERVICE
0000-0030 [W] 9525, [S] 11945 & [W] 15280 (E Asia)
0000-0100 5965 (S Asia), [W] 9580 (E Asia)
0000-0200 6195 (SE Asia), [W] 7265 (S Asia), [S] 9410 (W Asia & S Asia), 11750 (S America)
0000-0230 9590 (C America & S America), 9915 (S America)
0000-0300 [W] 9410 (C Asia & E Asia), 11955 (S Asia)
0000-0330 5970 (S America & C America), 6175 (N America)
0000-0700 5975 (N America & C America)
0030-0100 15280 (E Asia)
0100-0200 [W] 5965 (S Asia)
0100-0300 [S] 9605 (W Asia & S Asia), 17790 (E Asia)
0100-0330 [W] 6155 (C Asia), 15360 (SE Asia)
0200-0300 [S] 9410 (N Europe), [W] 9605 (W Asia & S Asia)
0200-0330 6135 (E Africa), [W] 7235 (S Asia)
0230-0330 7325 (S America), [S] 9895 (C America & S America)
0230-0430 [W] 9590 (C America & S America)
0300-0400 6005 (W Africa & S Africa), [S] 6180 (Europe), [W] 9605 (W Asia & S Asia), 12095 (E Africa)
0300-0430 [S] 9605 (W Asia & S Asia)
0300-0500 11955 (E Asia)
0300-0600 3255 (S Africa)

John McCarthy presents Outlook, one of the most enjoyable of the BBC World Service's offerings. Habit-forming, it covers everything from hard news to the goings-on of ordinary people in extraordinary circumstances.

BBC

0300-0800	*9600 (S Africa)*
0300-0815	W *3955 (Europe), 6190 (S Africa)*
0300-0830 ⬅	6195 (Europe)
0300-0900	*15280 (E Asia)*
0300-0915	*11760 (Mideast), 15310 (W Asia & S Asia)*
0300-2230	9410 (Europe)
0330-0409	S *9615 (E Africa)*
0330-0410	W *9610 (E Africa)*
0330-0430	W *6175 (N America),* 9610 (E Africa)
0330-0500	*11730 (E Africa),* W *17790 (E Asia)*
0400-0500	S *12095 (Europe),* W *12095 &* S *17640 (E Africa)*
0400-0715	7160 (W Africa & C Africa)
0400-0730	*6005 (W Africa), 6180 (Europe), 15575 &* W *15575 (W Asia)*
0430-0800 ⬅	6175 (C America)
0500-0615	*15420 (E Africa)*
0500-0700	*17640 (E Africa)*
0500-0800	*15360 (SE Asia & Australasia)*
0500-0915	*11955 (SE Asia & Australasia)*
0500-1130	*9740 (SE Asia)*
0500-1400	*17885 (E Africa)*
0500-2000	12095 (Europe)
0600-0730	W *11780 (Europe & N Africa),* S *15400 (W Africa),* S *15575 (Europe)*
0600-0800	*17790 (S Africa)*
0600-0810	W *7145 (Australasia)*
0600-0815	*11940 (S Africa)*

0615-0700	15420 (E Africa)
0700-0715	*11860 (W Africa & C Africa)*
0700-0730	W *9610 (W Africa), 17830 (Africa)*
0700-0800	W *5975 (N America & C America),* W *7325 &* W *17640 (Europe)*
0700-2000	15485 (W Europe & N Africa)
0730-0900	W Sa/Su *15575 (W Asia)*
0730-1000	*15400 (W Africa)*
0730-2100	*17830 (W Africa & C Africa)*
0800-0915	W *7325 (Europe)*
0800-1500	17640 (E Europe & Mideast)
0815-1000	Sa/Su *6190 &* Sa/Su *11940 (S Africa)*
0830-0915	W *6195 (Europe)*
0900-0930	*15575 (W Asia)*
0900-1000	W *7180,* S *9580 &* S *11765 (E Asia), 15190 (S America), 15360 (E Asia)*
0900-1030	*15280 (E Asia & Australasia), 17830 (SE Asia)*
0900-1615	*6195 (SE Asia), 17705 (N Africa)*
0900-1815	*11750 (S Asia)*
0915-1000	W *6065 & 11955 (E Asia)*
0930-1500	*15575 (Mideast & W Asia)*
1000-1100	S *5965 (E North Am), 15400 (Africa)*
1000-1130	Sa/Su *15190 (S America), 17790 (S Asia)*
1000-1400	*6195 (C America & N America), 11760 (Mideast), 15310 (W Asia & S Asia)*
1000-1615	*11940 (S Africa)*
1000-2200	*6190 (S Africa)*
1100-1130	*15400 (W Africa), 17790 & 17830 (S America)*
1100-1200	*5965 (E North Am)*
1100-1300	W *6065,* W *7180, 9580,* S *11765, 11955 & 15360 (E Asia)*
1100-1400	*15220 (Americas)*
1100-1700	*21660 (S Africa)*
1130-1200	S *9600 (Europe),* W *9635 (E Europe),* S *11680 (Europe),* S *11710 (E Europe),* S *11830 (W Asia),* S *11845 (E Europe & W Asia),* S *15115 (Europe & W Asia)*
1130-1615	*9740 (SE Asia & Australasia)*
1200-1300	S *9515 (E North Am)*
1200-1400	W *5965 (E North Am)*
1300-1415	*15420 (E Africa)*
1300-1600	W *9590 &* S *11865 (N America)*
1300-1615	W *5990 &* S *7180 (E Asia), 9515 (E North Am)*
1300-1700	*21470 (E Africa)*
1400-1415	*17740 (E Africa), M-F 21490 (E Africa & S Africa)*
1400-1430	*11860 (E Africa), Sa/Su 21490 (E Africa & S Africa)*
1400-1500	*15310 (S Asia)*
1400-1600	*15220 & 15260/11775 (N America)*
1400-1700	W *7205 (W Asia & S Asia), 17840 (Americas)*
1415-1430	Sa/Su *15420 & Sa/Su 17740 (E Africa)*
1430-1500	M-F *15400 (W Africa)*
1500-1515	Sa/Su *11860 (E Africa)*
1500-1700	S *5975 (W Asia & S Asia),* S *6195 (Europe), 15400 (W Africa)*
1515-1530	W *5875 (Europe), 11860 (E Africa),* W *12040 (Europe)*
1530-1615	W Su *5875 (Europe),* W M-F *7180 (E Asia)*
1600-1745	*3915 &* W *7135 (SE Asia)*

1615-1700	Sα *9515* (E North Am), *15420* (E Africa)
1615-1745	**S** *7180* (SE Asia)
1615-1800	**S** *3255* (S Africa), **W** *9510* (S Asia), **W** *11940* (S Africa)
1615-1830	**S** *9510 & 9740* (S Asia)
1700-1745	**S** *6005 & 9630* (E Africa)
1700-1800	**S** *17840* (W North Am & C America)
1700-1900	*15420* (E Africa), **W** *17840* (W North Am)
1700-1930	*15400* (W Africa & S Africa)
1700-2330	**W** 3955 (Europe)
1715-1830	*5975* (S Asia), *7160* (Mideast & W Asia)
1715-2200	*6180* (Europe)
1800-2000	**S** *11955* (Australasia)
1800-2200	*3255* (S Africa)
1800-2330 ◁	*6195* (Europe)
1830-2130	*9630* (E Africa)
1830-2200	*6005* (E Africa), *9740* (Australasia)
1900-2000	*5975* (W Asia), **S** *7160* (Mideast & W Asia)
1930-2100	**W** *15400* (S Africa)
1945-2000 ◁	*5875 & 7210* (Europe)
2000-2100	*11955* (Australasia), **W** 12095 (S Europe & Atlantic)
2000-2200	*7325* (Europe)
2000-2230	**S** *12095* (Europe)
2000-2400	*11750* (S America)
2030-2100 ◁	Sα/Su *6050* (E Europe)
2030-2100	**S** *9915* & **S** *11780* (E Europe)
2100-2200	*3915* (SE Asia), **W** *5990* & **W** *6120* (E Asia)
2100-2400	*5975* (N America & C America), *6195* (SE Asia), *11955* (SE Asia & Australasia)
2115-2130	M-F *15390* & M-F *17715* (C America)
2130-2145	Tu/F *11680* (Atlantic & S America)
2200-2230	**S** *7325* (Europe), **S** *9915* (S America)
2200-2300	**W** *5905* (E Asia), *9660* (Pacific), **S** *9890* (E Asia), *12080* (S Pacific)
2200-2400	*6175* (N America), **W** *7110* & **S** *9570* (SE Asia), *9590* (N America), 9915 (S America)
2230-2300	**W** 9410 (Europe)
2230-2400	9915 (S America)
2300-2400	**W** *7180*, **S** *7250*, **W** *9525*, **W** *9580* & **S** *11945* (E Asia)

USA

FAMILY RADIO—(S Asia)
1302-1502	*11550*

KAIJ, DALLAS TX—(N America)
0000-0700	5810
0700-0800	**W** 5810
1500-2230	15725
1900-2000	**S** 13815
2000-2400	13815

KJES, MESQUITE NM
1300-1400	11715 (E North Am)
1400-1500	11715 (W North Am)
1800-1900	15385 (Australasia)

KNLS-NEW LIFE SATION—(E Asia)
0800-0900	**W** 7365 & **S** 9615
1300-1400	7365

KTBN, SALT LAKE CITY UT—(E North Am)
0000-0100	**W** 7510 & **S** 15590
0100-1500	7510
1500-1600	**W** 7510 & **S** 15590
1600-2400	15590

KVOH-VOICE OF HOPE—(W North Am & C America)
0000-0330	Tu-Sα 17775
0000-0700	9975
1800-1900	Su 17775
1900-2100	Sα/Su 17775
2100-2200	Su 17775

KWHR, BIG ISLAND, HAWAII
0000-0100	Tu-Su 17510 (E Asia)
0100-0400	17510 (E Asia)
0400-0500	**W** 17510 (E Asia)
0400-0800	**S** 17880 (E Asia)
0500-0800	**W** 9930 (E Asia)
0800-0900	9930 (E Asia)
0900-1000	Su-F 9930 (E Asia)
1000-1100	9930 (E Asia)
1100-1200	Su-F 9930 (E Asia)
1300-1400	Sα 9930 (E Asia)
1430-1500	Sα/Su 9930 (E Asia)
1500-1600	9930 (E Asia)
1600-1800	6120 (Australasia)
1800-2000	13625 (Australasia)
2000-2100	**W** M-F 11980 & **S** M-F 15405 (E Asia)
2300-2330	M-F 17510 (E Asia)
2330-2400	Su-F 17510 (E Asia)

MONITOR RADIO INTERNATIONAL
0000-0057	M-Sα 7535 (E North Am), M-Sα 9430 (C America & S America)
0100-0157	7535 (N America), M-Sα 9430 (C America & S America)
0200-0257	5850 (W North Am), M-F 9430 (W North Am & C America)
0300-0357	5850 (W North Am), M-F 7535 (E Africa)
0400-0457	M-F 7535 (Europe), M-F 9840 (C Africa & S Africa)
0500-0557	Tu-F 7535 (Europe)
0600-0657 &	
0700-0757	Tu-F 7535 (W Europe)
0800-0857	Tu-Su 7535 (Europe), **S** *9845/9430*, 11550 & **W** *13840* (Australasia), Tu-Su *15665* (E Europe)
0900-0957	**S** M 7395 & Tu-F 7395 (S America), M-F 7535 (Europe), M-F *9430* (E Asia), *13840* (Australasia)
1000-1057	M-F 6095 (E North Am), M-F 7395 (S America)
1100-1157	6095 (E North Am), 7395 (C America & S America)
1200-1257	M-F 6095 (E North Am), M-Sα *9355* (E Asia), *9430* (Australasia), M-F 9455 (C America & S America)
1300-1357	6095 (N America), 9355 (S Asia), *9385* (E Asia), M-F 9455 (W North Am & C America)
1400-1457 &	
1500-1557	*9355* (E Asia & S Asia), **W** *9385* & **S** *12160* (SE Asia)
1600-1657	**W** M-F *9355* (E Europe), *9385* (S Africa), **S** M-F *15745/11550* (E Europe), M-Sα 21640 (E Africa)
1700-1757	**W** *9355* (E Europe), M-Sα *9385* (S Africa), **S** *15745/11550* (E Europe)
1700-1800	**W** 21640 (C Africa)
1800-1857	**W** *9355* (Europe & Mideast), *9385*

(S Africa), **W** M-F 11550/13770
(E Europe), **S** *13770/11550* (Europe &
Mideast), **S** M-F 15665 (E Europe),
17510 (S Africa)

1900-1957 **W** M-Sa *9355* (Europe & Mideast),
9385 (S Africa), **S** M-Sa *13770/11550*
(Europe & Mideast), **S** M-F 15665
(E Europe), M-F 17510 (W Africa)

2000-2057 **W** 5850/9355 & **W** M-F 7510 (Europe),
S *9570/11550* (Australasia), **S** M-F
13770 (W Europe)

2100-2157 **W** 5850/9355 (E North Am & Europe),
W 7510 (Europe), **S** 11645 (E North
Am), **S** 13770 (W Europe), *13840*
(Australasia)

2200-2257 Su-F 7510 (Europe), **W** *9430* (E Asia),
M-F 13770 (S America), Su-F *13840* &
S *15405* (E Asia)

2300-2357 M-F 7510 (S Europe & W Africa), **W**
9430 (E Asia), M-F 13770 (S America),
13840/13625 (SE Asia), **S** *15405*
(E Asia)

VOA-VOICE OF AMERICA

0000-0100 7215, **S** *9770* & **W** *9890* (SE Asia),
11695 (C America & S America), *11760*
(SE Asia), 15185 (Pacific & SE Asia),
15290 (E Asia), 17735 (E Asia &
Australasia), 17820 (E Asia)

0000-0200 5995, 6130, 7405, 9455, 9775 & 13740
(C America & S America)

0100-0300 7115, 7205, **W** *7215* & **S** *9635* (S Asia),
W *9740* (Mideast & S Asia), *11705*,
S *11725*, *15170*, *15250*, **W** *15370*,
17740 & **W** *21550* (S Asia)

0300-0400 **W** 6035 & **S** *6115* (E Africa & S Africa),
7105 (S Africa), 7290 (C Africa &
E Africa)

0300-0430 **S** *5980* (E Africa & S Africa), 7340
(Africa), **W** *9885* (E Africa)

0300-0500 6080 (S Africa), **W** 6125 (C Africa &
E Africa), **S** 7280 (Africa), **W** 7405
(W Africa & S Africa), **W** 7415 (Africa),
W 9575 (W Africa & S Africa), **S** *15300*
(E Africa)

0300-0630 4750/4950 (W Africa & C Africa)

0400-0430 *6145* (S Africa)

0400-0500 **W** 6035 (W Africa & S Africa), **W** 7180
(C Africa), **S** 7265 (S Africa & E Africa),
S 7290 (C Africa)

0400-0600 **W** 9775 (C Africa & E Africa)

0400-0700 *7170* (N Africa), **S** *11965* (E Europe &
Mideast)

0500-0600 **W** 7295 (W Africa), **W** 9700 (N Africa &
W Africa)

0500-0630 **S** *5970* (W Africa & C Africa), **W** *5990*
(W Africa), 6035 (W Africa & S Africa),
6080, **S** *7195* & **S** *9530* (W Africa),
S *9630* & *12080* (Africa)

0500-0700 ◻ *15205* (Mideast & S Asia)

0500-0700 **W** *11825* (Mideast)

0530-0630 **W** M-F *13710* (Africa)

0600-0630 **W** 7285 (W Africa), *11950* (E Africa),
W *15600* (C Africa & E Africa)

0600-0700 **S** *6140* (N Africa), *11805* (N Africa &
W Africa)

0630-0700 Sa/Su 4750/4950 & **S** Sa/Su *5970*
(W Africa & C Africa), **W** Sa/Su *5990*
(W Africa), Sa/Su 6035 (W Africa &
S Africa), Sa/Su *6080*, **S** Sa/Su *7195*,
W Sa/Su *7285* & **S** Sa/Su *9530* (W
Africa), **S** Sa/Su *9630* (Africa), Sa/Su
11950 (E Africa), Sa/Su *12080* (Africa),
W Sa/Su *15600* (C Africa & E Africa)

1000-1200 5985 (Pacific & Australasia), 6165, 7405
& 9590 (C America), *11720* (E Asia &
Australasia)

1000-1500 *15425* (SE Asia & Pacific)

1100-1300 *6110/6160* (SE Asia)

1100-1400 9645 (SE Asia & Australasia)

1100-1500 9760 (E Asia, S Asia & SE Asia),
W *11705* & *15160* (E Asia)

1200-1330 *11715* (E Asia & Australasia)

1300-1800 *6110/6160* (S Asia & SE Asia)

1400-1800 7125, 7215 & 9645 (S Asia), **W** *15205*
(Mideast & S Asia), **S** *15255* (Mideast),
15395 (S Asia)

1500-1700 **W** 9575 (Mideast & S Asia), 9760
(S Asia & SE Asia), **S** *15205* (Europe,
N Africa & Mideast)

1500-1800 **S** *9700* (Mideast)

1600-1630 Sa/Su *11920* & Sa/Su *12040* (E Africa),
Sa/Su *13710* (Africa), Sa/Su *15225*
(S Africa), Sa/Su *15445* (C Africa &
E Africa), Sa/Su *17895* (W Africa)

1600-1700 **W** Sa/Su *3970* (S Africa)

1600-1800 **W** *7120* (W Africa)

1600-2130 4750/4950 (W Africa & C Africa),
S *6035* (W Africa), **W** *11715* (S Africa)

1630-1700 **W** *11805* (E Europe), *15225* (S Africa),
15245 (Europe), Sa/Su *15410* (Africa),
S *17735* (E Europe)

1630-1800 *15445* (C Africa & E Africa), *17895*
(W Africa)

1630-1900 *13710* (Africa)

1630-2000 *11920* & *12040* (E Africa)

1700-1800 M-F *5990* & M-F *6045* (E Asia), **S** *7150*
(SE Asia & S Pacific), **S** *7170* (E Asia
& Australasia), **W** M-F *9525* (E Asia,
SE Asia & S Pacific), **S** M-F *9550* (SE
Asia), **W** M-F *9670* (E Asia & SE Asia),
M-F *9770* (E Asia, S Asia & SE Asia),
W M-F *11895* (SE Asia), **W** M-F *11945*
& **W** M-F *15255* (E Asia & Australasia),
15410 (Africa)

1700-1900 **S** *6040* (Mideast), **W** *6040* (N Africa &
Mideast), **S** *7415* (Africa)

1700-2100 **S** *9760* (N Africa & Mideast), **W** *9760*
(Mideast & S Asia)

1700-2200 **S** *15205* (Europe)

1800-1900 **W** M-F *4875* (S Africa), **S** *17895*
(W Africa)

1800-2130 **W** 7275 (W Africa), **S** *15410* (Africa),
W *15410* (W Africa & S Africa), 15580
(W Africa)

1900-2000 9525 (Australasia), *11870* (E Asia &
Australasia), *15180* (Pacific)

1900-2100 **S** *9770* (N Africa & Mideast)

1900-2130 **S** 7375, 7415, **W** *13710* & **S** *15445*
(Africa)

2000-2030 *11855* (W Africa)

2000-2100	*17755* (W Africa & C Africa)
2000-2130	17725 (W Africa)
2000-2200	**W** *15205* (Mideast & S Asia)
2100-2130	**W** *15445* (C Africa)
2100-2200	**S** *6040*, **W** *6070*, **S** *9535* & **W** *9595* (Mideast), *9760* (E Europe & Mideast), *11870* (E Asia & Australasia)
2100-2400	*15185* (Pacific & SE Asia), *17735* (E Asia & Australasia)
2123-2200	Su-F 15580 (W Africa)
2130-2200	Sa-F *4750/4950* (W Africa & C Africa), **S** Su-F *6035* & **W** Su-F *7275* (W Africa), **S** Su-F *7375* & Su-F *7415* (Africa), **W** Su-F *11715* (S Africa) & **W** Su-F *13710* & **S** Su-F *15410* (Africa), **W** Su-F *15410* (W Africa & S Africa), **S** Su-F *15445* (Africa), **W** Su-F *15445* (C Africa), Su-F *17725* (W Africa)
2200-2230	M-F *4750/4950* (W Africa & C Africa), **S** M-F *6035* & **W** M-F *7275* (W Africa), **S** M-F *7340*, **S** M-F *7375* & M-F *7415* (Africa), **W** M-F *11715* (S Africa), **W** M-F *12080* & **W** M-F *13710* (Africa)
2200-2400	*7215* (SE Asia), **S** *9705* (SE Asia & Australasia), **S** *9770* (SE Asia), **W** *9770* (SE Asia & Australasia), **W** *9890* & *11760* (SE Asia), *15305* (E Asia & Australasia), *17820* (E Asia)
2330-2400	6185 (SE Asia)

WEWN, BIRMINGHAM AL

0000-0100	7425 (N America), **W** 7520 & **S** 15375 (S America)
0000-1000	5825 (Europe)
0100-0200	**S** Su-F 7425 & **W** 7425 (N America)
0200-0300	**S** 7425 & **W** Su-F 7425 (N America)
0300-0400	7425 (N America)
0400-0500	**S** Tu-Su 7425 & **W** 7425 (N America)
0500-0600	**W** Tu-Su 7425 (N America)
0600-0700	**S** 7425 (N America)
0700-0800	7425 (N America), **W** 7465 (S America)
1000-1200	**W** 7465 (Europe)
1200-1300	6000 (C America & S America), **S** 15695 (Europe)
1200-1400	**W** 15115 (Europe)
1200-1500	**W** 7425 (W North Am)
1300-1400	15375 (S America)
1400-1600	**W** 15235 (Europe)
1500-1600	**W** M-Sa 7425 (W North Am)
1600-1800	**W** 15340 (Europe)
1600-2200	13615 (N America)
1800-2100	13695 (Europe)
1900-2200	15375 (S America)
2100-2200	**S** 13695 (Europe)
2100-2400	**W** 5825 (Europe)
2200-2400	**W** 7425 (N America), **S** 11820 (Europe), **S** 13615 (N America)
2300-2400	**W** 7520 & **S** 15375 (S America)

WGTG, MC CAYSVILLE GA—(North & C America)

1000-0400	9400

WJCR, UPTON KY

24 Hr	7490 (E North Am)
1500-0300 ⬛	13595 (W North Am & E Asia)

WMLK, BETHEL PA—(Eu, Mideast & N America)

0400-0900 &	
1700-2200	Su-F 9465

WORLD HARVEST RADIO

0000-0300	5745 (E North Am)
0145-0200	M 7315 (C America)
0200-0230	Tu-Su 7315 (C America)
0230-0400	7315 (C America)
0300-1000	5760/5745 (E North Am)
0400-0600	Tu-Su 7315 (C America)
0600-0800	7315 (C America)
0800-0900	Sa/Su 7315 (C America)
0900-1000	7315 (C America)
1000-1045	M-Sa 6040 (E North Am & C Am)
1045-1300	6040 (E North Am & C America)
1300-1315	15105 (C America)
1300-1500	6040 (E North Am)
1315-1330	Su-F 15105 (C America)
1330-1800	15105 (C America)
1500-2200	13760 (E North Am & W Europe)
1800-1815	9495 (N America & C America)
1815-1830	M-Sa 9495 (N America & C America)
1830-2300	9495 (N America & C America)
2200-2400	5745 (E North Am)
2300-2330	Su 9495 (N America & C America)
2330-2400	Sa/Su 9495 (N America & C America)

WRMI-RADIO MIAMI INTERNATIONAL—(C America)

0000-0200 ⬛	9955
1230-1500 ⬛	Su 9955
1500-2400 ⬛	Sa/Su 9955

WRNO WORLDWIDE—(E North Am)

0000-0300	7355
0400-0700 ⬛	7395
1400-1500	**S** 7355/15420
1500-2030	7355/15420
2030-2100	**S** W-M 7355/15420
2100-2130	**S** 7355/15420
2130-2200	**S** Tu/Th-Su 7355/15420 & **W** W-M 7355/15420
2200-2230	**W** 7355/15420
2200-2300	**S** F-Su 7355/15420
2230-2300	**W** Tu/Th-Su 7355/15420
2300-2400	**S** 7355 & **W** F-Su 7355

WVHA, GREENBUSH ME

0900-1100	**W** Sa 11695 & **S** Sa 13825 (Africa)
1130-1200	**W** Su 11695 & **S** Su 13825 (Africa)
1200-1300	**W** Su 11695 & **S** Su 13825 (Europe)
1300-1500	Sa 15745 (N America)
1400-1600	Su 15745 (Europe)
1800-1900	M-F 9930 (Africa)
1900-2000	Su-F 9930 (Africa)
1900-2100	**W** Su/Tu/Th 15745 (Africa)
2000-2200	M-F 9930 (Europe), Su 9930 (Africa)
2100-2200	**W** Tu/Th 15745 (Africa)
2200-2300	Su 5850 (Africa)

WWCR, NASHVILLE TN (N. America & Europe)

0000-0100	3215, 5065, 7435 & 13845
0100-0400	2390, 3215, 5065 & 5935
0400-1000	2390, 3210, 5065, 5935
1000-1100	5065, 5935 & 15685
1100-1200	5935 & 15685
1200-1300	13845 & 15685
1300-2200	12160, 13845 & 15685
2200-2300	7435, 9475, 12160 & 13845
2300-2400	5065, 7435, 9475 & 13845

WYFR-FAMILY RADIO

0000-0045	6085 (E North Am)

0100-0445	6065 (E North Am), 9505 (W North Am)
0400-0500	**S** 9985 (Europe)
0500-0600	**S** 11580 (Europe)
0500-0700	5985 (W North Am)
0500-0745	9985 (Europe)
0600-0745	7355 (Europe)
0700-0800	**W** 9455 & **S** 13695 (W Africa)
1000-1500	5950 (E North Am)
1100-1200	**S** 11830 (W North Am)
1100-1245	**W** 7355 (W North Am)
1200-1245	**S** 6015 (W North Am)
1200-1345	**W** 11970 (C America)
1200-1700	11830 (W North Am), **S** 17750 (C America)
1300-1400	13695 (E North Am)
1300-1445	**W** 9705 (W North Am)
1350-1700	**W** 17760 (C America)
1500-1700	**W** 15215 (W North Am)
1600-1700	21525 (C Africa & S Africa)
1600-1745	**S** 21745 (Europe)
1600-1800	**W** 17555 (Europe)
1600-1900	**W** 15566 & **S** 15695 (Europe)
1604-1700	**S** 11705 (W North Am)
1800-1900	*9805* (Europe)
1800-1945	17555 (Europe)
1945-2145	**S** 17555 (Europe)
2000-2045	21525 (C Africa & S Africa)
2000-2200	**W** 7355 (Europe)
2000-2245	**W** 15566 & **S** 17845 (W Africa)
2045-2245	**S** 21525 (C Africa & S Africa)
2100-2245	**W** 11580 (C Africa & S Africa)

UZBEKISTAN
RADIO TASHKENT
0100-0130	**W** 5955 (S Asia), **W** 5975 & **S** 7190 (Mideast & W Asia), **W** 7285 (Mideast), **S** 9715 (Mideast, W Asia & S Asia)
1200-1230 &	
1330-1400	**W** 5060 (S Asia), **W** 6025 & **S** 7285 (W Asia & S Asia), 9715 & **S** 15295 (S Asia)

VATICAN STATE
VATICAN RADIO
0140-0200	5980, **W** 7335, **S** 9650 & **S** 11935 (S Asia)
0250-0310	**W** 6095 & 7305 (E North Am), **S** 9605 (E North Am & C America)
0320-0350	7360 & 9660/5865 (E Africa)
0500-0530	**W** 7360 (E Africa), 9660 (Africa), 11625 & **S** 13765 (E Africa)
0600-0620 ←	4010/4005 (Europe), 6245/5860 (W Europe)
0630-0700	**W** 7360 (W Africa), **W** 9660 (Africa), **S** 11625 (W Africa), **W** 11625 (Africa), **S** 13765 (W Africa), **S** 15570 (Africa)
0730-0745 ←	M-Sa 4010/4005 (Europe), M-Sa 6245/5860 (W Europe), M-Sa 7250 & M-Sa 9645 (Europe), M-Sa 11740 (W Europe & N Africa), M-Sa 15210/15215 (Mideast)
1020-1030	M-Sa 17550 (Africa)
1120-1130 ←	M-Sa 6245 & M-Sa 7250 (Europe), M-Sa 11740 (W Europe), M-Sa 15210 (Mideast)
1120-1130	**W** 17585 (Africa)

1345-1405	**W** 9500, 11625 & **S** 13765 (Australasia), 15585 (SE Asia)
1545-1600	**W** 9500, 11640 & **S** 15585 (S Asia)
1600-1630	**W** Sa 9500, Sa 11640 & Sa 15585 (S Asia)
1600-1635	**W** Sa 9660 (E Africa)
1615-1630	**S** 7250 (N Europe), **S** 11810 (Mideast)
1715-1730 ←	6245 (Europe), 9645 (W Europe)
1715-1730	**W** 7250 (Mideast)
1730-1800	**W** 7305 & **W** 9660 (E Africa), 11625 (E Africa & S Africa), **S** 13765 (E Africa), **S** 15570 (Africa)
2000-2030	**W** 7355 & 9645 (Africa), 11625 & **S** 13765 (W Africa)
2050-2110 ←	3945/4005 (Europe), 5882/5885 (W Europe)
2245-2305	**W** 6150 (SE Asia), **W** 7305 (E Asia), 9600 & 11830 (Australasia)

VIETNAM
VOICE OF VIETNAM
0100-0300	**W** *5940* & **S** *7250* (E North Am)
1000-1030	9840, **W** 12020 & **S** 15010 (SE Asia)
1100-1130	7285 & 9730 (SE Asia)
1230-1300	9840, **W** 12020 & **S** 15010 (E Asia & Americas)
1330-1400	9840, **W** 12020 & **S** 15010 (SE Asia)
1600-1630	9840, **W** 12020 & **S** 15010 (Africa)
1800-1830, 1900-1930 & 2030-2100	9840, **W** 12020 & **S** 15010 (Europe)
2330-2400	9840, **W** 12020 & **S** 15010 (E Asia & Americas)

YEMEN
REPUBLIC OF YEMEN RADIO—(Mideast & E Africa)
0600-0700 & 1800-1900	9780

YUGOSLAVIA
RADIO YUGOSLAVIA
0000-0030	**S** M-Sa *9580* & **S** 11870 (E North Am)
0100-0130	**W** M-Sa *6195* & **W** M-Sa *7115* (E North Am)
0200-0230	**W** *6100* & **W** *7115* (W North Am)
0430-0500	**S** *9580* (W North Am)
1330-1400	*11835* (Australasia)
1930-2000 ←	*6100* (W Europe), *9720* (S Africa)
2030-2100	**S** *7230* (Australasia)
2130-2200	**W** *9595* (Australasia)
2200-2230 ←	*6100* & *6185* (W Europe)

ZAMBIA
CHRISTIAN VOICE—(S Africa)
0400-0700	3330/6065
0700-1600	6065
1600-2200	3330/4965

RADIO ZAMBIA-ZNBC
0250-0600	6165
0600-1430	6165/7235
1430-2200	6165

ZIMBABWE
ZIMBABWE BROADCASTING CORP
0300-0530	3396
0530-1700	5975
1700-2200	4828

Voices from Home—1997

Country-by-Country Guide to Native Broadcasts

*F*or some listeners, English
offerings are merely icing on
the cake. Their real interest
is in eavesdropping on broadcasts
for nativos—home folks. These
can be enjoyable regardless of
language, especially when they
offer the traditional music of other
cultures.

Some you'll hear, many you
won't—depending on your location
and receiving equipment. Keep in
mind that native-
language broadcasts
tend to be weaker
than those in English,
so you may need
more patience and
better hardware.
PASSPORT REPORTS
explains about this.

When to Tune

Some broadcasts come in best during the
day within world band segments from 9300
to 17900 kHz. However, those from Latin
America and Africa peak near or during
darkness, especially from 4700 to 5100
kHz. See "Best Times and Frequencies"
earlier in this book for solid guidance.

Times and days of the week are in
World Time, explained in "Setting Your
World Time Clock" earlier in the book, as
well as in the glossary; for local times, see
"Addresses PLUS." Midyear, some stations
are an hour earlier (◄▬) or later (▬►) for
summer savings time, typically April
through October. Stations may also extend
their hours during holidays or for sports
events.

Frequencies in *italics* may
be best, as they come from
relay transmitters that
might be near you.

Schedules Prepared
for Entire Year

To be as helpful as
possible throughout the
year, PASSPORT's sched-
ules consist not just of

observed activity and other factual data, but also that which we have creatively opined will take place. This latter material is original from us, and therefore will not be so exact as factual information.

Most frequencies are used year round. Those used only parttime are labeled **S** for summer (midyear), and **W** for winter.

ARGENTINA—Spanish
RADIO ARGENTINA-RAE
0000-0200	Tu-Sa 15345 (Americas)
1200-1400	M-F 11710 (S America)
1800-1900	M-F 15345 (Europe & N Africa)
2300-2400	M-F 15345 (Mideast & N Africa)

ARMENIA—Armenian
VOICE OF ARMENIA
0100-0130	⬜	9965 (S America)
1730-1830	⬜	4810 (E Europe, Mideast & W Asia), 4990 & 7480 (Mideast & N Africa)
1900-2000	**S**	7480 (Europe)
2000-2100		7480 (Europe)
2000-2200	⬜	4810 (E Europe, Mideast & W Asia), 4990 (Mideast & N Africa)
2100-2130	⬜	9965 (Europe & C America)
2115-2145	**S**	11615 (Europe)
2215-2245	⬜	9965 (Europe & C America)

AUSTRIA—German
RADIO AUSTRIA INTERNATIONAL
0000-0030 &	
0100-0130	9655 (E North Am), 9870 & 13730 (S America)
0200-0230	9655 (E North Am), 9870 (C America), 13730 (S America)
0300-0330	9870 (C America)
0400-0430	6155 & 13730 (Europe)
0430-0530	M-Sa 6155 & M-Sa 13730 (Europe)
0500-0530	*6015* (N America), **S** Su 6155 & **S** Su 13730 (Europe), M-Sa 15410 & M-Sa 17870 (Mideast)
0530-0600	**S** 6155 & **S** 13730 (Europe), **S** 15410 & **S** 17870 (Mideast)
0600-0630	*6015* (N America), 6155 & 13730 (Europe), 15410 & 17870 (Mideast)
0630-0700	**W** 6155 & **W** 13730 (Europe), **W** 15410 & **W** 17870 (Mideast)
0700-0730	6155 & 13730 (Europe), 15410 & 17870 (Mideast)
0800-0830	6155 & 13730 (Europe), 17870 (Australasia)
0830-0900	**S** 6155 & **S** 13730 (Europe), **S** 17870 (Australasia)
0900-0930	6155 & 13730 (Europe), 15450 (E Asia), 17870 (Australasia)
0930-1000	**S** Su 6155, **W** 6155, **S** Su 13730 & **W** 13730 (Europe), **S** Su 15450 & **W** 15450 (E Asia), **W** M-Sa 17870 & Su 17870 (Australasia)
1000-1030	6155 & 13730 (Europe), 15450 (E Asia), 17870 (Australasia)

1030-1100	**W** Su 6155 & **W** Su 13730 (Europe), **W** Su 17870 (Australasia)
1100-1130	6155 (Europe), 13730 (W Europe & E North Am), 15450 (E Asia)
1130-1200	**S** M-Sa 6155 (Europe), **S** M-Sa 15450 (E Asia)
1200-1230	6155 (Europe), 13730 (W Europe & E North Am)
1230-1300	**W** M-Sa 6155 (Europe), **W** M-Sa 13730 (W Europe & E North Am)
1300-1330 &	
1400-1430	6155 & 13730 (Europe)
1430-1500	**S** M-Sa 6155 & **S** M-Sa 13730 (Europe)
1500-1530	6155 (Europe), 9665 (Mideast), 11780 (S Asia & SE Asia), 13730 (Europe)
1530-1600	**S** Su 6155 & M-Sa 6155 (Europe), **S** Su 9665 & M-Sa 9665 (Mideast), **W** 11780 (S Asia & SE Asia), **S** Su 13730 & M-Sa 13730 (Europe)
1600-1630	6155 (Europe), 9665 (Mideast), 11780 (S Asia & SE Asia), 13730 (Europe)
1630-1700	**W** 6155 (Europe), **W** 9665 (Mideast), **W** 13730 (Europe)
1700-1730	6155 (Europe), 9665 (Mideast), 11780 (S Asia & SE Asia), 13730 (Europe)
1800-1830	5945 & 6155 (Europe), 9665 (Mideast)
1830-1900	M-Sa 5945 & M-Sa 6155 (Europe), M-Sa 9665 (Mideast)
1900-1930	5945 & 6155 (Europe), 9665 (Mideast), 13730 (S Africa)
1930-2000	**S** 5945 & **S** 6155 (Europe)
2000-2030 &	
2100-2130	5945 & 6155 (Europe), 9880 (S Europe & W Africa), 13730 (S Africa)
2200-2230	5945 & 6155 (Europe), 9870 (S Am)
2300-2330	9870 (S America)

BELGIUM
RADIO VLAANDEREN INTERNATIONAL
Dutch
0500-0600		**S** 7240 (S Europe), **S** 11640 (Africa)
0600-0700		**W** 5985 (Europe), **W** 9925 (Africa)
0700-0730	⬜	5985 (Europe), 9925/9920 (S Europe & Australasia)
0730-0830		**S** M-Sa 7190 (Europe)
0830-0900	⬜	M-Sa 6035 & M-Sa 9925 (Europe)
0830-0930		**W** M-Sa 9905 (Europe)
0900-0930	⬜	6035 & 9925 (Europe)
0900-1100	⬜	Su 17610/17595 (Africa)
0930-1100	⬜	Su 6035 & Su 9925 (Europe)
1000-1100		**S** 15545 (Africa)
1100-1130		**S** 11640 (Europe), **S** 17595/17690 (Africa)
1100-1200	⬜	M-Sa 6035 (Europe), 17610/17595 (Africa)
1100-1200		**W** 15510 (Africa)
1200-1230	⬜	6035 (Europe)
1200-1230		**W** 9925 (Europe), **S** 13610 (E North Am), **S** 15540 (SE Asia), **W** 17610/17595 (Africa)
1230-1300		**S** M-Sa 13610 (E North Am), **S** M-Sa 15540 (SE Asia)
1300-1330		**W** 13670 (E North Am)
1300-1700		**S** Su 11640 (Europe)
1330-1400		**W** M-Sa 13670 (E North Am)
1400-1530		**W** Su 5915 (Europe)

1400-1700 ⬅ Su 9925 (Europe), Su 17690 (Africa)
1430-1600 **S** Sa 9925 (Europe)
1530-1700 **W** Sa/Su 5915 (Europe)
1600-1630 **S** 9925 (S Europe & N Africa),
 S 13795 (Mideast), **S** 17640 (Africa)
1700-1730 **W** 9925 (Mideast), **W** 11765 (Africa)
1800-1830 ⬅ 5910 & 9925 (Europe)
1800-1830 **W** 9925 (Europe)
1800-2010 **S** W/Sa 13685 (Africa)
1900-2000 **S** 9925 (Europe), **S** 13645 (Africa)
1900-2110 **W** W/Sa 9940 (Africa)
2000-2030 **S** 9925 (Europe)
2000-2100 **W** 5910 (Europe), **W** 9925 (Africa)
2100-2130 ⬅ 5910 (Europe)
2100-2130 **W** 9925 (Europe), **W** Su 9925 (Africa)
2200-2300 **S** 9925 (E North Am), **S** 11690
 (S America)
2300-2400 **W** 5900 (E North Am), **W** 9925
 (S America)

French
0800-0830 ⬅ 6035 & 9925 (Europe), 15545 (Africa)
0930-1000 **S** M-Sa 15545 (Africa)
1030-1100 ⬅ M-Sa 6035 (Europe), M-Sa 17610/
 17595 (Africa)
1030-1100 **W** M-Sa 15510 (Africa)
1330-1400 **S** M-Sa 13610 (E North Am), **S** M-Sa
 15540 (SE Asia)
1430-1500 **W** M-Sa 13670 (E North Am)
1830-1900 **S** 13645 (Africa)
1930-2000 ⬅ 5910 (Europe)
1930-2000 **W** 9925 (Africa)
2130-2200 **S** 9925 (E North Am), **S** 13800
 (S America)
2230-2300 **W** 5900 (E North Am), **W** 9925
 (S America)

BRAZIL—Portuguese
RADIO NACIONAL DA AMAZONIA
0700-0800 ➡ M-F 6180, M-F 11780
0800-2400 ➡ 6180, 11780
RADIO BANDEIRANTES
24 Hr 6090, 9645, 11925
RADIO NACIONAL
1630-1750 15265 (Europe & W Africa)
1800-1920 17750 (Africa)

CANADA—French
CBC—(E North Am)
0100-0300 ⬅ M 9625
0300-0400 ⬅ Su 9625 & Tu-Sa 9625
1300-1310 &
1500-1555 ⬅ M-F 9625
1700-1715 ⬅ Su 9625
1900-1945 ⬅ M-F 9625
1900-2310 ⬅ Sa 9625
RADIO CANADA INTERNATIONAL
0000-0030 **S** Tu-Sa 9535 & **S** Tu-Sa 11940
 (C America & S America), **S** Tu-Sa
 13670 (S America)
0000-0100 **S** 5960 (E North Am)
0100-0130 **W** 9535 (C America & S America),
 W 11725 (S America)
0100-0200 ⬅ 9755 (E North Am & C America)
0130-0200 **W** Su/M 9535 (C America & S
 America), **W** Su/M 11725 (S America)
0230-0300 **S** Tu-Sa 6120 (E North Am &

C America), **S** Tu-Sa 9535 & **S** Tu-Sa
 11715 (C America & S America)
0300-0330 **W** 6025, **W** 9505, **S** 11835 & **S** 11970
 (Mideast)
0330-0400 **W** Tu-Sa 6010 (E North Am &
 C America), **W** Tu-Sa 9755 (C America)
0530-0600 **S** M-F 7295 (W Europe & N Africa),
 S M-F 15430 (Africa), **S** M-F 17840
 (Africa & Mideast)
0630-0700 ⬅ M-F 6050 (Europe)
0630-0700 **W** M-F 6150 (Europe), **W** M-F 9740
 (Africa), **W** M-F 9760 (Europe & N
 Africa), **W** M-F 11905 (Mideast)
1200-1230 **W** 6150 & **S** 9660 (E Asia), **W** 11730 &
 S 15195 (SE Asia)
1200-1300 **S** 15305 (E North Am & C America)
1300-1400 ⬅ 9650 (E North Am)
1300-1400 **W** 15425 (C America)
1300-1600 **S** Su 15305 (E North Am & C America)
1400-1500 **S** M-Sa 15305, **S** 15325 & **S** M-Sa
 17820 (Europe), **S** M-Sa 17895
 (W Europe & Africa)
1500-1600 ⬅ 11935 (Europe & Mideast)
1500-1600 **W** 9555 (Europe & Mideast), **W** 11915
 & **W** M-Sa 15325 (Europe), **W** 17820
 (W Europe & Africa)
1900-2000 **S** 5995 (Europe & Mideast), **S** 11700
 & **S** 13650 (Europe), **S** 13670 (Africa),
 S 15325 & **S** 17870 (Europe)
2000-2100 ⬅ 7235 (S Europe & N Africa), 15150 &
 17820 (Africa)
2000-2100 **W** 5925 (Europe), **W** 5995 (Europe &
 Mideast), **W** 9805 (W Europe & N
 Africa), **W** 11945 & **W** 13650 (Europe),
 W 13690 (Africa)
2130-2200 **S** 5995 (Europe & Mideast), **S** 11690
 & **S** 13650 (Europe), **S** 13670 (Africa),
 S 13740 (C America), **S** 15305 (C
 America & S America), **S** 17820 (Africa)
2230-2300 ⬅ 7235 (S Europe & N Africa), 9755 (E
 North Am & C America)
2230-2300 **W** 5960 (E North Am), **W** 5995 (Europe
 & N Africa), 11705 (SE Asia), **W** 11945
 (Europe), **W** 13690 (Africa), **S** 15305
 (C America & S America)

CHINA
CHINA RADIO INTERNATIONAL
Chinese
0200-0300 **W** 7820 (S America), 9690 (N America
 & C America), 9710 & 11695/11715 (N
 America), **S** 12055 & 15435 (S America)
0300-0400 9730 (W North Am)
0400-0500 9710 & 11695/11715 (N America)
0900-1000 9480 (E Asia), 9945 (SE Asia), 11695
 (Australasia), 11945 & 12015 (SE Asia),
 15100 & 15180 (E Asia), 15205 & 15260
 (SE Asia)
1000-1100 6590 (E Asia)
1300-1400 11945, 12015, 15205 & 15260 (SE Asia)
1500-1600 **W** 4020 (E Asia), 9457 (S Asia), 11910
 (S Asia & E Africa), **S** 15455 (S Asia)
1730-1830 **W** 4020 & 5250 (E Asia), 7110 & 7335
 (Europe & N Africa), **W** 7700 (N Africa
 & W Africa), 7800 (Europe & N Africa),
 S 9820 (N Africa & W Africa)

2000-2100	**W** 6955 (N Africa & W Africa), **W** 7125, **S** 7185, **W** 7435 & 7660 (E Europe), 7780 (W Africa), **S** 8345 (E Asia), 9620 (E Africa), 11445 (Africa), **S** 11650 (E Europe), *11790 (C Africa & E Africa)*
2100-2130 ⬅	*6165 (Europe)*
2230-2300	*9770 (C Africa & S Africa), 11790 (C Africa & E Africa)*
2230-2330	5220 (E Asia), 6140, **W** 7110 & 7230 (SE Asia), 8260 (E Asia), 9440 (SE Asia), 9535 (E Asia), **S** 11685, 12015 & 15400 (SE Asia)

Cantonese

0100-0200	**W** 7820 (S America), *9710 & 11695/11715* (N America), **S** 12055 (S America)
1000-1100	9945 (SE Asia), 15100 (E Asia)
1100-1200	11945, 12015, 15205 & 15260 (SE Asia)
1700-1800	6920, 9900 (S Asia & E Africa)
1900-2000	7780 (W Africa)

CHINA (TAIWAN)
BROADCASTING CORPORATION OF CHINA
Chinese

0000-0100	*5950 (E North Am), 11740 (C America), 11855 (W North Am)*, **S** 15125, 15270, *15440 (C America)*
0000-0400	7295
0000-0700	9280 (E Asia)
0000-0900	9610
0000-1700	11725, 11885
0100-1700	15125
1100-1200 &	
1300-1500	9610
2055-2400	11885, **S** 15125
2100-2400	11725, 15270
2200-2400	*5950 (E North Am), 9610, 11740 (C America), 11855 (W North Am), 15440 (C America)*

VOICE OF FREE CHINA
Chinese

0000-0100	**W** *9690,* **W** *11720,* **S** *15130 &* **S** *17805* (S America)
0100-0200	**W** *11825, 15215 &* **S** *17845* (S America)
0400-0500	5950 (E North Am & C America), 7130 (SE Asia), *9680 (W North Am)*, 11825, 15270 & 15345 (SE Asia)
0700-0800	7130 (SE Asia)
0900-1000	7445 (SE Asia), 9610 (Australasia), 11745 (E Asia), 11915, 15270 & 15345 (SE Asia)
1200-1300	11745 (E Asia), 15270 (SE Asia)
1900-2000	9955 (Mideast & N Africa), **W** *9985,* **S** *15600,* **S** *17750 &* **W** *17760* (Europe)

Cantonese

0100-0200	*5950 (E North Am), 15440 (C America)*
0300-0400	*11740 (C America)*
0500-0600	*5950 (E North Am & C America), 9680 (W North Am)*, 11825, 11915, 15270 & 15345 (SE Asia)
1000-1100	7285, 7445 & 11915 (SE Asia)
1100-1200	15270 (SE Asia)
1300-1400	11915 & 15345 (SE Asia)

VOICE OF ASIA
Chinese

0500-0700	7285 (E Asia)

0700-1100	9280 (E Asia)
0800-0900	7285 (E Asia)
1300-1445 &	
1450-1500	7445 (SE Asia)

Cantonese

0800-0900	7445 (E Asia)

CLANDESTINE (C. AMERICA)—
Spanish
"LA VOZ DEL CID"—(C America)

0400-0700 &	
1000-1410	6306
2200-0355	9941

COLOMBIA—Spanish
CARACOL COLOMBIA

24h	5077/5075

ECOS DEL ATRATO

1000-0400	5019

RADIO NACIONAL

1100-0500	4955

CROATIA—Croatian
CROATIAN RADIO

0000-0200	**W** 5895 (Europe)
0008-0100	**W** 5895 (Europe), **S** 7165 & **W** 7370 (E North Am)
0108-0200	**W** 5895 & **S** 7165 (Europe), **W** 7370 (E North Am)
0208-0300 ⬅	5895 (Europe & N America)
0208-0300	**S** 7165 (Europe)
0308-0400 ⬅	5895 (Europe & N America)
0308-0400	**S** 7165 (Europe)
0408-0500 ⬅	5895 (Europe & N America)
0408-0500	**S** 7165 (Europe)
0500-1130	**S** 7165 (Europe, Asia & Australasia), **S** 13830 (S America)
0508-0600 ⬅	5895 (Europe & N America)
0600-0700 ⬅	5895 (Europe)
0600-0700	**S** 5920 (Europe)
0600-1000	**W** 7370 (Europe & Australasia), **W** 13830 (Australasia)
0600-1230 ⬅	9830 (Europe)
0700-1600	5920 (Europe)
1000-1900	**W** 7370 (Europe)
1130-1800	**S** 7165 (Europe)
1230-1900 ⬅	13830 (N America)
1600-1900	**W** 5895 (Europe)
1808-2100	**S** 7165 (Europe)
1908-2000 ⬅	13830 (E North Am)
1908-2200	**W** 5895 & **W** 7370 (Europe)
2000-2100	11635 (N America)
2100-2108	**W** 11635 (N America)
2108-2200	**S** 7165 (Europe), 11635 (N America)
2200-2208	**W** 7370 (E North Am)
2208-2300 &	
2308-2400	**W** 5895 (Europe), **S** 7165 & **W** 7370 (E North Am)

CUBA—Spanish
RADIO HABANA

0000-0200	6180 (C America)
0000-0400	11970 (S America)
0000-0500	5965, **W** 6070 & **S** 9505 (C America), **W** 9505 (S America), 9550 & 11760 (C America), 11875 & **S** 15230 (S America)

1100-1300	11875 (S America)
1100-1400	9550 (C America & N America)
1100-1500	6000 & 11760 (C America)
1200-1500	**W** 6070/5965 & **S** 9505 (C America)
2100-2300	**W** 9820 (Europe & N Africa), 9830 USB (E North Am), 11760 & **S** 13680 (Europe & N Africa)

RADIO REBELDE

1030-0500	5025

CYPRUS

CYPRUS BROADCASTING CORP—(Europe)
Greek

2215-2245	F-Su 6180, **W** F-Su 7125, **S** F-Su 7205, **W** F-Su 9675 & **S** F-Su 9760

RADIO MONTE CARLO—(N America)
Arabic

0400-0420	▣ 5960 & 9755

DENMARK—Danish

RADIO DANMARK

0030-0055	**W** 5905 (S America), 7275 (SE Asia & Australasia), 7465 (E North Am & C America), **S** 9525 (S America)
0130-0155	**W** 6120 (N America), 7465 (E North Am & C America), **S** 9560 (N Am)
0230-0255	**W** 6120 (N America), **S** 7465 (E North Am), **W** 7465 (S America), **S** 9560 (N America)
0330-0355	**W** 5965 & 7165 (Mideast), 7465 (W North Am), **S** 9565 (Mideast)
0430-0455	**W** 5965 (E Europe), **W** 6040 (Mideast & E Africa), **W** 7305 (Mideast), **S** 7520 (W North Am), **S** 9565 & **S** 13805 (Mideast)
0530-0555	**W** 5965 (E Europe), **W** 6195 (W North Am), **W** 7180 (E Africa), **S** 7465 (E Europe), **S** 13805 (E Africa)
0630-0655	**W** 5965 & **S** 7180 (Europe), **W** 7180 (W Europe), **S** 7295 (Australasia), **S** 9590 (W Africa & Australasia), **W** 9590 (W Africa), **W** 11735 & **S** 13805 (E Africa)
0730-0755	**W** 5965 (Europe), **S** 7180 (W Europe), **W** 7180 (W Europe & Australasia), **S** 7295 (Australasia), 9590 (Europe), **S** 13805 (W Africa)
0830-0855	**W** 9590 & **W** 13800 (Australasia), **S** 15220 (Mideast), **S** 17855 (Australasia)
0930-0955	**S** 13800 (E Asia), **W** 15175 (Australasia), **W** 15230 (Mideast), **S** 17855 (Australasia)
1030-1055	**W** 7295 (Atlantic), **S** 9480 (Europe), **W** 11830 (W Europe), **S** 15220 (S America)
1130-1155	7295 (Europe), **W** 15270 (S America), **S** 17740 (C Africa)
1230-1255	9590 (Europe), **W** 9795 (E Asia), **W** 11850 (E North Am), **S** 13800 & **S** 15305 (E Asia), **S** 15480 (S America), **W** 15605 (SE Asia)
1330-1355	9590 (Europe), **W** 9795 (E Asia), **W** 11840 (N America), **S** 13800 (SE Asia & Australasia), **S** 15305 (E Asia), **S** 15340 (N America), **W** 15605 (SE Asia & Australasia)
1430-1455	**W** 11720 (S Asia), **W** 11840 (N America), *11850 (SE Asia)*, **S** 13800 (S Asia & SE Asia), **S** 15340 (N America)
1530-1555	**W** 9485 (W North Am), **W** 9520 & **W** 11730 (Mideast), **S** 11840 (W North Am), **S** 13805 & **S** 15230 (Mideast)
1630-1655	**W** 9590 (E Europe), **W** 11840 (E Africa & W North Am), **S** 11860 (S Asia), **S** 13805 (E Africa)
1630-1700	**S** 15340 (W North Am)
1730-1755	7485 & **S** 7485 (E Europe), **W** 7525 (W Europe), **W** 9590 (E Africa), **S** 11860 (S Asia), **S** 15220 (E Africa)
1830-1855	**W** 5960 (W Europe), **S** 7485 (Europe), **W** 7485 (W Africa), **S** 9590 (Mideast), **W** 9590 (C Africa), **S** 13805 (W Africa), **S** 15220 (C Africa)
1930-1955	**W** 5930 (Australasia), **W** 5960 & **S** 7485 (Europe), **W** 7485 (W Africa), **W** 9590 (C Africa), **S** 11860 (Australasia), **S** 13805 (C Africa), **S** 15220 (W Africa)
2030-2055	**S** 7485 (Europe & Mideast), **W** 7520 (Europe), **W** 9480 (W North Am), **S** 9590 (Australasia)
2100-2130	**W** 7315 (Australasia)
2130-2155	**W** 5960 (Atlantic), **S** 7205 & **W** 7315 (Australasia), **W** 9480 (E Asia), **S** 9495 (Australasia), **S** 9590 (Atlantic)

2230-2255	**W** *5960* (Australasia), **W** *6200* (E North Am), **W** *7115* (E Asia), **S** *9485* (Australasia), **S** *11840* (E North Am)
2330-2355	**W** *5905* (S America), 7275 (SE Asia & Australasia), **W** *7465* & **S** *9485* (E North Am)
2330-2400	**S** *7490* (S America)

DOMINICAN REPUBLIC—Spanish
RADIO CRISTAL INTERNATIONAL
2100-0300	5012

ECUADOR—Spanish
HCJB-VOICE OF THE ANDES
0000-0504	6050 (S America), 15140 (Americas)
1030-1500	11960 (Americas)
1030-2400	6050 (S America)
1500-2400	15140 (Americas)
2130-2200	21455 USB (Europe & Australasia)
2130-2230	**W** *12025* & **S** *15550* (Europe)

RADIO QUITO
0500-1030 (Irr) &	
1030-0500	4919

EGYPT—Arabic
RADIO CAIRO
0000-0045	15220 (C America & S America), 17770 (S America)
0030-0330	9900 (E North Am)
0330-0430	9900 (W North Am)
1015-1215	17745 (Mideast & S Asia)
1100-1130	17800 (C Africa & S Africa)
1245-1600	15220 (C Africa)
2000-2200	11990 (Australasia)
2345-2400	15220 (C America & S America), 17770 (S America)

REPUBLIC OF EGYPT RADIO
0000-0030 ◄	9700 (N Africa), 11665 (C Africa & E Africa), 15285 (Mideast)
0150-0700 ◄	12050 (Europe & E North Am)
0200-2200 ◄	9755 (N Africa & Mideast)
0300-0600 ◄	9850 (N Africa & Mideast)
0300-2400 ◄	15285 (Mideast)
0350-0700 ◄	9620 & 9770 (N Africa)
0350-1800 ◄	11665 (Mideast)
0350-2400 ◄	9800 (Mideast)
0600-1400 ◄	11980 (N Africa & Mideast)
0600-1410 ◄	15480
0700-1100 ◄	15115 (W Africa)
0700-1500 ◄	11785 (N Africa)
0700-1530 ◄	12050 (Europe, E North Am & E Africa)
1100-2400 ◄	9850 (N Africa)
1245-1900 ◄	17670 (N Africa)
1530-2400 ◄	12050 (Europe & N America)
1800-2400 ◄	9700 (N Africa)
1900-2400 ◄	11665 (C Africa & E Africa)

FINLAND—Finnish & Swedish
YLE RADIO FINLAND
0300-0330	**S** 6120 (E Europe)
0400-0430	**W** 6030 (E Europe)
0400-0530	**S** 9655 (E Europe), **S** 15440 (Mideast & E Africa)
0500-0630 ◄	6120 (Europe), 11755 (Mideast)
0500-0630	**W** 6015 (E Europe), **W** 9635 (Mideast & E Africa)

0530-0600	**S** 6120 (Europe)
0600-0700	**S** 11755 (Europe & W Africa)
0700-0800 ◄	9560 (Europe & W Africa)
0700-0800	**S** Su 6045 (E Europe)
0700-0830	**S** Sa/Su 11805 (W Africa & Australasia), **S** Sa/Su 15120 (E Asia & Australasia)
0700-0915	11755 (Europe & W Africa)
0700-1700 ◄	6120 (Europe)
0800-0930	**W** Sa/Su 9760 (Australasia), **W** Sa/Su 15330 (SE Asia & Australasia)
0900-1000	**S** 13645 & **S** 15235 (E Asia)
0915-0930	**W** 11755 (Europe & W Africa)
1000-1015	11755 (Europe & W Africa)
1000-1030	**W** 11805 (E Asia), **S** 13645 & **S** 15235 (SE Asia & Australasia)
1000-1100	**W** 13770 (E Asia)
1015-1100	**S** 11755 (Europe & W Africa)
1100-1130	**S** 11900 (N America), **W** 15240 (E Asia & SE Asia), **W** 17825 (SE Asia & Australasia)
1100-2130	11755 (Europe & W Africa)
1200-1230 ◄	15400 (N America)
1200-1230	**W** 11735 & **S** 11900 (N America)
1230-1300	**S** Su 11900 (N America)
1300-1330 ◄	15400 (N America)
1300-1330	**W** 11735 (N America), **S** 13645 & **S** 15185 (S Asia)
1330-1400 ◄	Su 15400 (N America)
1330-1400	**W** Su 11735 (N America)
1400-1430	**W** 11805 & **W** 15240 (S Asia)
1400-1500	**S** 11900 & **S** 15400 (N America)
1415-1430 ◄	6180 (E Europe)
1430-1600	**S** 9745 (E Europe)
1500-1530 ◄	6180 (E Europe)
1500-1600	**W** 11785 & **W** 13645 (N America)
1530-1700	**W** 6180 (E Europe)
1600-1630	**W** 11880 (Mideast)
1600-1700	**W** 9680 (Mideast), **S** 13645 (Mideast & E Africa), **S** 15145 (E Africa)
1600-2130	**S** 6120 (Europe)
1630-1700	**W** 11880 (E Africa & S Africa)
1700-1830	**W** 9730 (Europe & W Africa)
1700-2000	**S** 9855 & **S** 15440 (Europe & W Africa)
1700-2100	**W** 6120 (Europe & W Africa)

FRANCE—French
RADIO FRANCE INTERNATIONALE
0000-0030	**S** *15440* (SE Asia)
0000-0100	**W** 5920 (C America), **W** 7120 (S Asia & SE Asia), **S** 9790 (E North Am), 9800 (S America), **S** 9800 (N America), **S** 9805 (S Asia & SE Asia), **S** *11670* (C America), *12025* (SE Asia)
0000-0200	*9715* (S America), 9790 (C America)
0000-0300	5945 (E North Am)
0000-0900	3965 (W Europe)
0000-1900	**S** 11705 (Africa)
0100-0200	**W** *11600* & **S** *15440* (S Asia)
0100-0300	*9790* (N America)
0200-0300	5920 (C America), 9715 (S America), *9800* (N America & C America)
0300-0400	5945 (E Africa & Mideast), 7315 (Mideast)

Time	Left column
0300-0445	5990 (E Europe)
0300-0500	**S** 7280 (E Europe), **W** 7280 & **S** 9550 (Mideast), *9800* (C America)
0300-0600	6045 (E Europe)
0300-0700	9790 (Africa)
0300-0800	7135 (Africa)
0400-0500	*5920* (C America), 5925 (N Africa), **W** 5945 (E Africa & Mideast), **S** *6175* (S Africa), **W** 7315, *9805* & **S** 11685 (Mideast), **S** 11700 (E Africa)
0400-0600 ◄	9805 (E Africa)
0400-0600	**W** 3965 (E Europe), *4890* (C Africa), **S** 9745 (E Europe)
0445-0545	**W** 5990 (E Europe)
0500-0600	**S** 5955 (N Africa), **S** 9805 (E Europe), 11685 (Mideast), 11700 & **S** 15155 (E Africa)
0500-0700 ◄	11995 (E Africa)
0500-0700	**W** 5925, **W** 5945 & **S** 7305 (N Africa), **W** 9550 (Mideast), **S** 11790 (E Europe), **S** 15605 (Mideast)
0500-0800	7280 (E Europe)
0500-1600	6175 (Europe & N Africa)
0600-0700	**W** 5990, **W** 6045 & 9745 (E Europe), *9845* (W Africa), 15155 & **S** 17800 (E Africa)
0600-0800	**W** 11685 (Mideast), 11700 (Africa)
0600-1200	9805 (E Europe)
0700-0800	**W** 7305 & **S** 9845 (N Africa), 15605 (Mideast), 17800 (E Africa), **S** 17850 (Africa)
0700-0900 ◄	15135 (E Africa)
0700-0900	**W** 9745 (E Europe), 9790 (N Africa), 11790 (E Europe), 15315 (W Africa)
0700-1000	**W** 15155 (Mideast), **W** 21620 (E Africa)
0700-1300	11670 (E Europe)
0700-1700	15300 (Africa)
0800-0900	**W** 15155 (E Europe), **S** 17800 (E Africa)
0800-1000	**W** 17650 (Mideast)
0800-1200	15195 (E Europe), 15605 (Mideast & S Asia)
0800-1500	17620 (E Africa)
0800-1600	11845 (N Africa), 17850 (Africa)
0900-1100	**W** 17620 (W Africa), **S** 17795 (E Africa), **W** 21580 (C Africa & S Africa)
0900-1200	15155 (E Europe)
0900-1600	15315 (N Africa & W Africa)
1000-1300	21620 (E Africa)
1000-1400	17650 (Mideast)
1030-1125	*5220/4130* (E Asia)
1030-1130	**S** *9715* (S America), *9790* (C America), *11670* (S Africa), *11700* (Australasia), **W** *13625* & **W** *15435* (Irr) (S America), **S** 15530 (C America)
1030-1200	**W** *7140* & **S** *9650* (E Asia), **W** *9650* & **S** *11710* (SE Asia)
1100-1200	*11890* (SE Asia), *17795* (S Africa)
1100-1500	21580 (C Africa & S Africa)
1100-1600	17620 (W Africa)
1130-1200	15530 (C America), **W** *17575* (Irr) (N America)
1130-1300 ◄	11700 (E North Am)
1130-1300	**S** 15365 (E North Am), **W** *15515* (Irr) (C America)

Time	Right column
1200-1300	*11670* (C America), **S** *11670* (S America), *13640* (C America), **W** *15435* & **W** *17560* (Irr) (S America)
1200-1400	*9790* (C Africa)
1300-1400	9805, **S** 11615 & **W** 11670 (E Europe), *13625* (N America & C America), **W** 15155 (E Europe), **S** 17795 (E Africa)
1300-1500	15195 (E Europe), **W** 21620 (E Africa)
1300-1600	15365 (E North Am), 21685 (Irr) (W Africa)
1330-1400	**S** M-Sa *13640* (C America), *15435* (S America), M-Sa *15515* (C America), **W** *17560* (S America), **W** M-Sa *17860* (C America)
1400-1500	11615 & **S** 15155 (E Europe), **S** 15605 (Mideast), **W** *17575* (N America & C America)
1400-1600	**S** *13640* (C America), **W** 15460 (E Africa), **S** *15525* (N America), 17795 (E Africa)
1400-1800	**W** 9605 (E Europe)
1430-1600	**S** *15515*, **W** *17860* & **W** *21645* (C America)
1500-1600	**W** 9790 (N Africa), 11615 (Mideast), **W** 11670 & **S** 15195 (E Europe), **S** 15405 (S Asia & SE Asia), **W** *17575* (N America), **S** 21580 (C Africa & S Africa)
1500-1700	**W** 9790 (S Asia & SE Asia)
1500-1800	9495 (E Europe), **W** 11995 & **S** 17620 (E Africa)
1600-1700	**S** 12030 (S Asia & SE Asia), 17620 (W Africa)
1600-1800	9790 (N Africa), **S** 11670 (E Europe), **W** 11965 (W Africa)
1600-1900	**W** 7160 (N Africa), **S** *15525* & **W** *17630* (S America)
1600-2400	3965 (W Europe)
1700-1800	**W** 9790 (Africa), **S** 9805 (E Europe)
1700-1900	11705 (Africa)
1700-2000	**S** *17620* (W Africa)
1700-2200	6175 (Europe & N Africa), 15300 (Africa)
1730-1800	**S** 15210 (E Africa)
1730-1900	**W** 9485 & **S** 15460 (E Africa)
1800-1900	**W** 5900 & 7135 (E Europe), **W** 7315 (E Africa), 11965 (W Africa)
1800-2000	**S** 11995 (E Africa)
1800-2100	**S** 9605 (E Europe)
1800-2200	*7160* (C Africa), **S** 9495 (E Europe), 9790 (Africa)
1900-2000	**W** 7135 (E Europe)
1900-2100	**W** 6175 (E Europe), **S** 11965 (W Africa)
1900-2200	7160 (N Africa & W Africa), 7315 (Africa), 9485 (E Africa), **S** *17630* & **W** *21765* (S America)
2000-2100	5915 (E Europe)
2000-2400	**S** 11705 (Africa)
2100-2200	**S** 5900 & **W** 5915 (E Europe), **W** 5945 (E Africa & Mideast), **S** 9805 (E Europe)
2200-2300	**W** 5920 (C America), **W** 5945 (E North America), 9715 & 9800 (S America), **S** 11670 (C America), *13640/15190* (N America)
2200-2400	9790 (C America), **S** 9790 (E North America)

2300-2400   5945 (E North Am), **W** 7120 (S Asia & SE Asia), **W** 9570 (SE Asia), 9715 (S America), **S** 9805 (S Asia & SE Asia), 12025 & **S** 15440 (SE Asia)

FRENCH POLYNESIA—French
RFO-TAHITI—(Pacific)
24 Hr   15168

GABON—French
AFRIQUE NUMERO UN
0500-2300   9580 (C Africa)
0800-1600   17630 (E North Am & W Africa)
1600-1900   15475 (W Africa & E North Am)

GERMANY—German
BAYERISCHER RUNDFUNK
24 Hr   6085
DEUTSCHE WELLE
0000-0150   **S** 9730 (C America), **W** 11795 & **S** 15410 (S America)
0000-0155   7130 (S Europe, N Africa & S America), **S** 7275 (N Europe), **S** 9680 (S Asia), **W** 9690 (S Asia & SE Asia), **S** 9765 (S America), **W** 9765 (C America), **S** 11795 (S Asia & SE Asia), 13780 (S America), **W** 15275 (C America)
0000-0200   6075 (Europe), 9545 (S America)
0000-0300   **W** 7225 & **S** 9795 (S Asia)
0000-0355   **S** 9545 (N America & C America), **W** 11785 (W Africa & Americas)
0000-0555   3995 (Europe)
0000-0600   6100 (N America & C America)
0200-0350   **S** 7175 (E Africa)
0200-0355   **W** 7130 (N Africa & S America)
0200-0400   6145 (N America)
0200-0555   6075 (Europe & N America), **S** 9735 (N America)
0200-0600   **W** 9545 (E Africa & S Africa)
0200-0755   **S** 9545 (S Europe & W Asia)
0400-0555   **S** 6145 (N America), **W** 9735 (Mideast & Africa), **S** 11795 (Africa & Australasia)
0400-0600   6085 (N America & C America), **W** 7195 (S Africa), **W** 7235 (W Africa), 9535 (N America), **S** 9700 (S Africa), **S** 13780 (Mideast)
0500-0600   **S** 9735 (Australasia)
0555-0800   **W** 3995 (Europe)
0555-1800   6075 (Europe)
0600-0700   **W** 6140 (Europe)
0600-0755   **S** 15630 (Africa)
0600-0800   6185 (Australasia), **S** 15275 (Mideast), **W** 15630 (SE Asia & Australasia)
0600-0955   **W** 9670 (E Europe & W Asia), 9690, 9735 & 11795 (Australasia), **S** 11865 (E Europe & W Asia), **S** 21640 (Australasia)
0600-1000   **S** 12080 (E Europe), **W** 15275 (Africa), **S** 17580 & 17845 (SE Asia & Australasia)
0600-1755   **S** 13780 (Mideast), **W** 13780 (S Europe)
0600-2200   9545 (S Europe)
0700-1700   6140 (Europe)

0800-0955   **W** 11865 (E Asia), **W** 15630 (Australasia)
0800-1155   **S** 17525 (S Asia)
0800-1200   **S** 17560 (W Africa)
0800-1355   **S** 13780 (E Asia)
0900-1355   15135 (Africa)
1000-1355   **W** 9545 & **W** 11865 (E Asia), **W** 12080 & **S** 15275 (E Europe & W Asia), 21560 (Mideast)
1000-1400   **W** 7340 (E Asia), **S** 9545 (N Europe), **S** 12000 (E Asia), 17845 (S Asia & SE Asia), **S** 21640 (E Asia)
1000-1600   **W** 15275 (Mideast)
1100-1300   **S** 11765 (Europe)
1200-1355   **S** 11785 (E Europe), **S** 15275 (Americas), **W** 15275 (N America & C America)
1200-1400   **W** 11945 (Europe), **S** 17560 (Africa), **W** 17765 (S America), **S** 17845 (Mideast)
1400-1555   **W** 9595 (S Asia), **S** 17845 (S Asia & SE Asia)
1400-1600   **W** 7175 (E Europe & W Asia), 13790 (N America), **S** 15275 (E Africa & S Asia)
1400-1700   17715 (N America), 17765 (S America)
1400-1755   **S** 9425, **W** 9620 & **S** 11795 (S Asia), **S** 17560 (W Africa), **S** 21560 (Mideast & E Africa)
1400-1800   **W** 7315 (S Asia), **W** 11795 (Mideast), **S** 12055 (S Asia), **W** 15135 (Mideast & Africa)
1600-1755   **S** 9655 (S Asia), **S** 13780 (S Asia & SE Asia), **S** 15275 (E Africa & S Asia)
1600-1800   **W** 7175 (E Europe, W Asia & S Asia)
1600-2000   **W** 7445 (S Asia), **S** 9835 (Mideast & S Europe)
1800-1955   **S** 13610 (Africa)
1800-2000   **W** 3995 (Europe), **S** 15275 (E Africa, W Africa & S America)
1800-2155   **S** 9655 (SE Asia & Australasia), **W** 9735 (S Africa), **W** 11765 (SE Asia & Australasia), **S** 11795 (E Africa & S Africa), **S** 13780 (Africa), **W** 17860 (W Africa & Americas)
1800-2200   6075 (Europe & Africa), **S** 7185 (S Africa), **W** 7215 (Africa), **W** 11795 (W Africa & S America)
1800-2355   **S** 17860 (W Africa & S America)
2000-2120   17810 (Americas)
2000-2155   **S** 9545 (Africa), **W** 9545 & **S** 15275 (W Africa & S America)
2000-2400   3995 (Europe)
2120-2155   **W** 17810 (N America)
2120-2200   17810 (S America)
2200-2255   **S** 17810 (S America)
2200-2355   9715 (E Asia), **S** 11785 (S America)
2200-2400   **W** 5925 & **W** 6010 (E Asia), 6075 (Europe), 6100 (N America & C America), **S** 7315 (C America), **W** 7315 (S Asia & SE Asia), **S** 7340 (E Asia), 9545 (S America), **S** 9545 (N America & C America), **S** 9680 (S Asia), **W** 9690 (S Asia & SE Asia), **S** 9730 (C America), 9765 (S America), **W** 11785 (W Africa & Americas), **S** 11795 (S Asia & SE Asia), **W** 11795

& *13780* (S America), **W** *15275* (C America), **S** *15410* (S America)
DEUTSCHLANDRADIO—(Europe)
24 Hr   6005
RADIO BREMEN—(Europe)
24 Hr   6190
SUDDEUTSCHER R'FUNK—(Europe)
0455-2305 ▭ 6030
SUDWESTFUNK—(Europe)
24 Hr   7265

GREECE—Greek
FONI TIS HELLADAS
0000-0130 &
0200-0330   **W** 7448, **W** 9420 & 9935/6260 (N America)
0330-0345   9935/6260 (N America)
0400-0525   **W** 7450, 9425/9420, **W** 11645 & 15650 (Mideast)
0600-0745   7450, **S** 9425 & 11645 (Europe & Australasia)
0900-0950   15415/15630 (E Asia), 15650 (Australasia)
1000-1135   9425 & 9915 (Mideast)
1200-1230   **W** 9420 (Mideast), **W** 11645 & **W** 15650 (Africa)
1200-1235 &
1245-1350   **S** 15175 (Eu & N Am)
1300-1335 ▭ 15650 (Europe & N America)
1300-1335   **W** 9420 (Europe & N America), 11645 (C Asia)
1345-1450 ▭ 15650 (Europe & N America)
1345-1450   **W** 9420 (Europe & N America)
1400-1430   **S** 9420, 11645 & **S** 15630 (Mideast)
1500-1600   **W** 7450 (Europe), **S** 9375, 9420 & 11645 (E Europe)
1710-1725   **W** 7450, **S** 9375, 9425/9420 & **S** 11645 (E Europe)
1800-1840   11645 & 15150 (Africa)
1800-1900   **W** 7450, **W** 9395, **W** 9425 & **W** 11595 (Europe)
1900-2100   **W** 9420 (Europe)
1900-2150   7450 (Europe), **S** 9420/7430 (Europe, N America & Australasia)
2100-2235   9425 (Australasia)
2100-2250   **W** 6260 (Europe)
2200-2300   **W** 6260 (N America)
2200-2305   **S** 9395 (C America & S America), 11595 (S America)
2300-2335   **S** 9425 (C America & Australasia)
RADIO STATHMOS MAKEDONIAS
0500-1700   **S** 9935 (Europe)
0500-1730   **S** 11595 (Mideast)
0600-0800 ▭ 7430/6245 (Europe)
0600-1730   **W** 9935 (Mideast)
0600-1900   **W** 11595 (Europe)
1400-2200   7430 (Europe)
1500-2200   **S** 6260 (Europe)
1730-2200   9935 (Mideast)
1900-2300   **W** 6245 (Europe)
2200-2300   **W** 7430 (Europe), **W** 9935 (Mideast)

HOLLAND—Dutch
RADIO NEDERLAND
0000-0025   *7285, 9590,* **W** *12065* & **S** *13695* (SE Asia)

0130-0225   6020 (C America), *6165* (N America), **S** *9895* (E North Am), *15315/11695* (S America)
0330-0425   **S** *7310* & **W** *9860* (E Africa), *11655* (Mideast)
0530-0625   **W** *5995, 6165* & **S** *9715* (W North Am)
0530-0630   **S** 5945 (W Europe), **S** 7130 & **S** 9895 (Europe), **S** 11655 (E Europe & Mideast)
0530-0800   **S** *7395* (W Europe)
0630-0725   **W** 7130 (Europe), **S** *9615,* **W** *9715/ 9720,* **S** *9720* & **W** *11655/11660* (Australasia)
0630-0800   **S** 7240 (W Europe)
0630-0855   **W** 6020 (S Europe), **W** *7400* (Europe)
0630-1000   **S** 11935 (W Europe)
0630-1725   5955 (Europe), 9895 (S Europe)
0800-0925   **S** Sa 9590 (Europe)
0900-1025   Sa 7190 & **W** Sa 9860 (Europe)
0900-1255   **W** 11900 (W Europe)
1000-1045   *6020* (C America)
1000-1155   **S** 13700 (S Europe)

1030-1125	*9720*, **S** *9820* & **W** *11895* (Australasia), *17580* (SE Asia), *21480* (E Asia)
1330-1425	**W** *5930* & **S** *7260* (E Asia), **W** *7375* (E Asia & SE Asia), **S** *12065* (SE Asia), **W** *13770* (S Asia), **S** *15530* (SE Asia)
1430-1525	*7365*, **S** *7400* & **W** *13770* (S Asia)
1500-1725	**S** *7310* (W Europe), **S** *13700* (S Europe)
1600-1725	**W** 7300 & 9855 (Irr) (Europe)
1600-1825	**W** 6015 (S Europe & W Africa)
1630-1725	*6020* (S Africa), **S** *11655* (E Africa)
1730-1825	**W** 7300 (N Africa & Mideast), **S** 9860 (Mideast), **W** 9895 (E Africa), **S** 13700 (Mideast), **S** 15560 (S Africa & E Africa), *17605* & *21590* (W Africa)
1930-2025	**S** 6020 (W Europe & N Africa)
2030-2125	*6015* (S Africa), **S** *7120* (C Africa & S Africa), **W** 11655 & *15315* (W Africa), Su *15560* (S America), **S** *17605* (W Africa)
2030-2225	6020 (N Africa & W Africa)
2130-2225	*6030* & **S** *9895* (C America), **W** *11730* (E North Am), **S** 13700 (S America), **S** *15155* (E North Am), *15315* (S America)
2330-2400	*7285, 9590*, **W** *12065* & **S** *13695* (SE Asia)

HUNGARY—Hungarian
RADIO BUDAPEST

0000-0100 ⬅	M 9835 (S America)
0000-0100	**W** M 6165 (S America), **S** 9840 (N America), **W** M 11955 (S America)
0100-0200 ⬅	11870 (N America)
0100-0200	**W** 6190 & **W** 9850 (N America)
0130-0230	**S** 9840 (N America)
0230-0330 ⬅	11870 (N America)
0230-0330	**W** 5965 & **W** 9850 (N America)
0900-1000	**S** 15160 (Australasia)
1000-1100 ⬅	13695 & 17750 (Australasia)
1000-1100	**S** Su 15160 & **W** 15220 (Australasia)
1100-1200 ⬅	Su 13695 & Su 17750 (Australasia)
1100-1200	**S** Su 5970 (W Europe), **S** Su 11905 (N Europe), **W** Su 15220 (Australasia)
1200-1300 ⬅	Su 9835/9825 (Europe)
1200-1300	**W** Su 5945 (W Europe), **W** Su 7220 (N Europe), **W** Su 11910 (N Europe & E Europe)
1300-1400	**S** Su 11905 (N Europe)
1400-1500 ⬅	Su 5970 (W Europe), Su 9835 (Europe)
1400-1500	**W** Su 7220 (N Europe), **W** Su 11950 (N Europe & E Europe)
1800-1900	**S** 5975 (N Europe), **S** 7130 (W Europe)
1900-2000 ⬅	3975 (Europe), 9835 (W Europe)
1900-2000	**W** 5975 (N Europe), **W** 7250 (W Europe)
2000-2100	**S** 6140 (N Europe), **S** 7130 (W Europe)
2100-2200 ⬅	3975 (Europe), 9835 (W Europe)
2100-2200	**W** 5970 (N Europe), **W** 7185 (W Europe)
2200-2300	**S** 6085 & **S** 11910 (S America)
2300-2400 ⬅	9835 (S America)
2300-2400	**S** Su 6085, **W** 6165, **S** Su 11910 & **W** 11955 (S America)

IRAN—Persian
VO THE ISLAMIC REPUBLIC

| 0000-0030 | **W** 7100 & **S** 7130 (Mideast & Europe) |

0000-1230	15084
0130-1330	15365 (W Asia & S Asia)
1300-2400	15084
1630-1730	7230 (Europe)
1630-1930	6175/6005 & **W** 7180 (W Asia)
1630-2400	**W** 7100 & **S** 7130 (Mideast & Europe)

ISRAEL—Hebrew
RESHET BET

0000-0530	**S** 9388 (W Europe & E North Am)
0000-0700	**W** 7495 (W Europe & E North Am)
0300-1400	**S** 15615 (W Europe & E North Am)
0400-0700	**W** 9390 (W Europe & E North Am)
0445-2200	**S** 13750 (Europe)
0600-1730	**S** 17545 (Europe)
0700-1500	**W** 13755 (Europe)
0700-1725	**W** 11590 (W Europe & E North Am)
0800-0900 ⬅	Sa 13615 (E Europe)
1000-1200 ⬅	Su-F 13615 (E Europe)
1200-1400	**W** 15615 (E Europe)
1400-1600	**S** 11585 (W Europe & E North Am)
1500-1600	**S** 12077 (W Europe & E North Am)
1500-1900	**S** 15615 (W Europe & E North Am)
1700-2300	**W** 9388 & **W** 9390 (W Europe & E North Am)
1730-2400	**W** 7495 & **W** 9388 (W Europe & E North Am)
1900-2200	**S** 11588 (W Europe)

ITALY—Italian
RADIO ROMA-RAI INTERNATIONAL

0000-0050	6005 (E North Am), 9575 (S America), 9645/9675 (E North Am & C America), 11800 (N America & C America), 11880 (S America)
0130-0230	*6110* & *11765* (S America)
0130-0305	6005 (E North Am), 9575 (S America), 9645/9675 (N America & C America), 11800 (E North Am & C America), 11880 (S America)
0415-0425	5990/5975 (S Europe), 7275 (S Europe & N Africa)
0435-0510	**W** 9670, **W** 11800, **S** 11880 & **S** 15400 (E Africa)
1000-1100	*11925* (Australasia)
1320-1650	Su 21535 (S America), Su 21710 (C Africa & S Africa)
1400-1430	15245/15250 & 17780 (E North Am)
1500-1525	5990, 7290 & **S** 9670 (S Europe & N Africa)
1555-1625	5990, 7290 & 9755 (Europe)
1700-1800	7235, **S** 9535 & **W** 9710 (N Africa), 11840 & 15230 (Africa), *15320* (S Africa), 17870 (E Africa)
1830-1905	15245/15250 & 17780 (E North Am)
2230-2400	6005 (E North Am), 9575 (S America), 9645/9675 (E North Am & C America), 11800 (N America & C America), 11880 (S America)

RAI-RTV ITALIANA

2300-0500 ⬅	6060 (Europe, Mideast & N Africa)
0500-2300 ⬅	6060, 7175 & 9515 (Europe, N Africa & Mideast)
0600-1300	15240 (E Africa)
1320-1650	Su 9855 (Europe), Su 17780 (E North Am), Su 21520 (E Africa)

TELE RADIO STEREO—(Europe)
24 Hr   6012 (Irr)

JAPAN—Japanese
RADIO JAPAN/NHK

0000-0030	ⓦ 7140 & ⓦ 7225 (E Asia), 7295/11665 (SE Asia), ⓢ 9560 (E Asia), 11850 (Australasia), 17845/11875 (S Asia)
0000-0100	ⓦ 6055, 6155 & ⓢ 6180 (Europe)
0200-0300	5960 (E North Am), ⓦ 9605 (W North Am), ⓢ 9660 (S America), ⓢ 11790 (W North Am), 11840 (E Asia), 11860 (SE Asia), 11910 (E Asia), ⓦ 11950 (S America), ⓦ 11960 & ⓢ 15230 (W North Am), 17810 (SE Asia)
0200-0400	11885 (W North Am)
0300-0400	9515 (Europe, N Africa & Mideast), 11895 (C America)
0400-0500	5960 & ⓦ 6095 (Europe), 6110 (W North Am & C America), ⓢ 7230 (Europe), 11840 (E Asia), 17810 (SE Asia), 17820 (Mideast & N Africa)
0600-0700	5975 & 7230 (Europe), 11740 (SE Asia), 11920 (Australasia), ⓦ 11960 & ⓢ 15230 (W North Am), 21610 (SE Asia)
0800-0900	6070 (S America), ⓦ 6090 & ⓢ 9610 (E Asia), 9685 (S America), 11740 (SE Asia), 11850 & 11920 (Australasia), 15135 (W Africa), 15165 (Europe, N Africa & Mideast), 15190 & 17810 (SE Asia), 17815 (C Africa), 21610 (SE Asia)
0800-1400	ⓦ 7225 & ⓢ 9750 (E Asia)
0900-1400	11815 (SE Asia)
1000-1100	ⓦ 6090 (E Asia), ⓢ 6120 (E North Am), ⓢ 9610 (E Asia), 11730 (S Africa), 11850 (Australasia), ⓦ 11895 (S America), 15190 (SE Asia)
1200-1300	ⓦ 6090 (E Asia), ⓦ 6120 (E North Am), 7125 & ⓢ 9610 (E Asia), 15350 (SE Asia)
1300-1400	9535 & 11705 (W North Am), 11895 (S Asia), 15400 (W Africa), 21490 (C Africa)
1600-1700	6150/6035 (E Asia), ⓦ 7240 (S Asia), 9535 (W North Am), 9580 (SE Asia), ⓢ 11880/11930 (S Asia), 21700 (Europe, Mideast & Africa)
1800-1900	6150/6035 (E Asia), 7140 (Australasia), ⓦ 7280 (S Asia), 9535 (W North Am), 9580 (SE Asia), 11850 (Australasia), ⓢ 11880 (S Asia), 11930 (Mideast & N Africa)
2000-2100	6035 (Australasia), 7210 (Europe), 9535 (W North Am), 11850 (Australasia)
2000-2400	7295/11665 (SE Asia)
2100-2400	ⓦ 7225 (E Asia)
2200-2300	6055/6050, ⓦ 6140 & ⓢ 6165 (Europe), ⓦ 7125 (SE Asia), ⓦ 7140 (E Asia), ⓢ 9535 (SE Asia), ⓢ 9560 (E Asia), 9685 (S America), 11850 (Australasia)

RADIO TAMPA

0000-0800	3925, 9760
0000-1000	6115
0000-1300	3945
0000-1730	6055, 9595
0800-1730 &	
2020-2300	3925
2030-2400	6055, 9595
2300-2400	3925, 3945, 6115, 9760

JORDAN—Arabic
RADIO JORDAN

0000-0100 ⊟	15435 (S America)
0000-0210 ⊟	7180 (Mideast, SE Asia & Australasia), 11805 (S America), 11935 (W Europe & E North Am)
0400-0600 ⊟	9630 (N Africa & E Africa)
0400-0815	11810 (Mideast, SE Asia & Australasia)
0400-0900 ⊟	15290 (W Europe)
0600-0900 ⊟	11835 (E Europe)
0830-1130	11810 (Mideast, SE Asia & Australasia)
1100-1300 ⊟	15355 (N Africa & C America)
1200-1515 ⊟	15215 (Mideast, SE Asia & Australasia)
1300-1500 ⊟	17800 (W Europe)
1300-1630 ⊟	11705 (N Africa & E Africa)
1600-2100	9610 (Mideast, SE Asia & Australasia)
1630-1800 ⊟	11945 (E Europe)
1800-2200 ⊟	9830 (W Europe)
1900-2200 ⊟	11740 (E Europe)
1900-2400 ⊟	15435 (S America)
2100-2400 ⊟	7180 (Mideast, SE Asia & Australasia)
2200-2400 ⊟	11805 (S America), 11935 (W Europe & E North Am)

KOREA (REPUBLIC)—Korean
RADIO KOREA INTERNATIONAL

0000-0100	5975 (E Asia), 15575 (N America)
0100-0200	7275 (E Asia)
0300-0400	7275 (E Asia), 11725 & 11810 (S America), 15575 (N America)
0700-0800	ⓦ 7105 (W Europe), 7550 (Europe), ⓢ 9510 (W Europe), 15575 (Mideast & Africa)
0900-1100	5975 & 7275 (E Asia), 9570 (Australasia), 13670 (Europe)
1000-1100	6135 (E Asia)
1100-1130	6145 (E North Am), 9640 (E Asia), 9650 (E North Am), 11725 (S America)
1300-1400	9640 (E Asia), 13670 (SE Asia)
1700-1900	5975 (E Asia), 7550 & 15575 (Europe)
2100-2200	5975 & 7275 (E Asia), 9640 (SE Asia)
2300-2400	5975 (E Asia), 15575 (N America)

KUWAIT—Arabic
RADIO KUWAIT

0000-0530	11675 (W North Am)
0200-1305	6055 & 15495 (Mideast)
0400-0805	15505 (E Europe & W Asia)
0445-0930	15110 (S Asia & SE Asia)
0815-1740	15505 (W Africa & C Africa)
0900-1505	17885 (E Asia)
0930-1605	13620 (Europe & E North Am)
1315-1730	15110 (S Asia & SE Asia)
1315-2130	9880 (Mideast)
1615-1800	11990 (Europe & E North Am)
1745-2300	15505 (Europe & E North Am)
1800-2400	9855 (Europe & E North Am), 15495 (W Africa & C Africa)

LEBANON
VOICE OF LEBANON
Arabic & French
0355-2225 🔲 6550

LIBYA—Arabic
RADIO JAMAHIRIYA
0000-0345	15235 (W Africa & S America), 15415 (Europe), 17725/15435 (N Africa & Mideast)
1015-1630	17725/15435 (N Africa & Mideast)
1015-1700	15415 (Europe)
1015-2400	15235 (W Africa & S America)
1700-2400	17725/15435 (N Africa & Mideast)
1900-2400	15415 (Europe)

LITHUANIA—Lithuanian
LITHUANIAN RADIO—(Europe)
1000-1100 &
1100-1200 🔲 9710
RADIO VILNIUS
0000-0030	**S** *9560/6120* (E North Am)	
0900-0930	🔲 9710 (Europe)	

MEXICO—Spanish
RADIO EDUCACION
0000-1200   6185
RADIO MEXICO INTERNATIONAL—(W North Am & C America)
0000-0500,
1300-1700 &
2000-2400   5985 & 9705
RADIO MIL
24 Hr   6010 (Irr)

MOROCCO—Arabic, some French
RADIO MEDI UN—(Europe & N Africa)
0500-0100   9575
RTV MAROCAINE
0000-0500	11920 (N Africa & Mideast)
0945-2100	15345 (N Africa)
1100-1500	15335 (Europe)
1400-1700	17595 (Irr) (Europe & W Africa)
2200-2400	15335 (Europe)

NORWAY—Norwegian
RADIO NORWAY INTERNATIONAL
0000-0030	**W** 5905 (S America), 7275 (SE Asia & Australasia), 7465 (E North Am & C America), **S** 9525 (S America)
0100-0130	**W** 6120 (N America), **S** 7465 & **W** Tu-Su 7465 (E North Am & C America), **S** Tu-Su 9560 (N America)
0200-0230	**W** 6120 (N America), **S** 7465 (E North Am), **W** 7465 (S America), **S** 9560 (N America)
0300-0330	**W** 5965 & 7165 (Mideast), **S** 7465 & **W** Tu-Su 7465 (W North Am), **S** 9565 (Mideast)
0400-0430	**W** 5965 (E Europe), **W** 6040 (Mideast & E Africa), **W** 7305 (Mideast), **S** Tu-Su 7520 (W North Am), **S** 9565 & **S** 13805 (Mideast)
0500-0530	**W** 5965 (E Europe), **W** 6195 (W North Am), **W** 7180 (E Africa), **S** 7465 (E Europe), **S** 13805 (E Africa)

0600-0630	**W** 5965 & **S** 7180 (Europe), **W** 7180 (W Europe), **S** M-Sa 7295 (Australasia), **S** M-Sa 9590 (W Africa & Australasia), **W** 9590 (W Africa), **W** 11735 & **S** 13805 (E Africa)
0700-0730	**W** 5965 (Europe), **S** 7180 (W Europe), **W** M-Sa 7180 (W Europe & Australasia), **S** 7295 (Australasia), **S** 9590 (Europe), **W** 9590 & **S** 13805 (W Africa)
0800-0830	**W** 9590 & **W** 13800 (Australasia), **S** 15220 (Mideast), **S** M-Sa 17855 (Australasia)
0900-0930	**S** 13800 (E Asia), **W** 15175 (Australasia), **W** 15230 (Mideast), **S** 17855 (Australasia)
1000-1030	**W** 7295 (Atlantic), **S** 9480 (Europe), **W** 11830 (W Europe), **S** 15220 (S America)
1100-1130	**S** 7295 (Europe), **W** 15270 (S America), **S** 17740 (C Africa)
1200-1230	**S** M-Sa 9590 & **W** 9590 (Europe), **W** 9795 (E Asia), **W** 11850 (E North Am), **S** M-Sa 13800 & **S** M-Sa 15305 (E Asia), **S** 15480 (S America), **W** 15605 (SE Asia)
1300-1330	**S** 9590 & **W** M-Sa 9590 (Europe), **W** M-Sa 9795 (E Asia), **W** 11840 (N America), **S** M-Sa 13800 (SE Asia & Australasia), **S** 15305 (E Asia), **S** M-Sa 15340 (N America), **W** M-Sa 15605 (SE Asia & Australasia)
1400-1430	**W** 11720 (S Asia), **W** M-Sa 11840 (N America), 11850 (SE Asia), **S** 13800 (S Asia & SE Asia), **S** 15340 (N America)
1500-1530	**W** 9485 (W North Am), **W** M-Sa 9520 & **W** M-Sa 11730 (Mideast), **S** 11840 (W North Am), **S** 13805 & **S** 15230 (Mideast)
1600-1630	**W** 9590 (E Europe), **W** 11840 (E Africa), **W** 11840 (W North Am), **S** M-Sa 11860 (S Asia), **S** M-Sa 13805 (E Africa), **S** 15340 (W North Am)
1700-1730	7485 (E Europe), **W** 7525 (W Europe), **W** 9590 (E Africa), **S** 11860 (S Asia), **S** 15220 (E Africa)
1800-1830	**W** 5960 (W Europe), **S** M-Sa 7485 (Europe), **W** 7485 (W Africa), **S** M-Sa 9590 (Mideast), **W** 9590 (C Africa), **S** M-Sa 13805 (W Africa), **S** M-Sa 15220 (C Africa)
1900-1930	**W** M-Sa 5930 (Australasia), **W** M-Sa 5960 & **S** 7485 (Europe), **W** M-Sa 7485 (W Africa), **W** M-Sa 9590 (C Africa), **S** 11860 (Australasia), **S** 13805 (C Africa), **S** 15220 (W Africa)
2000-2030	**S** 7485 (Europe & Mideast), **W** 7520 (Europe), **W** 9480 (W North Am), **S** M-Sa 9590 (Australasia)
2100-2130	**W** 5960 (Atlantic & E North Am), **S** 7205 (Australasia), **S** 9480 (E Asia), **S** 9495 (Australasia), **S** 9590 (Atlantic)
2200-2230	**W** 5960 (Australasia), **W** M-Sa 6200 (E North Am), **W** M-Sa 7115 (E Asia),

	S M-Sa 9485 (Australasia), **S** 11840
	(E North Am)
2300-2330	**W** 5905 (S America), 7275 (SE Asia &
	Australasia), **W** 7465 (E North Am), **S**
	7490 (S America), **S** 9485 (E North Am)

OMAN—Arabic
RADIO OMAN
0200-0400	6085 (E Africa), 6120 (Mideast &
	W Asia)
0300-1800	7230 (Mideast & E Africa)
0400-0500	**W** 6085 & **S** 9540 (E Africa)
0400-0700	9735 (Mideast & W Asia)
0500-0800	9540 (E Africa)
0700-1800	**S** 11890 (Mideast & W Asia)
0800-1400	**W** 11890 (Mideast)
0800-1500	15375 (Mideast)
1400-1600	**W** 7170 (Mideast & W Asia)
1500-2145	9735 (Mideast)
1600-1800	**W** 6085 (Mideast & W Asia)
1800-2000	**S** 7230 (Mideast & E Africa)
1800-2145	6085 (Mideast & W Asia)

PARAGUAY—Spanish
RADIO ENCARNACION
| 0700-0300 ➡ | 11939 |

RADIO NACIONAL
0700-1700 ➡	9735 (S America & E North Am)
1700-2000 ➡	9735 (Irr) (S America)
2000-0300 ➡	9735 (S America & E North Am)

PHILIPPINES—Tagalog
RADYO PILIPINAS—(Mideast)
| 1730-1930 | **S** 11720, **W** 11815, 11890/9720 & 15190 |

POLAND—Polish
POLISH RADIO
1200-1225 ⬅	7270 (W Europe), 7285 (E Europe)
1530-1625	**S** 9670 (W Europe)
1630-1725 ⬅	6000 & 7145 (W Europe), 7285
	(E Europe)
1630-1725	**W** 11815 (W Europe)
2200-2255 ⬅	6035 (E Europe), 6095 (W Europe)

PORTUGAL—Portuguese
RDP INTERNATIONAL
0000-0330	6095/6130 (E North Am), 9600
	(S America), 9635 (C America &
	S America), 11840 (S America)
0330-0400	Su/M 6095/6130 & Su/M 9570 (E North
	Am), Su/M 9600 (S America), Su/M
	9635 (C America & S America), Su/M
	11840 (S America)
0600-0800 ⬅	M-F 6130/6155 (Europe)
0700-0800 ⬅	M-F 9780 (Europe)
0745-0900 ⬅	M-F 9630 (Europe)
0800-1000 ⬅	Sa/Su 17595 (SE Asia), Sa/Su 17680/
	15515 (E Africa & S Africa), Sa/Su
	21655 (W Africa & S America)
0800-1400 ⬅	6130 & 9780 (Europe)
0900-1030 ⬅	Sa/Su 9615 (Europe)
1000-1200 ⬅	17680/15515 (E Africa & S Africa),
	21655 (W Africa & S America), M-F
	21720 (E Africa & S Africa)
1200-1300 ⬅	M-F 17595 (SE Asia)

1200-1800 ⬅	Sa/Su 17680/15515 (E Africa &
	S Africa), Sa/Su 21655 (W Africa &
	S America)
1300-2100 ⬅	Sa/Su 15200 (E North Am), Sa/Su
	17745 (C America)
1400-1530 ⬅	M-F 21515 (Mideast & S Asia)
1400-1800 ⬅	Sa/Su 6130 & Sa/Su 9780 (Europe)
1600-1900 ⬅	Sa/Su 21515 (Mideast & S Asia)
1800-2100 ⬅	6130, 9780 & M-F 9815 (Europe), 15515
	(E Africa & S Africa), 21655 (W Africa
	& S America)
1900-2000 ⬅	Sa/Su 21515 (Irr) (Mideast & S Asia)
2000-2300	9570 (Irr) (E North Am)
2100-2300 ⬅	9780 (Irr) (Europe), 15515 (Irr) (E Africa
	& S Africa), 21655 (Irr) (W Africa &
	S America)
2100-2300	11840 (Irr) (S America)
2300-2330	9570 (E North Am)
2300-2400	6095/6130 (E North Am), 9600
	(S America), 9635 (C America &
	S America), 11840 (S America)

QATAR—Arabic
QATAR BROADCASTING SERVICE
0245-0706	**W** 7170, **W** 7210, **S** 9570/11740 & **S**
	9585 (Mideast & N Africa)
0707-1306	**W** 11820, **S** 15265, **W** 15395/17895 &
	S 17830 (Mideast & N Africa)
1307-1706	**W** 9535, **W** 11750 & **S** 17830 (Europe)
1307-2130	**S** 11740 (Europe)
1707-2130	**W** 7170/9570, **W** 7210 & **S** 9570/9585
	(Europe)

ROMANIA—Romanian
RADIO ROMANIA
0500-0800	9570 & **W** 11970 (Europe)
0600-0800	**S** 11940 (Europe)
0800-1500	15105 (Europe, N Africa & Mideast),
	W 17850 (Europe)
0800-1700	**S** 11790 (Europe)

RADIO ROMANIA INTERNATIONAL
0130-0200	5990 (E North Am), 6155, 9510, 9570 &
	11940 (N America)
0600-0614	**S** 9550, 9665, **W** 11775 & **S** 11810
	(Europe)
0715-0815	Su 15335 (S Asia & SE Asia), Su 15370
	& Su 17790 (Mideast & S Asia)
0815-0915	Su 15335 (W Africa), Su 15380 & **S** Su
	17720 (S Africa), Su 17790 (W Africa)
0915-1015	Su 9570 (Europe), Su 9590 & Su 9665
	(W Europe), **S** Su 11775 & **S** Su
	11810 (Europe & Atlantic), **W** Su 11940
	(Europe), **S** Su 11970 (Europe &
	Atlantic)
1300-1330	**S** 9510, **S** 11775, **W** 15335 & **W**
	17790 (Australasia)
1630-1700	**W** 7105, **W** 7195, **S** 9510, **W** 9665 &
	S 11775 (Mideast)
1730-1800	**W** 5990, **W** 7195, **S** 9510, **W** 9690 &
	S 11830 (Europe), **S** 11840 (N Europe)
2000-2030	**W** 6080 & **W** 7175 (Europe), **S** 9510 &
	S 11790 (W Europe)
2230-2300	9570, **W** 9580, **S** 11775 & **S** 11830 (S
	America)

2300-2400	W 5990 (C America), W 7175 (Australasia), 9570 (E North Am), 9750/9550 & S 11810 (Australasia), S 11830 & 11940 (N America)

SAUDI ARABIA—Arabic
BROADCASTING SERVICE OF THE KINGDOM

0300-0600	7150, 9555 (Mideast), 9620/9885 (N Africa), 9720 (W Asia), 11740/11935 (C Asia), W 11785, S 11870, S 17745/17780 & W 17745/17720 (C Asia)
0300-1700	9580 (Mideast & E Africa)
0300-2100	10990 (Irr) ISL & 10990 (Irr) ISU (Mideast)
0600-0700	7150
0600-0900	11710 (N Africa), 11950 (W Asia)
0600-1200	11820 (Mideast)
0900-1200	17880/17895 (SE Asia), 21495/21530 (E Asia & SE Asia)
0900-1500	15060 (N Africa)
1200-1500	15230/15175 (W Europe), 15380 (W Asia)
1200-1600	15165 (N Africa), 15280 (Mideast)
1500-1800	11780 (N Africa), 11910/11965 (W Europe), 11950 (W Asia)
1600-1800	9730 (C Africa), 11710 (N Africa), 11835 (Mideast)
1700-2100	6020 (Mideast & E Africa)
1800-2100	9705/9775 (W Asia), 11935 (N Africa)
1800-2300	9555 (N Africa), 9870 (W Europe)
2100-2300	3868 (Irr) USB (Mideast)

SINGAPORE
RADIO SINGAPORE INTERNATIONAL—(SE Asia)
Chinese

1100-1400	6000 & 6120

Malay

1100-1400	6135 & 7250

RADIO CORPORATION OF SINGAPORE
Chinese

0000-1100, 1400-1700 & 2300-2400	6000

Malay

0000-1100, 1400-1700 & 2200-2400	7250

SPAIN—Spanish
RADIO EXTERIOR DE ESPANA

0000-0100	Su/M 5970 (C America), Su/M 11815 (N America), Su/M 17870 (S America)
0000-0200	11945 (S America)
0000-0500	6055/11850 (N America & C America), 6125 & 9620 (S America)
0100-0400	Tu-Sa 3210 (C America), Tu-Sa 5970 (N America), Tu-Sa 5990 (S America)
0200-0500	9540 (N America & C America)
0500-0700	9650 (Australasia), 9685 (Europe), 9760 (Australasia), W 11890 (Mideast), 11920 (Europe), S 15125 (Mideast)
0600-0910	12035 (Europe)
0900-0910	17715 (S America)
0900-1200	Su 9620 (W Europe)
0900-1700	W 15110 & S 17890 (Mideast)

0900-1900	17755 (W Africa & S Africa)
0910-0940	Su-F 12035 (Europe), Su-F 17715 (S America)
0940-1515	12035 (Europe)
0940-1900	17715 (S America)
1000-1200	9620 (E Asia)
1100-1400	M-F 3210 (C America), M-F 9630 (N America), M-F 11815 (S America)
1200-1400	11910 (SE Asia)
1200-1515	9620 (W Europe)
1200-1800	17845/21570 (C America & S America)
1300-1800	Sa/Su 11815 (N America)
1400-1800	Sa/Su 5970 (C America), Sa/Su 17870/11880 (S America)
1515-1600	Sa/Su 9620 (W Europe), Sa/Su 12035 (Europe)
1600-1700	Su 9620 (W Europe), 12035 (Europe), M-Sa 15210 (W Africa & C Africa)
1700-2000	Sa/Su 6125 (W Europe)
1700-2235	7275 (Europe)
1800-1900	S Sa/Su 17845/21570 (C America & S America)
1800-2235	5970 (C America), 11815 (N America), 17870 (S America)
1900-2000	S Sa/Su 17845/15125 (C America & S America)
1900-2200	W 11880 & S 17870 (E North Am & C America)
2000-2100	Sa 6125 (W Europe), S Sa 17845/15125 (C America & S America)
2200-2235	11880 (E North Am & C America)
2200-2300	6130 (N Africa), W 9580 & S 15110 (Mideast)
2235-2255	Su 5970 (C America), Su 11815 (N America), Su 11880 (E North Am & C America), Su 17870 (S America)
2235-2300	Su 7275 (Europe)
2255-2400	5970 (C America), 11815 (N America), 11880 (E North Am & C America), 17870 (S America)
2300-2400	6125, 9620 & 11945 (S America)

SWEDEN—Swedish
RADIO SWEDEN

0000-0030	6065 & S 9810 (S America)
0100-0130	9695/9895 (SE Asia & Australasia), W 11695 (S Asia)
0200-0230 ◄	7120/7115 (N America)
0200-0230	S 9850 (N America)
0300-0330 ◄	7120/7115 (N America)
0300-0330	S 9850 (N America)
0400-0615	S M-F 9730 (Europe & N Africa)
0500-0715 ◄	M-F 6065 (Europe)
0500-0715	W M-F 9860 (Europe & N Africa)
0600-0800	S Sa 13625 (Africa)
0700-0900 ◄	Sa 6065 (Europe)
0700-0900	W Sa 9860 (Europe & N Africa), S Su 13625 & W Sa 15390 (Africa)
0800-1000 ◄	Su 6065 (Europe)
0800-1000	W Su 9860 (Europe & N Africa), W Su 15390 (Africa)
1030-1100	S 15230 (Europe & N Africa)
1100-1130 ◄	Sa/Su 6065 (Europe)
1100-1130	S 13740 (E Asia & Australasia), W 13775 (SE Asia & Australasia), 15120

(E Asia & Australasia), **[S]** 15240 (S Asia)

1130-1200 ◄	6065 (Europe), 11650 (E North Am)
1130-1200	**[W]** 9860 (Europe & N Africa)
1200-1230	**[S]** 13740, **[W]** 13775 & 15120 (E Asia & Australasia), 15240 (S Asia)
1300-1330	**[W]** 13775 (E Asia & Australasia), **[W]** 15120 (E Asia), **[W]** 15240 (S Asia)
1400-1430	**[S]** 15240 (E North Am)
1500-1530 ◄	11650 (N America)
1500-1530	**[W]** 15240 (E North Am)
1545-1600 ◄	6000 (E Europe), 6065 (Europe), 11650 (N America)
1545-1600	**[S]** 13765 (Mideast)
1545-1605	**[S]** 11650 (Europe & Africa)
1600-1645 ◄	Sa/Su 6065 (Europe)
1605-1615	**[S]** M-F 11650 (Europe & Africa), **[S]** M-F 13765 (Mideast)
1645-1705 ◄	6065 (Europe)
1645-1705	**[W]** 9670 (Europe & Africa), **[W]** 13700 (Mideast)
1705-1715 ◄	M-F 6065 (Europe)
1705-1715	**[W]** M-F 9670 (Europe & Africa), **[W]** M-F 13700 (Mideast)
1800-1830	**[S]** 15600 (Europe & Africa)
1900-1930 ◄	6065 (Europe & Mideast), 13690/13605 (Mideast)
1900-1930	**[W]** 9655 (Europe & N Africa)
1930-2000	**[W]** M-F 9655 (Europe & N Africa)
2000-2030 ◄	M-F 6065 (Europe)
2100-2130 ◄	6065 (Europe & Mideast), 9655 (Europe & Africa)
2200-2230 ◄	6065 (Europe), 9655 (Europe & Africa)

SWITZERLAND
SWISS RADIO INTERNATIONAL
French

0200-0230	6135 (E North Am), 9885 (E North Am & C America), *9905* (N America & C America)
0400-0445	**[S]** 9535 (S Europe & E Europe)
0430-0500	6135 (W North Am), 9885 (N America)
0500-0545 ◄	6165 (Europe & N Africa)
0500-0545	**[W]** 7410 (E Europe)
0530-0600	**[S]** 9535 (S Europe & E Europe)
0630-0700 ◄	6165 (Europe & N Africa)
0630-0700	**[W]** 7410 (E Europe), **[S]** 9535 (S Europe & E Europe), 9885 & **[S]** 11860 (W Africa), **[W]** 12070 & **[S]** 13635 (S Africa), **[W]** 13635 (W Africa)
0730-0800	**[W]** 7410 (E Europe)
0730-1100 ◄	6165 (Europe & N Africa)
0930-1000	*9885*, **[W]** 11640, 13685 & **[S]** 17515 (Australasia)
1130-1200	**[W]** 9885, **[W]** 11640, 13635, **[S]** 15415 & **[S]** 17515 (E Asia)
1200-1230 ◄	6165 (Europe & N Africa), 9535 (S Europe & W Europe)
1330-1400	*7230* (SE Asia), *7480* (E Asia), **[W]** 11640, 13635 & **[S]** 15480 (SE Asia)
1530-1600	**[W]** 9885 & 12075 (C Asia & S Asia), 13635 & **[S]** 15530 (W Asia & S Asia)
1830-1845 ◄	7510 (N Europe)
1830-1845	**[W]** 5850, 9885 & **[S]** 12075 (Mideast), 13635 (E Africa)

1930-2000 ◄	6165 (Europe & N Africa)
2030-2100	**[W]** *9770* (S Africa), **[S]** 9870 (Africa), 9885 (S Africa), 9905 & **[S]** 11640 (Africa), **[W]** 11640 (S Africa)
2215-2230	**[W]** 6135 (S America), 9885 (C America & S America), **[S]** 9905 & *11650* (S America)

German

0030-0100	6135 (E North Am), 9885 (E North Am & C America), *9905* (N America & C America)
0330-0400	6135 (W North Am), 9885 (N America), *9905* (N America & C America)
0500-0515	**[S]** 9535 (S Europe & E Europe)
0600-0615 ◄	6165 (Europe & N Africa)
0600-0615	**[W]** 7410 (E Europe)
0730-0800	9885 & **[S]** 11860 (W Africa), **[W]** 12070 & **[S]** 13635 (S Africa), **[W]** 13635 (W Africa)
1000-1030	*9885*, **[W]** 11640, 13685 & **[S]** 17515 (Australasia)
1130-1200 ◄	6165 (Europe & N Africa), 9535 (S Europe & W Europe)
1200-1230	**[W]** 9885, **[W]** 11640, 13635, **[S]** 15415 & **[S]** 17515 (E Asia)
1430-1445	*7230* (SE Asia), *7480* (E Asia), **[W]** 11640, 13635 & **[S]** 15480 (SE Asia)
1600-1630	**[W]** 9885 & 12075 (C Asia & S Asia), 13635 & **[S]** 15530 (W Asia & S Asia)
1600-1900 ◄	6165 (Europe & N Africa)
1730-1800	**[W]** 5850 (Mideast), **[W]** 7510 (N Europe), 9885 (Mideast), **[S]** 9905 (N Europe), **[S]** 12075 (Mideast), 13635 (E Africa)
2130-2200	**[S]** 9870 (Africa), 9885 (S Africa), **[W]** 9905 & **[S]** 11640 (Africa), **[W]** 11640 (S Africa)
2230-2300	**[W]** 6135 (S America), 9885 (C America & S America), **[S]** 9905 & *11650* (S America)

Italian

0300-0315	6135 (E North Am), 9885 (E North Am & C America), *9905* (N America & C America)
0445-0500	**[S]** 9535 (S Europe & E Europe)
0500-0530	6135 (W North Am), 9885 (N America), *9905* (N America & C America)
0545-0600 ◄	6165 (Europe & N Africa)
0545-0600	**[W]** 7410 (E Europe)
0600-0615	**[S]** 9535 (S Europe & E Europe)
0700-0715 ◄	6165 (Europe & N Africa)
0700-0715	**[W]** 7410 (E Europe)
0700-0730	9885 & **[S]** 11860 (W Africa), **[W]** 12070 & **[S]** 13635 (S Africa), **[W]** 13635 (W Africa)
0830-0900	*9885*, **[W]** 11640, 13685 & **[S]** 17515 (Australasia)
1230-1245	**[W]** 9885, **[W]** 11640, 13635, **[S]** 15415 & **[S]** 17515 (E Asia)
1230-1300 ◄	6165 (Europe & N Africa), 9535 (S Europe & W Europe)
1400-1430	*7230* (SE Asia), *7480* (E Asia), **[W]** 11640, 13635 & **[S]** 15480 (SE Asia)
1400-1600 ◄	6165 (Europe & N Africa)
1630-1645	**[W]** 9885 & 12075 (C Asia & S Asia), 13635 & **[S]** 15530 (W Asia & S Asia)

1800-1830	**W** 5850 (Mideast), **W** 7510 (N Europe), 9885 (Mideast), **S** 9905 (N Europe), **S** 12075 (Mideast), 13635 (E Africa)
1900-1930 ◀	6165 (Europe & N Africa)
2100-2130	**S** 9870 (Africa), 9885 (S Africa), **W** 9905 & **S** 11640 (Africa), **W** 11640 (S Africa)
2300-2330	**W** 6135 (S America), 9885 (C America & S America), **S** 9905 & *11650* (S America)

SYRIA—Arabic
RADIO DAMASCUS
0430-0530 ◀	9950 (Mideast)
1905-2100	12085 (Mideast)
2030-2130 ◀	9950 (Mideast)
2215-2315	12085 & 13610/15095 (S America)

SYRIAN BROADCASTING SERVICE
0600-1600 ◀	15095
0600-1700 ◀	12085

THAILAND—Thai
RADIO THAILAND
0100-0200	9655 & 11905 (Asia), **S** 15370 (N America)
0330-0430	9655 (Asia), **W** 11890 (W North Am), 11905 (Asia), **S** 15370 (W North Am)
1330-1400	**W** 7145 (E Asia), 9655 & 11905 (Asia), **S** 11955 (E Asia)
1800-1900	9655 (Asia), **S** 9690 & **W** 11855 (Mideast), 11905 (Asia)
2045-2115	9655 (Asia), **S** 9680, **S** 9755 & **W** 11805 (Europe), 11905 (Asia)

TUNISIA—Arabic
RTV TUNISIENNE
0400-0600	7475 (Europe), 12006 (N Africa & Mideast)
0500-1700	15450 (N Africa & Mideast)
0600-1400	17500 (N Africa & Mideast)
0600-1700	11730 (Europe)
1700-2330	7280 (N Africa & Mideast), 7475 (Europe), 12006 (N Africa & Mideast)

TURKEY—Turkish
VOICE OF TURKEY
0000-0400	**S** 11725 (Europe & N America)
0000-0800 ◀	9445 (Europe & E North Am), 9460 (Europe)
0000-0800	**W** 11710 (Europe & E North Am)
0000-1000 ◀	15385 (Europe)
24 Hr	11955 (Mideast)
0400-0700	**S** 9505 (Europe, N America & C America)
0400-0900	**S** 21715 (W Asia, S Asia & Australasia)
0500-1000 ◀	11925 & 15145 (W Asia)
0500-1000	**W** 9560 (W Asia, S Asia & Australasia)
0700-0900	**S** 13670 (Europe)
0800-2200 ◀	9460 (Europe & E North Am)
1000-1500	**S** F 15625 (N Africa & E Africa)
1000-1700 ◀	15350 (Europe)
1000-2300 ◀	9560 (W Asia, S Asia & Australasia)
1100-1600	**W** F 7150 (N Africa)
1300-1500	**S** 13670 (Europe)
1600-2200	**S** 7115 (N Africa & Mideast)

1600-2300 ◀	5980 (Europe)
1700-2300	**W** 7255 (Mideast & Africa)
1700-2400 ◀	15385 (Europe)
2100-2400	**S** 11725 (Europe & N America)
2200-2400 ◀	9445 (Europe & E North Am), 9460 (Europe)
2200-2400	**W** 11710 (Europe & E North Am)
2300-2350	**S** 11810 (Europe & E North Am)

UKRAINE—Ukrainian
RADIO UKRAINE
0000-0100	**S** 9560 (S Europe & N Africa), **S** 9875 (S Africa)
0000-0300	**S** 5915 (S Europe & N Africa), **S** 6020 (E Europe)
0000-0700	**S** 6010 (S Europe & N Africa)
0100-0200 ◀	5905 (S Europe & N Africa)
0100-0300	**S** 7150 & **S** 9550 (E North Am)
0100-0400 ◀	6080 (W Asia)
0100-0400	**W** 7205 (W Europe, W Africa & S America), **S** 9735 (E North Am)
0100-0500	**W** 6130 (S Europe & N Africa)
0100-0530	**S** 9685 (E North Am)
0100-0600	**S** 6090 (W Asia), **W** 7240 (W Europe), **S** 7285 (W Asia)
0100-0630	**W** 7135 (W Asia)
0100-1100	**S** 9620 (S Europe)
0130-0700	**W** 4860 (W Asia), **W** 6020 (W Europe & E North Am)
0200-0400	**W** 5915 (W Europe & E North Am), **W** 6010 (W Europe & C America), **W** 6055 (W North Am)
0200-0500	**W** 5905 (W Europe, W Africa & S America)
0300-0500	**S** 9640 (W Asia)
0300-1400	**S** 7420 (Europe)
0400-0800	**W** 6080 (W Asia)
0400-1700	**S** 6020 (E Europe)
0430-0830	**W** 9610
0500-0700	**W** 5915 (W Europe & E North Am), **W** 7205 (W Europe)
0500-0800	**W** 6010 (W Europe & C America)
0500-1000	9640 (W Asia)
0500-1700	**S** 7405 (N Europe)
0530-1030	**W** 12040 (Europe)
0600-1500	**S** 11720 (Europe), **W** 13720 (W Europe), **W** 17725 (W Africa, S America & Australasia)
0600-1600	**W** 11840 (S Europe & N Africa)
0600-1700	**S** 7320 & **S** 11980 (W Asia)
0700-1100	**W** 9620 (Europe)
0700-1130	**W** 13670 (W Asia)
0700-1600	**W** 11705 (W Europe)
0700-1700	**S** 13690 (W Europe)
0900-1330	**W** 11705
0900-1500	**W** 21480 (W Africa & S America)
0900-1800	**W** 6080 (W Asia)
1000-1100	**W** 9600 (W Asia)
1000-1500	**W** 9640 (W Asia)
1000-1700	**S** 9960 (W Europe & E North Am)
1100-1430	9600 (W Asia)
1100-1700	**S** 7180 (Europe)
1100-1800	**W** 9735 & **W** 9870 (W Europe & E North Am)
1130-1700	**W** 9620 (W Asia)

1200-1530	W 13670 (S Europe & N Africa)
1400-1600	W 6055
1400-1700	S 6130 (Europe), S 17790 (S America)
1430-1700	S 9600 (W Asia)
1500-1800	W 4795 (Europe)
1530-1800	W 6130 (S Europe & N Africa)
1600-1700	W 5905 (S Europe & N Africa), 11705 (W Europe)
1600-1800	W 6055 (Mideast & E Africa), W 7135 (W Asia)
1700-1800 ⟵	5905 (S Europe & N Africa)
1700-1800	W 11705 (W Europe)
1730-1800	W 4820 (Europe)
1800-2000	S 6010 (S Europe & N Africa), S 6020 (E Europe), S 6130 (Europe), S 9960 (W Europe & E North Am), S 11705 (W Europe), S 17790 (S America)
1900-2000	W 6010 (N Europe), W 7205 (W Europe), S 9875 (S Africa)
1900-2100 ⟵	5905 (S Europe & N Africa)
1900-2100	W 4795 & W 4820 (Europe), W 6020 (N Europe & E North Am), W 6055 (Mideast & E Africa), W 6080 (W Asia), W 6130 (W Europe, N Africa & E North Am), W 7135 (W Asia), W 7240 (W Europe)
2000-2100	W 6010 (N Europe, W Europe & C America), W 7205 (W Europe, W Africa & S America)
2100-2400	S 7150 & S 9550 (E North Am)
2200-2300	S 5915 & S 6010 (S Europe & N Africa), S 6020 (E Europe), S 7375 (Australasia), S 9560 (S Europe & N Africa), S 9875 (S Africa)
2300-2330	W 6020 (N Europe & E North Am)
2300-2400 ⟵	5905 (S Europe & N Africa), 6080 (W Asia)
2300-2400	W 4795 & W 4820 (Europe), W 5940 (S Europe & N Africa), W 6010 (N Europe, W Europe & C America), W 6055 (W North Am), W 6130 (W Europe, N Africa & E North Am), W 7135 (W Asia), W 7205 (W Europe, W Africa & S America), W 7240 (W Europe), W 9620 (W Africa & S America)

UNITED ARAB EMIRATES—Arabic
UAE RADIO FROM ABU DHABI

0000-0200	9605 & 9695 (E North Am), 9770 (W North Am), 9770 (Irr) (Europe)
0200-0400	S 6180 (Mideast), W 17770 (E Asia)
0200-0500	17855 (Australasia), W 21735 (E Asia)
0200-0600	W 9605 (Mideast), 9695 (Mideast & S Asia)
0500-0700	21735 (Australasia)
0500-1300	W 15285/15280 (Mideast)
0600-0800	W 13605 & S 15265 (Europe)
0700-1100	S 17760 (N Africa)
0800-1200	W 17885 (Europe)
0900-1100	W 15315, S 17825 & S 21735 (E Asia)
1100-1300	W 9605 & S 15315 (E Asia)
1100-1500	W 17760 & S 21630 (N Africa)
1200-1500	S 15380 (Mideast)

1200-1600	W 15265 (Europe)
1300-1700	11885 (Australasia), W 11970 (Mideast)
1500-1700	S 13605 (Mideast)
1500-1800	S 15265 (N Africa)
1500-2145	9605 (Mideast)
1600-2000	9695 (Mideast & S Asia)
1600-2145	9770 (Europe)
1700-2145	W 6180 (N Africa & Mideast), 11710 (Europe)
1900-2145	W 9780 (Irr)
2145-2400	9770 (Irr) (Europe)

UAE RADIO IN DUBAI

0000-0200	11795 (Irr) (Europe, E North Am & C America), 13675 (Irr) (E North Am & C America)
0230-0330	11945, 13675, 15400 & 21485 (E North Am & C America)
0400-0530	15435 (Australasia), 17830 (E Asia), 21700 (Australasia)
0600-1030, 1110-1330 & 1400-1600	13675 & 15395 (Europe), 17825/17630 (N Africa), 21605 (Europe)
1640-2055	11795, 13675 & 15395 (Europe), 17825/17630 (N Africa)
2055-2400	11795 (Irr) (Europe, E North Am & C America), 13675 (Irr) (E North Am & C America)

Entertainer Michael Feinstein tickles the ivories on the VOA's Talk to America, with hosts Meredith Buell and Barbara Klein.

VENEZUELA—Spanish
ECOS DEL TORBES
0900-1300	4980
1300-1900	9640
2000-0400	4980

RADIO TACHIRA
0130-0400	4830 (Irr)
1000-1300 &	
2000-0130	4830

RADIO VALERA
0300-0400	Tu-Su 4840 (Irr)
1000-0300	4840 (Irr)

VIETNAM—Vietnamese
VOICE OF VIETNAM
0000-0100	9840 & 🅂 15010 (E Asia & Americas)
0000-1700	12035
0300-0900	4960, 5924, 10059, 🖤 12020
0400-0500	🖤 7345 (W North Am)

1100-1600	4960, 5924, 10059
1700-1800	9840, 🖤 12020 & 🅂 15010 (Europe)
2100-2300	4960, 5924, 10059
2200-2400	12035

YUGOSLAVIA—Serbian
RADIO YUGOSLAVIA
0000-0030	🅂 Su 9580 (E North Am)
0030-0100	🖤 6195, 🖤 7115 & 🅂 9580 (E North Am)
0100-0130	🖤 Su 6195 & 🖤 Su 7115 (E North Am)
0130-0200	🖤 6195 & 🖤 7115 (E North Am)
1400-1430	11835 (Australasia)
1900-1930	🅂 Sa 7230 (Australasia)
1930-2030	🅂 7230 (Australasia)
2000-2030	⬅ Sa 6100 (W Europe)
2000-2030	🖤 Sa 9595 (Australasia)
2030-2100	⬅ 6100 (W Europe)
2030-2130	🖤 9595 (Australasia)
2330-2400	🅂 9580 (E North Am)

Carmelo Ciancio/VOA

Addresses PLUS—1997

E-Mail and Postal Addresses . . . *PLUS* World Wide Web Sites, Phones and Faxes, Contact Personnel, Bureaus, Future Plans, Items for Sale, Free Gifts . . . *PLUS* Summer and Winter Times in Each Country!

The rest of this book tells how stations reach you, but this section is different. It spins the bottle the other way by showing how you can reach the stations. It also reveals other ways that stations can inform and entertain you.

the listener reported hearing was, in fact, theirs. While they were at it, some would also throw in a free souvenir of their station—a calendar, perhaps, or a pennant or sticker.

This is still being done today. You can see how by looking under Verification in the glossary farther back in this book, then making use of Addresses PLUS for contact specifics.

"Applause" Replies

When radio was new, listeners sent in "applause" cards not only to let stations know about reception quality, but also how much their shows were—or were not—being appreciated. By way of saying "thanks," stations would reply with a letter or attractive card verifying ("QSLing" in radio lingo) that the station

Electronic Bazaar

Stations sell offbeat items, too. Besides the obvious, such as world band radios, some stations peddle native recordings, books, magazines, station T-shirts, ties, tote bags, aprons, caps, watches, clocks, pens, knives, letter openers, lighters, refrigerator magnets, keyrings and other collectables. One Miami-based station will even sell you airtime for a buck a minute!

How about *this* for a job? Overlooking palm and surf on the South Pacific island of Palau is the announcer for KHBN, the Voice of Hope. The station broadcasts to Asia and Australasia, but is heard far beyond.

High Adventure Ministries

Paying Postfolk

Most stations prefer to reply to listener correspondence—even e-mail—via the postal system. That way, they can send you printed schedules, verification cards and other "hands-on" souvenirs. Big stations usually do so for free, but smaller ones often want to be reimbursed for postage costs.

Most effective, especially for Latin American and Indonesian stations, is to enclose some unused (mint) stamps from the station's country. These are available from Plum's Airmail Postage, 12 Glenn Road, Flemington NJ 08822 USA, phone +1 (908) 788-1020, fax +1 (908) 782 2612. Too, you can try DX Stamp Service, 7661 Roder Parkway, Ontario NY 14519 USA;

or DX-QSL Associates, 434 Blair Road NW, Vienna VA 22180 USA.

One way to help ensure your return-postage stamps will be used as you intended is to stick them onto a pre-addressed return airmail envelope (self-addressed stamped envelope, or SASE).

You can also prompt reluctant stations by donating one U.S. dollar, preferably hidden from prying eyes by a piece of foil-covered carbon paper or the like. Registration helps, too, as cash tends to get stolen. Additionally, International Reply Coupons (IRCs), which recipients may exchange locally for air or surface stamps, are available at many post offices worldwide. Thing is, they're relatively costly, are not fully effective, and aren't accepted by postal authorities in all countries.

Stamp Out Crime

Yes, even in 1997 mail theft is a problem in several countries. We identify these, and for each one offer proven ways to avoid theft.

Remember that some postal employees are stamp collectors, and in certain countries they freely steal mail with unusual stamps. When in doubt, use everyday stamps or, even better, a postal meter.

¿Que Hora Es?

World Time, explained elsewhere in this book, is essential if you want to find out when your favorite station is on. But if you want to know what time it is in any given country, World Time and Addresses PLUS work together to give you the most accurate local times within each country.

How accurate? The United States' official expert on international local times tells us that her organization finds PASSPORT's local times to be the most accurate available from any source, anywhere.

So that you don't have to wrestle with seasonal changes in your own local time, we give local times for each country in terms of hours' difference from World Time, which stays the same year-round. For example, if you look below under "Algeria," you'll see that country is World Time +1; that is, one hour ahead of World Time. So, if World Time is 1200, the local time in Algeria is 1300 (1:00 PM). On the other hand, México City is World Time –6; that is, six hours behind World Time. If World Time is 1200, in México City it's 6:00 AM. And so it goes for each country in this section. Times shown in parentheses are for the middle of the year—roughly

April-October; specific dates of seasonal-time changeovers for individual countries can be obtained (U.S. callers only) by dialing toll-free (800) 342-5624.

Spotted Something New?

Has something changed since we went to press? A missing detail? Please let us know! Your update information, especially photocopies of material received from stations, are highly valued. Contact the IBS Editorial Office, Box 300, Penn's Park, PA 18943 USA, fax +1 (215) 598 3794, e-mail addresses@passport.com.

Many thanks to *Número Uno*, *Radio Nuevo Mundo*, *Cumbre DX*, *Ask-DX*, *India Broadbase* and *Relámpago DX* for their kind cooperation in the preparation of this section.

Using PASSPORT's Addresses PLUS Section

- **Stations included:** All stations known to reply, however erratically, or new stations which possibly may reply, to correspondence from listeners.
- **Giveaways:** If you want any of these, request politely in your correspondence. Available until supplies run out.
- **Address type:** Communications addresses are given. These sometimes differ from the physical locations given in the Blue Pages.
- **Leased-time programs:** Private non-political organizations that lease air time, but which possess no world band transmitters of their own, are not necessarily listed. However, they may be reached via the stations over which they are heard.
- **Unless otherwise indicated, stations:**
  — Reply regularly within six months to most listeners' correspondence in English.
  — Provide, upon request, free station schedules and verification ("QSL") postcards or letters (see "Verification"

in the glossary for further information). We specify when other items are available for free or for purchase.

— Do not require compensation for postage costs incurred in replying to you. Where compensation is required, details are provided.

- **Local times:** These are given in difference from World Time (UTC). For example, "World Time –5" means that if you subtract five hours from UTC, you'll get the local time in that country; so if it were 1100 World Time, it would be 0600 local time in that country. Times in

Tips for Effective Correspondence

Write to be read. Winning correspondence, on paper or by e-mail, is interesting and helpful from the recipient's point of view, yet friendly without being chummy. Comments on specific programs are almost always appreciated.

They don't know English? No problem. A basic form of translation service, performed by computer, is available for free via Globalink over the World Wide Web at http://www.globalink.com/xlate.html. That same organization—and many more, including some university language departments—will do translations by human beings, usually for a modest fee.

Incorporate language courtesies. Writing in the broadcaster's tongue is always a plus—this section of PASSPORT indicates when it is a requirement—but English is usually the next-best bet. In addition, when writing in any language to Spanish-speaking countries, remember that what gringos think of as the "last name" is actually written as the penultimate name. Thus, Juan Antonio Vargas García, which can also be written as Juan Antonio Vargas G., refers to Sr. Vargas; so your salutation should read, *Estimado Sr. Vargas*.

What's that "García" doing there, then? That's *mamita's* father's family name. Latinos more or less solved the problem of gender fairness in names long before the Anglos.

But, wait—what about Portuguese, used by all those lovely stations in Brazil? Same concept, but in reverse. *Mamá's* father's family name is penultimate, and the "real" last name is where English-speakers are used to it, at the end.

In Chinese, the "last" name comes first. However, when writing in English, Chinese names are sometimes reversed for the benefit of *weiguoren*—foreigners. Use your judgement. For example, "Li" is a common Chinese last name, so if you see "Li Dan," it's "Mr. Li." But if it's "Dan Li," and certainly if it's been anglicized into "Dan Lee," he's already one step ahead of you, and it's still "Mr. Li" (or Lee). Less widely known is that the same can also occur in Hungarian. For example, "Bartók Béla" for Béla Bartók.

If in doubt, fall back on the ever-safe "Dear Sir" or "Dear Madam," or use e-mail, where salutations are not expected. And be patient—replies by post usually take weeks, sometimes months. Slow responders, those that tend to take six months or more to reply, are cited in this section, as are erratic repliers.

(parentheses) are for the middle of the year—roughly April-October.

- **Fax numbers:** To help avoid confusion, fax numbers are given without hyphens, telephone numbers with hyphens, and are configured for international dialing once you add your country's international access code (011 in the United States and Canada, 010 in the United Kingdom, and so on). For domestic dialing within countries outside the United States, Canada and the Caribbean, replace the country code (1-3 digits preceded by a "+") by a zero.

- **E-mail addresses:** Given in Internet format. CompuServe users wishing to communicate with CompuServe addresses (those ending in @compuserve.com) should simply use the numeric address, replacing the dot with a comma. Thus, 74434.3020@compuserve.com (Internet format) becomes 74434,3020 (CompuServe format). Alternatively, CompuServe users wishing to communicate with a non-CompuServe Internet address (not ending in @compuserve.com) need to precede the address given in Addresses PLUS with *internet:* Too, periods, commas and semicolons at the end of an address are normal sentence punctuation, *not* part of that address. Individuals can often be reached by using their last name before the "@".

- **World Wide Web, FTP and Gopher URLs (site addresses):** Periods, commas and semicolons at the end of a URL are our normal sentence punctuation, not part of that address.

- **Web radio:** World band stations which also have RealAudio, StreamWorks or comparable Web audio programming are indicated by ☞. Stations that have Web audio programming, but which aren't on world band, are indicated by ☞.

AFGHANISTAN World Time +4:30
NOTE: Postal service to this country is occasionally suspended.
Radio Afghanistan, P.O. Box 544, Kabul, Afghanistan. Rarely replies.

ALBANIA World Time +1 (+2 midyear)
Radio Tirana, External Service, Rruga Ismail Qemali, Tirana, Albania. Phone: +355 (42) 23-239. Fax: (External Service) +355 (42) 23 650; (General Directorate) +355 (42) 26 203. Contact: Rifat Kryeziu, Director; Bardhyl Pollo, Director of External Services; Adriana Bislea, English Department; or Diana Koci; (Directorate) Itfan Mandija, General Directorate of Albanian RTV. Recent budget cutbacks have caused the once-vigorous Correspondence Section to be completely eliminated, so getting any sort of reply is unlikely. For example, staffers are now too few to fill the little remaining airtime with programs (music filler is used instead), even though they reportedly work seven days a week (and are paid only around $60 per month).

ALGERIA World Time +1 (+2 midyear)
Radio Algiers International—same details as "Radiodiffusion-Télévision Algerienne," below.
Radiodiffusion-Télévision Algerienne (ENRS)
NONTECHNICAL AND GENERAL TECHNICAL: 21 Boulevard el Chouhada, Algiers 16000, Algeria. Phone: +213 (2) 594-266. Fax: +213 (2) 605 814. Contact: (nontechnical) L. Zaghlami; Chaabane Lounakil, Head of International Arabic Section; Yahi Zéhira, Head of International Relations; or Relations Extérieures; (general technical) Direction Technique. Replies irregularly. French or Arabic preferred, but English accepted.
FREQUENCY MANAGEMENT OFFICE: Télédiffusion d'Algérie, route de Bainem, B.P. 50, Bouzareah, Algeria. Fax: +213 (2) 797 390 or +213 (2) 941 390. Contact: Mouloud Lahlou, Director General.

ANGOLA World Time +1
NOTE: Because of the unsettled conditions prevalent in Angola, except for the first three stations given below, few of the former stations have been active in recent years. Whether most will eventually be reactivated is unknown at this time.
A Voz da Resistência do Galo Negro (VORGAN) (Voice of the Resistance of the Black Cockerel), Free Angola Information Service, 1629 K Street NW, Suite 503, Washington DC 20006 USA. Phone: +1 (202) 775-0958. Fax: +1 (202) 785 8063. URL: (UNITA) http://www.sfiedi.fr/kup/index.html#anglais. Contact: Kalik Chaka, Director of Information; or Jardo Muekalia, Chief Representative to the United States. Pro-UNITA, led by Joseph Savimbi—once a rebel organization, but which is now considered to be part of the legitimate Angolan political structure. Transmits from Jamba in the central highlands of Angola.
Rádio Nacional de Angola, Cx. Postal 1329, Luanda, Angola. Fax: +244 (2) 391 234. Contact: Bernardino Costa, Public Opinion Office; Sra. Luiza Fancony, Diretora de Programas; Lourdes de Almeida, Chefe de Seção; or Cesar A.B. da Silva, Diretor Geral. Formerly replied occasionally to correspondence, preferably in Portuguese, but replies have been more difficult recently. $1, return postage or 2 IRCs most helpful.
Emissora Provincial de Benguela, Cx. Postal 19, Benguela, Angola. Contact: Simão Martíns Cuto, Responsável Administrativo; Carlos A.A. Gregório, Diretor; or José Cabral Sande. $1 or return postage required. Replies irregularly.
Emissora Provincial de Bié (if reactivated), C.P. 33, Kuito, Bié, Angola. Contact: José Cordeiro Chimo, O Diretor. Replies occasionally to correspondence in Portuguese.
Emissora Provincial de Moxico (if reactivated), Cx. Postal 74, Luena, Angola. Contact: Paulo Cahilo, Diretor. $1 or return postage required. Replies to correspondence in Portuguese. Other **Emissora Provincial** stations (if reactivated)—same address, etc., as Rádio Nacional, above.

ANTARCTICA World Time –2 (–3 midyear) Base Antárctica Esperanza; +13 McMurdo

AMERICAN FORCES ANTARCTIC NETWORK (AFAN) MCMURDO

NOTE: AFAN McMurdo has been essentially inoperative since 1992. Yet, according to Jeff Lutz, who was in Antarctica at the time, it did go on the air at least once, in 1995, to carry the Super Bowl football game, and thus there is the slim chance that it may be active at least every now and then. However, note that during the time the Super Bowl is aired the Antarctic is in round-the-clock daylight, so AFAN is unlikely to propagate more than 1,500 km or so on its established frequency of 6012 kHz (1 kW).

U.S NAVY: U.S. Navy Communication Station COMNAVSUPPOR-ANTARCTICA, McMurdo Station, FPO San Francisco CA 96601 USA.

GOVERNMENT CONTRACTOR: Antarctic Support Associates, 61 Inverness Drive East, Suite 300, Englewood CO 80112 USA. Phone: +1 (303) 790-8606. Fax: +1 (303) 792 2397. Contact: Andrew Wright.

Radio Nacional Arcángel San Gabriel—LRA 36, Base Antárctica Esperanza (Tierra de San Martín), 9411 Territorio Antárctico Argentino, Argentina. Contact: (general) Elizabeth Beltrán de Gallegos, Programación y Locución; (technical) Cristian Omar Guida. Return postage required. Replies irregularly to correspondence in Spanish. If no reply, try sending your correspondence (but don't write the station's name on your envelope) and 2 IRCs via the helpful Gabriel Iván Barrera, Casilla 2868, 1000-Buenos Aires, Argentina; fax +54 (1) 322 3351.

ANTIGUA World Time –4

BBC World Service—Caribbean Relay Station, P.O. Box 1203, St. John's, Antigua. Phone: +1 (809) 462-0994. Fax: +1 (809) 462 0436. Contact: (technical) G. Hoef, Manager; Roy Fleet; or R. Pratt, Company Engineer. Nontechnical correspondence should be sent to the BBC World Service in London (see).

Deutsche Welle—Relay Station Antigua—same address and contact as BBC World Service, above. Nontechnical correspondence should be sent to the Deutsche Welle in Germany (see).

ARGENTINA World Time –3 Buenos Aires and eastern provinces; –4 in some western provinces.

Radiodifusión Argentina al Exterior—RAE, C.C. 555 Correo Central, 1000-Buenos Aires, Argentina. Phone: +54 (1) 325-6368. Fax: +54 (1) 325 9433. Contact: (general) Paul F. Allen, Announcer, English Team; John Anthony Middleton, Head of the English Team; María Dolores López; Rodrigo Calderón, English Department; or Sandro Cenci, Chief, Italian Section; (administration) Marcela G.R. Campos, Directora; (technical) Gabriel Iván Barrera, DX Editor; or Patricia Menéndez. Free paper pennant and tourist literature. Return postage or $1 appreciated.

Radio Malargüe, Esq. Aldao 350, 5613-Malargüe, Argentina. Contact: Eduardo Vicente Lucero, Jefe Técnico; Nolasco H. Barrera, Interventor; or José Pandolfo, Departamento Administración. Free pennants. Return postage necessary. Prefers correspondence in Spanish.

Radio Nacional Buenos Aires, Maipú 555, 1000-Buenos Aires, Argentina. $1 helpful. Prefers correspondence in Spanish.

Radio Nacional Mendoza, Av. Emilio Civit 460, 5500-Mendoza, Argentina. Phone: (administrative) +54 (61) 38-15-27. Phone/fax: (general) +54 (61) 25-79-31. Fax: +54 (61) 38 05 96. Contact: (general/administrative) Lic. Jorge Horacio Parvanoff, Director; (technical) Juan Carlos Fernández, Jefe del Departamento Técnico. Free pamphlets and stickers. Replies to correspondence, preferably in Spanish, but English also accepted. Plans to replace transmitter.

Radio Rivadavia (when operating to Antarctica), Arenales 2467, 1124-Buenos Aires, Argentina. Fax: +54 (1) 824 6927.

ARMENIA World Time +3 (+4 midyear)

Armenian Radio—see Voice of Armenia for details.

Lutherische Stunde (religious program aired over Radio Intercontinental), Postfach 1162, D-27363 Sottrum, Germany.

Mitternachtsruf (religious program aired via Radio Intercontinental), Postfach 62, 79807 Lottstetten, Germany; Postfach 290, Eicholzstrasse 38, CH-8330 Pfaffikon, Switzerland; or P.O. Box 4389, W. Columbia, SC 29171 USA. Contact: Jonathan Malgo. Free stickers and promotional material.

Radio Intercontinental—see Voice of Armenia, below, for details.

Voice of Armenia, Radio Agency, Alek Manoukyan Street 5, 375025 Yerevan, Armenia. Phone: +7 (8852) 558-010. Fax: +7 (8852) 551 513. Contact: V. Voskanian, Deputy Editor-in-Chief; R. Abalian, Editor-in-Chief; or Levon Amamikian. Free postcards and stamps. Replies slowly.

ASCENSION World Time exactly

BBC World Service—Atlantic Relay Station, English Bay, Ascension (South Atlantic Ocean). Fax: +247 6117. Contact: (technical) Jeff Cant, Staff Manager; M.R. Watkins, A/Assistant Resident Engineer; or Nicola Nicholls, Transmitter Engineer. Nontechnical correspondence should be sent to the BBC World Service in London (see).

Radio Japan, Radio Roma and Voice of America/IBB—via BBC Ascension Relay Station—All correspondence should be directed to the regular addresses in Japan, Italy and the USA (see).

Voice of America/VOA-IBB—Ascension Relay Station—same details as "BBC World Service," above. Nontechnical correspondence should be directed to the regular VOA address (see USA).

AUSTRALIA World Time +11 (+10 midyear) Victoria (VIC), New South Wales (NSW), Australian Capital Territory (ACT) and Tasmania (TAS); +10:30 (+9:30 midyear) South Australia (SA); +10 Queensland (QLD); +9:30 Northern Territory (NT); +8 Western Australia (WA)

Australian Defence Forces Radio, Department of Defence, EMU (Electronic Media Unit) ANZAC Park West, APW 1-B-07, Reid, Canberra, ACT 2601, Australia. Phone: +61 (6) 266-6669. Fax: +61 (6) 266 6565. Contact: (general) Adam Iffland, Presenter; (technical) Hugh Mackenzie, Managing Presenter; or Brian Langshaw. SAE and 2 IRCs needed for a reply. Station replies to verification inquiries only. At last check, transmissions were emanating from a 40 kW single-sideband transmitter in Canberra at HMAS Harman.

Australian Broadcasting Corporation Northern Territory HF Service—ABC Darwin, Administrative Center for the Northern Territory Shortwave Service, ABC Box 9994, GPO Darwin NT 0820, Australia. Phone: +61 (89) 433-222, +61 (89) 433-229, or +61 (89) 433-231; (engineering) +61 (89) 433-210. Fax: +61 (89) 433 235 or +61 (89) 433 208. Contact: (general) Sue Camilleri, Broadcaster and Community Liaison Officer; Yvonne Corby; Christine Kakakios; or Fred McCue, Producer, "Mornings with Michael Mackenzie"; (technical) Peter Camilleri, Production Manager. Free stickers. Free "Traveller's Guide to ABC Radio." T-shirts US$20. Three IRCs or return postage helpful.

BBC World Service via Radio Australia—For verification direct from the Australian transmitters, contact Arie Schellars, Ass't. Transmission Manager, Master Control, at Radio Australia (see). Nontechnical correspondence should be sent to the BBC World Service in London (see).

CAAMA Radio—ABC, Central Australian Aboriginal Media Association, Bush Radio Service, P.O. Box 2924, Alice Springs NT 0871, Australia. Phone: +61 (89) 529-204. Fax: +61 (89) 529 214. Contact: Merridie Satoar, Department Manager; Mark Lillyman, News Director; or Owen Cole, CAAMA General Manager; (administration) Graham Archer, Station Manager; (technical) Warren Huck, Technician. Free stickers. Two IRCs or return postage helpful.

Radio Australia—ABC
STUDIOS AND MAIN OFFICES: GPO Box 428G, Melbourne VIC 3001, Australia. Phone: ("Openline" voice mail for listeners' messages and requests) +61 (3) 9626-1825; (general) +61 (3) 9626-1800; (management) +61 (3) 9626-1901; (technical) +61 (3) 9626 1912/3/4; (ABC programs) +61 (3) 9626-1916. Fax & Faxpoll: (general) +61 (3) 9626 1899; (management) +61 (3) 9626 1903; (technical) +61 (3) 9626 1917. E-mail: roz@radioaus.org.au or raust3@ozemail.com.au. URLs: (general) http://www.abc.net.au/ra/default.htm; (RealAudio in English) http://www.wrn.org/stations/abc.html; (overview) http://www.dca.gov.au/pubs/creative_nation/filmtv.htm. Contact: (general) Susan Jenkins, Correspondence Officer; Roger Broadbent, Head, English Language Programming; Judi Cooper, Business Development Manager; Derek White, General Manager, International Broadcasting; Ms. Lisa T. Breeze, Publicist; Denis Gibbons, Producer, "Feedback"; Catherine McCafferty, Audience Liaison; or Dan Gordon; (technical) Nigel Holmes, Transmission Manager, Transmission Management Unit; Arie Schellaars, Ass't. Transmission Manager, Master Control; or Neil Deer, Controller, Resources & Distribution. T-shirts available. On-air language courses available in English, Chinese and Vietnamese. Radio Australia's budget has been cut back substantially to help subsidize Australia Television's overseas operations, which were originally supposed to be paid for by advertising.
NEW YORK BUREAU, NONTECHNICAL: Room 2260, 630 Fifth Avenue, New York NY 10020 USA. Phone: (representative) +1 (212) 332-2540; or (correspondent) +1 (212) 332-2545. Fax: +1 (212) 332 2546. Contact: Maggie Jones, North American Representative.
LONDON BUREAU, NONTECHNICAL: 54 Portland Place, London W1N 4DY, United Kingdom. Phone: +44 (171) 631-4456. Fax: (administration) +44 (171) 323 0059, (news) +44 (171) 323 1125. Contact: Robert Bolton, Manager.
BANGKOK BUREAU, NONTECHNICAL: 209 Soi Hutayana off Soi Suanplu, South Sathorn Road, Bangkok 10120, Thailand. Fax: +66 (2) 287 2040. Contact: Nicholas Stuart.
Radio Rum Jungle—ABC (program studios), Top Aboriginal Bush Association, Corner Speed Street & Gap Road, Batchelor NT 0870, Australia. Phone: +61 (89) 523-433. Fax: +61 (89) 522 093. Contact: Mae-Mae Morrison, Announcer; Andrew Joshua, Chairman; or George Butler. Three IRCs or return postage helpful. May send free posters.
Radio VNG (official time station)
PRIMARY ADDRESS: National Standards Commission, P.O. Box 282, North Ryde, NSW 2113, Australia. Toll-free telephone number (Australia only) (008) 251-942. Phone: +61 (2) 888-3922. Fax: +61 (2) 888 3033. E-mail: richardb@ozemail.com.au. Contact: Dr. Richard Brittain, Secretary, National Time Committee. Station offers a free 16-page booklet about VNG and free promotional material. Free stickers and postcards. Three IRCs helpful.
ALTERNATIVE ADDRESS: VNG Users Consortium, GPO Box 1090, Canberra ACT 2601, Australia. Fax: +61 (6) 249 9969. Contact: Dr. Marion Leiba, Honorary Secretary. Three IRCs appreciated.

AUSTRIA World Time +1 (+2 midyear)
Radio Austria International
MAIN OFFICE: Würzburggasse 30, A-1136 Vienna, Austria. Phone: (general) +43 (1) 87878-2130; (voice mail) +43 (1) 87878-3636; (technical) +43 (1) 87878-2629. Fax: (general) +43 (1) 87878 4404; (technical) +43 (1) 87878 2773. E-mail: (general) info@rai.ping.at; ("Kurzwellen Panorama") kwp@rai.ping.at. URLs: (general) http://www.ping.at/rai/; (RealAudio in English and German) http://www.via.at/stations/orf.html. Contact: (general) Vera Bock, Listener's Service; "Postbox"/"Hörerbriefkasten" listeners' letters shows; ("Kurzwellen Panorama") Wolf Harranth, Editor; (administration) Prof. Paul Lendvai, Director; Dr. Edgar Sterbenz,

Deputy Director; (technical) Ing. Ernst Vranka, Frequency Management Department. Free stickers and program schedule twice a year, as well as quiz prizes. Mr. Harranth seeks collections of old verification cards and letters for the highly organized historical archives he is maintaining.
WASHINGTON NEWS BUREAU: 1206 Eaton Ct. NW, Washington DC 20007 USA. Phone: +1 (202) 822-9570. Contact: Franz R. Kössler.
Österreichischer Rundfunk—Blue Danube Radio, Argentinierstr. 30A, A-1040 Vienna, Austria. Phone: +43 (1) 50101-8901. Fax: +43 (1) 50101 8900. E-mail: (general) bdrtas@orf.at; (Webmaster) 100071.1652@compuserve.com. URL: (general) http://www.via.at/fobdr/; (RealAudio news weekdays, repeats weekends, in English, German and French) http://www.wrn.org/stations/danube.html. Contact: Andreas Rudas, Publicity Officer; Bernhard Bamgartner, Webmaster.

AZERBAIJAN World Time +3 (+4 midyear)
Azerbaijani Radio—see Radio Dada Gorgud for details.
Radio Dada Gorgud (Voice of Azerbaijan), Medhi Hüseyin küçási 1, 370011 Baku, Azerbaijan. Phone: +7 (8922) 398-585. Fax: +7 (8922) 395 452. Contact: Mrs. Tamam Bayatli-Öner, Director. Free postcards. $1 or return postage helpful. Replies occasionally to correspondence in English.

BAHRAIN World Time +3
Radio Bahrain, Broadcasting & Television, Ministry of Information, P.O. Box 702, Al Manāmah, Bahrain. Phone: (Arabic Service) +973 781-888; (English Service) +973 629-085. Fax: (Arabic Service) +973 681 544; (English Service) +973 780 911. Contact: A. Suliman (for director of broadcasting). $1 or IRC required. Replies irregularly.

BANGLADESH World Time +6
Radio Bangladesh
NONTECHNICAL CORRESPONDENCE: External Services, Shahbagh Post Box No. 2204, Dhaka 1000, Bangladesh. Phone: +880 (2) 504-348 or +880 (2) 503-688. Fax: +880 (2) 862 021. Contact: Quazi Mahmudur Rahman, Director, Liaison; Masudul Hasan, Deputy Director; Syed Zaman; A.K. Jahidul Huq, Assistant Director; Ashraf ul-Alam, Assistant for Director; or Mobarak Hossain Khan, Director.
TECHNICAL CORRESPONDENCE: National Broadcasting Authority, NBA House, 121 Kazi Nazrul Islam Avenue, Dhaka 1000, Bangladesh. Phone: +880 (2) 818-734 or +880 (2) 865-294. Fax: +880 (2) 817 850. Contact: Nurul Islam, Station Engineer, Research; Mohammed Romizuddin Bhuiya, Senior Engineer (Research Wing). Verifications not common from this office.

BELARUS World Time +2 (+3 midyear)
Belarussian Radio—see Radio Belarus for details.
Bible Focus (religious program aired over Radio Minsk), P.O. Box 205, Doncaster, DN10 6LZ, United Kingdom. Contact: Maurice Hinchliffe.
Die Antwort (religious program aired over Radio Minsk), Postfach 767, CH-1701 Freiburg, Switzerland. Phone: +41 (37) 281-717. Fax: +41 (37) 281 752. Contact: Rev. Hermann A. Parli, Director of Claropa Radio Center. *Die Antwort* quarterly newsletter for SF5.00 or DM6.00 per year. Calendar for SF10.00 or DM12.00.
Grodno Radio—see Radio Belarus for details.
Mogilev Radio—see Radio Belarus for details.
Radio Belarus, vul. Chyrvonaya 4, 220807 Minsk, Belarus. Phone: +7 (0172) 395-875, +7 (0172) 334-039 or +7 (0172) 333-922. Fax: +7 (0172) 366 643 or +7 (0172) 648 182. Contact: Michail Tondel, Chief Editor; or Jürgen Eberhardt. Free Belarus stamps.
Radio Minsk—see Radio Belarus for details.
Voice of Orthodoxy (program)
MINSK OFFICE: V. Pristavko, P.O. Box 17, 220012 Minsk, Belarus. Aired via transmission facilities of Radio Trans

Europe, Portugal, and the Voice of Hope, Lebanon. Correspondence and reception reports welcomed.
PARIS OFFICE: B.P. 416-08, F-75366 Paris Cedex 08, France. Contact: Valentin Korelsky, General Secretary.

BELGIUM   World Time +1 (+2 midyear)
📻 Radio Vlaanderen Internationaal
NOTE: According to a spokesperson for RVI, as of mid-1995 the station expects to make no further investment in shortwave equipment, as it considers it to be an "old, obsolete medium." However, discussions with RVI suggest that they may not be fully aware of certain variables for successfully reaching audiences—notably, the growth since the late Eighties in world band listening in such places as North America, where advanced-technology broadcasting and narrowcasting options are greater than anyplace else; and, at the other end of the economic-technological continuum, the paucity of affordable advanced-technology options in key parts of the world to which RVI transmits. Taken together, these suggest that this course of action may be reconsidered in due course if the station is to remain viable.
NONTECHNICAL AND GENERAL TECHNICAL: (English Department) Brussels Calling, P.O. Box 26, B-1000 Brussels, Belgium; (other departments) Belgische Radio en Televisie, Postbus 26, B-1000 Brussels, Belgium. Phone: +32 (2) 741-5611 or +32 (2) 741-3802. Fax: (administration and Dutch Service) +32 (2) 732 6295; (other language services) +32 (2) 734 8336. BBS: +32 (3) 825-3613. E-mail: rvi@brtn.be. URLs: (general) http://www.brtn.be/rvi/; or (RealAudio in English and Dutch) http://www.wrn.org/stations/rvi.html. Contact (general) Deanne Lehman, Producer, "P.O. Box 26" letterbox program; Liz Sanderson, Head, English Service; Maryse Jacob, Head, French Service; Martina Luxen, Head, German Service; Ximena Prieto, Head, Spanish Service; (administration) Monique Delvaux, Directeur; (general technical) Frans Vossen, Producer, "Radio World." For members of their Listeners' Club, there are free stickers, key rings, ballpoint pens and *Club Echo* Listeners' Club magazine—plus Club members can receive genuine QSL cards. Remarks and reception reports can also be sent to the following diplomatic addresses:
Nigeria Embassy: 1A, Bak Road, Ikoyi-Island, Lagos, Nigeria.
Argentina Embassy: Defensa 113, 8°Piso, 1065 Buenos Aires, Argentina.
India Embassy: 50 N Shanti Path Chanakyapuri, New Delhi 110021, India.
FREQUENCY MANAGEMENT OFFICE: BRTN, Ave. Reyerslaan 52, B-1043 Brussels, Belgium. Phone: +32 (2) 741-5571. Fax: +32 (2) 741 5567. Contact: Hugo Gauderis or Willy Devos.

BENIN   World Time +1
Office de Radiodiffusion et Télévision du Benin, La Voix de la Révolution, B.P. 366, Cotonou, Bénin; this address is for Cotonou and Parakou stations, alike. Contact: (Cotonou) Damien Zinsou Ala Hassa; Emile Desire Ologoudou, Directeur Generale; or Leonce Goohouede; (technical) Anastase Adjoko, Chef de Service Technique; (Radio Parakou, general) J. de Matha, Le Chef de la Station, or (Radio Parakou, technical) Léon Donou, Le Chef des Services Techniques. Return postage, $1 or IRC required. Replies irregularly and slowly to correspondence in French.

BHUTAN   World Time +7 (+6 midyear)
Bhutan Broadcasting Service
STATION: Department of Information and Broadcasting, Ministry of Communications, P.O. Box 101, Thimphu, Bhutan. Phone: +975 23-070. Fax: +975 23 073. Contact: (general) Ashi Renchen Chhoden, News and Current Affairs; Narda Gautam; or Sonam Tshong, Executive Director; (technical) C. Proden, Station Engineer; or Technical Head. Two IRCs, return postage or $1 required. Replies extremely irregularly; correspondence to the U.N. Mission (*see* following) may be more fruitful.

UNITED NATIONS MISSION: Permanent Mission of the Kingdom of Bhutan to the United Nations, Two United Nations Plaza, 27th Floor, New York NY 10017 USA. Fax: +1 (212) 826 2998. Contact: Mrs. Kunzang C. Namgyel, Third Secretary; Mrs. Sonam Yangchen, Attaché; Ms. Leki Wangmo, Second Secretary; Thinley Dorrji, Second Secretary; or Hari K. Chhetri, Second Secretary. Free newspapers and booklet on the history of Bhutan.

BOLIVIA   World Time −4
NOTE ON STATION IDENTIFICATIONS: Many Bolivian stations listed as "Radio..." may also announce as "Radio Emisora..." or "Radiodifusora..."
Galaxia Radiodifusión—*see* Radio Galaxia, below.
Hitachi Radiodifusión—*see* Radio Hitachi, below.
Paitití Radiodifusión—*see* Radio Paitití, below.
Radio Abaroa, Calle Nicanor Gonzalo Salvatierra 249, Riberalta, Beni, Bolivia. Contact: René Arias Pacheco, Director. Return postage or $1 required. Replies rarely to correspondence in Spanish.
Radio Animas, Chocaya, Animas, Potosí, Bolivia. Return postage or $1 required. Replies irregularly to correspondence in Spanish.
Radio Camargo—*see* Radio Emisoras Camargo, below.
Radio Centenario "La Nueva"
MAIN OFFICE: Casilla 818, Santa Cruz de la Sierra, Bolivia. Phone: +591 (3) 529-265. Fax: +591 (3) 524 747. Contact: Napoleón Ardaya Borja, Director. May send a calendar. Free stickers. Return postage or $1 required. Audio cassettes of contemporary Christian music and Bolivian folk music $10, including postage; CDs of Christian folk music $15, including postage. Replies to correspondence in English and Spanish.
U.S. BRANCH OFFICE: LATCOM, 1218 Croton Avenue, New Castle PA 16101 USA. Phone: +1 (412) 652-0101. Fax: +1 (412) 652 4654. Contact: Hope Cummins.
Radio Colonia—*see* Radio Televisión Colonia.
Radio Cosmos (when active), Casilla 1092, Cochabamba, Bolivia. Phone: +591 (42) 50-423. Fax: +591 (42) 51 173. Contact: Laureano Rojas, Jr. $1 or return postage required. Replies to correspondence in Spanish.
Radiodifusoras Integración—*see* Radio Integración, below.
Radiodifusoras Minería, Casilla de Correo 247, Oruro, Bolivia. Phone: +591 (52) 52-736. Contact: Dr. José Carlos Gómez Espinoza, Gerente y Director General; or Srta. Costa Colque Flores., Responsable del programa "Minería Cultural." Free pennants. Replies to correspondence in Spanish.
Radiodifusoras Trópico, Casilla 60, Trinidad, Beni, Bolivia. Contact: Eduardo Avila Alberdi, Director. Replies slowly to correspondence in Spanish. Return postage required for reply.
Radio Eco
MAIN ADDRESS: Correo Central, Reyes, Ballivián, Beni, Bolivia. Contact: Gonzalo Espinoza Cortés, Director. Free station literature. $1 or return postage required. Replies to correspondence in Spanish.
ALTERNATIVE ADDRESS: Rolmán Medina Méndez, Correo Central, Reyes, Ballivián, Bolivia.
Radio Eco San Borja (San Borja la Radio), Correo Central, San Borja, Ballivián, Beni, Bolivia. Contact: Gonzalo Espinoza Cortés, Director. Free station poster promised to correspondents. Return postage appreciated. Replies slowly to correspondence in Spanish.
Radio El Mundo, Casilla 1984, Santa Cruz de la Sierra, Bolivia. Phone: +591 (3) 464-646. Fax: +591 (3) 465 057. Contact: Freddy Banegas Carrasco, Gerente; Lic. José Luis Vélez Ocampo C., Director; or Lic. Juan Pablo Sainz, Gerente General. Free stickers and pennants. $1 or return postage required. Replies irregularly to correspondence in Spanish.
Radio Emisora Dos de Febrero (when active), Vaca Diez 400, Rurrenabaque, Beni, Bolivia. Contact: John Arze von Boeck. Free pennant, which is especially attractive. Replies occasionally to correspondence in Spanish.

Radio Emisora Galaxia—see Radio Galaxia, below.

Radio Emisora Padilla—see Radio Padilla, below.

Radio Emisora San Ignacio, Calle Ballivián s/n, San Ignacio de Moxos, Beni, Bolivia. Contact: Carlos Salvatierra Rivero, Gerente y Director. $1 or return postage necessary.

Radio Emisora Villamontes—see Radio Villamontes, below.

Radio Emisoras Camargo, Casilla 09, Camargo, Pcia. Nor-Cinti, Bolivia. Contact: Pablo García B., Gerente Propietario. Return postage or $1 required. Replies slowly to correspondence in Spanish.

Radio Emisoras Minería—see Radiodifusoras Minería.

Radio Estación Frontera—see Radio Frontera, below.

Radio Fides, Casilla 9143, La Paz, Bolivia. Fax: +591 (2) 379 030. Contact: Pedro Eduardo Pérez, Director; Felicia de Rojas, Secretaria; or Roxana Beltrán C. Replies occasionally to correspondence in Spanish.

Radio Frontera, Casilla 179, Cobija, Pando, Bolivia. Contact: Lino Miahuchi von Ancken, CP9AR. Free pennants. $1 or return postage necessary. Replies to correspondence in Spanish.

Radio Galaxia, Calle Beni s/n casi esquina Udarico Rosales, Guayaramerín, Beni, Bolivia. Contact: Dorián Arias, Gerente; Héber Hitachi Banegas, Director; or Carlos Arteaga Tacaná, Director-Dueño. Return postage or $1 required. Replies to correspondence in Spanish.

Radio Grigotá, Casilla 203, Santa Cruz de la Sierra, Bolivia. Phone/fax: +591 (3) 326 443. Fax: +591 (3) 362 795. Contact: (general) Víctor Hugo Arteaga B., Director General; (technical) Tania Martins de Arteaga, Gerente Administrativo. Free stickers, pins, pennants, key rings and posters. $1 or return postage required. Replies occasionally to correspondence in English, French, Portuguese and Spanish. May replace old Philips transmitter.

Radio Hitachi (Hitachi Radiodifusión), Calle Sucre 20, Guayaramerín, Beni, Bolivia. Contact: Héber Hitachi Banegas, Director. Return postage of $1 required.

Radio Illimani, Casilla 1042, La Paz, Bolivia. Phone: +591 (2) 376-364. Contact: Rubén D. Choque, Director; Lic. Manuel Liendo Rázuri, Gerente General. $1 required, and your letter should be registered and include a tourist brochure or postcard from where you live. Replies irregularly to friendly correspondence in Spanish.

Radio Integración, Casilla 7902, La Paz, Bolivia. Contact: Lic. Manuel Liendo Rázuri, Gerente General; Benjamín Juan Carlos Blanco Q., Director Ejecutivo; or Carmelo de la Cruz Huanca, Comunicador Social. Free pennants. Return postage required.

Radio Juan XXIII (Veintitrés), Avenida Santa Cruz al frente de la plaza principal, San Ignacio de Velasco, Santa Cruz, Bolivia. Phone: +591 (962) 2188. Contact: Fernando

Festival Queen of The *Campesinas*, right, displays garments typically worn by Quechua Indians in the mountains of Bolivia. Announcer is from Radio Televisión Colonia in Yapacani.

Manuel Picazo Torres, Director; or Pbro. Elías Cortezon, Director. Return postage or $1 required. Replies occasionally to correspondence in Spanish.

Radio La Cruz del Sur, Casilla 1408, La Paz, Bolivia. Contact: Pastor Rodolfo Moya Jiménez, Director. Pennant $1 or return postage. Replies slowly to correspondence in Spanish.

Radio La Palabra, Parroquia de Santa Ana de Yacuma, Beni, Bolivia. Phone: +591 (848) 2117. Contact: Padre Yosu Arketa, Director. Return postage necessary. Replies to correspondence in Spanish.

Radio La Plata, Casilla 276, Sucre, Bolivia. Phone: +591 (64) 31-616. Fax: +591 (64) 41 400. Contact: Freddy Donoso Bleichner.

Radio Libertad, Casilla 5324, La Paz, Bolivia. Phone: +591 (2) 365-154. Fax: +591 (2) 363 069. Contact: (general) Oscar Violetta Barrios; (technical) Lic. Teresa Sanjinés Lora, Gerente General. Depending upon what's on hand, pamphlets, stickers, pins, pennants, purses, pencil sharpeners, key rings and calendars. If blank cassette and $2 is sent, they will be happy to dub recording of local music. Sells T-shirts for $10. Return postage or $1 required for reply. Upon request, they will record for listeners any type of Bolivian music they have on hand, and send it to that listener for the cost of the cassette and postage; or, if the listener sends a cassette, for the cost of postage. Replies fairly regularly to correspondence in English and Spanish.

Radio López, Correo Central, Uyuni, Provincia Nor-López, Potosí, Bolivia. Experimental transmissions in Quechua run by Federación Regional Unica de Trabajadores Campesinos del Altiplano.

Radio Loyola, Casilla 40, Sucre, Bolivia. Phone: +591 (64) 30-222. Fax: +591 (64) 42 555. Contact: (general) Lic. José Weimar León G., Director; (technical) Tec. Norberto Rosales. Free stickers and pennants. Replies occasionally to correspondence in English, Italian and Spanish. Considering replacing 18-year-old transmitter.

Radio Mauro Núñez (when active), Centro de Estudios para el Desarrollo de Chuquisaca (CEDEC), Casilla 196, Sucre, Bolivia. Phone: +591 (64) 25-008. Fax: +591 (64) 32 628. Contact: Jorge A. Peñaranda Llanos; Dr. Vladimir Gutiérrez P., Director; or Jesús Urioste. Replies to correspondence in Spanish.

Radio Metropolitana, Casilla de Correo 8704, La Paz, Bolivia. Phone: +591 (2) 354-418, +591 (2) 375-953, +595 (2) 324-394 or +595 (2) 361-176. Fax: +591 (2) 356 785. Contact: Rodolfo Beltrán Rosales, Jefe de Prensa de "El Metropolicial"; or Carlos Palenque Avilés, Presidente Ejecutivo RTP. Free postcards and pennants. $1 or return postage necessary.

Radio Minería—see Radiodifusoras Minería.

Radio Movima, Calle Baptista No. 24, Santa Ana de Yacuma, Beni, Bolivia. Contact: Rubén Serrano López, Director; Javier Roca Díaz, Director Gerente; or Mavis Serrano, Directora. Return postage or $1 required. Replies irregularly to correspondence in Spanish.

Radio Nacional de Huanuni, Casilla 681, Oruro, Bolivia. Contact: Rafael Linneo Morales, Director General; or Alfredo Murillo, Director. Return postage or $1 required. Replies irregularly to correspondence in Spanish.

Radio Norte, Calle Warnes 195, 2do piso del Cine Escorpio, Montero, Santa Cruz, Bolivia. Phone: +591 (92) 20-970. Contact: Leonardo Arteaga Ríos, Director.

Radio Padilla, Padilla, Chuquisaca, Bolivia. Contact: Moisés Palma Salazar, Director. Return postage or $1 required. Replies to correspondence in Spanish.

Radio Paitití, Casilla 172, Guayaramerín, Beni, Bolivia. Contact: Armando Mollinedo Bacarreza, Director; Luis Carlos Santa Cruz Cuéllar, Director Gerente; or Ancir Vaca Cuéllar, Gerente-Propietario. Free pennants. Return postage or $3 required. Replies irregularly to correspondence in Spanish.

Radio Panamericana, Casilla 5263, La Paz, Bolivia. Con-

tact: Daniel Sánchez Rocha, Director. Replies irregularly, with correspondence in Spanish preferred. $1 or 2 IRCs helpful.

Radio Perla del Acre, Casilla 7, Cobija, Departamento de Pando, Bolivia. Return postage or $1 required. Replies irregularly to correspondence in Spanish.

Radio Pío XII (Doce), Casilla 434, Oruro, Bolivia. Phone: +591 (52) 53-168. Contact: Pbro. Roberto Durette, OMI, Director General. Return postage necessary. Replies occasionally to correspondence in Spanish.

Radio San Gabriel, Casilla 4792, La Paz, Bolivia. Phone: +591 (2) 355-371. Fax/phone: +591 (2) 321 174. Contact: Hno. José Canut Saurat, Director General; or Sra. Martha Portugal, Dpto. de Publicidad. $1 or return postage helpful. Free book on station, Aymara calendars and *La Voz del Pueblo Aymara* magazine. Replies fairly regularly to correspondence in Spanish. Station of the Hermanos de la Salle Catholic religious order.

Radio San Miguel, Casilla 102, Riberalta, Beni, Bolivia. Phone: +591 (852) 8268. Contact: Félix Alberto Rada Q., Director; or Gerin Pardo Molina, Director. Free stickers and pennants; has a different pennant each year. Return postage or $1 required. Replies irregularly to correspondence in Spanish. Feedback on program "Bolivia al Mundo" (aired 0200-0300 World Time) especially appreciated.

Radio Santa Ana, Calle Sucre No. 250, Santa Ana de Yacuma, Beni, Bolivia. Contact: Mario Roberto Suárez, Director; or Mariano Verdugo. Return postage or $1 required. Replies irregularly to correspondence in Spanish.

Radio Santa Cruz, Emisora del Instituto Radiofónico Fé y Alegría (IRFA), Casilla 672 (or 3213), Santa Cruz, Bolivia. Phone: +591 (3) 531-817. Fax: +591 (3) 532 257. Contact: Padre Francisco Flores, S.J., Director General; Srta. María Yolanda Marco, Secretaria; Señora Mirian Suárez, Productor, "Protagonista Ud.", Director General; Lic. Silvia Nava S. Free pamphlets, stickers and pennants. Return postage required. Replies to correspondence in English, French and Spanish.

Radio Sararenda, Casilla 7, Camiri, Santa Cruz, Bolivia. Phone: +595 (952) 2121. Contact: Freddy Lara Aguilar, Director; Kathy Arenas, Administradora. Free stickers and photos of Camiri. Replies to correspondence in Spanish.

Radio Televisión Colonia, Correo Central, Yapacani, Santa Cruz de la Sierra, Bolivia. Phone/fax: +591 (933) 61-64. Fax: +591 (933) 60-00. Contact: (general) Yrey Fausto Montaño Ustárez, Gerente Propietario; (technical) Ing. Rene Zambrana. Replies to correspondence in English, French, Italian, Japanese, Portuguese and Spanish. Free pamphlets, stickers, pins, pennants and small handicrafts made by local artisans. Sells *El Fin de la Corrupción en Bolivia* by Emiliano Zeballos for $10; CDs and audio cassettes of Yapacani and Bolivian folk music for (CDs) $20 each and (cassettes) $10 each; T-shirts $10; video cassettes $20; handicrafts by local artisans at various prices. Return postage required for reply.

Radio Villamontes, Avenida Méndez Arcos No. 156, Villamontes, Departamento de Tarija, Bolivia. Contact: Gerardo Rocabado Galarza, Director. $1 or return postage required.

BOSNIA-HERCEGOVINA   World Time +1 (+2 midyear)

Radio & Television of Bosnia-Hercegovina, Bulevar M. Selimovica 4, 71 000 Sarajevo, Bosnia-Hercegovina. Phone: +387 (71) 646-014 or +387 (71) 455-124. Fax: +387 (71) 645 142 or +387 (71) 455 104. Contact: Milenko Vockic, Director; Mr. N. Dizdarevic; or Mr. R. Basic.

BOTSWANA   World Time +2

Radio Botswana, Private Bag 0060, Gaborone, Botswana. Phone: +267 352-541. Phone: +267 352-541. Fax: +267 371 588 or +267 357 138. Contact: (general) Ted Makgekgenene, Director; or Monica Mphusu, Producer, "Maokaneng/Pleasure Mix"; (technical) Kingsley Reebang. Free stickers, pennants and pins. Return postage, $1 or 2 IRCs required. Replies slowly and irregularly.

Voice of America/VOA-IBB—Botswana Relay Station
TRANSMITTER SITE: Voice of America/IBB, Botswana Relay Station, Moepeng Hill, Selebi-Phikwe, Botswana. Phone: +267 810-932. Fax: +267 810 252. Contact: Dennis G. Brewer, Station Manager. This address for specialized technical correspondence only. All other correspondence should be directed to the regular VOA address (*see* USA).

BRAZIL   World Time –1 (–2 midyear) Atlantic Islands; –2 (–3 midyear) Eastern, including Brasília and Rio de Janeiro, plus the town of Barra do Garças; –3 (–4 midyear) Western; –4 (–5 midyear) Acre. Some northern states keep midyear time year round.
NOTE: Postal authorities recommend that, because of the level of theft in the Brazilian postal system, correspondence to Brazil be sent only via registered mail.

Emissora Rural A Voz do São Francisco, C.P. 8, 56301 Petrolina, Pernambuco, Brazil. Contact: Maria Letecia de Andrade Nunes. Return postage necessary. Replies to correspondence in Portuguese.

Rádio Alvorada (Londrina), Rua Sen. Souza Naves 9, 9 Andar, 86015 Londrina, Paraná, Brazil. Contact: Padre José Guidoreni, Diretor. Pennants $1 or return postage. Replies to correspondence in Portuguese.

Rádio Alvorada (Parintins), Travessa Leopoldo Neves 503, 69150 Parintins, Amazonas, Brazil. Contact: Raimunda Ribeira da Motta, Diretora. Return postage required. Replies occasionally to correspondence in Portuguese.

Rádio Anhanguera, C.P. 13, 74823-000 Goiânia, Goiás, Brazil. Contact: Rossana F. da Silva; or Eng. Domingos Vicente Tinoco. Return postage required. Replies to correspondence in Portuguese.

Rádio Aparecida, C.P. 14664, 03698 São Paulo SP, Brazil. Contact: Padre Cabral; Cassiano Macedo, Producer, "Encontro DX"; or João Climaco, Diretor Geral. Return postage or $1 required. Replies occasionally to correspondence in Portuguese.

Rádio Bandeirantes, C.P. 372, Rua Radiantes 13, Morumbí, 01059-970 São Paulo SP, Brazil. Fax: +55 (11) 843 5391. Contact: Samir Razuk, Diretor Geral; Carlos Newton; or Salomão Esper, Superintendente. Free stickers, pennants and canceled Brazilian stamps. $1 or return postage required.

Rádio Baré (when active), Avenida Santa Cruz Machado 170 A, 69010-070 Manaus, Amazonas, Brazil. Contact: Fernando A.B. Andrade, Diretor Programação e Produção. The Diretor is looking for radio catalogs.

Radiobrás—see Rádio Nacional da Amazônia and Rádio Nacional do Brasil.

Rádio Brasil, C.P. 625, 13101 Campinas, São Paulo SP, Brazil. Contact: Wilson Roberto Correa Viana, Gerente. Return postage required. Replies to correspondence in Portuguese.

Rádio Brasil Central, C.P. 330, 74001-970 Goiânia, Goiás, Brazil. Contact: Ney Raymundo Fernández, Coordinador Executivo; Sergio Rubens da Silva; or Arizio Pedro Soarez, Diretor Gerente. Free stickers. $1 or return postage required. Replies to correspondence in Portuguese.

Rádio Brasil Tropical, C.P. 405, 78005-970 Cuiabá, Mato Grosso, Brazil. Contact: Klecius Santos. Free stickers. $1 required. Replies to correspondence in Portuguese.

Rádio Caiari, C.P. 104, 78901 Porto Velho, Rondônia, Brazil. Contact: Carlos Alberto Diniz Martins, Diretor Geral. Free stickers. Return postage helpful. Replies irregularly to correspondence in Portuguese.

Rádio Canção Nova, C.P. 15, 12630 Cachoeira Paulista, São Paulo SP, Brazil. Contact: Benedita Luiza Rodrigues; or Valera Guimarães Massafera, Secretária. Free stickers, pennants and station brochure sometimes given upon request. $1 helpful.

Rádio Capixaba, C.P. 509, 29001 Vitória, Espírito Santo,

Brazil. Contact: Jairo Gouvea Maia, Diretor; or Sofrage do Benil. Replies occasionally to correspondence in Portuguese.

Rádio Carajá, C.P. 520, 75001-970 Anápolis, Goiás, Brazil. Contact: Nilson Silva Rosa, Diretor Geral. Return postage helpful. Replies to correspondence in Portuguese.

Rádio Clube do Pará, C.P. 533, 66001 Belém, Pará, Brazil. Contact: Edyr Paiva Proença, Diretor Geral; or José Almeida Lima de Sousa. Return postage required. Replies irregularly to correspondence in Portuguese.

Rádio Clube Marilia (when active), C.P. 325, Marilia, 17500 São Paulo SP, Brazil. Contact: Antonio Carlos Nasser. Return postage required. Replies to correspondence in Portuguese.

Rádio Clube de Rondonópolis, C.P. 190, Rondonópolis, Mato Grosso, Brazil. Contact: Canário Silva, Departamento Comercial; or Saúl Feliz, Gerente-Geral. Return postage helpful. Replies to correspondence in Portuguese.

Rádio Clube Varginha, C.P. 102, 37101 Varginha, Minas Gerais, Brazil. Contact: Juraci Viana. Return postage necessary. Replies slowly to correspondence in Portuguese.

Rádio Coari—see Rádio Educação Rural-Coari.

Rádio Cultura de Campos, C.P. 79, 28100-970 Campos, Rio de Janeiro, Brazil. $1 or return postage necessary. Replies to correspondence in Portuguese.

Rádio Cultura de Araraquara, Avenida Espanha 284, Araraquara 14800, São Paulo SP, Brazil. Contact: Antonio Carlos Rodrigues dos Santos. Return postage required. Replies slowly to correspondence in Portuguese.

Rádio Cultura do Pará, Avenida Almirante Barroso 735, 66065 Belém, Pará, Brazil. Contact: Ronald Pastor; or Augusto Proença, Diretor. Return postage required. Replies irregularly to correspondence in Portuguese.

Rádio Cultura Foz do Iguaçu, C.P. 312, 85890 Foz do Iguaçu, Paraná, Brazil. Contact: Ennes Mendes da Rocha, Gerente-Geral. Return postage necessary. Replies to correspondence in Portuguese. Carries Rádio Transamérica programming at night, but all technical correspondence should be sent to Rádio Cultura Foz do Iguaçu.

Rádio Cultura Ondas Tropicais, Rua Barcelos s/n esquina com Major Gabriel, 69020-060 Manaus, Brazil. Contact: Luíz Fernando de Souza Ferreira.

Rádio Cultura São Paulo, Rua Cenno Sbrighi 378, 05099 São Paulo SP, Brazil. Contact: Thais de Almeida Dias, Chefe de Produção e Programação; Sra. Maria Luíza Amaral Kfouri, Chefe de Produção; Valvenio Martins de Almeida; or José Munhoz, Coordenador. $1 or return postage required. Replies slowly to correspondence in Portuguese.

Rádio Difusora Cáceres, C.P. 297, 78200-000 Cáceres, Mato Grosso, Brazil. Contact: Sra. Maridalva Amaral Vignardi. $1 or return postage required. Replies occasionally to correspondence in Portuguese.

Rádio Difusora de Aquidauana, C.P. 18, 79200-000 Aquidauana, Mato Grosso do Sul, Brazil. Phone: +55 (67) 241-3956 or +55 (67) 241-3957. Contact: Primaz Aldo Bertoni, Diretor. Free tourist literature and used Brazilian stamps. $1 or return postage required. This station sometimes identifies during the program day as "Nova Difusora," but its sign-off announcement gives the official name as "Rádio Difusora, Aquidauana."

Rádio Difusora de Londrina, C.P. 1870, 86010 Londrina, Paraná, Brazil. Contact: Walter Roberto Manganoti, Gerente. Free tourist brochure, which sometimes seconds as a verification. $1 or return postage helpful. Replies irregularly to correspondence in Portuguese.

Rádio Difusora do Amazonas, C.P. 311, 69001 Manaus, Amazonas, Brazil. Contact: J. Joaquim Marinho, Diretor. Joaquim Marinho is a keen stamp collector and especially interested in Duck Hunting Permit Stamps. Will reply to correspondence in Portuguese or English. $1 or return postage helpful.

Rádio Difusora do Maranhão, C.P. 152, 65001 São Luíz, Maranhão, Brazil. Contact: Alonso Augusto Duque, BA, Presidente; José de Arimatéla Araújo, Diretor; or Fernando Souza, Gerente. Free tourist literature. Return postage required. Replies occasionally to correspondence in Portuguese.

Rádio Difusora Jataí, C.P. 33 (or Rua de José Carvalhos Bastos 542), 76801 Jataí, Goiás, Brazil. Contact: Zacarías Faleiros, Diretor Gerente.

Rádio Difusora Macapá (when active), C.P. 2929, 68901 Macapá, Amapá, Brazil. Contact: Francisco de Paulo Silva Santos or Rui Lobato. $1 or return postage required. Replies irregularly to correspondence in Portuguese.

Rádio Difusora Poços de Caldas, C.P. 937, 37701-970 Poços de Caldas, Minas Gerais, Brazil. Contact: Marco Aurelio C. Mendoça, Diretor. $1 or return postage helpful. Replies to correspondence in Portuguese.

Rádio Difusora Roraima, Rua Capitão Ene Garcez 830, 69300 Boa Vista, Roraima, Brazil. Contact: Francisco Geraldo França, Diretor Geral; Manuel Pinto Teixeira, Diretor; or Francisco Alves Vieira. Return postage required. Replies occasionally to correspondence in Portuguese.

Rádio Difusora "6 de Agosto," Rua Pio Nazário 31, 69930-000 Xapuri, Brazil. Contact: Francisco Evangelista de Abreu. Replies to correspondence in Portuguese.

Rádio Educação Rural—Campo Grande, C.P. 261, 79002-233 Campo Grande, Mato Grosso do Sul, Brazil. Phone: +55 (67) 384-3164, +55 (67) 382-2238 or +55 (67) 384-3345. Contact: Ailton Guerra, Gerente-Geral; Angelo Venturelli, Direcor; or Diácono Tomás Schwamborn. $1 or return postage required. Replies to correspondence in Portuguese.

Rádio Educação Rural—Coari, Praça São Sebastião 228, 69460 Coari, Amazonas, Brazil. Contact: Lino Rodrigues Pessoa, Diretor Comercial; Joaquim Florencio Coelho, Diretor Administrador da Comunidad Salgueiro; or Elijane Martins Correa. $1 or return postage helpful. Replies irregularly to correspondence in Portuguese.

Rádio Educadora Cariri, C.P. 57, 63101 Crato, Ceará, Brazil. Contact: Padre Gonçalo Farias Filho, Diretor Gerente.

Return postage or $1 helpful. Replies irregularly to correspondence in Portuguese.

Rádio Educadora da Bahia, Centro de Rádio, Rua Pedro Gama 413/E, Alto Sobradinho Federação, 40000 Salvador, Bahia, Brazil. Contact: Elza Correa Ramos; or Walter Sequieros R. Tanure. $1 or return postage required. May send local music CD. Replies to correspondence in Portuguese.

Rádio Educadora de Bragança (when active), Rua Barão do Rio Branco 1151, 68600 Bragança, Brazil. Contact: José Rosendo de S. Neto. $1 or return postage required. Replies to correspondence in Portuguese.

Rádio Educadora de Guajará Mirim, Praça Mario Correa No.90, CEP78957-000 Guajará Mirim, Estado de Rondônia, Brazil. Contact: Padre Isidoro José Moro. Return postage helpful. Replies to correspondence in Portuguese.

Rádio Gaúcha, Avenida Ipiranga 1075 2do andar, Azenha, 90060 Porto Alegre, Rio Grande do Sul, Brazil. Phone: +55 (51) 223-6600. Contact: Alexandre Amaral de Aguiar, News Editor; Almind Antonio Ranzlun, Diretor Gerente; or Geraldo Canali. Replies occasionally to correspondence, preferably in Portuguese.

Rádio Gazeta, Avenida Paulista 900, 01310 São Paulo SP, Brazil. Fax: +55 (11) 285 4895. Contact: Shakespeare Ettinger, Superv. Geral de Operação; Bernardo Leite da Costa; José Roberto Mignone Cheibub, General Manager; or Ing. Aníbal Horta Figueiredo. Free stickers. $1 or return postage necessary. Replies to correspondence in Portuguese.

Rádio Globo, Rua das Palmeiras 315, 01226 São Paulo SP, Brazil. Contact: Ademar Dutra, Locutor, "Programa Ademar Dutra"; or José Marques. Replies to correspondence, preferably in Portuguese.

Rádio Guaíba, Rua Caldas Junior 219, 90010-260 Porto Alegre, Rio Grande do Sul, Brazil. Return postage may be helpful.

Radio Guaraní, Avenida Assis Chateaubriand 499, Floresta, 30150-101 Belo Horizonte, Minas Gerais, Brazil. Contact: Junara Belo, Setor de Comunicaçoes. Replies slowly to correspondence in Portuguese. Return postage helpful.

Rádio Guarujá
STATION: C.P. 45, 88001 Florianópolis, Santa Catarina, Brazil. Contact: Acy Cabral Tieve, Diretor; Joana Sempre Bom Braz, Assessora de Marketing e Comunicação; or Rosa Michels de Souza. Return postage required. Replies irregularly to correspondence in Portuguese.
NEW YORK OFFICE: 45 West 46 Street, 5th Floor, Manhattan, NY 10036 USA.

Rádio Inconfidência, C.P. 1027, 30001 Belo Horizonte, Minas Gerais, Brazil. Fax: +55 (31) 296 3070. Contact: Isaias Lansky, Diretor; Manuel Emilio de Lima Torres, Diretor Superintendente; Jairo Antolio Lima, Diretor Artístico; or Eugenio Silva. Free stickers and postcards. $1 or return postage helpful.

Rádio Integração, Rua Alagoas 270, lotes 8 e 9, 69980 Cruzeiro do Sul, Acre, Brazil. Contact: Claudio Onofre Ferreiro. Return postage required. Replies to correspondence in Portuguese.

Rádio IPB AM, Rua Itajaí 473, Bairro Antonio Vendas, 79050 Campo Grande, Mato Grosso do Sul, Brazil. Contact: Iván Páez Barboza, Diretor Geral (hence, the station's name, "IPB"); Pastor Laercio Paula das Neves, Dirigente Estadual; Agenor Patrocinio S., Locutor; Pastor José Adão Hames; or Kelly Cristina Rodrigues da Silva, Secretária. Return postage required. Replies to correspondence in Portuguese.

Rádio Itatiaia, Rua Itatiaia 117, 31210-170 Belo Horizonte, Minas Gerais, Brazil. Fax: +55 (31) 446 2900. Contact: Lúcia Araújo Bessa, Assistente da Diretória.

Rádio Jornal "A Crítica," C.P. 2250, 69061-970 Manaus, Brazil.

Rádio Marajoara, Travessa Campos Sales 370, Centro, 66015 Belém, Pará, Brazil. Contact: Elizete Maria dos Santos

Pamplona, Diretora Geral; or Sra. Neide Carvalho, Secretária da Diretoria Executiva. Return postage required. Replies irregularly to correspondence in Portuguese.

Rádio Marumbí, C.P. 62 (C.P. 296 is the alternative box), 88010-970 Florianópolis, Santa Catarina, Brazil. Contact: Davi Campos, Diretor Artístico. $1 or return postage required. Replies to correspondence in Portuguese.

Rádio Meteorologia Paulista, C.P. 91, 14940-970 Ibitinga, São Paulo SP, Brazil. Contact: Roque de Rosa, Diretora. Replies to correspondence in Portuguese. $1 or return postage required.

Rádio Mundial, Rua da Consolação 2608, 1º Andar, CJ. 11, 01416-000 Consolação, São Paulo SP, Brazil. Fax: +55 (11) 258 5838 or +55 (11) 258 0152.

Rádio Nacional da Amazônia, Radiobrás, [domestic service], SCRN 702/3 Bloco B, Ed. Radiobrás, Brasília DF, Brazil. Fax: +55 (61) 321 7602. Contact: (general) Luíz Otavio de Castro Souza, Diretor; Fernando Gómez da Camara, Gerente de Escritório; or Januario Procopio Toledo, Diretor. Free stickers, but no verifications.

Rádio Nacional do Brasil—Radiobrás, External Service, C.P. 08840, CEP 70912-790, Brasília DF, Brazil. Fax: +55 (61) 321 7602. Contact: Renato Geraldo de Lima, Manager; Michael Brown, Announcer; or Gaby Hertha Einstoss, Correspondence Service. Free stickers. Correspondence welcomed in English and other languages. Unlike Radiobrás' domestic service (preceding entry), Radiobrás' External Service verifies regularly.

Rádio Nacional São Gabriel da Cachoeira, Avenida Alvaro Maia s/n, 69750-000 São Gabriel da Cachoeira, Amazonas, Brazil. Contact: Luíz dos Santos Franca, Gerente; or Valdir de Souza Marques. Return postage necessary. Replies to correspondence in Portuguese.

Rádio Nikkei, Rua Grumixamas 843, 04349 Jabaquara, São Paulo SP, Brazil. Contact: Paulo N. Miyagui, Presidente.

Rádio Novas de Paz, C.P. 22, 80001 Curitiba, Paraná, Brazil. Contact: João Falavinha Ienzen, Gerente. $1 or return postage required. Replies irregularly to correspondence in Portuguese.

Rádio Nova Visão
STUDIOS: Rua do Manifesto 1373, 04209-001 São Paulo, Brazil. Contact: Rev. Iván Nunes; or Marlene P. Nunes, Secretária. Return postage required. Replies to correspondence in Portuguese. Free stickers and non-data verifications. Relays Rádio Trans Mundial fulltime.
TRANSMITTER: C.P. 551, 97100 Santa Maria, Rio Grande do Sul, Brazil; or C.P. 6084, 90031 Porto Alegre, Rio Grande do Sul, Brazil. Reportedly issues full-data verifications, upon request, from this location. If no luck, try writing, in English or Dutch, to Tom van Ewijck in Holland, who is in contact with the transmitter site, via e-mail at egiaroll@cat.cce.usp.br.

Rádio Oito de Setembro, C.P. 8, 13691 Descalvado, São Paulo SP, Brazil. Contact: Adonias Gomes. Replies to corrrespondence in Portuguese.

Rádio Pioneira de Teresina, Rua 24 de Janeiro, 150 sul/ centro Teresina 64001-230, Piauí, Brazil. Contact: Luíz Eduardo Bastos; or Padre Tony Batista, Diretor. $1 or return postage required. Replies slowly to correspondence in Portuguese.

Rádio Portal da Amazônia (when active), Rua Dom Antônio Malan 674, 78010 Cuiabá, Mato Grosso, Brazil; also, C.P. 277, 78001 Cuiabá, Mato Grosso, Brazil. Contact: Celso Castilho, Gerente Geral; or Arnaldo Medina. Return postage required. Replies occasionally to correspondence in Portuguese.

Rádio Potí, C.P. 145, 59001-970 Natal, Rio Grande do Norte, Brazil. Contact: Cid Lobo. Return postage helpful. Replies slowly to correspondence in Portuguese.

Rádio Progresso, Estrada do Belmont s/n, Bº Nacional, 78000 Porto Velho, Rondônia, Brazil. Return postage required. Replies occasionally to correspondence in Portuguese.

Rádio Record
STATION: C.P. 7920, 04084-002 São Paulo SP, Brazil. Contact: Mário Luíz Catto, Diretor Geral. Free stickers. Return postage or $1 required. Replies occasionally to correspondence in Portuguese.
NEW YORK OFFICE: 630 Fifth Avenue, Room 2607, New York NY 10111 USA.

Rádio Ribeirão Preto, C.P 814, 14001-970 Ribeirão Preto, São Paulo SP, Brazil. Contact: Lucinda de Oliveira, Secretária; Luis Schiavone Junior; or Paulo Henríque Rocha da Silva. Replies to correspondence in Portuguese.

Rádio Rio Mar, Rua José Clemente 500, Manaus, Amazonas, Brazil. Replies to correspondence in Portuguese. $1 or return postage necessary.

Rádio Rural Santarém, Rua Floriano Peixoto 632, 68005-060 Santarém, Pará, Brazil. Contact: João Elias B. Bentes, Gerente Geral. Replies slowly to correspondence in Portuguese. Free stickers. Return postage or $1 required.

Rádio Sentinela, Travessa Ruy Barbosa 142, 68250 Obidos, Pará, Brazil. Contact: Max Hamoy or Maristela Hamoy. Return postage required. Replies occasionally to correspondence in Portuguese.

Rádio Timbira, Rua do Correio, s/n Bairro de Fátima, 65050 São Luís, Maranhão, Brazil. Contact: Sandoval Pimentel Silva, Diretor Geral. Free picture postcards. $1 helpful. Replies occasionally to correspondence in Portuguese; persist.

Rádio Transamérica—see Rádio Cultura Foz do Iguaçu.

Rádio Trans Mundial—see Rádio Nova Visão.

Rádio Tropical, C.P. 23, 78600-000 Barra do Garças, Mato Grosso, Brazil. Contact: Alacir Viera Cándido, Diretor e Presidente; or Walter Francisco Dorados, Diretor Artístico. $1 or return postage required. Replies slowly and rarely to correspondence in Portuguese.

Rádio Tupi, Rua Nadir Dias Figueiredo 1329, 02110 São Paulo SP, Brazil. Contact: Alfredo Raymundo Filho, Diretor Geral; Celso Rodrigues de Oliveira, Asesor Internacional da Presidencia; Montival da Silva Santos; or Elia Soares. Free stickers. Return postage required. Replies occasionally to correspondence in Portuguese.

Rádio Universo, C.P. 7133, 80001 Curitiba, Paraná, Brazil. Contact: Luíz Andreu Rúbio, Diretor. Replies occasionally to correspondence in Portuguese.

Rádio Verdes Florestas, C.P. 53, 69981-970 Cruzeiro do Sul, Acre, Brazil. Contact: Marlene Valente de Andrade. Return postage required. Replies occasionally to correspondence in Portuguese.

BULGARIA World Time +2 (+3 midyear)

Radio Horizont, Bulgarian Radio, 4 Dragan Tsankov Blvd., 1040 Sofia, Bulgaria. Phone: +359 (2) 65-28-71. Fax: (weekdays) +359 (2) 65 72 30. Contact: Borislav Djamdjiev, Director; Iassen Indjev, Executive Director; or Martin Minkov, Editor-in-Chief.

Radio Bulgaria
NONTECHNICAL AND TECHNICAL: P.O. Box 900, BG-1000, Sofia-Z, Bulgaria. Phone: +359 (2) 66-19-54. Fax: (general, usually weekdays only) +359 (2) 87 10 60, +359 (2) 87 10 61 or +359 (2) 65 05 60; (Managing Director) +359 (2) 66 22 15; (Frequency Manager) +359 (2) 963 4464. Contact: (general) Mrs. Iva Delcheva, English Section; Kristina Mihailova, In Charge of Listeners' Letters, English Section; or Svilen Stoicheff, Head of English Section; (administration and technical) Anguel H. Nedyalkov, Managing Director; (technical) Atanas Tzenov, Frequency Manager. Free tourist literature, postcards, stickers, T-shirts, bookmarks and pennants. Gold, silver and bronze diplomas for correspondents meeting certain requirements. Free sample copies of *Bulgaria* magazine. Replies regularly, but sometimes slowly. For concerns about frequency usage, contact BTC, below, with copies to Messrs. Nedyalkov and Tzenov of Radio Bulgaria.
FREQUENCY MANAGEMENT AND TRANSMISSION OPERATIONS: Bulgarian Telecommunications Company (BTC), Ltd.,

Randall Robinson, leader of Transafrica, answers questions over "VOA Today." The Voice of America, heard worldwide, ranks as one of the leading stations among African listeners.

Carmelo Ciancio, VOA

8 Totleben Blvd., 1606 Sofia, Bulgaria. Phone: +359 (2) 88-00-75. Fax: +359 (2) 87 58 85 or +359 (2) 80 25 80. Contact: Roumen Petkov, Frequency Manager; or Mrs. Margarita Krasteva, Radio Regulatory Department.

BURKINA FASO World Time exactly
Radiodiffusion-Télévision Burkina, B.P. 7029, Ouagadougou, Burkina Faso. Phone: +226 310-441. Contact: Raphael L. Onadia or M. Pierre Tassembedo. Replies irregularly to correspondence in French. IRC or return postage helpful.

BURMA—see MYANMAR.

BURUNDI World Time +2
La Voix de la Révolution, B.P. 1900, Bujumbura, Burundi. Phone: +257 22-37-42. Fax: +257 22 65 47 or +257 22 66 13. Contact: (general) Grégoire Barampumba, Head of News Section; or Frederic Havugiyaremye, Journaliste; (administration) Gérard Mfuranzima, Le Directeur de la Radio; or Didace Baranderetse, Directeur Général de la Radio; (technical) Abraham Makuza, Le Directeur Technique. $1 required.

CAMBODIA World Time +7
National Radio of Cambodia
STATION ADDRESS: Monivong Boulevard No. 106, Phnom Penh, Cambodia. Phone: +855 (23) 23-369 or +855 (23) 22-869. Fax: + 855 (23) 27 319. Contact: (general) Miss Hem Bory, English Announcer; Kem Yan, Chief of External Relations; or Touch Chhatha, Producer, Art Department; (administration) In Chhay, Chief of Overseas Service; Som Sarun, Chief of Home Service; Van Sunheng, Deputy Director General, Cambodian National Radio and Television; or Ieng Muli, Minister of Information; (technical) Oum Phin, Chief of Technical Department. Free program schedule. Replies irregularly and slowly. Do not include stamps, currency, IRCs or dutiable items in envelope. Registered letters stand a much better chance of getting through.

CAMEROON World Time +1
NOTE: Any CRTV outlet is likely to be verified by contacting via registered mail, in English or French with $2 enclosed, James Achanyi-Fontem, Head of Programming, CRTV, B.P. 986, Douala, Cameroon.
Cameroon Radio Television Corporation (CRTV)—Bafoussam (when active), B.P. 970, Bafoussam (Ouest), Cameroon. Contact: (general) Boten Celestin; (technical) Ndam Seidou, Chef Service Technique. IRC or return postage required. Replies irregularly in French to correspondence in English or French.
Cameroon Radio Television Corporation (CRTV)—Bertoua (when active), B.P. 230, Bertoua (Eastern), Cameroon. Rarely replies to correspondence, preferably in French. $1 required.
Cameroon Radio Television Corporation (CRTV)—Buea (when active), P.M.B., Buea (Sud-Ouest), Cameroon. Contact: Ononino Oli Isidore, Chef Service Technique. Three IRCs, $1 or return postage required.
Cameroon Radio Television Corporation (CRTV)—Douala, B.P. 986, Douala (Littoral), Cameroon. Contact: (technical) Emmanual Ekite, Technicien. Free pennants. Three IRCs or $1 required.
Cameroon Radio Television Corporation (CRTV)—Garoua, B.P. 103, Garoua (Nord/Adamawa), Cameroon. Contact: Kadeche Manguele. Free cloth pennants. Three IRCs or return postage required. Replies irregularly and slowly to correspondence in French.
Cameroon Radio Television Corporation (CRTV)—Yaoundé, B.P. 1634, Yaoundé (Centre-Sud), Cameroon. Phone: +237-21-40-77. Fax: +237 20 43 40. Contact: (technical or nontechnical) Gervais Mendo Ze, Le Directeur-Général; (technical) Francis Achu Samba, Le Directeur Technique. $1 required. Recorded musical cassettes 60 francs. Replies slowly to correspondence in French.

CANADA World Time –3:30 (–2:30 midyear) Newfoundland; –4 (–3 midyear) Atlantic; –5 (–4 midyear) Eastern, including Quebec and Ontario; –6 (–5 midyear) Central; except Saskatchewan; –6 Saskatchewan; –7 (–6 midyear) Mountain; –8 (–7 midyear) Pacific, including Yukon
BBC World Service via RCI/CBC—For verification direct from RCI's CBC shortwave transmitters, contact Radio Canada International (see below). Nontechnical correspondence should be sent to the BBC World Service in London (see).
Canadian Forces Network Radio—see Radio Canada International, below. Free pennants and calendars.
CBC Headquarters—English Programs, Box 500, Toronto ON, M5W 1E6, Canada. Phone: +1 (416) 975-3311. URLs: (general) http://www.cbc.ca/; (CBC Web sites and e-mail addresses) http://www.cbc.ca/aboutcbc/address/address.html. CBC prepares some of the programs heard over Radio Canada International (see).
CBC Headquarters—French Programs—see Radio Canada International, below. CBC prepares some of the programs heard over Radio Canada International.
CBC Northern Quebec Shortwave Service—see Radio Canada International, below.
CFCX-CIQC/CKOI
TRANSMITTER (CFCX); ALSO, STUDIOS FOR CIQC ENGLISH-LANGUAGE PROGRAMS: CFCX-CIQC, Radio Montréal, Mount Royal Broadcasting, Inc., 1200 McGill College Avenue, Suite 300, Montréal, Quebec, H3B 4G7 Canada. Phone: +1 (514) 766-2311, then press keys for appropriate department. Fax: +1 (514) 393 4659. Contact: Ted Silver, Programme Director; (technical) Kim Bickerdike, Technical Director. Correspondence welcomed in English or French.
FRENCH-LANGUAGE PROGRAM STUDIOS: CKOI, Metromedia CMR, Inc., 211 Gordon Avenue, Verdun, Quebec, H4G 2R2 Canada. Fax: (CKOI—Programming Dept.) +1 (514) 766 2474; (sister station CKVL) +1 (514) 761 0136. URL:

http://www.netmusik.com/Empire/empire_histo.html. Free stickers and possibly T-shirts. Correspondence in French preferred, but English and Spanish accepted.

CFRX-CFRB

📻*MAIN ADDRESS:* 2 St. Clair Avenue West, Toronto ON, M4V 1L6 Canada. Phone: (talkshow) +1 (416) 872-1010; (general) +1 (416) 924-5711. Fax: +1 (416) 924 9685. E-mail: iain@io.org. URL: (including RealAudio) http://www.io.org/~iain/CFRB/index.html. Contact: (nontechnical) Steve Kowch, Operations Manager; or Gary Slaight, President; (technical) Ian Sharp, Technician Supervision. Free station history sheet. Reception reports should be sent to verification address, below.

VERIFICATION ADDRESS: ODXA, P.O. Box 161, Station A, Willowdale ON, M2N 5S8 Canada. Phone/fax: +1 (905) 853 3169. E-mail: 73737.3453@compuserve.com. Contact: Stephen Canney, VA3ID. Free program schedules and ODXA information sheets. Reception reports are processed quickly if sent to this address, rather than to the station itself.

CFVP-CKMX, AM 1060, Standard Broadcasting, P.O. Box 2750, Stn. "M", Calgary AB, T2P 4P8 Canada. Phone: (general) +1 (403) 240-5800; (news) +1 (403) 240-5844; (technical) +1 (403) 240-5867. Fax: (general and technical) +1 (403) 240 5801; (news) +1 (403) 246 7099. Contact: (general) Gary Russell, General Manager; Beverley Van Tighem, Exec. Ass't.; (technical) Ken Pasolli, Technical Director.

CHNX-CHNS, P.O. Box 400, Halifax NS, B3J 2R2 Canada. Phone: +1 (902) 422-1651. Fax: +1 (902) 422 5330. Contact: (general) Troy Michaels, Operations Manager; or Morrisey Dunn, Host; (technical) Kurt J. Arsenault, Chief Engineer; or Wayne Harvey, Engineer. Return postage or $1 helpful. Replies irregularly.

CHU (official time and frequency station), Time and Frequency Standards, Bldg. M-36, National Research Council, Ottawa ON, K1A 0R6 Canada. Phone: (general) +1 (613) 993-5186; (administration) +1 (613) 993-1003 or +1 (613) 993-2704. Fax: +1 (613) 993 1394. E-mail: radio.chu@nrc.ca. URL: http://www.ems.nrc.ca. Contact: Dr. R.J. Douglas, Programme Leader. Official standard frequency and World Time station for Canada on 3330, 7335 and 14670 kHz. Brochure available upon request. Those with a personal computer, Bell 103 standard modem and appropriate software can get the exact time, via CHU's cesium clock, off the air from their computer; details available upon request.

CKZN-CBN, CBC, P.O. Box 12010, Station "A", St. John's NF, A1B 3T8 Canada. Phone: +1 (709) 576-5000. Fax: +1 (709) 576 5099. Contact: (general) John O'Mara, Manager of Communications; (technical) Elaine Janes, Engineering Assistant; or Shawn R. Williams, Manager, Regional Engineering, Newfoundland Region. Free CBC sticker and verification card with the history of Newfoundland included. Don't enclose money, stamps or IRCs with correspondence, as they will only have to be returned.

CKZU-CBU, CBC, P.O. Box 4600, Vancouver BC, V6B 4A2 Canada. Toll-free telephone (U.S & Canada only) (800) 961-6161. Phone: (general) +1 (604) 662-6000; (engineering) +1 (604) 662-6064. Fax: (general) +1 (604) 662 6350; (engineering) +1 (604) 662 6350. URL: http://www.cbc.ca. Contact: (general) Public Relations; (technical) Dave Newbury, Transmission Engineer.

📻**Radio Canada International**

NOTE: (Canadian Forces Network Radio and CBC Northern Quebec Service): The following RCI address, fax and e-mail information for the Main Office and Transmission Office is also valid for the Canadian Forces Network Radio and CBC Northern Quebec Shortwave Service, provided you make your communication to the attention of the particular service you seek to contact.

MAIN OFFICE: P.O. Box 6000, Montréal, Quebec, H3C 3A8 Canada. Phone: (general) +1 (514) 597-7555; (Audience Relations) +1 (514) 597-7555; (English and French programming) +1 (514) 597-7551; (Russian programming) +1 (514) 597-6866; (CBC's "As It Happens" Talkback Machine") +1 (416) 205-3331. Fax: (RCI) +1 (514) 284 0891; (Canadian Forces Network) +1 (514) 597 7893. E-mail: (general) rci@montreal.src.ca; (Audience Relations) rci@cam.org. URL: http://radioworks.cbc.ca/radio/rci/rci/html; (RealAudio in English) http://www.wrn.org/stations/rci.html. Contact: (general) Maggy Akerblom, Director of Audience Relations; Ousseynou Diop, Manager, English and French Programming; or André Courey, Producer/Host, the "Mailbag"; (administration) Terry Hargreaves, Executive Director; (technical—verifications) Bill Westenhaver, CIDX. Free stickers and other small station souvenirs. 50th Anniversary T-shirts, sweatshirts, watches, lapel pins and tote bags available for sale; write to the above address for a free illustrated flyer giving prices and ordering information. RCI has been given funding to continue basic operation through March 31, 1997.

CBC RECORD SALES: Various CBC items available in the United States from CBC Radio Works at toll-free telephone (800) 363-1530 (VISA/MC). Canadian CDs sold worldwide except North America, from International Sales, CBC Records, P.O. Box 500, Station "A", Toronto ON, M5W 1E6 Canada (VISA/MC), fax +1 (416) 975 3482; and within the United States from CBC/Allegro, 3434 SE Milwaukie Avenue, Portland OR 97202 USA, toll-free telephone (800) 288-2007, fax (503) 232 9504 (VISA/MC).

TRANSMISSION OFFICE: P.O. Box 6000, Montréal PQ, H3C 3A8 Canada. Phone: +1 (514) 597-7616/17/18/19/20. Fax: +1 (514) 284 9550 or +1 (514) 284 2052. Contact: (general) Gérald Théorêt, Frequency Manager; (administration) Jacques Bouliane, Chief Engineer. This office only for informing about transmitter-related problems (interference, modulation quality, etc.), especially by fax. Verifications not given out at this office; requests for verification should be sent to the main office, above.

TRANSMITTER SITE: CBC, P.O. Box 1200, Sackville NB, E0A 3C0 Canada. Phone: +1 (506) 536-2690/1. Fax: +1 (506) 536 2342. Contact: Marc Leblanc, Plant Manager. All correspondence not concerned with transmitting equipment should be directed to the appropriate address in Montréal, above. Free tours given during normal working hours.

LABOR REPRESENTATION AND RCI BOOSTERS' ORGANIZATION: Coalition to Restore Full RCI Funding, SCFP Local 675, 1250 de la Visitation, Montréal, Quebec, H2L 3B4 Canada. Phone: +1 (514) 844-2262. Fax: +1 (514) 521 3082. E-mail: rci@cam.org. Contact: Wojtek Gwiazda. Local 675 is active in maintaining RCI as an active force in international broadcasting, and welcomes correspondence from like-minded individuals and organizations.

WASHINGTON NEWS BUREAU: CBC, National Press Building, Suite 500, 529 14th Street NW, Washington DC 20045 USA. Phone: +1 (202) 638-3286. Fax: +1 (202) 783 9321. Contact: Jean-Louis Arcand, David Hall or Susan Murray.

LONDON NEWS BUREAU: CBC, 43-51 Great Titchfield Street, London W1P 8DD, England. Phone: +44 (171) 412-9200. Fax: +44 (171) 631 3095.

PARIS NEWS BUREAU: CBC, 17 avenue Matignon, F-75008 Paris, France. Phone: +33 (1) 43-59-11-85. Fax: +33 (1) 44 21 15 14.

Radio Monte-Carlo Middle East (via Radio Canada International)—see Cyprus.

Shortwave Classroom, Naismith Memorial Public School, P.O. Box 280, Almonte ON, K0A 1A0 Canada. Phone: (weekdays during school season) +1 (613) 256-3773; (other times) +1 (613) 256-2018. Fax: (during school season) +1 (613) 256 3825. E-mail: as167@freenet.carleton.ca. Contact: Neil Carleton, Organizer. *The Shortwave Classroom* newsletter, three times per year, for "$10 and an accompanying feature to share with teachers in the newsletter." Ongoing nonprofit volunteer project of teachers and others to use shortwave listening in the classroom to teach about global perspectives, media studies, world geography, languages, social studies and other subjects. Interested teachers and parents worldwide are invited to make contact.

CENTRAL AFRICAN REPUBLIC   World Time +1

Radio Centrafrique, Radiodiffusion-Télévision Centrafricaine, B.P. 940, Bangui, Central African Republic. Contact: (technical) Jacques Mbilo, Le Directeur des Services Techniques; or Michèl Bata, Services Techniques. Replies on rare occasion to correspondence in French; return postage required.

CHAD   World Time +1

Radiodiffusion Nationale Tchadienne—N'djamena, B.P. 892, N'Djamena, Chad. Contact: Djimadoum Ngoka Kilamian. Two IRCs or return postage required. Replies slowly to correspondence in French.

Radio Diffusion Nationale Tchadienne—Radio Abéché, B.P. 105, Abéché, Ouaddai, Chad. Return postage helpful. Replies rarely to correspondence in French.

Radiodiffusion Nationale Tchadienne—Radio Moundou, B.P. 122, Moundou, Logone, Chad. Contact: Dingantoudji N'Gana Esaie.

CHILE   World Time –3 (–4 midyear)

Radio Esperanza

OFFICE: Casilla 830, Temuco, Chile. Phone/fax: +56 (45) 240-161. Contact: (general) Juanita Cárcamo, Departamento de Programación; Eleazar Jara, Dpto. de Programación; Ramón Woerner, Publicidad; or Alberto Higueras Martínez, Locutor; (verifications) Juanita Carmaco M., Dpto. de Programacíon; (technical) Juan Luis Puentes, Dpto. Técnico. Free pennants, stickers, bookmarks and tourist information. Two IRCs or 2 U.S. stamps appreciated. Replies, usually quite slowly, to correspondence in Spanish or English.
STUDIO: Calle Luis Durand 03057, Temuco, Chile. Phone/fax: +56 (45) 240-161.

Radio Santa María, Apartado 1, Coyhaique, Chile. Phone: +56 (67) 23-23-98, +56 (67) 23-20-25 or +56 (67) 23-18-17. Fax: +56 (67) 23 13 06. Contact: Pedro Andrade Vera, Coordinador. $1 or return postage required. May send free tourist cards. Replies to correspondence in Spanish and Italian.

Radio Triunfal Evangélica, Costanera Sur 7209, Comuna de Cerro Navia, Santiago, Chile. Contact: Fernando González Segura, Obispo de la Misión Pentecostal Fundamentalista. Two IRCs required. Replies to correspondence in Spanish.

CHINA   World Time +8; still nominally +6 ("Urümqi Time") in the Xinjiang Uighur Autonomous Region, but in practice +8 is observed there, as well.

NOTE: China Radio International, the Central People's Broadcasting Station and certain regional outlets reply regularly to listeners' letters in a variety of languages. If a Chinese regional station does not respond to your correspondence within four months—and many will not, unless your letter is in Chinese or the regional dialect—try writing them c/o China Radio International.

Central People's Broadcasting Station (CPBS)—China National Radio, Zhongyang Renmin Guangbo Diantai, P.O. Box 4501, Beijing 100866, China. Phone: +86 (10) 609-2008, +86 (10) 801-2345 or +86 (10) 863-397. Fax: +86 (10) 851 6630. Contact: Wang Changquan, Audience Department, China National Radio. Tape recordings of music and news $5 plus postage. CPBS T-shirts $10 plus postage; also sells ties and other items with CPBS logo. No credit cards. Free stickers, pennants and other small souvenirs. Return postage helpful. Responds regularly to correspondence in English and Standard Chinese (Mandarin). Although in recent years this station has officially been called "China National Radio" in English-language documents, all on-air identifications in Standard Chinese continue to be "Zhongyang Renmin Guangbo Diantai" (Central People's Broadcasting Station).

CPBS-1 also airs Chinese-language programs co-produced by CPBS and Radio Canada International.

China Huayi Broadcasting Company, P.O. Box 251, Fuzhou City, Fujian 350001, China. Contact: Lin Hai Chun. Replies to correspondence in English and Chinese.

China National Radio—see Central People's Broadcasting Station/CPBS, above.

China Radio International

MAIN OFFICE, NON-CHINESE LANGUAGES SERVICE: 2 Fuxingmenwaidajie Street, Beijing 100866, China. Phone: (general) +86 (10) 609-2274; (English Dept.) +86 (10) 609-2760; (English News) +86 (10) 862-691; (current affairs) +86 (10) 801-3134; (administration) +86 (10) 851-3135. Fax: (Audience Relations) +86 (1) 851 3175 or (administration) +86 (1) 851 3174. Contact: (general) Yanling Zhang, Head of Audience Relations; Ms. Chen Lifang, Mrs. Fan Fuguang, Ms. Qi Guilin, Audience Relations, English Department; Richard D. Hutto, Advisor, English Department; Zhang Hong Quan, Reporter, General Editor's Office; Dai Mirong and Qui Mei, "Listeners' Letterbox"; Zang Guohua, or Deputy Director of English Service; (technical) Liu Yuzhou, Technical Director; or Ge Hongzhang, Frequency Manager; (research) Ms. Zhang Yanling; (administration) Zhang Zhenhua, Director General, China Radio International; Wang Guoqing, Assistant Director, China Radio International. Free bi-monthly *The Messenger* magazine, pennants, stickers, desk calendars, pins, hair ornaments and such small souvenirs as handmade papercuts. T-shirts $5 and CDs $15. Two-volume, 820-page set of *Day-to-Day Chinese* language-lesson books $15, including postage worldwide; contact Li Yi, English Department. Various other Chinese books (on arts, medicine, etc.) in English available from Chen Denong, CIBTC, P.O. Box 399, Beijing, China; fax +86 (10) 841 2023. To remain on *The Messenger* magazine mailing list, listeners should write to the station at least once a year. CRI is also relayed via shortwave transmitters in Brazil, Canada, France, French Guiana, Mali, Russia, Spain and Switzerland.
MAIN OFFICE, CHINESE LANGUAGES SERVICE: Box 565, Beijing, China. Prefers correspondence in Chinese (Mandarin), Cantonese, Hakka, Chaozhou or Amoy.
BONN NEWS BUREAU: Am Buchel 81, D-53173 Bonn, Germany. Contact: Ma Xuming.
HONG KONG NEWS BUREAU: 387 Queen's Road East, Hong Kong, China (place "China" in the address only for mail scheduled to arrive after June 30th, 1997). Contact: Zang Daolin, Bureau Chief; Zhang Xiujuan; or Zhang Jiaping.
WASHINGTON NEWS BUREAU: 2401 Calvert Street NW, Suite 1012, Washington DC 20008 USA. Phone: +1 (202) 387-6860. Phone/fax: +1 (202) 387-0459, but first call +1 (202) 387-6860 so fax can be switched on. Contact: Tang Minguo, Bureau Chief; Luo Qiao; or Dai Hongfeng.
NEW YORK NEWS BUREAU: 630 First Avenue #35K, New York NY 10016 USA. Fax: +1 (212) 889 2076. Contact: Liu Hui, Bureau Chief.
PARIS NEWS BUREAU: 7 rue Charles Lecocq, F-75015 Paris, France. Contact: Huang Liangde, Chef de Bureau; Jia Yanjing; or Xiong Wei.
SYDNEY NEWS BUREAU: 121/226 Sussex Street, Sydney NSW 2000, Australia. Contact: Xu Rongmao, Bureau Chief; or Shi Chungyong.
TOKYO NEWS BUREAU: Meith Fuyoku Nakameguro 2F3-10-3 Kamimeguro, Megoro-ku, Tokyo 153, Japan. Phone/fax: +81 (3) 3719-8414. Contact: Zhang Guo-qing, Bureau Chief.

Fujian People's Broadcasting Station, Fuzhou, Fujian, China. $1 helpful. Replies occasionally and usually slowly.

Gansu People's Broadcasting Station, Lanzhou, China. Contact: Li Mei. IRC helpful.

Guangxi People's Broadcasting Station, No. 12 Min Zu Avenue, Nanning, Guangxi 530022, China. Contact: Song Yue, Staffer; or Li Hai Li, Staffer. Free stickers and handmade papercuts. IRC helpful. Replies irregularly.

Heilongjiang People's Broadcasting Station, No. 115 Zhongshan Road, Harbin City, Heilongjiang, China. $1 or return postage helpful.

Honghe People's Broadcasting Station, Jianshe Donglu 32, Geji City 661400, Yunnan, China. Contact: Shen De-chun, Head of Station; or Mrs. Cheng Lin, Editor-in-Chief. Free travel brochures.

Hubei People's Broadcasting Station, No. 563 Jie Fang Avenue, Wuhan, Hubei, China.

Jiangxi People's Broadcasting Station, Nanchang, Jiangxi, China. Contact: Tang Ji Sheng, Editor, Chief Editor's Office. Free gold/red pins. Replies irregularly. Mr. Tang enjoys music, literature and stamps, so enclosing a small memento along these lines should help assure a speedy reply.

Nei Monggol (Inner Mongolia) People's Broadcasting Station, Hohhot, Nei Monggol Zizhiqu, China. Contact: Zhang Xiang-Quen, Secretary; or Liang Yan. Replies irregularly.

Qinghai People's Broadcasting Station, Xining, Qinghai, China. Contact: Liqing Fangfang. $1 helpful.

☞**Radio Television Hong Kong**, C.P.O. Box 70200, Kowloon Central Office (or 1A Broadcast Drive, Television House), Hong Kong, China (place "China" in the address only for mail scheduled to arrive after June 30th, 1997). Phone: +852 2339-7774. Fax: +852 2338 4151 or +852 2338 0279. E-mail: wingkili@vol.net. URLs: (including 28.8 kb RealAudio in English and Cantonese, but heavy graphics make for slow downloading) http://www.cuhk/rthk; (14.4 kb RealAudio in English with limited program choices, but downloads quickly) http://www.wrn.org/stations/rthk.html. Contact: (general) Jagjit Dillon; (technical) W.K. Li, Telecommunications Engineer. May broadcast brief weather reports every even two years, usually around late March or early April, on 3940 kHz or 7290 khz (e.g., sometime between 1000 and 1200 World Time) for the South China Sea Yacht Race, organised by the Royal Hong Kong Yacht Club, who can be contacted via fax: +852 (2) 572 5399.

HONG KONG TELECOM: P.O. Box 9896 GPO, Hong Kong, China; or Cape D-Aguilar Road, Shek O, Hong Kong (place "China" in the address only for mail scheduled to arrive after June 30th, 1997). Phone: +852 (2) 888 1128. Fax: +852 (2) 809 2434. Contact: Lui Kam Chuen, Assistant Engineer. Hong Kong Telecom is responsible for operating the transmitter used during the South China Sea Yacht Race (*see*) above. Reception reports may be sent to this address.

Sichuan People's Broadcasting Station, Chengdu, Sichuan, China. Replies occasionally.

Voice of Jinling, P.O. Box 268, Nanjing, Jiangsu 210002, China. Fax: +86 (25) 413 235. Contact: Strong Lee, Producer/ Host, "Window of Taiwan." Free stickers and calendars, plus Chinese-language color station brochure and information on the Nanjing Technology Import & Export Corporation. Replies to correspondence in Chinese and to simple correspondence in English. $1 or return postage helpful.

Voice of Pujiang, P.O. Box 3064, Shanghai 200002, China. Contact: Jiang Bimiao, Editor & Reporter.

Voice of the Strait, People's Liberation Army Broadcasting Centre, P.O. Box 187, Fuzhou, Fujian, China. Replies very irregularly.

Wenzhou People's Broadcasting Station, Wenzhou, China.

Xilingol People's Broadcasting Station, Xilinhot, Xilingol, China.

Xinjiang People's Broadcasting Station, No. 84 Tuanjie Lu (United Road), Urümqi, Xinjiang 830044, China. Contact: Zhao Ji-shu. Free tourist booklet, postcards and used Chinese stamps. Replies to correspondence in Chinese and to simple correspondence in English.

Xizang People's Broadcasting Station, Lhasa, Xizang (Tibet), China. Contact: Lobsang Chonphel, Announcer. Free stickers and brochures. Enclosing an English-language magazine may help with a reply.

Yunnan People's Broadcasting Station, No 73 Renmin Road (W), Central Building of Broadcasting & TV, Kunming, Yunnan 650031, China. Contact: Sheng Hongpeng or F.K. Fan. Free Chinese-language brochure on Yunnan Province, but no QSL cards. $1 or return postage helpful. Replies occasionally.

CHINA (TAIWAN)   World Time +8

☞**Broadcasting Corporation of China (BCC)**, 53 Jen'ai Road, Sec. 3, Taipei 10628, Taiwan. Phone: +886 (2) 771-0151. Fax: +886 (2) 751 9277. URL: (including RealAudio) http://www.bcc.com.tw/

Central Broadcasting System (CBS), 55 Pei'an Road, Tachih, Taipei 104, Taiwan. Phone: +886 (2) 591-8161. Contact: Lee Ming, Deputy Director. Free stickers.

Voice of Asia, P.O. Box 24-777, Taipei, Taiwan. Phone: +886 (2) 771-0151, X-2431. Fax: +886 (2) 751 9277. Contact: (general) Vivian Pu, Co-Producer, with Isaac Guo of "Letterbox"; or Ms. Chao Mei-Yi, Deputy Chief; (technical) Engineering Department. Free shopping bags, inflatable globes, coasters, calendars, stickers and booklets. T-shirts $5.

Voice of Free China, P.O. Box 24-38, Taipei 106, Taiwan. Phone: +886 (2) 752-2825 or +886 (2) 771-0151. Fax: +886 (2) 751 9277. URL: http://gio.gov.tw/info/yearbook/nf_html/ ch1603t.html. Contact: (general) Daniel Dong, Chief, Listeners' Service Section; Paula Chao, Producer, "Mailbag Time"; Yea-Wen Wang; or Phillip Wong, "Perspectives"; (administration) John C.T. Feng, Director; or Dong Yu-Ching, Deputy Director; (technical) Wen-Bin Tsai, Engineer, Engineering Department; Tai-Lau Ying, Engineering Department; Tien-Shen Kao; or Huang Shuh-shyun, Director, Engineering

Standing in front of Taipei's Imperial Museum are, with bag, Bob Crane of California's C. Crane, and Kevin Wang of Sangean. Although most of Sangean's production in Taiwan and China is OEM, they sell many radios under their own name.

Department. Free stickers, caps, shopping bags, *Voice of Free China Journal*, annual diary, "Let's Learn Chinese" language-learning course materials, booklets and other publications, and Taiwanese stamps. Station offers listeners a free Frisbee-type saucer if they return the "Request Card" sent to them by the station. T-shirts $5. VoFC programs are relayed to the Americas via WYFR's transmitters in Okeechobee, Florida, USA (*see*).
OSAKA NEWS BUREAU: C.P.O. Box 180, Osaka Central Post Office, Osaka 530-91, Japan.
TOKYO NEWS BUREAU: P.O Box 21, Azubu Post Office, Tokyo 106, Japan.
SAN FRANCISCO NEWS BUREAU: P.O. Box 192793, San Francisco CA 94119-2793 USA.

CLANDESTINE—*see* DISESTABLISHMENTARIAN.

COLOMBIA World Time –5
NOTE: Colombia, the country, is always spelled with two o's. It is never written as "Columbia."
Armonías del Caquetá, Apartado Aéreo 71, Florencia, Caquetá, Colombia. Phone: +57 (88) 352-080. Contact: Padre Alvaro Serna Alzate, Director. Replies rarely to correspondence in Spanish. Return postage required.
Caracol Arauca—*see* La Voz del Cinaruco.
Caracol Colombia (when active)
MAIN OFFICE: Apartado Aéreo 9291, Santafé de Bogotá, D.C., Colombia. Phone: +57 (1) 337-8866. Fax: +57 (1) 337

7126. Contact: Hernán Peláez Restrepo, Jefe Cadena Básica. Free stickers. Replies to correspondence in Spanish and English.
MIAMI OFFICE: 2100 Coral Way, Miami FL 33145 USA. Phone: +1 (305) 285-2477 or +1 (305) 285-1260. Fax: +1 (305) 858 5907.
Caracol Florencia, Apartado Aéreo 465, Florencia, Caquetá, Colombia. Phone: +57 (88) 352-199. Contact: Guillermo Rodríguez Herrara, Gerente; Vicente Delgado, Operador. Replies occasionally to correspondence in Spanish.
Caracol Villavicencio—*see* La Voz de los Centauros.
Ecos del Atrato, Apartado Aéreo 196, Quibdó, Chocó, Colombia. Phone: +57 (49) 711-450. Contact: Absalón Palacios Agualimpia, Administrador. Free pennants. Replies to correspondence in Spanish.
Ecos del Orinoco (when active), Gobernación del Vichada, Puerto Carreño, Vichada, Colombia.
La Voz de la Selva—*see* Caracol Florencia.
La Voz de los Centauros (Caracol Villavicencio), Cra. 31 No. 37-71 Of. 1001, Villavicencio, Meta, Colombia. Phone: +57 (86) 214-995. Fax: +57 (86) 623-954. Contact: Carlos Torres Leyva, Gerencia; or Olga Arenas, Administradora. Replies to correspondence in Spanish.
La Voz del Cinaruco (when active), Calle 19 No. 19-62, Arauca, Colombia. Contact: Efrahim Valera, Director. Pennants for return postage. Replies rarely to correspondence in Spanish; return postage required.

La Voz del Guainía (when active), Calle 6 con Carrera 3, Puerto Inírida, Guainía, Colombia. Contact: Luis Fernando Román Robayo, Director. Replies occasionally to correspondence in Spanish.

La Voz del Guaviare, Carrera 22 con Calle 9, San José del Guaviare, Colombia. Phone: +57 (986) 840-153/4. Fax: +57 (986) 840 102. Contact: Luis Fernando Román Robayo, Director General. Replies slowly to correspondence in Spanish.

La Voz del Llano, Calle 38 No. 30A-106, Villavicencio, Meta, Colombia. Phone: +57 (86) 624-102. Fax: +57 (86) 625 045. Contact: Alcides Antonio Jáuregui B., Director. Replies occasionally to correspondence in Spanish. $1 or return postage necessary.

La Voz del Río Arauca
STATION: Carrera 20 No. 19-09, Arauca, Colombia. Phone: +57 (818) 52-910. Contact: Jorge Flórez Rojas, Gerente; Luis Alfonso Riaño, Locutor; or Mario Falla, Periodista. $1 or return postage required. Replies occasionally to correspondence in Spanish; persist.
BOGOTÁ OFFICE: Cra. 10 No. 14-56, Of. 309/310, Santafé de Bogotá, D.C., Colombia.

La Voz del Yopal (when active), Calle 9 No. 22-63, Yopal, Casanare, Colombia. Phone: +57 (87) 558-382. Fax: +57 (87) 557 054. Contact: Pedro Antonio Socha Pérez, Gerente; or Marta Cecilia Socha Pérez, Subgerente. Return postage necessary. Replies to correspondence in Spanish.

Ondas del Meta (when active), Calle 38 No. 30A-106, Villavicencio, Meta, Colombia. Phone: +57 (86) 626-783. Fax: +57 (86) 625 045. Contact: Yolanda Plazas Agredo, Administradora. Free tourist literature. Return postage required. Replies irregularly and slowly to correspondence in Spanish. Plans to reactivate from a new antenna site.

Ondas del Orteguaza, Calle 16, No. 12-48, piso 2, Florencia, Caquetá, Colombia. Phone: +57 (88) 352-558. Contact: Jorge Daniel Santos Calderón, Gerente; or Sandra Liliana Vásquez, Secretaria. Free stickers. IRC, return postage or $1 required. Replies occasionally to correspondence in Spanish.

Radio Buenaventura (when active), Calle 1a. No. 2-39, Of. 301, Buenaventura, Valle, Colombia. Phone: +57 (224) 24-387. Contact: Mauricio Castaño Angulo, Gerente; or María Herlinda López Meza, Secretaria. Free stickers. Return postage or $1 required. Replies to correspondence in Spanish.

RCN (Radio Cadena Nacional)
MAIN OFFICE: Apartado Aéreo 4984, Santafé de Bogotá, D.C., Colombia. Contact: Antonio Pardo García, Gerente de Producción y Programación. Will verify all correct reports for stations in the RCN network. Spanish preferred and return postage necessary.

Radiodifusora Nacional de Colombia
MAIN ADDRESS: Edificio Inravisión, CAN, Av. Eldorado, Santafé de Bogotá, D.C., Colombia. Phone: +57 (1) 222-0415. Fax: +57 (1) 222 0409 or +57 (1) 222 8000. Contact: Jimmy García Camargo, Director; or Rubén Darío Acero. Tends to reply slowly.
CANAL INTERNACIONAL: Apartado Aéreo 93994, Santafé de Bogotá, D.C., Colombia. Contact: Jesús Valencia Sánchez.

Radio Macarena (when active), Calle 38 No. 32-41, piso 7, Edif. Santander, Villavicencio, Meta, Colombia. Phone: +57 (986) 626-780. Phone/fax: +57 (986) 624 507. Contact: (general) Pedro Rojas Velásquez; Carlos Alberto Pimienta, Gerente; (technical) Sra. Alba Nelly González de Rojas, Administradora. Sells religious audio cassettes for 3,000 pesos. Return postage required. Replies slowly to correspondence in Spanish. Considering installing a more powerful transmitter and Audimax audio processor.

Radio Melodía (Cadena Melodía) (when active), Apartado Aéreo 58721, Santafé de Bogotá, D.C., Colombia; or Apartado Aéreo 19823, Santafé de Bogotá, D.C., Colombia. Phone: +57 (1) 217-0423, +57 (1) 217-0720, +57 (1) 217-1334 or +57 (1) 217-1452. Fax: +57 (1) 248 8772. Contact: Gerardo Páez Mejía, Vicepresidente; Elvira Mejía de Pérez, Gerente General; or Gracilla Rodríguez, Asistente Gerencia. Stickers and pennants $1 or return postage.

Radio Mira, Apartado Aéreo 165, Tumaco, Nariño, Colombia. Phone: +57 (27) 272-452. Contact: Padre Jairo Arturo Ochoa Zea. Return postage required.

Radio Nueva Vida (when active), Apartado Aéreo 3068, Bucaramanga, Colombia. Phone: +57 (76) 443-195. Contact: Marco Antonio Caicedo, Director. Cassettes with biblical studies $3 each. Return postage. Replies to correspondence in Spanish.

Radio Santa Fé (if reactivated), Apartado Aéreo 9339, Santafé de Bogotá, D.C., Colombia. Phone: +57 (1) 345-6781. Fax: +57 (1) 249 6095. Contact: (general) César Augusto Duque; or Adolfo Bernal Mahé, Gerente Administrativo; (technical) Sra. María Luisa Mahé Vda. de Bernal, Gerente. Return postage appreciated. Replies slowly to correspondence in Spanish. Not likely to return to world band anytime soon, but in the past has left world band for an extended period, then returned, so who knows.

Radio Super (Bogotá) (when active), Calle 39A No. 18-12, Santafé de Bogotá, D.C., Colombia. Phone: +57 (1) 338-2166. Fax: +57 (1) 287 8678. Contact: Henry Pava Camelo, Director Gerente. Free posters. Return postage required.

Radio Super (Ibagué) (when active), Parque Murillo Toro 3-31, P. 3, Ibagué, Tolima, Colombia. Phone: +57 (82) 611-381. Fax: +57 (82) 611 471. Contact: Fidelina Caycedo Hernández; or Germán Acosta Ramos, Locutor Control. Free stickers. Return postage or $1 helpful. Replies irregularly to correspondence in Spanish.

CONGO   World Time +1
Radio Congo, Radiodiffusion-Télévision Congolaise, B.P. 2241, Brazzaville, Congo. Contact: (general) Antoine Ngongo, Rédacteur en chef; (administration) Albert Fayette Mikano, Directeur. $1 required. Replies irregularly to letters in French sent via registered mail.

COSTA RICA   World Time –6
Adventist World Radio, the Voice of Hope, AWR-PanAmerica, Apartado 1177, 4050 Alajuela, Costa Rica. Phone: +506 443-0474, +506 443-0920 or +506 443-0560. Fax +506 441 1282. E-mail: 74617.1577@compuserve.com or rmadvent@racsa.sol.cr. Contact: David Gregory, General Manager. Free stickers, calendars, Costa Rican stamps and religious printed matter. IRCS or $1 appreciated. Also, *see* AWR listings under Guam, Guatemala, Italy, Kenya, Russia and the USA.

Faro del Caribe Internacional y Misiónera—TIFC
MAIN OFFICE: Apartado 2710, 1000 San José, Costa Rica. Phone: +506 (226) 2573 or +506 (226) 2618. Fax: +506 (227) 1725. Contact: Carlos A. Rozotto Piedrasanta, Director Administrativo. Free stickers, pennants, books and bibles. $1 or IRCs helpful.
U.S. OFFICE, NONTECHNICAL: Misión Latinoamericana, P.O. Box 620485, Orlando FL 32862 USA.

Radio Casino, Apartado 287, 7301 Puerto Limón, Costa Rica. Contact: Max DeLeo, Announcer; Luis Grau Villalobos, Gerente; (technical) Ing. Jorge Pardo, Director Técnico; or Luis Muir, Técnico.

Radio Exterior de España—Cariari Relay Station, Cariari de Pococí, Costa Rica. Phone: +506 767-7308 or +506 767-7311. Fax: +506 225 2938.

Radio For Peace International (RFPI)
MAIN OFFICE: Apartado 88, Santa Ana, Costa Rica. Phone: +506 249-1821. Fax: +506 249 1095. E-mail: rfpicr@sol.racsa.co.cr. URL: http://www.clarke.net/pub/cwilkins/rfpi. Contact: (general) Debra Latham, General Manager of RFPI, Editor of *VISTA* and co-host of "RFPI Mailbag"; (programming) Joe Bernard, Program Coordinator; Willie Barrantes, Director, Spanish Department; María Suárez Toro and Katerina Anfossi Gómez, FIRE, Women's Programming; James Latham and Brad Heavner, hosts, "Far Right Radio Review"; (nontechnical or technical) James L.

Latham, Station Manager. Replies sometimes slow in coming because of the mail. Audio cassette presentations, in English or Spanish, from women's perspectives welcomed for replay over "FIRE" program. Quarterly *VISTA* newsletter, which includes schedules and program information, $35 annual membership ($50 family/organization) in "Friends of Radio for Peace International"; station commemorative T-shirts and rainforest T-shirts $20; thermo mugs $10 (VISA/MC). Actively solicits listener contributions—directly, as well as indirectly through well-wishers signing up with PeaceCOM's long distance telephone service (+1 541/345-3326), or making designated world band purchases from Grove Enterprises (800/438-8155). $1 or 3 IRCs appreciated. Limited number of places available for volunteer broadcasting and journalism interns; those interested should send résumé. If funding can be worked out, hopes to add a world band transmission facility in Salmon Arm, British Columbia, Canada. RFPI was created by United Nations Resolution 35/55 on December 5, 1980.
U.S. OFFICE, NONTECHNICAL: P.O. Box 20728, Portland OR 97294 USA. Phone: +1 (503) 252-3639. Fax: +1 (503) 255 5216. Contact: Dr. Richard Schneider, Chancellor CEO, University of Global Education (formerly World Peace University). Newsletter, T-shirts and so forth, as above. University of the Air courses (such as "Earth Mother Speaks" and "History of the U.N.") $25 each, or on audio cassette $75 each (VISA/MC).
Radio Reloj, Sistema Radiofónico H.B., Apartado 4334, 1000 San José, Costa Rica. Contact: Roger Barahona, Gerente; or Francisco Barahona Gómez. $1 required.
Radio Universidad de Costa Rica, San Pedro de Montes de Oca, 1000 San José, Costa Rica. Contact: Marco González Muñoz; or Nora Garita B., Directora. Free postcards, station brochure and stickers. Replies slowly to correspondence in Spanish or English. $1 or return postage required.

CÔTE D'IVOIRE   World Time exactly
Radiodiffusion Télévision Ivoirienne, B.P. 191, Abidjan 1, Côte d'Ivoire. Phone: +225 32-4800.

CROATIA   World Time +1 (+2 midyear)
Croatian Radio
MAIN OFFICE: Hrvatska Radio-Televizija (HRT), Prisavlje 3, 41000 Zagreb, Croatia. Phone: (technical) +385 (1) 616-3355. Fax: (technical) +385 (1) 616 3347. E-mail: (technical) zelimir.klasan@hrt.com.hr. URL: http://www.hrt.com.hr/oiv/hr_inoz.html. Contact: (general) Darko Kragovic; (technical) Zelimir Klasan. Free Croatian stamps. Subscriptions to *Croatian Voice*. $1 helpful. Replies irregularly and slowly.
WASHINGTON NEWS BUREAU: Croatian-American Association, 1912 Sunderland Place NW, Washington DC 20036 USA. Phone: +1 (202) 429-5543. Fax: +1 (202) 429 5545. URL: http://www.hrnet.org/CAA/. Contact: Bob Schneider, Director.
Hrvatska Radio-Televizija—see Croatian Radio, Studio Zagreb, above, for details.

CUBA   World Time −5 (−4 midyear)
Radio Habana Cuba, (general) P.O. Box 7026, Havana, Cuba; (technical) P.O. Box 6240, Havana 10600, Cuba. Phone: +53 (7) 49-547. Fax: +53 (7) 70 5810 or +53 (7) 79 5007. E-mail: (general) radiohc@tinored.cu; ("DXers Unlimited") acoro@tinored.cu. Contact: (general) Lourdes López, Head of Correspondence Dept.; Jorge Miyares, English Service; or Mike La Guardia, Senior Editor; (administration) Ms. Milagro Hernández Cuba, General Director; (technical) Arnaldo Coro Antich, ("Arnie Coro"), Producer, "DXers Unlimited"; or Luis Pruna Amer, Director Técnico. Free wallet and wall calendars, pennants, stickers, keychains and pins. DX Listeners' Club. Free sample *Granma International* newspaper. Contests with various prizes. Free Cuban news service via general e-mail address, above.
Radio Rebelde, Departamento de Relaciones Públicas, Apartado 6277, Havana 10600, Cuba. Contact: Noemí Cairo Marín, Secretaria, Relaciones Públicas; Iberlise González

Padua, Relaciones Públicas; or Jorge Luis Más Zabala, Director, Relaciones Públicas. Replies very slowly, with correspondence in Spanish preferred.

CYPRUS   World Time +2 (+3 midyear)
BBC World Service—East Mediterranean Relay, P.O. Box 219, Limassol, Cyprus. Nontechnical correspondence should be sent to the BBC World Service in London (see).
Cyprus Broadcasting Corporation, Broadcasting House, P.O. Box 4824, 1397 Nicosia, Cyprus. Phone: +357 (2) 422-231. Fax: +357 (2) 314 050. Contact: Dimitris Kiprianou, Director General. Free stickers. Replies occasionally, sometimes slowly. IRC or $1 helpful.
Radio Bayrak (if reactivated), Bayrak Radio & T.V. Corporation, P.O. Box 417, Lefko a, Mersin 10, Turkey. Contact: (technical) A. Ziya Dincer, Technical Director; (administration) Erdal Onurhan, Director General. Although not operating on world band for some years, now, one unconfirmed report indicates that they may eventually repair their shortwave transmitter and return to the air.
Radio Monte-Carlo Middle East, P.O. Box 2026, Nicosia, Cyprus. Contact: M. Pavlides, Chef de Station. This address for listeners to the RMC Arabic Service, which prepares its world band programs in Cyprus, but transmits them via facilities of Radio Canada International in Canada. For details of Radio Monte-Carlo's headquarters and other branch offices, see Monaco.

CZECH REPUBLIC   World Time +1 (+2 midyear)
☞**Radio Prague**, Czech Radio, Vinohradská 12, 120 99 Prague, Czech Republic. Phone: (general) +42 (2) 240-94608; (English Department) +42 (2) 242-18349. Fax: (general) +42 (2) 242 22236; (external programs, nontechnical and technical) +42 (2) 242 18239; (domestic and external programs, technical) +42 (2) 232 1020. E-mail: (general) cr@radio.cz; (English Department) english@radio.cz; (reception reports, Nora Mikes) nora@werich.radio.cz; (free news texts) robot@radio.cz, writing "Subscribe English" (or other desired language) within the subject line. URLs: (text and RealAudio in English, German, Spanish and French) http://www.radio.cz; (RealAudio in English and Czech) http://www.wrn.org/stations/prague.html; (text) http://town.hall.org/Archives/Mirrors/Prague; ftp://ftp.radio.cz; gopher://gopher.radio.cz. Contact: (general) Markéta Albrechtová; Lenka Adamová, "Mailbag"; Zdenek Dohnal; Nora Mikes, Listener Relations; L. Kubik; or Jan Valeška, Head of English Section; (administration) Dr. Richard Seeman, Director, Foreign Broadcasts; (technical, all programs) Oldrich Čip, Chief Engineer. Free stickers, key chains, and calendars; free Radio Prague Monitor Club "DX Diploma" for regular correspondents. Free books available for Czech-language course called "Check out Czech." Samples of *Welcome to the Czech Republic* and *Czech Life* available upon request from Orbis, Vinohradská 46, 120 41 Prague, Czech Republic.
RFE-RL—see USA.

DENMARK   World Time +1 (+2 midyear)
Radio ABC/Denmark, P.O. Box 174, DK-8900 Randers, Denmark. Phone: +45 8640-1222. Fax: +45 8640 5522. E-mail: mail@radioabc.dk. URL: http://www.radioabc.dk. Contact: Stig Hartvig Nielsen, General Manager. Replies to correspondence in English and Scandinavian languages. Verifies all correct reception reports. Free stickers. Return postage appreciated. Transmits Sundays via leased-time facilities in Kaliningrad, Russia (see Verification of Stations Using Transmitters in St. Petersburg and Kaliningrad, under "Russia").
Radio Danmark
MAIN OFFICE: Rosenørns Allé 22, DK-1999 Frederiksberg C, Denmark. Phone: (Danish-language 24-hour telephone tape recording for schedule information) +45 3520-5796 for Europe/Africa, +45 3520-5797 for Eastern Hemisphere, +45 3520-5798 for Western Hemisphere; (office) +45 3520-5785 or +45 3520-5761; (voice mail) +45 3520-5791; (Schionning) +45

3520-5786. Fax: + 45 3520 57 81. E-mail: (schedule and program matters) rdk@dr.dk; (technical) rdk.ek@login.dknet.dk. URL: http://www.mi.aau.dk/rdk/ or http://www.dr.dk. Contact: (general) Lulu Vittrup, Audience Communications; or Bjorn Schionning; (technical and Danish-language letterbox program) Erik Køie, Producer, "Stil Ind," and Technical Adviser; (technical) Dan Helto, Frequency Manager. Replies to correspondence in English or Danish. Will verify all correct reception reports if $1 or IRC is enclosed for return postage. Transmits via two transmitters of Radio Norway.

PRODUCTION OFFICE, ENGLISH PROGRAM: Box 666, DK-1506 Copenhagen, Denmark. E-mail: jui@dr.dk. Contact: Julian Isherwood, Producer, "Tune In" twice monthly (on Saturday) letterbox program; this program is authorized to continue through the end of 1996, and its fate thereafter is not known as of press time.

TRANSMISSION MANAGEMENT AUTHORITY: Telecom Denmark, Telegade 2, DK-2630 Taastrup, Denmark. Phone: +45 4252-9111, Ext. 5746. Fax: +45 4371 1143. Contact: Ib H. Lavrsen, Senior Engineer.

NORWEGIAN OFFICE, TECHNICAL: Details of reception quality may also be sent to the Engineering Department of Radio Norway International (*see*), which operates the transmitters currently used for Radio Danmark.

DISESTABLISHMENTARIAN

NOTE ON STATIONS WITHIN THE UNITED STATES AND COSTA RICA: In the United States and Costa Rica, disestablishmentarian programs are aired within the provisions of national law, and thus usually welcome correspondence and requests for free or paid materials. Virtually all such programs in the United States are aired over a variety of private stations—WWCR in Nashville, WRNO near New Orleans, WHRI in Noblesville, Indiana, WRMI in Miami and, arguably, KVOH in Los Angeles. (WINB no longer carries such programs, as it became inactive after a heated controversy resulting from its ties to the Christian Identity movement.)

These programs usually refer to themselves as "patriotic," and include such traditional and relatively benign ideologies as populism and politically conservative evangelism. Among these categories, some go out of their way to disassociate themselves from bigotry. However, other programs, with tiny but dedicated audiences, are survivalist, antisemitic, neo-fascist, ultra-nationalist or otherwise on the fringes of the political "right," including the much-publicized militia movement. Perhaps surprisingly, few are overtly racist, although racism is often implied.

These programs reflect the American climate of unfettered freedom of speech, as well as, in some cases, the more cynical American tradition of profiting from proselytization. ("Our society is about to be conquered by alien or internationalist forces. To cope with this, you'll need certain things, which we sell.") Thus, American disestablishmentarian programs often differ greatly from the sorts of broadcasting discourse allowed within the laws and traditions of most other countries.

Well removed from this genre is the relatively low-powered voice of Radio For Peace International (*see*), a largely American-staffed station in Costa Rica. RFPI airs disestablishmentarian-*cum*-social-conscience programs from the relatively internationalist perspective of the political "new left" that grew into prominence in North America and Europe during the late Sixties. It also regularly follows and reports on the aforementioned disestablishmentarian programs aired over stations within the United States.

NOTE ON STATIONS OUTSIDE THE UNITED STATES AND COSTA RICA: Outside the United States and Costa Rica, disestablishmentarian broadcasting activities, some of which are actually clandestine, are unusually subject to abrupt change or termination. Being operated by anti-establishment political and/or military organizations, these groups tend to be suspicious of outsiders' motives. Thus, they are most likely to reply to contacts from those who communicate in the station's native tongue, and who are perceived to be at least somewhat favorably disposed to their cause. Most will provide, upon request, printed matter in their native tongue on their cause.

For more detailed information on clandestine (but not disestablishmentarian) stations, refer to the annual publication, *Clandestine Stations List,* about $10 or 10 IRCs postpaid by air, published by the Danish Shortwave Clubs International, Tavleager 31, DK-2670 Greve, Denmark; phone (Denmark) +45 4290-2900; fax (via Germany) +49 6371 71790; e-mail 100413.2375@compuserve.com; its expert editor, Mathias Kropf of Germany, may be reached at e-mail 100144.232@compuserve.com. For CIA media contact information, *see* USA.

"Agenda Cuba," 7175 SW 8 Street, Suite 217, Miami FL 33144 USA. Contact: Pedro Solares. Program of the Agenda Cuba organization. Via WRMI, USA.

"Along the Color Line," Department of History, Columbia University, 611 Fayerweather Hall, New York NY 10027 USA. Phone: +1 (212) 854-7080. Fax: +1 (212) 854 7060. Contact: Dr. Manning Marable, Director of the Institute for Research in African-American Studies. Critiques a wide variety of domestic and international issues relevant to African-Americans. Via RFPI, Costa Rica.

"Al-Quds" (if reactivated), P.O. Box 5092, Damascus, Syria. Supports the operations of various anti-Arafat, anti-Israeli organizations, in particular the Popular Front for the Liberation of Palestine—General Command (PFLP-GC). Operates from Syria.

"Alternative Radio," P.O. Box 551, Boulder CO 80306 USA. Phone: +1 (303) 444-8788. Contact: David Barsamian. Critiques such issues as multiculturalism, the environment, racism, American foreign policy, the media and the rights of indigenous peoples. Via RFPI, Costa Rica.

"America First Radio," P.O. Box 15499, Pittsburgh PA 15237 USA. Phone: (talk show, toll-free within United States) (800) 518-5979; (Populist Party, toll-free within the United States) (800) 998-4451. Fax: +1 (412) 443 4240. Contact: Harry Bertram. Monthly *Populist Observer* newspaper $30/yr, or $19 for introductory subscription. Populist Party talk show, reflecting American nationalist and populist perspective. Via WWCR, USA.

☞**"American Dissident Voices,"** P.O. Box 90, Hillsboro WV 24946 USA (or P.O. Box 596, Boring OR 97009 USA). E-mail: (general) crusader@national.alliance; or triton @abs.zolute.org; (Strom) ka_strom@ix.netcom. URL: (includes TrueSpeech/WAV audio archives and text archives) http://www.natvan.com/ADV/ADVDIR.HTML; (usenet) alt.politics.nationalism.white. Contact: Kevin Alfred Strom, WB4AIO, Producer. $12 for audio cassette of any given program. $55 for latest book from Canadian neonazi Ernst Zündel. *Free Speech* publication $40 per year. $1 for catalog of books and tapes. Free bumper stickers, "Who Rules America?" pamphlet and sample copies of *Patriot Review* newsletter. Program of the National Alliance, the most prominent neonazi organization in the United States. In its publicity, it claims to support "ordinary straight White America"; according to *The New York Times,* the National Alliance also states, "We must have a racially clean area of the earth." The show sometimes features William Pierce, chairman and founder of the American Nazi Party. Pierce, under the pen name "Andrew Macdonald," is the author of *The Turner Diaries,* which is felt may have given accused bomber Timothy McVeigh the idea and pyrotechnic knowledge for the Oklahoma City bombing. Via WRNO, and before that believed to be behind the U.S. clandestine station, "Voice of Tomorrow," which became inactive not long before "American Dissident Voices" came on the air.

"American Way," P.O. Box 198, Hawthorne NJ 07507 USA. Phone: (sponsor, SDL Incorporated, toll-free in U.S.) (800)

468-2646. Contact: Andrew M. Gause. Opposes *inter alia* the "New World Order" and the Federal Reserve System. Sponsored by a gold-and-silver coin dealer. Via WWCR.

"Amnesty International Reports," KCRW Radio, 1990 Pico Boulevard, Santa Monica CA 90405 USA. Phone: +1 (310) 450-5183. Fax: +1 (310) 450 7172. URL: http://www.igc.apc.org/amnesty/. Each month, this program reports on Amnesty International's human-rights findings within three countries. Via RFPI, Costa Rica.

"A Voz da Resistencia do Galo Negro" ("Voice of the Resistence of the Black Cockerel")—see Angola.

"Baker Report," 2083 Springwood Road #300, York PA 17403 USA. Phone: (show, toll-free in United States) (800) 482-5560; (orders, toll-free in United States) (800) 782-4843; (general number/voice mail) +1 (717) 244-1110. Contact: Dr. Jeffrey "Jeff" Baker. Three months of *The Baker Report* periodical $24.95; also sells audio tapes of programs and other items. Anti-"New World Order," Freemasonry and the Illuminati, and distrustful of official versions of various events, including the Oklahoma City bombing. Via WWCR, USA.

"Battle Cry Sounding"
HEADQUARTERS: Command Post, ACMTC, P.O. Box 90, Berino NM 88024 USA. Fax: +1 (505) 882 7325. Contact: General James M. Green. Voice of the Aggressive Christianity Missions Training Corps, which seeks to eliminate churches, synagogues, mosques and central governments, thence to replace them with fundamentalist "warrior tribes"; also, operates Women's International Mobilization Movement. Publishes *Wisdom's Cry*, *Words of the Spirit* and *Battle Cry Sounding* periodicals, and offers various other publications, as well as video and audio tapes. Via facilities of WWCR and WRMI, USA.
AFRICA OFFICE: P.O. Box 2686, Jos North, Plateau State, Nigeria. Contact: Colonel Simon Agwale, Adjutant.

"British Israel World Federation (Canada)," 313 Sherbourne Street, Toronto On, M5A 2S3 Canada. Phone: (office, weekdays) +1 (416) 921-5996; (Nesbitt) +1 (705) 435-5044; (McConkey) +1 (705) 485-3486. Fax: +1 (416) 921 9511. Contact: Douglas Nesbitt or John McConkey. Offers *The Prophetic* magazine and 90-minute audio cassettes of past programs. Although located in Canada, this is the only British Israel office in North America, and thus serves the United States, as well. According to Kenneth Stern in *A Force upon the Plain*, "Christian Identity [see "Herald of Truth" and "Scriptures for America"] began as British Israelism, which traced its roots to mid-nineteenth-century claims that white Christians were the 'true Israelites,' that Jews were offspring of Satan, and that blacks and other minorities were . . . subhuman." Via WWCR, USA.

"CounterSpin," Fairness and Accuracy in Reporting, 130 W. 25th Street, New York NY 10001 USA. Phone: +1 (212) 633-6700. URL: http://www.fair.org/fair/counterspin. Media watchdog organization that reports on what it feels are propaganda, disinformation and other abuses of the media, as well as citing instances of "hard-hitting, independent reporting that cuts against the prevailing media grain." Via RFPI, Costa Rica.

"Democratic Voice of Burma" ("Democratic Myanmar a-Than")
STATION: DVB Radio, P.O. Box 6720, St. Olavs Plass, N-0130 Oslo, Norway. Phone: +47 (22) 20-0021. Phone/fax: +47 (22) 36-2525. E-mail: dvb@sn.no. Contact: (general) Dr. Anng Kin, Listener Liaison; Aye Chan Naing, Daily Editor; or Thida, host for "Songs Request Program"; (administration) Daw Khin Pyone, Manager; (technical) Technical Dept. Free stickers and booklets to be offered in the near future. Norwegian kroner requested for a reply, but presumably Norwegian mint stamps would also suffice. Programs produced by Burmese democratic movements, as well as professional and independent radio journalists, to provide informational and educational services for the democracy movement in-

side and outside Burma. Opposes the current Myanmar government. Transmits via the facilities of Radio Norway International.
AFFINITY GROUP URL: Although the "Democratic Voice of Burma" has no URL, an affinity Burmese exile news group, BurmaNet, does at E-mail: (BurmaNet News editor, Free Burma Coalition, USA) strider@igc.apc.org; (Web coordinator, Free Burma Coalition, USA) freeburma@pobox.com. URL: (BurmaNet News, USA) http://sunsite.unc.edu/freeburma/listservers.html.

"Duncan Long Show," USA Patriot Network, P.O. Box 430, Johnstown CO 80534 USA. Phone: (talk show, toll-free within U.S.) (800) 607-8255; (elsewhere) +1 (970) 587-5171; (order line, toll-free within U.S.) (800) 205-6245. Fax: +1 (970) 587 5450. E-mail: duncan@kansas.net. URL: http://www.kansas.net/~duncan. Contact: Duncan Long, Host; or "Don W." Network Manager. Free sample of *USA Patriot News* monthly newspaper/catalog, otherwise $16/six months. Sells survival gear, night-vision goggles, Taiwanese shortwave radios, books and NTSC videos. VISA/MC/AX. Survivalist/militia how-to show, detailing such things as how and where to obtain, modify and use firearms and other military-type gear for various types of situations, including conventional, guerilla/special, biological and chemical combat, as well as "target shooting." Via WWCR, USA.

"Executive Intelligence Review Talks," EIR News Service, P.O. Box 17390, Washington DC 20041 USA. Phone: (Executive Intelligence Review) +1 (202) 544-7010; (Schiller Institute) +1 (202) 544-7018; (21st Century Institute, general information) +1 (202) 639-6821; (21st Century Institute, subscription information) +1 (703) 777-9451; (Ben Franklin Bookstore for LaRouche publications) toll-free daytimes only within United States (800) 453-4108, elswhere +1 (703) 777-3661. Fax: +1 (202) 544 7105. E-mail: (technical) ralphgib@aol.com. E-mail & URL (Schiller Institute): http://www.erols.com/larouche/schiller.htm. Contact: (general) Mel Kanovsky, Frank Bell; or, asking correspondence to be forwarded, Lyndon LaRouche; (technical) Ralph Gibbons. Publishes *Executive Intelligence Review* newsletter, $896/year, and a wide variety of other periodicals and books. Supports former U.S. presidential candidate Lyndon LaRouche's populist political organization worldwide, including the Schiller Institute and 21st Century Institute of Political Action. Via WWCR, USA.

"Far Right Radio Review"—see RFPI, Costa Rica, for contact information. Critiques populist and politically rightist programs emanating from various privately owned world band stations in the United States.

"FIRE"—see RFPI, Costa Rica, for contact information. Award-winning multilingual (English and Spanish) feminist program produced by the Feminist International Radio Endeavour staff at RFPI, led by María Suárez. Financially supported by the Foundation for a Compassionate Society.
"Food Not Bombs Radio Network"
PRODUCTION FACILITY: 350 7th Avenue #35, San Francisco CA 94118 USA. Phone: +1 (415) 330-5030. Contact: Richard Edmondson, Producer. Via RFPI, Costa Rica.
ORGANIZATIONAL ADDRESS: Food Not Bombs, 3145 Gary Blvd. #12, San Francisco CA 94118 USA; also, temporarily can be reached at 25 Taylor Avenue, San Francisco CA 94118 USA. Phone: (toll-free in the U.S.) (800) 884-1136; (elsewhere) +1 (415) 351-1672. $10 for starter kit and 128-page book for starting a food recovery program; NTSC video $15. Food Not Bombs is a political activist group concerned with American homeless people, with the radio program focusing on what it views as "oppressive local, state and federal policies." The producer is a former homeless person.

☞**"For the People"**—see United Broadcasting Network, USA.

"Forum for Democracy"—see Radio Miami Internacional, USA, for address. Program of the Vietnam Restoration Party, based in California. Aired via KWHR, Hawaii, USA.

☞"Freedom's Call"—see WWCR, USA, for postal address. E-mail and biographical URL: http://www.talkamerica.com/bogritz.html. URL: (StreamWorks audio) http://www.talkamerica.com/. Contact: James "Bo" Gritz. Opposes gun control, the Federal income tax, the "New World Order," Zionism, alleged Jewish "control" of such institutions as the Federal Reserve System, and the United Nations. Disputes official accounts of such events as the Oklahoma City bombing. Gritz, a retired U.S. Green Beret lieutenant colonel, America's most-decorated Vietnam veteran and former presidential candidate of the Populist Party (see "Radio Free America"), is the character upon whom the movie character "Rambo" is understood to have been based. Gritz is also credited, along with Jack McLamb (see "Officer Jack McLamb

Show"), with being the key individual to persuade Randy Weaver to end the Ruby Ridge standoff. He leads two paramilitary/militia training organizations: Specially Prepared Individuals for Key Events (SPIKE), and the Idaho-based Constitutionalist Covenant Community. Via WWCR.

"Full Disclosure Live," Studio 303, The Superior Broadcasting Company, P.O. Box 1533, Oil City PA 16301 USA. Phone: (toll-free within the United States) (800) 825-5303; (elsewhere) +1 (814) 678-8801. URL: http://ripco.com:8080/~glr/glr.html. Contact: Glen Roberts. Free sample newsletter and catalog. Offers a variety of electronics and related publications. Conservative talk show concerning such topics as militias, political broadcasts and related communications, and eavesdropping. Via WWCR, USA.

Who Really Listens to "Rambo Radio"?

It happens every night, if establishment media reports are to be believed. Countless militia members, would-be terrorists and silent sympathizers sit glued to their world band radios and Internet screens—soaking up reports, instructions and ideological sustenance from what CBS' Dan Rather calls "right-wing hate groups."

Lurking Liberals

But purveyors of political dogmatism may be digging their own graves. Judging from mail and publications received at PASSPORT, it seems that the main audience may not consist of people nodding in agreement while cleaning their AK-47s. Instead, it appears to be made up of listeners reinforcing their own values of tolerance by being exposed firsthand to what certain disestablishmentarian groups are really thinking.

If you're one of these "lurking liberals," here are some relevant studies that are militantly anti-disestablishmentarian.

Talk America

James "Bo" Gritz, America's most-decorated Vietnam veteran and the real-life "Rambo," hosts "Freedom's Call" on world band and Web radio.

Comprehensive Book Details Movement

The first and most exhaustive is *A Force Upon the Plain*, by Kenneth S. Stern of the American Jewish Committee (1996, Simon & Schuster, ISBN 0-684-81916-3). This comprehensive 304-page book, thoroughly indexed for reference, covers a wide variety of groups and individuals associated with "the American militia movement and the politics of hate." It excels in analysis of why people think and act along these lines, and nowhere recommends that this complex issue be dealt with simply by suppressing speech.

Alas, the book's understanding of radio is depressingly limited. For example, Stern states flatly, "'Martians' is the shortwave term for 'minorities'," as though the shortwave spectrum were the private turf of bigots. Otherwise, *A Force Upon the Plain* is probably the best single place to turn for watchdog research on militia and kindred groups in the United States—and even beyond, such as Australia.

ADL Report Targets Shortwave

In 1996 the Anti-Defamation League of the B'nai B'rith in New York issued its own 23-page document, *Research Report: Poisoning the Airwaves: The Extremist Message of Hate on Shortwave Radio*, by Dorothy Rose. As the title suggests, this document, unlike the Stern book, zeroes in explicitly on disestablishmentarian shortwave programs, and only thus on groups and individuals involved. Given the ADL's reputation for scholarship, the report disappoints in its number of minor factual errors, but it does indicate who says what about whom, over which stations, as well as who seems to associate with whom.

Clearly, though, a key objective of this document is to cast doubt over the legality of disestablishmentarian programs. For example, it states, "broadcasters of hate may be circumventing the Federal Communications Commission by using shortwave frequencies whose transmissions 'are intended to be received directly by the general public in foreign countries' to spread propaganda clearly targeting domestic audiences."

Not indicated, aside from the uncertain legality of that regulation, is that the FCC already enforces it by ensuring that transmitter and antenna configurations are effective in reaching foreign targets, while also being maximally ineffective in reaching domestic targets. What the FCC doesn't attempt to do, but which the ADL report implies it should do, is to analyze program content to determine whether it is intended for domestic audiences—a ticklish task, indeed.

Shortwave being shortwave, no matter where an antenna is beamed, signals will also be received at reduced strength in many other parts of the world— including the United States. Yet, the FCC's approach is comparable to that of the official Voice of America, which by statute must target its programs to non-U.S. audiences.

Interestingly, the ADL's hardline position is of relatively recent vintage. Several years back, the first such operation, the neonazi "Voice of To-morrow" *(sic)*, was being aired clandestinely over an illegal transmitter in Virginia. The ADL, noting that the station had virtually no listenership, chose not to become involved. Obviously, the FCC decided to look the other way, too, perhaps figuring that the publicity resulting from a federal raid would do more to help neonazis than an occasional illegal broadcast at low power.

The ADL does not distribute *Poisoning the Airwaves* to the general public, but considers requests from qualified reporters, scholars and others. Contact the ADL Media Relations Department, 823 United Nations Plaza, New York NY 10017 USA, phone +1 (212) 490-2525. Or you may be able to order or borrow a copy, as we did, from someone who can get it, or visit an academic or other specialized library. Alternatively, you may be able to find it online via professional search organizations.

"Herald of Truth," P.O. Box 1021, Harrison AK 72602 USA. Phone: +1 (501) 741-1119. Contact: Pastor Bob Hallstrom. Free copies of broadcast transcripts and packet of information. Program of the Kingdom Identity Ministries, a Christian Identity organization believed to be associated with "Scriptures for America" (see), and reportedly descended from British Israelism (see "British Israel World Federation"). Vehemently opposes to what it calls "Jews, queers, aliens and minorities," and supports "white Christians," specifically those "Aryan Jacob Israel people" originating from Western Europe. Yet, also opposes a seemingly endless roster of conservative white Christian political leaders, including Rush Limbaugh and U.S. House Speaker Newt Gingrich, and claims the late U.S. President Franklin Roosevelt was a Jewish communist. Sells various books and audio cassettes, as well as the *Patriot Report* newsletter. Via WWCR and WRMI, USA; Christian Identity programs are also aired over other American world band stations, such as WRNO, but no longer via WINB, which is inactive.

"Hightower Radio," Saddle Burr Productions, P.O. Box 13516, Austin TX 78711 USA. Phone: +1 (512) 477-5588. Fax: +1 (512) 478 8536. E-mail: hightower@essential.org. URL: (text and RealAudio) http://www.essential.org/hightower/; (StreamWorks audio once or so a day) http://www.kpig.com/welcome.htm. Contact: Jim Hightower. The term "maverick" comes from the contrarian way Texas pioneer Samuel Maverick and certain of his descendants handled cattle and other matters. Hightower Radio is considered to be heir to that spirit, featuring former Texas Agriculture Commissioner Jim Hightower, something of an establishment Texas disestablishmentarian and a gen-yew-wine Lone Star liberal. Via RFPI, Costa Rica, and Web radio

"Holy Medina Radio" (when active)—see Radio Iraq International for contact information. Opposes the Saudi government.

"Hour of Courage," International Commerce Corporation, 135 S. Main Street, 7th Floor, Greenville SC 29601 USA. Phone: (toll-free within United States) (800) 327-8606. Fax: +1 (803) 232 9309. Contact: Ron Wilson. *Creatures from Jeckyll Island* book $25. Forsees a conspiracy to take over the United States, opposes gun control, and is distrustful of official versions of various events, such as Waco. Also predicts the coming of a "greatest financial catastrophe in the world," and suggests that to protect against its consequences,

...Continued

Little Station, Big Impact

Another watchdog can be found on world band radio, even if its signal is weak and chancy. The tiny Costa-Rica-based Radio for Peace International (RFPI), created by United Nations resolution, tirelessly documents these programs from a new-left perspective.

RFPI's "Far Right Radio Review," inaugurated in 1994, is aired regularly, as well as summarized quarterly in its newsletter, *VISTA*. Hosted by James Latham and Brad Heavner, "Far Right Radio Review" documents and critiques American disestablishmentarian programs, which they clearly would be happy to see yanked off the air.

According to RFPI, it feeds opinion about and information on these programs to over 30 news agencies, reportedly sometimes as a result of references by the ADL. As a result, Mr. Latham has become virtually the standard source for news gatherers covering shortwave disestablishmentarian operations.

Wiesenthal Center Monitors Programs

Other sources? Larger and specialized bookstores and libraries are adding titles regularly. Too, the Simon Wiesenthal Center in Los Angeles reportedly is rigorous in monitoring militia and other disestablishmentarian programs over American world band stations, although we were unable to confirm this. Like the ADL, the Wiesenthal Center also issues reports that are made available to selected reporters, scholars and others. It may be reached at +1 (310) 553-9036.

But perhaps the best place for serious researchers to look is in the juicy "Sources" appendix of *A Force Upon the Plain*. Running no less than 33 pages, this section is the ultimate guide to what's available for further reading—at least as of when the book went to press in 1996.

listeners purchase precious metals from its sponsoring organization, Atlantic Bullion and Coin. Theme song: "Dixie." Via WWCR and WHRI, USA.

"Hour of the Time"
PROGRAM AND HEADQUARTERS: Research Center, Citizens' Agency for Joint Intelligence (CAJI), P.O. Box 1420, Show Low AZ 85901 USA. Phone: (general) +1 (602) 337-2562; (sponsoring organization, toll-free in United States) (800) 289-2646. E-mail: caji@pobox.com. Contact: William Cooper. Opposes "New World Order," the United Nations and the Federal Reserve; favors militias to resist potentially oppressive government. Predicts financial catastrophe, and as protection suggests that listeners purchase gold and silver from its sponsoring organization, Swiss-America Trading. *Behold a Pale Horse* (Light Technology Publishing), a 1991 book by Cooper, covers his many claims, including about alien space invaders: "1 in 40 humans have been implanted with devices . . . aliens are building an army of implanted humans who can be activated and turned on us." Via WWCR, USA.
NEWSPAPER: Veritas, P.O. Box 3390, St. John's AZ 85936 USA. Phone: +1 (520) 337-2878. Prices range from $15 for six issues to $50 for 24 issues.
"Insight," The Progressive, 409 East Main Street, Madison WI 53703 USA. Phone: +1 (608) 257-4626. Fax: +1 (608) 257 3373. E-mail: progressive@peacenet.org. Contact: Matthew Rothschild, Editor. Radio outlet for *The Progressive* magazine, a disestablishmentarian publication founded in 1909. Via RFPI, Costa Rica.
"Intelligence Report," Wolverine Productions, P.O. Box 281, Augusta MI 49012 USA. Phone: +1 (616) 966-3002. Fax: +1 (616) 966 0742. Contact: (programs) John Stadtmiller or Mark Koernke; (administrative) Libby. Sells various tapes and publications. Opposes the "New World Order" and supports the militia and survivalist movements. Mark Koernke, from Dexter, Michigan, is the "Mark from Michigan" reported on extensively with respect to the Oklahoma City bombing. Reportedly affiliated with the "Voice of Liberty" program (see). Aired via WRMI, USA.
"Junta Patriótica Cubana"—see "Puerto Libre," below.
"La Voz de Alpha 66," 1714 Flagler Street, Miami FL 33135 USA. Contact: Diego Medina, Producer. Anti-Castro, anti-communist; privately supported by the Alpha 66 organization. Aired via such private American stations as WHRA.
"La Voz de la Fundación," 7300 NW 35 Terrace, Miami FL 33122 USA; or P.O. Box 440069, Miami FL 33144 USA. Contact: Ninoska Pérez Castellón, Executive Producer; (technical) Mariela Ferretti. URL: http://www.icanect.net~canfnet/english/prgvoz.htm. Free stickers. Anti-Castro, anti-communist; privately supported by the Cuban American National Foundation. Also, *see* Radio Martí, USA. Via Radio Miami Internacional and WHRI.
"La Voz del CID," 10021 SW 37th Terrace, Miami FL 33165 USA; if no result, try AFINSA Portugal, R Ricardo Jorge 53, 4000 Oporto, Portugal; Apartado de Correo 8130, 1000 San José, Costa Rica; or Apartado Postal 51403, Sabana Grande 1050, Caracas, Venezuela. Phone: (U.S.) +1 (305) 551-8484. Fax: (U.S.) +1 (305) 559 9365; (Portugal) +351 21 41 49 94. Contact: Alfredo Aspitia, Asistente de Prensa e Información; or Francisco Fernández. Anti-Castro, anti-communist; privately supported by Cuba Independiente y Democrática. Free political literature. Via their own clandestine transmitters in Central America, possibly Guatemala.
"La Voz Popular," Fernando García, Centro de Promoción Popular, Apartado 20-668, México D.F, Mexico; Arcoios, P.O. Box 835, Seattle WA 98111 USA; or Network in Solidarity with the People of Guatemala, 930 F Street NW, Suite 720, Washington DC 20004 USA. Contact: Julia Batres Lemus. Station of the Unidad Revolucionaria Nacional Guatemalteca (URNG) anti-Guatemalan-government rebels, which operates from the Sierra Madre mountains.

"Lightwave Mission Broadcasting"—*see* "Radio Newyork International."
"Making Contact"
PRODUCTION OFFICE: David Barsamian, P.O. Box 551, Boulder CO 80306 USA. Phone: +1 (303) 444-8788. Via RFPI, Costa Rica.
ORGANIZATION OFFICE: National Radio Project, 830 Los Trancos Road, Portola Valley CA 94028 USA. Phone: +1 (415) 851-7256. Focuses on social and political problems and solutions within the United States and beyond.
"Mujer Cubana"—*see* Radio Miami Internacional, USA, for contact information. Program of a group of Cuban woman exiles in Miami. Via WRMI, USA.
"National Radio of the Saharan Arab Democratic Republic,"—*see* "Voice of the Free Sahara," below, which is operated by the same group, the Frente Polisario.
"National Unity Radio"—*see* Sudan National Broadcasting Corporation for contact information.
"Norman Resnick Show," USA Patriot Network, P.O. Box 430, Johnstown CO 80534 USA. Phone: (talk show, toll-free within U.S.) (800) 607-8255; (elsewhere) +1 (970) 587-5171; (order line, toll-free within U.S.) (800) 205-6245. Fax: +1 (970) 587 5450. Contact: Norman "Dr. Norm" Resnick, Host; or "Don W.", Network Manager. Free sample of *USA Patriot News* monthly newspaper/catalog, otherwise $16/six months. Sells survival gear, night-vision goggles, Taiwanese shortwave radios, books and NTSC videos. VISA/MC/AX. Former professor Resnick states that he is "an observant, kosher Jew." He describes his program as discussing "educational, social, political and economic issues from a Constitutional perspective," with emphasis on the activities on the U.S. Bureau of Alcohol, Tobacco and Firearms. Opposed *inter alia* to the "New World Order" and gun control. Via WWCR, USA.
"Officer Jack McLamb Show," P.O. Box 8712, Phoenix AZ 85066 USA. Phone: (McLamb) +1 (602) 237-2533; (Swiss-America Trading, sponsor, toll-free within the United States) (800) 289-2646. URL: http://www.police-against-nwo.com/. Program and sister organization, Police Against the New World Order, are headed by former Phoenix police officer Jack McLamb. Supports activities to convert American police officers and military personnel over to view and act favorably towards militias, as well as similar groups and armed individuals. Sells *The Waco Whitewash, Vampire Killer 2000* and other publications. In *Vampire Killer 2000*, written by McLamb, he opposes, among many others, CBS News, financial interests of the Rothschild family, and gun control. McLamb is credited, along with "Bo" Gritz (*see* "Freedom's Call"), with being a key individual in persuading Randy Weaver to end the Ruby Ridge standoff. Via WHRI, USA.
"Overcomer" ("Voice of the Last Day Prophet of God"), P.O. Box 691, Walterboro SC 29488 USA. Phone: (toll-free in the United States) (800) 397-3892; (elsewhere) +1 (803) 538-8686. Contact: Brother R.G. Stair. Sample "Overcomer" newsletter and various pamphlets free upon request. Sells a Sangean shortwave radio for $50, plus other items of equipment and various publications at appropriate prices. Primarily a fundamentalist Christian program from an exceptionally pleasant Southern town, but disestablishmentarian in such things as its characterizations of homosexuals in general, as well as the supposed homosexual and heterosexual activities of priests and nuns within the Roman Catholic Church. Also opposes Freemasonry, U.S. aid to Israel and reported abuses of powers of U.S. Federal authorities. Invites listeners to write in, giving the name of the station over which "The Overcomer" was heard and the quality of reception. States that the program spends $55,000 per month on renting airtime over world band, satellite and local stations; at one point, tried in vain to go on the air via oceangoing craft. Via WRNO, WRMI and WGTG, USA.
"Preparedness Hour," USA Patriot Network, P.O. Box 430, Johnstown CO 80534 USA. Phone: (talk show, toll-free within

U.S.) (800) 607-8255; (elsewhere) +1 (970) 587-5171; (order line, toll-free within U.S.) (800) 205-6245. Fax: +1 (970) 587 5450. Contact: (general) Bob Speer, Host; or "Don W.", Network Manager; (sponsor) Jim Cedarstrom. Free sample of *USA Patriot News* monthly newspaper/catalog, $16/six months. Sells survival gear, night-vision goggles, Taiwanese shortwave radios, books and NTSC videos. VISA/MC/AX. Program concentrates on such survivalist skills as growing food, making soap and cheese, home childbirth and how to obtain and train mules or donkeys. Speer is described by his associates as a "SPIKE trainer" (Specially Prepared Individuals for Key Events) for retired U.S. Green Beret lieutenant colonel James "Bo" Gritz. Sponsored by Discount Gold, which urges listeners to invest in precious metals as an alternative to holding paper money or investments. Via WWCR, USA.

"Prophecy Club," P.O. Box 750234, Topeka KS 66675 USA. Phone/fax: (club) +1 (913) 478-1112; (sponsor, toll-free in U.S. only) (800) 525-9556. Contact: Stan Johnson, Director. Club, which takes no cards or phone orders, offers free sample newsletter and catalog; also sells newsletter subscriptions, as well as videos in NTSC format for $28.75 within the United States and $30 elsewhere, including shipping. Also offers audio cassettes for $5.75 (U.S.) or $6 (elsewhere). Sponsor accepts cards and sells similar items. Organization states that it is devoted to study and research on Bible prophecy. Programs oppose, *i.a.*, the "New World Order" and Freemasonry. Via WWCR and WHRI, USA, as well as various AM, FM and television stations.

"Protecting Your Wealth," 9188 E. San Salvador Drive #203, Scottsdale AZ 85258 USA. Phone: (program, toll-free within United States) (800) 598-1500; (sponsoring organization, toll-free within the United States) (800) 451-4452; (elsewhere) +1 (602) 451-0575. Fax: +1 (602) 451 4394. Contact: Mike Callahan or Eric Ceadarstrom. Opposed to the "New World Order" and groups involved in paper-based financial markets. Supports rural-based survivalism, and claims that the purpose of anti-terrorism and related American legislation is to extend government control over people so as to strip them of their assets. Alleges that paper money, bonds and securities are controlled by an elite that is about to create a second Great Depression, rendering those assets worthless. As an alternative, urges people to invest in the precious metals sold by their sponsoring organization, Viking International Trading, as well as to move to the countryside with their shortwave radios and to purchase hoardable foods sold by a sister firm. Via WWCR, USA.

"Radio Amahoro" ("Radio Voice of Peace for Rwanda") STATION OFFICE: Inter-Africa Group, P.O. Box 1631, Addis Ababa, Ethiopia.
SPONSORING ORGANIZATION: Centre Amani/Europep, rue du Noyer 322, B-1040 Brussels, Belgium. Fax: +32 (2) 735 3916. Contact: Tatien Musabyimana, Director; or Guy Theunis, Administrateur. Free stickers. Christian humanitarian organization seeking peace and reconciliation among Rwandan tribes and refugees. Via Afrique Numéro Un (see Gabon) and the Voice of Ethiopia (see).

"Radio Democrat International Nigeria," NALICON U.K, P.O. Box 9663, London SE1 3LZ, United Kingdom; or NALICON U.S.A, P.O. Box 175, Boston MA 02131 USA. Phone: (Boston) +1 (617) 364-4455. Fax: (London) +44 (171) 403 6985; (Boston) +1 (617) 364 7362. E-mail: (London) nalicon @postlin.demon.co.uk; (Boston) nalicon@nalicon.com. Station set up to disseminate information concerning democracy, human rights and the environment in Nigeria. Anti-Nigerian government. Created by London-based Nigerian exile group, NALICON (National Liberation Council of Nigeria). Requests broadcast material and funds to maintain a regular broadcasting schedule. Welcomes scripts, and recordings from listeners and supporters. Transmits via the South African facilities of Sentech.

"Radio Dniester International"—see "Moldavian Republic of Pridnestrovye."

"Radio Free America"
NETWORK: Sun Radio Network, 2857 Executive Drive, Clearwater FL 34622 USA. Phone: (call-in show, toll-free within U.S.) (800) 878-8255; (general) +1 (813) 572-9209. Contact: Tom Valentine, Host and Member of the Board of Liberty Lobby. Succeeds *Liberty Lobby* program aired two decades ago. Via WWCR and WHRI, USA.
SPONSORING ORGANIZATION: Liberty Lobby, 300 Independence Avenue SE, Washington DC 20003 USA. Phone: (executive offices) +1 (202) 546-5611; (newspaper) +1 (202) 544-1794; (video sales, toll-free within U.S.) (800) 596-4465; (book and newspaper sales, toll-free within U.S.) (800) 522-6292; (publication/video sales to other countries) +1 (941) 263-4101. Fax: +1 (202) 546 3626. Contact: (general) Don Markey, Public Affairs Associate; or Ted Gunderson, spokesman. (administration) Willis Carto, Founder. *The Spotlight* newspaper, which reportedly has a circulation of some 100,000, is nominally $38/year, but is sometimes offered over the air for less; sells *The Barnes Review*, a revisionist Holocaust publication; also offers books at various prices and NTSC videos for $23.95, including shipping. Audio tapes of past broadcasts $9. VISA/MC. Opposes the "New World Order" and various activities of the Bilderberg gathering, Trilateral Commission, U.S. Federal Reserve System, Israeli government and Anti-Defamation League of the B'nai B'rith. Expresses occasional interest in unorthodox medical treatments and UFOs. Prefers to call itself "populist," rather than "antisemetic"—the term attached to Liberty Lobby activities by much of the media, including PBS' "Frontline" and a wide variety of newspapers and newsmagazines. Supports the political aspirations of such conservative/populist figures as Pat Buchanan, but also expresses skepticism towards capitalism. Keeps close watch, with occasional live coverage, on sieges and other activities of such law-enforcement agencies as the U.S. Bureau of Alcohol, Tobacco and Firearms. The Liberty Lobby was founded in 1956 by Willis Carto, who more recently founded the Populist Party, which has featured David Duke and "Bo" Gritz as Presidential candidates.

"Radio Free Bougainville"
MAIN ADDRESS: 2 Griffith Avenue, Roseville NSW 2069, Australia. Phone/fax: +61 (2) 417-1066. E-mail: (Bougainville Freedom Movement) sashab@magna.com.au. URL: (Bougainville Freedom Movement) http://www.magna.com.au/~sashab/BFM.htm. Contact: Sam Voron, Australian Director. $5, AUS$5 or 5 IRCs required. Station's continued operation is totally dependent on the availability of local coconuts for power generation, currently the only form of power available for those living in the blockaded areas of the island of Bougainville. Station is opposed to the Papua New Guinea government, and supports armed struggle for complete independence and the "Bougainville Interim Government."
ALTERNATIVE ADDRESS: P.O. Box 1203, Honiara, Solomon Islands. Contact: Martin R. Miriori, Humanitarian Aid Coordinator. $1, AUS$2 or 3 IRCs required. No verification data issued from this address.

"Radio Free Somalia," 2 Griffith Avenue, Roseville NSW 2069, Australia. Phone/fax: +61 (2) 417-1066. Contact: Sam Voron, Australian Director. $5, AUS$5 or 5 IRCs required. Station is operated from Gaalkacyo in the Mudug region of northeastern Somalia by the Somali International Amateur Radio Club. Seeks volunteers and donations of radio equipment and airline tickets.

"Radio Liberty"—proposed American talk show which says it is concerned with "the battle for the survival of Western civilization" and supposed censorship of newscasts by "someone." Via KVOH.

"Radio Message of Freedom" ("Radyo Pyam-e Azadi"), GPO Box 857, University Town, Peshawar, Pakistan. Contact:

Qaribur Rehman Saeed, Director of Radio. Sponsored by the Islamic Party of Afghanistan rebel organization, headed by Golboddin Hekmatyar. Via its own transmitting facilities, once and possibly still located in Afghanistan.

"Radio Newyork International," 97 High Street, Kennebunk ME 04043 USA. Phone: (Weiner or McCormack) +1 (207) 985-7547; (Becker) +1 (316) 825-4264. E-mail: 74434.3020 @compuserve.com. Contact: Allan Weiner, Scott Becker or Anita McCormick. Two "RNI the Video" NTSC cassettes $24.95 each; two "Best of Voyages Broadcast Services" audio cassettes $14.95 each, or both $24.95. Also, Offshore Society sells T-shirts, tote bags and such. Last heard as an entertainment program, rather than the original disestablishmentarian offshore exercise. However, Weiner, along with partner Becker, plan to finish outfitting their new ship, the Electra, as a shortwave station under the name "Lightwave Mission Broadcasting," providing enough financial backing can be found, such as via contributions to their "Offshore Society."

"Radio of the Provisional Government of National Union and National Salvation of Cambodia," 212 E. 47th Street #24G, New York NY 10017 USA; or Permanent Mission of Democratic Cambodia to the United Nations, 747 3rd Avenue, 8th Floor, New York NY 10017 USA. Contact: Phobel Cheng, First Secretary, Permanent Mission of Cambodia to the United Nations. Khmer Rouge station. Operates from a clandestine site within Cambodia.

"Radio of the Saudi Opposition from Najd and Hijaz" ("Idha'at al-Mu'aradah al-Sa'udiyah fi Najd wa al-Hijaz")—see Radio Iraq International for contact information. Opposes the Saudi government.

"Radio Pridnestrovye"—see "Moldavian Republic of Pridnestrovye."

"Radiostantsiya Pamyat"—see Russia.

"Radio Revista Lux," 75 NW 22 Avenue, Miami FL 33125 USA. Contact: René L. Díaz. Program of the Union of Electrical Plant Workers of Cuba in Exile. Via WRMI, USA.

"Radio Voice of Peace for Rwanda"—see "Radio Amahoro," above.

"Radio Voice of the Mojahed"—see "Voice of the Mojahed," below.

"Republic of Iraq Radio, Voice of the Iraqi People" ("Idha'at al-Jamahiriya al-Iraqiya, Saut al-Sha'b al-Iraqi"), Broadcasting Service of the Kingdom of Saudi Arabia, P.O. Box 61718, Riyadh 11575, Saudi Arabia. Phone: +966 (1) 442-5170. Fax: +966 (1) 402 8177. Contact: Suliman A. Al-Samnan, Director of Frequency Management. Anti-Saddam Hussein "black" clandestine supported by CIA, British intelligence, the Gulf Cooperation Council and Saudi Arabia. The name of this station has changed periodically since its inception during the Gulf crisis. Via transmitters in Saudi Arabia.

"RFPI Reports"—see RFPI, Costa Rica, for contact information. News about human rights, social justice and the environment, mainly from Latin America and the Caribbean.

"Rush Limbaugh Show," EIB World Band, WABC, #2 Pennsylvania Avenue, New York NY 10121 USA; telephone (toll-free, USA only) (800) 282-2882, (elsewhere) +1 (212) 613-3800; fax (during working hours) +1 (212) 563 9166. E-mail 70277.2502@compuserve.com. Via WRNO, USA. Reception reports concerning this program can also be sent with 2 IRCs or an SASE directly to WRNO.

"Scriptures for America," P.O. Box 766, Laporte CO 80535 USA. Phone: +1 (307) 745-5913. Fax: +1 (307) 745 5914. URLs: ftp://ftp.netcom.com/pub/SF/SFA or http://www.ra.nilenet.com/~tmw/files/homo.html. Contact: Pastor Peter J. "Pete" Peters. "Introductory Packet" $2. A leader within the Christian Identity movement (also see "Herald of Truth" and "British Israel World Federation"). Peters vehemently opposes, inter alia, homosexuals, the Anti-Defamation League of the B'nai B'rith and other Jews and Jewish organizations, nonwhites, and international banking institutions. Also expresses suspicion of official and media re-

sponses to such events as the Oklahoma City bombing, and is supportive of militia activities. Like the relatively visible (e.g., advertising in U.S. World News & Report) Pastor Karl Schott of Christ's Gospel Fellowship/The Pathfinder in Spokane, Peters alleges that Christians whose ancestry is from selected parts of Europe are the true chosen people of Biblical prophecy. Free brochures and catalog of publications and recordings. Via WWCR and WRNO, USA.

"Second Opinion"—see "Insight," above, for contact information. Various thinkers propose solutions to world problems. Via Radio for Peace International, Costa Rica.

"Seventieth Week Magazine," P.O. Box 771, Gladewater TX 75647 USA. Contact: Ben McKnight. Free "Flash Bulletins" booklets. Opposes "New World Order," believes United Nations and UFOs are plotting to take over the United States and commit genocide against Christians and patriots, and distrusts official versions of various events, such as the Oklahoma City bombing. Via WWCR, USA.

"Steppin' Out of Babylon," 2804 Piedmont Avenue, Berkeley CA 94705 USA. Phone: +1 (510) 540-8850. Contact: Sue Supriano, Producer. Interviews with those protesting various conditions, including war, poverty and human-rights abuses. Via RFPI.

"Taking Back America," Eagle Radio Network, P.O. Box 209, Northfield Falls VT 05564. Phone: (general) +1 (802) 485-4170; (sponsor, "Lifeline" telephone network, toll-free in U.S.) (800) 311-2814. Fax: +1 (802) 485 4466. URL: http://www.orn.com/~drbs/Eagle/eagle.htm. Contact: Charles E. Collins or Richard Eutsler. Opposes the "New World Order," supports such third-party activities as the presidential candidacy of Charles E. Collins. Seems to be wanting for funds.

"This Way Out," Overnight Productions, P.O. Box 38327, Los Angeles CA 90038 USA. Phone: +1 (213) 874-0874. E-mail: tworadio@aol.com. URL: http://abacus.oxy.edu/QRD/www/media/radio/thiswayout/index.html or http://www.qrd.org/qrd/www/media/radio/thiswayout/helptwo.html. News, music, interviews and features from and about lesbians and gays, mainly but not exclusively within the United States. Via RFPI.

"Un Solo Pueblo" (when active)—see Radio Copán International, Honduras, for address; or write directly to the sponsoring organization at 8561 NW South River Drive, Suite 201, Medley FL 33166 USA; also, Organo del Centro de la Democracia Cubana, P.O. Box 161742, Miami FL 33116 USA. Anti-Castro, anti-communist; privately supported by the Coordinadora Social Demócrata Cubana.

"Vietnam Veterans Radio Network," 7807 N. Avalon, Kansas City MO 64152 USA. Contact: John ("Doc") Upton. This radio voice of the Vietnam Veterans Against the War mixes music, commentaries and sound bites concerning some of the more difficult aspects of the Vietnam War experience. Via RFPI.

"Voice of Arab Syria"—see Radio Iraq International for contact information.

"Voice of China" ("Zhongguo Zhi Yin Guangbo Diantai"), Democratization of China, P.O. Box 11663, Berkeley CA 94701 USA; Foundation for China in the 21st Century, P.O. Box 11696, Berkeley CA 94701 USA; or P.O. Box 79218, Monkok, Hong Kong (Hong Kong address valid no later than June 30th, 1997). Phone: +1 (510) 2843-5025. Fax: +1 (510) 2843 4370. Contact: Bang Tai Xu, Director. Mainly "overseas Chinese students" interested in the democratization of China. Financial support from the Foundation for China in the 21st Century. Have "picked up the mission" of the earlier Voice of June 4th, but have no organizational relationship with it. Transmits via facilities of the Central Broadcasting System, Taiwan (see).

"Voice of Eritrea"—see Radio Iraq International, Iraq, for contact information.

"Voice of Freedom" (if reactivated), 206 Carlton St., Toronto ON, Canada. Contact: Ernst Zündel. Neonazi, supporting

Adolf Hitler, the Third Reich and the NSDAP, as well as denying established Holocaust history. Although Zündel's program, formerly broadcast over WWCR and WRNO, is currently not aired over world band, he is sometimes heard on "American Dissident Voices" (see). Zündel, whose conviction in Canada for defaming a distinctly identifiable group was eventually overturned, has authored a number of books, including The Hitler We Loved, and Why.

"Voice of Iraq"—see Radio Damascus for contact information.

"Voice of Iraqi Kurdistan" ("Aira dangi Kurdestana Iraqa") (when active), P.O. Box 2443, Merrifield VA 22116 USA; P.O. Box 1504, London W7 3LX, United Kingdom; Kurdiska Riksförbundet, Hornsgatan 80, S-117 21 Stockholm, Sweden; or Kurdistan Press, Örnsvägen 6C, S-172 Sundbyberg, Sweden. Phone: (Stockholm) +46 (8) 668-6060 or +46 (8) 668-66088; (Sundbyberg) +46 (8) 298-332. Contact: (United States) Namat Sharif, Kurdistan Democratic Party. Sponsored by the Kurdistan Democratic Party, led by Masoud Barzani, and the National Democratic Iraqi Front. From its own transmitting facilities, reportedly once located in the Kurdish section of Iraq.

"Voice of Kashmir Freedom" ("Sada-i Hurriyat-i Kashmir"), P.O. Box 102, Muzaffarabad, Azad Kashmir, via Pakistan. Favors Azad Kashmiri independence from India; pro-Moslem, sponsored by the Kashmiri Mojahedin organization. From transmission facilities believed to be in Pakistan.

"Voice of Liberty," Box 1776, Liberty KY 42539 USA; or Box 3987, Rex GA 32073 USA. Phone: (call-in) toll-free in United States (800) 526-1776, or elsewhere +1 (404) 968-8865; (voice mail) +1 (404) 968-0330. Contact: Paul Parsons or Rick Tyler. Sells various audio cassettes, $50 starter kit and News Front newspaper. Supports the Voice of Liberty Patriots organization, and reportedly is affiliated with the Church of the Remnant and the "Intelligence Report" program (see). Opposed to certain practices of the Bureau of Alcohol, Tobacco and Firearms and various other law-enforcement organizations in the United States, abortion, and restrictions on firearms and Christian prayer. Via WWCR, USA.

"Voice of National Salvation" ("Gugugui Sori Pangsong"), Grenier Osawa 107, 40 Nando-cho, Shinjuku-ku, Tokyo, Japan. Phone: + 81 (3) 5261-0331. Fax: +81 (3) 5261 0332. Contact: Kuguk Chonson. Pro-North Korea, pro-Korean unification; supported by North Korean government. On the air since 1967, but not always under the same name. Via North Korean transmitters located in Pyongyang, Haeju and Wongsan.

"Voice of Oromo Liberation" ("Kun Segalee Bilisumma Oromooti"), Postfach 510610, D-13366 Berlin, Germany. Phone: +49 (30) 494-1036. Fax: +49 (30) 494 3372. Contact: Tayete Ferah, European Coordinator. Station of the Oromo Liberation Front of Ethiopia, an Oromo nationalist organization transmitting via facilities of Ukrainian Radio (see). Reply unlikely, but interesting correspondence with a suitable donation and SASE might trigger a favorable response.

"Voice of Palestine, Voice of the Palestinian Islamic Revolution" ("Saut al-Filistin, Saut al-Thowrah al-Islamiyah al-Filistiniyah")—see Voice of the Islamic Republic of Iran, over whose transmitters this program is clandestinely aired, for potential contact information. Supports the Islamic Resistance Movement, Hamas, which is anti-Arafat and anti-Israel.

"Voice of Peace," Inter-Africa Group, P.O. Box 1631, Addis Ababa, Ethiopia. Humanitarian organization, partially funded by UNICEF, seeking peace and reconciliation among warring factions in Somalia. Via the Voice of Ethiopia (see).

"Voice of Rebellious Iraq" ("Saut al-Iraq al-Tha'ir"), P.O. Box 11365/738, Tehran, Iran; P.O. Box 37155/146, Qom, Iran; or P.O. Box 36802, Damascus, Syria. Anti-Iraqi regime, supported by the Shi'ite-oriented Supreme Assembly of the Islamic Revolution of Iraq, led by Mohammed Baqir al-Hakim. Supported by the Iranian government and transmitted from Iranian soil.

"Voice of Southern Azerbaijan" ("Bura Janubi Azerbaijan Sasi"). Phone: (Holland) +31 (70) 319-2189. This Azeri-language station is operated by the National and Independent Front of Southern Azerbaijan, which is opposed to Iranian and Armenian influence in Azerbaijan.

"Voice of the Communist Party of Iran" ("Seda-ye Hezb-e Komunist-e Iran"), B.M. Box 2123, London WC1N 3XX, United Kingdom; or O.I.S., Box 50040, S-104 05 Stockholm, Sweden. Sponsored by the Communist Party of Iran (KOMALA, formerly Tudeh).

"Voice of the Crusader"—see "Voice of the Mojahed," below.

"Voice of the Free Sahara" ("La Voz del Sahara Libre, La Voz del Pueblo Sahel"), Sahara Libre, Frente Polisario, B.P. 10, El-Mouradia, 16000 Algiers, Algeria; Sahara Libre, Ambassade de la République Arabe Saharaui Démocratique, 1 Av. Franklin Roosevelt, 16000 Algiers, Algeria; or B.P. 10, Al-Mouradia, Algiers, Algeria. Phone (Algeria): +213 (2) 747-907. Fax, when operating (Algeria): +213 (2) 747 984. Contact: Mohamed Lamin Abdesalem; Mahafud Zein; or Sneiba Lehbib. Free stickers, booklets, cards, maps, paper flags and calendars. Two IRCs helpful. Pro-Polisario Front; supported by Algerian government and aired via the facilities of Radiodiffusion-Télévision Algerienne.

"Voice of the Iranian Revolution" ("Aira Dangi Shurashi Irana")—see "Voice of the Communist Party of Iran," above, for details.

"Voice of the Iraqi People"—see "Radio of the Iraqi Republic from Baghdad, Voice of the Iraqi People," above.

"Voice of the Islamic Revolution in Iraq"—see "Voice of Rebellious Iraq," above, for contact information. Affiliated with the Shi'ite-oriented Supreme Assembly of the Islamic Revolution of Iraq, led by Mohammed Baqir al-Hakim.

"Voice of the Martyrs" ("Radioemission der Hilfsaktion Martyrerkirche"), Postfach 5540, D-78434 Konstanz, Germany. Possibly linked with Internationale Radioarbeits-Gemeinschaft fur die Martyrerkirche, which previously broadcast via Radio Trans-Europe, Portugal, as Radio Stephanusbotschaft. Sometimes uses facilities of Radio Intercontinental, Armenia.

"Voice of the Mojahed" ("Seda-ye Mojahed ast")
PARIS BUREAU: Mojahedines de Peuple d'Iran, 17 rue des Gords, F-95430 Auvers-sur-Oise, France. Contact: Majid Taleghani. This is the only address known to reply to listener correspondence recently. According to Rich D'Angelo of suburban Philadelphia, station replies very irregularly and slowly to pre-prepared verification cards or letters. SASE probably helpful, with correspondence in French or Persian almost certainly preferable. Sponsored by the People's Mojahedin Organization of Iran (OMPI) and the National Liberation Army of Iran.
OTHER BUREAUS: M.I.S.S., B.M. Box 9720, London WC1N 3XX, United Kingdom; P.O. Box 951, London NW11 9EL, United Kingdom; or P.O. Box 3133, Baghdad, Iraq. Contact: A. Hossein.

"Voice of Tibet," Welhavensgate 1, N-0166 Oslo, Norway. Phone: +47 2211-4980. Fax: +47 2211 4988. E-mail: http://www.twics.com/~tsgjp/tibrad.html. Contact: Svein Wilhelmsen, Project Manager; Oystein Alme, Coordinator; or Kalsang Phuljung. Joint venture of the Norwegian Human Rights House, Norwegian Tibet Committee and World-View International. Programs, which are produced in Oslo, Norway, and elsewhere, focus on Tibetan culture, education, human rights and news from Tibet. Anti-Chinese control of Tibet. Those seeking a verification for this program should enclose a prepared card or letter. Return postage helpful. Transmits via the facilities of FEBA, Seychelles.

"Voz de la Ortodoxia," P.O. Box 35-1811, José Martí Station, Miami FL 33152 USA. Contact: Mario Jiménez. Program of the Partido Ortodoxo Cubano. Via WRMI, USA.

"WINGS," P.O. Box 33220, Austin TX 78764 USA. Phone/fax:

+1 (512) 416-9000. E-mail: wings@igc.apc.org. Contact: Frieda Werden, Producer. News program of the Women's International News Gathering Service, covering such issues as women's rights, women activists and movements for sociopolitical change. Via RFPI, Costa Rica.

"World of Prophecy," 1708 Patterson Road, Austin TX 78733 USA. Contact: Texe Marrs. Conservative Christian program opposing various forms of government regulation and control, such as of the environment. Via WWCR and WHRI, USA.

DJIBOUTI   World Time +3

Radiodiffusion-Télévision de Djibouti (if reactivated), B.P. 97, Djibouti. Return postage helpful. Correspondence in French preferred. This station is currently off the air due to transmitter failure. It is unlikely to come back on the air in the forseeable future, unless the French resuscitate the failed transmitter as part of the proposed, but as yet not approved, effort to install a Radio France Internationale relay in Djibouti.

DOMINICAN REPUBLIC   World Time –4

Emisora Onda Musical (when active), Palo Hincado 204 Altos, Apartado Postal 860, Santo Domingo, Dominican Republic. Contact: Mario Báez Asunción, Director. Replies occasionally to correspondence in Spanish. $1 helpful.

La N-103/Radio Norte (when active), Apartado Postal 320, Santiago, Dominican Republic. Contact: José Darío Pérez Díaz, Director; or Héctor Castillo, Gerente.

Radio Amanecer Internacional, Apartado Postal 1500, Santo Domingo, Dominican Republic. Contact: (general) Señora Ramona C. de Suberví, Directora; (technical) Ing. Sócrates Domínguez. $1 or return postage required. Replies slowly to correspondence in Spanish.

Radio Barahona (when active), Apartado 201, Barahona, Dominican Republic; or Gustavo Mejía Ricart No. 293, Apto. 2-B, Ens. Quisqueya, Santo Domingo, Dominican Republic. Contact: (general) Rodolfo Z. Lama Jaar, Administrador; (technical) Ing. Roberto Lama Sajour, Administrador General. Free stickers. Letters should be sent via registered mail. $1 or return postage helpful. Replies to correspondence in Spanish.

Radio Cima (when active), Apartado 804, Santo Domingo, Dominican Republic. Fax: +1 (809) 541 1088. Contact: Roberto Vargas, Director. Free pennants, postcards, coins and taped music. Roberto likes collecting stamps and coins.

Radio Cristal Internacional, Apartado Postal 894, Santo Domingo, Dominican Republic. Phone: +1 (809) 565-1460. Fax: +1 (809) 567 9107. Contact: (general) Fernando Hermón Gross, Director de Programas; (administration) Darío Badía, Presidente; or Héctor Badía, Director de Administración.

Radio Quisqueya (when active), Apartado Postal 363, Puerto Plata, Dominican Republic; or Apartado Postal 135-2, Santo Domingo, Dominican Republic. Contact: Lic. Gregory Castellanos Ruano, Director. Replies occasionally to correspondence in Spanish and English.

Radio Santiago (when active), Apartado 282, Santiago, Dominican Republic. Contact: Luis Felipe Moscos Finke, Gerente; Luis Felipe Moscos Cordero, Jefe Ingeniero; or Carlos Benoit, Announcer & Program Manager.

ECUADOR   World Time –5 (–4 sometimes, in times of drought); –6 Galapagos

NOTE: According to HCJB's excellent "DX Party Line," during periods of drought, such as caused by "El Niño," electricity rationing causes periods in which transmitters cannot operate because of inadequate hydroelectric power, as well as spikes which occasionally damage transmitters. Accordingly, many Ecuadorian stations tend to be irregular, or even entirely off the air, during drought conditions.

NOTE: According to veteran Dxer Harald Kuhl in Hard-Core-DX of Kotanet Communications Ltd., IRCs are exchangeable only in the cities of Quito and Guayaquil. Too, overseas airmail postage is very expensive now in Ecuador, so when in doubt enclosing $2 for return postage is appropriate.

Ecos del Oriente (when active), Sucre y 12 de Febrero, Lago Agrio, Sucumbíos, Ecuador. Phone: +593 (6) 830-141. Contact: Elsa Irene Velástegui, Secretaria. Sometimes includes free 20 sucre note (Ecuadorian currency) with reply. $2 or return postage required. Replies, often slowly, to correspondence in Spanish.

Emisora La Voz de Chinchipe—see Radio La Voz de Chinchipe.

Emisoras Gran Colombia (if reactivated), Casilla 17-01-2246, Quito, Ecuador (new physical address: Vasco de Contreras 689 y Pasaje "A", Quito, Ecuador). Phone: +593 (2) 443-147. Phone/fax: +593 (2) 442-951. Contact: Nancy Cevallos Castro, Gerente General. Return postage required. Replies to correspondence in Spanish. Their shortwave transmitter is out of order. While they would like to repair or replace it, for the time being they don't have the funds to do so, as they have just spent what extra money they had on new premises.

Emisoras Jesús del Gran Poder, Casilla 17-01-133, Quito, Ecuador. Phone: +593 (2) 513-077.

Emisoras Luz y Vida, Casilla 11-01-222, Loja, Ecuador. Phone: +593 (7) 570-426. Contact: Hermana (Sister) Ana Maza Reyes, Directora; or Lic. Guida Carrión H., Directora de Programas. Return postage required. Replies irregularly to correspondence in Spanish.

Escuelas Radiofónicas Populares del Ecuador (when active), Casilla 06-01-693, Riobamba, Ecuador. Fax: +593 (3) 961 625. Contact: Juan Pérez Sarmiento, Director Ejecutivo; or María Ercilia López, Secretaria. Free pennants and key rings. "Chimborazo" cassette of Ecuadorian music for 10,000 sucres plus postage; T-shirts for 12,000 sucres plus postage; and caps with station logo for 8,000 sucres plus postage. Return postage helpful. Replies to correspondence in Spanish.

Estéreo Carrizal (when active), Avenida Estudiantil, Quinta Velásquez, Calceta, Ecuador. Phone: +593 (5) 685-5470. Contact: Ovidio Velásquez Alcundia, Gerente General. Free book of Spanish-language poetry by owner. Replies to correspondence in Spanish.

HCJB, Voice of the Andes
STATION: Casilla 17-17-691, Villalengua 884, Quito, Pichincha, Ecuador. Phone: +593 (2) 466-808 (X-441 for the English Dept.). Fax: +593 (2) 447 263. E-mail: (English Dept.) english@hcjb.org.ec; (Spanish Dept.) spanish@hcjb.org.ec; (Japanese Dept.) japanese@hcjb.org.ec; (Frequency Management) irops@hcjb.org.ec. URL: http://www.hcjb.org.ec. Contact: (general) English (or other language) Department; Saludos Amigos—letterbox program; (administration) Glen Volkhardt, Director of Broadcasting; or John Beck, Director of International Radio; (technical) David Lewis, Frequency Manager. Free religious brochures, calendars, stickers and pennants; free e-mail The Andean Herald newsletter. Catch the Vision book $8, postpaid. IRC or unused U.S. or Canadian stamps appreciated for airmail reply.
INTERNATIONAL HEADQUARTERS: World Radio Missionary Fellowship, Inc., P.O. Box 39800, Colorado Springs CO 80949 USA. Phone: +1 (719) 590-9800. Fax: +1 (719) 590 9801. Contact: Andrew Braio, Public Information; (administration) Richard D. Jacquin, Director, International Operations. Various items sold via U.S. address—catalog available. This address is not a mail drop, so listeners' correspondence, except those concerned with purchasing HCJB items, should be directed to the usual Quito address.
TRANSMISSION ENGINEERING CENTER: 1718 W. Mishawaka Road, Elkhart IN 46517 USA. Phone: +1 (219) 294-8201. Fax: +1 (219) 294 8329. Contact: Dave Pasechnik, Project Manager; or Bob Moore, Engineering. This address only for those professionally concerned with the design and manufacture of transmitter and antenna equipment. Listeners' correspondence should be directed to the usual Quito address.
REGIONAL OFFICES: Although HCJB has over 20 regional offices throughout the world, the station wishes that all

listener correspondence be directed to the station in Quito, as the regional offices do not serve as mail drops for the station.

La Voz de los Caras, Casilla 13-01-629, Calle Montúfar 1012, Bahía de Caráquez, Manabí, Ecuador. Fax: +593 (4) 690 305. Contact: Ing. Marcelo A. Nevárez Faggioni, Director-General. Free 50th anniversary pennants, while they last. $2 or return postage required. Replies occasionally and slowly to correspondence in English and Spanish.

La Voz de Saquisilí—Radio Libertador (when active), Casilla 669, Saquisilí, Ecuador; or Calle 24 de Mayo, Saquisilí, Cotopaxi, Ecuador. Phone: +593 (3) 721-035. Contact: Eddy Roger Velástegui Mena, Director de Relaciones Públicas; Srta. Carmen Mena Corrales; or Sra. Arturo Mena Herrera, Gerente-Propietario. $2 or mint Ecuadorian stamps for return postage; IRCs difficult to exchange. Eddy Velástegui M. is the only reliable responder at this station; but, as he is away at college most of the time, replies to correspondence tend to be slow and irregular. Spanish strongly preferred.

La Voz del Napo, Misión Josefina, Tena, Napo, Ecuador. Phone: +593 (6) 886-422. Contact: Ramiro Cabrera, Director. Free pennants and stickers. $2 or return postage required. Replies occasionally to correspondence in Spanish.

La Voz del Río Tarqui, Manuel Vega 653 y Presidente Córdova, Cuenca, Ecuador. Phone: +593 (7) 822-132. Contact: Sra. Alicia Pulla Célleri, Administración; or Sra. Rosa María Pulla. Replies irregularly to correspondence in Spanish. Has ties with station WKDM in New York.

La Voz del Upano
STATION: Vicariato Apostólico de Méndez, Misión Salesiana, 10 de Agosto s/n, Macas, Ecuador; or Casilla 602, Quito, Ecuador. Phone: +593 (7) 700 186. Contact: P. Domingo Barrueco C., Director. Free pennants and calendars. On one occasion, not necessarily to be repeated, sent tape of Ecuadorian folk music for $2. Otherwise, $2 required. Replies to correspondence in Spanish.
QUITO OFFICE: Procura Salesiana, Equinoccio 623 y Queseras del Medio, Quito, Ecuador. Phone: +593 (2) 551-012.

Radio Bahá'í, "La Emisora de la Familia," Casilla 10-02-1464, Otavalo, Imbabura, Ecuador. Phone: +593 (6) 920-245. Fax: +593 (6) 922 504. Contact: (general) William Rodríguez Barreiro, Coordinador; or Juan Antonio Reascos, Locutor; (technical) Ing. Tom Dopps. Free information about the Bahá'í faith, which teaches the unity of all the races, nations and religions, and that the Earth is one country and mankind its citizens. Free pennants. Return postage appreciated. Replies regularly to correspondence in English or Spanish. Enclosing a family photo may help getting a reply. Station is property of the Instituto Nacional de Enseñanza de la Fe Bahá'í (National Spiritual Assembly of the Bahá'ís of Ecuador). Although there are many Bahá'í radio stations around the world, Radio Bahá'í in Ecuador is the only one on shortwave.

Radio Buen Pastor—see Radio "El Buen Pastor."

Radio Católica Nacional del Ecuador (when active), Av. América 1830 y Mercadillo (Apartado 540A), Quito, Ecuador. Phone: +593 (2) 545-770. Contact: John Sigüenza, Director; Sra. Yolanda de Suquitana, Secretaria; (technical) Sra. Gloria Cardozo, Technical Director. Free stickers. Return postage required. Replies to correspondence in Spanish.

Radio Católica Santo Domingo (if reactivated), Apartado Postal 17-24-0006, Santo Domingo de los Colorados, Pichincha, Ecuador. Contact: Nancy Moncada, Secretaria; Pedro Figueroa, Director de Programas; or Padre Gualberto Pérez Paredas, Director. Free pennants. Return postage or $2 helpful. Replies to correspondence in Spanish.

Radio Centro, Casilla 18-01-574, Ambato, Ecuador. Phone: +593 (3) 822-240 or +593 (3) 841-126. Fax: +593 (3) 829 824. Contact: Luis Alberto Gamboa Tello, Director Gerente; or Lic. María Elena de López. Free stickers. Return postage appreciated. Replies to correspondence in Spanish.

Radio Centinela del Sur (C.D.S. Internacional), Casilla 11-01-106, Loja, Ecuador. Fax: +593 (7) 562 270. Contact: (general) Marcos G. Coronel V., Director de Programas; (technical) José Coronel Illescas, Director Propietario. Return postage required. Replies rarely to correspondence in Spanish.

Radio Cumandá (if reactivated)
STATION: Principal y Espejo, Coca, Napo, Ecuador. Phone: +593 (6) 315-089. Contact: Angel Bonilla, Director.
OWNER: Luís Cordero 226, Machachi, Pichincha, Ecuador. Contact: José J. Quinga, Propietario.

Radiodifusora Cultural Católica La Voz del Upano—see La Voz del Upano, above.

Radiodifusora Cultural, La Voz del Napo—see La Voz del Napo, above.

Radio "El Buen Pastor," Asociación Cristiana de Indígenas Saraguros (ACIS), Reino de Quito y Azuay, Correo Central, Saraguro, Loja, Ecuador. Phone: +593 (2) 00-146. Contact: (general) Dean Pablo Davis, Sub-director; Segundo Poma, Director; Mark Vogan, OMS Missionary; Mike Schrode, OMS Ecuador Field Director; or Zoila Vacacela, Secretaria; (technical) Miguel Kelly. $2 or return postage in the form of mint Ecuadorian stamps required, as IRCs are difficult to exchange in Ecuador. Station is keen to receive reception reports; may respond to English, but correspondence in Spanish preferred.

Radio Federación Shuar (Shuara Tuntuiri), Casilla 17-01-1422, Quito, Ecuador. Phone/fax: +593 (2) 504-264. Contact: Manuel Jesús Vinza Chacucuy, Director; or Prof. Albino M. Utitiaj P., Director de Medios. Return postage or $2 required. Replies irregularly to correspondence in Spanish.

Radio Interoceánica (if reactivated), Santa Rosa de Quijos, Cantón El Chaco, Provincia de Napo, Ecuador. Contact: Byron Medina, Gerente; or Ing. Olaf Hegmuir. $2 or return postage required, and donations appreciated (station owned by Swedish Covenant Church). Replies slowly to correspondence in Spanish or Swedish. Station's shortwave transmitter needs repair, but funds are not forthcoming, so it's anybody's guess if it will ever return to the air.

Radio Jesús del Gran Poder—see Emisoras Jesús del Gran Poder, above.

Radio La Voz de Chinchipe, Calle 12 de Febrero, Barrio Central, Zumba, Zamora Chinchipe, Ecuador. Contact: Edgar Geovanny Jumbo Pineda, Director.

Radio La Voz del Río Tarqui—see La Voz del Rio Tarqui.

Radio Luz y Vida—see Emisoras Luz y Vida, above.

Radio Municipal (if activated on world band), Alcaldía Municipal de Quito, García Moreno 887 y Espejo, Quito, Ecuador. Contact: Miguel Arízaga Q., Director. Currently not on shortwave, but hopes to activate a 2 kW shortwave transmitter—its old mediumwave AM transmitter modified for world band—on 4750 kHz once the legalities are completed. If this station ever materializes, which is looking increasingly doubtful, it is expected to welcome correspondence from abroad, especially in Spanish.

Radio Nacional Espejo, Casilla 17-01-352, Quito, Ecuador. Phone: +593 (2) 21-366. Contact: Marco Caceido, Gerente; or Mercedes B. de Caceido, Secretaria. Replies irregularly to correspondence in English and Spanish.

Radio Nacional Progreso, Casilla V, Loja, Ecuador. Contact: José A. Guamán Guajala, Director del programa "Círculo Dominical." Replies irregularly to correspondence in Spanish, particularly for feedback on "Círculo Dominical" program aired Sundays from 1100 to 1300. Return postage required.

Radio Oriental, Casilla 260, Tena, Napo, Ecuador. Phone: +593 (6) 886-033 or +593 (6) 886-388. Contact: Luis Enrique Espín Espinosa, Gerente General. $2 or return postage helpful. Reception reports welcome.

Radio Popular de Cuenca (when active), Av. Loja 2408, Cuenca, Ecuador. Phone: +593 (7) 810-131. Contact: Sra. Manena Escondón Vda. de Villavicencio, Directora y Propietaria. Return postage or $2 required. Replies rarely to correspondence in Spanish.

Radio Quito, Casilla 17-21-1971, Quito, Ecuador. Phone/fax: +593 (2) 508-301. Contact: Xavier Almeida, Gerente General; or José Almeida, Subgerente. Free stickers. Return postage required. Replies slowly, but regularly.

Sistema de Emisoras Progreso—see Radio Nacional Progreso, above.

EGYPT World Time +2 (+3 midyear)

WARNING: MAIL THEFT. Feedback from PASSPORT readership indicates that money is sometimes stolen from envelopes sent to Radio Cairo.

Radio Cairo

NONTECHNICAL: P.O. Box 566, Cairo, Egypt. Contact: Mrs. Sahar Kalil, Director of English Service to North America & Producer, "Questions and Answers"; or Mrs. Magda Hamman, Secretary. Free stickers, postcards, stamps, maps, papyrus souvenirs, calendars and *External Services of Radio Cairo* book. Free booklet and individually tutored Arabic-language lessons with loaned textbooks from Kamila Abdullah, Director General, Arabic by Radio, Radio Cairo, P.O. Box 325, Cairo, Egypt. Arabic-language religious, cultural and language-learning audio and video tapes from the Egyptian Radio and Television Union sold via Sono Cairo Audio-Video, P.O. Box 2017, Cairo, Egypt; when ordering video tapes, inquire to ensure they function on the television standard (NTSC, PAL or SECAM) in your country. Once replied regularly, if slowly, but recently replies have been increasingly scarce. Comments welcomed about audio quality—*see TECHNICAL*, below. Avoid enclosing money (*see WARNING*, above). A new 500 kW shortwave transmitter is to be brought into service in the near future to improve reception.

NONTECHNICAL, HOLY KORAN RADIO: P.O. Box 1186, Cairo, Egypt. Contact: Abd al-Samad al Disuqi, Director. Operates only on 9755 kHz.

TECHNICAL: Broadcast Engineering Department, 24th Floor—TV Building (Maspiro), Egyptian Radio and Television Union, P.O. Box 1186/11151, Cairo, Egypt. Phone/fax: (propagation and monitoring office, set to automatically receive faxes outside normal working hours; otherwise, be prepared to request a switchover from voice to fax) +20 (2) 578-9491. Fax: (ERTU projects) +20 (2) 766 909. E-mail: to be inaugurated shortly. Contact: Dr. Eng. Abdoh Fayoumi, Head of Propagation and Monitoring; or Nivene W. Laurence, Engineer. Comments and suggestions on audio quality and level especially welcomed.

ENGLAND—see UNITED KINGDOM.

EQUATORIAL GUINEA World Time +1

Radio Africa

TRANSMISSION OFFICE: Apartado 851, Malabo, Isla Bioko, Equatorial Guinea.

U.S. OFFICE FOR CORRESPONDENCE AND VERIFICATIONS: Pan American Broadcasting, 20410 Town Center Lane #200, Cupertino CA 95014 USA. Phone: +1 (408) 996-2033. Fax: +1 (408) 252 6855. E-mail: pabcomain@aol.com. Contact: (listener correspondence) Terry Kraemer; (general) Carmen Jung, Office & Sales Administrator; or James Manero. $1 in cash or unused U.S. stamps, or 2 IRCs, required for reply.

Radio East Africa—same details as "Radio Africa," above.

Radio Nacional de Guinea Ecuatorial—Bata (Radio Bata), Apartado 749, Bata, Río Muni, Equatorial Guinea. Phone: +240 08-382. Contact: José Mba Obama, Director. If no response try sending your letter c/o Spanish Embassy, Bata, enclosing $1 for return postage. Spanish preferred.

Radio Nacional de Guinea Ecuatorial—Malabo (Radio Malabo), Apartado 195, Malabo, Isla Bioko, Equatorial Guinea. Phone: +240 92-260. Fax: +240 92 097. Contact: (general) Román Manuel Mané-Abaga, Jefe de Programación; Ciprano Somon Suakin; or Manuel Chema Lobede; (technical) Hermenegildo Moliko Chele, Jefe Servicios Técnicos de Radio y Televisión. $1 or return postage required. Replies irregularly to correspondence in Spanish.

ERITREA World Time +3

Voice of the Broad Masses of Eritrea (Dimisi Hafash), EPLF National Guidance, Information Department, Radio Branch, P.O. Box 872, Asmara, Eritrea; Ministry of Information and Culture, Technical Branch, P.O. Box 243, Asmara, Eritrea; EPLF National Guidance, Information Department, Radio Branch, P.O. Box 2571, Addis Ababa, Ethiopia; EPLF National Guidance, Information Department, Radio Branch, Sahel Eritrea, P.O. Box 891, Port Sudan, Sudan; or EPLF Desk for Nordic Countries, Torsplan 3, 1 tr, S-113 64 Stockholm, Sweden. Fax (Stockholm) +46 (8) 322 337. Contact: (Eritrea) Ghebreab Ghebremedhin; (Ethiopia and Sudan) Mehreteab Tesfa Giorgis. Return postage or $1 helpful. Free information on history of station, Ethiopian People's Liberation Front and Eritrea.

ESTONIA World Time +2 (+3 midyear)

Estonian Radio (Eesti Raadio)—same details as "Radio Estonia," below, except replace "Radio Estonia, External Service, The Estonian Broadcasting Company" with "Eesti Raadio."

Radio Estonia, External Service, The Estonian Broadcasting Company, 21 Gonsiori Street, EE-0100 Tallinn, Estonia. Phone: (general) +372 (2) 434-110/5; (English Service) +372 (2) 434-252. Fax: +372 (2) 434 457. E-mail: lastname@er.ee. URL: http://www.er.ee/er.html. Contact: (general) Silja Orusalu, Editor, I.C.A. Department; Harry Tiido; Mrs. Tiina Sillam, Head of English Service; Mrs. Kai Siidiratsep, Head of Service; Enno Turmen, Head of Swedish Service; Juri Vilosius, Head of Finnish Service; Mrs. Mari Maasik, Finnish Service; or Elena Rogova; (administration) Kusta Reinsoo, Deputy Head of External Service. Free pennants. $1 required. Replies occasionally.

Mary Kroszner

The Louvre has survived its latest addition, this time a glass pyramid by modernist I.M. Pei. Just as old and new architecture are synergistic in France, so is French radio. It's now available worldwide both on traditional world band radio and leading-edge Web radio.

ETHIOPIA   World Time +3

"Radio Amahoro"—see Disestablishmentarian listing earlier in this section.

Radio Ethiopia: (external service) P.O. Box 654; (domestic service) P.O. Box 1020—both in Addis Ababa, Ethiopia. Phone: (main office) +251 (1) 116-427; (engineering) +251 (1) 200-948. Fax: +251 (1) 552 263. Contact: (external service, general) Kahsai Tewoldemedhin, Program Director; Ms. Woinshet Woldeyes, Secretary, Audience Relations; Ms. Ellene Mocria, Head of Audience Relations; or Yohaness Ruphael, Producer, "Contact"; (administration) Kasa Miliko, Head of Station; (technical) Terefe Ghebre Medhin or Zegeye Solomon. Free stickers. Very poor replier.

Radio Fana (Radio Torch), P.O. Box 30702, Addis Ababa, Ethiopia. Contact: Mulugeta Gessese, General Manager; Mesfin Alemayehu, Head, External Relations; or Girma Lema, Head, Planning and Research Department. Station is autonomous and receives its income from non-governmental educational sponsorship. Seeks help with obtaining vehicles, recording equipment and training materials.

"Voice of Peace"—see Disestablishmentarian listing earlier in this section.

FINLAND   World Time +2 (+3 midyear)

YLE Radio Finland

MAIN OFFICE: Pl 78, Fin-00024 Helsinki, Finland. Phone: (general, 24-hour English speaking switchboard for both Radio Finland and Yleisradio Oy) +358 (9) 148-01; (international information) +358 (9) 148-03729 (administration) +358 (9) 148-04320 or +358 (9) 148-04316; (Technical Customer Service) +358 (9) 148-03213. Fax: (general) +358 (9) 148 1169; (international information) +358 (9) 148 03390; (Technical Affairs) +358 (9) 148 03588. E-mail: rfinland@yle.mailnet.fi

or yleus@aol.com. URL: http://www.yle.fi/fbc.radiofin.html. Contact—Radio Finland: (English) Eddy Hawkins; (Finnish & Swedish) Pertti Seppä; (German & French) Dr. Stefan Tschirpke; (Russian) Timo Uotila and Mrs. Eija Laitinen; (administration) Juhani Niinistö, Head of External Broadcasting; (technical) Technical Customer Service. Contact—Yleisradio Oy parent organization: (general) Marja Salusjärvi, Head of International PR; (administration) Arne Wessberg, Managing Director; or Tapio Siikala, Director for Domestic & International Radio. Sometimes provides free stickers and small souvenirs, as well as tourist and other magazines. Replies to correspondence, but doesn't provide verification data.

FREQUENCY PLANNING: Bureau of Network Planning, Pl 20, Fin-00024 Helsinki, Finland. Phone: +358 (9) 1480-2787. Fax: +358 (9) 148 5260. Contact: Esko Huuhka.

MEASURING STATION: Yleisradio, Fin-05400 Jokela, Finland. Phone: +358 (9) 282-006. Fax: +358 (14) 472 410. Contact: Ing. Kari Hautala.

NORTH AMERICAN OFFICE—LISTENER & MEDIA LIAISON: P.O. Box 462, Windsor CT 06095 USA. Phone: +1 (860) 688-5540 or +1 (860) 688-5098. Phone/fax: (24-hour toll-free within U.S. and Canada for recorded schedule and voice mail) (800) 221-9539. Fax: +1 (860) 688 0113. E-mail: yleus@aol.com. Contact: John Berky, YLE Finland Transcriptions. Free YLE North America newsletter.

FRANCE   World Time +1 (+2 midyear)

☞**France Info**, 116 Ave. du Président Kennedy, F-75016 Paris, France. Phone: +33 (1) 42-30-22-22. Fax: +33 (1) 42 30 14 88. E-mail: via URL. URL: (including RealAudio) http://www.radio-france.fr/france-info/index.htm.

🔊Radio France Internationale (RFI)

MAIN OFFICE: B.P. 9516, F-75016 Paris Cedex 16, France. Phone: (general) +33 (1) 42-30-22-22; (International Affairs and Program Placement) +33 (1) 44-30-89-31 or +33 (1) 44-30-89-49; (Service de la communication) +33 (1) 42-30-29-51; (Audience Relations) +33 (1) 44-30-89-69/70/71; (Media Relations) +33 (1) 42-30-29-85; (Développement et de la communication) +33 (1) 44-30-89-21; (*Fréquence* **Monde**) +33 (1) 42-30-10-86. Fax: (general) +33 (1) 42 30 30 71; (International Affairs and Program Placement) +33 (1) 44 30 89 20; (Audience Relations) +33 (1) 44 30 89 99; (other nontechnical) +33 (1) 42 30 44 81. E-mail: fenyo@eunet.fr. URLs: http://www-rfi.eunet.fr/rfil/html; (France Infonet RealAudio News) http://www.radio-france.fr/html/france_info.html; http://www.francelink.com; http://193.107.193.136/rfil.html; http://www.fnet.fr/; (RealAudio in English) http://www.wrn.org/stations/rfi.html. Contact: Simson Najovits, Chief, English Department; J.P. Charbonnier, Producer, "Lettres des Auditeurs"; Joël Amar, International Affairs/Program Placement Department; Arnaud Littardi, Directeur du développement et de la communication; Nicolas Levkov, Rédactions en Langues Etrangères; Daniel Franco, Rédaction en français; Mme. Anne Toulouse, Rédacteur en chef du Service Mondiale en français; Christine Berbudeau, Rédacteur en chef, *Fréquence* **Monde**; or Marc Verney, Attaché de Presse; (administration) Jean-Paul Cluzel, Président-Directeur Général; (technical) M. Raymond Pincon, Producer, "Le Courrier Technique." Free *Fréquence* **Monde** bi-monthly magazine in French upon request. Free souvenir keychains, pins, lighters, pencils, T-shirts and stickers have been received by some—especially when visiting the headquarters at 116 avenue du Président Kennedy, in the chichi 16th Arrondissement. Can provide supplementary materials for "Dites-moi tout" French-language course; write to the attention of Mme. Chantal de Grandpre, "Dites-moi tout." "Le Club des Auditeurs" French-language listener's club ("Club 9516" for English-language listeners); applicants must provide name, address and two passport-type photos, whereupon they will receive a membership card and the club bulletin. RFI hopes to install a shortwave broadcasting center in Djibouti, which if approved could be operational in the not-too-distant future. RFI exists primarily to defend and promote Francophone culture, but also provides meaningful information and cultural perspectives in non-French languages. The French government under both socialist and conservative leadership has given RFI consistent and substantial support, and with that support RFI has grown and continues to grow into a leading position in International broadcasting.

TRANSMISSION OFFICE, TECHNICAL: Direction de l'Equipment et de la Production, TDF—Groupe France Telecom, Ondes décamétriques, B.P. 518, F-92542 Montrouge Cedex, France. Phone: +33 (1) 46-57-77-83 or +33 (1) 49-65-11-61. Fax: +33 (1) 49 65 19 11 or +33 (1) 49 65 21 37. URL: http://www.francetelecom.com/. Contact: Daniel Bochent, Chef du service ondes décamétriques; Alain Meunier, service ondes décamétriques; Mme. Annick Tusseau; Mme. Christiane Bouvet; or M. Michel Azibert, chef internationale. This office only for informing about transmitter-related problems (interference, modulation quality, etc.), especially by fax. Verifications not given out at this office; requests for verification should be sent to the main office, above.

UNITED STATES PROMOTIONAL, SCHOOL LIAISON, PROGRAM PLACEMENT AND CULTURAL EXCHANGE OFFICES: *New Orleans:* Services Culturels, Suite 2105, Ambassade de France, 300 Poydras Street, New Orleans LA 70130 USA. Phone: +1 (504) 523-5394. Phone/fax: +1 (504) 529-7502. E-mail: asteg@on101.com. Contact: Adam-Anthony Steg, Attaché Audiovisuel. This office promotes RFI, especially to language teachers and others in the educational community within the southern United States, and arranges for bi-

national cultural exchanges. It also sets up RFI feeds to local radio stations within the southern United States.

New York: Audiovisual Bureau, Radio France Internationale, 972 Fifth Avenue, New York NY 10021 USA. Phone: +1 (212) 439-1452. Fax: +1 (212) 439 1455. Contact: Gérard Blondel or Julien Vin. This office promotes RFI, especially to language teachers and others within the educational community outside the southern United States, and arranges for bi-national cultural exchanges. It also sets up RFI feeds to local radio stations within much of the United States.

NEW YORK NEWS BUREAU: 1290 Avenue of the Americas, New York NY 10019 USA. Phone: +1 (212) 581-1771. Fax: +1 (212) 541 4309. Contact: Ms. Auberi Edler, reporter; or Bruno Albin, reporter.

WASHINGTON NEWS BUREAU: 529 14th Street NW, Suite 1126, Washington DC 20045 USA. Phone: +1 (202) 879-6706. Contact: Pierre J. Cayrol.

SAN FRANCISCO OFFICE, SCHEDULES: 2654 17th Avenue, San Francisco CA 94116 USA. Phone: +1 (415) 564-9968. Contact: George Poppin. Self-addressed stamped envelope or IRC required for reply. This address, a volunteer office, only provides RFI schedules to listeners. All other correspondence should be sent directly to the main office in Paris.

Voice of Orthodoxy—see Belarus.

FRENCH GUIANA   World Time –3

Radio France Internationale/Swiss Radio International—Guyane Relay Station, TDF, Montsinéry, French Guiana. Contact: (technical) Chef des Services Techniques, RFI Guyane. All correspondence concerning non-technical matters should be sent directly to the main addresses (*see*) for Radio France International in France and Swiss Radio International in Berne. Can consider replies only to technical correspondence in French.

RFO Guyane, Cayenne, French Guiana. Fax: +594 30 26 49. Free stickers. Replies occasionally and sometimes slowly; correspondence in French preferred, but English often okay.

FRENCH POLYNESIA   World Time –10 Tahiti

RFO Tahiti—Radio Tahiti (while still operating), B.P. 125, Papeete, Tahiti, French Polynesia. Fax: +689 413 155 or +689 425 041. Contact: (general) J.R. Bodin; (technical) Léon Siquin, Services Techniques. Free stickers, tourist brochures and broadcast-coverage map. Three IRCs, return postage, 5 francs or $1 helpful, but not mandatory. M. Siquin and his teenage sons Xavier and Philippe, all friendly and fluent in English, collect pins from radio/TV stations, memorabilia from the Chicago Bulls basketball team and other souvenirs of American pop culture; these make more appropriate enclosures than the usual postage-reimbursement items. This station, whose indigenous island programming of yore has become increasingly European and prosaic, once hoped to obtain new studios and transmitters. Alas, the effort came to naught. Now, only one of their three ancient world band transmitters continues to function regularly and, as a result, the station will abandon world band entirely sometime in the near future.

GABON   World Time +1

Afrique Numéro Un, B.P. 1, Libreville, Gabon. Fax: +241 742 133. Contact: (general) Gaston Didace Singangoye; or A. Letamba, Le Directeur des Programmes; (technical) Mme. Marguerite Bayimbi, Le Directeur [sic] Technique. Free calendars and bumper stickers. $1, 2 IRCs or return postage helpful. Replies very slowly.

RTV Gabonaise, B.P. 10150, Libreville, Gabon. Contact: André Ranaud-Renombo, Le Directeur Technique, Adjoint Radio. Free stickers. $1 required. Replies occasionally, but slowly, to correspondence in French.

GEORGIA   World Time +4

Georgian Radio, TV-Radio Tbilisi, ul. M. Kostava 68, 380071 Tbilisi, Republic of Georgia. Phone: (domestic service) +995

(8832) 368-362 or (external service) +995 (8832) 368-885. Fax: +995 (8832) 368 665. Contact: (external service) Helena Apkhadze, Foreign Editor; Tamar Shengelia; Mrs. Natia Datuaschwili, Secretary; or Maya Chihradze; (domestic service) Lia Uumlaelsa, Manager; or V. Khundadze, Acting Director of Television and Radio Department. Replies occasionally and slowly.

Republic of Abkhazia Radio, Abkhaz State Radio & TV Co., Aidgylara Street 34, Sukhum 384900, Republic of Abkhazia; however, as of press time, according to the station there is a total embargo on mail to the Republic of Abkhazia. Contact: G. Amkuab, General Director. A 1992 uprising in northwestern Georgia drove the majority of ethnic Georgians from the region. This area remains virtually autonomous from Georgia.

GERMANY World Time +1 (+2 midyear)

Adventist World Radio, the Voice of Hope—*see* USA and Italy.

Bayerischer Rundfunk, Rundfunkplatz 1, D-80300 Munich, Germany. Fax: +49 (89) 5900 2375. URL: http://www.br-online.de/. Contact: Dr. Gualtiero Guidi; or Jutta Paue, Engineering Adviser. Free stickers and 250-page program schedule book.

Canadian Forces Network Radio—*see* CANADA.

☞Deutsche Welle, Radio and TV International

MAIN OFFICE: Postfach 10 04 44, D-50588 Cologne, Germany. Phone: (general) +49 (221) 389-2001/2; (listener's mail) +49 (221) 389-2500; (Program Distribution) +49 (221) 389-2731; (technical) +49 (221) 389-3221 or +49 (221) 389-3228; (Public Relations) +49 (221) 3890. Fax: (general) +49 (221) 389 4155, +49 (221) 389 2080 or +49 (221) 389 3000; (listeners' mail) +49 (221) 389 2510; (English Service, general) +49 (221) 389 4599; (English Service, Current Affairs) +49 (221) 389 4554; (Public Relations) +49 (221) 389 2047; (Program Distribution) +49 (221) 389 2777; (technical) +49 (221) 389 3200. E-mail: (general) dw@dw.gmd.de; (schedule information) 100144.2133@compuserve.com; (specific individuals or programs) format is firstname.lastname @dw.gmd.de, so to reach, say, Harald Schuetz, it would be harald.schuetz@dw.gmd.de; (Program Distribution) 100302.2003@compuserve.com. URL: (general) http://www-dw.gmd.de/DW; (RealAudio and text in German and English) http://www.dmc.net/dw/dw.html or http://mainnet.dmc.net/dw.html; (RealAudio in English and German) http://www.wrn.org/stations/dw.html. Contact: (general) Ursula Fleck-Jerwin, Audience Mail Department; Ernst Peterssen, Head of Audience Research and Listeners' Mail; Dr. Wilhelm Nobel, Director of Public Relations; Dr. Jochen Thies, Head, English Service; or Dr. Burkhard Nowotny, Director of Media Department; (listener questions and comments) Harald Schuetz; ("German by Radio" language course) Herrad Meese; (administration) Dieter Weirich, Director General; (technical—head of engineering) Peter Senger, Chief Engi-

Deutsche Welle to Maintain North American Service

For many years after World War II, world band audiences in North America declined in number. Yet, during this same period, station after station added transmissions to North America.

However, starting in the mid-Eighties, the American world band audience started to grow significantly for the first time in decades. Yet, in a perverse twist of logic, some stations began cutting back on their operations beamed there. Partly, of course, this was due to the end of the Cold War. But a number of stations also reasoned that because North America had so many alternative media, shortwave "obviously" would no longer be able to hold listeners—even though direct and indirect audience measurements all pointed to exactly the opposite conclusion.

Along these lines, a Deutsche Welle press release in late 1995, echoing an earlier directive from its managing director, stated that "DW will end its [non-German-language] shortwave broadcasts in free and developed countries, such as western Europe, as of next year [1996]." Bad enough that this mentality would apply to western Europe, where some industry analysts see signs that shortwave listenership is poised to grow with the imminent rise of the next sunspot cycle. But what about all the other "free and developed countries"?

Grundig's North American office contacted Deutsche Welle for an explanation. Frau Silke Bröker of DW's Technical Advisory Service replied in 1996, "In principle, it can be said that at present there are no plans whatsoever to make any changes in the shortwave coverage of North America, as we are well aware of the fact that despite all new media and technologies shortwave has and will maintain its importance in international broadcasting."

neer; (technical—Radio Frequency Department) Peter Pischalka or Horst Scholz; (technical—Technical Advisory Service) Mrs. Silke Bröker. Free pennants, stickers, key chains, pens, *Deutsch—warum nicht?* language-course book, *Germany—A European Country and its People* book, and the excellent *DW-radio tune-in* magazine. Local Deutsche Welle Listeners' Clubs in selected countries. Operates via world band transmitters in Germany, Antigua, Canada, Madagascar, Portugal, Russia, Rwanda and Sri Lanka. Deutsche Welle is scheduled to move from Cologne to Berlin in the near future. Its Wertachtal and Nauen transmission facilities are currently being upgraded with additional 500 kW transmitters. DW's Jülich site is (in the former West) Germany, with a dozen 100 kW shortwave transmitters, is to cease operation in 1997, as the station now has more than enough higher-powered facilities available to it.

ELECTRONIC TRANSMISSION OFFICE FOR PROGRAM PREVIEWS: Infomedia, 25 rue du Lac, L-8808 Arsdorf, Luxembourg. Phone: +352 649-270. Fax: +352 649 271. This office will electronically transmit Deutsche Welle program previews to you upon request; be sure to provide either a dedicated fax number or an e-mail address so they can reply to you.

BRUSSELS NEWS BUREAU: International Press Center, 1 Boulevard Charlemagne, B-1040 Brussels, Belgium.

U.S./CANADIAN LISTENER CONTACT OFFICE: P.O. Box 50641, Washington DC 20091 USA.

RUSSIAN LISTENER CONTACT OFFICE: Nemezkaja Wolna, Abonentnyj jaschtschik 596, Glawpotschtamt, 190000 St. Petersburg, Russia.

TOKYO NEWS BUREAU: C.P.O. Box 132, Tokyo 100-91, Japan.

WASHINGTON NEWS BUREAU: P.O. Box 14163, Washington DC 20004 USA. Fax: +1 (202) 526 2255. Contact: Adnan Al-Katib, Correspondent.

Deutschland Radio-Berlin, Hans-Rosenthal-Platz 1, D-10825 Berlin Schönberg, Germany. Fax: +49 (30) 850 3390. Contact: Gerda Holunder. $1 or return postage required. Free stickers and postcards.

Radio Bremen, Heinrich Hertzstr. 13, D-28329 Bremen, Germany. Fax: +49 (421) 246 1010. URL: http://www.deutschland.de/rb/. Contact: Jim Senberg. Free stickers and shortwave guidebook.

Süddeutscher Rundfunk, Neckarstr. 230, D-70049 Stuttgart, Germany. Fax: +49 (711) 929 2600. Free stickers.

Südwestfunk, Hans Bredowstr., D-76530 Baden-Baden, Germany. Fax: +49 (722) 192 2010. URL: http://www.swf/de/. Contact: (technical) Prof. Dr. Hans Krankl, Chief Engineer.

Universell Leben (Universal Life)

HEADQUARTERS: Postfach 5643, D-97006 Würzburg, Germany. Phone: +49 (931) 3903-0. Fax: (general) +49 (931) 3903 233; (engineering) +49 (931) 3903 299. E-mail: ul-buero@t-online.de. URL: http://www.universelles-leben.org. Contact: Janet Wood, English Dept; "Living in the Spirit of God" listeners' letters program. Free stickers, publications and occasional small souvenirs. Transmits "The Word, The Cosmic Wave" (Das Wort, die kosmische Welle) via the Voice of Russia, WWCR (USA) and various other world band stations, as well as "Vida Universal" via Radio Miami Internacional and WHRI in the United States. Replies to correspondence in English, German or Spanish.

SALES OFFICE: Das WORT GmbH, Im Universelles Leben, Max-Braun-Str. 2, D-97828 Marktheidenfeld/Altfeld, Germany. Sells books, audio cassettes and videos related to broadcast material.

NORTH AMERICAN BUREAU: The Inner Religion, P.O. Box 3549, Woodbridge CT 06525 USA. Phone: +1 (203) 281-7771. Fax: +1 (203) 230 2703.

Voice of America/VOA-IBB Network Control Center (NCC), Ismaning. Fax: +49 (89) 964 739. Contact: (administration) James Lambert, Manager; (technical) Ing. Innozenz Kastner or Ing. Georg Pflaumbaum. This NCC location manages satellite interface in Germany for the IBB (*see*, USA).

GHANA   World Time exactly

WARNING—CONFIDENCE ARTISTS: Attempted correspondence with Radio Ghana may result in requests, perhaps resulting from mail theft, from skilled confidence artists for money, free electronic or other products, publications or immigration sponsorship. To help avoid this, correspondence to Radio Ghana should be sent via registered mail.

Radio Ghana, Ghana Broadcasting Corporation, P.O. Box 1633, Accra, Ghana. Fax: +233 (21) 773 227. Contact: (general) Maud Blankson-Mills, Head, Audience Research; Robinson Aryee, Head, English Section; Emmanuel Felli, Head, French Section; or Victor Markin, Producer, English Section; (administration) Mrs. Anna Sai, Assistant Director of Radio; (technical) E. Heneath, Propagation Department. Mr. Markin states that he is interested in reception reports, as well as feedback on the program he produces, "Health Update," so directing your correspondence to him may be the best bet. Otherwise, replies are increasingly scarce, but whomever you send your correspondence to, you should register it, and enclose an IRC, return postage or $1.

GREECE   World Time +2 (+3 midyear)

Foni tis Helladas (Voice of Greece)

NONTECHNICAL: Elliniki Radiophonia Tileorasi S.A., ERT-5 Program, Foni tis Helladas, P.O. Box 60019, GR-153 10 Aghia Paraskevi Attikis, Athens, Greece. Phone: +30 (1) 638-0381 or +30 (1) 600-9341. Fax: +30 (1) 600 9608. E-mail: daggel@leon.nrcps.ariadne-t.gr. URL: http://alpha.servicenet.ariadne-t.gr/Docs/Era5_1/html. Contact: Kosta Valetas, Director, Programs for Abroad. Free tourist literature.

TECHNICAL: Frequency Management Department, Elliniki Radiophonia Tileorasi S.A., General Technical Directorate, Direction of Engineering and Development, ERT-5th Program, P.O. Box 60019, GR-153 10 Aghia Paraskevi Attikis, Athens, Greece. Phone: +30 (1) 601-4700 or +30 (1) 639-6762. Fax: +30 (1) 639 0652 or +30 (1) 600 9608. E-mail: skalai@leon.nrcps.ariadne-t.gr. Contact: (general) Demetri H. Vafeas, Chief Engineer; Ing. Dionisios Angelogiannis; Frequency Manager; or Ing. Filotas Gianotas; (administration) Th. Kokossis, General Director; or Nicolas Yannakakis, Director. Taped reports not accepted.

Radiophonikos Stathmos Makedonias—ERT-3, Angelaki 2, GR-546 21 Thessaloniki, Greece. Phone: +30 (31) 264-800. Fax: +30 (31) 236 466. E-mail: charter3@compulink.gr. Contact: (general) Mrs. Tatiana Tsioli, Program Director; or Lefty Kongalides, Head of International Relations; (technical) Dimitrios Keramidas, Engineer. Free booklets and other small souvenirs.

Voice of America/VOA-IBB—Kaválla Relay Station. Phone: +30 (5) 912-2855. Fax: +30 (5) 913 1310. Contact: Michael Nardi, Relay Station Manager. These numbers for urgent technical matters only. Otherwise, does not welcome direct correspondence; *see* USA for acceptable VOA Washington address and related information.

Voice of America/VOA-IBB—Rhodes Relay Station. Phone: +30 (241) 24-731. Fax: +30 (241) 27 522. Contact: Wesley Robinson, Relay Station Manager. These numbers for urgent technical matters only. Otherwise, does not welcome direct correspondence; *see* USA for acceptable VOA Washington address and related information.

GUAM   World Time +10

Adventist World Radio, the Voice of Hope—KSDA
AWR-Asia, P.O. Box 7468, Agat, Guam 96928 USA. Phone: +671 585-2000. Fax: +671 565 2983. E-mail: 74617.2361@compuserv.com; 70673.2552@compuserve.com. URL: (limited RealAudio, plus text) http://ourworld.compuserve.com/homepages/awr_asia. Contact: (general) Lolita Colegado, Listener Mail Services; (technical) Elvin Vence, Engineer. Free stickers, quarterly *AWR Current*, program schedule and religious printed matter.

Also, *see* AWR listings under Costa Rica, Guatemala, Italy, Kenya, Russia and the USA.

Trans World Radio—KTWR

MAIN OFFICE, NONTECHNICAL: P.O. Box CC, Agana, Guam 96910 USA. Phone: +671 477-9701. Fax: +671 477 2838. E-mail: (general) wfrost@twr.hafa.net.gu; (technical) gzensen@twr.hafa.net.gu. URL: http://www.twr.org/guam.htm. Contact: (general) Karen Zeck, Listener Correspondence; James Elliott, Producer, "Friends in Focus" listeners' questions program; Wayne T. Frost, Program Director & Producer, "Pacific DX Report"; or Kathy Gregowski; (administration) Edward Stortro, Station Director; (technical) George Ross. Also, *see* USA. Free small publications. Plans to add, very shortly, a 100kW transmitter and a 7 MHz antenna.
FREQUENCY COORDINATION OFFICE: 1868 Halsey Drive, Asan, Guam 96922 USA. Phone: +671 828-8637. Fax: +671 828 8636. E-mail: ktwrfreq@twr.hafa.net.gu. Contact: George Zensen, Chief Engineer.
AUSTRALIAN OFFICE: G.P.O. Box 602D, Melbourne 3001, Australia. Phone: +61 (3) 9872-4606. Fax: +61 (3) 9874 8890. Contact: John Reeder, Director.
HONG KONG OFFICE: Unit 1, Block A, Room 901, 9/F, Po Lung Centre, 11 Wang Chiu Road, Kowloon Bay, Kowloon, Hong Kong. Contact: Joyce Lok, Programme Manager.
INDIA OFFICE: P.O. Box 4310, New Delhi-110 019, India. Contact: N. Emil Jebasingh, Vishwa Vani; or S. Stanley.
"ARDXC REPORT" PROGRAM: ARDXC, Box 227, Box Hill 3128 VIC, Australia. URL: http://www.eagles.bbs.net.au/~andrewt/ardxc/index/html. Return postage necessary.
SINGAPORE BUREAU, NONTECHNICAL: 273 Thomson Road, 03-03 Novena Gardens, Singapore 1130, Singapore.
TOKYO OFFICE: C.P.O. Box 1000, Tokyo Central Post Office, Tokyo 100-91, Japan. Fax: +81 (3) 3233 2650.

GUATEMALA   World Time –6

Adventist World Radio, the Voice of Hope—Unión Radio, Apartado Postal 51-C, Guatemala City, Guatemala. E-mail: mundi@guate.net. Contact: D. Rolando García P., Gerente General. Free tourist and religious literature and Guatemalan stamps. Return postage, 3 IRCs or $1 appreciated. Correspondence in Spanish preferred. Also, *see* AWR listings under Costa Rica, Guam, Italy, Kenya, Russia and the USA.

Radio Cultural—TGNA, Apartado de Correo 601, Guatemala City, Guatemala. Phone: +502 (2) 427-45 or +502 (2) 443-78. Contact: Mariela Posadas, QSL Secretary; or Wayne Berger, Chief Engineer. Free religious printed matter. Return postage or $1 appreciated.

La Voz de Atitlán—TGDS, Santiago Atitlán, Guatemala. Contact: Juan Ajtzip Alvarado, Director; José Miguel Pop Tziná; or Esteban Ajtzip Tziná, Director Ejecutivo. Return postage required. Replies to correspondence in Spanish.

La Voz de Nahualá, Nahualá, Sololá, Guatemala. Contact: (technical) Juan Fidel Lepe Juárez, Técnico Auxiliar; or F. Manuel Esquipulas Carrillo Tzep. Return postage required. Correspondence in Spanish preferred.

Radio Buenas Nuevas, 13020 San Sebastián, Huehuetenango, Guatemala. Contact: Israel G. Rodas Mérida, Gerente. $1 or return postage helpful. Free religious and station information in Spanish. Replies to correspondence in Spanish.

Radio Coatán, San Sebástian Coatán, Huehuetenango, Guatemala. Contact: Domingo Hernández, Director; or Virgilio José, Locutor.

Radio Chortís, Centro Social, 20004 Jocotán, Chiquimula, Guatemala. Contact: Padre Juan María Boxus, Director. $1 or return postage required. Replies irregularly to correspondence in Spanish.

Radio K'ekchi—TGVC, K'ekchi Baptist Association, 16015 Fray Bartolomé de las Casas, Alta Verapaz, Guatemala. Contact: Gilberto Sun Xicol, Gerente; Carlos Díaz Araújo, Director; Ancelmo Cuc Chub, Locutor y Director; or David

Daniel, Media Consultant. Free paper pennant. $1 or return postage required. Replies to correspondence in Spanish.

Radio Mam, Acu'Mam, Cabricán, Quetzaltenango, Guatemala. Contact: Porfirio Pérez, Director. Free stickers and pennants. $1 or return postage required. Replies irregularly to correspondence in Spanish. Donations permitting (the station is religious), they would like to get a new transmitter to replace the current unit, which is failing.

Radio Maya de Barillas—TGBA, 13026 Villa de Barillas, Huehuetenango, Guatemala. Contact: José Castañeda, Pastor Evangélico y Gerente. Free pennants and pins. $1 or return postage required. Replies occasionally to correspondence in Spanish and Indian languages.

Radio Tezulutlán—TGTZ, Apartado de Correo 19, 16901 Cobán, Guatemala. Contact: Sergio W. Godoy, Director; or Hno. Antonio Jacobs, Director Ejecutivo. Pennant for donation to specific bank account. $1 or return postage required. Replies to correspondence in Spanish.

GUINEA   World Time exactly

Radiodiffusion-Télévision Guinéenne, B.P. 391, Conakry, Guinea. Contact: (general) Yaoussou Diaby, Journaliste Sportif; (administration) Alpha Sylla, Directeur, Sofoniya I Centre de Transmission; (technical, studio) Mbaye Gagne, Chef de Studio; (technical, overall) Direction des Services Techniques. Return postage or $1 required. Replies very irregularly to correspondence in French.

GUYANA   World Time –3

Voice of Guyana, Guyana Broadcasting Corporation, P.O. Box 10760, Georgetown, Guyana. Phone: +592 (2) 587-34. Fax: +592 (2) 587 56, but persist as fax machine appears to be switched off much of the time. Contact: (technical) Roy Marshall, Senior Technician; or Shiroxley Goodman, Chief Engineer. $1 or IRC helpful. Sending a spare sticker from another station helps assure a reply.

HOLLAND (THE NETHERLANDS)   World Time +1 (+2 midyear)

☞Radio Nederland Wereldomroep (Radio Netherlands)
MAIN OFFICE: Postbus 222, 1200 JG Hilversum, The Netherlands. Phone: (general) +31 (35) 672-4211; (English Department) +31 (35) 672-4242; (Answerline) +31 (35) 672-4222; (Frequency Planning) +31 (35) 672-4425 or +31 (35) 672-4213; (Program Placement) +31 (35) 672-4258. Fax: (general) +31 (35) 672 4352, but indicate destination department on fax cover sheet; (Programme Directorate) +31 (35) 72 4252; (English Department) +31 (35) 672 4239; (Distribution & Frequency Planning Department) +31 (35) 672 4429 or +31 (35) 672 4207. E-mail: (general) letters@rnw.nl. ("Media Network") media@rnw.nl; (employee contact) firstname.lastname@rnw.nl; (miscellaneous) vonb@rnw.nl or von@pobox.work.com. URL: (text and audio in .wav) http://www.rnw.nl; http://www.xs4all.nl/~vonb/. Contact: (general) Jonathan Marks, Director of Programs; Rina Miller, Head English Department; Mike Shea, Network Manager English; Iris Walstra, English Correspondence; Diana Janssen, Producer, Media Network; Lee Martin, North American program placement; or Robert Chesal, Host, "Sounds Interesting" (include your telephone number); (administration) Lodewijk Bouwens, Director General; (technical, including for full-data verifications) Jan Willem Drexhage, Head of Distribution and Frequency Planning; or Ehard Goddijn. Full-data verification card if the report is correct and follows guidelines issued in the RNW flyer, "Writing Useful Reception Reports," available upon request. Semi-annual *On Target* newsletter also free upon request, as are stickers and booklets. RNW produces its own CDs, mainly of classical and world music. Visitors welcome, but it is helpful to call in advance. A New York office is expected to open shortly.
WASHINGTON NEWS BUREAU: 1773 Lanier Place, Apt. 1, Washington DC 20009 USA. Phone: +1 (202) 265-9530. Contact: Arnoud Hekkens.

Radio Budapest's English staff. From left, Mike Mitchell, Karl Kirk, Györgyi Jakobi, Enikő Zsuffa, Ágnes Kevi, Renáta Winkelbauer, Charlie Coutts, Sándor Laczkó, Nicholas Jenkins and Bálint Sebestyén. Not shown: Sándor Kőröspataki and Vera Sárkány.

LATIN AMERICAN OFFICE: (local correspondence only) Apartado 880-1007, Ventro Colón, Costa Rica. This address solely for correspondence to RNW's Costa Rican employees, who speak only Spanish. All other correspondence should be sent directly to Holland.

NEW DELHI OFFICE: (local correspondence only) P.O. Box 5257, Chanakya Puri Post Office, New Delhi-110 021, India. All non-local correspondence should be sent directly to Holland.

HONDURAS World Time −6

La Voz de la Mosquitia

STATION: Puerto Lempira, Región Mosquitia, Honduras. Contact: Sammy Simpson, Director; Sra. Wilkinson; or Larry Sexton. Free pennants.

U.S. OFFICE: Global Outreach, Box 1, Tupelo MS 38802 USA. Phone: +1 (601) 842-4615.

La Voz Evangélica—HRVC

MAIN OFFICE: Apartado Postal 3252, Tegucigalpa, M.D.C., Honduras. Phone: +504 34-3468/69/70. Fax: +504 33 3933. Contact: (general) Srta. Orfa Esther Durón Mendoza, Secretaria; Tereso Ramos, Director de Programación; or Modesto Palma, Jefe, Depto. Tráfico; (technical) Carlos Paguada, Director del Dpto. Técnico; (administration) Venancio Mejía, Gerente; Nelson Perdomo, Director. Free calendars. Three IRCs or $1 required. Replies to correspondence in English, Spanish, Portuguese and German.

REGIONAL OFFICE, SAN PEDRO SULA: Apartado 2336, San

Pedro Sula, Honduras. Phone: +504 57-5030. Contact: Hernán Miranda, Director.

REGIONAL OFFICE, LA CEIBA: Apartado 164, La Ceiba, Honduras. Phone: +504 43-2390. Contact: José Banegas, Director.

U.S. OFFICE: Conservative Baptist Home Mission Society, Box 828, Wheaton IL 60187 USA. Phone: +1 (708) 260-3800, ext. 1217. Fax: +1 (708) 653 4936. Contact: Jill W. Smith.

Radio Copán Internacional—HRJA

STATION: Apartado 955, Tegucigalpa, M.D.C., Honduras.

MIAMI OFFICE: P.O. Box 526852, Miami FL 33152 USA. Phone: +1 (305) 267-1728. Fax: +1 (305) 267 9253. E-mail: 71163.1735@compuserve.com. Contact: Jeff White. Sells airtime for $1 per minute to anybody in any language to say pretty much whatever they want.

Radio HRET

STATION: Primera Iglesia Bautista, Domicilio Conocido, Puerto Lempira, Gracias a Dios 33101, Honduras. Fax: +504 980 018. Contact: Leonardo Alvarez López, Locutor y Operador; Desiderio Williams, Locutor y Operador. Return postage necessary. Replies, sometimes slowly, to correspondence in Spanish. Currently installing new transmitter, which should be on the air very shortly, and redesigning their antenna.

NONTECHNICAL ENGLISH CORRESPONDENCE: David Daniell, Asesor de Comunicaciones, Apartado Postal 25, Bulevares, MX 53140, Mexico. Replies to correspondence in English and Spanish.

TECHNICAL ENGLISH CORRESPONDENCE: Ing. Larry Baysinger, 8000 Casualwood Ct., Louisville KY 40291 USA. Replies to correspondence in English and Spanish, but calls not accepted.

Radio Internacional, Apartado 1473, San Pedro Sula, Honduras. Phone: +504 528-181. Fax: +504 581 070. Contact: Víctor Antonio ("Tito") Handal, Gerente y Propietario; or Hugo Hernández y Claudia Susana Prieto, Locutores del "Desfile de Estrellas," aired Sunday at 0200-0500 World Time. Free stickers, stamps, postcards and one-lempira banknote. $1 helpful. Appears to reply regularly to correspondence in Spanish.

Radio Litoral (when active), La Ceiba, Atlántida Province, Honduras. Contact: José A. Mejía, Gerente y Propietario. Free postcards. $1 or return postage necessary. Replies to correspondence in Spanish.

Radio Luz y Vida—HRPC, Apartado 303, San Pedro Sula, Honduras. Fax: +504 57 0394. Contact: C. Paul Easley, Director; or, to have your letter read over the air, "English Friendship Program." Return postage or $1 appreciated.

Sani Radio (when active), Apartado 113, La Ceiba, Honduras. Contact: Jacinto Molina G., Director; or Mario S. Corzo. Return postage or $1 required.

HONG KONG   World Time +8

NOTE: Hong Kong is scheduled to revert to Chinese rule on July 1st, 1997. Thus, for all Hong Kong station information except the BBC World Service, look under "China."

BBC World Service—Hong Kong Relay, East Asia Relay Company Ltd, Tsang Tsui Broadcasting Station Nim Wan, Tuen Mun, New Territories, Hong Kong. Contact: Miles Ashton; (technical) Phillip Sandell, Resident Engineer. Nontechnical correspondence should be sent to the BBC World Service in London (see). The BBC will dismantle this facility, so it can't be used for jamming, before Hong Kong reverts to Chinese rule in 7/97 (also, see Thailand).

HUNGARY   World Time +1 (+2 midyear)

Radio Budapest

STATION OFFICES: Bródy Sándor utca 5-7, H-1800 Budapest, Hungary. Phone: (general) +36 (1) 138-7339, +36 (1) 138-8328, +36 (1) 138-7357 +36 (1) 138-8588, +36 (1) 138-7710 or +36 (1) 138-7723; (voice mail, English) +36 (1) 138-8320; (voice mail, German) +36 (1) 138-7325; (administration) +36 (1) 138-7503 or +36 (1) 138-8415; (technical) +36 (1) 138-7226 or +36 (1) 138-8923. Fax: (general) +36 (1) 138 8517; (administration) +36 (1) 138 8838; (technical) +36 (1) 138 7105. E-mail: (Radio Budapest, English) angol1@kaf.radio.hu; (Radio Budapest, German) nemetl@kaf.radio.hu; (Hungarian Information Resources) avadasz@bluemoon.sma.com. URLs: (RealAudio in English and Hungarian) http://www.wrn.org/stations/hungary.html; (general)) http://www.eunet.hu/radio; (shortwave program) http://www.glue.umd.edu/-gotthard/hir/entertainment/radio/; (North American Service via Hungarian Information Resources) http://mineral.umd.edu/hir/Entertainment/Radio/Shortwave. Contact: (English Language Service) Ágnes Kevi, Correspondence; Charles Taylor Coutts, Producer, "Gatepost" (listeners' letters' program) & Head of English Language Service; Louis Horváth, DX Editor; or Sándor Laczkó, Editor; (administration) Antal Réger, Director, Foreign Broadcasting; Dr. Zsuzsa Mészáros, Vice-Director, Foreign Broadcasting; János Szirányi, President, Magyar Rádió; or János Simkó, Vice President, Magyar Rádió; (technical) László Füszfás, Deputy Technical Director, Magyar Rádió, Külföldi Adások Főszerkesztősége; or Lajos Horváth, Műszaki Igazgatósá; (Hungarian Information Resources) Andrew Vadasz. Free Budapest International periodical, stickers, pennants, stamps and printed tourist and other material. Also, for those whose comments or program proposals are used over the air, T-shirts, baseball-style caps and ballpoint pens. RBSWC DX News bulletin free to all Radio Budapest Shortwave Club members. Advertisements considered.

TRANSMISSION AUTHORITY: Ministry of Transport, Communications & Water Management, P.O. Box 87, H-1400 Budapest, Hungary. Phone/fax: +36 (1) 156-3493. Fax: +36 (1) 461 3392. Contact: Ferenc Horváth, Frequency Manager, Radio Communications Engineering Services.

ICELAND   World Time exactly

Radio Alpha & Omega, Omega Television, P.O. Box 3340, 123 Reykjavík, Iceland. Phone: +354 (5) 67-6111. Fax: +354 (5) 68-3741. Contact: Eirikur Sigurbjoernson. This Christian station, which currently operates via leased-time transmission facilities in Jülich, Germany, sells tape recordings for $20.

Ríkisútvarpid, International Relations Department, Efstaleiti 1, 150 Reykjavík, Iceland. Phone: +354 (5) 15-3000. Fax: +354 (5) 15 3010. E-mail: heimirs@ruv.is. URL: http://www.ruv.is/. Contact: Dóra Ingvadóttir, Head of International Relations; or Heimir Steinsson, Webmaster.

INDIA   World Time +5:30

NOTE: The facility "New Broadcasting House" is being built to supplement the existing Broadcasting House on Parliament Street. It is to be used by the domestic and external services, alike, and is scheduled to be in full operation before 2001.

Ministry of Information & Broadcasting, Main Secretariat, A-Wing, Shastri Bhawan, New Delhi-110 001, India. Phone: (general) +91 (11) 384-340, +91 (11) 384-782 or +91 (11) 379-338; (Information & Broadcasting Secretary) +91 (11) 382-639. Fax: +91 (11) 383 513. Contact: (general) B. Ghose, Information & Broadcasting Secretary; (administration) K.P. Singh Deo, Minister for Information & Broadcasting.

Akashvani—Governing Body for All India Radio

ADMINISTRATION: Directorate General of All India Radio, Akashvani Bhawan, 1 Sansad Marg, New Delhi-110 001, India. Phone: (general) +91 (11) 371-0006; (Engineer-in-Chief) +91 (11) 371-0058; (Frequency Management) +91 (11) 371-0145; (Director General) +91 (11) 371-0300 or +91 (11) 371-4061. Fax: +91 (11) 371-1956. E-mail: (Web maintenance) rdair@giasd101.vsnl.net.in. URL: http://air.kode.net. Contact: (general) S.K. Kapoor, Director General; (technical) H.M. Joshi, Engineer-in-Chief; or S.A.S. Abidi, Assistant Director and Frequency Manager.

AUDIENCE RESEARCH: Audience Research Unit, All India Radio, Press Trust of India Building, 2nd floor, Sansad Marg, New Delhi-110 001, India. Phone: +91 (11) 371-0033. Contact: S.K. Khatri, Director.

INTERNATIONAL MONITORING STATION—MAIN OFFICE: International Monitoring Station, All India Radio, Dr. K.S. Krishnan Road, Todapur, New Delhi-110 097, India. Phone: (general) +91 (11) 581-461; (Control Room) +91 (11) 680-2362; (administration) +91 (11) 680-2306. Contact: S. Haider, Director.

INTERNATIONAL MONITORING STATION—FREQUENCY PLANNING: Central Monitoring Station, All India Radio, Ayanagar, New Delhi-100 047, India. Phone: +91 (11) 666-306. Contact: (technical) D.P. Chhabra, Assistant Resident Engineer (Frequency Planning).

All India Radio—Aizawl, Radio Tila, Tuikhuahtlang, Aizawl-796 001, Mizoram, India. Phone: +91 (3652) 2415. Contact: (technical) D.K. Sharma, Station Engineer.

All India Radio—Bangalore

HEADQUARTERS: see All India Radio—External Services Division.

AIR OFFICE NEAR TRANSMITTER: P.O. Box 5096, Bangalore-560 001, Karnataka, India. Phone: +91 (80) 261-243. Contact: (technical) C. Iyengar, Supervising Engineer.

All India Radio—Bhopal, Akashvani Bhawan, Shamla Hills, Bhopal-462 002, Madhya Pradesh, India. Phone: +91 (755) 540-041. Contact: (technical) C. Lal, Station Engineer.

All India Radio—Bombay

EXTERNAL SERVICES: see All India Radio—External Services Division.

DOMESTIC SERVICE: P.O. Box 13034, Bombay-400 020, India. Phone: +91 (22) 202-9853. Contact: (general) Sarla Mirchandani, Programme Executive, for Station Director; (technical) S. Sundaram, Supervising Engineer. Return postage helpful.

All India Radio—Calcutta, G.P.O. Box 696, Calcutta—700 001, West Bengal, India. Phone: +91 (33) 281-705. Contact: (technical) R.N. Dam, Supervising Engineer.

All India Radio—Delhi—see All India Radio—New Delhi.

All India Radio—External Services Division, Parliament Street, P.O. Box 500, New Delhi-110 001, India. Phone: +91 (11) 371-0057 or +91 (11) 371-5411. Contact: (general) P. M. Iyer, Director of External Services; A. S. Guin, Director of Frequency Assignments; or S.C. Panda, Audience Relations Officer; (technical) S.A.S. Abidi, Assistant Director Engineering (F.A.). E-mail: (Web maintenance) rdair@giasd101.vsnl.net.in. URL: http://air.kode.net/glance/external.htm. Free monthly *India Calling* magazine and stickers. Replies erratic. Except for stations listed below, correspondence to domestic stations is more likely to be responded to if it is sent via the External Services Division; request that your letter be forwarded to the appropriate domestic station.

All India Radio—Gangtok, Old MLA Hostel, Gangtok—737 101, Sikkim, India. Phone: +91 (11) 3592-226-36. Contact: (general) N.P. Yolmo, Station Director; (technical) Deepak Kumar, Station Engineer.

All India Radio—Gorakhpur

NEPALESE EXTERNAL SERVICE: see All India Radio—External Services Division.

DOMESTIC SERVICE: Post Bag 26, Gorakhpur-273 001, Uttar Pradesh, India. Phone: +91 (551) 337-401. Contact: (technical) Dr. S.M. Pradhan, Supervising Engineer.

All India Radio—Guwahati, P.O. Box 28, Chandmari, Guwahati-781 003, Assam, India. Phone: +91 (361) 540-135. Contact: (technical) P.C. Sanghi, Superintend Engineer.

All India Radio—Hyderabad, Rocklands, Saifabad, Hyderabad-500 004, Andhra Pradesh, India. Phone: +91 (842) 234-904. Contact: (technical) N. Srinivasan, Supervising Engineer.

All India Radio—Imphal, Palau Road, Imphal-795 001, Manipur, India. Phone: +91 (385) 220-534. Contact: (technical) M. Jayaraman, Supervising Engineer.

All India Radio—Itanagar, Naharlagun, Itanagar-791 110, Arunachal Pradesh, India. Phone: +91 (11) 3781-4485. Contact: J.T. Jirdoh, Station Director; or Suresh Naik, Superintending Engineer. Verifications direct from station are difficult, as engineering is done by staff visiting from the Regional Engineering Headquarters at AIR—Guwahati (see); that address might be worth contacting if all else fails.

All India Radio—Jaipur, 5 Park House, Mirza Ismail Road, Jaipur-302 001, Rajasthan, India. Phone: +91 (141) 366-263. Contact: (technical) S.C. Sharma, Station Engineer.

All India Radio—Jammu—see Radio Kashmir—Jammu.

All India Radio—Kohima, Kohima-797 001, Nagaland, India. Phone: +91 (3866) 2121. Contact: (technical) K.G. Talwar, Superintending Engineer; or K. Morang, Assistant Station Engineer. Return postage, $1 or IRC helpful.

All India Radio—Kurseong, Mehta Club Building, Kurseong-734 203, Darjeeling District, West Bengal, India. Phone: +91 (3554) 350. Contact: (general) George Kuruvilla, Assistant Director; (technical) R.K. Shina, Station Engineer.

All India Radio—Leh—see Radio Kashmir—Leh.

All India Radio—Lucknow, 18 Vidhan Sabha Marg, Lucknow-226 001, Uttar Pradesh, India. Phone: +91 (522) 244-130. Contact: R.K. Singh, Supervising Engineer. This station now appears to be replying via the External Services Division, New Delhi.

All India Radio—Madras

EXTERNAL SERVICES: see All India Radio—External Services Division.

DOMESTIC SERVICE: Kamrajar Salai, Mylapore, Madras-600 004, Tamil Nadu, India. Phone: +91 (44) 845-975. Contact: (technical) S. Bhatia, Supervising Engineer.

All India Radio—New Delhi, P.O. Box 70, New Delhi-110 011, India. Phone: (voice mail for information in English and Hindi about domestic programs) +91 (11) 376-1166; (general) +91 (11) 371-0113. Contact: (technical) G.C. Tyagi, Supervising Engineer. $1 helpful.

All India Radio—Panaji

HEADQUARTERS: see All India Radio—External Services Division, above.

AIR OFFICE NEAR TRANSMITTER: P.O. Box 220, Altinho, Panaji-403 001, Goa, India. Phone: +91 (832) 45-563. Contact: (technical) V.K. Singhla, Station Engineer; or G.N. Shetti, Assistant Engineer.

A second 250 kW transmitter is now coming into operation on 15290 kHz but, according to expert Indian radio researcher Manosij Guha, the station continues to be hampered by a lack of staff and an unstable electric supply.

All India Radio—Port Blair, Dilanipur, Port Blair-744 102, South Andaman, Andaman & Nicobar Islands, Union Territory, India. Phone: +91 (3192) 20-682. Contact: (general) P.L. Thakur; (technical) Yuvraj Bajaj, Station Engineer. Registering letter appears to be useful. Don't send any cash with your correspondence as it appears to be a violation of their foreign currency regulations.

All India Radio—Ranchi, 6 Ratu Road, Ranchi-834 001, Bihar, India. Phone: +91 (651) 302-358. Contact: (technical) H.N. Agarwal, Supervising Engineer.

All India Radio—Shillong, P.O. Box 14, Shillong-793 001, Meghalaya, India. Phone: +91 (364) 224-443 or +91 (364) 222-781. Contact: (general) C. Lalsaronga, Director NEIS; (technical) H.K. Agarwal, Supervising Engineer. Free booklet on station's history.

All India Radio—Shimla, Choura Maidan, Shimla-171 004, Himachal Pradesh, India. Phone: +91 (177) 4809. Contact: (technical) B.K. Upadhyay, Supervising Engineer; or P.K. Sood, Assistant Station Engineer. Return postage helpful.

All India Radio—Srinagar—see Radio Kashmir—Srinagar.

All India Radio—Thiruvananthapuram, P.O. Box 403, Bhakti Vilas, Vazuthacaud, Thiruvananthapuram-695 014, Kerala, India. Phone: +91 (471) 65-009. Contact: (technical) K.M. Georgekutty, Station Engineer.

Radio Kashmir—Jammu, Begum Haveli, Old Palace Road, Jammu-180 001, Jammu & Kashmir, India. Phone: +91 (191) 544-411. Contact: (technical) S.K. Sharma, Station Engineer.

Radio Kashmir—Leh, Leh-194 101, Ladakh District, Jammu & Kashmir, India. Phone: +91 (1982) 2263. Contact: (technical) L.K. Gandotar, Station Engineer.

Radio Kashmir—Srinagar, Sherwani Road, Srinagar—190 001, Jammu & Kashmir, India. Phone: +91 (194) 71-460. Contact: L. Rehman, Station Director.

Radio Tila—see All India Radio—Aizawl.

Trans World Radio

STUDIO: P.O. Box 4407, L-15, Green Park, New Delhi-110 016, India. Phone: +91 (11) 662-058. Fax: +91 (11) 686 8049. URL: http://www.twr.org/srilanka.htm. Contact: N. Emil Jebasingh, Director.

ON-AIR ADDRESS: P.O. Box 5, Andhra Pradesh, India.

INDONESIA World Time +7 Western: Waktu Indonesia Bagian Barat (Jawa, Sumatera); +8 Central: Waktu Indonesia Bagian Tengal (Bali, Kalimantan, Sulawesi, Nusa Tenggara); +9 Eastern: Waktu Indonesia Bagian Timur (Irian Jaya, Maluku).

NOTE: Except where otherwise indicated, Indonesian stations, especially those of the Radio Republik Indonesia (RRI) network, will reply to at least some correspondence in English. However, correspondence in Indonesian is more likely to ensure a reply.

Kang Guru II Radio English, Indonesia Australia Language Foundation, Kotak Pos 6756 JKSRB, Jakarta 12067,

Indonesia. E-mail: kangguru@server.indo.net.id. URL: http://www.indo.net.id/commercial/waterfall/kangguru.html. Contact: Greg Clough, Kang Guru Project Manager. This program is aired over various RRI outlets, including Jakarta and Sorong. Continuation of this project, currently sponsored by Australia's AusAID, will depend upon whether adequate supplementary funding can be made available.

Radio Pemerintah Daerah TK II—RPD Poso, Jalan Jenderal Sudirman 7, Poso, Sulawesi Tengah, Indonesia. Contact: Joseph Tinagari, Kepala Stasiun. Return postage necessary. Replies occasionally to correspondence in Indonesian.

Radio Pemerintah Daerah Kabupaten TK II—RPDK Berau, Jalan SA Maulana, Tanjungredeb, Kalimantan Timur, Indonesia. Contact: Kus Syariman. Return postage necessary.

Radio Pemerintah Daerah Kabupaten—RPDK Bolaang Mongondow, Jalan S. Parman 192, Kotamobagu, Sulawesi Utara, Indonesia. Replies occasionally to correspondence in Indonesian.

Radio Pemerintah Daerah Kabupaten TK II—RPDK Buol-Tolitoli, Jalan Mohamed Ismail Bantilan No. 4, Tolitoli 94511, Sulawesi Tengah, Indonesia. Contact: Said Rasjid, Kepala Studio; Wiraswasta, Operator/Penyiar; or Muh. Yasin, SM. Return postage required. Replies extremely irregularly to correspondence in Indonesian.

Radio Pemerintah Daerah Kabupaten TK II—RPDK Ende, Jalan Panglima Sudirman, Ende, Flores, Nusa Tenggara Timor, Indonesia. Contact: (technical) Thomas Keropong, YC9LHD. Return postage required.

Radio Pemerintah Daerah Kabupaten TK II—RPDK Manggarai, Ruteng, Flores, Nusa Tenggara Timur, Indonesia. Contact: Simon Saleh, B.A. Return postage required.

Radio Pemerintah Daerah Kabupaten TK II—RPDK Tapanuli Selatan, Kotak Pos No. 9, Padang-Sidempuan, Sumatera Utara, Indonesia. Return postage required.

Radio Republik Indonesia—RRI Ambon, Jalan Jenderal Akhmad Yani 1, Ambon, Maluku, Indonesia. Contact: Drs. H. Ali Amran or Pirla C. Noija, Kepala Seksi Siaran. A very poor replier to correspondence in recent years. Correspondence in Indonesian and return postage essential.

Radio Republik Indonesia—RRI Banda Aceh, Kotak Pos No. 112, Banda Aceh, Aceh, Indonesia. Contact: S.H. Rosa Kim. Return postage helpful.

Radio Republik Indonesia—RRI Bandung, Stasiun Regional 1, Kotak Pos No. 1055, Bandung 40010, Jawa Barat, Indonesia. Contact: Drs. Idrus Alkaf, Kepala Stasiun; Idrus Alkaf, Director; Mrs. Ati Kusmiati; or Eem Suhaemi, Kepala Seksi Siaran. Return postage or IRC helpful.

Radio Republik Indonesia—RRI Banjarmasin, Stasiun Nusantara 111, Kotak Pos No. 117, Banjarmasin 70234, Kalimantan Selatan, Indonesia. Contact: Jul Chaidir, Stasiun Kepala; or Harmyn Husein. Return postage or IRCs helpful.

Radio Republik Indonesia—RRI Bengkulu, Stasiun Regional 1, Kotak Pos No. 13 Kawat, Kotamadya Bengkulu, Indonesia. Contact: Drs. H. Harmyn Husein, Kepala Stasiun. Free picture postcards, decals and tourist literature. Return postage or 2 IRCs helpful.

Radio Republik Indonesia—RRI Biak, Kotak Pos No. 505, Biak, Irian Jaya, Indonesia.

Radio Republik Indonesia—RRI Bukittinggi, Stasiun Regional 1 Bukittinggi, Jalan Prof. Muhammad Yamin No. 199, Aurkuning, Bukittinggi 26131, Propinsi Sumatera Barat, Indonesia. Fax: +62 (752) 367 132. Contact: Mr. Effendi, Sekretaris; Zul Arifin Mukhtar, SH; or Samirwan Sarjana Hukum, Producer, "Phone in Program." Replies to correspondence in Indonesian or English. Return postage helpful.

Radio Republik Indonesia—RRI Denpasar, P.O. Box 31, Denpasar, Bali, Indonesia. Replies slowly to correspondence in Indonesian. Return postage or IRCs helpful.

Radio Republik Indonesia—RRI Dili, Stasiun Regional 1 Dili, Jalan Kaikoli, Kotak Pos 103, Dili 88000, Timor-Timur, Indonesia. Contact: Harry A. Silalahi, Kepala Stasiun;

Arnoldus Klau; or Paul J. Amalo, BA. Return postage or $1 helpful. Replies occasionally to correspondence in Indonesian.

Radio Republik Indonesia—RRI Fak Fak, Jalan Kapten P. Tendean, Kotak Pos No. 54, Fak-Fak 98601, Irian Jaya, Indonesia. Contact: A. Rachman Syukur, Kepala Stasiun; Bahrum Siregar; Aloys Ngotra, Kepala Seksi Siaran; or Richart Tan, Kepala Sub Seksi Siaran Kata. Return postage required. Replies occasionally.

Radio Republik Indonesia—RRI Gorontalo, Jalan Jenderal Sudirman, Gorontalo, Sulawesi Utara, Indonesia. Contact: Emod. Iskander, Kepala; or Saleh S. Thalib, Technical Manager. Return postage helpful. Replies occasionally, preferably to correspondence in Indonesian.

Radio Republik Indonesia—RRI Jakarta

STATION: Stasiun Nasional Jakarta, Kotak Pos No. 356, Jakarta, Jawa Barat, Indonesia. Contact: Drs.R. Baskara, Stasiun Kepala; or Syamsul Muin Harahap, Manager. Return postage helpful. Replies irregularly.

"DATELINE" ENGLISH PROGRAM: see Kang Guru II Radio English.

Radio Republik Indonesia—RRI Jambi, Jalan Jenderal A. Yani No. 5, Telanaipura, Jambi 36122, Propinsi Jambi, Indonesia. Contact: Marlis Ramali, Manager; M. Yazid, Kepala Siaran; or Bucnari Muhammad, Kepala Stasiun. Return postage helpful.

Radio Republik Indonesia—RRI Jayapura, Jalan Tasangkapura No. 23, Jayapura 99222, Irian Jaya, Indonesia. Contact: Harry Liborang, Direktorat Radio; or Dr. David Alex Siahainenia, Kepala. Return postage helpful.

Radio Republik Indonesia—RRI Kendari, Kotak Pos No. 7, Kendari 93111, Sulawesi Tenggara, Indonesia. Contact: H. Sjahbuddin, BA; or Drs. Supandi. Return postage required. Replies slowly to correspondence in Indonesian.

Radio Republik Indonesia—RRI Kupang (Regional I), Jalan Tompello No. 8, Kupang, Timor, Indonesia. Contact: Alfonsus Soetarno, BBA, Kepala Stasiun; Qustigap Bagang, Kepala Seksi Siaran; or Said Rasyid, Kepala Studio. Return postage helpful. Correspondence in Indonesian preferred. Replies occasionally.

Radio Republik Indonesia—RRI Madiun, Jalan Mayor Jenderal Panjaitan No. 10, Madiun, Jawa Timur, Indonesia. Fax: +62 (351) 4964. Contact: Imam Soeprapto, Kepala Seksi Siaran. Replies to correspondence in English or Indonesian. Return postage helpful.

Radio Republik Indonesia—RRI Malang, Kotak Pos No. 78, Malang 65112, Jawa Timur, Indonesia; or Jalan Candi Panggung No. 58, Mojolangu, Malang 65142, Indonesia. Contact: Drs.Tjutju Tjuar Na Adikorya, Kepala Stasiun; Ml. Mawahib, Kepala Seksi Siaran; or Dra Hartati Soekemi, Mengetahui. Return postage required. Free history and other booklets. Replies irregularly to correspondence in Indonesian.

Radio Republik Indonesia—RRI Manado, Kotak Pos No. 1110, Manado 95124 Propinsi Sulawesi Utara, Indonesia. Fax: +62 (431) 63 492. Contact: Costher H. Gulton, Kepala Stasiun. Free stickers and postcards. Return postage or $1 required. Replies occasionally to correspondence in Indonesian.

Radio Republik Indonesia—RRI Manokwari, Regional II, Jalan Merdeka No. 68, Manokwari, Irian Jaya, Indonesia. Contact: P.M. Tisera, Kepala Stasiun; or Nurdin Mokogintu. Return postage helpful.

Radio Republik Indonesia—RRI Mataram, Stasiun Regional I Mataram, Jalan Langko No. 83, Mataram 83114, Nusa Tenggara Barat, Indonesia. Contact: Drs. Hamid Djasman, Kepala; or Harnama, Ketua Dewan Pimpinan Harian. Free stickers. Return postage required. With sufficient return postage or small token gift, sometimes sends tourist information and Batik print. Replies to correspondence in Indonesian.

Radio Republik Indonesia—RRI Medan, Jalan Letkol

Martinus Lubis No. 5, Medan 20232, Sumatera, Indonesia. Phone: +62 (61) 324-222/441. Fax: +62 (61) 512 161. Contact: Kepala Stasiun, Ujamalul Abidin Ass; Drs. Syamsui Muin Harahap; Drs. S. Parlin Tobing, SH, Produsennya, "Kontak Pendengar"; Drs. H. Suryanta Saleh; or Suprato. Free stickers. Return postage required. Replies to correspondence in Indonesian.

Radio Republik Indonesia—RRI Merauke, Stasiun Regional 1, Kotak Pos No. 11, Merauke, Irian Jaya, Indonesia. Contact: (general) Achmad Ruskaya B.A., Kepala Stasiun, Drs.Tuanakotta Semuel, Kepala Seksi Siaran; or John Manuputty, Kepala Subseksi Pemancar; (technical) Daf'an Kubangun, Kepala Seksi Tehnik. Return postage helpful.

Radio Republik Indonesia—RRI Nabire, Kotak Pos No. 110, Jalan Merdeka 74 Nabire 98801, Irian Jaya, Indonesia. Contact: Muchtar Yushaputra, Kepala Stasiun. Free stickers and occasional free picture postcards. Return postage or IRCs helpful.

Radio Republik Indonesia—RRI Padang, Kotak Pos No. 77, Padang 25121, Sumatera Barat, Indonesia. Phone: +61 (751) 28-363. Contact: Marlis Ramali; Syair Siak, Kepala Stasiun; or Amir Hasan, Kepala Seksi Siaran. Return postage helpful.

Radio Republik Indonesia—RRI Palangkaraya, Jalan M. Husni Thamrin No. 1, Palangkaraya 73111, Kalimantan Tengah, Indonesia. Phone: +62 (514) 21-779. Fax: +62 (514) 21 778. Contact: Drs.Amiruddin; S. Polin; A.F. Herry Purwanto; Meyiwati SH; Supardal Djojosubrojo, Sarjana Hukum; Gumer Kamis; or Ricky D. Wader, Kepala Stasiun. Return postage helpful. Will respond to correspondence in Indonesian or English.

Radio Republik Indonesia—RRI Palembang, Jalan Radio No. 2, Km. 4, Palembang, Sumatera Selatan, Indonesia. Contact: Drs. H. Mursjid Noor, Kepala Stasiun; H.A. Syukri Ahkab, Kepala Seksi Siaran; or H.Iskandar Suradilaga. Return postage helpful. Replies slowly and occasionally.

Radio Republik Indonesia—RRI Palu, Jalan R.A. Kartini No. 39, 94112 Palu, Sulawesi Tengah, Indonesia. Phone: +62 (451) 21-621. Contact: Akson Boole; Untung Santoso; Nyonyah Netty Ch. Soriton, Kepala Seksi Siaran; or M. Hasjim, Head of Programming. Return postage required. Replies slowly to correspondence in Indonesian.

Radio Republik Indonesia—RRI Pekanbaru, Jalan Jenderal Sudirman No. 440, Kotak Pos 51, Pekanbaru, Riau, Indonesia. Phone: +62 (761) 22-081. Fax: +62 (761) 23 605. Contact: (general) Drs. Mukidi, Kepala Stasiun; Arisun Agus, Kepala Seksi Siaran; or Zainal Abbas; (technical) A. Hutasuhut, Kepala Seksi Teknik. Return postage helpful.

Radio Republik Indonesia—RRI Pontianak, Kotak Pos No. 6, Pontianak 78111, Kalimantan Barat, Indonesia. Contact: Daud Hamzah, Kepala Seksi Siaran; Achmad Ruskaya, BA; Drs. Effendi Afati, Producer, "Dalam Acara Kantong Surat"; Subagio, Kepala Sub Bagian Tata Usaha; Suryadharma, Kepala Sub Seksi Programa; or Muchlis Marzuki B.A. Return postage or $1 helpful. Replies some of the time to correspondence in Indonesian (preferred) or English.

Radio Republik Indonesia—RRI Samarinda, Kotak Pos No. 45, Samarinda, Kalimantan Timur 75001, Indonesia. Phone: +62 (541) 43-495. Fax: +62 (541) 41 693. Contact: Siti Thomah, Kepala Seksi Siaran; Tyranus Lenjau, English Announcer; S. Yati; Marthin Tapparan; or Sunendra, Kepala Stasiun. May send tourist brochures and maps. Return postage helpful. Replies to correspondence in Indonesian.

Radio Republik Indonesia—RRI Semarang, Kotak Pos No. 1073, Semarang Jateng, Jawa Tengah, Indonesia. Phone: +62 (24) 316 501. Contact: Djarwanto, SH; Drs. Sabeni, Doktorandus; Drs. Purwadi, Program Director; Dra. Endang Widiastuti, Kepala Sub Seksi Periklanan Jasa dan Hak Cipta; Bagus Giarto, Kepala Stasiun; or Mardanon, Kepala Teknik. Return postage helpful.

Radio Republik Indonesia—RRI Serui, Jalan Pattimura Kotak Pos 19, Serui 98211, Irian Jaya, Indonesia. Contact: Agus Raunsai, Kepala Stasiun; J. Lolouan, BA, Kepala Studio; Ketua Tim Pimpinan Harian, Kepala Seksi Siaran; or Drs. Jasran Abubakar. Replies occasionally to correspondence in Indonesian. IRC or return postage helpful.

Radio Republik Indonesia—RRI Sibolga, Jalan Ade Irma Suryani, Nasution No. 5, Sibolga, Sumatera Utara, Indonesia. Contact: Mrs. Laiya, Mrs. S. Sitoupul or B.A. Tanjung. Return postage required. Replies occasionally to correspondence in Indonesian.

Radio Republik Indonesia—RRI Sorong
STATION: Jalan Jenderal Achmad Yani No. 44, Klademak II, Kotak Pos 146, Sorong 98414, Irian Jaya, Indonesia. Phone: +62 (951) 21-003, +62 (951) 22-111, or +62 (951) 22-611. Contact: Drs. Sallomo Hamid; Tetty Rumbay S., Kasubsi Siaran Kata; Mrs. Tien Widarsanto, Resa Kasi Siaran; Ressa Molle; or Linda Rumbay. Return postage helpful.
"DATELINE" ENGLISH PROGRAM: See Kang Guru II Radio English.

Radio Republik Indonesia—RRI Sumenep, Jalan Urip Sumoharjo No. 26, Sumenep, Madura, Jawa Timur, Indonesia. Contact: Badarus Sjamsi, Kepala, Wseksi Siaran. Return postage helpful.

Radio Republik Indonesia—RRI Surabaya, Stasiun Regional 1, Kotak Pos No. 239, Surabaya 60271, Jawa Timur, Indonesia. Phone: +62 (31) 41-327. Fax: +62 (31) 42 351. Contact: Zainal Abbas, Kepala Stasiun; Drs.Agus Widjaja, Kepala Subseksi Programa Siaran; Usmany Johozua, Kepala Seksi Siaran; or Ny Koen Tarjadi. Return postage or IRCs helpful.

Radio Republik Indonesia—RRI Surakarta, Kotak Pos No. 40, Surakarta 57133, Jawa Tengah, Indonesia. Contact: H. Tomo, B.A., Head of Broadcasting. Return postage helpful.

Radio Republik Indonesia—RRI Tanjungkarang, Kotak Pos No. 24, Bandar Lampung 35213, Indonesia. Phone: +62 (721) 52-280. Fax: +62 (721) 62 767. Contact: Hi Hanafie Umar; Djarot Nursinggih, Tech. Transmission; Drs. Zulhaqqi Hafiz, Kepala Sub Seksi Periklanan; Asmara Haidar Manaf; or Sutakno, S.E., Kepala Stasiun. Return postage helpful. Replies in Indonesian to correspondence in English or Indonesian.

Radio Republik Indonesia—RRI Tanjung Pinang, Stasiun RRI Regional II Tanjung Pinang, Kotak Pos No. 8, Tanjung Pinang 29123, Riau, Indonesia. Contact: M. Yazid, Kepala Stasiun; Wan Suhardi, Produsennya, "Siaran Bahasa Melayu"; or Rosakim, Sarjana Hukum. Return postage helpful. Replies occasionally to correspondence in Indonesian or English.

Radio Republik Indonesia—RRI Ternate, Jalan Kedaton, Ternate (Ternate), Maluku, Indonesia. Contact: (general) Abd. Latief Kamarudin, Kepala Stasiun; (technical) Rusdy Bachmid, Head of Engineering; or Abubakar Alhadar. Return postage helpful.

Radio Republik Indonesia Tual, Tual, Kepulauan Kai, Maluku, Indonesia.

Radio Republik Indonesia—RRI Ujung Pandang, RRI Nusantara IV, Kotak Pos No. 103, Ujung Pandang, Sulawesi Selatan, Indonesia. Contact: H. Kamaruddin Alkaf Yasin, Head of Broadcasting Department; L.A. Rachim Ganie; or Drs. Bambang Pudjono. Return postage, $1 or IRCs helpful. Replies irregularly and sometimes slowly.

Radio Republik Indonesia—RRI Wamena, RRI Regional II, Kotak Pos No. 10, Wamena, Irian Jaya 99501, Indonesia. Contact: Yoswa Kumurawak, Penjab Subseksi Pemancar. Return postage helpful.

Radio Republik Indonesia—RRI Yogyakarta, Jalan Amat Jazuli 4, Kotak Pos 18, Yogyakarta 55224, Jawa Tengah, Indonesia. Fax: +62 (274) 2784. Contact: Phoenix Sudomo Sudaryo; Tris Mulyanti, Seksi Programa Siaran; Martono, ub. Kabid Penyelenggaraan Siaran; Mr. Kadis, Technical Department; or Drs. H. Hamdan Sjahbeni, Kepala Stasiun.

IRC, return postage or $1 helpful. Replies occasionally to correspondence in Indonesian or English.

Radio Siaran Pemerintah Daerah TK II—RSPD Halmahera Tengah, Soasio, Jalan A. Malawat, Soasio, Maluku Tengah 97812, Indonesia. Contact: Drs. S. Chalid A. Latif, Kepala Badan Pengelola.

Radio Siaran Pemerintah Daerah TK II—RSPD Sumba Timur, Jalan Gajah Mada No. 10 Hambala, Waingapu, Nusa Tenggara Timur 87112, Indonesia. Contact: Simon Petrus, Penanggung Jawab Operasional. Replies slowly and rarely to correspondence in Indonesian.

Radio Siaran Pemerintah Daerah Kabupaten TK II—RSPDK Maluku Tengah, Jalan Pattimura, Masohi, Seram, Maluku Tengah, Indonesia. Contact: Toto Pramurahardja, BA, Kepala Stasiun. Replies slowly to correspondence in Indonesian.

Radio Siaran Pemerintah Daerah Kabupaten Daerah TK II—RSPDKD Ngada, Jalan Soekarno-Hatta, Bjawa, Flores, Nusa Tenggara Tengah, Indonesia. Phone: +62 (384) 21-142. Contact: Drs. Petrud Tena, Kepala Studio.

Voice of Indonesia, Kotak Pos No. 1157, Jakarta 10001, Indonesia. Phone: +62 (21) 720-3467, +62 (21) 355-381 or +62 (21) 349-091. Fax: +61 (21) 345 7132. Contact: Anastasia Yasmine, Head of Foreign Affairs Section.

IRAN World Time +3:30
Voice of the Islamic Republic of Iran
MAIN OFFICE: IRIB External Services, P.O. Box 19395-6767, Tehran, Iran. Phone: (IRIB Public Relations) +98 (21) 204-001/2/3 and +98 (21) 204-6894/5. Fax: (external services) +98 (21) 204 1097 or +98 (21) 291 095; (IRIB Public Relations) +98 (21) 205 3305/7; (IRIB Central Administration) +98 (21) 204 1051; (technical) +98 (21) 654 841. Contact: (general) Hamid Yasamin, Public Affairs; Ali Larijani, Head; or Hameed Barimani, Producer, "Listeners Special"; (administration) J. Ghanbari, Director General; or J. Sarafraz, Deputy Managing Director; (technical) M. Ebrahim Vassigh, Frequency Manager. Free seven-volume set of books on Islam, magazines, calendars, book markers, tourist literature and postcards. Verifications require a minimum of two days' reception data, plus return postage. If English Service doesn't reply, then try writing the French Service in French.
ENGINEERING ACTIVITIES, TEHRAN: IRIB, P.O. Box 15875-4344, Tehran, Iran. Phone: +98 (21) 2196-6127. Fax: +98 (21) 204 1051; +98 (21) 2196 6268 or +98 (21) 172 924. Contact: Mrs. Niloufar Parviz.
ENGINEERING ACTIVITIES, HESSARAK/KARAJ: IRIB, P.O. Box 155, Hessarak/Karaj, Iran. Phone: +98 (21) 204-0008. Fax: +98 (21) 2196 6268. Contact: Mohsen Amiri.
BONN BUREAU, NONTECHNICAL: Puetzsir 34, 53129 Bonn, Postfach 150 140, D-53040 Bonn, Germany. Phone: +49 (228) 231-001. Fax: +49 (228) 231 002.
LONDON BUREAU, NONTECHNICAL: c/o WTN, IRIB, The Interchange Oval Road, Camden Lock, London NWI, United Kingdom. Phone: +44 (171) 284-3668. Fax: + 44 (171) 284 3669.
PARIS BUREAU, NONTECHNICAL: 27 rue de Liège, escalier B, 1e étage, porte D, F-75008 Paris, France. Phone: + 33 (1) 42-93-12-73. Fax: +33 (1) 42 93 05 13.
Mashhad Regional Radio, P.O. Box 555, Mashhad Center, Jomhoriye Eslame, Iran. Contact: J. Ghanbari, General Director.

IRAQ World Time +3 (+4 midyear)
Holy Medina Radio—see Radio Iraq International, below, for contact information.
Radio Iraq International (Idha'at al-Iraq al-Duwaliyah)
MAIN OFFICE: P.O. Box 8145, Baghdad, Iraq. Contact: Muzaffar 'Abd-al'-Al, Director; or Jamal Al-Samaraie, Head of Department. All broadcasting facilities in Iraq are currently suffering from severe operational difficulties.
INDIA ADDRESS: P.O. Box 3044, New Delhi 110003, India.

Radio of Iraq, Call of the Kinfolk (Idha'at al-Iraq, Nida' al-Ahl)—same details as "Radio Iraq International," above.
Voice of Arab Syria—see Radio Iraq International, above, for contact information.

IRELAND World Time exactly (+1 midyear)
Mid-West Radio
HEADQUARTERS: County Mayo Radio Limited, P.O. Box 1, Abbey Street, Ballyhaunis, Co. Mayo, Ireland. Phone: +353 (907) 30-553. Fax: +353 (907) 30 285. E-mail: soumayo@iol.ie. URL: http://www.mayo-ireland.ie/Mayo/Towns/BallyH/MWR/MWRsched.htm. Contact: P. Claffey, Managing Director; or J. O'Toole, Secretary. Broadcasts on world band occasionally, such as on St. Patrick's Day, to such places as North America, Europe, Africa and the Middle East, via facilities of the BBC World Service. Hopes to make service more regular, perhaps weekly, if funds permit. Correspondence welcomed.
WORLD BAND CORRESPONDENCE: Michael Commins, Murneen, Claremorris, Co. Mayo, Ireland. Phone: +353 (94) 81-531. Verifies reception reports with a special QSL card.
☞Radio Telefís Eireann (Irish Overseas Broadcasting), P.O. Box 4950, Dublin 1, Ireland. Phone, offices: (general) +353 (1) 208-3111; (Broadcasting Development) +353 (1) 208-2350. Phone, concise news bulletins: (United States, special charges apply) (900) 420-2411; (United Kingdom) +44 (891) 871-116; (Australia) +61 (55) 211-40. Phone, concise sports bulletins: (United States, special charges apply) (900) 420-2412; (United Kingdom) +44 (891) 871-117; (Australia) +61 (55) 211-41. Fax: (general) +353 (1) 208 3082; (Broadcasting Development) +353 (1) 208 3031. E-mail: boyd@tv.rte.ie. URLs: (general) http://www.rte.ie/; http://www.bess.tcd.ie/ireland/rte.html; (RealAudio in English and Gaelic) http://www.rte.ie/sounds.html; (RealAudio, some programs) http://www.wrn.org/stations/rte.html. Contact: Wesley Boyd, Director of Broadcast Development; Julie Hayde; or Bernie Pope, Reception. IRC appreciated. Via facilities of WWCR (USA) and the BBC (U.K.).

ISRAEL World Time +2 (+3 midyear)
Bezeq, The Israel Telecommunication Corp Ltd, Engineering & Planning Division, Radio & T.V. Broadcasting Section, P.O. Box 29555, 61 294 Tel-Aviv, Israel. Phone: +972 (3) 519-4479. Fax: +972 (3) 510 0696, +972 (3) 519 4614 or +972 (3) 515 1232. URL: http://www.bezeq.co.il/. Contact: Rafael Shamir, Radio Frequency Manager; Johanan Rotem, Frequency Manager; or Marian Kaminski, Head of AM Radio Broadcasting. Bezeq is responsible for transmitting the programs of the Israel Broadcasting Authority (IBA), which *inter alia* parents Kol Israel. This address only for pointing out transmitter-related problems (interference, modulation quality, network mixups, etc.), especially by fax, of transmitters based in Israel. Verifications not given out at this office; requests for verification should be sent to English Department of Kol Israel (see below).
Galei Zahal, Zahal, Military Mail No. 01005, Israel. Phone: +972 (3) 512-6666. Fax: +972 (3) 512 6760. Contact: Yitshak Pasternak, Director. Israeli law allows the Galei Zahal, as well as the Israel Broadcasting Authority, to air broadcasts beamed to outside Israel.
☞Kol Israel (Israel Radio, the Voice of Israel)
STUDIOS: Israel Broadcasting Authority, P.O. Box 1082, 91 010 Jerusalem, Israel. Phone: (general) +972 (2) 302-222; (Engineering Dept.) +972 (2) 535-051; (administration) +972 (2) 248-715. Fax: (English Service) +972 (2) 253 282; (Engineering Dept.) +972 (2) 388 821; (other) +972 (2) 248 392 or +972 (2) 302 327. E-mail: ask@israel-info.gov.il. URLs: (media and communications) gopher://israel-info.gov.il/00/cul/media/950900.med; (Foreign Ministry, general information on Israeli broadcasting) http://www.israel-mfa.gov.il; (RealAudio with English and Hebrew news, but only via download, then playback) http://www.artificia.com/html/news.cgi. Contact: (general) Sara Manobla, Head of English Service; Edmond Sehayeq, Head of Programming, Arabic,

Penguin

The sights and sounds of Italy are captured daily in English, Italian and other languages from Radio Roma. Operated by RAI, this powerful world band service is heard nearly everywhere.

Persian & Yemenite broadcasts; Yishai Eldar, Senior Editor, English Service; (administration) Shmuel Ben-Zvi, Director; (technical, frequency management) Raphael Kochanowski, Director of Liaison & Coordination, Engineering Dept. Various political, religious, tourist, immigration and language publications. IRC required for reply.
SAN FRANCISCO OFFICE, SCHEDULES: 2654 17th Avenue, San Francisco CA 94116 USA. Phone: +1 (415) 564-9968. Contact: George Poppin. Self-addressed stamped envelope or IRC required for reply. This address, a volunteer office, only provides Kol Israel schedules. All other correspondence should be sent directly to the main office in Jerusalem.

ITALY   World Time +1 (+2 midyear)
NOTE: The future of some Italian commercial world band stations is currently up in the air as a result of a government fee of approximately $20,000 per year nominally being levied upon private Italian broadcasters since 1996.
Adventist World Radio, the Voice of Hope, AWR-Europe, P.O. Box 383, 47100 Forlì, Italy. Phone: +39 (543) 766-655. Fax: +39 (543) 768 198. E-mail: awritaly@mbox.queen.it. Contact: Erika Gysin, Listener Mail Services. This office will verify reports for AWR broadcasts from Italy, Russia and Slovakia. Free religious printed matter, quarterly *AWR Current* newsletter, stickers, program schedules and other small souvenirs. At PASSPORT TO WORLD BAND RADIO press time, AWR had license applications pending in Italy for its existing station at Forli, as well as for a new facility in Argenta. Also, *see* AWR listings under Costa Rica, Guam, Guatemala, Kenya, Russia and USA.
DX PROGRAM: "Radio Magazine," produced by Dario Villani.
European Christian Radio, Postfach 500, A-2345 Brunn, Austria. Fax: +39 (2) 29 51 74 63. Contact: John Adams, Director; or C.R. Coleman, Station Manager. $1 or 2 IRCs required.

Italian Radio Relay Service, IRRS-Shortwave, Nexus IBA, C.P. 11028, I-20110 Milan MI, Italy. Phone: +39 (2) 214-614 or +39 (2) 266-6971. Fax: +39 (2) 706 38151. E-mail: (general) info@nexus.org; ("Hello There" program) ht@nexus.org; (reception reports of test transmissions) test@nexus.org; (other reception reports) reports@nexus.org; (International Public Access Radio, a joint venture of IRRS and WRMI, USA) IPAR@nexus.org; URLs: (general) http://www.nexus.org; (RealAudio) http://www.nexus.org/IRN/index.html; (schedules) http://www.nexus.org/nexus-iba/schedules; (International Public Access Radio) http://www.nexus.org/IPAR. Contact: (general) Alfredo E. Cotroneo, President & Producer of "Hello There"; (technical) Ms. Anna S. Boschetti, Verification Manager. Free station literature. Two IRCs or $1 helpful.
Radio Europa International, via Gerardi 6, I-25124 Brescia, Italy. Contact: Mariarosa Zahella. Replies irregularly, but return postage helpful.
Radio Europe, via Davanzati 8, I-20158 Milan MI, Italy. Phone: +39 (2) 3931-0347. Fax: +39 (2) 8645 0149. E-mail: 100135.54@compuserve.com. Contact: Dario Monferini, Foreign Relations Director; or Alex Bertini, General Manager. Pennants $5 and T-shirts $25. $30 for a lifetime membership to Radio Europe's Listeners' Club. Membership includes T-shirt, poster, stickers, flags, gadgets, and so forth, with a monthly drawing for prizes. Application forms available from station. Sells airtime for $20 per hour. Two IRCs or $1 return postage appreciated.
Radio Maria, Via Turati 7, I-22036 Erba, Italy.
Radiorama Radio, C.P. 873, I-34100 Trieste, Italy. Contact: Valerio G. Cavallo. Program over the Italian Radio Relay Service (*see*). Verifies directly.
Radio Roma-RAI International (external services)
MAIN OFFICE: External/Foreign Service, Centro RAI, Saxa

Rubra, I-00188 Rome, Italy; or P.O. Box 320, Correspondence Sector, 00100 Rome, Italy. Phone: +39 (6) 33-17-2360. Fax: +39 (6) 33 17 18 95 or +39 (6) 322 6070. E-mail: (experimental Web site in Italian) webmaster@rai.it. URLs: (Radio Roma) http://www.rai.it/raiintern/; (experimental RAI RealAudio service in Italian) http://www.rai.it/grr. Contact: (general) Rosaria Vassallo, Correspondence Sector; or Augusto Milana, Editor-in-Chief, Shortwave Programs in Foreign Languages; (administration) Angela Buttiglione, Managing Director; or Gabriella Tambroni, Assistant Director. Free stickers, banners, calendars and *RAI Calling from Rome* magazine. Can provide supplementary materials, including on VHS and CD-ROM, for Italian-language video course, "Viva l' italiano," with an audio equivalent soon to be offered, as well. Is constructing "a new, more powerful and sophisticated shortwave transmitting center" in Tuscany; when this is activated, RAI International plans to expand news, cultural items and music in Italian and various other language services—including Spanish, Portuguese, Italian, plus new services in Chinese and Japanese. Responses can be very slow.

SHORTWAVE FREQUENCY MONITORING OFFICE: RAI Monitoring Station, Centro di Controllo, Via Mirabellino 1, I-20052 Monza (MI), Italy. Phone: +39 (39) 388-389. Phone/fax (ask for fax): +39 (39) 386-222. Contact: Signora Giuseppina Moretti, Frequency Management.

ENGINEERING OFFICE, ROME: Via Teulada 66, I-00195 Rome, Italy. Phone: +39 (6) 331 70721. Fax: +39 (6) 331 75142 or +39 (6) 372 3376. Contact: Clara Isola.

ENGINEERING OFFICE, TURIN: Via Cernaia 33, I-10121 Turin, Italy. Phone: +39 (11) 810-2293. Fax: +39 (11) 575 9610. Contact: Giuseppe Allamano.

NEW YORK OFFICE, NONTECHNICAL: 1350 Avenue of the Americas —21st floor, New York NY 10019 USA. Phone: +1 (212) 468-2500. Fax: +1 (212) 765 1956. Contact: Umberto Bonetti, Deputy Director of Radio Division. RAI caps, aprons and tote bags for sale at Boutique RAI, c/o the aforementioned New York address.

SAN FRANCISCO OFFICE, SCHEDULES: 2654 17th Avenue, San Francisco CA 94116 USA. Phone: +1 (415) 564-9968. Contact: George Poppin. Self-addressed stamped envelope or IRC required for reply. This address, a volunteer office, only provides RAI schedules to listeners. All other correspondence should be sent directly to the main office in Rome.

Radio Speranza (when active), Largo San Giorgio 91, I-41100 Modena, Italy. Phone/fax: +39 (59) 230-373. Contact: Padre Cordioli Luigi, Missionario Redentorista. Free Italian-language newsletter. Replies enthusiastically to correspondence in Italian. Return postage appreciated. The Italian PTT may take this Catholic station off the air.

RTV Italiana-RAI (domestic services)
CALTANISSETTA: Radio Uno, Via Cerda 19, I-90139 Palermo, Sicily, Italy. Contact: Gestione Risorse, Transmission Quality Control. $1 required.
ROME: Notturno Italiano, Centro RAI, Saxa Rubra, I-00188 Rome, Italy. Fax: +39 (6) 322 6070.
Tele Radio Stereo—*see* Tele Radio Europe, above, for details.

IVORY COAST—*see* Côte d'Ivoire

JAPAN World Time +9
☞**JOAV—JWAVE FM**, 4-17-30 Hishiazabu, Hinatoku, Tokyo 106-88, Japan. Phone: (main office) +81 (3) 3797-1111; (advertising) +81 (3) 3797-7901. Fax: +81 (3) 3797-7935. URL: (audio) http://www.infojapan.com/JWAVE/. Contact: S. Suetsugu, Publicity; A. Takachio, Advertising Director; T. Sato, Manager, Administration & Programming; or T. Harukawa, C.E.O. Music station. Many items sold by radio shopping. VISA/MC.
NHK Fukuoka, 1-1-10 Ropponmatsu, Chuo-ku, Fukuoka-shi, Fukuoka, 810-77, Japan.
NHK Osaka, 3-43 Bamba-cho, Chuo-ku, Osaka 540-01 Japan. Fax: +81 (6) 941 0612. Contact: (technical) Technical Bureau. IRC or $1 helpful.

NHK Sapporo, 1-1-1 Ohdori Nishai, Chuo-ku, Sapporo 060, Japan. Fax: +81 (11) 232 5951.
NHK Tokyo/Shobu-Kuki, JOAK, 3047-1 Oaza-Sanga, Shoubu-cho, Minami Saitamagun, Saitama 346-01, Japan. Fax: +81 (3) 3481 4985 or +81 (480) 85 1508. IRC or $1 helpful. Replies occasionally. Letters should be sent via registered mail.
Radio Japan/NHK (external service)
MAIN OFFICE: 2-2-1 Jinnan, Shibuya-ku, Tokyo 150-01, Japan. Phone: (general) +81 (3) 3465-1111. Fax: (general) +81 (3) 3481 1350; ("Hello from Tokyo" and Production Center) +81 (3) 3465 0966; ("Media Roundup") +81 (3) 3481 1633; (News Department) + 81 (3) 3481 1462. E-mail: info@intl.nhk.or.jp. URLs: http://www.nhk.or.jp/rjnet; gopher://gopher.ntt.jp. Contact: (general) Akio Horikawa, Producer, "Hello from Tokyo"; Reiko Ijuin, Chief Producer, "Hello from Tokyo"; Mitsunori Matsumura, Director of Public Relations; Tsutomu Aoki, Director of Programming; Matsuo Sekino, Director of News Department; Kenji Sato, Director of Production Center; Mr. H. Misawa, Producer, "Media Roundup"; Takahisa Furukawa, English Announcer; H. Inagaki; H. Kawamoto; or Ms. Mari Kishi, Presenter, "Media Roundup"; (administration) Masaomi Sato, Director General. Free *Radio Japan News* publication, sundry other small souvenirs and "Let's Learn/Practice Japanese" language-course materials. Quizzes with prizes, including beautiful wall calendars and plastic fans, over "Media Roundup."
WASHINGTON NEWS BUREAU: NHK, 2030 M Street NW, Suite 706, Washington DC 20036 USA. Fax: +1 (202) 828 4571.
LONDON NEWS BUREAU: NHK General Bureau for Europe, 4 Millbank, Westminster, London SW1P 3JA, United Kingdom. Fax: +44 (171) 393 0193.
SYDNEY NEWS BUREAU: c/o SBS 14, Herbert Street, Artarmon NSW 2064, Australia. Fax: +61 (2) 9437 6105.
SINGAPORE NEWS BUREAU: NHK, 1 Scotts Road #15-06, Shaw Centre, Singapore 0922. Fax: +65 737 5251.
BANGKOK NEWS BUREAU: 6F MOT Building (Thai TV CH9), 222 Rama 9 Road, Bangkok 10310, Thailand. Fax: +66 (2) 253 2442.
Radio Tampa/NSB
MAIN OFFICE: Nihon Shortwave Broadcasting, 9-15 Akasaka 1-chome, Minato-ku, Tokyo 107, Japan. Fax: +81 (3) 3583 9062. Contact: H. Nagao, Public Relations; M. Teshima; Ms. Terumi Onoda; or H. Ono. Free stickers and Japanese stamps. $1 or IRC helpful.
NEW YORK NEWS BUREAU: 1325 Avenue of the Americas #2403, New York NY 10019 USA. Fax: +1 (212) 261 6449. Contact: Noboru Fukui, reporter.

JORDAN World Time +2 (+3 midyear)

Radio Jordan, P.O. Box 909, Amman, Jordan. Phone: +962 (6) 774-111. Fax: +962 (6) 788 115. URL: http://iconnect.com/jordan/radio.html. Contact: (general) Jawad Zada, Director of English Service & Producer of "Mailbag"; or Qasral Mushatta; (administrative) Radi Alkhas, General Director; or Muwaffaq al-Rahayifah, Director of Shortwave Services; (technical) Fawzi Saleh, Director of Engineering. Free stickers. Replies irregularly and slowly.

KAZAKHSTAN World Time +6 (+7 midyear)

Kazakh Radio, Kazakh Broadcasting Company, 175A Zheltoksan Street, 480013 Almaty, Kazakhstan. Phone: +7 (3272) 630-763 or +7 (3272) 635-629. Fax: + 7 (3272) 631 207. Contact: B. Shalakhmentov, Chairman; or S.D. Primbetov, Deputy Chairman.

Radio Almaty ("Radio Alma-Ata" and "Radio Almaty" in English Service, "Radio Kazakhstan" in Russian and some other services), 175A Zheltoksan Street, 480013 Almaty, Kazakhstan. Phone: +7 (3272) 637-694 or +7 (3272) 633-716. Fax: +7 (3272) 631 207. Contact: Mr. Gulnar. Correspondence welcomed in English, German, Russian, Korean and Kazakh. Station hopes to start up services in Chinese and Japanese, but not in the near future.

KENYA World Time +3

Adventist World Radio, The Voice of Hope, AWR Africa, P.O. Box 10114, Nairobi, Kenya. Phone: +254 (2) 713-961. Fax: +254 (2) 713 907. E-mail: 74532.1575@compuserve.com. Contact: Samuel Misiani, Associate Director, AWR-Africa. Free home study guides, program schedule and other small items. IRCs or $1 are appreciated. Also, *see* AWR listings under Costa Rica, Guam, Guatemala, Italy, Russia and the USA.

Kenya Broadcasting Corporation, P.O. Box 30456, Nairobi, Kenya. Fax: +254 (2) 220 675. Contact: (general) Henry Makokha, Liaison Office; (administration) Phillip Okundi, Managing Director; (technical) Augustine Kenyanjier Gochui; Lawrence Holnati, Engineering Division; or Manager Technical Services. IRC required. Replies irregularly.

KIRIBATI World Time +12

Radio Kiribati, P.O. Box 78, Bairiki, Tarawa, Republic of Kiribati. Fax: +686 21096. Contact: Atiota Bauro, Program Organiser; Mrs. Otiri Laboia; or Moia Tetoa, Producer, "Kaoti Ami Iango," a program devoted to listeners views; (administration) Teraku Tekanene, Managing Director; (technical) Trakaogo, Engineer-in-Charge; Tooto Kabwebwenibeia, Broadcast Engineer; or T. Fakaofo, Technical Staff. Cassettes of local songs available for purchase. $1 or return postage required for a reply (IRCs not accepted).

KOREA (DPR) World Time +9

Radio Pyongyang, External Service, Korean Central Broadcasting Station, Pyongyang, Democratic People's Republic of Korea (*not* "North Korea"). Phone: +850 (2) 812-301 or +850 (2) 36-344. Fax: +850 (2) 814 418. Phone and fax numbers valid only in those countries with direct telephone service to North Korea. Free book for German speakers to learn Korean, sundry other publications, pennants, calendars, newspapers, artistic prints and pins. Do not include dutiable items in your envelope. Replies are irregular, as mail from countries not having diplomatic relations with North Korea is sent via circuitous routes and apparently does not always arrive. Indeed, PASSPORT readers continue to report that mail to Radio Pyongyang in North Korea results in their receiving anti-communist literature from *South Korea*, which indicates that mail interdiction has not ceased. To get around this, one gambit is to send your correspondence to an associate in a country—such as China, Ukraine or India—having reasonable relations with North Korea, and ask that it be forwarded. Nevertheless, replies from this station appear to be increasingly common, including occasionally to the United States and other countries with which North Korea has no diplomatic relations.

Regional Korean Central Broadcasting Stations—Not known to reply, but a long-shot possibility is to try corresponding in Korean to: Korean Central Broadcasting Station, Ministry of Posts and Telecommunications, Chongsung-dong (Moranbong), Pyongyang, Democratic People's Republic of Korea. Fax: +850 (2) 812 301 (valid only in those countries with direct telephone service to North Korea). Contact: Chong Ha-chol, Chairman, Radio and Television Broadcasting Committee.

KOREA (REPUBLIC) World Time +9

Korean Broadcasting System (KBS), 18 Yoido-dong, Youngdungpo-gu, Seoul 150-790, Republic of Korea. Phone: +82 (2) 781-2410. Fax: +82 (2) 761 2499.

📻Radio Korea International

MAIN OFFICE: Overseas Service, Korean Broadcasting System, 18 Yoido-dong, Youngdungpo-gu, Seoul 150-790, Republic of Korea. Phone: (general) +82 (2) 781-3710 or +82 (2) 781-3721; (English Service) +82 (2) 781-3728/29/35; (Russian Service) +82 (2) 781-3714. Fax: +82 (2) 781 3799. E-mail: info@kbsnt.kbs.co.kr; webmaster@kbsnt.kbs.co.kr. URLs: (RealAudio in English and Korean) http://www.wrn.org/stations/kbs.html; (general, but relatively slow download because of extensive graphics) http://kbsnt.kbs.co.kr/; (History of Korea, relatively slow download) http://www.kbs.co.kr/pr/history.htm. Contact: (general) Chae Hong-Pyo, Director of English Service; Robert Gutnikov, English Service; Ms. Han Hee-joo, Producer/Host, "Shortwave Feedback"; Jong Kyong-Tae, Producer, Russian Service; H.A. Staiger, Deputy Head of German Service; Ms. Lee Hae-Ok, Japanese Service; or Ms. Kim Hae-Young, Producer, Japanese Service; (administration) Kim Joo-Chul, Executive Director; or Choi Jang-Hoon, Director. Free stickers, calendars, *Let's Learn Korean* book and a wide variety of other small souvenirs. *History of Korea* now available via Internet (*see* URL, above) and on CD-ROM (inquire).

WASHINGTON NEWS BUREAU: National Press Building, Suite 1076, 529 14th Street NW, Washington DC 20045 USA. Phone: +1 (202) 662-7345. Fax: +1 (202) 662 7347.

KUWAIT World Time +3

Ministry of Information, P.O. Box 193, 13002 Safat, Kuwait. Phone: +965 241-5301. Fax: +965 243 4511. Contact: Sheik Nasir Al-Sabah, Minister of Information.

Radio Kuwait, P.O. Box 397, 13004 Safat, Kuwait. Phone: +965 241-0301 or +965 242-3774. Fax: +965 241 5498, +965 245 6660 or +965 241 5946. Contact: (general) Manager, External Service; (technical) Nasser M. Al-Saffar, Controller, Frequency Management. Sometimes gives away stickers, calendars, pens or key chains.

KYRGYZSTAN World Time +5 (+6 midyear)

Kyrgyz Radio, Kyrgyz TV and Radio Center, Prospekt Moloday Gvardil 63, 720 300 Bishkek, Kyrgyzstan. Fax: +7 (3312) 257 930. Contact: A.I. Vitshkov or E.M. Abdukarimov.

LAOS World Time +7

Lao National Radio, Luang Prabang ("Sathani Withayu Kachaisiang Khueng Luang Prabang"), Luang Prabang, Laos; or B.P. 310, Vientiane, Laos. Return postage required (IRCs not accepted). Replies slowly and very rarely. Best bet is to write in Laotian or French directly to Luang Prabang, where the transmitter is located.

Lao National Radio, Vientiane, Laotian National Radio and Television, B.P. 310, Vientiane, Laos. Contact: Bounthan Inthasai, Deputy Managing Director. The external service of this station tends to be erratic.

LATVIA World Time +2 (+3 midyear)

Latvijas Radio, 8 Doma Laukums, LV-1505 Riga, Latvia. Phone: +371 (2) 206-722. Fax: +371 (2) 206 709. Contact: (general) Aivars Ginters, International Relations; or Ms. Darija Juškeviča, Program Director; (administration) Arnolds Klotins, Director General; (technical) Aigars Semevics, Technical Director. Replies to nontechnical correspondence in Latvian. Does not issue verification replies.

Radio Latvia, P.O. Box 266, LV-1098 Riga, Latvia. Phone: (director general) +371 (2) 206-747; (Program Director) +371 (2) 206-750; (secretary) +371 (2) 206-722. Fax: (International Relations) +371 (8) 820 216; (secretary) +371 (2) 206 709. Contact: (general) Ms. Fogita Cimcus, Chief Editor, English; (administration) Laimonas Tapinas, Director General; (technical, but not for verifications) Aigars Semevics, Technical Director. Free stickers and pennants. Unlike Latvijas Radio, preceding, Radio Latvia verifies regularly via the Chief Editor.

LEBANON   World Time +2 (+3 midyear)

NOTE: The government plans to rationalize the existing radio situation in Lebanon in the near future. As a result, some stations may be forced to leave the air or to alter the nature of their operations.

Radio Lebanon, Radio Liban (when operation commences), Ministry of Information, Beirut, Lebanon. Plans to inaugurate a major world band service, nominally sometime well into 1997.

Voice of Hope, P.O. Box 77, 10292 Metulla, Israel; or P.O. Box 3379, Limassol, Cyprus. Phone: (Israel) +972 (6) 959-174 or +972 (6) 959-889. Fax: (Israel) +972 (6) 997 827. Contact: Gary Hull, Station Manager; or Isaac Gronberg, Director. Free stickers. IRC requested.May send 214 page book *Voice of Hope* via USA headquarters *(see).* Hopes to raise power of current 10 kW facility (to Middle East) to 25 kW. Also, *see* KVOH—Voice of Hope/High Adventure Ministries, USA.

Voice of Lebanon, La Voix du Liban, B.P. 165271, Al-Ashrafiyah, Beirut, Lebanon. Phone/fax: +961 (1) 323-458. $1 required. Replies extremely irregularly to correspondence in French or Arabic, but usually willing to discuss significant matters by telephone. Operated by the Phalangist organization.

Voice of Orthodoxy—see Belarus.

LIBERIA   World Time exactly

NOTE: Currently, mail sent to Liberia is being returned as undeliverable.

ELBC, Liberian Broadcasting System, P.O. Box 10-594, 1000 Monrovia 10, Liberia. Phone: +231 22-4984 or +231 22-2758. Contact: Jesse B. Karnley, Director General, Broadcasting; or James Morlu, Deputy Director, Broadcasting. Operates on behalf of the Economic Community of West African States' peacekeeping force, ECOMOG.

Radio Liberia, Liberian Communications Network/KISS, P.O. Box 1103, Monrovia, Liberia. Phone: +231 22-6963. Fax: (during working hours) +231 22 6003. Contact: Issac P. Davis, Engineer-in-Charge.

LIBYA   World Time +1

Radio Jamahiriya

MAIN OFFICE: P.O. Box 4677 (or P.O. Box 4396), Tripoli, Libya. Contact: R. Cachia. Arabic preferred.

MALTA OFFICE: European Branch Office, P.O. Box 17, Hamrun, Malta. This office, which may still be in operation, has historically replied more consistently than has the main office.

LITHUANIA   World Time +2 (+3 midyear)

Lithuanian National Radio

STATION: Lietuvos Nacionalinis Radijas, Konarskio 49, LT-2674 Vilnius, Lithuania. Phone: +370 (2) 634-471. Fax: +370 (2) 660 526. Contact: Nerijus Maliukevicius, Director.

ADMINISTRATION: Lithuanian National Radio and Television Center, Konarskio 43, LT-2674 Vilnius, Lithuania. Phone: +370 (2) 633-182. Fax: +370 (2) 263 282. E-mail: lrtc@aiva.lt.

Radio Vilnius, Lietuvos Nacionalinis Radijas, Konarskio 49, LT-2674 Vilnius, Lithuania. Phone: +370 (2) 634-471. Fax: +370 (2) 660 526 or +370 (2) 221 5 71. Contact: Ms. Rasa Lukaite, "Letterbox"; Audrius Braukyla, Editor-in-Chief; or Ilonia Rukiene, Head of English Department. Free stickers, pennants, Lithuanian stamps and other souvenirs. Trans-

mits to North America via the facilities of Deutsche Welle in Germany *(see).*

MADAGASCAR   World Time +3

Radio Madagasikara, B.P. 1202, Antananarivo, Madagascar. Contact: Mlle. Rakotoniaina Soa Herimanitia, Secrétaire de Direction, a young lady who collects stamps; or Adolphe Andriakoto, Directeur. $1 required, and enclosing used stamps from various countries may help. Tape recordings accepted. Replies very rarely and slowly, preferably to friendly philatelist gentlemen who correspond in French.

Radio Nederland Wereldomroep—Madagascar Relay, B.P. 404, Antananarivo, Madagascar. Contact: (technical) Rahamefy Eddy, Technische Dienst.; or J.A. Ratobimiarana, Chief Engineer. Nontechnical correspondence should be sent to Radio Nederland Wereldomroep in Holland *(see).*

MALAWI   World Time +2

Malawi Broadcasting Corporation, P.O. Box 30133, Chichiri, Blantyre 3, Malawi. Fax: +265 671 353 or +265 671 257. Contact: Henry R. Chirwa, Head of Production; Ben M. Tembo, Head of Presentations; V.P. Idi, Acting Head of Presentations; P. Chinseu; or T.J. Sineta. Return postage or $1 helpful.

MALAYSIA   World Time +8

📻**RTM.net**—see Radio Malaysia, Kajang, below.

📻**Radio Malaysia, Kajang**, RTM, Angkasapuri, Bukit Putra, 50614 Kuala Lumpur, Peninsular Malaysia, Malaysia. Phone: +60 (3) 282-5333 or +60 (3) 282-4976. Fax: +60 (3) 282 5859. E-mail: rtml@asia.connect.com.my. URL: (general) http://www.asiaconnect.com.my/rtm-net/; (RealAudio for several domestic stations, plus special Internet programming) http://www.asiaconnect.com.my/rtm-net/live/. Contact (general) Ahmad Raphay, Director of Radio; (technical) Deputy Director Engineering; Abdullah Bin Shahadan, Engineer, Transmission & Monitoring; or Ong Poh, Chief Engineer. May sell T-shirts and key chains. Return postage required.

Radio Malaysia Kota Kinabalu, RTM, 88614 Kota Kinabalu, Sabah, Malaysia. Contact: Benedict Janil, Director of Broadcasting; or Hasbullah Latiff. Return postage required.

Radio Malaysia Sarawak (Kuching), RTM, Broadcasting House, Jalan P. Ramlee, 93614 Kuching, Sarawak, Malaysia. Phone: +60 (82) 248-422. Fax: +60 (82) 241 914. Contact: (general) Tuan Haji Ahmad Shafiee Haji Yaman, Director of Broadcasting; or Human Resources Development; (technical, but also nontechnical) Colin A. Minoi, Technical Correspondence; (technical) Kho Kwang Khoon, Deputy Director of Engineering. Return postage helpful.

Radio Malaysia Sarawak (Miri), RTM, Miri, Sarawak, Malaysia. Contact: Mohammed Nasir B. Mohammed. $1 or return postage helpful.

Radio Malaysia Sarawak (Sibu), RTM, Jabatan Penyiaran, Bangunan Penyiaran, 96009 Sibu, Sarawak, Malaysia. Contact: Clement Stia, Divisional Controller, Broadcasting Department. $1 or return postage required. Replies irregularly and slowly.

Voice of Islam—Program of the Voice of Malaysia *(see),* below.

Voice of Malaysia, Suara Malaysia, Wisma Radio, P.O. Box 11272-KL, 50740 Angkasapuri, Kuala Lumpur, Malaysia. Phone: +60 (3) 282-5333. Fax: +60 (3) 282 5859. Contact: (general) Mrs. Mahani bte Ujang, Supervisor, English Service; Hajjah Wan Chuk Othman, English Service; (administration) Santokh Singh Gill, Director; or Mrs. Adilan bte Omar, Assistant Director; (technical) Lin Chew, Director of Engineering. Free calendars and stickers. Two IRCs or return postage helpful. Replies slowly and irregularly.

MALI   World Time exactly

Radiodiffusion Télévision Malienne, B.P. 171, Bamako, Mali. Phone: +223 22-47-27. Fax: +223 22 42 05. Contact: Karamoko Issiaka Daman, Directeur des Programmes; (administration) Abdoulaye Sidibe, Directeur General. $1 or

IRC helpful. Replies slowly and irregularly to correspondence in French. English is accepted.

MALTA World Time +1 (+2 midyear)
Voice of the Mediterranean, P.O. Box 143, La Valletta, CMR 01, Malta. Phone: +356 220-950, +356 240-421 or +356 248-080. Fax: +356 241 501. Contact: (general) Ali Abdul Aziz El-Kish, Director of News and Programs; or Dr. Guido Saliba, Deputy Director of News and Programs; (German Service and listener contact) Ingrid Huettmann; (administration) Richard Vella Laurenti, Managing Director. Letters and recception reports welcomed in English, French, German or Arabic. Free monthly English newsletter upon request. Station, which went off the air for about three months when Deutsch Welle shut down its Malta facilities in mid-January, 1996, is a joint venture of the Libyan and Maltese governments. Currently, transmissions—beamed to Europe, East Asia and Australasia—are via leased-time facilities in Russia.

MAURITANIA World Time exactly
Office de Radiodiffusion-Télévision de Mauritanie, B.P. 200, Nouakchott, Mauritania. Fax: +222 (2) 51264. Contact: Madame Amir Feu; Lemrabott Boukhary; Madame Fatimetou Fall Dite Ami, Secretaire de Direction; or Mr. Hane Abou. Return postage or $1 required. Rarely replies.

MAURITIUS World Time +4
Mauritius Broadcasting Corporation, P.O. Box 48, Curepipe, Mauritius. Phone: +230 675-5001. Fax: +230 675 7332. Contact: S. Sunassee, Chief Technical Officer. Currently inactive on world band, but hopes to reactivate transmissions eventually on 4855 and 9710 kHz.

MEXICO World Time –6 (–5 midyear) Central, including D.F.; –7 (–6 midyear) Mountain; –8 (–7 midyear) Pacific
La Hora Exacta—XEQK, IMER, Margaritas 18, Col. Florida, 01030 México, D.F., Mexico. Contact: Gerardo Romero.
La Voz de Veracruz—XEFT, Apartado Postal 21, 91700-4H. Veracruz, Ver., Mexico. Contact: C.P. Miguel Rodríguez Sáez, Sub-Director; or Lic. Juan de Dios Rodríguez Díaz, Director-Gerente. Free tourist guide to Veracruz. Return postage, IRC or $1 probably helpful. Likely to reply to correspondence in Spanish.
Radio Educación—XEPPM, SPE-333/92, Apartado Postal 21-940, 04021 México, D.F., Mexico. Phone: (general) +52 (5) 559-8075 or +52 (5) 559-3102; (studio) +52 (5) 575-0919. Fax: +52 (5) 559 2301. Contact: (general) Lic. Susana E. Mejía Vázquez, Jefe del Dept. de Audiencia y Evaluación; or María Teresa Moya Malfavón, Directora de Producción y Planeación; (administration) Luis Ernesto Pi Orozco, Director General; (technical) Ing. Gustavo Carreño López, Subdirector, Dpto. Técnico. Free stickers, station photo and a copy of a local publication, *Audio Tinta Boletín Informativo*. Return postage or $1 required. Replies, sometimes slowly, to correspondence in English, Spanish, Italian or French.
Radio Huayacocotla—XEJN
STATION ADDRESS: "Radio Huaya," Dom. Gutierrez Najera s/n, Apartado Postal 13, 92600 Huayacocotla, Veracruz, Mexico. Phone: +52 (775) 8-0067. Fax: +52 (775) 8 0178. E-mail: framos@uibero.uia.mx. Contact: Juan Antonio Vázquez; Alfredo Zepeda; Martha Silvia Ortiz López, Director de Programas; or Felipe de Jesús Martínez Sosa. Return postage or $1 helpful. Replies irregularly to correspondence in Spanish.
SPONSORING ORGANIZATION: Fomento Cultural y Educativo, A.C. Miguel Laurent 340, Col. Del Valle, 03100 México, D.F., Mexico. Phone: +2 (5) 559-6000. Fax: +52 (5) 575 8357.
Radio México Internacional—XERMX, Grupo IMER, Instituto Méxicano de la Radio, Apartado Postal 21-300, 04201 México, D.F., Mexico. Phone: +52 (5) 628-1700. Fax: +52 (5) 604 8902. Contact: Lic. Juan Mort Martín del Campo, Gerente. Free stickers, post cards and stamps. Welcomes correspondence, including inquiries about Mexico, in Span-

ish, English, French and Italian. Has recently rehabilitated its transmission facilities.
Radio Mil—XEOI, NRM, Insurgentes Sur 1870, Col. Florida, 01030 México, D.F., Mexico. Phone: (station) +52 (5) 662-1000 or +52 (5) 662-1100; (Núcleo Radio Mil network) +52 (5) 662-6060, +52 (5) 663-0739 or +52 (5) 663 0590. Fax: (station) +52 (5) 662 0974; (Núcleo Radio Mil network) +52 (5) 662 0979. Contact: Guillermo Salas Vargas, Presidente; Srta. Cristina Stivalet, Gerente; or Zoila Quintanar Flores. Free stickers. $1 or return postage required.
Radio Universidad/UNAM—XEUDS, Apartado Postal No. 1817, 83000 Hermosillo, Sonora, Mexico. Contact: A. Merino M., Director; or Ing. Miguel Angel González Lopez, Subdirector de Ingenieria. Free tourist literature and stickers. $1 or return postage required. Replies irregularly to correspondence in Spanish.
Radio XEQQ, La Voz de la América Latina (on the rare occasions when operating), Sistema Radiópolis, Ayuntamiento 52, 06070 México D.F., Mexico; or Ejército Nacional No. 579 (6to piso), 11520 México, D.F., Mexico. Contact: (general) Sra. Martha Sandoval; (technical) Ing. Miguel Angel Barrientos, Director Técnico de Plantas Transmisoras. Free pennants. $1, IRC or return postage required. When operating, replies fairly regularly to correspondence in Spanish.
Radio XEUJ, Apartado Postal 62, 67700 Linares, Nuevo León, Mexico. Contact: (general) Marcelo Becerra González, Director General; or Joel Becerra Pecina; (technical) Ing. Gustavo Martínez de la Cruz. Free stickers, pennants and Mexican tourist cards. Replies irregularly to correspondence in Spanish, English or French. Considering replacing their transmitting equipment and extending hours of transmission.
Radio XEUW, Ocampo 119, 91700 Veracruz, Mexico. Contact: Ing. Baltazar Pazos de la Torre, Director General. Free pennants. Return postage required. Replies occasionally to correspondence in Spanish.
Tus Panteras—XEQM, Apartado Postal No. 217, 97000 Mérida, Yucatán, Mexico. Fax: +52 (99) 28 06 80. Contact: Arturo Iglesias Villalobos; L.C.C Roberto Domínguez Avila, Director General; or Ylmar Pacheco Gómez, Locutor. Replies irregularly to correspondence in Spanish.

"MOLDAVIAN REPUBLIC OF PRIDNESTROVYE" World Time +2 (+3 midyear)
NOTE: As direct mail service to this region is often nonexistent, the best way to contact the stations listed below is via Rumen Pankov, P.O. Box 199, BG-1000 Sofia-C, Bulgaria, enclosing 5 IRCs or $2, or 1 IRC and $1.
Radio Dniester International (external service, when operating), 45 - 25th October Street, 278000 Tiraspol, Pridnestrovye, C.I.S. Fax: (via Trans World Radio, Moscow, which leases transmission time from the Pridnestrovye PTT, which in turn also serves this organization) +7 (095) 368-3700. Contact: A. Komar, Chief Editor; or Marina Yagovitina, Announcer. Free postcards.
Radio Pridnestrovye, 10 Rosa Luxemburg Street, 278000 Tiraspol, Pridnestrovye, C.I.S.

MOLDOVA World Time +2 (+3 midyear)
Radio Moldova International
NOTE: As direct mail service to Moldova is often nonexistent, the best way to contact Radio Moldova International is via Rumen Pankov, P.O. Box 199, BG-1000 Sofia-C, Bulgaria, enclosing 5 IRCs or $2, or 1 IRC and $1.
GENERAL CORRESPONDENCE: If direct mail service is available from your location, try Str. Miorița 1, 277028 Chişinău, Moldova. Phone: +373 (2) 72-17-92, +373 (2) 72-33-79 or +373 (2) 72-33-85. Fax: +373 (2) 72 33 29 or +373 (2) 72 33 07. Contact: Constantin Marin, International Editor-in-Chief; Alexandru Dorogan, General Director of Radio Broadcasting; Daniel Lacky, Editor, English Service; Veleriu Vasilica, Director; or Raisa Gonciar. Transmits via facilities of Radio România International.

RECEPTION REPORTS: Should direct mail service be available from your location, try RMI-Monitoring Action, P.O. Box 9972, 277070 Chişinău-70, Moldova.

MONACO   World Time +1 (+2 midyear)
Radio Monte-Carlo
MAIN OFFICE: 16 Boulevard Princesse Charlotte, MC-98080 Monaco Cedex, Monaco. Phone: +377 (93) 15-16-17. Fax: +377 (93) 15 16 30 or +377 (93) 15 94 48. E-mail: via URL. URL: http://www.twr.org/monte.htm. Contact: Jacques Louret; Bernard Poizat, Service Diffusion; or Caroline Wilson, Director of Communication. Free stickers. This station is on world band only with its Arabic Service.
MAIN PARIS OFFICE, NONTECHNICAL: 12 rue Magellan, F-75008 Paris, France. Phone: +33 (1) 40-69-88-00. Fax: +33 (1) 40 69 88 55 or +33 (1) 45 00 92 45.
PARIS OFFICE (ARABIC SERVICE): 78 Avenue Raymond Poincairé, F-75008 Paris, France. Phone: +33 (1) 45-01-53-30.
CYPRUS OFFICE (ARABIC SERVICE)—see Cyprus.

Trans World Radio
STATION: B.P. 349, MC-98007 Monte-Carlo, Monaco. Phone: +377 (92) 16-56-00. Fax: +377 (92) 16 56 01. URL: http://www.twr.org/monte.htm. Contact: (general) Mrs. Jeanne Olson; (administration) Richard Olson, Station Manager; (technical) Bernhard Schraut, Frequency Coordinator. Free paper pennant. IRC or $1 helpful. Also, *see* USA.
GERMANY OFFICE: Evangeliums-Rundfunk, Postfach 1444, D-35573 Wetzlar, Germany. Phone: +49 (6441) 9570. Fax: +49 (6441) 9571. URL: http://www.jesus-online.de/erf/erf_home.htm. Contact: Jürgen Werth, Direktor.
HOLLAND OFFICE, NONTECHNICAL: Postbus 176, NL-3780 BD Voorthuizen, Holland. Phone: +31 (0) 34-29-27-27. Fax: +31 (0) 34 29 67 27. Contact: Beate Kiebel, Manager Broadcast Department; or Felix Widmer.
VIENNA OFFICE, TECHNICAL: Postfach 141, A-1235 Vienna, Austria. Phone: +43 (1) 865-2055. Fax: +43 (1) 865 2093. Contact: Helmut Menzel, Frequency Management Services.

MONGOLIA   World Time +8
Radio Ulaanbaatar, External Services, C.P.O. Box 365, Ulaanbaatar, Mongolia. Phone: +976 (1) 327-900 or +976 (1) 321-624. Fax: +976 (1) 323 096. Contact: (general) Mr. Bayasa, Mail Editor, English Department; N. Tuya, Head of English Department; or Ms. Tsegmid Burmaa, Japanese Department; (administration) Ch. Surenjav, Director; (technical) Ing. Ganhuu, Chief of Technical Department. Free pennants, postcards, newspapers and Mongolian stamps.

MOROCCO   World Time exactly
Radio Medi Un
MAIN OFFICE: B.P. 2055, Tangier, Morocco. Contact: J. Dryk, Responsable Haute Fréquence. Two IRCs helpful. Free stickers. Correspondence in French preferred.
PARIS BUREAU, NONTECHNICAL: 78 Avenue Raymond Poincaré, F-75016 Paris, France. Phone: +33 (1) 45-01-53-30. Correspondence in French preferred.
RTV Marocaine, RTM, 1 rue al-Brihi, Rabat, Morocco. Phone: +212 (7) 70-17-40. Fax +212 (7) 70 32 08. Contact: (nontechnical and technical) Mrs. Naaman Khadija, Ingénieur d'Etat en Télécommunication; (technical) Tanone Mohammed Jamaledine, Technical Director; Hammouda Mohamed, Engineer; or N. Read. Correspondence welcomed in English, French, Arabic or Berber—especially suggestions for times, languages and other relevant information concerning possible limited expansion of shortwave transmissions to new targets so Moroccan and North African affairs can be more widely disseminated and understood.
Voice of America/VOA-IBB—Morocco Relay Station, Briech. Phone: (office) +212 (9) 93-24-81; (transmitter) +212 (9) 93-22-00. Fax: +212 (9) 93 55 71. Contact: Wilfred Cooper, Manager. These numbers for urgent technical matters only. Otherwise, does not welcome direct correspondence; *see* USA for acceptable VOA Washington address and related information.

MOZAMBIQUE   World Time +2
Rádio Maputo (when active)—*see* Radio Moçambique, below.
Rádio Moçambique, C.P. 2000, Maputo, Mozambique. Phone: +258 (1) 42-18- 14. Fax: +258 (1) 42 18 16. Contact: (general) João de Sousa, Administrador e Diretor Comercial; Machado da Graça, Administrador para o Pelouro da Produção; Orlanda Mendes, Produtor, "Linha Direta"; or Marcos Cuembelo, Administrador e Diretor Financeiro; (administration) Manuel Veterano, Presidente do Conselho de Administração; (technical) Rufino de Matos, Administrador e Diretor Técnico. Free medallions and pens. Cassettes featuring local music $15. Return postage, $1 or 2 IRCs required. Replies to correspondence in Portuguese or English. Means are being studied by which Rádio Moçambique, which the Mozambique prime minister says "is going through difficult times," may be properly financed and thus remain on the air.

MYANMAR (BURMA)   World Time +6:30
Radio Myanmar
STATION: GPO Box 1432, Yangon-11181, Myanmar; or Pyay Road, Yangon-11041, Myanmar. Phone: +95 (1) 31-355. Fax: +95 (1) 30 211. Contact: U. Ko Ko Htway, Director, M.T.R.D.

NAMIBIA   World Time +3 (+2 midyear)
Radio Namibia/NBC, P.O. Box 321, Windhoek 9000, Namibia. Phone: +264 (61) 291-2209 or 264 (61) 291-3291. Fax: +264 (61) 291 2156 or +264 (61) 291 2291. Contact: P. Schachtschneider, Manager, Transmitter Maintenance. Free stickers.

NEPAL   World Time +5:45
Radio Nepal, P.O. Box 634, Singha Durbar, Kathmandu, Nepal. Phone: (general) +977 (1) 223-910 or +977 (1) 215-773; (engineering) +977 (1) 225-467. Fax: +977 (1) 221 952. Contact: (general) B.P. Shivakoti; R.J. Karlei; P. Sunuwar; or S.K. Pant, Producer, "Listener's Mail"; (technical) Ram S. Karki, Acting Director, Engineering. 3 IRCs necessary, but station urges that neither mint stamps nor cash be enclosed, as this invites theft by Nepalese postal employees.

NETHERLANDS ANTILLES   World Time –4
Radio Nederland Wereldomroep—Bonaire Relay, P.O. Box 45, Kralendijk, Netherlands Antilles. Nontechnical correspondence should be sent to Radio Nederland Wereldomroep in Holland (*see*).

NEW ZEALAND   World Time +13 (+12 midyear)
Kiwi Radio (unlicensed, but left alone by the government), P.O. Box 3103, Onekawa, Napier 4030, New Zealand. Phone: +64 (6) 834-4079. Contact: Graham J. Barclay. Free stickers, schedule etc. New Zealand tourist information free upon request. Kiwi Radio T-shirts and three history sets on cassette available for $23 airmail. Internet page coming soon. Return postage appreciated.
Radio New Zealand International (Te Reo Irirangi O Aotearoa, O Te Moana-nui-a-kiwa), P.O. Box 123, Wellington, New Zealand. Phone: +64 (4) 474-1437. Fax: +64 (4) 474 1433. E-mail: rnzi@actrix.gen.nz. URL: http://www.actrix.gen.nz/biz/rnzi. Contact: Florence de Ruiter, Listener Mail; Myra Oh, Producer, "Mailbox"; or Walter Zweifel, News Editor; (administration) Ms. Linden Clark, Manager; (technical) Adrian Sainsbury, Frequency Manager. Free stickers. Schedule/flyer about station, map of New Zealand and tourist literature available. English/Maori T-shirts for US$20; Sweatshirts $40; interesting variety of CDs, as well as music cassettes and spoken programs, in Domestic "Replay Radio" catalog (VISA/MC). Three IRCs for verification, one IRC for schedule/catalog.
Radio Reading Service—ZLXA, P.O. Box 360, Levin 5500, New Zealand. Phone: +64 (6) 368-2229. Fax: +64 (6) 368 0151. E-mail: little@levin.horowhenua.gen.nz. Contact: (general) Ron Harper; Ash Bell; Brian Stokoe, Program Supervisor; or Jim Meecham ZL2 BHF, Producer, "CQ Pacific, Radio

Radio New Zealand International is one of the grand little gems of the airwaves. Shown, from left, wearing RNZI sweatshirts, are Rosemary Hancock, listener; Doreen Sam, staffer from the Solomon Islands; Vanessa Johnson, listener; Walter Zweifel, Editor; Florence de Ruiter, Producer/Administrator; Moera Fiti-Tuilaepa, News; and Mary-Ann Reid, listener.

RNZI

about Radio"; (administration) Allen J. Little, Station Director. Free brochure, postcards and stickers. $1, return postage or 3 IRCs appreciated.

NICARAGUA World Time –6
Radio Miskut, Correo Central (Bragman's Bluff), Puerto Cabezas, R.A.A.N., Nicaragua. Fax: +505 (267) 3032. Contact: Evaristo Mercado Pérez, Director de Operación y de Programas. Audio cassettes of programs and Nicaraguan folk music $8 each, T-shirts $10, and *Resumen Mensual del Gobierno y Consejo Regional* and *Revista Informativa Detallada de las Gestiones y Logros* $10 per copy. Replies slowly and irregularly to correspondence in English and Spanish. $2 helpful, as is registering your letter.

NIGER World Time +1
La Voix du Sahel, O.R.T.N., B.P. 361, Niamey, Niger. Fax: +227 72 35 48. Contact: (general) Adamou Oumarou; Zakari Saley; Souley Boubacou; or Mounkaila Inazadan, Producer, "Inter-Jeunes Variétés"; (administration) Oumar Tiello, Directeur; (technical) Afo Sourou Victor. $1 helpful. Correspondence in French preferred. Correspondence by males with this station may result in requests for certain unusual types of magazines and photographs.

NIGERIA World Time +1
WARNING—MAIL THEFT: For the time being, correspondence from abroad to Nigerian addresses has a relatively high probability of being stolen.
WARNING—CONFIDENCE ARTISTS: For years, now, correspondence with Nigerian stations has sometimes resulted in letters from highly skilled "pen pal" confidence artists. These typically offer to send you large sums of money, if you will provide details of your bank account or similar information

(after which they clean out your account). Other scams are disguised as tempting business proposals; or requests for money, free electronic or other products, publications or immigration sponsorship. Persons thus approached should contact their country's diplomatic offices. For example, Americans should contact the Diplomatic Security Section of the Department of State [phone +1 (202) 647-4000], or an American embassy or consulate.
Radio Nigeria—Enugu, P.M.B. 1051, Enugu (Anambra), Nigeria. Contact: Louis Nnamuchi, Assistant Director Technical Services. Two IRCs, return postage or $1 required. Replies slowly.
Radio Nigeria—Ibadan, P.M.B. 5003, Ibadan, Oyo State, Nigeria. Contact: V.A. Kalejaiye, Technical Services Department. $1 or return postage required. Replies slowly.
Radio Nigeria—Kaduna, P.O. Box 250, Kaduna (Kaduna), Nigeria. Contact: Yusuf Garba or Johnson D. Allen. $1 or return postage required. Replies slowly.
Radio Nigeria—Lagos, P.M.B. 12504, Ikoyi, Lagos, Nigeria. Contact: Babatunde Olalekan Raji, Monitoring Unit. Two IRCs or return postage helpful. Replies slowly and irregularly.
Voice of Nigeria (when active), P.M.B. 40003 Falomo Post Office, Ikoyi, Lagos, Nigeria. Phone: +234 (1) 269-3078/3245/ 3075/. Fax: +234 (1) 269 1944. Contact: (general) Alhaji Lawal Yusuf Saulawa, Director Programmes; Mrs. Stella Bassey, Deputy Director Programmes; Alhaji Mohammed Okorejior, Acting Director News; or Livy Iwok, Editor; (administration) Alhaji Mallam Yaya Abubakar, Director General; Abubakar Jijiwa, Chairman; or Dr. Walter Ofonagoro, Minister of Information; (technical) J.O. Kurunmi, Deputy Director Engineering Services; or G.C. Ugwa, Director Engineering. Replies from station tend to be erratic, but continue to gener-

ate unsolicited correspondence from supposed "pen pals" (see WARNING—CONFIDENCE ARTISTS, above); faxes, which are much less likely to be intercepted, may be more fruitful. Two IRCs or return postage helpful.

NORTHERN MARIANA ISLANDS   World Time +10
Far East Broadcasting Company—KFBS Saipan
MAIN OFFICE: FEBC, P.O. Box 209, Saipan, Mariana Islands MP 96950 USA. Phone: +670 322-9088. Fax: +670 322 3060. E-mail: 3268568@mcimail.com. URL: http://febc.org. Contact: Chris Slabaugh, Field Director; Mike Adams; or Robert Springer. Replies sometimes take months. Also, *see* FEBC Radio International, USA.

Monitor Radio International—KHBI, P.O. Box 1387, Saipan, Mariana Islands (*see* USA). Phone: +670 234-6515. Fax: +670 234 5452. E-mail: (Station Manager) doming@khbi.csms.com. Contact: (nontechnical) Alexander U. Igisaiar; or Doming F. Villar, Station Manager; (technical) Jess Emmanuel Domingo. Free stickers. Return postage appreciated if writing to Saipan; no return postage necessary when writing to Boston. Visitors welcome, preferably from 9 to 4 Monday through Friday, but contact transmitter site before arrival in Saipan to make arrangements.

NORWAY   World Time +1 (+2 midyear)
Radio Norway International
MAIN OFFICE, NONTECHNICAL: Utgitt av Utenlandssendingen/NRK, N-0340 Oslo, Norway. Phone: (general) +47 (22) 45-84-41; (Norwegian-language 24-hour recording of schedule information +47 (22) 45-80-08 (Americas, Europe, Africa), +47 (22) 45-80-09 (elsewhere); (Radio Projects Dept.) +47 (22) 45-95-87. Fax: (general) +47 (22) 45 71 34 or +47 (22) 60 57 19; ("Listener's Corner" and Radio Projects Dept.) +47 (22) 45 72 29. E-mail: radionorway@nrk.no. URL: http://www.nrk.no/utenland/. Contact: (general) Kirsten Ruud Salomonsen, Head of External Broadcasting; (technical) Gundel Krauss Dahl, Head of Radio Projects. Free stickers and flags. Reportedly plans to add a second 500 kW transmitter at Sveio by early 1997.
FREQUENCY MANAGEMENT OFFICE: Statens Teleforvaltning, P.O. Box 447 Sentrum, N-0104 Oslo, Norway. Phone: +47 (22) 82-48-89. Fax: +47 (22) 82 48 91. E-mail: olav.grimdalen@nta.telemax.no or olavmo@sn.no. Contact: Olav Mo Grimdalen, Frequency Manager.
WASHINGTON NEWS BUREAU: Norwegian Broadcasting, 2030 M Street NW, Suite 700, Washington DC 20036 USA. Phone: +1 (202) 785-1481 or +1 (202) 785-1460. Contact: Bjorn Hansen or Gunnar Myklebust.
SINGAPORE NEWS BUREAU: NRK, 325 River Valley Road #01-04, Singapore.

OMAN   World Time +4
BBC World Service—Eastern Relay Station, P.O. Box 6898 (or 3716), Ruwi Post Office, Muscat, Oman. Contact: (technical) David P. Bones, Senior Transmitter Engineer; Tim Mullins, Senior Transmitter Engineer; Chris Dolman; or Dave Plater, G4MZY, Senior Transmitter Engineer. Nontechnical correspondence should be sent to the BBC World Service in London (see).

Radio Oman, P.O. Box 600, Muscat, Oman. Fax: +968 602 055 or +968 602 831. Contact: (general) Director General, Radio; (technical) Rashid Haroon Aljabry or A. Al-Sawafi. Replies irregularly, and responses can take anywhere from two weeks to two years. $1, return postage or 3 IRCs helpful.

PAKISTAN   World Time +5
Azad Kashmir Radio, Muzaffarabad, Azad Kashmir, Pakistan. Contact: (technical) M. Sajjad Ali Siddiqui, Director of Engineering; or Liaquatullah Khan, Engineering Manager. Registered mail helpful. Rarely replies to correspondence.
Pakistan Broadcasting Corporation—same address, fax and contact as "Radio Pakistan," below.
Radio Pakistan, P.O. Box 1393, Islamabad 44000, Pakistan.

Phone: +92 (51) 813-802 or +91 (51) 829-022. Fax: +92 (51) 811 861. Contact: (technical) Anwer Inayet Khan, Senior Broadcast Engineer, Room No. 324, Frequency Management Cell; Syed Abrar Hussain, Controller Frequency Management; Syed Asmat Ali Shah, Senior Broadcasting Engineer; or Nasirahmad Bajwa, Frequency Management. Free stickers, pennants and *Pakistan Calling* magazine. May also send pocket calendar. Plans to replace two 50 kW transmitters with 500 kW units if and when funding is forthcoming.

PALAU   World Time +9
KHBN—Voice of Hope, P.O. Box 66, Koror, Palau, Pacific Islands. Phone: +680 488-2162. Fax: +680 488 2163. Contact: (general) Joseph Tan, Station Manager; (technical) Joe Fay, Chief Engineer. Free stickers and publications. IRC requested. Also, *see* KVOH—Voice of Hope/High Adventure Ministries, USA.

PALESTINIAN AUTHORITY (West Bank and Gaza)   World Time +2 (+3 midyear)
Voice of Palestine—*see* Yemen.

PAPUA NEW GUINEA   World Time +10
National Broadcasting Commission of Papua New Guinea, P.O. Box 1359, Boroko, Papua New Guinea. Phone: +675 3253-022. Fax: +675 3255 403 or +675 3230 404. Contact: (general) Renagi Lohia, Chairman and C.E.O.; Francesca Maredei, Planning Officer; (technical) Bob Kabewa, Sr. Technical Officer. Two IRCs or return postage helpful. Replies irregularly.
Radio Bougainville, P.O. Box 35, Buka, North Solomons Province (NSP), Papua New Guinea. Fax: +675 939 912. Contact: Demas Kumaina, Provincial Programme Manager; Ms. Christine Talei, Assistant Provincial Manager; or Aloysius Laukai, Senior Programme Officer. Replies irregularly.
Radio Central, P.O. Box 1359, Boroko, NCD, Papua New Guinea. Contact: Steven Gamini, Station Manager; or Amos Langit, Technician. $1, 2 IRCs or return postage helpful. Replies irregularly.
Radio Eastern Highlands (Karai Bilong Kumul), P.O. Box 311, Goroka, EHP, Papua New Guinea. Fax: +675 722 841. Contact: Ignas Yanam, Technical Officer; or Kiri Nige, Engineering Division. $1 or return postage required. Replies irregularly.
Radio East New Britain, P.O. Box 393, Rabaul, ENBP, Papua New Guinea. Fax: +675 923 254. Contact: Esekia Mael, Station Manager; or Otto Malatane, Provincial Program Manager. Return postage required. Replies slowly.
Radio East Sepik, P.O. Box 65, Wewak, E.S.P., Papua New Guinea. Fax: +675 862 405. Contact: Elias Albert, Assistant Provincial Program Manager; or Luke Umbo, Station Manager.
Radio Enga, P.O. Box 300, Wabag, Enga Province, Papua New Guinea. Phone: +675 571 213. Fax: +675 571 069. Contact: (general) John Lyein Kur, Station Manager; or Robert Papuvo, Provincial Programme Manager; (technical) Felix Tumun K., Station Technician.
Radio Gulf, P.O. Box 36, Kerema, Gulf, Papua New Guinea. Contact: Robin Wainetta, Station Manager; or Timothy Akia, Provincial Program Manager.
Radio Madang, P.O. Box 2138, Yomba, Madang, Papua New Guinea. Fax: +675 822 360. Contact: (general) Simon Tiori, Station Manager; D. Boaging, Assistant Manager; Peter Charlie Yannum, Assistant Provincial Programme Manager; or James Steve Valakvi, Assistant Provincial Program Manager; (technical) Lloyd Guvil, Technician.
Radio Manus, P.O. Box 505, Lorengau, Manus, Papua New Guinea. Phone: +675 409-146. Fax: +675 409 079. Contact: (technical and nontechnical) John P. Mandrakamu, Provincial Program Manager. Return postage appreciated.
Radio Milne Bay, P.O. Box 111, Alotau, Milne Bay, Papua New Guinea. Contact: (general) Trevor Webumo, Assistant Manager; Simon Muraga, Station Manager; or Raka Petuely, Program Officer; (technical) Philip Maik, Technician.

Radio Morobe, P.O. Box 1262, Lae, Morobe, Papua New Guinea. Fax: +675 426 423. Contact: Ken L. Tropu, Assistant Program Manager; Peter W. Manua, Program Manager; or Aloysius R. Nase, Station Manager.

Radio New Ireland, P.O. Box 140, Kavieng, New Ireland, Papua New Guinea. Fax: +675 941 489. Contact: Otto A. Malatana, Station Manager; or Ruben Bale, Provincial Program Manager. Return postage or $1 helpful.

Radio Northern, Voice of Oro, P.O. Box 137, Popondetta, Oro, Papua New Guinea. Contact: Roma Tererembo, Assistant Provincial Programme Manager; or Misael Pendaia, Station Manager. Return postage required.

Radio Sandaun, P.O. Box 37, Vanimo, West Sepik, Papua New Guinea. Fax: +675 871 305. Contact: (nontechnical) Gabriel Deckwalen, Station Manager; Elias Rathley, Provincial Programme Manager; or Miss Norryne Pate, Secretary; (technical) Paia Ottawa, Technician. $1 helpful.

Radio Simbu, P.O. Box 228, Kundiawa, Chimbu, Papua New Guinea. Phone: +675 751-038 or +675 751-082. Fax: +675 751 012. Contact: (general) Tony Mill Waine, Provincial Programme Manager; Felix Tsiki; or Thomas Ghiyandiule, Producer, "Pasikam Long ol Pipel"; (technical) Gabriel Paiao, Station Technician. Cassette recordings $5. Free two-Kina banknotes.

Radio Southern Highlands, P.O. Box 104, Mendi, SHP, Papua New Guinea. Phone: +675 591-020 or +675 591-137. Fax: +675 591 017. Contact: (general) Andrew Meles, Programme Manager; Miriam Piapo, Programme Officer; Benard Kagaro, Programme Officer; Lucy Aluy, Programme Officer; or Nicholas Sambu, Producer, "Questions & Answers"; (technical) Ronald Helori, Station Technician. $1 or return postage helpful; or donate a wall poster of a rock band, singer or American landscape.

Radio United Bougainville, Public Awareness Campaign Unit, P.O. Box 268, Buka, Papua New Guinea. Fax: +675 968 001. Reportedly funded by the Bougainville Transitional Government, this essentially official station has been established to counter the rebel station, "Radio Free Bougainville" (see under Disestablishmentarian).

Radio Western, P.O. Box 23, Daru, Western Province, Papua New Guinea. Contact: (general) Geo Gedabing, Provincial Programme Manager; (technical) Samson Tobel, Technician. $1 or return postage required. Replies irregularly.

Radio Western Highlands, P.O. Box 311, Mount Hagen, WHP, Papua New Guinea. Fax: +675 521 279. Contact: (technical) Esau Okole, Technician. $1 or return postage helpful. Replies occasionally.

Radio West New Britain, P.O. Box 412, Kimbe, WNBP, Papua New Guinea. Fax: +675 935 600. Contact: Valuka Lowa, Provincial Station Manager; Lemeck Kuam, Producer, "Questions and Answers"; or Esekial Mael. Return postage required.

PARAGUAY   World Time –3 (–4 midyear)

La Voz del Chaco Paraguayo, Filadelfia, Dpto. de Boquerón, Chaco, Paraguay. This station, currently only on mediumwave AM, hopes to add a world band transmitter within the 60-meter (5 MHz) band. However, to date nothing concrete has come of this.

Radio Encarnación, Gral. Artigas casi Gral. B. Caballero, Encarnación, Paraguay. Phone: (general) +595 (71) 4376 or +595 (71) 3345; (press) +595 (71) 4120. Fax: +595 (71) 4099.

Radio Nacional, Calle Montevideo, esq. Estrella, Asunción, Paraguay. Phone: +595 (21) 449-213. Fax: +595 (21) 332 750. Contact: Carlos Tomás Montaner, Director Técnico. Free tourist brochure. $1 or return postage required. Replies, sometimes slowly, to correspondence in Spanish; the director, a former basketball player, is interested in basketball-related subjects.

PERU   World Time –5 year-round in Loreto, Cusco and Puno. Other departments sometimes move to World Time –4 for a few weeks of the year.

NOTE: Obtaining replies from Peruvian stations calls for

creativity, tact, patience—and the proper use of Spanish, not form letters and the like. There are nearly 150 world band stations operating from Perú on any given day. While virtually all of these may be reached simply by using as the address the station's city, as given in the Blue Pages, the following are the only stations known to be replying—even if only occasionally—to correspondence from abroad.

Estación C, Casilla de Correo 210, Moyobamba, San Martín, Peru.

Estación Soritor—see Radio Estelar.

Estación Tarapoto, Jirón Federico Sánchez 720, Tarapoto, Peru. Phone: +51 (94) 522-709. Contact: Luis Humberto Hidalgo Sánchez, Gerente General; or José Luna Paima, Announcer. Replies occasionally to correspondence in Spanish.

Estación Wari, Calle Nazareno 108, Ayacucho, Peru. Contact: Walter Muñoz Ynga I., Gerente.

Estación X (Equis), Jirón Mariscal Castilla s/n, Yurimaguas, Alto Amazonas, Peru.

Estación Yurimaguas (if reactivated), Calle Comercio 102, Yurimaguas, Loreto, Peru. Phone: + 51 (31) 2191. Contact: Adolfo Onjanma Tanchiva, Locutor/Director de Producción. Also, Prof. Ronald Ramírez Vela, Director del programa "Enseñanza, Aprendizaje," is interested in feedback on that program, aired Monday to Friday from 1100 to 1130 World Time. Return postage appreciated.

Frecuencia Líder (Radio Bambamarca), Jirón Jorge Chávez 416, Bambamarca, Hualgayoc, Cajamarca, Peru. Contact: (general) Valentín Peralta Díaz, Gerente; Irma Peralta Rojas; or Carlos Antonio Peralta Rojas; (technical) Oscar Lino Peralta Rojas. Free station photos. *La Historia de Bambamarca* book for 5 Soles; cassettes of Peruvian and Latin American folk music for 4 Soles each; T-shirts for 10 Soles each (sending US$1 per Sol should suffice and cover foreign postage costs, as well). Replies occasionally to correspondence in Spanish. Considering replacing their transmitter to improve reception.

Frecuencia San Ignacio, Jirón Villanueva Pinillos 330, San Ignacio, Cajamarca, Peru. Contact: Franklin R. Hoyos Cóndor, Director Gerente; Oscar Vásquez Chacón, Locutor; or Ignacio Gómez Torres, Técnico de Sonido. Replies to correspondence in Spanish. $1 or return postage necessary.

La Voz de la Selva—see Radio La Voz de la Selva.

La Voz de Celendín—see Radio Frecuencia VH, below.

La Voz de Sayapullo, Distrito de Sayapullo, Provincia de Cajabamba, Región Nor Oriental del Marañón, Peru.

La Voz del Marañon—see Radio La Voz del Marañon.

Onda Azul—see Radio Onda Azul, below.

Ondas del Suroriente—see Radio Ondas del Suroriente, below.

Radio Adventista Mundial—La Voz de la Esperanza, Jirón Dos de Mayo No. 218, Celendín, Cajamarca, Peru. Contact: Francísco Goicoechea Ortiz, Director; or Lucas Solano Oyarce, Director de Ventas.

Radio Altura (Cerro de Pasco), Casilla de Correo 140, Cerro de Pasco, Pasco, Peru. Contact: Oswaldo de la Cruz Vásquez, Gerente General. Replies to correspondence in Spanish.

Radio Altura (Huarmaca), Antonio Raymondi 3ra Cuadra, Distrito de Huarmaca, Provincia de Huancabamba, Piura, Peru.

Radio Amauta, Jirón Manuel Iglesias s/n, a pocos pasos de la Plazuela San Juan, San Pablo, Cajamarca, Nor Oriental del Marañón, Peru.

Radio América, Montero Rosas 1099 Santa Beatriz, Lima, Peru. Phone: +51 (14) 728-985. Fax: +51 (14) 719 909. Contact: Liliana Sugobono F., Directora.

Radio Ancash, Casilla de Correo 210, Huaraz, Peru. Phone: +51 (44) 721-381. Contact: Armando Moreno Romero, Gerente General. Replies to correspondence in Spanish.

Radio Andahuaylas, Jr. Ayacucho No. 248, Andahuaylas,

Folk festival organized by Radio Tayacaja in Peru is held on the campus of Nuestra Señora de Lourdes college.

Apurímac, Peru. Contact: Sr. Daniel Andréu C., Gerente. $1 required. Replies irregularly to correspondence in Spanish.
Radio Apurímac, Jirón Cusco 206 (or Ovalo El Olivo No. 23), Abancay, Apurímac, Peru. Contact: Antero Quispe Allca, Director General.
Radio Atahualpa (when active), Plaza Bolognesi s/n, Cajamarca, Peru; or Valle Riestra 1432, Urb. Colmenares Puerto Libre, Peru. Contact: José Suárez Suárez, Gerente.
Radio Atlántida
STATION: Jirón Arica 441, Iquitos, Loreto, Peru. Phone: +51 (94) 23-2276. Contact: Pablo Rojas Bardales.
LISTENER CORRESPONDENCE: Sra. Carmela López Paredes, Productor, "Trocha Turística," Jirón Arica 1083, Iquitos, Loreto, Peru. Free pennants and tourist information. $1 or return postage required. Replies to most correspondence in Spanish, the preferred language, and some correspondence in English. "Trocha Turística" is a bilingual (Spanish and English) tourist program aired weekdays 2300-2330.
Radio Ayaviri (La Voz de Melgar), Apartado 8, Ayaviri, Puno, Peru. Fax: +51 (54) 32 02 07, specify on fax "Anexo 127." Contact: (general) Sra. Corina Llaiqui Ochoa, Administradora; (technical) José Aristo Solórzano Mendoza, Director. Free pennants. Sells audio cassettes of local folk music for $5 plus postage; also exchanges music cassettes. Correspondence accepted in English, but Spanish preferred.
Radio Bahía, Jirón Alfonso Ugarte 309, Chimbote, Ancash, Peru. Contact: Margarita Rossel Soria, Administradora; or Miruna Cruz Rossel, Administradora.
Radio Cajamarca, Jirón La Mar 675, Cajamarca, Peru. Phone: +51 (44) 921-014. Contact: Porfirio Cruz Potosí.
Radio Chanchamayo, Jirón Tarma 551, La Merced, Junín, Peru.
Radio Chota, Apartado 3, Jirón Fernando Vega 690, Chota, Cajamarca, Peru. Contact: Aladino Gavadía Huamán, Administrador. $1 or return postage required. Replies slowly to correspondence in Spanish.

Radio 5264 (Cinco Mil Doscientos Sesenta y Cuatro), Jirón Ricardo Palma s/n, Chiriaco, Provincia Bagua, Dpto. Amazonas, Peru.
Radio Concordia, Av. La Paz 512-A, Arequipa, Peru. Contact: Pedro Pablo Acosta Fernández. Free stickers. Return postage required.
Radio Continental, Av. Independencia 56, Arequipa, Peru. Contact: Leonor Núñez Melgar. Free stickers. Replies slowly to correspondence in Spanish.
Radio CORA, Compañía Radiofónica Lima, S.A., Paseo de la República 144, Centro Cívico, Oficina 5, Lima 1, Peru. Fax: +51 (14) 336 134. Contact: (general) Juan Ramírez Lazo, Director Gerente; Dra. Lylian Ramírez M., Directora de Prensa y Programación; Juan Ramírez Lazo, Director Gerente; or Ms. Angelina María Abie; (technical) Srta. Sylvia Ramírez M., Directora Técnica. Free station sticky-label pads. Audio cassettes with extracts from their programs $20 plus $2 postage; women's hair bands $2 plus $1 postage. Two IRCs or $1 required. Replies slowly to correspondence in English, Spanish, French, Italian and Portuguese.
Radio Cosmos (when active), Jirón San Martín 484, Celendín, Provincia de Celendín, Departamento de Cajamarca, Peru. Return postage required. Correspondence in Spanish preferred.
Radio Cultural Amauta, Apartado 24, Huanta, Peru. Phone: +51 (64) 932-153. Contact: Vicente Saico Tinco.
Radio Cusco, Apartado 251, Cusco, Peru. Phone: +51 (84) 225-0851. Fax: +51 (84) 223 308. Contact: Sra. Juana Huamán Yépez, Administradora; or Raúl Siú Almonte, Gerente General; (technical) Benjamín Yábar Alvarez. Free pennants, postcards and key rings. Audio cassettes of Peruvian music $10 plus postage. $1 or return postage required. Replies irregularly to correspondence in English or Spanish. Station is looking for folk music recordings from around the world to use in their programs.
Radio Del Pacífico, Casilla de Correo 4236, Lima 1, Peru.

Contact: J. Petronio Allauca, Secretario, Depto. de Relaciones Públicas. $1 or return postage required. Replies occasionally to correspondence in Spanish.

Radiodifusoras Huancabamba, Calle Unión 409, Huancabamba, Piura, Peru.

Radio El Sol de los Andes, Jirón 2 de Mayo 257, Juliaca, Peru. Phone: +51 (54) 321-115. Phone/fax: +51 (54) 322-981. Contact: Armando Alarcón Velarde.

Radio Estación Uno, Barrio Altos, Distrito de Pucará, Provincia Jaén, Nor Oriental del Marañón, Peru.

Radio Estelar, Jirón Manuel del Aguila 301 (or Apartado Postal 26), Moyobamba, Peru. Contact: Ríder Jibaja Ramírez, Gerente Propietario.

Radio Frecuencia VH (La Voz de Celendín), Jirón José Gálvez 730, Celendín, Cajamarca, Peru. Contact: Fernando Vásquez Castro, Propietario.

Radio Frecuencia San Ignacio—see Frecuencia San Ignacio.

Radio Horizonte (Chachapoyas), Apartado 69 (or Jirón Santo Domingo 639), Chachapoyas, Amazonas, Peru. Phone: +51 (74) 757-793. Fax: +51 (74) 757 004. Contact: Sra. Rocío García Rubio, Ing. Electronico, Directora. Replies to correspondence in English, French, German and Spanish. $1 required.

Radio Horizonte (Chiclayo), Calle Incanto 387, Distrito José Leonardo Ortiz, Chiclayo, Peru. Phone: +51 (74) 222-486. Contact: Celia Purizaca Suxe, Secretaria. Return postage required. Sra. Purizaca collects music cassettes from all over the world.

Radio Huancabamba, Calle Unión 610-Barrio Chalaco, Huancabamba, Piura, Peru. Fax: +51 (74) 320 229, specifying "Radio Huancabamba" on fax. Contact: César Colunche Bustamante, Gerente Director Proprietario. Free picture postcards. Replies occasionally to correspondence in English, French, Italian, Portuguese and Spanish. Hopes to replace transmitter.

Radio Huanta 2000, Jirón Gervacio Santillana 455, Huanta, Peru. Phone: +51 (64) 932-105. Contact: Ronaldo Sapaico Maravi, Departamento Técnico; Sra. Lucila Orellana de Paz, Administradora. Free photo of staff. Return postage or $1 appreciated. Replies to correspondence in Spanish.

Radio Huarmaca, Av. Grau 454 (detrás de Inversiones La Loretana), Distrito de Huarmaca, Provincia de Huancabamba, Región Grau, Peru.

Radio Ilucán, Jirón Lima 290, Cutervo, Región Nororiental del Marañón, Peru. Phone: +51 (74) 220-205, Anexo 10. Contact: José Gálvez Salazar, Gerente Administrativo. $1 required. Replies occasionally to correspondence in Spanish, and seems to be friendly with Mr. Takayuki Inoue Nozaki.

Radio Imagen, Casilla de Correo 42, Tarapoto, San Martín, Peru; or Apartado 254, Tarapoto, San Martín, Peru. Contact: Adith Chumbe Vásquez, Secretaria; or Jaime Ríos Tapullima, Gerente General. Replies irregularly to correspondence in Spanish. $1 or return postage helpful.

Radio Imperial, Calle Ayabaca 339-341, Huancabamba, Piura, Peru. Contact: José Gabriel Correa Ruíz, Gerente. Replies occasionally to correspondence in Spanish. May not be active, as transmitter was sold to Radio Mi Frotera (see) in mid-1996.

Radio Inca del Perú (when active), Av. Manco Cápac No. 263, Baños del Inca, Cajamarca, Peru. Contact: Josué Gonzalo Urteaga V., Director Gerente. Replies slowly to correspondence in Spanish.

Radio Integración, Av. Seoane 200, Abancay, Apurímac, Peru. Contact: Zenón Hernán Farfán Cruzado, Propietario.

Radio Internacional del Perú, Jirón Bolognesi 532, San Pablo, Cajamarca, Peru.

Radio Jaén (La Voz de la Frontera), Calle Mariscal Castilla 439, Jaén, Cajamarca, Peru.

Radio Juliaca (La Decana), Apartado Postal 67, Juliaca, San Román, Puno, Peru. Contact: Alberto Quintanilla Ch., Director.

Radio La Hora, Av. Garcilazo 180, Cusco, Peru. Contact: Edmundo Montesinos Gallo, Gerente General. Free stickers, pins, pennants and postcards of Cusco. Return postage required. Replies occasionally to correspondence in Spanish. Hopes to increase transmitter power if and when the economic situation improves.

Radio La Inmaculada, Parroquia La Inmaculada Concepción, Frente de la Plaza de Armas, Santa Cruz, Provincia de Santa Cruz, Departamento de Cajamarca, Peru.

Radio Lajas, Jirón Rosendo Mendívil 589, Lajas, Chota, Cajamarca, Nor Oriental del Marañón, Peru. Contact: Alfonso Medina Burga, Gerente Propietario.

Radio La Merced, Calle Bolognesi s/n, Distrito de Tongod, Provincia de Santa Cruz, Cajamarca, Peru. Contact: Roberto Ramos Llatas, Director Gerente. $1 or return postage required. Formerly replied irregularly to correspondence in Spanish, but currently there is no postal delivery to the area.

Radio La Oroya, Apartado Postal No. 88, La Oroya, Provincia de Yauli, Departamento de Junín, Peru. Contact: Jacinto Manuel Figueroa Yauri, Gerente-Propietario. Free pennants. $1 or return postage necessary. Replies to correspondence in Spanish.

Radio Latina (when active), Av. Sáenz Peña 1558, Chiclayo, Lambayeque, Peru. Phone: +51 (74) 233-140. Contact: Carlos Tipara González, Director General.

Radio La Voz de Cutervo, Jirón María Elena Medina 644-650, Cutervo, Cajamarca, Peru.

Radio La Voz de Huamanga (if reactivated), Calle El Nazareno, 2do Pasaje No. 161, Ayacucho, Peru. Phone: +51 (64) 912-366. Contact: Sra. Aguida A. Valverde Gonzales. Free pennants and postcards.

Radio La Voz de La Selva, Casilla de Correo 207, Iquitos, Loreto, Peru. Phone: +51 (94) 241-515. Fax: +51 (94) 239 360. Contact: Julia Jauregui Rengifo, Directora; Marcelino Esteban Benito, Director; Pedro Sandoval Guzmán, Announcer; or Mery Blas Rojas. Replies to correspondence in Spanish.

Radio La Voz del Marañón, Jirón Bolognesi, Barrio La Alameda, Cajamarca, Nor Oriental del Marañón, Peru.

Radio La Voz de Oxapampa, Av. Mullenbruck 469, Oxapampa, Pasco, Peru. Contact: Pascual Villafranca Guzmán, Director Propietario.

Radio La Voz de San Antonio, Jirón Alfonso Ugarte 732, Bambamarca, Cajamarca, Peru. Contact: Valentín Mejía Vásquez, Director General; Mauricio Rodríguez R.; Wilmer Vásquez Campos, Encargado Administración; Walter Hugo Silva Bautista. $1 or return postage required. Replies to correspondence in Spanish.

Radio La Voz de Santa Cruz, Av. Zarumilla 190, Santa Cruz, Cajamarca, Peru.

Radio Libertad de Junín, Apartado 2, Junín, Peru. Contact: Mauro Chaccha G., Director Gerente. Replies slowly to correspondence in Spanish. Return postage necessary.

Radio Líder, Portal Belén 115, 2do piso, Cuzco, Peru. Contact: Mauro Calvo Acurio, Propietario.

Radio Los Andes, Huarmaca, Huancabamba, Grau, Peru. Contact: William Cerro Calderón.

Radio LTC (Radio Comercial Collao), Jirón Unión 242, Juliaca, Puno, Peru. Phone: +51 (54) 322-452 or +51 (54) 322-560. Fax: +51 (54) 322 570. Contact: Mario Leónidas Torres, Gerente General.

Radio Luz Universal, Baptist Mid-Missions, Apartado 368, Cusco, Peru.

Radio Luz y Sonido
STATION: Seminario Mayor San Teodoro, Jirón 2 de Mayo 1260 (or Jirón Dámaso Beraún 741, Apartado 280, Plaza de Armas), Huánuco, Peru. Phone: +51 (64) 512-394. Contact: Sor (Sister) María Milagros, S.J., Representante; Cirilo Damián, Willy Campos Soto, Seminaristas; or Prof. Jesús Abad Pereira, Director.

LISTENER CORRESPONDENCE: Orlando Bravo Jesús, Comunicador Social, Av. 28 de Agosto 307, Paucarbamba, Huánuco, Peru. Return postage or $1 required. Replies to correspondence in Spanish.

Radio Madre de Dios, Apartado 37, Puerto Maldonado, Madre de Dios, Peru. Phone: +51 (84) 571-050. Contact: Alcides Arguedas Márquez, Director del programa "Un Festival de Música Internacional," heard Mondays 0100 to 0200 World Time. Sr. Arguedas is interested in feedback for this letterbox program. Replies to correspondence in Spanish. $1 or return postage appreciated.

Radio Marañón, Apartado 50, Jaén (via Chiclayo), Peru. Phone/fax: +51 (74) 731-147. Contact: Padre Luis Távara Martín, S.J., Director. Return postage necessary. Replies slowly to correspondence in Spanish.

Radio Melodía, San Camilo 501A, Arequipa, Peru. Contact: J. Elba Alvarez de Delgado, Jefa Administración Personal y Financiera; or Deyssy Torres O. Free stickers, pennants and calendars. $1 or return postage necessary. Replies slowly to correspondence in Spanish.

Radio Mi Frontera, Calle San Ignacio 520, Distrito de Chirinos, Provincia de San Ignacio, Región Nor Oriental del Marañón, Peru.

Radio Mundial Adventista, Colegio Adventista de Titicaca, Casilla 4, Juliaca, Peru.—A new facility, AWR-Perú, with now 5 kW shortwave transmitter, is planned to go on the air in early 1997, assuming the last stages of planning and construction are successful.

Radio Mundo, Calle Tecte 245, Cusco, Peru. Phone: + 51 (84) 232-076. Fax: +51 (84) 233 076. Contact: Valentín Olivera Puelles, Gerente. Free postcards and stickers. Return postage necessary. Replies slowly to correspondence in Spanish.

Radio Municipal de Cangallo (when active), Concejo Provincial de Cangallo, Plaza Principal No. 02, Cangallo, Ayacucho, Peru. Contact: Nivardo Barbarán Agüero, Encargado Relaciones Públicas.

Radio Nacional del Perú
ADMINISTRATIVE OFFICE: Avenida José Gálvez 1040 Santa Beatriz, Lima, Peru. Fax: +51 (14) 726 799. Contact: Henry Aragón Ybarra, Gerente; or Rafael Mego Carrascal, Jefatura de la Administración. Replies occasionally, by letter or listener-prepared verification card, to correspondence in Spanish. Return postage required.
STUDIO ADDRESS: Av. Petit Thouars 447, Lima, Peru.

Radio Naylamp, Avenida Huamachuco 1080, 2do piso, Lambayeque, Peru. Phone: +51 (74) 283-353. Contact: Dr. Juan José Grández Vargas, Director Gerente; or Delicia Coronel Muñoz, who is interested in receiving postcards and the like. Feedback for Dr. J.J.'s weeknightly program "Buenas Tardes, Ecuador," from 0000 to 0100 World Time, appreciated. Free stickers, pennants and calendars. Return postage necessary.

Radio Nor Andina, Jirón José Gálvez 602, Celendín, Cajamarca, Peru. Contact: Misael Alcántara Guevara, Gerente; or Victor B. Vargas C., Departamento de Prensa. Free calendar. $1 required. Donations (registered mail best) sought for the Committee for Good Health for Children, headed by Sr. Alcántara, which is active in saving the lives of hungry youngsters in poverty-stricken Cajamarca Province. Replies irregularly to casual or technical correspondence in Spanish, but regularly to Children's Committee donors and helpful correspondence in Spanish.

Radio Nor Peruana, Emisora Municipal (when active), Jirón Ortiz Arrieta 588, 2do piso, Chachapoyas, Amazonas, Peru. Phone: +51 (44) 981-027. Contact: Fernando Serván Rocha, Director. Replies very slowly to correspondence in Spanish. Return postage necessary.

Radio Onda Azul, Apartado 210, Puno, Peru. Phone: +51 (54) 351-562. Fax: +51 (54) 352 233. Contact: (general) Mauricio Rodríguez R., Jefe de Producción y Programación; (technical) Marino Rojas Olazabal, Administrador. Free key rings, calendars and diaries. Return postage required. Replies to correspondence in Spanish.

Radio Onda Imperial, Calle Sacsayhuanan K-10, Urbanización Manuel Prado, Cusco, Peru.

Radio Ondas del Huallaga, Apartado 343, Jirón Leoncio Prado 723, Huánuco, Peru. Phone: +51 (64) 512-428. Contact: Flaviano Llanos M., Representante Legal. $1 or return postage required. Replies to correspondence in Spanish.

Radio Ondas del Río Mayo (while continued active), Jirón Huallaga 348, Nueva Cajamarca, San Martín, Peru. Contact: Edilberto Lucío Peralta Lozada, Gerente; or Víctor Huaras Rojas, Locutor. Free pennants. Return postage helpful. Replies slowly to correspondence in Spanish. Station was raided by the authorities in 1996, but went back on the air, anyway, as an act of defiance.

Radio Ondas del Suroriente, Jirón Ricardo Palma 510, Quillabamba, La Convención, Cusco, Peru.

Radio Oriente, Vicariato Apostólico, Calle Progreso 114, Yurimaguas, Loreto, Peru. Phone: +51 (94) 352-156. Phone/fax (ask to switch over to fax): +51 (94) 352-566. Contact: (general) Sra. Elisa Cancino Hidalgo; Juan Antonio López-Manzanares M., Director; (technical) Pedro Capo Moragues, Gerente Técnico. $1 or return postage required. Replies occasionally to correspondence in English, French, Spanish and Catalan.

Radio Origen, Avenida Augusto B. Leguía 196, Huancavelica, Peru. Contact: Oscar Andrez Alvarado Yalico, Director General y Propietario. $1 or return postage required. Replies occasionally to correspondence in Spanish.

Radio Paccha, Calle Mariscal Castilla 52, Paccha, Provincia de Chota, Departamento de Cajamarca, Peru.

Radio Paucartambo, Jirón Conde de las Lagunas, 2do piso, Frente al Hostal San José, Paucartambo, Pasco, Peru. Contact: Irwin Junio Berrios Pariona, Gerente General. Replies occasionally to correspondence in Spanish.

Radio Paucartambo, Emisora Municipal
STATION ADDRESS: Paucartambo, Cusco, Peru.
STAFFER ADDRESS: Manuel H. Loaiza Canal, Correo Central, Paucartambo, Cusco, Peru. Sr. Loaiza, who hosts the weeknightly music show, "El Bus Musical," heard from 2300-2400 World Time, seeks feedback on the program. Return postage or $1 required.

Radio Quillabamba, Centro de los Medios de la Comunicación Social, Quillabamba, La Convención, Cusco, Peru. Contact: Padre Francisco Panera, Director. Replies very irregularly to correspondence in Spanish.

Radio Reina de la Selva, Jirón Ayacucho 944, Plaza de Armas, Chachapoyas, Amazonas, Peru. Contact: José David Reina N., Director. Replies irregularly to correspondence in Spanish. Return postage necessary.

Radio San Francisco Solano, Parroquia de Sóndor, Calle San Miguel No. 207, Distrito de Sóndor, Huancabamba, Piura, Peru. Contact: Padre Manuel J. Rosas C., Vicario Parroquial. Station operated by the Franciscan Fathers. Replies to correspondence in Spanish. $1 helpful.

Radio San Ignacio (La Voz de la Frontera), Jirón Mercado 218, San Ignacio, Cajamarca, Peru. Contact: Pedro Alfonso Morales y Sáenz, Director General; Dr. Daniel Carrillo Mendoza, Asesor legal y jurídico.

Radio San Juan, Pasaje San Martín 300, Urbanización Alto Mochica, Trujillo, Peru. Phone: +51 (44) 263-592. Contact: Santiago López Valderrama, Gerente.

Radio San Martín (when active), Jirón Progreso 225, Tarapoto, San Martín, Peru. Contact: Fernando Tafur Arévalo, Gerente General. May send stickers and magazines. Return postage required. Replies occasionally to correspondence in Spanish.

Radio San Miguel, Av. Huayna Cápac 146, Huánchac, Cusco, Peru. Contact: Sra. Catalina Pérez de Alencastre, Gerente General; or Margarita Mercado. Replies to correspondence in Spanish.

Radio San Miguel Arcángel, Jirón Grau 493, San Miguel de Pallaques, Cajamarca, Peru.

Radio Santa Rosa, Casilla 4451, Lima 1, Peru. Phone: +51 (14) 277-488. Fax: +51 (14) 276 791. Contact: Padre Juan Sokolich Alvarado; or Lucy Palma Barreda. Free stickers and pennants. $1 or return postage necessary. 180-page book commemorating stations 35th anniversary $10. Replies to correspondence in Spanish.

Radio Satélite E.U.C., Jirón Cutervo No. 543, Cajamarca, Santa Cruz, Peru. Contact: Sabino Llamo Chávez, Gerente. Free tourist brochure. $1 or return postage required. Replies irregularly to correspondence in Spanish.

Radio Sicuani, Jirón 2 de Mayo 206, Sicuani, Canchis, Cusco, Peru; or P.O. Box 45, Sicuani, Peru. Contact: Mario Ochoa Vargas, Director.

Radio Soledad, Centro Minero de Retama, Distrito de Parcoy, Provincia de Pataz, La Libertad, Peru. Contact: Vicente Valdivieso, Locutor. Return postage necessary.

Radio Sudamérica, Jirón Ramón Castilla 704, 2^0 piso, Cutervo, Cajamarca, Peru. Contact: Jorge Paredes Guerra, Administrador; or Amadeo Mario Muñoz Guivar, Propietario.

Radio Tacna, Casilla de Correo 370, Tacna, Peru. Phone: +51 (54) 714-871.Fax: +51 (54) 723 745. Contact: (nontechnical and technical) Ing. Alfonso Cáceres Contreras, Sub-Gerente/Jefe Técnico; (administration) Yolanda Vda. de Cáceres C., Directora Gerente. Free stickers and samples of Correo local newspaper. $1 or return postage helpful. Audio cassettes of Peruvian and other music $2 plus postage. Replies irregularly to correspondence in English and Spanish.

Radio Tarma, Casilla de Correo 167, Tarma, Peru. Contact: Mario Monteverde Pumareda, Gerente General. Sometimes sends 100 Inti banknote in return when $1 enclosed. Free stickers. $1 or return postage required. Replies irregularly to correspondence in Spanish.

Radio Tayacaja, Correo Central, Distrito de Pampas, Tayacaja, Huancavelica, Peru. Phone: +51 (64) 22-02-17, Anexo 238. Contact: (general) J. Jorge Flores Cárdenas; (technical) Ing. Larry Guido Flores Lezama. Free stickers and pennants. Replies to correspondence in Spanish. Hopes to replace transmitter.

Radio Tingo María, Jirón Callao 115 (or Av. Raimondi No. 592), Casilla de Correo 25, Tingo María, Leoncio Prado, Peru. Contact: Gina A. de la Cruz Ricalde, Administradora; or Ricardo Abad Vásquez, Gerente. Free brochures. $1 required. Replies slowly to correspondence in Spanish.

Radio Tropical, S.A., Casilla de Correo 31, Tarapoto, Peru. Fax: +51 (94) 522 155. Contact: Mery A. Rengifo Tenazoa; or Luis F. Mori Roatogui, Gerente. Free stickers, occasionally free pennants, and station history booklet. $1 or return postage required. Replies occasionally to correspondence in Spanish.

Radio Unión, Apartado 833, Lima 27, Peru. Phone: +51 (14) 408-657. Fax: +51 (14) 407 594. Contact: Juan Carlos Sologuren, Dpto. de Administración, who collects stamps. Free satin pennants and stickers. IRC required, and enclosing used or new stamps from various countries is especially appreciated. Replies irregularly to correspondence and tape recordings, especially from young women, with Spanish preferred.

Radio Victoria, Av. Tacna 225 4to piso, Lima 1, Peru. Fax: +51 (14) 427-1195. This station is owned by the Brazilian-run Pentecostal Church "Dios Es Amor." Their program "La Voz de la Liberación" is produced locally and aired over numerous Peruvian shortwave stations.

Radio Villa Rica
GENERAL CORRESPONDENCE: Jirón Virrey Toledo 544, Huancavelica, Peru. Contact: Srta. Maritza Pozo Manrique. Free informative pamphlets. Local storybooks and poems from Huancavelica $15; cassettes of Peruvian and Andean regional music $20; also sells cloth and wooden folk articles. Replies occasionally to correspondence in Spanish.

TECHNICAL CORRESPONDENCE: Apartado 92, Huancavelica, Peru. Contact: Fidel Hilario Huamani, Director. $3 required in return postage for a reply to a reception report from abroad.

Radio Visión 2000 (when active), Radiodifusora Comercial Visión 2000, Jirón Prolongación Mariscal Sucre s/n, Bambamarca, Hualgayoc, Cajamacra, Peru. Contact: Víctor Marino Tello Cruzado, Propietario. Return postage required. Replies slowly to correspondence in Spanish.

PHILIPPINES   World Time +8

NOTE: Philippine stations sometimes send publications with lists of Philippine young ladies seeking "pen pal" courtships.

Far East Broadcasting Company—FEBC Radio International (External Service)
MAIN OFFICE: P.O. Box 1, Valenzuela, Metro Manila 0560, Philippines. Phone: +63 (2) 292-5603, or +63 (2) 292-9403. Fax: +63 (2) 292 9430, but lacks funds to provide faxed replies. E-mail: (English Department) english@febc.jmf.org.ph; (Peter McIntyre, Host "DX Dial") dx@febc.jmf.org.ph or pm@febc.jfm.org.ph; (Jane Colley) jane@febc.jmf.org.ph; (Roger Foyle) foyle@febc.jmf.org.ph; (Mrs. Fay Olympia) alvarez@febc.jmf.org.ph; (Christine Johnson) cjohnson@febc.jmf.org.ph; (Larry Podmore) lpodmore@febc.jmf.org.ph. URL: http://www.febc.org/febchome.html. Contact: (general) Peter McIntyre, Manager, International Operations Division & Producer, "DX Dial"; Jane Colley, Head, Audience Relations; Roger P. Foyle, Audience Relations Counsellor & Acting DX Secretary; Ella McIntyre, Producer, "Mailbag" and "Let's Hear from You"; Fay Olympia, English Programme Supervisor; Ms. Madini Tluanga, Producer, "Good Morning from Manila"; Christine D. Johnson, Head, Overseas English Service; David Miller, Chief News Editor, FEB-News Bureau; (administration) Carlos Peña, Managing Director; (engineering) Ing. Renato Valentin, Frequency Manager; Larry Podmore, IBG Chief Engineer. Free stickers, calendar cards and DX Club Registration. Three IRCs appreciated for airmail reply. Plans to add a new 100 kW shortwave transmitter.
NEW DELHI BUREAU, NONTECHNICAL: c/o FEBA, Box 6, New Delhi-110 001, India.

Far East Broadcasting Company (Domestic Service), Bgy. Bayanan Baco Radyo DZB2, c/o ONF Calapan, Orr. Mindoro 5200, Philippines. Contact: (general) Dangio Onday, Program Supervisor/OIC; (technical) Danilo Flores, Broadcast Technician.

Radyo Pilipinas, the Voice of Democracy, Philippine Broadcasting Service, 4th Floor, PIA Building, Visayas Avenue, 1100 Quezon City, Metro Manila, Philippines. Phone: (general) +63 (2) 924-2620 or +63 (2) 924-2548; (engineering) +63 (2) 924-2268. Fax: +63 (2) 924 2745. Contact: (nontechnical) Evelyn Salvador Agato, Officer-in-Charge; Mercy Lumba; Leo Romano, Producer, "Listeners and Friends"; or Richard Lorenzo, Production Coordinator; (technical) Danilo Alberto, Supervisor; or Mike Pangilinan, Engineer. Free postcards & stickers.

Radio Veritas Asia
STUDIOS AND ADMINISTRATIVE HEADQUARTERS: P.O. Box 2642, Quezon City 1166, Philippines. Phone: +63 (2) 900-012. Fax: +63 (2) 907 436. Contact: Ms. Cleofe R. Labindao, Audience Relations Supervisor; or Msgr. Pietro Nguyen Van Tai, Program Director; (administration) Ms. Erlinda G. So, Manager; (technical) Ing. Floremundo L. Kiguchi, Technical Director; or Frequency and Monitoring Department. Free caps, T-shirts, stickers, pennants, rulers, pens, postcards and calendars.
TRANSMITTER SITE: Radio Veritas Asia, Palauig, Zambales, Philippines. Contact: Fr. Hugo Delbaere, CICM, Technical Consultant.
BRUSSELS BUREAUS AND MAIL DROPS: Catholic Radio and Television Network, 32-34 Rue de l' Association, B-1000 Brussels, Belgium; or UNDA, 12 Rue de l'Orme, B-1040 Brussels, Belgium.

Voice of America/VOA-IBB—Poro and Tinang Relay Stations. Phone: +63 (2) 813-0470/1/2. Fax: +63 (2) 813 0469. Contact: Frank Smith, Manager; or David Strawman, Deputy Manager. These numbers for urgent technical matters only. Otherwise, does not welcome direct correspondence; see USA for acceptable VOA Washington address and related information.

PIRATE

Pirate radio stations are usually one-person operations airing home-brew entertainment and/or iconoclastic viewpoints. In order to avoid detection by the authorities, they tend to appear irregularly, with little concern for the niceties of conventional program scheduling. Most are found in Europe chiefly on weekends, and mainly during evenings in North America, often just above 6200 kHz, just below 7000 kHz and just above 7375 kHz. These *sub rosa* stations and their addresses are subject to unusually abrupt change or termination, sometimes as a result of forays—increasingly common in such countries as the United States—by radio authorities.

Two worthy sources of current addresses and other information on American pirate radio activity are: *The Pirate Radio Directory*, by Andrew Yoder and George Zeller [Tiare Publications, P.O. Box 493, Lake Geneva WI 53147 USA, U.S. toll-free phone (800) 420-0579; or for specific inquiries, fax author Zeller directly at +1 (216) 696 0770], an excellent annual reference; and A*C*E, Box 11201, Shawnee Mission KS 66207 USA (URL: http://www.access.digex.net/~cps/ACE.html), a club which publishes a periodical ($20/year U.S., US$21 Canada, $27 elsewhere) for serious pirate radio enthusiasts. Pirate information is also available via URL http://www.ttn.nai.net/ (subject "Monday Night Jive").

A show on a specialized form of American pirate activity—low-powered local (usually FM) stations—is "Micro-Radio in the U.S.," aired over Radio for Peace International, Costa Rica, some Mondays at 2130 and some Thursdays at 2200 World Time on 6200 or 7385 kHz, plus 15050 kHz.

For Europirate DX try:

SRSNEWS, Swedish Report Service, Ostra Porten 29, S-442 54 Ytterby, Sweden. E-mail: srs@ice.warp.slink.se. URL: http://www-pp.kdt.net/jonny/index.html.

Pirate Connection, Kämnärsvägen 13D:220, S-226 46 Lund, Sweden. Six issues annually for about $23. Related to SRSNEWS, above.

Pirate Chat, 21 Green Park, Bath, Avon, BA1 1HZ, United Kingdom.

FRS Goes DX, P.O. Box 2727, 6049 ZG Herten, Holland

Free-DX, 3 Greenway, Harold Park, Romford, Essex, RM3 OHH, United Kingdom.

FRC-Finland, P.O. Box 82, SF-40101 Jyvaskyla, Finland.

Pirate Express, Postfach 220342, Wuppertal, Germany.

For up-to-date listener discussions and other pirate-radio information on the Internet, the usenet URLs are: alt.radio.pirate and rec.radio.pirate.

POLAND   World Time +1 (+2 midyear)

Polish Radio Warsaw

STATION: External Service, P.O. Box 46, 00-977 Warsaw, Poland. Phone: (general) +48 (22) 645-9305; (English Section) +48 (22) 645-9262; (German Section) +48 (22) 645-9333; (placement liaison) +48 (2) 645-9002. Fax: (general and administration) +48 (22) 645 5917 or +48 (22) 645 5919; (placement liaison) +48 (2) 645 5906. URL: (RealAudio in English and Polish) http://www.wrn.org/stations/poland.html; (text in Polish) http://www.radio.com.pl/. Contact: (general) Rafa Kiepuszewski, Head, English Section & Producer, "Postbag"; or Ann Plapan, Corresponding Secretary; (administration) Jerzy M. Nowakowski, Managing Director; Bogumi a Berdychowska, Deputy Director; Maciej Lętowski, Executive Manager. Free stickers, pens, key rings and possibly T-shirts. DX Listeners' Club. Plans to use Russian relay facilities.

TRANSMISSION AUTHORITY: PAR (National Radiocommunication Agency), ul. Kasprzaka 18/20, 01-211 Warsaw,

Poland. Phone: +48 (22) 658-5140. Fax: +48 (22) 658 5175. Contact: Ms. Filomena Grodzicka, Ms. Urszula Rzepa or Jan Kondej.

Radio Maryja, ul. Zwirki i Wigury 80, 87-100 Torun, Poland. Phone: +48 (56) 36-580/2. Fax: +48 (56) 36 572. Contact: Rafak Kiepuszenski, Editor. Direct replies appear not to be forthcoming, at least to correspondence in English. A Catholic station, Radio Maryja has been under investigation since March, 1996, by Polish government authorities for alleged financial transgressions.

PORTUGAL   World Time +1 (+2 midyear); Azores World Time −1 (World Time midyear)

RDP International—Rádio Portugal, Box 1011, Lisbon 1001, Portugal. Phone: (main office) +351 (1) 347-5065/8; (engineering) +351 (1) 387-1109. Fax: (main office) +351 (1) 347 4475; (engineering) +351 (1) 387 1381. Contact: (general) "Listeners' Mailbag," English Service; or Arlindo de Carvalho; (administration) José Manuel Nunes, Chairman; (technical) Winnie Almeida, DX Producer/Host, English Section; Eng. Francisco Mascarenhas; or Rui de Jesus, Frequency Manager. Free stickers, paper pennants and calendars. May send literature from the Portuguese National Tourist Office.

Rádio Renascença, Rua Ivens 14, 1294 Lisbon Codex, Portugal. Phone: +351 (1) 347-5270. Fax: +351 (1) 342 2658. Contact: C. Pabil, Director-Manager.

Radio Trans Europe (transmission facilities), 6° esq., Rua Braamcamp 84, 1200 Lisbon, Portugal. Transmitter located at Sines.

Voice of Orthodoxy—see Belarus.

QATAR   World Time +3

Qatar Broadcasting Service, P.O. Box 3939, Doha, Qatar. Phone: +974 86-48-05. Fax: +974 82 28 88. Contact: Jassem Mohamed Al-Qattan, Head of Public Relations. May send booklet on Qatar Broadcasting Service. Rarely replies, but return postage helpful.

ROMANIA   World Time +2 (+3 midyear)

Radio România International

STATION: P.O. Box 111, RO-70756 Bucharest, Romania; or Romanian embassies worldwide. Phone: (general) +40 (1) 312-3645; (engineering) +40 (1) 312-1057. Fax: (general) +40 (1) 223 2613 [if no connection, try via office of the Director General of Radio România, but mark fax "Pentru RRI"; that fax is +40 (1) 222 5641]; (Engineering Services) +40 (1) 312 1056/7 or +40 (1) 615 6992. E-mail: rri@radio.ror.ro. URL: (general) http://indis.ici.ro/romania/news/rri.html; (RealAudio) in English) http://www.wrn.org/stations/romania/html. Contact: (communications in English, Romanian or German) Frederica Dochinoiu, Sorin Gugonea or Dan Balamat, "Listeners' Letterbox"; (radio enthusiasts' issues, English only) "DX Mailbag," English Department; (communications in French or Romanian) Doru Vasile Ionescu, Director; (technical) Ms. Sorin Floricu, Radu Ianculescu or Marius Nisipeanu, Engineering Services. Free stickers, pennants, posters, pins and assorted other items. Can provide supplementary materials for "Romanian by Radio" course on audio cassettes. Listeners' Club. Annual contests. Replies slowly but regularly. Concerns about frequency management should be directed to the PTT (see below), with copies to the Romanian Autonomous Company (see farther below) and to a suitable official at RRI.

TRANSMISSION AND FREQUENCY MANAGEMENT, PTT: General Directorate of Regulations, Ministry of Communications, 14a Al. Libertatii, 70060 Bucharest, Romania. Phone: +40 (1) 400-1060. Fax: +40 (1) 400 1230. Contact: Mrs. Elena Danila.

TRANSMISSION AND FREQUENCY MANAGEMENT, AUTONOMOUS COMPANY: Romanian Autonomous Company for Radio Communications, 14a Al. Libertatii, 70060 Bucharest, Romania. Phone: +40 (1) 400-1228. Contact: Mr. Marian Ionita.

RUSSIA (Times given for republics, oblasts and krays):

- World Time +2 (+3 midyear) Kaliningradskaya;
- World Time +3 (+4 midyear) Arkhangel'skaya (incl. Nenetskiy), Astrakhanskaya, Belgorodskaya, Bryanskaya, Ivanovskaya, Kaluzhskaya, Karelia, Kirovskaya, Komi, Kostromskaya, Kurskaya, Lipetskaya, Moscovskaya, Murmanskaya, Nizhegorodskaya, Novgorodskaya, Orlovskaya, Penzenskaya, Pskovskaya, Riazanskaya, Samarskaya, Sankt-Peterburgskaya, Smolenskaya, Tambovskaya, Tulskaya, Tverskaya, Vladimirskaya, Vologodskaya, Volgogradskaya, Voronezhskaya, Yaroslavskaya;
- World Time +4 (+5 midyear) Checheno-Ingushia, Chuvashia, Dagestan, Kabardino-Balkaria, Kalmykia, Krasnodarskiy, Mari-Yel, Mordovia, Severnaya Osetia, Stavropolskiy, Tatarstan, Udmurtia;
- World Time +5 (+6 midyear) Bashkortostan, Chelyabinskaya, Kurganskaya, Orenburgskaya, Permskaya, Yekaterinburgskaya, Tyumenskaya;
- World Time +6 (+7 midyear) Altayskiy, Omskaya;
- World Time +7 (+8 midyear) Kemerovskaya, Krasnoyarskiy (incl. Evenkiyskiy), Novosibirskaya, Tomskaya, Tuva;
- World Time +8 (+9 midyear) Buryatia, Irkutskaya;
- World Time +9 (+10 midyear) Amurskaya, Chitinskaya, Sakha (West);
- World Time +10 (+11 midyear) Khabarovskiy, Primorskiy, Sakha (Center), Yevreyskaya;
- World Time +11 (+12 midyear) Magadanskaya (exc. Chukotskiy, Sakha (East), Sakhalinskaya;
- World Time +12 (+13 midyear) Chukotskiy, Kamchatskaya, Koryakskiy;
- World Time +13 (+14 midyear) all points east of longtitude 172.30 E.

WARNING—MAIL THEFT: Airmail correspondence containing funds or IRCs from North America and Japan may not arrive safely even if sent by registered air mail, as such mail enters via Moscow Airport. However, funds sent from Europe, North America and Japan via surface mail enter via St. Petersburg, and thus stand a better chance of arriving safely. Airmail service is otherwise now almost on a par with that of other advanced countries.

VERIFICATION OF STATIONS USING TRANSMITTERS IN ST. PETERSBURG AND KALININGRAD: Transmissions of certain world band stations—such as the Voice of Russia, Golos Rossii, Mayak and China Radio International—when emanating from transmitters located in St. Petersburg and Kaliningrad, may be verified directly from: World Band Verification QSL Service, The State Enterprise for Broadcasting and Radio Communications No. 2 (GPR-2), ul. Akademika Pavlova 13A, 197376 St. Petersburg, Russia. Fax: +7 (812) 234 2971 during working hours. Contact: Mikhail V. Sergeyev, Chief Engineer; or Mikhail Timofeyev, verifier. Free stickers. Two IRCs required for a reply, which upon request includes a copy of "Broadcast Schedule," which gives transmission details (excluding powers) for all transmissions emanating from three distinct transmitter locations: Kaliningrad-Bolshakovo, St. Petersburg and St. Petersburg-Popovka. This organization—which has 26 shortwave, three longwave, 15 mediumwave AM and nine FM transmitters—relays broadcasts for clients for the equivalent of about $0.70-1.00 per kW/hour.

Government Radio Agencies

C.I.S. FREQUENCY MANAGEMENT ENGINEERING OFFICE: The Main Centre for Control of Broadcasting Networks, ul. Nikolskaya 7, 103012 Moscow, Russia. +7 (095) 921-2501. Fax: +7 (095) 956 7546 or +7 (095) 921 1624. Contact: (general) Mrs. Antonia Ostakhova or Ms. Margarita Ovetchkina; (administration) Anatoliy T. Titov, Chief Director. This office plans the frequency usage for transmitters throughout much of the C.I.S. Correspondence should be concerned only with significant technical observations or engineering suggestions concerning frequency management improvement—not regular requests for verifications. Correspondence in Russian preferred, but English accepted.

STATE ENTERPRISE FOR BROADCASTING AND RADIO COMMUNICATIONS NO. 2 (GPR-2)—see VERIFICATION OF STATIONS USING TRANSMITTERS IN ST. PETERSBURG AND KALININGRAD, above.

STATE RADIO COMPANY: AS "Radioagency Co., Pyatnitskaya 25, 113326 Moscow, Russia. Phone: (Khlebnikov and Petrunicheva) +7 (095) 233-6474; (Komissarova) +7 (095) 233-6660; (Staviskaia) +7 (095) 233-7003. Fax: (Khlebnikov, Petrunicheva and Komissarova) +7 (095) 233 1342; (Staviskaia) +7 (095) 230 2828 or +7 (095) 233 7648. Contact: Valentin Khlebnikov, Mrs. Maris Petrunicheva, Mrs. Lyudmila Komissarova or Mrs. Rachel Staviskaia.

STATE TRANSMISSION AUTHORITY: Russian Ministry of Telecommunication, ul. Tverskaya 7, 103375 Moscow, Russia. Phone: +7 (095) 201-6568. Fax: +7 (095) 292 7086 or +7 (095) 292 7128. Contact: Anatoly C. Batiouchkine.

STATE TV AND RADIO COMPANY: Russian State TV & Radio Company, ul. Yamskogo 5, Polya 19/21, 125124 Moscow, Russia. Phone: +7 (095) 213-1054, +7 (095) 213-1054 or +7 (095) 250-0511. Fax: +7 (095) 250 0105. Contact: Ivan Sitilenlov.

Adventist World Radio, the Voice of Hope, AWR-Russia, The Voice of Hope Media Center, P.O. Box 170, 300000 Tula-Centre, Russia. Fax: +7 (087) 233 1218. Contact: Peter Kulakov, Manager; or Igor Revtov, AWR Coordinator. Free home study Bible guides and other religious material, including some small souvenirs. Often reception reports are redirected to the AWR Europe office (see under Italy). Also, see AWR listings under Costa Rica, Guam, Guatemala, Italy, Kenya and the USA.

Adygey Radio (Radio Maykop), ul. Zhukovskogo 24, 352700 Maykop, Republic of Adygeya, Russia.

Arkhangel'sk Radio, Dom Radio, ul. Popova 2, 163000 Arkhangel'sk, Arkhangel'skaya Oblast, Russia; or U1PR, Valentin G. Kalasnikov, ul. Suvorov 2, kv. 16, Arkhangel'sk, Arkhangel'skaya Oblast, Russia. Replies irregularly to correspondence in Russian.

Bashkir Radio, ul. Gafuri 9, 450076 Ufa, Bashkortostan, Russia.

Buryat Radio, Dom Radio, ul. Erbanova 7, 670000 Ulan-Ude, Republic of Buryatia, Russia. Contact: Z.A. Telin or L.S. Shikhanova.

Chita Radio, ul. Kostushko-Grigorovicha 27, 672090 Chita, Chitinskaya Oblast, Russia. Contact: (technical) V.A. Klimov, Chief Engineer; V.A. Moorzin, Head of Broadcasting; or A.A. Anufriyev.

FEBC Russia, P.O. Box 2128, Khabarovsk 680020, Russia.

Golos Rossii, ul. Pyatnitskaya 25, 113326 Moscow, Russia. Phone: +7 (095) 233-6868. Fax: +7 (095) 233 6449 or +7 (095) 973 2000. Contact: Oleg Maksimovich Poptsov, Chairman of All-Russian State Teleradio Broadcasting Company. Correspondence in Russian preferred. For verification of reception from transmitters located in St. Petersburg and Kaliningrad, *see NOTE,* above, shortly after the country heading, "RUSSIA."

Islamskaya Volna (Islamic Wave), Islamic Center of Moscow Region, Moscow Jami Mosque, Vypolzov per. 7, 129090 Moscow, Russia. Phone: +7 (095) 233-6423/6, +7 (095) 233-6629 or +7 (095) 281-4904. Contact: Sheikh Ravil Gainutdin. Return postage necessary.

Kabardino-Balkar Radio (Radio Nalchik), ul. Nogmova 38, 360000 Nalchik, Republic of Kabardino-Balkariya, Russia.

Kala Alturaia (Voice of Assyria)—see Voice of Russia.

Kamchatka Radio, RTV Center, Dom Radio, ul. Sovietskaya 62-G, 683000 Petropavlovsk-Kamchatskiy, Kamchatskaya Oblast, Russia. Contact: A. Borodin, Chief OTK; or V.I. Aibabin. $1 required. Replies in Russian to correspondence in Russian or English.

Khabarovsk Radio, RTV Center, ul. Lenina 71, 680013 Khabarovsk, Khabarovskiy Kray, Russia; or Dom Radio, pl.

Slavy, 682632 Khabarovsk, Khabarovskiy Kray, Russia. Contact: (technical) V.N. Kononov, Glavnyy Inzhener.

Khanty-Mansiysk Radio, Dom Radio, ul. Mira 7, 626200 Khanty-Mansiysk, Khanty-Mansiyskiy Autonomous Okrug, Tyumenskaya Oblast, Russia. Contact: (technical) Vladimir Sokolov, Engineer.

Koryak Radio, ul. Obukhova 4, 684620 Palana, Koryakskiy Khrebet, Russia.

Krasnoyarsk Radio, RTV Center, Sovietskaya 128, 660017 Krasnoyarsk, Krasnoyarskiy Kray, Russia. Contact: Valeriy Korotchenko; or Anatoliy A. Potehin, RAØAKE. Free local information booklets in English/Russian. Replies in Russian to correspondence in English or Russian. Return postage helpful.

Magadan Radio, RTV Center, ul. Kommuny 8/12, 685013 Magadan, Magadanskaya Oblast, Russia. Contact: Viktor Loktionov or V.G. Kuznetsov. Return postage helpful. May reply to correspondence in Russian.

Mariy Radio, Mari Yel, ul. Osipenko 50, 424014 Yoshkar-Ola, Russia.

Mayak—see Radio Odin and Mayak, below.

Mukto Probaho—see Thailand.

Murmansk Radio, sopka Varnichnaya, 183042 Murmansk, Murmanskaya Oblast, Russia; or RTV Center, Sopka Varnichaya, 183042 Murmansk, Murmanskaya Oblast, Russia.

Northern European Radio Relay Service (NERRS) (when inaugurated), World Band Verification QSL Service, The State Enterprise for Broadcasting and Radio Communications No. 2 (GPR-2), ul. Akademika Pavlova 13A, 197376 St. Petersburg, Russia. Fax: +7 (812) 234 2971. This planned operation hopes to air non-controversial commercial world band programs to Europe.

Primorsk Radio, RTV Center, ul. Uborevieha 20A, 690000 Vladivostok, Primorskiy Kray, Russia. Contact: A.G. Giryuk. Return postage helpful.

Radio Alef (joint project of Voice of Russia and the Jewish Children's Association "Banim Banot"), P.O. Box 72, 123154 Moscow, Russia.

Radio Kudymkar, 617240 Kudymkar, Komi-Permytskiy Autonomous Okrug, Permskaya Oblast, Russia.

Radio Lena, ul. Semena Dezhneva 75-4, Radiocenter, 677002 Yakutsk, Russia.

Radio Maykop—see Adygey Radio, above.

Radio Nalchik—see Radio Kabardino-Balkar, above.

Radio Novaya Volna (New Wave Radio, when operating; an independent program last traced over Radio Odin and Golos Rossii), ul. Akademika Koroleva 19, 127427 Moscow, Russia. Fax: +7 (095) 215 0847. Contact: Vladimir Razin, Editor-in-Chief.

Radio Odin and **Mayak**, ul. Akademika Koroleva 12, 127427 Moscow, Russia. Phone: (general) +7 (095) 217-9340; (English Service) +7 (095) 233-6578; (administration) +7 (095) 217-7888. Fax: +7 (095) 215 0847. Contact: (administration) Vladimir Povolyayev, Director. Correspondence in Russian preferred, but English increasingly accepted. For verification of reception from transmitters located in St. Petersburg and Kaliningrad, see NOTE, above, shortly after the country heading, "RUSSIA."

Radio Pamyat—see Radiostantsiya Pamyat, below.

Radio Perm, ul. Teknicheskaya 21, 614600 Perm, Permskaya Oblast, Russia.

Radio Radonezh (when active), Studio 158, ul. Paytnickay 25, 113326 Moscow, Russia. Phone: +7 (095) 233-7258. Phone/fax: +7 (095) 233-6356. Contact: Anton Parshin, Announcer. Although this Orthodox Church station's logo shows Radiostansiya Radonezh, it consistently identifies as Radio Radonezh.

Radio Rossii (Russia's Radio), Room 121, ul. Yamskogo 5-R, Polya 19/21, 125124 Moscow, Russia. Phone: +7 (095) 213-1054 or +7 (095) 250-0511. Fax: +7 (095) 250 0105 or +7 (095)

233 6449. Contact: Sergei Yerofeyev, Director of International Operations [sic]; or Sergei Davidov, Director. Free English-language information sheet. For verification of reception from transmitters located in St. Petersburg and Kaliningrad, see NOTE, above, shortly after the country heading, "RUSSIA."

Radio Rossii-Nostalgie

MOSCOW OFFICE: Phone: +7 (095) 956-1245. French-managed leased-time program aired over a variety of Russian transmitters.

PARIS HEADQUARTERS: 9-11 Rue Franquet, F-75015 Paris, France. Phone: +33 (1) 53-68-80-00. Fax: +33 (1) 45 32 10 31. Contact: (technical) Hervé Pichat, Chef Technique.

Radio Samorodinka, P.O. Box 898, Center, 101000 Moscow, Russia. Contact: L.S. Shiskin, Editor. This station may be licensed as other than a regular broadcaster.

Radio Seven, ul. Gagarina 6-A, 443079 Samara, Samaraskaya Oblast, Russia. Contact: A.P. Nenashjev; or Mrs. A.S. Shamsutdinova, Editor.

Radio Slavyanka, kv. 160, ul. Marshala Shaposhnikova 14, 103168 Moscow, Russia.

Radio Yunost, ul. Pyatnitskaya 25, 113326 Moscow, Russia. Fax: +7 (095) 233 6244. Contact: Yevgeniy Vasilyevich Pavlov, Director General. Although this station's logo shows Radiostansiya Yunost, it consistently identifies as Radio Yunost.

Radiostantsiya Atlantika (program of Murmansk Radio, aired via Golos Rossii), per. Rusanova 7-A, 183767 Murmansk, Russia.

Radiostantsiya Pamyat (Memory Radio Station, if reactivated), ul. Valovaya, d.32, kv.4, 113054 Moscow, Russia; or P.O. Box 23, 113535 Moscow, Russia. Phone/fax: +7 (095) 237-3971. Contact: (general) Dimitriy Vasilyev, Director; (technical) Yuri Oleggovich Miroliubov, Radio Operator. Audio cassettes of broadcasts for $2 each. Correspondence in Russian preferred, with 2 IRCs being requested for a reply; verification cards feature monarchist and Czarist-era themes. Station of the Pamyat National Patriotic Front, whose "memories" are of monarchist and fascist eras.

Radiostantsiya Tikhiy Okean (program of Primorsk Radio, also aired via Voice of Russia transmitters), RTV Center, ul. Uborevieha 20A, 690000 Vladivostok, Primorskiy Kray, Russia.

Radiostantsiya Yakutsk, ul. Semena Dezhneva 75/2, Radiocenter, 677000 Yakutsk, Russia.

Radiostantsiya Yunost—see Radio Yunost.

Sakha Radio, Dom Radio, ul. Ordzhonikidze 48, 677007 Yakutsk, Sakha (Yakutia) Republic, Russia. Fax: +7 (095) 230 2919. Contact: (general) Alexandra Borisova; Lia Sharoborina, Advertising Editor; or Albina Danilova, Producer, "Your Letters"; (technical) Sergei Bobnev, Technical Director. Russian books $15; audio cassettes $10. Free station stickers and original Yakutian souvenirs. Replies to correspondence in English.

Sakhalin Radio, Dom Radio, ul. Komsomolskaya 209, 693000 Yuzhno-Sakhalinsk, Sakhalin Is., Sakhalinskaya Oblast, Russia. Contact: V. Belyaev, Chairman of Sakhalinsk RTV Committee.

Tyumen' Radio, RTV Center, ul. Permyakova 6, 625013 Tyumen', Tyumenskaya Oblast, Russia. Contact: (technical) V.D. Kizerov, Engineer, Technical Center. Sometimes replies to correspondence in Russian. Return postage helpful.

Voice of Russia, ul. Pyatnitskaya 25, Moscow 113326, Russia. Phone: (World Service) +7 (095) 233-6980 or +7 (095) 233-6586; (International Relations) +7 (095) 233-7801; (Programmes Directorate) +7 (095) 233-6793; (Commercial Dept.) +7 (095) 233-7934; (Audience Research) +7 (095) 233-6278; (Chairman's Secretariat) +7 (095) 233-6331; (News) +7 (095) 233-6513. Fax: (general and administration) +7 (095) 230 2828; (World Service) +7 (095) 233 7693; (International Relations) +7 (095) 233 7648; (News) +7 (095) 233 7567; (technical) +7 (095) 233 1342. E-mail: (general) lettes@vor.ru; (administrative) chairman@vor.ru; (backup e-mail address) root@avrora.msk.ru. URL: http://www.vor.ru. Contact: (English Service—listeners' questions to be answered over the air) Joe Adamov; (English Service—all other general correspondence) Ms. Olga Troshina, World Service Letters Department; (general correspondence, all languages) Victor Kopytin, Director of International Relations Department; Vladimir Zhamkin, Editor-in-Chief; Yevgeny Nilov, Deputy Editor-in-Chief; Anatoly Morozov, Deputy Editor-in-Chief; (Japanese) Yelena Sopova, Japanese Department; (verifications, all services) Mrs. Eugenia Stepanova, c/o English Service; (administration) Yuri Minayev, First Deputy Chairman, Voice of Russia; Armen Oganesyan, Chairman, World Service, Voice of Russia; (technical) Valentin Khleknikov, Frequency Coordinator; Leonid Maevski, Engineering Services; or Maria Petrunicheva, Engineering Services. For verification of reception from transmitters located in St. Petersburg and Kaliningrad, see NOTE, above, shortly after the country heading, "RUSSIA." For verification from transmitters in Khabarovsk, you can also write directly to the Voice of Russia, Dom Radio, Lenina 4, Khabarovsk 680020, Russia. For engineering correspondence concerning frequency management problems, besides "technical," preceding, see NOTE on C.I.S. Frequency Management towards the beginning of this "Russia" listing. Free stickers, booklets and sundry other souvenirs occasionally available upon request. Sells audio cassettes of Russian folk and classical music, as well as a Russian language-learning course. Although not officially a part of the Voice of Russia, an organization selling Russian art and handcrafts that sprung from contacts made with the Voice of Russia is "Cheiypouka," Box 266, Main St., Stonington ME 04681 USA; phone +1 (207) 367-5021.

Voice of Assyria (Kala Alturaia)—See Voice of Russia.

RWANDA   World Time +2
Deutsche Welle—Relay Station Kigali—Correspondence should be directed to the main offices in Cologne, Germany (see).
Radio Rwanda, B.P. 404, Kigali, Rwanda. Fax: +250 (7) 6185. Contact: Marcel Singirankabo. $1 required. Rarely replies, with correspondence in French preferred.

SAO TOME E PRINCIPE   World Time exactly
Voice of America/VOA-IBB—São Tomé Relay Station, P.O. Box 522, São Tomé, São Tomé e Príncipe. Phone: +23 912 22-800. Fax: +23 912 22 435. Contact: Jack Fisher, Relay Manager. These numbers for timely and significant technical matters only. All other communications should be directed to the usual VOA address in Washington (see USA).

SAUDI ARABIA   World Time +3
Broadcasting Service of The Kingdom of Saudi Arabia, P.O. Box 61718, Riyadh 11575, Saudi Arabia. Phone: (general) +966 (1) 404-2795; (administration) +966 (1) 442-5493; (technical) +966 (1) 442-5170. Fax: (general) +966 (1) 402 8177; (Frequency Management) +966 (1) 404 1692. Contact: (general) Mutlaq A. Albegami, European Service Manager; (technical) Sulaiman Samnan, Director of Frequency Management; or A. Shah, Department of Frequency Management. Free travel information and book on Saudi history.
Radio Islam from Holy Mecca (Idha'at Islam min Mecca al-Mukarama)—program with the same contact details as Broadcasting Service of the Kingdom of Saudi Arabia, above.

SENEGAL   World Time exactly
Office de Radiodiffusion-Télévision du Sénégal, B.P. 1765, Dakar, Senegal. Phone: +221 23-63-49. Fax: + 221 22 34 90. Contact: (technical) Joseph Nesseim, Directeur des Services Techniques. Free stickers and Senegalese stamps. Return postage, $1 or 2 IRCs required; as Mr. Nesseim collects stamps, unusual stamps may be even more appreciated. Replies to correspondence in French.

SEYCHELLES   World Time +4
BBC World Service—Indian Ocean Relay Station, P.O. Box 448, Victoria, Mahé, Seychelles; or Grand Anse, Mahé, Seychelles. Phone: +248 78-269. Fax: +248 78 500. Contact: (administration) Peter J. Loveday, Station Manager; (technical) Peter Lee, Resident Engineer; Nigel Bird, Resident Engineer; or Steve Welch, Assistant Resident Engineer. Nontechnical correspondence should be sent to the BBC World Service in London (see).
Far East Broadcasting Association—FEBA Radio
MAIN OFFICE: P.O. Box 234, Mahé, Seychelles, Indian Ocean. Phone: (main office) +248 241-215; (engineering) +248 241-353. E-mail: spepper@febaradio.org.uk. URL: http://www.febc.org/febchome.html. Contact: Station Director; or Richard Whittington, Schedule Engineer. Free stickers, pennants and station information sheet. $1 or one IRC helpful. Also, see FEBC Radio International—USA and United Kingdom.
CANADIAN OFFICE: 6850 Antrim Avenue, Burnaby BC, V5J 4M4 Canada. Fax: +1 (604) 430 5272. E-mail: dpatter@axionet.com.
INDIA OFFICE: FEBA India, P.O. Box 2526, 7 Commissariat Road, Bangalore-560 025, India. Fax: +91 (80) 584 701. E-mail: 6186706@mcimail.com. Contact: Peter Muthl Raj.

SIERRA LEONE   World Time exactly
Sierra Leone Broadcasting Service, New England, Freetown, Sierra Leone. Phone: +232 (22) 240-123; +232 (22) 240-173; +232 (22) 240-497; or +232 (22) 241-919. Fax: +232 (22) 240 922. Contact: (general) Joshua Nicol, Special Assistant to the Director of Broadcasting; (technical) Emmanuel B. Ehirim, Project Engineer.

SINGAPORE   World Time +8
BBC World Service—Far Eastern Relay Station, P.O. Box 434, 26 Olive Road, Singapore. Phone: + 65 260-1511. Fax: +65 669 0834. Contact: (technical) Far East Resident Engineer. Nontechnical correspondence should be sent to the BBC World Service in London (see).
Radio Corporation of Singapore, Farrer Road, P.O. Box 968, Singapore 9128 Singapore. Phone: +65 251-8622 or +65 359-7340. Fax: +65 256 9556 or +65 256 9338. URL: http://155.69.60.55:8000/rsi/index.htm. Contact: (general) Lillian Tan, Public Relations Division; Lim Heng Tow, Manager, International & Community Relations; B. Padhmanabhan, Assistant Vice President; Tan Eng Lai, Promotion Executive; Hui Wong, Producer/Presenter; Lucy Leong; or Karamjit Kaur, Senior Controller; (administration) Anthony Chia, Director General; (technical) Asaad Samir, V.P. Engineering; or Lee Wai Meng. Free regular and Post-It stickers, pens, umbrellas, mugs, towels, wallets and lapel pins. Do not include currency in envelope.
Radio Japan via Singapore—For verification direct from the Singaporean transmitters, contact the BBC World Service—Far Eastern Relay Station (see above) Nontechnical correspondence should be sent to Radio Japan in Tokyo (see).
Radio Singapore International, Farrer Road, P.O. Box 5300, Singapore 912899, Singapore. Phone: (general) +1 65 359-7662; (programme listings) +65 353-5300; (publicity) +65 350-3708 or +65 256-0401. Fax: +65 259 1357 or +65 259 1380. E-mail: radiosi@singnet.com.sg. URL: http://www.rsi.com.sg. Contact: (general) Anushia Kanagabasai, Producer, "You Asked For It"; Belinda Yeo, Producer, "Dateline RSI"; or Mrs. Sakuntala Gupta, Programme Manager, English Service; (administration) S. Chandra Mohan, Station Director; (technical) Selena Kaw, Office of the Administrative Executive; or Yong Wui Pin, Engineer. Free souvenir T-shirts and key chains to selected listeners. Do not include currency in envelope.

SLOVAK REPUBLIC (Slovakia)   World Time +1 (+2 mid-year)

Radio Slovakia International, Slovenský Rozhlas, Vysielanie do Zahraničia, Mýtna 1, 812 90 Bratislava, Slovak Republic. Phone: (Chief Editor) +42 (7) 49-62-81; (Deputy Chief Editor) +42 (7) 49-62-82; (English Section) +42 (7) 49-80-75; (Slovak Section) +42 (7) 49-82-47; (French Section) +42 (7) 49-82-67; (German Section) +42 (7) 49-62-83. Phone/fax: (technical) +42 (7) 49-76-59. Fax: (French and English Sections) +42 (7) 49 82 67; (English Section) +42 (7) 49 62 82; (other language sections) +42 (7) 49 82 47; (technical) +42 (7) 39 89 23. E-mail: (provisional address set up by a friendly radio enthusiast) xavcom@xs4all.nl. URL: (provisional Web site set up by a friendly radio enthusiast) http://www.xs4all.nl/~xavcom/rozhlas/. Contact: Helga Dingová, Director of English Broadcasting; Alan Jones, Producer "Listeners' Tribune"; (administration) PhDr. Karol Palkovič, Head of External Broadcasting; (technical) Edita Chocholatá, Frequency Co-ordinator; Jozef Krátky, Ing. "Slovak Lesson" course, but no accompanying printed materials. Free stickers, pennants, pocket calendars and other small souvenirs and publications. Reader feedback suggests station may not always receive mail addressed to it; so, if you get no reply, keep trying.

SOLOMON ISLANDS   World Time +11

Solomon Islands Broadcasting Corporation, P.O. Box 654, Honiara, Solomon Islands. Phone: +677 20051. Fax: +677 23159. Contact: (general) Julian Maka'a, Producer, "Listeners From Far Away"; Alison Ofotalau, Voice Performer; Cornelius Teasi; John Babera; or Program Director; (administration) James Kilua, General Manager; (technical) George Tora, Chief Engineer. IRC or $1 helpful. Problems with the domestic mail system may cause delays.

SOMALIA   World Time +3

Radio Mogadishu—Currently, there are three stations operating under the rubric Radio Mogadishu. None are known to reply to listener correspondence.

SOMALILAND   World Time +3

NOTE: "Somaliland," claimed as a independent nation, is diplomatically recognized only as part of Somalia.

Radio Hargeisa (when active), P.O. Box 14, Hargeisa, Somaliland, Somalia. Contact: Sulayman Abdel-Rahman, announcer. Most likely to respond to correspondence in Somali or Arabic. As of 1994, Radio Hargeisa was supposedly in the process of installing a new 25 kW shortwave transmitter; however, since then, they been continuing to make do with their usual, and highly erratic, mobile transmitter.

SOUTH AFRICA   World Time +2

BBC World Service via South Africa—For verification direct from the South African transmitters, contact Sentech (see below). Nontechnical correspondence should be sent to the BBC World Service in London (see).

Channel Africa, P.O. Box 91313, Auckland Park 2006, Republic of South Africa. Phone: + 27 (11) 714-2551 or +27 (11) 714-3942; (technical) +27 (11) 714-3409. Fax: (general) + 27 (11) 714 2546, +27 (11) 714 4956 or +27 (11) 714 6377; (technical) +27 (11) 714 5812. URL: (general, including news about South Africa) http://www.sabc.co.za/units/chanafr/index.html; (RealAudio in English) http://www.wrn.org/stations/africa/html; (technical) see Sentech, below. Contact: (general) Tony Machilika, Head of English Service; Robert Michel, Head of Research and Strategic Planning; Lionel Williams, Executive Editor; Flame Nieuwenhuizen, Acting Executive Editor; or Noeleen Vorster, Corporate Communications Manager; (technical) Mrs. H. Meyer, Supervisor Operations; or Lucienne Libotte, Technology Operations. T-shirts $11 and watches $25. Prices do not include shipping and handling. Free *Share* newsletter from the Department of Foreign Affairs, stickers and calendars. Reception reports

are best directed to Sentech (*see below*), which operates the transmission facilities.

Sentech (Pty) Ltd, Shortwave Services, Private Bag X06, Honeydew 2040, South Africa. Phone: (shortwave) +27 (11) 475-1596 or +27 (11) 471-4658; (general) +27 (11) 475-5600. Fax: +27 (11) 475 5112 or +27 (11) 471 4605. E-mail: (Otto) ottok@sentech.co.za; (Smuts) smutsn@sentech.co.za. URL: (shortwave) http://www.sentech.co.za/meyerton.html; (general, homepage) http://www.sentech.co.za/. Contact: Mr. N. Smuts, Managing Director; or Kathy Otto. Sentech is currently issuing its own verification cards, and is the best place to direct reception reports for all South African world band stations. Four additional 100 kW Brown Boveri transmitters are expected to be on the air shortly for use to such nearby targets as Mozambique, Zambia and Zimbabwe.

South African Broadcasting Corporation, P.O. Box 91312, Auckland Park 2006, Republic of South Africa. Phone: (technical) +27 (11) 714-3409. Fax: (general) +27 (11) 714 5055; (technical) +27 (11) 714 3106 or +27 (11) 714 5812. E-mail: lastname@sabc.co.za. URL: http://www.sabc.co.za. Contact: *Radio Oranje:* Hennie Klopper, Announcer; or Christo Olivier; Oranje has recently been sold to a private investor and its continued operation on shortwave is uncertain; *RADIO 2000:* J.H. Odendaal, Transmitter Manager; *All networks:* Karel van der Merwe, Head of Radio. Free stickers and ballpoint pens. Reception reports are best directed to Sentech (*see above*), which operates the transmission facilities.

SPAIN   World Time +1 (+2 midyear)

Radio Exterior de España (Spanish National Radio)
MAIN OFFICE: Apartado 156.202, E-28080 Madrid, Spain. Phone: +34 (1) 346-1081/1083/1149/1160. Fax: +34 (1) 346 1813/1815. Contact: Pilar Salvador M., Relaciones con la Audiencia REE; Nuria Alonso Veiga, Head of Information Service; or Penelope Eades, Foreign Language Programmer. Free stickers, calendars, pennants and tourist information.
RUSSIAN OFFICE: P.O. Box 88, 109044 Moscow, Russia.
Costa Rican Relay Facility—see Costa Rica.
WASHINGTON NEWS BUREAU: National Press Building, 529 14th Street NW, Suite 1288, Washington DC 20045 USA. Phone: +1 (202) 783-0768. Contact: Luz María Rodríguez.

SRI LANKA   World Time +6:30 (formerly +5:30, to which it may revert should there be an end to the electricity shortage resulting from the current drought)

Deutsche Welle—Relay Station Sri Lanka, 92/2 Rt. Hon. D.S. Senanayake Mwts, Colombo 8, Sri Lanka. Nontechnical correspondence should be sent to the Deutsche Welle in Germany (*see*).

Radio Japan/NHK, c/o SLBC, P.O. Box 574, Torrington Square, Colombo 7, Sri Lanka. This address for technical correspondence only. General nontechnical listener correspondence should be sent to the usual Radio Japan address in Japan. News-oriented correspondence may also be sent to the NHK Bangkok Bureau (see Radio Japan, Japan).

Sri Lanka Broadcasting Corporation, P.O. Box 574, Colombo 7, Sri Lanka. Phone: (domestic service) +94 (1) 697-491; (external service) +94 (1) 695-661. Fax: +94 (1) 695 488. E-mail: brzcast1@sri.lanka.net. Contact: N. Jayaweera, Director of Audience Research; Lal Herath, Deputy Director General of Broadcasting; or Icumar Ratnayake, Controller, "Mailbag Program"; (SLBC administration) Newton Gunaratne, Deputy Director-General; (technical) H.M.N.R. Jayawardena, Frequency Engineer.

Voice of America/VOA-IBB—Colombo (Ekala) Relay Station, 228/1 Galle Road, Colombo 4, Sri Lanka. Phone: +94 (1) 585-0119. Fax: +94 (1) 502 675. Contact: David M. Sites, Relay Station Manager. This address, which verifies correct reception reports for the Ekala station, is for technical correspondence only. This site is to be replaced in 1997 by another and much-larger facility in Sri Lanka; all correspondence concerning that new facility, as well as all nontechnical correspondence, should be directed to the regular VOA address (see USA).

ST. HELENA   World Time exactly

Radio St. Helena (when operating once each year), Broadway House, Main Street, Jamestown, Island of St. Helena, South Atlantic Ocean. Phone: +290 4669. Fax: +290 4542. URLs: http://www.algonet.se/~ltd/sthelena; or (Radio St. Helena Day Coordinator, Sweden) http://www.webcom.com/ harvest/glo_hig.html. Contact: (general) Tony Leo, Station Manager; (listeners' questions) Ralph Peters, Presenter, "Evening Shuttle." $1, required. Is on the air on world band only once each year—"Radio St Helena Day"—usually late October (e.g., October 27, 1996), on 11092.5 kHz in the upper-sideband (USB) mode.

SUDAN   World Time +2

National Unity Radio—see Sudan National Broadcasting Corporation, below, for details.

Sudan National Broadcasting Corporation, P.O. Box 572, Omdurman, Sudan. Phone: +249 (11) 53-151 or +249 (11) 52-100. Contact: (general) Mohammed Elfatih El Sumoal; (technical) Abbas Sidig, Director General, Engineering and Technical Affairs; Mohammed Elmahdi Khalil, Administrator, Engineering and Technical Affairs; or Adil Didahammed, Engineering Department. Replies irregularly. Return postage necessary.

SURINAME   World Time –3

Radio Apintie, Postbus 595, Paramaribo, Suriname. Phone: +597 40-05-00. Fax: +597 40 06 84. Contact: Ch. E. Vervuurt, Director. Free pennant. Return postage or $1 required.

SWAZILAND   World Time +2

Swaziland Commercial Radio
NONTECHNICAL CORRESPONDENCE: P.O. Box 5569, Rivonia 2128, Transvaal, South Africa. Phone: +27 (11) 884-8400. Fax: +27 (11) 883 1982. Contact: Rob Vickers, Manager—Religion. IRC helpful. Replies irregularly.
TECHNICAL CORRESPONDENCE: P.O. Box 99, Amsterdam 2375, South Africa. Contact: Guy Doult, Chief Engineer.
SOUTH AFRICA BUREAU: P.O. Box 1586, Alberton 1450, Republic of South Africa. Phone: +27 (11) 434-4333. Fax: +27 (11) 434 4777.

Trans World Radio—Swaziland
MAIN OFFICE: P.O. Box 64, Manzini, Swaziland. Phone: +268 52-781/2/3. Fax: +268 55 333. E-mail: (James Burnett) jburnett.twr.org; (technical) sstavrop@twr.org. URL: http:// www.twr.org/swazi.htm. Contact: (general) Dawn-Lynn Prediger, DX Secretary; Mrs. L. Stavropoulos; Greg Shaw, Follow-up Department; Peter A. Prediger, Station Director; or Program Manager; (technical) Chief Engineer; or James Burnett, Regional Engineer. Free stickers, postcards and calendars. May swap canceled stamps. $1, return postage or 3 IRCs required. Plans to upgrade its transmitter power from 25 kW to 50 kW. Also, see USA.
AFRICA REGIONAL OFFICE: P.O. Box 4232, Kempton Park, 1610 South Africa. Contact: Stephen Boakye-Yiadom, African Regional Director.
KENYA OFFICE: P.O. Box 21514 Nairobi, Kenya.
MALAWI OFFICE: P. O. Box 52 Lilongwe, Malawi.
SOUTH AFRICA OFFICE: P.O. Box 36000, Menlo Park 0102, Republic of South Africa.
ZIMBABWE OFFICE: P.O. Box H-74, Hatfield, Harare, Zimbabwe.

SWEDEN   World Time +1 (+2 midyear)

IBRA Radio (program)
MAIN OFFICE: International Broadcasting Association, Box 396, S-105 36 Stockholm, Sweden. Fax: +46 (8) 579 029. URL: http://193.14.201.40/ibra/sanding/index.html. Free pennants and stickers, plus green-on-white IBRA T-shirt available. IBRA Radio is heard as a program over various world band radio stations, including the Voice of Hope, Lebanon, Trans World Radio, Monaco, and the Voice of Russia.

CANADA OFFICE: P.O. Box 444, Niagara Falls ON, L2E 6T8 Canada.
CYPRUS OFFICE: P.O. Box 7420, 3315 Limassol, Cyprus. Contact: Rashad Saleem. Free schedules, calendars and stickers.

☞Radio Sweden

MAIN OFFICE: S-105 10 Stockholm, Sweden. Phone: (general) +46 (8) 784-7281, +46 (8) 784-7288 or +46 (8) 784-5000; (listener voice mail) +46 (8) 784-7287; (Technical Department) +46 (8) 784-7286. Fax: (general) +46 (8) 667-6283; (audience contact and Technical Department) +46 (8) 660-2990; (polling to receive schedule) +46 (8) 667-3701. E-mail: info@rs.sr.se. URL: (RealAudio in Swedish, and text): http://www.sr.se/rs/index.htm; (RealAudio in English) http://www.wrn.org/stations/rs.html; (MediaScan) http://www.sr.se/rs/english/media/media.htm; (Wood) http://www.abc.se/~m8914; (English Service) ftp.funet.fi:pub/sounds/radiosweden/mediascan. Contact: (general) Alan Pryke, Host, "In Touch with Stockholm" [include your telephone number]; Sarah Roxström, Head, English Service; Greta Grandin, Program Assistant, English Service; George Wood, Producer, MediaScan; Olimpia Seldon, Assistant to the Director; or Charlotte Adler, Public Relations & Information; (administration) Hans Wachholz, Director; (technical) Rolf Erik Beckman, Head, Technical Department. T-shirts (two sizes) $12 or £8. Payment for T-shirts may be by international money order, Swedish postal giro account No. 43 36 56-6 or internationally negotiable bank check.
TRANSMISSION AUTHORITY: TERACOM, Svensk Rundradio AB, P.O. Box 17666, S-118 92 Stockholm, Sweden. Phone: (Nilsson) +46 (8) 671-2066; (Gustavfsson) +46 (8) 671-2061. Fax: (Nilsson and Gustavfsson) +46 (8) 671 2060 or +46 (8) 671 2080; (Sonesson) +46 (42) 342 268 or +46 (8) 671 2084. E-mail: mni@teracom.se. Contact: (Frequency Planning Dept.—head office): Magnus Nilsson, Ms. Clara Gustavfsson or Lars Sonesson. Free stickers; sometimes free T-shirts to those monitoring during special test transmissions. Seeks monitoring feedback for new frequency usages.
NEW YORK NEWS BUREAU: Swedish Broadcasting, 825 Third Avenue, New York NY 10022 USA. Phone: +1 (212) 688-6872 or +1 (212) 643-8855. Fax: +1 (212) 594 6413. Contact: Elizabeth Johansson or Ann Hedengren.
WASHINGTON NEWS BUREAU: Swedish Broadcasting, 2030 M Street NW, Suite 700, Washington DC 20036 USA. Phone: +1 (202) 785-1727. Contact: Folke Rydén, Lisa Carlsson or Steffan Ekendahl.

SWITZERLAND   World Time +1 (+2 midyear)

Die Antwort—see Belarus.

European Broadcasting Union, Case Postal 67, CH-1218 Grand-Saconnex GE, Switzerland. Phone: +41 (22) 717-2111. Fax: +41 (22) 717 2710. URL: http://www.ebu.ch. Contact: Frank Kozamernik.

International Telecommunication Union, Place des Nations, CH-1211 Geneva 20, Switzerland. Phone: +41 (22) 730-5111. Fax: +41 (22) 733 7256. URL: (ITU newsletter) http://www.itu.ch. The ITU is the world's official regulatory body for all telecommunication activities, including world band radio. Offers a wide range of official multilingual telecommunication publications in print and/or digital formats. Of primary interest to world band is the monthly *HF Tentative Broadcasting Schedule* (via diskette for about 1,056 SFR/year) of the ITU's "International Frequency Registration Board" (IFRB); however, this publication's usefulness has decreased considerably in recent years, as it covers only official segments (see Best Times and Frequencies elsewhere in this book for official and unofficial segment parameters and planned implementation dates for changed parameters).

Red Cross Broadcasting Service, Département de la Communication, CICR/ICRC, 19 Avenue de la Paix, CH-1202 Geneva, Switzerland. Phone: +41 (22) 734-6001. Fax: +41 (22) 733 2057 or +41 (22) 734 8280. Contact: Patrick Piper,

Head; Elisabeth Copson, "Red Crossroads"; or Carlos Bauverd, Chef, Division de la Presse. Free stickers, wall calendar and station information. IRC appreciated. Free program cassettes to interested radio stations. As of September, 1995, the RCBS has been reorganized to have shorter, but more frequent, broadcasts.

Swiss Radio International

MAIN OFFICE: Giacomettistrasse 1, CH-3000 Berne 15, Switzerland. Phone: +41 (31) 350-9222. Fax: (general) +41 (31) 350 9569; (administration) +41 (31) 350 9744 or +41 (31) 350 9581; (Communication and Marketing) +41 (31) 350 9544; (Programme Department) +41 (31) 350 9569. URL: http://www.srg-ssr.ch/SRI/. Contact: (general) Nancy Thöny, Listeners' Letters, English Programmes; Marlies Schmutz, Listeners' Letters, German Programmes; Thérèse Schafter, Listeners' Letters, French Programmes; Esther Niedhammer, Listeners' Letters, Italian Programmes; Beatrice Lombard, Promotion; Giovanni D'Amico, Audience Officer; (administration) Ulrich Kündig, General Manager; Nicolas Lombard, Deputy General Manager; Walter Fankhauser, Head, Communication & Marketing Services; Rose-Marie Malinverni, Head, Editorial Co-ordination Unit; Ron Grünig, Head, English Programmes; James Jeanneret, Head, German Programmes; Philippe Zahne, Head, French Programmes; Fabio Mariani, Head, Italian Programmes; (technical) Paul Badertscher, Head, Engineering Services; Bob Zanotti. Free station flyers, posters, stickers and pennants. Sells CDs of Swiss music, plus audio and video (PAL/NTSC) cassettes; also, Swiss watches and clocks, microphone lighters, letter openers, books, T-shirts, sweatshirts and Swiss Army knives. VISA/EURO/AX or cash, but no personal checks. For catalog, write Nicolas D. Lombard, Head, SRI Enterprises, c/o the above address, or fax +41 (31) 350 9581. Station plans to introduce a new world band relay facility for South East Asia, likely in 1997.

TRANSMISSION AUTHORITY: Division Radiodiffusion, Swiss Telecom PTT, Speichergaße 6, CH-3030 Berne, Switzerland. Phone: +41 (31) 338-3490. Fax: +41 (31) 338 6554. Contact: (general) Ing. Ulrich Wegmüller, Frequency Coordinator; (administration) Dr. Walter G. Tiedweg, Head Radio Division.

WASHINGTON NEWS BUREAU: 2030 M Street NW, Washington DC 20554 USA. Phone: (general) +1 (202) 775-0894 or +1 (202) 429-9668; (French-language radio) +1 (202) 296-0277; (German-language radio) +1 (202) 7477. Fax: +1 (202) 833 2777. Contact: Christophe Erbeck, reporter.

United Nations Radio, Room G209, Palais des Nations, CH-1211 Geneva 10, Switzerland. Phone: +41 (22) 917-4222. Fax: +41 (22) 917 0123. E-mail: audio-visual@un.org. URLs: (RealAudio) http://www.nexus.org/IRN/index.html; http://www.wrn.org/stations/un.html.

SYRIA   World Time +2 (+3 midyear)

Radio Damascus, Syrian Radio & Television, Ommayad Square, Damascus, Syria. Phone: +963 (11) 720-700. Contact: Mr. Afaf, Director General; Lisa Arslanian; or Mrs. Wafa Ghawi. Free stickers, paper pennants and *The Syria Times* newspaper. Replies can be highly erratic, but as of late have been more regular, if sometimes slow.

"Voice of Iraq"—see Radio Damascus, above, for contact information.

TAHITI—see FRENCH POLYNESIA.

TAJIKISTAN   World Time +6

Radio Dushanbe, Radio House, 31 Chapayev Street, 735025 Dushanbe, Tajikistan. Contact: Gulom Makhmudovich, Deputy Chairman; Raisamuhtan Dinova Vuncha, English Service; or Mrs. Raisa Muhutdinova, Editor-in-Chief, English Department. Correspondence in Russian, Farsi, Dari, Tajik or Uzbek preferred. Used Russian stamps appreciated, for whatever reason, but return postage not really necessary.

Radio Pay-i 'Ajam-see Radio Dushanbe for details.

Tajik Radio, Radio House, 31 Chapayev Street, 735025 Dushanbe, Tajikistan. Contact: Mirbobo Mirrakhimov, Chairman of State Television and Radio Corporation. Correspondence in Russian, Tajik or Uzbek preferred.

TANZANIA   World Time +3

Radio Tanzania, Director of Broadcasting, P.O. Box 9191, Dar es Salaam, Tanzania. Phone: +255 (51) 38-015. Fax: +255 (51) 29 416. Contact: (general) Mrs. Deborah Mwenda, Acting Head of External Service; Abdul Ngarawa, Acting Controller of Programs; B.M. Kapinga, Director of Broadcasting; or Ahmed Jongo, Producer, "Your Answer"; (technical) Head of Research & Planning. Replies to correspondence in English.

Radio Tanzania Zanzibar, P.O. Box 1178, Zanzibar, Tanzania. Phone: +255 (54) 31-088. Fax: +255 (54) 57 207. Contact: (general) Yusuf Omar Chunda, Director Department of Information and Broadcasting; or Ali Bakari Muombwa, Messenger, Dispatch Room; (technical) Nassor M. Suleiman, Maintenance Engineer. $1 return postage helpful.

THAILAND   World Time +7

BBC World Service—Thai Relay Station, **Mukto Probaho**, GPO Box 1605, Bangkok 10501, Thailand. Contact: Sk Abdullah. Correspondence in English and reception reports welcomed. Members' Club. This daily Bengali-language Christian religious program/listener-response show, produced by a studio associated with IBRA Radio (see Sweden), is aired via transmission facilities of the Voice of Russia. Sometimes verifies via IBRA Radio in Sweden.

Radio Thailand World Service, 236 Vibhavadi Rangsit Highway, Din Daeng, Iiuaykhwang, Bangkok 10400, Thailand. Phone: +66 (2) 277-0122, +66 (2) 277-1814 or +66 (2) 277-1840. Fax: +66 (2) 277 7095 or +66 (2) 271 3514. Contact: Mrs. Amporn Samosorn, Chief of External Services; or Patra Lamjiack. Free pennants. Replies irregularly, especially to those who persist.

Voice of America/VOA-IBB—Relay Station Thailand, Udon Thani, Thailand. Phone: +66 (42) 271-490/1. Only matters of urgent importance should be directed to this site. All other correspondence should be directed to the regular VOA address in Washington (see USA).

TOGO   World Time exactly

Radio Lomé, Lomé, Togo. Return postage, $1 or 2 IRCs helpful. French preferred.

TONGA   World Time +13

Tonga Broadcasting Commission (if and when antenna, destroyed by a cyclone, is ever repaired or replaced), A3Z, P.O. Box 36, Nuku'alofa, Tonga. Fax: +676 22670 or +676 24417. Contact: (general) Robina Nakao, Producer, "Dedication Program"; Mateaki Heimuli, Controller of Programs; or Tavake Fusimalohi, General Manager; (technical) M. Indiran, Chief Engineer; or Kifitoni Sikulu, Controller, Technical Services.

TUNISIA   World Time +1

Radiodiffusion Télévision Tunisienne, Radio Sfax, 71 Avenue de la Liberté, Tunis, Tunisia. Phone: +216 (1) 287-300. Fax: +216 (1) 781 058. Contact: Mongai Caffai, Director General; Mohamed Abdelkafi, Director; or Smaoui Sadok, Le Sous-Directeur Technique. Replies irregularly and slowly to correspondence in French or Arabic; indeed, as of late correspondence has often been returned unopened.

TURKEY   World Time +2 (+3 midyear)

Radyo Çinarli, Çinarli Anadolu Teknik ve Endüstri Meslek Lisesi Deneme Radyosu, Çinarli, 35.110 İzmir, Turkey. Phone: +90 (232) 486-6434; (technical) +90 (232) 461-7442. Fax: +90 (232) 435 1032. Contact: (general) Ahmet Ayaydin, School Manager; (technical) Göksel Uysal, Technical Manager. Station is run by the local technical institute. Free studio photos and, occasionally, other small souvenirs. Correspondence in English accepted.

Turkish Radio-Television Corporation—Voice of Turkey
MAIN OFFICE, NONTECHNICAL: P.K. 333, 06.443 Yenisehir Ankara, Turkey. Phone: (general) +90 (312) 490-9800/9806/9808/9809; (English Department) +90 (312) 490-9842. Fax: +90 (312) 490 9845/6. Contact: (English) Osman Erkan, Host, "Letterbox" and Head of English Department; (other languages) Rafet Esit, Foreign Languages Section Chief; (administration) Savaş Kiratli, Head of the External Services Dept.; or A. Akad Gukuriva, Deputy Director General; (technical) Mete Coşkun. Free stickers, pennants, women's embroidery artwork swatches and tourist literature.
MAIN OFFICE, TECHNICAL (FOR EMIRLER AND ÇAKIRLAR TRANSMITTER SITES): Gene Mudurluk Teknik, TRT Sitesi, Kkat : 5/C, Or-An, 06.450 Ankara, Turkey. Phone: +90 (312) 490-1730/2. Fax: +90 (312) 490 1733. Contact: Turgay Cakimci, Frequency Manager; or Vural Tekel , Deputy Director General, Engineering; or Ms. F. Elvan Boratav, International Technical Relations Department.
OR-AN OFFICE: Diş Yayınlar Dairesi Başkanlığı, Turan Güneş Bulvarı, Or-An Çankaya, Ankara, Turkey.
SAN FRANCISCO OFFICE, SCHEDULES: 2654 17th Avenue, San Francisco CA 94116 USA. Phone: +1 (415) 564-9968. Contact: George Poppin. Self-addressed stamped envelope or IRC required for reply. This address, a volunteer office, only provides TRT schedules to listeners. All other correspondence should be sent directly to Ankara.
Türkiye Polis Radyosu (Turkish Police Radio), T.C. Içişleri Bakanliği, Emniyet Genel Müdürlüğü, Ankara, Turkey. Contact: Station Director. Tourist literature for return postage. Replies irregularly.
Meteoroloji Sesi Radyosu (Voice of Meteorology), T.C. Tarim Bakanliği, Devlet Meteoroloji İşler , Genel Müdürlüğü, P.K. 401, Ankara, Turkey. Phone: +90 (312) 359-7545, X-281. Fax: +90 (312) 314 1196. Contact: (nontechnical) Gühekin Takinalp; or Abdullah Gölpinar; (technical) Mehmet Örmeci, Director General. Free tourist literature. Return postage helpful.

TURKMENISTAN World Time +5
"Turkmen Milliyet"—see Turkmen Radio, below.
Turkmen Radio, Ulitsa Mollanepsa 3, 744000 Ashgabat, Turkmenistan. Phone: +7 (3632) 251-515. Fax: +7 (3632) 251 421. Contact: K. Karayev; or Yu M. Pashaev, Deputy Chairman of State Television and Radio Company; (technical) A.A Armanklichev, Deputy Chief, Technical Department.

UGANDA World Time +3
Radio Uganda
GENERAL OFFICE: P.O. Box 7142, Kampala, Uganda. Phone: +256 (41) 254-461, +256 (41) 242-316 or +256 (41) 245-376. Fax: +256 (41) 256 888. Contact: Kikulwe Rashid Harolin or A.K. Mlamizo. $1 or return postage required. Replies infrequently and slowly.
ENGINEERING OFFICE: P.O. Box 2038, Kampala, Uganda. Contact: Yona Hamala, Chief Engineer. Four IRCs or $1 required. Enclosing a self addressed envelope may also help to get a reply.

UKRAINE World Time +2 (+3 midyear)
WARNING-MAIL THEFT: For the time being, letters to Ukrainian stations, especially containing funds or IRCs, are more likely to arrive safely if sent by registered mail.
For Those at Sea, (Dly Tech, Kto v More), Krymskoye Radio, ul. Krymskaya d. 6, 333000 Simferopol, Ukraine. Contact: Konstantin Lepin, who collects stamps and is a fan of American jazz. Via Golos Rossii, Russia (see).
Government Transmission Authority: RRT/Concern of Broadcasting, Radiocommunication & Television, 10 Dorogajtshaya St., 254112 Kiev, Ukraine. Phone: +380 (44) 226-2262 or +380 (44) 440-8688. Fax: +380 (44) 440 8722. Contact: Alexey Karpenko, Nikolai P. Kyryliuk or Mrs. Liudmila Deretskaya.
Radio Ukraine International [see NOTE, following], ul. Kreshchatik 26, 252001 Kiev, Ukraine. Phone: +380 (44) 229-

4586, +380 (44) 229-2870 or +380 (44) 229-1757. Fax: +380 (44) 229 4585. Contact: (administration) Viktor I. Naburusko, Editor-in-Chief; (technical) see Ukrainian Radio, below. Free stickers, calendars and Ukrainian stamps.
NOTE: Temporarily operating from reserve studios at the Ukrainian Radio's Technical Center, Pervomayskyy Street, Kiev, while extensive damage from a 1996 fire is being repaired. Mail and communications lines presumably will be forwarded during this period, but if these fail try the temporary address. Replies irregularly.
Radio Lugansk, ul. Dem'ochina 25, 348000 Lugansk, Ukraine. Contact: A.N. Mospanova.
Ukrainian Radio [see NOTE, following], ul. Kreshchatik 26, 252001 Kiev, Ukraine. Phone: +380 (44) 229-1285. Fax: (administration) +380 (44) 229 1170 or +380 (44) 229 4557; (technical) +380 (44) 220 6733. Contact: (administration) Vladimir Reznikov, General Manager, Ukrainian Radio; Vasyl Yurychek, Vice President of State Television and Radio Company; or Zinovy Kulik, Chairman of the Ukrainian State Committee for Television and Radio Broadcasting; (technical) Anatoly Ivanov, Frequency Coordination, Engineering Services.
NOTE: Temporarily operating from reserve studios at the Ukrainian Radio's Technical Center, Pervomayskyy Street, Kiev, while extensive damage from a 1996 fire is being repaired. Mail and communications lines presumably will be forwarded during this period, but if these fail try the temporary address. Replies irregularly.

UNITED ARAB EMIRATES World Time +4
Capital Radio—see UAE Radio from Abu Dhabi, below, for details.
UAE Radio from Abu Dhabi, Ministry of Information & Culture, P.O. Box 63, Abu Dhabi, United Arab Emirates. Phone: +971 (2) 451-000. Fax: (station) +971 (2) 451 155; (Ministry of Information & Culture) +971 (2) 452 504. Contact: (general) Aïda Hamza, Director, Foreign Language Services; or Abdul Hadi Mubarak, Producer, "Live Program"; (technical) Ibrahim Rashid, Director General, Technical Department; or Fauzi Saleh, Chief Engineer. Free stickers, postcards and stamps. Do not enclose money with correspondence.
UAE Radio in Dubai, P.O. Box 1695, Dubai, United Arab Emirates. Phone: +971 (4) 370-255. Fax: +971 (4) 374 111 +971 (4) 370 283 or +971 (4) 371 079. Contact: Ms. Khulud Halaby; or Sameer Aga, Producer, "Cassette Club Cinarabic"; (technical) K.F. Fenner, Chief Engineer—Radio; or Ahmed Al Muhaideb, Assistant Controller, Engineering. Free pennants. Replies irregularly.

UNITED KINGDOM World Time exactly (+1 midyear)
Adventist World Radio, the Voice of Hope—see USA.
BBC Monitoring, Caversham Park, Reading RG4 8TZ, United Kingdom. Phone: (general) +44 (1734) 472-742; (Marketing) +44 (1734) 469-289 or +44 (7134) 469-391; (Customer Service) +44 (1734) 469-332, +44 (1734) 469-389, or +44 (1734) 469-355; (Technical Operations) +44 (1734) 469-357; (World Media—Broadcast Schedules/monitoring) +44 (1734) 469-261/2; (Editorial—former USSR) +44 (1734) 469-244/290; (Editorial—Central Europe & Balkans) +44 (1734) 469-245; (Editorial—Asia/Pacific) +44 (1734) 469-246; (Editorial—Middle East, Africa & Latin America) +44 (1734) 469-248/388/389. Fax: (general) +44 (1734) 461 954; (World Media—Broadcasting Schedules/monitoring) +44 (1734) 461 993; (Marketing/Customer service) +44 (1734) 463 823 or +44 (1734) 461 020; (Technical Operations) +44 (1734) 462 414; (editorial) +44 (1734) 483 036. E-mail: (World Media—Broadcasting Schedules/monitoring) 100437.173@compuserve.com; (Marketing) 100431.2524@compuserve.com; (Customer Service) csu@mon.bbc.co.uk; (editorial queries) media@mon.bbc.co.uk; (World Media—Broadcasting Schedules/monitoring) chris_greenway@mon.bbc.co.uk; (monitoring) kenny@mon.bbc.co.uk. URLs: (Sample pages of World Media) http://www.bbc.co.uk/caversham/

homepage.html; (introduction) http://www.monitor.bbc.co.uk/ Welcome.html. Contact: (Marketing) Marian Martin, Marketing Executive; (Customer Service) Stephen Innes, Customer Service Manager; (World Media—Broadcasting Schedules/ monitoring) Chris Greenway, Manager, World Media—Broadcasting Schedules; Al Bolton, Monitor, Research Unit; or Dave Kenny, Monitor, Research Unit; (administration) Andrew Hills, Director; (technical) Keith Gough, Manager, Technical Operations. BBC Monitoring produces the weekly publication *World Media*, which is available in two parts: *Broadcasting News* (news and developments in the international broadcasting industry) and *Broadcasting Schedules* (provides schedules for international, domestic, clandestine and religious radio and TV stations worldwide). Both available on yearly subscription, costing £390.00 (*Broadcasting News* only), £105.00 (*Broadcasting Schedules* only) and £445.00 (Combined *Broadcasting News* and *Schedules*). Prices exclude postage overseas. *World Media* is also available online through the Internet or via a direct dial-in bulletin board at an annual cost of £550.00 (*News & Schedules*), £425.00 (*News* only) and £130.00 (*Schedules*) only). VISA/MC/ AX. The Technical Operations Unit provides detailed observations of broadcasts on the long, medium and short wave bands. This unit provides tailored channel occupancy observations, reception reports, *Broadcast Schedules Database* (constantly updated on over 100 countries) and the *Broadcast Research Log* (a record of broadcasting developments compiled daily). BBC Monitoring works in conjunction with the Foreign Broadcast Information Service (*see* USA).

BBC World Service

MAIN OFFICE, NONTECHNICAL: P.O. Box 76, Bush House, Strand, London WC2B 4PH, United Kingdom. Phone: (general) +44 (171) 240-3456; (International Broadcasting & Audience Research) +44 (171) 257-8141; (Press Office) +44 (171) 257-2947/1; (administration) +44 (171) 257-2057. Fax: (Audience Correspondence) +44 (171) 257 8258; ("Write On" listeners' letters program) +44 (171) 497 0287; (International Broadcasting & Audience Research) +44 (171) 257-8254; (Press Office) +44 (171) 240 8760; (administration) +44 (171) 379 6841. E-mail: (general listener correspondence) worldservice.letters@bbc.co.uk; (general BBC inquiries concerning domestic and external services) correspondence@bbc.co.uk; ("New Ideas") newideas@bbc-sci.demon.co.uk; (other specific programs) format is typically programname@bbc.co.uk, so for example the "Write On" correspondence program is writeon@bbc.co.uk, and so on; (specific individuals) for individuals at Bush House, the format is firstname.lastname@bbc.co.uk; (BBC World Service Science, Industry and Medicine Unit) editor@bbc-sci.demon.co.uk; (Polish service) polska.sekcja@ bbc.co.uk. URLs: (general, including snippets of RealAudio) http:// www.bbc.co.uk/worldservice/; (World Service program information) http://www.bbc.co.uk/worldservice/schedules/; (frequency database by language/stream and country) http:// www.bbc.co.uk/worldservice/freq.html. Contact: ("Write On") Paddy Feeny, Presenter; Ernest Warburton, Editor, World Service in English; Graham L. Mytton, Head of International Broadcasting & Audience Research; Fritz Groothues, Head, Strategy Development; or Neil Curry, Director, "The World"; (administration) Sam Younger, Managing Director. Offers *BBC On Air* magazine (*see* below). Also, *see* Antigua, Ascension, Oman, Seychelles, Singapore and Thailand, which are where technical correspondence concerning these BBC relay transmissions should be sent if you seek a reply with full verification data, as no such data are provided via the London address. The present facility at Masirah, Oman, is scheduled to be replaced in 2001 by a new site at Al-Ashkharah, also in Oman, which is to include four 300 kW shortwave transmitters.

MAIN OFFICE, TECHNICAL: BBC World Service Coverage Department, Reception Analysis Unit, N.E. Wing, P.O. Box 76, Bush House, Strand, London WC2B 4PH, United Kingdom. Phone: (Reception Analysis) +44 (171) 257-2155; (Control Room) +44 (171) 257-2672. Fax: (Reception Analysis) +44 (171) 240 8926; (Control Room) +44 (171) 379 3205; (administration) +44 (1524) 822 2225. Contact: (Reception Analysis/ frequency management) Geoffery S. Spells, Senior Engineer; Michael Still, Engineer; or David Chambers, Engineer; (Control Room) Ashley Jones, Engineer; (administration) Dennis Thompson, Chief Assistant to the Chief Engineer. These offices generally respond only to other broadcast-engineering entities, or to technical reception reports from those interested or involved in regular technical monitoring. Normal listener correspondence should be directed to the Main Office—Nontechnical (*see* above).

PARIS OFFICE: 155 rue du Faubourg-St. Honoré, F-75008 Paris, France. Phone: +33 (1) 45-61-97-00 or +33 (1) 45-63-15-88. Fax: +33 (1) 45 63 67 12.

BERLIN OFFICE: Savignyplatz 6, Berlin 12, Germany.

SINGAPORE ADDRESS: P.O. Box 434, Maxwell Road Post Office, Singapore 9008, Singapore. Fax: +65 253 8131.

AUSTRALIA OFFICE: Suite 101, 80 William Street, East Sydney, NSW 2011, Australia. Fax: 61 (2) 9361 0853. Contact: (general) Michelle Rowland; or Marilyn Eccles, Information Desk. BBC World Service—Publication and Product Sales

BBC ENGLISH magazine, P.O. Box 96, Cambridge, United Kingdom. Publication aids in the learning of English.

BBC TOPICAL TAPES, P.O. Box 76, Bush House, Strand, London WC2B 4PH, United Kingdom. Sells audio cassettes of BBC programs.

BBC WORLD SERVICE SHOP, Bush House Arcade, Strand, London WC2B 4PH, United Kingdom. Phone: +44 (171) 257-2576. Fax: (mail order) +44 (171) 497 0498; (retail store) +44 (171) 240 4811. Numerous audio/video (video PAL/VHS only) cassettes, publications (including PASSPORT TO WORLD BAND RADIO), portable world band radios, T-shirts, sweatshirts and other BBC souvenirs available by mail from BBC World Service Shop; for Mail Order details, contact the above London address (VISA/MC/AX/Access).

BBC ON AIR monthly magazine, Room 227 NW, Bush House, Strand, London WC2B 4PH, United Kingdom; 30 Broad Street, Denville NJ 07834 USA. Phone: (Editorial Office) +44 (171) 257-2875 or +44 (171) 257-2803; (Editor) +44 (171) 257-2150; (Circulation Manager) +44 (171) 257-2855; (advertising) +44 (171) 257-2873; (subscription voice mail outside North America) +44 (171) 257-2211; (subscription sales toll-free within the United States) (800) 875-2997; (subscription sales within Canada) +1 (201) 627-2997. Fax: +44 (171) 240 4899. E-mail: worldservice.letters@bbc.co.uk. Contact: (editorial) Vicky Payne, Editor; (subscriptions) Rosemarie Reid, Circulation Manager; (advertising) Paul Cosgrove. Subscription $30 or £18 per year. VISA/MC/AX/Barclay/EURO/Access.

Bessemer Broadcasting (when reactivated), 52 Hampton Road, Fir Vale, Sheffield S5 7AN, United Kingdom. Phone/ fax: +44 (0114) 243-5838. Contact: Trefor Morgan, General Manager. This experimental station has been granted a second 12-month test and development license from the U.K. Radio Communication Agency. Station is a joint venture of the Chapel Green Community College and its radio society, Hately Antenna Technology of Aberdeen, and Bessemer Broadcasting. Reception reports are welcome. Return postage necessary. Although the station is not yet back on the air, it is expected to be on the air once more starting sometime in 1997, possibly 24-hours daily from south Yorkshire near Sheffield or Rotherham, on 2404.5 or 5750 kHz, with a power of 0.32 kW.

Far East Broadcasting Association (FEBA), Ivy Arch Road, Worthing, West Sussex BN14 8BX, United Kingdom. Phone: +44 (1903) 237-281. Fax: +44 (1903) 205 294. E-mail: user@febaradio.co.uk. URLs: http://www.febc.org or http:// www.febaradio.org.uk. Contact: Tony Ford. This office is the headquarters for FEBA worldwide.

Best-selling author and former CBS correspondent Charles Kuralt still graces the airwaves with his perceptive wit. Here, he appears on a "Talk to America" interview for the premiere of "This I Believe," a cooperative effort between the Voice of America and Disney.

Carmelo Ciancio, VOA

Bible Focus—*see* Belarus.

☞**World Radio Network Ltd**, Wyvil Court, 10 Wyvil Road, London SW8 2TY, United Kingdom. Phone: +44 (171) 896-9000. Fax: + 44 (171) 896 9007. E-mail: (general) online@wrn.org or wrn@cityscape.co.uk; (Cohen) jeffc@wrn.org. URLs: (general and web radio) http://www.wrn.org; (sound files) http://town.org/radio/wrn.html. Contact: Karl Miosga, Managing Director; or Jeffrey Cohen, President. Provides Web RealAudio and SteamWorks, plus program placement via satellite in various countries for nearly two dozen international broadcasters.

UNITED NATIONS World Time –5 (–4 midyear)
☞**United Nations Radio**, R/S-850, United Nations, New York NY 10017 USA; or write the station over which UN Radio was heard (Radio Myanmar, Radio Cairo, China Radio International, Sierra Leone Broadcasting Service, Radio Zambia, Radio Tanzania, Polish Radio Warsaw, HCJB/Ecuador, IRRS/Italy, All India Radio, RFPI/Costa Rica). Fax: +1 (212) 963 1307. E-mail: audio-visual@un.org. URLs: (RealAudio) http://www.nexus.org/IRN/index.html; http://www.wrn.org/stations/un.html. Contact: (general) Sylvester E. Rowe, Chief, Radio and Video Service; or Ayman El-Amir, Chief, Radio Section, Department of Public Information; (technical and nontechnical) Sandra Guy, Secretary. Free stamps and *UN Frequency* publication.
GENEVA OFFICE: see Switzerland.
PARIS OFFICE: UNESCO Radio, 7 Pl.de Fontenoy, 75018 Paris, France. Fax: +33 (1) 45 67 30 72. Contact: Erin Faherty, Executive Radio Producer.

URUGUAY World Time –3
Emisora Ciudad de Montevideo, Canelones 2061, 11200 Montevideo, Uruguay. Contact: Jorge Yizmeyian.
La Voz de Artigas (when active), Av. Lecueder 483, 55000 Artigas, Uruguay. Phone: +598 (642) 2447 or +598 (642) 3445. Fax: +598 (642) 4744. Contact: (general) Sra. Solange Murillo Ricciardi, Co-Propietario; (technical) Roberto Murillo Ricciardi. Free stickers and pennants. Replies to correspondence in English, Spanish, French, Italian and Portuguese.
Radiodifusion Nacional-*see* SODRE, below. Plans to replace transmitter.

☞**Radio Monte Carlo**, Av. 18 de Julio 1224, 11100 Montevideo, Uruguay. E-mail: cx20@netgate.comintur.com.uy. URL: (text, plus perhaps eventually RealAudio) http://netgate.comintur.com.uy/cx20/index.htm. Contact: Ana Ferreira de Errázquin, Secretaria, Departamento de Prensa de la Cooperativa de Radioemisoras; Déborah Ibarra, Secretaria; Emilia Sánchez Vega, Secretaria; or Ulises Graceras. Correspondence in Spanish preferred.
Radio Oriental—Same as Radio Monte Carlo, above.
SODRE
PUBLICITY AND TECHNICAL: Radiodifusión Nacional, Casilla 1412, 11000 Montevideo, Uruguay. Contact: (general) Roberto Belo, Radioactividades Producer; (publicity) Daniel Ayala González, Publicidad; (technical) Francisco Escobar, Depto. Técnico.
OTHER: "Radioactividades," Casilla 801 (or Casilla 6541), 11000 Montevideo, Uruguay. Fax: +598 (2) 48 71 27. Contact: Daniel Muñoz Faccioli.

USA World Time –4 Atlantic, including Puerto Rico and Virgin Islands; –5 (–4 midyear) Eastern, excluding Indiana; –5 Indiana, except northwest and southwest portions; –6 (–5 midyear) Central, including northwest and southwest Indiana; –7 (–6 midyear) Mountain, except Arizona; –7 Arizona; –8 (–7 midyear) Pacific; –9 (–8 midyear) Alaska, except Aleutian Islands; –10 (–9 midyear) Aleutian Islands; –10 Hawaii; –11 Samoa
Note on Disestablishmentarian Programs: Contact and related information for many American politically oriented shows that are of an anti-establishment bent are listed separately earlier in this chapter, under Disestablishmentarian, following the entries for Denmark.
Adventist World Radio, the Voice of Hope
WORLD HEADQUARTERS: 12501 Old Columbia Pike, Silver Spring MD 20904 USA. Phone: +1 (301) 680-6304. Fax: +1 (301) 680 6303. E-mail: 74617.1621@compuserve.com. Contact: (general) Gordon Retzer, President. Most correspondence and all reception reports are best sent to the station where the transmission you heard actually emanated (*see* Costa Rica, Guam, Guatemala, Italy, which includes Slovakia transmissions and Russia), rather than to the World Headquarters. Free religious printed matter, pennants, stickers, program schedules and other small souvenirs. IRC or $1 appreciated.
INTERNATIONAL RELATIONS: P.O. Box 29235, Indianapolis IN 46229 USA. Phone/fax: +1 (317) 891-8540. Contact: Dr. Adrian M. Peterson, International Liaison. Free sample of *Radio News Bulletin* for shortwave enthusiasts, as well as other publications, with regular news releases and technical information. Issues some special verification cards. QSL stamps also available from this address in return for reception reports.
DX PROGRAM: "Wavescan," prepared by Adrian Peterson (*see* preceding); aired on all AWR facilities.
LISTENER NEWSLETTER: Current, published quarterly by AWR, is available through AWR stations: Costa Rica, Guam and Italy. Free, but IRCs appreciated.
PUBLIC RELATIONS & DEVELOPMENT: AWR, c/o Newbold College, Binfield, Bracknell, Berks. RG42 4AN, United Kingdom. Phone: +44 (1344) 401-401. Fax: +44 (1344) 304 169. E-mail: 74617.2230@compuserve.com. Contact: Andrea Steele, Director Public Relations & Development. Also, *see* AWR listings under Costa Rica, Guam, Guatemala, Italy, Kenya and Russia.
FREQUENCY MANAGEMENT OFFICE: AWR-Europe, Postfach 100252, D-64202 Darmstadt, Germany. Phone: +49 (6151) 390-90. Fax: +49 (6151) 390-913. Contact: Claudius Dedio, Frequency Manager. Implied by various reports is that this office will shortly be merged into the Public Relations & Development Office in the United Kingdom (*see* preceding entry) or AWR's Italian facility (*see*).
Asia Pacific Network (APN), 1201 Connecticut Avenue

NW, 4th floor, Washington DC 20036 USA. Phone: (general) +1 (202) 457-6975; (president) +1 (202) 457-6948. Fax: +1 (202) 457 6996. Contact: (administration) Richard Richter, President; Craig Perry, Vice President; Daniel Southerland, Executive Editor. APN, created in 1996, is funded as a private nonprofit U.S. corporation by a grant from the Broadcasting Board of Governors (see).

AudioNet, 2929 Elm Street, Dallas TX 75226 USA. Phone: (general) +1 (214) 748-6660; (Public Relations) +1 (214) 748-6660, X-120. Fax: +1 (214) 748 6657. E-mail: webmaster@audionet.com. URL: http://audionet.com/. Contact: (general) Laura Boyd, Public Relations; (administration) Mark Cuban, President. Currently the world's major supplier of Web radio broadcast audio over the Internet, using RealAudio.

BBC World Service via WYFR—Family Radio—For verification direct from WYFR's transmitters, contact WYFR—Family Radio (see below). Nontechnical correspondence should be sent to the BBC World Service in London (see).

Broadcasting Board of Governors (BBG), 330 Independence Avenue SW, Room 3360, Washington DC 20547 USA. Phone: +1 (202) 401-3736. Fax: +1 (202) 401 3376. Contact: (general) Kathleen Harrington, Public Relations; (administration) David Burke, Chairman. The BBG, created in 1994 and headed by nine members nominated by the President, is the oversight agency for all official non-military United States international broadcasting operations, including the VOA, RFE-RL, Radio Martí and Asia Pacific Network.

Central Intelligence Agency, Washington DC 20505 USA. Phone: (press liason) +1 (703) 482-7668; (general) +1 (703) 482-1100. URLs: (general) http://www.odci.gov/cia/; (Public Affairs) http://www.odci.gov/cia/public_affairs/pas.html. Contact: (general) Dennis Boxx, Director, Public Affairs; Kent Harrington, Press Liason; (administration) Nora Slatkin, Executive Director. Although the CIA is not believed to be operating any broadcasting stations at present, it is known to have done so in the past, usually in the form of "black" clandestine stations, and could do so again in the future. Additionally, the Agency is reliably reported to have funded a variety of organizations over the years, and may still be funding a relatively small number of organizations today, which operate, control or influence world band programs and stations. Also, see Foreign Broadcast Information Service, below.

C-SPAN, 400 N Capitol Street NW, Suite 650, Washington DC 20001 USA. Phone: +1 (202) 626-4863 or +1 (202) 737-3220. Fax: +1 (202) 737 3323. URL: http://www.c-span.org/. Contact: Thomas Patton, Audio Network; or Rayne Pollack, Manager, Press Relations. Relays selected international radio broadcasts over cable systems within the United States.

Disestablishmentarian Programs—see Disestablishmentarian listing earlier in this chapter, following the entries for "Denmark."

FEBC Radio International

INTERNATIONAL HEADQUARTERS: Far East Broadcasting Company, Inc., P.O. Box 1, La Mirada CA 90637 USA. Phone: +1 (310) 947-4651. Fax: +1 (310) 943 0160. E-mail: 3350911@mcimail.com; febc-usa@xc.org. URL: http://febc.org. Operates world band stations in the Northern Mariana Islands, the Philippines and the Seychelles.

UNITED KINGDOM OFFICE: FEBA Radio, Ivy Arch Road, Worthing, West Sussex BN14 8BX, United Kingdom. Phone: +44 (903) 237-281. Fax: +44 (903) 205 294.

Federal Communications Commission

ORGANIZATION: 2000 M Street NW, Washington DC 20554 USA (a scheduled move to the Portals complex in southwest Washington appears to have been postponed, if not deferred indefinitely, because of a lack of funds). Phone: (toll-free for licensed or prospective private broadcasters within the United States) (888) 322-8255; (general) +1 (202) 418-0200; (public affairs) +1 (202) 418-0500; (public affairs, recorded listing of

releases and texts) +1 (202) 418-2222; (international bureau, technical) + 1 (202) 739-0509; (international bureau, administration) +1 (202) 418-0420; (international bureau, legal) +1 (202) 739-0415; (international bureau, notifications and WARC) +1 (202) 418-2156. Fax: (public affairs) +1 (202) 418 2809; (international bureau, technical) +1 (202) 887 6124 or +1 (202) 418 0398; (international bureau, administration) +1 (202) 418 2818; (international bureau, legal) +1 (202) 887 0175. E-mail: fccinfo@fcc.gov. URLs: (shortwave broadcasting, direct) http://www.fcc.gov/ib/pnd/neg/hf_web/hf.html; (shortwave broadcasting via welcome page) http://www.fcc.Welcome.html, then follow the links to the International Bureau, Hot Topics and HF-Broadcasting; (general) http://fcc.gov/; (FTP) ftp://ftp.fcc.gov (shortwave broadcasting files can be downloaded from /pub/Bureaus/International/). Contact: (public affairs) Patricia Chew or Sharon Hurd; (international bureau, technical) Thomas E. Polzin, James Ballis or Charles Magnuson, Planning and Negotiations Division, International Bureau, Room 892; (international bureau, legal) Rod Porter, Esq., Deputy International Bureau Chief, Suite 800; (international bureau, notifications and WARC) Charles Breig, Chief. The FCC, whose International Bureau has recently been functioning exceptionally well, regulates all private broadcasting within the United States, and is not affiliated with the Voice of America/IBB. However, the FCC as a whole is being drastically downsized to save funds, and in the process plans no longer to concern itself with complaints from the public about powerline and other illegal electrical interference to radio receivers.

POTENTIAL OF DOMESTIC SHORTWAVE BROADCASTING: In 1995, the International Bureau discovered, to its surprise, that there may not be a valid legal basis for the present FCC rule prohibiting domestic shortwave broadcasting. (Currently, private U.S. world band stations must be configured to broadcast internationally, a relatively costly proposition.) Although the Bureau has no plans to act on its own in this regard, it may do so should forces within the broadcasting industry—such as AM stations wishing to increase audience size via low-power regional shortwave simulcasting—demonstrate a strong interest in having the rule-making procedure opened on that issue.

Foreign Broadcast Information Service, P.O. Box 2604, Washington DC 20013 USA. Phone: +1 (202) 338-6735. Parented by the CIA (see, above) and working in concert with BBC Monitoring (see United Kingdom) and selected other organizations, the F.B.I.S., with listening posts in various countries outside the United States, monitors broadcasts worldwide for intelligence-gathering purposes. However, it never engages in broadcasting or jamming of any sort, directly or indirectly.

Government Broadcasting Regulatory Authority—For private international broadcasting, see Federal Communications Commission, above; also, see the non-governmental National Association of Shortwave Broadcasters, below. For non-military governmentasl international broadcasting, see Broadcasting Board of Governors (BBG).

International Broadcasting Bureau (IBB)—see Voice of America/VOA. Also, RFE-RL (engineering).

Jacobs (George) and Associates, Inc., 8701 Georgia Avenue, Suite 410, Silver Spring MD 20910 USA. Phone: +1 (301) 587-8800. Fax: +1 (301) 587 8801. E-mail: gjacobs@clark.net. URL: http://www.clark.net/pub/gjacobs/gja.html. Contact: (technical) Bob German or Mrs. Anne Case; (administration) George Jacobs, P.E. This firm provides frequency management and other engineering services for a variety of private U.S. world band stations, but does not correspond with the general public.

KAIJ

ADMINISTRATION OFFICE: Two-if-by-Sea Broadcasting Co., 22720 SE 410th St., Enumclaw WA 89022 USA. Phone/fax: (Mike Parker, California) +1 (818) 606-1254; (Washington

State office, if and when operating) +1 (206) 825 4517. Contact: Mike Parker (mark envelope, "please forward"). Relays programs of Dr. Gene Scott. Replies occasionally. *STUDIO:* Faith Center, 1615 S. Glendale Avenue, Glendale CA 91025 USA. Phone: +1 (818) 246-8121. Contact: Dr. Gene Scott, President.
TRANSMITTER: RR#3 Box 120, Frisco TX 75034 USA (physical location: Highway 380, 3.6 miles west of State Rt. 289, near Denton TX). Phone: +1 (214) 346-2758. Contact: Walt Green or Fred Bethel. Station encourages mail to be sent to administration office, which seldom replies, or the studio (*see above*).

KFXX—1520 AM Sports Radio, 4614 SW Kelly Avenue, Portland OR 97201 USA. Phone: (toll-free within U.S.) (800) 932-5399; (main office/advertising) +1 (503) 223-1441; (studio) +1 (503) 733-5399. Fax: +1 (503) 227-5466 or +1 (503) 223-6909. E-mail: kfxx@kfxx.com. URL: (RealAudio) http://www.kfxx.com/, http://207.113.204.163/pub/kfxx/kfxx.htm or http://www.audionet.com/. Contact: Angie Buss, Publicity/Advertising; Lori Shannon, Director of I.S. Operations; or Tom Baker, C.E.O. Sports talk. 24 hours. Sells articles.

KGEI—Voice of Friendship—The original owners discontinued transmission from Redwood City, California, during last half of 1994 because of the high cost of operation at that location. However, another organization, the Calvary Chapel of Costa Mesa, California, hopes to reactivate operation from near Twin Falls, Idaho, in the United States, although they have not as yet filed an application with the Federal Communications Commission. They plan to use the KGEI—Voice of Friendship call sign and the aging California 250 kW transmitter, donated by the former owners, for religious transmissions to Latin America, especially Mexico.

KGON—92.3 FM, 4614 SW Kelly Avenue, Portland Oregon 97201 USA. Phone: (toll-free within U.S.) (800) 222-1441; (main office/advertising) +1 (503) 223-1441; (studio) +1 (503) 733-5466. Fax: +1 (503) 227 5466. E-mail: kgon@kgon.com. URL: (RealAudio) http://www.kgon.com/, http://207.113.204.163/pub/kgon/kgon.htm or http://www.audionet.com/. Contact: Christy Croghan, Publicity/Advertising; Lori Shannon, Director of I.S. Operations; or Tom Baker, C.E.O. Classic rock station. 24 hours. Return postage necessary.

KJES—King Jesus Eternal Savior
STATION: The Lord's Ranch, Star Route Box 300, Mesquite NM 88048 USA. Phone: +1 (505) 233-3725. Fax: +1 (505) 233 3019. Contact: Michael Reuter, Manager. $1 or return postage required.
SPONSORING ORGANIZATION: Our Lady's Youth Center, P.O. Box 1422, El Paso TX 79948 USA. Phone: +1 (915) 533-9122.

KLIF—570 AM, 3500 Maple Avenue #1600, Dallas TX 75219-3901 USA. Phone: (toll-free within U.S.) (800) 583-1570; (main office) +1 (214) 526-2400; (advertising) +1 (214) 520-4308. Fax: +1 (214) 520 4343. E-mail: danhgm@ix.netcom.com. URL: (RealAudio) http://www.klif.com/ or http://www.audionet.com/pub/klif/kliflive.htm. Contact: Susan Fine, Publicity; Jim Quick, Advertising Director; Jim Tyler, Web Director; Diana Underwood, Special Projects Coordinator; or Dan Holyburton, General Manager. Talk radio. 24 hours. Free program guides, station information, magnets and key chains.

KNLS—New Life Station
OPERATIONS CENTER: 605 Bradley Ct., Franklin TN 37067 USA (letters sent to the Alaska transmitter site are usually forwarded to Franklin). Phone: +1 (615) 371-8707. Fax: +1 (615) 371 8791. E-mail: knls@aol.com. URL: http://www.hax.com/wcb/linksaaa.htm. Contact: (general) Wesley Jones, Manager, Follow-Up Department; or Steven Towell, Senior Producer, English Language Service; (technical) Michael Osborne, Production Manager and Webeditor. Free quarterly newsletter, pennants, stickers, English-language

and Russian-language religious tapes and literature, and English-language learning course materials for Russian speakers. Free information about Alaska. DX books and bibles available; 2 IRCs appreciated for each book. Special, individually numbered, limited edition, verification cards issued for each new transmission period. Swaps canceled stamps from different countries to help listeners round out their stamp collections. Accepts faxed reports. Return postage helpful.
TRANSMITTER SITE: P.O. Box 473, Anchor Point AK 99556 USA. Phone: +1 (907) 235-8262. Fax: +1 (907) 235 2326. Contact: (technical) Kevin Chambers, Engineer.

KNRK—94.7 FM, 4614 SW Kelly Avenue, Portland OR 97201 USA. Phone: (toll-free within the U.S.) (800) 777-0947; (main office/advertising) +1 (503) 223-1441; (studio) +1 (503) 733-5470. Fax: +1 (503) 221 0004 or +1 (503) 223 6909. E-mail: knrk@knrk.com. URL: (RealAudio) OR—http://www.knrk.com/, http://207.113.204.163/pub/knrk/knrk.htm or http://www.audionet.com/. Contact: Elliott Moore, Publicity/Advertising; Lori Shannon, Director of I.S. Operations; or Tom Baker, C.E.O. Alternative programming. 24 hours. Return postage necessary.

KPLX—99.5 FM, 3500 Maple Avenue #1600, Dallas TX 75219-3901 USA. Phone: (toll-free within the U.S.) (800) 999-5759; (main office) +1 (214) 526-2400; (advertising) +1 (214) 520-4315. Fax: +1 (214) 520 4343. URL: (RealAudio) http://www.kplx.com/ or http://www.audionet.com/pub/kplx/kplx.com. Contact: Susan Fine, Publicity; Bob Saunders, Advertising Director; Jim Tyler, Web Director; Diana Underwood, Special Projects Coordinator; or Dan Holyburton, General Manager. Country radio. 24 hours. Free T-shirts, key chains, contest prizes, station information and concert guides.

KPRC—Houston Super Talk, 11767 Katy Freeway, Houston TX 77079 USA. Phone: (main office/advertising) +1 (713) 588-4800. Fax: +1 (713) 588 4821. URL:(RealAudio) http://www.audionet.com/ or http://207.113.204.163/pub/supertalk/supertalk.htm. Contact: Bonny English, Advertising Director; or Dan Patrick, Publicity & General Manager. Talk radio. 24 hours. $1 required for return postage.

KTBN—Trinity Broadcasting Network:
GENERAL CORRESPONDENCE: P.O. Box A, Santa Ana CA 92711 USA. Phone: +1 (714) 832-2950. Fax: +1 (714) 731 4196 or +1 (714) 665 2101. E-mail: (general) tbntalk@tbn.com; or chiser@tbn.org; (verifications) chiser@tbn.org. URL: http://www.tbn.org. Contact: Cheryl Gilroy, Secretary; Alice Fields; Jay Jones, Producer, "Music of Praise"; or Programming Department. Monthly TBN newsletter. Religious merchandise sold. Return postage helpful.
TECHNICAL CORRESPONDENCE: Engineering/QSL Department, 2442 Michelle Drive, Tustin CA 92680 USA. Phone: +1 (714) 665-2145. Fax: +1 (714) 730 0661. Contact: Chris Hiser, QSL Manager; or Ben Miller, WB5TLZ, Vice President of Engineering.

KVOH—High Adventure Radio
MAIN OFFICE: P.O. Box 100, Simi Valley CA 93062 USA. Phone: (High Adventure Ministries) +1 (805) 520-9460; (KVOH) +1 (805) 527-6529. Fax: (general) +1 (805) 520 7823 or +1 (805) 527 3871. E-mail: 73223.1040@compuserve.com. URL: http://www.webcom.com/harvest/glo_hig.html. Contact: (general, High Adventure Ministries) John Tayloe, President; James Baker, International Sales Director; (listeners' communications) Peter Darg or Listeners' Letterbox"; (administration, High Adventure Ministries) George Otis, President and Chairman; (administration, KVOH) Paul Johnson, General Manager, KVOH; (technical) Mike Baugh, Network Chief Engineer. Free *Voice of Hope* book, "High Adventure Ministries" pamphlet and sample "Voice of Hope" broadcast tape. Also, *see* Lebanon. Replies as time permits. As of August, 1995, has been accepting *inter alia* politically oriented disestablishmentarian programs for leased-time broadcast. *VICTORIA, AUSTRALIA OFFICE, NONTECHNICAL:* P.O. Box

295 Vermont, Victoria 3133, Australia. Phone: +61 (3) 9801-4648. Fax: +61 (3) 9887 1145. Contact: Roger Pearce, Director.
CALIFORNIA BRANCH OFFICE, NONTECHNICAL: P.O. Box 7466, Van Nuys, CA 91409 USA.
CANADA OFFICE, NONTECHNICAL: Box 425, Station "E", Toronto, M6H 4E3 Canada. Phone/fax: +1 (416) 898-5447. Contact: Don McLaughlin, Director.
U.K. OFFICE, NONTECHNICAL: Box 109, Hereford HR4-9XR, United Kingdom. Contact: Paul Ogle, Director. Phone: +44 (0432) 359-099. Fax: +44 (0432) 263 408. Contact: Peter Darg, Director.
WESTERN AUSTRALIA OFFICE, NONTECHNICAL: 79 Sycamore Drive, Duncraig WA 6023, Australia. Phone: +61 (9) 448-7088. Fax: +61 (9) 345 5407. Contact: Caron Hedgeland, Director.
SINGAPORE OFFICE, NONTECHNICAL: Orchard Point Box 796, Singapore 9123, Singapore.Phone: + 65 737-1682. Fax: +65 737 7723. Contact: Judi Hooi, Director.

KWHR-World Harvest Radio:
ADMINISTRATION OFFICE: see WHRI, USA, below.
TRANSMITTER: Although located 6 miles southwest of Naalehu, 8 miles north of South Cape, and 2000 feet west of South Point (Ka La) Road (the antennas are easily visible from this road) on otherwise friendly Big Island, Hawaii, the folks at this rural transmitter site maintain no post office box in or near Naalehu, and their telephone number is unlisted, reportedly because of hostile phone calls from a local individual. Best bet is to contact them via their administration office (*see* WHRI, below), or to drive in unannounced (it's just off South Point Road) the next time you vacation on lovely Big Island. If you learn more, please let us know!

☞**KWNK—Sports Radio 670**, 6633 Fallbrook Avenue #700, West Hills CA 91307 USA. Phone: (main office) +1 (818) 887-1855; (studio) +1 (213) 613-0670. E-mail: sports670@aol.com. URL: (RealAudio) http://207.113.204.163/pub/kwnk/kwnk.htm or http://www.audionet.com/; (general) http://www.sports670.com. Contact: Tom Murray, Advertising Manager; Bill Manning, Operations Manager; or William Cabranes, C.E.O. Sports talk station. 24 hours. Various giveaways. Sells T-shirts, hats and advertising products. Return postage necessary.

Leinwoll (Stanley)—Telecommunication Consultant, 305 E. 86th Street, Suite 21S-W, New York NY 10028 USA. Phone: +1 (212) 987-0456. Fax: +1 (212) 987 3532. Contact: Stanley Leinwoll, President. This firm provides frequency management and other engineering services for a variety of private U.S. world band stations, but does not correspond with the general public.

Monitor Radio International, Shortwave World Service (all locations), P.O. Box 860, Boston MA 02123 USA. Phone: (general, toll-free within U.S.) (800) 288-7090 or (general elsewhere) +1 (617) 450-2929 [with either number, extension 2060 for schedules or 2929 for Shortwave Helpline]; (listener line) +1 (617) 450-7777. Fax: +1 (617) 450 2283. E-mail: (general) radio@csps.com; (letters and reception reports) letterbox@csms.com; (technical questions) letterbox-tech@csms.com. URL: http://www.freerange.com/csmonitor; or http://town. hall.org/radio/Monitor/index.html. Contact: Catherine Aitken-Smith, Director of International Broadcasting, Herald Broadcasting Syndicate; Lisa Dale, Host, "Letterbox"; or Tina Hammers, Response Supervisor. Free stickers and information on Christian Science religion. *Christian Science Monitor* newspaper and full line of Christian Science books available from 1 Norway Street, Boston MA 02115 USA. *Science and Health with Key to the Scriptures* by Mary Baker Eddy available in English $14.95 paperback ($16.95 in French, German, Portuguese or Spanish paperback; $24.95 in Czech or Russian hardcover) from Science and Health, P.O. Box 1875, Boston MA 02117 USA. Also, *see* Northern Mariana Islands.

Monitor Radio International, Shortwave World Service—WSHB Cypress Creek, Rt. 2, Box 107A, Pineland SC 29934 USA. Phone: (general) +1 (803) 625-5555; (station manager) +1 (803) 625-5551; (engineer) +1 (803) 625-5554. Fax: +1 (803) 625 5559. E-mail: (station manager) cee@wshb.csms.com; (engineer) tony@wshb.csms.com; (QSL coordinator) judy@wshb.csms.com. Contact: (technical) Antonio L. (Tony") Kobatake, Chief Transmitter/Service Engineer; C. Ed Evans, Senior Station Manager; or Judy P. Cooke, QSL Coordinator. Visitors welcome from 9 to 4 Monday through Friday; for other times, contact transmitter site beforehand to make arrangements. This address for technical feedback on South Carolina transmissions only; other inquiries should be directed to the usual Boston address.

National Association of Shortwave Broadcasters
HEADQUARTERS: 11185 Columbia Pike, Silver Spring MD 20901 USA. Phone: +1 (301) 593-5409. Fax: +1 (301) 681 0099. Contact: Tulio R. Haylock, Secretary-Treasurer. Association of most private U.S. world band stations, as well as a group of other international broadcasters, equipment manufacturers and organizations related to shortwave broadcasting. Includes committees on various subjects, such as digital shortwave radio. Interfaces with the Federal Communications Commission's International Bureau and other broadcasting-related organizations to advance the interests of its members. Publishes *NASB Newsletter* for members and associate members; free sample upon request on letterhead of an appropriate organization. Annual one-day convention held near Washington DC's National Airport early each spring; non-members wishing to attend should contact the Secretary-Treasurer in advance; convention fee typically $50 per person.
MEMBERSHIP OFFICE: 276 N. Bobwhite, Orange CA 92669 USA. Phone/fax: (membership information) +1 (714) 771-1843. Contact: William E. "Ted" Haney, Membership Chairman, NASB. Full Membership (only for private U.S. shortwave broadcasters) $500 or more /year; Associate Membership (other organizations, subject to approval): $500/year.

☞**National Public Radio**, 635 Massachusetts Avenue NW, Washington DC 20001 USA. Phone: (general) +1 (202) 414-2000; (audience services) +1 (202) 414-3232. E-mail: uspubrad@npr.org. URLs: (including RealAudio) http://www.npr.org; (RealAudio) http://www.wrn.org/stations/npr.html.

☞**Net Radio Network**, 43 S.E. Main Street Suite 149, Minneapolis MN 55414 USA. Phone: (main office) +1 (612) 378-2211. Fax: +1 (612) 378 9540. URL: (audio) http://www.netradio.net or http://www.audionet.com/netradio. Contact: Scott Goldberg, Publicity; Tom Harrold, Advertising Director; Nathan Wright, Director of Internet Presence; or Rob Griggs, C.E.O. Specialises in Rock, Classic and Country music. 24 hours. Free T-shirts, hats and computers.

Public Radio International, 100 North Sixth Street, Suite 900A, Minneapolis MN 55403 USA. Phone: (general) +1 (612) 338-5000, (New Business Development) +1 (612) 330-9238. Fax: +1 (612) 330 9222. URL: http://www.pri.org/. Contact: Beth Talisman, Senior Manager, New Business Development. Makes available selected international broadcasts for those PRI radio stations within the United States which choose to air them in whole or in part, often after having taped them for later replay. Interestingly, PRI's placement of international programs seems to have increased, rather than decreased, the interest in world band listening within the United States.

Radio Martí, Office of Cuba Broadcasting, 400 6th Street SW, Washington DC 20547 USA. Phone: +1 (202) 401-7013. Fax: +1 (202) 401 3340. E-mail: (technical) rseifert@usia.gov. Contact: (general) Rolando Bonachea, Director of Radio; or Agustín Alles, Director of News; (technical) Rick Seifert, Engineering Supervisor; or Mike Pallone, Technical Director. This station, which reportedly is friendly to the Cuban American National Foundation (*see* "La Voz de la Fundación," under Disestablishmentarian), is in the process of moving to new facilities in Miami.

RFE-RL

PRAGUE HEADQUARTERS: Vinohradská 1, 110 00 Prague 1, Czech Republic. Phone: (switchboard) +42 (2) 2112-1111 or +42 (2) 2422-752; (President) +42 (2) 2112-3000/3001; (Technical Operations) +42 (2) 2112-3700; (Broadcast Operations) +42 (2) 2112-3550. Fax: (President) +42 (2) 2112 3002; (Broadcast Operations) +42 (2) 2112 3586; (news & current affairs) +42 (2) 2112 3600; (information services) +42 (2) 2112 2006. E-mail: lastname@rferl.org. URL: http://www.rferl.org/BD/index.html. Contact: Kevin Klose, President; Tom Morgan, Director of Technical Operations; Luke Springer, Director of Broadcast Operations; or Robert McMahon, Director of News & Current Affairs.

WASHINGTON OFFICE: 1201 Connecticut Avenue NW, Washington DC 20036 USA. Phone: (general) +1 (202) 457-6900; (news) +1 (202) 457-6953; (engineering) +1 (202) 457-6965. Fax: +1 (202) 457 6992; (engineering) +1 (202) 457 6995. E-mail: and URL: *see* above. Contact: (general) Jane Lester, Secretary of the Corporation; (news) Oleh Zwadiuk, Washington Bureau Chief; (engineering) David Walcutt, Broadcast Operations Liaison Officer. This organization has wound down considerably from its Cold War days, with its remaining transmission facilities now being a part of the International Broadcasting Bureau (IBB), *see.*

Trans World Radio, International Headquarters, P.O. Box 8700, Cary NC 27512 USA. Phone: +1 (919) 460-3700. Fax: +1 (919) 460 3702. URL: http://www.twr.org/. Contact: (general) John Vaught, Public Relations; Rosemarie Jaszka, Director, Public Relations; or Mark Christensen; (technical) Glenn W. Sink, Assistant Vice President, International Operations. Free "Towers to Eternity" publication for those living in the U.S. Technical correspondence should be sent directly to the country where the transmitter is located—Guam, Monaco, Swaziland.

☞**United Broadcasting Network**, Telford Hotel, 3 River Street, White Springs FL 32096 USA. Phone: (24-hour toll-free order line, within U.S. only) (800) 888-9999; (toll-free within U.S. for other contacts) (800) 825-5937; (elsewhere) +1 (904) 397-4145 or +1 (904) 397-4288; (UBN station affiliate contact) +1 (904) 397-4300; (front desk) +1 (904) 397-1000. Fax: +1 (904) 397 4149. E-mail: ubn@audionet.com. URL: (RealAudio) http://www.audionet.com/. Contact: Kent Phillips, Producer; Chuck Harder, Host; or Dianne Harder, Administrator. Free monthly *Station Listing & Program Guide* Flyer. Annual membership, including quarterly *For the People Magazine* and *Lemons* book $15. Bi-weekly *News Reporter* newspaper $19/year. NTSC videos of past FTP broadcasts $23.95. T-shirts and golf shirts $9.95-21.95 plus shipping. Sells a wide variety of books from its "For the People Bookstore"; free catalog upon request. VISA/MC. Sells U.S.-made tabletop radio similar to Drake SW1 reviewed in PASSPORT REPORTS *(see).* The "For The People" talk show, aired over UBN, espouses American populism, a philosophy going back to 1891. FTP's governing non-profit organization supports trade restrictions, freedom of health-care choice and progressive taxes on high incomes, while opposing racism and antisemitism. Live afternoons and on tape evenings (local time) via WHRI, USA. A non-talk-show version of FTP is now on television Stateside. FTP is researching the feasibility of setting up one or two of its own 50 kW shortwave transmitters within the United States.

United States Information Agency (USIA)—see Voice of America/VOA-IBB, below.

☞**Voice of America/VOA-IBB—All Transmitter Locations**

MAIN OFFICE, NONTECHNICAL: United States Information Agency (USIA), International Broadcasting Bureau (IBB), 330 Independence Avenue SW, Washington DC 20547 USA. If contacting the VOA directly is impractical, write c/o the American Embassy or USIS Center in your country. Phone:

(to hear VOA-English live) +1 (202) 619-1979; (Office of External Affairs) +1 (202) 619-2358 or +1 (202) 619-2039; (Audience Mail Division) +1 (202) 619-2770; (Africa Division) +1 (202) 619-1666 or +1 (202) 619-2879; ("Communications World") +1 (202) 619-3047; (Office of Research) +1 (202) 619-4965; (Computer Services) +1 (202) 619-2020; (administration) +1 (202) 619-1088. Fax: (general information for listeners outside the United States) +1 (202) 376 1066; (Public Liaison for listeners within the United States) +1 (202) 619 1241; (Office of External Affairs) +1 (202) 205 0634 or +1 (202) 205 2875; (Africa Division) +1 (202) 619 1664; ("Communications World," Audience Mail Division and Office of Research) +1 (202) 619 0211; (administration) +1 (202) 619 0085; ("Communications World") +1 (202) 619 2543. E-mail: (general inquires outside the United States) letters@voa.gov; (reception reports from outside the United States) qsl@voa.gov; (reception reports from within the United States) qsl-usa@voa.gov; ("Communications World") ke@voa.gov; (Office of Research) gmackenz@usia.gov. URLs: (text only) http://www.voa.gov/text-only.html; (text, plus audio in .au and .wav) http://www.voa.gov; gopher://gopher.voa.gov; ftp://ftp.voa.gov; (RealAudio) http://www.voa.gov/programs/audio/realaudio or http://www.wrn.org/stations/voa.html. Contact: Mrs. Betty Lacy Thompson, Chief, Audience Mail Division, B/K. G759A Cohen; Leo Sarkisian; Rita Rochelle, Africa Division; Kim Andrew Elliott, Producer, "Communications World"; Chris Kern, Chief of Computer Services; or George Mackenzie, Audience Research Officer; (administration) Geoffrey Cowan, Director (at least until 1/96). Free stickers and calendars. Free "Music Time in Africa" calendar, to non-U.S. addresses only, from Mrs. Rita Rochelle, Africa Division, Room 1622. If you're an American and miffed because you can't receive these goodies from the VOA, don't blame the station—they're only following the law. The VOA occasionally hosts international broadcasting conventions, and as of 1996 has been accepting limited supplemental funding from the U.S. Agency for International Development (AID).

MAIN OFFICE, TECHNICAL: United States Information Agency (USIA), International Broadcasting Bureau (IBB), 330 Independence Avenue SW, Washington DC 20547 USA. Contact: Mrs. Irene Greene, QSL Desk, Audience Mail Division, Room G-759-C; (administration) Robert Kamosa, Head, IBB-Engineering. E-mail: qsl@voa.gov. Also, *see* Ascension, Botswana, Greece, Morocco, Philippines, São Tomé e Principe, Sri Lanka and Thailand.

FREQUENCY AND MONITORING OFFICE, TECHNICAL: SW B/EOF:Frequency Management & Monitoring Division, United States Information Agency (USIA), International Broadcasting Bureau (IBB), 4605 Cohen Bldg., 330 Independence Avenue SW, Washington DC 20547 USA. Phone: +1 (202) 619-1669 or +1 (202) 619-1675. Fax: +1 (202) 619 1680 or +1 (202) 619 1781. E-mail: ferguson@beng.voa.gov. URL: http://voa.his.com/. Contact: Daniel Ferguson. Enclosing pre-addressed labels will help secure a reply.

LABOR REPRESENTATION: AFGE Local 1812/USIA, 301 4th Street SW, Room 348, Washington DC 20547 USA. Phone: +1 (202) 619-4759. Contact: Stacey Rose-Blass. Local 1812 is active in trying to maintain the VOA as an active force in international broadcasting.

Voice of America/VOA-IBB—Delano Relay Station, Rt. 1, Box 1350, Delano CA 93215 USA. Phone: +1 (805) 725-0150 or +1 (805) 861-4136. Fax: +1 (805) 725 6511. Contact: (technical) Jim O'Neill, Engineer; or Gene Pitts, Manager. Nontechnical correspondence should be sent to the VOA address in Washington.

Voice of America/VOA-IBB—Greenville Relay Station, P.O. Box 1826, Greenville NC 27834 USA. Phone: +1 (919) 758-2171 or +1 (919) 752-7115. Fax: +1 (919) 752 5959. Contact: (technical) Bruce Hunter, Manager. Nontechnical correspondence should be sent to the VOA address in Washington.

☞**WBAL—Baltimore**, 3800 Hooper Avenue, Baltimore MD

21211 USA. Phone: (toll-free within the U.S.) (800) 767-9225; (main office/advertising) +1 (410 467-3000; (studio) +1 (410) 467-9225. Fax: +1 (410) 338 6694. E-mail: (general) webman@wbal.com; (news) news@wbal.com; or (programming) programming@wbal.com. URL: (RealAudio) http://wbal.com/, http://www.wbal.com/, http://207.113.204.163/pub/wbal/wbal.htm or http://www.audionet.com. Contact: (publicity) Mary France; or Christopher Beauchamp, Web Director. News, talk and sports station. 24 hours.

WEWN—EWTN Worldwide Catholic Radio
STATION OFFICE: Eternal Word Radio Network (EWTN), Catholic Radio Service, P.O. Box 100234, Birmingham AL 35210 USA. Phone: (toll-free within U.S.) (800) 585-9396; (elsewhere) +1 (205) 672-7200. Fax: +1 (205) 672 9988. E-mail: (general) 70413.40@compuserve.com; (listener feedback) viewer.response@ewtn.com. URLs: (station) http://www.ewtn.com/wewn.htm or http://www.catholic.org/wewn/wewn.html; (EWTN) http://www.ewtn.com; (news update) http://www.ewtn.com/news.htm. Contact: (general) Mrs. Gwen Carr, Office Manager; W. Glen Tapley, Director of Network Radio Operations; or Father John Mary Klobacher, Chaplain, co-host of "Live Wire" call-in program; (marketing) Scott Hults, Director of Radio Marketing and Program Development; (administration) William Steltemeier, President; (technical) Frank Phillips, Vice President of Radio; Gary Gagnon, Frequency Manager; Joseph A. Dentici, Engineer; or Matt Cadak, Chief Engineer. Listener correspondence welcomed; responds to correspondence on-air and by mail. Free Gabriel's Horn newsletter and bumper stickers; also, free At Mary's Knee quarterly newsletter for children. Sells numerous religious publications ranging from $2 to $20, as well as T-shirts ($10-12), sweatshirts ($20); list available upon request (VISA/MC). IRC or return postage appreciated for correspondence. Volunteers needed for placing articles or ads in parish or Diocesan publications, as well as other parish activities. Although a Catholic entity, WEWN is not an official station of the Vatican, which operates its own Vatican Radio (see). Rather, WEWN reflects the activities of Mother M. Angelica and the Eternal Word Foundation, Inc. Donations and bequests accepted by the Eternal Word Foundation. TRANSMISSION FACILITY: P.O. Box 176, Vandiver AL 35176 USA. Phone and fax: see Station Office, above. Contact: Bernard Lockhart, Marketing Manager; or Norman Williams, Manager, Planning & Installation.
RELIGIOUS ORDER and EWTN ORGANIZATIONAL HEADQUARTERS: Our Lady of The Angels Monastery, 5817 Old Leeds Road, Birmingham AL 35210 USA. Phone: +1 (205) 956-5987. Fax: +1 (205) 951 0142.

WGTG—With Glory to God, Box 1131, Copperhill TN 37317 USA; or 2710 Hawk Drive, Marietta GA 30066 USA. Phone/fax: +1 (706) 492-5944. Contact: (general) Roseanne Frantz, Program Director; or "Mail Bag"; (technical) Dave Frantz, Chief Engineer. $1 or 3 IRCs for verification response. WGTG is a family-run Christian station supported by listener donations. Comments on reception quality, and especially audio quality, are welcomed. SASE appreciated. Hopes to add four more AM/SSB transmitters, nominally of 50 kW apiece.
PROGRAM PROVIDER: Fundamental Broadcasting Network (FBN), Morehead City NC 28557 USA. Phone: +1 (919) 240-1600. Fax: + (919) 726 2251. Contact: Pastor Clyde Eborn. A nonprofit organization, FBN feeds program material to WGTG via satellite.

WHRI—World Harvest Radio, WHRI/KWHR, LeSEA Broadcasting, P.O. Box 12, South Bend IN 46624 USA. Phone: +1 (219) 291-8200. Fax: (station) +1 (219) 291 9043. URL: http://www.whri.com. Contact: (listener contact) Loren Holycross; (general) Joe Brashier, Vice President; Joe Hill, Operations Manager; or Robert Willinger; (technical) Douglas Garlinger, Chief Engineer. Free stickers. WHRI T-shirts $12 from 61300 S. Ironwood Road, South Bend IN 46614 USA. In late 1996, World Harvest Radio inaugurated a monthly contest for the

two best taped reception reports of their stations. Each month, winners receive a World Harvest Radio T-shirt and a copy of the 1997 edition of PASSPORT TO WORLD BAND RADIO. Return postage appreciated. Carries programs from various political organizations; these may be contacted either directly (see Disestablishmentarian, earlier in this chapter) or via WHRI.

WINB—World International Broadcasters (if reactivated), World International Broadcast Network, P.O. Box 88, Red Lion PA 17356 USA. Phone: (general) +1 (717) 244-5360; (administration) +1 (717) 246-1681; (studio) +1 (717) 244-3145. Fax: +1 (717) 244 9316. Contact: (general) Mrs. Sally Spyker, Correspondence Secretary; John Stockdale, Manager; Clyde H. Campbell, C.F.O.; or John H. Norris, Owner; (technical) Fred W. Wise, Technical Director. Return postage helpful outside United States. No giveaways or items for sale. No decision has been made whether to repair WINB's transmitter and antennas, which reportedly are in poor condition, perhaps because of the former and bitter controversy concerning this station's one-time association with Christian Identity leader Pastor Pete Peters (see "Scriptures for America" under Disestablishmentarian).

WJCR—Jesus Christ Radio, P.O. Box 91, Upton KY 42784 USA. Phone: +1 (502) 369-8614. Contact: (general) Pastor Don Powell, President; Gerri Powell; Trish Powell; or A.L. Burile; (technical) Louis Tate, Chief Engineer. Free religious printed matter. Return postage or $1 appreciated. Actively solicits listener contributions.

WMLK—Assemblies of Yahweh, P.O. Box C, Bethel PA 19507 USA. Toll free telephone (U.S only) +1 (800) 523 3827; (elsewhere) +1 (717) 933-4518. Contact: (general) Elder Jacob O. Meyer, Manager & Producer of "The Open Door to the Living World"; (technical) Gary McAvin, Engineer. Free Yahweh magazine, stickers and religious material. Bibles, audio tapes and religious paperback books offered. Replies slowly, but enclosing return postage, $1 or IRCs sometimes helps speed things up. Plans to increase transmitter power to 100 kW.

WRMI—Radio Miami Internacional
MAIN OFFICE: P.O. Box 526852, Miami FL 33152 USA. Phone: +1 (305) 267-1728. Fax: +1 (305) 267 9253. E-mail: (general) 71163.1735@compuserve.com; radiomiami@aol.com; (International Public Access Radio, a joint venture of WRMI and IRRS of Italy) IPAR@nexus.org. URL: (International Public Access Radio) http://www.nexus.org/IPAR. Contact: (general) Jeff White, Producer, "Viva Miami!"; (technical) Indalecio

A growing number of stations are privately owned, such as America's World Harvest Radio in Indiana. Here, Joe Hill, Operations Manager, stands before its state-of-the-art hardware.

"Kiko" Espinosa, Chief Engineer. Free station stickers and tourist brochures. Sells PASSPORT TO WORLD BAND RADIO $23-33 (Depending where in the world it is sent), Grundig Yacht Boy 400 radios $205-220 (ditto), T-shirts $15 (worldwide), baseball-style hats $10 (worldwide)—all postpaid by airmail. No cards. Sells "public access" airtime to nearly anyone to say virtually anything for $1 or more per minute. Radio Miami Internacional also acts as a broker for Cuban and Vietnamese exile programs aired via U.S. stations KWHR, WHRI and WRNO. Technical correspondence may be sent to either WRMI or the station over which the program was heard. Hopes to add one or more new antennas and an additional 50 kW transmitter in the foreseeable future.
VENEZUELA OFFICE: Apartado 2122, Valencia 2001, Venezuela. Phone:/fax: + 58 (45) 810-362. Contact: Yoslen Silva.

☞**WRLT—FM Radio Lightning 100**, L&C Tower, Floor 30, 401 Church Street, Nashville TN 37219 USA. Phone: (main office/advertising) +1 (615) 242-5600; (studio) +1 (615) 737-0100. Fax: +1 (615) 242 9877. E-mail: comments@wrlt.com. URL: (RealAudio) http://wrlt.com/, http://www.wrlt.com/ or http://www.audionet.com/. Contact: Judy McNutt, Publicity; Roger Bertolini, Vice President & Advertising Director; or Lester Turner, C.E.O. Adult alternative programming. 24 hours. Return postage necessary.

WRNO, Box 100, New Orleans LA 70181 USA; or 4539 I-10 Service Road North, Metairie LA 70006 USA. Phone: +1 (504) 889-2424. Fax: +1 (504) 889 0602. URL: http://www.wrnoworldwide.com/. Contact: Joseph Mark Costello III, General Manager; or Paul Heingarten, Operations Manager. Single copy of program guide for 2 IRCs or an SASE. Stickers available for SASE. T-shirts available for $10. Sells World Band radios. Carries programs from various organizations; these may be contacted either directly (*see* Disestablishmentarian, earlier in this section) or via WRNO. Correct reception reports verified for 2 IRCs or an SASE. Frequently offers limited edition verification cards to those sending in reception reports.

WSHB—*see* Monitor Radio International, above.

☞**WTEM—Sports Talk 570 AM**, 11300 Rockville Pike, Bethesda MD 20852 USA. Phone: (main office) +1 (301) 770-5700; (advertising) +1 (301) 231-3507; (studio) +1 (301) 231-0570. Fax: +1 (301) 881 8030 or +1 (301) 881 8025. URL: (RealAudio)—http://www.wtem.com/, http://207.113.204.163/pub/wtem/wtem.htm or http://www.audionet.com/. Contact: Steve Perkins, Marketing Manager. Sports talk station. 24 hours.

WVHA—World Voice of Historic Adventism:
ADMINISTRATION STUDIO: Prophecy Countdown, Inc., P.O. Box 1844, 1701 Robie Avenue, Mount Dora FL 32757 USA. Phone: (toll-free phone, USA only) (800) 447-5683; (elsewhere) +1 (352) 735-1844. Fax: +1 (352) 735 4055. Contact: (general) Pastor John Osborne, Founder/Speaker; (administration) Kathleen Greenfield, Board Chairman & WVHA Acting Director; (technical) Gordon Simkin, Chief Engineer & Producer, "DXTRA." This station is not affiliated with Adventist World Radio or its parent organization. Various free publications and postcards. Sells books, CDs and audio cassettes, as well as video recordings (NTSC and PAL formats); VISA/MC/AX/Discover. Plans to add a log periodic antenna for North America, two curtain antennas for South America and two 100kW transmitters, funds permitting. Should this come to pass, they then plan to add a shortwave facility in Hawaii. Concerning this, Rev. Osborne stated, "A representative from [antenna manufacturer] TCI and I recently combed the islands of Hawaii, and have found the perfect location for a shortwave radio station to reach the other half of the world. As soon as WVHA is on sound financial footing, we plan to move on our Hawaii project."
TRANSMITTER: P.O. Box A, Olamon ME 04467 USA. Phone: +1 (207) 732-9842 or +1 (207) 832-6189. Fax: +1 (207) 732 5475. Contact: (general) Rita Knight; (technical) Mary Lee Mottram. WVHA indicates that it provides over 100 local

families with free food. Although it is engaged in a difference of opinion with local authorities concerning its tax-free status, the station states that it has offered to "compensate the town for their tax shortfall should the [legal] decision weigh in our favor."

WWCR—World Wide Christian Radio, F.W. Robbert Broadcasting Co., 1300 WWCR Avenue, Nashville TN 37218 USA. Phone: (general) +1 (615) 255-1300. Fax: +1 (615) 255 1311. E-mail: (general) wwcr@aol.com; or nmks01b@prodigy.com; (head of operations) wwcrl@aol.com; or nmks01b@prodigy.com; ("World Wide Country Radio") nmks01d@prodigy.com; ("Spectrum") spectrum@orn.com. URLs: http://www.wwcr.com; ("Spectrum") http://www.orn.com~spectrum/. Contact: (general) Chuck Adair, Sales Representative; or John Mondary; (administration) George McClintock, K4BTY, General Manager; or Adam W. Lock, Sr., WA2JAL, Head of Operations; (technical) Watt Hairston, Chief Engineer. Free program guide, updated monthly. Return postage helpful. Replies as time permits. Carries programs from various political organizations; these may be contacted directly (*see* Disestablishmentarian, earlier in this chapter).

WWV/WWVB (official time and frequency stations), Frequency-Time Broadcast Services Section, Time and Frequency Division, NIST, Mail Station 847, 325 Broadway, Boulder CO 80303 USA. Phone: (tape recording of latest shortwave technical propagation data and forecast) +1 (303) 497-3235; (live WWV audio) +1 (303) 499-7111; (Broadcast Manager) +1 (303) 497-3281; (Public Affairs) +1 (303) 497-3246; (Institute for Telecommunications Sciences) +1 (303) 497-3484. Phone/fax: (technical, call first before trying to fax) +1 (303) 497-3914. Fax: (Public Affairs) +1 (303) 497 3371. Contact: (general) Fred P. McGehan, Public Affairs Officer; (administration) Roger Beehler, Broadcast Manager; (technical) John B. Milton, Engineer-in-Charge; or Matt Deutsch, Engineer. Along with branch sister station WWVH in Hawaii (*see* below), WWV and WWVB are the official time and frequency stations of the United States, operating over longwave (WWVB) on 60 kHz, and over shortwave (WWV) on 2500, 5000, 10000, 15000 and 20000 kHz. Free Special Publication 432 "NIST Time & Frequency Services" pamphlet. Don't enclose return postage, money or IRCs, as they will only have to be returned by station. Plans to increase power of WWVB, currently 13 kW, before end of decade.

WWVH (official time and frequency station), NIST—Hawaii, P.O. Box 417, Kekaha, Kauai HI 96752 USA. Phone: +1 (808) 335-4361; (live audio) +1 (808) 335-4363. Fax: +1 (808) 335 4747. Contact: (technical) Dean T. Okayama, Engineer-in-Charge. E-mail: None planned. Along with headquarters sister stations WWV and WWVB (*see* preceding), WWVH is the official time and frequency station of the United States, operating on 2500, 5000, 10000 and 15000 kHz. Free Special Publication 432 "NIST Time & Frequency Services" pamphlet.

WYFR—Family Radio
NONTECHNICAL: Family Stations, Inc., 290 Hegenberger Road, Oakland CA 94621 USA. Phone: (toll-free, U.S. only) (800) 543-1495; (elsewhere) +1 (510) 568-6200. Fax: +1 (510) 562 1023. E-mail: famradio@lanminds.com. URL: (Family Radio Network) http://www.familyradio.com. Contact: Shortwave Department. Free gospel tracts (33 languages), books, booklets, quarterly *Family Radio News* magazine and frequency schedule. 2 IRCs helpful.
TECHNICAL: WYFR-Family Radio, 10400 NW 240th Street, Okeechobee FL 34972 USA. Phone: +1 (941) 763-0281. Fax: +1 (941) 763 8867. Contact: Dan Elyea, Engineering Manager.

☞**XTRA—AM**, 4891 Pacific Highway, San Diego 92110 CA USA. Phone: (main office) +1 (619) 291-9191; (studio) +1 (619) 291-2912. Fax: +1 (619) 294 2916 or +1 (619) 291 5622. E-mail: feedback@xtrasports.com. URL: (AudioNet) http://www.audionet.com; (general) http://www.xtrasports.com. Contact: Jeanne Zelasko, Publicity; Beth Lynch, Advertising; Howard Freedman, V.P. Operations; or Randy Michaels, C.E.O. All-sports station. 24 hours. Return postage required.

UZBEKISTAN   World Time +5
WARNING—MAIL THEFT: Due to increasing local mail theft, Radio Tashkent suggests that those wishing to correspond should try using one of the drop-mailing addresses listed below.

Radio Tashkent
STATION: 49 Khorezm Street, 740047 Tashkent, Uzbekistan. Phone: +7 (3712) 441-210. Fax: +7 (3712) 440 021. Contact: V. Danchev, Correspondence Section; Lenora Hannanowa; Zulfiya Ibragimova; Mrs. G. Babadjanova, Chief Director of Programs; or Mrs. Florida Perevertailo, Producer, "At Listeners' Request." Free pennants, badges, wallet calendars and postcards. Books in English by Uzbek writers are apparently available for purchase. Station offers free membership to two clubs: The "Salum Aleikum Listeners' Club" is open to anyone who asks to join, whereas "Radio Tashkent DX Club" is open to listeners who send in ten reception reports that are verified by the station. Station has tentative plans to expand its Southeast Asian Service.
LONDON OFFICE: 72 Wigmore Street, London W18 9L, United Kingdom.
FRANKFURT OFFICE: Radio Taschkent, c/o Uzbekistan Airways, Merkurhaus, Raum 215, Hauptbahnhof 10, D-60329 Frankfurt, Germany.
BANGKOK OFFICE: 848-850 Ramapur Road, Bangkok 10050, Thailand.
Uzbek Radio—see Radio Tashkent for details.

VANUATU   World Time +12 (+11 midyear)
Radio Vanuatu, Information & Public Relations, P.M.B. 049, Port Vila, Vanuatu. Phone: +678 22-999. Fax: +678 22 026. Contact: Ambong Thompson, Head of Programs; or Allan Kalfabun, Sales & Marketing Consultant, who is interested in exchanging letters and souvenirs from other countries; (technical) K.J. Page, Principal Engineer. Recently, this station has occasionally been subject to censorship by the prime minister.

VATICAN CITY STATE   World Time +1 (+2 midyear)
Vatican Radio
MAIN AND PROMOTION OFFICES: 00120 Città del Vaticano, Vatican City State. Phone: (general) +39 (6) 698-83551; (Promotion Office and schedules) +39 (6) 698-83045 or +39 (6) 698-83463; (technical) +39 (6) 698-85258 or +39 (6) 988-3995. Fax: (general) +39 (6) 698 84565 or +39 (6) 698 83237; (technical) +39 (6) 698 85125 or +39 (6) 698 85062. E-mail: mc6778@mclinkit. URL: (RealAudio in English, German and French, plus text) http://wrn.org/vatican-radio/. Contact: (general) Elisabetta Vitalini Sacconi, Promotion Office and schedules; Eileen O'Neill, Head of Program Development, English Service; Fr. Lech Rynkiewicz; Fr. Federico Lombardi, S.J., Program Manager; P. Moreau, Ufficio Promozione; Solange de Maillardoz, International Relations; or Veronica Scarisbrick, Producer, "On the Air;" (administration) Fr. Pasquale Borgomeo, S.J., Direttore Generale; (technical) Umberto Tolaini, Frequency Manager, Direzione Tecnica; Sergio Salvatori, Assistant Frequency Manager, Direzione Tecnica; Eugenio Matis SJ, Technical Director; or Giovanni Serra, Frequency Management Department. Correspondence sought on religious and programming matters, rather than the technical minutiae of radio. Free station stickers and paper pennants. Music CDs $13; *Pope John Paul II: The Pope of the Rosary* double CD/cassette $19.98 plus shipping; "Sixty Years...a Single Day" PAL video on Vatican Radio for 15,000 lire, including postage, from the Promotion Office. Vatican Radio's annual budget is $10 million.
TOKYO OFFICE: 2-10-10 Shiomi, Koto-ku, Tokyo 135, Japan. Fax: +81 (3) 5632 4457.

VENEZUELA   World Time –4
NOTE: According to radio writer/traveler Don Moore, Venezuelan stations are cutting back on their hours of operation to save electricity during the current period of economic recession.

Ecos del Torbes, Apartado 152, San Cristóbal 5001-A, Táchira, Venezuela. Phone: +58 (76) 438-244. Contact: (general) Daphne González Zerpa, Directora; (technical) Ing. Iván Escobar S., Jefe Técnico.
Radio Amazonas Internacional, Av. Simón Bolívar 4, Puerto Ayacucho 7101, Amazonas, Venezuela.
Radio Frontera (when active), Edificio Radio, San Antonio del Táchira, Táchira, Venezuela. Phone: +58 (76) 782-92. Fax: +58 (76) 785 08. Contact: Modesto Marchena, Gerente General. May reply to correspondence in Spanish. $1 or return postage suggested. If no reply, try sending your reports to Venezuelan DXer Antonio J. Contín, Calle Los Lirios #1219, Urbanización Miraflores 4013, Cabimas, Estado Zulia, Venezuela. In return for this service he requests you send $2-3 and would like any spare Latin American pennants and stickers you might have.
Radio Mundial Los Andes (Radio Los Andes 1040) (if reactivated), Calle 44 No. 3-57, Mérida, Venezuela. Phone: +58 (74) 639-286. May reply to correspondence in Spanish. $1 or return postage suggested.
Radio Nacional de Venezuela
MAIN OFFICE: Apartado 3979, Caracas 1050, Venezuela (although transmitter site is at Campo Carabobo near Valencia, some three hours drive away from Caracas). Phone: +58 (2) 745-166. Contact: Martin G. Delfin, English News Director; Jaime Alsina, Director; Ing. Dionisio Atencio; or Sra. Haydee Briceno, Gerente. Free 50th anniversary stickers, while they last, and other small souvenirs. If no response, try Apartado 50700, Caracas 1050, Venezuela. Although station has been virtually inaudible on its fundamental frequency for some time, now, it has been heard during 1996 on spurious frequencies; thus, it would appear that it is, or at least was until recently, still active.
MIAMI POSTAL ADDRESS: Jet Cargo International, M-7, P.O. Box 020010, Miami FL 33102 USA. Contact: Martin G. Delfin, English News Director.
Radio Occidente, Carrera 4a. No. 6-46, Tovar 5143, Mérida, Venezuela.
Radio Rumbos (when active)
MAIN ADDRESS: Apartado 2618, Caracas 1010A, Venezuela. Phone: +58 (2) 261-0666. Fax: +58 (2) 335 164. Contact: (general) Andrés Felipe Serrano, Vice-Presidente; (technical) Ing. José Corrales; or Jaime L. Ferguson, Departamento Técnico. Free pamphlets, keychains and stickers. $1 or IRC required. Replies occasionally to correspondence in Spanish.
MIAMI ADDRESS: P.O. Box 020010, Miami FL 33102 USA.
Radio Táchira, Apartado 152, San Cristóbal 5001-A, Táchira, Venezuela. Phone: +58 (76) 430-009. Contact: Desirée González Zerpa, Directora; Sra. Albertina, Secretaria; or Eleázar Silva Malavé, Gerente.
Radio Valera, Av. 10 No. 9-31, Valera 3102, Trujillo, Venezuela. Phone: +58 (71) 53-744. Replies to correspondence in Spanish. Return postage required. This station has been on the same world band frequency for almost 50 years, which is a record for Latin America. If no response try via Antonio J. Contín. (*see* Radio Frontera, above).

VIETNAM   World Time +7
Bac Thai Broadcasting Service—contact via Voice of Vietnam—Overseas Service, below.
Lai Chau Broadcasting Service—contact via Voice of Vietnam—Overseas Service, below.
Lam Dong Broadcasting Service, Da Lat, Vietnam. Contact: Hoang Van Trung. Replies slowly to correspondence in Vietnamese, but French may also suffice.
Son La Broadcasting Service, Son La, Vietnam. Contact: Nguyen Hang, Director. Replies slowly to correspondence in Vietnamese, but French may also suffice.
Voice of Vietnam—Domestic Service (Đài Tiếng Nói Việt Nam, TNVN)—Addresses and contact numbers as for all sections of Voice of Vietnam—Overseas Service, below. Contact: Phan Quang, Director General.

Automatic Gain Control (AGC). Smooths out fluctuations in signal strength brought about by fading, a regular occurrence with world band signals.

AV. A Voz—Portuguese for "The Voice." In PASSPORT, this term is also used to represent "The Voice of."

Bandwidth. A key variable that determines selectivity (see), bandwidth is the amount of radio signal at –6 dB a radio's circuitry will let pass through, and thus be heard. With world band channel spacing at 5 kHz, the best single bandwidths are usually in the vicinity of 3 to 6 kHz. Better radios offer two or more selectable bandwidths: one of 5 to 7 kHz or so for when a station is in the clear, and one or more others between 2 to 4 kHz for when a station is hemmed in by other stations next to it. Proper selectivity is a key determinant of the aural quality of what you hear.

Baud. Measurement of the speed by which radioteletype (see), radiofax (see) and other digital data are transmitted. Baud is properly written entirely in lower case, and thus is abbreviated as b (baud), kb (kilobaud) or Mb (Megabaud). Baud rate standards are usually set by the international CCITT regulatory body.

BC. Broadcasting, Broadcasting Company, Broadcasting Corporation.

Broadcast. A radio or television transmission meant for the general public. *Compare* Utility Stations, Hams.

BS. Broadcasting Station, Broadcasting Service.

Cd. Ciudad—Spanish for "City."

Channel. An everyday term to indicate where a station is supposed to be located on the dial. World band channels are spaced exactly 5 kHz apart. Stations operating outside this norm are "off-channel" (for these, PASSPORT provides resolution to better than 1 kHz to aid in station identification).

Chugging, Chuffing. The sound made by some synthesized tuning systems when the tuning knob is turned. Called "chugging" or "chuffing," as it is suggestive of the rhythmic "chug, chug" sound of a steam engine or "chugalug" gulping.

Cl. Club, Clube.

Cult. Cultura, Cultural.

Default. The setting at which a control of a digitally operated electronic device, including many world band radios, normally operates, and to which it will eventually return.

Dipole Antenna. See Passive Antenna.

Digital Frequency Display, Digital Tuning. See Synthesizer.

Digital Signal Processing. Technique in which computer-type circuitry is used to enhance the readability or other characteristics of an analog audio signal. Used on a very few world band supersets; also available as an add-on accessory.

Domestic Service. See DS.

DS. Domestic Service—Broadcasting intended primarily for audiences in the broadcaster's home country. However, some domestic programs are beamed on world band to expatriates and other kinfolk abroad, as well as interested foreigners. *Compare* ES.

DSP. See Digital Signal Processing.

DX, DXers, DXing. From an old telegraph term "to DX"; that is, to communicate over a great distance. Thus, DXers are those who specialize in finding distant or exotic stations that are considered to be rare catches. Few world band listeners are considered to be regular DXers, but many others seek out DX stations every now and then—usually by bandscanning, which is greatly facilitated by PASSPORT's Blue Pages.

Dynamic Range. The ability of a receiver to handle weak signals in the presence of strong competing signals within or near the same world band segment (see World Band Spectrum). Sets with inferior dynamic range sometimes "overload," especially with external antennas, causing a mishmash of false signals up and down—and even beyond—the segment being received.

Earliest Heard (or Latest Heard). See key at the bottom of

each Blue Page. If the PASSPORT monitoring team cannot establish the definite sign-on (or sign-off) time of a station, the earliest (or latest) time that the station could be traced is indicated by a left-facing or right-facing "arrowhead flag." This means that the station almost certainly operates beyond the time shown by that "flag." It also means that, unless you live relatively close to the station, you're unlikely to be able to hear it beyond that "flagged" time.

EBS. Economic Broadcasting Station, a type of station found in China.

ECSS. Exalted-carrier selectable sideband, a term no longer in general use except to refer to manually and carefully tuning in a conventional AM-mode signal using the receiver's single-sideband circuitry. See Synchronous Detector.

Ed, Educ. Educational, Educação, Educadora.

Electrical Noise. See Noise.

Em. Emissora, Emisora, Emissor, Emetteur—in effect, "station" in various languages.

Enhanced Fidelity. Radios with good audio performance and certain types of high-tech circuitry can improve upon the fidelity of world band reception. Among the newer fidelity-enhancing techniques is synchronous detection (see). Another potential technological advance to enhance fidelity is digital world band transmission, which is actively being researched in the United States and elsewhere.

EP. Emissor Provincial—Portuguese for "Provincial Station."

ER. Emissor Regional—Portuguese for "Regional Station."

Ergonomics. How handy and comfortable—intuitive—a set is to operate, especially hour after hour.

ES. External Service—Broadcasting intended primarily for audiences abroad. *Compare* DS.

External Service. See ES.

F. Friday.

Fax. See Radiofax.

Feeder, Shortwave. A utility transmission from the broadcaster's home country to a relay site or placement facility some distance away. Although these specialized transmissions carry world band programming, they are not intended to be received by the general public. Many world band radios can process these quasi-broadcasts anyway. Feeders operate in lower sideband (LSB), upper sideband (USB) or independent sideband (termed ISL if heard on the lower side, ISU if heard on the upper side) modes. Most shortwave feeders have by now been replaced by satellite feeders. See Single Sideband, Utility Stations.

Frequency. The standard term to indicate where a station is located on the dial—regardless of whether it is "on-channel" or "off-channel" (see Channel). Measured in kilohertz (kHz) or Megahertz (MHz), which differ only in the placement of a decimal; e.g., 5975 kHz is the same as 5.975 MHz. Either measurement is equally valid, but to minimize confusion PASSPORT and most stations designate frequencies only in kHz.

Frequency Synthesizer. See Synthesizer, Frequency.

Front-End Selectivity. The ability of the initial stage of receiving circuitry to admit only limited frequency ranges into succeeding stages of circuitry. Good front-end selectivity keeps signals from other, powerful bands or segments from being superimposed upon the frequency range you're tuning. For example, a receiver with good front-end selectivity will receive only shortwave signals within the range 3200-3400 kHz. However, a receiver with mediocre front-end selectivity might allow powerful local mediumwave AM stations from 520-1700 kHz to be heard "ghosting in" between 3200 and 3400 kHz, along with the desired shortwave signals. Obviously, mediumwave AM signals don't belong on shortwave. Receivers with inadequate front-end selectivity can benefit by the addition of a preselector (see).

GMT. Greenwich Mean Time—See World Time.

Hams. Government-licensed amateur radio hobbyists who *transmit* to each other by radio, often by single sideband

The Seventh-day Adventist Church is unusually active on world band, including from Russia, where they operate the Zaokskaya Seminariya between Tula and Moscow.

(see), for pleasure within special amateur bands. Many of these bands are within the shortwave spectrum (see). This is the same spectrum used by world band radio, but world band and ham radio, which laymen sometimes confuse with each other, are two very separate entities. The easiest way is to think of hams as making something like phone calls, whereas world band stations are like long-distance versions of ordinary FM or mediumwave AM stations.

Harmonic, Harmonic Radiation, Harmonic Signal. Weak spurious repeat of a signal in multiple(s) of the fundamental, or "real," frequency. Thus, the third harmonic of a medium-wave AM station on 1120 kHz might be heard faintly on 4480 kHz within the world band spectrum. Stations almost always try to avoid harmonic radiation, but in rare cases have been known to amplify a harmonic signal so they can operate inexpensively on a second frequency. Also, see Subharmonic.

Hash. Electrical noise. See Noise.

High Fidelity. See Enhanced Fidelity.

Image Rejection. A key type of spurious-signal rejection (see).

Independent Sideband. See Single Sideband.

Interference. Sounds from other signals, notably on adjacent channels or the same channel ("co-channel"), that are disturbing the one you are trying to hear. Worthy radios reduce interference by having good selectivity (see). Nearby television sets and cable television wiring may also generate a special type of radio interference called TVI, a "growl" usually heard every 15 kHz or so.

International Telecommunication Union (ITU). The regulatory body, headquartered in Geneva, for all international telecommunications, including world band radio. Sometimes incorrectly referred to as the "International Telecommunications Union." In recent years, the ITU has become increasingly ineffective as a regulatory body for world band, with much of its former role having been taken up by groups of affiliated international broadcasters voluntarily coordinating their schedules a number of times each year.

Inverted-L Antenna. See Passive Antenna.

Ionosphere. See Propagation.

Irr. Irregular operation or hours of operation; i.e., schedule tends to be unpredictable.

ISB. Independent sideband. See Single Sideband.

ISL. Independent sideband, lower. See Feeder.

ISU. Independent sideband, upper. See Feeder.

ITU. See International Telecommunication Union.

Jamming. Deliberate interference to a transmission with the intent of discouraging listening. Jamming is practiced much less now than it was during the Cold War.

Keypad. On a world band radio, like a computer, a keypad can be used to control many variables. However, unlike a computer, the keypad on most world band radios consists of ten numeric or multifunction keys, usually supplemented by two more keys, as on a telephone keypad. Keypads are used primarily so you can enter a station's frequency for reception, and the best keypads have real keys (not a membrane) in the standard telephone format of 3×4 with "zero" under the "8" key. Many keypads are also used for presets, but this means you have to remember code numbers for stations (e.g., BBC 5975 kHz is "07"); handier radios either have separate keys for presets, or use LCD-displayed "pages" to access presets.

kHz. Kilohertz, the most common unit for measuring where a station is on the world band dial. Formerly known as "kilocycles per second," or kc/s. 1,000 kilohertz equals one Megahertz.

Kilohertz. See kHz.

kW. Kilowatt(s), the most common unit of measurement for transmitter power (see).

LCD. Liquid-crystal display. LCDs, if properly designed, are fairly easily seen in bright light, but require side lighting (also called "backlighting") under darker conditions. LCDs, being gray on gray, also tend to have mediocre contrast, and sometimes can be read from only a certain angle or angles, but they consume nearly no battery power.

LED. Light-emitting diode. LEDs are very easily read in the dark or in normal room light, but consume battery power and are hard to read in bright light.

Loc. Local.

Location. The physical location of a station's transmitter, which may be different from the studio location. Transmitter location is useful as a guide to reception quality. For example, if you're in eastern North America and wish to listen to the Voice of Russia, a transmitter located in St. Petersburg will almost certainly provide better reception than one located in Siberia.

Longwave Band. The 148.5–283.5 kHz portion of the low-frequency (LF) radio spectrum used in Europe, the Near East, North Africa, Russia and Mongolia for domestic broadcasting. As a practical matter, these longwave signals, which have nothing to do with world band or other shortwave signals, are not usually audible in other parts of the world.

Longwire Antenna. See Passive Antenna.

LSB. Lower Sideband. See Feeder, Single Sideband.

LV. La Voix, La Voz—French and Spanish for "The Voice." In PASSPORT, this term is also used to represent "The Voice of."

M. Monday.

Mediumwave Band, Mediumwave AM Band. See AM Band.

Megahertz. See MHz.

Memory, Memories. See Preset.

Meters. An outdated unit of measurement used for individual world band segments of the shortwave spectrum. The frequency range covered by a given meters designation—also known as "wavelength"—can be gleaned from the following formula: $frequency\ (kHz) = 299{,}792 \div meters$. Thus, 49 meters comes out to a frequency of 6118 kHz—well within the range of frequencies included in that segment (see World Band Spectrum). Inversely, meters can be derived from the following: $meters = 299{,}792 \div frequency\ (kHz)$.

MHz. Megahertz, a common unit to measure where a station is on the dial. Formerly known as "Megacycles per second," or Mc/s. One Megahertz equals 1,000 kilohertz.

Mode. Method of transmission of radio signals. World band radio broadcasts are almost always in the analog AM mode, the same mode used in the mediumwave AM band (see). The AM mode consists of three components: two "sidebands" and one "carrier." Each sideband contains the same programming as the other, and the carrier carries no programming, so a few stations have experimented with the single-sideband (SSB) mode. SSB contains only one sideband, either the lower sideband (LSB) or upper sideband (USB), and a reduced carrier. It requires special radio circuitry to be demodulated, or made intelligible, which is the main reason SSB has not succeeded, and is not expected to succeed, as a world band mode. There are yet other modes used on shortwave, but not for world band. These include CW (Morse-type code), radiofax, RTTY (radioteletype) and narrow-band FM used by utility and ham stations. Narrowband FM is not used for music, and is different from usual FM. See Single Sideband, ISB, ISL, ISU, LSB and USB.

N. New, Nueva, Nuevo, Nouvelle, Nacional, National, Nationale.

Nac. Nacional. Spanish and Portuguese for "National."

Nat, Natl, Nat'l. National, Nationale.

Noise. Static, buzzes, pops and the like caused by the earth's atmosphere (typically lightning), and to a lesser extent by galactic noise. Also, electrical noise emanates from such man-made sources as electric blankets, fish-tank heaters, heating pads, electrical and gasoline motors, light dimmers, flickering light bulbs, non-incandescent lights, computers and computer peripherals, office machines, electrical fences, and faulty electrical utility wiring and related components.

Other. Programs are in a language other than one of the world's primary languages.

Overloading. See Dynamic Range.

Passive Antenna. An antenna that is not electronically amplified. Typically, these are mounted outdoors, although the "tape-measure" type that comes as an accessory with some portables is usually strung indoors. For world band reception, virtually all outboard models for consumers are made from wire. The two most common designs are the inverted-L (so-called "longwire") and trapped dipole (either horizontal or sloper). These antennas are preferable to active antennas (see), and are reviewed in detail in the Radio Database International White Paper, PASSPORT *Evaluation of Popular Outdoor Antennas (Unamplified)*.

PBS. People's Broadcasting Station.

PLL (Phase-Locked Loop). With world band receivers, a PLL circuit means that the radio can be tuned digitally, often using a number of handy tuning techniques, such as a keypad and presets (see).

Power. Transmitter power *before* amplification by the antenna, expressed in kilowatts (kW). The present range of world band powers is 0.01 to 1,000 kW.

Power Lock. See Travel Power Lock.

PR. People's Republic.

Preselector. A device—typically outboard, but sometimes inboard—that effectively limits the range of frequencies which can enter a receiver's circuitry or the circuitry of an active antenna (see); that is, which improves front-end selectivity (see). For example, a preselector may let in the range 15000-16000 kHz, thus helping ensure that your receiver or active antenna will encounter no problems within that range caused by signals from, say, 5800-6200 kHz or local mediumwave AM signals (520-1705 kHz). This range usually can be varied, manually or automatically, according to the frequency to which the receiver is being tuned. A preselector may be passive (unamplified) or active (amplified).

Preset. Allows you to select a station pre-stored in a radio's memory. The handiest presets require only one push of a button, as on a car radio.

Propagation. World band signals travel, like a basketball, up and down from the station to your radio. The "floor" below is the earth's surface, whereas the "player's hand" on high is the *ionosphere*, a gaseous layer that envelops the planet. While the earth's surface remains pretty much the same from day to day, the ionosphere—nature's own passive "satellite"—varies in how it propagates radio signals, depending on how much sunlight hits the "bounce points."

Thus, some world band segments do well mainly by day, whereas others are best by night. During winter there's less sunlight, so the "night bands" become unusually active, whereas the "day bands" become correspondingly less useful (see World Band Spectrum). Day-to-day changes in the sun's weather also cause short-term changes in world band radio reception; this explains why some days you can hear rare signals.

Additionally, the 11-year sunspot cycle has a long-term effect on propagation. Currently, the sunspot cycle is exiting its trough. This means that while the upper world band segments have been less active than usual in recent years, there will be a significant and welcome improvement in world band reception towards the end of the decade and beyond.

PS. Provincial Station, Pangsong.

Pto. Puerto, Porto.

QSL. See Verification.

R. Radio, Radiodiffusion, Radiodifusora, Radiodifusão, Radiophonikos, Radiostantsiya, Radyo, Radyosu, and so forth.

Radiofax, Radio Facsimile. Like ordinary telefax (facsimile by telephone lines), but by radio.

Radioteletype (RTTY). Characters, but not illustrations, transmitted by radio. See Baud.

Receiver. Synonym for a radio, but sometimes—especially when called a "communications receiver"—implying a radio with superior tough-signal performance.

Reduced Carrier. See Single Sideband.

Reg. Regional.

Relay. A retransmission facility, often highlighted in "Worldwide Broadcasts in English" and "Voices from Home" in PASSPORT's WorldScan® section. Relay facilities are generally considered to be located outside the broadcaster's country. Being closer to the target audience, they usually provide superior reception. See Feeder.

Rep. Republic, République, República.

RN. See R and N.

RS. Radio Station, Radiostantsiya, Radiostudiya, Radiophonikos Stathmos.

RT, RTV. Radiodiffusion Télévision, Radio Télévision, and so forth.

RTTY. See Radioteletype.

S. As an icon **S**: aired summer (midyear) only. As an ordinary letter: San, Santa, Santo, São, Saint, Sainte. Also, South.

Sa. Saturday.

Scan, Scanning. Circuitry within a radio that allows it to bandscan or memory-scan automatically.

Segments. See Shortwave Spectrum.

Selectivity. The ability of a radio to reject interference (see) from signals on adjacent channels. Thus, also known as adjacent-channel rejection, a key variable in radio quality. Also, see "Bandwidth" and "Synchronous Detector".

Sensitivity. The ability of a radio to receive weak signals; thus, also known as weak-signal sensitivity. Of special importance if you're listening during the day, or if you're located in such parts of the world as Western North America, Hawaii and Australasia, where signals tend to be relatively weak.

Shortwave Spectrum. The shortwave spectrum—also known as the High Frequency (HF) spectrum—is, strictly speaking, that portion of the radio spectrum from 3-30 MHz (3,000-30,000 kHz). However, common usage places it from 2.3-30 MHz (2,000-30,000 kHz). World band operates on shortwave within 14 discrete segments between 2.3-26.1 MHz, with the rest of the shortwave spectrum being occupied by hams (see) and utility stations (see). Also, see World Band Spectrum, as well as the detailed "Best Times and Frequencies" piece elsewhere in this edition.

Sideband. See Mode.

Single Sideband, Independent Sideband. Spectrum- and power-conserving modes of transmission commonly used by utility stations and hams. Few broadcasters use, or are expected ever to use, these modes. Many world band radios are already capable of demodulating single-sideband transmissions, and some can even process independent-sideband signals. Certain single-sideband transmissions operate with a minimum of carrier reduction, which allows them to be listened to, albeit with some distortion, on ordinary radios not equipped to demodulate single sideband. Properly designed synchronous detectors (see) may prevent such distortion. See Feeder, Mode.

Site. See Location.

Slew Controls. Elevator-button-type up and down controls to tune a radio. On many radios with synthesized tuning, slewing is used in lieu of tuning by knob. Better is when slew controls are complemented by a tuning knob, which is more versatile.

Sloper Antenna. See Passive Antenna.

SPR. Spurious (false) extra signal from a transmitter actually operating on another frequency. One such type is harmonic (see).

Spurious-Signal Rejection. The ability of a radio receiver not to produce false, or "ghost," signals that might otherwise interfere with the clarity of the station you're trying to hear. See Image Rejection.

St, Sta, Sto. Abbreviations for words that mean "Saint."

Static. See Noise.

Su. Sunday.

Subharmonic. A harmonic heard at 1 times the operating frequency. Thus, the subharmonic of a station on 3360 kHz might be heard faintly on 5040 kHz. Also, see Harmonic.

Synchronous Detector. World band radios are increasingly coming equipped with this high-tech circuit that greatly reduces fading distortion. Better synchronous detectors also allow for selectable sideband; that is, the ability to select the clearer of the two sidebands of a world band or other AM-mode signal. See Mode.

Synchronous Selectable Sideband. See Synchronous Detector.

Synthesizer, Frequency. Simple radios often use archaic needle-and-dial tuning that makes it difficult to find a desired channel or to tell which station you are hearing, except by ear. Other models utilize a digital frequency synthesizer to tune in signals without your having to hunt and peck. Among other things, such synthesizers allow for push-button tuning and presets, and display the exact frequency digitally—pluses that make tuning in the world considerably easier. Virtually a "must" feature.

Target. Where a transmission is beamed.

Th. Thursday.

Travel Power Lock. Control to disable the on/off switch to prevent a radio from switching on accidentally.

Transmitter Power. See Power.

Trapped Dipole Antenna. See Passive Antenna.

Tu. Tuesday.

Universal Day. See World Time.

Universal Time. See World Time.

USB. Upper Sideband. See Feeder, Single Sideband.

UTC. See World Time.

Utility Stations. Most signals within the shortwave spectrum are not world band stations. Rather, they are utility stations—radio telephones, ships at sea, aircraft and the like—that transmit strange sounds (growls, gurgles, dih-dah sounds, etc.) point-to-point and are not intended to be heard by the general public. Compare Broadcast, Hams and Feeders.

v. Variable frequency; i.e., one that is unstable or drifting because of a transmitter malfunction or to avoid jamming.

Verification. A card or letter from a station verifying that a listener indeed heard that particular station. In order to stand a chance of qualifying for a verification card or letter, you need to provide the station heard with the following information in a three-number "SIO" code, in which "SIO 555" is best and "SIO 111" is worst:

- **S**ignal strength, with 5 being of excellent quality, comparable to that of a local mediumwave AM station, and 1 being inaudible or at least so weak as to be virtually unintelligible. 2 (faint, but somewhat intelligible), 3 (moderate strength) and 4 (good strength) represent the signal-strength levels usually encountered with world band stations.
- **I**nterference from other stations, with 5 indicating no interference whatsoever, and 1 indicating such extreme interference that the desired signal is virtually drowned out. 2 (heavy interference), 3 (moderate interference) and 4 (slight interference) represent the differing degrees of interference more typically encountered with world band signals. If possible, indicate the names of the interfering station(s) and the channel(s) they are on. Otherwise, at least describe what the interference sounds like.

- **O**verall quality of the signal, with 5 being best, 1 worst.
- In addition to providing SIO findings, you should indicate which programs you've heard, as well as comments on how you liked or disliked those programs. Refer to the "Addresses PLUS" section of this edition for information on where and to whom your report should be sent, and whether return postage should be included.
- Because of the time involved in listening, few stations wish to receive tape recordings of their transmissions.

Vo. Voice of.

W. As an icon **W**: aired winter only. As a regular letter: Wednesday.

Wavelength. See Meters.

Weak-Signal Sensitivity. See Sensitivity.

World Band Radio. Similar to regular mediumwave AM band and FM band radio, except that world band stations can be heard over enormous distances and thus often carry news, music and entertainment programs created especially for audiences abroad. Some world band stations have audiences of up to 120 million each day. Some 600 million people worldwide are believed to listen to world band radio.

World Band Spectrum. See "Best Times and Frequencies" elsewhere in this edition.

World Day. See World Time.

World Time. Also known as Coordinated Universal Time (UTC), Greenwich Mean Time (GMT) and Zulu time (Z). With nearly 170 countries on world band radio, if each announced its own local time you would need a calculator to figure it all out. To get around this, a single international time—World Time—is used. The difference between World Time and local time is detailed in the "Addresses PLUS" section of this edition, the "Compleat Idiot's Guide to Getting Started" and especially in the last page of this edition. It is also determined simply by listening to World Time announcements given on the hour by world band stations—or minute by minute by WWV and WWVH in the United States on such frequencies as 5000, 10000 and 15000 kHz, or CHU in Canada on 3330, 7335 and 14670 kHz. A 24-hour clock format is used, so "1800 World Time" means 6:00 PM World Time. If you're in, say, North America, Eastern Time is five hours behind World Time winters and four hours behind World Time summers, so 1800 World Time would be 1:00 PM EST or 2:00 PM EDT. The easiest solution is to use a 24-hour clock set to World Time. Many radios already have these built in, and World Time clocks are also available as accessories. World Time also applies to the days of the week. So if it's 9:00 PM (21:00) Wednesday in New York during the winter, it's 0200 *Thursday* World Time.

WS. World Service.

Printed in USA

1997 DIRECTORY OF ADVERTISERS

Passport's Blue Pages—1997

Channel-by-Channel Guide to World Band Schedules

250 kW of power. These clues suggest this is probably what you're hearing, even if you're not in Europe. It also shows that English will be on in ten minutes.

Schedules for Entire Year

Times and days of the week are in World Time; for local times, see Addresses PLUS. Some stations are shown as one hour earlier (◀■) or later (■▶) midyear—typically April through October. Stations may also extend their hours during holidays or for sports events.

To be as helpful as possible throughout the year, PASSPORT'S Blue Pages include not just observed activity and factual schedules, but also that which we have creatively opined will take place. This predictive information is original from us, and although it's a useful bonus, it's inherently not so exact as factual data.

Passport's Blue Pages Help Identify Stations

But just dialing around can be frustrating if you don't have a "map"—PASSPORT'S Blue Pages. Say, you've stumbled across something Asian-sounding on 7410 kHz at 2035 World Time. PASSPORT'S Blue Pages show All India Radio in Hindi beamed to Western Europe, with a hefty

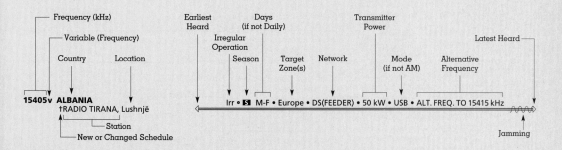

Frequency (kHz)		Earliest Heard	Days (if not Daily)	Transmitter Power	
Variable (Frequency)		Irregular Operation			Latest Heard
Country	Location		Season	Target Zone(s)	Network	Mode (if not AM)	Alternative Frequency

15405v ALBANIA †RADIO TIRANA, Lushnjë
— Station
— New or Changed Schedule

Irr • S M-F • Europe • DS(FEEDER) • 50 kW • USB • ALT. FREQ. TO 15415 kHz

Jamming

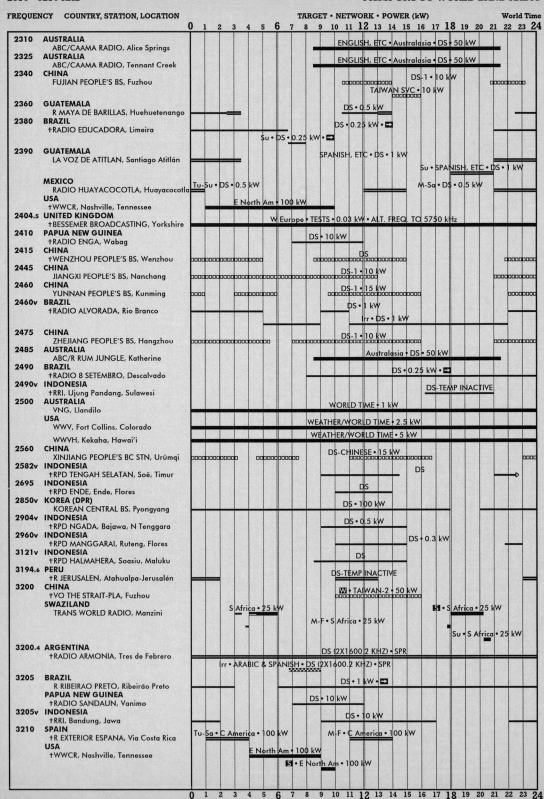

FREQUENCY	COUNTRY, STATION, LOCATION	TARGET • NETWORK • POWER (kW)
2310	**AUSTRALIA** ABC/CAAMA RADIO, Alice Springs	ENGLISH, ETC • Australasia • DS • 50 kW
2325	**AUSTRALIA** ABC/CAAMA RADIO, Tennant Creek	ENGLISH, ETC • Australasia • DS • 50 kW
2340	**CHINA** FUJIAN PEOPLE'S BS, Fuzhou	DS-1 • 10 kW / TAIWAN SVC • 10 kW
2360	**GUATEMALA** R MAYA DE BARILLAS, Huehuetenango	DS • 0.5 kW
2380	**BRAZIL** †RADIO EDUCADORA, Limeira	DS • 0.25 kW • ➡ / Su • DS • 0.25 kW • ➡
2390	**GUATEMALA** LA VOZ DE ATITLAN, Santiago Atitlán	SPANISH, ETC • DS • 1 kW / Su • SPANISH, ETC • DS • 1 kW
	MEXICO RADIO HUAYACOCOTLA, Huayacocotla	Tu-Su • DS • 0.5 kW / M-Sa • DS • 0.5 kW
	USA †WWCR, Nashville, Tennessee	E North Am • 100 kW
2404.5	**UNITED KINGDOM** †BESSEMER BROADCASTING, Yorkshire	W Europe • TESTS • 0.03 kW • ALT. FREQ. TO 5750 kHz
2410	**PAPUA NEW GUINEA** †RADIO ENGA, Wabag	DS • 10 kW
2415	**CHINA** †WENZHOU PEOPLE'S BS, Wenzhou	DS
2445	**CHINA** JIANGXI PEOPLE'S BS, Nanchang	DS-1 • 10 kW
2460	**CHINA** YUNNAN PEOPLE'S BS, Kunming	DS-1 • 15 kW
2460v	**BRAZIL** †RADIO ALVORADA, Rio Branco	DS • 1 kW / Irr • DS • 1 kW
2475	**CHINA** ZHEJIANG PEOPLE'S BS, Hangzhou	DS-1 • 10 kW
2485	**AUSTRALIA** ABC/R RUM JUNGLE, Katherine	Australasia • DS • 50 kW
2490	**BRAZIL** †RADIO 8 SETEMBRO, Descalvado	DS • 0.25 kW • ➡
2490v	**INDONESIA** †RRI, Ujung Pandang, Sulawesi	DS-TEMP INACTIVE
2500	**AUSTRALIA** VNG, Llandilo	WORLD TIME • 1 kW
	USA WWV, Fort Collins, Colorado	WEATHER/WORLD TIME • 2.5 kW
	WWVH, Kekaha, Hawai'i	WEATHER/WORLD TIME • 5 kW
2560	**CHINA** XINJIANG PEOPLE'S BC STN, Urümqi	DS-CHINESE • 15 kW
2582v	**INDONESIA** †RPD TENGAH SELATAN, Soë, Timur	DS
2695	**INDONESIA** †RPD ENDE, Ende, Flores	DS
2850v	**KOREA (DPR)** KOREAN CENTRAL BS, Pyongyang	DS • 100 kW
2904v	**INDONESIA** †RPD NGADA, Bajawa, N Tenggara	DS • 0.5 kW
2960v	**INDONESIA** †RPD MANGGARAI, Ruteng, Flores	DS • 0.3 kW
3121v	**INDONESIA** †RPD HALMAHERA, Soasiu, Maluku	DS
3194.6	**PERU** †R JERUSALEN, Atahualpa-Jerusalén	DS-TEMP INACTIVE
3200	**CHINA** †VO THE STRAIT-PLA, Fuzhou	🅦 • TAIWAN-2 • 50 kW
	SWAZILAND TRANS WORLD RADIO, Manzini	S Africa • 25 kW / 🆂 • S Africa • 25 kW / M-F • S Africa • 25 kW / Su • S Africa • 25 kW
3200.4	**ARGENTINA** †RADIO ARMONIA, Tres de Febrero	DS (2X1600.2 KHZ) • SPR / Irr • ARABIC & SPANISH • DS (2X1600.2 KHZ) • SPR
3205	**BRAZIL** R RIBEIRAO PRETO, Ribeirão Preto	DS • 1 kW • ➡
	PAPUA NEW GUINEA †RADIO SANDAUN, Vanimo	DS • 10 kW
3205v	**INDONESIA** †RRI, Bandung, Jawa	DS • 10 kW
3210	**SPAIN** †R EXTERIOR ESPANA, Via Costa Rica	Tu-Sa • C America • 100 kW / M-F • C America • 100 kW
	USA †WWCR, Nashville, Tennessee	E North Am • 100 kW / 🆂 • E North Am • 100 kW

FREQUENCY   COUNTRY, STATION, LOCATION   TARGET • NETWORK • POWER (kW)   World Time

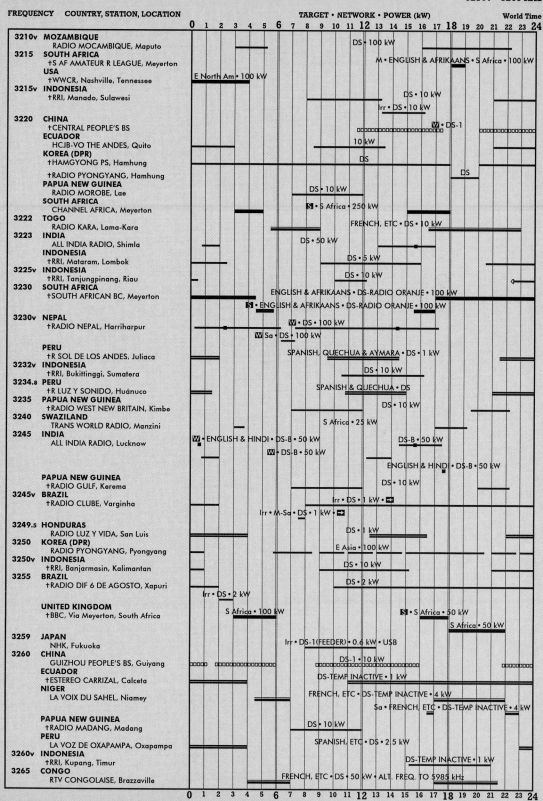

FREQUENCY	COUNTRY, STATION, LOCATION
3210v	MOZAMBIQUE
	RADIO MOCAMBIQUE, Maputo
3215	SOUTH AFRICA
	†S AF AMATEUR R LEAGUE, Meyerton
	USA
	†WWCR, Nashville, Tennessee
3215v	INDONESIA
	†RRI, Manado, Sulawesi
3220	CHINA
	†CENTRAL PEOPLE'S BS
	ECUADOR
	HCJB-VO THE ANDES, Quito
	KOREA (DPR)
	†HAMGYONG PS, Hamhung
	†RADIO PYONGYANG, Hamhung
	PAPUA NEW GUINEA
	RADIO MOROBE, Lae
	SOUTH AFRICA
	CHANNEL AFRICA, Meyerton
3222	TOGO
	RADIO KARA, Lama-Kara
3223	INDIA
	ALL INDIA RADIO, Shimla
	INDONESIA
	†RRI, Mataram, Lombok
3225v	INDONESIA
	†RRI, Tanjungpinang, Riau
3230	SOUTH AFRICA
	†SOUTH AFRICAN BC, Meyerton
3230v	NEPAL
	†RADIO NEPAL, Harriharpur
	PERU
	†R SOL DE LOS ANDES, Juliaca
3232v	INDONESIA
	†RRI, Bukittinggi, Sumatera
3234.8	PERU
	†R LUZ Y SONIDO, Huánuco
3235	PAPUA NEW GUINEA
	†RADIO WEST NEW BRITAIN, Kimbe
3240	SWAZILAND
	TRANS WORLD RADIO, Manzini
3245	INDIA
	ALL INDIA RADIO, Lucknow
	PAPUA NEW GUINEA
	†RADIO GULF, Kerema
3245v	BRAZIL
	†RADIO CLUBE, Varginha
3249.5	HONDURAS
	RADIO LUZ Y VIDA, San Luis
3250	KOREA (DPR)
	RADIO PYONGYANG, Pyongyang
3250v	INDONESIA
	†RRI, Banjarmasin, Kalimantan
3255	BRAZIL
	†RADIO DIF 6 DE AGOSTO, Xapuri
	UNITED KINGDOM
	†BBC, Via Meyerton, South Africa
3259	JAPAN
	NHK, Fukuoka
3260	CHINA
	GUIZHOU PEOPLE'S BS, Guiyang
	ECUADOR
	†ESTEREO CARRIZAL, Calceta
	NIGER
	LA VOIX DU SAHEL, Niamey
	PAPUA NEW GUINEA
	†RADIO MADANG, Madang
	PERU
	LA VOZ DE OXAPAMPA, Oxapampa
3260v	INDONESIA
	†RRI, Kupang, Timur
3265	CONGO
	RTV CONGOLAISE, Brazzaville

Chart data (TARGET • NETWORK • POWER):
- MOZAMBIQUE, RADIO MOCAMBIQUE: DS • 100 kW
- SOUTH AFRICA, S AF AMATEUR R LEAGUE: M • ENGLISH & AFRIKAANS • S Africa • 100 kW
- USA, WWCR: E North Am • 100 kW
- INDONESIA, RRI Manado: DS • 10 kW; Irr • DS • 10 kW
- CHINA, CENTRAL PEOPLE'S BS: W • DS-1
- ECUADOR, HCJB: 10 kW
- KOREA (DPR), HAMGYONG PS: DS
- RADIO PYONGYANG: DS
- PAPUA NEW GUINEA, RADIO MOROBE: DS • 10 kW
- SOUTH AFRICA, CHANNEL AFRICA: S • S Africa • 250 kW
- TOGO, RADIO KARA: FRENCH, ETC • DS • 10 kW
- INDIA, ALL INDIA RADIO Shimla: DS • 50 kW
- INDONESIA, RRI Mataram: DS • 5 kW
- INDONESIA, RRI Tanjungpinang: DS • 10 kW
- SOUTH AFRICA, SOUTH AFRICAN BC: ENGLISH & AFRIKAANS • DS-RADIO ORANJE • 100 kW; S • ENGLISH & AFRIKAANS • DS-RADIO ORANJE • 100 kW
- NEPAL, RADIO NEPAL: W • DS • 100 kW; W Sa • DS • 100 kW
- PERU, R SOL DE LOS ANDES: SPANISH, QUECHUA & AYMARA • DS • 1 kW
- INDONESIA, RRI Bukittinggi: DS • 10 kW
- PERU, R LUZ Y SONIDO: SPANISH & QUECHUA • DS
- PAPUA NEW GUINEA, RADIO WEST NEW BRITAIN: DS • 10 kW
- SWAZILAND, TRANS WORLD RADIO: S Africa • 25 kW
- INDIA, ALL INDIA RADIO Lucknow: W • ENGLISH & HINDI • DS-B • 50 kW; W • DS-B • 50 kW; DS-B • 50 kW; ENGLISH & HINDI • DS-B • 50 kW
- PAPUA NEW GUINEA, RADIO GULF: DS • 10 kW
- BRAZIL, RADIO CLUBE: Irr • DS • 1 kW • ; Irr • M-Sa • DS • 1 kW •
- HONDURAS, RADIO LUZ Y VIDA: DS • 1 kW
- KOREA (DPR), RADIO PYONGYANG: E Asia • 100 kW
- INDONESIA, RRI Banjarmasin: DS • 10 kW
- BRAZIL, RADIO DIF 6 DE AGOSTO: DS • 2 kW; Irr • DS • 2 kW
- UNITED KINGDOM, BBC: S Africa • 100 kW; S • S Africa • 50 kW; S Africa • 50 kW
- JAPAN, NHK: Irr • DS-1 (FEEDER) • 0.6 kW • USB
- CHINA, GUIZHOU PEOPLE'S BS: DS-1 • 10 kW
- ECUADOR, ESTEREO CARRIZAL: DS-TEMP INACTIVE • 1 kW
- NIGER, LA VOIX DU SAHEL: FRENCH, ETC • DS-TEMP INACTIVE • 4 kW; Sa • FRENCH, ETC • DS-TEMP INACTIVE • 4 kW
- PAPUA NEW GUINEA, RADIO MADANG: DS • 10 kW
- PERU, LA VOZ DE OXAPAMPA: SPANISH, ETC • DS • 2.5 kW
- INDONESIA, RRI Kupang: DS-TEMP INACTIVE • 1 kW
- CONGO, RTV CONGOLAISE: FRENCH, ETC • DS • 50 kW • ALT. FREQ. TO 5985 kHz

ENGLISH ▬   ARABIC ⁓⁓   CHINESE ▫▫▫   FRENCH ▭▭   GERMAN ▬▬   RUSSIAN ═══   SPANISH ▬▬   OTHER ▭

FREQUENCY   COUNTRY, STATION, LOCATION

TARGET • NETWORK • POWER (kW)

World Time

0 1 2 3 4 5 6 7 8 9 10 11 12 13 14 15 16 17 18 19 20 21 22 23 24

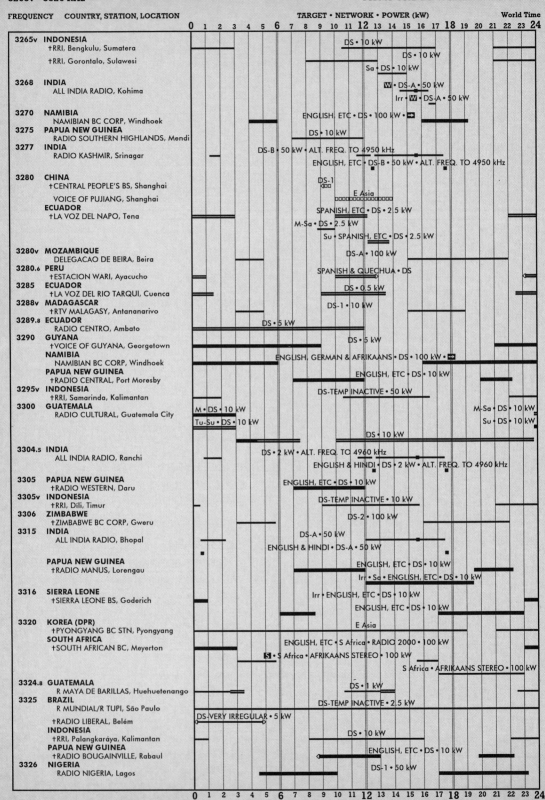

Frequency	Country, Station, Location	Target • Network • Power
3265v	INDONESIA	
	†RRI, Bengkulu, Sumatera	DS • 10 kW
	†RRI, Gorontalo, Sulawesi	DS • 10 kW / Sa • DS • 10 kW
3268	INDIA	
	ALL INDIA RADIO, Kohima	W • DS-A • 50 kW / Irr • W • DS-A • 50 kW
3270	NAMIBIA	
	NAMIBIAN BC CORP, Windhoek	ENGLISH, ETC • DS • 100 kW • ⇨
3275	PAPUA NEW GUINEA	
	RADIO SOUTHERN HIGHLANDS, Mendi	DS • 10 kW
3277	INDIA	
	RADIO KASHMIR, Srinagar	DS-B • 50 kW • ALT. FREQ. TO 4950 kHz / ENGLISH, ETC • DS-B • 50 kW • ALT. FREQ. TO 4950 kHz
3280	CHINA	
	†CENTRAL PEOPLE'S BS, Shanghai	DS-1
	VOICE OF PUJIANG, Shanghai	E Asia
	ECUADOR	
	†LA VOZ DEL NAPO, Tena	SPANISH, ETC • DS • 2.5 kW / M-Sa • DS • 2.5 kW / Su • SPANISH, ETC • DS • 2.5 kW
3280v	MOZAMBIQUE	
	DELEGACAO DE BEIRA, Beira	DS-A • 100 kW
3280.6	PERU	
	†ESTACION WARI, Ayacucho	SPANISH & QUECHUA • DS
3285	ECUADOR	
	†LA VOZ DEL RIO TARQUI, Cuenca	DS • 0.5 kW
3288v	MADAGASCAR	
	†RTV MALAGASY, Antananarivo	DS-1 • 10 kW
3289.8	ECUADOR	
	RADIO CENTRO, Ambato	DS • 5 kW
3290	GUYANA	
	†VOICE OF GUYANA, Georgetown	DS • 5 kW
	NAMIBIA	
	NAMIBIAN BC CORP, Windhoek	ENGLISH, GERMAN & AFRIKAANS • DS • 100 kW • ⇨
	PAPUA NEW GUINEA	
	†RADIO CENTRAL, Port Moresby	ENGLISH, ETC • DS • 10 kW
3295v	INDONESIA	
	†RRI, Samarinda, Kalimantan	DS-TEMP INACTIVE • 50 kW
3300	GUATEMALA	
	RADIO CULTURAL, Guatemala City	M • DS • 10 kW / Tu-Su • DS • 10 kW / M-Sa • DS • 10 kW / Su • DS • 10 kW / DS • 10 kW
3304.5	INDIA	
	ALL INDIA RADIO, Ranchi	DS • 2 kW • ALT. FREQ. TO 4960 kHz / ENGLISH & HINDI • DS • 2 kW • ALT. FREQ. TO 4960 kHz
3305	PAPUA NEW GUINEA	
	†RADIO WESTERN, Daru	ENGLISH, ETC • DS • 10 kW
3305v	INDONESIA	
	†RRI, Dili, Timur	DS-TEMP INACTIVE • 10 kW
3306	ZIMBABWE	
	†ZIMBABWE BC CORP, Gweru	DS-2 • 100 kW
3315	INDIA	
	ALL INDIA RADIO, Bhopal	DS-A • 50 kW / ENGLISH & HINDI • DS-A • 50 kW
	PAPUA NEW GUINEA	
	†RADIO MANUS, Lorengau	ENGLISH, ETC • DS • 10 kW / Irr • Sa • ENGLISH, ETC • DS • 10 kW
3316	SIERRA LEONE	
	†SIERRA LEONE BS, Goderich	Irr • ENGLISH, ETC • DS • 10 kW / ENGLISH, ETC • DS • 10 kW
3320	KOREA (DPR)	
	†PYONGYANG BC STN, Pyongyang	E Asia
	SOUTH AFRICA	
	†SOUTH AFRICAN BC, Meyerton	ENGLISH, ETC • S Africa • RADIO 2000 • 100 kW / S • S Africa • AFRIKAANS STEREO • 100 kW / S Africa • AFRIKAANS STEREO • 100 kW
3324.8	GUATEMALA	
	R MAYA DE BARILLAS, Huehuetenango	DS • 1 kW
3325	BRAZIL	
	R MUNDIAL/R TUPI, São Paulo	DS-TEMP INACTIVE • 2.5 kW
	†RADIO LIBERAL, Belém	DS-VERY IRREGULAR • 5 kW
	INDONESIA	
	†RRI, Palangkaráya, Kalimantan	DS • 10 kW
	PAPUA NEW GUINEA	
	†RADIO BOUGAINVILLE, Rabaul	ENGLISH, ETC • DS • 10 kW
3326	NIGERIA	
	RADIO NIGERIA, Lagos	DS-1 • 50 kW

0 1 2 3 4 5 6 7 8 9 10 11 12 13 14 15 16 17 18 19 20 21 22 23 24

SEASONAL **S** OR **W**   1-HR TIMESHIFT MIDYEAR ⇦ OR ⇨   JAMMING / OR ∧   EARLIEST HEARD ◁   LATEST HEARD ▷   NEW FOR 1997 †

FREQUENCY   COUNTRY, STATION, LOCATION   TARGET • NETWORK • POWER (kW)   World Time

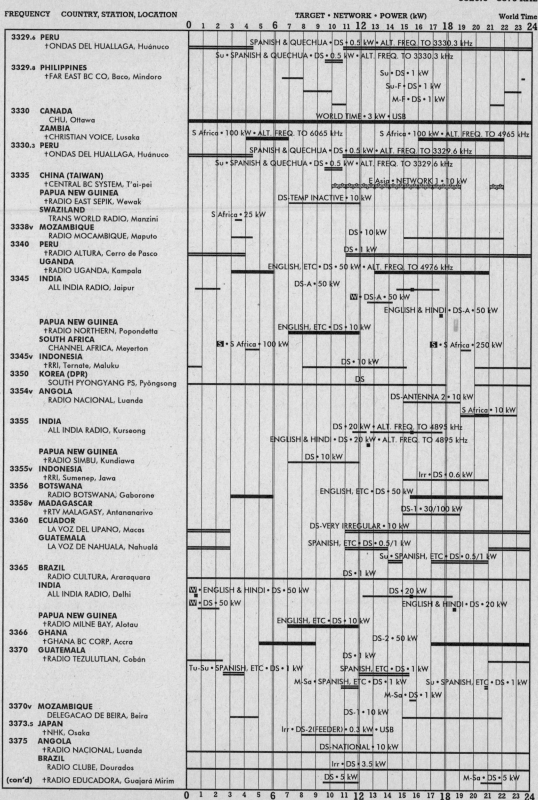

0 1 2 3 4 5 6 7 8 9 10 11 12 13 14 15 16 17 18 19 20 21 22 23 24

Frequency	Country, Station, Location	Details
3329.6	**PERU** †ONDAS DEL HUALLAGA, Huánuco	SPANISH & QUECHUA • DS • 0.5 kW • ALT. FREQ. TO 3330.3 kHz / Su • SPANISH & QUECHUA • DS • 0.5 kW • ALT. FREQ. TO 3330.3 kHz
3329.8	**PHILIPPINES** †FAR EAST BC CO, Baco, Mindoro	Su • DS • 1 kW / Su-F • DS • 1 kW / M-F • DS • 1 kW
3330	**CANADA** CHU, Ottawa	WORLD TIME • 3 kW • USB
	ZAMBIA †CHRISTIAN VOICE, Lusaka	S Africa • 100 kW • ALT. FREQ. TO 6065 kHz S Africa • 100 kW • ALT. FREQ. TO 4965 kHz
3330.3	**PERU** †ONDAS DEL HUALLAGA, Huánuco	SPANISH & QUECHUA • DS • 0.5 kW • ALT. FREQ. TO 3329.6 kHz / Su • SPANISH & QUECHUA • DS • 0.5 kW • ALT. FREQ. TO 3329.6 kHz
3335	**CHINA (TAIWAN)** †CENTRAL BC SYSTEM, T'ai-pei	E Asia • NETWORK 1 • 10 kW
	PAPUA NEW GUINEA †RADIO EAST SEPIK, Wewak	DS-TEMP INACTIVE • 10 kW
	SWAZILAND TRANS WORLD RADIO, Manzini	S Africa • 25 kW
3338v	**MOZAMBIQUE** RADIO MOCAMBIQUE, Maputo	DS • 10 kW
3340	**PERU** †RADIO ALTURA, Cerro de Pasco	DS • 1 kW
	UGANDA †RADIO UGANDA, Kampala	ENGLISH, ETC • DS • 50 kW • ALT. FREQ. TO 4976 kHz
3345	**INDIA** ALL INDIA RADIO, Jaipur	DS-A • 50 kW / W • DS-A • 50 kW / ENGLISH & HINDI • DS-A • 50 kW
	PAPUA NEW GUINEA †RADIO NORTHERN, Popondetta	ENGLISH, ETC • DS • 10 kW
	SOUTH AFRICA CHANNEL AFRICA, Meyerton	S • S Africa • 100 kW S • S Africa • 250 kW
3345v	**INDONESIA** †RRI, Ternate, Maluku	DS • 10 kW
3350	**KOREA (DPR)** SOUTH PYONGYANG PS, Pyŏngsong	DS
3354v	**ANGOLA** RADIO NACIONAL, Luanda	DS-ANTENNA 2 • 10 kW S Africa • 10 kW
3355	**INDIA** ALL INDIA RADIO, Kurseong	DS • 20 kW • ALT. FREQ. TO 4895 kHz / ENGLISH & HINDI • DS • 20 kW • ALT. FREQ. TO 4895 kHz
	PAPUA NEW GUINEA †RADIO SIMBU, Kundiawa	DS • 10 kW
3355v	**INDONESIA** †RRI, Sumenep, Jawa	Irr • DS • 0.6 kW
3356	**BOTSWANA** RADIO BOTSWANA, Gaborone	ENGLISH, ETC • DS • 50 kW
3358v	**MADAGASCAR** †RTV MALAGASY, Antananarivo	DS-1 • 30/100 kW
3360	**ECUADOR** LA VOZ DEL UPANO, Macas	DS-VERY IRREGULAR • 10 kW
	GUATEMALA LA VOZ DE NAHUALA, Nahualá	SPANISH, ETC • DS • 0.5/1 kW / Su • SPANISH, ETC • DS • 0.5/1 kW
3365	**BRAZIL** RADIO CULTURA, Araraquara	DS • 1 kW
	INDIA ALL INDIA RADIO, Delhi	W • ENGLISH & HINDI • DS • 50 kW DS • 20 kW / W • DS • 50 kW ENGLISH & HINDI • DS • 20 kW
	PAPUA NEW GUINEA †RADIO MILNE BAY, Alotau	ENGLISH, ETC • DS • 10 kW
3366	**GHANA** †GHANA BC CORP, Accra	DS-2 • 50 kW
3370	**GUATEMALA** †RADIO TEZULUTLAN, Cobán	DS • 1 kW / Tu-Su • SPANISH, ETC • DS • 1 kW SPANISH, ETC • DS • 1 kW / M-Sa • SPANISH, ETC • DS • 1 kW Su • SPANISH, ETC • DS • 1 kW / M-Sa • DS • 1 kW
3370v	**MOZAMBIQUE** DELEGACAO DE BEIRA, Beira	DS-1 • 10 kW
3373.5	**JAPAN** †NHK, Osaka	Irr • DS-2(FEEDER) • 0.3 kW • USB
3375	**ANGOLA** †RADIO NACIONAL, Luanda	DS-NATIONAL • 10 kW
	BRAZIL RADIO CLUBE, Dourados	Irr • DS • 3.5 kW
(con'd)	†RADIO EDUCADORA, Guajará Mirim	DS • 5 kW M-Sa • DS • 5 kW

0 1 2 3 4 5 6 7 8 9 10 11 12 13 14 15 16 17 18 19 20 21 22 23 24

ENGLISH ▬   ARABIC ⁵⁵⁵   CHINESE □□□   FRENCH ▬   GERMAN ▬   RUSSIAN ═   SPANISH ▬   OTHER ▬

FREQUENCY   COUNTRY, STATION, LOCATION

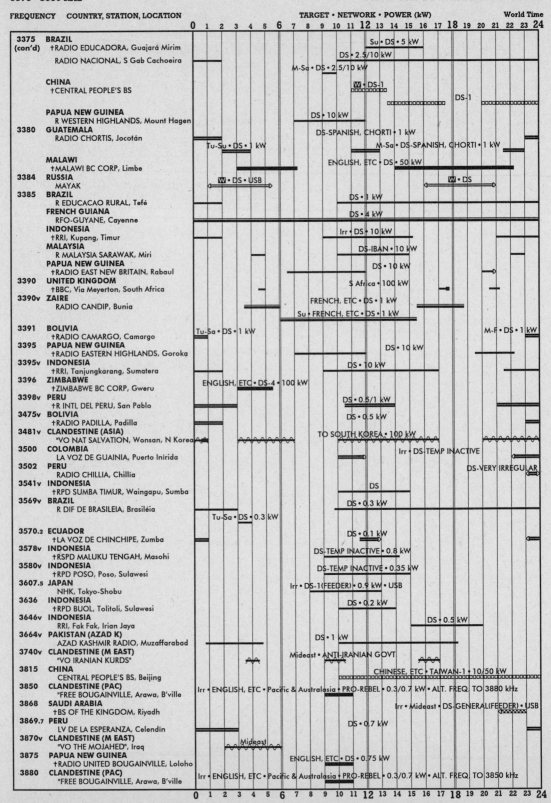

FREQUENCY   COUNTRY, STATION, LOCATION   TARGET • NETWORK • POWER (kW)   World Time

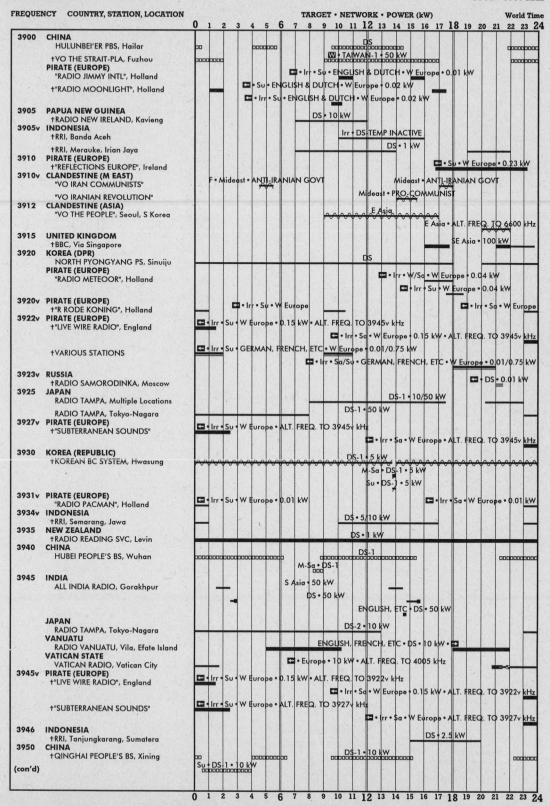

FREQUENCY	COUNTRY, STATION, LOCATION	Schedule / Notes
3900	**CHINA**	
	HULUNBEI'ER PBS, Hailar	DS
		W • TAIWAN-1 • 50 kW
	†VO THE STRAIT-PLA, Fuzhou	
	PIRATE (EUROPE)	
	"RADIO JIMMY INTL", Holland	• Irr • Su • ENGLISH & DUTCH • W Europe • 0.01 kW
	†"RADIO MOONLIGHT", Holland	• Su • ENGLISH & DUTCH • W Europe • 0.02 kW
		• Irr • Su • ENGLISH & DUTCH • W Europe • 0.02 kW
3905	**PAPUA NEW GUINEA**	
	†RADIO NEW IRELAND, Kavieng	DS • 10 kW
3905v	**INDONESIA**	
	†RRI, Banda Aceh	Irr • DS • TEMP INACTIVE
	†RRI, Merauke, Irian Jaya	DS • 1 kW
3910	**PIRATE (EUROPE)**	
	†"REFLECTIONS EUROPE", Ireland	• Su • W Europe • 0.23 kW
3910v	**CLANDESTINE (M EAST)**	
	"VO IRAN COMMUNISTS"	F • Mideast • ANTI-IRANIAN GOVT Mideast • ANTI-IRANIAN GOVT
	"VO IRANIAN REVOLUTION"	Mideast • PRO-COMMUNIST
3912	**CLANDESTINE (ASIA)**	
	"VO THE PEOPLE", Seoul, S Korea	E Asia
		E Asia • ALT. FREQ. TO 6600 kHz
3915	**UNITED KINGDOM**	
	†BBC, Via Singapore	SE Asia • 100 kW
3920	**KOREA (DPR)**	
	NORTH PYONGYANG PS, Sinuiju	DS
	PIRATE (EUROPE)	
	"RADIO METEOOR", Holland	• Irr • W/Sa • W Europe • 0.04 kW
		• Irr • Su • W Europe • 0.04 kW
3920v	**PIRATE (EUROPE)**	
	†"R RODE KONING", Holland	• Irr • Su • W Europe • Irr • Sa • W Europe
3922v	**PIRATE (EUROPE)**	
	†"LIVE WIRE RADIO", England	• Irr • Su • W Europe • 0.15 kW • ALT. FREQ. TO 3945v kHz
		• Irr • Sa • W Europe • 0.15 kW • ALT. FREQ. TO 3945v kHz
	†VARIOUS STATIONS	• Irr • Su • GERMAN, FRENCH, ETC • W Europe • 0.01/0.75 kW
		• Irr • Sa/Su • GERMAN, FRENCH, ETC • W Europe • 0.01/0.75 kW
3923v	**RUSSIA**	
	†RADIO SAMORODINKA, Moscow	• DS • 0.01 kW
3925	**JAPAN**	
	RADIO TAMPA, Multiple Locations	DS-1 • 10/50 kW
	RADIO TAMPA, Tokyo-Nagara	DS-1 • 50 kW
3927v	**PIRATE (EUROPE)**	
	†"SUBTERRANEAN SOUNDS"	• Irr • Su • W Europe • ALT. FREQ. TO 3945v kHz
		• Irr • Sa • W Europe • ALT. FREQ. TO 3945v kHz
3930	**KOREA (REPUBLIC)**	
	†KOREAN BC SYSTEM, Hwasung	DS-1 • 5 kW
		M-Sa • DS-1 • 5 kW
		Su • DS-1 • 5 kW
3931v	**PIRATE (EUROPE)**	
	"RADIO PACMAN", Holland	• Irr • Su • W Europe • 0.01 kW • Irr • Sa • W Europe • 0.01 kW
3934v	**INDONESIA**	
	†RRI, Semarang, Jawa	DS • 5/10 kW
3935	**NEW ZEALAND**	
	†RADIO READING SVC, Levin	DS • 1 kW
3940	**CHINA**	
	HUBEI PEOPLE'S BS, Wuhan	DS-1
		M-Sa • DS-1
3945	**INDIA**	
	ALL INDIA RADIO, Gorakhpur	S Asia • 50 kW
		DS • 50 kW
		ENGLISH, ETC • DS • 50 kW
	JAPAN	
	RADIO TAMPA, Tokyo-Nagara	DS-2 • 10 kW
	VANUATU	
	RADIO VANUATU, Vila, Efate Island	ENGLISH, FRENCH, ETC • DS • 10 kW
	VATICAN STATE	
	VATICAN RADIO, Vatican City	• Europe • 10 kW • ALT. FREQ. TO 4005 kHz
3945v	**PIRATE (EUROPE)**	
	†"LIVE WIRE RADIO", England	• Irr • Su • W Europe • 0.15 kW • ALT. FREQ. TO 3922v kHz
		• Irr • Sa • W Europe • 0.15 kW • ALT. FREQ. TO 3922v kHz
	†"SUBTERRANEAN SOUNDS"	• Irr • Su • W Europe • ALT. FREQ. TO 3927v kHz
		• Irr • Sa • W Europe • ALT. FREQ. TO 3927v kHz
3946	**INDONESIA**	
	†RRI, Tanjungkarang, Sumatera	DS • 2.5 kW
3950	**CHINA**	
	†QINGHAI PEOPLE'S BS, Xining	DS-1 • 10 kW
(con'd)		Su • DS-1 • 10 kW

0 1 2 3 4 5 6 7 8 9 10 11 12 13 14 15 16 17 18 19 20 21 22 23 24

ENGLISH ▬▬   ARABIC ≶≶≶   CHINESE □□□   FRENCH ▬▬   GERMAN ▬▬   RUSSIAN ══   SPANISH ▬▬   OTHER ▬▬

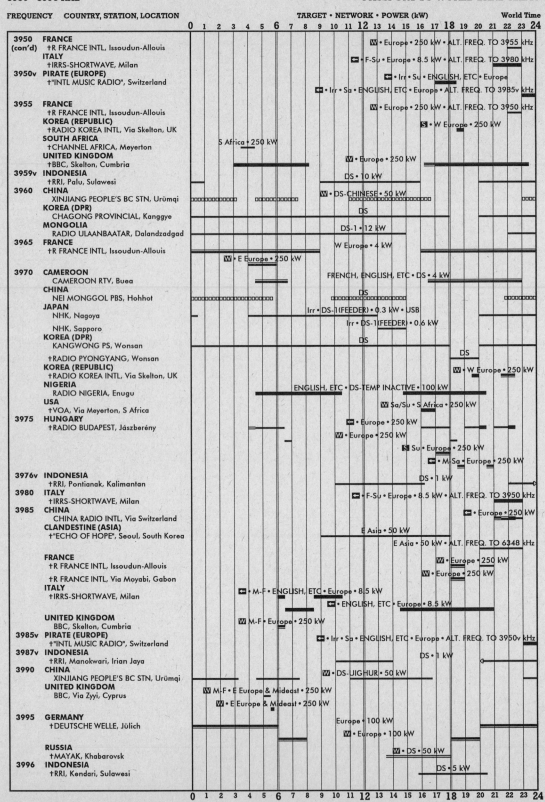

FREQUENCY   COUNTRY, STATION, LOCATION

TARGET • NETWORK • POWER (kW)

World Time

3950
(con'd)   **FRANCE**
    †R FRANCE INTL, Issoudun-Allouis   W • Europe • 250 kW • ALT. FREQ. TO 3955 kHz
    ITALY
    †IRRS-SHORTWAVE, Milan   • F-Su • Europe • 8.5 kW • ALT. FREQ. TO 3980 kHz
3950v **PIRATE (EUROPE)**
    †"INTL MUSIC RADIO", Switzerland   • Irr • Su • ENGLISH, ETC • Europe
    • Irr • Sa • ENGLISH, ETC • Europe • ALT. FREQ. TO 3985v kHz

3955   **FRANCE**
    †R FRANCE INTL, Issoudun-Allouis   W • Europe • 250 kW • ALT. FREQ. TO 3950 kHz
    KOREA (REPUBLIC)
    †RADIO KOREA INTL, Via Skelton, UK   S • W Europe • 250 kW
    SOUTH AFRICA
    †CHANNEL AFRICA, Meyerton   S Africa • 250 kW
    UNITED KINGDOM
    †BBC, Skelton, Cumbria   W • Europe • 250 kW
3959v **INDONESIA**
    †RRI, Palu, Sulawesi   DS • 10 kW
3960   **CHINA**
    XINJIANG PEOPLE'S BC STN, Urümqi   W • DS-CHINESE • 50 kW
    KOREA (DPR)
    CHAGONG PROVINCIAL, Kanggye   DS
    MONGOLIA
    RADIO ULAANBAATAR, Dalandzadgad   DS-1 • 12 kW
3965   **FRANCE**
    †R FRANCE INTL, Issoudun-Allouis   W Europe • 4 kW
    W • E Europe • 250 kW

3970   **CAMEROON**
    CAMEROON RTV, Buea   FRENCH, ENGLISH, ETC • DS • 4 kW
    CHINA
    NEI MONGGOL PBS, Hohhot   DS
    JAPAN
    NHK, Nagoya   Irr • DS-1(FEEDER) • 0.3 kW • USB

    NHK, Sapporo   Irr • DS-1(FEEDER) • 0.6 kW
    KOREA (DPR)
    KANGWONG PS, Wonsan   DS

    †RADIO PYONGYANG, Wonsan   DS
    KOREA (REPUBLIC)
    †RADIO KOREA INTL, Via Skelton, UK   W • W Europe • 250 kW
    NIGERIA
    RADIO NIGERIA, Enugu   ENGLISH, ETC • DS-TEMP INACTIVE • 100 kW
    USA
    †VOA, Via Meyerton, S Africa   W • Sa/Su • S Africa • 250 kW
3975   **HUNGARY**
    †RADIO BUDAPEST, Jászberény   • Europe • 250 kW
    W • Europe • 250 kW
    S • Su • Europe • 250 kW
    • M-Sa • Europe • 250 kW

3976v **INDONESIA**
    †RRI, Pontianak, Kalimantan   DS • 1 kW
3980   **ITALY**
    †IRRS-SHORTWAVE, Milan   • F-Su • Europe • 8.5 kW • ALT. FREQ. TO 3950 kHz
3985   **CHINA**
    CHINA RADIO INTL, Via Switzerland   • Europe • 250 kW
    CLANDESTINE (ASIA)
    †"ECHO OF HOPE", Seoul, South Korea   E Asia • 50 kW
    E Asia • 50 kW • ALT. FREQ. TO 6348 kHz

    FRANCE
    †R FRANCE INTL, Issoudun-Allouis   W • Europe • 250 kW

    †R FRANCE INTL, Via Moyabi, Gabon   W • Europe • 250 kW
    ITALY
    †IRRS-SHORTWAVE, Milan   • M-F • ENGLISH, ETC • Europe • 8.5 kW
    • ENGLISH, ETC • Europe • 8.5 kW

    UNITED KINGDOM
    BBC, Skelton, Cumbria   W • M-F • Europe • 250 kW
3985v **PIRATE (EUROPE)**
    †"INTL MUSIC RADIO", Switzerland   • Irr • Sa • ENGLISH, ETC • Europe • ALT. FREQ. TO 3950v kHz
3987v **INDONESIA**
    †RRI, Manokwari, Irian Jaya   DS • 1 kW
3990   **CHINA**
    XINJIANG PEOPLE'S BC STN, Urümqi   W • DS-UIGHUR • 50 kW
    UNITED KINGDOM
    BBC, Via Zyyi, Cyprus   W • M-F • E Europe & Mideast • 250 kW
    W • E Europe & Mideast • 250 kW

3995   **GERMANY**
    †DEUTSCHE WELLE, Jülich   Europe • 100 kW
    W • Europe • 100 kW

    RUSSIA
    †MAYAK, Khabarovsk   W • DS • 50 kW
3996   **INDONESIA**
    †RRI, Kendari, Sulawesi   DS • 5 kW

FREQUENCY   COUNTRY, STATION, LOCATION   TARGET • NETWORK • POWER (kW)   World Time

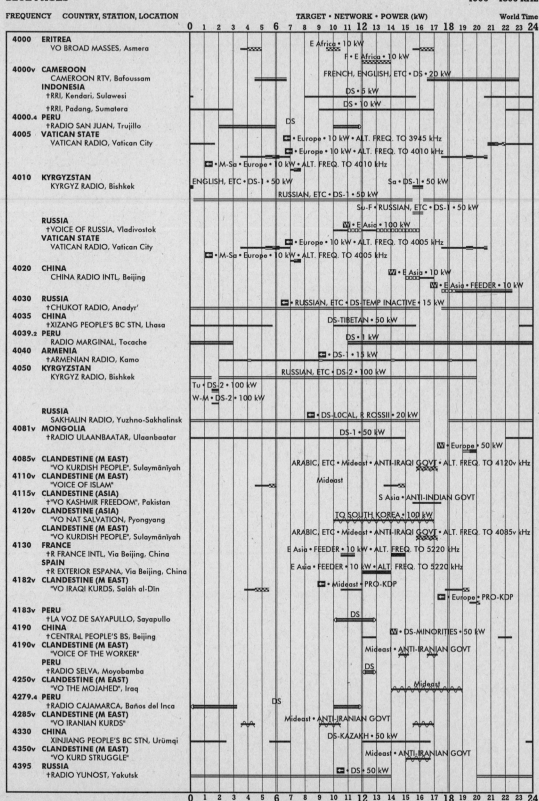

FREQUENCY	COUNTRY, STATION, LOCATION	TARGET • NETWORK • POWER (kW)
4000	**ERITREA** VO BROAD MASSES, Asmera	E Africa • 10 kW / F • E Africa • 10 kW
4000v	**CAMEROON** CAMEROON RTV, Bafoussam	FRENCH, ENGLISH, ETC • DS • 20 kW
	INDONESIA †RRI, Kendari, Sulawesi	DS • 5 kW
	†RRI, Padang, Sumatera	DS • 10 kW
4000.4	**PERU** †RADIO SAN JUAN, Trujillo	DS
4005	**VATICAN STATE** VATICAN RADIO, Vatican City	⊡ • Europe • 10 kW • ALT. FREQ. TO 3945 kHz / ⊡ • Europe • 10 kW • ALT. FREQ. TO 4010 kHz / ⊡ • M-Sa • Europe • 10 kW • ALT. FREQ. TO 4010 kHz
4010	**KYRGYZSTAN** KYRGYZ RADIO, Bishkek	ENGLISH, ETC • DS-1 • 50 kW Sa • DS-1 • 50 kW / RUSSIAN, ETC • DS-1 • 50 kW / Su-F • RUSSIAN, ETC • DS-1 • 50 kW
	RUSSIA †VOICE OF RUSSIA, Vladivostok	W • E Asia • 100 kW
	VATICAN STATE VATICAN RADIO, Vatican City	⊡ • Europe • 10 kW • ALT. FREQ. TO 4005 kHz / ⊡ • M-Sa • Europe • 10 kW • ALT. FREQ. TO 4005 kHz
4020	**CHINA** CHINA RADIO INTL, Beijing	W • E Asia • 10 kW / W • E Asia • FEEDER • 10 kW
4030	**RUSSIA** †CHUKOT RADIO, Anadyr'	⊡ • RUSSIAN, ETC • DS-TEMP INACTIVE • 15 kW
4035	**CHINA** †XIZANG PEOPLE'S BC STN, Lhasa	DS-TIBETAN • 50 kW
4039.2	**PERU** RADIO MARGINAL, Tocache	DS • 1 kW
4040	**ARMENIA** †ARMENIAN RADIO, Kamo	⊡ • DS-1 • 15 kW
4050	**KYRGYZSTAN** KYRGYZ RADIO, Bishkek	RUSSIAN, ETC • DS-2 • 100 kW / Tu • DS-2 • 100 kW / W-M • DS-2 • 100 kW
	RUSSIA SAKHALIN RADIO, Yuzhno-Sakhalinsk	⊡ • DS-LOCAL, R ROSSII • 20 kW
4081v	**MONGOLIA** †RADIO ULAANBAATAR, Ulaanbaatar	DS-1 • 50 kW / W • Europe • 50 kW
4085v	**CLANDESTINE (M EAST)** "VO KURDISH PEOPLE", Sulaymānīyah	ARABIC, ETC • Mideast • ANTI-IRAQI GOVT • ALT. FREQ. TO 4120v kHz
4110v	**CLANDESTINE (M EAST)** "VOICE OF ISLAM"	Mideast
4115v	**CLANDESTINE (ASIA)** †"VO KASHMIR FREEDOM", Pakistan	S Asia • ANTI-INDIAN GOVT
4120v	**CLANDESTINE (ASIA)** "VO NAT SALVATION, Pyongyang	TO SOUTH KOREA • 100 kW
	CLANDESTINE (M EAST) "VO KURDISH PEOPLE", Sulaymānīyah	ARABIC, ETC • Mideast • ANTI-IRAQI GOVT • ALT. FREQ. TO 4085v kHz
4130	**FRANCE** †R FRANCE INTL, Via Beijing, China	E Asia • FEEDER • 10 kW • ALT. FREQ. TO 5220 kHz
	SPAIN †R EXTERIOR ESPANA, Via Beijing, China	E Asia • FEEDER • 10 kW • ALT. FREQ. TO 5220 kHz
4182v	**CLANDESTINE (M EAST)** "VO IRAQI KURDS, Salāh al-Dīn	⊡ • Mideast • PRO-KDP / ⊡ • Europe • PRO-KDP
4183v	**PERU** †LA VOZ DE SAYAPULLO, Sayapullo	DS
4190	**CHINA** †CENTRAL PEOPLE'S BS, Beijing	W • DS-MINORITIES • 50 kW
4190v	**CLANDESTINE (M EAST)** "VOICE OF THE WORKER"	Mideast • ANTI-IRANIAN GOVT
	PERU †RADIO SELVA, Moyobamba	DS
4250v	**CLANDESTINE (M EAST)** "VO THE MOJAHED", Iraq	Mideast
4279.4	**PERU** †RADIO CAJAMARCA, Baños del Inca	DS
4285v	**CLANDESTINE (M EAST)** "VO IRANIAN KURDS"	Mideast • ANTI-IRANIAN GOVT
4330	**CHINA** XINJIANG PEOPLE'S BC STN, Urümqi	DS-KAZAKH • 50 kW
4350v	**CLANDESTINE (M EAST)** "VO KURD STRUGGLE"	Mideast • ANTI-IRANIAN GOVT
4395	**RUSSIA** †RADIO YUNOST, Yakutsk	⊡ • DS • 50 kW

ENGLISH ▬▬   ARABIC ⋙⋙   CHINESE □□□   FRENCH ═══   GERMAN ▰▰▰   RUSSIAN ▭▭▭   SPANISH ══   OTHER ───

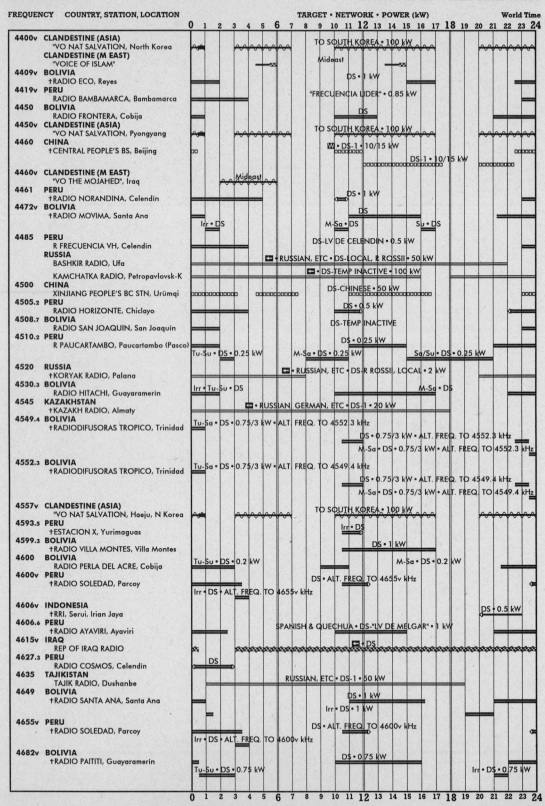

FREQUENCY   COUNTRY, STATION, LOCATION   TARGET • NETWORK • POWER (kW)   World Time

Frequency	Country, Station, Location	Network/Notes
4400v	CLANDESTINE (ASIA) "VO NAT SALVATION, North Korea	TO SOUTH KOREA • 100 kW
	CLANDESTINE (M EAST) "VOICE OF ISLAM"	Mideast
4409v	BOLIVIA †RADIO ECO, Reyes	DS • 1 kW
4419v	PERU RADIO BAMBAMARCA, Bambamarca	"FRECUENCIA LIDER" • 0.85 kW
4450	BOLIVIA RADIO FRONTERA, Cobija	DS
4450v	CLANDESTINE (ASIA) "VO NAT SALVATION, Pyongyang	TO SOUTH KOREA • 100 kW
4460	CHINA †CENTRAL PEOPLE'S BS, Beijing	W • DS-1 • 10/15 kW / DS-1 • 10/15 kW
4460v	CLANDESTINE (M EAST) "VO THE MOJAHED", Iraq	Mideast
4461	PERU †RADIO NORANDINA, Celendín	DS • 1 kW
4472v	BOLIVIA †RADIO MOVIMA, Santa Ana	DS / Irr • DS / M-Sa • DS / Su • DS
4485	PERU R FRECUENCIA VH, Celendín	DS-LV DE CELENDIN • 0.5 kW
	RUSSIA BASHKIR RADIO, Ufa	RUSSIAN, ETC • DS-LOCAL, R ROSSII • 50 kW
	KAMCHATKA RADIO, Petropavlovsk-K	DS-TEMP INACTIVE • 100 kW
4500	CHINA XINJIANG PEOPLE'S BC STN, Urümqi	DS-CHINESE • 50 kW
4505.2	PERU RADIO HORIZONTE, Chiclayo	DS • 0.5 kW
4508.7	BOLIVIA RADIO SAN JOAQUIN, San Joaquín	DS-TEMP INACTIVE
4510.2	PERU R PAUCARTAMBO, Paucartambo (Pasco)	DS • 0.25 kW / Tu-Su • DS • 0.25 kW / M-Sa • DS • 0.25 kW / Sa/Su • DS • 0.25 kW
4520	RUSSIA †KORYAK RADIO, Palana	RUSSIAN, ETC • DS-R ROSSII, LOCAL • 2 kW
4530.3	BOLIVIA RADIO HITACHI, Guayaramerín	Irr • Tu-Su • DS / M-Sa • DS
4545	KAZAKHSTAN †KAZAKH RADIO, Almaty	RUSSIAN, GERMAN, ETC • DS-1 • 20 kW
4549.4	BOLIVIA †RADIODIFUSORAS TROPICO, Trinidad	Tu-Sa • DS • 0.75/3 kW • ALT. FREQ. TO 4552.3 kHz / DS • 0.75/3 kW • ALT. FREQ. TO 4552.3 kHz / M-Sa • DS • 0.75/3 kW • ALT. FREQ. TO 4552.3 kHz
4552.3	BOLIVIA †RADIODIFUSORAS TROPICO, Trinidad	Tu-Sa • DS • 0.75/3 kW • ALT. FREQ. TO 4549.4 kHz / DS • 0.75/3 kW • ALT. FREQ. TO 4549.4 kHz / M-Sa • DS • 0.75/3 kW • ALT. FREQ. TO 4549.4 kHz
4557v	CLANDESTINE (ASIA) "VO NAT SALVATION, Haeju, N Korea	TO SOUTH KOREA • 100 kW
4593.5	PERU †ESTACION X, Yurimaguas	Irr • DS
4599.3	BOLIVIA †RADIO VILLA MONTES, Villa Montes	DS • 1 kW
4600	BOLIVIA RADIO PERLA DEL ACRE, Cobija	Tu-Su • DS • 0.2 kW / M-Sa • DS • 0.2 kW
4600v	PERU †RADIO SOLEDAD, Parcoy	DS • ALT. FREQ. TO 4655v kHz / Irr • DS • ALT. FREQ. TO 4655v kHz
4606v	INDONESIA †RRI, Serui, Irian Jaya	DS • 0.5 kW
4606.6	PERU †RADIO AYAVIRI, Ayaviri	SPANISH & QUECHUA • DS-"LV DE MELGAR" • 1 kW
4615v	IRAQ REP OF IRAQ RADIO	DS
4627.3	PERU RADIO COSMOS, Celendín	DS
4635	TAJIKISTAN TAJIK RADIO, Dushanbe	RUSSIAN, ETC • DS-1 • 50 kW
4649	BOLIVIA †RADIO SANTA ANA, Santa Ana	DS • 1 kW / Irr • DS • 1 kW
4655v	PERU †RADIO SOLEDAD, Parcoy	DS • ALT. FREQ. TO 4600v kHz / Irr • DS • ALT. FREQ. TO 4600v kHz
4682v	BOLIVIA †RADIO PAITITI, Guayaramerín	DS • 0.75 kW / Tu-Su • DS • 0.75 kW / Irr • DS • 0.75 kW

0 1 2 3 4 5 6 7 8 9 10 11 12 13 14 15 16 17 18 19 20 21 22 23 24

FREQUENCY   COUNTRY, STATION, LOCATION

TARGET • NETWORK • POWER (kW)

World Time

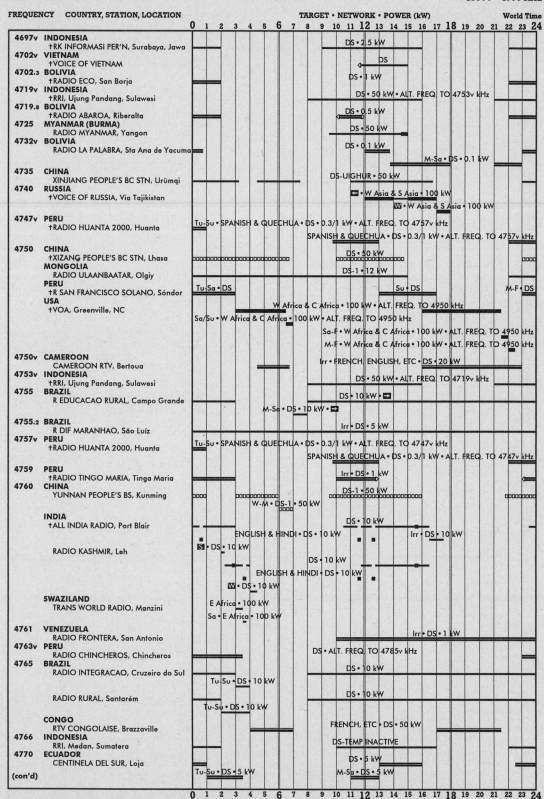

Frequency	Country, Station, Location	Annotation
4697v	INDONESIA †RK INFORMASI PER'N, Surabaya, Jawa	DS • 2.5 kW
4702v	VIETNAM †VOICE OF VIETNAM	DS
4702.3	BOLIVIA †RADIO ECO, San Borja	DS • 1 kW
4719v	INDONESIA †RRI, Ujung Pandang, Sulawesi	DS • 50 kW • ALT. FREQ. TO 4753v kHz
4719.8	BOLIVIA †RADIO ABAROA, Riberalta	DS • 0.5 kW
4725	MYANMAR (BURMA) RADIO MYANMAR, Yangon	DS • 50 kW
4732v	BOLIVIA RADIO LA PALABRA, Sta Ana de Yacuma	DS • 0.1 kW; M-Sa • DS • 0.1 kW
4735	CHINA XINJIANG PEOPLE'S BC STN, Urümqi	DS-UIGHUR • 50 kW
4740	RUSSIA †VOICE OF RUSSIA, Via Tajikistan	W Asia & S Asia • 100 kW; W • W Asia & S Asia • 100 kW
4747v	PERU †RADIO HUANTA 2000, Huanta	Tu-Su • SPANISH & QUECHUA • DS • 0.3/1 kW • ALT. FREQ. TO 4757v kHz; SPANISH & QUECHUA • DS • 0.3/1 kW • ALT. FREQ. TO 4757v kHz
4750	CHINA †XIZANG PEOPLE'S BC STN, Lhasa	DS • 50 kW
	MONGOLIA RADIO ULAANBAATAR, Olgiy	DS-1 • 12 kW
	PERU †R SAN FRANCISCO SOLANO, Sóndor	Tu-Sa • DS; Su • DS; M-F • DS
	USA †VOA, Greenville, NC	W Africa & C Africa • 100 kW • ALT. FREQ. TO 4950 kHz; Sa/Su • W Africa & C Africa • 100 kW • ALT. FREQ. TO 4950 kHz; Sa-F • W Africa & C Africa • 100 kW • ALT. FREQ. TO 4950 kHz; M-F • W Africa & C Africa • 100 kW • ALT. FREQ. TO 4950 kHz
4750v	CAMEROON CAMEROON RTV, Bertoua	Irr • FRENCH, ENGLISH, ETC • DS • 20 kW
4753v	INDONESIA †RRI, Ujung Pandang, Sulawesi	DS • 50 kW • ALT. FREQ. TO 4719v kHz
4755	BRAZIL R EDUCACAO RURAL, Campo Grande	DS • 10 kW; M-Sa • DS • 10 kW
4755.2	BRAZIL R DIF MARANHAO, São Luíz	Irr • DS • 5 kW
4757v	PERU †RADIO HUANTA 2000, Huanta	Tu-Su • SPANISH & QUECHUA • DS • 0.3/1 kW • ALT. FREQ. TO 4747v kHz; SPANISH & QUECHUA • DS • 0.3/1 kW • ALT. FREQ. TO 4747v kHz
4759	PERU †RADIO TINGO MARIA, Tinga Maria	Irr • DS • 1 kW
4760	CHINA YUNNAN PEOPLE'S BS, Kunming	DS-1 • 50 kW; W-M • DS-1 • 50 kW
	INDIA †ALL INDIA RADIO, Port Blair	DS • 10 kW; ENGLISH & HINDI • DS • 10 kW; Irr • DS • 10 kW
	RADIO KASHMIR, Leh	S • DS • 10 kW; DS • 10 kW; ENGLISH & HINDI • DS • 10 kW; W • DS • 10 kW
	SWAZILAND TRANS WORLD RADIO, Manzini	E Africa • 100 kW; Sa • E Africa • 100 kW
4761	VENEZUELA RADIO FRONTERA, San Antonio	Irr • DS • 1 kW
4763v	PERU RADIO CHINCHEROS, Chincheros	DS • ALT. FREQ. TO 4785v kHz
4765	BRAZIL RADIO INTEGRACAO, Cruzeiro do Sul	DS • 10 kW; Tu-Su • DS • 10 kW
	RADIO RURAL, Santarém	DS • 10 kW; Tu-Su • DS • 10 kW
	CONGO RTV CONGOLAISE, Brazzaville	FRENCH, ETC • DS • 50 kW
4766	INDONESIA RRI, Medan, Sumatera	DS-TEMP INACTIVE
4770	ECUADOR CENTINELA DEL SUR, Loja	DS • 5 kW; Tu-Su • DS • 5 kW; M-Sa • DS • 5 kW

(con'd)

ENGLISH ▬ ARABIC ⧓ CHINESE ▢▢▢ FRENCH ▬ GERMAN ▬ RUSSIAN ═ SPANISH ▬ OTHER ▬

FREQUENCY   COUNTRY, STATION, LOCATION   TARGET • NETWORK • POWER (kW)   World Time

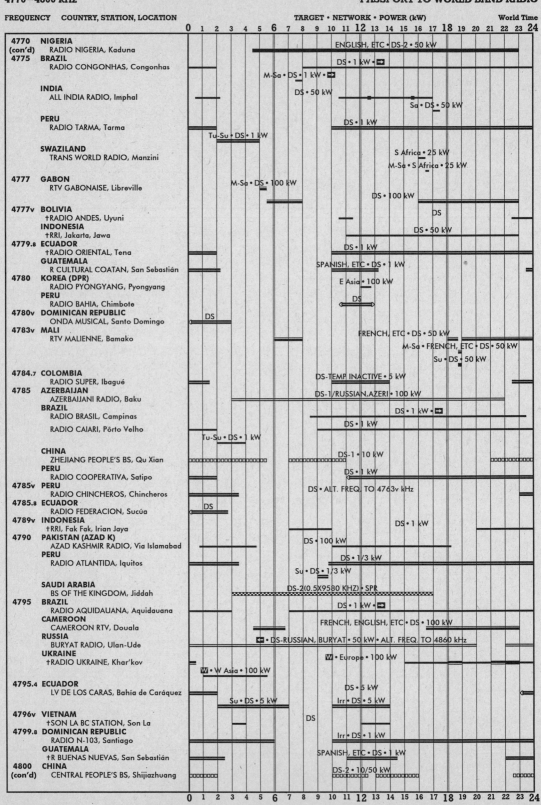

4770	**NIGERIA**	
(con'd)	RADIO NIGERIA, Kaduna	ENGLISH, ETC • DS-2 • 50 kW
4775	**BRAZIL**	
	RADIO CONGONHAS, Congonhas	DS • 1 kW • ▄▶
		M-Sa • DS • 1 kW • ▄▶
	INDIA	
	ALL INDIA RADIO, Imphal	DS • 50 kW
		Sa • DS • 50 kW
	PERU	
	RADIO TARMA, Tarma	DS • 1 kW
		Tu-Su • DS • 1 kW
	SWAZILAND	
	TRANS WORLD RADIO, Manzini	S Africa • 25 kW
		M-Sa • S Africa • 25 kW
4777	**GABON**	
	RTV GABONAISE, Libreville	M-Sa • DS • 100 kW
		DS • 100 kW
4777v	**BOLIVIA**	
	†RADIO ANDES, Uyuni	DS
	INDONESIA	
	†RRI, Jakarta, Jawa	DS • 50 kW
4779.8	**ECUADOR**	
	†RADIO ORIENTAL, Tena	DS • 1 kW
	GUATEMALA	
	R CULTURAL COATAN, San Sebastián	SPANISH, ETC • DS • 1 kW
4780	**KOREA (DPR)**	
	RADIO PYONGYANG, Pyongyang	E Asia • 100 kW
	PERU	
	RADIO BAHIA, Chimbote	DS
4780v	**DOMINICAN REPUBLIC**	
	ONDA MUSICAL, Santo Domingo	DS
4783v	**MALI**	
	RTV MALIENNE, Bamako	FRENCH, ETC • DS • 50 kW
		M-Sa • FRENCH, ETC • DS • 50 kW
		Su • DS • 50 kW
4784.7	**COLOMBIA**	
	RADIO SUPER, Ibagué	DS-TEMP INACTIVE • 5 kW
4785	**AZERBAIJAN**	
	AZERBAIJANI RADIO, Baku	DS-1/RUSSIAN, AZERI • 100 kW
	BRAZIL	
	RADIO BRASIL, Campinas	DS • 1 kW • ▄▶
	RADIO CAIARI, Pôrto Velho	DS • 1 kW
		Tu-Su • DS • 1 kW
	CHINA	
	ZHEJIANG PEOPLE'S BS, Qu Xian	DS-1 • 10 kW
	PERU	
	RADIO COOPERATIVA, Satipo	DS • 1 kW
4785v	**PERU**	
	RADIO CHINCHEROS, Chincheros	DS • ALT. FREQ. TO 4763v kHz
4785.8	**ECUADOR**	
	RADIO FEDERACION, Sucúa	DS
4789v	**INDONESIA**	
	†RRI, Fak Fak, Irian Jaya	DS • 1 kW
4790	**PAKISTAN (AZAD K)**	
	AZAD KASHMIR RADIO, Via Islamabad	DS • 100 kW
	PERU	
	RADIO ATLANTIDA, Iquitos	DS • 1/3 kW
		Su • DS • 1/3 kW
	SAUDI ARABIA	
	BS OF THE KINGDOM, Jiddah	DS-2(0.5X9580 KHZ) • SPR
4795	**BRAZIL**	
	RADIO AQUIDAUANA, Aquidauana	DS • 1 kW • ▄▶
	CAMEROON	
	CAMEROON RTV, Douala	FRENCH, ENGLISH, ETC • DS • 100 kW
	RUSSIA	
	BURYAT RADIO, Ulan-Ude	▄▶ • DS-RUSSIAN, BURYAT • 50 kW • ALT. FREQ. TO 4860 kHz
	UKRAINE	
	†RADIO UKRAINE, Khar'kov	W • Europe • 100 kW
		W • W Asia • 100 kW
4795.4	**ECUADOR**	
	LV DE LOS CARAS, Bahía de Caráquez	DS • 5 kW
		Su • DS • 5 kW
		Irr • DS • 5 kW
4796v	**VIETNAM**	
	†SON LA BC STATION, Son La	DS
4799.8	**DOMINICAN REPUBLIC**	
	RADIO N-103, Santiago	Irr • DS • 1 kW
	GUATEMALA	
	†R BUENAS NUEVAS, San Sebastián	SPANISH, ETC • DS • 1 kW
4800	**CHINA**	
(con'd)	CENTRAL PEOPLE'S BS, Shijiazhuang	DS-2 • 10/50 kW

FREQUENCY   COUNTRY, STATION, LOCATION   TARGET • NETWORK • POWER (kW)   World Time

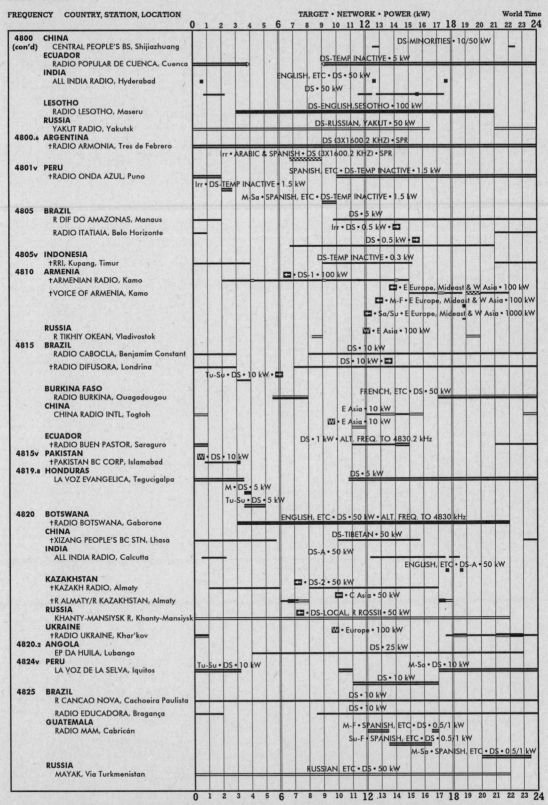

Frequency	Country, Station, Location	Target • Network • Power
4800 (con'd)	**CHINA** CENTRAL PEOPLE'S BS, Shijiazhuang	DS-MINORITIES • 10/50 kW
	ECUADOR RADIO POPULAR DE CUENCA, Cuenca	DS-TEMP INACTIVE • 5 kW
	INDIA ALL INDIA RADIO, Hyderabad	ENGLISH, ETC • DS • 50 kW; DS • 50 kW
	LESOTHO RADIO LESOTHO, Maseru	DS-ENGLISH, SESOTHO • 100 kW
	RUSSIA YAKUT RADIO, Yakutsk	DS-RUSSIAN, YAKUT • 50 kW
4800.6	**ARGENTINA** †RADIO ARMONIA, Tres de Febrero	DS (3X1600.2 KHZ) • SPR; Irr • ARABIC & SPANISH • DS (3X1600.2 KHZ) • SPR
4801v	**PERU** †RADIO ONDA AZUL, Puno	SPANISH, ETC • DS-TEMP INACTIVE • 1.5 kW; Irr • DS-TEMP INACTIVE • 1.5 kW; M-Sa • SPANISH, ETC • DS-TEMP INACTIVE • 1.5 kW
4805	**BRAZIL** R DIF DO AMAZONAS, Manaus	DS • 5 kW
	RADIO ITATIAIA, Belo Horizonte	Irr • DS • 0.5 kW •; DS • 0.5 kW •
4805v	**INDONESIA** †RRI, Kupang, Timur	DS-TEMP INACTIVE • 0.3 kW
4810	**ARMENIA** †ARMENIAN RADIO, Kamo	• DS-1 • 100 kW
	†VOICE OF ARMENIA, Kamo	• E Europe, Mideast & W Asia • 100 kW; • M-F • E Europe, Mideast & W Asia • 100 kW; • Sa/Su • E Europe, Mideast & W Asia • 1000 kW
	RUSSIA R TIKHIY OKEAN, Vladivostok	• E Asia • 100 kW
4815	**BRAZIL** RADIO CABOCLA, Benjamim Constant	DS • 10 kW
	†RADIO DIFUSORA, Londrina	DS • 10 kW •; Tu-Su • DS • 10 kW •
	BURKINA FASO RADIO BURKINA, Ouagadougou	FRENCH, ETC • DS • 50 kW
	CHINA CHINA RADIO INTL, Togtoh	E Asia • 10 kW; • E Asia • 10 kW
	ECUADOR †RADIO BUEN PASTOR, Saraguro	DS • 1 kW • ALT. FREQ. TO 4830.2 kHz
4815v	**PAKISTAN** †PAKISTAN BC CORP, Islamabad	• DS • 10 kW
4819.8	**HONDURAS** LA VOZ EVANGELICA, Tegucigalpa	DS • 5 kW; M • DS • 5 kW; Tu-Su • DS • 5 kW
4820	**BOTSWANA** †RADIO BOTSWANA, Gaborone	ENGLISH, ETC • DS • 50 kW • ALT. FREQ. TO 4830 kHz
	CHINA †XIZANG PEOPLE'S BC STN, Lhasa	DS-TIBETAN • 50 kW
	INDIA ALL INDIA RADIO, Calcutta	DS-A • 50 kW; ENGLISH, ETC • DS-A • 50 kW
	KAZAKHSTAN †KAZAKH RADIO, Almaty	• DS-2 • 50 kW
	†R ALMATY/R KAZAKHSTAN, Almaty	• C Asia • 50 kW
	RUSSIA KHANTY-MANSIYSK R, Khanty-Mansiysk	• DS-LOCAL, R ROSSII • 50 kW
	UKRAINE †RADIO UKRAINE, Khar'kov	• Europe • 100 kW
4820.2	**ANGOLA** EP DA HUILA, Lubango	DS • 25 kW
4824v	**PERU** LA VOZ DE LA SELVA, Iquitos	Tu-Su • DS • 10 kW; M-Sa • DS • 10 kW; DS • 10 kW
4825	**BRAZIL** R CANCAO NOVA, Cachoeira Paulista	DS • 10 kW
	RADIO EDUCADORA, Bragança	DS • 10 kW
	GUATEMALA RADIO MAM, Cabricán	M-F • SPANISH, ETC • DS • 0.5/1 kW; Su-F • SPANISH, ETC • DS • 0.5/1 kW; M-Sa • SPANISH, ETC • DS • 0.5/1 kW
	RUSSIA MAYAK, Via Turkmenistan	RUSSIAN, ETC • DS • 50 kW

ENGLISH ▬   ARABIC ⁞⁞⁞   CHINESE □□□   FRENCH ▬   GERMAN ▬   RUSSIAN ═   SPANISH ▬   OTHER ▬

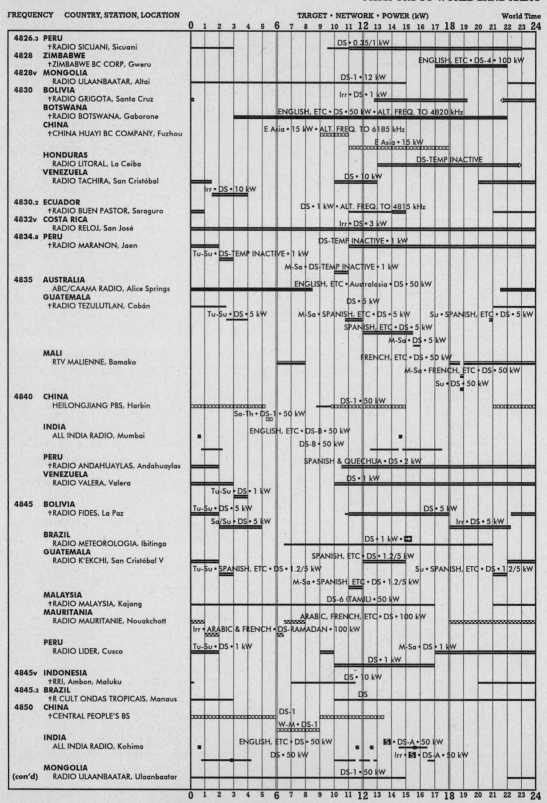

FREQUENCY   COUNTRY, STATION, LOCATION   TARGET • NETWORK • POWER (kW)   World Time

Frequency	Country, Station, Location	Details
4826.3	PERU †RADIO SICUANI, Sicuani	DS • 0.35/1 kW
4828	ZIMBABWE †ZIMBABWE BC CORP, Gweru	ENGLISH, ETC • DS-4 • 100 kW
4828v	MONGOLIA RADIO ULAANBAATAR, Altai	DS-1 • 12 kW
4830	BOLIVIA †RADIO GRIGOTA, Santa Cruz	Irr • DS • 1 kW
	BOTSWANA †RADIO BOTSWANA, Gaborone	ENGLISH, ETC • DS • 50 kW • ALT. FREQ. TO 4820 kHz
	CHINA †CHINA HUAYI BC COMPANY, Fuzhou	E Asia • 15 kW • ALT. FREQ. TO 6185 kHz / E Asia • 15 kW
	HONDURAS RADIO LITORAL, La Ceiba	DS-TEMP INACTIVE
	VENEZUELA RADIO TACHIRA, San Cristóbal	DS • 10 kW / Irr • DS • 10 kW
4830.2	ECUADOR †RADIO BUEN PASTOR, Saraguro	DS • 1 kW • ALT. FREQ. TO 4815 kHz
4832v	COSTA RICA RADIO RELOJ, San José	Irr • DS • 3 kW
4834.8	PERU †RADIO MARANON, Jaen	DS-TEMP INACTIVE • 1 kW / Tu-Su • DS-TEMP INACTIVE • 1 kW / M-Sa • DS-TEMP INACTIVE • 1 kW
4835	AUSTRALIA ABC/CAAMA RADIO, Alice Springs	ENGLISH, ETC • Australasia • DS • 50 kW
	GUATEMALA †RADIO TEZULUTLAN, Cobán	DS • 5 kW / Tu-Su • DS • 5 kW / M-Sa • SPANISH, ETC • DS • 5 kW / Su • SPANISH, ETC • DS • 5 kW / SPANISH, ETC • DS • 5 kW / M-Sa • DS • 5 kW
	MALI RTV MALIENNE, Bamako	FRENCH, ETC • DS • 50 kW / M-Sa • FRENCH, ETC • DS • 50 kW / Su • DS • 50 kW
4840	CHINA HEILONGJIANG PBS, Harbin	DS-1 • 50 kW / Sa-Th • DS-1 • 50 kW
	INDIA ALL INDIA RADIO, Mumbai	ENGLISH, ETC • DS-B • 50 kW / DS-B • 50 kW
	PERU †RADIO ANDAHUAYLAS, Andahuaylas	SPANISH & QUECHUA • DS • 2 kW
	VENEZUELA RADIO VALERA, Valera	DS • 1 kW / Tu-Su • DS • 1 kW
4845	BOLIVIA †RADIO FIDES, La Paz	Tu-Su • DS • 5 kW / DS • 5 kW / Sa/Su • DS • 5 kW / Irr • DS • 5 kW
	BRAZIL RADIO METEOROLOGIA, Ibitinga	DS • 1 kW • ⇨
	GUATEMALA RADIO K'EKCHI, San Cristóbal V	SPANISH, ETC • DS • 1.2/5 kW / Tu-Su • SPANISH, ETC • DS • 1.2/5 kW / Su • SPANISH, ETC • DS • 1.2/5 kW / M-Sa • SPANISH, ETC • DS • 1.2/5 kW
	MALAYSIA †RADIO MALAYSIA, Kajang	DS-6 (TAMIL) • 50 kW
	MAURITANIA RADIO MAURITANIE, Nouakchott	ARABIC, FRENCH, ETC • DS • 100 kW / Irr • ARABIC & FRENCH • DS-RAMADAN • 100 kW
	PERU RADIO LIDER, Cusco	Tu-Su • DS • 1 kW / M-Sa • DS • 1 kW / DS • 1 kW
4845v	INDONESIA †RRI, Ambon, Maluku	DS • 10 kW
4845.3	BRAZIL †R CULT ONDAS TROPICAIS, Manaus	DS
4850	CHINA †CENTRAL PEOPLE'S BS	DS-1 / W-M • DS-1
	INDIA ALL INDIA RADIO, Kohima	ENGLISH, ETC • DS • 50 kW / 𝕊 • DS-A • 50 kW / DS • 50 kW / Irr • 𝕊 • DS-A • 50 kW
(con'd)	MONGOLIA RADIO ULAANBAATAR, Ulaanbaatar	DS-1 • 50 kW

FREQUENCY   COUNTRY, STATION, LOCATION

TARGET • NETWORK • POWER (kW)

World Time

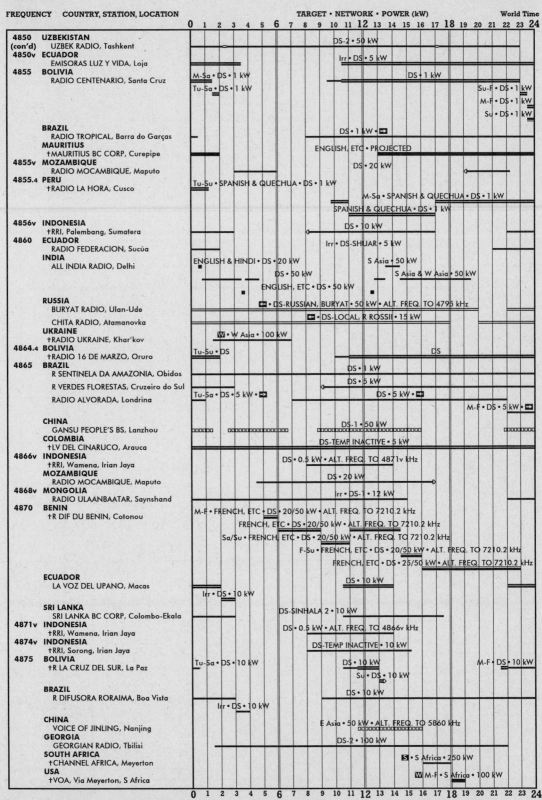

FREQUENCY	COUNTRY, STATION, LOCATION	Schedule details
4850 (con'd)	UZBEKISTAN — UZBEK RADIO, Tashkent	DS-2 • 50 kW
4850v	ECUADOR — EMISORAS LUZ Y VIDA, Loja	Irr • DS • 5 kW
4855	BOLIVIA — RADIO CENTENARIO, Santa Cruz	M-Sa • DS • 1 kW / DS • 1 kW / Tu-Sa • DS • 1 kW / Su-F • DS • 1 kW / M-F • DS • 1 kW / Su • DS • 1 kW
	BRAZIL — RADIO TROPICAL, Barra do Garças	DS • 1 kW • ▭
	MAURITIUS — †MAURITIUS BC CORP, Curepipe	ENGLISH, ETC • PROJECTED
4855v	MOZAMBIQUE — RADIO MOCAMBIQUE, Maputo	DS • 20 kW
4855.4	PERU — †RADIO LA HORA, Cusco	Tu-Su • SPANISH & QUECHUA • DS • 1 kW / M-Sa • SPANISH & QUECHUA • DS • 1 kW / SPANISH & QUECHUA • DS • 1 kW
4856v	INDONESIA — †RRI, Palembang, Sumatera	DS • 10 kW
4860	ECUADOR — RADIO FEDERACION, Sucúa	Irr • DS-SHUAR • 5 kW
	INDIA — ALL INDIA RADIO, Delhi	ENGLISH & HINDI • DS • 20 kW / S Asia • 50 kW / DS • 50 kW / S Asia & W Asia • 50 kW / ENGLISH, ETC • DS • 50 kW
	RUSSIA — BURYAT RADIO, Ulan-Ude	▭ • DS-RUSSIAN, BURYAT • 50 kW • ALT. FREQ. TO 4795 kHz
	CHITA RADIO, Atamanovka	▭ • DS-LOCAL, R ROSSII • 15 kW
	UKRAINE — †RADIO UKRAINE, Khar'kov	W • W Asia • 100 kW
4864.4	BOLIVIA — †RADIO 16 DE MARZO, Oruro	Tu-Su • DS / DS
4865	BRAZIL — R SENTINELA DA AMAZONIA, Obidos	DS • 1 kW
	R VERDES FLORESTAS, Cruzeiro do Sul	DS • 5 kW
	RADIO ALVORADA, Londrina	Tu-Sa • DS • 5 kW • ▭ / DS • 5 kW • ▭ / M-F • DS • 5 kW • ▭
	CHINA — GANSU PEOPLE'S BS, Lanzhou	DS-1 • 50 kW
	COLOMBIA — †LV DEL CINARUCO, Arauca	DS-TEMP INACTIVE • 5 kW
4866v	INDONESIA — †RRI, Wamena, Irian Jaya	DS • 0.5 kW • ALT. FREQ. TO 4871v kHz
	MOZAMBIQUE — RADIO MOCAMBIQUE, Maputo	DS • 20 kW
4868v	MONGOLIA — RADIO ULAANBAATAR, Saynshand	Irr • DS-1 • 12 kW
4870	BENIN — †R DIF DU BENIN, Cotonou	M-F • FRENCH, ETC • DS • 20/50 kW • ALT. FREQ. TO 7210.2 kHz / FRENCH, ETC • DS • 20/50 kW • ALT. FREQ. TO 7210.2 kHz / Sa/Su • FRENCH, ETC • DS • 20/50 kW • ALT. FREQ. TO 7210.2 kHz / F-Su • FRENCH, ETC • DS • 20/50 kW • ALT. FREQ. TO 7210.2 kHz / FRENCH, ETC • DS • 25/50 kW • ALT. FREQ. TO 7210.2 kHz
	ECUADOR — LA VOZ DEL UPANO, Macas	DS • 10 kW / Irr • DS • 10 kW
	SRI LANKA — SRI LANKA BC CORP, Colombo-Ekala	DS-SINHALA 2 • 10 kW
4871v	INDONESIA — †RRI, Wamena, Irian Jaya	DS • 0.5 kW • ALT. FREQ. TO 4866v kHz
4874v	INDONESIA — †RRI, Sorong, Irian Jaya	DS-TEMP INACTIVE • 10 kW
4875	BOLIVIA — †R LA CRUZ DEL SUR, La Paz	Tu-Sa • DS • 10 kW / DS • 10 kW / Su • DS • 10 kW / M-F • DS • 10 kW
	BRAZIL — R DIFUSORA RORAIMA, Boa Vista	DS • 10 kW / Irr • DS • 10 kW
	CHINA — VOICE OF JINLING, Nanjing	E Asia • 50 kW • ALT. FREQ. TO 5860 kHz
	GEORGIA — GEORGIAN RADIO, Tbilisi	DS-2 • 100 kW
	SOUTH AFRICA — †CHANNEL AFRICA, Meyerton	S • S Africa • 250 kW
	USA — †VOA, Via Meyerton, S Africa	W • M-F • S Africa • 100 kW

ENGLISH ▬   ARABIC ⚏⚏   CHINESE ▫▫▫   FRENCH ═   GERMAN ▭   RUSSIAN ══   SPANISH ▬   OTHER ─

| FREQUENCY | COUNTRY, STATION, LOCATION | TARGET • NETWORK • POWER (kW) | World Time |

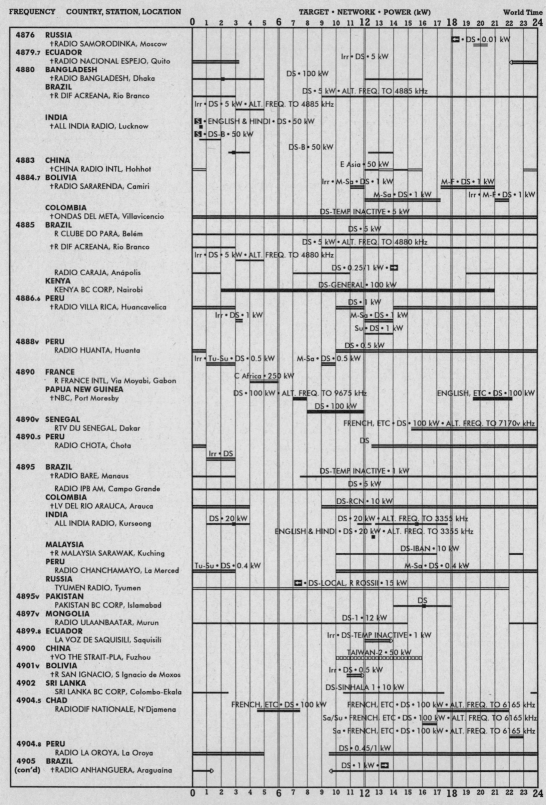

FREQUENCY   COUNTRY, STATION, LOCATION   TARGET • NETWORK • POWER (kW)   World Time

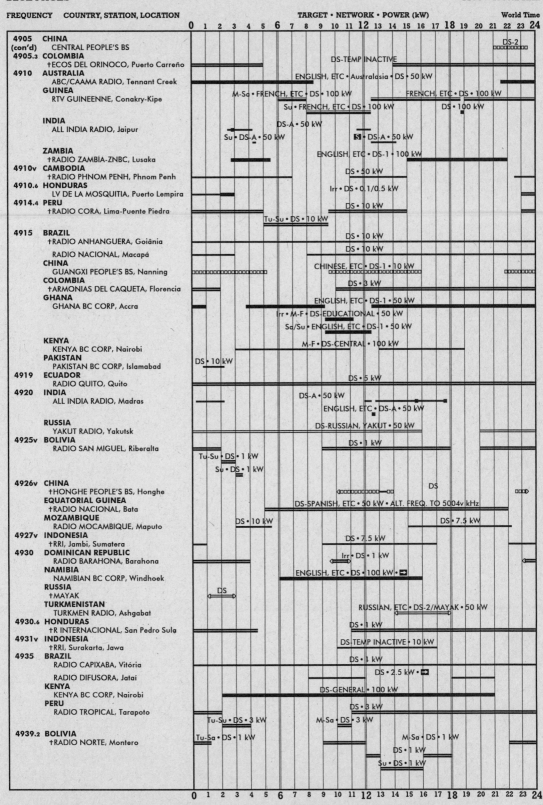

Frequency	Country, Station, Location	Notes
4905 (con'd)	**CHINA** CENTRAL PEOPLE'S BS	DS-2
4905.3	**COLOMBIA** †ECOS DEL ORINOCO, Puerto Carreño	DS-TEMP INACTIVE
4910	**AUSTRALIA** ABC/CAAMA RADIO, Tennant Creek	ENGLISH, ETC • Australasia • DS • 50 kW
	GUINEA RTV GUINEENNE, Conakry-Kipe	M-Sa • FRENCH, ETC • DS • 100 kW / FRENCH, ETC • DS • 100 kW / Su • FRENCH, ETC • DS • 100 kW / DS • 100 kW
	INDIA ALL INDIA RADIO, Jaipur	DS-A • 50 kW / Su • DS-A • 50 kW / S • DS-A • 50 kW
	ZAMBIA †RADIO ZAMBIA-ZNBC, Lusaka	ENGLISH, ETC • DS-1 • 100 kW
4910v	**CAMBODIA** †RADIO PHNOM PENH, Phnom Penh	DS • 50 kW
4910.6	**HONDURAS** LV DE LA MOSQUITIA, Puerto Lempira	Irr • DS • 0.1/0.5 kW
4914.4	**PERU** †RADIO CORA, Lima-Puente Piedra	DS • 10 kW / Tu-Su • DS • 10 kW
4915	**BRAZIL** †RADIO ANHANGUERA, Goiânia	DS • 10 kW
	RADIO NACIONAL, Macapá	DS • 10 kW
	CHINA GUANGXI PEOPLE'S BS, Nanning	CHINESE, ETC • DS-1 • 10 kW
	COLOMBIA †ARMONIAS DEL CAQUETA, Florencia	DS • 3 kW
	GHANA GHANA BC CORP, Accra	ENGLISH, ETC • DS-1 • 50 kW / Irr • M-F • DS-EDUCATIONAL • 50 kW / Sa/Su • ENGLISH, ETC • DS-1 • 50 kW
	KENYA KENYA BC CORP, Nairobi	M-F • DS-CENTRAL • 100 kW
	PAKISTAN PAKISTAN BC CORP, Islamabad	DS • 10 kW
4919	**ECUADOR** RADIO QUITO, Quito	DS • 5 kW
4920	**INDIA** ALL INDIA RADIO, Madras	DS-A • 50 kW / ENGLISH, ETC • DS-A • 50 kW
	RUSSIA YAKUT RADIO, Yakutsk	DS-RUSSIAN, YAKUT • 50 kW
4925v	**BOLIVIA** RADIO SAN MIGUEL, Riberalta	DS • 1 kW / Tu-Su • DS • 1 kW / Su • DS • 1 kW
4926v	**CHINA** †HONGHE PEOPLE'S BS, Honghe	DS
	EQUATORIAL GUINEA †RADIO NACIONAL, Bata	DS-SPANISH, ETC • 50 kW • ALT. FREQ. TO 5004v kHz
	MOZAMBIQUE RADIO MOCAMBIQUE, Maputo	DS • 10 kW / DS • 7.5 kW
4927v	**INDONESIA** †RRI, Jambi, Sumatera	DS • 7.5 kW
4930	**DOMINICAN REPUBLIC** RADIO BARAHONA, Barahona	Irr • DS • 1 kW
	NAMIBIA NAMIBIAN BC CORP, Windhoek	ENGLISH, ETC • DS • 100 kW • ➡
	RUSSIA †MAYAK	DS
	TURKMENISTAN TURKMEN RADIO, Ashgabat	RUSSIAN, ETC • DS-2/MAYAK • 50 kW
4930.6	**HONDURAS** †R INTERNACIONAL, San Pedro Sula	DS • 1 kW
4931v	**INDONESIA** †RRI, Surakarta, Jawa	DS-TEMP INACTIVE • 10 kW
4935	**BRAZIL** RADIO CAPIXABA, Vitória	DS • 1 kW
	RADIO DIFUSORA, Jataí	DS • 2.5 kW • ➡
	KENYA KENYA BC CORP, Nairobi	DS-GENERAL • 100 kW
	PERU RADIO TROPICAL, Tarapoto	DS • 3 kW / Tu-Su • DS • 3 kW / M-Sa • DS • 3 kW
4939.2	**BOLIVIA** †RADIO NORTE, Montero	Tu-Sa • DS • 1 kW / M-Sa • DS • 1 kW / DS • 1 kW / Su • DS • 1 kW

0 1 2 3 4 5 6 7 8 9 10 11 12 13 14 15 16 17 18 19 20 21 22 23 24

ENGLISH ▬▬   ARABIC ▧▧▧   CHINESE □□□   FRENCH ══   GERMAN ▬▬   RUSSIAN ══   SPANISH ══   OTHER ──

| FREQUENCY | COUNTRY, STATION, LOCATION | TARGET • NETWORK • POWER (kW) | World Time |

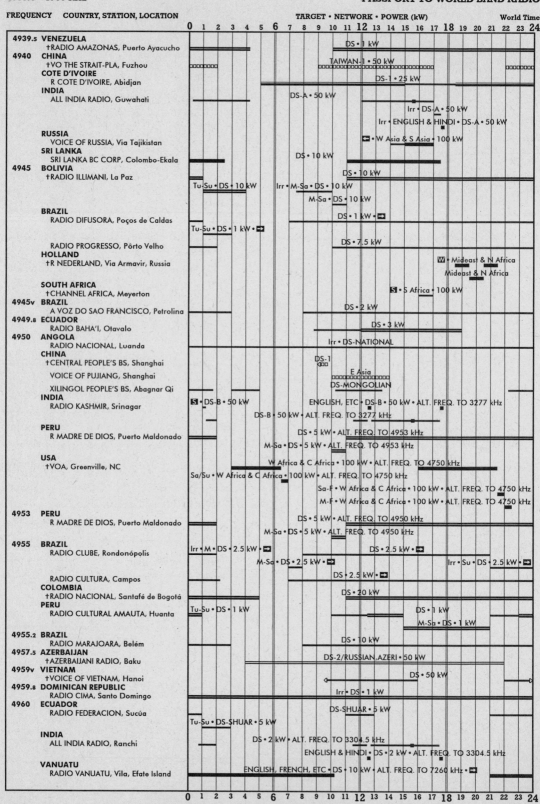

4939.5 VENEZUELA
†RADIO AMAZONAS, Puerto Ayacucho — DS • 1 kW

4940 CHINA
†VO THE STRAIT-PLA, Fuzhou — TAIWAN-1 • 50 kW

COTE D'IVOIRE
R COTE D'IVOIRE, Abidjan — DS-1 • 25 kW

INDIA
ALL INDIA RADIO, Guwahati — DS-A • 50 kW / Irr • DS-A • 50 kW / Irr • ENGLISH & HINDI • DS-A • 50 kW

RUSSIA
VOICE OF RUSSIA, Via Tajikistan — W Asia & S Asia • 100 kW

SRI LANKA
SRI LANKA BC CORP, Colombo-Ekala — DS • 10 kW

4945 BOLIVIA
†RADIO ILLIMANI, La Paz — DS • 10 kW / Tu-Su • DS • 10 kW / Irr • M-Sa • DS • 10 kW / M-Sa • DS • 10 kW

BRAZIL
RADIO DIFUSORA, Poços de Caldas — DS • 1 kW • ⇨ / Tu-Su • DS • 1 kW • ⇨

RADIO PROGRESSO, Pôrto Velho — DS • 7.5 kW

HOLLAND
†R NEDERLAND, Via Armavir, Russia — W • Mideast & N Africa / Mideast & N Africa

SOUTH AFRICA
†CHANNEL AFRICA, Meyerton — S • S Africa • 100 kW

4945v BRAZIL
A VOZ DO SAO FRANCISCO, Petrolina — DS • 2 kW

4949.8 ECUADOR
RADIO BAHA'I, Otavalo — DS • 3 kW

4950 ANGOLA
RADIO NACIONAL, Luanda — Irr • DS-NATIONAL

CHINA
†CENTRAL PEOPLE'S BS, Shanghai — DS-1

VOICE OF PUJIANG, Shanghai — E Asia

XILINGOL PEOPLE'S BS, Abagnar Qi — DS-MONGOLIAN

INDIA
RADIO KASHMIR, Srinagar — S • DS-B • 50 kW / ENGLISH, ETC • DS-B • 50 kW • ALT. FREQ. TO 3277 kHz / DS-B • 50 kW • ALT. FREQ. TO 3277 kHz

PERU
R MADRE DE DIOS, Puerto Maldonado — DS • 5 kW • ALT. FREQ. TO 4953 kHz / M-Sa • DS • 5 kW • ALT. FREQ. TO 4953 kHz

USA
†VOA, Greenville, NC — W Africa & C Africa • 100 kW • ALT. FREQ. TO 4750 kHz / Sa/Su • W Africa & C Africa • 100 kW • ALT. FREQ. TO 4750 kHz / Sa-F • W Africa & C Africa • 100 kW • ALT. FREQ. TO 4750 kHz / M-F • W Africa & C Africa • 100 kW • ALT. FREQ. TO 4750 kHz

4953 PERU
R MADRE DE DIOS, Puerto Maldonado — DS • 5 kW • ALT. FREQ. TO 4950 kHz / M-Sa • DS • 5 kW • ALT. FREQ. TO 4950 kHz

4955 BRAZIL
RADIO CLUBE, Rondonópolis — Irr • M • DS • 2.5 kW • ⇨ / DS • 2.5 kW • ⇨ / M-Sa • DS • 2.5 kW • ⇨ / Irr • Su • DS • 2.5 kW • ⇨

RADIO CULTURA, Campos — DS • 2.5 kW • ⇨

COLOMBIA
†RADIO NACIONAL, Santafé de Bogotá — DS • 20 kW

PERU
RADIO CULTURAL AMAUTA, Huanta — Tu-Su • DS • 1 kW / DS • 1 kW / M-Sa • DS • 1 kW

4955.2 BRAZIL
RADIO MARAJOARA, Belém — DS • 10 kW

4957.5 AZERBAIJAN
†AZERBAIJANI RADIO, Baku — DS-2/RUSSIAN, AZERI • 50 kW

4959v VIETNAM
†VOICE OF VIETNAM, Hanoi — DS • 50 kW

4959.8 DOMINICAN REPUBLIC
RADIO CIMA, Santo Domingo — Irr • DS • 1 kW

4960 ECUADOR
RADIO FEDERACION, Sucúa — DS-SHUAR • 5 kW / Tu-Su • DS-SHUAR • 5 kW

INDIA
ALL INDIA RADIO, Ranchi — DS • 2 kW • ALT. FREQ. TO 3304.5 kHz / ENGLISH & HINDI • DS • 2 kW • ALT. FREQ. TO 3304.5 kHz

VANUATU
RADIO VANUATU, Vila, Efate Island — ENGLISH, FRENCH, ETC • DS • 10 kW • ALT. FREQ. TO 7260 kHz • ⇨

FREQUENCY   COUNTRY, STATION, LOCATION   TARGET • NETWORK • POWER (kW)   World Time

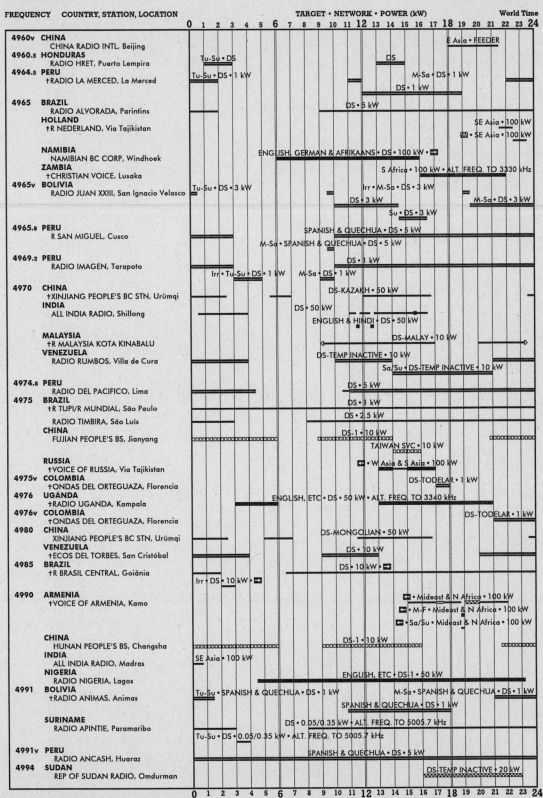

Frequency	Country, Station, Location	Notes
4960v	CHINA — CHINA RADIO INTL, Beijing	E Asia • FEEDER
4960.5	HONDURAS — RADIO HRET, Puerto Lempira	Tu-Su • DS; DS
4964.5	PERU — †RADIO LA MERCED, La Merced	Tu-Su • DS • 1 kW; M-Sa • DS • 1 kW; DS • 1 kW
4965	BRAZIL — RADIO ALVORADA, Parintins	DS • 5 kW
	HOLLAND — †R NEDERLAND, Via Tajikistan	SE Asia • 100 kW; W • SE Asia • 100 kW
	NAMIBIA — NAMIBIAN BC CORP, Windhoek	ENGLISH, GERMAN & AFRIKAANS • DS • 100 kW • ⇨
	ZAMBIA — †CHRISTIAN VOICE, Lusaka	S Africa • 100 kW • ALT. FREQ. TO 3330 kHz
4965v	BOLIVIA — RADIO JUAN XXIII, San Ignacio Velasco	Tu-Su • DS • 3 kW; Irr • M-Sa • DS • 3 kW; DS • 3 kW; M-Sa • DS • 3 kW; Su • DS • 3 kW
4965.8	PERU — R SAN MIGUEL, Cusco	SPANISH & QUECHUA • DS • 5 kW; M-Sa • SPANISH & QUECHUA • DS • 5 kW
4969.2	PERU — RADIO IMAGEN, Tarapoto	DS • 1 kW; Irr • Tu-Su • DS • 1 kW; M-Sa • DS • 1 kW
4970	CHINA — †XINJIANG PEOPLE'S BC STN, Urümqi	DS-KAZAKH • 50 kW
	INDIA — ALL INDIA RADIO, Shillong	DS • 50 kW; ENGLISH & HINDI • DS • 50 kW
	MALAYSIA — †R MALAYSIA KOTA KINABALU	DS-MALAY • 10 kW
	VENEZUELA — RADIO RUMBOS, Villa de Cura	DS-TEMP INACTIVE • 10 kW; Sa/Su • DS-TEMP INACTIVE • 10 kW
4974.8	PERU — RADIO DEL PACIFICO, Lima	DS • 5 kW
4975	BRAZIL — †R TUPI/R MUNDIAL, São Paulo	DS • 1 kW
	RADIO TIMBIRA, São Luís	DS • 2.5 kW
	CHINA — FUJIAN PEOPLE'S BS, Jianyang	DS-1 • 10 kW; TAIWAN SVC • 10 kW
	RUSSIA — †VOICE OF RUSSIA, Via Tajikistan	⇨ • W Asia & S Asia • 100 kW
4975v	COLOMBIA — †ONDAS DEL ORTEGUAZA, Florencia	DS-TODELAR • 1 kW
4976	UGANDA — †RADIO UGANDA, Kampala	ENGLISH, ETC • DS • 50 kW • ALT. FREQ. TO 3340 kHz
4976v	COLOMBIA — †ONDAS DEL ORTEGUAZA, Florencia	DS-TODELAR • 1 kW
4980	CHINA — XINJIANG PEOPLE'S BC STN, Urümqi	DS-MONGOLIAN • 50 kW
	VENEZUELA — †ECOS DEL TORBES, San Cristóbal	DS • 10 kW
4985	BRAZIL — †R BRASIL CENTRAL, Goiânia	DS • 10 kW • ⇨; Irr • DS • 10 kW • ⇨
4990	ARMENIA — †VOICE OF ARMENIA, Kamo	⇨ • Mideast & N Africa • 100 kW; ⇨ • M-F • Mideast & N Africa • 100 kW; ⇨ • Sa/Su • Mideast & N Africa • 100 kW
	CHINA — HUNAN PEOPLE'S BS, Changsha	DS-1 • 10 kW
	INDIA — ALL INDIA RADIO, Madras	SE Asia • 100 kW
	NIGERIA — RADIO NIGERIA, Lagos	ENGLISH, ETC • DS-1 • 50 kW
4991	BOLIVIA — †RADIO ANIMAS, Animas	Tu-Su • SPANISH & QUECHUA • DS • 1 kW; M-Sa • SPANISH & QUECHUA • DS • 1 kW; SPANISH & QUECHUA • DS • 1 kW
	SURINAME — RADIO APINTIE, Paramaribo	DS • 0.05/0.35 kW • ALT. FREQ. TO 5005.7 kHz; Tu-Su • DS • 0.05/0.35 kW • ALT. FREQ. TO 5005.7 kHz
4991v	PERU — RADIO ANCASH, Huaraz	SPANISH & QUECHUA • DS • 5 kW
4994	SUDAN — REP OF SUDAN RADIO, Omdurman	DS-TEMP INACTIVE • 20 kW

0 1 2 3 4 5 6 7 8 9 10 11 12 13 14 15 16 17 18 19 20 21 22 23 24

ENGLISH ▬▬   ARABIC ⩘⩘⩘   CHINESE □□□   FRENCH ▭▭   GERMAN ▬▬   RUSSIAN ▬▬   SPANISH ▬▬   OTHER ▬▬

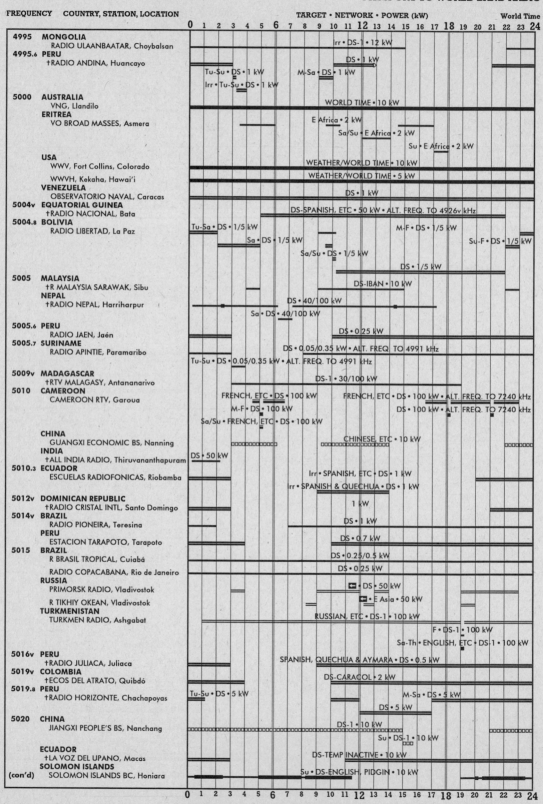

FREQUENCY   COUNTRY, STATION, LOCATION

TARGET • NETWORK • POWER (kW)

World Time

FREQUENCY	COUNTRY, STATION, LOCATION	TARGET • NETWORK • POWER (kW)
4995	**MONGOLIA** RADIO ULAANBAATAR, Choybalsan	Irr • DS-1 • 12 kW
4995.6	**PERU** †RADIO ANDINA, Huancayo	DS • 1 kW / Tu-Su • DS • 1 kW / M-Sa • DS • 1 kW / Irr • Tu-Su • DS • 1 kW
5000	**AUSTRALIA** VNG, Llandilo	WORLD TIME • 10 kW
	ERITREA VO BROAD MASSES, Asmera	E Africa • 2 kW / Sa/Su • E Africa • 2 kW / Su • E Africa • 2 kW
	USA WWV, Fort Collins, Colorado	WEATHER/WORLD TIME • 10 kW
	WWVH, Kekaha, Hawai'i	WEATHER/WORLD TIME • 5 kW
	VENEZUELA OBSERVATORIO NAVAL, Caracas	DS • 1 kW
5004v	**EQUATORIAL GUINEA** †RADIO NACIONAL, Bata	DS-SPANISH, ETC • 50 kW • ALT. FREQ. TO 4926v kHz
5004.8	**BOLIVIA** RADIO LIBERTAD, La Paz	Tu-Sa • DS • 1/5 kW / M-F • DS • 1/5 kW / Su-F • DS • 1/5 kW / Sa • DS • 1/5 kW / Sa/Su • DS • 1/5 kW / DS • 1/5 kW
5005	**MALAYSIA** †R MALAYSIA SARAWAK, Sibu	DS-IBAN • 10 kW
	NEPAL †RADIO NEPAL, Harriharpur	DS • 40/100 kW / Sa • DS • 40/100 kW
5005.6	**PERU** RADIO JAEN, Jaén	DS • 0.25 kW
5005.7	**SURINAME** RADIO APINTIE, Paramaribo	DS • 0.05/0.35 kW • ALT. FREQ TO 4991 kHz / Tu-Su • DS • 0.05/0.35 kW • ALT. FREQ. TO 4991 kHz
5009v	**MADAGASCAR** †RTV MALAGASY, Antananarivo	DS-1 • 30/100 kW
5010	**CAMEROON** CAMEROON RTV, Garoua	FRENCH, ETC • DS • 100 kW / FRENCH, ETC • DS • 100 kW • ALT. FREQ. TO 7240 kHz / M-F • DS • 100 kW / DS • 100 kW • ALT. FREQ. TO 7240 kHz / Sa/Su • FRENCH, ETC • DS • 100 kW
	CHINA GUANGXI ECONOMIC BS, Nanning	CHINESE, ETC • 10 kW
	INDIA †ALL INDIA RADIO, Thiruvananthapuram	DS • 50 kW
5010.3	**ECUADOR** ESCUELAS RADIOFONICAS, Riobamba	Irr • SPANISH, ETC • DS • 1 kW / Irr • SPANISH & QUECHUA • DS • 1 kW
5012v	**DOMINICAN REPUBLIC** †RADIO CRISTAL INTL, Santo Domingo	1 kW
5014v	**BRAZIL** RADIO PIONEIRA, Teresina	DS • 1 kW
	PERU ESTACION TARAPOTO, Tarapoto	DS • 0.7 kW
5015	**BRAZIL** R BRASIL TROPICAL, Cuiabá	DS • 0.25/0.5 kW
	RADIO COPACABANA, Rio de Janeiro	DS • 0.25 kW
	RUSSIA PRIMORSK RADIO, Vladivostok	⊡ • DS • 50 kW
	R TIKHIY OKEAN, Vladivostok	⊡ • E Asia • 50 kW
	TURKMENISTAN TURKMEN RADIO, Ashgabat	RUSSIAN, ETC • DS-1 • 100 kW / F • DS-1 • 100 kW / Sa-Th • ENGLISH, ETC • DS-1 • 100 kW
5016v	**PERU** †RADIO JULIACA, Juliaca	SPANISH, QUECHUA & AYMARA • DS • 0.5 kW
5019v	**COLOMBIA** †ECOS DEL ATRATO, Quibdó	DS-CARACOL • 2 kW
5019.8	**PERU** †RADIO HORIZONTE, Chachapoyas	Tu-Su • DS • 5 kW / M-Sa • DS • 5 kW / DS • 5 kW
5020	**CHINA** JIANGXI PEOPLE'S BS, Nanchang	DS-1 • 10 kW / Su • DS-1 • 10 kW
	ECUADOR †LA VOZ DEL UPANO, Macas	DS-TEMP INACTIVE • 10 kW
	SOLOMON ISLANDS	
(con'd)	SOLOMON ISLANDS BC, Honiara	Su • DS-ENGLISH, PIDGIN • 10 kW

FREQUENCY   COUNTRY, STATION, LOCATION

TARGET • NETWORK • POWER (kW)

World Time

0 1 2 3 4 5 6 7 8 9 10 11 12 13 14 15 16 17 18 19 20 21 22 23 24

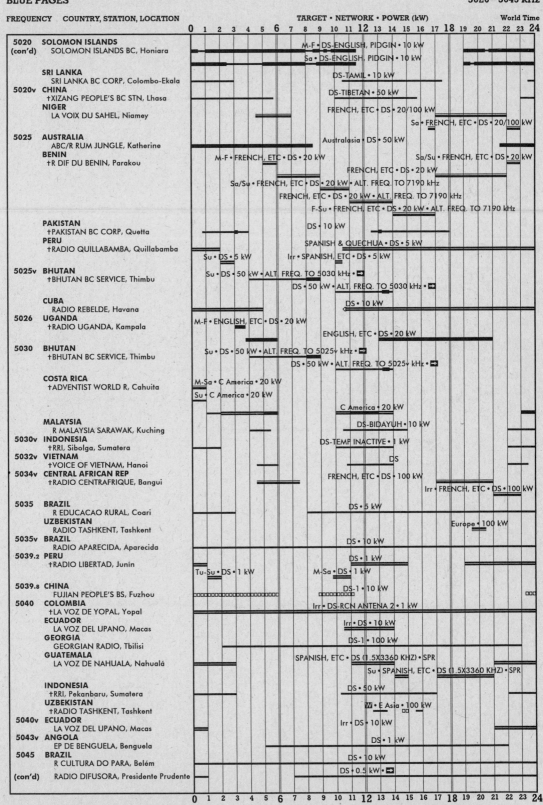

Frequency	Country / Station / Location	Details
5020 (con'd)	**SOLOMON ISLANDS** SOLOMON ISLANDS BC, Honiara	M-F • DS-ENGLISH, PIDGIN • 10 kW Sa • DS-ENGLISH, PIDGIN • 10 kW
	SRI LANKA SRI LANKA BC CORP, Colombo-Ekala	DS-TAMIL • 10 kW
5020v	**CHINA** †XIZANG PEOPLE'S BC STN, Lhasa	DS-TIBETAN • 50 kW
	NIGER LA VOIX DU SAHEL, Niamey	FRENCH, ETC • DS • 20/100 kW Sa • FRENCH, ETC • DS • 20/100 kW
5025	**AUSTRALIA** ABC/R RUM JUNGLE, Katherine	Australasia • DS • 50 kW
	BENIN †R DIF DU BENIN, Parakou	M-F • FRENCH, ETC • DS • 20 kW Sa/Su • FRENCH, ETC • DS • 20 kW FRENCH, ETC • DS • 20 kW Sa/Su • FRENCH, ETC • DS • 20 kW • ALT. FREQ. TO 7190 kHz FRENCH, ETC • DS • 20 kW • ALT. FREQ. TO 7190 kHz F-Su • FRENCH, ETC • DS • 20 kW • ALT. FREQ. TO 7190 kHz
	PAKISTAN †PAKISTAN BC CORP, Quetta	DS • 10 kW
	PERU †RADIO QUILLABAMBA, Quillabamba	SPANISH & QUECHUA • DS • 5 kW Su • DS • 5 kW Irr • SPANISH, ETC • DS • 5 kW
5025v	**BHUTAN** †BHUTAN BC SERVICE, Thimbu	Su • DS • 50 kW • ALT. FREQ. TO 5030 kHz • ▶ DS • 50 kW • ALT. FREQ. TO 5030 kHz • ▶
	CUBA RADIO REBELDE, Havana	DS • 10 kW
5026	**UGANDA** †RADIO UGANDA, Kampala	M-F • ENGLISH, ETC • DS • 20 kW ENGLISH, ETC • DS • 20 kW
5030	**BHUTAN** †BHUTAN BC SERVICE, Thimbu	Su • DS • 50 kW • ALT. FREQ. TO 5025v kHz • ▶ DS • 50 kW • ALT. FREQ. TO 5025v kHz • ▶
	COSTA RICA †ADVENTIST WORLD R, Cahuita	M-Sa • C America • 20 kW Su • C America • 20 kW C America • 20 kW
	MALAYSIA R MALAYSIA SARAWAK, Kuching	DS-BIDAYUH • 10 kW
5030v	**INDONESIA** †RRI, Sibolga, Sumatera	DS-TEMP INACTIVE • 1 kW
5032v	**VIETNAM** †VOICE OF VIETNAM, Hanoi	DS
5034v	**CENTRAL AFRICAN REP** †RADIO CENTRAFRIQUE, Bangui	FRENCH, ETC • DS • 100 kW Irr • FRENCH, ETC • DS • 100 kW
5035	**BRAZIL** R EDUCACAO RURAL, Coari	DS • 5 kW
	UZBEKISTAN RADIO TASHKENT, Tashkent	Europe • 100 kW
5035v	**BRAZIL** RADIO APARECIDA, Aparecida	DS • 10 kW
5039.2	**PERU** †RADIO LIBERTAD, Junín	DS • 1 kW Tu-Su • DS • 1 kW M-Sa • DS • 1 kW
5039.8	**CHINA** FUJIAN PEOPLE'S BS, Fuzhou	DS-1 • 10 kW
5040	**COLOMBIA** †LA VOZ DE YOPAL, Yopal	Irr • DS-RCN ANTENA 2 • 1 kW
	ECUADOR LA VOZ DEL UPANO, Macas	Irr • DS • 10 kW
	GEORGIA GEORGIAN RADIO, Tbilisi	DS-1 • 100 kW
	GUATEMALA LA VOZ DE NAHUALA, Nahualá	SPANISH, ETC • DS (1.5X3360 KHZ) • SPR Su • SPANISH, ETC • DS (1.5X3360 KHZ) • SPR
	INDONESIA †RRI, Pekanbaru, Sumatera	DS • 50 kW
	UZBEKISTAN †RADIO TASHKENT, Tashkent	W • E Asia • 100 kW
5040v	**ECUADOR** LA VOZ DEL UPANO, Macas	Irr • DS • 10 kW
5043v	**ANGOLA** EP DE BENGUELA, Benguela	DS • 1 kW
5045	**BRAZIL** R CULTURA DO PARA, Belém	DS • 10 kW
(con'd)	RADIO DIFUSORA, Presidente Prudente	DS • 0.5 kW • ▶

0 1 2 3 4 5 6 7 8 9 10 11 12 13 14 15 16 17 18 19 20 21 22 23 24

ENGLISH ▬   ARABIC ▨   CHINESE ▯▯▯   FRENCH ══   GERMAN ▬▬   RUSSIAN ═══   SPANISH ▬▬   OTHER ▬

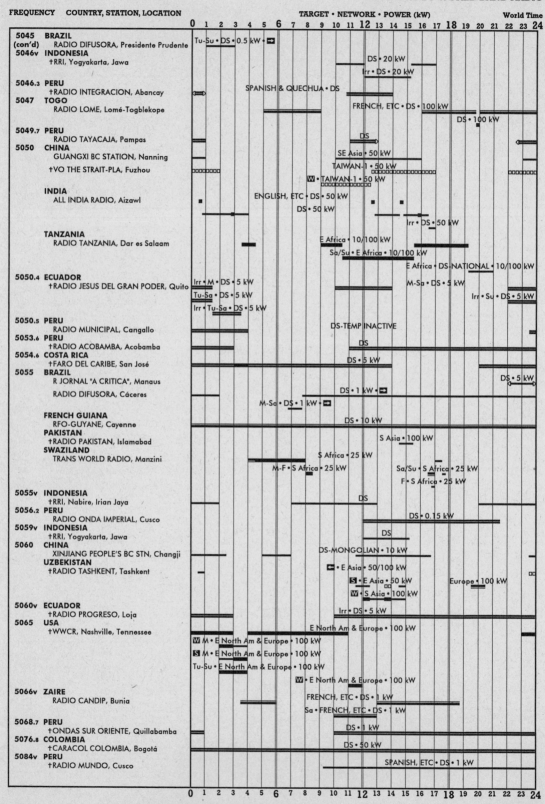

FREQUENCY   COUNTRY, STATION, LOCATION

TARGET • NETWORK • POWER (kW)

World Time

0 1 2 3 4 5 6 7 8 9 10 11 12 13 14 15 16 17 18 19 20 21 22 23 24

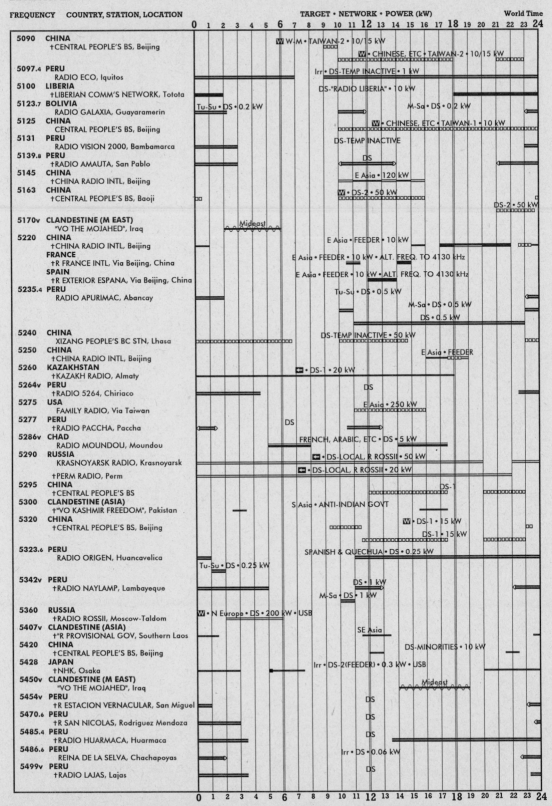

Frequency	Country, Station, Location	Target • Network • Power
5090	**CHINA** †CENTRAL PEOPLE'S BS, Beijing	W • W-M • TAIWAN-2 • 10/15 kW / W • CHINESE, ETC • TAIWAN-2 • 10/15 kW
5097.4	**PERU** RADIO ECO, Iquitos	Irr • DS-TEMP INACTIVE • 1 kW
5100	**LIBERIA** †LIBERIAN COMM'S NETWORK, Totota	DS-"RADIO LIBERIA" • 10 kW
5123.7	**BOLIVIA** RADIO GALAXIA, Guayaramerin	Tu-Su • DS • 0.2 kW / M-Sa • DS • 0.2 kW
5125	**CHINA** CENTRAL PEOPLE'S BS, Beijing	W • CHINESE, ETC • TAIWAN-1 • 10 kW
5131	**PERU** RADIO VISION 2000, Bambamarca	DS-TEMP INACTIVE
5139.8	**PERU** †RADIO AMAUTA, San Pablo	DS
5145	**CHINA** †CHINA RADIO INTL, Beijing	E Asia • 120 kW
5163	**CHINA** †CENTRAL PEOPLE'S BS, Baoji	W • DS-2 • 50 kW / DS-2 • 50 kW
5170v	**CLANDESTINE (M EAST)** "VO THE MOJAHED", Iraq	Mideast
5220	**CHINA** †CHINA RADIO INTL, Beijing	E Asia • FEEDER • 10 kW
	FRANCE †R FRANCE INTL, Via Beijing, China	E Asia • FEEDER • 10 kW • ALT. FREQ. TO 4130 kHz
	SPAIN †R EXTERIOR ESPANA, Via Beijing, China	E Asia • FEEDER • 10 kW • ALT. FREQ. TO 4130 kHz
5235.4	**PERU** RADIO APURIMAC, Abancay	Tu-Su • DS • 0.5 kW / M-Sa • DS • 0.5 kW / DS • 0.5 kW
5240	**CHINA** XIZANG PEOPLE'S BC STN, Lhasa	DS-TEMP INACTIVE • 50 kW
5250	**CHINA** †CHINA RADIO INTL, Beijing	E Asia • FEEDER
5260	**KAZAKHSTAN** †KAZAKH RADIO, Almaty	DS-1 • 20 kW
5264v	**PERU** †RADIO 5264, Chiriaco	DS
5275	**USA** FAMILY RADIO, Via Taiwan	E Asia • 250 kW
5277	**PERU** †RADIO PACCHA, Paccha	DS
5286v	**CHAD** RADIO MOUNDOU, Moundou	FRENCH, ARABIC, ETC • DS • 5 kW
5290	**RUSSIA** KRASNOYARSK RADIO, Krasnoyarsk	DS-LOCAL, R ROSSII • 50 kW
	†PERM RADIO, Perm	DS-LOCAL, R ROSSII • 20 kW
5295	**CHINA** †CENTRAL PEOPLE'S BS	DS-1
5300	**CLANDESTINE (ASIA)** †"VO KASHMIR FREEDOM", Pakistan	S Asia • ANTI-INDIAN GOVT
5320	**CHINA** †CENTRAL PEOPLE'S BS, Beijing	W • DS-1 • 15 kW / DS-1 • 15 kW
5323.6	**PERU** RADIO ORIGEN, Huancavelica	SPANISH & QUECHUA • DS • 0.25 kW / Tu-Su • DS • 0.25 kW
5342v	**PERU** †RADIO NAYLAMP, Lambayeque	DS • 1 kW / M-Sa • DS • 1 kW
5360	**RUSSIA** †RADIO ROSSII, Moscow-Taldom	W • N Europe • DS • 200 kW • USB
5407v	**CLANDESTINE (ASIA)** †"R PROVISIONAL GOV", Southern Laos	SE Asia
5420	**CHINA** †CENTRAL PEOPLE'S BS, Beijing	DS-MINORITIES • 10 kW
5428	**JAPAN** †NHK, Osaka	Irr • DS-2(FEEDER) • 0.3 kW • USB
5450v	**CLANDESTINE (M EAST)** "VO THE MOJAHED", Iraq	Mideast
5454v	**PERU** †R ESTACION VERNACULAR, San Miguel	DS
5470.6	**PERU** †R SAN NICOLAS, Rodriguez Mendoza	DS
5485.4	**PERU** †RADIO HUARMACA, Huarmaca	DS
5486.6	**PERU** REINA DE LA SELVA, Chachapoyas	Irr • DS • 0.06 kW
5499v	**PERU** †RADIO LAJAS, Lajas	DS

0 1 2 3 4 5 6 7 8 9 10 11 12 13 14 15 16 17 18 19 20 21 22 23 24

ENGLISH ▬   ARABIC ⋙   CHINESE ▭▭▭   FRENCH ▬   GERMAN ▬   RUSSIAN ═   SPANISH ▬   OTHER ▬

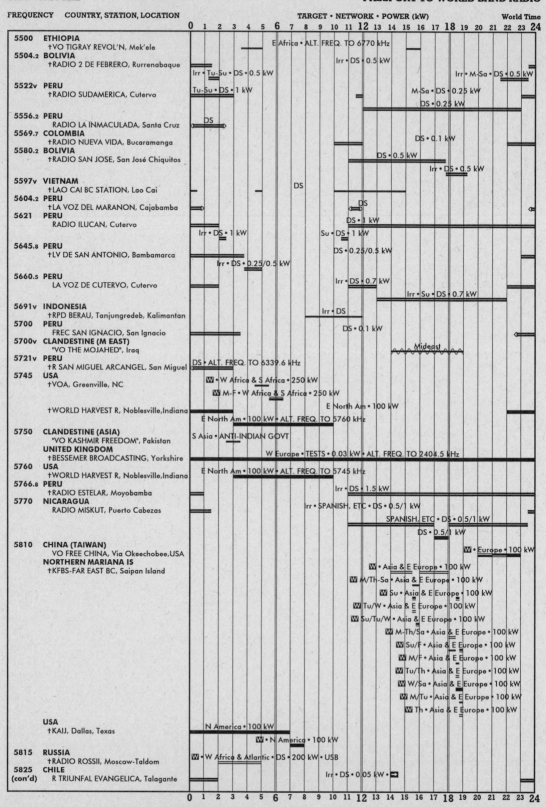

FREQUENCY   COUNTRY, STATION, LOCATION

TARGET • NETWORK • POWER (kW)

World Time

Frequency	Country, Station, Location	Details
5500	**ETHIOPIA** †VO TIGRAY REVOL'N, Mek'ele	E Africa • ALT. FREQ. TO 6770 kHz
5504.2	**BOLIVIA** †RADIO 2 DE FEBRERO, Rurrenabaque	Irr • DS • 0.5 kW / Irr • Tu-Su • DS • 0.5 kW / Irr • M-Sa • DS • 0.5 kW
5522v	**PERU** †RADIO SUDAMERICA, Cutervo	Tu-Su • DS • 1 kW / M-Sa • DS • 0.25 kW / DS • 0.25 kW
5556.2	**PERU** RADIO LA INMACULADA, Santa Cruz	DS
5569.7	**COLOMBIA** †RADIO NUEVA VIDA, Bucaramanga	DS • 0.1 kW
5580.2	**BOLIVIA** †RADIO SAN JOSE, San José Chiquitos	DS • 0.5 kW / Irr • DS • 0.5 kW
5597v	**VIETNAM** †LAO CAI BC STATION, Lao Cai	DS
5604.2	**PERU** †LA VOZ DEL MARANON, Cajabamba	DS
5621	**PERU** RADIO ILUCAN, Cutervo	DS • 1 kW / Irr • DS • 1 kW / Su • DS • 1 kW
5645.8	**PERU** †LV DE SAN ANTONIO, Bambamarca	DS • 0.25/0.5 kW / Irr • DS • 0.25/0.5 kW
5660.5	**PERU** LA VOZ DE CUTERVO, Cutervo	Irr • DS • 0.7 kW / Irr • Su • DS • 0.7 kW
5691v	**INDONESIA** †RPD BERAU, Tanjungredeb, Kalimantan	Irr • DS
5700	**PERU** FREC SAN IGNACIO, San Ignacio	DS • 0.1 kW
5700v	**CLANDESTINE (M EAST)** "VO THE MOJAHED", Iraq	Mideast
5721v	**PERU** †R SAN MIGUEL ARCANGEL, San Miguel	DS • ALT. FREQ. TO 6339.6 kHz
5745	**USA** †VOA, Greenville, NC	W • W Africa & S Africa • 250 kW / W M-F • W Africa & S Africa • 250 kW
	†WORLD HARVEST R, Noblesville, Indiana	E North Am • 100 kW / E North Am • 100 kW • ALT. FREQ. TO 5760 kHz
5750	**CLANDESTINE (ASIA)** "VO KASHMIR FREEDOM", Pakistan	S Asia • ANTI-INDIAN GOVT
	UNITED KINGDOM †BESSEMER BROADCASTING, Yorkshire	W Europe • TESTS • 0.03 kW • ALT. FREQ. TO 2404.5 kHz
5760	**USA** †WORLD HARVEST R, Noblesville, Indiana	E North Am • 100 kW • ALT. FREQ. TO 5745 kHz
5766.8	**PERU** †RADIO ESTELAR, Moyobamba	Irr • DS • 1.5 kW
5770	**NICARAGUA** RADIO MISKUT, Puerto Cabezas	Irr • SPANISH, ETC • DS • 0.5/1 kW / SPANISH, ETC • DS • 0.5/1 kW / DS • 0.5/1 kW
5810	**CHINA (TAIWAN)** VO FREE CHINA, Via Okeechobee, USA	W • Europe • 100 kW
	NORTHERN MARIANA IS †KFBS-FAR EAST BC, Saipan Island	W • Asia & E Europe • 100 kW / W M/Th-Sa • Asia & E Europe • 100 kW / W Su • Asia & E Europe • 100 kW / W Tu/W • Asia & E Europe • 100 kW / W Su/Tu/W • Asia & E Europe • 100 kW / W M-Th/Sa • Asia & E Europe • 100 kW / W Su/F • Asia & E Europe • 100 kW / W M/F • Asia & E Europe • 100 kW / W Tu/Th • Asia & E Europe • 100 kW / W W/Sa • Asia & E Europe • 100 kW / W M/Tu • Asia & E Europe • 100 kW / W Th • Asia & E Europe • 100 kW
	USA †KAIJ, Dallas, Texas	N America • 100 kW / W • N America • 100 kW
5815	**RUSSIA** †RADIO ROSSII, Moscow-Taldom	W • W Africa & Atlantic • DS • 200 kW • USB
5825 (con'd)	**CHILE** R TRIUNFAL EVANGELICA, Talagante	Irr • DS • 0.05 kW

FREQUENCY   COUNTRY, STATION, LOCATION   TARGET • NETWORK • POWER (kW)   World Time

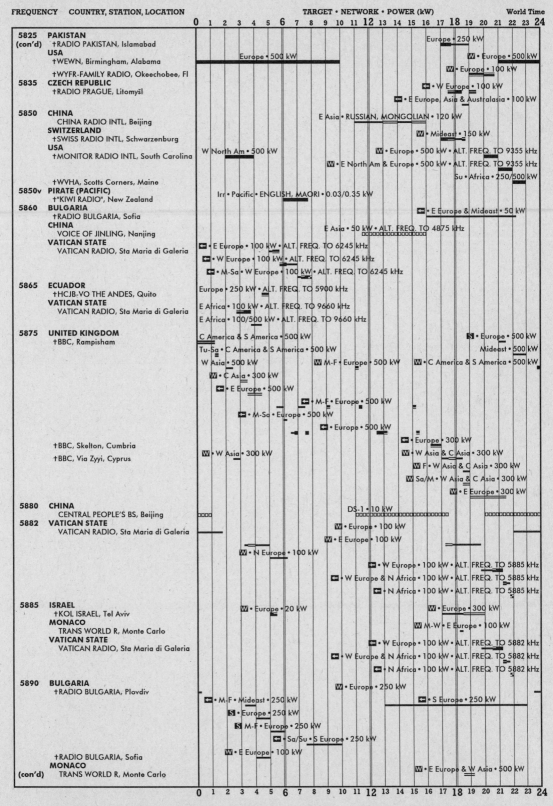

Frequency	Country, Station, Location	Target • Network • Power
5825 (con'd)	**PAKISTAN** †RADIO PAKISTAN, Islamabad	Europe • 250 kW
	USA †WEWN, Birmingham, Alabama	Europe • 500 kW / W • Europe • 500 kW
	†WYFR-FAMILY RADIO, Okeechobee, Fl	W • Europe • 100 kW
5835	**CZECH REPUBLIC** †RADIO PRAGUE, Litomyšl	W Europe • 100 kW / E Europe, Asia & Australasia • 100 kW
5850	**CHINA** CHINA RADIO INTL, Beijing	E Asia • RUSSIAN, MONGOLIAN • 120 kW
	SWITZERLAND †SWISS RADIO INTL, Schwarzenburg	W • Mideast • 150 kW
	USA †MONITOR RADIO INTL, South Carolina	W North Am • 500 kW / W • Europe • 500 kW • ALT. FREQ. TO 9355 kHz / W • E North Am & Europe • 500 kW • ALT. FREQ. TO 9355 kHz / Su • Africa • 250/500 kW
	†WVHA, Scotts Corners, Maine	
5850v	**PIRATE (PACIFIC)** †"KIWI RADIO", New Zealand	Irr • Pacific • ENGLISH, MAORI • 0.03/0.35 kW
5860	**BULGARIA** †RADIO BULGARIA, Sofia	E Europe & Mideast • 50 kW
	CHINA VOICE OF JINLING, Nanjing	E Asia • 50 kW • ALT. FREQ. TO 4875 kHz
	VATICAN STATE VATICAN RADIO, Sta Maria di Galeria	E Europe • 100 kW • ALT. FREQ. TO 6245 kHz / W Europe • 100 kW • ALT. FREQ. TO 6245 kHz / M-Sa • W Europe • 100 kW • ALT. FREQ. TO 6245 kHz
5865	**ECUADOR** †HCJB-VO THE ANDES, Quito	Europe • 250 kW • ALT. FREQ. TO 5900 kHz
	VATICAN STATE VATICAN RADIO, Sta Maria di Galeria	E Africa • 100 kW • ALT. FREQ. TO 9660 kHz / E Africa • 100/500 kW • ALT. FREQ. TO 9660 kHz
5875	**UNITED KINGDOM** †BBC, Rampisham	C America & S America • 500 kW / S • Europe • 500 kW / Tu-Sa • C America & S America • 500 kW / Mideast • 500 kW / W Asia • 500 kW / W • M-F • Europe • 500 kW / W • C America & S America • 500 kW / W • C Asia • 300 kW / E Europe • 500 kW / M-F • Europe • 500 kW / M-Sa • Europe • 500 kW / Europe • 500 kW
	†BBC, Skelton, Cumbria	Europe • 300 kW / W • W Asia • 300 kW / W • W Asia & C Asia • 300 kW
	†BBC, Via Zyyi, Cyprus	W F • W Asia & C Asia • 300 kW / W Sa/M • W Asia & C Asia • 300 kW / W • E Europe • 300 kW
5880	**CHINA** CENTRAL PEOPLE'S BS, Beijing	DS-1 • 10 kW
5882	**VATICAN STATE** VATICAN RADIO, Sta Maria di Galeria	W • Europe • 100 kW / W • E Europe • 100 kW / W • N Europe • 100 kW / W Europe • 100 kW • ALT. FREQ. TO 5885 kHz / W Europe & N Africa • 100 kW • ALT. FREQ. TO 5885 kHz / N Africa • 100 kW • ALT. FREQ. TO 5885 kHz
5885	**ISRAEL** †KOL ISRAEL, Tel Aviv	W • Europe • 20 kW / W • Europe • 300 kW
	MONACO TRANS WORLD R, Monte Carlo	W M-W • E Europe • 100 kW
	VATICAN STATE VATICAN RADIO, Sta Maria di Galeria	W Europe • 100 kW • ALT. FREQ. TO 5882 kHz / W Europe & N Africa • 100 kW • ALT. FREQ. TO 5882 kHz / N Africa • 100 kW • ALT. FREQ. TO 5882 kHz
5890	**BULGARIA** †RADIO BULGARIA, Plovdiv	W • Europe • 250 kW / M-F • Mideast • 250 kW / S Europe • 250 kW / S • Europe • 250 kW / M-F • Europe • 250 kW / Sa/Su • S Europe • 250 kW
	†RADIO BULGARIA, Sofia	W • E Europe • 100 kW
(con'd)	**MONACO** TRANS WORLD R, Monte Carlo	W • E Europe & W Asia • 500 kW

ENGLISH ▬▬   ARABIC ෴   CHINESE ☐☐☐   FRENCH ▭▭   GERMAN ▬▬   RUSSIAN ══   SPANISH ▬▬   OTHER ▬

FREQUENCY   COUNTRY, STATION, LOCATION

TARGET • NETWORK • POWER (kW)

World Time

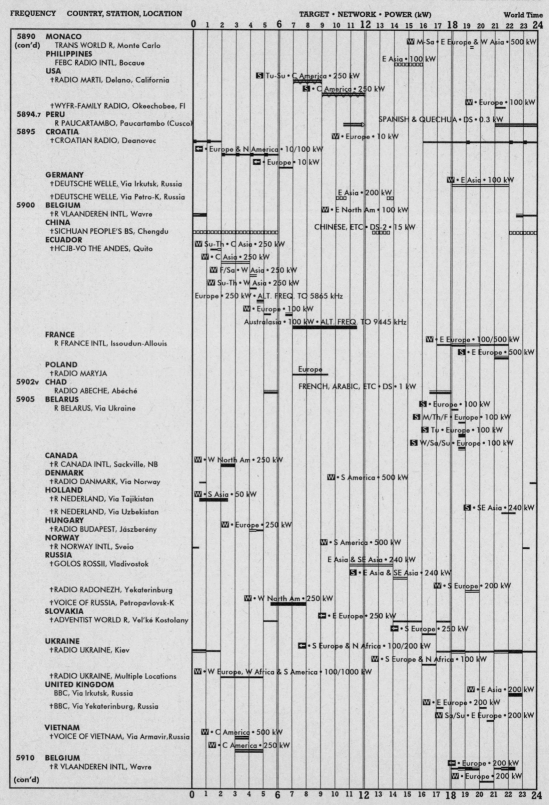

5890	MONACO
(con'd)	TRANS WORLD R, Monte Carlo
	PHILIPPINES
	FEBC RADIO INTL, Bocaue
	USA
	†RADIO MARTI, Delano, California
	†WYFR-FAMILY RADIO, Okeechobee, Fl
5894.7	**PERU**
	R PAUCARTAMBO, Paucartambo (Cusco)
5895	**CROATIA**
	†CROATIAN RADIO, Deanovec
	GERMANY
	†DEUTSCHE WELLE, Via Irkutsk, Russia
	†DEUTSCHE WELLE, Via Petro-K, Russia
5900	**BELGIUM**
	†R VLAANDEREN INTL, Wavre
	CHINA
	†SICHUAN PEOPLE'S BS, Chengdu
	ECUADOR
	†HCJB-VO THE ANDES, Quito
	FRANCE
	R FRANCE INTL, Issoudun-Allouis
	POLAND
	†RADIO MARYJA
5902v	**CHAD**
	RADIO ABECHE, Abéché
5905	**BELARUS**
	R BELARUS, Via Ukraine
	CANADA
	†R CANADA INTL, Sackville, NB
	DENMARK
	†RADIO DANMARK, Via Norway
	HOLLAND
	†R NEDERLAND, Via Tajikistan
	†R NEDERLAND, Via Uzbekistan
	HUNGARY
	†RADIO BUDAPEST, Jászberény
	NORWAY
	†R NORWAY INTL, Sveio
	RUSSIA
	†GOLOS ROSSII, Vladivostok
	†RADIO RADONEZH, Yekaterinburg
	†VOICE OF RUSSIA, Petropavlovsk-K
	SLOVAKIA
	†ADVENTIST WORLD R, Vel'ké Kostolany
	UKRAINE
	†RADIO UKRAINE, Kiev
	†RADIO UKRAINE, Multiple Locations
	UNITED KINGDOM
	BBC, Via Irkutsk, Russia
	†BBC, Via Yekaterinburg, Russia
	VIETNAM
	†VOICE OF VIETNAM, Via Armavir, Russia
5910	**BELGIUM**
	†R VLAANDEREN INTL, Wavre
(con'd)	

Labels within chart:
- M-Sa • E Europe & W Asia • 500 kW
- E Asia • 100 kW
- Tu-Su • C America • 250 kW
- C America • 250 kW
- Europe • 100 kW
- SPANISH & QUECHUA • DS • 0.3 kW
- Europe • 10 kW
- Europe & N America • 10/100 kW
- Europe • 10 kW
- E Asia • 100 kW
- E Asia • 200 kW
- E North Am • 100 kW
- CHINESE, ETC • DS-2 • 15 kW
- Su-Th • C Asia • 250 kW
- C Asia • 250 kW
- F/Sa • W Asia • 250 kW
- Su-Th • W Asia • 250 kW
- Europe • 250 kW • ALT. FREQ. TO 5865 kHz
- Europe • 100 kW
- Australasia • 100 kW • ALT. FREQ. TO 9445 kHz
- E Europe • 100/500 kW
- E Europe • 500 kW
- Europe
- FRENCH, ARABIC, ETC • DS • 1 kW
- Europe • 100 kW
- M/Th/F • Europe • 100 kW
- Tu • Europe • 100 kW
- W/Sa/Su • Europe • 100 kW
- W North Am • 250 kW
- S America • 500 kW
- S Asia • 50 kW
- SE Asia • 240 kW
- Europe • 250 kW
- S America • 500 kW
- E Asia & SE Asia • 240 kW
- E Asia & SE Asia • 240 kW
- S Europe • 200 kW
- W North Am • 250 kW
- E Europe • 250 kW
- S Europe • 250 kW
- S Europe & N Africa • 100/200 kW
- S Europe & N Africa • 100 kW
- W Europe, W Africa & S America • 100/1000 kW
- E Asia • 200 kW
- E Europe • 200 kW
- Sa/Su • E Europe • 200 kW
- C America • 500 kW
- C America • 250 kW
- Europe • 200 kW
- Europe • 200 kW

FREQUENCY   COUNTRY, STATION, LOCATION   TARGET • NETWORK • POWER (kW)   World Time

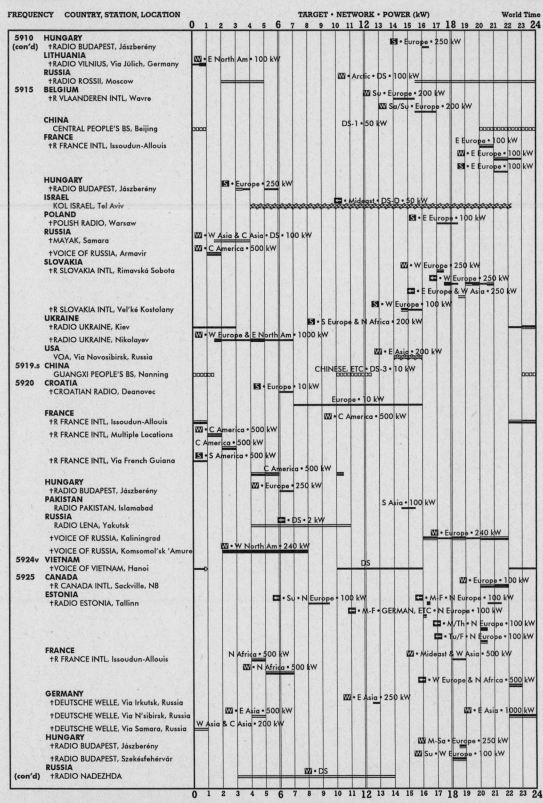

5910
(con'd) HUNGARY
  †RADIO BUDAPEST, Jászberény — S • Europe • 250 kW
  LITHUANIA
  †RADIO VILNIUS, Via Jülich, Germany — W • E North Am • 100 kW
  RUSSIA
  †RADIO ROSSII, Moscow — W • Arctic • DS • 100 kW

5915 BELGIUM
  †R VLAANDEREN INTL, Wavre — W Su • Europe • 200 kW / W Sa/Su • Europe • 200 kW

  CHINA
  CENTRAL PEOPLE'S BS, Beijing — DS-1 • 50 kW
  FRANCE
  †R FRANCE INTL, Issoudun-Allouis — E Europe • 100 kW / W • E Europe • 100 kW / S • E Europe • 100 kW

  HUNGARY
  †RADIO BUDAPEST, Jászberény — S • Europe • 250 kW
  ISRAEL
  KOL ISRAEL, Tel Aviv — • Mideast • DS-D • 50 kW
  POLAND
  †POLISH RADIO, Warsaw — S • E Europe • 100 kW
  RUSSIA
  †MAYAK, Samara — W • W Asia & C Asia • DS • 100 kW
  †VOICE OF RUSSIA, Armavir — W • C America • 500 kW
  SLOVAKIA
  †R SLOVAKIA INTL, Rimavská Sobota — W • W Europe • 250 kW / • W Europe • 250 kW / • E Europe & W Asia • 250 kW

  †R SLOVAKIA INTL, Vel'ké Kostolany — S • W Europe • 100 kW
  UKRAINE
  †RADIO UKRAINE, Kiev — S • S Europe & N Africa • 200 kW
  †RADIO UKRAINE, Nikolayev — W • W Europe & E North Am • 1000 kW
  USA
  VOA, Via Novosibirsk, Russia — W • E Asia • 200 kW
5919.5 CHINA
  GUANGXI PEOPLE'S BS, Nanning — CHINESE, ETC • DS-3 • 10 kW
5920 CROATIA
  †CROATIAN RADIO, Deanovec — S • Europe • 10 kW
  Europe • 10 kW

  FRANCE
  †R FRANCE INTL, Issoudun-Allouis — W • C America • 500 kW
  †R FRANCE INTL, Multiple Locations — W • C America • 500 kW
  C America • 500 kW
  †R FRANCE INTL, Via French Guiana — S • S America • 500 kW
  C America • 500 kW

  HUNGARY
  †RADIO BUDAPEST, Jászberény — W • Europe • 250 kW
  PAKISTAN
  RADIO PAKISTAN, Islamabad — S Asia • 100 kW
  RUSSIA
  RADIO LENA, Yakutsk — • DS • 2 kW
  †VOICE OF RUSSIA, Kaliningrad — W • Europe • 240 kW
  †VOICE OF RUSSIA, Komsomol'sk 'Amure — W • W North Am • 240 kW
5924v VIETNAM
  †VOICE OF VIETNAM, Hanoi — DS
5925 CANADA
  †R CANADA INTL, Sackville, NB — W • Europe • 100 kW
  ESTONIA
  †RADIO ESTONIA, Tallinn — • Su • N Europe • 100 kW / • M-F • N Europe • 100 kW / • M-F • GERMAN, ETC • N Europe • 100 kW / • M/Th • N Europe • 100 kW / • Tu/F • N Europe • 100 kW

  FRANCE
  †R FRANCE INTL, Issoudun-Allouis — N Africa • 500 kW / W • N Africa • 500 kW / W • Mideast & W Asia • 500 kW / • W Europe & N Africa • 500 kW

  GERMANY
  †DEUTSCHE WELLE, Via Irkutsk, Russia — W • E Asia • 250 kW
  †DEUTSCHE WELLE, Via N'sibirsk, Russia — W • E Asia • 500 kW / W • E Asia • 1000 kW
  †DEUTSCHE WELLE, Via Samara, Russia — W Asia & C Asia • 200 kW
  HUNGARY
  †RADIO BUDAPEST, Jászberény — W M-Sa • Europe • 250 kW
  †RADIO BUDAPEST, Szekésfehérvár — W Su • W Europe • 100 kW
  RUSSIA
  (con'd) †RADIO NADEZHDA — W • DS

ENGLISH ▬   ARABIC ⧓   CHINESE ☐☐☐   FRENCH ▭   GERMAN ▬   RUSSIAN ═   SPANISH ▬   OTHER ▬

FREQUENCY   COUNTRY, STATION, LOCATION

TARGET • NETWORK • POWER (kW)

World Time

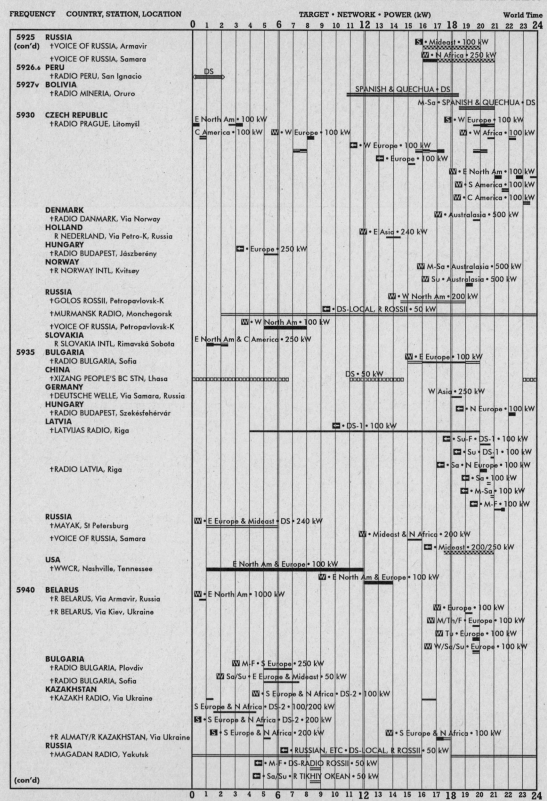

5925	**RUSSIA**	
(con'd)	†VOICE OF RUSSIA, Armavir	**S** • Mideast • 100 kW
	†VOICE OF RUSSIA, Samara	**W** • N Africa • 250 kW
5926.6	**PERU**	
	†RADIO PERU, San Ignacio	DS
5927v	**BOLIVIA**	
	†RADIO MINERIA, Oruro	SPANISH & QUECHUA • DS / M-Sa • SPANISH & QUECHUA • DS
5930	**CZECH REPUBLIC**	
	†RADIO PRAGUE, Litomyšl	E North Am • 100 kW / C America • 100 kW / **W** • W Europe • 100 kW / **S** • W Europe • 100 kW / **W** • W Africa • 100 kW / • W Europe • 100 kW / • Europe • 100 kW / **W** • E North Am • 100 kW / **W** • S America • 100 kW / **W** • C America • 100 kW
	DENMARK	
	†RADIO DANMARK, Via Norway	**W** • Australasia • 500 kW
	HOLLAND	
	R NEDERLAND, Via Petro-K, Russia	**W** • E Asia • 240 kW
	HUNGARY	
	†RADIO BUDAPEST, Jászberény	• Europe • 250 kW
	NORWAY	
	†R NORWAY INTL, Kvitsøy	**W** M-Sa • Australasia • 500 kW / **W** Su • Australasia • 500 kW
	RUSSIA	
	†GOLOS ROSSII, Petropavlovsk-K	**W** • W North Am • 200 kW
	†MURMANSK RADIO, Monchegorsk	• DS-LOCAL, R ROSSII • 50 kW
	†VOICE OF RUSSIA, Petropavlovsk-K	**W** • W North Am • 100 kW
	SLOVAKIA	
	R SLOVAKIA INTL, Rimavská Sobota	E North Am & C America • 250 kW
5935	**BULGARIA**	
	†RADIO BULGARIA, Sofia	**W** • E Europe • 100 kW
	CHINA	
	†XIZANG PEOPLE'S BC STN, Lhasa	DS • 50 kW
	GERMANY	
	†DEUTSCHE WELLE, Via Samara, Russia	W Asia • 250 kW
	HUNGARY	
	†RADIO BUDAPEST, Székésfehérvár	• N Europe • 100 kW
	LATVIA	
	†LATVIJAS RADIO, Riga	• DS-1 • 100 kW / • Su-F • DS-1 • 100 kW / • Su • DS-1 • 100 kW / • Sa • N Europe • 100 kW / • Sa • 100 kW / • M-Sa • 100 kW
	†RADIO LATVIA, Riga	• M-F • 100 kW
	RUSSIA	
	†MAYAK, St Petersburg	**W** • E Europe & Mideast • DS • 240 kW
	†VOICE OF RUSSIA, Samara	**W** • Mideast & N Africa • 200 kW / • Mideast • 200/250 kW
	USA	
	†WWCR, Nashville, Tennessee	E North Am & Europe • 100 kW / **W** • E North Am & Europe • 100 kW
5940	**BELARUS**	
	†R BELARUS, Via Armavir, Russia	**W** • E North Am • 1000 kW
	†R BELARUS, Via Kiev, Ukraine	**W** • Europe • 100 kW / **W** M/Th/F • Europe • 100 kW / **W** Tu • Europe • 100 kW / **W** W/Sa/Su • Europe • 100 kW
	BULGARIA	
	†RADIO BULGARIA, Plovdiv	**W** M-F • S Europe • 250 kW
	†RADIO BULGARIA, Sofia	**W** Sa/Su • E Europe & Mideast • 50 kW
	KAZAKHSTAN	
	†KAZAKH RADIO, Via Ukraine	**W** • S Europe & N Africa • DS-2 • 100 kW / S Europe & N Africa • DS-2 • 100/200 kW / **S** • S Europe & N Africa • DS-2 • 200 kW
	†R ALMATY/R KAZAKHSTAN, Via Ukraine	**S** • S Europe & N Africa • 200 kW / **W** • S Europe & N Africa • 100 kW
	RUSSIA	
	†MAGADAN RADIO, Yakutsk	• RUSSIAN, ETC • DS-LOCAL, R ROSSII • 50 kW / • M-F • DS-RADIO ROSSII • 50 kW / • Sa/Su • R TIKHIY OKEAN • 50 kW
(con'd)		

FREQUENCY   COUNTRY, STATION, LOCATION

TARGET • NETWORK • POWER (kW)

World Time

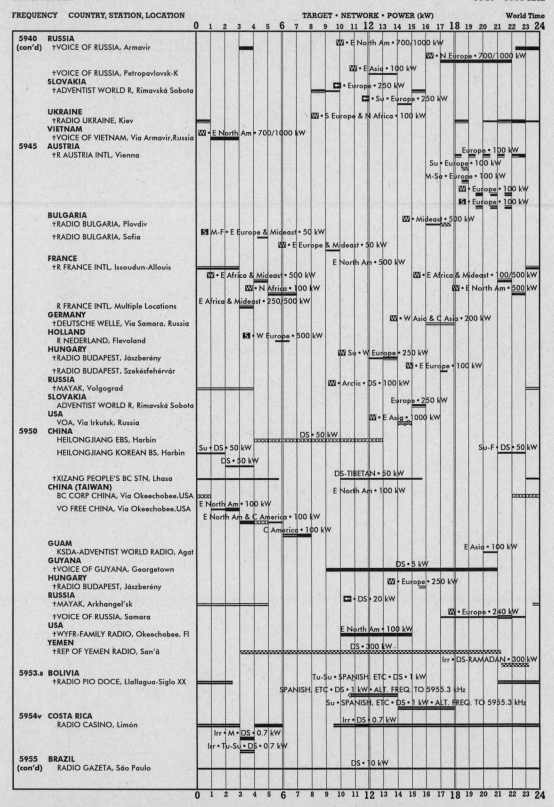

Frequency	Country, Station, Location	Notes
5940 (con'd)	**RUSSIA** †VOICE OF RUSSIA, Armavir	W • E North Am • 700/1000 kW / W • N Europe • 700/1000 kW
	†VOICE OF RUSSIA, Petropavlovsk-K	W • E Asia • 100 kW
	SLOVAKIA †ADVENTIST WORLD R, Rimavská Sobota	• Europe • 250 kW / • Su • Europe • 250 kW
	UKRAINE †RADIO UKRAINE, Kiev	W • S Europe & N Africa • 100 kW
	VIETNAM †VOICE OF VIETNAM, Via Armavir, Russia	W • E North Am • 700/1000 kW
5945	**AUSTRIA** †R AUSTRIA INTL, Vienna	Europe • 100 kW / Su • Europe • 100 kW / M-Sa • Europe • 100 kW / W • Europe • 100 kW / S • Europe • 100 kW
	BULGARIA †RADIO BULGARIA, Plovdiv	W • Mideast • 500 kW
	†RADIO BULGARIA, Sofia	S M-F • E Europe & Mideast • 50 kW / W • E Europe & Mideast • 50 kW
	FRANCE †R FRANCE INTL, Issoudun-Allouis	E North Am • 500 kW / W • E Africa & Mideast • 500 kW / W • N Africa • 100 kW / W • E Africa & Mideast • 100/500 kW / W • E North Am • 500 kW
	R FRANCE INTL, Multiple Locations	E Africa & Mideast • 250/500 kW
	GERMANY †DEUTSCHE WELLE, Via Samara, Russia	W • W Asia & C Asia • 200 kW
	HOLLAND R NEDERLAND, Flevoland	S • W Europe • 500 kW
	HUNGARY †RADIO BUDAPEST, Jászberény	W Su • W Europe • 250 kW
	†RADIO BUDAPEST, Szekésfehérvár	W • E Europe • 100 kW
	RUSSIA †MAYAK, Volgograd	W • Arctic • DS • 100 kW
	SLOVAKIA ADVENTIST WORLD R, Rimavská Sobota	Europe • 250 kW
	USA VOA, Via Irkutsk, Russia	W • E Asia • 1000 kW
5950	**CHINA** HEILONGJIANG EBS, Harbin	DS • 50 kW
	HEILONGJIANG KOREAN BS, Harbin	Su • DS • 50 kW / Su-F • DS • 50 kW / DS • 50 kW
	†XIZANG PEOPLE'S BC STN, Lhasa	DS-TIBETAN • 50 kW
	CHINA (TAIWAN) BC CORP CHINA, Via Okeechobee, USA	E North Am • 100 kW / E North Am • 100 kW
	VO FREE CHINA, Via Okeechobee, USA	E North Am & C America • 100 kW / C America • 100 kW
	GUAM KSDA-ADVENTIST WORLD RADIO, Agat	E Asia • 100 kW
	GUYANA †VOICE OF GUYANA, Georgetown	DS • 5 kW
	HUNGARY †RADIO BUDAPEST, Jászberény	W • Europe • 250 kW
	RUSSIA †MAYAK, Arkhangel'sk	• DS • 20 kW
	†VOICE OF RUSSIA, Samara	W • Europe • 240 kW
	USA †WYFR-FAMILY RADIO, Okeechobee, Fl	E North Am • 100 kW
	YEMEN †REP OF YEMEN RADIO, San'ā	DS • 300 kW / Irr • DS-RAMADAN • 300 kW
5953.8	**BOLIVIA** †RADIO PIO DOCE, Llallagua-Siglo XX	Tu-Su • SPANISH, ETC • DS • 1 kW / SPANISH, ETC • DS • 1 kW • ALT. FREQ. TO 5955.3 kHz / Su • SPANISH, ETC • DS • 1 kW • ALT. FREQ. TO 5955.3 kHz
5954v	**COSTA RICA** RADIO CASINO, Limón	Irr • DS • 0.7 kW / Irr • M • DS • 0.7 kW / Irr • Tu-Su • DS • 0.7 kW
5955 (con'd)	**BRAZIL** RADIO GAZETA, São Paulo	DS • 10 kW

ENGLISH ▬   ARABIC ▨   CHINESE ▫▫▫   FRENCH ▬   GERMAN ▬   RUSSIAN ▬   SPANISH ▬   OTHER ▬

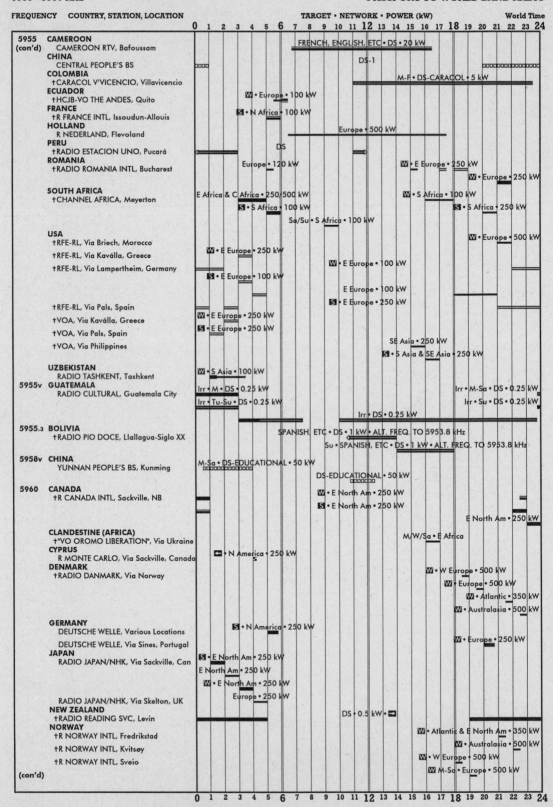

FREQUENCY   COUNTRY, STATION, LOCATION   TARGET • NETWORK • POWER (kW)   World Time

5955	**CAMEROON**	
(con'd)	CAMEROON RTV, Bafoussam	FRENCH, ENGLISH, ETC • DS • 20 kW
	CHINA	
	CENTRAL PEOPLE'S BS	DS-1
	COLOMBIA	
	†CARACOL V'VICENCIO, Villavicencio	M-F • DS-CARACOL • 5 kW
	ECUADOR	
	†HCJB-VO THE ANDES, Quito	W • Europe • 100 kW
	FRANCE	
	†R FRANCE INTL, Issoudun-Allouis	S • N Africa • 100 kW
	HOLLAND	
	R NEDERLAND, Flevoland	Europe • 500 kW
	PERU	
	†RADIO ESTACION UNO, Pucará	DS
	ROMANIA	
	†RADIO ROMANIA INTL, Bucharest	Europe • 120 kW W • E Europe • 250 kW W • Europe • 250 kW
	SOUTH AFRICA	
	†CHANNEL AFRICA, Meyerton	E Africa & C Africa • 250/500 kW W • S Africa • 100 kW
		S • S Africa • 100 kW S • S Africa • 250 kW
		Sa/Su • S Africa • 100 kW
	USA	
	†RFE-RL, Via Briech, Morocco	W • Europe • 500 kW
	†RFE-RL, Via Kaválla, Greece	W • E Europe • 250 kW
	†RFE-RL, Via Lampertheim, Germany	W • E Europe • 100 kW
		S • E Europe • 100 kW
		E Europe • 100 kW
	†RFE-RL, Via Pals, Spain	S • E Europe • 250 kW
	†VOA, Via Kaválla, Greece	W • E Europe • 250 kW
	†VOA, Via Pals, Spain	S • E Europe • 250 kW
	†VOA, Via Philippines	SE Asia • 250 kW
		S • S Asia & SE Asia • 250 kW
	UZBEKISTAN	
	RADIO TASHKENT, Tashkent	W • S Asia • 100 kW
5955v	**GUATEMALA**	
	RADIO CULTURAL, Guatemala City	Irr • M • DS • 0.25 kW Irr • M-Sa • DS • 0.25 kW
		Irr • Tu-Su • DS • 0.25 kW Irr • Su • DS • 0.25 kW
		Irr • DS • 0.25 kW
5955.3	**BOLIVIA**	
	†RADIO PIO DOCE, Llallagua-Siglo XX	SPANISH, ETC • DS • 1 kW • ALT. FREQ. TO 5953.8 kHz
		Su • SPANISH, ETC • DS • 1 kW • ALT. FREQ. TO 5953.8 kHz
5958v	**CHINA**	
	YUNNAN PEOPLE'S BS, Kunming	M-Sa • DS-EDUCATIONAL • 50 kW
		DS-EDUCATIONAL • 50 kW
5960	**CANADA**	
	†R CANADA INTL, Sackville, NB	W • E North Am • 250 kW
		S • E North Am • 250 kW
		E North Am • 250 kW
	CLANDESTINE (AFRICA)	
	†"VO OROMO LIBERATION", Via Ukraine	M/W/Sa • E Africa
	CYPRUS	
	R MONTE CARLO, Via Sackville, Canada	• N America • 250 kW
	DENMARK	
	†RADIO DANMARK, Via Norway	W • W Europe • 500 kW
		W • Europe • 500 kW
		W • Atlantic • 350 kW
		W • Australasia • 500 kW
	GERMANY	
	DEUTSCHE WELLE, Various Locations	S • N America • 250 kW
	DEUTSCHE WELLE, Via Sines, Portugal	W • Europe • 250 kW
	JAPAN	
	RADIO JAPAN/NHK, Via Sackville, Can	S • E North Am • 250 kW
		E North Am • 250 kW
		W • E North Am • 250 kW
	RADIO JAPAN/NHK, Via Skelton, UK	Europe • 250 kW
	NEW ZEALAND	
	†RADIO READING SVC, Levin	DS • 0.5 kW •
	NORWAY	
	†R NORWAY INTL, Fredrikstad	W • Atlantic & E North Am • 350 kW
	†R NORWAY INTL, Kvitsøy	W • Australasia • 500 kW
	†R NORWAY INTL, Sveio	W • W Europe • 500 kW
		W • M-Sa • Europe • 500 kW
(con'd)		

FREQUENCY   COUNTRY, STATION, LOCATION   TARGET • NETWORK • POWER (kW)   World Time

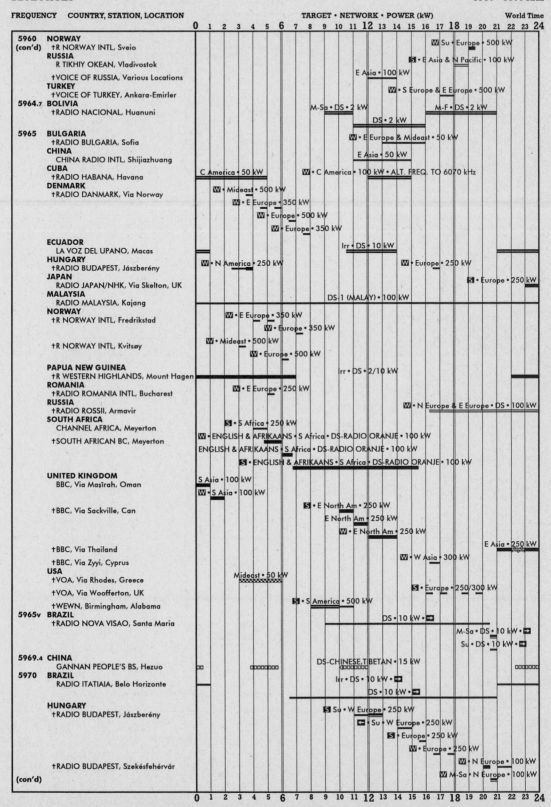

FREQUENCY	COUNTRY, STATION, LOCATION	TARGET • NETWORK • POWER (kW)
5960 (con'd)	NORWAY †R NORWAY INTL, Sveio	W Su • Europe • 500 kW
	RUSSIA R TIKHIY OKEAN, Vladivostok	S • E Asia & N Pacific • 100 kW
	†VOICE OF RUSSIA, Various Locations	E Asia • 100 kW
	TURKEY †VOICE OF TURKEY, Ankara-Emirler	W • S Europe & E Europe • 500 kW
5964.7	BOLIVIA †RADIO NACIONAL, Huanuni	M-Sa • DS • 2 kW M-F • DS • 2 kW DS • 2 kW
5965	BULGARIA †RADIO BULGARIA, Sofia	W • E Europe & Mideast • 50 kW
	CHINA CHINA RADIO INTL, Shijiazhuang	E Asia • 50 kW
	CUBA †RADIO HABANA, Havana	C America • 50 kW W • C America • 100 kW • ALT. FREQ. TO 6070 kHz
	DENMARK †RADIO DANMARK, Via Norway	W • Mideast • 500 kW W • E Europe • 350 kW W • Europe • 500 kW W • Europe • 350 kW
	ECUADOR LA VOZ DEL UPANO, Macas	Irr • DS • 10 kW
	HUNGARY †RADIO BUDAPEST, Jászberény	W • N America • 250 kW W • Europe • 250 kW
	JAPAN RADIO JAPAN/NHK, Via Skelton, UK	S • Europe • 250 kW
	MALAYSIA RADIO MALAYSIA, Kajang	DS-1 (MALAY) • 100 kW
	NORWAY †R NORWAY INTL, Fredrikstad	W • E Europe • 350 kW W • Europe • 350 kW
	†R NORWAY INTL, Kvitsøy	W • Mideast • 500 kW W • Europe • 500 kW
	PAPUA NEW GUINEA †R WESTERN HIGHLANDS, Mount Hagen	Irr • DS • 2/10 kW
	ROMANIA †RADIO ROMANIA INTL, Bucharest	W • E Europe • 250 kW
	RUSSIA †RADIO ROSSII, Armavir	W • N Europe & E Europe • DS • 100 kW
	SOUTH AFRICA CHANNEL AFRICA, Meyerton	S • S Africa • 250 kW
	†SOUTH AFRICAN BC, Meyerton	W • ENGLISH & AFRIKAANS • S Africa • DS-RADIO ORANJE • 100 kW ENGLISH & AFRIKAANS • S Africa • DS-RADIO ORANJE • 100 kW S • ENGLISH & AFRIKAANS • S Africa • DS-RADIO ORANJE • 100 kW
	UNITED KINGDOM BBC, Via Maşīrah, Oman	S Asia • 100 kW W • S Asia • 100 kW
	†BBC, Via Sackville, Can	S • E North Am • 250 kW E North Am • 250 kW W • E North Am • 250 kW
	†BBC, Via Thailand	E Asia • 250 kW
	†BBC, Via Zyyi, Cyprus	W • W Asia • 300 kW
	USA †VOA, Via Rhodes, Greece	Mideast • 50 kW
	†VOA, Via Woofferton, UK	S • Europe • 250/300 kW
	†WEWN, Birmingham, Alabama	S • S America • 500 kW
5965v	BRAZIL †RADIO NOVA VISAO, Santa Maria	DS • 10 kW • ▣ M-Sa • DS • 10 kW • ▣ Su • DS • 10 kW • ▣
5969.4	CHINA GANNAN PEOPLE'S BS, Hezuo	DS-CHINESE, TIBETAN • 15 kW
5970	BRAZIL RADIO ITATIAIA, Belo Horizonte	Irr • DS • 10 kW • ▣ DS • 10 kW • ▣
	HUNGARY †RADIO BUDAPEST, Jászberény	S Su • W Europe • 250 kW ▣ • Su • W Europe • 250 kW S • Europe • 250 kW W • Europe • 250 kW
	†RADIO BUDAPEST, Székésfehérvár	W • N Europe • 100 kW W M-Sa • N Europe • 100 kW
(con'd)		

        0 1 2 3 4 5 6 7 8 9 10 11 12 13 14 15 16 17 18 19 20 21 22 23 24

ENGLISH ▬   ARABIC �   CHINESE □□□   FRENCH ▬▬   GERMAN ▬▬   RUSSIAN ══   SPANISH ▬▬   OTHER ▬

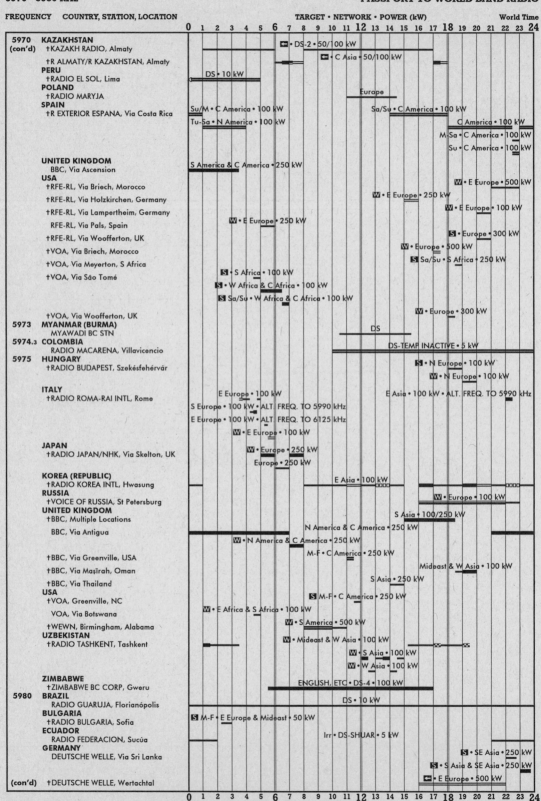

FREQUENCY	COUNTRY, STATION, LOCATION

TARGET • NETWORK • POWER (kW)   World Time

5970 **KAZAKHSTAN**
(con'd) †KAZAKH RADIO, Almaty — DS-2 • 50/100 kW
  †R ALMATY/R KAZAKHSTAN, Almaty — C Asia • 50/100 kW
  PERU
  †RADIO EL SOL, Lima — DS • 10 kW
  POLAND
  †RADIO MARYJA — Europe
  SPAIN
  †R EXTERIOR ESPANA, Via Costa Rica — Su/M • C America • 100 kW / Sa/Su • C America • 100 kW / Tu-Sa • N America • 100 kW / C America • 100 kW / M-Sa • C America • 100 kW / Su • C America • 100 kW

  UNITED KINGDOM
  BBC, Via Ascension — S America & C America • 250 kW
  USA
  †RFE-RL, Via Briech, Morocco — W • E Europe • 500 kW
  †RFE-RL, Via Holzkirchen, Germany — W • E Europe • 250 kW
  †RFE-RL, Via Lampertheim, Germany — W • E Europe • 100 kW
  RFE-RL, Via Pals, Spain — W • E Europe • 250 kW
  †RFE-RL, Via Woofferton, UK — S • Europe • 300 kW
  †VOA, Via Briech, Morocco — W • Europe • 500 kW
  †VOA, Via Meyerton, S Africa — S Sa/Su • S Africa • 250 kW
  †VOA, Via São Tomé — S • S Africa • 100 kW / S • W Africa & C Africa • 100 kW / S Sa/Su • W Africa & C Africa • 100 kW

  †VOA, Via Woofferton, UK — W • Europe • 300 kW
5973 **MYANMAR (BURMA)**
  MYAWADI BC STN — DS
5974.3 **COLOMBIA**
  RADIO MACARENA, Villavicencio — DS-TEMP INACTIVE • 5 kW
5975 **HUNGARY**
  †RADIO BUDAPEST, Szekésfehérvár — S • N Europe • 100 kW / W • N Europe • 100 kW

  ITALY
  †RADIO ROMA-RAI INTL, Rome — E Europe • 100 kW / E Asia • 100 kW • ALT. FREQ. TO 5990 kHz / S Europe • 100 kW • ALT. FREQ. TO 5990 kHz / E Europe • 100 kW • ALT. FREQ. TO 6125 kHz / W • E Europe • 100 kW

  JAPAN
  †RADIO JAPAN/NHK, Via Skelton, UK — W • Europe • 250 kW / Europe • 250 kW

  KOREA (REPUBLIC)
  †RADIO KOREA INTL, Hwasung — E Asia • 100 kW
  RUSSIA
  †VOICE OF RUSSIA, St Petersburg — W • Europe • 100 kW
  UNITED KINGDOM
  †BBC, Multiple Locations — S Asia • 100/250 kW
  BBC, Via Antigua — N America & C America • 250 kW

  †BBC, Via Greenville, USA — W • N America & C America • 250 kW
  †BBC, Via Maşīrah, Oman — M-F • C America • 250 kW / Mideast & W Asia • 100 kW
  †BBC, Via Thailand — S Asia • 250 kW
  USA
  †VOA, Greenville, NC — S M-F • C America • 250 kW
  VOA, Via Botswana — W • E Africa & S Africa • 100 kW
  †WEWN, Birmingham, Alabama — W • S America • 500 kW
  UZBEKISTAN
  †RADIO TASHKENT, Tashkent — W • Mideast & W Asia • 100 kW / W • S Asia • 100 kW / W • W Asia • 100 kW

  ZIMBABWE
  †ZIMBABWE BC CORP, Gweru — ENGLISH, ETC • DS-4 • 100 kW
5980 **BRAZIL**
  RADIO GUARUJA, Florianópolis — DS • 10 kW
  BULGARIA
  †RADIO BULGARIA, Sofia — S M-F • E Europe & Mideast • 50 kW
  ECUADOR
  RADIO FEDERACION, Sucúa — Irr • DS-SHUAR • 5 kW
  GERMANY
  DEUTSCHE WELLE, Via Sri Lanka — S • SE Asia • 250 kW / S • S Asia & SE Asia • 250 kW

(con'd) †DEUTSCHE WELLE, Wertachtal — E Europe • 500 kW

FREQUENCY   COUNTRY, STATION, LOCATION   TARGET • NETWORK • POWER (kW)   World Time

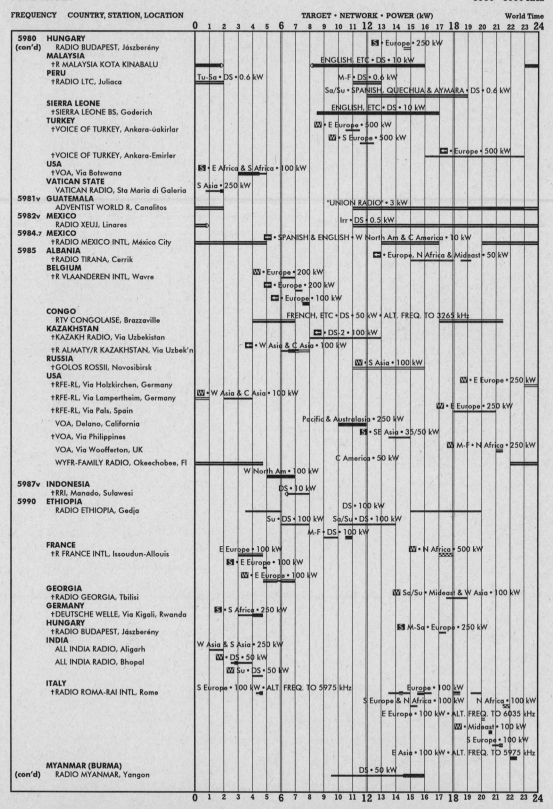

Frequency	Country, Station, Location	Target • Network • Power
5980 (con'd)	**HUNGARY** RADIO BUDAPEST, Jászberény	Ⓢ • Europe • 250 kW
	MALAYSIA †R MALAYSIA KOTA KINABALU	ENGLISH, ETC • DS • 10 kW
	PERU †RADIO LTC, Juliaca	Tu-Sa • DS • 0.6 kW / M-F • DS • 0.6 kW / Sa/Su • SPANISH, QUECHUA & AYMARA • DS • 0.6 kW
	SIERRA LEONE †SIERRA LEONE BS, Goderich	ENGLISH, ETC • DS • 10 kW
	TURKEY †VOICE OF TURKEY, Ankara-úakirlar	W • E Europe • 500 kW / W • S Europe • 500 kW
	†VOICE OF TURKEY, Ankara-Emirler	⬅ • Europe • 500 kW
	USA †VOA, Via Botswana	Ⓢ • E Africa & S Africa • 100 kW
	VATICAN STATE VATICAN RADIO, Sta Maria di Galeria	S Asia • 250 kW
5981v	**GUATEMALA** ADVENTIST WORLD R, Canalitos	"UNION RADIO" • 3 kW
5982v	**MEXICO** RADIO XEUJ, Linares	Irr • DS • 0.5 kW
5984.7	**MEXICO** †RADIO MEXICO INTL, México City	⬅ • SPANISH & ENGLISH • W North Am & C America • 10 kW
5985	**ALBANIA** †RADIO TIRANA, Cerrik	⬅ • Europe, N Africa & Mideast • 50 kW
	BELGIUM †R VLAANDEREN INTL, Wavre	W • Europe • 200 kW / ⬅ • Europe • 200 kW / ⬅ • Europe • 100 kW
	CONGO RTV CONGOLAISE, Brazzaville	FRENCH, ETC • DS • 50 kW • ALT. FREQ. TO 3265 kHz
	KAZAKHSTAN †KAZAKH RADIO, Via Uzbekistan	⬅ • DS-2 • 100 kW
	†R ALMATY/R KAZAKHSTAN, Via Uzbek'n	⬅ • W Asia & C Asia • 100 kW
	RUSSIA †GOLOS ROSSII, Novosibirsk	W • S Asia • 100 kW
	USA †RFE-RL, Via Holzkirchen, Germany	W • E Europe • 250 kW
	†RFE-RL, Via Lampertheim, Germany	W • W Asia & C Asia • 100 kW
	†RFE-RL, Via Pals, Spain	W • E Europe • 250 kW
	VOA, Delano, California	Pacific & Australasia • 250 kW
	†VOA, Via Philippines	Ⓢ • SE Asia • 35/50 kW
	VOA, Via Woofferton, UK	W M-F • N Africa • 250 kW / C America • 50 kW
	WYFR-FAMILY RADIO, Okeechobee, Fl	W North Am • 100 kW
5987v	**INDONESIA** †RRI, Manado, Sulawesi	DS • 10 kW
5990	**ETHIOPIA** RADIO ETHIOPIA, Gedja	DS • 100 kW / Su • DS • 100 kW / Sa/Su • DS • 100 kW / M-F • DS • 100 kW
	FRANCE †R FRANCE INTL, Issoudun-Allouis	E Europe • 100 kW / Ⓢ • E Europe • 100 kW / W • E Europe • 100 kW / W • N Africa • 500 kW
	GEORGIA †RADIO GEORGIA, Tbilisi	W Sa/Su • Mideast & W Asia • 100 kW
	GERMANY †DEUTSCHE WELLE, Via Kigali, Rwanda	Ⓢ • S Africa • 250 kW
	HUNGARY †RADIO BUDAPEST, Jászberény	Ⓢ M-Sa • Europe • 250 kW
	INDIA ALL INDIA RADIO, Aligarh	W Asia & S Asia • 250 kW
	ALL INDIA RADIO, Bhopal	W • DS • 50 kW / W Su • DS • 50 kW
	ITALY †RADIO ROMA-RAI INTL, Rome	S Europe • 100 kW • ALT. FREQ. TO 5975 kHz / Europe • 100 kW / S Europe & N Africa • 100 kW / N Africa • 100 kW / E Europe • 100 kW • ALT. FREQ. TO 6035 kHz / W • Mideast • 100 kW / S Europe • 100 kW / E Asia • 100 kW • ALT. FREQ. TO 5975 kHz
(con'd)	**MYANMAR (BURMA)** RADIO MYANMAR, Yangon	DS • 50 kW

ENGLISH ▬▬   ARABIC ⧖⧖⧖   CHINESE ▫▫▫   FRENCH ▬▬   GERMAN ▬▬   RUSSIAN ══   SPANISH ▬▬   OTHER ▬▬

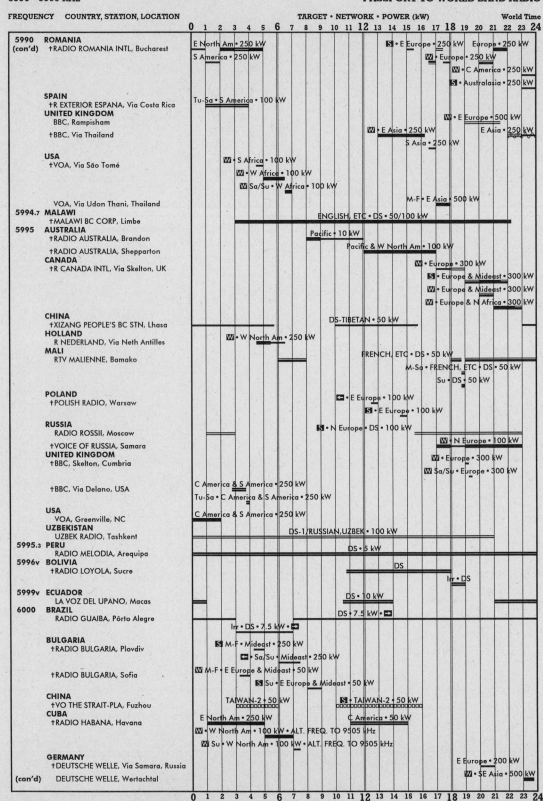

FREQUENCY   COUNTRY, STATION, LOCATION   TARGET • NETWORK • POWER (kW)   World Time

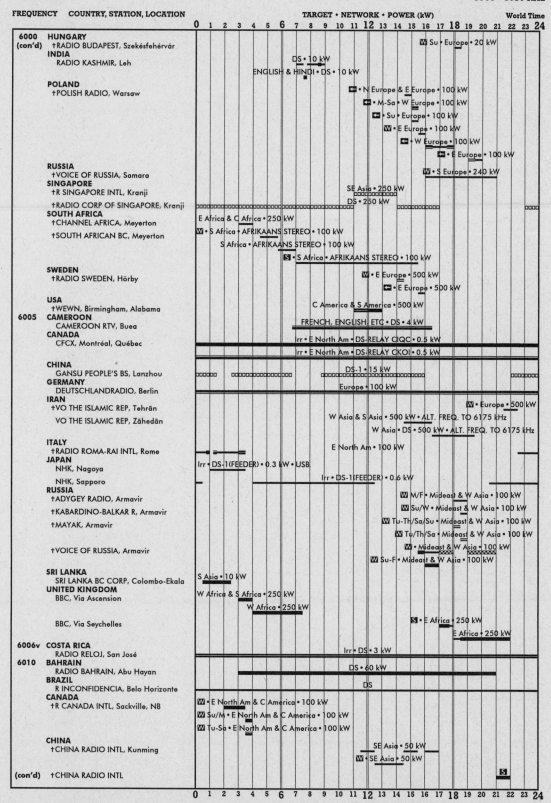

FREQUENCY	COUNTRY, STATION, LOCATION	TARGET • NETWORK • POWER (kW)
6000 (con'd)	**HUNGARY** †RADIO BUDAPEST, Székésfehérvár	W • Su • Europe • 20 kW
	INDIA RADIO KASHMIR, Leh	DS • 10 kW ENGLISH & HINDI • DS • 10 kW
	POLAND †POLISH RADIO, Warsaw	☐ • N Europe & E Europe • 100 kW ☐ • M-Sa • W Europe • 100 kW ☐ • Su • Europe • 100 kW W • E Europe • 100 kW ☐ • W Europe • 100 kW ☐ • E Europe • 100 kW
	RUSSIA †VOICE OF RUSSIA, Samara	W • S Europe • 240 kW
	SINGAPORE †R SINGAPORE INTL, Kranji	SE Asia • 250 kW
	†RADIO CORP OF SINGAPORE, Kranji	DS • 250 kW
	SOUTH AFRICA †CHANNEL AFRICA, Meyerton	E Africa & C Africa • 250 kW
	†SOUTH AFRICAN BC, Meyerton	W • S Africa • AFRIKAANS STEREO • 100 kW S Africa • AFRIKAANS STEREO • 100 kW S • S Africa • AFRIKAANS STEREO • 100 kW
	SWEDEN †RADIO SWEDEN, Hörby	W • E Europe • 500 kW ☐ • E Europe • 500 kW
	USA †WEWN, Birmingham, Alabama	C America & S America • 500 kW
6005	**CAMEROON** CAMEROON RTV, Buea	FRENCH, ENGLISH, ETC • DS • 4 kW
	CANADA CFCX, Montréal, Québec	Irr • E North Am • DS-RELAY CIQC • 0.5 kW Irr • E North Am • DS-RELAY CKOI • 0.5 kW
	CHINA GANSU PEOPLE'S BS, Lanzhou	DS-1 • 15 kW
	GERMANY DEUTSCHLANDRADIO, Berlin	Europe • 100 kW
	IRAN †VO THE ISLAMIC REP, Tehrān	W • Europe • 500 kW
	VO THE ISLAMIC REP, Zāhedān	W Asia & S Asia • 500 kW • ALT. FREQ. TO 6175 kHz W Asia • DS • 500 kW • ALT. FREQ. TO 6175 kHz
	ITALY †RADIO ROMA-RAI INTL, Rome	E North Am • 100 kW
	JAPAN NHK, Nagoya	Irr • DS-1 (FEEDER) • 0.3 kW • USB
	NHK, Sapporo	Irr • DS-1 (FEEDER) • 0.6 kW
	RUSSIA †ADYGEY RADIO, Armavir	W • M/F • Mideast & W Asia • 100 kW
	†KABARDINO-BALKAR R, Armavir	W • Su/W • Mideast & W Asia • 100 kW
	†MAYAK, Armavir	W • Tu-Th/Sa/Su • Mideast & W Asia • 100 kW W • Tu/Th/Sa • Mideast & W Asia • 100 kW
	†VOICE OF RUSSIA, Armavir	W • Mideast & W Asia • 100 kW W • Su-F • Mideast & W Asia • 100 kW
	SRI LANKA SRI LANKA BC CORP, Colombo-Ekala	S Asia • 10 kW
	UNITED KINGDOM BBC, Via Ascension	W Africa & S Africa • 250 kW W Africa • 250 kW
	BBC, Via Seychelles	S • E Africa • 250 kW E Africa • 250 kW
6006v	**COSTA RICA** RADIO RELOJ, San José	Irr • DS • 3 kW
6010	**BAHRAIN** RADIO BAHRAIN, Abu Hayan	DS • 60 kW
	BRAZIL R INCONFIDENCIA, Belo Horizonte	DS
	CANADA †R CANADA INTL, Sackville, NB	W • E North Am & C America • 100 kW W • Su/M • E North Am & C America • 100 kW W • Tu-Sa • E North Am & C America • 100 kW
	CHINA †CHINA RADIO INTL, Kunming	SE Asia • 50 kW W • SE Asia • 50 kW
(con'd)	†CHINA RADIO INTL	S

ENGLISH ▬▬   ARABIC ⧢⧢   CHINESE □□□   FRENCH ▬▬   GERMAN ▬▬   RUSSIAN ═══   SPANISH ▬▬   OTHER ▬▬

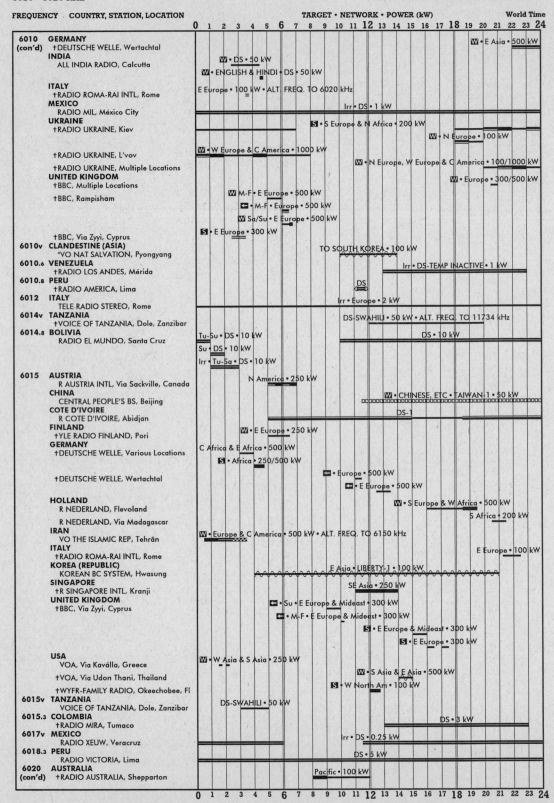

FREQUENCY   COUNTRY, STATION, LOCATION   TARGET • NETWORK • POWER (kW)   World Time

6010 **GERMANY**
(con'd)   †DEUTSCHE WELLE, Wertachtal   W • E Asia • 500 kW
      INDIA
         ALL INDIA RADIO, Calcutta   W • DS • 50 kW
           W • ENGLISH & HINDI • DS • 50 kW
      ITALY
         †RADIO ROMA-RAI INTL, Rome   E Europe • 100 kW • ALT. FREQ. TO 6020 kHz
      MEXICO
         RADIO MIL, México City   Irr • DS • 1 kW
      UKRAINE
         †RADIO UKRAINE, Kiev   S • S Europe & N Africa • 200 kW
           W • N Europe • 100 kW
         †RADIO UKRAINE, L'vov   W • W Europe & C America • 1000 kW
         †RADIO UKRAINE, Multiple Locations   W • N Europe, W Europe & C America • 100/1000 kW
      UNITED KINGDOM
         †BBC, Multiple Locations   W • Europe • 300/500 kW
         †BBC, Rampisham   W M-F • E Europe • 500 kW
           • M-F • Europe • 500 kW
           W Sa/Su • E Europe • 500 kW
         †BBC, Via Zyyi, Cyprus   S • E Europe • 300 kW
6010v **CLANDESTINE (ASIA)**
         "VO NAT SALVATION, Pyongyang   TO SOUTH KOREA • 100 kW
6010.6 **VENEZUELA**
         †RADIO LOS ANDES, Mérida   Irr • DS-TEMP INACTIVE • 1 kW
6010.8 **PERU**
         †RADIO AMERICA, Lima   DS
6012 **ITALY**
         TELE-RADIO STEREO, Rome   Irr • Europe • 2 kW
6014v **TANZANIA**
         †VOICE OF TANZANIA, Dole, Zanzibar   DS-SWAHILI • 50 kW • ALT. FREQ. TO 11734 kHz
6014.8 **BOLIVIA**
         RADIO EL MUNDO, Santa Cruz   Tu-Su • DS • 10 kW   DS • 10 kW
           Su • DS • 10 kW
           Irr • Tu-Sa • DS • 10 kW

6015 **AUSTRIA**
         R AUSTRIA INTL, Via Sackville, Canada   N America • 250 kW
      CHINA
         CENTRAL PEOPLE'S BS, Beijing   W • CHINESE, ETC • TAIWAN-1 • 50 kW
      COTE D'IVOIRE
         R COTE D'IVOIRE, Abidjan   DS-1
      FINLAND
         †YLE RADIO FINLAND, Pori   W • E Europe • 250 kW
      GERMANY
         †DEUTSCHE WELLE, Various Locations   C Africa & E Africa • 500 kW
           S • Africa • 250/500 kW
         †DEUTSCHE WELLE, Wertachtal   • Europe • 500 kW
           • E Europe • 500 kW
      HOLLAND
         R NEDERLAND, Flevoland   W • S Europe & W Africa • 500 kW
         R NEDERLAND, Via Madagascar   S Africa • 200 kW
      IRAN
         VO THE ISLAMIC REP, Tehrān   W • Europe & C America • 500 kW • ALT. FREQ. TO 6150 kHz
      ITALY
         †RADIO ROMA-RAI INTL, Rome   E Europe • 100 kW
      KOREA (REPUBLIC)
         KOREAN BC SYSTEM, Hwasung   E Asia • LIBERTY-1 • 100 kW
      SINGAPORE
         †R SINGAPORE INTL, Kranji   SE Asia • 250 kW
      UNITED KINGDOM
         †BBC, Via Zyyi, Cyprus   • Su • E Europe & Mideast • 300 kW
           • M-F • E Europe & Mideast • 300 kW
           S • E Europe & Mideast • 300 kW
           S • E Europe • 300 kW
      USA
         VOA, Via Kaválla, Greece   W • W Asia & S Asia • 250 kW
         †VOA, Via Udon Thani, Thailand   W • S Asia & E Asia • 500 kW
         †WYFR-FAMILY RADIO, Okeechobee, Fl   S • W North Am • 100 kW
6015v **TANZANIA**
         VOICE OF TANZANIA, Dole, Zanzibar   DS-SWAHILI • 50 kW
6015.3 **COLOMBIA**
         †RADIO MIRA, Tumaco   DS • 3 kW
6017v **MEXICO**
         RADIO XEUW, Veracruz   Irr • DS • 0.25 kW
6018.3 **PERU**
         RADIO VICTORIA, Lima   DS • 5 kW
6020 **AUSTRALIA**
(con'd)   †RADIO AUSTRALIA, Shepparton   Pacific • 100 kW

SEASONAL S OR W   1-HR TIMESHIFT MIDYEAR ⬅ OR ➡   JAMMING / OR /\   EARLIEST HEARD ◁   LATEST HEARD ▷   NEW FOR 1997 †

FREQUENCY   COUNTRY, STATION, LOCATION

TARGET • NETWORK • POWER (kW)

World Time

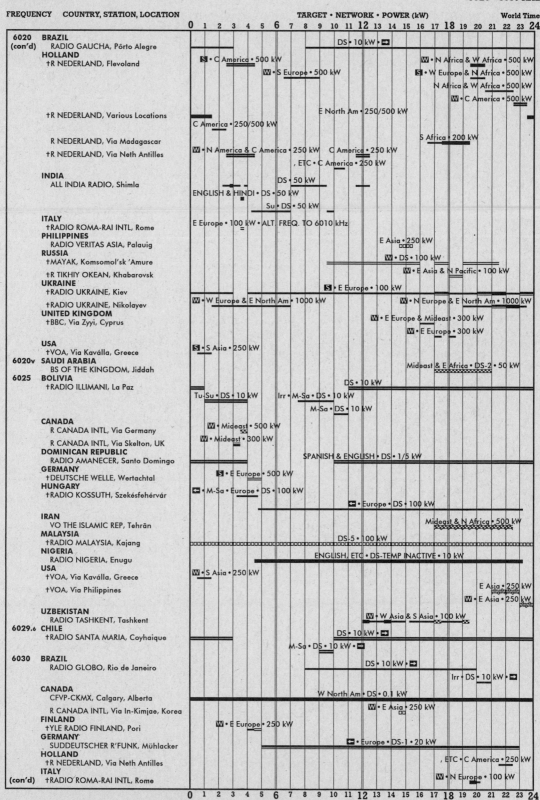

FREQUENCY	COUNTRY, STATION, LOCATION	
6020 (con'd)	**BRAZIL** RADIO GAUCHA, Pôrto Alegre	DS • 10 kW
	HOLLAND †R NEDERLAND, Flevoland	S • C America • 500 kW / W • S Europe • 500 kW / W • N Africa & W Africa • 500 kW / S • W Europe & N Africa • 500 kW / N Africa & W Africa • 500 kW / W • C America • 500 kW
	†R NEDERLAND, Various Locations	E North Am • 250/500 kW / C America • 250/500 kW
	R NEDERLAND, Via Madagascar	S Africa • 200 kW
	†R NEDERLAND, Via Neth Antilles	W • N America & C America • 250 kW C America • 250 kW / , ETC • C America • 250 kW
	INDIA ALL INDIA RADIO, Shimla	DS • 50 kW / ENGLISH & HINDI • DS • 50 kW / Su • DS • 50 kW
	ITALY †RADIO ROMA-RAI INTL, Rome	E Europe • 100 kW • ALT FREQ. TO 6010 kHz
	PHILIPPINES RADIO VERITAS ASIA, Palauig	E Asia • 250 kW
	RUSSIA †MAYAK, Komsomol'sk 'Amure	W • DS • 100 kW
	†R TIKHIY OKEAN, Khabarovsk	W • E Asia & N Pacific • 100 kW
	UKRAINE †RADIO UKRAINE, Kiev	S • E Europe • 100 kW
	†RADIO UKRAINE, Nikolayev	W • W Europe & E North Am • 1000 kW W • N Europe & E North Am • 1000 kW
	UNITED KINGDOM †BBC, Via Zyyi, Cyprus	W • E Europe & Mideast • 300 kW / W • E Europe • 300 kW
	USA †VOA, Via Kaválla, Greece	S • S Asia • 250 kW
6020v	**SAUDI ARABIA** BS OF THE KINGDOM, Jiddah	Mideast & E Africa • DS-2 • 50 kW
6025	**BOLIVIA** †RADIO ILLIMANI, La Paz	DS • 10 kW / Tu-Su • DS • 10 kW Irr • M-Sa • DS • 10 kW / M-Sa • DS • 10 kW
	CANADA R CANADA INTL, Via Germany	W • Mideast • 500 kW
	R CANADA INTL, Via Skelton, UK	W • Mideast • 300 kW
	DOMINICAN REPUBLIC RADIO AMANECER, Santo Domingo	SPANISH & ENGLISH • DS • 1/5 kW
	GERMANY †DEUTSCHE WELLE, Wertachtal	S • E Europe • 500 kW
	HUNGARY †RADIO KOSSUTH, Székésfehérvár	M-Sa • Europe • DS • 100 kW / • Europe • DS • 100 kW
	IRAN VO THE ISLAMIC REP, Tehrān	Mideast & N Africa • 500 kW
	MALAYSIA †RADIO MALAYSIA, Kajang	DS-5 • 100 kW
	NIGERIA RADIO NIGERIA, Enugu	ENGLISH, ETC • DS-TEMP INACTIVE • 10 kW
	USA †VOA, Via Kaválla, Greece	W • S Asia • 250 kW
	†VOA, Via Philippines	E Asia • 250 kW / W • E Asia • 250 kW
	UZBEKISTAN RADIO TASHKENT, Tashkent	W • W Asia & S Asia • 100 kW
6029.6	**CHILE** †RADIO SANTA MARIA, Coyhaique	DS • 10 kW / M-Sa • DS • 10 kW
6030	**BRAZIL** RADIO GLOBO, Rio de Janeiro	DS • 10 kW / Irr • DS • 10 kW
	CANADA CFVP-CKMX, Calgary, Alberta	W North Am • DS • 0.1 kW
	R CANADA INTL, Via In-Kimjae, Korea	W • E Asia • 250 kW
	FINLAND †YLE RADIO FINLAND, Pori	W • E Europe • 250 kW
	GERMANY SUDDEUTSCHER R'FUNK, Mühlacker	• Europe • DS-1 • 20 kW
	HOLLAND †R NEDERLAND, Via Neth Antilles	, ETC • C America • 250 kW
(con'd)	**ITALY** †RADIO ROMA-RAI INTL, Rome	W • N Europe • 100 kW

ENGLISH ▬   ARABIC ⟋⟍⟋   CHINESE □□□   FRENCH ══   GERMAN ▬▬   RUSSIAN ══   SPANISH ▬▬   OTHER ▬

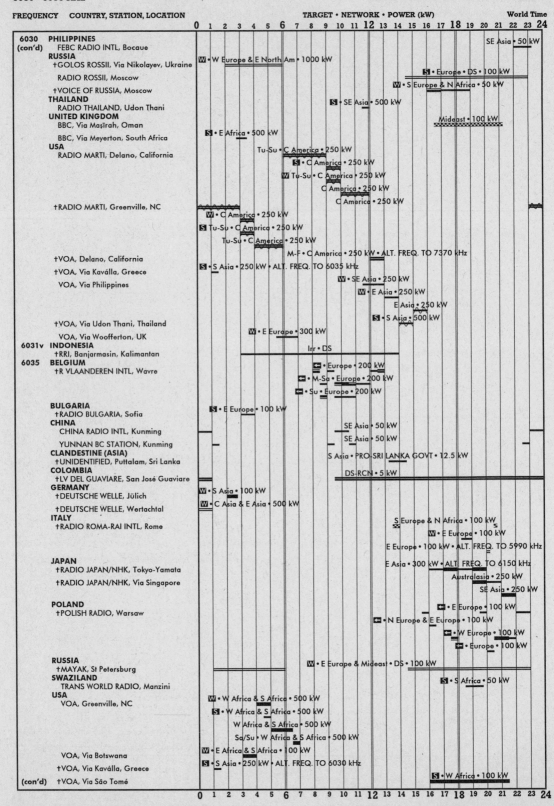

FREQUENCY	COUNTRY, STATION, LOCATION	TARGET • NETWORK • POWER (kW)	World Time

6030 **PHILIPPINES**
(con'd) FEBC RADIO INTL, Bocaue — SE Asia • 50 kW
RUSSIA
†GOLOS ROSSII, Via Nikolayev, Ukraine — W • W Europe & E North Am • 1000 kW
RADIO ROSSII, Moscow — S • Europe • DS • 100 kW
†VOICE OF RUSSIA, Moscow — W • S Europe & N Africa • 50 kW
THAILAND
RADIO THAILAND, Udon Thani — S • SE Asia • 500 kW
UNITED KINGDOM
BBC, Via Maşīrah, Oman — Mideast • 100 kW
BBC, Via Meyerton, South Africa — S • E Africa • 500 kW
USA
RADIO MARTI, Delano, California — Tu-Su • C America • 250 kW
— S • C America • 250 kW
— W Tu-Su • C America • 250 kW
— C America • 250 kW
— C America • 250 kW
†RADIO MARTI, Greenville, NC — W • C America • 250 kW
— S Tu-Su • C America • 250 kW
— Tu-Su • C America • 250 kW
— M-F • C America • 250 kW • ALT. FREQ. TO 7370 kHz
†VOA, Delano, California — S • S Asia • 250 kW • ALT. FREQ. TO 6035 kHz
†VOA, Via Kaválla, Greece — W • SE Asia • 250 kW
VOA, Via Philippines — W • E Asia • 250 kW
— E Asia • 250 kW
— S • S Asia • 500 kW
†VOA, Via Udon Thani, Thailand — W • E Europe • 300 kW
VOA, Via Woofferton, UK
6031v **INDONESIA**
†RRI, Banjarmasin, Kalimantan — Irr • DS
6035 **BELGIUM**
†R VLAANDEREN INTL, Wavre — • Europe • 200 kW
— • M-Sa • Europe • 200 kW
— • Su • Europe • 200 kW
BULGARIA
†RADIO BULGARIA, Sofia — S • E Europe • 100 kW
CHINA
CHINA RADIO INTL, Kunming — SE Asia • 50 kW
YUNNAN BC STATION, Kunming — SE Asia • 50 kW
CLANDESTINE (ASIA)
†UNIDENTIFIED, Puttalam, Sri Lanka — S Asia • PRO-SRI LANKA GOVT • 12.5 kW
COLOMBIA
†LV DEL GUAVIARE, San José Guaviare — DS-RCN • 5 kW
GERMANY
†DEUTSCHE WELLE, Jülich — W • S Asia • 100 kW
†DEUTSCHE WELLE, Wertachtal — W • C Asia & E Asia • 500 kW
ITALY
†RADIO ROMA-RAI INTL, Rome — S Europe & N Africa • 100 kW
— W • E Europe • 100 kW
— E Europe • 100 kW • ALT. FREQ. TO 5990 kHz
— E Asia • 300 kW • ALT. FREQ. TO 6150 kHz
JAPAN
†RADIO JAPAN/NHK, Tokyo-Yamata — Australasia • 250 kW
†RADIO JAPAN/NHK, Via Singapore — SE Asia • 250 kW
POLAND
†POLISH RADIO, Warsaw — • E Europe • 100 kW
— • N Europe & E Europe • 100 kW
— • W Europe • 100 kW
— • Europe • 100 kW
RUSSIA
†MAYAK, St Petersburg — W • E Europe & Mideast • DS • 100 kW
SWAZILAND
TRANS WORLD RADIO, Manzini — S • S Africa • 50 kW
USA
VOA, Greenville, NC — W • W Africa & S Africa • 500 kW
— S • W Africa & S Africa • 500 kW
— W Africa & S Africa • 500 kW
— Sa/Su • W Africa & S Africa • 500 kW
VOA, Via Botswana — W • E Africa & S Africa • 100 kW
†VOA, Via Kaválla, Greece — S • S Asia • 250 kW • ALT. FREQ. TO 6030 kHz
(con'd) †VOA, Via São Tomé — S • W Africa • 100 kW

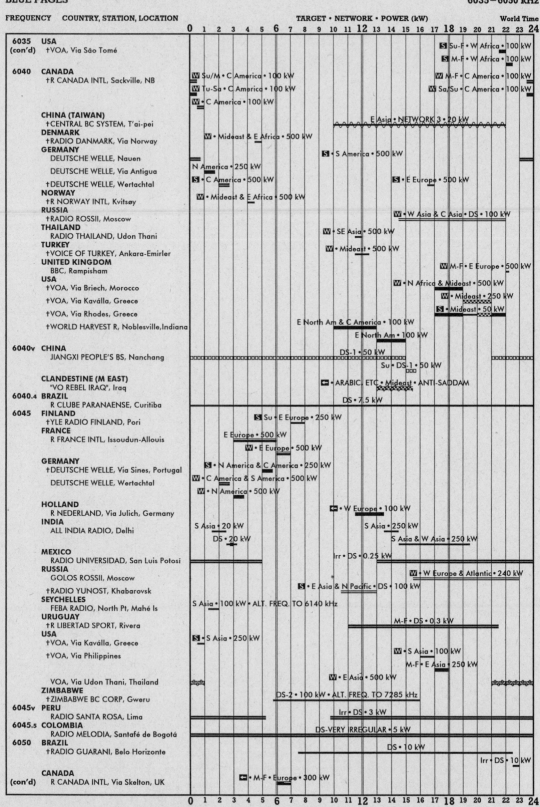

FREQUENCY   COUNTRY, STATION, LOCATION   TARGET • NETWORK • POWER (kW)   World Time

6035 (con'd)	USA — †VOA, Via São Tomé
6040	CANADA — †R CANADA INTL, Sackville, NB
	CHINA (TAIWAN) — †CENTRAL BC SYSTEM, T'ai-pei
	DENMARK — †RADIO DANMARK, Via Norway
	GERMANY — DEUTSCHE WELLE, Nauen
	DEUTSCHE WELLE, Via Antigua
	†DEUTSCHE WELLE, Wertachtal
	NORWAY — †R NORWAY INTL, Kvitsøy
	RUSSIA — †RADIO ROSSII, Moscow
	THAILAND — RADIO THAILAND, Udon Thani
	TURKEY — †VOICE OF TURKEY, Ankara-Emirler
	UNITED KINGDOM — BBC, Rampisham
	USA — †VOA, Via Briech, Morocco
	†VOA, Via Kaválla, Greece
	†VOA, Via Rhodes, Greece
	†WORLD HARVEST R, Noblesville, Indiana
6040v	CHINA — JIANGXI PEOPLE'S BS, Nanchang
	CLANDESTINE (M EAST) — "VO REBEL IRAQ", Iraq
6040.4	BRAZIL — R CLUBE PARANAENSE, Curitiba
6045	FINLAND — †YLE RADIO FINLAND, Pori
	FRANCE — R FRANCE INTL, Issoudun-Allouis
	GERMANY — †DEUTSCHE WELLE, Via Sines, Portugal
	DEUTSCHE WELLE, Wertachtal
	HOLLAND — R NEDERLAND, Via Julich, Germany
	INDIA — ALL INDIA RADIO, Delhi
	MEXICO — RADIO UNIVERSIDAD, San Luis Potosí
	RUSSIA — GOLOS ROSSII, Moscow
	†RADIO YUNOST, Khabarovsk
	SEYCHELLES — FEBA RADIO, North Pt, Mahé Is
	URUGUAY — †R LIBERTAD SPORT, Rivera
	USA — †VOA, Via Kaválla, Greece
	†VOA, Via Philippines
	VOA, Via Udon Thani, Thailand
	ZIMBABWE — †ZIMBABWE BC CORP, Gweru
6045v	PERU — RADIO SANTA ROSA, Lima
6045.5	COLOMBIA — RADIO MELODIA, Santafé de Bogotá
6050	BRAZIL — †RADIO GUARANI, Belo Horizonte
(con'd)	CANADA — R CANADA INTL, Via Skelton, UK

Transmission schedule entries:

- 6035 USA †VOA, Via São Tomé: S Su-F • W Africa • 100 kW; S M-F • W Africa • 100 kW
- 6040 CANADA †R CANADA INTL, Sackville, NB: W Su/M • C America • 100 kW; W Tu-Sa • C America • 100 kW; W • C America • 100 kW; W M-F • C America • 100 kW; W Sa/Su • C America • 100 kW
- CHINA (TAIWAN) †CENTRAL BC SYSTEM: E Asia • NETWORK 3 • 20 kW
- DENMARK †RADIO DANMARK, Via Norway: W • Mideast & E Africa • 500 kW
- GERMANY DEUTSCHE WELLE, Nauen: S • S America • 500 kW
- DEUTSCHE WELLE, Via Antigua: N America • 250 kW
- †DEUTSCHE WELLE, Wertachtal: S • C America • 500 kW; S • E Europe • 500 kW
- NORWAY †R NORWAY INTL, Kvitsøy: W • Mideast & E Africa • 500 kW
- RUSSIA †RADIO ROSSII, Moscow: W • W Asia & C Asia • DS • 100 kW
- THAILAND RADIO THAILAND: W • SE Asia • 500 kW
- TURKEY †VOICE OF TURKEY: W • Mideast • 500 kW
- UNITED KINGDOM BBC, Rampisham: W M-F • E Europe • 500 kW
- USA †VOA, Via Briech, Morocco: W • N Africa & Mideast • 500 kW
- †VOA, Via Kaválla, Greece: W • Mideast • 250 kW
- †VOA, Via Rhodes, Greece: S • Mideast • 50 kW
- †WORLD HARVEST R: E North Am & C America • 100 kW; E North Am • 100 kW
- 6040v CHINA JIANGXI PEOPLE'S BS: DS-1 • 50 kW; Su • DS-1 • 50 kW
- CLANDESTINE (M EAST) "VO REBEL IRAQ": ARABIC, ETC • Mideast • ANTI-SADDAM
- 6040.4 BRAZIL R CLUBE PARANAENSE: DS • 7.5 kW
- 6045 FINLAND †YLE RADIO FINLAND: S Su • E Europe • 250 kW
- FRANCE R FRANCE INTL: E Europe • 500 kW; W • E Europe • 500 kW
- GERMANY †DEUTSCHE WELLE, Via Sines: S • N America & C America • 250 kW
- DEUTSCHE WELLE, Wertachtal: W • C America & S America • 500 kW; W • N America • 500 kW
- HOLLAND R NEDERLAND: • W Europe • 100 kW
- INDIA ALL INDIA RADIO: S Asia • 20 kW; DS • 20 kW; S Asia • 250 kW; S Asia & W Asia • 250 kW
- MEXICO RADIO UNIVERSIDAD: Irr • DS • 0.25 kW
- RUSSIA GOLOS ROSSII: W • W Europe & Atlantic • 240 kW
- †RADIO YUNOST: S • E Asia & N Pacific • DS • 100 kW
- SEYCHELLES FEBA RADIO: S Asia • 100 kW • ALT. FREQ. TO 6140 kHz
- URUGUAY †R LIBERTAD SPORT: M-F • DS • 0.3 kW
- USA †VOA, Via Kaválla, Greece: S • S Asia • 250 kW
- †VOA, Via Philippines: W • S Asia • 100 kW; M-F • E Asia • 250 kW
- VOA, Via Udon Thani, Thailand: W • E Asia • 500 kW
- ZIMBABWE †ZIMBABWE BC CORP: DS-2 • 100 kW • ALT. FREQ. TO 7285 kHz
- 6045v PERU RADIO SANTA ROSA: Irr • DS • 3 kW
- 6045.5 COLOMBIA RADIO MELODIA: DS-VERY IRREGULAR • 5 kW
- 6050 BRAZIL †RADIO GUARANI: DS • 10 kW; Irr • DS • 10 kW
- CANADA R CANADA INTL, Via Skelton, UK: • M-F • Europe • 300 kW

ENGLISH ▬   ARABIC ≋   CHINESE ▫▫▫   FRENCH ▬   GERMAN ▬   RUSSIAN ═   SPANISH ▬   OTHER ▬

FREQUENCY   COUNTRY, STATION, LOCATION   · · · TARGET • NETWORK • POWER (kW) · · · World Time

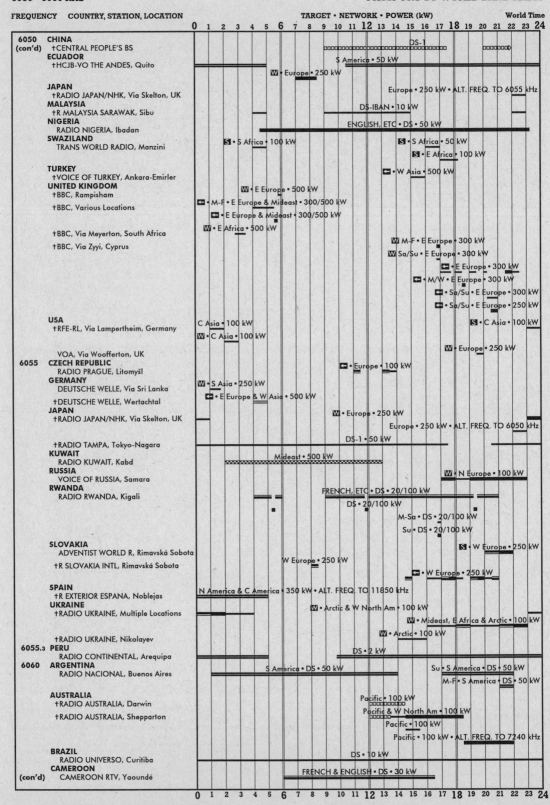

6050
(con'd) **CHINA**
　　†CENTRAL PEOPLE'S BS — DS-1
　ECUADOR
　　†HCJB-VO THE ANDES, Quito — S America • 50 kW
　　　W • Europe • 250 kW
　JAPAN
　　†RADIO JAPAN/NHK, Via Skelton, UK — Europe • 250 kW • ALT. FREQ. TO 6055 kHz
　MALAYSIA
　　†R MALAYSIA SARAWAK, Sibu — DS-IBAN • 10 kW
　NIGERIA
　　RADIO NIGERIA, Ibadan — ENGLISH, ETC • DS • 50 kW
　SWAZILAND
　　TRANS WORLD RADIO, Manzini — S • S Africa • 100 kW
　　　S • S Africa • 50 kW
　　　S • E Africa • 100 kW
　TURKEY
　　†VOICE OF TURKEY, Ankara-Emirler — • W Asia • 500 kW
　UNITED KINGDOM
　　†BBC, Rampisham — W • E Europe • 500 kW
　　†BBC, Various Locations — • M-F • E Europe & Mideast • 300/500 kW
　　　• E Europe & Mideast • 300/500 kW
　　†BBC, Via Meyerton, South Africa — W • E Africa • 500 kW
　　†BBC, Via Zyyi, Cyprus — W M-F • E Europe • 300 kW
　　　W Sa/Su • E Europe • 300 kW
　　　• E Europe • 300 kW
　　　• M/W • E Europe • 300 kW
　　　• Sa/Su • E Europe • 300 kW
　　　• Sa/Su • E Europe • 250 kW
　USA
　　†RFE-RL, Via Lampertheim, Germany — C Asia • 100 kW
　　　W • C Asia • 100 kW
　　　S • C Asia • 100 kW
　　VOA, Via Woofferton, UK — W • Europe • 250 kW
6055 **CZECH REPUBLIC**
　　RADIO PRAGUE, Litomyšl — • Europe • 100 kW
　GERMANY
　　DEUTSCHE WELLE, Via Sri Lanka — W • S Asia • 250 kW
　　†DEUTSCHE WELLE, Wertachtal — • E Europe & W Asia • 500 kW
　JAPAN
　　†RADIO JAPAN/NHK, Via Skelton, UK — W • Europe • 250 kW
　　　Europe • 250 kW • ALT. FREQ. TO 6050 kHz
　　†RADIO TAMPA, Tokyo-Nagara — DS-1 • 50 kW
　KUWAIT
　　RADIO KUWAIT, Kabd — Mideast • 500 kW
　RUSSIA
　　VOICE OF RUSSIA, Samara — W • N Europe • 100 kW
　RWANDA
　　RADIO RWANDA, Kigali — FRENCH, ETC • DS • 20/100 kW
　　　DS • 20/100 kW
　　　M-Sa • DS • 20/100 kW
　　　Su • DS • 20/100 kW
　SLOVAKIA
　　ADVENTIST WORLD R, Rimavská Sobota — S • W Europe • 250 kW
　　†R SLOVAKIA INTL, Rimavská Sobota — W Europe • 250 kW
　　　• W Europe • 250 kW
　SPAIN
　　†R EXTERIOR ESPANA, Noblejas — N America & C America • 350 kW • ALT. FREQ. TO 11850 kHz
　UKRAINE
　　†RADIO UKRAINE, Multiple Locations — W • Arctic & W North Am • 100 kW
　　　W • Mideast, E Africa & Arctic • 100 kW
　　†RADIO UKRAINE, Nikolayev — W • Arctic • 100 kW
6055.3 **PERU**
　　RADIO CONTINENTAL, Arequipa — DS • 2 kW
6060 **ARGENTINA**
　　RADIO NACIONAL, Buenos Aires — S America • DS • 50 kW
　　　Su • S America • DS • 50 kW
　　　M-F • S America • DS • 50 kW
　AUSTRALIA
　　†RADIO AUSTRALIA, Darwin — Pacific • 100 kW
　　†RADIO AUSTRALIA, Shepparton — Pacific & W North Am • 100 kW
　　　Pacific • 100 kW
　　　Pacific • 100 kW • ALT. FREQ. TO 7240 kHz
　BRAZIL
　　RADIO UNIVERSO, Curitiba — DS • 10 kW
　CAMEROON
(con'd) CAMEROON RTV, Yaoundé — FRENCH & ENGLISH • DS • 30 kW

SEASONAL S OR W   1-HR TIMESHIFT MIDYEAR ⊡ OR ⊡   JAMMING / OR ∧   EARLIEST HEARD ◁   LATEST HEARD ▷   NEW FOR 1997 †

FREQUENCY   COUNTRY, STATION, LOCATION

TARGET • NETWORK • POWER (kW)   World Time

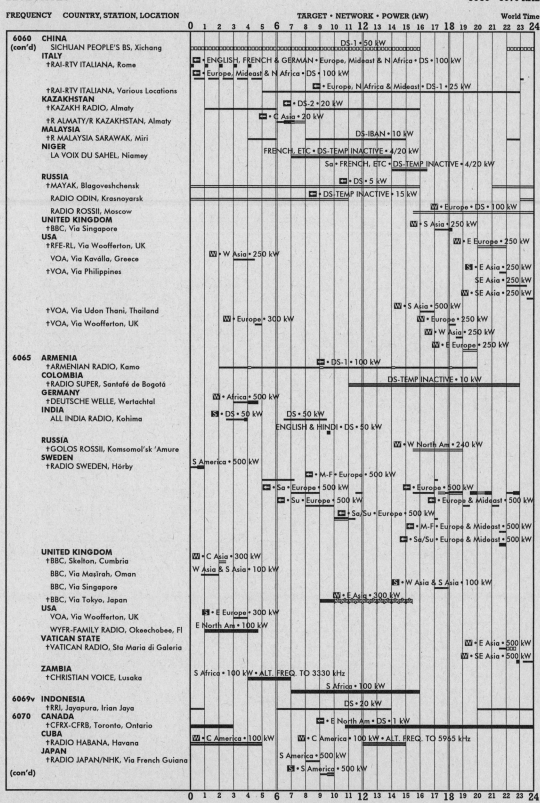

Frequency	Country, Station, Location	Target • Network • Power
6060 (con'd)	**CHINA** SICHUAN PEOPLE'S BS, Xichang	DS-1 • 50 kW
	ITALY †RAI-RTV ITALIANA, Rome	ENGLISH, FRENCH & GERMAN • Europe, Mideast & N Africa • DS • 100 kW
		Europe, Mideast & N Africa • DS • 100 kW
	†RAI-RTV ITALIANA, Various Locations	Europe, N Africa & Mideast • DS-1 • 25 kW
	KAZAKHSTAN †KAZAKH RADIO, Almaty	DS-2 • 20 kW
	†R ALMATY/R KAZAKHSTAN, Almaty	C Asia • 20 kW
	MALAYSIA †R MALAYSIA SARAWAK, Miri	DS-IBAN • 10 kW
	NIGER LA VOIX DU SAHEL, Niamey	FRENCH, ETC • DS-TEMP INACTIVE • 4/20 kW
		Sa • FRENCH, ETC • DS-TEMP INACTIVE • 4/20 kW
	RUSSIA †MAYAK, Blagoveshchensk	DS • 5 kW
	RADIO ODIN, Krasnoyarsk	DS-TEMP INACTIVE • 15 kW
	RADIO ROSSII, Moscow	W • Europe • DS • 100 kW
	UNITED KINGDOM †BBC, Via Singapore	W • S Asia • 250 kW
	USA †RFE-RL, Via Woofferton, UK	W • E Europe • 250 kW
	VOA, Via Kaválla, Greece	W • W Asia • 250 kW
	†VOA, Via Philippines	S • E Asia • 250 kW
		SE Asia • 250 kW
		W • SE Asia • 250 kW
	†VOA, Via Udon Thani, Thailand	W • S Asia • 500 kW
	†VOA, Via Woofferton, UK	W • Europe • 300 kW
		W • Europe • 250 kW
		W • W Asia • 250 kW
		W • E Europe • 250 kW
6065	**ARMENIA** †ARMENIAN RADIO, Kamo	DS-1 • 100 kW
	COLOMBIA †RADIO SUPER, Santafé de Bogotá	DS-TEMP INACTIVE • 10 kW
	GERMANY †DEUTSCHE WELLE, Wertachtal	W • Africa • 500 kW
	INDIA ALL INDIA RADIO, Kohima	S • DS • 50 kW
		DS • 50 kW
		ENGLISH & HINDI • DS • 50 kW
	RUSSIA †GOLOS ROSSII, Komsomol'sk 'Amure	W • W North Am • 240 kW
	SWEDEN †RADIO SWEDEN, Hörby	S America • 500 kW
		M-F • Europe • 500 kW
		Sa • Europe • 500 kW
		Europe • 500 kW
		Su • Europe • 500 kW
		Europe & Mideast • 500 kW
		Sa/Su • Europe • 500 kW
		M-F • Europe & Mideast • 500 kW
		Sa/Su • Europe & Mideast • 500 kW
	UNITED KINGDOM †BBC, Skelton, Cumbria	W • C Asia • 300 kW
	BBC, Via Maşīrah, Oman	W Asia & S Asia • 100 kW
	BBC, Via Singapore	S • W Asia & S Asia • 100 kW
	†BBC, Via Tokyo, Japan	W • E Asia • 300 kW
	USA VOA, Via Woofferton, UK	S • E Europe • 300 kW
	WYFR-FAMILY RADIO, Okeechobee, Fl	E North Am • 100 kW
	VATICAN STATE †VATICAN RADIO, Sta Maria di Galeria	W • E Asia • 500 kW
		W • SE Asia • 500 kW
	ZAMBIA †CHRISTIAN VOICE, Lusaka	S Africa • 100 kW • ALT. FREQ. TO 3330 kHz
		S Africa • 100 kW
6069v	**INDONESIA** †RRI, Jayapura, Irian Jaya	DS • 20 kW
6070	**CANADA** †CFRX-CFRB, Toronto, Ontario	E North Am • DS • 1 kW
	CUBA †RADIO HABANA, Havana	W • C America • 100 kW
		W • C America • 100 kW • ALT. FREQ. TO 5965 kHz
	JAPAN †RADIO JAPAN/NHK, Via French Guiana	S America • 500 kW
		S • S America • 500 kW
(con'd)		

ENGLISH ▬   ARABIC ⌇⌇⌇   CHINESE ▫▫▫   FRENCH ══   GERMAN ▬▬   RUSSIAN ══   SPANISH ══   OTHER ──

FREQUENCY	COUNTRY, STATION, LOCATION	TARGET • NETWORK • POWER (kW)	World Time

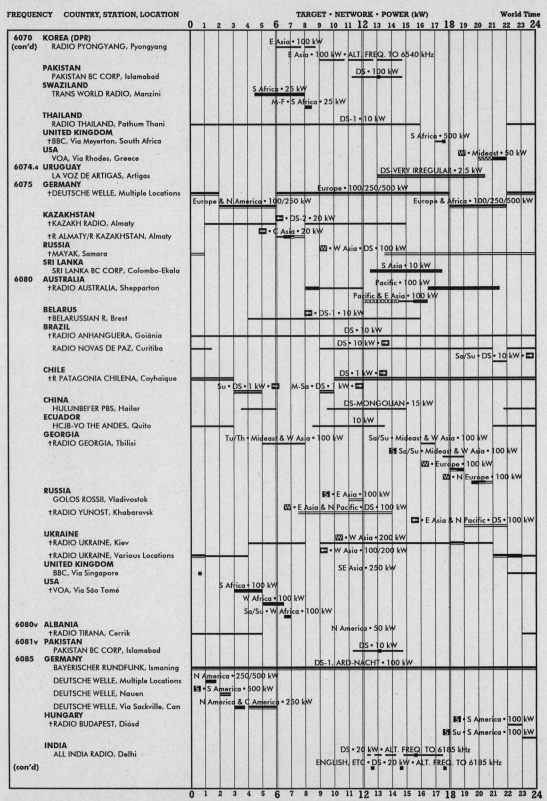

6070 **KOREA (DPR)**
(con'd) RADIO PYONGYANG, Pyongyang — E Asia • 100 kW
— E Asia • 100 kW • ALT. FREQ. TO 6540 kHz

PAKISTAN
PAKISTAN BC CORP, Islamabad — DS • 100 kW
SWAZILAND
TRANS WORLD RADIO, Manzini — S Africa • 25 kW
M-F • S Africa • 25 kW

THAILAND
RADIO THAILAND, Pathum Thani — DS-1 • 10 kW
UNITED KINGDOM
†BBC, Via Meyerton, South Africa — S Africa • 500 kW
USA
VOA, Via Rhodes, Greece — W • Mideast • 50 kW
6074.4 **URUGUAY**
LA VOZ DE ARTIGAS, Artigas — DS • VERY IRREGULAR • 2.5 kW
6075 **GERMANY**
†DEUTSCHE WELLE, Multiple Locations — Europe • 100/250/500 kW
Europe & N America • 100/250 kW   Europe & Africa • 100/250/500 kW

KAZAKHSTAN
†KAZAKH RADIO, Almaty — DS-2 • 20 kW
†R ALMATY/R KAZAKHSTAN, Almaty — C Asia • 20 kW
RUSSIA
†MAYAK, Samara — W • W Asia • DS • 100 kW
SRI LANKA
SRI LANKA BC CORP, Colombo-Ekala — S Asia • 10 kW
6080 **AUSTRALIA**
†RADIO AUSTRALIA, Shepparton — Pacific • 100 kW
Pacific & E Asia • 100 kW

BELARUS
†BELARUSSIAN R, Brest — DS-1 • 10 kW
BRAZIL
†RADIO ANHANGUERA, Goiânia — DS • 10 kW
RADIO NOVAS DE PAZ, Curitiba — DS • 10 kW
Sa/Su • DS • 10 kW

CHILE
†R PATAGONIA CHILENA, Coyhaique — DS • 1 kW
Su • DS • 1 kW   M-Sa • DS • 1 kW
CHINA
HULUNBEI'ER PBS, Hailar — DS-MONGOLIAN • 15 kW
ECUADOR
HCJB-VO THE ANDES, Quito — 10 kW
GEORGIA
†RADIO GEORGIA, Tbilisi — Tu/Th • Mideast & W Asia • 100 kW   Sa/Su • Mideast & W Asia • 100 kW
S Sa/Su • Mideast & W Asia • 100 kW
W • Europe • 100 kW
W • N Europe • 100 kW

RUSSIA
GOLOS ROSSII, Vladivostok — S • E Asia • 100 kW
†RADIO YUNOST, Khabarovsk — W • E Asia & N Pacific • DS • 100 kW
E Asia & N Pacific • DS • 100 kW

UKRAINE
†RADIO UKRAINE, Kiev — W • W Asia • 200 kW
†RADIO UKRAINE, Various Locations — W • W Asia • 100/200 kW
UNITED KINGDOM
BBC, Via Singapore — SE Asia • 250 kW
USA
†VOA, Via São Tomé — S Africa • 100 kW
W Africa • 100 kW
Sa/Su • W Africa • 100 kW

6080v **ALBANIA**
†RADIO TIRANA, Cerrik — N America • 50 kW
6081v **PAKISTAN**
PAKISTAN BC CORP, Islamabad — DS • 10 kW
6085 **GERMANY**
BAYERISCHER RUNDFUNK, Ismaning — DS-1, ARD-NACHT • 100 kW
DEUTSCHE WELLE, Multiple Locations — N America • 250/500 kW
DEUTSCHE WELLE, Nauen — S • S America • 500 kW
DEUTSCHE WELLE, Via Sackville, Can — N America & C America • 250 kW
HUNGARY
†RADIO BUDAPEST, Diósd — S • S America • 100 kW
S Su • S America • 100 kW

INDIA
ALL INDIA RADIO, Delhi — DS • 20 kW • ALT. FREQ. TO 6185 kHz
ENGLISH, ETC • DS • 20 kW • ALT. FREQ. TO 6185 kHz

(con'd)

FREQUENCY   COUNTRY, STATION, LOCATION   TARGET • NETWORK • POWER (kW)   World Time

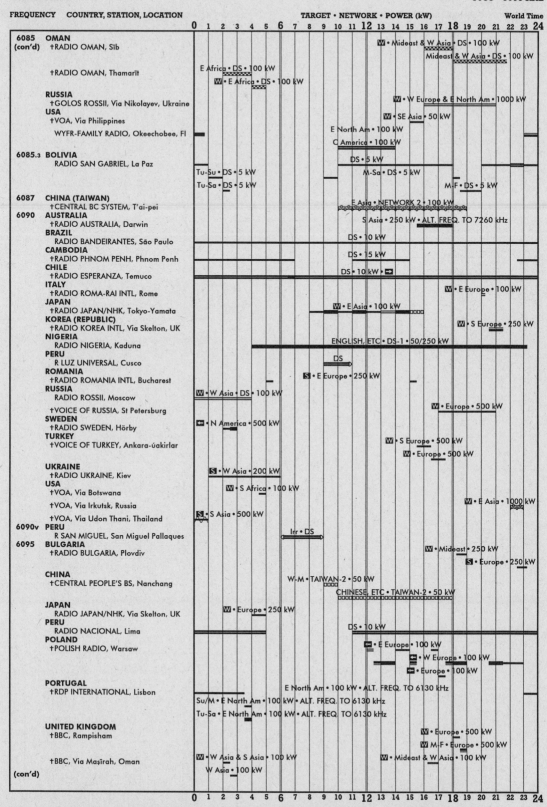

6085 (con'd) OMAN
  †RADIO OMAN, Sīb — W • Mideast & W Asia • DS • 100 kW; Mideast & W Asia • DS • 100 kW
  †RADIO OMAN, Thamarīt — E Africa • DS • 100 kW; W • E Africa • DS • 100 kW

RUSSIA
  †GOLOS ROSSII, Via Nikolayev, Ukraine — W • W Europe & E North Am • 1000 kW
USA
  †VOA, Via Philippines — W • SE Asia • 50 kW
  WYFR-FAMILY RADIO, Okeechobee, Fl — E North Am • 100 kW; C America • 100 kW

6085.3 BOLIVIA
  RADIO SAN GABRIEL, La Paz — DS • 5 kW; Tu-Su • DS • 5 kW; M-Sa • DS • 5 kW; Tu-Sa • DS • 5 kW; M-F • DS • 5 kW

6087 CHINA (TAIWAN)
  †CENTRAL BC SYSTEM, T'ai-pei — E Asia • NETWORK 2 • 100 kW
6090 AUSTRALIA
  †RADIO AUSTRALIA, Darwin — S Asia • 250 kW • ALT. FREQ. TO 7260 kHz
BRAZIL
  RADIO BANDEIRANTES, São Paulo — DS • 10 kW
CAMBODIA
  †RADIO PHNOM PENH, Phnom Penh — DS • 15 kW
CHILE
  †RADIO ESPERANZA, Temuco — DS • 10 kW •
ITALY
  †RADIO ROMA-RAI INTL, Rome — W • E Europe • 100 kW
JAPAN
  †RADIO JAPAN/NHK, Tokyo-Yamata — W • E Asia • 100 kW
KOREA (REPUBLIC)
  †RADIO KOREA INTL, Via Skelton, UK — W • S Europe • 250 kW
NIGERIA
  RADIO NIGERIA, Kaduna — ENGLISH, ETC • DS-1 • 50/250 kW
PERU
  R LUZ UNIVERSAL, Cusco — DS
ROMANIA
  †RADIO ROMANIA INTL, Bucharest — S • E Europe • 250 kW
RUSSIA
  RADIO ROSSII, Moscow — W • W Asia • DS • 100 kW
  †VOICE OF RUSSIA, St Petersburg — W • Europe • 500 kW
SWEDEN
  †RADIO SWEDEN, Hörby — N America • 500 kW
TURKEY
  †VOICE OF TURKEY, Ankara-úakirlar — W • S Europe • 500 kW; W • Europe • 500 kW
UKRAINE
  †RADIO UKRAINE, Kiev — S • W Asia • 200 kW
USA
  †VOA, Via Botswana — W • S Africa • 100 kW
  †VOA, Via Irkutsk, Russia — W • E Asia • 1000 kW
  †VOA, Via Udon Thani, Thailand — S • S Asia • 500 kW
6090v PERU
  R SAN MIGUEL, San Miguel Pallaques — Irr • DS
6095 BULGARIA
  †RADIO BULGARIA, Plovdiv — W • Mideast • 250 kW; S • Europe • 250 kW

CHINA
  †CENTRAL PEOPLE'S BS, Nanchang — W-M • TAIWAN-2 • 50 kW; CHINESE, ETC • TAIWAN-2 • 50 kW

JAPAN
  RADIO JAPAN/NHK, Via Skelton, UK — W • Europe • 250 kW
PERU
  RADIO NACIONAL, Lima — DS • 10 kW
POLAND
  †POLISH RADIO, Warsaw — • E Europe • 100 kW; • W Europe • 100 kW; • Europe • 100 kW

PORTUGAL
  †RDP INTERNATIONAL, Lisbon — E North Am • 100 kW • ALT. FREQ. TO 6130 kHz; Su/M • E North Am • 100 kW • ALT. FREQ. TO 6130 kHz; Tu-Sa • E North Am • 100 kW • ALT. FREQ. TO 6130 kHz

UNITED KINGDOM
  †BBC, Rampisham — W • Europe • 500 kW; W M-F • Europe • 500 kW
  †BBC, Via Maşīrah, Oman — W • W Asia & S Asia • 100 kW; W Asia • 100 kW; W • Mideast & W Asia • 100 kW

(con'd)

ENGLISH ▬   ARABIC ▨   CHINESE ▱   FRENCH ▬   GERMAN ▬   RUSSIAN ▬   SPANISH ▬   OTHER ▬

FREQUENCY   COUNTRY, STATION, LOCATION   TARGET • NETWORK • POWER (kW)   World Time

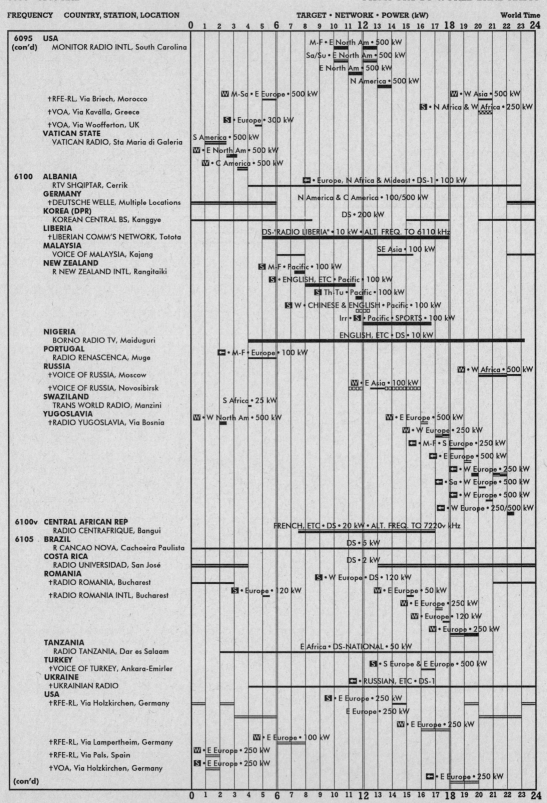

6095   **USA**
(con'd)   MONITOR RADIO INTL, South Carolina
- M-F • E North Am • 500 kW
- Sa/Su • E North Am • 500 kW
- E North Am • 500 kW
- N America • 500 kW

†RFE-RL, Via Briech, Morocco   W • M-Sa • E Europe • 500 kW   W • W Asia • 500 kW

†VOA, Via Kaválla, Greece   S • N Africa & W Africa • 250 kW

†VOA, Via Woofferton, UK   S • Europe • 300 kW

VATICAN STATE
   VATICAN RADIO, Sta Maria di Galeria
- S America • 500 kW
- W • E North Am • 500 kW
- W • C America • 500 kW

6100   **ALBANIA**
   RTV SHQIPTAR, Cerrik   • Europe, N Africa & Mideast • DS-1 • 100 kW

GERMANY
   †DEUTSCHE WELLE, Multiple Locations   N America & C America • 100/500 kW

KOREA (DPR)
   KOREAN CENTRAL BS, Kanggye   DS • 200 kW

LIBERIA
   †LIBERIAN COMM'S NETWORK, Totota   DS • "RADIO LIBERIA" • 10 kW • ALT. FREQ. TO 6110 kHz

MALAYSIA
   VOICE OF MALAYSIA, Kajang   SE Asia • 100 kW

NEW ZEALAND
   R NEW ZEALAND INTL, Rangitaiki
- S • M-F • Pacific • 100 kW
- S • ENGLISH, ETC • Pacific • 100 kW
- S • Th-Tu • Pacific • 100 kW
- S W • CHINESE & ENGLISH • Pacific • 100 kW
- Irr • S • Pacific • SPORTS • 100 kW

NIGERIA
   BORNO RADIO TV, Maiduguri   ENGLISH, ETC • DS • 10 kW

PORTUGAL
   RADIO RENASCENCA, Muge   • M-F • Europe • 100 kW

RUSSIA
   †VOICE OF RUSSIA, Moscow   W • W Africa • 500 kW

   †VOICE OF RUSSIA, Novosibirsk   W • E Asia • 100 kW

SWAZILAND
   TRANS WORLD RADIO, Manzini   S Africa • 25 kW

YUGOSLAVIA
   †RADIO YUGOSLAVIA, Via Bosnia
- W • W North Am • 500 kW
- W • E Europe • 500 kW
- W • W Europe • 250 kW
- • M-F • S Europe • 250 kW
- • E Europe • 500 kW
- • W Europe • 250 kW
- • Sa • W Europe • 500 kW
- • W Europe • 500 kW
- • W Europe • 250/500 kW

6100v   **CENTRAL AFRICAN REP**
   RADIO CENTRAFRIQUE, Bangui   FRENCH, ETC • DS • 20 kW • ALT. FREQ. TO 7220v kHz

6105   **BRAZIL**
   R CANCAO NOVA, Cachoeira Paulista   DS • 5 kW

COSTA RICA
   RADIO UNIVERSIDAD, San José   DS • 2 kW

ROMANIA
   †RADIO ROMANIA, Bucharest   S • W Europe • DS • 120 kW

   †RADIO ROMANIA INTL, Bucharest
- S • Europe • 120 kW
- W • E Europe • 50 kW
- W • E Europe • 250 kW
- W • Europe • 120 kW
- W • Europe • 250 kW

TANZANIA
   RADIO TANZANIA, Dar es Salaam   E Africa • DS-NATIONAL • 50 kW

TURKEY
   †VOICE OF TURKEY, Ankara-Emirler   S • S Europe & E Europe • 500 kW

UKRAINE
   †UKRAINIAN RADIO   • RUSSIAN, ETC • DS-1

USA
   †RFE-RL, Via Holzkirchen, Germany
- S • E Europe • 250 kW
- E Europe • 250 kW
- W • E Europe • 250 kW

   †RFE-RL, Via Lampertheim, Germany   W • E Europe • 100 kW

   †RFE-RL, Via Pals, Spain   W • E Europe • 250 kW

   †VOA, Via Holzkirchen, Germany   S • E Europe • 250 kW

   • E Europe • 250 kW

(con'd)

FREQUENCY   COUNTRY, STATION, LOCATION   TARGET • NETWORK • POWER (kW)   World Time

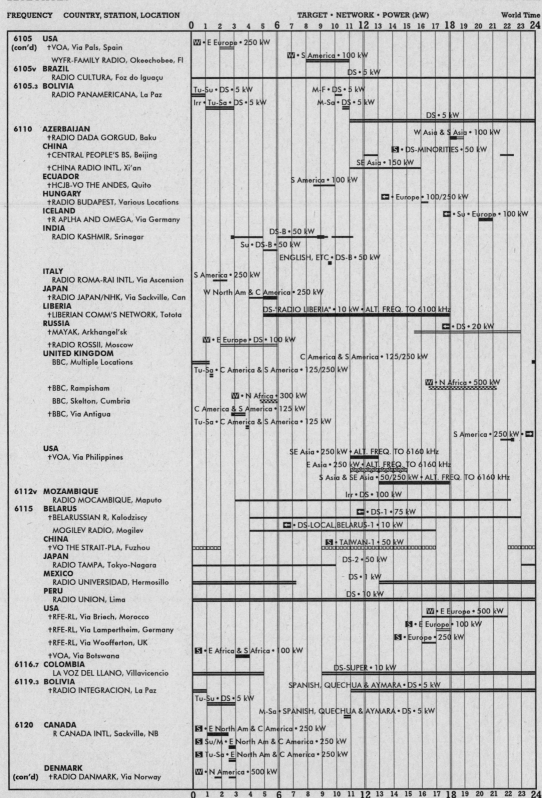

Frequency	Country, Station, Location	Target • Network • Power
6105 (con'd)	USA · †VOA, Via Pals, Spain	W • E Europe • 250 kW
		W • S America • 100 kW
	WYFR-FAMILY RADIO, Okeechobee, Fl	
6105v	BRAZIL · RADIO CULTURA, Foz do Iguaçu	DS • 5 kW
6105.3	BOLIVIA · RADIO PANAMERICANA, La Paz	Tu-Su • DS • 5 kW M-F • DS • 5 kW
		Irr • Tu-Sa • DS • 5 kW M-Sa • DS • 5 kW
		DS • 5 kW
6110	AZERBAIJAN · †RADIO DADA GORGUD, Baku	W Asia & S Asia • 100 kW
	CHINA · †CENTRAL PEOPLE'S BS, Beijing	S • DS-MINORITIES • 50 kW
	†CHINA RADIO INTL, Xi'an	SE Asia • 150 kW
	ECUADOR · †HCJB-VO THE ANDES, Quito	S America • 100 kW
	HUNGARY · †RADIO BUDAPEST, Various Locations	• Europe • 100/250 kW
	ICELAND · †R APLHA AND OMEGA, Via Germany	• Su • Europe • 100 kW
	INDIA · RADIO KASHMIR, Srinagar	DS-B • 50 kW
		Su • DS-B • 50 kW
		ENGLISH, ETC • DS-B • 50 kW
	ITALY · RADIO ROMA-RAI INTL, Via Ascension	S America • 250 kW
	JAPAN · †RADIO JAPAN/NHK, Via Sackville, Can	W North Am & C America • 250 kW
	LIBERIA · †LIBERIAN COMM'S NETWORK, Totota	DS-"RADIO LIBERIA" • 10 kW • ALT. FREQ. TO 6100 kHz
	RUSSIA · †MAYAK, Arkhangel'sk	• DS • 20 kW
	†RADIO ROSSII, Moscow	W • E Europe • DS • 100 kW
	UNITED KINGDOM · BBC, Multiple Locations	C America & S America • 125/250 kW
		Tu-Sa • C America & S America • 125/250 kW
	†BBC, Rampisham	W • N Africa • 500 kW
	BBC, Skelton, Cumbria	W • N Africa • 300 kW
	†BBC, Via Antigua	C America & S America • 125 kW
		Tu-Sa • C America & S America • 125 kW
		S America • 250 kW •
	USA · †VOA, Via Philippines	SE Asia • 250 kW • ALT. FREQ. TO 6160 kHz
		E Asia • 250 kW • ALT. FREQ. TO 6160 kHz
		S Asia & SE Asia • 50/250 kW • ALT. FREQ. TO 6160 kHz
6112v	MOZAMBIQUE · RADIO MOCAMBIQUE, Maputo	Irr • DS • 100 kW
6115	BELARUS · †BELARUSSIAN R, Kalodziscy	• DS-1 • 75 kW
	MOGILEV RADIO, Mogilev	• DS-LOCAL BELARUS-1 • 10 kW
	CHINA · †VO THE STRAIT-PLA, Fuzhou	S • TAIWAN-1 • 50 kW
	JAPAN · RADIO TAMPA, Tokyo-Nagara	DS-2 • 50 kW
	MEXICO · RADIO UNIVERSIDAD, Hermosillo	DS • 1 kW
	PERU · RADIO UNION, Lima	DS • 10 kW
	USA · †RFE-RL, Via Briech, Morocco	W • E Europe • 500 kW
	†RFE-RL, Via Lampertheim, Germany	S • E Europe • 100 kW
	†RFE-RL, Via Woofferton, UK	S • Europe • 250 kW
	†VOA, Via Botswana	S • E Africa & S Africa • 100 kW
6116.7	COLOMBIA · LA VOZ DEL LLANO, Villavicencio	DS-SUPER • 10 kW
6119.3	BOLIVIA · †RADIO INTEGRACION, La Paz	SPANISH, QUECHUA & AYMARA • DS • 5 kW
		Tu-Su • DS • 5 kW
		M-Sa • SPANISH, QUECHUA & AYMARA • DS • 5 kW
6120	CANADA · R CANADA INTL, Sackville, NB	S • E North Am & C America • 250 kW
		S • Su/M • E North Am & C America • 250 kW
		S • Tu-Sa • E North Am & C America • 250 kW
(con'd)	DENMARK · †RADIO DANMARK, Via Norway	W • N America • 500 kW

0 1 2 3 4 5 6 7 8 9 10 11 12 13 14 15 16 17 18 19 20 21 22 23 24

ENGLISH ▬   ARABIC ⬚⬚⬚   CHINESE ⬚⬚⬚   FRENCH ▬   GERMAN ▬   RUSSIAN ═   SPANISH ▬   OTHER ▬

| FREQUENCY | COUNTRY, STATION, LOCATION | TARGET • NETWORK • POWER (kW) | World Time |

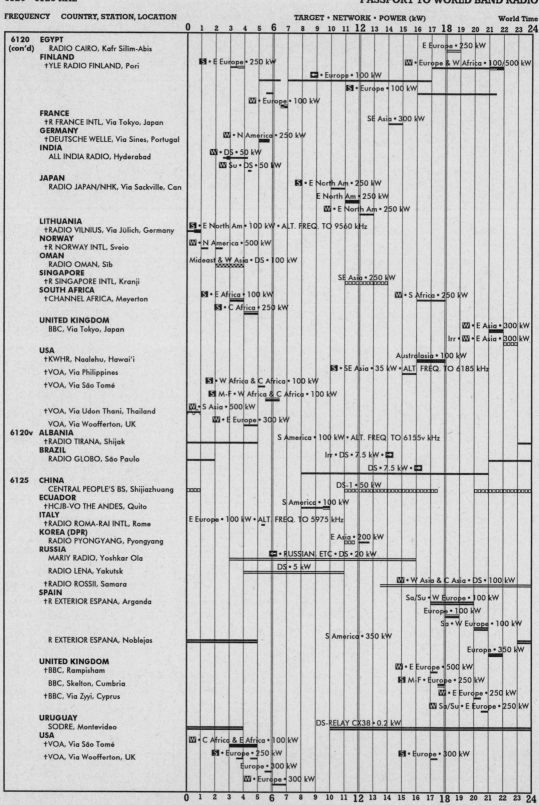

6120 (con'd)
- **EGYPT** — RADIO CAIRO, Kafr Silim-Abis — E Europe • 250 kW
- **FINLAND** — †YLE RADIO FINLAND, Pori — S • E Europe • 250 kW — W • Europe & W Africa • 100/500 kW — ⬌ • Europe • 100 kW — S • Europe • 100 kW — W • Europe • 100 kW
- **FRANCE** — †R FRANCE INTL, Via Tokyo, Japan — SE Asia • 300 kW
- **GERMANY** — †DEUTSCHE WELLE, Via Sines, Portugal — W • N America • 250 kW
- **INDIA** — ALL INDIA RADIO, Hyderabad — W • DS • 50 kW — W Su • DS • 50 kW
- **JAPAN** — RADIO JAPAN/NHK, Via Sackville, Can — S • E North Am • 250 kW — E North Am • 250 kW — W • E North Am • 250 kW
- **LITHUANIA** — †RADIO VILNIUS, Via Jülich, Germany — S • E North Am • 100 kW • ALT. FREQ. TO 9560 kHz
- **NORWAY** — †R NORWAY INTL, Sveio — W • N America • 500 kW
- **OMAN** — RADIO OMAN, Sib — Mideast & W Asia • DS • 100 kW
- **SINGAPORE** — †R SINGAPORE INTL, Kranji — SE Asia • 250 kW
- **SOUTH AFRICA** — †CHANNEL AFRICA, Meyerton — S • E Africa • 100 kW — W • S Africa • 250 kW — S • C Africa • 250 kW
- **UNITED KINGDOM** — BBC, Via Tokyo, Japan — W • E Asia • 300 kW — Irr • W • E Asia • 300 kW
- **USA** — †KWHR, Naalehu, Hawai'i — Australasia • 100 kW
  - †VOA, Via Philippines — S • SE Asia • 35 kW • ALT FREQ. TO 6185 kHz
  - †VOA, Via São Tomé — S • W Africa & C Africa • 100 kW — M-F • W Africa & C Africa • 100 kW
  - †VOA, Via Udon Thani, Thailand — W • S Asia • 500 kW
  - VOA, Via Woofferton, UK — W • E Europe • 300 kW

6120v
- **ALBANIA** — †RADIO TIRANA, Shijak — S America • 100 kW • ALT. FREQ TO 6155v kHz
- **BRAZIL** — RADIO GLOBO, São Paulo — Irr • DS • 7.5 kW • ⬌ — DS • 7.5 kW • ⬌

6125
- **CHINA** — CENTRAL PEOPLE'S BS, Shijiazhuang — DS-1 • 50 kW
- **ECUADOR** — †HCJB-VO THE ANDES, Quito — S America • 100 kW
- **ITALY** — †RADIO ROMA-RAI INTL, Rome — E Europe • 100 kW • ALT. FREQ. TO 5975 kHz
- **KOREA (DPR)** — RADIO PYONGYANG, Pyongyang — E Asia • 200 kW
- **RUSSIA** — MARIY RADIO, Yoshkar Ola — ⬌ • RUSSIAN, ETC • DS • 20 kW
  - RADIO LENA, Yakutsk — DS • 5 kW
  - †RADIO ROSSII, Samara — W • W Asia & C Asia • DS • 100 kW
- **SPAIN** — †R EXTERIOR ESPANA, Arganda — Sa/Su • W Europe • 100 kW — Europe • 100 kW — Sa • W Europe • 100 kW
  - R EXTERIOR ESPANA, Noblejas — S America • 350 kW — Europe • 350 kW
- **UNITED KINGDOM** — †BBC, Rampisham — W • E Europe • 500 kW
  - BBC, Skelton, Cumbria — S • M-F • Europe • 250 kW
  - †BBC, Via Zyyi, Cyprus — W • E Europe • 250 kW — W Sa/Su • E Europe • 250 kW
- **URUGUAY** — SODRE, Montevideo — DS-RELAY CX38 • 0.2 kW
- **USA** — †VOA, Via São Tomé — W • C Africa & E Africa • 100 kW
  - †VOA, Via Woofferton, UK — S • Europe • 250 kW — Europe • 300 kW — W • Europe • 300 kW — S • Europe • 300 kW

FREQUENCY   COUNTRY, STATION, LOCATION

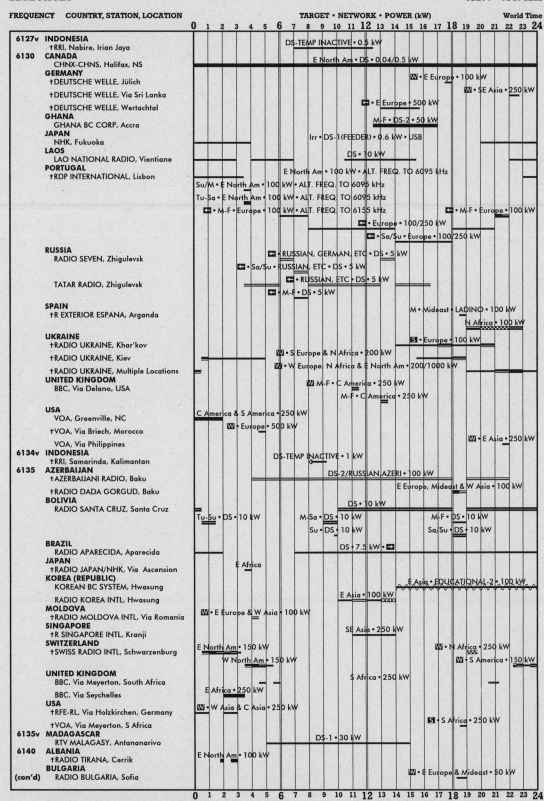

Frequency	Country, Station, Location	Target • Network • Power (kW)
6127v	INDONESIA †RRI, Nabire, Irian Jaya	DS-TEMP INACTIVE • 0.5 kW
6130	CANADA CHNX-CHNS, Halifax, NS	E North Am • DS • 0.04/0.5 kW
	GERMANY †DEUTSCHE WELLE, Jülich	W • E Europe • 100 kW
	†DEUTSCHE WELLE, Via Sri Lanka	W • SE Asia • 250 kW
	†DEUTSCHE WELLE, Wertachtal	E Europe • 500 kW
	GHANA GHANA BC CORP, Accra	M-F • DS-2 • 50 kW
	JAPAN NHK, Fukuoka	Irr • DS-1 (FEEDER) • 0.6 kW • USB
	LAOS LAO NATIONAL RADIO, Vientiane	DS • 10 kW
	PORTUGAL †RDP INTERNATIONAL, Lisbon	E North Am • 100 kW • ALT. FREQ. TO 6095 kHz
		Su/M • E North Am • 100 kW • ALT. FREQ. TO 6095 kHz
		Tu-Sa • E North Am • 100 kW • ALT. FREQ. TO 6095 kHz
		M-F • Europe • 100 kW • ALT. FREQ. TO 6155 kHz / M-F • Europe • 100 kW
		• Europe • 100/250 kW
		Sa/Su • Europe • 100/250 kW
	RUSSIA RADIO SEVEN, Zhigulevsk	RUSSIAN, GERMAN, ETC • DS • 5 kW
		Sa/Su • RUSSIAN, ETC • DS • 5 kW
	TATAR RADIO, Zhigulevsk	RUSSIAN, ETC • DS • 5 kW
		M-F • DS • 5 kW
	SPAIN †R EXTERIOR ESPANA, Arganda	M • Mideast • LADINO • 100 kW
		N Africa • 100 kW
	UKRAINE †RADIO UKRAINE, Khar'kov	S • Europe • 100 kW
	†RADIO UKRAINE, Kiev	W • S Europe & N Africa • 200 kW
	†RADIO UKRAINE, Multiple Locations	W • W Europe, N Africa & E North Am • 200/1000 kW
	UNITED KINGDOM BBC, Via Delano, USA	W M-F • C America • 250 kW
		M-F • C America • 250 kW
	USA VOA, Greenville, NC	C America & S America • 250 kW
	†VOA, Via Briech, Morocco	W • Europe • 500 kW
	VOA, Via Philippines	W • E Asia • 250 kW
6134v	INDONESIA †RRI, Samarinda, Kalimantan	DS-TEMP INACTIVE • 1 kW
6135	AZERBAIJAN †AZERBAIJANI RADIO, Baku	DS-2/RUSSIAN, AZERI • 100 kW
	†RADIO DADA GORGUD, Baku	E Europe, Mideast & W Asia • 100 kW
	BOLIVIA RADIO SANTA CRUZ, Santa Cruz	DS • 10 kW
		Tu-Su • DS • 10 kW / M-Sa • DS • 10 kW / M-F • DS • 10 kW
		Su • DS • 10 kW / Sa/Su • DS • 10 kW
	BRAZIL RADIO APARECIDA, Aparecida	DS • 7.5 kW •
	JAPAN †RADIO JAPAN/NHK, Via Ascension	E Africa
	KOREA (REPUBLIC) KOREAN BC SYSTEM, Hwasung	E Asia • EDUCATIONAL-2 • 100 kW
	RADIO KOREA INTL, Hwasung	E Asia • 100 kW
	MOLDOVA †RADIO MOLDOVA INTL, Via Romania	W • E Europe & W Asia • 100 kW
	SINGAPORE †R SINGAPORE INTL, Kranji	SE Asia • 250 kW
	SWITZERLAND †SWISS RADIO INTL, Schwarzenburg	E North Am • 150 kW
		W North Am • 150 kW
		W • N Africa • 250 kW
		W • S America • 150 kW
	UNITED KINGDOM BBC, Via Meyerton, South Africa	S Africa • 250 kW
	BBC, Via Seychelles	E Africa • 250 kW
	USA †RFE-RL, Via Holzkirchen, Germany	W • W Asia & C Asia • 250 kW
	†VOA, Via Meyerton, S Africa	S • S Africa • 250 kW
6135v	MADAGASCAR RTV MALAGASY, Antananarivo	DS-1 • 30 kW
6140	ALBANIA †RADIO TIRANA, Cerrik	E North Am • 100 kW
(con'd)	BULGARIA RADIO BULGARIA, Sofia	W • E Europe & Mideast • 50 kW

ENGLISH ▬   ARABIC ▨   CHINESE ▢▢▢   FRENCH ▬   GERMAN ▬   RUSSIAN ▬   SPANISH ▬   OTHER ▬

FREQUENCY   COUNTRY, STATION, LOCATION

TARGET • NETWORK • POWER (kW)

World Time

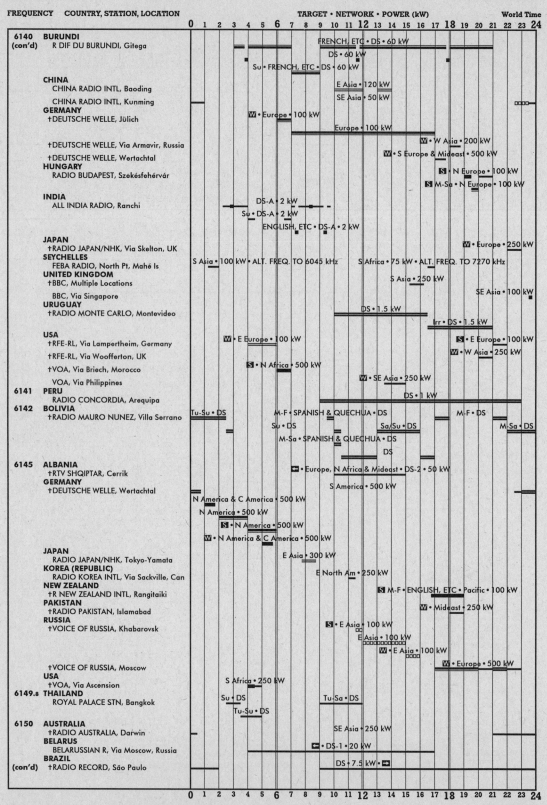

FREQUENCY   COUNTRY, STATION, LOCATION

TARGET • NETWORK • POWER (kW)

World Time

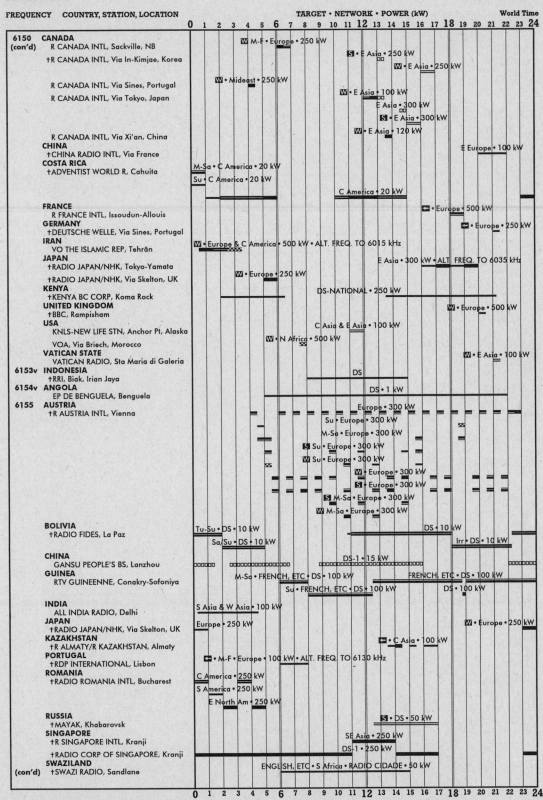

FREQUENCY	COUNTRY, STATION, LOCATION
6150 (con'd)	**CANADA** R CANADA INTL, Sackville, NB
	†R CANADA INTL, Via In-Kimjae, Korea
	R CANADA INTL, Via Sines, Portugal
	R CANADA INTL, Via Tokyo, Japan
	R CANADA INTL, Via Xi'an, China
	CHINA
	†CHINA RADIO INTL, Via France
	COSTA RICA
	†ADVENTIST WORLD R, Cahuita
	FRANCE R FRANCE INTL, Issoudun-Allouis
	GERMANY †DEUTSCHE WELLE, Via Sines, Portugal
	IRAN VO THE ISLAMIC REP, Tehrān
	JAPAN †RADIO JAPAN/NHK, Tokyo-Yamata
	†RADIO JAPAN/NHK, Via Skelton, UK
	KENYA †KENYA BC CORP, Koma Rock
	UNITED KINGDOM †BBC, Rampisham
	USA KNLS-NEW LIFE STN, Anchor Pt, Alaska
	VOA, Via Briech, Morocco
	VATICAN STATE VATICAN RADIO, Sta Maria di Galeria
6153v	**INDONESIA** †RRI, Biak, Irian Jaya
6154v	**ANGOLA** EP DE BENGUELA, Benguela
6155	**AUSTRIA** †R AUSTRIA INTL, Vienna
	BOLIVIA †RADIO FIDES, La Paz
	CHINA GANSU PEOPLE'S BS, Lanzhou
	GUINEA RTV GUINEENNE, Conakry-Sofoniya
	INDIA ALL INDIA RADIO, Delhi
	JAPAN †RADIO JAPAN/NHK, Via Skelton, UK
	KAZAKHSTAN †R ALMATY/R KAZAKHSTAN, Almaty
	PORTUGAL †RDP INTERNATIONAL, Lisbon
	ROMANIA †RADIO ROMANIA INTL, Bucharest
	RUSSIA †MAYAK, Khabarovsk
	SINGAPORE †R SINGAPORE INTL, Kranji
	†RADIO CORP OF SINGAPORE, Kranji
	SWAZILAND
(con'd)	†SWAZI RADIO, Sandlane

Program listings (target • network • power):

- W • M-F • Europe • 250 kW
- S • E Asia • 250 kW
- W • E Asia • 250 kW
- W • Mideast • 250 kW
- W • E Asia • 100 kW
- E Asia • 300 kW
- S • E Asia • 300 kW
- W • E Asia • 120 kW
- E Europe • 100 kW
- M-Sa • C America • 20 kW
- Su • C America • 20 kW
- C America • 20 kW
- • Europe • 500 kW
- • Europe • 250 kW
- W • Europe & C America • 500 kW • ALT. FREQ. TO 6015 kHz
- E Asia • 300 kW • ALT. FREQ. TO 6035 kHz
- W • Europe • 250 kW
- DS-NATIONAL • 250 kW
- W • Europe • 500 kW
- C Asia & E Asia • 100 kW
- W • N Africa • 500 kW
- W • E Asia • 100 kW
- DS
- DS • 1 kW
- Europe • 300 kW
- Su • Europe • 300 kW
- M-Sa • Europe • 300 kW
- S • Su • Europe • 300 kW
- W • Su • Europe • 300 kW
- W • Europe • 300 kW
- S • Europe • 300 kW
- S • M-Sa • Europe • 300 kW
- W • M-Sa • Europe • 300 kW
- Tu-Su • DS • 10 kW
- DS • 10 kW
- Sa/Su • DS • 10 kW
- Irr • DS • 10 kW
- DS-1 • 15 kW
- M-Sa • FRENCH, ETC • DS • 100 kW
- FRENCH, ETC • DS • 100 kW
- Su • FRENCH, ETC • DS • 100 kW
- DS • 100 kW
- S Asia & W Asia • 100 kW
- Europe • 250 kW
- W • Europe • 250 kW
- • C Asia • 100 kW
- • M-F • Europe • 100 kW • ALT. FREQ. TO 6130 kHz
- C America • 250 kW
- S America • 250 kW
- E North Am • 250 kW
- S • DS • 50 kW
- SE Asia • 250 kW
- DS-1 • 250 kW
- ENGLISH, ETC • S Africa • RADIO CIDADE • 50 kW

FREQUENCY   COUNTRY, STATION, LOCATION

TARGET • NETWORK • POWER (kW)   World Time

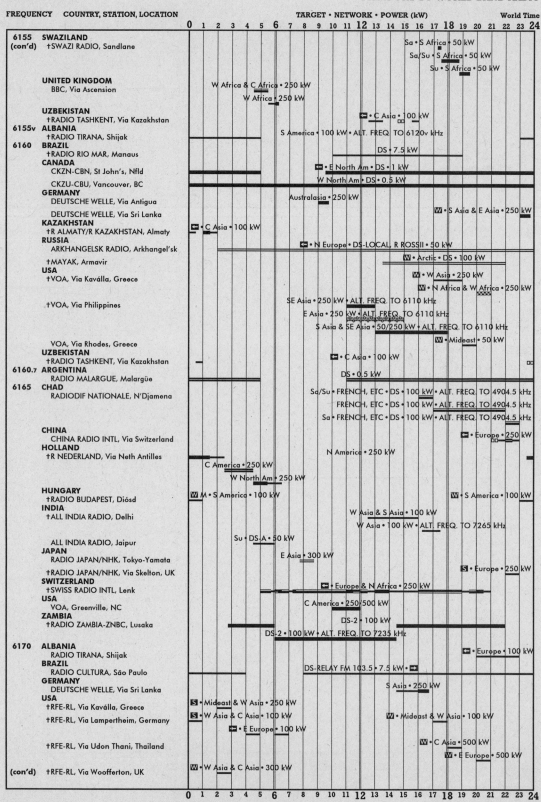

6155 (con'd)	**SWAZILAND**	†SWAZI RADIO, Sandlane	Sa • S Africa • 50 kW / Sa/Su • S Africa • 50 kW / Su • S Africa • 50 kW
	UNITED KINGDOM	BBC, Via Ascension	W Africa & C Africa • 250 kW / W Africa • 250 kW
	UZBEKISTAN	†RADIO TASHKENT, Via Kazakhstan	• C Asia • 100 kW
6155v	**ALBANIA**	†RADIO TIRANA, Shijak	S America • 100 kW • ALT. FREQ. TO 6120v kHz
6160	**BRAZIL**	†RADIO RIO MAR, Manaus	DS • 7.5 kW
	CANADA	CKZN-CBN, St John's, Nfld	E North Am • DS • 1 kW
		CKZU-CBU, Vancouver, BC	W North Am • DS • 0.5 kW
	GERMANY	DEUTSCHE WELLE, Via Antigua	Australasia • 250 kW
		DEUTSCHE WELLE, Via Sri Lanka	W • S Asia & E Asia • 250 kW
	KAZAKHSTAN	†R ALMATY/R KAZAKHSTAN, Almaty	• C Asia • 100 kW
	RUSSIA	ARKHANGELSK RADIO, Arkhangel'sk	• N Europe • DS-LOCAL, R ROSSII • 50 kW
		†MAYAK, Armavir	W • Arctic • DS • 100 kW
	USA	†VOA, Via Kaválla, Greece	W • W Asia • 250 kW / W • N Africa & W Africa • 250 kW
		†VOA, Via Philippines	SE Asia • 250 kW • ALT. FREQ. TO 6110 kHz / E Asia • 250 kW • ALT. FREQ. TO 6110 kHz / S Asia & SE Asia • 50/250 kW • ALT. FREQ. TO 6110 kHz / W • Mideast • 50 kW
		VOA, Via Rhodes, Greece	
	UZBEKISTAN	†RADIO TASHKENT, Via Kazakhstan	• C Asia • 100 kW
6160.7	**ARGENTINA**	RADIO MALARGÜE, Malargüe	DS • 0.5 kW
6165	**CHAD**	RADIODIF NATIONALE, N'Djamena	Sa/Su • FRENCH, ETC • DS • 100 kW • ALT. FREQ. TO 4904.5 kHz / FRENCH, ETC • DS • 100 kW • ALT. FREQ. TO 4904.5 kHz / Sa • FRENCH, ETC • DS • 100 kW • ALT. FREQ. TO 4904.5 kHz
	CHINA	CHINA RADIO INTL, Via Switzerland	• Europe • 250 kW
	HOLLAND	†R NEDERLAND, Via Neth Antilles	N America • 250 kW / C America • 250 kW / W North Am • 250 kW
	HUNGARY	†RADIO BUDAPEST, Diósd	W M • S America • 100 kW / W • S America • 100 kW
	INDIA	†ALL INDIA RADIO, Delhi	W Asia & S Asia • 100 kW / W Asia • 100 kW • ALT. FREQ. TO 7265 kHz
		ALL INDIA RADIO, Jaipur	Su • DS-A • 50 kW
	JAPAN	RADIO JAPAN/NHK, Tokyo-Yamata	E Asia • 300 kW
		†RADIO JAPAN/NHK, Via Skelton, UK	S • Europe • 250 kW
	SWITZERLAND	†SWISS RADIO INTL, Lenk	• Europe & N Africa • 250 kW
	USA	VOA, Greenville, NC	C America • 250/500 kW
	ZAMBIA	†RADIO ZAMBIA-ZNBC, Lusaka	DS-2 • 100 kW / DS-2 • 100 kW • ALT. FREQ. TO 7235 kHz
6170	**ALBANIA**	RADIO TIRANA, Shijak	• Europe • 100 kW
	BRAZIL	RADIO CULTURA, São Paulo	DS-RELAY FM 103.5 • 7.5 kW •
	GERMANY	DEUTSCHE WELLE, Via Sri Lanka	S Asia • 250 kW
	USA	†RFE-RL, Via Kaválla, Greece	S • Mideast & W Asia • 250 kW
		†RFE-RL, Via Lampertheim, Germany	S • W Asia & C Asia • 100 kW / W • Mideast & W Asia • 100 kW / • E Europe • 100 kW
		†RFE-RL, Via Udon Thani, Thailand	W • C Asia • 500 kW / W • E Europe • 500 kW
(con'd)		†RFE-RL, Via Woofferton, UK	W • W Asia & C Asia • 300 kW

FREQUENCY   COUNTRY, STATION, LOCATION

TARGET • NETWORK • POWER (kW)

World Time

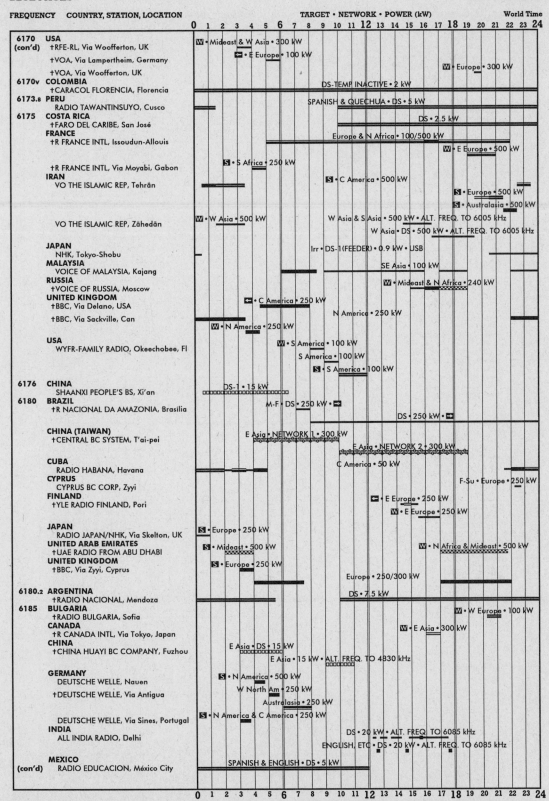

Frequency	Country, Station, Location	Target • Network • Power
6170 (con'd)	**USA** †RFE-RL, Via Woofferton, UK	W • Mideast & W Asia • 300 kW
	†VOA, Via Lampertheim, Germany	• E Europe • 100 kW
	†VOA, Via Woofferton, UK	W • Europe • 300 kW
6170v	**COLOMBIA** †CARACOL FLORENCIA, Florencia	DS-TEMP INACTIVE • 2 kW
6173.8	**PERU** RADIO TAWANTINSUYO, Cusco	SPANISH & QUECHUA • DS • 5 kW
6175	**COSTA RICA** †FARO DEL CARIBE, San José	DS • 2.5 kW
	FRANCE †R FRANCE INTL, Issoudun-Allouis	Europe & N Africa • 100/500 kW
		W • E Europe • 500 kW
	†R FRANCE INTL, Via Moyabi, Gabon	S • S Africa • 250 kW
	IRAN VO THE ISLAMIC REP, Tehrān	S • C America • 500 kW
		S • Europe • 500 kW
		S • Australasia • 500 kW
	VO THE ISLAMIC REP, Zāhedān	W • W Asia • 500 kW W Asia & S Asia • 500 kW • ALT. FREQ. TO 6005 kHz
		W Asia • DS • 500 kW • ALT. FREQ. TO 6005 kHz
	JAPAN NHK, Tokyo-Shobu	Irr • DS-1 (FEEDER) • 0.9 kW • USB
	MALAYSIA VOICE OF MALAYSIA, Kajang	SE Asia • 100 kW
	RUSSIA †VOICE OF RUSSIA, Moscow	W • Mideast & N Africa • 240 kW
	UNITED KINGDOM †BBC, Via Delano, USA	• C America • 250 kW
	†BBC, Via Sackville, Can	N America • 250 kW
		W • N America • 250 kW
	USA WYFR-FAMILY RADIO, Okeechobee, Fl	W • S America • 100 kW
		S America • 100 kW
		S • S America • 100 kW
6176	**CHINA** SHAANXI PEOPLE'S BS, Xi'an	DS-1 • 15 kW
6180	**BRAZIL** †R NACIONAL DA AMAZONIA, Brasilia	M-F • DS • 250 kW •
		DS • 250 kW •
	CHINA (TAIWAN) †CENTRAL BC SYSTEM, T'ai-pei	E Asia • NETWORK 1 • 300 kW
		E Asia • NETWORK 2 • 300 kW
	CUBA RADIO HABANA, Havana	C America • 50 kW
	CYPRUS CYPRUS BC CORP, Zyyi	F-Su • Europe • 250 kW
	FINLAND †YLE RADIO FINLAND, Pori	• E Europe • 250 kW
		W • E Europe • 250 kW
	JAPAN RADIO JAPAN/NHK, Via Skelton, UK	S • Europe • 250 kW
	UNITED ARAB EMIRATES †UAE RADIO FROM ABU DHABI	S • Mideast • 500 kW W • N Africa & Mideast • 500 kW
	UNITED KINGDOM †BBC, Via Zyyi, Cyprus	S • Europe • 250 kW
		Europe • 250/300 kW
6180.2	**ARGENTINA** †RADIO NACIONAL, Mendoza	DS • 7.5 kW
6185	**BULGARIA** †RADIO BULGARIA, Sofia	W • W Europe • 100 kW
	CANADA †R CANADA INTL, Via Tokyo, Japan	W • E Asia • 300 kW
	CHINA †CHINA HUAYI BC COMPANY, Fuzhou	E Asia • DS • 15 kW
		E Asia • 15 kW • ALT. FREQ. TO 4830 kHz
	GERMANY DEUTSCHE WELLE, Nauen	S • N America • 500 kW
	†DEUTSCHE WELLE, Via Antigua	W North Am • 250 kW
		Australasia • 250 kW
	DEUTSCHE WELLE, Via Sines, Portugal	S • N America & C America • 250 kW
	INDIA ALL INDIA RADIO, Delhi	DS • 20 kW • ALT. FREQ. TO 6085 kHz
		ENGLISH, ETC • DS • 20 kW • ALT. FREQ. TO 6085 kHz
	MEXICO (con'd) RADIO EDUCACION, México City	SPANISH & ENGLISH • DS • 5 kW

0 1 2 3 4 5 6 7 8 9 10 11 12 13 14 15 16 17 18 19 20 21 22 23 24

ENGLISH ▬   ARABIC ⌇⌇   CHINESE □□□   FRENCH ══   GERMAN ▬▬   RUSSIAN ══   SPANISH ══   OTHER ──

FREQUENCY   COUNTRY, STATION, LOCATION

TARGET • NETWORK • POWER (kW)

World Time

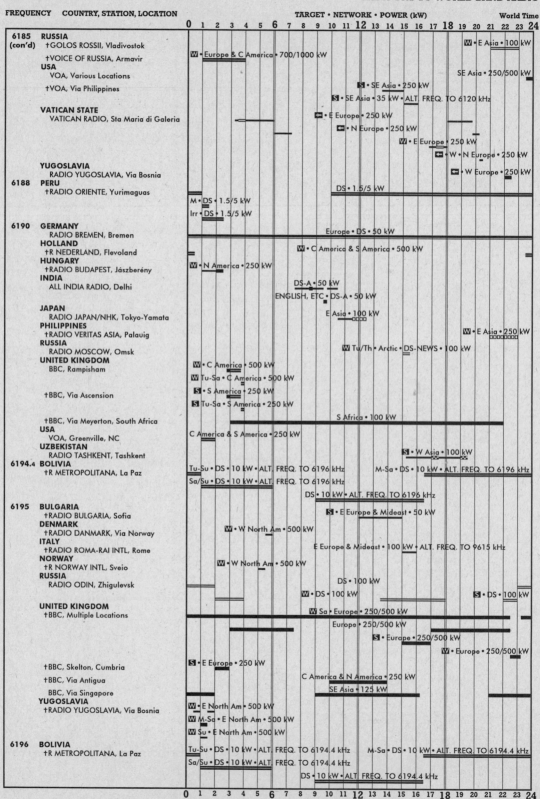

FREQUENCY	COUNTRY, STATION, LOCATION	Details
6185 (con'd)	**RUSSIA** †GOLOS ROSSII, Vladivostok	W • Europe & C America • 700/1000 kW; W • E Asia • 100 kW
	†VOICE OF RUSSIA, Armavir	
	USA VOA, Various Locations	SE Asia • 250/500 kW
	†VOA, Via Philippines	S • SE Asia • 250 kW; S • SE Asia • 35 kW • ALT. FREQ. TO 6120 kHz
	VATICAN STATE VATICAN RADIO, Sta Maria di Galeria	E Europe • 250 kW; N Europe • 250 kW; W • E Europe • 250 kW; W • N Europe • 250 kW; W Europe • 250 kW
	YUGOSLAVIA RADIO YUGOSLAVIA, Via Bosnia	
6188	**PERU** †RADIO ORIENTE, Yurimaguas	DS • 1.5/5 kW; M • DS • 1.5/5 kW; Irr • DS • 1.5/5 kW
6190	**GERMANY** RADIO BREMEN, Bremen	Europe • DS • 50 kW
	HOLLAND †R NEDERLAND, Flevoland	W • C America & S America • 500 kW
	HUNGARY †RADIO BUDAPEST, Jászberény	W • N America • 250 kW
	INDIA ALL INDIA RADIO, Delhi	DS-A • 50 kW; ENGLISH, ETC • DS-A • 50 kW
	JAPAN RADIO JAPAN/NHK, Tokyo-Yamata	E Asia • 100 kW
	PHILIPPINES †RADIO VERITAS ASIA, Palauig	W • E Asia • 250 kW
	RUSSIA RADIO MOSCOW, Omsk	W Tu/Th • Arctic • DS-NEWS • 100 kW
	UNITED KINGDOM BBC, Rampisham	W • C America • 500 kW; W Tu-Sa • C America • 500 kW; S • S America • 250 kW; S Tu-Sa • S America • 250 kW
	†BBC, Via Ascension	
	†BBC, Via Meyerton, South Africa	S Africa • 100 kW
	USA VOA, Greenville, NC	C America & S America • 250 kW
	UZBEKISTAN RADIO TASHKENT, Tashkent	S • W Asia • 100 kW
6194.4	**BOLIVIA** †R METROPOLITANA, La Paz	Tu-Su • DS • 10 kW • ALT. FREQ. TO 6196 kHz; M-Sa • DS • 10 kW • ALT. FREQ. TO 6196 kHz; Sa/Su • DS • 10 kW • ALT. FREQ. TO 6196 kHz; DS • 10 kW • ALT. FREQ. TO 6196 kHz
6195	**BULGARIA** †RADIO BULGARIA, Sofia	S • E Europe & Mideast • 50 kW
	DENMARK †RADIO DANMARK, Via Norway	W • W North Am • 500 kW
	ITALY †RADIO ROMA-RAI INTL, Rome	E Europe & Mideast • 100 kW • ALT. FREQ. TO 9615 kHz
	NORWAY †R NORWAY INTL, Sveio	W • W North Am • 500 kW
	RUSSIA RADIO ODIN, Zhigulevsk	DS • 100 kW; W • DS • 100 kW; S • DS • 100 kW
	UNITED KINGDOM †BBC, Multiple Locations	W Sa • Europe • 250/500 kW; Europe • 250/500 kW; S • Europe • 250/500 kW; W • Europe • 250/500 kW
	†BBC, Skelton, Cumbria	S • E Europe • 250 kW
	†BBC, Via Antigua	C America & N America • 250 kW
	BBC, Via Singapore	SE Asia • 125 kW
	YUGOSLAVIA †RADIO YUGOSLAVIA, Via Bosnia	W • E North Am • 500 kW; W M-Sa • E North Am • 500 kW; W Su • E North Am • 500 kW
6196	**BOLIVIA** †R METROPOLITANA, La Paz	Tu-Su • DS • 10 kW • ALT. FREQ. TO 6194.4 kHz; M-Sa • DS • 10 kW • ALT. FREQ. TO 6194.4 kHz; Sa/Su • DS • 10 kW • ALT. FREQ. TO 6194.4 kHz; DS • 10 kW • ALT. FREQ. TO 6194.4 kHz

FREQUENCY   COUNTRY, STATION, LOCATION

TARGET • NETWORK • POWER (kW)

World Time

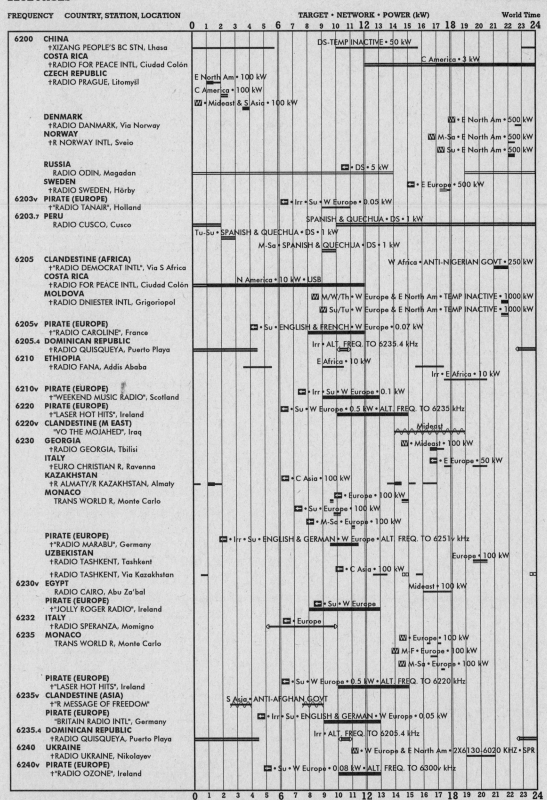

Freq	Country / Station
6200	**CHINA** †XIZANG PEOPLE'S BC STN, Lhasa — DS-TEMP INACTIVE • 50 kW
	COSTA RICA †RADIO FOR PEACE INTL, Ciudad Colón — C America • 3 kW
	CZECH REPUBLIC †RADIO PRAGUE, Litomyšl — E North Am • 100 kW / C America • 100 kW / W • Mideast & S Asia • 100 kW
	DENMARK †RADIO DANMARK, Via Norway — W • E North Am • 500 kW
	NORWAY †R NORWAY INTL, Sveio — W M-Sa • E North Am • 500 kW / W Su • E North Am • 500 kW
	RUSSIA RADIO ODIN, Magadan — DS • 5 kW
	SWEDEN †RADIO SWEDEN, Hörby — E Europe • 500 kW
6203v	**PIRATE (EUROPE)** †"RADIO TANAIR", Holland — Irr • Su • W Europe • 0.05 kW
6203.7	**PERU** RADIO CUSCO, Cusco — SPANISH & QUECHUA • DS • 1 kW / Tu-Su • SPANISH & QUECHUA • DS • 1 kW / M-Sa • SPANISH & QUECHUA • DS • 1 kW
6205	**CLANDESTINE (AFRICA)** †"RADIO DEMOCRAT INTL", Via S Africa — W Africa • ANTI-NIGERIAN GOVT • 250 kW
	COSTA RICA †RADIO FOR PEACE INTL, Ciudad Colón — N America • 10 kW • USB
	MOLDOVA †RADIO DNIESTER INTL, Grigoriopol — W M/W/Th • W Europe & E North Am • TEMP INACTIVE • 1000 kW / W Su/Tu • W Europe & E North Am • TEMP INACTIVE • 1000 kW
6205v	**PIRATE (EUROPE)** †"RADIO CAROLINE", France — Su • ENGLISH & FRENCH • W Europe • 0.07 kW
6205.4	**DOMINICAN REPUBLIC** †RADIO QUISQUEYA, Puerto Playa — Irr • ALT. FREQ. TO 6235.4 kHz
6210	**ETHIOPIA** †RADIO FANA, Addis Ababa — E Africa • 10 kW / Irr • E Africa • 10 kW
6210v	**PIRATE (EUROPE)** †"WEEKEND MUSIC RADIO", Scotland — Irr • Su • W Europe • 0.1 kW
6220	**PIRATE (EUROPE)** †"LASER HOT HITS", Ireland — Su • W Europe • 0.5 kW • ALT. FREQ. TO 6235 kHz
6220v	**CLANDESTINE (M EAST)** "VO THE MOJAHED", Iraq — Mideast
6230	**GEORGIA** †RADIO GEORGIA, Tbilisi — W • Mideast • 100 kW
	ITALY †EURO CHRISTIAN R, Ravenna — E Europe • 50 kW
	KAZAKHSTAN †R ALMATY/R KAZAKHSTAN, Almaty — C Asia • 100 kW
	MONACO TRANS WORLD R, Monte Carlo — Europe • 100 kW / Su • Europe • 100 kW / M-Sa • Europe • 100 kW
	PIRATE (EUROPE) †"RADIO MARABU", Germany — Irr • Su • ENGLISH & GERMAN • W Europe • ALT. FREQ. TO 6251v kHz
	UZBEKISTAN †RADIO TASHKENT, Tashkent — Europe • 100 kW
	†RADIO TASHKENT, Via Kazakhstan — C Asia • 100 kW
6230v	**EGYPT** RADIO CAIRO, Abu Za'bal — Mideast • 100 kW
	PIRATE (EUROPE) †"JOLLY ROGER RADIO", Ireland — Su • W Europe
6232	**ITALY** †RADIO SPERANZA, Momigno — Europe
6235	**MONACO** TRANS WORLD R, Monte Carlo — W • Europe • 100 kW / W M-F • Europe • 100 kW / W M-Sa • Europe • 100 kW
	PIRATE (EUROPE) †"LASER HOT HITS", Ireland — Su • W Europe • 0.5 kW • ALT. FREQ. TO 6220 kHz
6235v	**CLANDESTINE (ASIA)** †"R MESSAGE OF FREEDOM" — S Asia • ANTI-AFGHAN GOVT
	PIRATE (EUROPE) "BRITAIN RADIO INTL", Germany — Irr • Su • ENGLISH & GERMAN • W Europe • 0.05 kW
6235.4	**DOMINICAN REPUBLIC** †RADIO QUISQUEYA, Puerto Playa — Irr • ALT. FREQ. TO 6205.4 kHz
6240	**UKRAINE** †RADIO UKRAINE, Nikolayev — W • W Europe & E North Am • 2X6130·6020 KHZ • SPR
6240v	**PIRATE (EUROPE)** †"RADIO OZONE", Ireland — Su • W Europe • 0.08 kW • ALT. FREQ. TO 6300v kHz

ENGLISH ▬   ARABIC ∿∿∿   CHINESE □□□   FRENCH ══   GERMAN ══   RUSSIAN ══   SPANISH ══   OTHER ──

FREQUENCY   COUNTRY, STATION, LOCATION

TARGET • NETWORK • POWER (kW)

World Time

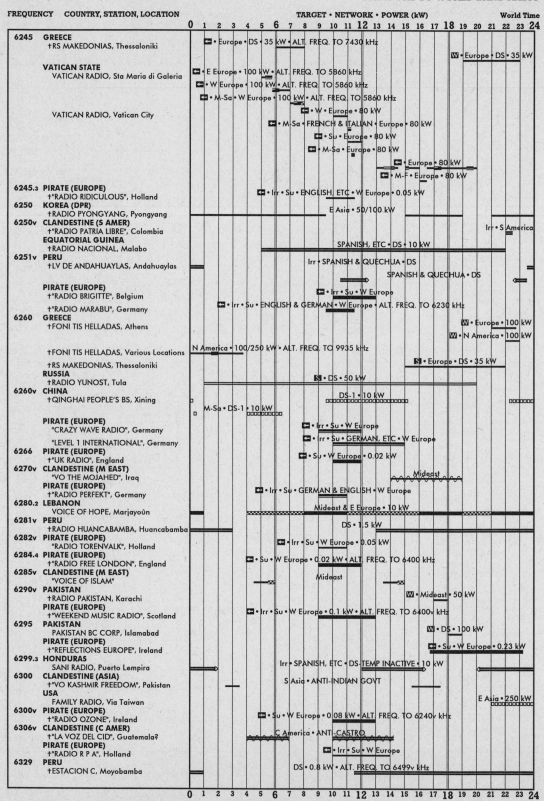

6245	GREECE	
	†RS MAKEDONIAS, Thessaloniki	⬅ • Europe • DS • 35 kW • ALT. FREQ. TO 7430 kHz
		🅦 • Europe • DS • 35 kW
	VATICAN STATE	
	VATICAN RADIO, Sta Maria di Galeria	⬅ • E Europe • 100 kW • ALT. FREQ. TO 5860 kHz
		⬅ • W Europe • 100 kW • ALT. FREQ. TO 5860 kHz
		⬅ • M-Sa • W Europe • 100 kW • ALT. FREQ. TO 5860 kHz
	VATICAN RADIO, Vatican City	⬅ • W • Europe • 80 kW
		⬅ • M-Sa • FRENCH & ITALIAN • Europe • 80 kW
		⬅ • Su • Europe • 80 kW
		⬅ • M-Sa • Europe • 80 kW
		⬅ • Europe • 80 kW
		⬅ • M-F • Europe • 80 kW
6245.3	PIRATE (EUROPE)	
	†"RADIO RIDICULOUS", Holland	⬅ • Irr • Su • ENGLISH, ETC • W Europe • 0.05 kW
6250	KOREA (DPR)	
	†RADIO PYONGYANG, Pyongyang	E Asia • 50/100 kW
6250v	CLANDESTINE (S AMER)	
	†"RADIO PATRIA LIBRE", Colombia	Irr • S America
	EQUATORIAL GUINEA	
	†RADIO NACIONAL, Malabo	SPANISH, ETC • DS • 10 kW
6251v	PERU	
	†LV DE ANDAHUAYLAS, Andahuaylas	Irr • SPANISH & QUECHUA • DS
		SPANISH & QUECHUA • DS
	PIRATE (EUROPE)	
	†"RADIO BRIGITTE", Belgium	⬅ • Irr • Su • W Europe
	†"RADIO MARABU", Germany	⬅ • Irr • Su • ENGLISH & GERMAN • W Europe • ALT. FREQ. TO 6230 kHz
6260	GREECE	
	†FONI TIS HELLADAS, Athens	🅦 • Europe • 100 kW
		🅦 • N America • 100 kW
	†FONI TIS HELLADAS, Various Locations	N America • 100/250 kW • ALT. FREQ. TO 9935 kHz
	†RS MAKEDONIAS, Thessaloniki	🆂 • Europe • DS • 35 kW
	RUSSIA	
	†RADIO YUNOST, Tula	🆂 • DS • 50 kW
6260v	CHINA	
	†QINGHAI PEOPLE'S BS, Xining	DS-1 • 10 kW
		M-Sa • DS-1 • 10 kW
	PIRATE (EUROPE)	
	"CRAZY WAVE RADIO", Germany	⬅ • Irr • Su • W Europe
	"LEVEL 1 INTERNATIONAL", Germany	⬅ • Irr • Su • GERMAN, ETC • W Europe
6266	PIRATE (EUROPE)	
	†"UK RADIO", England	⬅ • Su • W Europe • 0.02 kW
6270v	CLANDESTINE (M EAST)	
	"VO THE MOJAHED", Iraq	Mideast
	PIRATE (EUROPE)	
	†"RADIO PERFEKT", Germany	⬅ • Irr • Su • GERMAN & ENGLISH • W Europe
6280.2	LEBANON	
	VOICE OF HOPE, Marjayoûn	Mideast & E Europe • 10 kW
6281v	PERU	
	†RADIO HUANCABAMBA, Huancabamba	DS • 1.5 kW
6282v	PIRATE (EUROPE)	
	"RADIO TORENVALK", Holland	⬅ • Irr • Su • W Europe • 0.05 kW
6284.4	PIRATE (EUROPE)	
	†"RADIO FREE LONDON", England	⬅ • Su • W Europe • 0.02 kW • ALT. FREQ. TO 6400 kHz
6285v	CLANDESTINE (M EAST)	
	"VOICE OF ISLAM"	Mideast
6290v	PAKISTAN	
	†RADIO PAKISTAN, Karachi	🅦 • Mideast • 50 kW
	PIRATE (EUROPE)	
	†"WEEKEND MUSIC RADIO", Scotland	⬅ • Irr • Su • W Europe • 0.1 kW • ALT. FREQ. TO 6400 kHz
6295	PAKISTAN	
	PAKISTAN BC CORP, Islamabad	🅦 • DS • 100 kW
	PIRATE (EUROPE)	
	†"REFLECTIONS EUROPE", Ireland	⬅ • Su • W Europe • 0.23 kW
6299.3	HONDURAS	
	SANI RADIO, Puerto Lempira	Irr • SPANISH, ETC • DS • TEMP INACTIVE • 10 kW
6300	CLANDESTINE (ASIA)	
	†"VO KASHMIR FREEDOM", Pakistan	S Asia • ANTI-INDIAN GOVT
	USA	
	FAMILY RADIO, Via Taiwan	E Asia • 250 kW
6300v	PIRATE (EUROPE)	
	†"RADIO OZONE", Ireland	⬅ • Su • W Europe • 0.08 kW • ALT. FREQ. TO 6240v kHz
6306v	CLANDESTINE (C AMER)	
	†"LA VOZ DEL CID", Guatemala?	C America • ANTI-CASTRO
	PIRATE (EUROPE)	
	†"RADIO R P A", Holland	⬅ • Irr • Su • W Europe
6329	PERU	
	†ESTACION C, Moyobamba	DS • 0.8 kW • ALT. FREQ. TO 6499v kHz

FREQUENCY   COUNTRY, STATION, LOCATION   TARGET • NETWORK • POWER (kW)   World Time

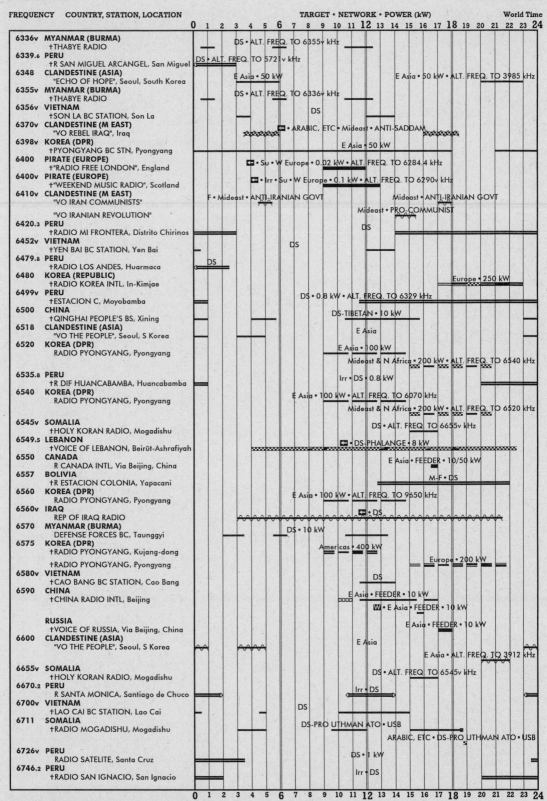

Frequency	Country, Station, Location	Target • Network • Power
6336v	**MYANMAR (BURMA)** †THABYE RADIO	DS • ALT. FREQ. TO 6355v kHz
6339.6	**PERU** †R SAN MIGUEL ARCANGEL, San Miguel	DS • ALT. FREQ. TO 5721v kHz
6348	**CLANDESTINE (ASIA)** "ECHO OF HOPE", Seoul, South Korea	E Asia • 50 kW / E Asia • 50 kW • ALT. FREQ. TO 3985 kHz
6355v	**MYANMAR (BURMA)** †THABYE RADIO	DS • ALT. FREQ. TO 6336v kHz
6356v	**VIETNAM** †SON LA BC STATION, Son La	DS
6370v	**CLANDESTINE (M EAST)** "VO REBEL IRAQ", Iraq	ARABIC, ETC • Mideast • ANTI-SADDAM
6398v	**KOREA (DPR)** †PYONGYANG BC STN, Pyongyang	E Asia • 50 kW
6400	**PIRATE (EUROPE)** †"RADIO FREE LONDON", England	Su • W Europe • 0.02 kW • ALT. FREQ. TO 6284.4 kHz
6400v	**PIRATE (EUROPE)** †"WEEKEND MUSIC RADIO", Scotland	Irr • Su • W Europe • 0.1 kW • ALT. FREQ. TO 6290v kHz
6410v	**CLANDESTINE (M EAST)** "VO IRAN COMMUNISTS"	F • Mideast • ANTI-IRANIAN GOVT / Mideast • ANTI-IRANIAN GOVT
	"VO IRANIAN REVOLUTION"	Mideast • PRO-COMMUNIST
6420.3	**PERU** †RADIO MI FRONTERA, Distrito Chirinos	DS
6452v	**VIETNAM** †YEN BAI BC STATION, Yen Bai	DS
6479.8	**PERU** †RADIO LOS ANDES, Huarmaca	DS
6480	**KOREA (REPUBLIC)** †RADIO KOREA INTL, In-Kimjae	Europe • 250 kW
6499v	**PERU** †ESTACION C, Moyobamba	DS • 0.8 kW • ALT. FREQ. TO 6329 kHz
6500	**CHINA** †QINGHAI PEOPLE'S BS, Xining	DS-TIBETAN • 10 kW
6518	**CLANDESTINE (ASIA)** "VO THE PEOPLE", Seoul, S Korea	E Asia
6520	**KOREA (DPR)** RADIO PYONGYANG, Pyongyang	E Asia • 100 kW / Mideast & N Africa • 200 kW • ALT. FREQ. TO 6540 kHz
6535.8	**PERU** †R DIF HUANCABAMBA, Huancabamba	Irr • DS • 0.8 kW
6540	**KOREA (DPR)** RADIO PYONGYANG, Pyongyang	E Asia • 100 kW • ALT. FREQ. TO 6070 kHz / Mideast & N Africa • 200 kW • ALT. FREQ. TO 6520 kHz
6545v	**SOMALIA** †HOLY KORAN RADIO, Mogadishu	DS • ALT. FREQ. TO 6655v kHz
6549.5	**LEBANON** †VOICE OF LEBANON, Beirŭt-Ashrafiyah	DS-PHALANGE • 8 kW
6550	**CANADA** R CANADA INTL, Via Beijing, China	E Asia • FEEDER • 10/50 kW
6557	**BOLIVIA** †R ESTACION COLONIA, Yapacani	M-F • DS
6560	**KOREA (DPR)** RADIO PYONGYANG, Pyongyang	E Asia • 100 kW • ALT. FREQ. TO 9650 kHz
6560v	**IRAQ** REP OF IRAQ RADIO	DS
6570	**MYANMAR (BURMA)** DEFENSE FORCES BC, Taunggyi	DS • 10 kW
6575	**KOREA (DPR)** †RADIO PYONGYANG, Kujang-dong	Americas • 400 kW
	†RADIO PYONGYANG, Pyongyang	Europe • 200 kW
6580v	**VIETNAM** †CAO BANG BC STATION, Cao Bang	DS
6590	**CHINA** †CHINA RADIO INTL, Beijing	E Asia • FEEDER • 10 kW / W • E Asia • FEEDER • 10 kW
	RUSSIA †VOICE OF RUSSIA, Via Beijing, China	E Asia • FEEDER • 10 kW
6600	**CLANDESTINE (ASIA)** "VO THE PEOPLE", Seoul, S Korea	E Asia / E Asia • ALT. FREQ. TO 3912 kHz
6655v	**SOMALIA** †HOLY KORAN RADIO, Mogadishu	DS • ALT. FREQ. TO 6545v kHz
6670.2	**PERU** R SANTA MONICA, Santiago de Chuco	Irr • DS
6700	**VIETNAM** †LAO CAI BC STATION, Lao Cai	DS
6711	**SOMALIA** †RADIO MOGADISHU, Mogadishu	DS-PRO UTHMAN ATO • USB / ARABIC, ETC • DS-PRO UTHMAN ATO • USB
6726v	**PERU** RADIO SATELITE, Santa Cruz	DS • 1 kW
6746.2	**PERU** †RADIO SAN IGNACIO, San Ignacio	Irr • DS

ENGLISH ▬▬   ARABIC ﹏﹏   CHINESE ▫▫▫   FRENCH ══   GERMAN ▬▬   RUSSIAN ══   SPANISH ══   OTHER ▬▬

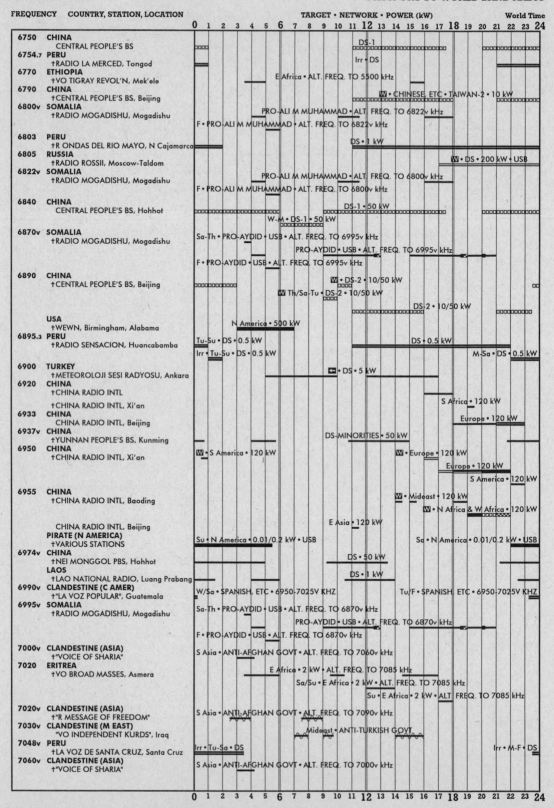

FREQUENCY　　COUNTRY, STATION, LOCATION　　　　　　TARGET • NETWORK • POWER (kW)　　　　World Time

0 1 2 3 4 5 6 7 8 9 10 11 12 13 14 15 16 17 18 19 20 21 22 23 24

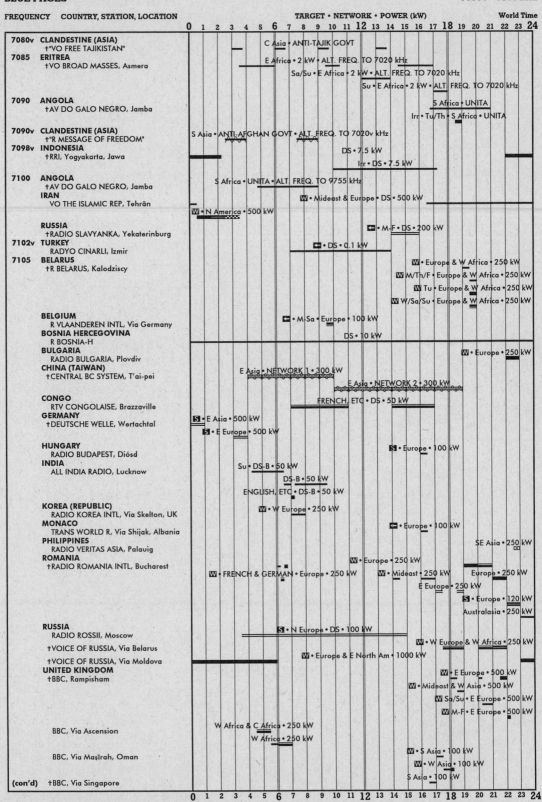

Frequency	Country, Station, Location	Target • Network • Power
7080v	CLANDESTINE (ASIA) †"VO FREE TAJIKISTAN"	C Asia • ANTI-TAJIK GOVT
7085	ERITREA †VO BROAD MASSES, Asmera	E Africa • 2 kW • ALT. FREQ. TO 7020 kHz; Sa/Su • E Africa • 2 kW • ALT. FREQ. TO 7020 kHz; Su • E Africa • 2 kW • ALT. FREQ. TO 7020 kHz
7090	ANGOLA †AV DO GALO NEGRO, Jamba	S Africa • UNITA; Irr • Tu/Th • S Africa • UNITA
7090v	CLANDESTINE (ASIA) †"R MESSAGE OF FREEDOM"	S Asia • ANTI-AFGHAN GOVT • ALT. FREQ. TO 7020v kHz
7098v	INDONESIA †RRI, Yogyakarta, Jawa	DS • 7.5 kW; Irr • DS • 7.5 kW
7100	ANGOLA †AV DO GALO NEGRO, Jamba	S Africa • UNITA • ALT. FREQ. TO 9755 kHz
	IRAN VO THE ISLAMIC REP, Tehrān	W • Mideast & Europe • DS • 500 kW; W • N America • 500 kW
	RUSSIA †RADIO SLAVYANKA, Yekaterinburg	M-F • DS • 200 kW
7102v	TURKEY RADYO CINARLI, Izmir	DS • 0.1 kW
7105	BELARUS †R BELARUS, Kalodziscy	W • Europe & W Africa • 250 kW; W M/Th/F • Europe & W Africa • 250 kW; W Tu • Europe & W Africa • 250 kW; W W/Sa/Su • Europe & W Africa • 250 kW
	BELGIUM R VLAANDEREN INTL, Via Germany	M-Sa • Europe • 100 kW
	BOSNIA HERCEGOVINA R BOSNIA-H	DS • 10 kW
	BULGARIA RADIO BULGARIA, Plovdiv	W • Europe • 250 kW
	CHINA (TAIWAN) †CENTRAL BC SYSTEM, T'ai-pei	E Asia • NETWORK 1 • 300 kW; E Asia • NETWORK 2 • 300 kW
	CONGO RTV CONGOLAISE, Brazzaville	FRENCH, ETC • DS • 50 kW
	GERMANY †DEUTSCHE WELLE, Wertachtal	S • E Asia • 500 kW; S • E Europe • 500 kW
	HUNGARY RADIO BUDAPEST, Diósd	S • Europe • 100 kW
	INDIA ALL INDIA RADIO, Lucknow	Su • DS-B • 50 kW; DS-B • 50 kW; ENGLISH, ETC • DS-B • 50 kW
	KOREA (REPUBLIC) RADIO KOREA INTL, Via Skelton, UK	W • W Europe • 250 kW
	MONACO TRANS WORLD R, Via Shijak, Albania	Europe • 100 kW
	PHILIPPINES RADIO VERITAS ASIA, Palauig	SE Asia • 250 kW
	ROMANIA †RADIO ROMANIA INTL, Bucharest	W • Europe • 250 kW; W • FRENCH & GERMAN • Europe • 250 kW; W • Mideast • 250 kW; Europe • 250 kW; E Europe • 250 kW; S • Europe • 120 kW; Australasia • 250 kW
	RUSSIA RADIO ROSSII, Moscow	S • N Europe • DS • 100 kW
	†VOICE OF RUSSIA, Via Belarus	W • W Europe & W Africa • 250 kW
	†VOICE OF RUSSIA, Via Moldova	W • Europe & E North Am • 1000 kW
	UNITED KINGDOM †BBC, Rampisham	W • E Europe • 500 kW; W • Mideast & W Asia • 500 kW; W Sa/Su • E Europe • 500 kW; W M-F • E Europe • 500 kW
	BBC, Via Ascension	W Africa & C Africa • 250 kW; W Africa • 250 kW
	BBC, Via Maşīrah, Oman	W • S Asia • 100 kW; W • W Asia • 100 kW; S Asia • 100 kW
(con'd)	†BBC, Via Singapore	

0 1 2 3 4 5 6 7 8 9 10 11 12 13 14 15 16 17 18 19 20 21 22 23 24

ENGLISH ▬　ARABIC ░░░　CHINESE □□□　FRENCH ══　GERMAN ═══　RUSSIAN ══　SPANISH ═══　OTHER ▬

FREQUENCY   COUNTRY, STATION, LOCATION

TARGET • NETWORK • POWER (kW)   World Time

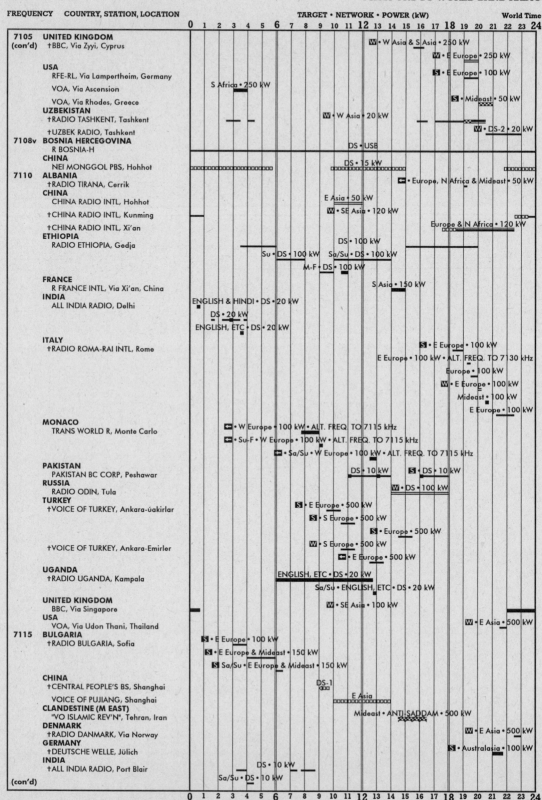

FREQUENCY	COUNTRY, STATION, LOCATION	Details
7105 (con'd)	UNITED KINGDOM †BBC, Via Zyyi, Cyprus	W • W Asia & S Asia • 250 kW; W • E Europe • 250 kW
	USA RFE-RL, Via Lampertheim, Germany	S • E Europe • 100 kW
	VOA, Via Ascension	S Africa • 250 kW
	VOA, Via Rhodes, Greece	S • Mideast • 50 kW
	UZBEKISTAN †RADIO TASHKENT, Tashkent	W • W Asia • 20 kW
	†UZBEK RADIO, Tashkent	W • DS-2 • 20 kW
7108v	BOSNIA HERCEGOVINA R BOSNIA-H	DS • USB
	CHINA NEI MONGGOL PBS, Hohhot	DS • 15 kW
7110	ALBANIA †RADIO TIRANA, Cerrik	⇨ • Europe, N Africa & Mideast • 50 kW
	CHINA CHINA RADIO INTL, Hohhot	E Asia • 50 kW
	†CHINA RADIO INTL, Kunming	W • SE Asia • 120 kW
	†CHINA RADIO INTL, Xi'an	Europe & N Africa • 120 kW
	ETHIOPIA RADIO ETHIOPIA, Gedja	DS • 100 kW; Su • DS • 100 kW; Sa/Su • DS • 100 kW; M-F • DS • 100 kW
	FRANCE R FRANCE INTL, Via Xi'an, China	S Asia • 150 kW
	INDIA ALL INDIA RADIO, Delhi	ENGLISH & HINDI • DS • 20 kW; DS • 20 kW; ENGLISH, ETC • DS • 20 kW
	ITALY †RADIO ROMA-RAI INTL, Rome	S • E Europe • 100 kW; E Europe • 100 kW • ALT. FREQ. TO 7130 kHz; Europe • 100 kW; W • E Europe • 100 kW; Mideast • 100 kW; E Europe • 100 kW
	MONACO TRANS WORLD R, Monte Carlo	⇨ • W Europe • 100 kW • ALT. FREQ. TO 7115 kHz; ⇨ • Su-F • W Europe • 100 kW • ALT. FREQ. TO 7115 kHz; ⇨ • Sa/Su • W Europe • 100 kW • ALT. FREQ. TO 7115 kHz
	PAKISTAN PAKISTAN BC CORP, Peshawar	DS • 10 kW; S • DS • 10 kW
	RUSSIA RADIO ODIN, Tula	W • DS • 100 kW
	TURKEY †VOICE OF TURKEY, Ankara-úakirlar	S • E Europe • 500 kW; S • S Europe • 500 kW; S • Europe • 500 kW; W • S Europe • 500 kW
	†VOICE OF TURKEY, Ankara-Emirler	⇨ • E Europe • 500 kW
	UGANDA †RADIO UGANDA, Kampala	ENGLISH, ETC • DS • 20 kW; Sa/Su • ENGLISH, ETC • DS • 20 kW
	UNITED KINGDOM BBC, Via Singapore	W • SE Asia • 100 kW
	USA VOA, Via Udon Thani, Thailand	W • E Asia • 500 kW
7115	BULGARIA †RADIO BULGARIA, Sofia	S • E Europe • 100 kW; S • E Europe & Mideast • 150 kW; S • Sa/Su • E Europe & Mideast • 150 kW
	CHINA †CENTRAL PEOPLE'S BS, Shanghai	DS-1
	VOICE OF PUJIANG, Shanghai	E Asia
	CLANDESTINE (M EAST) "VO ISLAMIC REV'N", Tehran, Iran	Mideast • ANTI-SADDAM • 500 kW
	DENMARK †RADIO DANMARK, Via Norway	W • E Asia • 500 kW
	GERMANY †DEUTSCHE WELLE, Jülich	S • Australasia • 100 kW
	INDIA †ALL INDIA RADIO, Port Blair	DS • 10 kW; Sa/Su • DS • 10 kW
(con'd)		

FREQUENCY   COUNTRY, STATION, LOCATION   TARGET • NETWORK • POWER (kW)   World Time

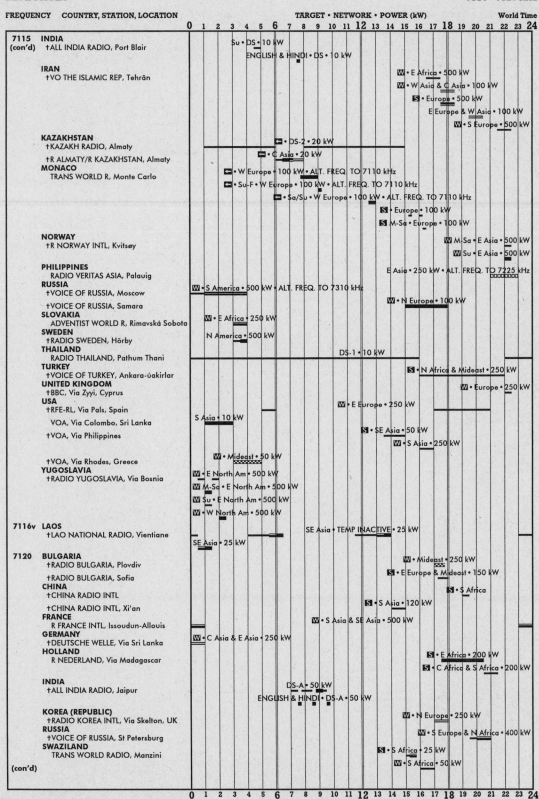

FREQUENCY	COUNTRY, STATION, LOCATION	TARGET • NETWORK • POWER (kW)
7115 (con'd)	**INDIA** †ALL INDIA RADIO, Port Blair	Su • DS • 10 kW / ENGLISH & HINDI • DS • 10 kW
	IRAN †VO THE ISLAMIC REP, Tehrān	W • E Africa • 500 kW / W • W Asia & C Asia • 100 kW / S • Europe • 500 kW / E Europe & W Asia • 100 kW / W • S Europe • 500 kW
	KAZAKHSTAN †KAZAKH RADIO, Almaty	DS-2 • 20 kW
	†R ALMATY/R KAZAKHSTAN, Almaty	C Asia • 20 kW
	MONACO TRANS WORLD R, Monte Carlo	W • W Europe • 100 kW • ALT. FREQ. TO 7110 kHz / Su-F • W Europe • 100 kW • ALT. FREQ. TO 7110 kHz / Sa/Su • W Europe • 100 kW • ALT. FREQ. TO 7110 kHz / S • Europe • 100 kW / S M-Sa • Europe • 100 kW
	NORWAY †R NORWAY INTL, Kvitsøy	W M-Sa • E Asia • 500 kW / W Su • E Asia • 500 kW
	PHILIPPINES RADIO VERITAS ASIA, Palauig	E Asia • 250 kW • ALT. FREQ. TO 7225 kHz
	RUSSIA †VOICE OF RUSSIA, Moscow	W • S America • 500 kW • ALT. FREQ. TO 7310 kHz
	†VOICE OF RUSSIA, Samara	W • N Europe • 100 kW
	SLOVAKIA ADVENTIST WORLD R, Rimavská Sobota	W • E Africa • 250 kW
	SWEDEN †RADIO SWEDEN, Hörby	N America • 500 kW
	THAILAND RADIO THAILAND, Pathum Thani	DS-1 • 10 kW
	TURKEY †VOICE OF TURKEY, Ankara-úakirlar	S • N Africa & Mideast • 250 kW
	UNITED KINGDOM †BBC, Via Zyyi, Cyprus	W • Europe • 250 kW
	USA †RFE-RL, Via Pals, Spain	W • E Europe • 250 kW
	VOA, Via Colombo, Sri Lanka	S Asia • 10 kW
	†VOA, Via Philippines	S • SE Asia • 50 kW / W • S Asia • 250 kW
	†VOA, Via Rhodes, Greece	W • Mideast • 50 kW
	YUGOSLAVIA †RADIO YUGOSLAVIA, Via Bosnia	W • E North Am • 500 kW / W M-Sa • E North Am • 500 kW / W Su • E North Am • 500 kW / W • W North Am • 500 kW
7116v	**LAOS** †LAO NATIONAL RADIO, Vientiane	SE Asia • TEMP INACTIVE • 25 kW / SE Asia • 25 kW
7120	**BULGARIA** †RADIO BULGARIA, Plovdiv	W • Mideast • 250 kW
	†RADIO BULGARIA, Sofia	S • E Europe & Mideast • 150 kW
	CHINA †CHINA RADIO INTL	S • S Africa
	†CHINA RADIO INTL, Xi'an	S • S Asia • 120 kW
	FRANCE R FRANCE INTL, Issoudun-Allouis	W • S Asia & SE Asia • 500 kW
	GERMANY †DEUTSCHE WELLE, Via Sri Lanka	W • C Asia & E Asia • 250 kW
	HOLLAND R NEDERLAND, Via Madagascar	S • E Africa • 200 kW / S • C Africa & S Africa • 200 kW
	INDIA †ALL INDIA RADIO, Jaipur	DS-A • 50 kW / ENGLISH & HINDI • DS-A • 50 kW
	KOREA (REPUBLIC) †RADIO KOREA INTL, Via Skelton, UK	W • N Europe • 250 kW
	RUSSIA †VOICE OF RUSSIA, St Petersburg	W • S Europe & N Africa • 400 kW
	SWAZILAND TRANS WORLD RADIO, Manzini	S • S Africa • 25 kW / W • S Africa • 50 kW
(con'd)		

ENGLISH ▬   ARABIC ෴   CHINESE ▫▫▫   FRENCH ═══   GERMAN ▬▬   RUSSIAN ══   SPANISH ▬▬   OTHER ▬

FREQUENCY   COUNTRY, STATION, LOCATION   TARGET • NETWORK • POWER (kW)   World Time

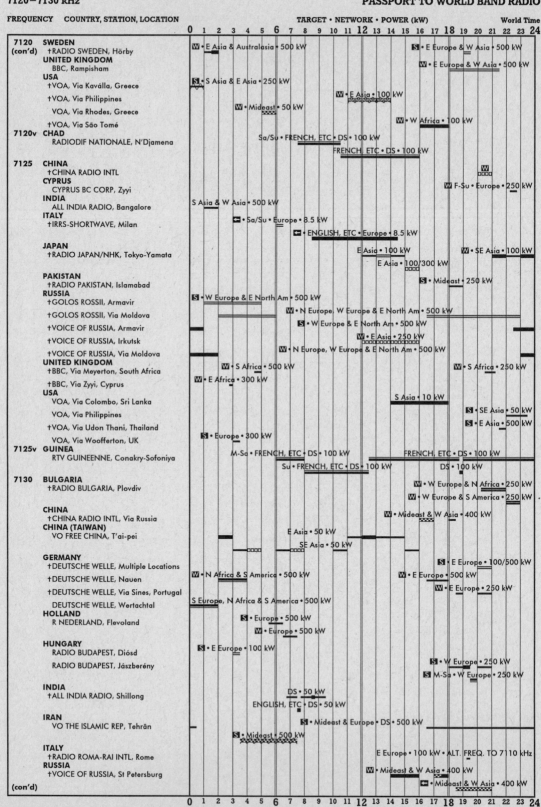

7120 (con'd)
- **SWEDEN** — †RADIO SWEDEN, Hörby — W • E Asia & Australasia • 500 kW — S • E Europe & W Asia • 500 kW
- **UNITED KINGDOM** — BBC, Rampisham — W • E Europe & W Asia • 500 kW
- **USA**
  - †VOA, Via Kavála, Greece — S • S Asia & E Asia • 250 kW
  - †VOA, Via Philippines — W • E Asia • 100 kW
  - VOA, Via Rhodes, Greece — W • Mideast • 50 kW
  - †VOA, Via São Tomé — W • W Africa • 100 kW

7120v CHAD — RADIODIF NATIONALE, N'Djamena — Sa/Su • FRENCH, ETC • DS • 100 kW — FRENCH, ETC • DS • 100 kW

7125 CHINA
- †CHINA RADIO INTL — W
- **CYPRUS** — CYPRUS BC CORP, Zyyi — W F-Su • Europe • 250 kW
- **INDIA** — ALL INDIA RADIO, Bangalore — S Asia & W Asia • 500 kW
- **ITALY** — †IRRS-SHORTWAVE, Milan — Sa/Su • Europe • 8.5 kW — ENGLISH, ETC • Europe • 8.5 kW
- **JAPAN** — †RADIO JAPAN/NHK, Tokyo-Yamata — E Asia • 100 kW — W • SE Asia • 100 kW — E Asia • 100/300 kW
- **PAKISTAN** — †RADIO PAKISTAN, Islamabad — S • Mideast • 250 kW
- **RUSSIA**
  - †GOLOS ROSSII, Armavir — S • W Europe & E North Am • 500 kW
  - †GOLOS ROSSII, Via Moldova — W • N Europe, W Europe & E North Am • 500 kW
  - †VOICE OF RUSSIA, Armavir — S • W Europe & E North Am • 500 kW
  - †VOICE OF RUSSIA, Irkutsk — W • E Asia • 250 kW
  - †VOICE OF RUSSIA, Via Moldova — W • N Europe, W Europe & E North Am • 500 kW
- **UNITED KINGDOM**
  - †BBC, Via Meyerton, South Africa — W • S Africa • 500 kW — W • S Africa • 250 kW
  - †BBC, Via Zyyi, Cyprus — W • E Africa • 300 kW
- **USA**
  - VOA, Via Colombo, Sri Lanka — S Asia • 10 kW
  - VOA, Via Philippines — S • SE Asia • 50 kW
  - †VOA, Via Udon Thani, Thailand — S • E Asia • 500 kW
  - VOA, Via Woofferton, UK — S • Europe • 300 kW

7125v GUINEA — RTV GUINEENNE, Conakry-Sofoniya — M-Sa • FRENCH, ETC • DS • 100 kW — FRENCH, ETC • DS • 100 kW — Su • FRENCH, ETC • DS • 100 kW — DS • 100 kW

7130 BULGARIA
- †RADIO BULGARIA, Plovdiv — W • W Europe & N Africa • 250 kW — W • W Europe & S America • 250 kW
- **CHINA** — †CHINA RADIO INTL, Via Russia — W • Mideast & W Asia • 400 kW
- **CHINA (TAIWAN)** — VO FREE CHINA, T'ai-pei — E Asia • 50 kW — SE Asia • 50 kW
- **GERMANY**
  - †DEUTSCHE WELLE, Multiple Locations — S • E Europe • 100/500 kW
  - †DEUTSCHE WELLE, Nauen — W • N Africa & S America • 500 kW — W • E Europe • 500 kW
  - †DEUTSCHE WELLE, Via Sines, Portugal — W • E Europe • 250 kW
  - DEUTSCHE WELLE, Wertachtal — S Europe, N Africa & S America • 500 kW
- **HOLLAND** — R NEDERLAND, Flevoland — S • Europe • 500 kW — W • Europe • 500 kW
- **HUNGARY**
  - RADIO BUDAPEST, Diósd — S • E Europe • 100 kW
  - RADIO BUDAPEST, Jászberény — S • W Europe • 250 kW — S M-Sa • W Europe • 250 kW
- **INDIA** — †ALL INDIA RADIO, Shillong — DS • 50 kW — ENGLISH, ETC • DS • 50 kW
- **IRAN** — VO THE ISLAMIC REP, Tehrān — S • Mideast & Europe • DS • 500 kW — S • Mideast • 500 kW
- **ITALY** — †RADIO ROMA-RAI INTL, Rome — E Europe • 100 kW • ALT. FREQ. TO 7110 kHz
- **RUSSIA** — †VOICE OF RUSSIA, St Petersburg — W • Mideast & W Asia • 400 kW — Mideast & W Asia • 400 kW

(con'd)

FREQUENCY   COUNTRY, STATION, LOCATION   TARGET • NETWORK • POWER (kW)   World Time

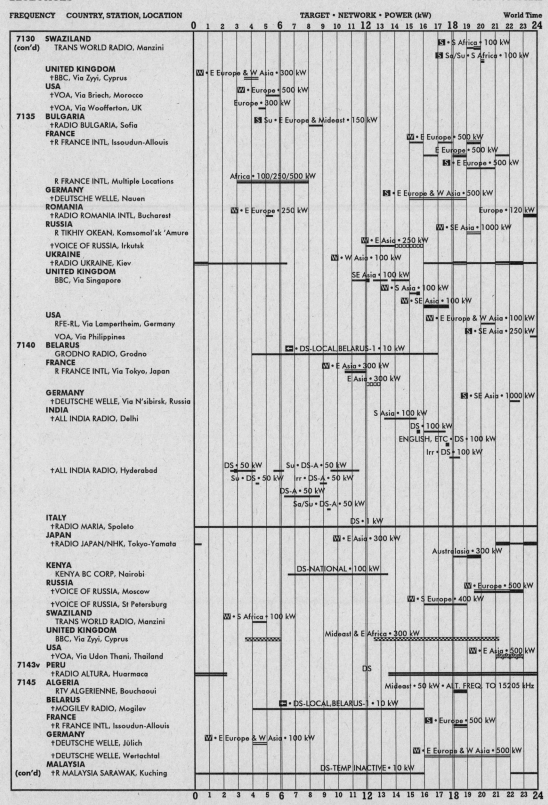

7130	SWAZILAND		S • S Africa • 100 kW
(con'd)	TRANS WORLD RADIO, Manzini		S • Sa/Su • S Africa • 100 kW
	UNITED KINGDOM		
	†BBC, Via Zyyi, Cyprus	W • E Europe & W Asia • 300 kW
	USA		
	†VOA, Via Briech, Morocco	W • Europe • 500 kW
	†VOA, Via Woofferton, UK	Europe • 300 kW
7135	BULGARIA		
	†RADIO BULGARIA, Sofia	S • Su • E Europe & Mideast • 150 kW
	FRANCE		
	†R FRANCE INTL, Issoudun-Allouis	W • E Europe • 500 kW
		E Europe • 500 kW
		S • E Europe • 500 kW
	R FRANCE INTL, Multiple Locations	Africa • 100/250/500 kW
	GERMANY		
	†DEUTSCHE WELLE, Nauen	S • E Europe & W Asia • 500 kW
	ROMANIA		
	†RADIO ROMANIA INTL, Bucharest	W • E Europe • 250 kW · Europe • 120 kW
	RUSSIA		
	R TIKHIY OKEAN, Komsomol'sk 'Amure	W • SE Asia • 1000 kW
	†VOICE OF RUSSIA, Irkutsk	W • E Asia • 250 kW
	UKRAINE		
	†RADIO UKRAINE, Kiev	W • W Asia • 100 kW
	UNITED KINGDOM		
	BBC, Via Singapore	SE Asia • 100 kW
		W • S Asia • 100 kW
		W • SE Asia • 100 kW
	USA		
	RFE-RL, Via Lampertheim, Germany	W • E Europe & W Asia • 100 kW
	VOA, Via Philippines	S • SE Asia • 250 kW
7140	BELARUS		
	GRODNO RADIO, Grodno	DS-LOCAL,BELARUS-1 • 10 kW
	FRANCE		
	R FRANCE INTL, Via Tokyo, Japan	W • E Asia • 300 kW
		E Asia • 300 kW
	GERMANY		
	†DEUTSCHE WELLE, Via N'sibirsk, Russia	S • SE Asia • 1000 kW
	INDIA		
	†ALL INDIA RADIO, Delhi	S Asia • 100 kW
		DS • 100 kW
		ENGLISH, ETC • DS • 100 kW
		Irr • DS • 100 kW
	†ALL INDIA RADIO, Hyderabad	DS • 50 kW · Su • DS-A • 50 kW
		Su • DS • 50 kW · Irr • DS-A • 50 kW
		DS-A • 50 kW
		Sa/Su • DS-A • 50 kW
	ITALY		
	†RADIO MARIA, Spoleto	DS • 1 kW
	JAPAN		
	†RADIO JAPAN/NHK, Tokyo-Yamata	W • E Asia • 300 kW
		Australasia • 300 kW
	KENYA		
	KENYA BC CORP, Nairobi	DS-NATIONAL • 100 kW
	RUSSIA		
	†VOICE OF RUSSIA, Moscow	W • Europe • 500 kW
	†VOICE OF RUSSIA, St Petersburg	W • S Europe • 400 kW
	SWAZILAND		
	TRANS WORLD RADIO, Manzini	W • S Africa • 100 kW
	UNITED KINGDOM		
	BBC, Via Zyyi, Cyprus	Mideast & E Africa • 300 kW
	USA		
	†VOA, Via Udon Thani, Thailand	W • E Asia • 500 kW
7143v	PERU		
	†RADIO ALTURA, Huarmaca	DS
7145	ALGERIA		
	RTV ALGERIENNE, Bouchaoui	Mideast • 50 kW • ALT. FREQ. TO 15205 kHz
	BELARUS		
	†MOGILEV RADIO, Mogilev	DS-LOCAL,BELARUS-1 • 10 kW
	FRANCE		
	†R FRANCE INTL, Issoudun-Allouis	S • Europe • 500 kW
	GERMANY		
	†DEUTSCHE WELLE, Jülich	W • E Europe & W Asia • 100 kW
	†DEUTSCHE WELLE, Wertachtal	W • E Europe & W Asia • 500 kW
	MALAYSIA		
(con'd)	†R MALAYSIA SARAWAK, Kuching	DS-TEMP INACTIVE • 10 kW

ENGLISH ▬   ARABIC ░   CHINESE □□□   FRENCH ▬▬   GERMAN ▬   RUSSIAN ═   SPANISH ▬   OTHER ▬

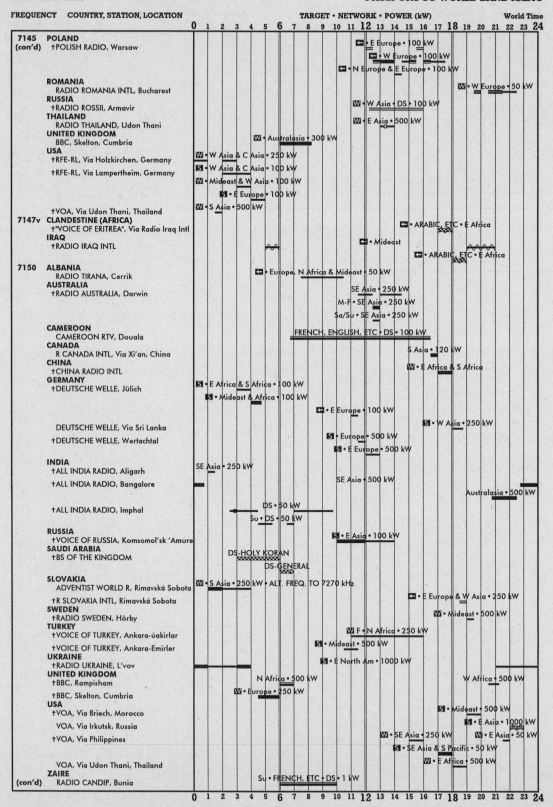

FREQUENCY   COUNTRY, STATION, LOCATION

TARGET • NETWORK • POWER (kW)

World Time

0 1 2 3 4 5 6 7 8 9 10 11 12 13 14 15 16 17 18 19 20 21 22 23 24

7145 (con'd)	**POLAND** †POLISH RADIO, Warsaw	⬌ • E Europe • 100 kW / ⬌ • W Europe • 100 kW / ⬌ • N Europe & E Europe • 100 kW
	ROMANIA RADIO ROMANIA INTL, Bucharest	W • W Europe • 50 kW
	RUSSIA †RADIO ROSSII, Armavir	W • W Asia • DS • 100 kW
	THAILAND RADIO THAILAND, Udon Thani	W • E Asia • 500 kW
	UNITED KINGDOM BBC, Skelton, Cumbria	W • Australasia • 300 kW
	USA †RFE-RL, Via Holzkirchen, Germany	W • W Asia & C Asia • 250 kW / S • W Asia & C Asia • 100 kW
	†RFE-RL, Via Lampertheim, Germany	W • Mideast & W Asia • 100 kW / S • E Europe • 100 kW
	†VOA, Via Udon Thani, Thailand	W • S Asia • 500 kW
7147v	**CLANDESTINE (AFRICA)** †"VOICE OF ERITREA", Via Radio Iraq Intl	⬌ • ARABIC, ETC • E Africa
	IRAQ †RADIO IRAQ INTL	⬌ • Mideast / ⬌ • ARABIC, ETC • E Africa
7150	**ALBANIA** RADIO TIRANA, Cerrik	⬌ • Europe, N Africa & Mideast • 50 kW
	AUSTRALIA †RADIO AUSTRALIA, Darwin	SE Asia • 250 kW / M-F • SE Asia • 250 kW / Sa/Su • SE Asia • 250 kW
	CAMEROON CAMEROON RTV, Douala	FRENCH, ENGLISH, ETC • DS • 100 kW
	CANADA R CANADA INTL, Via Xi'an, China	S Asia • 120 kW
	CHINA †CHINA RADIO INTL	W • E Africa & S Africa
	GERMANY †DEUTSCHE WELLE, Jülich	S • E Africa & S Africa • 100 kW / S • Mideast & Africa • 100 kW / ⬌ • E Europe • 100 kW / S • W Asia • 250 kW
	DEUTSCHE WELLE, Via Sri Lanka	S • Europe • 500 kW
	†DEUTSCHE WELLE, Wertachtal	S • E Europe • 500 kW
	INDIA †ALL INDIA RADIO, Aligarh	SE Asia • 250 kW
	†ALL INDIA RADIO, Bangalore	SE Asia • 500 kW / Australasia • 500 kW
	†ALL INDIA RADIO, Imphal	DS • 50 kW / Su • DS • 50 kW
	RUSSIA †VOICE OF RUSSIA, Komsomol'sk 'Amure	S • E Asia • 100 kW
	SAUDI ARABIA †BS OF THE KINGDOM	DS-HOLY KORAN / DS-GENERAL
	SLOVAKIA ADVENTIST WORLD R, Rimavská Sobota	W • S Asia • 250 kW • ALT. FREQ. TO 7270 kHz
	†R SLOVAKIA INTL, Rimavská Sobota	⬌ • E Europe & W Asia • 250 kW
	SWEDEN †RADIO SWEDEN, Hörby	W • Mideast • 500 kW
	TURKEY †VOICE OF TURKEY, Ankara-úakirlar	W • F • N Africa • 250 kW
	†VOICE OF TURKEY, Ankara-Emirler	S • Mideast • 500 kW
	UKRAINE †RADIO UKRAINE, L'vov	S • E North Am • 1000 kW
	UNITED KINGDOM †BBC, Rampisham	N Africa • 500 kW / W Africa • 500 kW
	†BBC, Skelton, Cumbria	W • Europe • 250 kW
	USA †VOA, Via Briech, Morocco	S • Mideast • 500 kW
	VOA, Via Irkutsk, Russia	S • E Asia • 1000 kW
	†VOA, Via Philippines	W • SE Asia • 250 kW / W • E Asia • 50 kW / S • SE Asia & S Pacific • 50 kW
	VOA, Via Udon Thani, Thailand	W • E Africa • 500 kW
(con'd)	**ZAIRE** RADIO CANDIP, Bunia	Su • FRENCH, ETC • DS • 1 kW

0 1 2 3 4 5 6 7 8 9 10 11 12 13 14 15 16 17 18 19 20 21 22 23 24

FREQUENCY	COUNTRY, STATION, LOCATION	TARGET • NETWORK • POWER (kW)	World Time

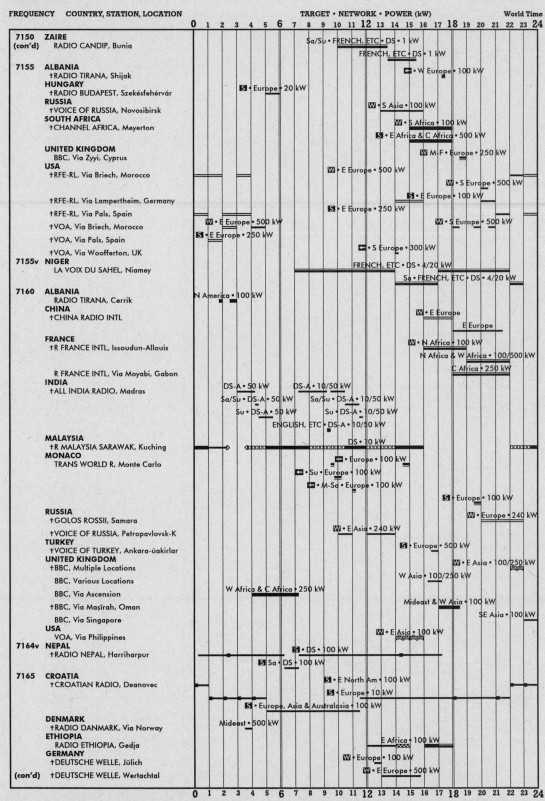

Contents (frequency / country / station / location):

- **7150** (con'd) — **ZAIRE**, RADIO CANDIP, Bunia
  - Sa/Su • FRENCH, ETC • DS • 1 kW
  - FRENCH, ETC • DS • 1 kW
- **7155** — **ALBANIA**, †RADIO TIRANA, Shijak
  - W • W Europe • 100 kW
  - **HUNGARY**, †RADIO BUDAPEST, Székésfehérvár
    - S • Europe • 20 kW
  - **RUSSIA**, †VOICE OF RUSSIA, Novosibirsk
    - W • S Asia • 100 kW
  - **SOUTH AFRICA**, †CHANNEL AFRICA, Meyerton
    - W • S Africa • 100 kW
    - S • E Africa & C Africa • 500 kW
  - **UNITED KINGDOM**, BBC, Via Zyyi, Cyprus
    - W M-F • Europe • 250 kW
  - **USA**, †RFE-RL, Via Briech, Morocco
    - W • E Europe • 500 kW
    - W • S Europe • 500 kW
  - †RFE-RL, Via Lampertheim, Germany
    - S • E Europe • 100 kW
  - †RFE-RL, Via Pals, Spain
    - S • E Europe • 250 kW
  - †VOA, Via Briech, Morocco
    - W • E Europe • 500 kW
    - W • S Europe • 500 kW
  - †VOA, Via Pals, Spain
    - S • E Europe • 250 kW
  - †VOA, Via Woofferton, UK
    - • S Europe • 300 kW
- **7155v** — **NIGER**, LA VOIX DU SAHEL, Niamey
  - FRENCH, ETC • DS • 4/20 kW
  - Sa • FRENCH, ETC • DS • 4/20 kW
- **7160** — **ALBANIA**, RADIO TIRANA, Cerrik
  - N America • 100 kW
  - **CHINA**, †CHINA RADIO INTL
    - W • E Europe
    - E Europe
  - **FRANCE**, †R FRANCE INTL, Issoudun-Allouis
    - W • N Africa • 100 kW
    - N Africa & W Africa • 100/500 kW
  - R FRANCE INTL, Via Moyabi, Gabon
    - C Africa • 250 kW
  - **INDIA**, †ALL INDIA RADIO, Madras
    - DS-A • 50 kW
    - DS-A • 10/50 kW
    - Sa/Su • DS-A • 50 kW
    - Sa/Su • DS-A • 10/50 kW
    - Su • DS-A • 50 kW
    - Su • DS-A • 10/50 kW
    - ENGLISH, ETC • DS-A • 10/50 kW
  - **MALAYSIA**, †R MALAYSIA SARAWAK, Kuching
    - DS • 10 kW
  - **MONACO**, TRANS WORLD R, Monte Carlo
    - • Europe • 100 kW
    - • Su • Europe • 100 kW
    - • M-Sa • Europe • 100 kW
    - S • Europe • 100 kW
  - **RUSSIA**, †GOLOS ROSSII, Samara
    - W • Europe • 240 kW
  - †VOICE OF RUSSIA, Petropavlovsk-K
    - W • E Asia • 240 kW
  - **TURKEY**, †VOICE OF TURKEY, Ankara-úakirlar
    - S • Europe • 500 kW
  - **UNITED KINGDOM**, †BBC, Multiple Locations
    - W • E Asia • 100/250 kW
  - BBC, Various Locations
    - W Asia • 100/250 kW
  - BBC, Via Ascension
    - W Africa & C Africa • 250 kW
  - †BBC, Via Maṣīrah, Oman
    - Mideast & W Asia • 100 kW
  - BBC, Via Singapore
    - SE Asia • 100 kW
  - **USA**, VOA, Via Philippines
    - W • E Asia • 100 kW
- **7164v** — **NEPAL**, †RADIO NEPAL, Harriharpur
  - S • DS • 100 kW
  - S Sa • DS • 100 kW
- **7165** — **CROATIA**, †CROATIAN RADIO, Deanovec
  - S • E North Am • 100 kW
  - S • Europe • 10 kW
  - S • Europe, Asia & Australasia • 100 kW
  - **DENMARK**, †RADIO DANMARK, Via Norway
    - Mideast • 500 kW
  - **ETHIOPIA**, RADIO ETHIOPIA, Gedja
    - E Africa • 100 kW
  - **GERMANY**, †DEUTSCHE WELLE, Jülich
    - W • Europe • 100 kW
- (con'd) — †DEUTSCHE WELLE, Wertachtal
  - W • E Europe • 500 kW

ENGLISH ▬▬   ARABIC ∿∿∿   CHINESE □□□   FRENCH ══   GERMAN ▬▬   RUSSIAN ══   SPANISH ▬▬   OTHER ──

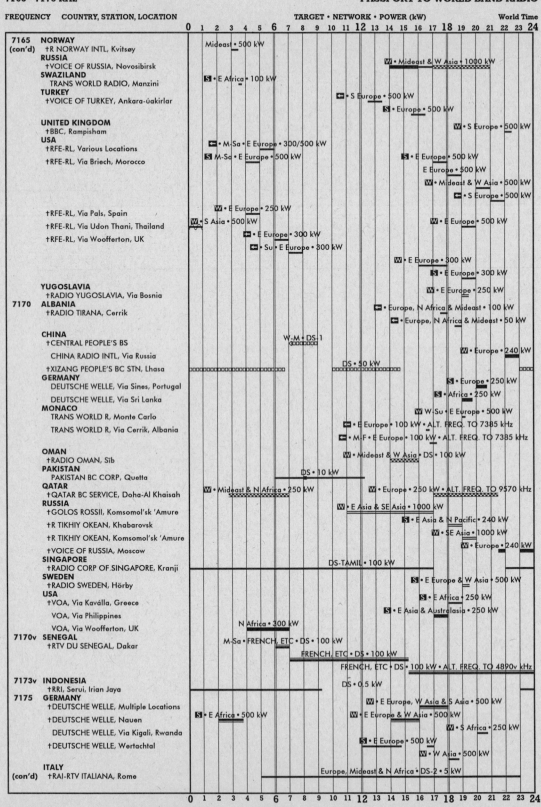

FREQUENCY	COUNTRY, STATION, LOCATION	TARGET • NETWORK • POWER (kW)	World Time

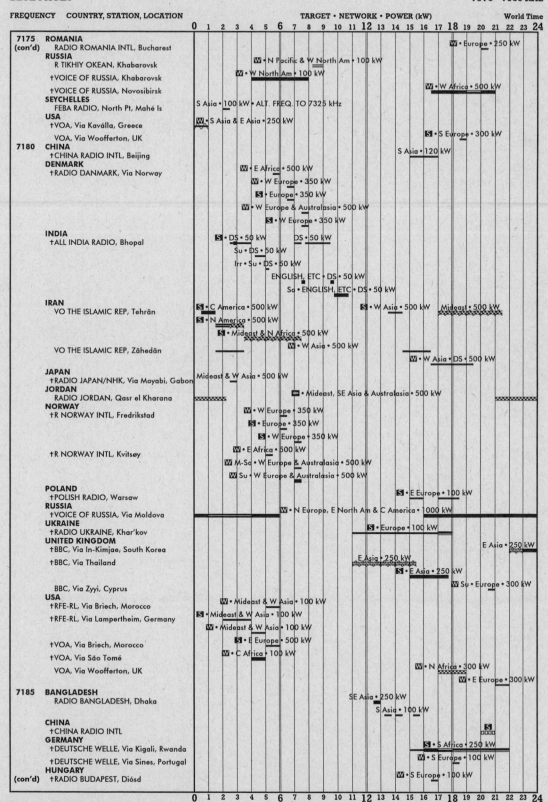

Frequency	Country, Station, Location	Target • Network • Power
7175 (con'd)	**ROMANIA** — RADIO ROMANIA INTL, Bucharest	W • Europe • 250 kW
	RUSSIA — R TIKHIY OKEAN, Khabarovsk	W • N Pacific & W North Am • 100 kW
	†VOICE OF RUSSIA, Khabarovsk	W • W North Am • 100 kW
	†VOICE OF RUSSIA, Novosibirsk	W • W Africa • 500 kW
	SEYCHELLES — FEBA RADIO, North Pt, Mahé Is	S Asia • 100 kW • ALT. FREQ. TO 7325 kHz
	USA — †VOA, Via Kaválla, Greece	W • S Asia & E Asia • 250 kW
	VOA, Via Woofferton, UK	S • S Europe • 300 kW
7180	**CHINA** — †CHINA RADIO INTL, Beijing	S Asia • 120 kW
	DENMARK — †RADIO DANMARK, Via Norway	W • E Africa • 500 kW
		W • W Europe • 350 kW
		S • Europe • 350 kW
		W • W Europe & Australasia • 500 kW
		S • W Europe • 350 kW
	INDIA — †ALL INDIA RADIO, Bhopal	S • DS • 50 kW DS • 50 kW
		Su • DS • 50 kW
		Irr • Su • DS • 50 kW
		ENGLISH, ETC • DS • 50 kW
		Sa • ENGLISH, ETC • DS • 50 kW
	IRAN — VO THE ISLAMIC REP, Tehrān	S • C America • 500 kW S • W Asia • 500 kW Mideast • 500 kW
		S • N America • 500 kW
		S • Mideast & N Africa • 500 kW
		W • W Asia • 500 kW
	VO THE ISLAMIC REP, Zāhedān	W • W Asia • DS • 500 kW
	JAPAN — †RADIO JAPAN/NHK, Via Moyabi, Gabon	Mideast & W Asia • 500 kW
	JORDAN — RADIO JORDAN, Qasr el Kharana	• Mideast, SE Asia & Australasia • 500 kW
	NORWAY — †R NORWAY INTL, Fredrikstad	W • W Europe • 350 kW
		S • Europe • 350 kW
		S • W Europe • 350 kW
	†R NORWAY INTL, Kvitsøy	W • E Africa • 500 kW
		W M-Sa • W Europe & Australasia • 500 kW
		W Su • W Europe & Australasia • 500 kW
	POLAND — †POLISH RADIO, Warsaw	S • E Europe • 100 kW
	RUSSIA — †VOICE OF RUSSIA, Via Moldova	W • N Europe, E North Am & C America • 1000 kW
	UKRAINE — †RADIO UKRAINE, Khar'kov	S • Europe • 100 kW
	UNITED KINGDOM — †BBC, Via In-Kimjae, South Korea	E Asia • 250 kW
	†BBC, Via Thailand	E Asia • 250 kW
		S • E Asia • 250 kW
	BBC, Via Zyyi, Cyprus	W Su • Europe • 300 kW
	USA — †RFE-RL, Via Briech, Morocco	W • Mideast & W Asia • 100 kW
	†RFE-RL, Via Lampertheim, Germany	S • Mideast & W Asia • 100 kW
		W • Mideast & W Asia • 100 kW
	†VOA, Via Briech, Morocco	S • E Europe • 500 kW
	†VOA, Via São Tomé	W • C Africa • 100 kW
	VOA, Via Woofferton, UK	W • N Africa • 300 kW
		W • E Europe • 300 kW
7185	**BANGLADESH** — RADIO BANGLADESH, Dhaka	SE Asia • 250 kW
		S Asia • 100 kW
	CHINA — †CHINA RADIO INTL	S
	GERMANY — †DEUTSCHE WELLE, Via Kigali, Rwanda	S • S Africa • 250 kW
	†DEUTSCHE WELLE, Via Sines, Portugal	W • S Europe • 100 kW
	HUNGARY (con'd) — †RADIO BUDAPEST, Diósd	W • S Europe • 100 kW

0 1 2 3 4 5 6 7 8 9 10 11 12 13 14 15 16 17 18 19 20 21 22 23 24

ENGLISH ▬ ARABIC ⨯⨯⨯ CHINESE ▫▫▫ FRENCH ═ GERMAN ▭▭ RUSSIAN ══ SPANISH ▬ OTHER ▬

FREQUENCY   COUNTRY, STATION, LOCATION

TARGET • NETWORK • POWER (kW)

World Time

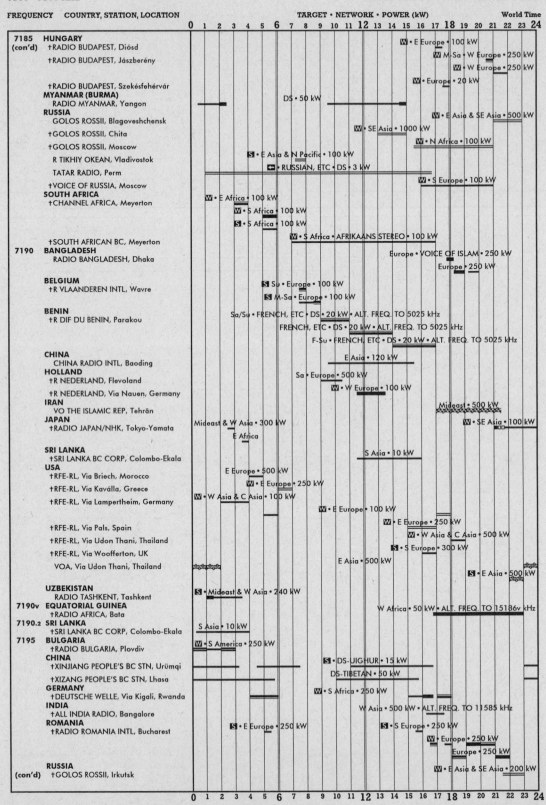

7185	**HUNGARY**
(con'd)	†RADIO BUDAPEST, Diósd — W • E Europe • 100 kW
	†RADIO BUDAPEST, Jászberény — W • M-Sa • W Europe • 250 kW / W • W Europe • 250 kW
	†RADIO BUDAPEST, Szekésfehérvár — W • Europe • 20 kW
	MYANMAR (BURMA)
	RADIO MYANMAR, Yangon — DS • 50 kW
	RUSSIA
	GOLOS ROSSII, Blagoveshchensk — W • E Asia & SE Asia • 500 kW
	†GOLOS ROSSII, Chita — W • SE Asia • 1000 kW
	†GOLOS ROSSII, Moscow — W • N Africa • 100 kW
	R TIKHIY OKEAN, Vladivostok — S • E Asia & N Pacific • 100 kW
	TATAR RADIO, Perm — RUSSIAN, ETC • DS • 3 kW
	†VOICE OF RUSSIA, Moscow — W • S Europe • 100 kW
	SOUTH AFRICA
	†CHANNEL AFRICA, Meyerton — W • E Africa • 100 kW / W • S Africa • 100 kW / S • S Africa • 100 kW
	†SOUTH AFRICAN BC, Meyerton — W • S Africa • AFRIKAANS STEREO • 100 kW
7190	**BANGLADESH**
	RADIO BANGLADESH, Dhaka — Europe • VOICE OF ISLAM • 250 kW / Europe • 250 kW
	BELGIUM
	†R VLAANDEREN INTL, Wavre — S • Su • Europe • 100 kW / S • M-Sa • Europe • 100 kW
	BENIN
	†R DIF DU BENIN, Parakou — Sa/Su • FRENCH, ETC • DS • 20 kW • ALT. FREQ. TO 5025 kHz / FRENCH, ETC • DS • 20 kW • ALT. FREQ. TO 5025 kHz / F-Su • FRENCH, ETC • DS • 20 kW • ALT. FREQ. TO 5025 kHz
	CHINA
	CHINA RADIO INTL, Baoding — E Asia • 120 kW
	HOLLAND
	†R NEDERLAND, Flevoland — Sa • Europe • 500 kW
	†R NEDERLAND, Via Nauen, Germany — W • W Europe • 100 kW
	IRAN
	VO THE ISLAMIC REP, Tehrän — Mideast • 500 kW
	JAPAN
	†RADIO JAPAN/NHK, Tokyo-Yamata — Mideast & W Asia • 300 kW / E Africa / W • SE Asia • 100 kW
	SRI LANKA
	†SRI LANKA BC CORP, Colombo-Ekala — S Asia • 10 kW
	USA
	†RFE-RL, Via Briech, Morocco — E Europe • 500 kW
	†RFE-RL, Via Kaválla, Greece — W • E Europe • 250 kW
	†RFE-RL, Via Lampertheim, Germany — W • W Asia & C Asia • 100 kW / W • E Europe • 100 kW
	†RFE-RL, Via Pals, Spain — W • E Europe • 250 kW
	†RFE-RL, Via Udon Thani, Thailand — W • W Asia & C Asia • 500 kW
	†RFE-RL, Via Woofferton, UK — S • S Europe • 300 kW
	VOA, Via Udon Thani, Thailand — E Asia • 500 kW / S • E Asia • 500 kW
	UZBEKISTAN
	RADIO TASHKENT, Tashkent — S • Mideast & W Asia • 240 kW
7190v	**EQUATORIAL GUINEA**
	†RADIO AFRICA, Bata — W Africa • 50 kW • ALT. FREQ. TO 15186v kHz
7190.2	**SRI LANKA**
	†SRI LANKA BC CORP, Colombo-Ekala — S Asia • 10 kW
7195	**BULGARIA**
	†RADIO BULGARIA, Plovdiv — W • S America • 250 kW
	CHINA
	†XINJIANG PEOPLE'S BC STN, Urümqi — S • DS-UIGHUR • 15 kW
	†XIZANG PEOPLE'S BC STN, Lhasa — DS-TIBETAN • 50 kW
	GERMANY
	†DEUTSCHE WELLE, Via Kigali, Rwanda — W • S Africa • 250 kW
	INDIA
	†ALL INDIA RADIO, Bangalore — W Asia • 500 kW • ALT. FREQ. TO 11585 kHz
	ROMANIA
	†RADIO ROMANIA INTL, Bucharest — S • E Europe • 250 kW / S • S Europe • 250 kW / W • Europe • 250 kW / Europe • 250 kW
	RUSSIA
(con'd)	†GOLOS ROSSII, Irkutsk — W • E Asia & SE Asia • 200 kW

FREQUENCY   COUNTRY, STATION, LOCATION   TARGET • NETWORK • POWER (kW)   World Time

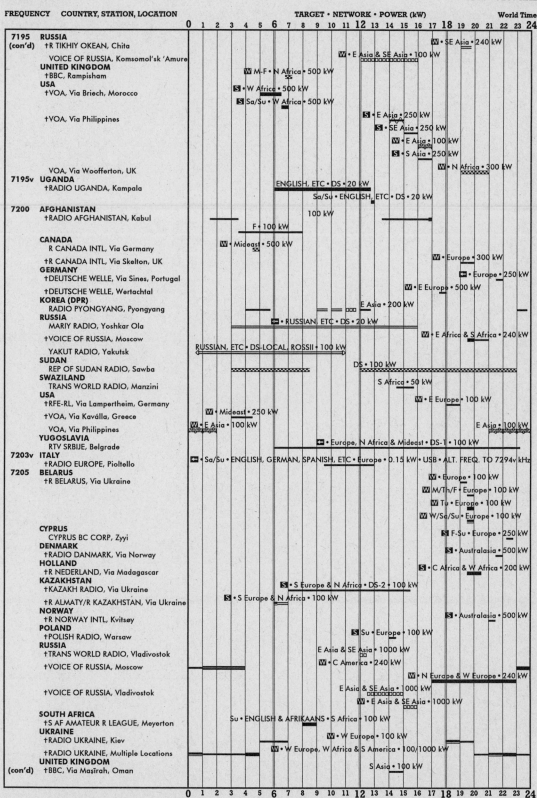

FREQUENCY	COUNTRY, STATION, LOCATION	TARGET • NETWORK • POWER (kW)
7195 (con'd)	**RUSSIA** †R TIKHIY OKEAN, Chita	W • SE Asia • 240 kW
	VOICE OF RUSSIA, Komsomol'sk 'Amure	W • E Asia & SE Asia • 100 kW
	UNITED KINGDOM †BBC, Rampisham	W • M-F • N Africa • 500 kW
	USA †VOA, Via Briech, Morocco	S • W Africa • 500 kW S • Sa/Su • W Africa • 500 kW
	†VOA, Via Philippines	S • E Asia • 250 kW S • SE Asia • 250 kW W • E Asia • 100 kW S • S Asia • 250 kW
	VOA, Via Woofferton, UK	W • N Africa • 300 kW
7195v	**UGANDA** †RADIO UGANDA, Kampala	ENGLISH, ETC • DS • 20 kW Sa/Su • ENGLISH, ETC • DS • 20 kW
7200	**AFGHANISTAN** †RADIO AFGHANISTAN, Kabul	100 kW F • 100 kW
	CANADA R CANADA INTL, Via Germany	W • Mideast • 500 kW
	†R CANADA INTL, Via Skelton, UK	W • Europe • 300 kW
	GERMANY †DEUTSCHE WELLE, Via Sines, Portugal	• Europe • 250 kW
	†DEUTSCHE WELLE, Wertachtal	W • E Europe • 500 kW
	KOREA (DPR) RADIO PYONGYANG, Pyongyang	E Asia • 200 kW
	RUSSIA MARIY RADIO, Yoshkar Ola	• RUSSIAN, ETC • DS • 20 kW
	†VOICE OF RUSSIA, Moscow	W • E Africa & S Africa • 240 kW
	YAKUT RADIO, Yakutsk	RUSSIAN, ETC • DS-LOCAL, ROSSII • 100 kW
	SUDAN REP OF SUDAN RADIO, Sawba	DS • 100 kW
	SWAZILAND TRANS WORLD RADIO, Manzini	S Africa • 50 kW
	USA †RFE-RL, Via Lampertheim, Germany	W • E Europe • 100 kW
	†VOA, Via Kaválla, Greece	W • Mideast • 250 kW
	VOA, Via Philippines	W • E Asia • 100 kW E Asia • 100 kW
	YUGOSLAVIA RTV SRBIJE, Belgrade	• Europe, N Africa & Mideast • DS-1 • 100 kW
7203v	**ITALY** †RADIO EUROPE, Pioltello	• Sa/Su • ENGLISH, GERMAN, SPANISH, ETC • Europe • 0.15 kW • USB • ALT. FREQ. TO 7294v kHz
7205	**BELARUS** †R BELARUS, Via Ukraine	W • Europe • 100 kW W • M/Th/F • Europe • 100 kW W • Tu • Europe • 100 kW W • W/Sa/Su • Europe • 100 kW
	CYPRUS CYPRUS BC CORP, Zyyi	S • F-Su • Europe • 250 kW
	DENMARK †RADIO DANMARK, Via Norway	S • Australasia • 500 kW
	HOLLAND †R NEDERLAND, Via Madagascar	S • C Africa & W Africa • 200 kW
	KAZAKHSTAN †KAZAKH RADIO, Via Ukraine	S • S Europe & N Africa • DS-2 • 100 kW
	†R ALMATY/R KAZAKHSTAN, Via Ukraine	S • S Europe & N Africa • 100 kW
	NORWAY †R NORWAY INTL, Kvitsøy	S • Australasia • 500 kW
	POLAND †POLISH RADIO, Warsaw	S • Su • Europe • 100 kW
	RUSSIA †TRANS WORLD RADIO, Vladivostok	E Asia & SE Asia • 1000 kW
	†VOICE OF RUSSIA, Moscow	W • C America • 240 kW W • N Europe & W Europe • 240 kW
	†VOICE OF RUSSIA, Vladivostok	E Asia & SE Asia • 1000 kW W • E Asia & SE Asia • 1000 kW
	SOUTH AFRICA †S AF AMATEUR R LEAGUE, Meyerton	Su • ENGLISH & AFRIKAANS • S Africa • 100 kW
	UKRAINE †RADIO UKRAINE, Kiev	W • W Europe • 100 kW
	†RADIO UKRAINE, Multiple Locations	W • W Europe, W Africa & S America • 100/1000 kW
	UNITED KINGDOM (con'd) †BBC, Via Maşirah, Oman	S Asia • 100 kW

ENGLISH ▬   ARABIC ▨   CHINESE ▢▢▢   FRENCH ▭▭   GERMAN ▬   RUSSIAN ══   SPANISH ▬   OTHER ▬

FREQUENCY	COUNTRY, STATION, LOCATION	TARGET • NETWORK • POWER (kW)	World Time

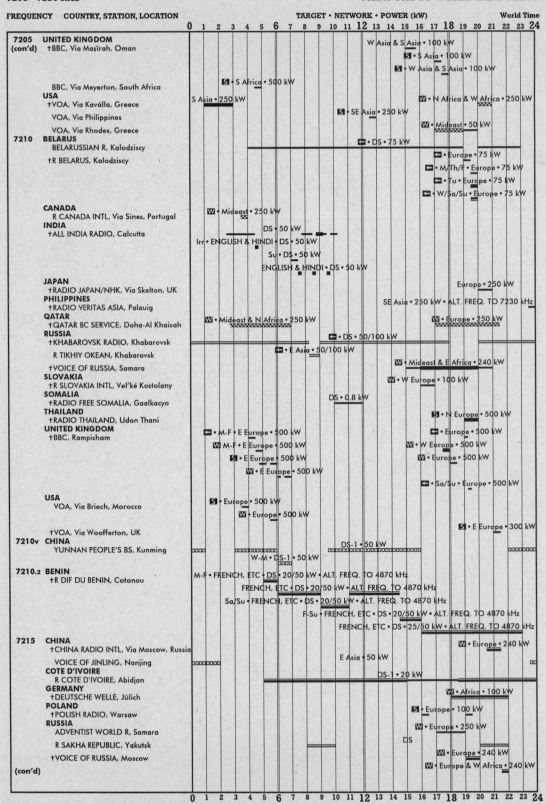

7205 UNITED KINGDOM
(con'd) †BBC, Via Maşīrah, Oman
    W Asia & S Asia • 100 kW
    S • S Asia • 100 kW
    S • W Asia & S Asia • 100 kW

  BBC, Via Meyerton, South Africa
    S • S Africa • 500 kW
USA
  †VOA, Via Kaválla, Greece   S Asia • 250 kW   W • N Africa & W Africa • 250 kW
  VOA, Via Philippines   S • SE Asia • 250 kW
  VOA, Via Rhodes, Greece   W • Mideast • 50 kW

7210 BELARUS
  BELARUSSIAN R, Kalodziscy   • DS • 75 kW
  †R BELARUS, Kalodziscy   • Europe • 75 kW
    • M/Th/F • Europe • 75 kW
    • Tu • Europe • 75 kW
    • W/Sa/Su • Europe • 75 kW

CANADA
  R CANADA INTL, Via Sines, Portugal   W • Mideast • 250 kW
INDIA
  †ALL INDIA RADIO, Calcutta   DS • 50 kW
    Irr • ENGLISH & HINDI • DS • 50 kW
    Su • DS • 50 kW
    ENGLISH & HINDI • DS • 50 kW

JAPAN
  †RADIO JAPAN/NHK, Via Skelton, UK   Europe • 250 kW
PHILIPPINES
  †RADIO VERITAS ASIA, Palauig   SE Asia • 250 kW • ALT. FREQ. TO 7230 kHz
QATAR
  †QATAR BC SERVICE, Doha-Al Khaisah   W • Mideast & N Africa • 250 kW   W • Europe • 250 kW
RUSSIA
  †KHABAROVSK RADIO, Khabarovsk   • DS • 50/100 kW
  R TIKHIY OKEAN, Khabarovsk   • E Asia • 50/100 kW
  †VOICE OF RUSSIA, Samara   W • Mideast & E Africa • 240 kW
SLOVAKIA
  †R SLOVAKIA INTL, Vel'ké Kostolany   W • W Europe • 100 kW
SOMALIA
  †RADIO FREE SOMALIA, Gaalkacyo   DS • 0.8 kW
THAILAND
  †RADIO THAILAND, Udon Thani   S • N Europe • 500 kW
UNITED KINGDOM
  †BBC, Rampisham   • M-F • E Europe • 500 kW   • Europe • 500 kW
    W • M-F • E Europe • 500 kW   W • W Europe • 500 kW
    S • E Europe • 500 kW   W • Europe • 500 kW
    W • E Europe • 500 kW
    • Sa/Su • Europe • 500 kW

USA
  VOA, Via Briech, Morocco   S • Europe • 500 kW
    W • Europe • 500 kW
  †VOA, Via Woofferton, UK   S • E Europe • 300 kW
7210v CHINA
  YUNNAN PEOPLE'S BS, Kunming   DS-1 • 50 kW
    W-M • DS-1 • 50 kW
7210.2 BENIN
  †R DIF DU BENIN, Cotonou   M-F • FRENCH, ETC • DS • 20/50 kW • ALT. FREQ. TO 4870 kHz
    FRENCH, ETC • DS • 20/50 kW • ALT. FREQ. TO 4870 kHz
    Sa/Su • FRENCH, ETC • DS • 20/50 kW • ALT. FREQ. TO 4870 kHz
    F-Su • FRENCH, ETC • DS • 20/50 kW • ALT. FREQ. TO 4870 kHz
    FRENCH, ETC • DS • 25/50 kW • ALT. FREQ. TO 4870 kHz

7215 CHINA
  †CHINA RADIO INTL, Via Moscow, Russia   W • Europe • 240 kW
  VOICE OF JINLING, Nanjing   E Asia • 50 kW
COTE D'IVOIRE
  R COTE D'IVOIRE, Abidjan   DS-1 • 20 kW
GERMANY
  †DEUTSCHE WELLE, Jülich   W • Africa • 100 kW
POLAND
  †POLISH RADIO, Warsaw   S • Europe • 100 kW
RUSSIA
  ADVENTIST WORLD R, Samara   W • Europe • 250 kW
  R SAKHA REPUBLIC, Yakutsk   DS
  †VOICE OF RUSSIA, Moscow   W • Europe • 240 kW
    W • Europe & W Africa • 240 kW

(con'd)

FREQUENCY   COUNTRY, STATION, LOCATION

TARGET • NETWORK • POWER (kW)

World Time

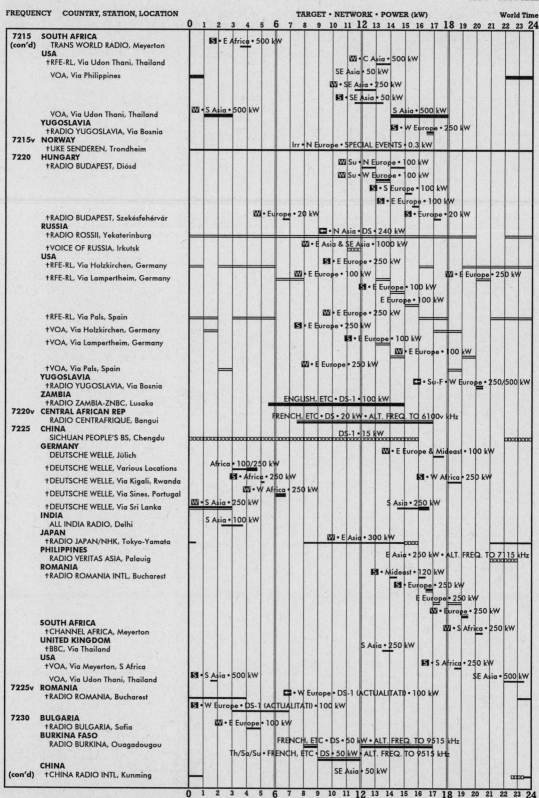

Frequency	Country, Station, Location	Target • Network • Power
7215 (con'd)	**SOUTH AFRICA** †TRANS WORLD RADIO, Meyerton	S • E Africa • 500 kW
	USA †RFE-RL, Via Udon Thani, Thailand	W • C Asia • 500 kW
	VOA, Via Philippines	SE Asia • 50 kW / W • SE Asia • 250 kW / S • SE Asia • 50 kW
	VOA, Via Udon Thani, Thailand	W • S Asia • 500 kW / S Asia • 500 kW
	YUGOSLAVIA †RADIO YUGOSLAVIA, Via Bosnia	S • W Europe • 250 kW
7215v	**NORWAY** †UKE SENDEREN, Trondheim	Irr • N Europe • SPECIAL EVENTS • 0.3 kW
7220	**HUNGARY** †RADIO BUDAPEST, Diósd	W Su • N Europe • 100 kW / W Su • W Europe • 100 kW / S • S Europe • 100 kW / S • E Europe • 100 kW
	†RADIO BUDAPEST, Szekésfehérvár	W • Europe • 20 kW / S • Europe • 20 kW
	RUSSIA †RADIO ROSSII, Yekaterinburg	N Asia • DS • 240 kW
	†VOICE OF RUSSIA, Irkutsk	W • E Asia & SE Asia • 1000 kW
	USA †RFE-RL, Via Holzkirchen, Germany	S • E Europe • 250 kW
	†RFE-RL, Via Lampertheim, Germany	W • E Europe • 100 kW / W • E Europe • 250 kW / S • E Europe • 100 kW / E Europe • 100 kW
	†RFE-RL, Via Pals, Spain	W • E Europe • 250 kW
	†VOA, Via Holzkirchen, Germany	S • E Europe • 250 kW
	†VOA, Via Lampertheim, Germany	S • E Europe • 100 kW / W • E Europe • 100 kW
	†VOA, Via Pals, Spain	W • E Europe • 250 kW
	YUGOSLAVIA †RADIO YUGOSLAVIA, Via Bosnia	• Su-F • W Europe • 250/500 kW
	ZAMBIA †RADIO ZAMBIA-ZNBC, Lusaka	ENGLISH, ETC • DS-1 • 100 kW
7220v	**CENTRAL AFRICAN REP** RADIO CENTRAFRIQUE, Bangui	FRENCH, ETC • DS • 20 kW • ALT. FREQ. TO 6100v kHz
7225	**CHINA** SICHUAN PEOPLE'S BS, Chengdu	DS-1 • 15 kW
	GERMANY DEUTSCHE WELLE, Jülich	W • E Europe & Mideast • 100 kW
	†DEUTSCHE WELLE, Various Locations	Africa • 100/250 kW
	†DEUTSCHE WELLE, Via Kigali, Rwanda	S • Africa • 250 kW / S • W Africa • 250 kW
	†DEUTSCHE WELLE, Via Sines, Portugal	W • W Africa • 250 kW
	†DEUTSCHE WELLE, Via Sri Lanka	W • S Asia • 250 kW / S Asia • 250 kW
	INDIA ALL INDIA RADIO, Delhi	S Asia • 100 kW
	JAPAN †RADIO JAPAN/NHK, Tokyo-Yamata	W • E Asia • 300 kW
	PHILIPPINES RADIO VERITAS ASIA, Palauig	E Asia • 250 kW • ALT. FREQ. TO 7115 kHz
	ROMANIA †RADIO ROMANIA INTL, Bucharest	S • Mideast • 120 kW / S • Europe • 250 kW / E Europe • 250 kW / W • Europe • 250 kW
	SOUTH AFRICA †CHANNEL AFRICA, Meyerton	W • S Africa • 250 kW
	UNITED KINGDOM †BBC, Via Thailand	S Asia • 250 kW
	USA †VOA, Via Meyerton, S Africa	S • S Africa • 250 kW
	VOA, Via Udon Thani, Thailand	S • S Asia • 500 kW / SE Asia • 500 kW
7225v	**ROMANIA** †RADIO ROMANIA, Bucharest	• W Europe • DS-1 (ACTUALITATI) • 100 kW / S • W Europe • DS-1 (ACTUALITATI) • 100 kW
7230	**BULGARIA** †RADIO BULGARIA, Sofia	W • E Europe • 100 kW
	BURKINA FASO RADIO BURKINA, Ouagadougou	FRENCH, ETC • DS • 50 kW • ALT. FREQ. TO 9515 kHz / Th/Sa/Su • FRENCH, ETC • DS • 50 kW • ALT. FREQ. TO 9515 kHz
CHINA (con'd)	†CHINA RADIO INTL, Kunming	SE Asia • 50 kW

ENGLISH ▬   ARABIC ≈≈≈   CHINESE □□□   FRENCH ▬▬   GERMAN ▬   RUSSIAN ══   SPANISH ▬   OTHER ▬

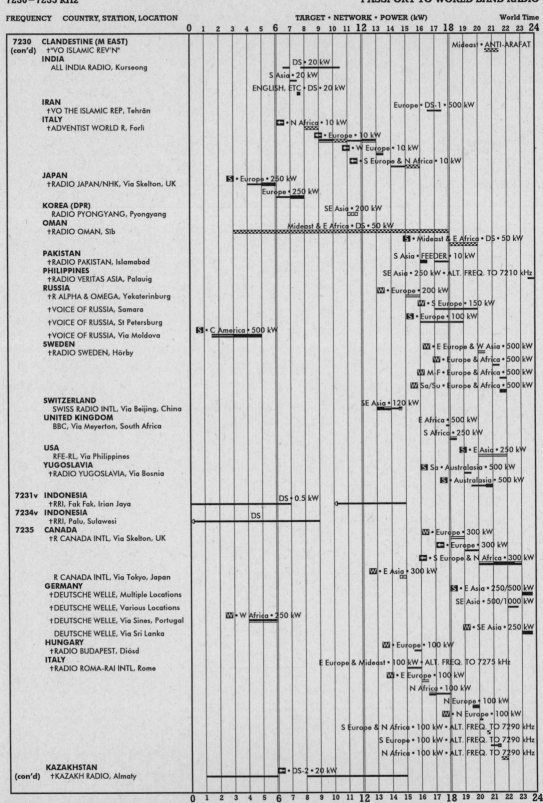

FREQUENCY	COUNTRY, STATION, LOCATION	TARGET • NETWORK • POWER (kW)	World Time

7230 CLANDESTINE (M EAST)
(con'd) †"VO ISLAMIC REV'N" — Mideast • ANTI-ARAFAT
INDIA
ALL INDIA RADIO, Kurseong — DS • 20 kW / S Asia • 20 kW / ENGLISH, ETC • DS • 20 kW
IRAN
†VO THE ISLAMIC REP, Tehrān — Europe • DS-1 • 500 kW
ITALY
†ADVENTIST WORLD R, Forlì — • N Africa • 10 kW / • Europe • 10 kW / • W Europe • 10 kW / • S Europe & N Africa • 10 kW
JAPAN
†RADIO JAPAN/NHK, Via Skelton, UK — S • Europe • 250 kW / Europe • 250 kW
KOREA (DPR)
RADIO PYONGYANG, Pyongyang — SE Asia • 200 kW
OMAN
†RADIO OMAN, Sīb — Mideast & E Africa • DS • 50 kW / S • Mideast & E Africa • DS • 50 kW
PAKISTAN
†RADIO PAKISTAN, Islamabad — S Asia • FEEDER • 10 kW
PHILIPPINES
†RADIO VERITAS ASIA, Palauig — SE Asia • 250 kW • ALT. FREQ. TO 7210 kHz
RUSSIA
†R ALPHA & OMEGA, Yekaterinburg — W • Europe • 200 kW
†VOICE OF RUSSIA, Samara — W • S Europe • 150 kW
†VOICE OF RUSSIA, St Petersburg — S • Europe • 100 kW
†VOICE OF RUSSIA, Via Moldova — S • C America • 500 kW
SWEDEN
†RADIO SWEDEN, Hörby — W • E Europe & W Asia • 500 kW / W • Europe & Africa • 500 kW / W M-F • Europe & Africa • 500 kW / W Sa/Su • Europe & Africa • 500 kW
SWITZERLAND
SWISS RADIO INTL, Via Beijing, China — SE Asia • 120 kW
UNITED KINGDOM
BBC, Via Meyerton, South Africa — E Africa • 500 kW / S Africa • 250 kW
USA
RFE-RL, Via Philippines — S • E Asia • 250 kW
YUGOSLAVIA
†RADIO YUGOSLAVIA, Via Bosnia — S Sa • Australasia • 500 kW / S • Australasia • 500 kW

7231v INDONESIA
†RRI, Fak Fak, Irian Jaya — DS • 0.5 kW
7234v INDONESIA
†RRI, Palu, Sulawesi — DS
7235 CANADA
†R CANADA INTL, Via Skelton, UK — W • Europe • 300 kW / • Europe • 300 kW / • S Europe & N Africa • 300 kW

R CANADA INTL, Via Tokyo, Japan — W • E Asia • 300 kW
GERMANY
†DEUTSCHE WELLE, Multiple Locations — S • E Asia • 250/500 kW
†DEUTSCHE WELLE, Various Locations — SE Asia • 500/1000 kW
†DEUTSCHE WELLE, Via Sines, Portugal — W • W Africa • 250 kW
DEUTSCHE WELLE, Via Sri Lanka — W • SE Asia • 250 kW
HUNGARY
†RADIO BUDAPEST, Diósd — W • Europe • 100 kW
ITALY
†RADIO ROMA-RAI INTL, Rome — E Europe & Mideast • 100 kW • ALT. FREQ. TO 7275 kHz / W • E Europe • 100 kW / N Africa • 100 kW / N Europe • 100 kW / W • N Europe • 100 kW / S Europe & N Africa • 100 kW • ALT. FREQ. TO 7290 kHz / S Europe • 100 kW • ALT. FREQ. TO 7290 kHz / N Africa • 100 kW • ALT. FREQ. TO 7290 kHz

KAZAKHSTAN
(con'd) †KAZAKH RADIO, Almaty — • DS-2 • 20 kW

FREQUENCY   COUNTRY, STATION, LOCATION

TARGET • NETWORK • POWER (kW)

World Time

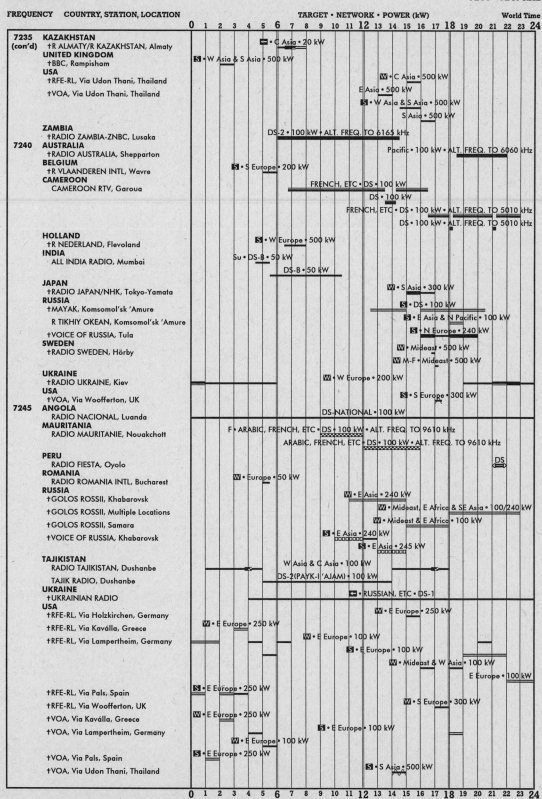

Frequency	Country, Station, Location	Target • Network • Power
7235 (con'd)	**KAZAKHSTAN**	
	†R ALMATY/R KAZAKHSTAN, Almaty	C Asia • 20 kW
	UNITED KINGDOM	
	†BBC, Rampisham	W Asia & S Asia • 500 kW
	USA	
	†RFE-RL, Via Udon Thani, Thailand	C Asia • 500 kW
	†VOA, Via Udon Thani, Thailand	E Asia • 500 kW / W Asia & S Asia • 500 kW / S Asia • 500 kW
	ZAMBIA	
	†RADIO ZAMBIA-ZNBC, Lusaka	DS-2 • 100 kW • ALT. FREQ. TO 6165 kHz
7240	**AUSTRALIA**	
	†RADIO AUSTRALIA, Shepparton	Pacific • 100 kW • ALT. FREQ. TO 6060 kHz
	BELGIUM	
	†R VLAANDEREN INTL, Wavre	S Europe • 200 kW
	CAMEROON	
	CAMEROON RTV, Garoua	FRENCH, ETC • DS • 100 kW / DS • 100 kW / FRENCH, ETC • DS • 100 kW • ALT. FREQ. TO 5010 kHz / DS • 100 kW • ALT. FREQ. TO 5010 kHz
	HOLLAND	
	†R NEDERLAND, Flevoland	W Europe • 500 kW
	INDIA	
	ALL INDIA RADIO, Mumbai	Su • DS-B • 50 kW / DS-B • 50 kW
	JAPAN	
	†RADIO JAPAN/NHK, Tokyo-Yamata	S Asia • 300 kW
	RUSSIA	
	†MAYAK, Komsomol'sk 'Amure	DS • 100 kW
	R TIKHIY OKEAN, Komsomol'sk 'Amure	E Asia & N Pacific • 100 kW
	†VOICE OF RUSSIA, Tula	N Europe • 240 kW
	SWEDEN	
	†RADIO SWEDEN, Hörby	Mideast • 500 kW / M-F • Mideast • 500 kW
	UKRAINE	
	†RADIO UKRAINE, Kiev	W Europe • 200 kW
	USA	
	†VOA, Via Woofferton, UK	S Europe • 300 kW
7245	**ANGOLA**	
	RADIO NACIONAL, Luanda	DS-NATIONAL • 100 kW
	MAURITANIA	
	RADIO MAURITANIE, Nouakchott	F • ARABIC, FRENCH, ETC • DS • 100 kW • ALT. FREQ. TO 9610 kHz / ARABIC, FRENCH, ETC • DS • 100 kW • ALT. FREQ. TO 9610 kHz
	PERU	
	RADIO FIESTA, Oyolo	DS
	ROMANIA	
	RADIO ROMANIA INTL, Bucharest	W • Europe • 50 kW
	RUSSIA	
	†GOLOS ROSSII, Khabarovsk	W • E Asia • 240 kW
	†GOLOS ROSSII, Multiple Locations	W • Mideast, E Africa & SE Asia • 100/240 kW
	†GOLOS ROSSII, Samara	W • Mideast & E Africa • 100 kW
	†VOICE OF RUSSIA, Khabarovsk	S • E Asia • 240 kW / S • E Asia • 245 kW
	TAJIKISTAN	
	RADIO TAJIKISTAN, Dushanbe	W Asia & C Asia • 100 kW
	TAJIK RADIO, Dushanbe	DS-2(PAYK-I 'AJAM) • 100 kW
	UKRAINE	
	†UKRAINIAN RADIO	RUSSIAN, ETC • DS-1
	USA	
	†RFE-RL, Via Holzkirchen, Germany	W • E Europe • 250 kW
	†RFE-RL, Via Kaválla, Greece	W • E Europe • 250 kW
	†RFE-RL, Via Lampertheim, Germany	W • E Europe • 100 kW / S • E Europe • 100 kW / W • Mideast & W Asia • 100 kW / E Europe • 100 kW
	†RFE-RL, Via Pals, Spain	S • E Europe • 250 kW
	†RFE-RL, Via Woofferton, UK	W • S Europe • 300 kW
	†VOA, Via Kaválla, Greece	W • E Europe • 250 kW
	†VOA, Via Lampertheim, Germany	S • E Europe • 100 kW
	†VOA, Via Pals, Spain	W • E Europe • 100 kW / S • E Europe • 250 kW
	†VOA, Via Udon Thani, Thailand	S • S Asia • 500 kW

0 1 2 3 4 5 6 7 8 9 10 11 12 13 14 15 16 17 18 19 20 21 22 23 24

ENGLISH ▬   ARABIC ⧓⧓⧓   CHINESE □□□   FRENCH ▬▬   GERMAN ▬▬   RUSSIAN ══   SPANISH ▬▬   OTHER ▬▬

FREQUENCY	COUNTRY, STATION, LOCATION	TARGET • NETWORK • POWER (kW)	World Time

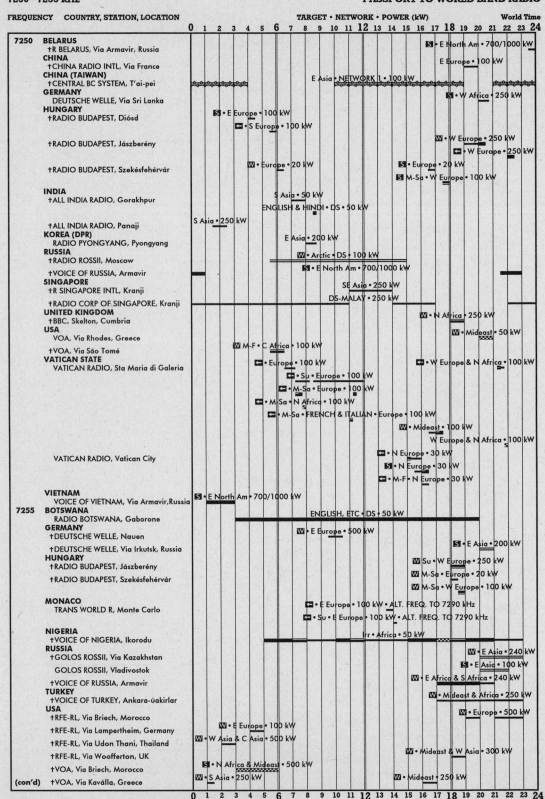

7250 BELARUS
†R BELARUS, Via Armavir, Russia — S • E North Am • 700/1000 kW
CHINA
†CHINA RADIO INTL, Via France — E Europe • 100 kW
CHINA (TAIWAN)
†CENTRAL BC SYSTEM, T'ai-pei — E Asia • NETWORK 1 • 100 kW
GERMANY
DEUTSCHE WELLE, Via Sri Lanka — S • W Africa • 250 kW
HUNGARY
†RADIO BUDAPEST, Diósd — S • E Europe • 100 kW / • S Europe • 100 kW
†RADIO BUDAPEST, Jászberény — W • W Europe • 250 kW / • W Europe • 250 kW
†RADIO BUDAPEST, Székésfehérvár — W • Europe • 20 kW / S • Europe • 20 kW / M-Sa • W Europe • 100 kW
INDIA
†ALL INDIA RADIO, Gorakhpur — S Asia • 50 kW / ENGLISH & HINDI • DS • 50 kW
†ALL INDIA RADIO, Panaji — S Asia • 250 kW
KOREA (DPR)
RADIO PYONGYANG, Pyongyang — E Asia • 200 kW
RUSSIA
†RADIO ROSSII, Moscow — W • Arctic • DS • 100 kW
†VOICE OF RUSSIA, Armavir — S • E North Am • 700/1000 kW
SINGAPORE
†R SINGAPORE INTL, Kranji — SE Asia • 250 kW
†RADIO CORP OF SINGAPORE, Kranji — DS-MALAY • 250 kW
UNITED KINGDOM
†BBC, Skelton, Cumbria — W • N Africa • 250 kW
USA
VOA, Via Rhodes, Greece — W • Mideast • 50 kW
†VOA, Via São Tomé — W M-F • C Africa • 100 kW
VATICAN STATE
VATICAN RADIO, Sta Maria di Galeria — • Europe • 100 kW / • W Europe & N Africa • 100 kW / • Su • Europe • 100 kW / • M-Sa • Europe • 100 kW / • M-Sa • N Africa • 100 kW / • M-Sa • FRENCH & ITALIAN • Europe • 100 kW / W • Mideast • 100 kW / W Europe & N Africa • 100 kW
VATICAN RADIO, Vatican City — • N Europe • 30 kW / S • N Europe • 30 kW / • M-F • N Europe • 30 kW
VIETNAM
VOICE OF VIETNAM, Via Armavir, Russia — S • E North Am • 700/1000 kW

7255 BOTSWANA
RADIO BOTSWANA, Gaborone — ENGLISH, ETC • DS • 50 kW
GERMANY
†DEUTSCHE WELLE, Nauen — W • E Europe • 500 kW
†DEUTSCHE WELLE, Via Irkutsk, Russia — S • E Asia • 200 kW
HUNGARY
†RADIO BUDAPEST, Jászberény — W Su • W Europe • 250 kW
†RADIO BUDAPEST, Székésfehérvár — W M-Sa • Europe • 20 kW / W M-Sa • W Europe • 100 kW
MONACO
TRANS WORLD R, Monte Carlo — • E Europe • 100 kW • ALT. FREQ. TO 7290 kHz / • Su • E Europe • 100 kW • ALT. FREQ. TO 7290 kHz
NIGERIA
†VOICE OF NIGERIA, Ikorodu — Irr • Africa • 50 kW
RUSSIA
†GOLOS ROSSII, Via Kazakhstan — W • E Asia • 240 kW
GOLOS ROSSII, Vladivostok — S • E Asia • 100 kW
†VOICE OF RUSSIA, Armavir — W • E Africa & S Africa • 240 kW
TURKEY
†VOICE OF TURKEY, Ankara-úakirlar — W • Mideast & Africa • 250 kW
USA
†RFE-RL, Via Briech, Morocco — W • Europe • 500 kW
†RFE-RL, Via Lampertheim, Germany — W • E Europe • 100 kW
†RFE-RL, Via Udon Thani, Thailand — W • W Asia & C Asia • 500 kW
†RFE-RL, Via Woofferton, UK — W • Mideast & W Asia • 300 kW
†VOA, Via Briech, Morocco — S • N Africa & Mideast • 500 kW
(con'd) †VOA, Via Kaválla, Greece — W • S Asia • 250 kW / W • Mideast • 250 kW

FREQUENCY   COUNTRY, STATION, LOCATION   TARGET • NETWORK • POWER (kW)   World Time

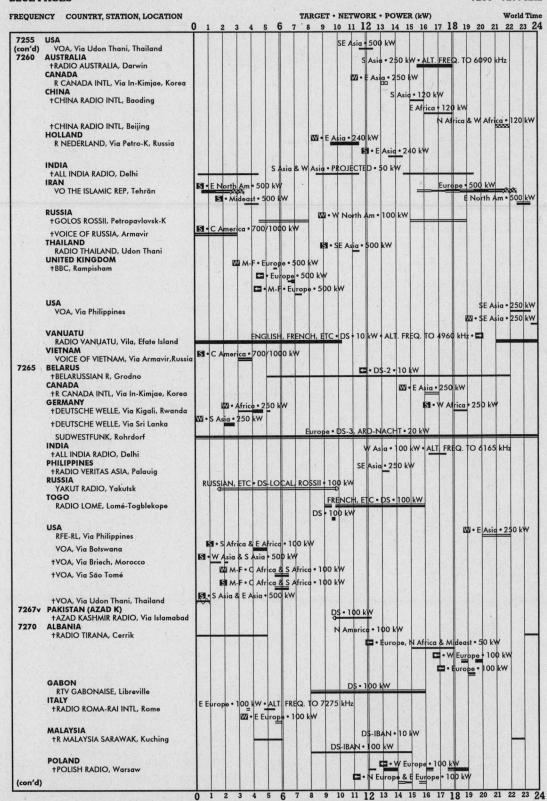

Frequency	Country, Station, Location	Target • Network • Power (kW)
7255 (con'd)	**USA** VOA, Via Udon Thani, Thailand	SE Asia • 500 kW
7260	**AUSTRALIA** †RADIO AUSTRALIA, Darwin	S Asia • 250 kW • ALT. FREQ. TO 6090 kHz
	CANADA R CANADA INTL, Via In-Kimjae, Korea	W • E Asia • 250 kW
	CHINA †CHINA RADIO INTL, Baoding	S Asia • 120 kW / E Africa • 120 kW / N Africa & W Africa • 120 kW
	†CHINA RADIO INTL, Beijing	
	HOLLAND R NEDERLAND, Via Petro-K, Russia	W • E Asia • 240 kW / S • E Asia • 240 kW
	INDIA †ALL INDIA RADIO, Delhi	S Asia & W Asia • PROJECTED • 50 kW
	IRAN VO THE ISLAMIC REP, Tehrān	S • E North Am • 500 kW / Europe • 500 kW / S • Mideast • 500 kW / E North Am • 500 kW
	RUSSIA †GOLOS ROSSII, Petropavlovsk-K	W • W North Am • 100 kW
	†VOICE OF RUSSIA, Armavir	S • C America • 700/1000 kW
	THAILAND RADIO THAILAND, Udon Thani	S • SE Asia • 500 kW
	UNITED KINGDOM †BBC, Rampisham	W M-F • Europe • 500 kW / ▪ • Europe • 500 kW / ▪ • M-F • Europe • 500 kW
	USA VOA, Via Philippines	SE Asia • 250 kW / W • SE Asia • 250 kW
	VANUATU RADIO VANUATU, Vila, Efate Island	ENGLISH, FRENCH, ETC • DS • 10 kW • ALT. FREQ. TO 4960 kHz • ▪
	VIETNAM VOICE OF VIETNAM, Via Armavir, Russia	S • C America • 700/1000 kW
7265	**BELARUS** †BELARUSSIAN R, Grodno	▪ • DS-2 • 10 kW
	CANADA †R CANADA INTL, Via In-Kimjae, Korea	W • E Asia • 250 kW
	GERMANY †DEUTSCHE WELLE, Via Kigali, Rwanda	W • Africa • 250 kW / S • W Africa • 250 kW
	†DEUTSCHE WELLE, Via Sri Lanka	W • S Asia • 250 kW
	SUDWESTFUNK, Rohrdorf	Europe • DS-3, ARD-NACHT • 20 kW
	INDIA †ALL INDIA RADIO, Delhi	W Asia • 100 kW • ALT. FREQ. TO 6165 kHz
	PHILIPPINES †RADIO VERITAS ASIA, Palauig	SE Asia • 250 kW
	RUSSIA YAKUT RADIO, Yakutsk	RUSSIAN, ETC • DS-LOCAL, ROSSII • 100 kW
	TOGO RADIO LOME, Lomé-Togblekope	FRENCH, ETC • DS • 100 kW / DS • 100 kW
	USA RFE-RL, Via Philippines	W • E Asia • 250 kW
	VOA, Via Botswana	S • S Africa & E Africa • 100 kW
	†VOA, Via Briech, Morocco	S • W Asia & S Asia • 500 kW
	†VOA, Via São Tomé	W M-F • C Africa & S Africa • 100 kW / S M-F • C Africa & S Africa • 100 kW
	†VOA, Via Udon Thani, Thailand	S • S Asia & E Asia • 500 kW
7267v	**PAKISTAN (AZAD K)** †AZAD KASHMIR RADIO, Via Islamabad	DS • 100 kW
7270	**ALBANIA** †RADIO TIRANA, Cerrik	N America • 100 kW / ▪ • Europe, N Africa & Mideast • 50 kW / ▪ • W Europe • 100 kW / ▪ • Europe • 100 kW
	GABON RTV GABONAISE, Libreville	DS • 100 kW
	ITALY †RADIO ROMA-RAI INTL, Rome	E Europe • 100 kW • ALT. FREQ. TO 7275 kHz / W • E Europe • 100 kW
	MALAYSIA †R MALAYSIA SARAWAK, Kuching	DS-IBAN • 10 kW / DS-IBAN • 100 kW
	POLAND †POLISH RADIO, Warsaw	▪ • W Europe • 100 kW / ▪ • N Europe & E Europe • 100 kW
(con'd)		

ENGLISH ▬   ARABIC ∽∽∽   CHINESE □□□   FRENCH ═   GERMAN ▬   RUSSIAN ══   SPANISH ══   OTHER ─

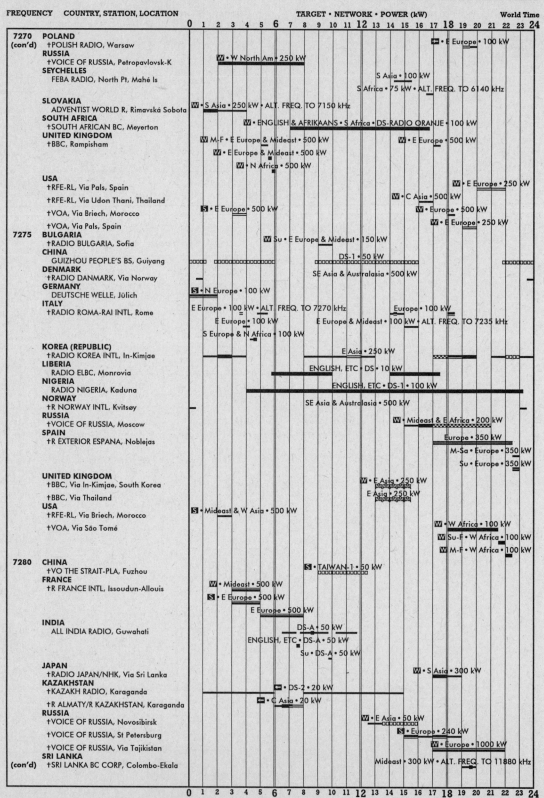

FREQUENCY   COUNTRY, STATION, LOCATION   TARGET • NETWORK • POWER (kW)   World Time

7270 **POLAND**
(con'd)   †POLISH RADIO, Warsaw — ▭ • E Europe • 100 kW
   RUSSIA
     †VOICE OF RUSSIA, Petropavlovsk-K — W • W North Am • 250 kW
   SEYCHELLES
     FEBA RADIO, North Pt, Mahé Is — S Asia • 100 kW / S Africa • 75 kW • ALT. FREQ. TO 6140 kHz
   SLOVAKIA
     ADVENTIST WORLD R, Rimavská Sobota — W • S Asia • 250 kW • ALT. FREQ. TO 7150 kHz
   SOUTH AFRICA
     †SOUTH AFRICAN BC, Meyerton — W • ENGLISH & AFRIKAANS • S Africa • DS-RADIO ORANJE • 100 kW
   UNITED KINGDOM
     †BBC, Rampisham — W • M-F • E Europe & Mideast • 500 kW / W • E Europe • 500 kW
        W • E Europe & Mideast • 500 kW
        W • N Africa • 500 kW
   USA
     †RFE-RL, Via Pals, Spain — W • E Europe • 250 kW
     †RFE-RL, Via Udon Thani, Thailand — W • C Asia • 500 kW
     †VOA, Via Briech, Morocco — S • E Europe • 500 kW / W • Europe • 500 kW
     †VOA, Via Pals, Spain — W • E Europe • 250 kW

7275 **BULGARIA**
     †RADIO BULGARIA, Sofia — W • Su • E Europe & Mideast • 150 kW
   CHINA
     GUIZHOU PEOPLE'S BS, Guiyang — DS-1 • 50 kW
   DENMARK
     †RADIO DANMARK, Via Norway — SE Asia & Australasia • 500 kW
   GERMANY
     DEUTSCHE WELLE, Jülich — S • N Europe • 100 kW
   ITALY
     †RADIO ROMA-RAI INTL, Rome — E Europe • 100 kW • ALT. FREQ. TO 7270 kHz / Europe • 100 kW
        E Europe • 100 kW / E Europe & Mideast • 100 kW • ALT. FREQ. TO 7235 kHz
        S Europe & N Africa • 100 kW
   KOREA (REPUBLIC)
     †RADIO KOREA INTL, In-Kimjae — E Asia • 250 kW
   LIBERIA
     RADIO ELBC, Monrovia — ENGLISH, ETC • DS • 10 kW
   NIGERIA
     RADIO NIGERIA, Kaduna — ENGLISH, ETC • DS-1 • 100 kW
   NORWAY
     †R NORWAY INTL, Kvitsøy — SE Asia & Australasia • 500 kW
   RUSSIA
     †VOICE OF RUSSIA, Moscow — W • Mideast & E Africa • 200 kW
   SPAIN
     †R EXTERIOR ESPANA, Noblejas — Europe • 350 kW
        M-Sa • Europe • 350 kW
        Su • Europe • 350 kW
   UNITED KINGDOM
     †BBC, Via In-Kimjae, South Korea — W • E Asia • 250 kW
     †BBC, Via Thailand — E Asia • 250 kW
   USA
     †RFE-RL, Via Briech, Morocco — S • Mideast & W Asia • 500 kW
     †VOA, Via São Tomé — W • W Africa • 100 kW
        W • Su-F • W Africa • 100 kW
        W • M-F • W Africa • 100 kW

7280 **CHINA**
     †VO THE STRAIT-PLA, Fuzhou — S • TAIWAN-1 • 50 kW
   FRANCE
     †R FRANCE INTL, Issoudun-Allouis — W • Mideast • 500 kW
        S • E Europe • 500 kW
        E Europe • 500 kW
   INDIA
     ALL INDIA RADIO, Guwahati — DS-A • 50 kW
        ENGLISH, ETC • DS-A • 50 kW
        Su • DS-A • 50 kW
   JAPAN
     †RADIO JAPAN/NHK, Via Sri Lanka — W • S Asia • 300 kW
   KAZAKHSTAN
     †KAZAKH RADIO, Karaganda — ▭ • DS-2 • 20 kW
     †R ALMATY/R KAZAKHSTAN, Karaganda — ▭ • C Asia • 20 kW
   RUSSIA
     †VOICE OF RUSSIA, Novosibirsk — W • E Asia • 50 kW
     †VOICE OF RUSSIA, St Petersburg — S • Europe • 240 kW
     †VOICE OF RUSSIA, Via Tajikistan — W • Europe • 1000 kW
   SRI LANKA
(con'd)   †SRI LANKA BC CORP, Colombo-Ekala — Mideast • 300 kW • ALT. FREQ. TO 11880 kHz

SEASONAL **S** OR **W**   1-HR TIMESHIFT MIDYEAR ▭ OR ▭   JAMMING / OR ∧   EARLIEST HEARD ◁   LATEST HEARD ▷   NEW FOR 1997 †

FREQUENCY	COUNTRY, STATION, LOCATION	TARGET • NETWORK • POWER (kW)	World Time

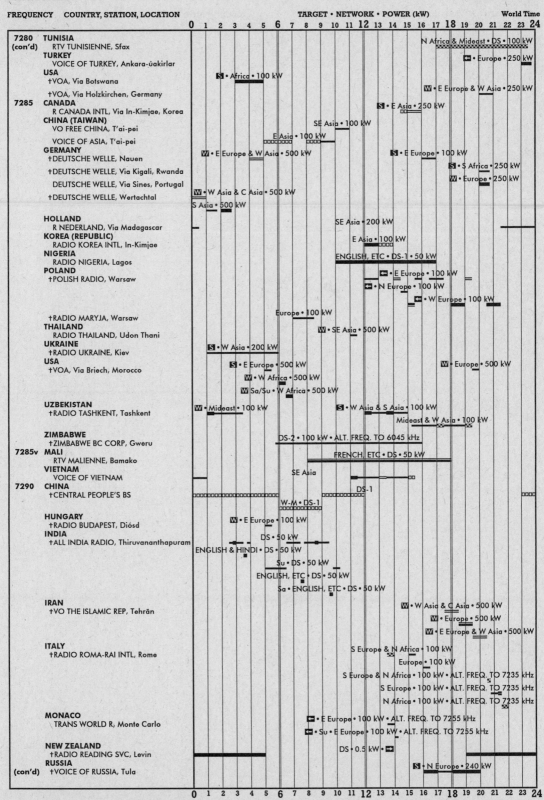

7280	**TUNISIA**	
(con'd)	RTV TUNISIENNE, Sfax	N Africa & Mideast • DS • 100 kW
	TURKEY	
	VOICE OF TURKEY, Ankara-úakirlar	▣ • Europe • 250 kW
	USA	
	†VOA, Via Botswana	⑤ • Africa • 100 kW
	†VOA, Via Holzkirchen, Germany	Ⓦ • E Europe & W Asia • 250 kW
7285	**CANADA**	
	R CANADA INTL, Via In-Kimjae, Korea	⑤ • E Asia • 250 kW
	CHINA (TAIWAN)	
	VO FREE CHINA, T'ai-pei	SE Asia • 100 kW
	VOICE OF ASIA, T'ai-pei	E Asia • 100 kW
	GERMANY	
	†DEUTSCHE WELLE, Nauen	Ⓦ • E Europe & W Asia • 500 kW
	†DEUTSCHE WELLE, Via Kigali, Rwanda	⑤ • E Europe • 100 kW
	DEUTSCHE WELLE, Via Sines, Portugal	⑤ • S Africa • 250 kW
		Ⓦ • Europe • 250 kW
	†DEUTSCHE WELLE, Wertachtal	Ⓦ • W Asia & C Asia • 500 kW
		S Asia • 500 kW
	HOLLAND	
	R NEDERLAND, Via Madagascar	SE Asia • 200 kW
	KOREA (REPUBLIC)	
	RADIO KOREA INTL, In-Kimjae	E Asia • 100 kW
	NIGERIA	
	RADIO NIGERIA, Lagos	ENGLISH, ETC • DS-1 • 50 kW
	POLAND	
	†POLISH RADIO, Warsaw	▣ • E Europe • 100 kW
		▣ • N Europe • 100 kW
		▣ • W Europe • 100 kW
	†RADIO MARYJA, Warsaw	Europe • 100 kW
	THAILAND	
	RADIO THAILAND, Udon Thani	Ⓦ • SE Asia • 500 kW
	UKRAINE	
	†RADIO UKRAINE, Kiev	⑤ • W Asia • 200 kW
	USA	
	†VOA, Via Briech, Morocco	⑤ • E Europe • 500 kW
		Ⓦ • Europe • 500 kW
		Ⓦ • W Africa • 500 kW
		Ⓦ Sa/Su • W Africa • 500 kW
	UZBEKISTAN	
	†RADIO TASHKENT, Tashkent	Ⓦ • Mideast • 100 kW
		⑤ • W Asia & S Asia • 100 kW
		Mideast & W Asia • 100 kW
	ZIMBABWE	
	†ZIMBABWE BC CORP, Gweru	DS-2 • 100 kW • ALT. FREQ. TO 6045 kHz
7285v	**MALI**	
	RTV MALIENNE, Bamako	FRENCH, ETC • DS • 50 kW
	VIETNAM	
	VOICE OF VIETNAM	SE Asia
7290	**CHINA**	DS-1
	†CENTRAL PEOPLE'S BS	
	HUNGARY	W-M • DS-1
	†RADIO BUDAPEST, Diósd	Ⓦ • E Europe • 100 kW
	INDIA	DS • 50 kW
	†ALL INDIA RADIO, Thiruvananthapuram	ENGLISH & HINDI • DS • 50 kW
		Su • DS • 50 kW
		ENGLISH, ETC • DS • 50 kW
		Sa • ENGLISH, ETC • DS • 50 kW
	IRAN	
	†VO THE ISLAMIC REP, Tehrān	Ⓦ • W Asia & C Asia • 500 kW
		Ⓦ • Europe • 500 kW
		Ⓦ • E Europe & W Asia • 500 kW
	ITALY	
	†RADIO ROMA-RAI INTL, Rome	S Europe & N Africa • 100 kW
		Europe • 100 kW
		S Europe & N Africa • 100 kW • ALT. FREQ. TO 7235 kHz
		S Europe • 100 kW • ALT. FREQ. TO 7235 kHz
		N Africa • 100 kW • ALT. FREQ. TO 7235 kHz
	MONACO	
	TRANS WORLD R, Monte Carlo	▣ • E Europe • 100 kW • ALT. FREQ. TO 7255 kHz
		▣ • Su • E Europe • 100 kW • ALT. FREQ. TO 7255 kHz
	NEW ZEALAND	
	†RADIO READING SVC, Levin	DS • 0.5 kW • ▣
	RUSSIA	
(con'd)	†VOICE OF RUSSIA, Tula	⑤ • N Europe • 240 kW

FREQUENCY   COUNTRY, STATION, LOCATION   TARGET • NETWORK • POWER (kW)   World Time

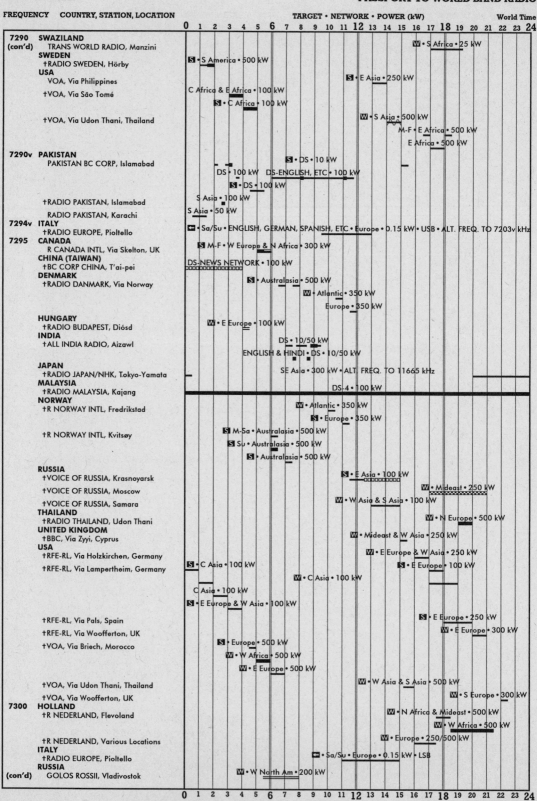

Frequency	Country, Station, Location	Target • Network • Power
7290 (con'd)	**SWAZILAND** TRANS WORLD RADIO, Manzini	W • S Africa • 25 kW
	SWEDEN †RADIO SWEDEN, Hörby	S • S America • 500 kW
	USA VOA, Via Philippines	S • E Asia • 250 kW
	†VOA, Via São Tomé	C Africa & E Africa • 100 kW; S • C Africa • 100 kW
	†VOA, Via Udon Thani, Thailand	W • S Asia • 500 kW; M-F • E Africa • 500 kW; E Africa • 500 kW
7290v	**PAKISTAN** PAKISTAN BC CORP, Islamabad	S • DS • 10 kW; DS • 100 kW; DS-ENGLISH, ETC • 100 kW; S • DS • 100 kW
	†RADIO PAKISTAN, Islamabad	S Asia • 100 kW
	RADIO PAKISTAN, Karachi	S Asia • 50 kW
7294v	**ITALY** †RADIO EUROPE, Pioltello	Sa/Su • ENGLISH, GERMAN, SPANISH, ETC • Europe • 0.15 kW • USB • ALT. FREQ. TO 7203v kHz
7295	**CANADA** R CANADA INTL, Via Skelton, UK	S • M-F • W Europe & N Africa • 300 kW
	CHINA (TAIWAN) †BC CORP CHINA, T'ai-pei	DS-NEWS NETWORK • 100 kW
	DENMARK †RADIO DANMARK, Via Norway	S • Australasia • 500 kW; W • Atlantic • 350 kW; Europe • 350 kW
	HUNGARY †RADIO BUDAPEST, Diósd	W • E Europe • 100 kW
	INDIA †ALL INDIA RADIO, Aizawl	DS • 10/50 kW; ENGLISH & HINDI • DS • 10/50 kW
	JAPAN †RADIO JAPAN/NHK, Tokyo-Yamata	SE Asia • 300 kW • ALT. FREQ. TO 11665 kHz
	MALAYSIA †RADIO MALAYSIA, Kajang	DS-4 • 100 kW
	NORWAY †R NORWAY INTL, Fredrikstad	W • Atlantic • 350 kW; S • Europe • 350 kW
	†R NORWAY INTL, Kvitsøy	S • M-Sa • Australasia • 500 kW; S • Su • Australasia • 500 kW; S • Australasia • 500 kW
	RUSSIA †VOICE OF RUSSIA, Krasnoyarsk	S • E Asia • 100 kW
	†VOICE OF RUSSIA, Moscow	W • Mideast • 250 kW
	†VOICE OF RUSSIA, Samara	W • W Asia & S Asia • 100 kW
	THAILAND †RADIO THAILAND, Udon Thani	W • N Europe • 500 kW
	UNITED KINGDOM †BBC, Via Zyyi, Cyprus	W • Mideast & W Asia • 250 kW
	USA †RFE-RL, Via Holzkirchen, Germany	W • E Europe & W Asia • 250 kW
	†RFE-RL, Via Lampertheim, Germany	S • C Asia • 100 kW; S • E Europe • 100 kW; W • C Asia • 100 kW; C Asia • 100 kW; S • E Europe & W Asia • 100 kW
	†RFE-RL, Via Pals, Spain	S • E Europe • 250 kW
	†RFE-RL, Via Woofferton, UK	W • E Europe • 300 kW
	†VOA, Via Briech, Morocco	S • Europe • 500 kW; W • W Africa • 500 kW; W • E Europe • 500 kW
	†VOA, Via Udon Thani, Thailand	W • W Asia & S Asia • 500 kW
	†VOA, Via Woofferton, UK	W • S Europe • 300 kW
7300	**HOLLAND** †R NEDERLAND, Flevoland	W • N Africa & Mideast • 500 kW; W • W Africa • 500 kW
	†R NEDERLAND, Various Locations	W • Europe • 250/500 kW
	ITALY †RADIO EUROPE, Pioltello	Sa/Su • Europe • 0.15 kW • LSB
	RUSSIA (con'd) GOLOS ROSSII, Vladivostok	W • W North Am • 200 kW

FREQUENCY   COUNTRY, STATION, LOCATION   TARGET • NETWORK • POWER (kW)   World Time

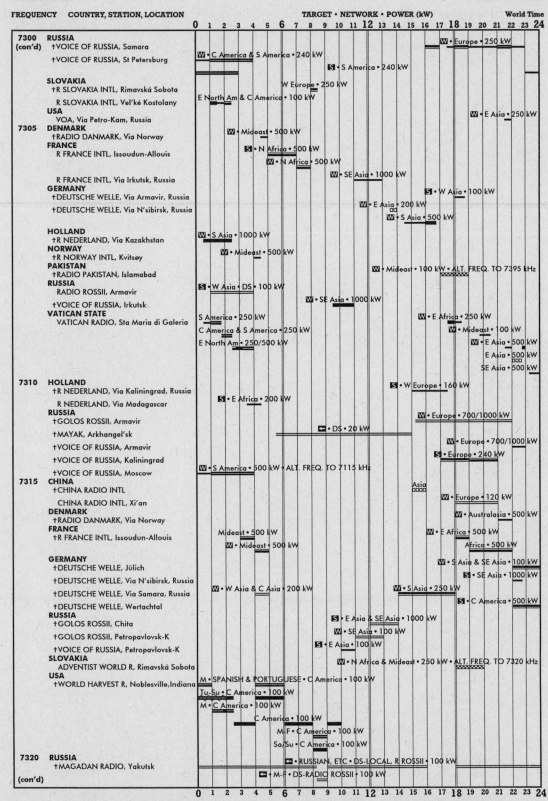

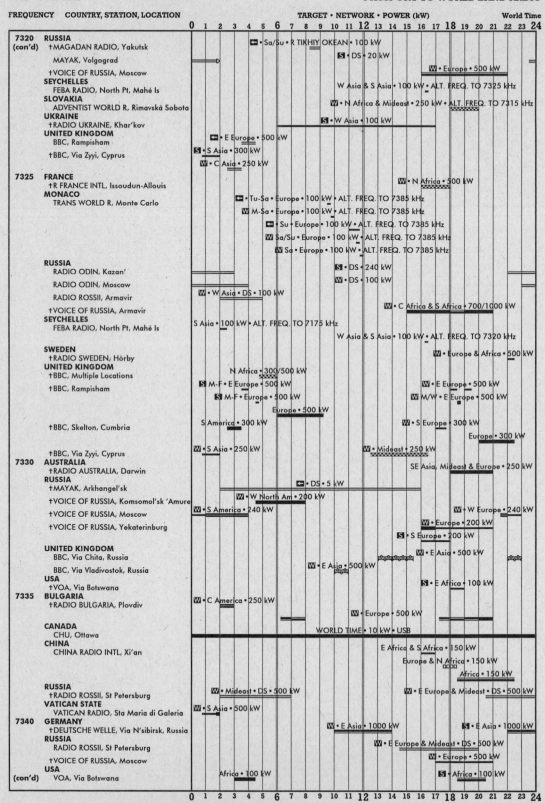

FREQUENCY   COUNTRY, STATION, LOCATION

TARGET • NETWORK • POWER (kW)

World Time

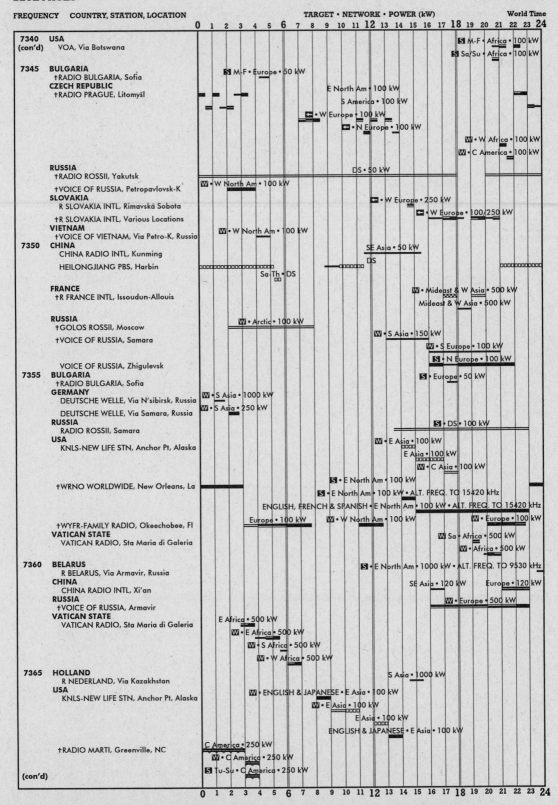

Frequency	Country, Station, Location
7340 (con'd)	**USA** — VOA, Via Botswana
7345	**BULGARIA** — †RADIO BULGARIA, Sofia
	CZECH REPUBLIC — †RADIO PRAGUE, Litomyšl
	RUSSIA — †RADIO ROSSII, Yakutsk
	†VOICE OF RUSSIA, Petropavlovsk-K
	SLOVAKIA — R SLOVAKIA INTL, Rimavská Sobota
	†R SLOVAKIA INTL, Various Locations
	VIETNAM — †VOICE OF VIETNAM, Via Petro-K, Russia
7350	**CHINA** — CHINA RADIO INTL, Kunming
	HEILONGJIANG PBS, Harbin
	FRANCE — †R FRANCE INTL, Issoudun-Allouis
	RUSSIA — †GOLOS ROSSII, Moscow
	†VOICE OF RUSSIA, Samara
	VOICE OF RUSSIA, Zhigulevsk
7355	**BULGARIA** — †RADIO BULGARIA, Sofia
	GERMANY — DEUTSCHE WELLE, Via N'sibirsk, Russia
	DEUTSCHE WELLE, Via Samara, Russia
	RUSSIA — RADIO ROSSII, Samara
	USA — KNLS-NEW LIFE STN, Anchor Pt, Alaska
	†WRNO WORLDWIDE, New Orleans, La
	†WYFR-FAMILY RADIO, Okeechobee, Fl
	VATICAN STATE — VATICAN RADIO, Sta Maria di Galeria
7360	**BELARUS** — R BELARUS, Via Armavir, Russia
	CHINA — CHINA RADIO INTL, Xi'an
	RUSSIA — †VOICE OF RUSSIA, Armavir
	VATICAN STATE — VATICAN RADIO, Sta Maria di Galeria
7365	**HOLLAND** — R NEDERLAND, Via Kazakhstan
	USA — KNLS-NEW LIFE STN, Anchor Pt, Alaska
	†RADIO MARTI, Greenville, NC
(con'd)	

Bar chart annotations:

- VOA, Via Botswana: S M-F • Africa • 100 kW; S Sa/Su • Africa • 100 kW
- RADIO BULGARIA, Sofia: S M-F • Europe • 50 kW
- RADIO PRAGUE, Litomyšl: E North Am • 100 kW; S America • 100 kW; • W Europe • 100 kW; • N Europe • 100 kW; W • W Africa • 100 kW; W • C America • 100 kW
- RADIO ROSSII, Yakutsk: DS • 50 kW
- VOICE OF RUSSIA, Petropavlovsk-K: W • W North Am • 100 kW
- R SLOVAKIA INTL, Rimavská Sobota: • W Europe • 250 kW
- R SLOVAKIA INTL, Various Locations: • W Europe • 100/250 kW
- VOICE OF VIETNAM, Via Petro-K, Russia: W • W North Am • 100 kW
- CHINA RADIO INTL, Kunming: SE Asia • 50 kW
- HEILONGJIANG PBS, Harbin: DS; Sa-Th • DS
- R FRANCE INTL, Issoudun-Allouis: W • Mideast & W Asia • 500 kW; Mideast & W Asia • 500 kW
- GOLOS ROSSII, Moscow: W • Arctic • 100 kW
- VOICE OF RUSSIA, Samara: W • S Asia • 150 kW; W • S Europe • 100 kW; S • N Europe • 100 kW
- VOICE OF RUSSIA, Zhigulevsk: S • Europe • 50 kW
- DEUTSCHE WELLE, Via N'sibirsk, Russia: W • S Asia • 1000 kW
- DEUTSCHE WELLE, Via Samara, Russia: W • S Asia • 250 kW
- RADIO ROSSII, Samara: S • DS • 100 kW
- KNLS-NEW LIFE STN, Anchor Pt, Alaska: W • E Asia • 100 kW; E Asia • 100 kW; W • C Asia • 100 kW
- WRNO WORLDWIDE, New Orleans, La: S • E North Am • 100 kW; S • E North Am • 100 kW • ALT. FREQ. TO 15420 kHz; ENGLISH, FRENCH & SPANISH • E North Am • 100 kW • ALT. FREQ. TO 15420 kHz
- WYFR-FAMILY RADIO, Okeechobee, Fl: Europe • 100 kW; W • W North Am • 100 kW; W • Europe • 100 kW
- VATICAN RADIO, Sta Maria di Galeria: W Sa • Africa • 500 kW; W • Africa • 500 kW
- R BELARUS, Via Armavir, Russia: S • E North Am • 1000 kW • ALT. FREQ. TO 9530 kHz
- CHINA RADIO INTL, Xi'an: SE Asia • 120 kW; Europe • 120 kW
- VOICE OF RUSSIA, Armavir: W • Europe • 500 kW
- VATICAN RADIO, Sta Maria di Galeria: E Africa • 500 kW; W • E Africa • 500 kW; W • S Africa • 500 kW; W • W Africa • 500 kW
- R NEDERLAND, Via Kazakhstan: S Asia • 1000 kW
- KNLS-NEW LIFE STN, Anchor Pt, Alaska: W • ENGLISH & JAPANESE • E Asia • 100 kW; W • E Asia • 100 kW; E Asia • 100 kW; ENGLISH & JAPANESE • E Asia • 100 kW
- RADIO MARTI, Greenville, NC: C America • 250 kW; W • C America • 250 kW; S Tu-Su • C America • 250 kW

ENGLISH ▬   ARABIC ⌇⌇⌇   CHINESE ▫▫▫   FRENCH ═══   GERMAN ▬▬   RUSSIAN ═══   SPANISH ▬▬   OTHER ▬

FREQUENCY   COUNTRY, STATION, LOCATION   TARGET • NETWORK • POWER (kW)   World Time

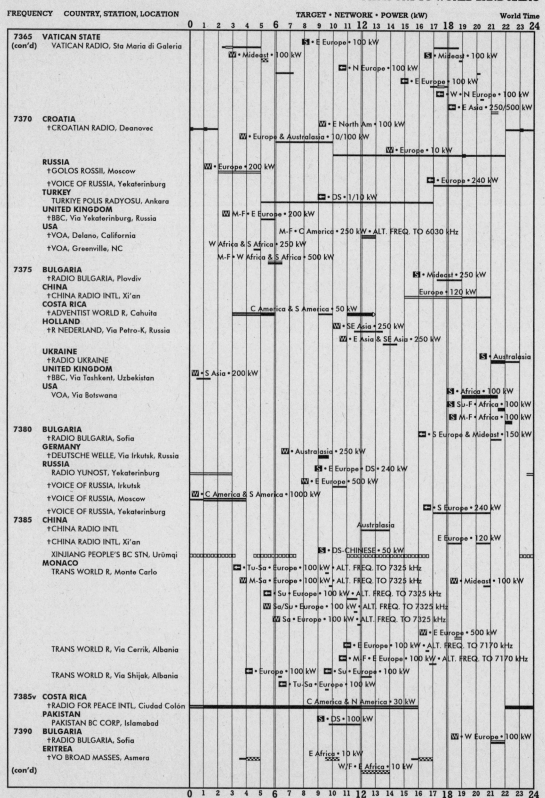

Frequency	Country, Station, Location	Target • Network • Power
7365 (con'd)	**VATICAN STATE**	
	VATICAN RADIO, Sta Maria di Galeria	S • E Europe • 100 kW
		W • Mideast • 100 kW
		S • Mideast • 100 kW
		• N Europe • 100 kW
		• E Europe • 100 kW
		• W • N Europe • 100 kW
		• E Asia • 250/500 kW
7370	**CROATIA**	
	†CROATIAN RADIO, Deanovec	W • E North Am • 100 kW
		W • Europe & Australasia • 10/100 kW
		W • Europe • 10 kW
	RUSSIA	
	†GOLOS ROSSII, Moscow	W • Europe • 200 kW
	†VOICE OF RUSSIA, Yekaterinburg	• Europe • 240 kW
	TURKEY	
	TURKIYE POLIS RADYOSU, Ankara	• DS • 1/10 kW
	UNITED KINGDOM	
	†BBC, Via Yekaterinburg, Russia	W • M-F • E Europe • 200 kW
	USA	
	†VOA, Delano, California	M-F • C America • 250 kW • ALT. FREQ. TO 6030 kHz
	†VOA, Greenville, NC	W Africa & S Africa • 250 kW
		M-F • W Africa & S Africa • 500 kW
7375	**BULGARIA**	
	†RADIO BULGARIA, Plovdiv	S • Mideast • 250 kW
	CHINA	
	†CHINA RADIO INTL, Xi'an	Europe • 120 kW
	COSTA RICA	
	†ADVENTIST WORLD R, Cahuita	C America & S America • 50 kW
	HOLLAND	
	†R NEDERLAND, Via Petro-K, Russia	W • SE Asia • 250 kW
		W • E Asia & SE Asia • 250 kW
	UKRAINE	
	†RADIO UKRAINE	S • Australasia
	UNITED KINGDOM	
	†BBC, Via Tashkent, Uzbekistan	W • S Asia • 200 kW
	USA	
	VOA, Via Botswana	S • Africa • 100 kW
		S • Su-F • Africa • 100 kW
		S • M-F • Africa • 100 kW
7380	**BULGARIA**	
	†RADIO BULGARIA, Sofia	• S Europe & Mideast • 150 kW
	GERMANY	
	†DEUTSCHE WELLE, Via Irkutsk, Russia	W • Australasia • 250 kW
	RUSSIA	
	RADIO YUNOST, Yekaterinburg	S • E Europe • DS • 240 kW
	†VOICE OF RUSSIA, Irkutsk	W • E Europe • 500 kW
	†VOICE OF RUSSIA, Moscow	W • C America & S America • 1000 kW
	†VOICE OF RUSSIA, Yekaterinburg	• S Europe • 240 kW
7385	**CHINA**	
	†CHINA RADIO INTL	Australasia
	†CHINA RADIO INTL, Xi'an	E Europe • 120 kW
	XINJIANG PEOPLE'S BC STN, Urümqi	S • DS-CHINESE • 50 kW
	MONACO	
	TRANS WORLD R, Monte Carlo	• Tu-Sa • Europe • 100 kW • ALT. FREQ. TO 7325 kHz
		W • M-Sa • Europe • 100 kW • ALT. FREQ. TO 7325 kHz
		W • Mideast • 100 kW
		• Su • Europe • 100 kW • ALT. FREQ. TO 7325 kHz
		W • Sa/Su • Europe • 100 kW • ALT. FREQ. TO 7325 kHz
		W • Sa • Europe • 100 kW • ALT. FREQ. TO 7325 kHz
		W • E Europe • 500 kW
	TRANS WORLD R, Via Cerrik, Albania	• E Europe • 100 kW • ALT. FREQ. TO 7170 kHz
		• M-F • E Europe • 100 kW • ALT. FREQ. TO 7170 kHz
	TRANS WORLD R, Via Shijak, Albania	• Europe • 100 kW
		• Su • Europe • 100 kW
		• Tu-Sa • Europe • 100 kW
7385v	**COSTA RICA**	
	†RADIO FOR PEACE INTL, Ciudad Colón	C America & N America • 30 kW
	PAKISTAN	
	PAKISTAN BC CORP, Islamabad	S • DS • 100 kW
7390	**BULGARIA**	
	†RADIO BULGARIA, Sofia	W • W Europe • 100 kW
	ERITREA	
	†VO BROAD MASSES, Asmera	E Africa • 10 kW
		W/F • E Africa • 10 kW
(con'd)		

FREQUENCY   COUNTRY, STATION, LOCATION   TARGET • NETWORK • POWER (kW)   World Time

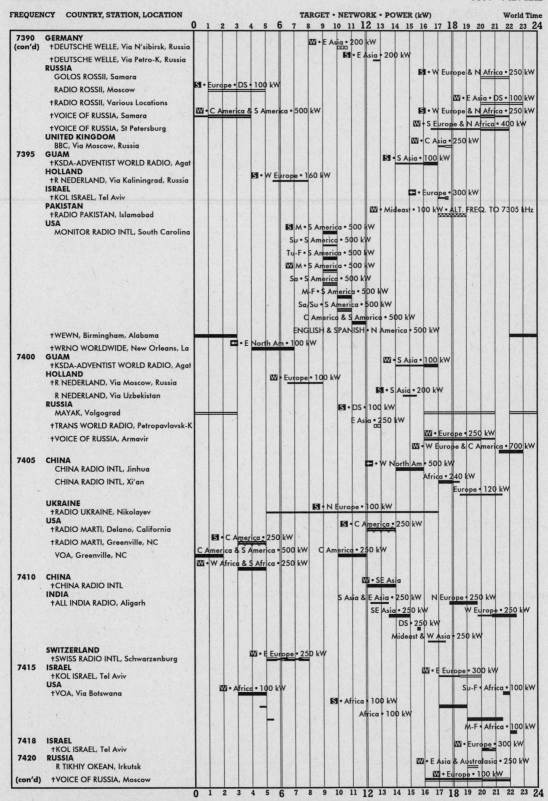

Frequency	Country, Station, Location	Target • Network • Power
7390 (con'd)	**GERMANY**	
	†DEUTSCHE WELLE, Via N'sibirsk, Russia	W • E Asia • 200 kW
	†DEUTSCHE WELLE, Via Petro-K, Russia	S • E Asia • 200 kW
	RUSSIA	
	GOLOS ROSSII, Samara	S • W Europe & N Africa • 250 kW
	RADIO ROSSII, Moscow	S • Europe • DS • 100 kW
	†RADIO ROSSII, Various Locations	W • E Asia • DS • 100 kW
	†VOICE OF RUSSIA, Samara	W • C America & S America • 500 kW / S • W Europe & N Africa • 250 kW
	†VOICE OF RUSSIA, St Petersburg	W • S Europe & N Africa • 400 kW
	UNITED KINGDOM	
	BBC, Via Moscow, Russia	W • C Asia • 250 kW
7395	**GUAM**	
	†KSDA-ADVENTIST WORLD RADIO, Agat	S • S Asia • 100 kW
	HOLLAND	
	†R NEDERLAND, Via Kaliningrad, Russia	S • W Europe • 160 kW
	ISRAEL	
	†KOL ISRAEL, Tel Aviv	← • Europe • 300 kW
	PAKISTAN	
	†RADIO PAKISTAN, Islamabad	W • Mideast • 100 kW • ALT. FREQ. TO 7305 kHz
	USA	
	MONITOR RADIO INTL, South Carolina	S • M • S America • 500 kW
		Su • S America • 500 kW
		Tu-F • S America • 500 kW
		W • M • S America • 500 kW
		Sa • S America • 500 kW
		M-F • S America • 500 kW
		Sa/Su • S America • 500 kW
		C America & S America • 500 kW
		ENGLISH & SPANISH • N America • 500 kW
	†WEWN, Birmingham, Alabama	
	†WRNO WORLDWIDE, New Orleans, La	← • E North Am • 100 kW
7400	**GUAM**	
	†KSDA-ADVENTIST WORLD RADIO, Agat	W • S Asia • 100 kW
	HOLLAND	
	†R NEDERLAND, Via Moscow, Russia	W • Europe • 100 kW
	R NEDERLAND, Via Uzbekistan	S • S Asia • 200 kW
	RUSSIA	
	MAYAK, Volgograd	S • DS • 100 kW
	†TRANS WORLD RADIO, Petropavlovsk-K	E Asia • 250 kW
	†VOICE OF RUSSIA, Armavir	W • Europe • 250 kW / W • W Europe & C America • 700 kW
7405	**CHINA**	
	CHINA RADIO INTL, Jinhua	← • W North Am • 500 kW
	CHINA RADIO INTL, Xi'an	Africa • 240 kW / Europe • 120 kW
	UKRAINE	
	†RADIO UKRAINE, Nikolayev	S • N Europe • 100 kW
	USA	
	†RADIO MARTI, Delano, California	S • C America • 250 kW
	†RADIO MARTI, Greenville, NC	S • C America • 250 kW
	VOA, Greenville, NC	C America & S America • 500 kW / C America • 250 kW / W • W Africa & S Africa • 250 kW
7410	**CHINA**	
	†CHINA RADIO INTL	W • SE Asia
	INDIA	
	†ALL INDIA RADIO, Aligarh	S Asia & E Asia • 250 kW / N Europe • 250 kW / SE Asia • 250 kW / W Europe • 250 kW / DS • 250 kW / Mideast & W Asia • 250 kW
	SWITZERLAND	
	†SWISS RADIO INTL, Schwarzenburg	W • E Europe • 250 kW
7415	**ISRAEL**	
	†KOL ISRAEL, Tel Aviv	W • E Europe • 300 kW
	USA	
	†VOA, Via Botswana	W • Africa • 100 kW / Su-F • Africa • 100 kW / S • Africa • 100 kW / Africa • 100 kW / M-F • Africa • 100 kW
7418	**ISRAEL**	
	†KOL ISRAEL, Tel Aviv	W • Europe • 300 kW
7420	**RUSSIA**	
	R TIKHIY OKEAN, Irkutsk	W • E Asia & Australasia • 250 kW
(con'd)	†VOICE OF RUSSIA, Moscow	W • Europe • 100 kW

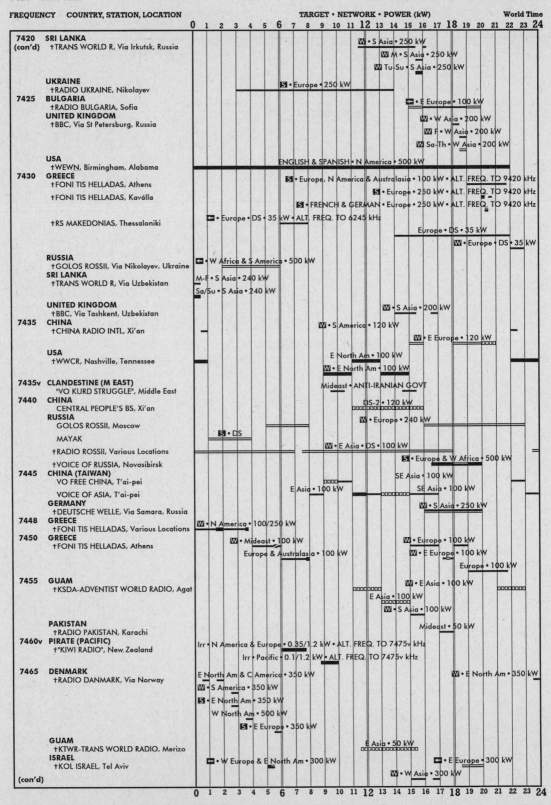

FREQUENCY   COUNTRY, STATION, LOCATION

TARGET • NETWORK • POWER (kW)

World Time

Frequency	Country, Station, Location	Listing
7420 (con'd)	SRI LANKA †TRANS WORLD R, Via Irkutsk, Russia	W • S Asia • 250 kW / W M • S Asia • 250 kW / W Tu-Su • S Asia • 250 kW
	UKRAINE †RADIO UKRAINE, Nikolayev	S • Europe • 250 kW
7425	BULGARIA †RADIO BULGARIA, Sofia	E Europe • 100 kW
	UNITED KINGDOM †BBC, Via St Petersburg, Russia	W • W Asia • 200 kW / W F • W Asia • 200 kW / W Sa-Th • W Asia • 200 kW
	USA †WEWN, Birmingham, Alabama	ENGLISH & SPANISH • N America • 500 kW
7430	GREECE †FONI TIS HELLADAS, Athens	S • Europe, N America & Australasia • 100 kW • ALT. FREQ. TO 9420 kHz / S • Europe • 250 kW • ALT. FREQ. TO 9420 kHz
	†FONI TIS HELLADAS, Kaválla	S • FRENCH & GERMAN • Europe • 250 kW • ALT. FREQ. TO 9420 kHz
	†RS MAKEDONIAS, Thessaloniki	Europe • DS • 35 kW • ALT. FREQ. TO 6245 kHz / Europe • DS • 35 kW / W • Europe • DS • 35 kW
	RUSSIA †GOLOS ROSSII, Via Nikolayev, Ukraine	W Africa & S America • 500 kW
	SRI LANKA †TRANS WORLD R, Via Uzbekistan	M-F • S Asia • 240 kW / Sa/Su • S Asia • 240 kW
	UNITED KINGDOM †BBC, Via Tashkent, Uzbekistan	W • S Asia • 200 kW
7435	CHINA †CHINA RADIO INTL, Xi'an	W • S America • 120 kW / W • E Europe • 120 kW
	USA †WWCR, Nashville, Tennessee	E North Am • 100 kW / W • E North Am • 100 kW
7435v	CLANDESTINE (M EAST) "VO KURD STRUGGLE", Middle East	Mideast • ANTI-IRANIAN GOVT
7440	CHINA CENTRAL PEOPLE'S BS, Xi'an	DS-2 • 120 kW
	RUSSIA GOLOS ROSSII, Moscow	W • Europe • 240 kW
	MAYAK	S • DS
	†RADIO ROSSII, Various Locations	W • E Asia • DS • 100 kW
	†VOICE OF RUSSIA, Novosibirsk	S • Europe & W Africa • 500 kW
7445	CHINA (TAIWAN) VO FREE CHINA, T'ai-pei	SE Asia • 100 kW
	VOICE OF ASIA, T'ai-pei	E Asia • 100 kW / SE Asia • 100 kW
	GERMANY †DEUTSCHE WELLE, Via Samara, Russia	W • S Asia • 250 kW
7448	GREECE †FONI TIS HELLADAS, Various Locations	W • N America • 100/250 kW
7450	GREECE †FONI TIS HELLADAS, Athens	W • Mideast • 100 kW / W • Europe • 100 kW / Europe & Australasia • 100 kW / W • E Europe • 100 kW / Europe • 100 kW
7455	GUAM †KSDA-ADVENTIST WORLD RADIO, Agat	W • E Asia • 100 kW / E Asia • 100 kW / W • S Asia • 100 kW / Mideast • 50 kW
	PAKISTAN †RADIO PAKISTAN, Karachi	
7460v	PIRATE (PACIFIC) †"KIWI RADIO", New Zealand	Irr • N America & Europe • 0.35/1.2 kW • ALT. FREQ. TO 7475v kHz / Irr • Pacific • 0.1/1.2 kW • ALT. FREQ. TO 7475v kHz
7465	DENMARK †RADIO DANMARK, Via Norway	E North Am & C America • 350 kW / W • S America • 350 kW / S • E North Am • 350 kW / W North Am • 500 kW / S • E Europe • 350 kW / W • E North Am • 350 kW
	GUAM †KTWR-TRANS WORLD RADIO, Merizo	E Asia • 50 kW
	ISRAEL †KOL ISRAEL, Tel Aviv	W Europe & E North Am • 300 kW / E Europe • 300 kW / W • W Asia • 300 kW
(con'd)		

FREQUENCY   COUNTRY, STATION, LOCATION   TARGET • NETWORK • POWER (kW)   World Time

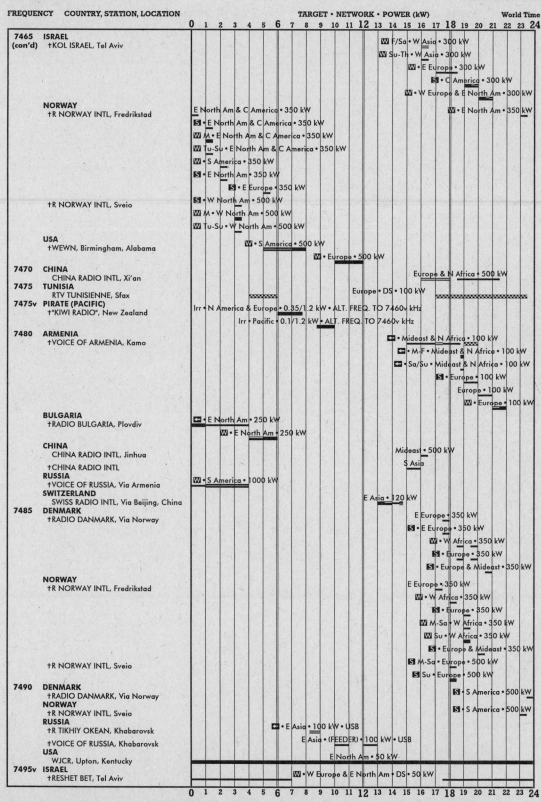

Frequency	Country, Station, Location	Target • Network • Power (kW)
7465 (con'd)	**ISRAEL** †KOL ISRAEL, Tel Aviv	W F/Sa • W Asia • 300 kW; W Su-Th • W Asia • 300 kW; W • E Europe • 300 kW; S • C America • 300 kW; W • W Europe & E North Am • 300 kW; W • E North Am • 350 kW
	NORWAY †R NORWAY INTL, Fredrikstad	E North Am & C America • 350 kW; S • E North Am & C America • 350 kW; W M • E North Am & C America • 350 kW; W Tu-Su • E North Am & C America • 350 kW; W • S America • 350 kW; S • E North Am • 350 kW; S • E Europe • 350 kW
	†R NORWAY INTL, Sveio	S • W North Am • 500 kW; W M • W North Am • 500 kW; W Tu-Su • W North Am • 500 kW
	USA †WEWN, Birmingham, Alabama	W • S America • 500 kW; W • Europe • 500 kW
7470	**CHINA** CHINA RADIO INTL, Xi'an	Europe & N Africa • 500 kW
7475	**TUNISIA** RTV TUNISIENNE, Sfax	Europe • DS • 100 kW
7475v	**PIRATE (PACIFIC)** †"KIWI RADIO", New Zealand	Irr • N America & Europe • 0.35/1.2 kW • ALT. FREQ. TO 7460v kHz; Irr • Pacific • 0.1/1.2 kW • ALT. FREQ. TO 7460v kHz
7480	**ARMENIA** †VOICE OF ARMENIA, Kamo	• Mideast & N Africa • 100 kW; • M-F • Mideast & N Africa • 100 kW; • Sa/Su • Mideast & N Africa • 100 kW; S • Europe • 100 kW; Europe • 100 kW; W • Europe • 100 kW
	BULGARIA †RADIO BULGARIA, Plovdiv	• E North Am • 250 kW; W • E North Am • 250 kW
	CHINA CHINA RADIO INTL, Jinhua	Mideast • 500 kW
	†CHINA RADIO INTL	S Asia
	RUSSIA †VOICE OF RUSSIA, Via Armenia	W • S America • 1000 kW
	SWITZERLAND SWISS RADIO INTL, Via Beijing, China	E Asia • 120 kW
7485	**DENMARK** †RADIO DANMARK, Via Norway	E Europe • 350 kW; S • E Europe • 350 kW; W • W Africa • 350 kW; S • Europe • 350 kW; S • Europe & Mideast • 350 kW
	NORWAY †R NORWAY INTL, Fredrikstad	E Europe • 350 kW; W • W Africa • 350 kW; S • Europe • 350 kW; W M-Sa • W Africa • 350 kW; W Su • W Africa • 350 kW; S • Europe & Mideast • 350 kW
	†R NORWAY INTL, Sveio	S M-Sa • Europe • 500 kW; S Su • Europe • 500 kW
7490	**DENMARK** †RADIO DANMARK, Via Norway	S • S America • 500 kW
	NORWAY †R NORWAY INTL, Sveio	S • S America • 500 kW
	RUSSIA †R TIKHIY OKEAN, Khabarovsk	• E Asia • 100 kW • USB
	†VOICE OF RUSSIA, Khabarovsk	E Asia • (FEEDER) • 100 kW • USB
	USA WJCR, Upton, Kentucky	E North Am • 50 kW
7495v	**ISRAEL** †RESHET BET, Tel Aviv	W • W Europe & E North Am • DS • 50 kW

FREQUENCY   COUNTRY, STATION, LOCATION   TARGET • NETWORK • POWER (kW)   World Time

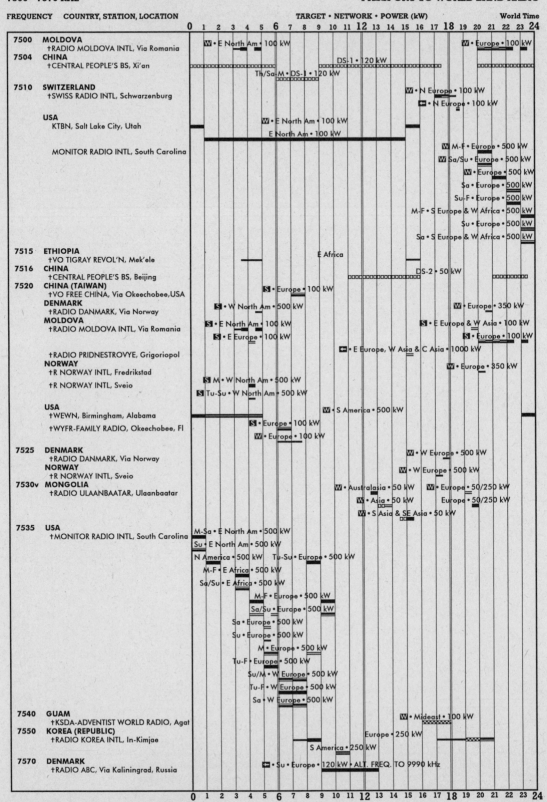

Frequency	Country, Station, Location	Program details
7500	**MOLDOVA** †RADIO MOLDOVA INTL, Via Romania	W • E North Am • 100 kW / W • Europe • 100 kW
7504	**CHINA** †CENTRAL PEOPLE'S BS, Xi'an	DS-1 • 120 kW / Th/Sa-M • DS-1 • 120 kW
7510	**SWITZERLAND** †SWISS RADIO INTL, Schwarzenburg	W • N Europe • 100 kW / W • N Europe • 100 kW
	USA KTBN, Salt Lake City, Utah	W • E North Am • 100 kW / E North Am • 100 kW
	MONITOR RADIO INTL, South Carolina	W • M-F • Europe • 500 kW / W • Sa/Su • Europe • 500 kW / W • Europe • 500 kW / Sa • Europe • 500 kW / Su-F • Europe • 500 kW / M-F • S Europe & W Africa • 500 kW / Su • Europe • 500 kW / Sa • S Europe & W Africa • 500 kW
7515	**ETHIOPIA** †VO TIGRAY REVOL'N, Mek'ele	E Africa
7516	**CHINA** †CENTRAL PEOPLE'S BS, Beijing	DS-2 • 50 kW
7520	**CHINA (TAIWAN)** †VO FREE CHINA, Via Okeechobee, USA	S • Europe • 100 kW
	DENMARK †RADIO DANMARK, Via Norway	S • W North Am • 500 kW / W • Europe • 350 kW
	MOLDOVA †RADIO MOLDOVA INTL, Via Romania	S • E North Am • 100 kW / S • E Europe & W Asia • 100 kW / S • E Europe • 100 kW / S • Europe • 100 kW
	†RADIO PRIDNESTROVYE, Grigoriopol	⇨ • E Europe, W Asia & C Asia • 1000 kW
	NORWAY †R NORWAY INTL, Fredrikstad	W • Europe • 350 kW
	†R NORWAY INTL, Sveio	S M • W North Am • 500 kW / S Tu-Su • W North Am • 500 kW
	USA †WEWN, Birmingham, Alabama	W • S America • 500 kW
	†WYFR-FAMILY RADIO, Okeechobee, Fl	S • Europe • 100 kW / W • Europe • 100 kW
7525	**DENMARK** †RADIO DANMARK, Via Norway	W • W Europe • 500 kW
	NORWAY †R NORWAY INTL, Sveio	W • W Europe • 500 kW
7530v	**MONGOLIA** †RADIO ULAANBAATAR, Ulaanbaatar	W • Australasia • 50 kW / W • Europe • 50/250 kW / W • Asia • 50 kW / Europe • 50/250 kW / W • S Asia & SE Asia • 50 kW
7535	**USA** †MONITOR RADIO INTL, South Carolina	M-Sa • E North Am • 500 kW / Su • E North Am • 500 kW / N America • 500 kW / Tu-Su • Europe • 500 kW / M-F • E Africa • 500 kW / Sa/Su • E Africa • 500 kW / M-F • Europe • 500 kW / Sa/Su • Europe • 500 kW / Sa • Europe • 500 kW / Su • Europe • 500 kW / M • Europe • 500 kW / Tu-F • Europe • 500 kW / Su/M • W Europe • 500 kW / Tu-F • W Europe • 500 kW / Sa • W Europe • 500 kW
7540	**GUAM** †KSDA-ADVENTIST WORLD RADIO, Agat	W • Mideast • 100 kW
7550	**KOREA (REPUBLIC)** †RADIO KOREA INTL, In-Kimjae	Europe • 250 kW / S America • 250 kW
7570	**DENMARK** †RADIO ABC, Via Kaliningrad, Russia	⇨ • Su • Europe • 120 kW • ALT. FREQ. TO 9990 kHz

SEASONAL **S** OR **W**   1-HR TIMESHIFT MIDYEAR ⇦ OR ⇨   JAMMING / OR ∧   EARLIEST HEARD ◁   LATEST HEARD ▷   NEW FOR 1997 †

FREQUENCY   COUNTRY, STATION, LOCATION

TARGET • NETWORK • POWER (kW)   World Time

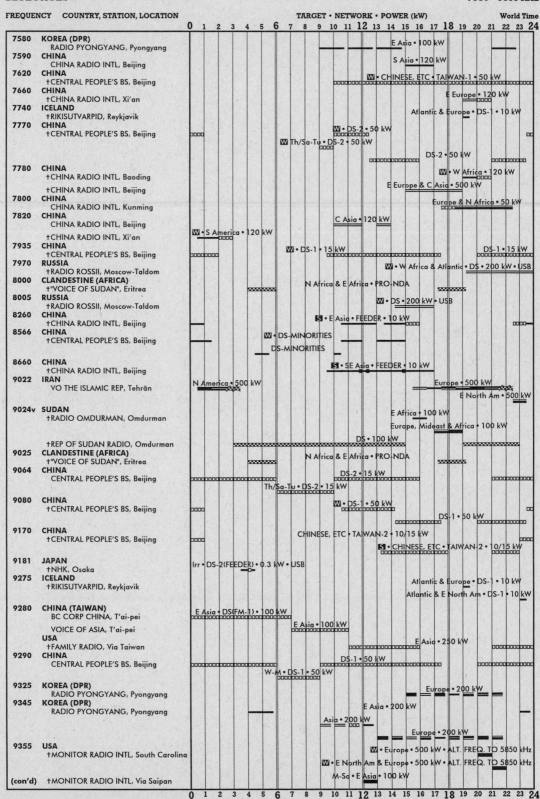

7580	**KOREA (DPR)**	E Asia • 100 kW
	RADIO PYONGYANG, Pyongyang	
7590	**CHINA**	S Asia • 120 kW
	CHINA RADIO INTL, Beijing	
7620	**CHINA**	W • CHINESE, ETC • TAIWAN-1 • 50 kW
	†CENTRAL PEOPLE'S BS, Beijing	
7660	**CHINA**	E Europe • 120 kW
	†CHINA RADIO INTL, Xi'an	
7740	**ICELAND**	Atlantic & Europe • DS-1 • 10 kW
	†RIKISUTVARPID, Reykjavik	
7770	**CHINA**	W • DS-2 • 50 kW
	†CENTRAL PEOPLE'S BS, Beijing	W Th/Sa-Tu • DS-2 • 50 kW
		DS-2 • 50 kW
7780	**CHINA**	W • W Africa • 120 kW
	†CHINA RADIO INTL, Baoding	
	†CHINA RADIO INTL, Beijing	E Europe & C Asia • 500 kW
7800	**CHINA**	Europe & N Africa • 50 kW
	CHINA RADIO INTL, Kunming	
7820	**CHINA**	C Asia • 120 kW
	CHINA RADIO INTL, Beijing	
	†CHINA RADIO INTL, Xi'an	W • S America • 120 kW
7935	**CHINA**	W • DS-1 • 15 kW · DS-1 • 15 kW
	†CENTRAL PEOPLE'S BS, Beijing	
7970	**RUSSIA**	W • W Africa & Atlantic • DS • 200 kW • USB
	†RADIO ROSSII, Moscow-Taldom	
8000	**CLANDESTINE (AFRICA)**	N Africa & E Africa • PRO-NDA
	†"VOICE OF SUDAN", Eritrea	
8005	**RUSSIA**	W • DS • 200 kW • USB
	†RADIO ROSSII, Moscow-Taldom	
8260	**CHINA**	S • E Asia • FEEDER • 10 kW
	†CHINA RADIO INTL, Beijing	
8566	**CHINA**	W • DS-MINORITIES
	†CENTRAL PEOPLE'S BS, Beijing	DS-MINORITIES
8660	**CHINA**	S • SE Asia • FEEDER • 10 kW
	†CHINA RADIO INTL, Beijing	
9022	**IRAN**	N America • 500 kW · Europe • 500 kW
	VO THE ISLAMIC REP, Tehrān	E North Am • 500 kW
9024v	**SUDAN**	E Africa • 100 kW
	†RADIO OMDURMAN, Omdurman	Europe, Mideast & Africa • 100 kW
	†REP OF SUDAN RADIO, Omdurman	DS • 100 kW
9025	**CLANDESTINE (AFRICA)**	N Africa & E Africa • PRO-NDA
	†"VOICE OF SUDAN", Eritrea	
9064	**CHINA**	DS-2 • 15 kW
	CENTRAL PEOPLE'S BS, Beijing	Th/Sa-Tu • DS-2 • 15 kW
9080	**CHINA**	W • DS-1 • 50 kW
	†CENTRAL PEOPLE'S BS, Beijing	DS-1 • 50 kW
9170	**CHINA**	CHINESE, ETC • TAIWAN-2 • 10/15 kW
	†CENTRAL PEOPLE'S BS, Beijing	S • CHINESE, ETC • TAIWAN-2 • 10/15 kW
9181	**JAPAN**	Irr • DS-2(FEEDER) • 0.3 kW • USB
	†NHK, Osaka	
9275	**ICELAND**	Atlantic & Europe • DS-1 • 10 kW
	†RIKISUTVARPID, Reykjavik	Atlantic & E North Am • DS-1 • 10 kW
9280	**CHINA (TAIWAN)**	E Asia • DS(FM-1) • 100 kW
	BC CORP CHINA, T'ai-pei	
	VOICE OF ASIA, T'ai-pei	E Asia • 100 kW
	USA	E Asia • 250 kW
	†FAMILY RADIO, Via Taiwan	
9290	**CHINA**	DS-1 • 50 kW
	CENTRAL PEOPLE'S BS, Beijing	W-M • DS-1 • 50 kW
9325	**KOREA (DPR)**	Europe • 200 kW
	RADIO PYONGYANG, Pyongyang	
9345	**KOREA (DPR)**	E Asia • 200 kW
	RADIO PYONGYANG, Pyongyang	Asia • 200 kW
		Europe • 200 kW
9355	**USA**	W • Europe • 500 kW • ALT. FREQ. TO 5850 kHz
	†MONITOR RADIO INTL, South Carolina	W • E North Am & Europe • 500 kW • ALT. FREQ. TO 5850 kHz
(con'd)	†MONITOR RADIO INTL, Via Saipan	M-Sa • E Asia • 100 kW

ENGLISH ▬   ARABIC ⧓   CHINESE ▭▭   FRENCH ▭   GERMAN ▬   RUSSIAN ═   SPANISH ▬   OTHER ▬

FREQUENCY   COUNTRY, STATION, LOCATION

TARGET • NETWORK • POWER (kW)   World Time

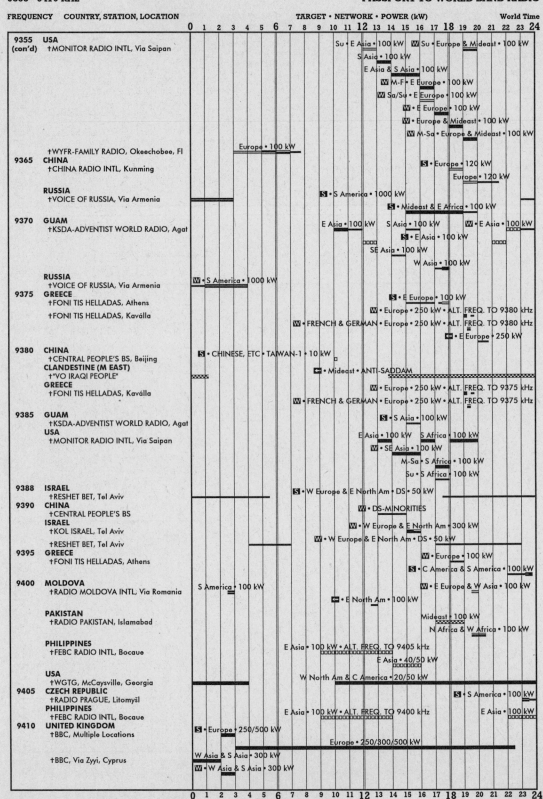

FREQUENCY   COUNTRY, STATION, LOCATION   TARGET • NETWORK • POWER (kW)   World Time

Freq	Country / Station / Location	Schedule
9415	**BULGARIA** †RADIO BULGARIA, Plovdiv	S America • 500 kW
	ECUADOR †HCJB-VO THE ANDES, Quito	E Asia • 250 kW
9420	**GREECE** †FONI TIS HELLADAS, Athens	W • N America • 100 kW; W • Mideast • 100 kW; W • Europe • 100 kW; W • ARABIC & ENGLISH • Mideast • 100 kW; W • Europe & N America • 100 kW; S • Mideast • 100 kW; S • Europe, N America & Australasia • 100 kW • ALT. FREQ. TO 7430 kHz
	†FONI TIS HELLADAS, Kaválla	Mideast • 250 kW • ALT. FREQ. TO 9425 kHz; E Europe • 250 kW; E Europe • 250 kW • ALT. FREQ. TO 9425 kHz; S • Europe • 250 kW • ALT. FREQ. TO 7430 kHz; S • FRENCH & GERMAN • Europe • 250 kW • ALT. FREQ. TO 7430 kHz
	SEYCHELLES FEBA RADIO, North Pt, Mahé Is	S Th • S Africa • 75 kW; S Africa • 75 kW; E Africa & Mideast • 100 kW; Su/Tu/F • E Africa & Mideast • 100 kW; C Africa & S Africa • 75 kW • ALT. FREQ. TO 9565 kHz; W • C Africa & S Africa • 75 kW • ALT. FREQ. TO 9565 kHz
9425	**CZECH REPUBLIC** †RADIO PRAGUE, Litomyšl	W • S Asia & SE Asia • 100 kW
	GERMANY †DEUTSCHE WELLE, Nauen	S • S Asia • 500 kW
	GREECE †FONI TIS HELLADAS, Athens	S • Europe & Australasia • 100 kW; S • E Europe • 100 kW; Mideast • 100 kW; E Europe • 100 kW; W • Europe • 100 kW; S • C America & Australasia • 100 kW; W • C America & S America • 100 kW; W • C America • 100 kW
	†FONI TIS HELLADAS, Kaválla	Mideast • 250 kW • ALT. FREQ. TO 9420 kHz; E Europe • 250 kW • ALT. FREQ. TO 9420 kHz; Australasia • 250 kW
	MONACO TRANS WORLD R, Via Cerrik, Albania	W Asia • 100 kW
9430	**BULGARIA** †RADIO BULGARIA, Plovdiv	S • Mideast • 250 kW; W • N Africa & W Africa • 500 kW; W • W Africa & S America • 500 kW
	CZECH REPUBLIC †RADIO PRAGUE, Litomyšl	W • E Africa • 100 kW; W • Mideast & E Africa • 100 kW; W • C Africa • 100 kW; W • Australasia • 100 kW; W • W Africa & S America • 100 kW; S • W Africa • 100 kW
	GUAM †KTWR-TRANS WORLD RADIO, Merizo	S • S Asia • 100 kW; SE Asia • 100 kW
	SWEDEN †RADIO SWEDEN, Hörby	S • Europe & Africa • 500 kW; S M-F • Europe & Africa • 500 kW; S Sa/Su • Europe & Africa • 500 kW
	USA MONITOR RADIO INTL, South Carolina	M-Sa • C America & S America • 500 kW; Su • C America & S America • 500 kW; M-F • W North Am & C America • 500 kW; Sa/Su • W North Am & C America • 500 kW
	†MONITOR RADIO INTL, Via Saipan	S • Australasia • 100 kW • ALT. FREQ. TO 9845 kHz; W • E Asia • 100 kW; M-F • E Asia • 100 kW; Sa/Su • E Asia • 100 kW; Australasia • 100 kW
9435	**ISRAEL** †KOL ISRAEL, Tel Aviv	S • Europe • 20 kW; W • W Asia • 300 kW; W F/Sa • W Asia • 300 kW; W Su-Th • W Asia • 300 kW; Europe • 300 kW; W Europe & E North Am • 300 kW

(con'd)

ENGLISH ▬ ARABIC ⁓ CHINESE ▫▫▫ FRENCH ═ GERMAN ▬ RUSSIAN ═ SPANISH ▬ OTHER ▬

FREQUENCY   COUNTRY, STATION, LOCATION

TARGET • NETWORK • POWER (kW)

World Time

0 1 2 3 4 5 6 7 8 9 10 11 12 13 14 15 16 17 18 19 20 21 22 23 24

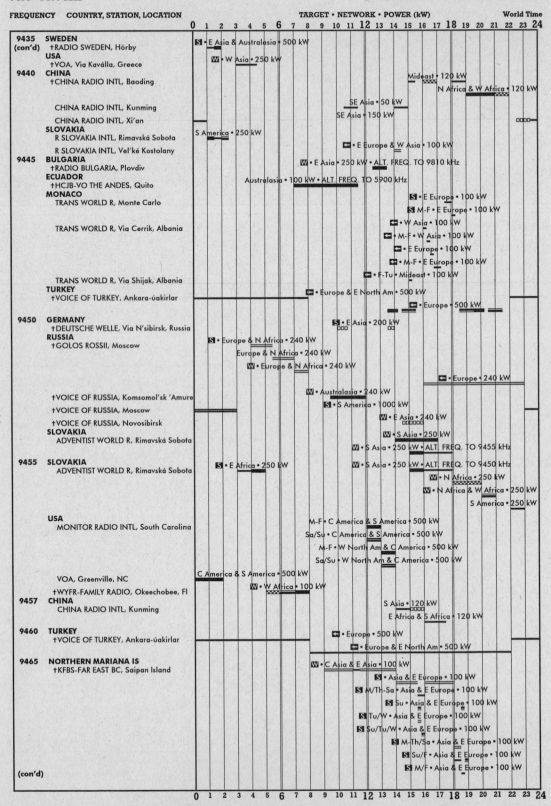

9435 (con'd)	SWEDEN †RADIO SWEDEN, Hörby	S • E Asia & Australasia • 500 kW
	USA †VOA, Via Kaválla, Greece	W • W Asia • 250 kW
9440	CHINA †CHINA RADIO INTL, Baoding	Mideast • 120 kW / N Africa & W Africa • 120 kW
	CHINA RADIO INTL, Kunming	SE Asia • 50 kW
	CHINA RADIO INTL, Xi'an	SE Asia • 150 kW
	SLOVAKIA R SLOVAKIA INTL, Rimavská Sobota	S America • 250 kW
	R SLOVAKIA INTL, Vel'ké Kostolany	E Europe & W Asia • 100 kW
9445	BULGARIA †RADIO BULGARIA, Plovdiv	W • E Asia • 250 kW • ALT. FREQ. TO 9810 kHz
	ECUADOR †HCJB-VO THE ANDES, Quito	Australasia • 100 kW • ALT. FREQ. TO 5900 kHz
	MONACO TRANS WORLD R, Monte Carlo	S • E Europe • 100 kW / S M-F • E Europe • 100 kW
	TRANS WORLD R, Via Cerrik, Albania	• W Asia • 100 kW / • M-F • W Asia • 100 kW / • E Europe • 100 kW / • M-F • E Europe • 100 kW
	TRANS WORLD R, Via Shijak, Albania	• F-Tu • Mideast • 100 kW
	TURKEY †VOICE OF TURKEY, Ankara-úakirlar	• Europe & E North Am • 500 kW / • Europe • 500 kW
9450	GERMANY †DEUTSCHE WELLE, Via N'sibirsk, Russia	S • E Asia • 200 kW
	RUSSIA †GOLOS ROSSII, Moscow	S • Europe & N Africa • 240 kW / Europe & N Africa • 240 kW / W • Europe & N Africa • 240 kW / • Europe • 240 kW
	†VOICE OF RUSSIA, Komsomol'sk 'Amure	W • Australasia • 240 kW
	†VOICE OF RUSSIA, Moscow	S • S America • 1000 kW
	†VOICE OF RUSSIA, Novosibirsk	W • E Asia • 240 kW
	SLOVAKIA ADVENTIST WORLD R, Rimavská Sobota	W • S Asia • 250 kW / W • S Asia • 250 kW • ALT. FREQ. TO 9455 kHz
9455	SLOVAKIA ADVENTIST WORLD R, Rimavská Sobota	S • E Africa • 250 kW / W • S Asia • 250 kW • ALT. FREQ. TO 9450 kHz / W • N Africa • 250 kW / W • N Africa & W Africa • 250 kW / S America • 250 kW
	USA MONITOR RADIO INTL, South Carolina	M-F • C America & S America • 500 kW / Sa/Su • C America & S America • 500 kW / M-F • W North Am & C America • 500 kW / Sa/Su • W North Am & C America • 500 kW
	VOA, Greenville, NC	C America & S America • 500 kW
	†WYFR-FAMILY RADIO, Okeechobee, Fl	W • W Africa • 100 kW
9457	CHINA CHINA RADIO INTL, Kunming	S Asia • 120 kW / E Africa & S Africa • 120 kW
9460	TURKEY †VOICE OF TURKEY, Ankara-úakirlar	• Europe • 500 kW / • Europe & E North Am • 500 kW
9465	NORTHERN MARIANA IS †KFBS-FAR EAST BC, Saipan Island	W • C Asia & E Asia • 100 kW / S • Asia & E Europe • 100 kW / S M/Th-Sa • Asia & E Europe • 100 kW / S Su • Asia & E Europe • 100 kW / S Tu/W • Asia & E Europe • 100 kW / S Su/Tu/W • Asia & E Europe • 100 kW / S M-Th/Sa • Asia & E Europe • 100 kW / S Su/F • Asia & E Europe • 100 kW / S M/F • Asia & E Europe • 100 kW

(con'd)

0 1 2 3 4 5 6 7 8 9 10 11 12 13 14 15 16 17 18 19 20 21 22 23 24

SEASONAL S OR W   1-HR TIMESHIFT MIDYEAR ⇥ OR ⇤   JAMMING / OR ∧   EARLIEST HEARD ◁   LATEST HEARD ▷   NEW FOR 1997 †

FREQUENCY   COUNTRY, STATION, LOCATION   TARGET • NETWORK • POWER (kW)   World Time

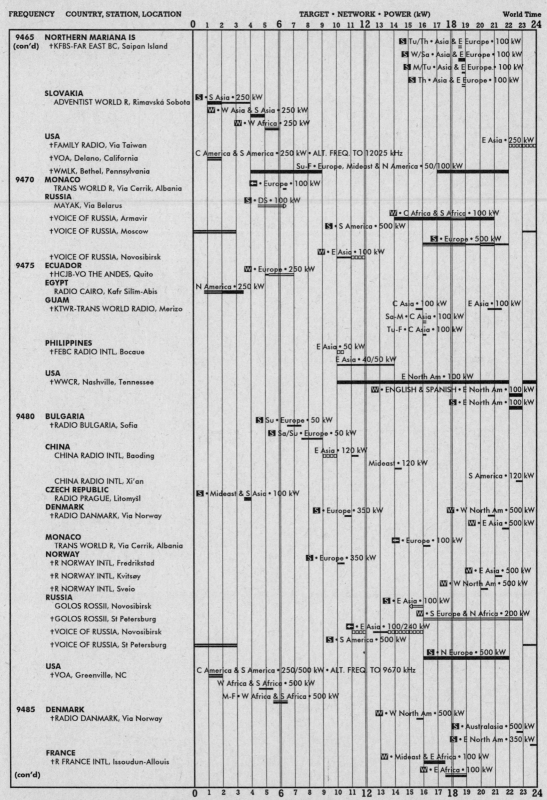

Frequency	Country / Station / Location	Target • Network • Power
9465 (con'd)	NORTHERN MARIANA IS — †KFBS-FAR EAST BC, Saipan Island	S Tu/Th • Asia & E Europe • 100 kW; S W/Sa • Asia & E Europe • 100 kW; S M/Tu • Asia & E Europe • 100 kW; S Th • Asia & E Europe • 100 kW
	SLOVAKIA — ADVENTIST WORLD R, Rimavská Sobota	S • S Asia • 250 kW; W • W Asia & S Asia • 250 kW; W • W Africa • 250 kW
	USA — †FAMILY RADIO, Via Taiwan	E Asia • 250 kW
	†VOA, Delano, California	C America & S America • 250 kW • ALT. FREQ. TO 12025 kHz
	†WMLK, Bethel, Pennsylvania	Su-F • Europe, Mideast & N America • 50/100 kW
9470	MONACO — TRANS WORLD R, Via Cerrik, Albania	• Europe • 100 kW
	RUSSIA — MAYAK, Via Belarus	S • DS • 100 kW
	†VOICE OF RUSSIA, Armavir	W • C Africa & S Africa • 100 kW
	†VOICE OF RUSSIA, Moscow	S • S America • 500 kW; S • Europe • 500 kW
	†VOICE OF RUSSIA, Novosibirsk	W • E Asia • 100 kW
9475	ECUADOR — †HCJB-VO THE ANDES, Quito	W • Europe • 250 kW
	EGYPT — RADIO CAIRO, Kafr Silīm-Abis	N America • 250 kW
	GUAM — †KTWR-TRANS WORLD RADIO, Merizo	C Asia • 100 kW; E Asia • 100 kW; Sa-M • C Asia • 100 kW; Tu-F • C Asia • 100 kW
	PHILIPPINES — †FEBC RADIO INTL, Bocaue	E Asia • 50 kW; E Asia • 40/50 kW
	USA — †WWCR, Nashville, Tennessee	E North Am • 100 kW; W • ENGLISH & SPANISH • E North Am • 100 kW; S • E North Am • 100 kW
9480	BULGARIA — †RADIO BULGARIA, Sofia	S Su • Europe • 50 kW; S Sa/Su • Europe • 50 kW
	CHINA — CHINA RADIO INTL, Baoding	E Asia • 120 kW; Mideast • 120 kW
	CHINA RADIO INTL, Xi'an	S America • 120 kW
	CZECH REPUBLIC — RADIO PRAGUE, Litomyšl	S • Mideast & S Asia • 100 kW
	DENMARK — †RADIO DANMARK, Via Norway	S • Europe • 350 kW; W • W North Am • 500 kW; W • E Asia • 500 kW
	MONACO — TRANS WORLD R, Via Cerrik, Albania	• Europe • 100 kW
	NORWAY — †R NORWAY INTL, Fredrikstad	S • Europe • 350 kW
	†R NORWAY INTL, Kvitsøy	W • E Asia • 500 kW
	†R NORWAY INTL, Sveio	W • W North Am • 500 kW
	RUSSIA — GOLOS ROSSII, Novosibirsk	S • E Asia • 100 kW
	†GOLOS ROSSII, St Petersburg	• S Europe & N Africa • 200 kW
	†VOICE OF RUSSIA, Novosibirsk	• E Asia • 100/240 kW
	†VOICE OF RUSSIA, St Petersburg	S • S America • 500 kW; S • N Europe • 500 kW
	USA — †VOA, Greenville, NC	C America & S America • 250/500 kW • ALT. FREQ. TO 9670 kHz; W Africa & S Africa • 500 kW; M-F • W Africa & S Africa • 500 kW
9485	DENMARK — †RADIO DANMARK, Via Norway	W • W North Am • 500 kW; S • Australasia • 500 kW; S • E North Am • 350 kW
	FRANCE — †R FRANCE INTL, Issoudun-Allouis	W • Mideast & E Africa • 100 kW; W • E Africa • 100 kW
(con'd)		

ENGLISH ▬   ARABIC ⁍⁍⁍   CHINESE ▫▫▫   FRENCH ══   GERMAN ▬▬   RUSSIAN ══   SPANISH ▬▬   OTHER ▬

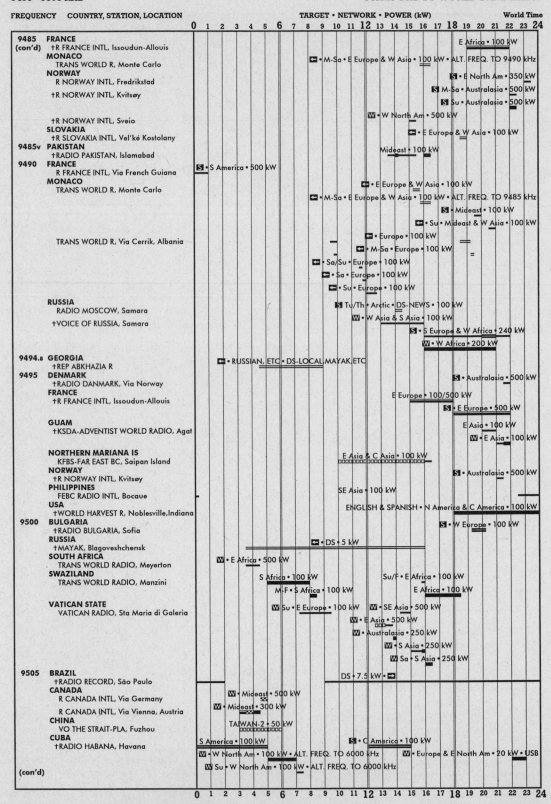

FREQUENCY   COUNTRY, STATION, LOCATION   TARGET • NETWORK • POWER (kW)   World Time

9485	FRANCE
(con'd)	†R FRANCE INTL, Issoudun-Allouis — E Africa • 100 kW
	MONACO
	TRANS WORLD R, Monte Carlo — M-Sa • E Europe & W Asia • 100 kW • ALT. FREQ. TO 9490 kHz
	NORWAY
	R NORWAY INTL, Fredrikstad — E North Am • 350 kW
	†R NORWAY INTL, Kvitsøy — M-Sa • Australasia • 500 kW
	Su • Australasia • 500 kW
	†R NORWAY INTL, Sveio — W • W North Am • 500 kW
	SLOVAKIA
	†R SLOVAKIA INTL, Vel'ké Kostolany — E Europe & W Asia • 100 kW
9485v	PAKISTAN
	†RADIO PAKISTAN, Islamabad — Mideast • 100 kW
9490	FRANCE
	R FRANCE INTL, Via French Guiana — S • S America • 500 kW
	MONACO
	TRANS WORLD R, Monte Carlo — E Europe & W Asia • 100 kW
	M-Sa • E Europe & W Asia • 100 kW • ALT. FREQ. TO 9485 kHz
	Mideast • 100 kW
	Su • Mideast & W Asia • 100 kW
	Europe • 100 kW
	M-Sa • Europe • 100 kW
	TRANS WORLD R, Via Cerrik, Albania — Sa/Su • Europe • 100 kW
	Sa • Europe • 100 kW
	Su • Europe • 100 kW
	RUSSIA
	RADIO MOSCOW, Samara — Tu/Th • Arctic • DS-NEWS • 100 kW
	W • W Asia & S Asia • 100 kW
	†VOICE OF RUSSIA, Samara — S Europe & W Africa • 240 kW
	W • W Africa • 200 kW
9494.8	GEORGIA
	†REP ABKHAZIA R — RUSSIAN, ETC • DS-LOCAL, MAYAK, ETC
9495	DENMARK
	†RADIO DANMARK, Via Norway — Australasia • 500 kW
	FRANCE
	†R FRANCE INTL, Issoudun-Allouis — E Europe • 100/500 kW
	E Europe • 500 kW
	GUAM
	†KSDA-ADVENTIST WORLD RADIO, Agat — E Asia • 100 kW
	W • E Asia • 100 kW
	NORTHERN MARIANA IS
	KFBS-FAR EAST BC, Saipan Island — E Asia & C Asia • 100 kW
	NORWAY
	†R NORWAY INTL, Kvitsøy — Australasia • 500 kW
	PHILIPPINES
	FEBC RADIO INTL, Bocaue — SE Asia • 100 kW
	USA
	†WORLD HARVEST R, Noblesville, Indiana — ENGLISH & SPANISH • N America & C America • 100 kW
9500	BULGARIA
	†RADIO BULGARIA, Sofia — W Europe • 100 kW
	RUSSIA
	†MAYAK, Blagoveshchensk — DS • 5 kW
	SOUTH AFRICA
	TRANS WORLD RADIO, Meyerton — W • E Africa • 500 kW
	SWAZILAND
	TRANS WORLD RADIO, Manzini — S Africa • 100 kW
	Su/F • E Africa • 100 kW
	M-F • S Africa • 100 kW
	E Africa • 100 kW
	VATICAN STATE
	VATICAN RADIO, Sta Maria di Galeria — Su • E Europe • 100 kW
	W • SE Asia • 500 kW
	W • E Asia • 500 kW
	W • Australasia • 250 kW
	W • S Asia • 250 kW
	W Sa • S Asia • 250 kW
9505	BRAZIL
	†RADIO RECORD, São Paulo — DS • 7.5 kW
	CANADA
	R CANADA INTL, Via Germany — W • Mideast • 500 kW
	R CANADA INTL, Via Vienna, Austria — W • Mideast • 300 kW
	CHINA
	VO THE STRAIT-PLA, Fuzhou — TAIWAN-2 • 50 kW
	CUBA
	†RADIO HABANA, Havana — S America • 100 kW
	C America • 100 kW
	W • Europe & E North Am • 20 kW • USB
	W • W North Am • 100 kW • ALT. FREQ. TO 6000 kHz
	W Su • W North Am • 100 kW • ALT. FREQ. TO 6000 kHz
(con'd)	

FREQUENCY   COUNTRY, STATION, LOCATION

TARGET • NETWORK • POWER (kW)   World Time

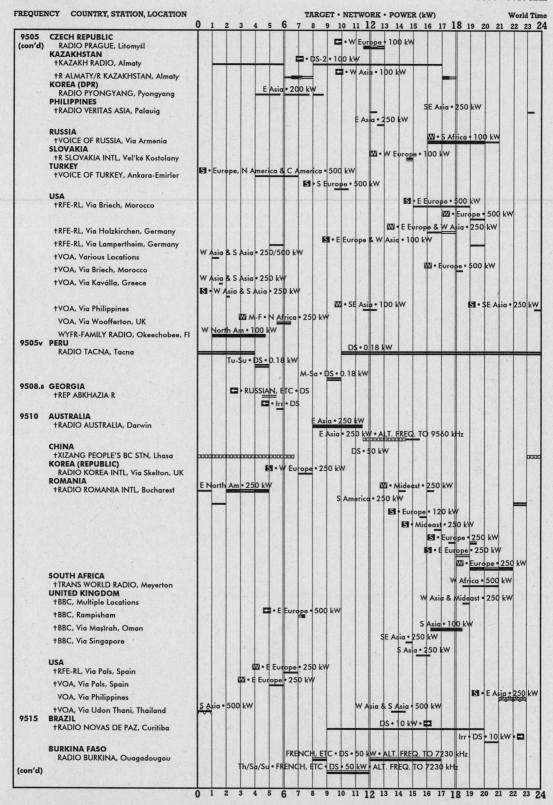

Frequency	Country, Station, Location	Target • Network • Power
9505 (con'd)	**CZECH REPUBLIC** — RADIO PRAGUE, Litomyšl	• W Europe • 100 kW
	KAZAKHSTAN †KAZAKH RADIO, Almaty	• DS-2 • 100 kW
	†R ALMATY/R KAZAKHSTAN, Almaty	• W Asia • 100 kW
	KOREA (DPR) RADIO PYONGYANG, Pyongyang	E Asia • 200 kW
	PHILIPPINES †RADIO VERITAS ASIA, Palauig	SE Asia • 250 kW / E Asia • 250 kW
	RUSSIA †VOICE OF RUSSIA, Via Armenia	W • S Africa • 100 kW
	SLOVAKIA †R SLOVAKIA INTL, Vel'ké Kostolany	W • W Europe • 100 kW
	TURKEY †VOICE OF TURKEY, Ankara-Emirler	S • Europe, N America & C America • 500 kW / S • S Europe • 500 kW
	USA †RFE-RL, Via Briech, Morocco	S • E Europe • 500 kW / W • Europe • 500 kW
	†RFE-RL, Via Holzkirchen, Germany	W • E Europe & W Asia • 250 kW
	†RFE-RL, Via Lampertheim, Germany	S • E Europe & W Asia • 100 kW
	†VOA, Various Locations	W Asia & S Asia • 250/500 kW
	†VOA, Via Briech, Morocco	W Asia & S Asia • 250 kW / W • Europe • 500 kW
	†VOA, Via Kaválla, Greece	S • W Asia & S Asia • 250 kW
	†VOA, Via Philippines	W • SE Asia • 100 kW / S • SE Asia • 250 kW
	VOA, Via Woofferton, UK	W • M-F • N Africa • 250 kW
	WYFR-FAMILY RADIO, Okeechobee, Fl	W North Am • 100 kW
9505v	**PERU** RADIO TACNA, Tacna	DS • 0.18 kW / Tu-Su • DS • 0.18 kW / M-Sa • DS • 0.18 kW
9508.8	**GEORGIA** †REP ABKHAZIA R	• RUSSIAN, ETC • DS / • Irr • DS
9510	**AUSTRALIA** †RADIO AUSTRALIA, Darwin	E Asia • 250 kW / E Asia • 250 kW • ALT. FREQ. TO 9560 kHz
	CHINA †XIZANG PEOPLE'S BC STN, Lhasa	DS • 50 kW
	KOREA (REPUBLIC) RADIO KOREA INTL, Via Skelton, UK	S • W Europe • 250 kW
	ROMANIA †RADIO ROMANIA INTL, Bucharest	E North Am • 250 kW / W • Mideast • 250 kW / S America • 250 kW / S • Europe • 120 kW / S • Mideast • 250 kW / S • Europe • 250 kW / S • E Europe • 250 kW / W • Europe • 250 kW
	SOUTH AFRICA †TRANS WORLD RADIO, Meyerton	W Africa • 500 kW
	UNITED KINGDOM †BBC, Multiple Locations	W Asia & Mideast • 250 kW
	†BBC, Rampisham	• E Europe • 500 kW
	†BBC, Via Maşīrah, Oman	S Asia • 100 kW
	†BBC, Via Singapore	SE Asia • 250 kW / S Asia • 250 kW
	USA †RFE-RL, Via Pals, Spain	W • E Europe • 250 kW
	†VOA, Via Pals, Spain	W • E Europe • 250 kW
	VOA, Via Philippines	S • E Asia • 250 kW
	†VOA, Via Udon Thani, Thailand	S Asia • 500 kW / W Asia & S Asia • 500 kW
9515	**BRAZIL** †RADIO NOVAS DE PAZ, Curitiba	DS • 10 kW • / Irr • DS • 10 kW •
	BURKINA FASO RADIO BURKINA, Ouagadougou	FRENCH, ETC • DS • 50 kW • ALT. FREQ. TO 7230 kHz / Th/Sa/Su • FRENCH, ETC • DS • 50 kW • ALT. FREQ. TO 7230 kHz
(con'd)		

ENGLISH ▬   ARABIC ⁓⁓⁓   CHINESE ▭▭▭   FRENCH ▬▬   GERMAN ▬▬   RUSSIAN ══   SPANISH ▬▬   OTHER ▬▬

FREQUENCY   COUNTRY, STATION, LOCATION   TARGET • NETWORK • POWER (kW)   World Time

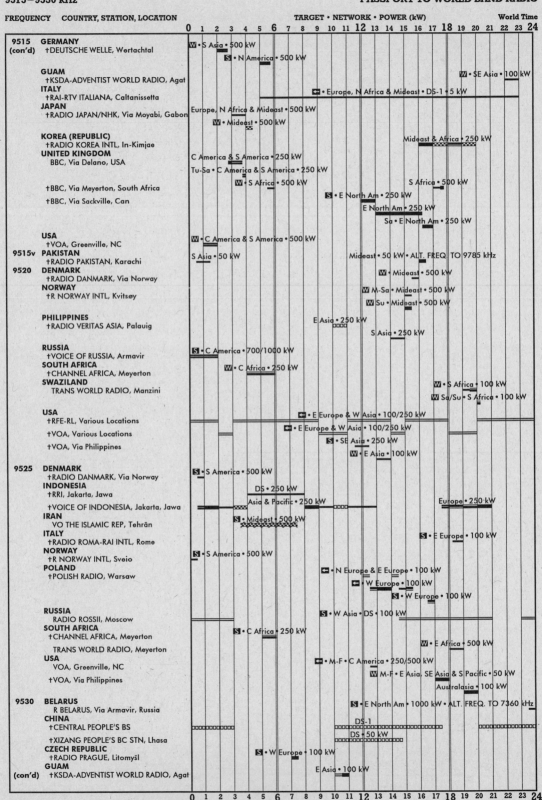

Frequency	Country, Station, Location	Schedule
9515 (con'd)	**GERMANY** †DEUTSCHE WELLE, Wertachtal	W • S Asia • 500 kW / S • N America • 500 kW
	GUAM †KSDA-ADVENTIST WORLD RADIO, Agat	W • SE Asia • 100 kW
	ITALY †RAI-RTV ITALIANA, Caltanissetta	• Europe, N Africa & Mideast • DS-1 • 5 kW
	JAPAN †RADIO JAPAN/NHK, Via Moyabi, Gabon	Europe, N Africa & Mideast • 500 kW / W • Mideast • 500 kW
	KOREA (REPUBLIC) †RADIO KOREA INTL, In-Kimjae	Mideast & Africa • 250 kW
	UNITED KINGDOM BBC, Via Delano, USA	C America & S America • 250 kW / Tu-Sa • C America & S America • 250 kW / W • S Africa • 500 kW
	†BBC, Via Meyerton, South Africa	S Africa • 500 kW
	†BBC, Via Sackville, Can	S • E North Am • 250 kW / E North Am • 250 kW / Sa • E North Am • 250 kW
	USA †VOA, Greenville, NC	W • C America & S America • 500 kW
9515v	**PAKISTAN** †RADIO PAKISTAN, Karachi	S Asia • 50 kW / Mideast • 50 kW • ALT. FREQ. TO 9785 kHz
9520	**DENMARK** †RADIO DANMARK, Via Norway	W • Mideast • 500 kW
	NORWAY †R NORWAY INTL, Kvitsøy	W M-Sa • Mideast • 500 kW / W Su • Mideast • 500 kW
	PHILIPPINES †RADIO VERITAS ASIA, Palauig	E Asia • 250 kW / S Asia • 250 kW
	RUSSIA †VOICE OF RUSSIA, Armavir	S • C America • 700/1000 kW
	SOUTH AFRICA †CHANNEL AFRICA, Meyerton	W • C Africa • 250 kW
	SWAZILAND TRANS WORLD RADIO, Manzini	W • S Africa • 100 kW / W Sa/Su • S Africa • 100 kW
	USA †RFE-RL, Various Locations	• E Europe & W Asia • 100/250 kW
	†VOA, Various Locations	• E Europe & W Asia • 100/250 kW
	†VOA, Via Philippines	S • SE Asia • 250 kW / W • E Asia • 100 kW
9525	**DENMARK** †RADIO DANMARK, Via Norway	S • S America • 500 kW
	INDONESIA †RRI, Jakarta, Jawa	DS • 250 kW
	†VOICE OF INDONESIA, Jakarta, Jawa	Asia & Pacific • 250 kW / Europe • 250 kW
	IRAN VO THE ISLAMIC REP, Tehrān	S • Mideast • 500 kW
	ITALY †RADIO ROMA-RAI INTL, Rome	S • E Europe • 100 kW
	NORWAY †R NORWAY INTL, Sveio	S • S America • 500 kW
	POLAND †POLISH RADIO, Warsaw	• N Europe & E Europe • 100 kW / • W Europe • 100 kW / S • W Europe • 100 kW
	RUSSIA RADIO ROSSII, Moscow	S • W Asia • DS • 100 kW
	SOUTH AFRICA †CHANNEL AFRICA, Meyerton	S • C Africa • 250 kW
	TRANS WORLD RADIO, Meyerton	W • E Africa • 500 kW
	USA VOA, Greenville, NC	• M-F • C America • 250/500 kW
	†VOA, Via Philippines	W M-F • E Asia, SE Asia & S Pacific • 50 kW / Australasia • 100 kW
9530	**BELARUS** R BELARUS, Via Armavir, Russia	S • E North Am • 1000 kW • ALT. FREQ. TO 7360 kHz
	CHINA †CENTRAL PEOPLE'S BS	DS-1
	†XIZANG PEOPLE'S BC STN, Lhasa	DS • 50 kW
	CZECH REPUBLIC †RADIO PRAGUE, Litomyšl	S • W Europe • 100 kW
(con'd)	**GUAM** †KSDA-ADVENTIST WORLD RADIO, Agat	E Asia • 100 kW

| FREQUENCY | COUNTRY, STATION, LOCATION | TARGET • NETWORK • POWER (kW) | World Time |

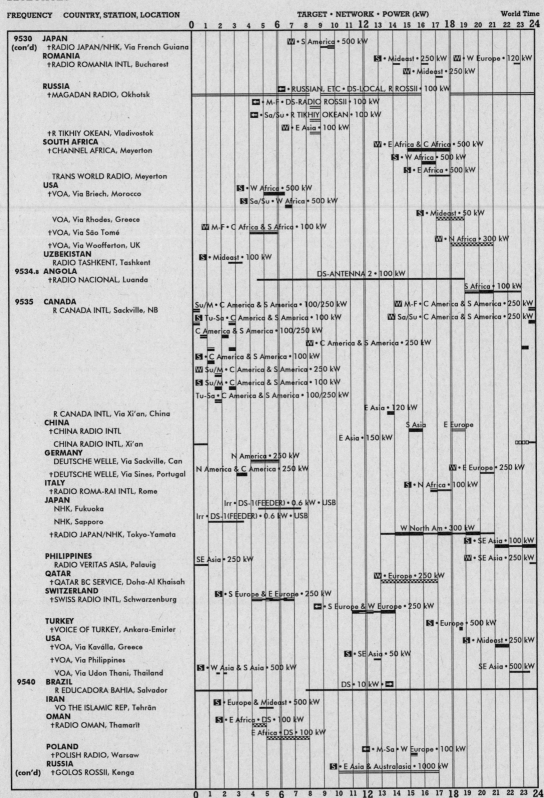

9530
(con'd) JAPAN
  †RADIO JAPAN/NHK, Via French Guiana — W • S America • 500 kW
ROMANIA
  †RADIO ROMANIA INTL, Bucharest — S • Mideast • 250 kW   W • W Europe • 120 kW
    W • Mideast • 250 kW
RUSSIA
  †MAGADAN RADIO, Okhotsk — RUSSIAN, ETC • DS-LOCAL, R ROSSII • 100 kW
    M-F • DS-RADIO ROSSII • 100 kW
    Sa/Su • R TIKHIY OKEAN • 100 kW
  †R TIKHIY OKEAN, Vladivostok — W • E Asia • 100 kW
SOUTH AFRICA
  †CHANNEL AFRICA, Meyerton — W • E Africa & C Africa • 500 kW
    S • W Africa • 500 kW
    S • E Africa • 500 kW
  TRANS WORLD RADIO, Meyerton
USA
  †VOA, Via Briech, Morocco — S • W Africa • 500 kW
    S Sa/Su • W Africa • 500 kW
  VOA, Via Rhodes, Greece — S • Mideast • 50 kW
  †VOA, Via São Tomé — W M-F • C Africa & S Africa • 100 kW
  †VOA, Via Woofferton, UK — W • N Africa • 300 kW
UZBEKISTAN
  RADIO TASHKENT, Tashkent — S • Mideast • 100 kW

9534.8 ANGOLA
  †RADIO NACIONAL, Luanda — DS-ANTENNA 2 • 100 kW
    S Africa • 100 kW

9535 CANADA
  R CANADA INTL, Sackville, NB — Su/M • C America & S America • 100/250 kW   W M-F • C America & S America • 250 kW
    S Tu-Sa • C America & S America • 100 kW   W Sa/Su • C America & S America • 250 kW
    C America & S America • 100/250 kW
    W • C America & S America • 250 kW
    S • C America & S America • 100 kW
    W Su/M • C America & S America • 250 kW
    S Su/M • C America & S America • 100 kW
    Tu-Sa • C America & S America • 100/250 kW
  R CANADA INTL, Via Xi'an, China — E Asia • 120 kW
CHINA
  †CHINA RADIO INTL — S Asia   E Europe
  CHINA RADIO INTL, Xi'an — E Asia • 150 kW
GERMANY
  DEUTSCHE WELLE, Via Sackville, Can — N America • 250 kW
  †DEUTSCHE WELLE, Via Sines, Portugal — N America & C America • 250 kW   W • E Europe • 250 kW
ITALY
  †RADIO ROMA-RAI INTL, Rome — S • N Africa • 100 kW
JAPAN
  NHK, Fukuoka — Irr • DS-1(FEEDER) • 0.6 kW • USB
  NHK, Sapporo — Irr • DS-1(FEEDER) • 0.6 kW • USB
  †RADIO JAPAN/NHK, Tokyo-Yamata — W North Am • 300 kW
    S • SE Asia • 100 kW
PHILIPPINES
  RADIO VERITAS ASIA, Palauig — SE Asia • 250 kW
    W • SE Asia • 250 kW
QATAR
  †QATAR BC SERVICE, Doha-Al Khaisah — W • Europe • 250 kW
SWITZERLAND
  †SWISS RADIO INTL, Schwarzenburg — S • S Europe & E Europe • 250 kW
    S Europe & W Europe • 250 kW
TURKEY
  †VOICE OF TURKEY, Ankara-Emirler — S • Europe • 500 kW
USA
  †VOA, Via Kaválla, Greece — S • Mideast • 250 kW
  †VOA, Via Philippines — S • SE Asia • 50 kW
  VOA, Via Udon Thani, Thailand — SE Asia • 500 kW
    S • W Asia & S Asia • 500 kW

9540 BRAZIL
  R EDUCADORA BAHIA, Salvador — DS • 10 kW
IRAN
  VO THE ISLAMIC REP, Tehrān — S • Europe & Mideast • 500 kW
OMAN
  †RADIO OMAN, Thamarīt — S • E Africa • DS • 100 kW
    E Africa • DS • 100 kW
POLAND
  †POLISH RADIO, Warsaw — M-Sa • W Europe • 100 kW
RUSSIA
(con'd) †GOLOS ROSSII, Kenga — S • E Asia & Australasia • 1000 kW

ENGLISH ▬   ARABIC ▨▨▨   CHINESE ▫▫▫   FRENCH ▭▭   GERMAN ▬▬   RUSSIAN ═══   SPANISH ▬   OTHER ▬

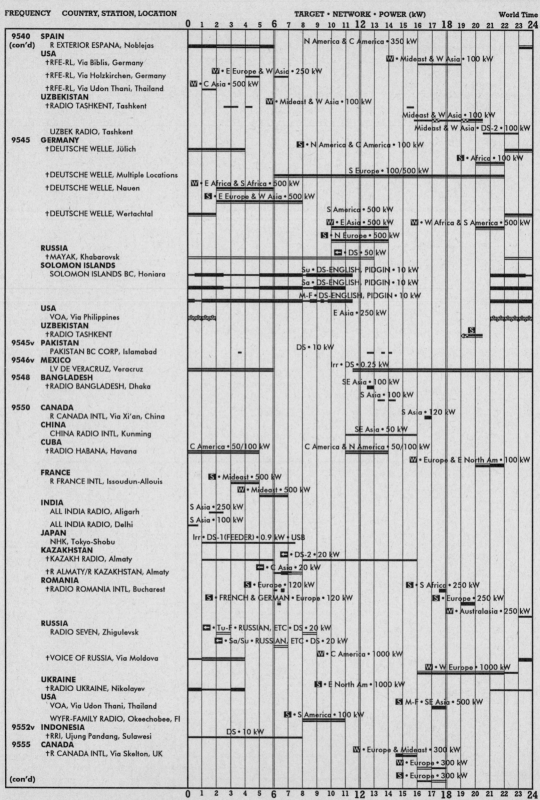

FREQUENCY   COUNTRY, STATION, LOCATION

TARGET • NETWORK • POWER (kW)

World Time

FREQUENCY	COUNTRY, STATION, LOCATION	TARGET • NETWORK • POWER (kW)
9540 (con'd)	SPAIN — R EXTERIOR ESPANA, Noblejas	N America & C America • 350 kW
	USA	
	†RFE-RL, Via Biblis, Germany	W • Mideast & W Asia • 100 kW
	†RFE-RL, Via Holzkirchen, Germany	W • E Europe & W Asia • 250 kW
	†RFE-RL, Via Udon Thani, Thailand	W • C Asia • 500 kW
	UZBEKISTAN	
	†RADIO TASHKENT, Tashkent	W • Mideast & W Asia • 100 kW
		Mideast & W Asia • 100 kW
	UZBEK RADIO, Tashkent	Mideast & W Asia • DS-2 • 100 kW
9545	GERMANY	
	†DEUTSCHE WELLE, Jülich	S • N America & C America • 100 kW
		S • Africa • 100 kW
	†DEUTSCHE WELLE, Multiple Locations	S Europe • 100/500 kW
	†DEUTSCHE WELLE, Nauen	W • E Africa & S Africa • 500 kW
		S • E Europe & W Asia • 500 kW
	†DEUTSCHE WELLE, Wertachtal	S America • 500 kW
		W • E Asia • 500 kW W • W Africa & S America • 500 kW
		S • N Europe • 500 kW
	RUSSIA	
	†MAYAK, Khabarovsk	◁ • DS • 50 kW
	SOLOMON ISLANDS	
	SOLOMON ISLANDS BC, Honiara	Su • DS-ENGLISH, PIDGIN • 10 kW
		Sa • DS-ENGLISH, PIDGIN • 10 kW
		M-F • DS-ENGLISH, PIDGIN • 10 kW
	USA	
	VOA, Via Philippines	E Asia • 250 kW
	UZBEKISTAN	
	†RADIO TASHKENT	S
9545v	PAKISTAN	
	PAKISTAN BC CORP, Islamabad	DS • 10 kW
9546v	MEXICO	
	LV DE VERACRUZ, Veracruz	Irr • DS • 0.25 kW
9548	BANGLADESH	
	†RADIO BANGLADESH, Dhaka	SE Asia • 100 kW
		S Asia • 100 kW
9550	CANADA	
	R CANADA INTL, Via Xi'an, China	S Asia • 120 kW
	CHINA	
	CHINA RADIO INTL, Kunming	SE Asia • 50 kW
	CUBA	
	†RADIO HABANA, Havana	C America • 50/100 kW C America & N America • 50/100 kW
		W • Europe & E North Am • 100 kW
	FRANCE	
	R FRANCE INTL, Issoudun-Allouis	S • Mideast • 500 kW
		W • Mideast • 500 kW
	INDIA	
	ALL INDIA RADIO, Aligarh	S Asia • 250 kW
	ALL INDIA RADIO, Delhi	S Asia • 100 kW
	JAPAN	
	NHK, Tokyo-Shobu	Irr • DS-1 (FEEDER) • 0.9 kW • USB
	KAZAKHSTAN	
	†KAZAKH RADIO, Almaty	◁ • DS-2 • 20 kW
	†R ALMATY/R KAZAKHSTAN, Almaty	◁ • C Asia • 20 kW
	ROMANIA	
	†RADIO ROMANIA INTL, Bucharest	S • Europe • 120 kW S • S Africa • 250 kW
		S • FRENCH & GERMAN • Europe • 120 kW S • Europe • 250 kW
		W • Australasia • 250 kW
	RUSSIA	
	RADIO SEVEN, Zhigulevsk	◁ • Tu-F • RUSSIAN, ETC • DS • 20 kW
		◁ • Sa/Su • RUSSIAN, ETC • DS • 20 kW
	†VOICE OF RUSSIA, Via Moldova	W • C America • 1000 kW
		W • W Europe • 1000 kW
	UKRAINE	
	†RADIO UKRAINE, Nikolayev	S • E North Am • 1000 kW
	USA	
	VOA, Via Udon Thani, Thailand	S • M-F • SE Asia • 500 kW
	WYFR-FAMILY RADIO, Okeechobee, Fl	S • S America • 100 kW
9552v	INDONESIA	
	†RRI, Ujung Pandang, Sulawesi	DS • 10 kW
9555	CANADA	
	†R CANADA INTL, Via Skelton, UK	W • Europe & Mideast • 300 kW
		W • Europe • 300 kW
		S • Europe • 300 kW

(con'd)

FREQUENCY COUNTRY, STATION, LOCATION

TARGET • NETWORK • POWER (kW)

World Time

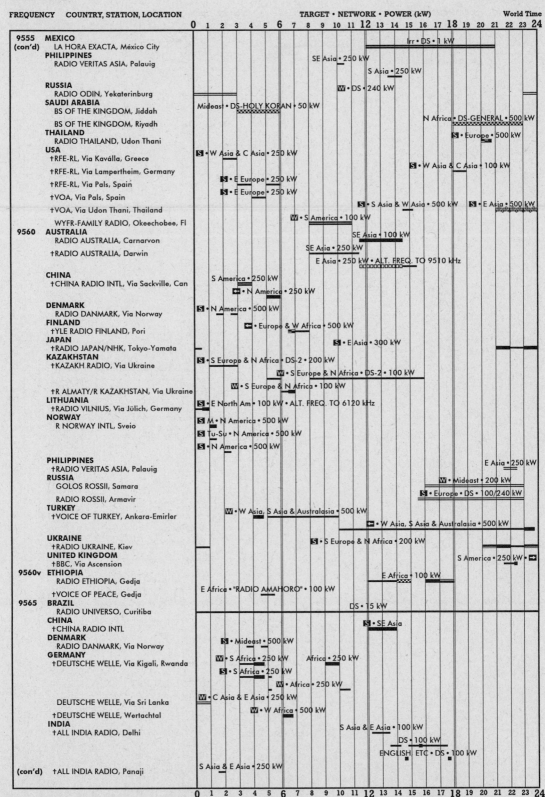

Frequency	Country / Station / Location	Target • Network • Power
9555 (con'd)	**MEXICO** LA HORA EXACTA, México City	Irr • DS • 1 kW
	PHILIPPINES RADIO VERITAS ASIA, Palauig	SE Asia • 250 kW / S Asia • 250 kW
	RUSSIA RADIO ODIN, Yekaterinburg	W • DS • 240 kW
	SAUDI ARABIA BS OF THE KINGDOM, Jiddah	Mideast • DS-HOLY KORAN • 50 kW
	BS OF THE KINGDOM, Riyadh	N Africa • DS-GENERAL • 500 kW
	THAILAND RADIO THAILAND, Udon Thani	S • Europe • 500 kW
	USA †RFE-RL, Via Kaválla, Greece	S • W Asia & C Asia • 250 kW
	†RFE-RL, Via Lampertheim, Germany	S • W Asia & C Asia • 100 kW
	†RFE-RL, Via Pals, Spain	S • E Europe • 250 kW
	†VOA, Via Pals, Spain	S • E Europe • 250 kW
	†VOA, Via Udon Thani, Thailand	S • S Asia & W Asia • 500 kW / S • E Asia • 500 kW
	WYFR-FAMILY RADIO, Okeechobee, Fl	W • S America • 100 kW
9560	**AUSTRALIA** RADIO AUSTRALIA, Carnarvon	SE Asia • 100 kW
	†RADIO AUSTRALIA, Darwin	SE Asia • 250 kW / E Asia • 250 kW • ALT. FREQ. TO 9510 kHz
	CHINA †CHINA RADIO INTL, Via Sackville, Can	S America • 250 kW / N America • 250 kW
	DENMARK RADIO DANMARK, Via Norway	S • N America • 500 kW
	FINLAND †YLE RADIO FINLAND, Pori	• Europe & W Africa • 500 kW
	JAPAN †RADIO JAPAN/NHK, Tokyo-Yamata	S • E Asia • 300 kW
	KAZAKHSTAN †KAZAKH RADIO, Via Ukraine	S • S Europe & N Africa • DS-2 • 200 kW / W • S Europe & N Africa • DS-2 • 100 kW
	†R ALMATY/R KAZAKHSTAN, Via Ukraine	W • S Europe & N Africa • 100 kW
	LITHUANIA †RADIO VILNIUS, Via Jülich, Germany	S • E North Am • 100 kW • ALT. FREQ. TO 6120 kHz
	NORWAY R NORWAY INTL, Sveio	S M • N America • 500 kW / S Tu-Su • N America • 500 kW / S • N America • 500 kW
	PHILIPPINES †RADIO VERITAS ASIA, Palauig	E Asia • 250 kW
	RUSSIA GOLOS ROSSII, Samara	W • Mideast • 200 kW
	RADIO ROSSII, Armavir	S • Europe • DS • 100/240 kW
	TURKEY †VOICE OF TURKEY, Ankara-Emirler	W • W Asia, S Asia & Australasia • 500 kW / • W Asia, S Asia & Australasia • 500 kW
	UKRAINE †RADIO UKRAINE, Kiev	S • S Europe & N Africa • 200 kW
	UNITED KINGDOM †BBC, Via Ascension	S America • 250 kW •
9560v	**ETHIOPIA** RADIO ETHIOPIA, Gedja	E Africa • 100 kW
	†VOICE OF PEACE, Gedja	E Africa • "RADIO AMAHORO" • 100 kW
9565	**BRAZIL** RADIO UNIVERSO, Curitiba	DS • 15 kW
	CHINA †CHINA RADIO INTL	S • SE Asia
	DENMARK RADIO DANMARK, Via Norway	S • Mideast • 500 kW
	GERMANY †DEUTSCHE WELLE, Via Kigali, Rwanda	W • S Africa • 250 kW / Africa • 250 kW / S • S Africa • 250 kW / W • Africa • 250 kW
	DEUTSCHE WELLE, Via Sri Lanka	W • C Asia & E Asia • 250 kW
	†DEUTSCHE WELLE, Wertachtal	W • W Africa • 500 kW
	INDIA †ALL INDIA RADIO, Delhi	S Asia & E Asia • 100 kW / DS • 100 kW / ENGLISH ETC • DS • 100 kW
(con'd)	†ALL INDIA RADIO, Panaji	S Asia & E Asia • 250 kW

FREQUENCY   COUNTRY, STATION, LOCATION   TARGET • NETWORK • POWER (kW)   World Time

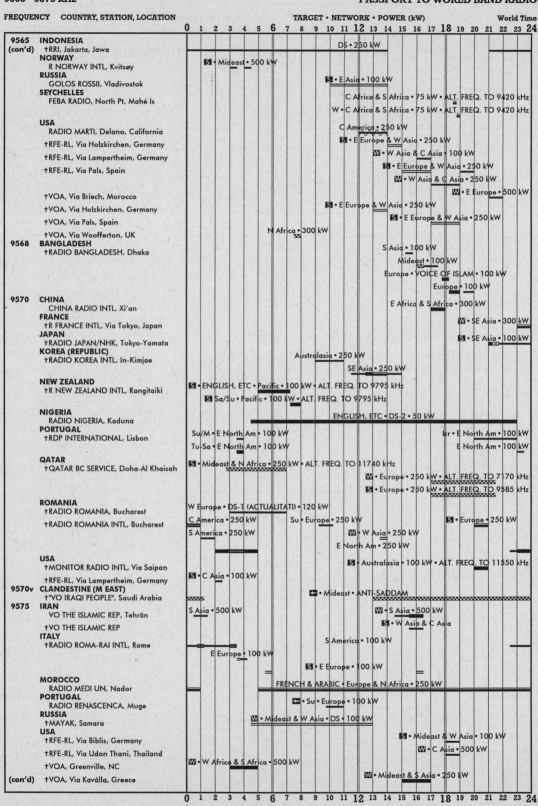

Frequency	Country, Station, Location	Target • Network • Power (kW)
9565 (con'd)	**INDONESIA** †RRI, Jakarta, Jawa	DS • 250 kW
	NORWAY R NORWAY INTL, Kvitsøy	S • Mideast • 500 kW
	RUSSIA GOLOS ROSSII, Vladivostok	S • E Asia • 100 kW
	SEYCHELLES FEBA RADIO, North Pt, Mahé Is	C Africa & S Africa • 75 kW • ALT. FREQ. TO 9420 kHz
		W • C Africa & S Africa • 75 kW • ALT. FREQ. TO 9420 kHz
	USA RADIO MARTI, Delano, California	C America • 250 kW
	†RFE-RL, Via Holzkirchen, Germany	S • E Europe & W Asia • 250 kW
	†RFE-RL, Via Lampertheim, Germany	W • W Asia & C Asia • 100 kW
	†RFE-RL, Via Pals, Spain	S • E Europe & W Asia • 250 kW
		W • W Asia & C Asia • 250 kW
		W • E Europe • 500 kW
	†VOA, Via Briech, Morocco	S • E Europe & W Asia • 250 kW
	†VOA, Via Holzkirchen, Germany	S • E Europe & W Asia • 250 kW
	†VOA, Via Pals, Spain	
	†VOA, Via Woofferton, UK	N Africa • 300 kW
9568	**BANGLADESH** †RADIO BANGLADESH, Dhaka	S Asia • 100 kW
		Mideast • 100 kW
		Europe • VOICE OF ISLAM • 100 kW
		Europe • 100 kW
9570	**CHINA** CHINA RADIO INTL, Xi'an	E Africa & S Africa • 300 kW
	FRANCE †R FRANCE INTL, Via Tokyo, Japan	W • SE Asia • 300 kW
	JAPAN †RADIO JAPAN/NHK, Tokyo-Yamata	S • SE Asia • 100 kW
	KOREA (REPUBLIC) †RADIO KOREA INTL, In-Kimjae	Australasia • 250 kW
		SE Asia • 250 kW
	NEW ZEALAND †R NEW ZEALAND INTL, Rangitaiki	S • ENGLISH, ETC • Pacific • 100 kW • ALT. FREQ. TO 9795 kHz
		S • Sa/Su • Pacific • 100 kW • ALT. FREQ. TO 9795 kHz
	NIGERIA RADIO NIGERIA, Kaduna	ENGLISH, ETC • DS-2 • 50 kW
	PORTUGAL †RDP INTERNATIONAL, Lisbon	Su/M • E North Am • 100 kW
		Irr • E North Am • 100 kW
		Tu-Sa • E North Am • 100 kW
		E North Am • 100 kW
	QATAR †QATAR BC SERVICE, Doha-Al Khaisah	S • Mideast & N Africa • 250 kW • ALT. FREQ. TO 11740 kHz
		W • Europe • 250 kW • ALT. FREQ. TO 7170 kHz
		S • Europe • 250 kW • ALT. FREQ. TO 9585 kHz
	ROMANIA †RADIO ROMANIA, Bucharest	W Europe • DS-1 (ACTUALITATI) • 120 kW
	†RADIO ROMANIA INTL, Bucharest	C America • 250 kW
		Su • Europe • 250 kW
		Europe • 250 kW
		S America • 250 kW
		W • W Asia • 250 kW
		E North Am • 250 kW
	USA †MONITOR RADIO INTL, Via Saipan	S • Australasia • 100 kW • ALT. FREQ. TO 11550 kHz
	†RFE-RL, Via Lampertheim, Germany	S • C Asia • 100 kW
9570v	**CLANDESTINE (M EAST)** †"VO IRAQI PEOPLE", Saudi Arabia	• Mideast • ANTI-SADDAM
9575	**IRAN** VO THE ISLAMIC REP, Tehrān	S Asia • 500 kW
		W • S Asia • 500 kW
	†VO THE ISLAMIC REP	S • W Asia & C Asia
	ITALY †RADIO ROMA-RAI INTL, Rome	S America • 100 kW
		E Europe • 100 kW
		S • E Europe • 100 kW
	MOROCCO RADIO MEDI UN, Nador	FRENCH & ARABIC • Europe & N Africa • 250 kW
	PORTUGAL RADIO RENASCENCA, Muge	• Su • Europe • 100 kW
	RUSSIA †MAYAK, Samara	W • Mideast & W Asia • DS • 100 kW
	USA †RFE-RL, Via Biblis, Germany	S • Mideast & W Asia • 100 kW
	†RFE-RL, Via Udon Thani, Thailand	W • C Asia • 500 kW
	†VOA, Greenville, NC	W • W Africa & S Africa • 500 kW
(con'd)	†VOA, Via Kaválla, Greece	W • Mideast & S Asia • 250 kW

0 1 2 3 4 5 6 7 8 9 10 11 12 13 14 15 16 17 18 19 20 21 22 23 24

SEASONAL **S** OR **W**   1-HR TIMESHIFT MIDYEAR ⇦ OR ⇨   JAMMING / OR /\   EARLIEST HEARD ◁   LATEST HEARD ▷   NEW FOR 1997 †

FREQUENCY   COUNTRY, STATION, LOCATION   TARGET • NETWORK • POWER (kW)   World Time

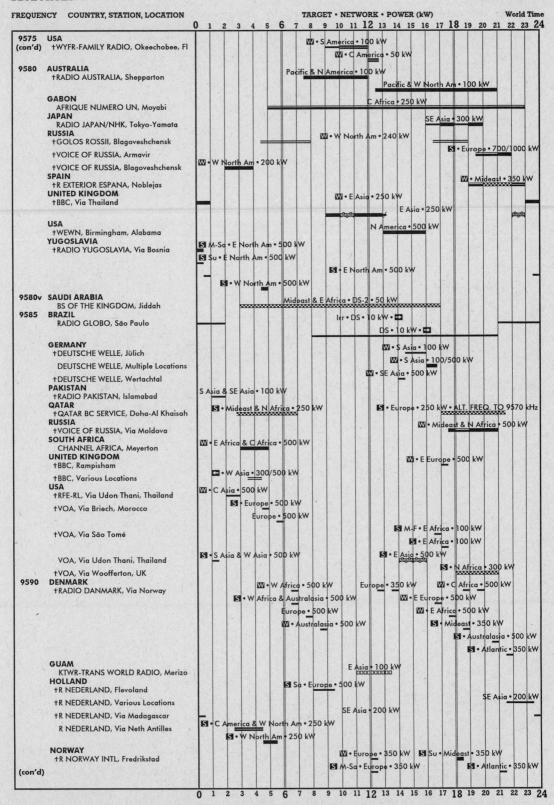

Frequency	Country, Station, Location	Target • Network • Power
9575 (con'd)	**USA** †WYFR-FAMILY RADIO, Okeechobee, Fl	W • S America • 100 kW; W • C America • 50 kW
9580	**AUSTRALIA** †RADIO AUSTRALIA, Shepparton	Pacific & N America • 100 kW; Pacific & W North Am • 100 kW
	GABON AFRIQUE NUMERO UN, Moyabi	C Africa • 250 kW
	JAPAN RADIO JAPAN/NHK, Tokyo-Yamata	SE Asia • 300 kW
	RUSSIA †GOLOS ROSSII, Blagoveshchensk	W • W North Am • 240 kW
	†VOICE OF RUSSIA, Armavir	S • Europe • 700/1000 kW
	†VOICE OF RUSSIA, Blagoveshchensk	W • W North Am • 200 kW
	SPAIN †R EXTERIOR ESPANA, Noblejas	W • Mideast • 350 kW
	UNITED KINGDOM †BBC, Via Thailand	W • E Asia • 250 kW; E Asia • 250 kW
	USA †WEWN, Birmingham, Alabama	N America • 500 kW
	YUGOSLAVIA †RADIO YUGOSLAVIA, Via Bosnia	S • M-Sa • E North Am • 500 kW; S • Su • E North Am • 500 kW; S • E North Am • 500 kW; S • W North Am • 500 kW
9580v	**SAUDI ARABIA** BS OF THE KINGDOM, Jiddah	Mideast & E Africa • DS-2 • 50 kW
9585	**BRAZIL** RADIO GLOBO, São Paulo	Irr • DS • 10 kW; DS • 10 kW
	GERMANY †DEUTSCHE WELLE, Jülich	W • S Asia • 100 kW
	DEUTSCHE WELLE, Multiple Locations	W • S Asia • 100/500 kW
	†DEUTSCHE WELLE, Wertachtal	W • SE Asia • 500 kW
	PAKISTAN †RADIO PAKISTAN, Islamabad	S Asia & SE Asia • 100 kW
	QATAR †QATAR BC SERVICE, Doha-Al Khaisah	S • Mideast & N Africa • 250 kW; S • Europe • 250 kW • ALT. FREQ. TO 9570 kHz
	RUSSIA †VOICE OF RUSSIA, Via Moldova	W • Mideast & N Africa • 500 kW
	SOUTH AFRICA CHANNEL AFRICA, Meyerton	W • E Africa & C Africa • 500 kW
	UNITED KINGDOM †BBC, Rampisham	S • E Europe • 500 kW
	†BBC, Various Locations	W Asia • 300/500 kW
	USA †RFE-RL, Via Udon Thani, Thailand	W • C Asia • 500 kW
	†VOA, Via Briech, Morocco	S • Europe • 500 kW; Europe • 500 kW
	†VOA, Via São Tomé	S • M-F • E Africa • 100 kW; S • E Africa • 100 kW
	VOA, Via Udon Thani, Thailand	S • S Asia & W Asia • 500 kW; S • E Asia • 500 kW
	†VOA, Via Woofferton, UK	S • N Africa • 300 kW
9590	**DENMARK** †RADIO DANMARK, Via Norway	W • W Africa • 500 kW; Europe • 350 kW; W • C Africa • 500 kW; S • W Africa & Australasia • 500 kW; W • E Europe • 500 kW; Europe • 500 kW; W • E Africa • 500 kW; W • Australasia • 500 kW; S • Mideast • 350 kW; S • Australasia • 500 kW; S • Atlantic • 350 kW
	GUAM KTWR-TRANS WORLD RADIO, Merizo	E Asia • 100 kW
	HOLLAND †R NEDERLAND, Flevoland	S • Sa • Europe • 500 kW
	†R NEDERLAND, Various Locations	SE Asia • 200 kW
	†R NEDERLAND, Via Madagascar	SE Asia • 200 kW
	R NEDERLAND, Via Neth Antilles	S • C America & W North Am • 250 kW; S • W North Am • 250 kW
	NORWAY †R NORWAY INTL, Fredrikstad	W • Europe • 350 kW; S • Su • Mideast • 350 kW; S • M-Sa • Europe • 350 kW; S • Atlantic • 350 kW
(con'd)		

ENGLISH ▬   ARABIC ⋙   CHINESE ▫▫▫   FRENCH ═   GERMAN ▭   RUSSIAN ═   SPANISH ▬   OTHER ▬

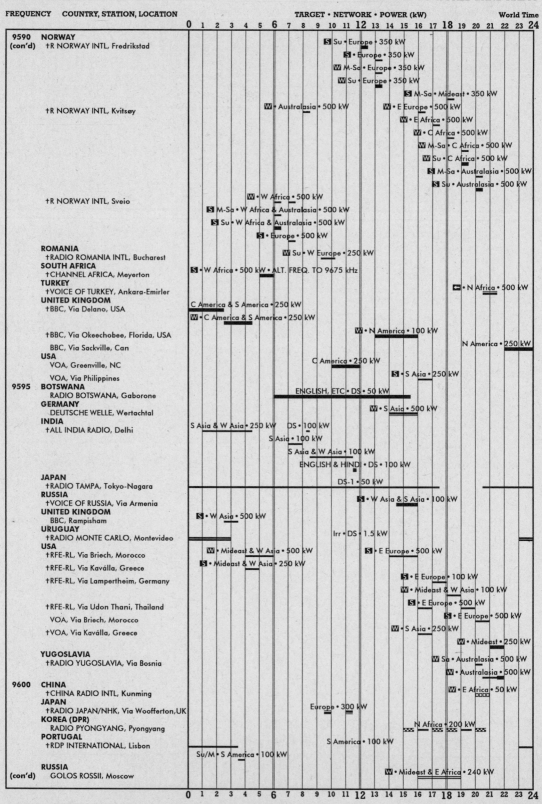

FREQUENCY	COUNTRY, STATION, LOCATION	TARGET • NETWORK • POWER (kW)	World Time

9590 NORWAY
(con'd) †R NORWAY INTL, Fredrikstad
— S Su • Europe • 350 kW
— S • Europe • 350 kW
— W M-Sa • Europe • 350 kW
— W Su • Europe • 350 kW

†R NORWAY INTL, Kvitsøy
— S M-Sa • Mideast • 350 kW
— W • Australasia • 500 kW
— W • E Europe • 500 kW
— W • E Africa • 500 kW
— W • C Africa • 500 kW
— W M-Sa • C Africa • 500 kW
— W Su • C Africa • 500 kW
— S M-Sa • Australasia • 500 kW
— S Su • Australasia • 500 kW

†R NORWAY INTL, Sveio
— W • W Africa • 500 kW
— S M-Sa • W Africa & Australasia • 500 kW
— S Su • W Africa & Australasia • 500 kW
— S • Europe • 500 kW

ROMANIA
†RADIO ROMANIA INTL, Bucharest
— W Su • W Europe • 250 kW
SOUTH AFRICA
†CHANNEL AFRICA, Meyerton
— S • W Africa • 500 kW • ALT. FREQ. TO 9675 kHz
TURKEY
†VOICE OF TURKEY, Ankara-Emirler
— ⊟ • N Africa • 500 kW
UNITED KINGDOM
†BBC, Via Delano, USA
— C America & S America • 250 kW
— W • C America & S America • 250 kW

†BBC, Via Okeechobee, Florida, USA
— W • N America • 100 kW
BBC, Via Sackville, Can
— N America • 250 kW
USA
VOA, Greenville, NC
— C America • 250 kW
VOA, Via Philippines
— S • S Asia • 250 kW
9595 BOTSWANA
RADIO BOTSWANA, Gaborone
— ENGLISH, ETC • DS • 50 kW
GERMANY
DEUTSCHE WELLE, Wertachtal
— W • S Asia • 500 kW
INDIA
†ALL INDIA RADIO, Delhi
— S Asia & W Asia • 250 kW   DS • 100 kW
— S Asia • 100 kW
— S Asia & W Asia • 100 kW
— ENGLISH & HINDI • DS • 100 kW
JAPAN
†RADIO TAMPA, Tokyo-Nagara
— DS-1 • 50 kW
RUSSIA
†VOICE OF RUSSIA, Via Armenia
— S • W Asia & S Asia • 100 kW
UNITED KINGDOM
BBC, Rampisham
— S • W Asia • 500 kW
URUGUAY
†RADIO MONTE CARLO, Montevideo
— Irr • DS • 1.5 kW
USA
†RFE-RL, Via Briech, Morocco
— W • Mideast & W Asia • 500 kW   S • E Europe • 500 kW
†RFE-RL, Via Kaválla, Greece
— S • Mideast & W Asia • 250 kW
†RFE-RL, Via Lampertheim, Germany
— S • E Europe • 100 kW
— W • Mideast & W Asia • 100 kW
†RFE-RL, Via Udon Thani, Thailand
— S • E Europe • 500 kW
VOA, Via Briech, Morocco
— S • E Europe • 500 kW
†VOA, Via Kaválla, Greece
— W • S Asia • 250 kW
— W • Mideast • 250 kW
YUGOSLAVIA
†RADIO YUGOSLAVIA, Via Bosnia
— W Sa • Australasia • 500 kW
— W • Australasia • 500 kW
9600 CHINA
†CHINA RADIO INTL, Kunming
— W • E Africa • 50 kW
JAPAN
†RADIO JAPAN/NHK, Via Woofferton, UK
— Europe • 300 kW
KOREA (DPR)
RADIO PYONGYANG, Pyongyang
— N Africa • 200 kW
PORTUGAL
†RDP INTERNATIONAL, Lisbon
— S America • 100 kW
— Su/M • S America • 100 kW

RUSSIA
(con'd) GOLOS ROSSII, Moscow
— W • Mideast & E Africa • 240 kW

FREQUENCY   COUNTRY, STATION, LOCATION   TARGET • NETWORK • POWER (kW)   World Time

0 1 2 3 4 5 6 7 8 9 10 11 12 13 14 15 16 17 18 19 20 21 22 23 24

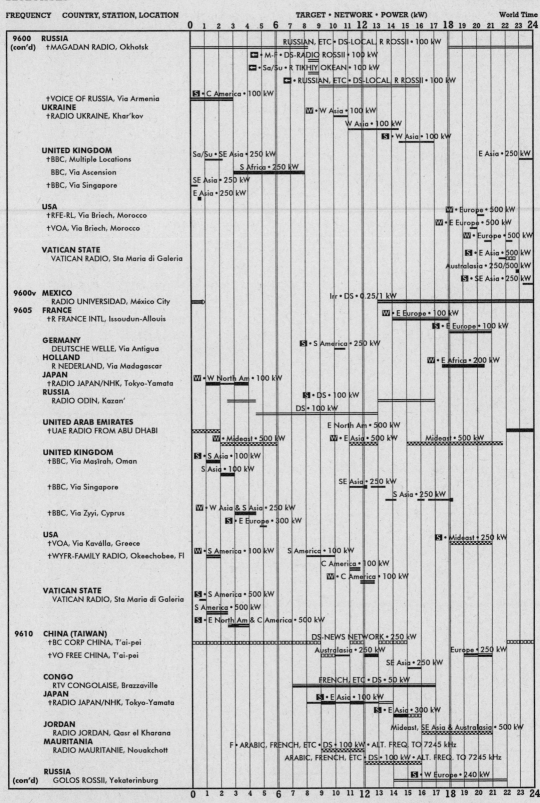

9600	RUSSIA	
(con'd)	†MAGADAN RADIO, Okhotsk	RUSSIAN, ETC • DS-LOCAL, R ROSSII • 100 kW
		M-F • DS-RADIO ROSSII • 100 kW
		Sa/Su • R TIKHIY OKEAN • 100 kW
		RUSSIAN, ETC • DS-LOCAL, R ROSSII • 100 kW
	†VOICE OF RUSSIA, Via Armenia	S • C America • 100 kW
	UKRAINE	
	†RADIO UKRAINE, Khar'kov	W • W Asia • 100 kW
		W Asia • 100 kW
		S • W Asia • 100 kW
	UNITED KINGDOM	
	†BBC, Multiple Locations	Sa/Su • SE Asia • 250 kW E Asia • 250 kW
	BBC, Via Ascension	S Africa • 250 kW
	†BBC, Via Singapore	SE Asia • 250 kW
		E Asia • 250 kW
	USA	
	†RFE-RL, Via Briech, Morocco	W • Europe • 500 kW
	†VOA, Via Briech, Morocco	W • E Europe • 500 kW
		W • Europe • 500 kW
	VATICAN STATE	
	VATICAN RADIO, Sta Maria di Galeria	S • E Asia • 500 kW
		Australasia • 250/500 kW
		S • SE Asia • 250 kW
9600v	MEXICO	
	RADIO UNIVERSIDAD, México City	Irr • DS • 0.25/1 kW
9605	FRANCE	
	†R FRANCE INTL, Issoudun-Allouis	W • E Europe • 100 kW
		S • E Europe • 100 kW
	GERMANY	
	DEUTSCHE WELLE, Via Antigua	S • S America • 250 kW
	HOLLAND	
	R NEDERLAND, Via Madagascar	W • E Africa • 200 kW
	JAPAN	
	†RADIO JAPAN/NHK, Tokyo-Yamata	W • W North Am • 100 kW
	RUSSIA	
	RADIO ODIN, Kazan'	S • DS • 100 kW
		DS • 100 kW
	UNITED ARAB EMIRATES	
	†UAE RADIO FROM ABU DHABI	E North Am • 500 kW
		W • Mideast • 500 kW W • E Asia • 500 kW Mideast • 500 kW
	UNITED KINGDOM	
	†BBC, Via Maşīrah, Oman	S • S Asia • 100 kW
		S Asia • 100 kW
	†BBC, Via Singapore	SE Asia • 250 kW
		S Asia • 250 kW
	†BBC, Via Zyyi, Cyprus	W • W Asia & S Asia • 250 kW
		S • E Europe • 300 kW
	USA	
	†VOA, Via Kaválla, Greece	S • Mideast • 250 kW
	†WYFR-FAMILY RADIO, Okeechobee, Fl	S • S America • 100 kW S America • 100 kW
		C America • 100 kW
		W • C America • 100 kW
	VATICAN STATE	
	VATICAN RADIO, Sta Maria di Galeria	S • S America • 500 kW
		S America • 500 kW
		S • E North Am & C America • 500 kW
9610	CHINA (TAIWAN)	
	†BC CORP CHINA, T'ai-pei	DS-NEWS NETWORK • 250 kW
	†VO FREE CHINA, T'ai-pei	Australasia • 250 kW Europe • 250 kW
		SE Asia • 250 kW
	CONGO	
	RTV CONGOLAISE, Brazzaville	FRENCH, ETC • DS • 50 kW
	JAPAN	
	†RADIO JAPAN/NHK, Tokyo-Yamata	S • E Asia • 100 kW
		S • E Asia • 300 kW
	JORDAN	
	RADIO JORDAN, Qasr el Kharana	Mideast, SE Asia & Australasia • 500 kW
	MAURITANIA	
	RADIO MAURITANIE, Nouakchott	F • ARABIC, FRENCH, ETC • DS • 100 kW • ALT. FREQ. TO 7245 kHz
		ARABIC, FRENCH, ETC • DS • 100 kW • ALT. FREQ. TO 7245 kHz
	RUSSIA	
(con'd)	GOLOS ROSSII, Yekaterinburg	S • W Europe • 240 kW

0 1 2 3 4 5 6 7 8 9 10 11 12 13 14 15 16 17 18 19 20 21 22 23 24

ENGLISH ▬▬   ARABIC ≋≋≋   CHINESE □□□   FRENCH ▭▭   GERMAN ▬▬   RUSSIAN ══   SPANISH ▬▬   OTHER ▬▬

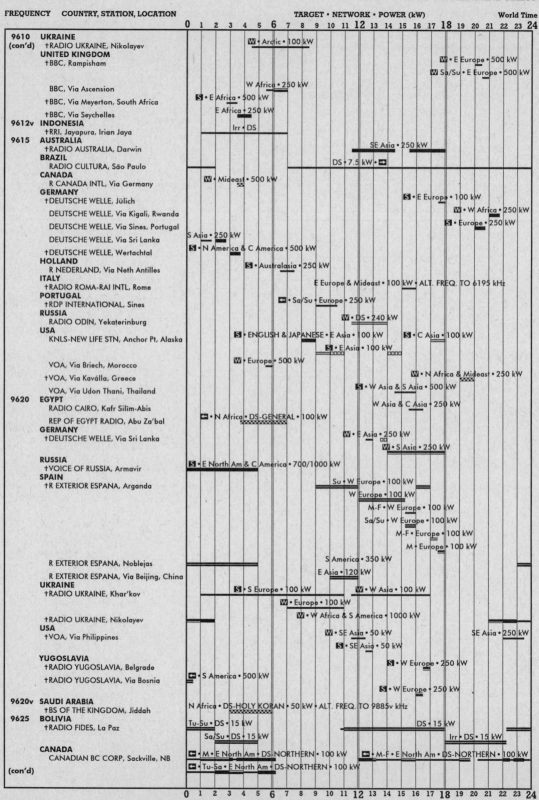

FREQUENCY   COUNTRY, STATION, LOCATION   **TARGET • NETWORK • POWER (kW)**   **World Time**

World Time scale: 0 1 2 3 4 5 6 7 8 9 10 11 12 13 14 15 16 17 18 19 20 21 22 23 24

9610
(con'd)

- UKRAINE
  - †RADIO UKRAINE, Nikolayev — W • Arctic • 100 kW
- UNITED KINGDOM
  - †BBC, Rampisham — W • E Europe • 500 kW; W Sa/Su • E Europe • 500 kW
  - BBC, Via Ascension — W Africa • 250 kW
  - †BBC, Via Meyerton, South Africa — S • E Africa • 500 kW
  - †BBC, Via Seychelles — E Africa • 250 kW

9612v
- INDONESIA
  - †RRI, Jayapura, Irian Jaya — Irr • DS

9615
- AUSTRALIA
  - †RADIO AUSTRALIA, Darwin — SE Asia • 250 kW
- BRAZIL
  - RADIO CULTURA, São Paulo — DS • 7.5 kW •
- CANADA
  - R CANADA INTL, Via Germany — W • Mideast • 500 kW
- GERMANY
  - †DEUTSCHE WELLE, Jülich — S • E Europe • 100 kW
  - DEUTSCHE WELLE, Via Kigali, Rwanda — W • W Africa • 250 kW
  - DEUTSCHE WELLE, Via Sines, Portugal — S • Europe • 250 kW
  - DEUTSCHE WELLE, Via Sri Lanka — S Asia • 250 kW
  - †DEUTSCHE WELLE, Wertachtal — S • N America & C America • 500 kW
- HOLLAND
  - R NEDERLAND, Via Neth Antilles — S • Australasia • 250 kW
- ITALY
  - †RADIO ROMA-RAI INTL, Rome — E Europe & Mideast • 100 kW • ALT. FREQ. TO 6195 kHz
- PORTUGAL
  - †RDP INTERNATIONAL, Sines — Sa/Su • Europe • 250 kW
- RUSSIA
  - RADIO ODIN, Yekaterinburg — W • DS • 240 kW
- USA
  - KNLS-NEW LIFE STN, Anchor Pt, Alaska — S • ENGLISH & JAPANESE • E Asia • 100 kW; S • C Asia • 100 kW; S • E Asia • 100 kW
  - VOA, Via Briech, Morocco — W • Europe • 500 kW
  - †VOA, Via Kaválla, Greece — W • N Africa & Mideast • 250 kW
  - VOA, Via Udon Thani, Thailand — S • W Asia & S Asia • 500 kW

9620
- EGYPT
  - RADIO CAIRO, Kafr Silim-Abis — W Asia & C Asia • 250 kW
  - REP OF EGYPT RADIO, Abu Za'bal — N Africa • DS-GENERAL • 100 kW
- GERMANY
  - †DEUTSCHE WELLE, Via Sri Lanka — W • E Asia • 250 kW; W • S Asia • 250 kW
- RUSSIA
  - †VOICE OF RUSSIA, Armavir — S • E North Am & C America • 700/1000 kW
- SPAIN
  - †R EXTERIOR ESPANA, Arganda — Su • W Europe • 100 kW; W Europe • 100 kW; M-F • W Europe • 100 kW; Sa/Su • W Europe • 100 kW; M-F • Europe • 100 kW; M • Europe • 100 kW
  - R EXTERIOR ESPANA, Noblejas — S America • 350 kW
  - R EXTERIOR ESPANA, Via Beijing, China — E Asia • 120 kW
- UKRAINE
  - †RADIO UKRAINE, Khar'kov — S • S Europe • 100 kW; W • W Asia • 100 kW; W • Europe • 100 kW
  - †RADIO UKRAINE, Nikolayev — W • W Africa & S America • 1000 kW
- USA
  - †VOA, Via Philippines — W • SE Asia • 50 kW; S • SE Asia • 50 kW; SE Asia • 250 kW
- YUGOSLAVIA
  - †RADIO YUGOSLAVIA, Belgrade — S • W Europe • 250 kW
  - †RADIO YUGOSLAVIA, Via Bosnia — S America • 500 kW; S • W Europe • 250 kW

9620v
- SAUDI ARABIA
  - †BS OF THE KINGDOM, Jiddah — N Africa • DS-HOLY KORAN • 50 kW • ALT. FREQ. TO 9885v kHz

9625
- BOLIVIA
  - †RADIO FIDES, La Paz — Tu-Su • DS • 15 kW; DS • 15 kW; Sa/Su • DS • 15 kW; Irr • DS • 15 kW
- CANADA
  - CANADIAN BC CORP, Sackville, NB — M • E North Am • DS-NORTHERN • 100 kW; M-F • E North Am • DS-NORTHERN • 100 kW; Tu-Sa • E North Am • DS-NORTHERN • 100 kW

(con'd)

FREQUENCY   COUNTRY, STATION, LOCATION   TARGET • NETWORK • POWER (kW)   World Time

0 1 2 3 4 5 6 7 8 9 10 11 12 13 14 15 16 17 18 19 20 21 22 23 24

9625   **CANADA**
(con'd)   CANADIAN BC CORP, Sackville, NB
- Su • E North Am • DS-NORTHERN • 100 kW
- Sa • E North Am • DS-NORTHERN • 100 kW
- Sa • ENGLISH & FRENCH • E North Am • DS-NORTHERN • 100 kW
- M-F • ENGLISH, FRENCH, ETC • E North Am • DS-NORTHERN • 100 kW

     CHINA
       †CHINA RADIO INTL, Kunming — W • S Asia • 120 kW
     ROMANIA
       †RADIO ROMANIA INTL, Bucharest — Europe • 250 kW   Europe • 120 kW
       S • W Europe • 250 kW

     RUSSIA
       GOLOS ROSSII, Yekaterinburg — W • E Asia & Australasia • 100 kW
     USA
       †RFE-RL, Via Biblis, Germany — S • Mideast & W Asia • 100 kW
       W • E Europe • 500 kW
       RFE-RL, Via Briech, Morocco — S • E Europe • 100 kW
       †RFE-RL, Via Lampertheim, Germany — W • E Europe • 100 kW

       †RFE-RL, Via Pals, Spain
- W • W Asia & C Asia • 250 kW
- S • E Europe • 300 kW
- S • W Asia & C Asia • 250 kW
- W Asia & C Asia • 250 kW
- E Europe • 250 kW
- W • E Europe • 250 kW
- S • E Europe & W Asia • 250 kW
- W • E Europe • 300 kW

       †RFE-RL, Via Woofferton, UK
       †VOA, Via Lampertheim, Germany — W • E Europe • 100 kW
       WYFR-FAMILY RADIO, Okeechobee, Fl — S • S America • 100 kW

9630   **BRAZIL**
       RADIO APARECIDA, Aparecida — DS • 10 kW •
     CHINA (TAIWAN)
       †CENTRAL BC SYSTEM, T'ai-pei — E Asia • NETWORK 2 • 300 kW
     INDONESIA
       †RRI, Jakarta, Jawa — DS • 250 kW
     JORDAN
       RADIO JORDAN, Qasr el Kharana — • N Africa & E Africa • 500 kW
     PORTUGAL
       †RDP INTERNATIONAL, Sines — • M-F • Europe • 250 kW
     RUSSIA
       GOLOS ROSSII, Serpukhov — S • Europe & W Africa • 250 kW
       †VOICE OF RUSSIA, Via Moldova — W • W Africa • 500 kW
     SPAIN
       R EXTERIOR ESPANA, Via Costa Rica — M-F • N America • 100 kW
     TURKEY
       †VOICE OF TURKEY, Ankara-Emirler
- • W Asia • 500 kW
- • W Asia & S Asia • 500 kW

     UNITED KINGDOM
       BBC, Via Seychelles — E Africa • 250 kW
     USA
       †VOA, Via Botswana
- S • Africa • 100 kW
- S • Sa/Su • Africa • 100 kW

9635   **FINLAND**
       †YLE RADIO FINLAND, Pori — W • Mideast & E Africa • 500 kW
     GUAM
       †KSDA-ADVENTIST WORLD RADIO, Agat — S • SE Asia • 100 kW
     PORTUGAL
       †RDP INTERNATIONAL, Lisbon
- C America & S America • 100 kW
- Su/M • C America & S America • 100 kW

     RUSSIA
       †VOICE OF RUSSIA, Via Kazakhstan — W • Mideast • 240 kW
     TURKEY
       †VOICE OF TURKEY, Ankara-Emirler — S • S Europe • 500 kW
     UNITED KINGDOM
       †BBC, Multiple Locations — W • Europe • 250/500 kW
       †BBC, Rampisham — W Su • Europe • 500 kW
       †BBC, Via Zyyi, Cyprus
- S • E Europe • 250 kW   W • Europe • 250 kW
- E Europe • 250 kW
- W • E Europe • 250 kW

     USA
       †RFE-RL, Via Pals, Spain — S • E Europe • 250 kW
       †VOA, Via Philippines — W • E Asia • 250 kW
       VOA, Via Udon Thani, Thailand — S • S Asia • 500 kW

9635v   **MALI**
       RTV MALIENNE, Bamako — FRENCH, ETC • DS • 50 kW
9638v   **MOZAMBIQUE**
       DELEGACAO DE BEIRA, Beira — DS-B • 100 kW

0 1 2 3 4 5 6 7 8 9 10 11 12 13 14 15 16 17 18 19 20 21 22 23 24

ENGLISH ▬   ARABIC ⌇⌇⌇   CHINESE ▫▫▫   FRENCH ═   GERMAN ▬   RUSSIAN ═   SPANISH ▬   OTHER ▬

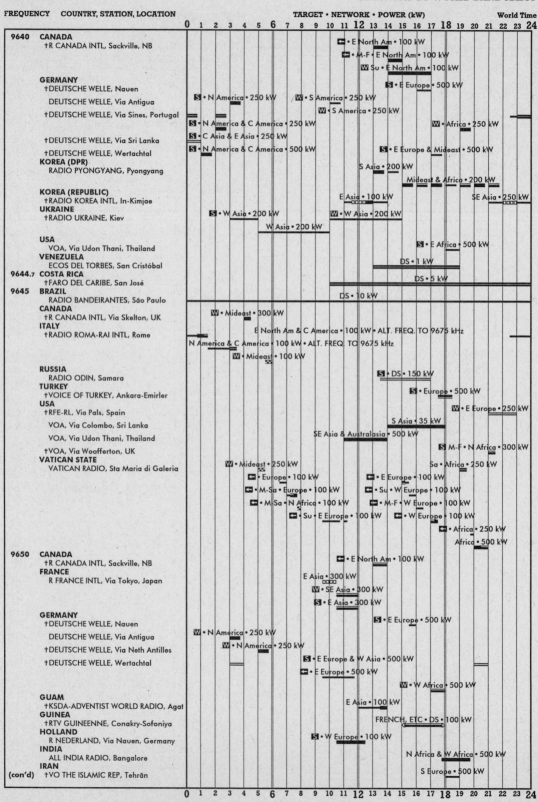

FREQUENCY	COUNTRY, STATION, LOCATION	TARGET • NETWORK • POWER (kW)	World Time

9640 CANADA
†R CANADA INTL, Sackville, NB
- ◨ • E North Am • 100 kW
- ◨ • M-F • E North Am • 100 kW
- W Su • E North Am • 100 kW

GERMANY
†DEUTSCHE WELLE, Nauen
- S • E Europe • 500 kW

DEUTSCHE WELLE, Via Antigua
- S • N America • 250 kW
- W • S America • 250 kW

†DEUTSCHE WELLE, Via Sines, Portugal
- W • S America • 250 kW
- S • N America & C America • 250 kW
- W • Africa • 250 kW

†DEUTSCHE WELLE, Via Sri Lanka
- S • C Asia & E Asia • 250 kW

†DEUTSCHE WELLE, Wertachtal
- S • N America & C America • 500 kW
- S • E Europe & Mideast • 500 kW

KOREA (DPR)
RADIO PYONGYANG, Pyongyang
- S Asia • 200 kW
- Mideast & Africa • 200 kW

KOREA (REPUBLIC)
†RADIO KOREA INTL, In-Kimjae
- E Asia • 100 kW
- SE Asia • 250 kW

UKRAINE
†RADIO UKRAINE, Kiev
- S • W Asia • 200 kW
- W • W Asia • 200 kW
- W Asia • 200 kW

USA
VOA, Via Udon Thani, Thailand

VENEZUELA
ECOS DEL TORBES, San Cristóbal
- S • E Africa • 500 kW
- DS • 1 kW

9644.7 COSTA RICA
†FARO DEL CARIBE, San José
- DS • 5 kW

9645 BRAZIL
RADIO BANDEIRANTES, São Paulo
- DS • 10 kW

CANADA
†R CANADA INTL, Via Skelton, UK
- W • Mideast • 300 kW

ITALY
†RADIO ROMA-RAI INTL, Rome
- E North Am & C America • 100 kW • ALT. FREQ. TO 9675 kHz
- N America & C America • 100 kW • ALT. FREQ. TO 9675 kHz
- W • Mideast • 100 kW

RUSSIA
RADIO ODIN, Samara
- S • DS • 150 kW

TURKEY
†VOICE OF TURKEY, Ankara-Emirler
- S • Europe • 500 kW

USA
†RFE-RL, Via Pals, Spain
- W • E Europe • 250 kW

VOA, Via Colombo, Sri Lanka
- S Asia • 35 kW

VOA, Via Udon Thani, Thailand
- SE Asia & Australasia • 500 kW

†VOA, Via Woofferton, UK
- S • M-F • N Africa • 300 kW

VATICAN STATE
VATICAN RADIO, Sta Maria di Galeria
- W • Mideast • 250 kW
- Sa • Africa • 250 kW
- ◨ • Europe • 100 kW
- ◨ • E Europe • 100 kW
- ◨ • M-Sa • Europe • 100 kW
- ◨ • Su • W Europe • 100 kW
- ◨ • M-Sa • N Africa • 100 kW
- ◨ • M-F • W Europe • 100 kW
- ◨ • Su • E Europe • 100 kW
- ◨ • W Europe • 100 kW
- ◨ • Africa • 250 kW
- Africa • 500 kW

9650 CANADA
†R CANADA INTL, Sackville, NB
- ◨ • E North Am • 100 kW

FRANCE
R FRANCE INTL, Via Tokyo, Japan
- E Asia • 300 kW
- W • SE Asia • 300 kW
- S • E Asia • 300 kW

GERMANY
†DEUTSCHE WELLE, Nauen
- S • E Europe • 500 kW

DEUTSCHE WELLE, Via Antigua
- W • N America • 250 kW

†DEUTSCHE WELLE, Via Neth Antilles
- W • N America • 250 kW

†DEUTSCHE WELLE, Wertachtal
- S • E Europe & W Asia • 500 kW
- ◨ • E Europe • 500 kW
- W • W Africa • 500 kW

GUAM
†KSDA-ADVENTIST WORLD RADIO, Agat
- E Asia • 100 kW

GUINEA
†RTV GUINEENNE, Conakry-Sofoniya
- FRENCH, ETC • DS • 100 kW

HOLLAND
R NEDERLAND, Via Nauen, Germany
- S • W Europe • 100 kW

INDIA
ALL INDIA RADIO, Bangalore
- N Africa & W Africa • 500 kW

IRAN
(con'd) †VO THE ISLAMIC REP, Tehrān
- S Europe • 500 kW

FREQUENCY   COUNTRY, STATION, LOCATION   TARGET • NETWORK • POWER (kW)   World Time

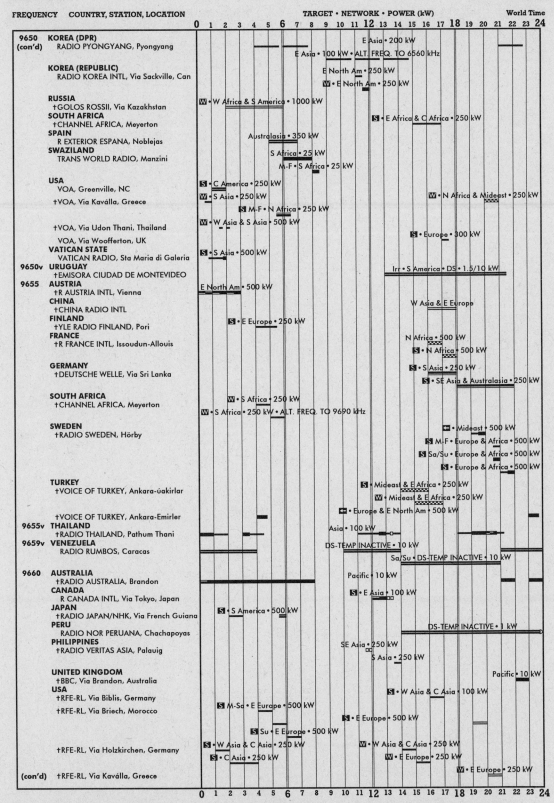

Frequency	Country, Station, Location	Target • Network • Power
9650 (con'd)	KOREA (DPR) — RADIO PYONGYANG, Pyongyang	E Asia • 200 kW; E Asia • 100 kW • ALT. FREQ. TO 6560 kHz
	KOREA (REPUBLIC) — RADIO KOREA INTL, Via Sackville, Can	E North Am • 250 kW; W • E North Am • 250 kW
	RUSSIA — †GOLOS ROSSII, Via Kazakhstan	W • W Africa & S America • 1000 kW
	SOUTH AFRICA — †CHANNEL AFRICA, Meyerton	S • E Africa & C Africa • 250 kW
	SPAIN — R EXTERIOR ESPANA, Noblejas	Australasia • 350 kW
	SWAZILAND — TRANS WORLD RADIO, Manzini	S Africa • 25 kW; M-F • S Africa • 25 kW
	USA — VOA, Greenville, NC	S • C America • 250 kW
	†VOA, Via Kaválla, Greece	W • S Asia • 250 kW; S • M-F • N Africa • 250 kW; W • N Africa & Mideast • 250 kW
	†VOA, Via Udon Thani, Thailand	W • W Asia & S Asia • 500 kW
	VOA, Via Woofferton, UK	S • Europe • 300 kW
	VATICAN STATE — VATICAN RADIO, Sta Maria di Galeria	S • S Asia • 500 kW
9650v	URUGUAY — †EMISORA CIUDAD DE MONTEVIDEO	Irr • S America • DS • 1.5/10 kW
9655	AUSTRIA — †R AUSTRIA INTL, Vienna	E North Am • 500 kW
	CHINA — †CHINA RADIO INTL	W Asia & E Europe
	FINLAND — †YLE RADIO FINLAND, Pori	S • E Europe • 250 kW
	FRANCE — †R FRANCE INTL, Issoudun-Allouis	N Africa • 500 kW; S • N Africa • 500 kW
	GERMANY — †DEUTSCHE WELLE, Via Sri Lanka	S • S Asia • 250 kW; S • SE Asia & Australasia • 250 kW
	SOUTH AFRICA — †CHANNEL AFRICA, Meyerton	W • S Africa • 250 kW; W • S Africa • 250 kW • ALT. FREQ. TO 9690 kHz
	SWEDEN — †RADIO SWEDEN, Hörby	• Mideast • 500 kW; S • M-F • Europe & Africa • 500 kW; S • Sa/Su • Europe & Africa • 500 kW; S • Europe & Africa • 500 kW
	TURKEY — †VOICE OF TURKEY, Ankara-úakirlar	S • Mideast & E Africa • 250 kW; W • Mideast & E Africa • 250 kW
	†VOICE OF TURKEY, Ankara-Emirler	• Europe & E North Am • 500 kW
9655v	THAILAND — †RADIO THAILAND, Pathum Thani	Asia • 100 kW
9659v	VENEZUELA — RADIO RUMBOS, Caracas	DS-TEMP INACTIVE • 10 kW; Sa/Su • DS-TEMP INACTIVE • 10 kW
9660	AUSTRALIA — †RADIO AUSTRALIA, Brandon	Pacific • 10 kW
	CANADA — R CANADA INTL, Via Tokyo, Japan	S • E Asia • 100 kW
	JAPAN — †RADIO JAPAN/NHK, Via French Guiana	S • S America • 500 kW
	PERU — RADIO NOR PERUANA, Chachapoyas	DS-TEMP INACTIVE • 1 kW
	PHILIPPINES — †RADIO VERITAS ASIA, Palauig	SE Asia • 250 kW; S Asia • 250 kW
	UNITED KINGDOM — †BBC, Via Brandon, Australia	Pacific • 10 kW
	USA — †RFE-RL, Via Biblis, Germany	S • W Asia & C Asia • 100 kW
	†RFE-RL, Via Briech, Morocco	S • M-Sa • E Europe • 500 kW; S • E Europe • 500 kW; S • Su • E Europe • 500 kW
	†RFE-RL, Via Holzkirchen, Germany	S • W Asia & C Asia • 250 kW; S • C Asia • 250 kW; W • W Asia & C Asia • 250 kW; W • E Europe • 250 kW
(con'd)	†RFE-RL, Via Kaválla, Greece	W • E Europe • 250 kW

FREQUENCY   COUNTRY, STATION, LOCATION   TARGET • NETWORK • POWER (kW)   World Time

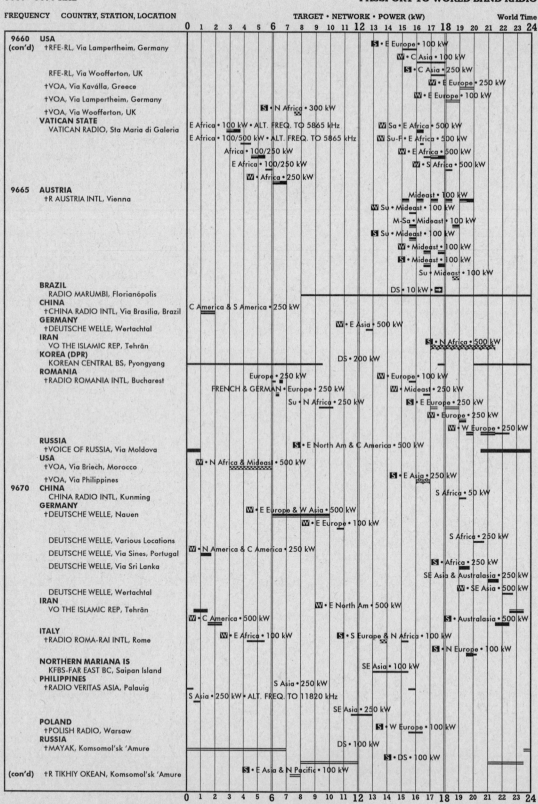

Frequency	Country, Station, Location	Target • Network • Power (kW)
9660 (con'd)	**USA**	
	†RFE-RL, Via Lampertheim, Germany	Ⓢ • E Europe • 100 kW
		Ⓦ • C Asia • 100 kW
	RFE-RL, Via Woofferton, UK	Ⓢ • C Asia • 250 kW
	†VOA, Via Kaválla, Greece	Ⓦ • E Europe • 250 kW
	†VOA, Via Lampertheim, Germany	Ⓦ • E Europe • 100 kW
	†VOA, Via Woofferton, UK	Ⓢ • N Africa • 300 kW
	VATICAN STATE	
	VATICAN RADIO, Sta Maria di Galeria	E Africa • 100 kW • ALT. FREQ. TO 5865 kHz
		Ⓦ Sa • E Africa • 500 kW
		E Africa • 100/500 kW • ALT. FREQ. TO 5865 kHz
		Ⓦ Su-F • E Africa • 500 kW
		Africa • 100/250 kW
		Ⓦ • E Africa • 500 kW
		E Africa • 100/250 kW
		Ⓦ • S Africa • 500 kW
		Ⓦ • Africa • 250 kW
9665	**AUSTRIA**	
	†R AUSTRIA INTL, Vienna	Mideast • 100 kW
		Ⓦ Su • Mideast • 100 kW
		M-Sa • Mideast • 100 kW
		Ⓢ Su • Mideast • 100 kW
		Ⓦ • Mideast • 100 kW
		Ⓢ • Mideast • 100 kW
		Su • Mideast • 100 kW
	BRAZIL	
	RADIO MARUMBI, Florianópolis	DS • 10 kW • ▭
	CHINA	
	†CHINA RADIO INTL, Via Brasilia, Brazil	C America & S America • 250 kW
	GERMANY	
	†DEUTSCHE WELLE, Wertachtal	Ⓦ • E Asia • 500 kW
	IRAN	
	VO THE ISLAMIC REP, Tehrān	Ⓢ • N Africa • 500 kW
	KOREA (DPR)	
	KOREAN CENTRAL BS, Pyongyang	DS • 200 kW
	ROMANIA	
	†RADIO ROMANIA INTL, Bucharest	Europe • 250 kW
		Ⓦ • Europe • 100 kW
		FRENCH & GERMAN • Europe • 250 kW
		Ⓦ • Mideast • 250 kW
		Su • N Africa • 250 kW
		Ⓢ • E Europe • 250 kW
		Ⓦ • Europe • 250 kW
		Ⓦ • W Europe • 250 kW
	RUSSIA	
	†VOICE OF RUSSIA, Via Moldova	Ⓢ • E North Am & C America • 500 kW
	USA	
	†VOA, Via Briech, Morocco	Ⓦ • N Africa & Mideast • 500 kW
	†VOA, Via Philippines	Ⓢ • E Asia • 250 kW
9670	**CHINA**	
	CHINA RADIO INTL, Kunming	S Africa • 50 kW
	GERMANY	
	†DEUTSCHE WELLE, Nauen	Ⓦ • E Europe & W Asia • 500 kW
		Ⓦ • E Europe • 100 kW
	DEUTSCHE WELLE, Various Locations	Ⓦ • N America & C America • 250 kW
	DEUTSCHE WELLE, Via Sines, Portugal	S Africa • 250 kW
	DEUTSCHE WELLE, Via Sri Lanka	Ⓢ • Africa • 250 kW
		SE Asia & Australasia • 250 kW
	DEUTSCHE WELLE, Wertachtal	Ⓦ • SE Asia • 500 kW
	IRAN	
	VO THE ISLAMIC REP, Tehrān	Ⓦ • E North Am • 500 kW
		Ⓦ • C America • 500 kW
		Ⓢ • Australasia • 500 kW
	ITALY	
	†RADIO ROMA-RAI INTL, Rome	Ⓦ • E Africa • 100 kW
		Ⓢ • S Europe & N Africa • 100 kW
		Ⓢ • N Europe • 100 kW
	NORTHERN MARIANA IS	
	KFBS-FAR EAST BC, Saipan Island	SE Asia • 100 kW
	PHILIPPINES	
	†RADIO VERITAS ASIA, Palauig	S Asia • 250 kW
		S Asia • 250 kW • ALT. FREQ. TO 11820 kHz
		SE Asia • 250 kW
	POLAND	
	†POLISH RADIO, Warsaw	Ⓢ • W Europe • 100 kW
	RUSSIA	
	†MAYAK, Komsomol'sk 'Amure	DS • 100 kW
		Ⓢ • DS • 100 kW
(con'd)	†R TIKHIY OKEAN, Komsomol'sk 'Amure	Ⓢ • E Asia & N Pacific • 100 kW

FREQUENCY   COUNTRY, STATION, LOCATION   TARGET • NETWORK • POWER (kW)   World Time

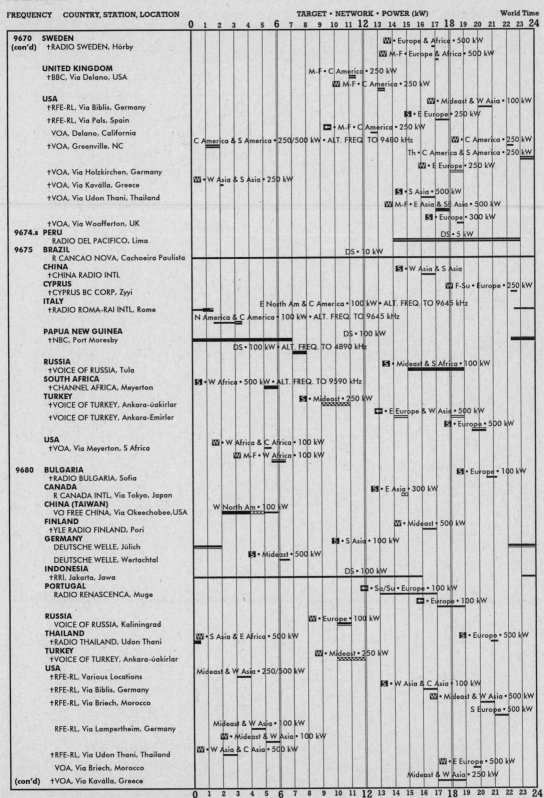

Frequency	Country / Station / Location	Target • Network • Power
9670 (con'd)	**SWEDEN** — †RADIO SWEDEN, Hörby	W • Europe & Africa • 500 kW; W M-F • Europe & Africa • 500 kW
	UNITED KINGDOM — †BBC, Via Delano, USA	M-F • C America • 250 kW; W M-F • C America • 250 kW
	USA — †RFE-RL, Via Biblis, Germany	W • Mideast & W Asia • 100 kW; S • E Europe • 250 kW
	†RFE-RL, Via Pals, Spain	M-F • C America • 250 kW
	VOA, Delano, California	C America & S America • 250/500 kW • ALT. FREQ. TO 9480 kHz; W • C America • 250 kW
	†VOA, Greenville, NC	Th • C America & S America • 250 kW
	†VOA, Via Holzkirchen, Germany	W • E Europe • 250 kW
	†VOA, Via Kavála, Greece	W • W Asia & S Asia • 250 kW
	†VOA, Via Udon Thani, Thailand	S • S Asia • 500 kW; W M-F • E Asia & SE Asia • 500 kW; S • Europe • 300 kW
	†VOA, Via Woofferton, UK	
9674.8	**PERU** — RADIO DEL PACIFICO, Lima	DS • 5 kW
9675	**BRAZIL** — R CANCAO NOVA, Cachoeira Paulista	DS • 10 kW
	CHINA — †CHINA RADIO INTL	S • W Asia & S Asia
	CYPRUS — †CYPRUS BC CORP, Zyyi	W F-Su • Europe • 250 kW
	ITALY — †RADIO ROMA-RAI INTL, Rome	E North Am & C America • 100 kW • ALT. FREQ. TO 9645 kHz; N America & C America • 100 kW • ALT. FREQ. TO 9645 kHz
	PAPUA NEW GUINEA — †NBC, Port Moresby	DS • 100 kW; DS • 100 kW • ALT. FREQ. TO 4890 kHz
	RUSSIA — †VOICE OF RUSSIA, Tula	S • Mideast & S Africa • 100 kW
	SOUTH AFRICA — †CHANNEL AFRICA, Meyerton	S • W Africa • 500 kW • ALT. FREQ. TO 9590 kHz
	TURKEY — †VOICE OF TURKEY, Ankara-úakirlar	S • Mideast • 250 kW
	†VOICE OF TURKEY, Ankara-Emirler	S • E Europe & W Asia • 500 kW; S • Europe • 500 kW
	USA — †VOA, Via Meyerton, S Africa	W • W Africa & C Africa • 100 kW; W M-F • W Africa • 100 kW
9680	**BULGARIA** — †RADIO BULGARIA, Sofia	S • Europe • 100 kW
	CANADA — R CANADA INTL, Via Tokyo, Japan	S • E Asia • 300 kW
	CHINA (TAIWAN) — VO FREE CHINA, Via Okeechobee, USA	W North Am • 100 kW
	FINLAND — †YLE RADIO FINLAND, Pori	W • Mideast • 500 kW
	GERMANY — DEUTSCHE WELLE, Jülich	S • S Asia • 100 kW
	DEUTSCHE WELLE, Wertachtal	S • Mideast • 500 kW
	INDONESIA — †RRI, Jakarta, Jawa	DS • 100 kW
	PORTUGAL — RADIO RENASCENCA, Muge	Sa/Su • Europe • 100 kW; Europe • 100 kW
	RUSSIA — VOICE OF RUSSIA, Kaliningrad	W • Europe • 100 kW
	THAILAND — †RADIO THAILAND, Udon Thani	W • S Asia & E Africa • 500 kW; S • Europe • 500 kW
	TURKEY — †VOICE OF TURKEY, Ankara-úakirlar	W • Mideast • 250 kW
	USA — †RFE-RL, Various Locations	Mideast & W Asia • 250/500 kW
	†RFE-RL, Via Biblis, Germany	S • W Asia & C Asia • 100 kW
	†RFE-RL, Via Briech, Morocco	W • Mideast & W Asia • 500 kW; S Europe • 500 kW
	RFE-RL, Via Lampertheim, Germany	Mideast & W Asia • 100 kW; W • Mideast & W Asia • 100 kW
	†RFE-RL, Via Udon Thani, Thailand	W • W Asia & C Asia • 500 kW
	VOA, Via Briech, Morocco	W • E Europe • 500 kW
(con'd)	†VOA, Via Kavála, Greece	Mideast & W Asia • 250 kW

ENGLISH ■■   ARABIC ⊠⊠   CHINESE □□□   FRENCH ══   GERMAN ▬▬   RUSSIAN ══   SPANISH ▬   OTHER ──

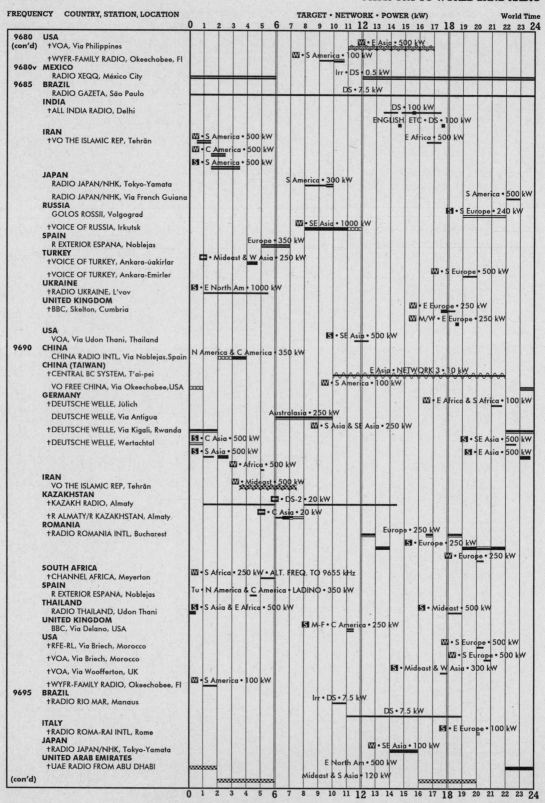

FREQUENCY   COUNTRY, STATION, LOCATION   TARGET • NETWORK • POWER (kW)   World Time

Frequency	Country, Station, Location	Target • Network • Power
9680 (con'd)	USA	
	†VOA, Via Philippines	W • E Asia • 500 kW
	†WYFR-FAMILY RADIO, Okeechobee, Fl	W • S America • 100 kW
9680v	MEXICO	
	RADIO XEQQ, México City	Irr • DS • 0.5 kW
9685	BRAZIL	
	RADIO GAZETA, São Paulo	DS • 7.5 kW
	INDIA	
	†ALL INDIA RADIO, Delhi	DS • 100 kW / ENGLISH ETC • DS • 100 kW
	IRAN	
	†VO THE ISLAMIC REP, Tehrān	W • S America • 500 kW / E Africa • 500 kW
		W • C America • 500 kW
		S • S America • 500 kW
	JAPAN	
	RADIO JAPAN/NHK, Tokyo-Yamata	S America • 300 kW
	RADIO JAPAN/NHK, Via French Guiana	S America • 500 kW
	RUSSIA	
	GOLOS ROSSII, Volgograd	S • S Europe • 240 kW
	†VOICE OF RUSSIA, Irkutsk	W • SE Asia • 1000 kW
	SPAIN	
	R EXTERIOR ESPANA, Noblejas	Europe • 350 kW
	TURKEY	
	†VOICE OF TURKEY, Ankara-úakirlar	Mideast & W Asia • 250 kW
	†VOICE OF TURKEY, Ankara-Emirler	W • S Europe • 500 kW
	UKRAINE	
	†RADIO UKRAINE, L'vov	S • E North Am • 1000 kW
	UNITED KINGDOM	
	†BBC, Skelton, Cumbria	W • E Europe • 250 kW / W M/W • E Europe • 250 kW
	USA	
	VOA, Via Udon Thani, Thailand	S • SE Asia • 500 kW
9690	CHINA	
	CHINA RADIO INTL, Via Noblejas, Spain	N America & C America • 350 kW
	CHINA (TAIWAN)	
	†CENTRAL BC SYSTEM, T'ai-pei	E Asia • NETWORK 3 • 10 kW
	VO FREE CHINA, Via Okeechobee, USA	W • S America • 100 kW
	GERMANY	
	†DEUTSCHE WELLE, Jülich	W • E Africa & S Africa • 100 kW
	DEUTSCHE WELLE, Via Antigua	Australasia • 250 kW
	†DEUTSCHE WELLE, Via Kigali, Rwanda	W • S Asia & SE Asia • 250 kW
	†DEUTSCHE WELLE, Wertachtal	S • C Asia • 500 kW / S • SE Asia • 500 kW
		S • S Asia • 500 kW / S • E Asia • 500 kW
		W • Africa • 500 kW
	IRAN	
	VO THE ISLAMIC REP, Tehrān	W • Mideast • 500 kW
	KAZAKHSTAN	
	†KAZAKH RADIO, Almaty	DS-2 • 20 kW
	†R ALMATY/R KAZAKHSTAN, Almaty	C Asia • 20 kW
	ROMANIA	
	†RADIO ROMANIA INTL, Bucharest	Europe • 250 kW / S • Europe • 250 kW / W • Europe • 250 kW
	SOUTH AFRICA	
	†CHANNEL AFRICA, Meyerton	W • S Africa • 250 kW • ALT. FREQ. TO 9655 kHz
	SPAIN	
	R EXTERIOR ESPANA, Noblejas	Tu • N America & C America • LADINO • 350 kW
	THAILAND	
	RADIO THAILAND, Udon Thani	S • S Asia & E Africa • 500 kW / S • Mideast • 500 kW
	UNITED KINGDOM	
	BBC, Via Delano, USA	S M-F • C America • 250 kW
	USA	
	†RFE-RL, Via Briech, Morocco	W • S Europe • 500 kW
	†VOA, Via Briech, Morocco	W • S Europe • 500 kW
	†VOA, Via Woofferton, UK	S • Mideast & W Asia • 300 kW
	†WYFR-FAMILY RADIO, Okeechobee, Fl	W • S America • 100 kW
9695	BRAZIL	
	†RADIO RIO MAR, Manaus	Irr • DS • 7.5 kW / DS • 7.5 kW
	ITALY	
	†RADIO ROMA-RAI INTL, Rome	S • E Europe • 100 kW
	JAPAN	
	†RADIO JAPAN/NHK, Tokyo-Yamata	W • SE Asia • 100 kW
	UNITED ARAB EMIRATES	
	†UAE RADIO FROM ABU DHABI	E North Am • 500 kW / Mideast & S Asia • 120 kW
(con'd)		

FREQUENCY   COUNTRY, STATION, LOCATION   TARGET • NETWORK • POWER (kW)   World Time

0 1 2 3 4 5 6 7 8 9 10 11 12 13 14 15 16 17 18 19 20 21 22 23 24

Frequency	Country, Station, Location	Target • Network • Power
9695 (con'd)	**USA**	
	†RFE-RL, Via Lampertheim, Germany	W • E Europe • 100 kW / W • W Asia & C Asia • 100 kW
	†RFE-RL, Via Pals, Spain	W • C Asia • 250 kW
	†RFE-RL, Via Udon Thani, Thailand	W • C Asia • 500 kW
	RFE-RL, Via Woofferton, UK	S • E Europe • 300 kW
	†VOA, Via Briech, Morocco	W • Mideast & W Asia • 500 kW
9700	**BULGARIA**	
	†RADIO BULGARIA, Plovdiv	E North Am & C America • 500 kW / Europe • 500 kW
		W • Europe • 500 kW / Europe • 150 kW
	†RADIO BULGARIA, Sofia	
	CHINA	
	CHINA RADIO INTL, Xi'an	Mideast & S Asia • 150 kW
	EGYPT	
	REP OF EGYPT RADIO, Abu Za'bal	N Africa • DS-VO THE ARABS • 100 kW
	GERMANY	
	†DEUTSCHE WELLE, Jülich	W • E Europe • 100 kW
	†DEUTSCHE WELLE, Various Locations	C America & S America • 250/500 kW
	†DEUTSCHE WELLE, Via Kigali, Rwanda	S • S Africa • 250 kW
	DEUTSCHE WELLE, Via Sri Lanka	S • W Asia • 250 kW
	†DEUTSCHE WELLE, Wertachtal	S America • 500 kW
	HOLLAND	
	R NEDERLAND, Via Neth Antilles	S • Australasia • 250 kW
	INDIA	
	†ALL INDIA RADIO, Aligarh	S Asia • 250 kW / DS • 250 kW
	NEW ZEALAND	
	†R NEW ZEALAND INTL, Rangitaiki	W Sa/Su • Pacific • 100 kW
		W • ENGLISH, ETC • Pacific • 100 kW
		W Th-Tu • Pacific • 100 kW
		W • CHINESE & ENGLISH • Pacific • 100 kW
	USA	
	†RFE-RL, Via Briech, Morocco	S • E Europe • 500 kW
	†VOA, Via Kaválla, Greece	W • N Africa & W Africa • 250 kW
	†VOA, Via Philippines	S • Mideast • 250 kW / W • S Asia • 250 kW
9705	**INDIA**	
	†ALL INDIA RADIO, Aligarh	SE Asia • 250 kW
	INDONESIA	
	†RRI, Pontianak, Kalimantan	DS
	KAZAKHSTAN	
	†KAZAKH RADIO, Almaty	DS-2 • 20 kW
	†R ALMATY/R KAZAKHSTAN, Almaty	C Asia • 20 kW
	MEXICO	
	†RADIO MEXICO INTL, México City	SPANISH & ENGLISH • W North Am & C America • 10 kW
	NIGER	
	†LA VOIX DU SAHEL, Niamey	FRENCH, ETC • DS • 100 kW / Sa • FRENCH, ETC • DS • 100 kW
	RUSSIA	
	†GOLOS ROSSII, Vladivostok	W • E Asia & SE Asia • 250 kW
	USA	
	†RFE-RL, Via Briech, Morocco	S • E Europe • 500 kW
	RFE-RL, Via Holzkirchen, Germany	S • C Asia • 250 kW
	†RFE-RL, Via Lampertheim, Germany	S • E Europe • 100 kW / W • E Europe • 100 kW
	RFE-RL, Via Pals, Spain	S • E Europe • 250 kW
	VOA, Via Briech, Morocco	S • E Europe • 500 kW
	†VOA, Via Kaválla, Greece	W • N Africa & W Africa • 250 kW
	VOA, Via Udon Thani, Thailand	W • W Asia & S Asia • 250 kW
	†VOA, Via Woofferton, UK	S • SE Asia & Australasia • 500 kW / W • E Europe • 250 kW
	WYFR-FAMILY RADIO, Okeechobee, Fl	W • C America • 100 kW / W • W North Am • 100 kW / S • C America & W North Am • 50 kW
9705v	**ETHIOPIA**	
	†RADIO ETHIOPIA, Gedja	DS • 100 kW / Su • DS • 100 kW / Sa/Su • DS • 100 kW / M-F • DS • 100 kW
	SAUDI ARABIA	
	†BS OF THE KINGDOM, Jiddah	W Asia • DS-HOLY KORAN • 50 kW • ALT. FREQ. TO 9775v kHz
9710 (con'd)	**AUSTRALIA**	
	†RADIO AUSTRALIA, Shepparton	Pacific & E Asia • 100 kW

0 1 2 3 4 5 6 7 8 9 10 11 12 13 14 15 16 17 18 19 20 21 22 23 24

ENGLISH ▬ ARABIC ▨ CHINESE ▫▫▫ FRENCH ═ GERMAN ▬▬ RUSSIAN ═ SPANISH ▬ OTHER ▬

FREQUENCY   COUNTRY, STATION, LOCATION   TARGET • NETWORK • POWER (kW)   World Time

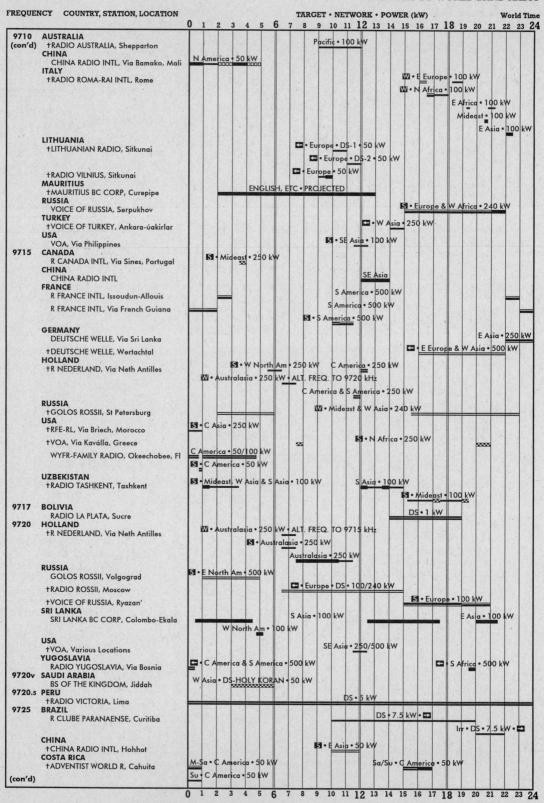

9710	AUSTRALIA
(con'd)	†RADIO AUSTRALIA, Shepparton — Pacific • 100 kW
	CHINA
	CHINA RADIO INTL, Via Bamako, Mali — N America • 50 kW
	ITALY
	†RADIO ROMA-RAI INTL, Rome — W • E Europe • 100 kW; W • N Africa • 100 kW; E Africa • 100 kW; Mideast • 100 kW; E Asia • 100 kW
	LITHUANIA
	†LITHUANIAN RADIO, Sitkunai — • Europe • DS-1 • 50 kW; • Europe • DS-2 • 50 kW
	†RADIO VILNIUS, Sitkunai — • Europe • 50 kW
	MAURITIUS
	†MAURITIUS BC CORP, Curepipe — ENGLISH, ETC • PROJECTED
	RUSSIA
	VOICE OF RUSSIA, Serpukhov — S • Europe & W Africa • 240 kW
	TURKEY
	†VOICE OF TURKEY, Ankara-úakirlar — • W Asia • 250 kW
	USA
	VOA, Via Philippines — S • SE Asia • 100 kW
9715	CANADA
	R CANADA INTL, Via Sines, Portugal — S • Mideast • 250 kW
	CHINA
	CHINA RADIO INTL — SE Asia
	FRANCE
	R FRANCE INTL, Issoudun-Allouis — S America • 500 kW
	R FRANCE INTL, Via French Guiana — S America • 500 kW; S • S America • 500 kW
	GERMANY
	DEUTSCHE WELLE, Via Sri Lanka — E Asia • 250 kW
	†DEUTSCHE WELLE, Wertachtal — • E Europe & W Asia • 500 kW
	HOLLAND
	†R NEDERLAND, Via Neth Antilles — S • W North Am • 250 kW; C America • 250 kW; W • Australasia • 250 kW • ALT. FREQ. TO 9720 kHz; C America & S America • 250 kW
	RUSSIA
	†GOLOS ROSSII, St Petersburg — W • Mideast & W Asia • 240 kW
	USA
	†RFE-RL, Via Briech, Morocco — S • C Asia • 250 kW
	†VOA, Via Kaválla, Greece — S • N Africa • 250 kW
	WYFR-FAMILY RADIO, Okeechobee, Fl — C America • 50/100 kW; S • C America • 50 kW
	UZBEKISTAN
	†RADIO TASHKENT, Tashkent — S • Mideast, W Asia & S Asia • 100 kW; S Asia • 100 kW; S • Mideast • 100 kW
9717	BOLIVIA
	RADIO LA PLATA, Sucre — DS • 1 kW
9720	HOLLAND
	†R NEDERLAND, Via Neth Antilles — W • Australasia • 250 kW • ALT. FREQ. TO 9715 kHz; S • Australasia • 250 kW; Australasia • 250 kW
	RUSSIA
	GOLOS ROSSII, Volgograd — S • E North Am • 500 kW
	†RADIO ROSSII, Moscow — • Europe • DS • 100/240 kW
	†VOICE OF RUSSIA, Ryazan' — S • Europe • 100 kW
	SRI LANKA
	SRI LANKA BC CORP, Colombo-Ekala — S Asia • 100 kW; E Asia • 100 kW
	USA
	†VOA, Various Locations — W North Am • 100 kW; SE Asia • 250/500 kW
	YUGOSLAVIA
	RADIO YUGOSLAVIA, Via Bosnia — • C America & S America • 500 kW; • S Africa • 500 kW
9720v	SAUDI ARABIA
	BS OF THE KINGDOM, Jiddah — W Asia • DS-HOLY KORAN • 50 kW
9720.5	PERU
	†RADIO VICTORIA, Lima — DS • 5 kW
9725	BRAZIL
	R CLUBE PARANAENSE, Curitiba — DS • 7.5 kW • ; Irr • DS • 7.5 kW •
	CHINA
	†CHINA RADIO INTL, Hohhot — S • E Asia • 50 kW
	COSTA RICA
	†ADVENTIST WORLD R, Cahuita — M-Sa • C America • 50 kW; Sa/Su • C America • 50 kW; Su • C America • 50 kW
(con'd)	

FREQUENCY   COUNTRY, STATION, LOCATION   TARGET • NETWORK • POWER (kW)   World Time

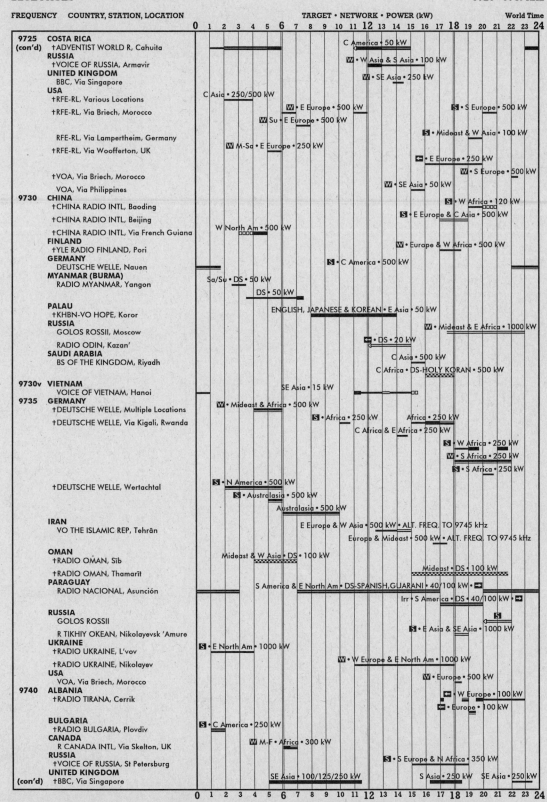

FREQUENCY	COUNTRY, STATION, LOCATION	TARGET • NETWORK • POWER (kW)
9725 (con'd)	COSTA RICA †ADVENTIST WORLD R, Cahuita	C America • 50 kW
	RUSSIA †VOICE OF RUSSIA, Armavir	W • W Asia & S Asia • 100 kW
	UNITED KINGDOM BBC, Via Singapore	W • SE Asia • 250 kW
	USA †RFE-RL, Various Locations	C Asia • 250/500 kW
	†RFE-RL, Via Briech, Morocco	W • E Europe • 500 kW · S • S Europe • 500 kW
		W Su • E Europe • 500 kW
	RFE-RL, Via Lampertheim, Germany	S • Mideast & W Asia • 100 kW
	†RFE-RL, Via Woofferton, UK	W M-Sa • E Europe • 250 kW
		• E Europe • 250 kW
	†VOA, Via Briech, Morocco	W • S Europe • 500 kW
	VOA, Via Philippines	W • SE Asia • 50 kW
9730	CHINA †CHINA RADIO INTL, Baoding	S • W Africa • 120 kW
	†CHINA RADIO INTL, Beijing	S • E Europe & C Asia • 500 kW
	†CHINA RADIO INTL, Via French Guiana	W North Am • 500 kW
	FINLAND †YLE RADIO FINLAND, Pori	W • Europe & W Africa • 500 kW
	GERMANY DEUTSCHE WELLE, Nauen	S • C America • 500 kW
	MYANMAR (BURMA) RADIO MYANMAR, Yangon	Sa/Su • DS • 50 kW
		DS • 50 kW
	PALAU †KHBN-VO HOPE, Koror	ENGLISH, JAPANESE & KOREAN • E Asia • 50 kW
	RUSSIA GOLOS ROSSII, Moscow	W • Mideast & E Africa • 1000 kW
	RADIO ODIN, Kazan'	• DS • 20 kW
	SAUDI ARABIA BS OF THE KINGDOM, Riyadh	C Asia • 500 kW
		C Africa • DS-HOLY KORAN • 500 kW
9730v	VIETNAM VOICE OF VIETNAM, Hanoi	SE Asia • 15 kW
9735	GERMANY †DEUTSCHE WELLE, Multiple Locations	W • Mideast & Africa • 500 kW
	†DEUTSCHE WELLE, Via Kigali, Rwanda	S • Africa • 250 kW Africa • 250 kW
		C Africa & E Africa • 250 kW
		S • W Africa • 250 kW
		W • S Africa • 250 kW
		S • S Africa • 250 kW
	†DEUTSCHE WELLE, Wertachtal	S • N America • 500 kW
		S • Australasia • 500 kW
		Australasia • 500 kW
	IRAN VO THE ISLAMIC REP, Tehrān	E Europe & W Asia • 500 kW • ALT. FREQ. TO 9745 kHz
		Europe & Mideast • 500 kW • ALT. FREQ. TO 9745 kHz
	OMAN †RADIO OMAN, Sīb	Mideast & W Asia • DS • 100 kW
	†RADIO OMAN, Thamarīt	Mideast • DS • 100 kW
	PARAGUAY RADIO NACIONAL, Asunción	S America & E North Am • DS-SPANISH,GUARANI • 40/100 kW •
		Irr • S America • DS • 40/100 kW •
	RUSSIA GOLOS ROSSII	S
	R TIKHIY OKEAN, Nikolayevsk 'Amure	S • E Asia & SE Asia • 1000 kW
	UKRAINE †RADIO UKRAINE, L'vov	S • E North Am • 1000 kW
	†RADIO UKRAINE, Nikolayev	W • W Europe & E North Am • 1000 kW
	USA VOA, Via Briech, Morocco	W • Europe • 500 kW
9740	ALBANIA †RADIO TIRANA, Cerrik	• W Europe • 100 kW
		• Europe • 100 kW
	BULGARIA †RADIO BULGARIA, Plovdiv	S • C America • 250 kW
	CANADA R CANADA INTL, Via Skelton, UK	W M-F • Africa • 300 kW
	RUSSIA †VOICE OF RUSSIA, St Petersburg	S • S Europe & N Africa • 350 kW
	UNITED KINGDOM	
(con'd)	†BBC, Via Singapore	SE Asia • 100/125/250 kW S Asia • 250 kW SE Asia • 250 kW

ENGLISH ▬▬   ARABIC ⋙   CHINESE □□□   FRENCH ▭▭   GERMAN ▭▭   RUSSIAN ═══   SPANISH ▭▭   OTHER ▬▬

FREQUENCY   COUNTRY, STATION, LOCATION   TARGET • NETWORK • POWER (kW)   World Time

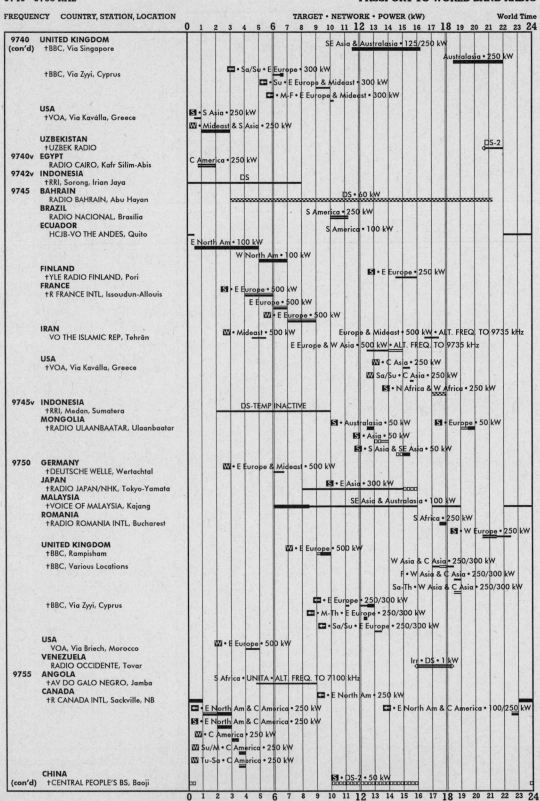

FREQUENCY	COUNTRY, STATION, LOCATION
9740 (con'd)	**UNITED KINGDOM** †BBC, Via Singapore
	†BBC, Via Zyyi, Cyprus
	USA †VOA, Via Kaválla, Greece
	UZBEKISTAN †UZBEK RADIO
9740v	**EGYPT** RADIO CAIRO, Kafr Silim-Abis
9742v	**INDONESIA** †RRI, Sorong, Irian Jaya
9745	**BAHRAIN** RADIO BAHRAIN, Abu Hayan
	BRAZIL RADIO NACIONAL, Brasília
	ECUADOR HCJB-VO THE ANDES, Quito
	FINLAND †YLE RADIO FINLAND, Pori
	FRANCE †R FRANCE INTL, Issoudun-Allouis
	IRAN VO THE ISLAMIC REP, Tehrän
	USA †VOA, Via Kaválla, Greece
9745v	**INDONESIA** †RRI, Medan, Sumatera
	MONGOLIA †RADIO ULAANBAATAR, Ulaanbaatar
9750	**GERMANY** †DEUTSCHE WELLE, Wertachtal
	JAPAN †RADIO JAPAN/NHK, Tokyo-Yamata
	MALAYSIA †VOICE OF MALAYSIA, Kajang
	ROMANIA †RADIO ROMANIA INTL, Bucharest
	UNITED KINGDOM †BBC, Rampisham
	†BBC, Various Locations
	†BBC, Via Zyyi, Cyprus
	USA VOA, Via Briech, Morocco
	VENEZUELA RADIO OCCIDENTE, Tovar
9755	**ANGOLA** †AV DO GALO NEGRO, Jamba
	CANADA †R CANADA INTL, Sackville, NB
(con'd)	**CHINA** †CENTRAL PEOPLE'S BS, Baoji

Schedule bar annotations:

- †BBC, Via Singapore: SE Asia & Australasia • 125/250 kW; Australasia • 250 kW
- †BBC, Via Zyyi, Cyprus: Sa/Su • E Europe • 300 kW; Su • E Europe & Mideast • 300 kW; M-F • E Europe & Mideast • 300 kW
- †VOA, Via Kaválla, Greece: S • S Asia • 250 kW; W • Mideast & S Asia • 250 kW
- †UZBEK RADIO: DS-2
- RADIO CAIRO: C America • 250 kW
- †RRI, Sorong: DS
- RADIO BAHRAIN: DS • 60 kW
- RADIO NACIONAL, Brasília: S America • 250 kW
- HCJB-VO THE ANDES: S America • 100 kW; E North Am • 100 kW; W North Am • 100 kW
- †YLE RADIO FINLAND: S • E Europe • 250 kW
- †R FRANCE INTL: S • E Europe • 500 kW; E Europe • 500 kW; W • E Europe • 500 kW
- VO THE ISLAMIC REP: W • Mideast • 500 kW; Europe & Mideast • 500 kW • ALT. FREQ. TO 9735 kHz; E Europe & W Asia • 500 kW • ALT. FREQ. TO 9735 kHz
- †VOA, Via Kaválla, Greece: W • C Asia • 250 kW; W Sa/Su • C Asia • 250 kW; S • N Africa & W Africa • 250 kW
- †RRI, Medan: DS-TEMP INACTIVE
- †RADIO ULAANBAATAR: S • Australasia • 50 kW; S • Europe • 50 kW; S • Asia • 50 kW; S • S Asia & SE Asia • 50 kW
- †DEUTSCHE WELLE: W • E Europe & Mideast • 500 kW
- †RADIO JAPAN/NHK: S • E Asia • 300 kW
- †VOICE OF MALAYSIA: SE Asia & Australasia • 100 kW
- †RADIO ROMANIA INTL: S Africa • 250 kW; S • W Europe • 250 kW
- †BBC, Rampisham: W • E Europe • 500 kW
- †BBC, Various Locations: W Asia & C Asia • 250/300 kW; F • W Asia & C Asia • 250/300 kW; Sa-Th • W Asia & C Asia • 250/300 kW
- †BBC, Via Zyyi, Cyprus: E Europe • 250/300 kW; M-Th • E Europe • 250/300 kW; Sa/Su • E Europe • 250/300 kW
- VOA, Via Briech, Morocco: W • E Europe • 500 kW
- RADIO OCCIDENTE: Irr • DS • 1 kW
- †AV DO GALO NEGRO: S Africa • UNITA • ALT. FREQ. TO 7100 kHz
- †R CANADA INTL: S • E North Am • 250 kW; E North Am & C America • 250 kW; E North Am & C America • 100/250 kW; S • E North Am & C America • 250 kW; W • C America • 250 kW; W Su/M • C America • 250 kW; W Tu-Sa • C America • 250 kW
- †CENTRAL PEOPLE'S BS: S • DS-2 • 50 kW

FREQUENCY　　COUNTRY, STATION, LOCATION　　　　　TARGET • NETWORK • POWER (kW)　　　　World Time

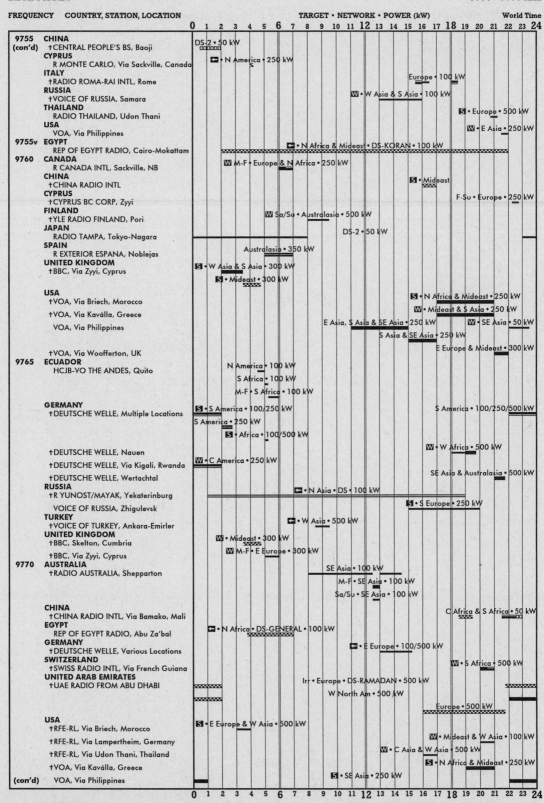

Frequency	Country, Station, Location	Target • Network • Power
9755 (con'd)	**CHINA** †CENTRAL PEOPLE'S BS, Baoji	DS-2 • 50 kW
	CYPRUS R MONTE CARLO, Via Sackville, Canada	N America • 250 kW
	ITALY †RADIO ROMA-RAI INTL, Rome	Europe • 100 kW
	RUSSIA †VOICE OF RUSSIA, Samara	W • W Asia & S Asia • 100 kW
	THAILAND RADIO THAILAND, Udon Thani	S • Europe • 500 kW
	USA VOA, Via Philippines	W • E Asia • 250 kW
9755v	**EGYPT** REP OF EGYPT RADIO, Cairo-Mokattam	N Africa & Mideast • DS-KORAN • 100 kW
9760	**CANADA** R CANADA INTL, Sackville, NB	W • M-F • Europe & N Africa • 250 kW
	CHINA †CHINA RADIO INTL	S • Mideast
	CYPRUS †CYPRUS BC CORP, Zyyi	F-Su • Europe • 250 kW
	FINLAND †YLE RADIO FINLAND, Pori	W • Sa/Su • Australasia • 500 kW
	JAPAN RADIO TAMPA, Tokyo-Nagara	DS-2 • 50 kW
	SPAIN R EXTERIOR ESPANA, Noblejas	Australasia • 350 kW
	UNITED KINGDOM †BBC, Via Zyyi, Cyprus	S • W Asia & S Asia • 300 kW / S • Mideast • 300 kW
	USA †VOA, Via Briech, Morocco	S • N Africa & Mideast • 250 kW
	†VOA, Via Kaválla, Greece	W • Mideast & S Asia • 250 kW
	VOA, Via Philippines	E Asia, S Asia & SE Asia • 250 kW / W • SE Asia • 50 kW / S Asia & SE Asia • 250 kW
	†VOA, Via Woofferton, UK	E Europe & Mideast • 300 kW
9765	**ECUADOR** HCJB-VO THE ANDES, Quito	N America • 100 kW / S Africa • 100 kW / M-F • S Africa • 100 kW
	GERMANY †DEUTSCHE WELLE, Multiple Locations	S • S America • 100/250 kW / S America • 250 kW / S America • 100/250/500 kW / S • Africa • 100/500 kW
	†DEUTSCHE WELLE, Nauen	W • W Africa • 500 kW
	†DEUTSCHE WELLE, Via Kigali, Rwanda	W • C America • 250 kW / SE Asia & Australasia • 500 kW
	†DEUTSCHE WELLE, Wertachtal	
	RUSSIA †R YUNOST/MAYAK, Yekaterinburg	N Asia • DS • 100 kW
	VOICE OF RUSSIA, Zhigulevsk	S • S Europe • 250 kW
	TURKEY †VOICE OF TURKEY, Ankara-Emirler	W Asia • 500 kW
	UNITED KINGDOM †BBC, Skelton, Cumbria	W • Mideast • 300 kW
	†BBC, Via Zyyi, Cyprus	W • M-F • E Europe • 300 kW
9770	**AUSTRALIA** †RADIO AUSTRALIA, Shepparton	SE Asia • 100 kW / M-F • SE Asia • 100 kW / Sa/Su • SE Asia • 100 kW
	CHINA †CHINA RADIO INTL, Via Bamako, Mali	C Africa & S Africa • 50 kW
	EGYPT REP OF EGYPT RADIO, Abu Za'bal	N Africa • DS-GENERAL • 100 kW
	GERMANY †DEUTSCHE WELLE, Various Locations	E Europe • 100/500 kW
	SWITZERLAND †SWISS RADIO INTL, Via French Guiana	W • S Africa • 500 kW
	UNITED ARAB EMIRATES †UAE RADIO FROM ABU DHABI	Irr • Europe • DS-RAMADAN • 500 kW / W North Am • 500 kW / Europe • 500 kW
	USA †RFE-RL, Via Briech, Morocco	S • E Europe & W Asia • 500 kW
	†RFE-RL, Via Lampertheim, Germany	W • Mideast & W Asia • 100 kW
	†RFE-RL, Via Udon Thani, Thailand	W • C Asia & W Asia • 500 kW
	†VOA, Via Kaválla, Greece	S • N Africa & Mideast • 250 kW
(con'd)	VOA, Via Philippines	S • SE Asia • 250 kW

ENGLISH ▬　**ARABIC** sss　**CHINESE** ▭▭▭　**FRENCH** ══　**GERMAN** ▬▬　**RUSSIAN** ══　**SPANISH** ▬▬　**OTHER** ▬

FREQUENCY   COUNTRY, STATION, LOCATION   TARGET • NETWORK • POWER (kW)   World Time

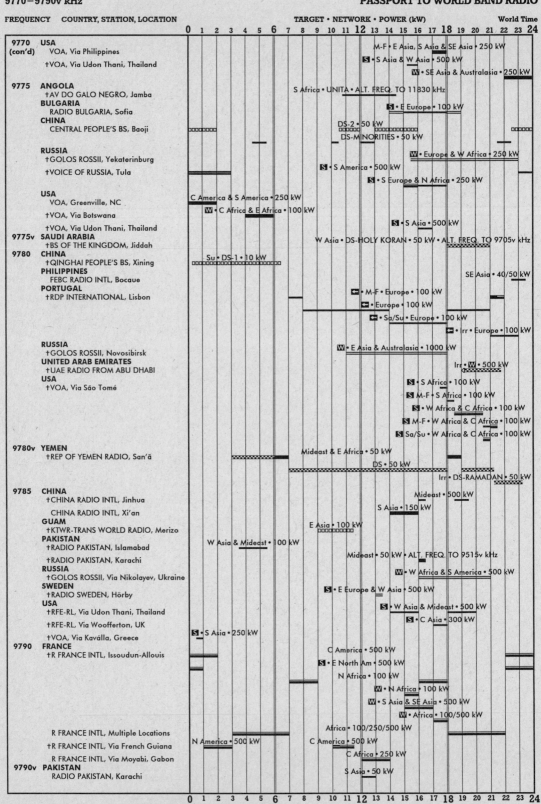

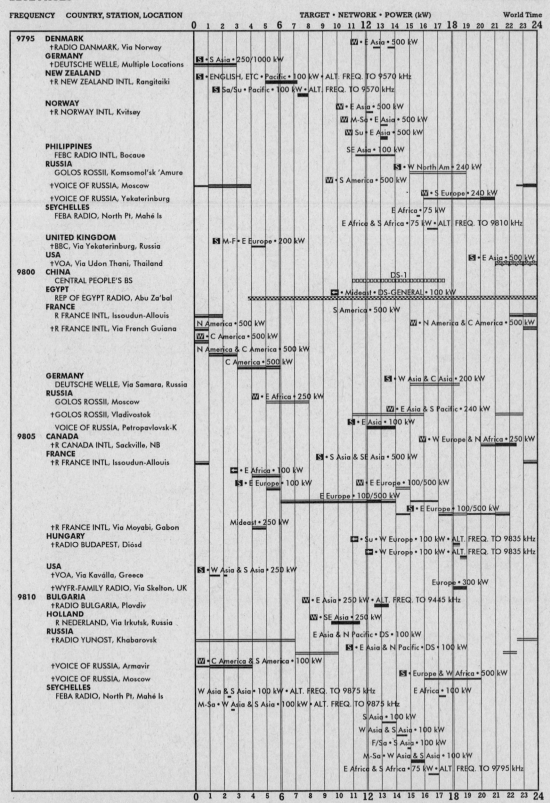

FREQUENCY　　COUNTRY, STATION, LOCATION

9795	**DENMARK**	W • E Asia • 500 kW
	†RADIO DANMARK, Via Norway	
	GERMANY	S • S Asia • 250/1000 kW
	†DEUTSCHE WELLE, Multiple Locations	
	NEW ZEALAND	S • ENGLISH, ETC • Pacific • 100 kW • ALT. FREQ. TO 9570 kHz
	†R NEW ZEALAND INTL, Rangitaiki	S • Sa/Su • Pacific • 100 kW • ALT. FREQ. TO 9570 kHz
	NORWAY	W • E Asia • 500 kW
	†R NORWAY INTL, Kvitsøy	W • M-Sa • E Asia • 500 kW
		W • Su • E Asia • 500 kW
	PHILIPPINES	SE Asia • 100 kW
	FEBC RADIO INTL, Bocaue	
	RUSSIA	S • W North Am • 240 kW
	GOLOS ROSSII, Komsomol'sk 'Amure	
	†VOICE OF RUSSIA, Moscow	W • S America • 500 kW
	†VOICE OF RUSSIA, Yekaterinburg	W • S Europe • 240 kW
	SEYCHELLES	E Africa • 75 kW
	FEBA RADIO, North Pt, Mahé Is	E Africa & S Africa • 75 kW • ALT. FREQ. TO 9810 kHz
	UNITED KINGDOM	S • M-F • E Europe • 200 kW
	†BBC, Via Yekaterinburg, Russia	
	USA	S • E Asia • 500 kW
	†VOA, Via Udon Thani, Thailand	
9800	**CHINA**	DS-1
	CENTRAL PEOPLE'S BS	
	EGYPT	☐ • Mideast • DS-GENERAL • 100 kW
	REP OF EGYPT RADIO, Abu Za'bal	
	FRANCE	S America • 500 kW
	R FRANCE INTL, Issoudun-Allouis	N America • 500 kW
	†R FRANCE INTL, Via French Guiana	W • N America & C America • 500 kW
		W • C America • 500 kW
		N America & C America • 500 kW
		C America • 500 kW
	GERMANY	S • W Asia & C Asia • 200 kW
	DEUTSCHE WELLE, Via Samara, Russia	
	RUSSIA	W • E Africa • 250 kW
	GOLOS ROSSII, Moscow	
	†GOLOS ROSSII, Vladivostok	W • E Asia & S Pacific • 240 kW
	VOICE OF RUSSIA, Petropavlovsk-K	S • E Asia • 100 kW
9805	**CANADA**	W • W Europe & N Africa • 250 kW
	†R CANADA INTL, Sackville, NB	
	FRANCE	S • S Asia & SE Asia • 500 kW
	†R FRANCE INTL, Issoudun-Allouis	☐ • E Africa • 100 kW
		S • E Europe • 100 kW
		W • E Europe • 100/500 kW
		E Europe • 100/500 kW
		S • E Europe • 100/500 kW
	†R FRANCE INTL, Via Moyabi, Gabon	Mideast • 250 kW
	HUNGARY	☐ • Su • W Europe • 100 kW • ALT. FREQ. TO 9835 kHz
	†RADIO BUDAPEST, Diósd	☐ • W Europe • 100 kW • ALT. FREQ. TO 9835 kHz
	USA	S • W Asia & S Asia • 250 kW
	†VOA, Via Kaválla, Greece	
	†WYFR-FAMILY RADIO, Via Skelton, UK	Europe • 300 kW
9810	**BULGARIA**	W • E Asia • 250 kW • ALT. FREQ. TO 9445 kHz
	†RADIO BULGARIA, Plovdiv	
	HOLLAND	W • SE Asia • 250 kW
	R NEDERLAND, Via Irkutsk, Russia	
	RUSSIA	E Asia & N Pacific • DS • 100 kW
	†RADIO YUNOST, Khabarovsk	S • E Asia & N Pacific • DS • 100 kW
	†VOICE OF RUSSIA, Armavir	W • C America & S America • 100 kW
	†VOICE OF RUSSIA, Moscow	S • Europe & W Africa • 500 kW
	SEYCHELLES	W Asia & S Asia • 100 kW • ALT. FREQ. TO 9875 kHz
	FEBA RADIO, North Pt, Mahé Is	E Africa • 100 kW
		M-Sa • W Asia & S Asia • 100 kW • ALT. FREQ. TO 9875 kHz
		S Asia • 100 kW
		W Asia & S Asia • 100 kW
		F/Sa • S Asia • 100 kW
		M-Sa • W Asia & S Asia • 100 kW
		E Africa & S Africa • 75 kW • ALT. FREQ. TO 9795 kHz

FREQUENCY   COUNTRY, STATION, LOCATION

TARGET • NETWORK • POWER (kW)

World Time

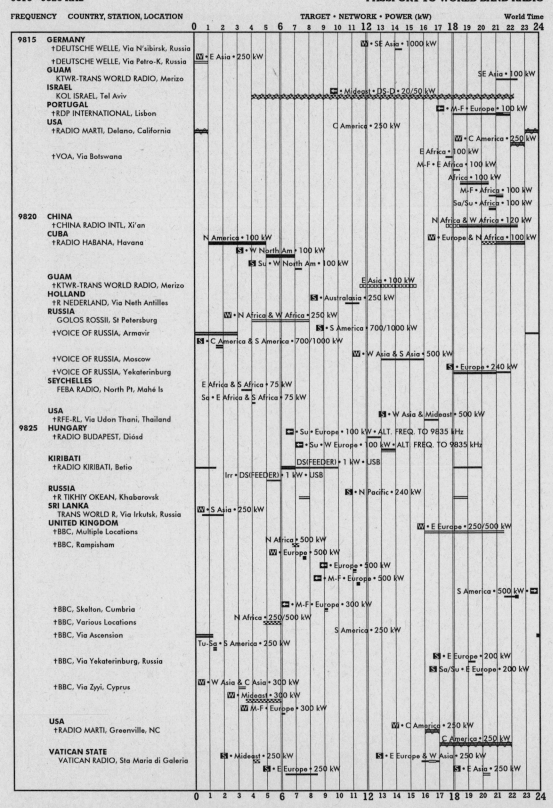

9815 GERMANY
  †DEUTSCHE WELLE, Via N'sibirsk, Russia — W • SE Asia • 1000 kW
  †DEUTSCHE WELLE, Via Petro-K, Russia — W • E Asia • 250 kW
  GUAM
  KTWR-TRANS WORLD RADIO, Merizo — SE Asia • 100 kW
  ISRAEL
  KOL ISRAEL, Tel Aviv — ⬚ • Mideast • DS-D • 20/50 kW
  PORTUGAL
  †RDP INTERNATIONAL, Lisbon — ⬚ • M-F • Europe • 100 kW
  USA
  †RADIO MARTI, Delano, California — C America • 250 kW / W • C America • 250 kW
  †VOA, Via Botswana — E Africa • 100 kW / M-F • E Africa • 100 kW / Africa • 100 kW / M-F • Africa • 100 kW / Sa/Su • Africa • 100 kW

9820 CHINA
  †CHINA RADIO INTL, Xi'an — N Africa & W Africa • 120 kW
  CUBA
  †RADIO HABANA, Havana — N America • 100 kW / W • Europe & N Africa • 100 kW / S • W North Am • 100 kW / S • Su • W North Am • 100 kW
  GUAM
  †KTWR-TRANS WORLD RADIO, Merizo — E Asia • 100 kW
  HOLLAND
  †R NEDERLAND, Via Neth Antilles — S • Australasia • 250 kW
  RUSSIA
  GOLOS ROSSII, St Petersburg — W • N Africa & W Africa • 250 kW
  †VOICE OF RUSSIA, Armavir — S • S America • 700/1000 kW / S • C America & S America • 700/1000 kW
  †VOICE OF RUSSIA, Moscow — W • W Asia & S Asia • 500 kW
  †VOICE OF RUSSIA, Yekaterinburg — S • Europe • 240 kW
  SEYCHELLES
  FEBA RADIO, North Pt, Mahé Is — E Africa & S Africa • 75 kW / Sa • E Africa & S Africa • 75 kW
  USA
  †RFE-RL, Via Udon Thani, Thailand — S • W Asia & Mideast • 500 kW

9825 HUNGARY
  †RADIO BUDAPEST, Diósd — ⬚ • Su • Europe • 100 kW • ALT. FREQ. TO 9835 kHz / ⬚ • Su • W Europe • 100 kW • ALT. FREQ. TO 9835 kHz
  KIRIBATI
  †RADIO KIRIBATI, Betio — DS(FEEDER) • 1 kW • USB / Irr • DS(FEEDER) • 1 kW • USB
  RUSSIA
  †R TIKHIY OKEAN, Khabarovsk — S • N Pacific • 240 kW
  SRI LANKA
  TRANS WORLD R, Via Irkutsk, Russia — W • S Asia • 250 kW
  UNITED KINGDOM
  †BBC, Multiple Locations — W • E Europe • 250/500 kW
  †BBC, Rampisham — N Africa • 500 kW / W • Europe • 500 kW / ⬚ • Europe • 500 kW / ⬚ • M-F • Europe • 500 kW / S America • 500 kW • ⬚
  †BBC, Skelton, Cumbria — ⬚ • M-F • Europe • 300 kW
  †BBC, Various Locations — N Africa • 250/500 kW / S America • 250 kW
  †BBC, Via Ascension — Tu-Sa • S America • 250 kW
  †BBC, Via Yekaterinburg, Russia — S • E Europe • 200 kW / S • Sa/Su • E Europe • 200 kW
  †BBC, Via Zyyi, Cyprus — W • W Asia & C Asia • 300 kW / W • Mideast • 300 kW / W • M-F • Europe • 300 kW
  USA
  †RADIO MARTI, Greenville, NC — W • C America • 250 kW / C America • 250 kW
  VATICAN STATE
  VATICAN RADIO, Sta Maria di Galeria — S • Mideast • 250 kW / S • E Europe & W Asia • 250 kW / S • E Europe • 250 kW / S • E Asia • 250 kW

FREQUENCY   COUNTRY, STATION, LOCATION   TARGET • NETWORK • POWER (kW)   World Time

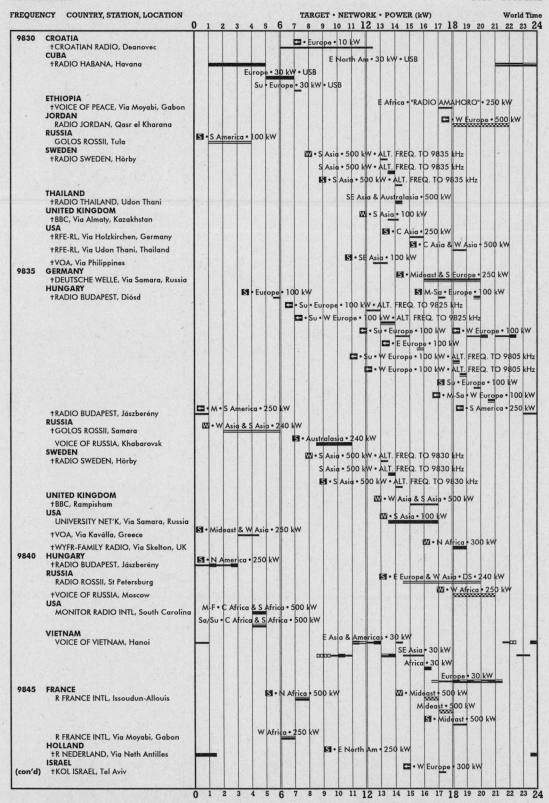

Freq	Country / Station / Location	Target • Network • Power
9830	**CROATIA**	
	†CROATIAN RADIO, Deanovec	Europe • 10 kW
	CUBA	
	†RADIO HABANA, Havana	E North Am • 30 kW • USB
		Europe • 30 kW • USB
		Su • Europe • 30 kW • USB
	ETHIOPIA	
	†VOICE OF PEACE, Via Moyabi, Gabon	E Africa • "RADIO AMAHORO" • 250 kW
	JORDAN	
	RADIO JORDAN, Qasr el Kharana	W Europe • 500 kW
	RUSSIA	
	GOLOS ROSSII, Tula	S America • 100 kW
	SWEDEN	
	†RADIO SWEDEN, Hörby	W • S Asia • 500 kW • ALT. FREQ. TO 9835 kHz
		S Asia • 500 kW • ALT. FREQ. TO 9835 kHz
		S • S Asia • 500 kW • ALT. FREQ. TO 9835 kHz
	THAILAND	
	†RADIO THAILAND, Udon Thani	SE Asia & Australasia • 500 kW
	UNITED KINGDOM	
	†BBC, Via Almaty, Kazakhstan	W • S Asia • 100 kW
	USA	
	†RFE-RL, Via Holzkirchen, Germany	S • C Asia • 250 kW
	†RFE-RL, Via Udon Thani, Thailand	S • C Asia & W Asia • 500 kW
	†VOA, Via Philippines	S • SE Asia • 100 kW
9835	**GERMANY**	
	†DEUTSCHE WELLE, Via Samara, Russia	S • Mideast & S Europe • 250 kW
	HUNGARY	
	†RADIO BUDAPEST, Diósd	S • Europe • 100 kW
		M-Sa • Europe • 100 kW
		Su • Europe • 100 kW • ALT. FREQ. TO 9825 kHz
		Su • W Europe • 100 kW • ALT. FREQ. TO 9825 kHz
		Su • Europe • 100 kW W Europe • 100 kW
		E Europe • 100 kW
		Su • W Europe • 100 kW • ALT. FREQ. TO 9805 kHz
		W Europe • 100 kW • ALT. FREQ. TO 9805 kHz
		Su • Europe • 100 kW
		M-Sa • W Europe • 100 kW
	†RADIO BUDAPEST, Jászberény	M • S America • 250 kW S America • 250 kW
	RUSSIA	
	†GOLOS ROSSII, Samara	W • W Asia & S Asia • 240 kW
	VOICE OF RUSSIA, Khabarovsk	S • Australasia • 240 kW
	SWEDEN	
	†RADIO SWEDEN, Hörby	W • S Asia • 500 kW • ALT. FREQ. TO 9830 kHz
		S Asia • 500 kW • ALT. FREQ. TO 9830 kHz
		S • S Asia • 500 kW • ALT. FREQ. TO 9830 kHz
	UNITED KINGDOM	
	†BBC, Rampisham	W • W Asia & S Asia • 500 kW
	USA	
	UNIVERSITY NET'K, Via Samara, Russia	W • S Asia • 100 kW
	†VOA, Via Kaválla, Greece	S • Mideast & W Asia • 250 kW
	†WYFR-FAMILY RADIO, Via Skelton, UK	W • N Africa • 300 kW
9840	**HUNGARY**	
	†RADIO BUDAPEST, Jászberény	S • N America • 250 kW
	RUSSIA	
	RADIO ROSSII, St Petersburg	S • E Europe & W Asia • DS • 240 kW
	†VOICE OF RUSSIA, Moscow	W • W Africa • 250 kW
	USA	
	MONITOR RADIO INTL, South Carolina	M-F • C Africa & S Africa • 500 kW
		Sa/Su • C Africa & S Africa • 500 kW
	VIETNAM	
	VOICE OF VIETNAM, Hanoi	E Asia & Americas • 30 kW
		SE Asia • 30 kW
		Africa • 30 kW
		Europe • 30 kW
9845	**FRANCE**	
	R FRANCE INTL, Issoudun-Allouis	S • N Africa • 500 kW
		W • Mideast • 500 kW
		Mideast • 500 kW
		S • Mideast • 500 kW
	R FRANCE INTL, Via Moyabi, Gabon	W Africa • 250 kW
	HOLLAND	
	†R NEDERLAND, Via Neth Antilles	S • E North Am • 250 kW
	ISRAEL	
(con'd)	†KOL ISRAEL, Tel Aviv	W Europe • 300 kW

ENGLISH ▬   ARABIC ⋙   CHINESE ▫▫▫   FRENCH ▬   GERMAN ▬   RUSSIAN ═   SPANISH ▬   OTHER ▬

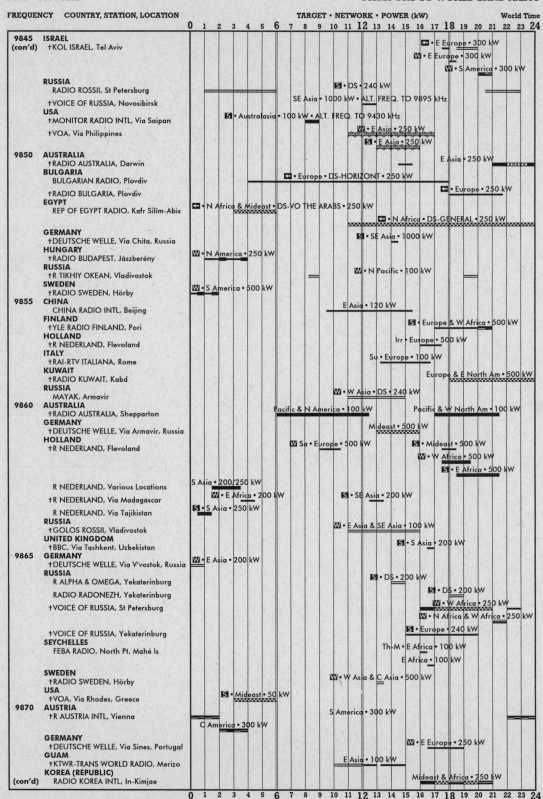

FREQUENCY   COUNTRY, STATION, LOCATION

TARGET • NETWORK • POWER (kW)

World Time

0 1 2 3 4 5 6 7 8 9 10 11 12 13 14 15 16 17 18 19 20 21 22 23 24

9845   ISRAEL
(con'd)   †KOL ISRAEL, Tel Aviv — E Europe • 300 kW / W • E Europe • 300 kW / W • S America • 300 kW

RUSSIA
RADIO ROSSII, St Petersburg — S • DS • 240 kW
†VOICE OF RUSSIA, Novosibirsk — SE Asia • 1000 kW • ALT. FREQ. TO 9895 kHz
USA
†MONITOR RADIO INTL, Via Saipan — S • Australasia • 100 kW • ALT. FREQ. TO 9430 kHz
†VOA, Via Philippines — W • E Asia • 250 kW / S • E Asia • 250 kW

9850   AUSTRALIA
†RADIO AUSTRALIA, Darwin — E Asia • 250 kW
BULGARIA
BULGARIAN RADIO, Plovdiv — Europe • DS-HORIZONT • 250 kW
†RADIO BULGARIA, Plovdiv — Europe • 250 kW
EGYPT
REP OF EGYPT RADIO, Kafr Silim-Abis — N Africa & Mideast • DS-VO THE ARABS • 250 kW / N Africa • DS-GENERAL • 250 kW
GERMANY
†DEUTSCHE WELLE, Via Chita, Russia — S • SE Asia • 1000 kW
HUNGARY
†RADIO BUDAPEST, Jászberény — W • N America • 250 kW
RUSSIA
†R TIKHIY OKEAN, Vladivostok — W • N Pacific • 100 kW
SWEDEN
†RADIO SWEDEN, Hörby — W • S America • 500 kW
9855   CHINA
CHINA RADIO INTL, Beijing — E Asia • 120 kW
FINLAND
†YLE RADIO FINLAND, Pori — S • Europe & W Africa • 500 kW
HOLLAND
†R NEDERLAND, Flevoland — Irr • Europe • 500 kW
ITALY
†RAI-RTV ITALIANA, Rome — Su • Europe • 100 kW
KUWAIT
†RADIO KUWAIT, Kabd — Europe & E North Am • 500 kW
RUSSIA
MAYAK, Armavir — W • W Asia • DS • 240 kW
9860   AUSTRALIA
†RADIO AUSTRALIA, Shepparton — Pacific & N America • 100 kW / Pacific & W North Am • 100 kW
GERMANY
†DEUTSCHE WELLE, Via Armavir, Russia — Mideast • 500 kW
HOLLAND
†R NEDERLAND, Flevoland — W Sa • Europe • 500 kW / S • Mideast • 500 kW / W • W Africa • 500 kW / S • E Africa • 500 kW

R NEDERLAND, Various Locations — S Asia • 200/250 kW
†R NEDERLAND, Via Madagascar — W • E Africa • 200 kW / S • SE Asia • 200 kW
R NEDERLAND, Via Tajikistan — S • S Asia • 250 kW
RUSSIA
†GOLOS ROSSII, Vladivostok — W • E Asia & SE Asia • 100 kW
UNITED KINGDOM
†BBC, Via Tashkent, Uzbekistan — S • S Asia • 200 kW
9865   GERMANY
†DEUTSCHE WELLE, Via V'vostok, Russia — W • E Asia • 200 kW
RUSSIA
R ALPHA & OMEGA, Yekaterinburg — S • DS • 200 kW
RADIO RADONEZH, Yekaterinburg — S • DS • 200 kW / W • W Africa • 250 kW
†VOICE OF RUSSIA, St Petersburg — W • N Africa & W Africa • 250 kW

†VOICE OF RUSSIA, Yekaterinburg — S • Europe • 240 kW
SEYCHELLES
FEBA RADIO, North Pt, Mahé Is — Th-M • E Africa • 100 kW / E Africa • 100 kW

SWEDEN
†RADIO SWEDEN, Hörby — W • W Asia & C Asia • 500 kW
USA
†VOA, Via Rhodes, Greece — S • Mideast • 50 kW
9870   AUSTRIA
†R AUSTRIA INTL, Vienna — S America • 300 kW / C America • 300 kW

GERMANY
†DEUTSCHE WELLE, Via Sines, Portugal — W • E Europe • 250 kW
GUAM
†KTWR-TRANS WORLD RADIO, Merizo — E Asia • 100 kW
KOREA (REPUBLIC)
(con'd)   RADIO KOREA INTL, In-Kimjae — Mideast & Africa • 250 kW

0 1 2 3 4 5 6 7 8 9 10 11 12 13 14 15 16 17 18 19 20 21 22 23 24

SEASONAL S OR W   1-HR TIMESHIFT MIDYEAR ⊏ OR ⊐   JAMMING / OR /\   EARLIEST HEARD ◁   LATEST HEARD ▷   NEW FOR 1997 †

FREQUENCY　　COUNTRY, STATION, LOCATION　　　　　　TARGET • NETWORK • POWER (kW)　　　World Time

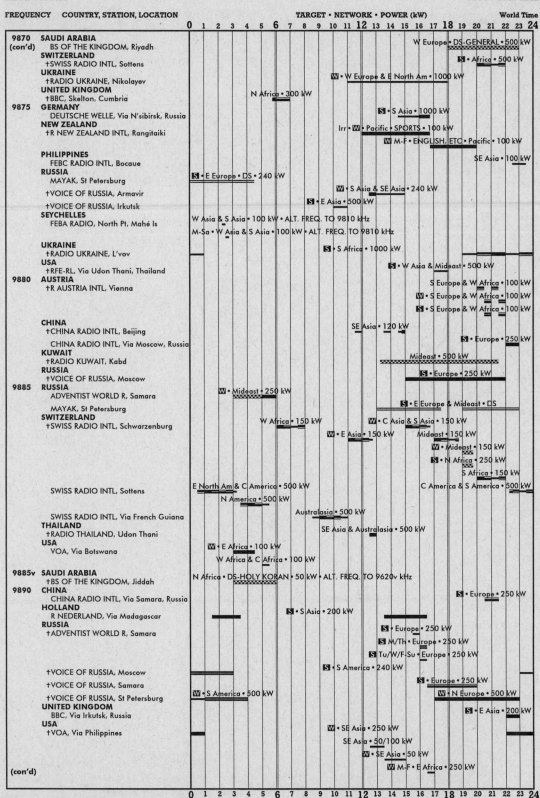

9870 SAUDI ARABIA
(con'd)　　BS OF THE KINGDOM, Riyadh　　　　　　　　　W Europe • DS-GENERAL • 500 kW
　　　SWITZERLAND
　　　†SWISS RADIO INTL, Sottens　　　　　　　　　　　S • Africa • 500 kW
　　　UKRAINE
　　　†RADIO UKRAINE, Nikolayev　　　　　　W • W Europe & E North Am • 1000 kW
　　　UNITED KINGDOM
　　　†BBC, Skelton, Cumbria　　　　　　N Africa • 300 kW
9875 GERMANY
　　　DEUTSCHE WELLE, Via N'sibirsk, Russia　　　S • S Asia • 1000 kW
　　　NEW ZEALAND
　　　†R NEW ZEALAND INTL, Rangitaiki　　　Irr • W • Pacific • SPORTS • 100 kW
　　　　　　　　　　　　　　　　　　W M-F • ENGLISH, ETC • Pacific • 100 kW
　　　PHILIPPINES
　　　FEBC RADIO INTL, Bocaue　　　　　　　　　　　SE Asia • 100 kW
　　　RUSSIA
　　　MAYAK, St Petersburg　　　S • E Europe • DS • 240 kW
　　　†VOICE OF RUSSIA, Armavir　　　　　W • S Asia & SE Asia • 240 kW
　　　†VOICE OF RUSSIA, Irkutsk　　　　S • E Asia • 500 kW
　　　SEYCHELLES
　　　FEBA RADIO, North Pt, Mahé Is　　W Asia & S Asia • 100 kW • ALT. FREQ. TO 9810 kHz
　　　　　　　　　M-Sa • W Asia & S Asia • 100 kW • ALT. FREQ. TO 9810 kHz
　　　UKRAINE
　　　†RADIO UKRAINE, L'vov　　　　S • S Africa • 1000 kW
　　　USA
　　　†RFE-RL, Via Udon Thani, Thailand　　　S • W Asia & Mideast • 500 kW
9880 AUSTRIA
　　　†R AUSTRIA INTL, Vienna　　　　　　S Europe & W Africa • 100 kW
　　　　　　　　　　　　　　　W • S Europe & W Africa • 100 kW
　　　　　　　　　　　　　　　S • S Europe & W Africa • 100 kW
　　　CHINA
　　　†CHINA RADIO INTL, Beijing　　　SE Asia • 120 kW
　　　CHINA RADIO INTL, Via Moscow, Russia　　　S • Europe • 250 kW
　　　KUWAIT
　　　†RADIO KUWAIT, Kabd　　　　　　Mideast • 500 kW
　　　RUSSIA
　　　†VOICE OF RUSSIA, Moscow　　　　S • Europe • 250 kW
9885 RUSSIA
　　　ADVENTIST WORLD R, Samara　　W • Mideast • 250 kW
　　　MAYAK, St Petersburg　　　　　　S • E Europe & Mideast • DS
　　　SWITZERLAND
　　　†SWISS RADIO INTL, Schwarzenburg　　W Africa • 150 kW　　W • C Asia & S Asia • 150 kW
　　　　　　　　　　　　　　W • E Asia • 150 kW　　Mideast • 150 kW
　　　　　　　　　　　　　　　　　　W • Mideast • 150 kW
　　　　　　　　　　　　　　　　　S • N Africa • 250 kW
　　　　　　　　　　　　　　　　　　S Africa • 150 kW
　　　SWISS RADIO INTL, Sottens　　E North Am & C America • 500 kW　　C America & S America • 500 kW
　　　　　　　　　　　　N America • 500 kW
　　　SWISS RADIO INTL, Via French Guiana　　Australasia • 500 kW
　　　THAILAND
　　　†RADIO THAILAND, Udon Thani　　SE Asia & Australasia • 500 kW
　　　USA
　　　VOA, Via Botswana　　　W • E Africa • 100 kW
　　　　　　　　　　　W Africa & C Africa • 100 kW
9885v SAUDI ARABIA
　　　†BS OF THE KINGDOM, Jiddah　　N Africa • DS-HOLY KORAN • 50 kW • ALT. FREQ. TO 9620v kHz
9890 CHINA
　　　CHINA RADIO INTL, Via Samara, Russia　　　S • Europe • 250 kW
　　　HOLLAND
　　　R NEDERLAND, Via Madagascar　　　S • S Asia • 200 kW
　　　RUSSIA
　　　†ADVENTIST WORLD R, Samara　　　S • Europe • 250 kW
　　　　　　　　　　　　　　　S M/Th • Europe • 250 kW
　　　　　　　　　　　　　　S Tu/W/F-Su • Europe • 250 kW
　　　†VOICE OF RUSSIA, Moscow　　　S • S America • 240 kW
　　　†VOICE OF RUSSIA, Samara　　　　S • Europe • 250 kW
　　　†VOICE OF RUSSIA, St Petersburg　　W • S America • 500 kW　　W • N Europe • 500 kW
　　　UNITED KINGDOM
　　　BBC, Via Irkutsk, Russia　　　　　S • E Asia • 200 kW
　　　USA
　　　†VOA, Via Philippines　　　W • SE Asia • 250 kW
　　　　　　　　　　　　SE Asia • 50/100 kW
　　　　　　　　　　　W • SE Asia • 50 kW
　　　　　　　　　　　W M-F • E Africa • 250 kW
(con'd)

ENGLISH ▬　　ARABIC ∽∽∽　　CHINESE □□□　　FRENCH ▬▬　　GERMAN ▬▬　　RUSSIAN ══　　SPANISH ▬▬　　OTHER ▬▬

FREQUENCY   COUNTRY, STATION, LOCATION

TARGET • NETWORK • POWER (kW)

World Time

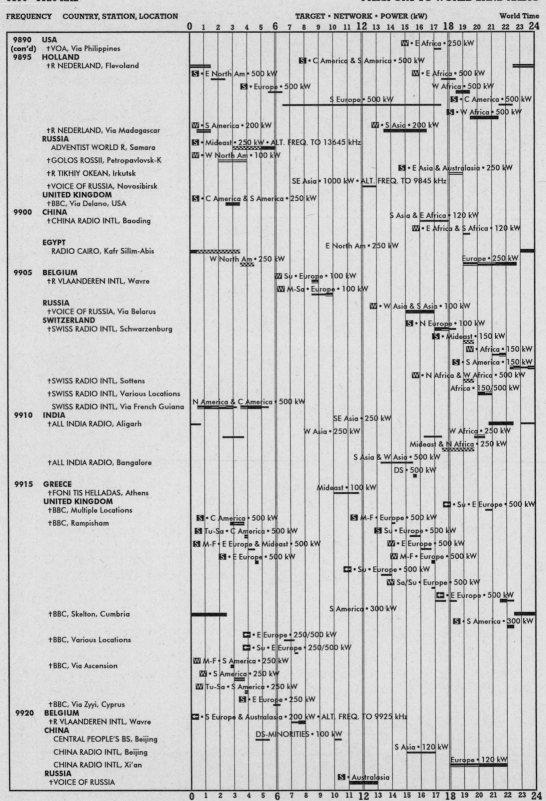

9890	**USA**
(con'd)	†VOA, Via Philippines — W • E Africa • 250 kW
9895	**HOLLAND**
	†R NEDERLAND, Flevoland — S • C America & S America • 500 kW
	S • E North Am • 500 kW
	S • Europe • 500 kW
	S Europe • 500 kW
	W • E Africa • 500 kW
	W Africa • 500 kW
	S • C America • 500 kW
	S • W Africa • 500 kW
	†R NEDERLAND, Via Madagascar — W • S America • 200 kW / W • S Asia • 200 kW
	RUSSIA
	ADVENTIST WORLD R, Samara — S • Mideast • 250 kW • ALT. FREQ. TO 13645 kHz
	†GOLOS ROSSII, Petropavlovsk-K — W • W North Am • 100 kW
	†R TIKHIY OKEAN, Irkutsk — S • E Asia & Australasia • 250 kW
	†VOICE OF RUSSIA, Novosibirsk — SE Asia • 1000 kW • ALT. FREQ. TO 9845 kHz
	UNITED KINGDOM
	†BBC, Via Delano, USA — S • C America & S America • 250 kW
9900	**CHINA**
	†CHINA RADIO INTL, Baoding — S Asia & E Africa • 120 kW
	W • E Africa & S Africa • 120 kW
	EGYPT
	RADIO CAIRO, Kafr Silim-Abis — E North Am • 250 kW
	W North Am • 250 kW
	Europe • 250 kW
9905	**BELGIUM**
	†R VLAANDEREN INTL, Wavre — W Su • Europe • 100 kW
	W M-Sa • Europe • 100 kW
	RUSSIA
	†VOICE OF RUSSIA, Via Belarus — W • W Asia & S Asia • 100 kW
	SWITZERLAND
	†SWISS RADIO INTL, Schwarzenburg — S • N Europe • 100 kW
	S • Mideast • 150 kW
	W • Africa • 150 kW
	S • S America • 150 kW
	†SWISS RADIO INTL, Sottens — W • N Africa & W Africa • 500 kW
	†SWISS RADIO INTL, Various Locations — Africa • 150/500 kW
	SWISS RADIO INTL, Via French Guiana — N America & C America • 500 kW
9910	**INDIA**
	†ALL INDIA RADIO, Aligarh — SE Asia • 250 kW
	W Asia • 250 kW
	W Africa • 250 kW
	Mideast & N Africa • 250 kW
	†ALL INDIA RADIO, Bangalore — S Asia & W Asia • 500 kW
	DS • 500 kW
9915	**GREECE**
	†FONI TIS HELLADAS, Athens — Mideast • 100 kW
	UNITED KINGDOM
	†BBC, Multiple Locations — ⟐ • Su • E Europe • 500 kW
	†BBC, Rampisham — S • C America • 500 kW
	S • M-F • Europe • 500 kW
	S Tu-Sa • C America • 500 kW
	S • Su • Europe • 500 kW
	S M-F • E Europe & Mideast • 500 kW
	W • E Europe • 500 kW
	S • E Europe • 500 kW
	W M-F • Europe • 500 kW
	⟐ • Su • Europe • 500 kW
	W Sa/Su • Europe • 500 kW
	⟐ • E Europe • 500 kW
	†BBC, Skelton, Cumbria — S America • 300 kW
	S • S America • 300 kW
	†BBC, Various Locations — ⟐ • E Europe • 250/500 kW
	⟐ • Su • E Europe • 250/500 kW
	†BBC, Via Ascension — W M-F • S America • 250 kW
	W • S America • 250 kW
	W Tu-Sa • S America • 250 kW
	†BBC, Via Zyyi, Cyprus — S • E Europe • 250 kW
9920	**BELGIUM**
	†R VLAANDEREN INTL, Wavre — ⟐ • S Europe & Australasia • 200 kW • ALT. FREQ. TO 9925 kHz
	CHINA
	CENTRAL PEOPLE'S BS, Beijing — DS-MINORITIES • 100 kW
	CHINA RADIO INTL, Beijing — S Asia • 120 kW
	CHINA RADIO INTL, Xi'an — Europe • 120 kW
	RUSSIA
	†VOICE OF RUSSIA — S • Australasia

SEASONAL S OR W   1-HR TIMESHIFT MIDYEAR ⟐ OR ⟐   JAMMING / OR ∧   EARLIEST HEARD ◁   LATEST HEARD ▷   NEW FOR 1997 †

FREQUENCY   COUNTRY, STATION, LOCATION

TARGET • NETWORK • POWER (kW)

World Time

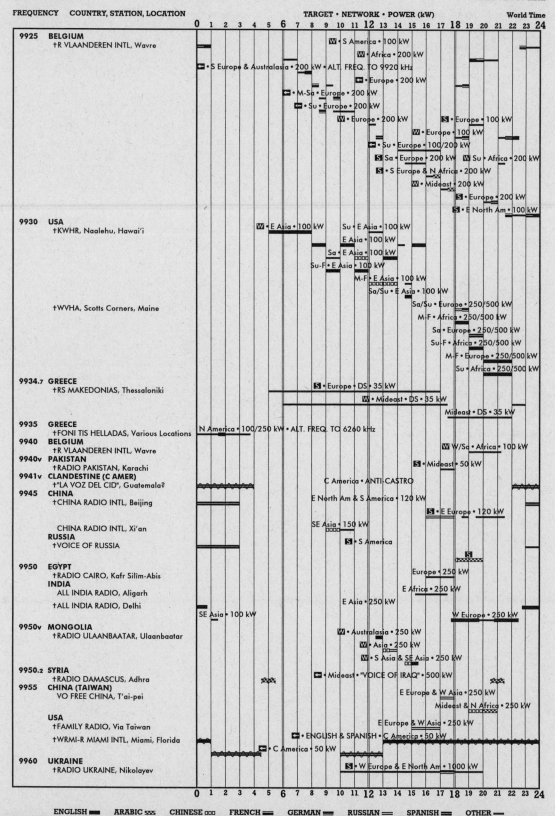

9925	**BELGIUM**
	†R VLAANDEREN INTL, Wavre
9930	**USA**
	†KWHR, Naalehu, Hawai'i
	†WVHA, Scotts Corners, Maine
9934.7	**GREECE**
	†RS MAKEDONIAS, Thessaloniki
9935	**GREECE**
	†FONI TIS HELLADAS, Various Locations
9940	**BELGIUM**
	†R VLAANDEREN INTL, Wavre
9940v	**PAKISTAN**
	†RADIO PAKISTAN, Karachi
9941v	**CLANDESTINE (C AMER)**
	†"LA VOZ DEL CID", Guatemala?
9945	**CHINA**
	†CHINA RADIO INTL, Beijing
	CHINA RADIO INTL, Xi'an
	RUSSIA
	†VOICE OF RUSSIA
9950	**EGYPT**
	†RADIO CAIRO, Kafr Silim-Abis
	INDIA
	ALL INDIA RADIO, Aligarh
	†ALL INDIA RADIO, Delhi
9950v	**MONGOLIA**
	†RADIO ULAANBAATAR, Ulaanbaatar
9950.2	**SYRIA**
	†RADIO DAMASCUS, Adhra
9955	**CHINA (TAIWAN)**
	VO FREE CHINA, T'ai-pei
	USA
	†FAMILY RADIO, Via Taiwan
	†WRMI-R MIAMI INTL, Miami, Florida
9960	**UKRAINE**
	†RADIO UKRAINE, Nikolayev

Chart annotations (by frequency):

9925 BELGIUM †R VLAANDEREN INTL, Wavre: W • S America • 100 kW; W • Africa • 200 kW; • S Europe & Australasia • 200 kW • ALT. FREQ. TO 9920 kHz; • Europe • 200 kW; • M-Sa • Europe • 200 kW; • Su • Europe • 200 kW; W • Europe • 200 kW; S • Europe • 100 kW; W • Europe • 100 kW; • Su • Europe • 100/200 kW; S • Sa • Europe • 200 kW; W • Su • Africa • 200 kW; S • S Europe & N Africa • 200 kW; W • Mideast • 200 kW; • Europe • 200 kW; S • E North Am • 100 kW

9930 USA †KWHR, Naalehu, Hawai'i: W • E Asia • 100 kW; Su • E Asia • 100 kW; E Asia • 100 kW; Sa • E Asia • 100 kW; Su-F • E Asia • 100 kW; M-F • E Asia • 100 kW; Sa/Su • E Asia • 100 kW

†WVHA, Scotts Corners, Maine: Sa/Su • Europe • 250/500 kW; M-F • Africa • 250/500 kW; Sa • Europe • 250/500 kW; Su-F • Africa • 250/500 kW; M-F • Europe • 250/500 kW; Su • Africa • 250/500 kW

9934.7 GREECE †RS MAKEDONIAS, Thessaloniki: S • Europe • DS • 35 kW; W • Mideast • DS • 35 kW; Mideast • DS • 35 kW

9935 GREECE †FONI TIS HELLADAS: N America • 100/250 kW • ALT. FREQ. TO 6260 kHz

9940 BELGIUM †R VLAANDEREN INTL, Wavre: W • W/Sa • Africa • 100 kW

9940v PAKISTAN †RADIO PAKISTAN, Karachi: S • Mideast • 50 kW

9941v CLANDESTINE (C AMER): C America • ANTI-CASTRO

9945 CHINA †CHINA RADIO INTL, Beijing: E North Am & S America • 120 kW; S • E Europe • 120 kW

CHINA RADIO INTL, Xi'an: SE Asia • 150 kW

RUSSIA †VOICE OF RUSSIA: S • S America

9950 EGYPT †RADIO CAIRO, Kafr Silim-Abis: Europe • 250 kW

INDIA ALL INDIA RADIO, Aligarh: E Africa • 250 kW

†ALL INDIA RADIO, Delhi: E Asia • 250 kW; SE Asia • 100 kW; W Europe • 250 kW

9950v MONGOLIA †RADIO ULAANBAATAR: W • Australasia • 250 kW; W • Asia • 250 kW; W • S Asia & SE Asia • 250 kW

9950.2 SYRIA †RADIO DAMASCUS, Adhra: • Mideast • "VOICE OF IRAQ" • 500 kW

9955 CHINA (TAIWAN) VO FREE CHINA, T'ai-pei: E Europe & W Asia • 250 kW; Mideast & N Africa • 250 kW

USA †FAMILY RADIO, Via Taiwan: E Europe & W Asia • 250 kW

†WRMI-R MIAMI INTL, Miami, Florida: • ENGLISH & SPANISH • C America • 50 kW; • C America • 50 kW

9960 UKRAINE †RADIO UKRAINE, Nikolayev: S • W Europe & E North Am • 1000 kW

ENGLISH ▬▬   ARABIC ≋≋≋   CHINESE □□□   FRENCH ▭▭   GERMAN ▬   RUSSIAN ═══   SPANISH ▬   OTHER ──

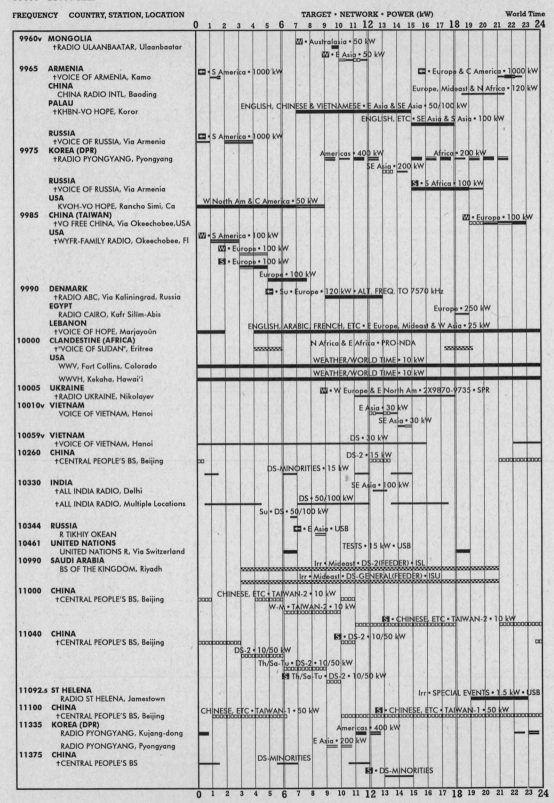

FREQUENCY   COUNTRY, STATION, LOCATION

TARGET • NETWORK • POWER (kW)

World Time

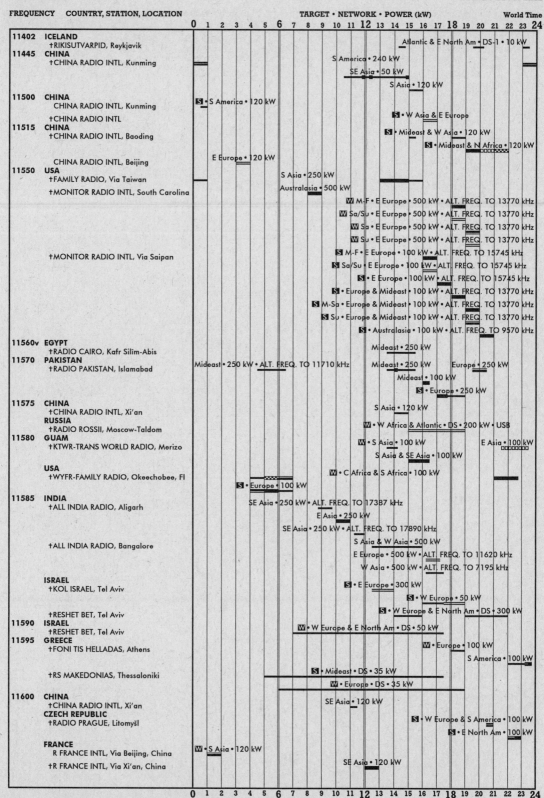

Frequency	Country, Station, Location	Details
11402	**ICELAND** †RIKISUTVARPID, Reykjavik	Atlantic & E North Am • DS-1 • 10 kW
11445	**CHINA** †CHINA RADIO INTL, Kunming	S America • 240 kW / SE Asia • 50 kW / S Asia • 120 kW
11500	**CHINA** CHINA RADIO INTL, Kunming	S • S America • 120 kW
	†CHINA RADIO INTL	S • W Asia & E Europe
11515	**CHINA** †CHINA RADIO INTL, Baoding	S • Mideast & W Asia • 120 kW / S • Mideast & N Africa • 120 kW
	CHINA RADIO INTL, Beijing	E Europe • 120 kW
11550	**USA** †FAMILY RADIO, Via Taiwan	S Asia • 250 kW
	†MONITOR RADIO INTL, South Carolina	Australasia • 500 kW
	†MONITOR RADIO INTL, Via Saipan	W • M-F • E Europe • 500 kW • ALT. FREQ. TO 13770 kHz / W • Sa/Su • E Europe • 500 kW • ALT. FREQ. TO 13770 kHz / W • Sa • E Europe • 500 kW • ALT. FREQ. TO 13770 kHz / W • Su • E Europe • 500 kW • ALT. FREQ. TO 13770 kHz / S • M-F • E Europe • 100 kW • ALT. FREQ. TO 15745 kHz / S • Sa/Su • E Europe • 100 kW • ALT. FREQ. TO 15745 kHz / S • E Europe • 100 kW • ALT. FREQ. TO 15745 kHz / S • Europe & Mideast • 100 kW • ALT. FREQ. TO 13770 kHz / S • M-Sa • Europe & Mideast • 100 kW • ALT. FREQ. TO 13770 kHz / S • Su • Europe & Mideast • 100 kW • ALT. FREQ. TO 13770 kHz / S • Australasia • 100 kW • ALT. FREQ. TO 9570 kHz
11560v	**EGYPT** †RADIO CAIRO, Kafr Silīm-Abis	Mideast • 250 kW
11570	**PAKISTAN** †RADIO PAKISTAN, Islamabad	Mideast • 250 kW • ALT. FREQ. TO 11710 kHz / Mideast • 250 kW / Europe • 250 kW / Mideast • 100 kW / S • Europe • 250 kW
11575	**CHINA** †CHINA RADIO INTL, Xi'an	S Asia • 120 kW
	RUSSIA †RADIO ROSSII, Moscow-Taldom	W • W Africa & Atlantic • DS • 200 kW • USB
11580	**GUAM** †KTWR-TRANS WORLD RADIO, Merizo	W • S Asia • 100 kW / E Asia • 100 kW / S Asia & SE Asia • 100 kW
	USA †WYFR-FAMILY RADIO, Okeechobee, Fl	W • C Africa & S Africa • 100 kW / S • Europe • 100 kW
11585	**INDIA** †ALL INDIA RADIO, Aligarh	SE Asia • 250 kW • ALT. FREQ. TO 17387 kHz / E Asia • 250 kW
	†ALL INDIA RADIO, Bangalore	SE Asia • 250 kW • ALT. FREQ. TO 17890 kHz / S Asia & W Asia • 500 kW / E Europe • 500 kW • ALT. FREQ. TO 11620 kHz / W Asia • 500 kW • ALT. FREQ. TO 7195 kHz
	ISRAEL †KOL ISRAEL, Tel Aviv	S • E Europe • 300 kW / S • W Europe • 50 kW
	†RESHET BET, Tel Aviv	S • W Europe & E North Am • DS • 300 kW
11590	**ISRAEL** †RESHET BET, Tel Aviv	W • W Europe & E North Am • DS • 50 kW
11595	**GREECE** †FONI TIS HELLADAS, Athens	W • Europe • 100 kW / S America • 100 kW
	†RS MAKEDONIAS, Thessaloniki	S • Mideast • DS • 35 kW / W • Europe • DS • 35 kW
11600	**CHINA** †CHINA RADIO INTL, Xi'an	SE Asia • 120 kW
	CZECH REPUBLIC †RADIO PRAGUE, Litomyšl	S • W Europe & S America • 100 kW / S • E North Am • 100 kW
	FRANCE R FRANCE INTL, Via Beijing, China	W • S Asia • 120 kW
	†R FRANCE INTL, Via Xi'an, China	SE Asia • 120 kW

ENGLISH ▬   ARABIC ≈≈≈   CHINESE □□□   FRENCH ═══   GERMAN ▬▬   RUSSIAN ══   SPANISH ▬▬▬   OTHER ───

FREQUENCY   COUNTRY, STATION, LOCATION   TARGET • NETWORK • POWER (kW)   World Time

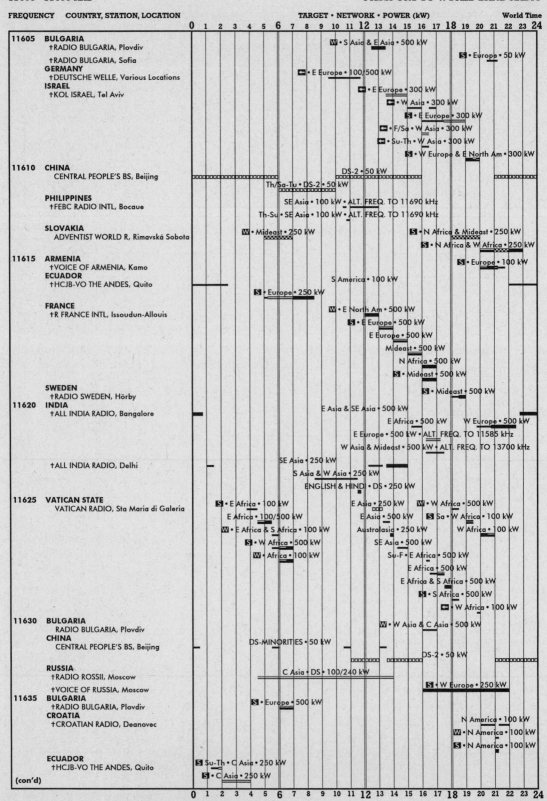

11605 **BULGARIA**
　　　†RADIO BULGARIA, Plovdiv — W • S Asia & E Asia • 500 kW
　　　†RADIO BULGARIA, Sofia — S • Europe • 50 kW
　　　GERMANY
　　　†DEUTSCHE WELLE, Various Locations — • E Europe • 100/500 kW
　　　ISRAEL
　　　†KOL ISRAEL, Tel Aviv — • E Europe • 300 kW
　　　　　• W Asia • 300 kW
　　　　　S • E Europe • 300 kW
　　　　　• F/Sa • W Asia • 300 kW
　　　　　• Su-Th • W Asia • 300 kW
　　　　　S • W Europe & E North Am • 300 kW

11610 **CHINA**
　　　CENTRAL PEOPLE'S BS, Beijing — DS-2 • 50 kW
　　　　　Th/Sa-Tu • DS-2 • 50 kW
　　　PHILIPPINES
　　　†FEBC RADIO INTL, Bocaue — SE Asia • 100 kW • ALT. FREQ. TO 11690 kHz
　　　　　Th-Su • SE Asia • 100 kW • ALT. FREQ. TO 11690 kHz
　　　SLOVAKIA
　　　ADVENTIST WORLD R, Rimavská Sobota — W • Mideast • 250 kW
　　　　　S • N Africa & Mideast • 250 kW
　　　　　S • N Africa & W Africa • 250 kW

11615 **ARMENIA**
　　　†VOICE OF ARMENIA, Kamo — S • Europe • 100 kW
　　　ECUADOR
　　　†HCJB-VO THE ANDES, Quito — S America • 100 kW
　　　FRANCE
　　　†R FRANCE INTL, Issoudun-Allouis — S • Europe • 250 kW
　　　　　W • E North Am • 500 kW
　　　　　S • E Europe • 500 kW
　　　　　E Europe • 500 kW
　　　　　Mideast • 500 kW
　　　　　N Africa • 500 kW
　　　　　S • Mideast • 500 kW
　　　　　S • Mideast • 500 kW
　　　SWEDEN
　　　†RADIO SWEDEN, Hörby
11620 **INDIA**
　　　†ALL INDIA RADIO, Bangalore — E Asia & SE Asia • 500 kW
　　　　　E Africa • 500 kW
　　　　　W Europe • 500 kW
　　　　　E Europe • 500 kW • ALT. FREQ. TO 11585 kHz
　　　　　W Asia & Mideast • 500 kW • ALT. FREQ. TO 13700 kHz
　　　†ALL INDIA RADIO, Delhi — SE Asia • 250 kW
　　　　　S Asia & W Asia • 250 kW
　　　　　ENGLISH & HINDI • DS • 250 kW

11625 **VATICAN STATE**
　　　VATICAN RADIO, Sta Maria di Galeria — S • E Africa • 100 kW
　　　　　E Asia • 250 kW
　　　　　W • W Africa • 500 kW
　　　　　E Africa • 100/500 kW
　　　　　E Asia • 500 kW
　　　　　S • Sa • W Africa • 100 kW
　　　　　W • E Africa & S Africa • 100 kW
　　　　　Australasia • 250 kW
　　　　　W Africa • 100 kW
　　　　　S • W Africa • 500 kW
　　　　　SE Asia • 500 kW
　　　　　W • Africa • 100 kW
　　　　　Su-F • E Africa • 500 kW
　　　　　E Africa • 500 kW
　　　　　E Africa & S Africa • 500 kW
　　　　　S • S Africa • 500 kW
　　　　　• W Africa • 100 kW

11630 **BULGARIA**
　　　RADIO BULGARIA, Plovdiv — W • W Asia & C Asia • 500 kW
　　　CHINA
　　　CENTRAL PEOPLE'S BS, Beijing — DS-MINORITIES • 50 kW
　　　　　DS-2 • 50 kW
　　　RUSSIA
　　　†RADIO ROSSII, Moscow — C Asia • DS • 100/240 kW
　　　†VOICE OF RUSSIA, Moscow — S • W Europe • 250 kW
11635 **BULGARIA**
　　　†RADIO BULGARIA, Plovdiv — S • Europe • 500 kW
　　　CROATIA
　　　†CROATIAN RADIO, Deanovec — N America • 100 kW
　　　　　W • N America • 100 kW
　　　　　S • N America • 100 kW
　　　ECUADOR
　　　†HCJB-VO THE ANDES, Quito — S Su-Th • C Asia • 250 kW
　　　　　S • C Asia • 250 kW

(con'd)

FREQUENCY   COUNTRY, STATION, LOCATION   TARGET • NETWORK • POWER (kW)   World Time

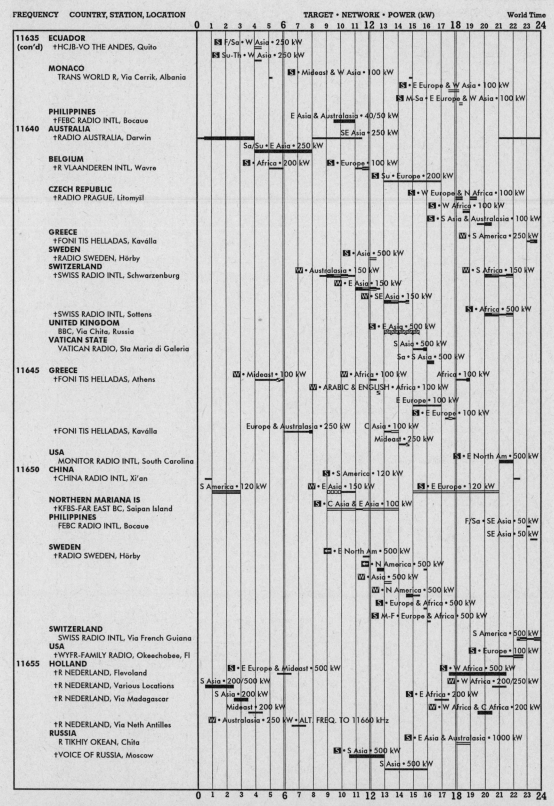

Frequency	Country, Station, Location	Schedule
11635 (con'd)	**ECUADOR** †HCJB-VO THE ANDES, Quito	S F/Sa • W Asia • 250 kW; S Su-Th • W Asia • 250 kW
	MONACO TRANS WORLD R, Via Cerrik, Albania	S • Mideast & W Asia • 100 kW; S • E Europe & W Asia • 100 kW; S M-Sa • E Europe & W Asia • 100 kW
	PHILIPPINES †FEBC RADIO INTL, Bocaue	E Asia & Australasia • 40/50 kW
11640	**AUSTRALIA** †RADIO AUSTRALIA, Darwin	SE Asia • 250 kW; Sa/Su • E Asia • 250 kW
	BELGIUM †R VLAANDEREN INTL, Wavre	S • Africa • 200 kW; S • Europe • 100 kW; S Su • Europe • 200 kW
	CZECH REPUBLIC †RADIO PRAGUE, Litomyšl	S • W Europe & N Africa • 100 kW; S • W Africa • 100 kW; S • S Asia & Australasia • 100 kW
	GREECE †FONI TIS HELLADAS, Kaválla	W • S America • 250 kW
	SWEDEN †RADIO SWEDEN, Hörby	S • Asia • 500 kW
	SWITZERLAND †SWISS RADIO INTL, Schwarzenburg	W • Australasia • 150 kW; W • E Asia • 150 kW; W • SE Asia • 150 kW; W • S Africa • 150 kW
	†SWISS RADIO INTL, Sottens	S • Africa • 500 kW
	UNITED KINGDOM BBC, Via Chita, Russia	S • E Asia • 500 kW
	VATICAN STATE VATICAN RADIO, Sta Maria di Galeria	S Asia • 500 kW; Sa • S Asia • 500 kW
11645	**GREECE** †FONI TIS HELLADAS, Athens	W • Mideast • 100 kW; W • Africa • 100 kW; W • ARABIC & ENGLISH • Africa • 100 kW; Africa • 100 kW; E Europe • 100 kW; S • E Europe • 100 kW
	†FONI TIS HELLADAS, Kaválla	Europe & Australasia • 250 kW; C Asia • 100 kW; Mideast • 250 kW
	USA MONITOR RADIO INTL, South Carolina	S • E North Am • 500 kW
11650	**CHINA** †CHINA RADIO INTL, Xi'an	S • S America • 120 kW; S America • 120 kW; W • E Asia • 150 kW; S • E Europe • 120 kW
	NORTHERN MARIANA IS †KFBS-FAR EAST BC, Saipan Island	S • C Asia & E Asia • 100 kW
	PHILIPPINES FEBC RADIO INTL, Bocaue	F/Sa • SE Asia • 50 kW; SE Asia • 50 kW
	SWEDEN †RADIO SWEDEN, Hörby	• E North Am • 500 kW; • N America • 500 kW; W • Asia • 500 kW; W • N America • 500 kW; S • Europe & Africa • 500 kW; S M-F • Europe & Africa • 500 kW
	SWITZERLAND SWISS RADIO INTL, Via French Guiana	S America • 500 kW
	USA †WYFR-FAMILY RADIO, Okeechobee, Fl	S • Europe • 100 kW
11655	**HOLLAND** †R NEDERLAND, Flevoland	S • E Europe & Mideast • 500 kW; S • W Africa • 500 kW
	†R NEDERLAND, Various Locations	S Asia • 200/500 kW; W • W Africa • 200/250 kW
	†R NEDERLAND, Via Madagascar	S Asia • 200 kW; S • E Africa • 200 kW; Mideast • 200 kW; W • W Africa & C Africa • 200 kW
	†R NEDERLAND, Via Neth Antilles	W • Australasia • 250 kW • ALT. FREQ. TO 11660 kHz
	RUSSIA R TIKHIY OKEAN, Chita	S • E Asia & Australasia • 1000 kW
	†VOICE OF RUSSIA, Moscow	S • S Asia • 500 kW; S Asia • 500 kW

ENGLISH ▬▬   ARABIC ≈≈≈   CHINESE □□□   FRENCH ▬▬   GERMAN ▬▬   RUSSIAN ▬▬   SPANISH ▬▬   OTHER ▬▬

FREQUENCY   COUNTRY, STATION, LOCATION   TARGET • NETWORK • POWER (kW)   World Time

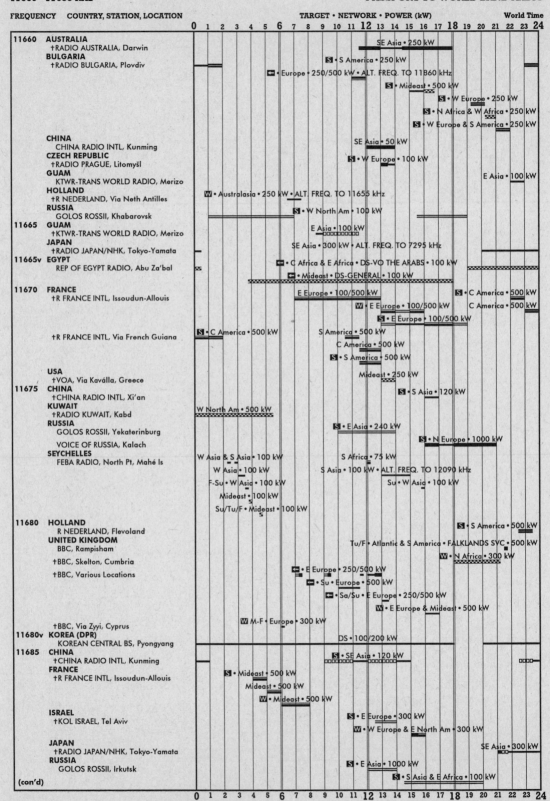

FREQUENCY	COUNTRY, STATION, LOCATION	TARGET • NETWORK • POWER (kW) / World Time

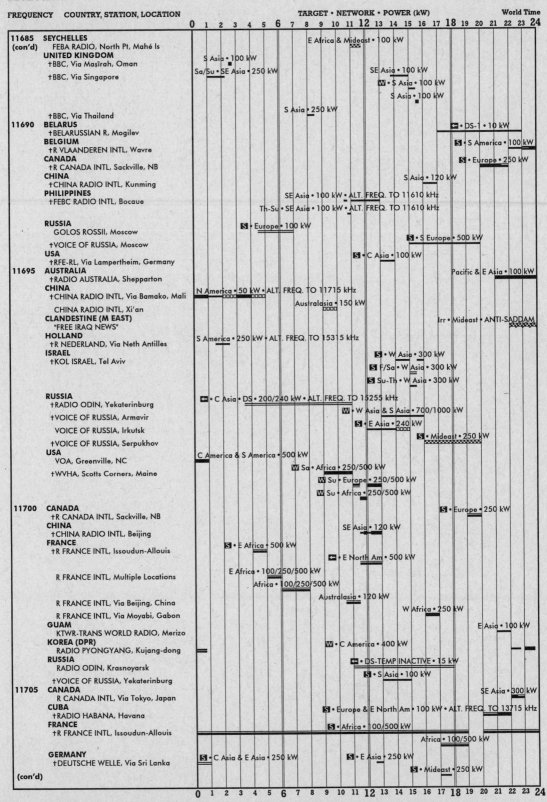

11685 (con'd) **SEYCHELLES**
  FEBA RADIO, North Pt, Mahé Is — E Africa & Mideast • 100 kW
UNITED KINGDOM
  †BBC, Via Maşīrah, Oman — S Asia • 100 kW / Sa/Su • SE Asia • 250 kW
  †BBC, Via Singapore — SE Asia • 100 kW / W • S Asia • 100 kW / S Asia • 100 kW
  †BBC, Via Thailand — S Asia • 250 kW

11690 **BELARUS**
  †BELARUSSIAN R, Mogilev — DS-1 • 10 kW
BELGIUM
  †R VLAANDEREN INTL, Wavre — S • S America • 100 kW
CANADA
  †R CANADA INTL, Sackville, NB — S • Europe • 250 kW
CHINA
  †CHINA RADIO INTL, Kunming — S Asia • 120 kW
PHILIPPINES
  †FEBC RADIO INTL, Bocaue — SE Asia • 100 kW • ALT. FREQ. TO 11610 kHz / Th-Su • SE Asia • 100 kW • ALT. FREQ. TO 11610 kHz
RUSSIA
  GOLOS ROSSII, Moscow — S • Europe • 100 kW
  †VOICE OF RUSSIA, Moscow — S • S Europe • 500 kW
USA
  †RFE-RL, Via Lampertheim, Germany — S • C Asia • 100 kW

11695 **AUSTRALIA**
  †RADIO AUSTRALIA, Shepparton — Pacific & E Asia • 100 kW
CHINA
  †CHINA RADIO INTL, Via Bamako, Mali — N America • 50 kW • ALT. FREQ. TO 11715 kHz
  CHINA RADIO INTL, Xi'an — Australasia • 150 kW
CLANDESTINE (M EAST)
  "FREE IRAQ NEWS" — Irr • Mideast • ANTI-SADDAM
HOLLAND
  †R NEDERLAND, Via Neth Antilles — S America • 250 kW • ALT. FREQ. TO 15315 kHz
ISRAEL
  †KOL ISRAEL, Tel Aviv — S • W Asia • 300 kW / S F/Sa • W Asia • 300 kW / S Su-Th • W Asia • 300 kW
RUSSIA
  †RADIO ODIN, Yekaterinburg — C Asia • DS 200/240 kW • ALT. FREQ. TO 15255 kHz
  †VOICE OF RUSSIA, Armavir — W • W Asia & S Asia • 700/1000 kW
  VOICE OF RUSSIA, Irkutsk — S • E Asia • 240 kW
  †VOICE OF RUSSIA, Serpukhov — S • Mideast • 250 kW
USA
  VOA, Greenville, NC — C America & S America • 500 kW
  †WVHA, Scotts Corners, Maine — W Sa • Africa • 250/500 kW / W Su • Europe • 250/500 kW / W Su • Africa • 250/500 kW

11700 **CANADA**
  †R CANADA INTL, Sackville, NB — S • Europe • 250 kW
CHINA
  †CHINA RADIO INTL, Beijing — SE Asia • 120 kW
FRANCE
  †R FRANCE INTL, Issoudun-Allouis — S • E Africa • 500 kW / E North Am • 500 kW
  R FRANCE INTL, Multiple Locations — E Africa • 100/250/500 kW / Africa • 100/250/500 kW
  R FRANCE INTL, Via Beijing, China — Australasia • 120 kW
  R FRANCE INTL, Via Moyabi, Gabon — W Africa • 250 kW
GUAM
  KTWR-TRANS WORLD RADIO, Merizo — E Asia • 100 kW
KOREA (DPR)
  RADIO PYONGYANG, Kujang-dong — W • C America • 400 kW
RUSSIA
  RADIO ODIN, Krasnoyarsk — DS-TEMP INACTIVE • 15 kW
  †VOICE OF RUSSIA, Yekaterinburg — S • S Asia • 100 kW

11705 **CANADA**
  R CANADA INTL, Via Tokyo, Japan — SE Asia • 300 kW
CUBA
  †RADIO HABANA, Havana — S • Europe & E North Am • 100 kW • ALT. FREQ. TO 13715 kHz
FRANCE
  †R FRANCE INTL, Issoudun-Allouis — S • Africa • 100/500 kW / Africa • 100/500 kW
GERMANY
  †DEUTSCHE WELLE, Via Sri Lanka — S • C Asia & E Asia • 250 kW / S • E Asia • 250 kW / S • Mideast • 250 kW

(con'd)

FREQUENCY   COUNTRY, STATION, LOCATION   TARGET • NETWORK • POWER (kW)   World Time

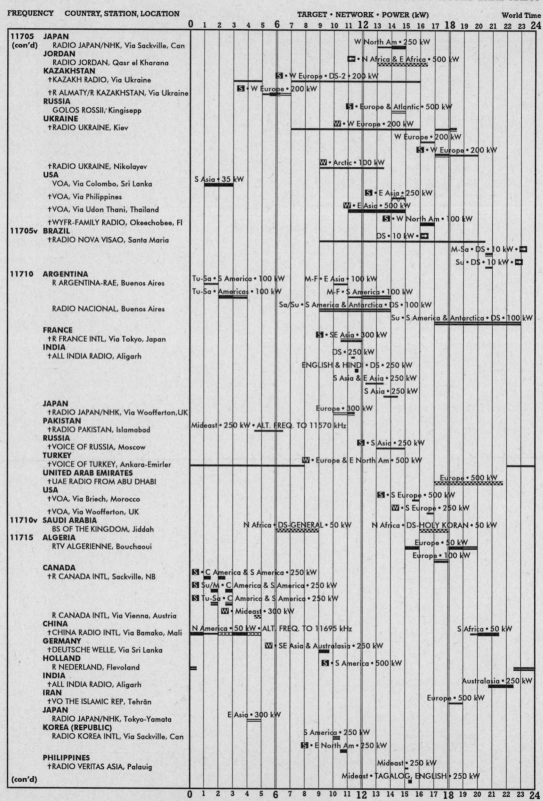

11705 **JAPAN**		
(con'd) RADIO JAPAN/NHK, Via Sackville, Can		W North Am • 250 kW
JORDAN		
RADIO JORDAN, Qasr el Kharana		N Africa & E Africa • 500 kW
KAZAKHSTAN		
†KAZAKH RADIO, Via Ukraine	S • W Europe • DS-2 • 200 kW	
†R ALMATY/R KAZAKHSTAN, Via Ukraine	S • W Europe • 200 kW	
RUSSIA		
GOLOS ROSSII, Kingisepp		S • Europe & Atlantic • 500 kW
UKRAINE		
†RADIO UKRAINE, Kiev	W • W Europe • 200 kW	
		W Europe • 200 kW
		S • W Europe • 200 kW
†RADIO UKRAINE, Nikolayev	W • Arctic • 100 kW	
USA		
VOA, Via Colombo, Sri Lanka	S Asia • 35 kW	
†VOA, Via Philippines		S • E Asia • 250 kW
†VOA, Via Udon Thani, Thailand		W • E Asia • 500 kW
†WYFR-FAMILY RADIO, Okeechobee, Fl		S • W North Am • 100 kW
11705v **BRAZIL**		
†RADIO NOVA VISAO, Santa Maria		DS • 10 kW • ➡
		M-Sa • DS • 10 kW • ➡
		Su • DS • 10 kW • ➡
11710 **ARGENTINA**		
R ARGENTINA-RAE, Buenos Aires	Tu-Sa • S America • 100 kW M-F • E Asia • 100 kW	
	Tu-Sa • Americas • 100 kW M-F • S America • 100 kW	
RADIO NACIONAL, Buenos Aires	Sa/Su • S America & Antarctica • DS • 100 kW	
		Su • S America & Antarctica • DS • 100 kW
FRANCE		
†R FRANCE INTL, Via Tokyo, Japan	S • SE Asia • 300 kW	
INDIA		
†ALL INDIA RADIO, Aligarh	DS • 250 kW	
	ENGLISH & HINDI • DS • 250 kW	
	S Asia & E Asia • 250 kW	
	S Asia • 250 kW	
JAPAN		
†RADIO JAPAN/NHK, Via Woofferton, UK	Europe • 300 kW	
PAKISTAN		
†RADIO PAKISTAN, Islamabad	Mideast • 250 kW • ALT. FREQ. TO 11570 kHz	
RUSSIA		
†VOICE OF RUSSIA, Moscow	S • S Asia • 250 kW	
TURKEY		
†VOICE OF TURKEY, Ankara-Emirler	W • Europe & E North Am • 500 kW	
UNITED ARAB EMIRATES		
†UAE RADIO FROM ABU DHABI		Europe • 500 kW
USA		
†VOA, Via Briech, Morocco		S • S Europe • 500 kW
†VOA, Via Woofferton, UK		W • S Europe • 250 kW
11710v **SAUDI ARABIA**		
BS OF THE KINGDOM, Jiddah	N Africa • DS-GENERAL • 50 kW N Africa • DS-HOLY KORAN • 50 kW	
11715 **ALGERIA**		
RTV ALGERIENNE, Bouchaoui		Europe • 50 kW
		Europe • 100 kW
CANADA		
†R CANADA INTL, Sackville, NB	S • C America & S America • 250 kW	
	S • Su/M • C America & S America • 250 kW	
	S • Tu-Sa • C America & S America • 250 kW	
R CANADA INTL, Via Vienna, Austria	W • Mideast • 300 kW	
CHINA		
†CHINA RADIO INTL, Via Bamako, Mali	N America • 50 kW • ALT. FREQ. TO 11695 kHz S Africa • 50 kW	
GERMANY		
†DEUTSCHE WELLE, Via Sri Lanka	W • SE Asia & Australasia • 250 kW	
HOLLAND		
R NEDERLAND, Flevoland	▭ S • S America • 500 kW	
INDIA		
†ALL INDIA RADIO, Aligarh		Australasia • 250 kW
IRAN		
†VO THE ISLAMIC REP, Tehrān		Europe • 500 kW
JAPAN		
RADIO JAPAN/NHK, Tokyo-Yamata	E Asia • 300 kW	
KOREA (REPUBLIC)		
RADIO KOREA INTL, Via Sackville, Can	S America • 250 kW	
	S • E North Am • 250 kW	
PHILIPPINES		
†RADIO VERITAS ASIA, Palauig	Mideast • 250 kW	
	Mideast • TAGALOG, ENGLISH • 250 kW	
(con'd)		

FREQUENCY   COUNTRY, STATION, LOCATION

TARGET • NETWORK • POWER (kW)   World Time

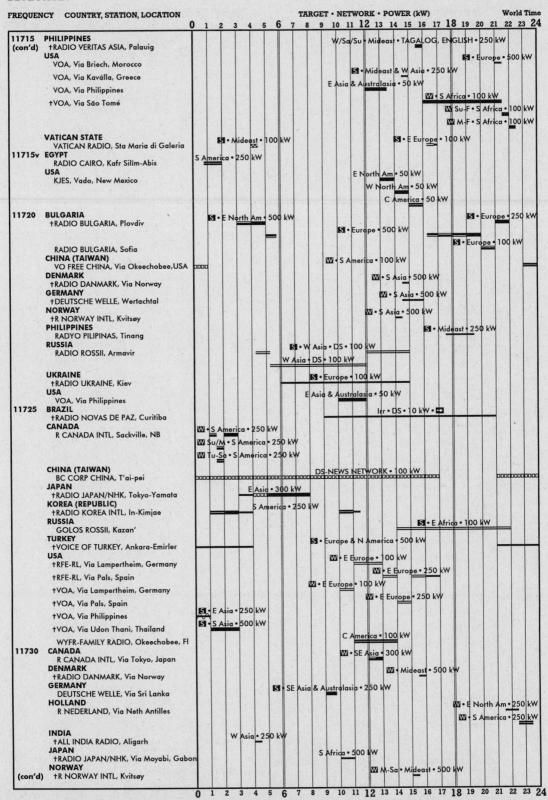

Frequency	Country, Station, Location	Details
11715 (con'd)	**PHILIPPINES** †RADIO VERITAS ASIA, Palauig	W/Sa/Su • Mideast • TAGALOG, ENGLISH • 250 kW
	USA VOA, Via Briech, Morocco	S • Europe • 500 kW
	VOA, Via Kaválla, Greece	S • Mideast & W Asia • 250 kW
	VOA, Via Philippines	E Asia & Australasia • 50 kW
	†VOA, Via São Tomé	W • S Africa • 100 kW / W Su-F • S Africa • 100 kW / W M-F • S Africa • 100 kW
	VATICAN STATE VATICAN RADIO, Sta Maria di Galeria	S • Mideast • 100 kW / S • E Europe • 100 kW
11715v	**EGYPT** RADIO CAIRO, Kafr Silim-Abis	S America • 250 kW
	USA KJES, Vado, New Mexico	E North Am • 50 kW / W North Am • 50 kW / C America • 50 kW
11720	**BULGARIA** †RADIO BULGARIA, Plovdiv	S • E North Am • 500 kW / S • Europe • 500 kW / S • Europe • 250 kW / S • Europe • 100 kW
	RADIO BULGARIA, Sofia	
	CHINA (TAIWAN) VO FREE CHINA, Via Okeechobee,USA	W • S America • 100 kW
	DENMARK †RADIO DANMARK, Via Norway	W • S Asia • 500 kW
	GERMANY †DEUTSCHE WELLE, Wertachtal	W • S Asia • 500 kW
	NORWAY †R NORWAY INTL, Kvitsøy	W • S Asia • 500 kW
	PHILIPPINES RADYO PILIPINAS, Tinang	S • Mideast • 250 kW
	RUSSIA RADIO ROSSII, Armavir	S • W Asia • DS • 100 kW / W Asia • DS • 100 kW
	UKRAINE †RADIO UKRAINE, Kiev	S • Europe • 100 kW
	USA VOA, Via Philippines	E Asia & Australasia • 50 kW
11725	**BRAZIL** †RADIO NOVAS DE PAZ, Curitiba	Irr • DS • 10 kW • ▭
	CANADA R CANADA INTL, Sackville, NB	W • S America • 250 kW / W Su/M • S America • 250 kW / W Tu-Sa • S America • 250 kW
	CHINA (TAIWAN) BC CORP CHINA, T'ai-pei	DS-NEWS NETWORK • 100 kW
	JAPAN †RADIO JAPAN/NHK, Tokyo-Yamata	E Asia • 300 kW
	KOREA (REPUBLIC) †RADIO KOREA INTL, In-Kimjae	S America • 250 kW
	RUSSIA GOLOS ROSSII, Kazan'	S • E Africa • 100 kW
	TURKEY †VOICE OF TURKEY, Ankara-Emirler	S • Europe & N America • 500 kW
	USA †RFE-RL, Via Lampertheim, Germany	W • E Europe • 100 kW
	†RFE-RL, Via Pals, Spain	W • E Europe • 250 kW
	†VOA, Via Lampertheim, Germany	W • E Europe • 100 kW
	†VOA, Via Pals, Spain	W • E Europe • 250 kW
	†VOA, Via Philippines	S • E Asia • 250 kW
	†VOA, Via Udon Thani, Thailand	S • S Asia • 500 kW
	WYFR-FAMILY RADIO, Okeechobee, Fl	C America • 100 kW
11730	**CANADA** R CANADA INTL, Via Tokyo, Japan	W • SE Asia • 300 kW
	DENMARK †RADIO DANMARK, Via Norway	W • Mideast • 500 kW
	GERMANY DEUTSCHE WELLE, Via Sri Lanka	S • SE Asia & Australasia • 250 kW
	HOLLAND R NEDERLAND, Via Neth Antilles	W • E North Am • 250 kW / W • S America • 250 kW
	INDIA †ALL INDIA RADIO, Aligarh	W Asia • 250 kW
	JAPAN †RADIO JAPAN/NHK, Via Moyabi, Gabon	S Africa • 500 kW
(con'd)	**NORWAY** †R NORWAY INTL, Kvitsøy	W M-Sa • Mideast • 500 kW

ENGLISH ▬ ARABIC ⠿ CHINESE ▯▯▯ FRENCH ═ GERMAN ▬ RUSSIAN ═ SPANISH ▬ OTHER ─

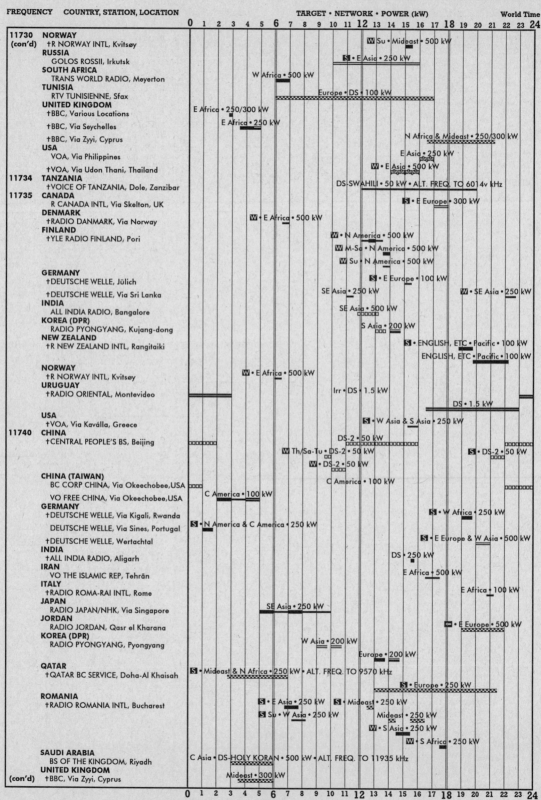

FREQUENCY   COUNTRY, STATION, LOCATION

TARGET • NETWORK • POWER (kW)   World Time

11730	NORWAY
(con'd)	†R NORWAY INTL, Kvitsøy	W • Su • Mideast • 500 kW
	RUSSIA	
	GOLOS ROSSII, Irkutsk	S • E Asia • 250 kW
	SOUTH AFRICA	
	TRANS WORLD RADIO, Meyerton	W Africa • 500 kW
	TUNISIA	
	RTV TUNISIENNE, Sfax	Europe • DS • 100 kW
	UNITED KINGDOM	
	†BBC, Various Locations	E Africa • 250/300 kW
	†BBC, Via Seychelles	E Africa • 250 kW
	†BBC, Via Zyyi, Cyprus	N Africa & Mideast • 250/300 kW
	USA	
	VOA, Via Philippines	E Asia • 250 kW
	†VOA, Via Udon Thani, Thailand	W • E Asia • 500 kW
11734	TANZANIA	
	†VOICE OF TANZANIA, Dole, Zanzibar	DS-SWAHILI • 50 kW • ALT. FREQ. TO 6014v kHz
11735	CANADA	
	R CANADA INTL, Via Skelton, UK	S • E Europe • 300 kW
	DENMARK	
	†RADIO DANMARK, Via Norway	W • E Africa • 500 kW
	FINLAND	
	†YLE RADIO FINLAND, Pori	W • N America • 500 kW
		W M-Sa • N America • 500 kW
		W Su • N America • 500 kW
	GERMANY	
	†DEUTSCHE WELLE, Jülich	S • E Europe • 100 kW
	†DEUTSCHE WELLE, Via Sri Lanka	SE Asia • 250 kW W • SE Asia • 250 kW
	INDIA	
	ALL INDIA RADIO, Bangalore	SE Asia • 500 kW
	KOREA (DPR)	
	RADIO PYONGYANG, Kujang-dong	S Asia • 200 kW
	NEW ZEALAND	
	†R NEW ZEALAND INTL, Rangitaiki	S • ENGLISH, ETC • Pacific • 100 kW
		ENGLISH, ETC • Pacific • 100 kW
	NORWAY	
	†R NORWAY INTL, Kvitsøy	W • E Africa • 500 kW
	URUGUAY	
	†RADIO ORIENTAL, Montevideo	Irr • DS • 1.5 kW DS • 1.5 kW
	USA	
	†VOA, Via Kaválla, Greece	S • W Asia & S Asia • 250 kW
11740	CHINA	
	†CENTRAL PEOPLE'S BS, Beijing	DS-2 • 50 kW
		W Th/Sa-Tu • DS-2 • 50 kW S • DS-2 • 50 kW
		W • DS-2 • 50 kW
	CHINA (TAIWAN)	
	BC CORP CHINA, Via Okeechobee, USA	C America • 100 kW
	VO FREE CHINA, Via Okeechobee, USA	C America • 100 kW
	GERMANY	
	†DEUTSCHE WELLE, Via Kigali, Rwanda	S • W Africa • 250 kW
	DEUTSCHE WELLE, Via Sines, Portugal	S • N America & C America • 250 kW
	†DEUTSCHE WELLE, Wertachtal	S • E Europe & W Asia • 500 kW
	INDIA	
	†ALL INDIA RADIO, Aligarh	DS • 250 kW
	IRAN	
	VO THE ISLAMIC REP, Tehrān	E Africa • 500 kW
	ITALY	
	†RADIO ROMA-RAI INTL, Rome	E Africa • 100 kW
	JAPAN	
	RADIO JAPAN/NHK, Via Singapore	SE Asia • 250 kW
	JORDAN	
	RADIO JORDAN, Qasr el Kharana	• E Europe • 500 kW
	KOREA (DPR)	
	RADIO PYONGYANG, Pyongyang	W Asia • 200 kW
		Europe • 200 kW
	QATAR	
	†QATAR BC SERVICE, Doha-Al Khaisah	S • Mideast & N Africa • 250 kW • ALT. FREQ. TO 9570 kHz
		S • Europe • 250 kW
	ROMANIA	
	†RADIO ROMANIA INTL, Bucharest	S • E Asia • 250 kW S • Mideast • 250 kW
		S Su • W Asia • 250 kW Mideast • 250 kW
		W • S Asia • 250 kW
		W • S Africa • 250 kW
	SAUDI ARABIA	
	BS OF THE KINGDOM, Riyadh	C Asia • DS-HOLY KORAN • 500 kW • ALT. FREQ. TO 11935 kHz
	UNITED KINGDOM	
(con'd)	†BBC, Via Zyyi, Cyprus	Mideast • 300 kW

FREQUENCY   COUNTRY, STATION, LOCATION

TARGET • NETWORK • POWER (kW)

World Time

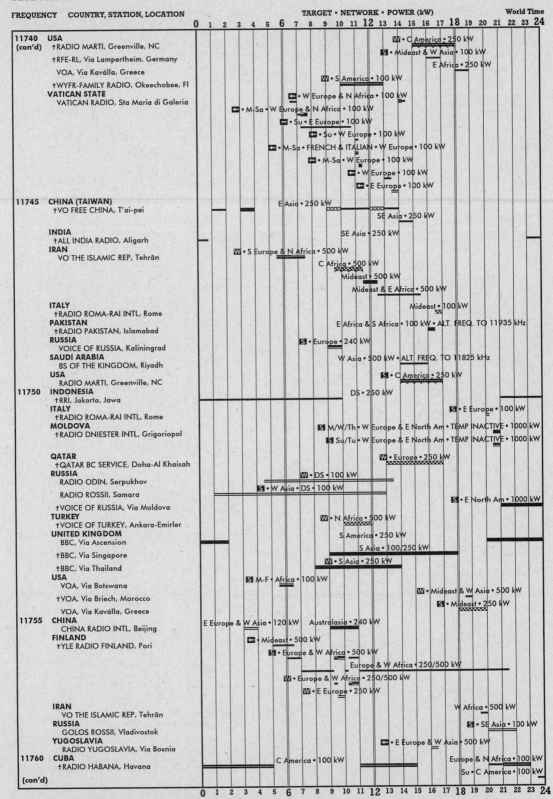

Frequency	Country, Station, Location	Target • Network • Power
11740 (con'd)	**USA**	
	†RADIO MARTI, Greenville, NC	W • C America • 250 kW
		S • Mideast & W Asia • 100 kW
	†RFE-RL, Via Lampertheim, Germany	E Africa • 250 kW
	VOA, Via Kaválla, Greece	
	†WYFR-FAMILY RADIO, Okeechobee, Fl	W • S America • 100 kW
	VATICAN STATE	
	VATICAN RADIO, Sta Maria di Galeria	W Europe & N Africa • 100 kW
		• M-Sa • W Europe & N Africa • 100 kW
		• Su • E Europe • 100 kW
		• Su • W Europe • 100 kW
		• M-Sa • FRENCH & ITALIAN • W Europe • 100 kW
		• M-Sa • W Europe • 100 kW
		• W Europe • 100 kW
		• E Europe • 100 kW
11745	**CHINA (TAIWAN)**	E Asia • 250 kW
	†VO FREE CHINA, T'ai-pei	SE Asia • 250 kW
	INDIA	
	†ALL INDIA RADIO, Aligarh	SE Asia • 250 kW
	IRAN	
	VO THE ISLAMIC REP, Tehrān	W • S Europe & N Africa • 500 kW
		C Africa • 500 kW
		Mideast • 500 kW
		Mideast & E Africa • 500 kW
	ITALY	
	†RADIO ROMA-RAI INTL, Rome	Mideast • 100 kW
	PAKISTAN	
	†RADIO PAKISTAN, Islamabad	E Africa & S Africa • 100 kW • ALT. FREQ. TO 11935 kHz
	RUSSIA	
	VOICE OF RUSSIA, Kaliningrad	S • Europe • 240 kW
	SAUDI ARABIA	
	BS OF THE KINGDOM, Riyadh	W Asia • 500 kW • ALT. FREQ. TO 11825 kHz
	USA	
	RADIO MARTI, Greenville, NC	S • C America • 250 kW
11750	**INDONESIA**	DS • 250 kW
	†RRI, Jakarta, Jawa	
	ITALY	
	†RADIO ROMA-RAI INTL, Rome	S • E Europe • 100 kW
	MOLDOVA	
	†RADIO DNIESTER INTL, Grigoriopol	S M/W/Th • W Europe & E North Am • TEMP INACTIVE • 1000 kW
		S Su/Tu • W Europe & E North Am • TEMP INACTIVE • 1000 kW
	QATAR	
	†QATAR BC SERVICE, Doha-Al Khaisah	W • Europe • 250 kW
	RUSSIA	
	RADIO ODIN, Serpukhov	W • DS • 100 kW
	RADIO ROSSII, Samara	S • W Asia • DS • 100 kW
	†VOICE OF RUSSIA, Via Moldova	S • E North Am • 1000 kW
	TURKEY	
	†VOICE OF TURKEY, Ankara-Emirler	W • N Africa • 500 kW
	UNITED KINGDOM	
	BBC, Via Ascension	S America • 250 kW
	†BBC, Via Singapore	S Asia • 100/250 kW
	†BBC, Via Thailand	W • S Asia • 250 kW
	USA	
	VOA, Via Botswana	S M-F • Africa • 100 kW
	†VOA, Via Briech, Morocco	W • Mideast & W Asia • 500 kW
	VOA, Via Kaválla, Greece	S • Mideast • 250 kW
11755	**CHINA**	E Europe & W Asia • 120 kW Australasia • 240 kW
	CHINA RADIO INTL, Beijing	
	FINLAND	
	†YLE RADIO FINLAND, Pori	• Mideast • 500 kW
		S • Europe & W Africa • 500 kW
		Europe & W Africa • 250/500 kW
		W • Europe & W Africa • 250/500 kW
		W • E Europe • 250 kW
	IRAN	
	VO THE ISLAMIC REP, Tehrān	W Africa • 500 kW
	RUSSIA	
	GOLOS ROSSII, Vladivostok	S • SE Asia • 100 kW
	YUGOSLAVIA	
	RADIO YUGOSLAVIA, Via Bosnia	• E Europe & W Asia • 500 kW
11760	**CUBA**	C America • 100 kW Europe & N Africa • 100 kW
	†RADIO HABANA, Havana	Su • C America • 100 kW
(con'd)		

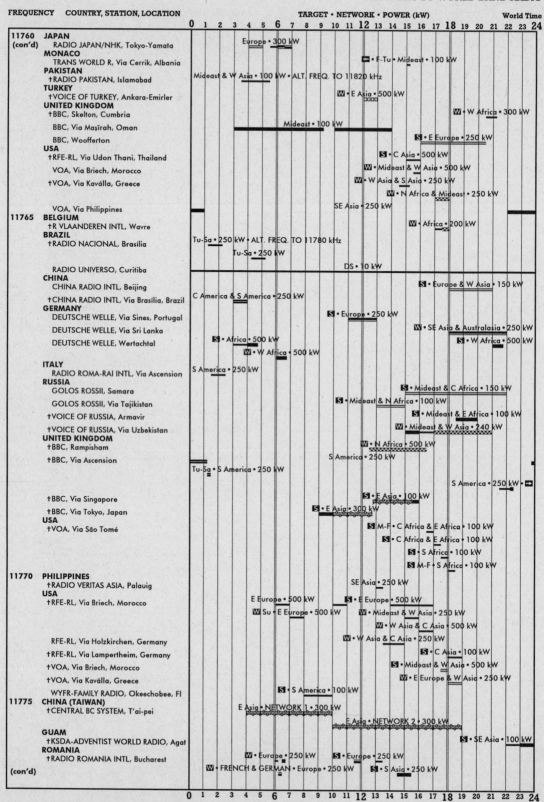

FREQUENCY   COUNTRY, STATION, LOCATION

TARGET • NETWORK • POWER (kW)

World Time

11760 JAPAN	
(con'd) RADIO JAPAN/NHK, Tokyo-Yamata	Europe • 300 kW
MONACO	
TRANS WORLD R, Via Cerrik, Albania	• F-Tu • Mideast • 100 kW
PAKISTAN	
†RADIO PAKISTAN, Islamabad	Mideast & W Asia • 100 kW • ALT. FREQ. TO 11820 kHz
TURKEY	
†VOICE OF TURKEY, Ankara-Emirler	W • E Asia • 500 kW
UNITED KINGDOM	
†BBC, Skelton, Cumbria	W • W Africa • 300 kW
BBC, Via Maşirah, Oman	Mideast • 100 kW
BBC, Woofferton	S • E Europe • 250 kW
USA	
†RFE-RL, Via Udon Thani, Thailand	S • C Asia • 500 kW
VOA, Via Briech, Morocco	W • Mideast & W Asia • 500 kW
†VOA, Via Kaválla, Greece	W • W Asia & S Asia • 250 kW
	W • N Africa & Mideast • 250 kW
VOA, Via Philippines	SE Asia • 250 kW
11765 BELGIUM	
†R VLAANDEREN INTL, Wavre	W • Africa • 200 kW
BRAZIL	
†RADIO NACIONAL, Brasília	Tu-Sa • 250 kW • ALT. FREQ. TO 11780 kHz
	Tu-Sa • 250 kW
RADIO UNIVERSO, Curitiba	DS • 10 kW
CHINA	
CHINA RADIO INTL, Beijing	S • Europe & W Asia • 150 kW
†CHINA RADIO INTL, Via Brasília, Brazil	C America & S America • 250 kW
GERMANY	
DEUTSCHE WELLE, Via Sines, Portugal	S • Europe • 250 kW
DEUTSCHE WELLE, Via Sri Lanka	W • SE Asia & Australasia • 250 kW
DEUTSCHE WELLE, Wertachtal	S • Africa • 500 kW W • W Africa • 500 kW
	W • W Africa • 500 kW
ITALY	
RADIO ROMA-RAI INTL, Via Ascension	S America • 250 kW
RUSSIA	
GOLOS ROSSII, Samara	S • Mideast & C Africa • 150 kW
GOLOS ROSSII, Via Tajikistan	S • Mideast & N Africa • 100 kW
†VOICE OF RUSSIA, Armavir	S • Mideast & E Africa • 100 kW
†VOICE OF RUSSIA, Via Uzbekistan	W • Mideast & W Asia • 240 kW
UNITED KINGDOM	
†BBC, Rampisham	W • N Africa • 500 kW
†BBC, Via Ascension	S America • 250 kW
	Tu-Sa • S America • 250 kW
	S America • 250 kW •
†BBC, Via Singapore	S • E Asia • 100 kW
†BBC, Via Tokyo, Japan	S • E Asia • 300 kW
USA	
†VOA, Via São Tomé	S • M-F • C Africa & E Africa • 100 kW
	S • C Africa & E Africa • 100 kW
	S • S Africa • 100 kW
	S • M-F • S Africa • 100 kW
11770 PHILIPPINES	
†RADIO VERITAS ASIA, Palauig	SE Asia • 250 kW
USA	
†RFE-RL, Via Briech, Morocco	E Europe • 500 kW S • E Europe • 500 kW
	W Su • E Europe • 500 kW W • Mideast & W Asia • 250 kW
	W • W Asia & C Asia • 500 kW
RFE-RL, Via Holzkirchen, Germany	W • W Asia & C Asia • 250 kW
†RFE-RL, Via Lampertheim, Germany	S • C Asia • 100 kW
†VOA, Via Briech, Morocco	S • Mideast & W Asia • 500 kW
†VOA, Via Kaválla, Greece	W • E Europe & W Asia • 250 kW
WYFR-FAMILY RADIO, Okeechobee, Fl	S • S America • 100 kW
11775 CHINA (TAIWAN)	
†CENTRAL BC SYSTEM, T'ai-pei	E Asia • NETWORK 1 • 300 kW
	E Asia • NETWORK 2 • 300 kW
GUAM	
†KSDA-ADVENTIST WORLD RADIO, Agat	S • SE Asia • 100 kW
ROMANIA	
†RADIO ROMANIA INTL, Bucharest	W • Europe • 250 kW S • Europe • 250 kW
(con'd)	W • FRENCH & GERMAN • Europe • 250 kW S • S Asia • 250 kW

FREQUENCY　　COUNTRY, STATION, LOCATION　　　　　　　TARGET • NETWORK • POWER (kW)　　　　　World Time

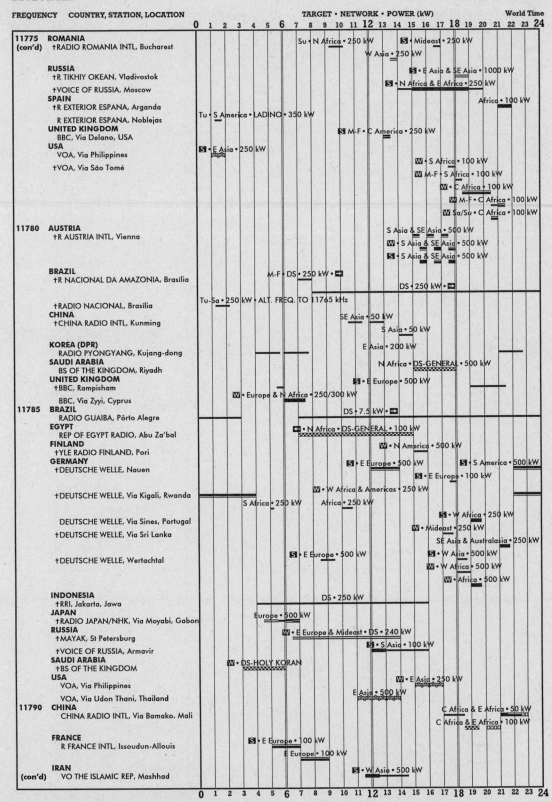

Frequency	Country / Station / Location	Target • Network • Power
11775 (con'd)	**ROMANIA** †RADIO ROMANIA INTL, Bucharest	Su • N Africa • 250 kW; S Mideast • 250 kW; W Asia • 250 kW
	RUSSIA †R TIKHIY OKEAN, Vladivostok	S • E Asia & SE Asia • 1000 kW
	†VOICE OF RUSSIA, Moscow	S • N Africa & E Africa • 250 kW; Africa • 100 kW
	SPAIN †R EXTERIOR ESPANA, Arganda	Tu • S America • LADINO • 350 kW
	R EXTERIOR ESPANA, Noblejas	
	UNITED KINGDOM BBC, Via Delano, USA	S M-F • C America • 250 kW
	USA VOA, Via Philippines	S • E Asia • 250 kW
	†VOA, Via São Tomé	W • S Africa • 100 kW; W M-F • S Africa • 100 kW; W • C Africa • 100 kW; W M-F • C Africa • 100 kW; W Sa/Su • C Africa • 100 kW
11780	**AUSTRIA** †R AUSTRIA INTL, Vienna	S Asia & SE Asia • 500 kW; W • S Asia & SE Asia • 500 kW; S • S Asia & SE Asia • 500 kW
	BRAZIL †R NACIONAL DA AMAZONIA, Brasilia	M-F • DS • 250 kW • ; DS • 250 kW •
	†RADIO NACIONAL, Brasilia	Tu-Sa • 250 kW • ALT. FREQ. TO 11765 kHz
	CHINA †CHINA RADIO INTL, Kunming	SE Asia • 50 kW; S Asia • 50 kW
	KOREA (DPR) RADIO PYONGYANG, Kujang-dong	E Asia • 200 kW
	SAUDI ARABIA BS OF THE KINGDOM, Riyadh	N Africa • DS-GENERAL • 500 kW
	UNITED KINGDOM †BBC, Rampisham	S • E Europe • 500 kW
	BBC, Via Zyyi, Cyprus	W • Europe & N Africa • 250/300 kW
11785	**BRAZIL** RADIO GUAIBA, Pôrto Alegre	DS • 7.5 kW •
	EGYPT REP OF EGYPT RADIO, Abu Za'bal	• N Africa • DS-GENERAL • 100 kW
	FINLAND †YLE RADIO FINLAND, Pori	W • N America • 500 kW
	GERMANY †DEUTSCHE WELLE, Nauen	S • E Europe • 500 kW; S • S America • 500 kW; S • E Europe • 100 kW
	†DEUTSCHE WELLE, Via Kigali, Rwanda	W • W Africa & Americas • 250 kW; S Africa • 250 kW; Africa • 250 kW
	DEUTSCHE WELLE, Via Sines, Portugal	S • W Africa • 250 kW
	†DEUTSCHE WELLE, Via Sri Lanka	W • Mideast • 250 kW; SE Asia & Australasia • 250 kW
	†DEUTSCHE WELLE, Wertachtal	S • E Europe • 500 kW; S • W Asia • 500 kW; W • W Africa • 500 kW; W • Africa • 500 kW
	INDONESIA †RRI, Jakarta, Jawa	DS • 250 kW
	JAPAN †RADIO JAPAN/NHK, Via Moyabi, Gabon	Europe • 500 kW
	RUSSIA †MAYAK, St Petersburg	W • E Europe & Mideast • DS • 240 kW
	†VOICE OF RUSSIA, Armavir	S • S Asia • 100 kW
	SAUDI ARABIA †BS OF THE KINGDOM	W • DS-HOLY KORAN
	USA VOA, Via Philippines	W • E Asia • 250 kW
	VOA, Via Udon Thani, Thailand	E Asia • 500 kW
11790	**CHINA** CHINA RADIO INTL, Via Bamako, Mali	C Africa & E Africa • 50 kW; C Africa & E Africa • 100 kW
	FRANCE R FRANCE INTL, Issoudun-Allouis	S • E Europe • 100 kW; E Europe • 100 kW
(con'd)	**IRAN** VO THE ISLAMIC REP, Mashhad	S • W Asia • 500 kW

FREQUENCY   COUNTRY, STATION, LOCATION   TARGET • NETWORK • POWER (kW)   World Time

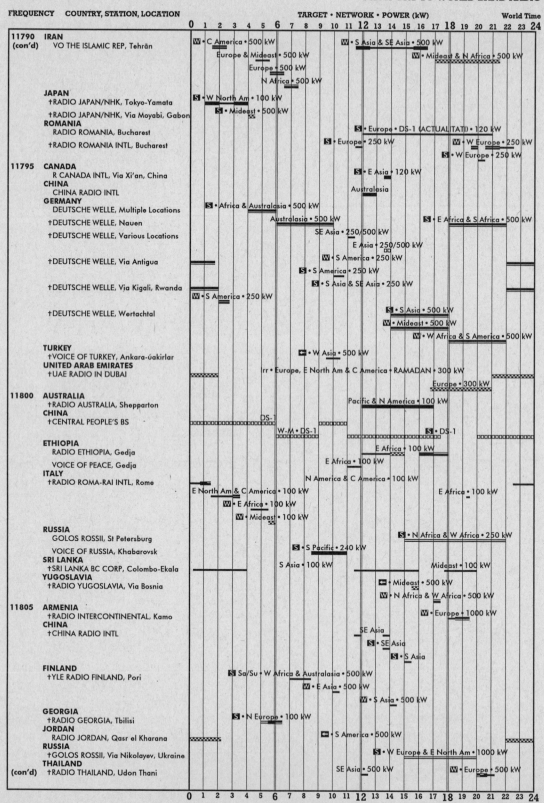

FREQUENCY   COUNTRY, STATION, LOCATION

TARGET • NETWORK • POWER (kW)

World Time

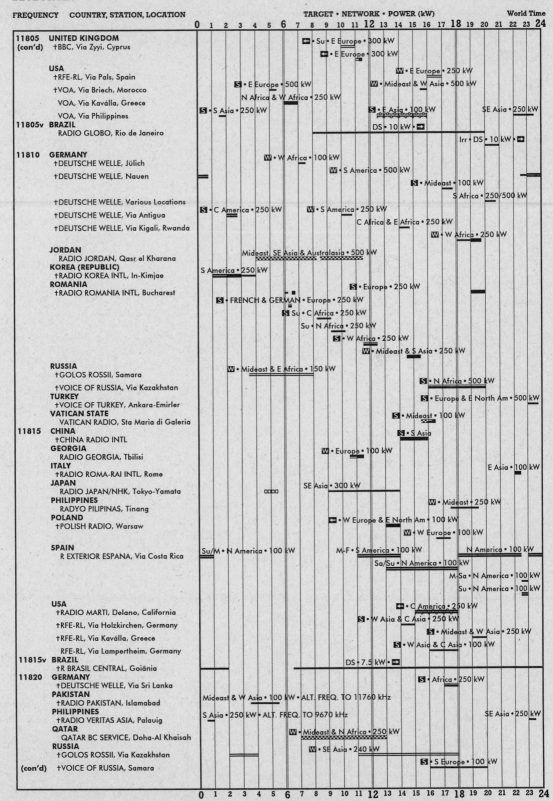

Frequency	Country, Station, Location
11805 (con'd)	**UNITED KINGDOM** †BBC, Via Zyyi, Cyprus
	USA †RFE-RL, Via Pals, Spain
	†VOA, Via Briech, Morocco
	VOA, Via Kaválla, Greece
	VOA, Via Philippines
11805v	**BRAZIL** RADIO GLOBO, Rio de Janeiro
11810	**GERMANY** †DEUTSCHE WELLE, Jülich
	†DEUTSCHE WELLE, Nauen
	†DEUTSCHE WELLE, Various Locations
	†DEUTSCHE WELLE, Via Antigua
	†DEUTSCHE WELLE, Via Kigali, Rwanda
	JORDAN RADIO JORDAN, Qasr el Kharana
	KOREA (REPUBLIC) †RADIO KOREA INTL, In-Kimjae
	ROMANIA †RADIO ROMANIA INTL, Bucharest
	RUSSIA †GOLOS ROSSII, Samara
	†VOICE OF RUSSIA, Via Kazakhstan
	TURKEY †VOICE OF TURKEY, Ankara-Emirler
	VATICAN STATE VATICAN RADIO, Sta Maria di Galeria
11815	**CHINA** †CHINA RADIO INTL
	GEORGIA RADIO GEORGIA, Tbilisi
	ITALY †RADIO ROMA-RAI INTL, Rome
	JAPAN RADIO JAPAN/NHK, Tokyo-Yamata
	PHILIPPINES RADYO PILIPINAS, Tinang
	POLAND †POLISH RADIO, Warsaw
	SPAIN R EXTERIOR ESPANA, Via Costa Rica
	USA †RADIO MARTI, Delano, California
	†RFE-RL, Via Holzkirchen, Germany
	†RFE-RL, Via Kaválla, Greece
	RFE-RL, Via Lampertheim, Germany
11815v	**BRAZIL** †R BRASIL CENTRAL, Goiânia
11820	**GERMANY** †DEUTSCHE WELLE, Via Sri Lanka
	PAKISTAN †RADIO PAKISTAN, Islamabad
	PHILIPPINES †RADIO VERITAS ASIA, Palauig
	QATAR QATAR BC SERVICE, Doha-Al Khaisah
	RUSSIA †GOLOS ROSSII, Via Kazakhstan
(con'd)	†VOICE OF RUSSIA, Samara

Target • Network • Power annotations:

- • Su • E Europe • 300 kW
- • E Europe • 300 kW
- W • E Europe • 250 kW
- S • E Europe • 500 kW
- W • Mideast & W Asia • 500 kW
- N Africa & W Africa • 250 kW
- S • S Asia • 250 kW
- S • E Asia • 100 kW   SE Asia • 250 kW
- DS • 10 kW •
- Irr • DS • 10 kW •
- W • W Africa • 100 kW
- W • S America • 500 kW
- S • Mideast • 100 kW
- S Africa • 250/500 kW
- S • C America • 250 kW
- W • S America • 250 kW
- C Africa & E Africa • 250 kW
- W • W Africa • 250 kW
- Mideast, SE Asia & Australasia • 500 kW
- S America • 250 kW
- S • Europe • 250 kW
- S • FRENCH & GERMAN • Europe • 250 kW
- S • Su • C Africa • 250 kW
- Su • N Africa • 250 kW
- S • W Africa • 250 kW
- W • Mideast & S Asia • 250 kW
- W • Mideast & E Africa • 150 kW
- S • N Africa • 500 kW
- S • Europe & E North Am • 500 kW
- S • Mideast • 100 kW
- S • S Asia
- W • Europe • 100 kW
- E Asia • 100 kW
- SE Asia • 300 kW
- W • Mideast • 250 kW
- • W Europe & E North Am • 100 kW
- W • W Europe • 100 kW
- Su/M • N America • 100 kW   M-F • S America • 100 kW   N America • 100 kW
- Sa/Su • N America • 100 kW
- M-Sa • N America • 100 kW
- Su • N America • 100 kW
- • C America • 250 kW
- S • W Asia & C Asia • 250 kW
- S • Mideast & W Asia • 250 kW
- S • W Asia & C Asia • 100 kW
- DS • 7.5 kW •
- S • Africa • 250 kW
- Mideast & W Asia • 100 kW • ALT. FREQ. TO 11760 kHz
- S Asia • 250 kW • ALT. FREQ. TO 9670 kHz   SE Asia • 250 kW
- W • Mideast & N Africa • 250 kW
- W • SE Asia • 240 kW
- S • S Europe • 100 kW

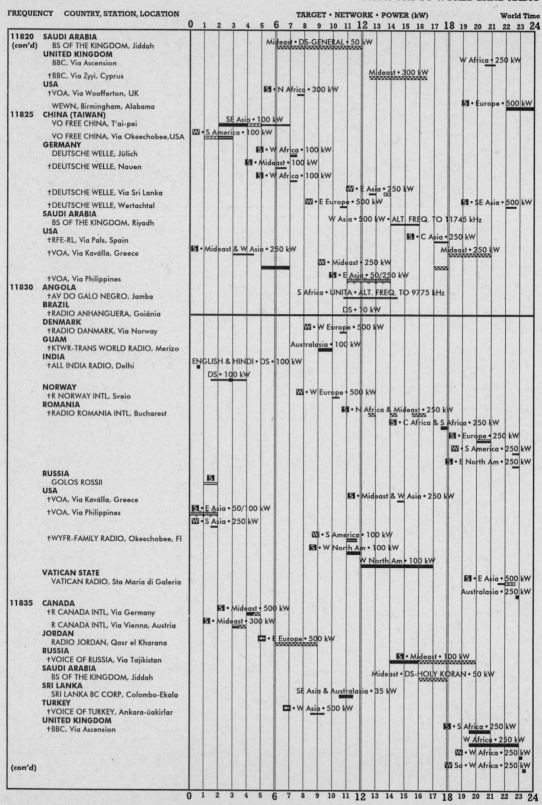

FREQUENCY	COUNTRY, STATION, LOCATION	TARGET • NETWORK • POWER (kW)	World Time

11820 SAUDI ARABIA
(con'd)   BS OF THE KINGDOM, Jiddah — Mideast • DS-GENERAL • 50 kW
UNITED KINGDOM
   BBC, Via Ascension — W Africa • 250 kW
   †BBC, Via Zyyi, Cyprus — Mideast • 300 kW
USA
   †VOA, Via Woofferton, UK — S • N Africa • 300 kW
   WEWN, Birmingham, Alabama — S • Europe • 500 kW
11825 CHINA (TAIWAN)
   VO FREE CHINA, T'ai-pei — SE Asia • 100 kW
   VO FREE CHINA, Via Okeechobee, USA — W • S America • 100 kW
GERMANY
   DEUTSCHE WELLE, Jülich — S • W Africa • 100 kW
   †DEUTSCHE WELLE, Nauen — S • Mideast • 100 kW
   — S • W Africa • 100 kW
   †DEUTSCHE WELLE, Via Sri Lanka — W • E Asia • 250 kW
   †DEUTSCHE WELLE, Wertachtal — W • E Europe • 500 kW
   — S • SE Asia • 500 kW
SAUDI ARABIA
   BS OF THE KINGDOM, Riyadh — W Asia • 500 kW • ALT. FREQ. TO 11745 kHz
USA
   †RFE-RL, Via Pals, Spain — S • C Asia • 250 kW
   †VOA, Via Kaválla, Greece — S • Mideast & W Asia • 250 kW
   — Mideast • 250 kW
   — W • Mideast • 250 kW
   †VOA, Via Philippines — S • E Asia • 50/250 kW
11830 ANGOLA
   †AV DO GALO NEGRO, Jamba — S Africa • UNITA • ALT. FREQ. TO 9775 kHz
BRAZIL
   †RADIO ANHANGUERA, Goiânia — DS • 10 kW
DENMARK
   †RADIO DANMARK, Via Norway — W • W Europe • 500 kW
GUAM
   †KTWR-TRANS WORLD RADIO, Merizo — Australasia • 100 kW
INDIA
   †ALL INDIA RADIO, Delhi — ENGLISH & HINDI • DS • 100 kW
   — DS • 100 kW
NORWAY
   †R NORWAY INTL, Sveio — W • W Europe • 500 kW
ROMANIA
   †RADIO ROMANIA INTL, Bucharest — S • N Africa & Mideast • 250 kW
   — S • C Africa & S Africa • 250 kW
   — S • Europe • 250 kW
   — W • S America • 250 kW
   — S • E North Am • 250 kW
RUSSIA
   GOLOS ROSSII — S
USA
   †VOA, Via Kaválla, Greece — S • Mideast & W Asia • 250 kW
   †VOA, Via Philippines — S • E Asia • 50/100 kW
   — W • S Asia • 250 kW
   †WYFR-FAMILY RADIO, Okeechobee, Fl — W • S America • 100 kW
   — S • W North Am • 100 kW
   — W North Am • 100 kW
VATICAN STATE
   VATICAN RADIO, Sta Maria di Galeria — S • E Asia • 500 kW
   — Australasia • 250 kW
11835 CANADA
   †R CANADA INTL, Via Germany — S • Mideast • 500 kW
   R CANADA INTL, Via Vienna, Austria — S • Mideast • 300 kW
JORDAN
   RADIO JORDAN, Qasr el Kharana — ⮂ • E Europe • 500 kW
RUSSIA
   †VOICE OF RUSSIA, Via Tajikistan — S • Mideast • 100 kW
SAUDI ARABIA
   BS OF THE KINGDOM, Jiddah — Mideast • DS-HOLY KORAN • 50 kW
SRI LANKA
   SRI LANKA BC CORP, Colombo-Ekala — SE Asia & Australasia • 35 kW
TURKEY
   †VOICE OF TURKEY, Ankara-úakirlar — ⮂ • W Asia • 500 kW
UNITED KINGDOM
   †BBC, Via Ascension — S • S Africa • 250 kW
   — W Africa • 250 kW
   — W • W Africa • 250 kW
   — W Sa • W Africa • 250 kW

(con'd)

FREQUENCY　　COUNTRY, STATION, LOCATION　　　　　　TARGET • NETWORK • POWER (kW)　　　World Time

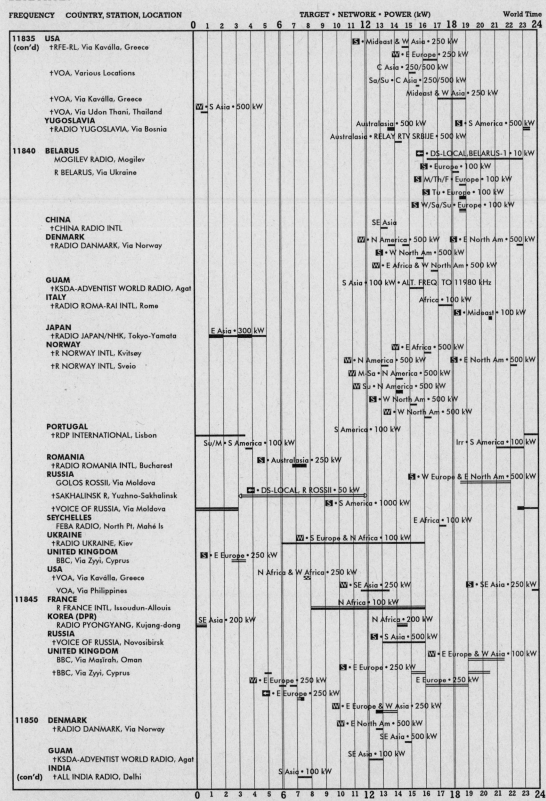

Frequency	Country, Station, Location	Schedule
11835 (con'd)	**USA**	
	†RFE-RL, Via Kaválla, Greece	S • Mideast & W Asia • 250 kW
		• E Europe • 250 kW
	†VOA, Various Locations	C Asia • 250/500 kW
		Sa/Su • C Asia • 250/500 kW
		Mideast & W Asia • 250 kW
	†VOA, Via Kaválla, Greece	
	†VOA, Via Udon Thani, Thailand	W • S Asia • 500 kW
	YUGOSLAVIA	Australasia • 500 kW S • S America • 500 kW
	†RADIO YUGOSLAVIA, Via Bosnia	Australasia • RELAY RTV SRBIJE • 500 kW
11840	**BELARUS**	
	MOGILEV RADIO, Mogilev	• DS-LOCAL, BELARUS-1 • 10 kW
	R BELARUS, Via Ukraine	S • Europe • 100 kW
		S M/Th/F • Europe • 100 kW
		S Tu • Europe • 100 kW
		S W/Sa/Su • Europe • 100 kW
	CHINA	
	†CHINA RADIO INTL	SE Asia
	DENMARK	
	†RADIO DANMARK, Via Norway	W • N America • 500 kW S • E North Am • 500 kW
		S • W North Am • 500 kW
		W • E Africa & W North Am • 500 kW
	GUAM	
	†KSDA-ADVENTIST WORLD RADIO, Agat	S Asia • 100 kW • ALT. FREQ. TO 11980 kHz
	ITALY	
	†RADIO ROMA-RAI INTL, Rome	Africa • 100 kW
		S • Mideast • 100 kW
	JAPAN	
	†RADIO JAPAN/NHK, Tokyo-Yamata	E Asia • 300 kW
	NORWAY	
	†R NORWAY INTL, Kvitsøy	W • E Africa • 500 kW
		W • N America • 500 kW S • E North Am • 500 kW
	†R NORWAY INTL, Sveio	W M-Sa • N America • 500 kW
		W Su • N America • 500 kW
		S • W North Am • 500 kW
		W • W North Am • 500 kW
	PORTUGAL	
	†RDP INTERNATIONAL, Lisbon	S America • 100 kW
		Su/M • S America • 100 kW Irr • S America • 100 kW
	ROMANIA	
	†RADIO ROMANIA INTL, Bucharest	S • Australasia • 250 kW
	RUSSIA	
	GOLOS ROSSII, Via Moldova	S • W Europe & E North Am • 500 kW
	†SAKHALINSK R, Yuzhno-Sakhalinsk	• DS-LOCAL, R ROSSII • 50 kW
	†VOICE OF RUSSIA, Via Moldova	S • S America • 1000 kW
	SEYCHELLES	
	FEBA RADIO, North Pt, Mahé Is	E Africa • 100 kW
	UKRAINE	
	†RADIO UKRAINE, Kiev	W • S Europe & N Africa • 100 kW
	UNITED KINGDOM	
	BBC, Via Zyyi, Cyprus	S • E Europe • 250 kW
	USA	
	†VOA, Via Kaválla, Greece	N Africa & W Africa • 250 kW
	VOA, Via Philippines	W • SE Asia • 250 kW S • SE Asia • 250 kW
11845	**FRANCE**	
	R FRANCE INTL, Issoudun-Allouis	N Africa • 100 kW
	KOREA (DPR)	
	RADIO PYONGYANG, Kujang-dong	SE Asia • 200 kW N Africa • 200 kW
	RUSSIA	
	†VOICE OF RUSSIA, Novosibirsk	S • S Asia • 500 kW
	UNITED KINGDOM	
	BBC, Via Maşīrah, Oman	W • E Europe & W Asia • 100 kW
	†BBC, Via Zyyi, Cyprus	S • E Europe • 250 kW
		E Europe • 250 kW
		W • E Europe • 250 kW
		• E Europe • 250 kW
		W • E Europe & W Asia • 250 kW
11850	**DENMARK**	
	†RADIO DANMARK, Via Norway	W • E North Am • 500 kW
		SE Asia • 500 kW
	GUAM	
	†KSDA-ADVENTIST WORLD RADIO, Agat	SE Asia • 100 kW
	INDIA	
(con'd)	†ALL INDIA RADIO, Delhi	S Asia • 100 kW

0 1 2 3 4 5 6 7 8 9 10 11 12 13 14 15 16 17 18 19 20 21 22 23 24

ENGLISH ▬▬　ARABIC ⁓⁓　CHINESE □□□　FRENCH ▭▭　GERMAN ▬▬　RUSSIAN ══　SPANISH ▬▬　OTHER ──

FREQUENCY   COUNTRY, STATION, LOCATION

TARGET • NETWORK • POWER (kW)

World Time

0 1 2 3 4 5 6 7 8 9 10 11 12 13 14 15 16 17 18 19 20 21 22 23 24

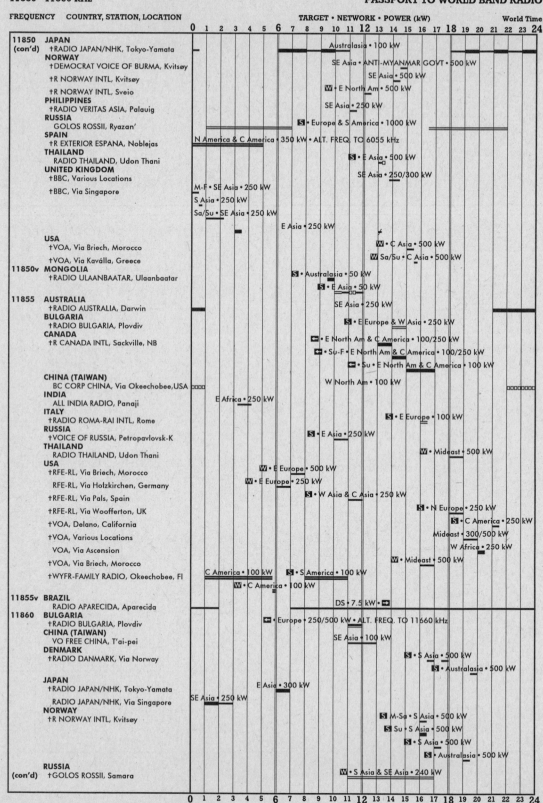

FREQUENCY	COUNTRY, STATION, LOCATION	TARGET • NETWORK • POWER (kW)
11850 (con'd)	JAPAN †RADIO JAPAN/NHK, Tokyo-Yamata	Australasia • 100 kW
	NORWAY †DEMOCRAT VOICE OF BURMA, Kvitsøy	SE Asia • ANTI-MYANMAR GOVT • 500 kW
	†R NORWAY INTL, Kvitsøy	SE Asia • 500 kW
	†R NORWAY INTL, Sveio	W • E North Am • 500 kW
	PHILIPPINES †RADIO VERITAS ASIA, Palauig	SE Asia • 250 kW
	RUSSIA GOLOS ROSSII, Ryazan'	S • Europe & S America • 1000 kW
	SPAIN †R EXTERIOR ESPANA, Noblejas	N America & C America • 350 kW • ALT. FREQ. TO 6055 kHz
	THAILAND RADIO THAILAND, Udon Thani	S • E Asia • 500 kW
	UNITED KINGDOM †BBC, Various Locations	SE Asia • 250/300 kW
	†BBC, Via Singapore	M-F • SE Asia • 250 kW
		S Asia • 250 kW
		Sa/Su • SE Asia • 250 kW
		E Asia • 250 kW
	USA †VOA, Via Briech, Morocco	W • C Asia • 500 kW
	†VOA, Via Kaválla, Greece	W Sa/Su • C Asia • 500 kW
11850v	MONGOLIA †RADIO ULAANBAATAR, Ulaanbaatar	S • Australasia • 50 kW
		S • E Asia • 50 kW
11855	AUSTRALIA †RADIO AUSTRALIA, Darwin	SE Asia • 250 kW
	BULGARIA †RADIO BULGARIA, Plovdiv	S • E Europe & W Asia • 250 kW
	CANADA †R CANADA INTL, Sackville, NB	⟷ • E North Am & C America • 100/250 kW
		⟷ • Su-F • E North Am & C America • 100/250 kW
		⟷ • Su • E North Am & C America • 100 kW
	CHINA (TAIWAN) BC CORP CHINA, Via Okeechobee,USA	W North Am • 100 kW
	INDIA ALL INDIA RADIO, Panaji	E Africa • 250 kW
	ITALY †RADIO ROMA-RAI INTL, Rome	S • E Europe • 100 kW
	RUSSIA †VOICE OF RUSSIA, Petropavlovsk-K	S • E Asia • 250 kW
	THAILAND RADIO THAILAND, Udon Thani	W • Mideast • 500 kW
	USA †RFE-RL, Via Briech, Morocco	W • E Europe • 500 kW
	RFE-RL, Via Holzkirchen, Germany	W • E Europe • 250 kW
	†RFE-RL, Via Pals, Spain	S • W Asia & C Asia • 250 kW
	†RFE-RL, Via Woofferton, UK	S • N Europe • 250 kW
	†VOA, Delano, California	S • C America • 250 kW
	†VOA, Various Locations	Mideast • 300/500 kW
	VOA, Via Ascension	W Africa • 250 kW
	†VOA, Via Briech, Morocco	W • Mideast • 500 kW
	†WYFR-FAMILY RADIO, Okeechobee, Fl	C America • 100 kW / S • S America • 100 kW / W • C America • 100 kW
11855v	BRAZIL RADIO APARECIDA, Aparecida	DS • 7.5 kW • ⟷
11860	BULGARIA †RADIO BULGARIA, Plovdiv	⟷ • Europe • 250/500 kW • ALT. FREQ. TO 11660 kHz
	CHINA (TAIWAN) VO FREE CHINA, T'ai-pei	SE Asia • 100 kW
	DENMARK †RADIO DANMARK, Via Norway	S • S Asia • 500 kW
		S • Australasia • 500 kW
	JAPAN †RADIO JAPAN/NHK, Tokyo-Yamata	E Asia • 300 kW
	RADIO JAPAN/NHK, Via Singapore	SE Asia • 250 kW
	NORWAY †R NORWAY INTL, Kvitsøy	S M-Sa • S Asia • 500 kW
		S Su • S Asia • 500 kW
		S • S Asia • 500 kW
		S • Australasia • 500 kW
	RUSSIA (con'd) †GOLOS ROSSII, Samara	W • S Asia & SE Asia • 240 kW

0 1 2 3 4 5 6 7 8 9 10 11 12 13 14 15 16 17 18 19 20 21 22 23 24

SEASONAL S OR W   1-HR TIMESHIFT MIDYEAR ⟷ OR ⟷   JAMMING / OR ∧   EARLIEST HEARD ◁   LATEST HEARD ▷   NEW FOR 1997 †

FREQUENCY   COUNTRY, STATION, LOCATION

TARGET • NETWORK • POWER (kW)

World Time

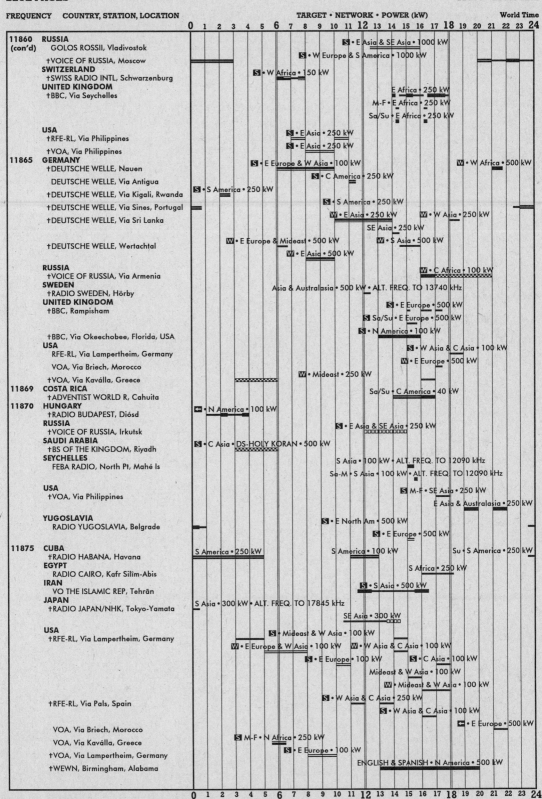

Frequency	Country, Station, Location	Target • Network • Power
11860 (con'd)	**RUSSIA**	
	GOLOS ROSSII, Vladivostok	S • E Asia & SE Asia • 1000 kW
	†VOICE OF RUSSIA, Moscow	S • W Europe & S America • 1000 kW
	SWITZERLAND	
	†SWISS RADIO INTL, Schwarzenburg	S • W Africa • 150 kW
	UNITED KINGDOM	
	†BBC, Via Seychelles	E Africa • 250 kW
		M-F • E Africa • 250 kW
		Sa/Su • E Africa • 250 kW
	USA	
	†RFE-RL, Via Philippines	S • E Asia • 250 kW
	†VOA, Via Philippines	S • E Asia • 250 kW
11865	**GERMANY**	
	†DEUTSCHE WELLE, Nauen	S • E Europe & W Asia • 100 kW W • W Africa • 500 kW
	DEUTSCHE WELLE, Via Antigua	S • C America • 250 kW
	†DEUTSCHE WELLE, Via Kigali, Rwanda	S • S America • 250 kW
	†DEUTSCHE WELLE, Via Sines, Portugal	S • S America • 250 kW
	†DEUTSCHE WELLE, Via Sri Lanka	W • E Asia • 250 kW W • W Asia • 250 kW
		SE Asia • 250 kW
	†DEUTSCHE WELLE, Wertachtal	W • E Europe & Mideast • 500 kW W • S Asia • 500 kW
		W • E Asia • 500 kW
	RUSSIA	
	†VOICE OF RUSSIA, Via Armenia	W • C Africa • 100 kW
	SWEDEN	
	†RADIO SWEDEN, Hörby	Asia & Australasia • 500 kW • ALT. FREQ. TO 13740 kHz
	UNITED KINGDOM	
	†BBC, Rampisham	S • E Europe • 500 kW
		S Sa/Su • E Europe • 500 kW
	†BBC, Via Okeechobee, Florida, USA	S • N America • 100 kW
	USA	
	RFE-RL, Via Lampertheim, Germany	S • W Asia & C Asia • 100 kW
	VOA, Via Briech, Morocco	W • E Europe • 500 kW
	†VOA, Via Kaválla, Greece	W • Mideast • 250 kW
11869	**COSTA RICA**	
	†ADVENTIST WORLD R, Cahuita	Sa/Su • C America • 40 kW
11870	**HUNGARY**	
	†RADIO BUDAPEST, Diósd	← • N America • 100 kW
	RUSSIA	
	†VOICE OF RUSSIA, Irkutsk	S • E Asia & SE Asia • 250 kW
	SAUDI ARABIA	
	†BS OF THE KINGDOM, Riyadh	S • C Asia • DS-HOLY KORAN • 500 kW
	SEYCHELLES	
	FEBA RADIO, North Pt, Mahé Is	S Asia • 100 kW • ALT. FREQ. TO 12090 kHz
		Sa-M • S Asia • 100 kW • ALT. FREQ. TO 12090 kHz
	USA	
	†VOA, Via Philippines	S M-F • SE Asia • 250 kW
		E Asia & Australasia • 250 kW
	YUGOSLAVIA	
	RADIO YUGOSLAVIA, Belgrade	S • E North Am • 500 kW
		S • E Europe • 500 kW
11875	**CUBA**	
	†RADIO HABANA, Havana	S America • 250 kW S America • 100 kW Su • S America • 250 kW
	EGYPT	
	RADIO CAIRO, Kafr Silim-Abis	S Africa • 250 kW
	IRAN	
	VO THE ISLAMIC REP, Tehrān	S • S Asia • 500 kW
	JAPAN	
	†RADIO JAPAN/NHK, Tokyo-Yamata	S Asia • 300 kW • ALT. FREQ. TO 17845 kHz
		SE Asia • 300 kW
	USA	
	†RFE-RL, Via Lampertheim, Germany	S • Mideast & W Asia • 100 kW
		W • E Europe & W Asia • 100 kW W • W Asia & C Asia • 100 kW
		S • E Europe • 100 kW S • C Asia • 100 kW
		Mideast & W Asia • 100 kW
		W • Mideast & W Asia • 100 kW
	†RFE-RL, Via Pals, Spain	S • W Asia & C Asia • 250 kW
		S • W Asia & C Asia • 100 kW
	VOA, Via Briech, Morocco	← • E Europe • 500 kW
	VOA, Via Kaválla, Greece	S M-F • N Africa • 250 kW
	†VOA, Via Lampertheim, Germany	S • E Europe • 100 kW
	†WEWN, Birmingham, Alabama	ENGLISH & SPANISH • N America • 500 kW

ENGLISH ▬   ARABIC ⧓⧓⧓   CHINESE ▫▫▫   FRENCH ▬▬   GERMAN ▬▬   RUSSIAN ▭▭   SPANISH ▭▭   OTHER ▬

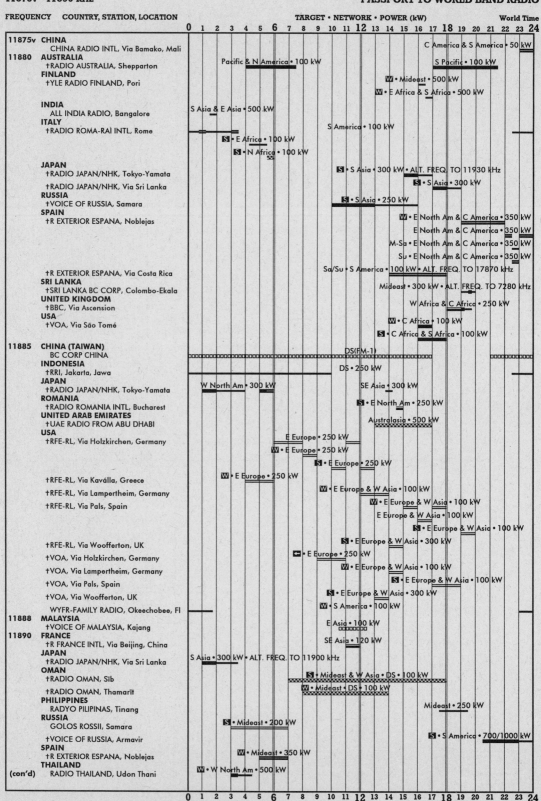

FREQUENCY   COUNTRY, STATION, LOCATION   TARGET • NETWORK • POWER (kW)   World Time

11875v	**CHINA**
	CHINA RADIO INTL, Via Bamako, Mali — C America & S America • 50 kW
11880	**AUSTRALIA**
	†RADIO AUSTRALIA, Shepparton — Pacific & N America • 100 kW / S Pacific • 100 kW
	FINLAND
	†YLE RADIO FINLAND, Pori — W • Mideast • 500 kW
	W • E Africa & S Africa • 500 kW
	INDIA
	ALL INDIA RADIO, Bangalore — S Asia & E Asia • 500 kW
	ITALY
	†RADIO ROMA-RAI INTL, Rome — S America • 100 kW
	S • E Africa • 100 kW
	S • N Africa • 100 kW
	JAPAN
	†RADIO JAPAN/NHK, Tokyo-Yamata — S • S Asia • 300 kW • ALT. FREQ. TO 11930 kHz
	†RADIO JAPAN/NHK, Via Sri Lanka — S • S Asia • 300 kW
	RUSSIA
	†VOICE OF RUSSIA, Samara — S • S Asia • 250 kW
	SPAIN
	†R EXTERIOR ESPANA, Noblejas — W • E North Am & C America • 350 kW
	E North Am & C America • 350 kW
	M-Sa • E North Am & C America • 350 kW
	Su • E North Am & C America • 350 kW
	†R EXTERIOR ESPANA, Via Costa Rica — Sa/Su • S America • 100 kW • ALT. FREQ. TO 17870 kHz
	SRI LANKA
	†SRI LANKA BC CORP, Colombo-Ekala — Mideast • 300 kW • ALT. FREQ. TO 7280 kHz
	UNITED KINGDOM
	†BBC, Via Ascension — W Africa & C Africa • 250 kW
	USA
	†VOA, Via São Tomé — W • C Africa • 100 kW
	S • C Africa & S Africa • 100 kW
11885	**CHINA (TAIWAN)**
	BC CORP CHINA — DS(FM-1)
	INDONESIA
	†RRI, Jakarta, Jawa — DS • 250 kW
	JAPAN
	†RADIO JAPAN/NHK, Tokyo-Yamata — W North Am • 300 kW / SE Asia • 300 kW
	ROMANIA
	†RADIO ROMANIA INTL, Bucharest — S • E North Am • 250 kW
	UNITED ARAB EMIRATES
	†UAE RADIO FROM ABU DHABI — Australasia • 500 kW
	USA
	†RFE-RL, Via Holzkirchen, Germany — E Europe • 250 kW
	W • E Europe • 250 kW
	S • E Europe • 250 kW
	†RFE-RL, Via Kaválla, Greece — W • E Europe • 250 kW
	†RFE-RL, Via Lampertheim, Germany — W • E Europe & W Asia • 100 kW
	†RFE-RL, Via Pals, Spain — W • E Europe & W Asia • 100 kW
	E Europe & W Asia • 100 kW
	S • E Europe & W Asia • 100 kW
	†RFE-RL, Via Woofferton, UK — S • E Europe & W Asia • 300 kW
	†VOA, Via Holzkirchen, Germany — E Europe • 250 kW
	†VOA, Via Lampertheim, Germany — W • E Europe & W Asia • 100 kW
	†VOA, Via Pals, Spain — S • E Europe & W Asia • 100 kW
	†VOA, Via Woofferton, UK — S • E Europe & W Asia • 300 kW
	WYFR-FAMILY RADIO, Okeechobee, Fl — W • S America • 100 kW
11888	**MALAYSIA**
	†VOICE OF MALAYSIA, Kajang — E Asia • 100 kW
11890	**FRANCE**
	†R FRANCE INTL, Via Beijing, China — SE Asia • 120 kW
	JAPAN
	†RADIO JAPAN/NHK, Via Sri Lanka — S Asia • 300 kW • ALT. FREQ. TO 11900 kHz
	OMAN
	†RADIO OMAN, Sīb — S • Mideast & W Asia • DS • 100 kW
	†RADIO OMAN, Thamarīt — W • Mideast • DS • 100 kW
	PHILIPPINES
	RADYO PILIPINAS, Tinang — Mideast • 250 kW
	RUSSIA
	GOLOS ROSSII, Samara — S • Mideast • 200 kW
	†VOICE OF RUSSIA, Armavir — S • S America • 700/1000 kW
	SPAIN
	†R EXTERIOR ESPANA, Noblejas — W • Mideast • 350 kW
	THAILAND
(con'd)	RADIO THAILAND, Udon Thani — W • W North Am • 500 kW

FREQUENCY　　COUNTRY, STATION, LOCATION　　　　　　TARGET • NETWORK • POWER (kW)　　　World Time

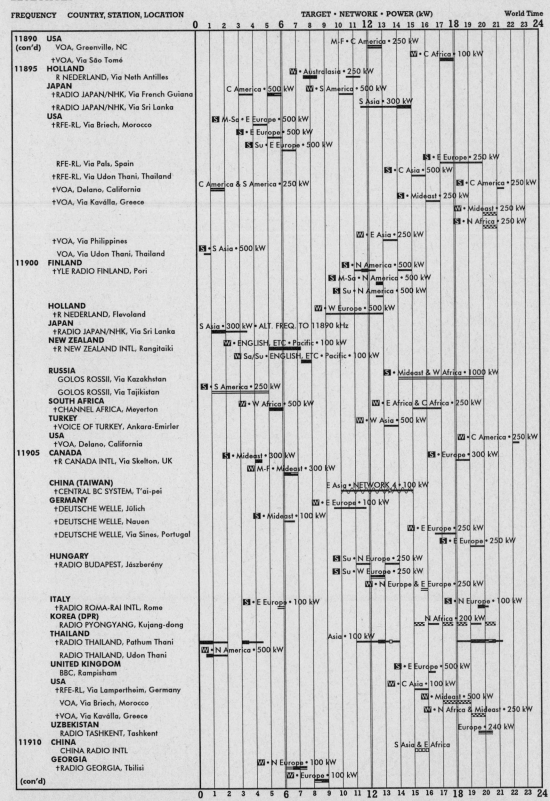

Frequency	Country, Station, Location	Schedule
11890 (con'd)	**USA** VOA, Greenville, NC	M-F • C America • 250 kW
	†VOA, Via São Tomé	W • C Africa • 100 kW
11895	**HOLLAND** R NEDERLAND, Via Neth Antilles	W • Australasia • 250 kW
	JAPAN †RADIO JAPAN/NHK, Via French Guiana	C America • 500 kW / W • S America • 500 kW
	†RADIO JAPAN/NHK, Via Sri Lanka	S Asia • 300 kW
	USA †RFE-RL, Via Briech, Morocco	S M-Sa • E Europe • 500 kW / S • E Europe • 500 kW / S Su • E Europe • 500 kW
	RFE-RL, Via Pals, Spain	S • E Europe • 250 kW
	†RFE-RL, Via Udon Thani, Thailand	S • C Asia • 500 kW / S • C America • 250 kW
	†VOA, Delano, California	C America & S America • 250 kW
	†VOA, Via Kaválla, Greece	S • Mideast • 250 kW / W • Mideast • 250 kW / S • N Africa • 250 kW
	†VOA, Via Philippines	W • E Asia • 250 kW
	VOA, Via Udon Thani, Thailand	S • S Asia • 500 kW
11900	**FINLAND** †YLE RADIO FINLAND, Pori	S • N America • 500 kW / S M-Sa • N America • 500 kW / S Su • N America • 500 kW
	HOLLAND †R NEDERLAND, Flevoland	W • W Europe • 500 kW
	JAPAN †RADIO JAPAN/NHK, Via Sri Lanka	S Asia • 300 kW • ALT. FREQ. TO 11890 kHz
	NEW ZEALAND †R NEW ZEALAND INTL, Rangitaiki	W • ENGLISH, ETC • Pacific • 100 kW / W Sa/Su • ENGLISH, ETC • Pacific • 100 kW
	RUSSIA GOLOS ROSSII, Via Kazakhstan	S • Mideast & W Africa • 1000 kW
	GOLOS ROSSII, Via Tajikistan	S • S America • 250 kW
	SOUTH AFRICA †CHANNEL AFRICA, Meyerton	W • W Africa • 500 kW / W • E Africa & C Africa • 250 kW
	TURKEY †VOICE OF TURKEY, Ankara-Emirler	W • W Asia • 500 kW
	USA †VOA, Delano, California	W • C America • 250 kW
11905	**CANADA** †R CANADA INTL, Via Skelton, UK	S • Mideast • 300 kW / W M-F • Mideast • 300 kW / S • Europe • 300 kW
	CHINA (TAIWAN) †CENTRAL BC SYSTEM, T'ai-pei	E Asia • NETWORK 4 • 100 kW
	GERMANY †DEUTSCHE WELLE, Jülich	W • E Europe • 100 kW
	†DEUTSCHE WELLE, Nauen	S • Mideast • 100 kW
	†DEUTSCHE WELLE, Via Sines, Portugal	W • E Europe • 250 kW / S • E Europe • 250 kW
	HUNGARY †RADIO BUDAPEST, Jászberény	S Su • N Europe • 250 kW / S Su • W Europe • 250 kW / W • N Europe & E Europe • 250 kW
	ITALY †RADIO ROMA-RAI INTL, Rome	S • E Europe • 100 kW / S • N Europe • 100 kW
	KOREA (DPR) RADIO PYONGYANG, Kujang-dong	N Africa • 200 kW
	THAILAND †RADIO THAILAND, Pathum Thani	Asia • 100 kW
	RADIO THAILAND, Udon Thani	W • N America • 500 kW
	UNITED KINGDOM BBC, Rampisham	S • E Europe • 500 kW
	USA †RFE-RL, Via Lampertheim, Germany	W • C Asia • 100 kW
	VOA, Via Briech, Morocco	W • Mideast • 500 kW
	†VOA, Via Kaválla, Greece	W • N Africa & Mideast • 250 kW
	UZBEKISTAN RADIO TASHKENT, Tashkent	Europe • 240 kW
11910	**CHINA** CHINA RADIO INTL	S Asia & E Africa
	GEORGIA †RADIO GEORGIA, Tbilisi	W • N Europe • 100 kW / W • Europe • 100 kW

(con'd)

ENGLISH ▬　ARABIC ⧓⧓⧓　CHINESE □□□　FRENCH ═　GERMAN ▬▬　RUSSIAN ══　SPANISH ═　OTHER ─

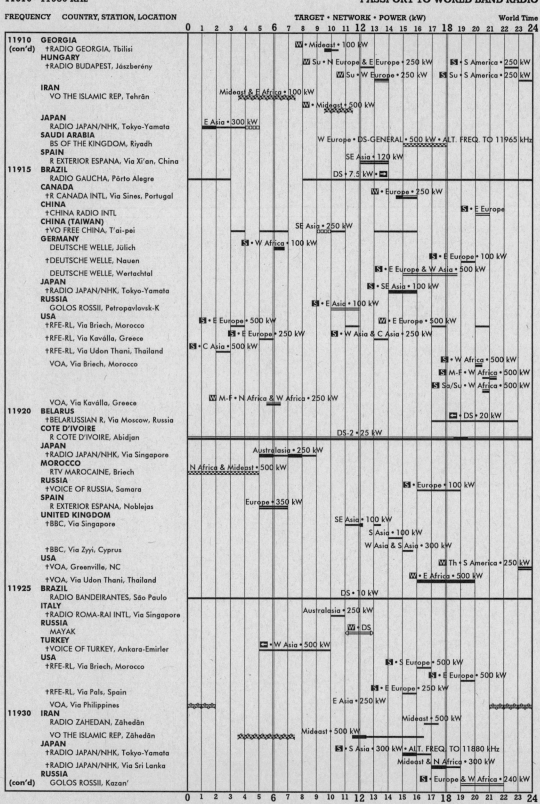

FREQUENCY   COUNTRY, STATION, LOCATION

TARGET • NETWORK • POWER (kW)

World Time

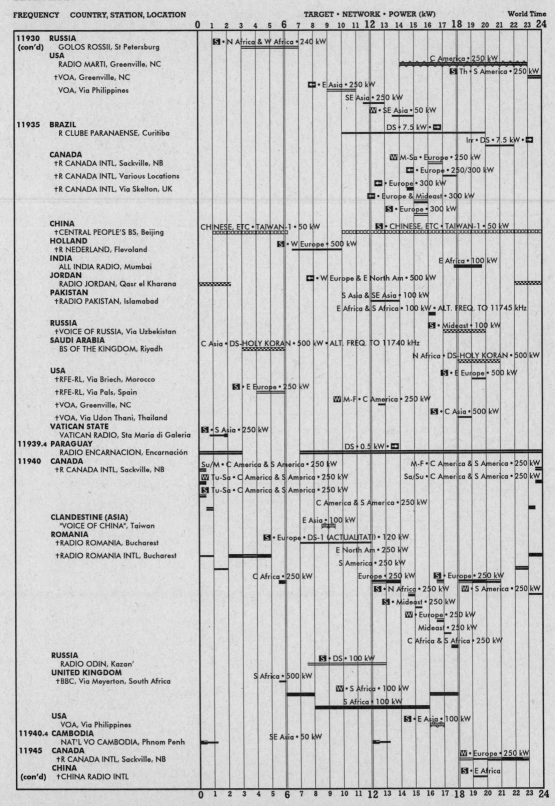

FREQUENCY	COUNTRY, STATION, LOCATION
11930 (con'd)	RUSSIA
	GOLOS ROSSII, St Petersburg
	USA
	RADIO MARTI, Greenville, NC
	†VOA, Greenville, NC
	VOA, Via Philippines
11935	BRAZIL
	R CLUBE PARANAENSE, Curitiba
	CANADA
	†R CANADA INTL, Sackville, NB
	†R CANADA INTL, Various Locations
	†R CANADA INTL, Via Skelton, UK
	CHINA
	†CENTRAL PEOPLE'S BS, Beijing
	HOLLAND
	†R NEDERLAND, Flevoland
	INDIA
	ALL INDIA RADIO, Mumbai
	JORDAN
	RADIO JORDAN, Qasr el Kharana
	PAKISTAN
	†RADIO PAKISTAN, Islamabad
	RUSSIA
	†VOICE OF RUSSIA, Via Uzbekistan
	SAUDI ARABIA
	BS OF THE KINGDOM, Riyadh
	USA
	†RFE-RL, Via Briech, Morocco
	†RFE-RL, Via Pals, Spain
	†VOA, Greenville, NC
	†VOA, Via Udon Thani, Thailand
	VATICAN STATE
	VATICAN RADIO, Sta Maria di Galeria
11939.4	PARAGUAY
	RADIO ENCARNACION, Encarnación
11940	CANADA
	†R CANADA INTL, Sackville, NB
	CLANDESTINE (ASIA)
	"VOICE OF CHINA", Taiwan
	ROMANIA
	†RADIO ROMANIA, Bucharest
	†RADIO ROMANIA INTL, Bucharest
	RUSSIA
	RADIO ODIN, Kazan'
	UNITED KINGDOM
	†BBC, Via Meyerton, South Africa
	USA
	VOA, Via Philippines
11940.4	CAMBODIA
	NAT'L VO CAMBODIA, Phnom Penh
11945	CANADA
	†R CANADA INTL, Sackville, NB
	CHINA
(con'd)	†CHINA RADIO INTL

ENGLISH ▬ ARABIC ⠶⠶ CHINESE ⠿⠿ FRENCH ═ GERMAN ▬ RUSSIAN ═ SPANISH ▭ OTHER ▬

FREQUENCY   COUNTRY, STATION, LOCATION

TARGET • NETWORK • POWER (kW)

World Time

0 1 2 3 4 5 6 7 8 9 10 11 12 13 14 15 16 17 18 19 20 21 22 23 24

11945 CHINA
(con'd) †CHINA RADIO INTL, Xi'an — SE Asia • 150 kW
GERMANY
DEUTSCHE WELLE, Via Antigua — W • C America • 250 kW
†DEUTSCHE WELLE, Via Sines, Portugal — W • Europe • 250 kW
†DEUTSCHE WELLE, Wertachtal — S • S Asia • 500 kW
JORDAN
RADIO JORDAN, Qasr el Kharana — • E Europe • 500 kW
RUSSIA
†VOICE OF RUSSIA, Via Moldova — S • Mideast & E Africa • 1000 kW
W • Mideast & C Africa • 1000 kW
SPAIN
R EXTERIOR ESPANA, Noblejas — S America • 350 kW
TURKEY
†VOICE OF TURKEY, Ankara-Emirler — • N Africa • 500 kW
UNITED ARAB EMIRATES
UAE RADIO IN DUBAI — E North Am & C America • 300 kW
UNITED KINGDOM
†BBC, Via Tokyo, Japan — E Asia • 300 kW
USA
VOA, Delano, California — S • M-F • C America • 250 kW
VOA, Via Philippines — W • M-F • E Asia & Australasia • 250 kW

11950 GERMANY
†DEUTSCHE WELLE, Via Sines, Portugal — W • E Europe • 250 kW
HUNGARY
†RADIO BUDAPEST, Jászberény — W • Su • N Europe & E Europe • 250 kW
JAPAN
†RADIO JAPAN/NHK, Via French Guiana — W • S America • 500 kW
KAZAKHSTAN
†KAZAKH RADIO, Almaty — • RUSSIAN, GERMAN, ETC • DS-1 • 100 kW
SAUDI ARABIA
BS OF THE KINGDOM, Jiddah — W Asia • DS-GENERAL • 50 kW
USA
†RFE-RL, Via Woofferton, UK — S • E Europe • 250 kW
†VOA, Via Kaválla, Greece — E Africa • 250 kW
Sa/Su • E Africa • 250 kW
S • N Africa • 250 kW

11950v CHINA
†XIZANG PEOPLE'S BC STN, Lhasa — DS-TIBETAN • 50 kW
11954.8 ANGOLA
RADIO NACIONAL, Luanda — DS-NATIONAL • 100 kW
11955 CANADA
R CANADA INTL, Via Tokyo, Japan — E Asia • 300 kW
HUNGARY
†RADIO BUDAPEST, Jászberény — W • M • S America • 250 kW   W • S America • 250 kW
THAILAND
RADIO THAILAND, Udon Thani — S • E Asia • 500 kW
TURKEY
†VOICE OF TURKEY, Ankara-úakirlar — Mideast • 250 kW
UNITED KINGDOM
†BBC, Via Singapore — S Asia • 250 kW   SE Asia & Australasia • 125 kW
SE Asia • 250 kW   Australasia • 250 kW
†BBC, Via Thailand — E Asia • 250 kW
†BBC, Via Zyyi, Cyprus — • E Europe • 250 kW
• Su • E Europe • 250 kW
USA
VOA, Via Kaválla, Greece — S • Mideast • 250 kW
11960 BELARUS
R BELARUS, Kalodziscy — S • Europe & W Africa • 250 kW
S • M/Th/F • Europe & W Africa • 250 kW
S • Tu • Europe & W Africa • 250 kW
S • W/Sa/Su • Europe & W Africa • 250 kW
ECUADOR
†HCJB-VO THE ANDES, Quito — N America & S America • 50 kW   W • Europe • 100 kW
IRAN
VO THE ISLAMIC REP, Tehrän — S • W Asia • 500 kW
JAPAN
†RADIO JAPAN/NHK, Tokyo-Yamata — W • W North Am • 300 kW
RUSSIA
VOICE OF RUSSIA, Khabarovsk — S • E Asia & SE Asia • 100 kW
VOICE OF RUSSIA, Via Belarus — S • Europe & W Africa • 250 kW
S • Europe • 100 kW
USA
†VOA, Delano, California — Th • C America & S America • 250 kW
VOA, Via Kaválla, Greece — W • W Asia & S Asia • 250 kW
VOA, Via Rhodes, Greece — W • Mideast • 50 kW
11960v MALI
RTV MALIENNE, Bamako — FRENCH, ETC • DS • 50 kW

0 1 2 3 4 5 6 7 8 9 10 11 12 13 14 15 16 17 18 19 20 21 22 23 24

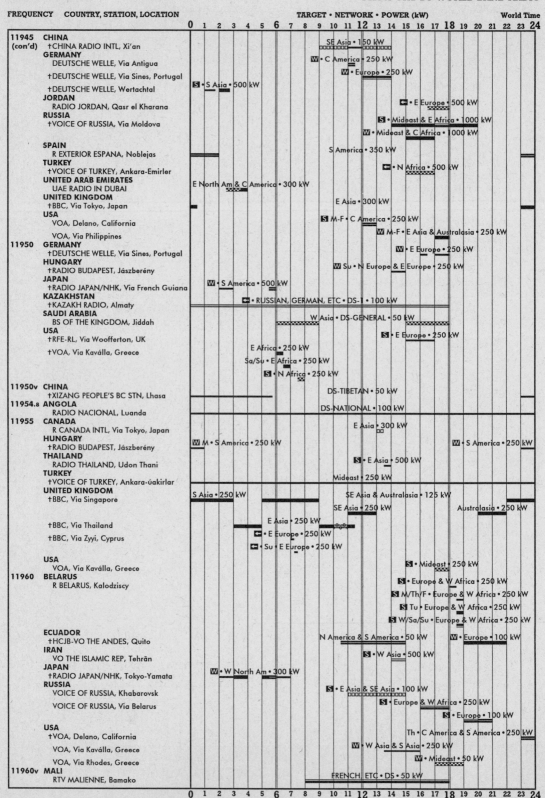

FREQUENCY   COUNTRY, STATION, LOCATION

TARGET • NETWORK • POWER (kW)   World Time

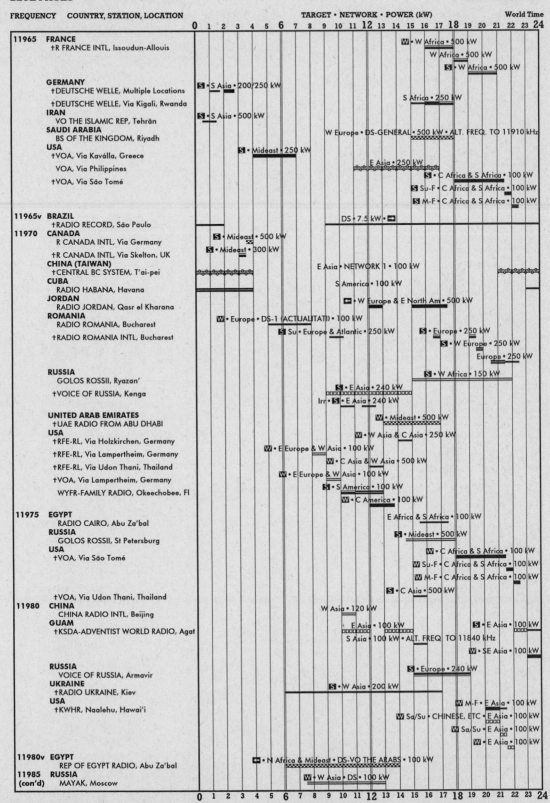

Frequency	Country, Station, Location	Target • Network • Power
11965	**FRANCE** †R FRANCE INTL, Issoudun-Allouis	S • W Africa • 500 kW / W Africa • 500 kW / S • W Africa • 500 kW
	GERMANY †DEUTSCHE WELLE, Multiple Locations	S • S Asia • 200/250 kW
	†DEUTSCHE WELLE, Via Kigali, Rwanda	S Africa • 250 kW
	IRAN VO THE ISLAMIC REP, Tehrān	S • S Asia • 500 kW
	SAUDI ARABIA BS OF THE KINGDOM, Riyadh	W Europe • DS-GENERAL • 500 kW • ALT. FREQ. TO 11910 kHz
	USA †VOA, Via Kaválla, Greece	S • Mideast • 250 kW
	VOA, Via Philippines	E Asia • 250 kW
	†VOA, Via São Tomé	S • C Africa & S Africa • 100 kW / S Su-F • C Africa & S Africa • 100 kW / S M-F • C Africa & S Africa • 100 kW
11965v	**BRAZIL** †RADIO RECORD, São Paulo	DS • 7.5 kW
11970	**CANADA** R CANADA INTL, Via Germany	S • Mideast • 500 kW
	†R CANADA INTL, Via Skelton, UK	S • Mideast • 300 kW
	CHINA (TAIWAN) †CENTRAL BC SYSTEM, T'ai-pei	E Asia • NETWORK 1 • 100 kW
	CUBA RADIO HABANA, Havana	S America • 100 kW
	JORDAN RADIO JORDAN, Qasr el Kharana	W Europe & E North Am • 500 kW
	ROMANIA RADIO ROMANIA, Bucharest	W • Europe • DS-1 (ACTUALITATI) • 100 kW
	†RADIO ROMANIA INTL, Bucharest	S Su • Europe & Atlantic • 250 kW / S • Europe • 250 kW / S • W Europe • 250 kW / Europe • 250 kW
	RUSSIA GOLOS ROSSII, Ryazan'	S • W Africa • 150 kW
	†VOICE OF RUSSIA, Kenga	S • E Asia • 240 kW / Irr • S • E Asia • 240 kW
	UNITED ARAB EMIRATES †UAE RADIO FROM ABU DHABI	W • Mideast • 500 kW
	USA †RFE-RL, Via Holzkirchen, Germany	W • W Asia & C Asia • 250 kW
	†RFE-RL, Via Lampertheim, Germany	W • E Europe & W Asia • 100 kW
	†RFE-RL, Via Udon Thani, Thailand	W • C Asia & W Asia • 500 kW
	†VOA, Via Lampertheim, Germany	W • E Europe & W Asia • 100 kW
	WYFR-FAMILY RADIO, Okeechobee, Fl	S • S America • 100 kW / W • C America • 100 kW
11975	**EGYPT** RADIO CAIRO, Abu Za'bal	E Africa & S Africa • 100 kW
	RUSSIA GOLOS ROSSII, St Petersburg	S • Mideast • 500 kW
	USA †VOA, Via São Tomé	W • C Africa & S Africa • 100 kW / W Su-F • C Africa & S Africa • 100 kW / W M-F • C Africa & S Africa • 100 kW
	†VOA, Via Udon Thani, Thailand	S • C Asia • 500 kW
11980	**CHINA** CHINA RADIO INTL, Beijing	W Asia • 120 kW
	GUAM †KSDA-ADVENTIST WORLD RADIO, Agat	E Asia • 100 kW / S • E Asia • 100 kW / S Asia • 100 kW • ALT. FREQ. TO 11840 kHz / W • SE Asia • 100 kW
	RUSSIA VOICE OF RUSSIA, Armavir	S • Europe • 240 kW
	UKRAINE †RADIO UKRAINE, Kiev	S • W Asia • 200 kW
	USA †KWHR, Naalehu, Hawai'i	W M-F • E Asia • 100 kW / W Sa/Su • CHINESE, ETC • E Asia • 100 kW / W Sa/Su • E Asia • 100 kW / W • E Asia • 100 kW
11980v	**EGYPT** REP OF EGYPT RADIO, Abu Za'bal	N Africa & Mideast • DS-VO THE ARABS • 100 kW
11985 (con'd)	**RUSSIA** MAYAK, Moscow	W • W Asia • DS • 100 kW

ENGLISH ▬ ARABIC ▨ CHINESE ▭▭ FRENCH ═ GERMAN ▬ RUSSIAN ═ SPANISH ═ OTHER ─

FREQUENCY   COUNTRY, STATION, LOCATION   TARGET • NETWORK • POWER (kW)   World Time

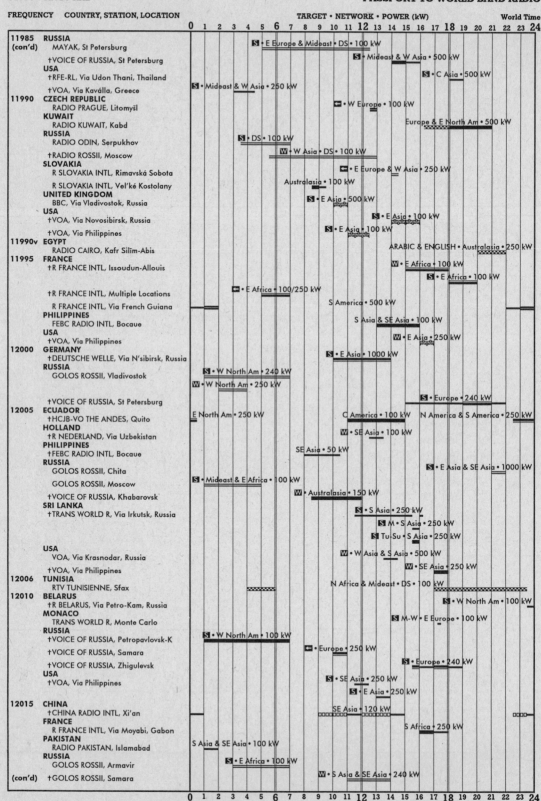

Frequency	Country, Station, Location	Target • Network • Power
11985 (con'd)	**RUSSIA** MAYAK, St Petersburg	S • E Europe & Mideast • DS • 100 kW
	†VOICE OF RUSSIA, St Petersburg	S • Mideast & W Asia • 500 kW
	USA †RFE-RL, Via Udon Thani, Thailand	S • C Asia • 500 kW
	†VOA, Via Kaválla, Greece	S • Mideast & W Asia • 250 kW
11990	**CZECH REPUBLIC** RADIO PRAGUE, Litomyšl	• W Europe • 100 kW
	KUWAIT RADIO KUWAIT, Kabd	Europe & E North Am • 500 kW
	RUSSIA RADIO ODIN, Serpukhov	S • DS • 100 kW
	†RADIO ROSSII, Moscow	W • W Asia • DS • 100 kW
	SLOVAKIA R SLOVAKIA INTL, Rimavská Sobota	• E Europe & W Asia • 250 kW
	R SLOVAKIA INTL, Vel'ké Kostolany	Australasia • 100 kW
	UNITED KINGDOM BBC, Via Vladivostok, Russia	• E Asia • 500 kW
	USA †VOA, Via Novosibirsk, Russia	S • E Asia • 100 kW
	†VOA, Via Philippines	S • E Asia • 100 kW
11990v	**EGYPT** RADIO CAIRO, Kafr Silīm-Abis	ARABIC & ENGLISH • Australasia • 250 kW
11995	**FRANCE** †R FRANCE INTL, Issoudun-Allouis	W • E Africa • 100 kW
		S • E Africa • 100 kW
	†R FRANCE INTL, Multiple Locations	• E Africa • 100/250 kW
	R FRANCE INTL, Via French Guiana	S America • 500 kW
	PHILIPPINES FEBC RADIO INTL, Bocaue	S Asia & SE Asia • 100 kW
	USA †VOA, Via Philippines	W • E Asia • 250 kW
12000	**GERMANY** †DEUTSCHE WELLE, Via N'sibirsk, Russia	S • E Asia • 1000 kW
	RUSSIA GOLOS ROSSII, Vladivostok	S • W North Am • 240 kW / W • W North Am • 250 kW
	†VOICE OF RUSSIA, St Petersburg	S • Europe • 240 kW
12005	**ECUADOR** †HCJB-VO THE ANDES, Quito	E North Am • 250 kW / C America • 100 kW / N America & S America • 250 kW
	HOLLAND †R NEDERLAND, Via Uzbekistan	W • SE Asia • 100 kW
	PHILIPPINES †FEBC RADIO INTL, Bocaue	SE Asia • 50 kW
	RUSSIA GOLOS ROSSII, Chita	S • E Asia & SE Asia • 1000 kW
	GOLOS ROSSII, Moscow	S • Mideast & E Africa • 100 kW
	†VOICE OF RUSSIA, Khabarovsk	W • Australasia • 150 kW
	SRI LANKA †TRANS WORLD R, Via Irkutsk, Russia	S • S Asia • 250 kW
		S M • S Asia • 250 kW
		S Tu-Su • S Asia • 250 kW
	USA VOA, Via Krasnodar, Russia	W • W Asia & S Asia • 500 kW
	†VOA, Via Philippines	W • SE Asia • 250 kW
12006	**TUNISIA** RTV TUNISIENNE, Sfax	N Africa & Mideast • DS • 100 kW
12010	**BELARUS** †R BELARUS, Via Petro-Kam, Russia	S • W North Am • 100 kW
	MONACO TRANS WORLD R, Monte Carlo	S M-W • E Europe • 100 kW
	RUSSIA †VOICE OF RUSSIA, Petropavlovsk-K	S • W North Am • 100 kW
	†VOICE OF RUSSIA, Samara	• Europe • 250 kW
	†VOICE OF RUSSIA, Zhigulevsk	S • Europe • 240 kW
	USA †VOA, Via Philippines	S • SE Asia • 250 kW
		S • E Asia • 250 kW
12015	**CHINA** †CHINA RADIO INTL, Xi'an	SE Asia • 120 kW
	FRANCE R FRANCE INTL, Via Moyabi, Gabon	S Africa • 250 kW
	PAKISTAN RADIO PAKISTAN, Islamabad	S Asia & SE Asia • 100 kW
	RUSSIA GOLOS ROSSII, Armavir	S • E Africa • 100 kW
(con'd)	†GOLOS ROSSII, Samara	W • S Asia & SE Asia • 240 kW

FREQUENCY   COUNTRY, STATION, LOCATION   TARGET • NETWORK • POWER (kW)   World Time

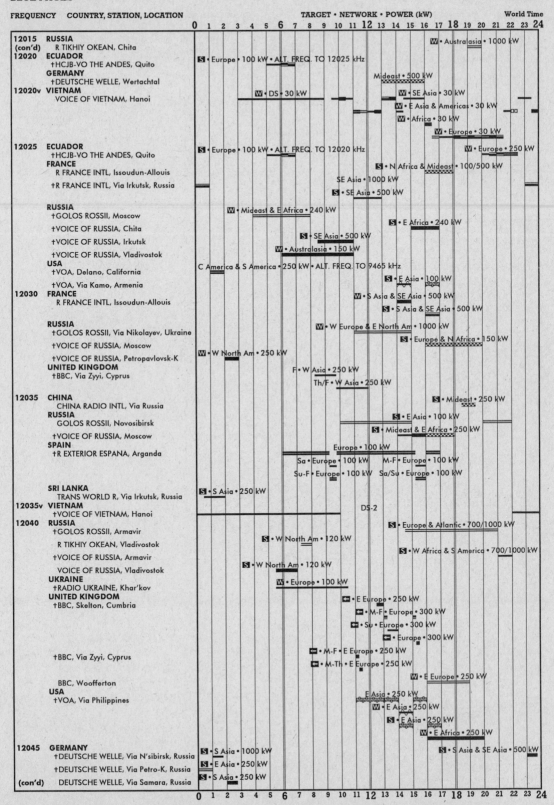

Frequency	Country, Station, Location
12015 (con'd)	**RUSSIA** R TIKHIY OKEAN, Chita — W • Australasia • 1000 kW
12020	**ECUADOR** †HCJB-VO THE ANDES, Quito — S • Europe • 100 kW • ALT. FREQ. TO 12025 kHz
	GERMANY †DEUTSCHE WELLE, Wertachtal — Mideast • 500 kW
12020v	**VIETNAM** VOICE OF VIETNAM, Hanoi — W • DS • 30 kW; W • SE Asia • 30 kW; W • E Asia & Americas • 30 kW; W • Africa • 30 kW; W • Europe • 30 kW
12025	**ECUADOR** †HCJB-VO THE ANDES, Quito — S • Europe • 100 kW • ALT. FREQ. TO 12020 kHz; W • Europe • 250 kW
	FRANCE R FRANCE INTL, Issoudun-Allouis — S • N Africa & Mideast • 100/500 kW
	†R FRANCE INTL, Via Irkutsk, Russia — SE Asia • 1000 kW; S • SE Asia • 500 kW
	RUSSIA †GOLOS ROSSII, Moscow — W • Mideast & E Africa • 240 kW
	†VOICE OF RUSSIA, Chita — S • E Africa • 240 kW
	†VOICE OF RUSSIA, Irkutsk — S • SE Asia • 500 kW
	†VOICE OF RUSSIA, Vladivostok — W • Australasia • 150 kW
	USA †VOA, Delano, California — C America & S America • 250 kW • ALT. FREQ. TO 9465 kHz
	†VOA, Via Kamo, Armenia — S • E Asia • 100 kW
12030	**FRANCE** R FRANCE INTL, Issoudun-Allouis — W • S Asia & SE Asia • 500 kW; S • S Asia & SE Asia • 500 kW
	RUSSIA †GOLOS ROSSII, Via Nikolayev, Ukraine — W • W Europe & E North Am • 1000 kW; S • Europe & N Africa • 150 kW
	†VOICE OF RUSSIA, Moscow
	†VOICE OF RUSSIA, Petropavlovsk-K — W • W North Am • 250 kW
	UNITED KINGDOM †BBC, Via Zyyi, Cyprus — F • W Asia • 250 kW; Th/F • W Asia • 250 kW
12035	**CHINA** CHINA RADIO INTL, Via Russia — S • Mideast • 250 kW
	RUSSIA GOLOS ROSSII, Novosibirsk — S • E Asia • 100 kW; S • Mideast & E Africa • 250 kW
	†VOICE OF RUSSIA, Moscow
	SPAIN †R EXTERIOR ESPANA, Arganda — Europe • 100 kW; Sa • Europe • 100 kW; M-F • Europe • 100 kW; Su-F • Europe • 100 kW; Sa/Su • Europe • 100 kW
	SRI LANKA TRANS WORLD R, Via Irkutsk, Russia — S • S Asia • 250 kW
12035v	**VIETNAM** †VOICE OF VIETNAM, Hanoi — DS-2
12040	**RUSSIA** †GOLOS ROSSII, Armavir — S • Europe & Atlantic • 700/1000 kW
	R TIKHIY OKEAN, Vladivostok — S • W North Am • 120 kW; S • W Africa & S America • 700/1000 kW
	†VOICE OF RUSSIA, Armavir
	VOICE OF RUSSIA, Vladivostok — S • W North Am • 120 kW
	UKRAINE †RADIO UKRAINE, Khar'kov — W • Europe • 100 kW
	UNITED KINGDOM †BBC, Skelton, Cumbria — • E Europe • 250 kW; • M-F • Europe • 300 kW; • Su • Europe • 300 kW; • Europe • 300 kW
	†BBC, Via Zyyi, Cyprus — • M-F • E Europe • 250 kW; • M-Th • E Europe • 250 kW
	BBC, Woofferton — W • E Europe • 250 kW
	USA †VOA, Via Philippines — E Asia • 250 kW; W • E Asia • 250 kW; S • E Asia • 250 kW; W • E Africa • 250 kW
12045	**GERMANY** †DEUTSCHE WELLE, Via N'sibirsk, Russia — S • S Asia • 1000 kW; S • S Asia & SE Asia • 500 kW
	†DEUTSCHE WELLE, Via Petro-K, Russia — S • E Asia • 250 kW
(con'd)	DEUTSCHE WELLE, Via Samara, Russia — S • S Asia • 250 kW

ENGLISH ▬   ARABIC ▩   CHINESE ▭   FRENCH ▬   GERMAN ▬   RUSSIAN ═   SPANISH ▬   OTHER ▬

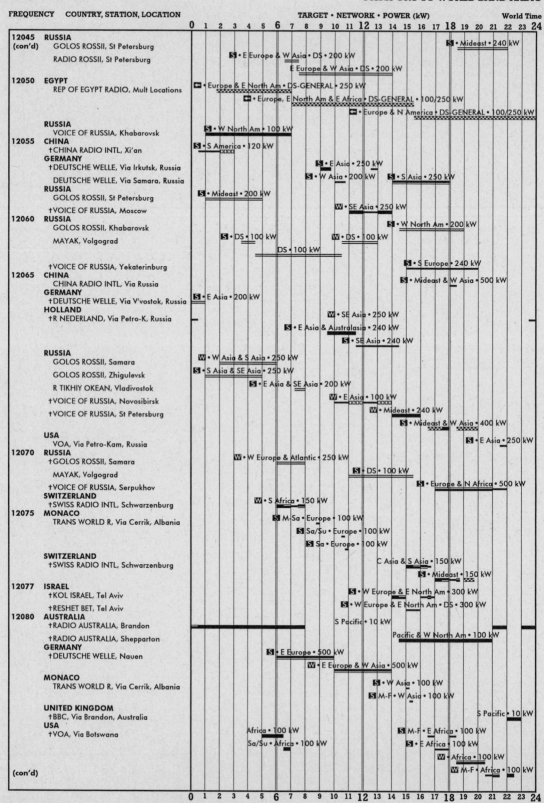

FREQUENCY   COUNTRY, STATION, LOCATION   TARGET • NETWORK • POWER (kW)   World Time

12045   **RUSSIA**
(con'd)   GOLOS ROSSII, St Petersburg   S • Mideast • 240 kW
       RADIO ROSSII, St Petersburg   S • E Europe & W Asia • DS • 200 kW
       E Europe & W Asia • DS • 200 kW

12050   **EGYPT**
       REP OF EGYPT RADIO, Mult Locations   Europe & E North Am • DS-GENERAL • 250 kW
       Europe, E North Am & E Africa • DS-GENERAL • 100/250 kW
       Europe & N America • DS-GENERAL • 100/250 kW

       RUSSIA
       VOICE OF RUSSIA, Khabarovsk   S • W North Am • 100 kW
12055   **CHINA**
       †CHINA RADIO INTL, Xi'an   S • S America • 120 kW
       GERMANY
       †DEUTSCHE WELLE, Via Irkutsk, Russia   S • E Asia • 250 kW
       DEUTSCHE WELLE, Via Samara, Russia   S • W Asia • 200 kW   S • S Asia • 250 kW
       RUSSIA
       GOLOS ROSSII, St Petersburg   S • Mideast • 200 kW
       †VOICE OF RUSSIA, Moscow   W • SE Asia • 250 kW
12060   **RUSSIA**
       GOLOS ROSSII, Khabarovsk   S • W North Am • 200 kW
       MAYAK, Volgograd   S • DS • 100 kW   W • DS • 100 kW
       DS • 100 kW

       †VOICE OF RUSSIA, Yekaterinburg   S • S Europe • 240 kW
12065   **CHINA**
       CHINA RADIO INTL, Via Russia   S • Mideast & W Asia • 500 kW
       GERMANY
       †DEUTSCHE WELLE, Via V'vostok, Russia   S • E Asia • 200 kW
       HOLLAND
       †R NEDERLAND, Via Petro-K, Russia   W • SE Asia • 250 kW
       S • E Asia & Australasia • 240 kW
       S • SE Asia • 240 kW

       RUSSIA
       GOLOS ROSSII, Samara   W • W Asia & S Asia • 250 kW
       GOLOS ROSSII, Zhigulevsk   S • S Asia & SE Asia • 250 kW
       R TIKHIY OKEAN, Vladivostok   S • E Asia & SE Asia • 200 kW
       †VOICE OF RUSSIA, Novosibirsk   W • E Asia • 100 kW
       †VOICE OF RUSSIA, St Petersburg   W • Mideast • 240 kW
       S • Mideast & W Asia • 400 kW

       USA
       VOA, Via Petro-Kam, Russia   S • E Asia • 250 kW
12070   **RUSSIA**
       †GOLOS ROSSII, Samara   W • W Europe & Atlantic • 250 kW
       MAYAK, Volgograd   S • DS • 100 kW
       †VOICE OF RUSSIA, Serpukhov   S • Europe & N Africa • 500 kW
       SWITZERLAND
       †SWISS RADIO INTL, Schwarzenburg   W • S Africa • 150 kW
12075   **MONACO**
       TRANS WORLD R, Via Cerrik, Albania   S • M-Sa • Europe • 100 kW
       S • Sa/Su • Europe • 100 kW
       S • Sa • Europe • 100 kW

       SWITZERLAND
       †SWISS RADIO INTL, Schwarzenburg   C Asia & S Asia • 150 kW
       S • Mideast • 150 kW
12077   **ISRAEL**
       †KOL ISRAEL, Tel Aviv   S • W Europe & E North Am • 300 kW
       †RESHET BET, Tel Aviv   S • W Europe & E North Am • DS • 300 kW
12080   **AUSTRALIA**
       †RADIO AUSTRALIA, Brandon   S Pacific • 10 kW
       †RADIO AUSTRALIA, Shepparton   Pacific & W North Am • 100 kW
       GERMANY
       †DEUTSCHE WELLE, Nauen   S • E Europe • 500 kW
       W • E Europe & W Asia • 500 kW

       MONACO
       TRANS WORLD R, Via Cerrik, Albania   S • W Asia • 100 kW
       S M-F • W Asia • 100 kW

       UNITED KINGDOM
       †BBC, Via Brandon, Australia   S Pacific • 10 kW
       USA
       †VOA, Via Botswana   Africa • 100 kW   S M-F • E Africa • 100 kW
       Sa/Su • Africa • 100 kW   S • E Africa • 100 kW
       W • Africa • 100 kW
       W M-F • Africa • 100 kW

(con'd)

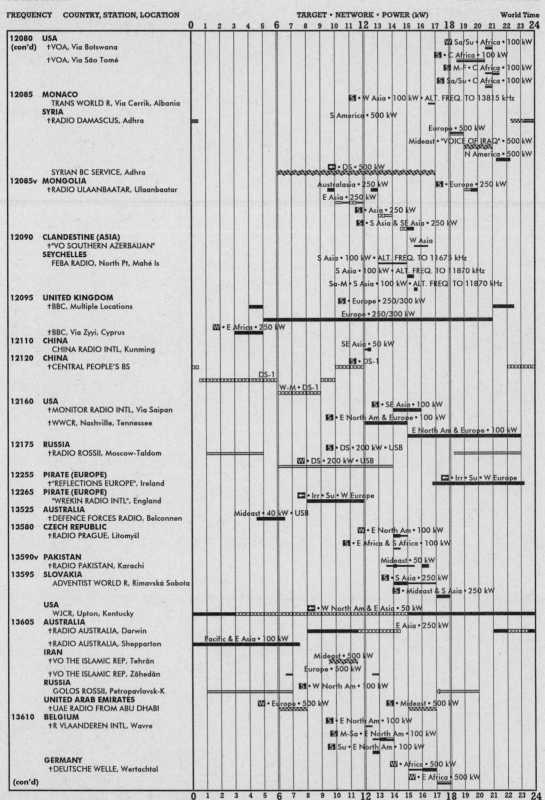

FREQUENCY   COUNTRY, STATION, LOCATION   TARGET • NETWORK • POWER (kW)   World Time

12080 (con'd)	**USA**	
	†VOA, Via Botswana	W Sa/Su • Africa • 100 kW
	†VOA, Via São Tomé	S • C Africa • 100 kW
		S • M–F • C Africa • 100 kW
		S • Sa/Su • C Africa • 100 kW
12085	**MONACO**	
	TRANS WORLD R, Via Cerrik, Albania	S • W Asia • 100 kW • ALT. FREQ. TO 13815 kHz
	SYRIA	
	†RADIO DAMASCUS, Adhra	S America • 500 kW
		Europe • 500 kW
		Mideast • "VOICE OF IRAQ" • 500 kW
		N America • 500 kW
	SYRIAN BC SERVICE, Adhra	← • DS • 500 kW
12085v	**MONGOLIA**	
	†RADIO ULAANBAATAR, Ulaanbaatar	Australasia • 250 kW
		S • Europe • 250 kW
		E Asia • 250 kW
		S • Asia • 250 kW
		S • S Asia & SE Asia • 250 kW
12090	**CLANDESTINE (ASIA)**	
	†"VO SOUTHERN AZERBAIJAN"	W Asia
	SEYCHELLES	
	FEBA RADIO, North Pt, Mahé Is	S Asia • 100 kW • ALT. FREQ. TO 11675 kHz
		S Asia • 100 kW • ALT. FREQ. TO 11870 kHz
		Sa–M • S Asia • 100 kW • ALT. FREQ. TO 11870 kHz
12095	**UNITED KINGDOM**	
	†BBC, Multiple Locations	S • Europe • 250/300 kW
		Europe • 250/300 kW
	†BBC, Via Zyyi, Cyprus	W • E Africa • 250 kW
12110	**CHINA**	
	CHINA RADIO INTL, Kunming	SE Asia • 50 kW
12120	**CHINA**	
	†CENTRAL PEOPLE'S BS	S • DS-1
		DS-1
		DS-1
		W–M • DS-1
12160	**USA**	
	†MONITOR RADIO INTL, Via Saipan	S • SE Asia • 100 kW
	†WWCR, Nashville, Tennessee	S • E North Am & Europe • 100 kW
		E North Am & Europe • 100 kW
12175	**RUSSIA**	
	†RADIO ROSSII, Moscow-Taldom	S • DS • 200 kW • USB
		W • DS • 200 kW • USB
12255	**PIRATE (EUROPE)**	
	†"REFLECTIONS EUROPE", Ireland	← • Irr • Su • W Europe
12265	**PIRATE (EUROPE)**	
	"WREKIN RADIO INTL", England	← • Irr • Su • W Europe
13525	**AUSTRALIA**	
	†DEFENCE FORCES RADIO, Belconnen	Mideast • 40 kW • USB
13580	**CZECH REPUBLIC**	
	†RADIO PRAGUE, Litomyšl	W • E North Am • 100 kW
		S • E Africa & S Africa • 100 kW
13590v	**PAKISTAN**	
	†RADIO PAKISTAN, Karachi	Mideast • 50 kW
13595	**SLOVAKIA**	
	ADVENTIST WORLD R, Rimavská Sobota	S • S Asia • 250 kW
		S • Mideast & S Asia • 250 kW
	USA	
	WJCR, Upton, Kentucky	← • W North Am & E Asia • 50 kW
13605	**AUSTRALIA**	
	†RADIO AUSTRALIA, Darwin	E Asia • 250 kW
	†RADIO AUSTRALIA, Shepparton	Pacific & E Asia • 100 kW
	IRAN	
	†VO THE ISLAMIC REP, Tehrān	Mideast • 500 kW
	†VO THE ISLAMIC REP, Zāhedān	Europe • 500 kW
	RUSSIA	
	GOLOS ROSSII, Petropavlovsk-K	S • W North Am • 100 kW
	UNITED ARAB EMIRATES	
	†UAE RADIO FROM ABU DHABI	W • Europe • 500 kW
		S • Mideast • 500 kW
13610	**BELGIUM**	
	†R VLAANDEREN INTL, Wavre	S • E North Am • 100 kW
		S • M–Sa • E North Am • 100 kW
		S • Su • E North Am • 100 kW
	GERMANY	
	†DEUTSCHE WELLE, Wertachtal	W • Africa • 500 kW
		W • E Africa • 500 kW
(con'd)		

ENGLISH ▬   ARABIC ᵡᵡᵡ   CHINESE ▭▭▭   FRENCH ▬   GERMAN ▬   RUSSIAN ══   SPANISH ▬   OTHER ▬

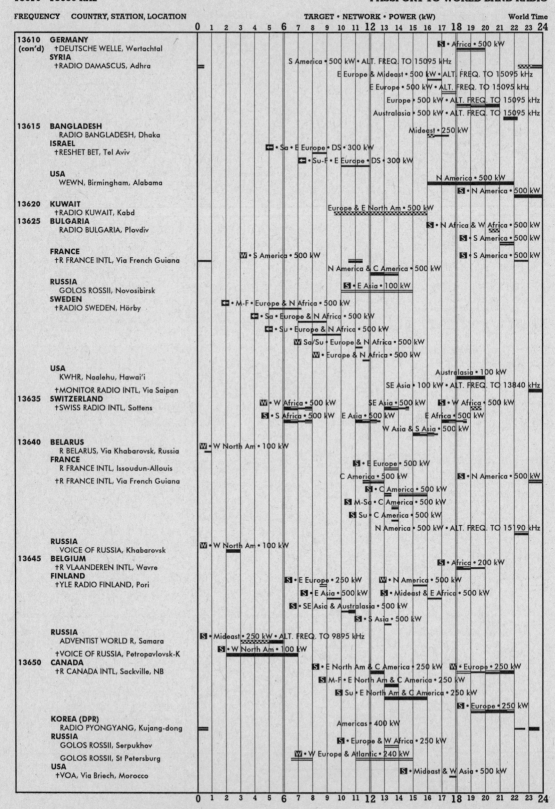

FREQUENCY   COUNTRY, STATION, LOCATION   TARGET • NETWORK • POWER (kW)   World Time

Frequency	Country, Station, Location	Target • Network • Power
13660	UNITED KINGDOM BBC, Rampisham	• Su • Europe • 500 kW
	†BBC, Skelton, Cumbria	Mideast • 300 kW / N Africa • 300 kW / N Africa • 300 kW
	BBC, Via Zyyi, Cyprus	W • N Africa • 300 kW
13665	PAKISTAN †RADIO PAKISTAN, Karachi	S Asia • 50 kW
	RUSSIA VOICE OF RUSSIA, Petropavlovsk-K	S • W North Am • 100 kW
	USA †RADIO MARTI, Greenville, NC	S • C America • 250 kW
13670	BELGIUM †R VLAANDEREN INTL, Wavre	W • E North Am • 100 kW / W M-Sa • E North Am • 100 kW / W Su • E North Am • 100 kW
	CANADA †R CANADA INTL, Sackville, NB	S Su/M • S America • 250 kW / S • Europe • 250 kW / S Tu-Sa • S America • 250 kW / S • Africa • 250 kW / S • S America • 250 kW / S • C America & S America • 250 kW
	CLANDESTINE (M EAST) †"VO IRAQI PEOPLE", Saudi Arabia	Irr • Mideast • ANTI-SADDAM
	KOREA (REPUBLIC) †RADIO KOREA INTL, In-Kimjae	Europe • 250 kW / SE Asia • 100 kW
	RUSSIA †VOICE OF RUSSIA, Via Armenia	W • W Africa • 100 kW
	TURKEY †VOICE OF TURKEY, Ankara-Emirler	S • Europe • 500 kW
	UKRAINE †RADIO UKRAINE, Kiev	W • W Asia • 200 kW / W • S Europe & N Africa • 200 kW
	USA †VOA, Via Botswana	S M-F • C Africa & S Africa • 100 kW / S • C Africa & S Africa • 100 kW
13675	UNITED ARAB EMIRATES †UAE RADIO IN DUBAI	Irr • E North Am & C America • RAMADAN • 300 kW / E North Am & C America • 300 kW / Europe • 300 kW
13680	CUBA †RADIO HABANA, Havana	S • Europe & N Africa • 100 kW
	RUSSIA GOLOS ROSSII, St Petersburg	S • W Europe & Atlantic • 240 kW
13685	BELGIUM †R VLAANDEREN INTL, Wavre	S W/Sa • Africa • 100 kW
	CHINA CHINA RADIO INTL, Via French Guiana	S America • 500 kW
	SWITZERLAND SWISS RADIO INTL, Various Locations	Australasia • 500 kW
13690	CANADA R CANADA INTL, Sackville, NB	W • Africa • 250 kW
	GERMANY †DEUTSCHE WELLE, Nauen	S • Mideast • 100 kW
	DEUTSCHE WELLE, Various Locations	Mideast • 100 kW / W • E Africa • 250 kW
	†DEUTSCHE WELLE, Via Sri Lanka	S • S Asia • 500 kW
	†DEUTSCHE WELLE, Wertachtal	S • W Asia • 500 kW
	UKRAINE †RADIO UKRAINE, Kiev	S • W Europe • 200 kW
13695	HOLLAND R NEDERLAND, Via Irkutsk, Russia	S • SE Asia • 250 kW
	HUNGARY RADIO BUDAPEST, Diósd	• Australasia • 100 kW / • Su • Australasia • 100 kW
	USA †WEWN, Birmingham, Alabama	W • Europe • 500 kW / Europe • 500 kW / S • Europe • 500 kW
	†WYFR-FAMILY RADIO, Okeechobee, Fl	S • W Africa • 100 kW / E North Am • 100 kW
13700	HOLLAND R NEDERLAND, Flevoland	S • S Europe • 500 kW / S • S America • 500 kW / Mideast & S Asia • 500 kW / W • S Asia • 500 kW / S • Mideast • 500 kW / S • W Africa • 500 kW

(con'd)

ENGLISH ▬ ARABIC ⋙ CHINESE ⊡⊡⊡ FRENCH ▬ GERMAN ▬ RUSSIAN ═ SPANISH ▬ OTHER ▬

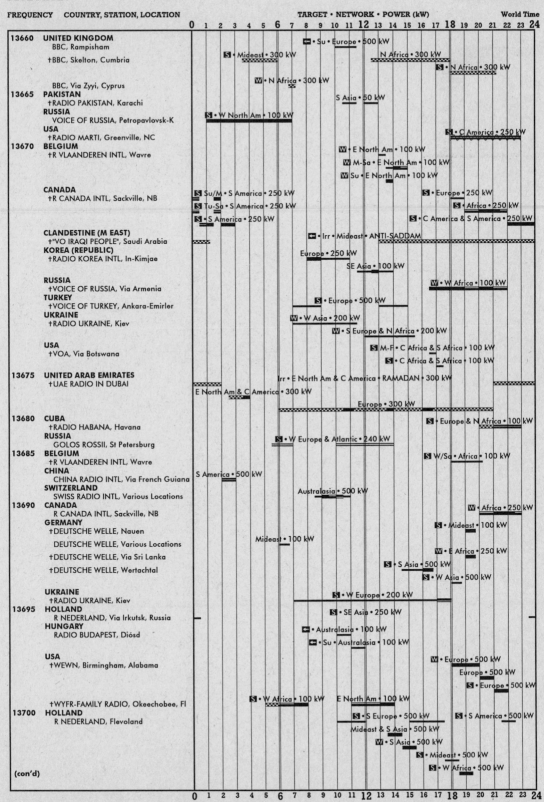

FREQUENCY   COUNTRY, STATION, LOCATION

TARGET • NETWORK • POWER (kW)

World Time

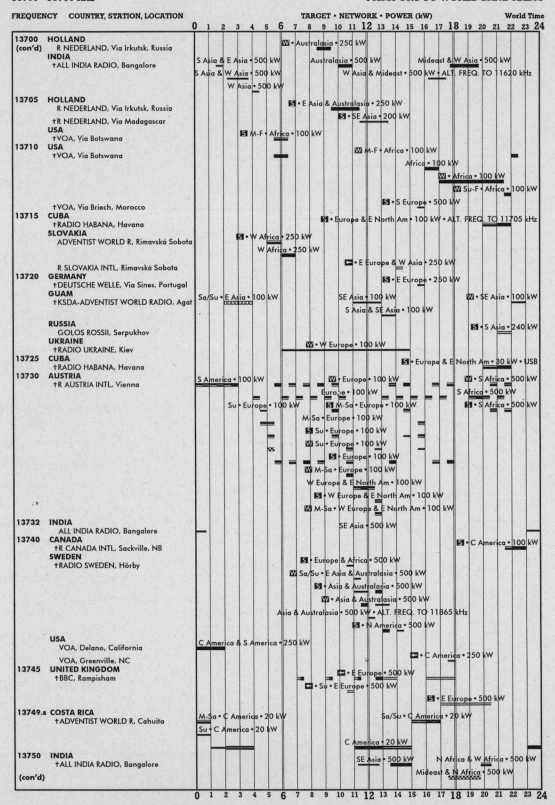

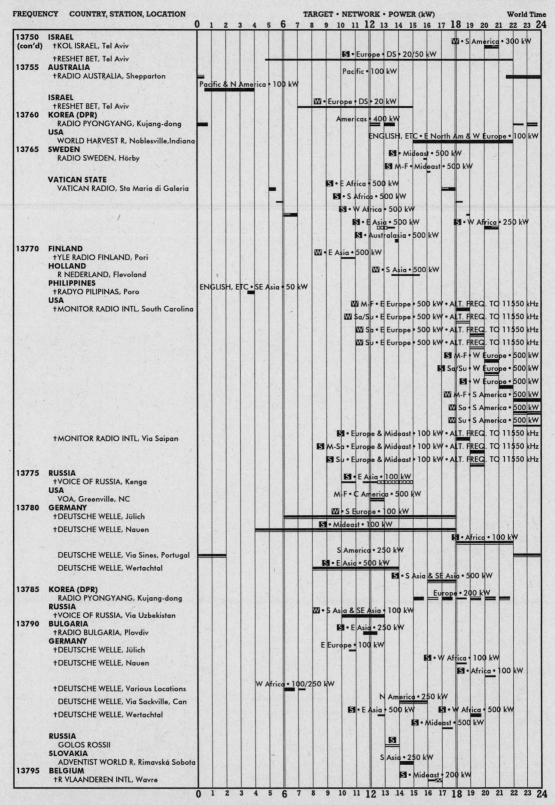

FREQUENCY	COUNTRY, STATION, LOCATION	TARGET • NETWORK • POWER (kW)	World Time

13750 ISRAEL
(con'd) †KOL ISRAEL, Tel Aviv — W • S America • 300 kW
  †RESHET BET, Tel Aviv — S • Europe • DS 20/50 kW

13755 AUSTRALIA
  †RADIO AUSTRALIA, Shepparton — Pacific • 100 kW / Pacific & N America • 100 kW

ISRAEL
  †RESHET BET, Tel Aviv — W • Europe • DS • 20 kW

13760 KOREA (DPR)
  RADIO PYONGYANG, Kujang-dong — Americas • 400 kW

USA
  WORLD HARVEST R, Noblesville, Indiana — ENGLISH, ETC • E North Am & W Europe • 100 kW

13765 SWEDEN
  RADIO SWEDEN, Hörby — S • Mideast • 500 kW
  — S M-F • Mideast • 500 kW

VATICAN STATE
  VATICAN RADIO, Sta Maria di Galeria — S • E Africa • 500 kW
  — S • S Africa • 500 kW
  — S • W Africa • 500 kW
  — S • E Asia • 500 kW   S • W Africa • 250 kW
  — S • Australasia • 500 kW

13770 FINLAND
  †YLE RADIO FINLAND, Pori — W • E Asia • 500 kW

HOLLAND
  R NEDERLAND, Flevoland — W • S Asia • 500 kW

PHILIPPINES
  †RADYO PILIPINAS, Poro — ENGLISH, ETC • SE Asia • 50 kW

USA
  †MONITOR RADIO INTL, South Carolina — W M-F • E Europe • 500 kW • ALT. FREQ. TO 11550 kHz
  — W Sa/Su • E Europe • 500 kW • ALT. FREQ. TO 11550 kHz
  — W Sa • E Europe • 500 kW • ALT. FREQ. TO 11550 kHz
  — W Su • E Europe • 500 kW • ALT. FREQ. TO 11550 kHz
  — S M-F • W Europe • 500 kW
  — S Sa/Su • W Europe • 500 kW
  — S • W Europe • 500 kW
  — W M-F • S America • 500 kW
  — W Sa • S America • 500 kW
  — W Su • S America • 500 kW

  †MONITOR RADIO INTL, Via Saipan — S • Europe & Mideast • 100 kW • ALT. FREQ. TO 11550 kHz
  — S M-Sa • Europe & Mideast • 100 kW • ALT. FREQ. TO 11550 kHz
  — S Su • Europe & Mideast • 100 kW • ALT. FREQ. TO 11550 kHz

13775 RUSSIA
  †VOICE OF RUSSIA, Kenga — S • E Asia • 100 kW

USA
  VOA, Greenville, NC — M-F • C America • 500 kW

13780 GERMANY
  †DEUTSCHE WELLE, Jülich — W • S Europe • 100 kW
  †DEUTSCHE WELLE, Nauen — S • Mideast • 100 kW
  — S • Africa • 100 kW

  DEUTSCHE WELLE, Via Sines, Portugal — S America • 250 kW
  DEUTSCHE WELLE, Wertachtal — S • E Asia • 500 kW   S • S Asia & SE Asia • 500 kW

13785 KOREA (DPR)
  RADIO PYONGYANG, Kujang-dong — Europe • 200 kW

RUSSIA
  †VOICE OF RUSSIA, Via Uzbekistan — W • S Asia & SE Asia • 100 kW

13790 BULGARIA
  †RADIO BULGARIA, Plovdiv — S • E Asia • 250 kW

GERMANY
  †DEUTSCHE WELLE, Jülich — E Europe • 100 kW
  †DEUTSCHE WELLE, Nauen — S • W Africa • 100 kW
  — S • Africa • 100 kW

  †DEUTSCHE WELLE, Various Locations — W Africa • 100/250 kW
  DEUTSCHE WELLE, Via Sackville, Can — N America • 250 kW
  †DEUTSCHE WELLE, Wertachtal — S • E Asia • 500 kW   S • W Africa • 500 kW
  — S • Mideast • 500 kW

RUSSIA
  GOLOS ROSSII — S

SLOVAKIA
  ADVENTIST WORLD R, Rimavská Sobota — S Asia • 250 kW

13795 BELGIUM
  †R VLAANDEREN INTL, Wavre — S • Mideast • 200 kW

ENGLISH ▬ ARABIC ⌇⌇ CHINESE ▫▫▫ FRENCH ▭▭ GERMAN ▬▬ RUSSIAN ══ SPANISH ▬▬ OTHER ▭

FREQUENCY	COUNTRY, STATION, LOCATION	TARGET • NETWORK • POWER (kW)	World Time

World Time: 0 1 2 3 4 5 6 7 8 9 10 11 12 13 14 15 16 17 18 19 20 21 22 23 24

13800 BELGIUM
R VLAANDEREN INTL, Wavre — S • S America • 100 kW

DENMARK
†RADIO DANMARK, Via Norway
- W • Australasia • 500 kW
- S • E Asia • 500 kW
- S • SE Asia & Australasia • 500 kW
- S • S Asia & SE Asia • 500 kW

NORWAY
†R NORWAY INTL, Kvitsøy
- W • Australasia • 500 kW
- S • E Asia • 500 kW
- S M-Sa • E Asia • 500 kW
- S Su • E Asia • 500 kW
- S M-Sa • SE Asia & Australasia • 500 kW
- S Su • SE Asia & Australasia • 500 kW
- S • S Asia & SE Asia • 500 kW

13805 DENMARK
†RADIO DANMARK, Via Norway
- S • Mideast • 500 kW
- S • E Africa • 500 kW
- S • W Africa • 500 kW
- S • C Africa • 500 kW

NORWAY
†R NORWAY INTL, Kvitsøy
- S • Mideast • 500 kW
- S • E Africa • 500 kW
- S • W Africa • 500 kW
- S M-Sa • E Africa • 500 kW
- S Su • E Africa • 500 kW
- S • C Africa • 500 kW
- S M-Sa • W Africa • 500 kW
- S Su • W Africa • 500 kW

13815 MONACO
TRANS WORLD R, Via Cerrik, Albania — S • W Asia • 100 kW • ALT. FREQ. TO 12085 kHz

RUSSIA
†VOICE OF RUSSIA, Via Moldova — S • N Africa & W Africa • 1000 kW

USA
†KAIJ, Dallas, Texas — S • N America • 100 kW
N America • 100 kW

13820 USA
†RADIO MARTI, Delano, California
- C America • 250 kW
- C America • 250 kW

†RADIO MARTI, Greenville, NC — S • C America • 250 kW

13825 USA
†WVHA, Scotts Corners, Maine
- S Sa • Africa • 250/500 kW
- S Su • Europe • 250/500 kW
- S Su • Africa • 250/500 kW

13830 CROATIA
†CROATIAN RADIO, Deanovec
- S • S America • 2.5 kW
- W • Australasia • 2.5 kW
- ⬌ • N America • 100 kW
- ⬌ • E North Am • 100 kW

13840 GUAM
†KSDA-ADVENTIST WORLD RADIO, Agat — S • Mideast • 100 kW

USA
†MONITOR RADIO INTL, Via Saipan
- W • Australasia • 100 kW
- Australasia • 100 kW
- Sa • E Asia • 100 kW
- Su-F • E Asia • 100 kW
- SE Asia • 100 kW • ALT. FREQ. TO 13625 kHz

13845 USA
†WWCR, Nashville, Tennessee
- W North Am • 100 kW
- S • W North Am • 100 kW

13860 ICELAND
RIKISUTVARPID, Reykjavik
- Atlantic & Europe • DS-1 • 10 kW
- Atlantic & E North Am • DS-1 • 10 kW

14670 CANADA
CHU, Ottawa — WORLD TIME • 3 kW • USB

15000 USA
WWV, Fort Collins, Colorado — WEATHER/WORLD TIME • 10 kW

WWVH, Kekaha, Hawai'i — WEATHER/WORLD TIME • 10 kW

15010v VIETNAM
VOICE OF VIETNAM, Ha Son Binh
- S • E Asia & Americas • 30 kW
- S • SE Asia • 30 kW
- S • Africa • 30 kW
- S • Europe • 30 kW

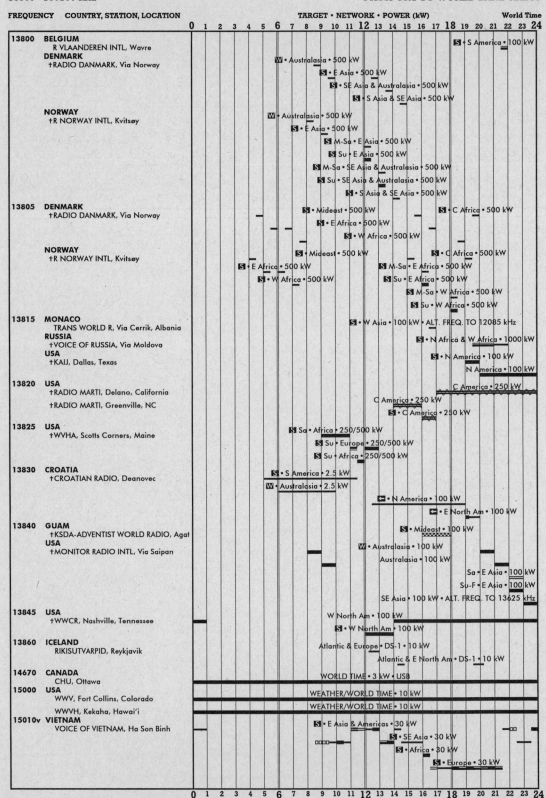

World Time: 0 1 2 3 4 5 6 7 8 9 10 11 12 13 14 15 16 17 18 19 20 21 22 23 24

SEASONAL S OR W   1-HR TIMESHIFT MIDYEAR ⬅ OR ➡   JAMMING / OR ⋀   EARLIEST HEARD ◁   LATEST HEARD ▷   NEW FOR 1997 †

FREQUENCY　　COUNTRY, STATION, LOCATION　　　　　　TARGET • NETWORK • POWER (kW)　　　　World Time

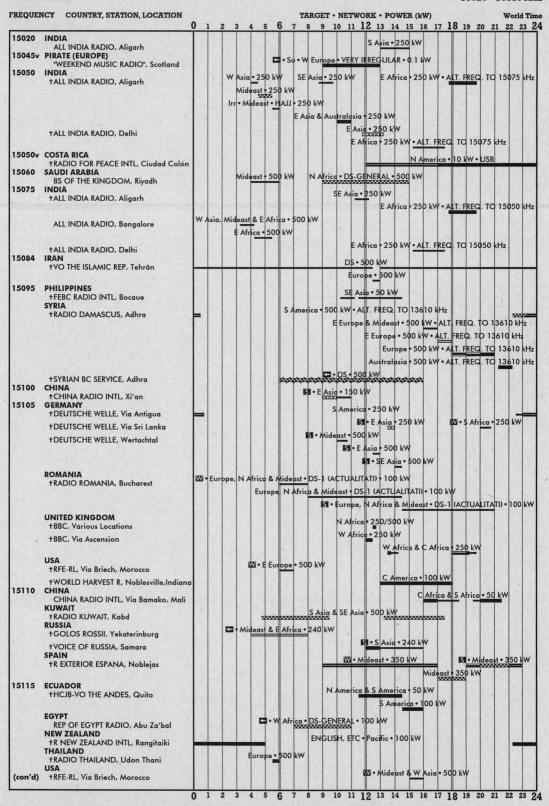

Frequency	Country / Station / Location	Schedule
15020	**INDIA** ALL INDIA RADIO, Aligarh	S Asia • 250 kW
15045v	**PIRATE (EUROPE)** "WEEKEND MUSIC RADIO", Scotland	• Su • W Europe • VERY IRREGULAR • 0.1 kW
15050	**INDIA** †ALL INDIA RADIO, Aligarh	W Asia • 250 kW / SE Asia • 250 kW / E Africa • 250 kW • ALT. FREQ. TO 15075 kHz
		Mideast • 250 kW
		Irr • Mideast • HAJJ • 250 kW
		E Asia & Australasia • 250 kW
	†ALL INDIA RADIO, Delhi	E Asia • 250 kW
		E Africa • 250 kW • ALT. FREQ. TO 15075 kHz
15050v	**COSTA RICA** †RADIO FOR PEACE INTL, Ciudad Colón	N America • 10 kW • USB
15060	**SAUDI ARABIA** BS OF THE KINGDOM, Riyadh	Mideast • 500 kW / N Africa • DS-GENERAL • 500 kW
15075	**INDIA** †ALL INDIA RADIO, Aligarh	SE Asia • 250 kW
		E Africa • 250 kW • ALT. FREQ. TO 15050 kHz
	ALL INDIA RADIO, Bangalore	W Asia, Mideast & E Africa • 500 kW
		E Africa • 500 kW
	†ALL INDIA RADIO, Delhi	E Africa • 250 kW • ALT. FREQ. TO 15050 kHz
15084	**IRAN** †VO THE ISLAMIC REP, Tehrān	DS • 500 kW
		Europe • 500 kW
15095	**PHILIPPINES** †FEBC RADIO INTL, Bocaue	SE Asia • 50 kW
	SYRIA †RADIO DAMASCUS, Adhra	S America • 500 kW • ALT. FREQ. TO 13610 kHz
		E Europe & Mideast • 500 kW • ALT. FREQ. TO 13610 kHz
		E Europe • 500 kW • ALT. FREQ. TO 13610 kHz
		Europe • 500 kW • ALT. FREQ. TO 13610 kHz
		Australasia • 500 kW • ALT. FREQ. TO 13610 kHz
	†SYRIAN BC SERVICE, Adhra	• DS • 500 kW
15100	**CHINA** †CHINA RADIO INTL, Xi'an	• E Asia • 150 kW
15105	**GERMANY** †DEUTSCHE WELLE, Via Antigua	S America • 250 kW
	†DEUTSCHE WELLE, Via Sri Lanka	• E Asia • 250 kW / • S Africa • 250 kW
	†DEUTSCHE WELLE, Wertachtal	• Mideast • 500 kW
		• E Asia • 500 kW
		• SE Asia • 500 kW
	ROMANIA †RADIO ROMANIA, Bucharest	• Europe, N Africa & Mideast • DS-1 (ACTUALITATI) • 100 kW
		Europe, N Africa & Mideast • DS-1 (ACTUALITATI) • 100 kW
		• Europe, N Africa & Mideast • DS-1 (ACTUALITATI) • 100 kW
	UNITED KINGDOM †BBC, Various Locations	N Africa • 250/500 kW
	†BBC, Via Ascension	W Africa • 250 kW
		W Africa & C Africa • 250 kW
	USA †RFE-RL, Via Briech, Morocco	• E Europe • 500 kW
	†WORLD HARVEST R, Noblesville, Indiana	C America • 100 kW
15110	**CHINA** CHINA RADIO INTL, Via Bamako, Mali	C Africa & S Africa • 50 kW
	KUWAIT †RADIO KUWAIT, Kabd	S Asia & SE Asia • 500 kW
	RUSSIA †GOLOS ROSSII, Yekaterinburg	• Mideast & E Africa • 240 kW
	†VOICE OF RUSSIA, Samara	• S Asia • 240 kW
	SPAIN †R EXTERIOR ESPANA, Noblejas	• Mideast • 350 kW / • Mideast • 350 kW
		Mideast • 350 kW
15115	**ECUADOR** †HCJB-VO THE ANDES, Quito	N America & S America • 50 kW
		S America • 100 kW
	EGYPT REP OF EGYPT RADIO, Abu Za'bal	• W Africa • DS-GENERAL • 100 kW
	NEW ZEALAND †R NEW ZEALAND INTL, Rangitaiki	ENGLISH, ETC • Pacific • 100 kW
	THAILAND †RADIO THAILAND, Udon Thani	Europe • 500 kW
(con'd)	**USA** †RFE-RL, Via Briech, Morocco	• Mideast & W Asia • 500 kW

ENGLISH ▬　ARABIC ░░░　CHINESE □□□　FRENCH ▬　GERMAN ▬　RUSSIAN ═　SPANISH ▬　OTHER ▬

FREQUENCY   COUNTRY, STATION, LOCATION

TARGET • NETWORK • POWER (kW)

World Time

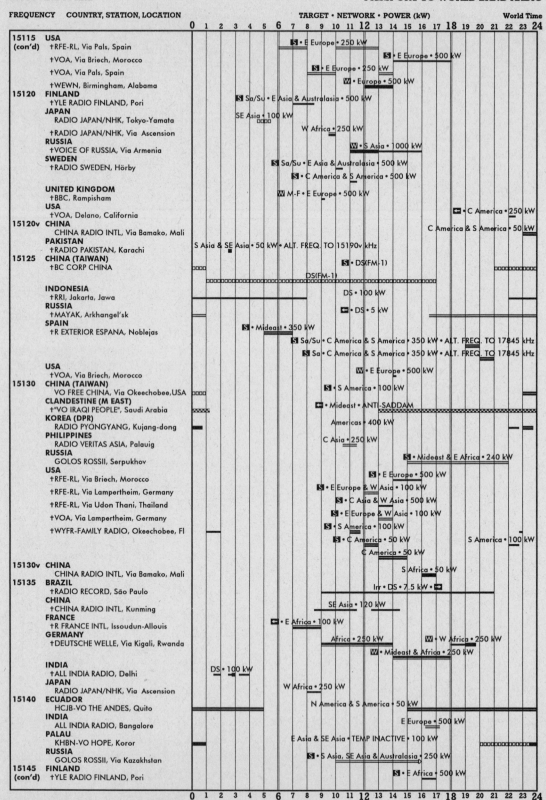

FREQUENCY	COUNTRY, STATION, LOCATION	Schedule
15115 (con'd)	USA †RFE-RL, Via Pals, Spain	S • E Europe • 250 kW / S • E Europe • 500 kW
	†VOA, Via Briech, Morocco	S • E Europe • 250 kW
	†VOA, Via Pals, Spain	W • Europe • 500 kW
	†WEWN, Birmingham, Alabama	
15120	FINLAND †YLE RADIO FINLAND, Pori	S Sa/Su • E Asia & Australasia • 500 kW
	JAPAN RADIO JAPAN/NHK, Tokyo-Yamata	SE Asia • 100 kW
	†RADIO JAPAN/NHK, Via Ascension	W Africa • 250 kW
	RUSSIA †VOICE OF RUSSIA, Via Armenia	W • S Asia • 1000 kW
	SWEDEN †RADIO SWEDEN, Hörby	S Sa/Su • E Asia & Australasia • 500 kW / S • C America & S America • 500 kW
	UNITED KINGDOM †BBC, Rampisham	W M-F • E Europe • 500 kW
	USA †VOA, Delano, California	C America • 250 kW
15120v	CHINA CHINA RADIO INTL, Via Bamako, Mali	C America & S America • 50 kW
	PAKISTAN †RADIO PAKISTAN, Karachi	S Asia & SE Asia • 50 kW • ALT. FREQ. TO 15190v kHz
15125	CHINA (TAIWAN) †BC CORP CHINA	S • DS(FM-1) / DS(FM-1)
	INDONESIA †RRI, Jakarta, Jawa	DS • 100 kW
	RUSSIA †MAYAK, Arkhangel'sk	DS • 5 kW
	SPAIN †R EXTERIOR ESPANA, Noblejas	S • Mideast • 350 kW / S Sa/Su • C America & S America • 350 kW • ALT. FREQ. TO 17845 kHz / S Sa • C America & S America • 350 kW • ALT. FREQ. TO 17845 kHz
	USA †VOA, Via Briech, Morocco	W • E Europe • 500 kW
15130	CHINA (TAIWAN) VO FREE CHINA, Via Okeechobee, USA	S • S America • 100 kW
	CLANDESTINE (M EAST) †"VO IRAQI PEOPLE", Saudi Arabia	• Mideast • ANTI-SADDAM
	KOREA (DPR) RADIO PYONGYANG, Kujang-dong	Americas • 400 kW
	PHILIPPINES RADIO VERITAS ASIA, Palauig	C Asia • 250 kW
	RUSSIA GOLOS ROSSII, Serpukhov	S • Mideast & E Africa • 240 kW
	USA †RFE-RL, Via Briech, Morocco	S • E Europe • 500 kW
	†RFE-RL, Via Lampertheim, Germany	S • E Europe & W Asia • 100 kW
	†RFE-RL, Via Udon Thani, Thailand	S • C Asia & W Asia • 500 kW
	†VOA, Via Lampertheim, Germany	S • E Europe & W Asia • 100 kW
	†WYFR-FAMILY RADIO, Okeechobee, Fl	S • S America • 100 kW / S • C America • 50 kW / S America • 100 kW / C America • 50 kW
15130v	CHINA CHINA RADIO INTL, Via Bamako, Mali	S Africa • 50 kW
15135	BRAZIL †RADIO RECORD, São Paulo	Irr • DS • 7.5 kW •
	CHINA †CHINA RADIO INTL, Kunming	SE Asia • 120 kW
	FRANCE †R FRANCE INTL, Issoudun-Allouis	• E Africa • 100 kW
	GERMANY †DEUTSCHE WELLE, Via Kigali, Rwanda	Africa • 250 kW / W • W Africa • 250 kW / W • Mideast & Africa • 250 kW
	INDIA †ALL INDIA RADIO, Delhi	DS • 100 kW
	JAPAN RADIO JAPAN/NHK, Via Ascension	W Africa • 250 kW
15140	ECUADOR HCJB-VO THE ANDES, Quito	N America & S America • 50 kW
	INDIA ALL INDIA RADIO, Bangalore	E Europe • 500 kW
	PALAU KHBN-VO HOPE, Koror	E Asia & SE Asia • TEMP INACTIVE • 100 kW
	RUSSIA GOLOS ROSSII, Via Kazakhstan	S • S Asia, SE Asia & Australasia • 250 kW
15145 (con'd)	FINLAND †YLE RADIO FINLAND, Pori	S • E Africa • 500 kW

FREQUENCY   COUNTRY, STATION, LOCATION   TARGET • NETWORK • POWER (kW)   World Time

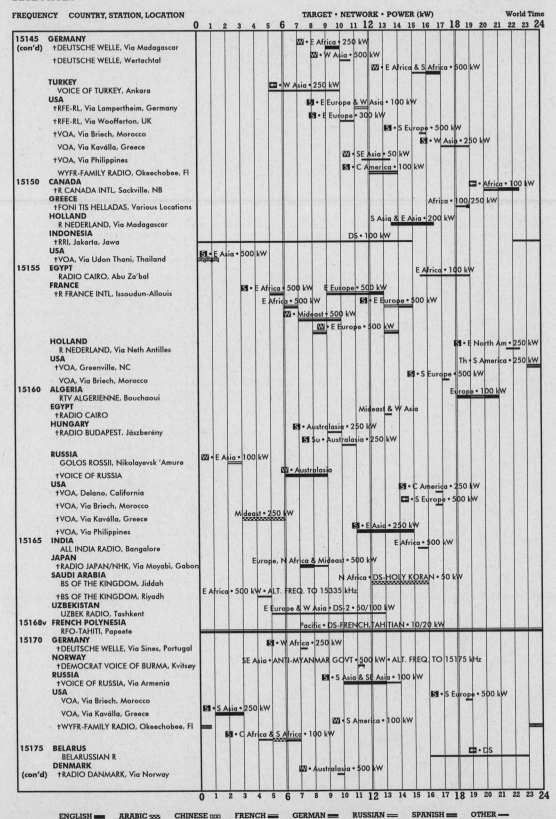

Frequency	Country, Station, Location	Target • Network • Power
15145 (con'd)	**GERMANY**	
	†DEUTSCHE WELLE, Via Madagascar	W • E Africa • 250 kW
	†DEUTSCHE WELLE, Wertachtal	W • W Asia • 500 kW
		W • E Africa & S Africa • 500 kW
	TURKEY	
	VOICE OF TURKEY, Ankara	W Asia • 250 kW
	USA	
	†RFE-RL, Via Lampertheim, Germany	S • E Europe & W Asia • 100 kW
	†RFE-RL, Via Woofferton, UK	S • E Europe • 300 kW
	†VOA, Via Briech, Morocco	S • S Europe • 500 kW
	VOA, Via Kavála, Greece	S • W Asia • 250 kW
	†VOA, Via Philippines	W • SE Asia • 50 kW
	WYFR-FAMILY RADIO, Okeechobee, Fl	S • C America • 100 kW
15150	**CANADA**	
	†R CANADA INTL, Sackville, NB	Africa • 100 kW
	GREECE	
	†FONI TIS HELLADAS, Various Locations	Africa • 100/250 kW
	HOLLAND	
	R NEDERLAND, Via Madagascar	S Asia & E Asia • 200 kW
	INDONESIA	
	†RRI, Jakarta, Jawa	DS • 100 kW
	USA	
	†VOA, Via Udon Thani, Thailand	S • E Asia • 500 kW
15155	**EGYPT**	
	RADIO CAIRO, Abu Za'bal	E Africa • 100 kW
	FRANCE	
	†R FRANCE INTL, Issoudun-Allouis	S • E Africa • 500 kW E Europe • 500 kW
		E Africa • 500 kW S • E Europe • 500 kW
		W • Mideast • 500 kW
		W • E Europe • 500 kW
	HOLLAND	
	R NEDERLAND, Via Neth Antilles	S • E North Am • 250 kW
	USA	
	†VOA, Greenville, NC	Th • S America • 250 kW
	VOA, Via Briech, Morocco	S • S Europe • 500 kW
15160	**ALGERIA**	
	RTV ALGERIENNE, Bouchaoui	Europe • 100 kW
	EGYPT	
	†RADIO CAIRO	Mideast & W Asia
	HUNGARY	
	†RADIO BUDAPEST, Jászberény	S • Australasia • 250 kW
		S Su • Australasia • 250 kW
	RUSSIA	
	GOLOS ROSSII, Nikolayevsk 'Amure	W • E Asia • 100 kW
	†VOICE OF RUSSIA	W • Australasia
	USA	
	†VOA, Delano, California	S • C America • 250 kW
	†VOA, Via Briech, Morocco	S • S Europe • 500 kW
	†VOA, Via Kavála, Greece	Mideast • 250 kW
	†VOA, Via Philippines	S • E Asia • 250 kW
15165	**INDIA**	
	ALL INDIA RADIO, Bangalore	E Africa • 500 kW
	JAPAN	
	†RADIO JAPAN/NHK, Via Moyabi, Gabon	Europe, N Africa & Mideast • 500 kW
	SAUDI ARABIA	
	BS OF THE KINGDOM, Jiddah	N Africa • DS-HOLY KORAN • 50 kW
	†BS OF THE KINGDOM, Riyadh	E Africa • 500 kW • ALT. FREQ. TO 15335 kHz
	UZBEKISTAN	
	UZBEK RADIO, Tashkent	E Europe & W Asia • DS-2 • 50/100 kW
15168v	**FRENCH POLYNESIA**	
	RFO-TAHITI, Papeete	Pacific • DS-FRENCH, TAHITIAN • 10/20 kW
15170	**GERMANY**	
	†DEUTSCHE WELLE, Via Sines, Portugal	S • W Africa • 250 kW
	NORWAY	
	†DEMOCRAT VOICE OF BURMA, Kvitsøy	SE Asia • ANTI-MYANMAR GOVT • 500 kW • ALT. FREQ. TO 15175 kHz
	RUSSIA	
	†VOICE OF RUSSIA, Via Armenia	S • S Asia & SE Asia • 100 kW
	USA	
	VOA, Via Briech, Morocco	S • S Europe • 500 kW
	VOA, Via Kavála, Greece	S • S Asia • 250 kW
		W • S America • 100 kW
	†WYFR-FAMILY RADIO, Okeechobee, Fl	S • C Africa & S Africa • 100 kW
15175	**BELARUS**	
	BELARUSSIAN R	DS
(con'd)	**DENMARK**	
	†RADIO DANMARK, Via Norway	W • Australasia • 500 kW

FREQUENCY   COUNTRY, STATION, LOCATION

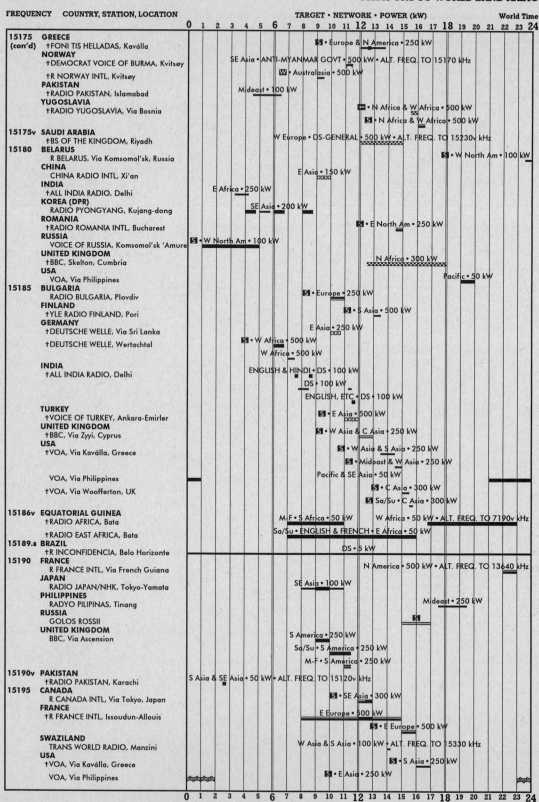

	TARGET • NETWORK • POWER (kW)
15175 GREECE	
(con'd) †FONI TIS HELLADAS, Kaválla	Ⓢ • Europe & N America • 250 kW
NORWAY	
†DEMOCRAT VOICE OF BURMA, Kvitsøy	SE Asia • ANTI-MYANMAR GOVT • 500 kW • ALT. FREQ. TO 15170 kHz
†R NORWAY INTL, Kvitsøy	Ⓦ • Australasia • 500 kW
PAKISTAN	
†RADIO PAKISTAN, Islamabad	Mideast • 100 kW
YUGOSLAVIA	
†RADIO YUGOSLAVIA, Via Bosnia	• N Africa & W Africa • 500 kW
	Ⓢ • N Africa & W Africa • 500 kW
15175v SAUDI ARABIA	
†BS OF THE KINGDOM, Riyadh	W Europe • DS-GENERAL • 500 kW • ALT. FREQ. TO 15230v kHz
15180 BELARUS	
R BELARUS, Via Komsomol'sk, Russia	Ⓢ • W North Am • 100 kW
CHINA	
CHINA RADIO INTL, Xi'an	E Asia • 150 kW
INDIA	
†ALL INDIA RADIO, Delhi	E Africa • 250 kW
KOREA (DPR)	
RADIO PYONGYANG, Kujang-dong	SE Asia • 200 kW
ROMANIA	
†RADIO ROMANIA INTL, Bucharest	Ⓢ • E North Am • 250 kW
RUSSIA	
VOICE OF RUSSIA, Komsomol'sk 'Amure	Ⓢ • W North Am • 100 kW
UNITED KINGDOM	
†BBC, Skelton, Cumbria	N Africa • 300 kW
USA	
VOA, Via Philippines	Pacific • 50 kW
15185 BULGARIA	
RADIO BULGARIA, Plovdiv	Ⓢ • Europe • 250 kW
FINLAND	
†YLE RADIO FINLAND, Pori	Ⓢ • S Asia • 500 kW
GERMANY	
†DEUTSCHE WELLE, Via Sri Lanka	E Asia • 250 kW
†DEUTSCHE WELLE, Wertachtal	Ⓢ • W Africa • 500 kW
	W Africa • 500 kW
INDIA	
†ALL INDIA RADIO, Delhi	ENGLISH & HINDI • DS • 100 kW
	DS • 100 kW
	ENGLISH, ETC • DS • 100 kW
TURKEY	
†VOICE OF TURKEY, Ankara-Emirler	Ⓢ • E Asia • 500 kW
UNITED KINGDOM	
†BBC, Via Zyyi, Cyprus	Ⓢ • W Asia & C Asia • 250 kW
USA	
†VOA, Via Kaválla, Greece	Ⓢ • W Asia & S Asia • 250 kW
	Ⓢ • Mideast & W Asia • 250 kW
VOA, Via Philippines	Pacific & SE Asia • 50 kW
†VOA, Via Woofferton, UK	Ⓢ • C Asia • 300 kW
	Ⓢ • Sa/Su • C Asia • 300 kW
15186v EQUATORIAL GUINEA	
†RADIO AFRICA, Bata	M-F • S Africa • 50 kW W Africa • 50 kW • ALT. FREQ. TO 7190v kHz
†RADIO EAST AFRICA, Bata	Sa/Su • ENGLISH & FRENCH • E Africa • 50 kW
15189.8 BRAZIL	
†R INCONFIDENCIA, Belo Horizonte	DS • 5 kW
15190 FRANCE	
R FRANCE INTL, Via French Guiana	N America • 500 kW • ALT. FREQ. TO 13640 kHz
JAPAN	
RADIO JAPAN/NHK, Tokyo-Yamata	SE Asia • 100 kW
PHILIPPINES	
RADYO PILIPINAS, Tinang	Mideast • 250 kW
RUSSIA	
GOLOS ROSSII	Ⓢ
UNITED KINGDOM	
BBC, Via Ascension	S America • 250 kW
	Sa/Su • S America • 250 kW
	M-F • S America • 250 kW
15190v PAKISTAN	
†RADIO PAKISTAN, Karachi	S Asia & SE Asia • 50 kW • ALT. FREQ. TO 15120v kHz
15195 CANADA	
R CANADA INTL, Via Tokyo, Japan	Ⓢ • SE Asia • 300 kW
FRANCE	
†R FRANCE INTL, Issoudun-Allouis	E Europe • 500 kW
	Ⓢ • E Europe • 500 kW
SWAZILAND	
TRANS WORLD RADIO, Manzini	W Asia & S Asia • 100 kW • ALT. FREQ. TO 15330 kHz
USA	
†VOA, Via Kaválla, Greece	Ⓢ • S Asia • 250 kW
VOA, Via Philippines	Ⓢ • E Asia • 250 kW

FREQUENCY　　COUNTRY, STATION, LOCATION

TARGET • NETWORK • POWER (kW)

World Time

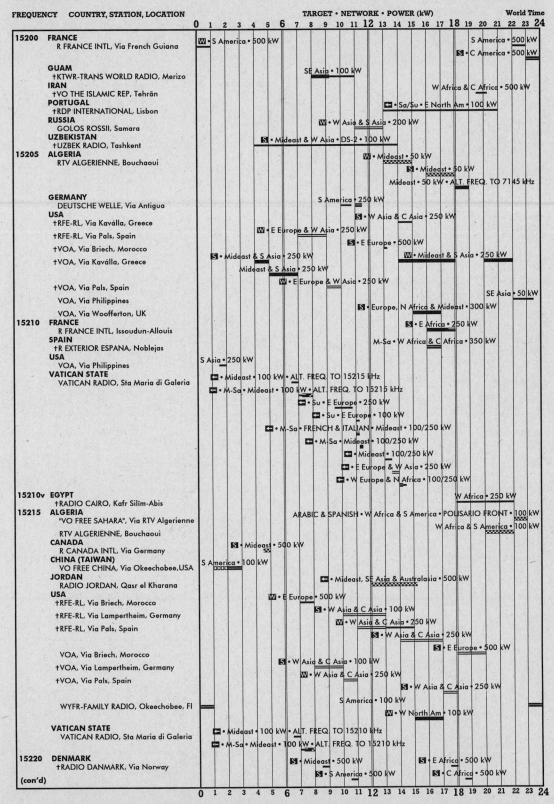

Freq	Country, Station, Location	Entry
15200	**FRANCE** R FRANCE INTL, Via French Guiana	S America • 500 kW / S America • 500 kW / C America • 500 kW
	GUAM †KTWR-TRANS WORLD RADIO, Merizo	SE Asia • 100 kW
	IRAN †VO THE ISLAMIC REP, Tehrān	W Africa & C Africa • 500 kW
	PORTUGAL †RDP INTERNATIONAL, Lisbon	Sa/Su • E North Am • 100 kW
	RUSSIA GOLOS ROSSII, Samara	W • W Asia & S Asia • 200 kW
	UZBEKISTAN †UZBEK RADIO, Tashkent	S • Mideast & W Asia • DS-2 • 100 kW
15205	**ALGERIA** RTV ALGERIENNE, Bouchaoui	W • Mideast • 50 kW / S • Mideast • 50 kW / Mideast • 50 kW • ALT. FREQ. TO 7145 kHz
	GERMANY DEUTSCHE WELLE, Via Antigua	S America • 250 kW
	USA †RFE-RL, Via Kaválla, Greece	S • W Asia & C Asia • 250 kW
	†RFE-RL, Via Pals, Spain	W • E Europe & W Asia • 250 kW
	†VOA, Via Briech, Morocco	S • E Europe • 500 kW
	†VOA, Via Kaválla, Greece	S • Mideast & S Asia • 250 kW / W • Mideast & S Asia • 250 kW
	†VOA, Via Pals, Spain	Mideast & S Asia • 250 kW
	VOA, Via Philippines	W • E Europe & W Asia • 250 kW / SE Asia • 50 kW
	VOA, Via Woofferton, UK	S • Europe, N Africa & Mideast • 300 kW
15210	**FRANCE** R FRANCE INTL, Issoudun-Allouis	S • E Africa • 250 kW
	SPAIN †R EXTERIOR ESPANA, Noblejas	M-Sa • W Africa & C Africa • 350 kW
	USA VOA, Via Philippines	S Asia • 250 kW
	VATICAN STATE VATICAN RADIO, Sta Maria di Galeria	• Mideast • 100 kW • ALT. FREQ. TO 15215 kHz / • M-Sa • Mideast • 100 kW • ALT. FREQ. TO 15215 kHz / • Su • E Europe • 250 kW / • Su • E Europe • 100 kW / • M-Sa • FRENCH & ITALIAN • Mideast • 100/250 kW / • M-Sa • Mideast • 100/250 kW / • Mideast • 100/250 kW / • E Europe & W Asia • 250 kW / • W Europe & N Africa • 100/250 kW
15210v	**EGYPT** †RADIO CAIRO, Kafr Silim-Abis	W Africa • 250 kW
15215	**ALGERIA** "VO FREE SAHARA", Via RTV Algerienne	ARABIC & SPANISH • W Africa & S America • POLISARIO FRONT • 100 kW / W Africa & S America • 100 kW
	RTV ALGERIENNE, Bouchaoui	S • Mideast • 500 kW
	CANADA R CANADA INTL, Via Germany	S America • 100 kW
	CHINA (TAIWAN) VO FREE CHINA, Via Okeechobee, USA	
	JORDAN RADIO JORDAN, Qasr el Kharana	• Mideast, SE Asia & Australasia • 500 kW
	USA †RFE-RL, Via Briech, Morocco	W • E Europe • 500 kW
	†RFE-RL, Via Lampertheim, Germany	S • W Asia & C Asia • 100 kW
	†RFE-RL, Via Pals, Spain	W • W Asia & C Asia • 250 kW / S • W Asia & C Asia • 250 kW / S • E Europe • 500 kW
	VOA, Via Briech, Morocco	S • W Asia & C Asia • 100 kW
	†VOA, Via Lampertheim, Germany	W • W Asia & C Asia • 250 kW
	†VOA, Via Pals, Spain	S • W Asia & C Asia • 250 kW
	WYFR-FAMILY RADIO, Okeechobee, Fl	S America • 100 kW / W • W North Am • 100 kW
	VATICAN STATE VATICAN RADIO, Sta Maria di Galeria	• Mideast • 100 kW • ALT. FREQ. TO 15210 kHz / • M-Sa • Mideast • 100 kW • ALT. FREQ. TO 15210 kHz
15220	**DENMARK** †RADIO DANMARK, Via Norway	S • Mideast • 500 kW / S • E Africa • 500 kW / S • S America • 500 kW / S • C Africa • 500 kW
(con'd)		

ENGLISH ▬　ARABIC ⌇⌇⌇　CHINESE ▫▫▫　FRENCH ▬▬　GERMAN ▬　RUSSIAN ══　SPANISH ▭▭　OTHER ▬

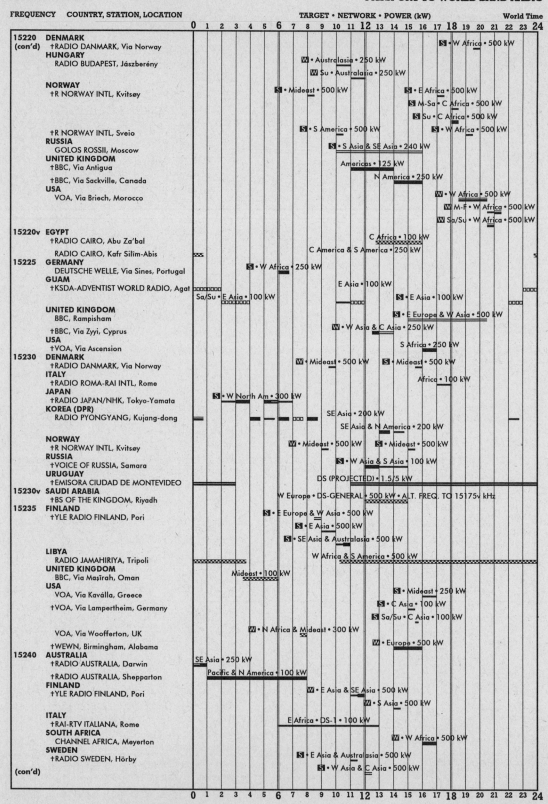

FREQUENCY   COUNTRY, STATION, LOCATION

TARGET • NETWORK • POWER (kW)

World Time

15220	**DENMARK**
(con'd)	†RADIO DANMARK, Via Norway — S • W Africa • 500 kW
	HUNGARY
	RADIO BUDAPEST, Jászberény — W • Australasia • 250 kW
	W • Su • Australasia • 250 kW
	NORWAY
	†R NORWAY INTL, Kvitsøy — S • Mideast • 500 kW / S • E Africa • 500 kW
	S • M-Sa • C Africa • 500 kW
	S • Su • C Africa • 500 kW
	†R NORWAY INTL, Sveio — S • S America • 500 kW / S • W Africa • 500 kW
	RUSSIA
	GOLOS ROSSII, Moscow — S • S Asia & SE Asia • 240 kW
	UNITED KINGDOM
	†BBC, Via Antigua — Americas • 125 kW
	†BBC, Via Sackville, Canada — N America • 250 kW
	USA
	VOA, Via Briech, Morocco — W • W Africa • 500 kW
	W • M-F • W Africa • 500 kW
	W • Sa/Su • W Africa • 500 kW
15220v	**EGYPT**
	†RADIO CAIRO, Abu Za'bal — C Africa • 100 kW
	RADIO CAIRO, Kafr Silim-Abis — C America & S America • 250 kW
15225	**GERMANY**
	DEUTSCHE WELLE, Via Sines, Portugal — S • W Africa • 250 kW
	GUAM
	†KSDA-ADVENTIST WORLD RADIO, Agat — E Asia • 100 kW
	Sa/Su • E Asia • 100 kW / S • E Asia • 100 kW
	UNITED KINGDOM
	BBC, Rampisham — S • E Europe & W Asia • 500 kW
	†BBC, Via Zyyi, Cyprus — W • W Asia & C Asia • 250 kW
	USA
	†VOA, Via Ascension — S Africa • 250 kW
15230	**DENMARK**
	†RADIO DANMARK, Via Norway — W • Mideast • 500 kW / S • Mideast • 500 kW
	ITALY
	†RADIO ROMA-RAI INTL, Rome — Africa • 100 kW
	JAPAN
	†RADIO JAPAN/NHK, Tokyo-Yamata — S • W North Am • 300 kW
	KOREA (DPR)
	RADIO PYONGYANG, Kujang-dong — SE Asia • 200 kW
	SE Asia & N America • 200 kW
	NORWAY
	†R NORWAY INTL, Kvitsøy — W • Mideast • 500 kW / S • Mideast • 500 kW
	RUSSIA
	†VOICE OF RUSSIA, Samara — S • W Asia & S Asia • 100 kW
	URUGUAY
	†EMISORA CIUDAD DE MONTEVIDEO — DS (PROJECTED) • 1.5/5 kW
15230v	**SAUDI ARABIA**
	†BS OF THE KINGDOM, Riyadh — W Europe • DS-GENERAL • 500 kW • ALT. FREQ. TO 15175v kHz
15235	**FINLAND**
	†YLE RADIO FINLAND, Pori — S • E Europe & W Asia • 500 kW
	S • E Asia • 500 kW
	S • SE Asia & Australasia • 500 kW
	LIBYA
	RADIO JAMAHIRIYA, Tripoli — W Africa & S America • 500 kW
	UNITED KINGDOM
	BBC, Via Maṣīrah, Oman — Mideast • 100 kW
	USA
	VOA, Via Kaválla, Greece — S • Mideast • 250 kW
	†VOA, Via Lampertheim, Germany — S • C Asia • 100 kW
	S • Sa/Su • C Asia • 100 kW
	VOA, Via Woofferton, UK — W • N Africa & Mideast • 300 kW
	†WEWN, Birmingham, Alabama — W • Europe • 500 kW
15240	**AUSTRALIA**
	†RADIO AUSTRALIA, Darwin — SE Asia • 250 kW
	†RADIO AUSTRALIA, Shepparton — Pacific & N America • 100 kW
	FINLAND
	†YLE RADIO FINLAND, Pori — W • E Asia & SE Asia • 500 kW
	W • S Asia • 500 kW
	ITALY
	†RAI-RTV ITALIANA, Rome — E Africa • DS-1 • 100 kW
	SOUTH AFRICA
	CHANNEL AFRICA, Meyerton — W • W Africa • 500 kW
	SWEDEN
	†RADIO SWEDEN, Hörby — S • E Asia & Australasia • 500 kW
	S • W Asia & C Asia • 500 kW
(con'd)	

FREQUENCY   COUNTRY, STATION, LOCATION

TARGET • NETWORK • POWER (kW)   World Time

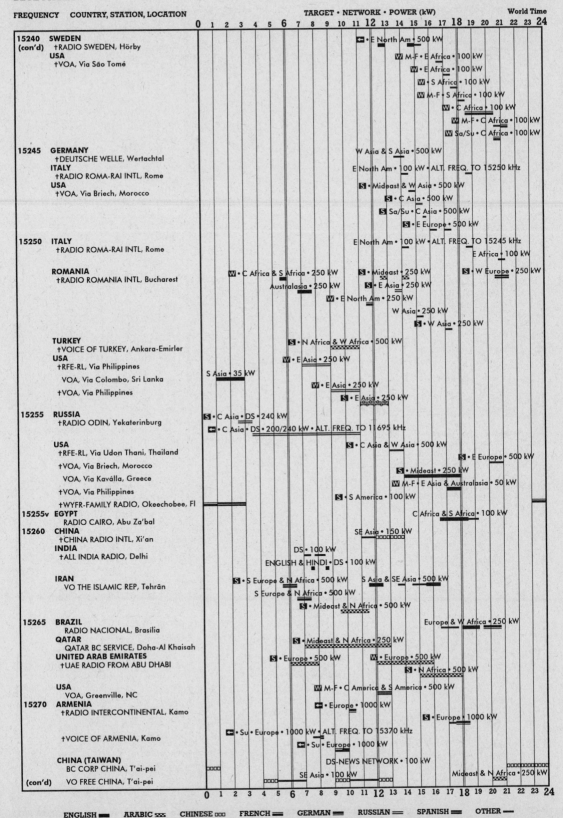

FREQUENCY	COUNTRY, STATION, LOCATION	TARGET • NETWORK • POWER (kW)
15240 (con'd)	**SWEDEN** †RADIO SWEDEN, Hörby	E North Am • 500 kW
	USA †VOA, Via São Tomé	W • M-F • E Africa • 100 kW / W • E Africa • 100 kW / W • S Africa • 100 kW / W • M-F • S Africa • 100 kW / W • C Africa • 100 kW / W • M-F • C Africa • 100 kW / W • Sa/Su • C Africa • 100 kW
15245	**GERMANY** †DEUTSCHE WELLE, Wertachtal	W Asia & S Asia • 500 kW
	ITALY †RADIO ROMA-RAI INTL, Rome	E North Am • 100 kW • ALT. FREQ. TO 15250 kHz
	USA †VOA, Via Briech, Morocco	S • Mideast & W Asia • 500 kW / S • C Asia • 500 kW / S • Sa/Su • C Asia • 500 kW / S • E Europe • 500 kW
15250	**ITALY** †RADIO ROMA-RAI INTL, Rome	E North Am • 100 kW • ALT. FREQ. TO 15245 kHz / E Africa • 100 kW
	ROMANIA †RADIO ROMANIA INTL, Bucharest	W • C Africa & S Africa • 250 kW / S • Mideast • 250 kW / S • W Europe • 250 kW / Australasia • 250 kW / S • E Asia • 250 kW / W • E North Am • 250 kW / W Asia • 250 kW / S • W Asia • 250 kW
	TURKEY †VOICE OF TURKEY, Ankara-Emirler	S • N Africa & W Africa • 500 kW / W • E Asia • 250 kW
	USA †RFE-RL, Via Philippines	
	VOA, Via Colombo, Sri Lanka	S Asia • 35 kW
	†VOA, Via Philippines	W • E Asia • 250 kW / S • E Asia • 250 kW
15255	**RUSSIA** †RADIO ODIN, Yekaterinburg	S • C Asia • DS • 240 kW / C Asia • DS • 200/240 kW • ALT. FREQ. TO 11695 kHz
	USA †RFE-RL, Via Udon Thani, Thailand	S • C Asia & W Asia • 500 kW / S • E Europe • 500 kW
	†VOA, Via Briech, Morocco	S • Mideast • 250 kW
	VOA, Via Kaválla, Greece	W • M-F • E Asia & Australasia • 50 kW
	†VOA, Via Philippines	
	†WYFR-FAMILY RADIO, Okeechobee, Fl	S • S America • 100 kW
15255v	**EGYPT** RADIO CAIRO, Abu Za'bal	C Africa & S Africa • 100 kW
15260	**CHINA** †CHINA RADIO INTL, Xi'an	SE Asia • 150 kW
	INDIA †ALL INDIA RADIO, Delhi	DS • 100 kW / ENGLISH & HINDI • DS • 100 kW
	IRAN VO THE ISLAMIC REP, Tehrān	S • S Europe & N Africa • 500 kW / S Asia & SE Asia • 500 kW / S Europe & N Africa • 500 kW / S • Mideast & N Africa • 500 kW
15265	**BRAZIL** RADIO NACIONAL, Brasilia	Europe & W Africa • 250 kW
	QATAR QATAR BC SERVICE, Doha-Al Khaisah	S • Mideast & N Africa • 250 kW
	UNITED ARAB EMIRATES †UAE RADIO FROM ABU DHABI	S • Europe • 500 kW / S • Europe • 500 kW / S • N Africa • 500 kW
	USA VOA, Greenville, NC	W • M-F • C America & S America • 500 kW
15270	**ARMENIA** †RADIO INTERCONTINENTAL, Kamo	S • Europe • 1000 kW / S • Europe • 1000 kW
	†VOICE OF ARMENIA, Kamo	S • Su • Europe • 1000 kW • ALT. FREQ. TO 15370 kHz / S • Su • Europe • 1000 kW
	CHINA (TAIWAN) BC CORP CHINA, T'ai-pei	DS-NEWS NETWORK • 100 kW
(con'd)	VO FREE CHINA, T'ai-pei	SE Asia • 100 kW / Mideast & N Africa • 250 kW

ENGLISH ▬▬ ARABIC ⊠⊠⊠ CHINESE □□□ FRENCH ══ GERMAN ▬▬▬ RUSSIAN ══ SPANISH ▬▬▬ OTHER ▬

FREQUENCY   COUNTRY, STATION, LOCATION

TARGET • NETWORK • POWER (kW)

World Time

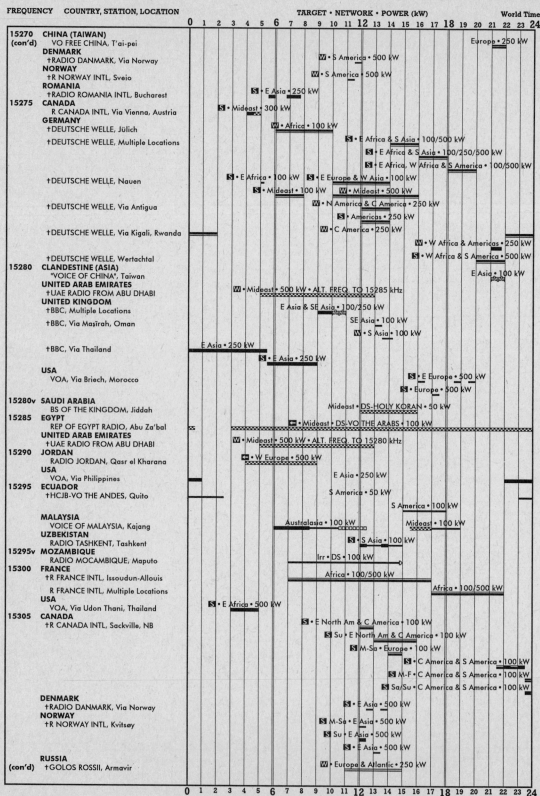

Frequency	Country / Station / Location	Target • Network • Power
15270 (con'd)	CHINA (TAIWAN) — VO FREE CHINA, T'ai-pei	Europe • 250 kW
	DENMARK — †RADIO DANMARK, Via Norway	W • S America • 500 kW
	NORWAY — †R NORWAY INTL, Sveio	W • S America • 500 kW
	ROMANIA — †RADIO ROMANIA INTL, Bucharest	S • E Asia • 250 kW
15275	CANADA — R CANADA INTL, Via Vienna, Austria	S • Mideast • 300 kW
	GERMANY — †DEUTSCHE WELLE, Jülich	W • Africa • 100 kW
	†DEUTSCHE WELLE, Multiple Locations	S • E Africa & S Asia • 100/500 kW
		S • E Africa & S Asia • 100/250/500 kW
		S • E Africa, W Africa & S America • 100/500 kW
	†DEUTSCHE WELLE, Nauen	S • E Africa • 100 kW / S • E Europe & W Asia • 100 kW / S • Mideast • 100 kW / W • Mideast • 500 kW
	†DEUTSCHE WELLE, Via Antigua	W • N America & C America • 250 kW
		S • Americas • 250 kW
	†DEUTSCHE WELLE, Via Kigali, Rwanda	W • C America • 250 kW
	†DEUTSCHE WELLE, Wertachtal	W • W Africa & Americas • 250 kW / S • W Africa & S America • 500 kW
15280	CLANDESTINE (ASIA) — "VOICE OF CHINA", Taiwan	E Asia • 100 kW
	UNITED ARAB EMIRATES — †UAE RADIO FROM ABU DHABI	W • Mideast • 500 kW • ALT. FREQ. TO 15285 kHz
	UNITED KINGDOM — †BBC, Multiple Locations	E Asia & SE Asia • 100/250 kW
	†BBC, Via Maṣīrah, Oman	SE Asia • 100 kW
		W • S Asia • 100 kW
	†BBC, Via Thailand	E Asia • 250 kW
		S • E Asia • 250 kW
	USA — VOA, Via Briech, Morocco	S • E Europe • 500 kW
		S • Europe • 500 kW
15280v	SAUDI ARABIA — BS OF THE KINGDOM, Jiddah	Mideast • DS-HOLY KORAN • 50 kW
15285	EGYPT — REP OF EGYPT RADIO, Abu Za'bal	• Mideast • DS-VO THE ARABS • 100 kW
	UNITED ARAB EMIRATES — †UAE RADIO FROM ABU DHABI	W • Mideast • 500 kW • ALT. FREQ. TO 15280 kHz
15290	JORDAN — RADIO JORDAN, Qasr el Kharana	• W Europe • 500 kW
	USA — VOA, Via Philippines	E Asia • 250 kW
15295	ECUADOR — †HCJB-VO THE ANDES, Quito	S America • 50 kW
		S America • 100 kW
	MALAYSIA — VOICE OF MALAYSIA, Kajang	Australasia • 100 kW / Mideast • 100 kW
	UZBEKISTAN — RADIO TASHKENT, Tashkent	S • S Asia • 100 kW
15295v	MOZAMBIQUE — RADIO MOCAMBIQUE, Maputo	Irr • DS • 100 kW
15300	FRANCE — †R FRANCE INTL, Issoudun-Allouis	Africa • 100/500 kW
	R FRANCE INTL, Multiple Locations	Africa • 100/500 kW
	USA — VOA, Via Udon Thani, Thailand	S • E Africa • 500 kW
15305	CANADA — †R CANADA INTL, Sackville, NB	S • E North Am & C America • 100 kW
		S Su • E North Am & C America • 100 kW
		S M-Sa • Europe • 100 kW
		S • C America & S America • 100 kW
		S M-F • C America & S America • 100 kW
		S Sa/Su • C America & S America • 100 kW
	DENMARK — †RADIO DANMARK, Via Norway	S • E Asia • 500 kW
	NORWAY — †R NORWAY INTL, Kvitsøy	S M-Sa • E Asia • 500 kW
		S Su • E Asia • 500 kW
		S • E Asia • 500 kW
	RUSSIA (con'd) — †GOLOS ROSSII, Armavir	W • Europe & Atlantic • 250 kW

FREQUENCY   COUNTRY, STATION, LOCATION

TARGET • NETWORK • POWER (kW)

World Time

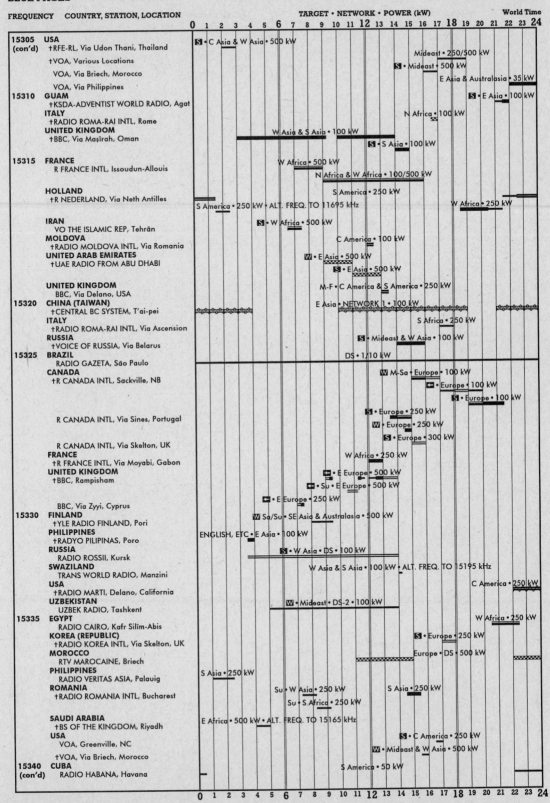

Frequency	Country, Station, Location
15305 (con'd)	**USA**
	†RFE-RL, Via Udon Thani, Thailand — S • C Asia & W Asia • 500 kW
	†VOA, Various Locations — Mideast • 250/500 kW
	VOA, Via Briech, Morocco — S • Mideast • 500 kW
	VOA, Via Philippines — E Asia & Australasia • 35 kW
15310	**GUAM** †KSDA-ADVENTIST WORLD RADIO, Agat — S • E Asia • 100 kW
	ITALY †RADIO ROMA-RAI INTL, Rome — N Africa • 100 kW
	UNITED KINGDOM †BBC, Via Maṣīrah, Oman — W Asia & S Asia • 100 kW / S • S Asia • 100 kW
15315	**FRANCE** R FRANCE INTL, Issoudun-Allouis — W Africa • 500 kW / N Africa & W Africa • 100/500 kW
	HOLLAND †R NEDERLAND, Via Neth Antilles — S America • 250 kW / S America • 250 kW • ALT. FREQ. TO 11695 kHz / W Africa • 250 kW
	IRAN VO THE ISLAMIC REP, Tehrān — S • W Africa • 500 kW
	MOLDOVA †RADIO MOLDOVA INTL, Via Romania — C America • 100 kW
	UNITED ARAB EMIRATES †UAE RADIO FROM ABU DHABI — W • E Asia • 500 kW / S • E Asia • 500 kW
	UNITED KINGDOM BBC, Via Delano, USA — M-F • C America & S America • 250 kW
15320	**CHINA (TAIWAN)** †CENTRAL BC SYSTEM, T'ai-pei — E Asia • NETWORK 1 • 100 kW
	ITALY †RADIO ROMA-RAI INTL, Via Ascension — S Africa • 250 kW
	RUSSIA †VOICE OF RUSSIA, Via Belarus — S • Mideast & W Asia • 100 kW
15325	**BRAZIL** RADIO GAZETA, São Paulo — DS • 1/10 kW
	CANADA †R CANADA INTL, Sackville, NB — W M-Sa • Europe • 100 kW / • Europe • 100 kW / S • Europe • 100 kW
	R CANADA INTL, Via Sines, Portugal — S • Europe • 250 kW / W • Europe • 250 kW / S • Europe • 300 kW
	R CANADA INTL, Via Skelton, UK
	FRANCE †R FRANCE INTL, Via Moyabi, Gabon — W Africa • 250 kW
	UNITED KINGDOM †BBC, Rampisham — • E Europe • 500 kW / • Su • E Europe • 500 kW
	BBC, Via Zyyi, Cyprus — • E Europe • 250 kW
15330	**FINLAND** †YLE RADIO FINLAND, Pori — W Sa/Su • SE Asia & Australasia • 500 kW
	PHILIPPINES †RADYO PILIPINAS, Poro — ENGLISH, ETC • E Asia • 100 kW
	RUSSIA RADIO ROSSII, Kursk — S • W Asia • DS • 100 kW
	SWAZILAND TRANS WORLD RADIO, Manzini — W Asia & S Asia • 100 kW • ALT. FREQ. TO 15195 kHz
	USA †RADIO MARTI, Delano, California — C America • 250 kW
	UZBEKISTAN UZBEK RADIO, Tashkent — W • Mideast • DS-2 • 100 kW
15335	**EGYPT** RADIO CAIRO, Kafr Silīm-Abis — W Africa • 250 kW
	KOREA (REPUBLIC) †RADIO KOREA INTL, Via Skelton, UK — S • Europe • 250 kW
	MOROCCO RTV MAROCAINE, Briech — Europe • DS • 500 kW
	PHILIPPINES RADIO VERITAS ASIA, Palauig — S Asia • 250 kW
	ROMANIA †RADIO ROMANIA INTL, Bucharest — Su • W Asia • 250 kW / S Asia • 250 kW / Su • S Africa • 250 kW
	SAUDI ARABIA †BS OF THE KINGDOM, Riyadh — E Africa • 500 kW • ALT. FREQ. TO 15165 kHz
	USA VOA, Greenville, NC — S • C America • 250 kW
	†VOA, Via Briech, Morocco — W • Mideast & W Asia • 500 kW
15340 (con'd)	**CUBA** RADIO HABANA, Havana — S America • 50 kW

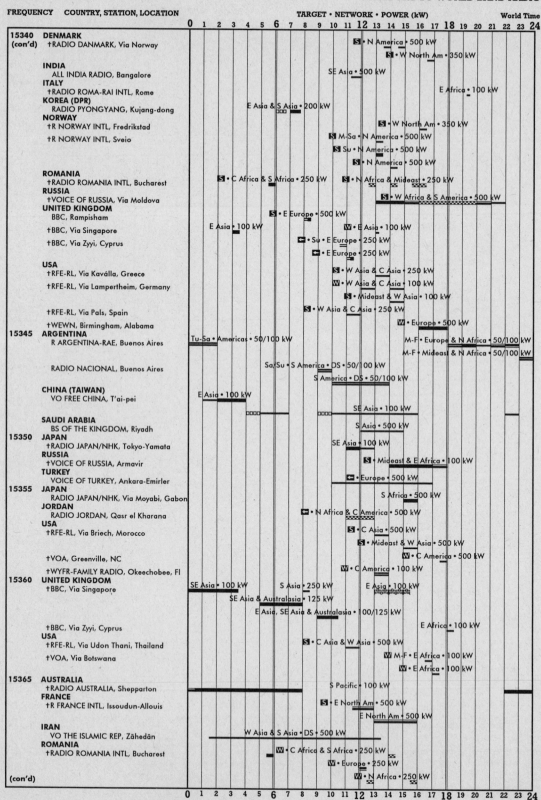

FREQUENCY	COUNTRY, STATION, LOCATION	TARGET • NETWORK • POWER (kW) / World Time
15340 (con'd)	**DENMARK** †RADIO DANMARK, Via Norway	S • N America • 500 kW; S • W North Am • 350 kW
	INDIA ALL INDIA RADIO, Bangalore	SE Asia • 500 kW
	ITALY †RADIO ROMA-RAI INTL, Rome	E Africa • 100 kW
	KOREA (DPR) RADIO PYONGYANG, Kujang-dong	E Asia & S Asia • 200 kW
	NORWAY †R NORWAY INTL, Fredrikstad	S • W North Am • 350 kW
	†R NORWAY INTL, Sveio	S • M-Sa • N America • 500 kW; S • Su • N America • 500 kW; S • N America • 500 kW
	ROMANIA †RADIO ROMANIA INTL, Bucharest	S • C Africa & S Africa • 250 kW; S • N Africa & Mideast • 250 kW
	RUSSIA †VOICE OF RUSSIA, Via Moldova	S • W Africa & S America • 500 kW
	UNITED KINGDOM BBC, Rampisham	S • E Europe • 500 kW
	†BBC, Via Singapore	E Asia • 100 kW; W • E Asia • 100 kW
	†BBC, Via Zyyi, Cyprus	• Su • E Europe • 250 kW; • E Europe • 250 kW
	USA †RFE-RL, Via Kaválla, Greece	S • W Asia & C Asia • 250 kW
	†RFE-RL, Via Lampertheim, Germany	W • W Asia & C Asia • 100 kW
	†RFE-RL, Via Pals, Spain	S • Mideast & W Asia • 100 kW; S • W Asia & C Asia • 250 kW
	†WEWN, Birmingham, Alabama	W • Europe • 500 kW
15345	**ARGENTINA** R ARGENTINA-RAE, Buenos Aires	Tu-Sa • Americas • 50/100 kW; M-F • Europe & N Africa • 50/100 kW; M-F • Mideast & N Africa • 50/100 kW
	RADIO NACIONAL, Buenos Aires	Sa/Su • S America • DS • 50/100 kW; S America • DS • 50/100 kW
	CHINA (TAIWAN) VO FREE CHINA, T'ai-pei	E Asia • 100 kW; SE Asia • 100 kW
	SAUDI ARABIA BS OF THE KINGDOM, Riyadh	S Asia • 500 kW
15350	**JAPAN** †RADIO JAPAN/NHK, Tokyo-Yamata	SE Asia • 100 kW
	RUSSIA †VOICE OF RUSSIA, Armavir	S • Mideast & E Africa • 100 kW
	TURKEY VOICE OF TURKEY, Ankara-Emirler	• Europe • 500 kW
15355	**JAPAN** RADIO JAPAN/NHK, Via Moyabi, Gabon	S Africa • 500 kW
	JORDAN RADIO JORDAN, Qasr el Kharana	• N Africa & C America • 500 kW
	USA †RFE-RL, Via Briech, Morocco	S • C Asia • 500 kW; S • Mideast & W Asia • 500 kW
	†VOA, Greenville, NC	W • C America • 500 kW
	†WYFR-FAMILY RADIO, Okeechobee, Fl	W • C America • 100 kW
15360	**UNITED KINGDOM** †BBC, Via Singapore	SE Asia • 100 kW; S Asia • 250 kW; E Asia • 100 kW; SE Asia & Australasia • 125 kW; E Asia, SE Asia & Australasia • 100/125 kW
	†BBC, Via Zyyi, Cyprus	E Africa • 100 kW
	USA †RFE-RL, Via Udon Thani, Thailand	S • C Asia & W Asia • 500 kW
	†VOA, Via Botswana	W M-F • E Africa • 100 kW; W • E Africa • 100 kW
15365	**AUSTRALIA** †RADIO AUSTRALIA, Shepparton	S Pacific • 100 kW
	FRANCE †R FRANCE INTL, Issoudun-Allouis	S • E North Am • 500 kW; E North Am • 500 kW
	IRAN VO THE ISLAMIC REP, Zāhedān	W Asia & S Asia • DS • 500 kW
	ROMANIA †RADIO ROMANIA INTL, Bucharest	W • C Africa & S Africa • 250 kW; W • Europe • 250 kW; W • N Africa • 250 kW
(con'd)		

FREQUENCY   COUNTRY, STATION, LOCATION

TARGET • NETWORK • POWER (kW)

World Time

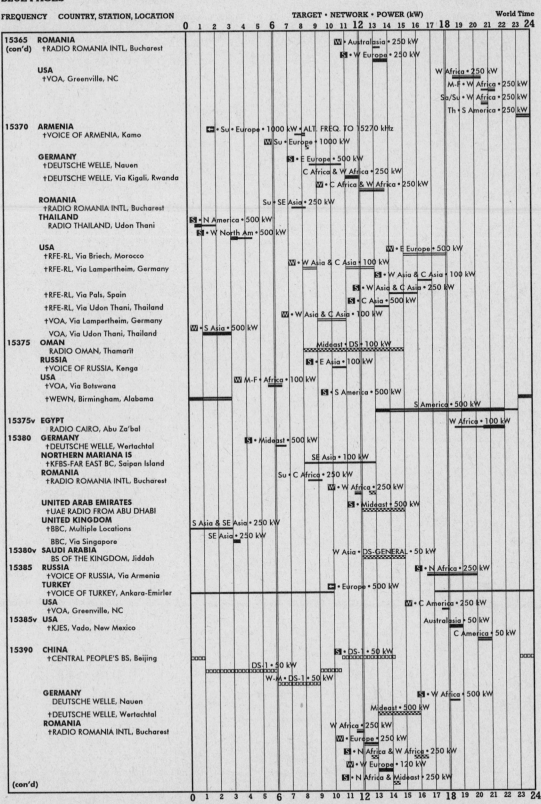

FREQUENCY	COUNTRY, STATION, LOCATION	Schedule (World Time 0–24)
15365 (con'd)	**ROMANIA** †RADIO ROMANIA INTL, Bucharest	W • Australasia • 250 kW ; S • W Europe • 250 kW
	USA †VOA, Greenville, NC	W Africa • 250 kW ; M-F • W Africa • 250 kW ; Sa/Su • W Africa • 250 kW ; Th • S America • 250 kW
15370	**ARMENIA** †VOICE OF ARMENIA, Kamo	Su • Europe • 1000 kW • ALT. FREQ. TO 15270 kHz ; W Su • Europe • 1000 kW
	GERMANY †DEUTSCHE WELLE, Nauen	S • E Europe • 500 kW ; C Africa & W Africa • 250 kW
	†DEUTSCHE WELLE, Via Kigali, Rwanda	W • C Africa & W Africa • 250 kW
	ROMANIA †RADIO ROMANIA INTL, Bucharest	Su • SE Asia • 250 kW
	THAILAND RADIO THAILAND, Udon Thani	S • N America • 500 kW ; S • W North Am • 500 kW
	USA †RFE-RL, Via Briech, Morocco	W • E Europe • 500 kW
	†RFE-RL, Via Lampertheim, Germany	W • W Asia & C Asia • 100 kW ; S • W Asia & C Asia • 100 kW
	†RFE-RL, Via Pals, Spain	S • W Asia & C Asia • 250 kW
	†RFE-RL, Via Udon Thani, Thailand	S • C Asia • 500 kW
	†VOA, Via Lampertheim, Germany	W • W Asia & C Asia • 100 kW
	VOA, Via Udon Thani, Thailand	W • S Asia • 500 kW
15375	**OMAN** RADIO OMAN, Thamarīt	Mideast • DS • 100 kW
	RUSSIA †VOICE OF RUSSIA, Kenga	S • E Asia • 100 kW
	USA †VOA, Via Botswana	W M-F • Africa • 100 kW
	†WEWN, Birmingham, Alabama	S • S America • 500 kW ; S America • 500 kW
15375v	**EGYPT** RADIO CAIRO, Abu Za'bal	W Africa • 100 kW
15380	**GERMANY** †DEUTSCHE WELLE, Wertachtal	S • Mideast • 500 kW
	NORTHERN MARIANA IS †KFBS-FAR EAST BC, Saipan Island	SE Asia • 100 kW
	ROMANIA †RADIO ROMANIA INTL, Bucharest	Su • C Africa • 250 kW ; W • W Africa • 250 kW
	UNITED ARAB EMIRATES †UAE RADIO FROM ABU DHABI	S • Mideast • 500 kW
	UNITED KINGDOM †BBC, Multiple Locations	S Asia & SE Asia • 250 kW ; SE Asia • 250 kW
	BBC, Via Singapore	
15380v	**SAUDI ARABIA** BS OF THE KINGDOM, Jiddah	W Asia • DS-GENERAL • 50 kW
15385	**RUSSIA** †VOICE OF RUSSIA, Via Armenia	S • N Africa • 250 kW
	TURKEY †VOICE OF TURKEY, Ankara-Emirler	Europe • 500 kW
	USA †VOA, Greenville, NC	W • C America • 250 kW
15385v	**USA** †KJES, Vado, New Mexico	Australasia • 50 kW ; C America • 50 kW
15390	**CHINA** †CENTRAL PEOPLE'S BS, Beijing	S • DS-1 • 50 kW ; DS-1 • 50 kW ; W-M • DS-1 • 50 kW
	GERMANY DEUTSCHE WELLE, Nauen	S • W Africa • 500 kW
	†DEUTSCHE WELLE, Wertachtal	Mideast • 500 kW
	ROMANIA †RADIO ROMANIA INTL, Bucharest	W Africa • 250 kW ; W • Europe • 250 kW ; S • N Africa & W Africa • 250 kW ; W • W Europe • 120 kW ; S • N Africa & Mideast • 250 kW

(con'd)

ENGLISH ▬   ARABIC ⧖   CHINESE ⬚   FRENCH ═   GERMAN ▬   RUSSIAN ═   SPANISH ▬   OTHER ▬

FREQUENCY   COUNTRY, STATION, LOCATION

TARGET • NETWORK • POWER (kW)

World Time

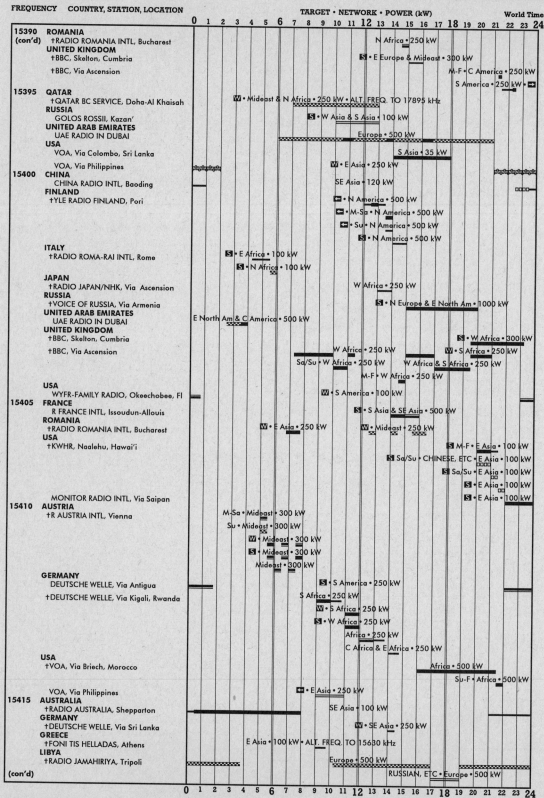

SEASONAL ⓈOR Ⓦ   1-HR TIMESHIFT MIDYEAR ⇦ OR ⇨   JAMMING / OR /\   EARLIEST HEARD ◁   LATEST HEARD ▷   NEW FOR 1997 †

FREQUENCY COUNTRY, STATION, LOCATION

TARGET • NETWORK • POWER (kW)

World Time

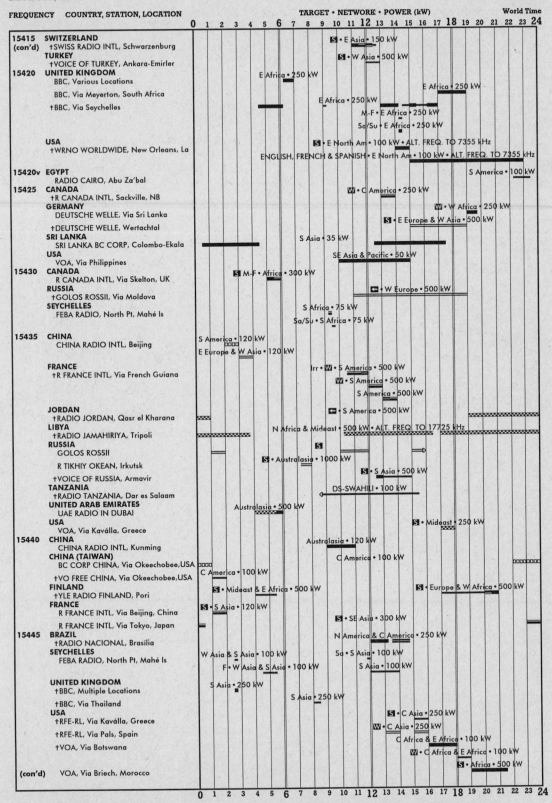

FREQUENCY	COUNTRY, STATION, LOCATION
15415	**SWITZERLAND**
(con'd)	†SWISS RADIO INTL, Schwarzenburg
	TURKEY
	†VOICE OF TURKEY, Ankara-Emirler
15420	**UNITED KINGDOM**
	BBC, Various Locations
	BBC, Via Meyerton, South Africa
	†BBC, Via Seychelles
	USA
	†WRNO WORLDWIDE, New Orleans, La
15420v	**EGYPT**
	RADIO CAIRO, Abu Za'bal
15425	**CANADA**
	†R CANADA INTL, Sackville, NB
	GERMANY
	DEUTSCHE WELLE, Via Sri Lanka
	†DEUTSCHE WELLE, Wertachtal
	SRI LANKA
	SRI LANKA BC CORP, Colombo-Ekala
	USA
	VOA, Via Philippines
15430	**CANADA**
	R CANADA INTL, Via Skelton, UK
	RUSSIA
	†GOLOS ROSSII, Via Moldova
	SEYCHELLES
	FEBA RADIO, North Pt, Mahé Is
15435	**CHINA**
	CHINA RADIO INTL, Beijing
	FRANCE
	†R FRANCE INTL, Via French Guiana
	JORDAN
	†RADIO JORDAN, Qasr el Kharana
	LIBYA
	†RADIO JAMAHIRIYA, Tripoli
	RUSSIA
	GOLOS ROSSII
	R TIKHIY OKEAN, Irkutsk
	†VOICE OF RUSSIA, Armavir
	TANZANIA
	†RADIO TANZANIA, Dar es Salaam
	UNITED ARAB EMIRATES
	UAE RADIO IN DUBAI
	USA
	VOA, Via Kaválla, Greece
15440	**CHINA**
	CHINA RADIO INTL, Kunming
	CHINA (TAIWAN)
	BC CORP CHINA, Via Okeechobee,USA
	†VO FREE CHINA, Via Okeechobee,USA
	FINLAND
	†YLE RADIO FINLAND, Pori
	FRANCE
	R FRANCE INTL, Via Beijing, China
	R FRANCE INTL, Via Tokyo, Japan
15445	**BRAZIL**
	†RADIO NACIONAL, Brasilia
	SEYCHELLES
	FEBA RADIO, North Pt, Mahé Is
	UNITED KINGDOM
	†BBC, Multiple Locations
	†BBC, Via Thailand
	USA
	†RFE-RL, Via Kaválla, Greece
	†RFE-RL, Via Pals, Spain
	†VOA, Via Botswana
(con'd)	VOA, Via Briech, Morocco

Target/Network/Power annotations (left to right):

- SWISS RADIO INTL: S • E Asia • 150 kW
- VOICE OF TURKEY: S • W Asia • 500 kW
- BBC, Various Locations: E Africa • 250 kW
- BBC, Via Meyerton: E Africa • 250 kW
- BBC, Via Seychelles: E Africa • 250 kW; M-F • E Africa • 250 kW; Sa/Su • E Africa • 250 kW
- WRNO WORLDWIDE: S • E North Am • 100 kW • ALT. FREQ. TO 7355 kHz; ENGLISH, FRENCH & SPANISH • E North Am • 100 kW • ALT. FREQ. TO 7355 kHz
- RADIO CAIRO: S America • 100 kW
- R CANADA INTL, Sackville: W • C America • 250 kW
- DEUTSCHE WELLE, Via Sri Lanka: W • W Africa • 250 kW
- DEUTSCHE WELLE, Wertachtal: S • E Europe & W Asia • 500 kW
- SRI LANKA BC CORP: S Asia • 35 kW
- VOA, Via Philippines: SE Asia & Pacific • 50 kW
- R CANADA INTL, Via Skelton: S • M-F • Africa • 300 kW
- GOLOS ROSSII, Via Moldova: W Europe • 500 kW
- FEBA RADIO: S Africa • 75 kW; Sa/Su • S Africa • 75 kW
- CHINA RADIO INTL, Beijing: S America • 120 kW; E Europe & W Asia • 120 kW
- R FRANCE INTL, Via French Guiana: Irr • W • S America • 500 kW; W • S America • 500 kW; S America • 500 kW
- RADIO JORDAN: S America • 500 kW
- RADIO JAMAHIRIYA: N Africa & Mideast • 500 kW • ALT. FREQ. TO 17725 kHz
- R TIKHIY OKEAN, Irkutsk: S • Australasia • 1000 kW
- VOICE OF RUSSIA, Armavir: S Asia • 500 kW
- RADIO TANZANIA: DS-SWAHILI • 100 kW
- UAE RADIO IN DUBAI: Australasia • 500 kW
- VOA, Via Kaválla: S • Mideast • 250 kW
- CHINA RADIO INTL, Kunming: Australasia • 120 kW
- BC CORP CHINA: C America • 100 kW
- VO FREE CHINA: C America • 100 kW
- YLE RADIO FINLAND: S • Mideast & E Africa • 500 kW; S • Europe & W Africa • 500 kW
- R FRANCE INTL, Via Beijing: S • S Asia • 120 kW
- R FRANCE INTL, Via Tokyo: S • SE Asia • 300 kW
- RADIO NACIONAL, Brasilia: N America & C America • 250 kW
- FEBA RADIO: W Asia & S Asia • 100 kW; Sa • S Asia • 100 kW; F • W Asia & S Asia • 100 kW; S Asia • 100 kW
- BBC, Multiple Locations: S Asia • 250 kW
- BBC, Via Thailand: S Asia • 250 kW
- RFE-RL, Via Kaválla: S • C Asia • 250 kW
- RFE-RL, Via Pals: W • C Asia • 250 kW
- VOA, Via Botswana: C Africa & E Africa • 100 kW; W • C Africa & E Africa • 100 kW
- VOA, Via Briech: S • Africa • 500 kW

ENGLISH ▬ ARABIC ▨ CHINESE ▫▫▫ FRENCH ══ GERMAN ▬▬ RUSSIAN ═ SPANISH ▭ OTHER ▬

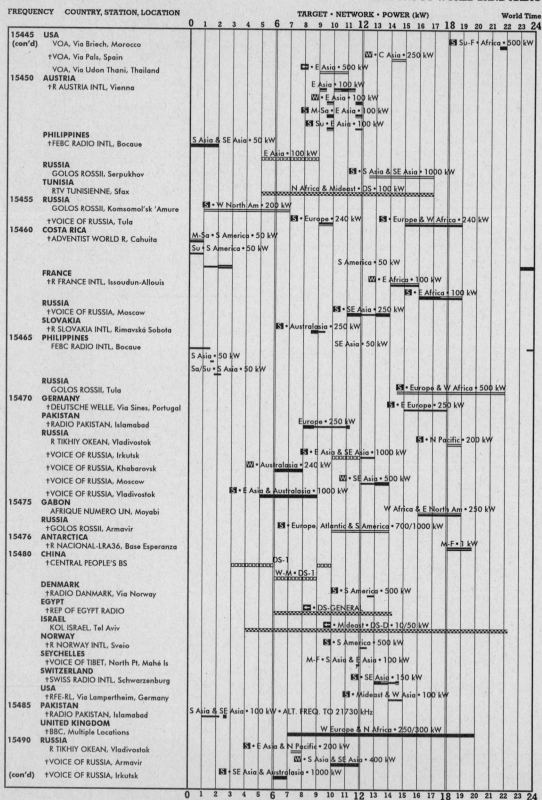

FREQUENCY	COUNTRY, STATION, LOCATION
15445 (con'd)	**USA** — VOA, Via Briech, Morocco
	†VOA, Via Pals, Spain
	VOA, Via Udon Thani, Thailand
15450	**AUSTRIA** — †R AUSTRIA INTL, Vienna
	PHILIPPINES — †FEBC RADIO INTL, Bocaue
	RUSSIA — GOLOS ROSSII, Serpukhov
	TUNISIA — RTV TUNISIENNE, Sfax
15455	**RUSSIA** — GOLOS ROSSII, Komsomol'sk 'Amure
	†VOICE OF RUSSIA, Tula
15460	**COSTA RICA** — †ADVENTIST WORLD R, Cahuita
	FRANCE — †R FRANCE INTL, Issoudun-Allouis
	RUSSIA — †VOICE OF RUSSIA, Moscow
	SLOVAKIA — †R SLOVAKIA INTL, Rimavská Sobota
15465	**PHILIPPINES** — FEBC RADIO INTL, Bocaue
	RUSSIA — GOLOS ROSSII, Tula
15470	**GERMANY** — †DEUTSCHE WELLE, Via Sines, Portugal
	PAKISTAN — †RADIO PAKISTAN, Islamabad
	RUSSIA — R TIKHIY OKEAN, Vladivostok
	†VOICE OF RUSSIA, Irkutsk
	†VOICE OF RUSSIA, Khabarovsk
	†VOICE OF RUSSIA, Moscow
	†VOICE OF RUSSIA, Vladivostok
15475	**GABON** — AFRIQUE NUMERO UN, Moyabi
	RUSSIA — †GOLOS ROSSII, Armavir
15476	**ANTARCTICA** — †R NACIONAL-LRA36, Base Esperanza
15480	**CHINA** — †CENTRAL PEOPLE'S BS
	DENMARK — †RADIO DANMARK, Via Norway
	EGYPT — †REP OF EGYPT RADIO
	ISRAEL — KOL ISRAEL, Tel Aviv
	NORWAY — †R NORWAY INTL, Sveio
	SEYCHELLES — †VOICE OF TIBET, North Pt, Mahé Is
	SWITZERLAND — †SWISS RADIO INTL, Schwarzenburg
	USA — †RFE-RL, Via Lampertheim, Germany
15485	**PAKISTAN** — †RADIO PAKISTAN, Islamabad
	UNITED KINGDOM — †BBC, Multiple Locations
15490	**RUSSIA** — R TIKHIY OKEAN, Vladivostok
	†VOICE OF RUSSIA, Armavir
(con'd)	†VOICE OF RUSSIA, Irkutsk

Schedule entries (TARGET • NETWORK • POWER):

- VOA, Via Briech: Su-F • Africa • 500 kW
- VOA, Via Pals: W • C Asia • 250 kW
- VOA, Via Udon Thani: E Asia • 500 kW
- R AUSTRIA INTL: E Asia • 100 kW; W • E Asia • 100 kW; S • M-Sa • E Asia • 100 kW; S • Su • E Asia • 100 kW
- FEBC RADIO INTL: S Asia & SE Asia • 50 kW
- GOLOS ROSSII, Serpukhov: E Asia • 100 kW
- GOLOS ROSSII: S • S Asia & SE Asia • 1000 kW
- RTV TUNISIENNE: N Africa & Mideast • DS • 100 kW
- GOLOS ROSSII, Komsomol'sk: S • W North Am • 200 kW
- VOICE OF RUSSIA, Tula: S • Europe • 240 kW; S • Europe & W Africa • 240 kW
- ADVENTIST WORLD R: M-Sa • S America • 50 kW; Su • S America • 50 kW; S America • 50 kW
- R FRANCE INTL: W • E Africa • 100 kW; S • E Africa • 100 kW
- VOICE OF RUSSIA, Moscow: S • SE Asia • 250 kW
- R SLOVAKIA INTL: S • Australasia • 250 kW
- FEBC RADIO INTL, Bocaue: SE Asia • 50 kW
- GOLOS ROSSII, Tula: S Asia • 50 kW; Sa/Su • S Asia • 50 kW
- S • Europe & W Africa • 500 kW
- DEUTSCHE WELLE: S • E Europe • 250 kW
- RADIO PAKISTAN: Europe • 250 kW
- R TIKHIY OKEAN: S • N Pacific • 200 kW
- VOICE OF RUSSIA, Irkutsk: S • E Asia & SE Asia • 1000 kW
- VOICE OF RUSSIA, Khabarovsk: W • Australasia • 240 kW
- VOICE OF RUSSIA, Moscow: W • SE Asia • 500 kW
- VOICE OF RUSSIA, Vladivostok: S • E Asia & Australasia • 1000 kW
- AFRIQUE NUMERO UN: W Africa & E North Am • 250 kW
- GOLOS ROSSII, Armavir: S • Europe, Atlantic & S America • 700/1000 kW
- R NACIONAL-LRA36: M-F • 1 kW
- CENTRAL PEOPLE'S BS: DS-1; W-M • DS-1
- RADIO DANMARK: S • S America • 500 kW
- REP OF EGYPT RADIO: DS-GENERAL
- KOL ISRAEL: Mideast • DS-D • 10/50 kW
- R NORWAY INTL: S • S America • 500 kW
- VOICE OF TIBET: M-F • S Asia & E Asia • 100 kW
- SWISS RADIO INTL: S • SE Asia • 150 kW
- RFE-RL: S • Mideast & W Asia • 100 kW
- RADIO PAKISTAN, Islamabad: S Asia & SE Asia • 100 kW • ALT. FREQ. TO 21730 kHz
- BBC: W Europe & N Africa • 250/300 kW
- R TIKHIY OKEAN, Vladivostok: S • E Asia & N Pacific • 200 kW
- VOICE OF RUSSIA, Armavir: W • S Asia & SE Asia • 400 kW
- VOICE OF RUSSIA, Irkutsk: S • SE Asia & Australasia • 1000 kW

World Time scale: 0 1 2 3 4 5 6 7 8 9 10 11 12 13 14 15 16 17 18 19 20 21 22 23 24

SEASONAL S OR W   1-HR TIMESHIFT MIDYEAR ⊟ OR ⊞   JAMMING / OR ∧   EARLIEST HEARD ◁   LATEST HEARD ▷   NEW FOR 1997 †

FREQUENCY   COUNTRY, STATION, LOCATION   TARGET • NETWORK • POWER (kW)   World Time

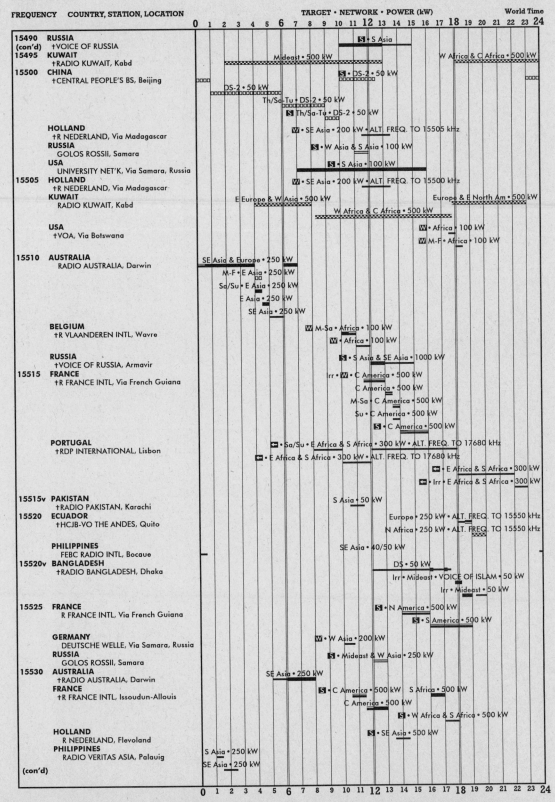

ENGLISH ▬   ARABIC ⸎⸎⸎   CHINESE ▫▫▫   FRENCH ▬▬   GERMAN ▬▬   RUSSIAN ══   SPANISH ▬▬   OTHER ▬

FREQUENCY   COUNTRY, STATION, LOCATION

TARGET • NETWORK • POWER (kW)

World Time

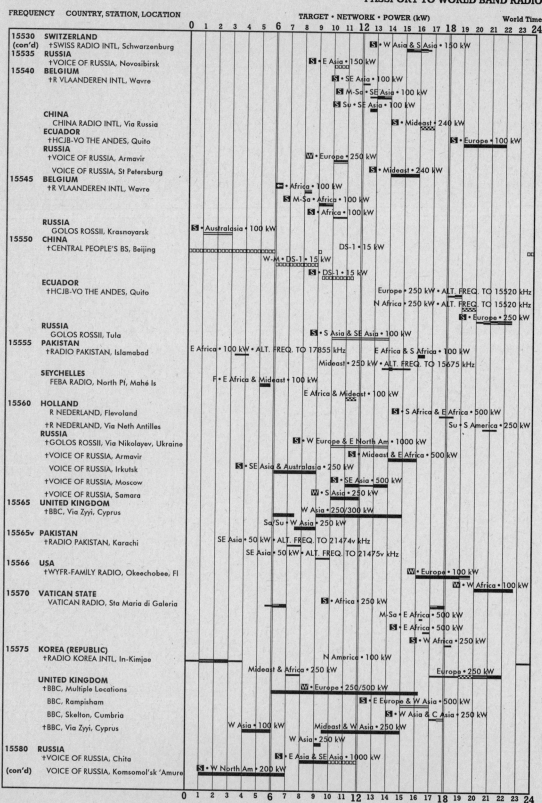

FREQUENCY	COUNTRY, STATION, LOCATION
15530 (con'd)	SWITZERLAND †SWISS RADIO INTL, Schwarzenburg
15535	RUSSIA †VOICE OF RUSSIA, Novosibirsk
15540	BELGIUM †R VLAANDEREN INTL, Wavre
	CHINA CHINA RADIO INTL, Via Russia
	ECUADOR †HCJB-VO THE ANDES, Quito
	RUSSIA †VOICE OF RUSSIA, Armavir
	VOICE OF RUSSIA, St Petersburg
15545	BELGIUM †R VLAANDEREN INTL, Wavre
	RUSSIA GOLOS ROSSII, Krasnoyarsk
15550	CHINA †CENTRAL PEOPLE'S BS, Beijing
	ECUADOR †HCJB-VO THE ANDES, Quito
	RUSSIA GOLOS ROSSII, Tula
15555	PAKISTAN †RADIO PAKISTAN, Islamabad
	SEYCHELLES FEBA RADIO, North Pt, Mahé Is
15560	HOLLAND R NEDERLAND, Flevoland
	†R NEDERLAND, Via Neth Antilles RUSSIA †GOLOS ROSSII, Via Nikolayev, Ukraine
	†VOICE OF RUSSIA, Armavir
	VOICE OF RUSSIA, Irkutsk
	VOICE OF RUSSIA, Moscow
	†VOICE OF RUSSIA, Samara
15565	UNITED KINGDOM †BBC, Via Zyyi, Cyprus
15565v	PAKISTAN †RADIO PAKISTAN, Karachi
15566	USA †WYFR-FAMILY RADIO, Okeechobee, Fl
15570	VATICAN STATE VATICAN RADIO, Sta Maria di Galeria
15575	KOREA (REPUBLIC) †RADIO KOREA INTL, In-Kimjae
	UNITED KINGDOM †BBC, Multiple Locations
	BBC, Rampisham
	BBC, Skelton, Cumbria
	†BBC, Via Zyyi, Cyprus
15580	RUSSIA †VOICE OF RUSSIA, Chita
(con'd)	VOICE OF RUSSIA, Komsomol'sk 'Amure

Station schedule notes (bars):

- SWISS RADIO INTL: S • W Asia & S Asia • 150 kW
- VOICE OF RUSSIA, Novosibirsk: S • E Asia • 150 kW
- R VLAANDEREN INTL: S • SE Asia • 100 kW
- S M-Sa • SE Asia • 100 kW
- S Su • SE Asia • 100 kW
- CHINA RADIO INTL: S • Mideast • 240 kW
- HCJB-VO THE ANDES: S • Europe • 100 kW
- VOICE OF RUSSIA, Armavir: W • Europe • 250 kW
- VOICE OF RUSSIA, St Petersburg: S • Mideast • 240 kW
- R VLAANDEREN INTL: • Africa • 100 kW
- S M-Sa • Africa • 100 kW
- S • Africa • 100 kW
- GOLOS ROSSII, Krasnoyarsk: S • Australasia • 100 kW
- CENTRAL PEOPLE'S BS: DS-1 • 15 kW
- W-M • DS-1 • 15 kW
- S • DS-1 • 15 kW
- HCJB-VO THE ANDES: Europe • 250 kW • ALT. FREQ. TO 15520 kHz
- N Africa • 250 kW • ALT. FREQ. TO 15520 kHz
- S • Europe • 250 kW
- GOLOS ROSSII, Tula: S • S Asia & SE Asia • 100 kW
- RADIO PAKISTAN, Islamabad: E Africa • 100 kW • ALT. FREQ. TO 17855 kHz
- E Africa & S Africa • 100 kW
- Mideast • 250 kW • ALT. FREQ. TO 15675 kHz
- FEBA RADIO: F • E Africa & Mideast • 100 kW
- E Africa & Mideast • 100 kW
- R NEDERLAND, Flevoland: S • S Africa & E Africa • 500 kW
- R NEDERLAND, Via Neth Antilles: Su • S America • 250 kW
- GOLOS ROSSII, Via Nikolayev: S • W Europe & E North Am • 1000 kW
- VOICE OF RUSSIA, Armavir: S • Mideast & E Africa • 500 kW
- VOICE OF RUSSIA, Irkutsk: S • SE Asia & Australasia • 250 kW
- VOICE OF RUSSIA, Moscow: S • SE Asia • 500 kW
- VOICE OF RUSSIA, Samara: W • S Asia • 250 kW
- BBC, Via Zyyi, Cyprus: W Asia • 250/300 kW
- Sa/Su • W Asia • 250 kW
- RADIO PAKISTAN, Karachi: SE Asia • 50 kW • ALT. FREQ. TO 21474v kHz
- SE Asia • 50 kW • ALT. FREQ. TO 21475v kHz
- WYFR-FAMILY RADIO: W • Europe • 100 kW
- W • W Africa • 100 kW
- VATICAN RADIO: S • Africa • 250 kW
- M-Sa • E Africa • 500 kW
- S • E Africa • 500 kW
- S • W Africa • 250 kW
- RADIO KOREA INTL: N America • 100 kW
- Mideast & Africa • 250 kW
- Europe • 250 kW
- BBC, Multiple Locations: W • Europe • 250/500 kW
- BBC, Rampisham: S • E Europe & W Asia • 500 kW
- BBC, Skelton, Cumbria: S • W Asia & C Asia • 250 kW
- BBC, Via Zyyi, Cyprus: W Asia • 100 kW
- Mideast & W Asia • 250 kW
- W Asia • 250 kW
- VOICE OF RUSSIA, Chita: S • E Asia & SE Asia • 1000 kW
- VOICE OF RUSSIA, Komsomol'sk: S • W North Am • 200 kW

FREQUENCY   COUNTRY, STATION, LOCATION   TARGET • NETWORK • POWER (kW)   World Time

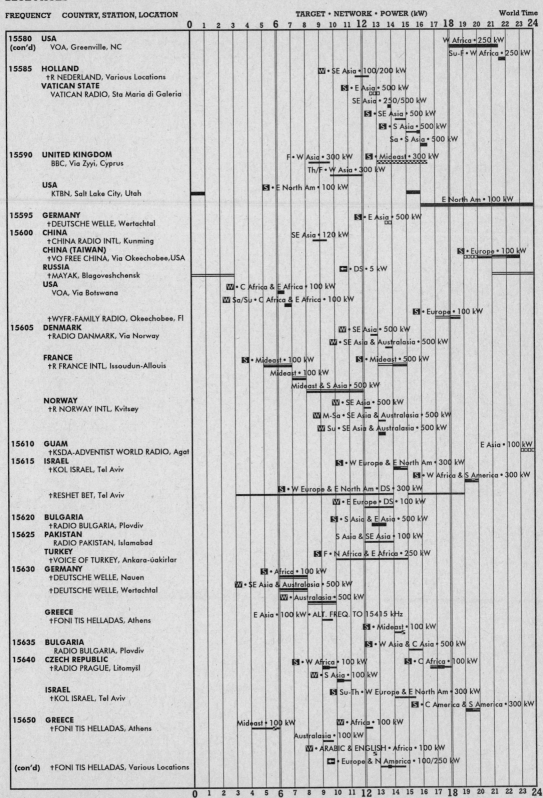

Frequency	Country, Station, Location	Target • Network • Power
15580 (con'd)	**USA** VOA, Greenville, NC	W Africa • 250 kW — Su-F • W Africa • 250 kW
15585	**HOLLAND** †R NEDERLAND, Various Locations **VATICAN STATE** VATICAN RADIO, Sta Maria di Galeria	W • SE Asia • 100/200 kW — S • E Asia • 500 kW — SE Asia • 250/500 kW — S • SE Asia • 500 kW — S • S Asia • 500 kW — Sa • S Asia • 500 kW
15590	**UNITED KINGDOM** BBC, Via Zyyi, Cyprus	F • W Asia • 300 kW — S • Mideast • 300 kW — Th/F • W Asia • 300 kW
	USA KTBN, Salt Lake City, Utah	S • E North Am • 100 kW — E North Am • 100 kW
15595	**GERMANY** †DEUTSCHE WELLE, Wertachtal	S • E Asia • 500 kW
15600	**CHINA** †CHINA RADIO INTL, Kunming	SE Asia • 120 kW
	CHINA (TAIWAN) †VO FREE CHINA, Via Okeechobee,USA	S • Europe • 100 kW
	RUSSIA †MAYAK, Blagoveshchensk	DS • 5 kW
	USA VOA, Via Botswana	W • C Africa & E Africa • 100 kW — W Sa/Su • C Africa & E Africa • 100 kW
	†WYFR-FAMILY RADIO, Okeechobee, Fl	S • Europe • 100 kW
15605	**DENMARK** †RADIO DANMARK, Via Norway	W • SE Asia • 500 kW — W • SE Asia & Australasia • 500 kW
	FRANCE †R FRANCE INTL, Issoudun-Allouis	S • Mideast • 100 kW — S • Mideast • 500 kW — Mideast • 100 kW — Mideast & S Asia • 500 kW
	NORWAY †R NORWAY INTL, Kvitsøy	W • SE Asia • 500 kW — W M-Sa • SE Asia & Australasia • 500 kW — W Su • SE Asia & Australasia • 500 kW
15610	**GUAM** †KSDA-ADVENTIST WORLD RADIO, Agat	E Asia • 100 kW
15615	**ISRAEL** †KOL ISRAEL, Tel Aviv	S • W Europe & E North Am • 300 kW — S • W Africa & S America • 300 kW — S • W Europe & E North Am • DS • 300 kW
	†RESHET BET, Tel Aviv	W • E Europe • DS • 100 kW
15620	**BULGARIA** †RADIO BULGARIA, Plovdiv	S • S Asia & E Asia • 500 kW
15625	**PAKISTAN** RADIO PAKISTAN, Islamabad	S Asia & SE Asia • 100 kW
	TURKEY †VOICE OF TURKEY, Ankara-úakirlar	S F • N Africa & E Africa • 250 kW
15630	**GERMANY** †DEUTSCHE WELLE, Nauen	S • Africa • 100 kW — W • SE Asia & Australasia • 500 kW
	†DEUTSCHE WELLE, Wertachtal	W • Australasia • 500 kW
	GREECE †FONI TIS HELLADAS, Athens	E Asia • 100 kW • ALT. FREQ. TO 15415 kHz — S • Mideast • 100 kW
15635	**BULGARIA** RADIO BULGARIA, Plovdiv	S • W Asia & C Asia • 500 kW
15640	**CZECH REPUBLIC** †RADIO PRAGUE, Litomyšl	S • W Africa • 100 kW — S • C Africa • 100 kW — W • S Asia • 100 kW
	ISRAEL †KOL ISRAEL, Tel Aviv	S Su-Th • W Europe & E North Am • 300 kW — S • C America & S America • 300 kW
15650	**GREECE** †FONI TIS HELLADAS, Athens	Mideast • 100 kW — W • Africa • 100 kW — Australasia • 100 kW — W • ARABIC & ENGLISH • Africa • 100 kW — Europe & N America • 100/250 kW
(con'd)	†FONI TIS HELLADAS, Various Locations	

ENGLISH ▬   ARABIC ≈≈≈   CHINESE □□□   FRENCH ══   GERMAN ▬▬   RUSSIAN ══   SPANISH ▬▬   OTHER ──

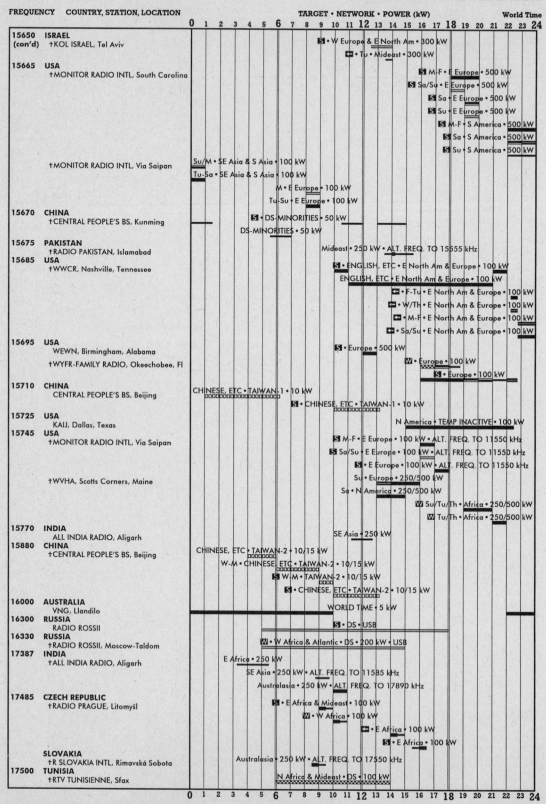

FREQUENCY   COUNTRY, STATION, LOCATION

TARGET • NETWORK • POWER (kW)

World Time

15650 ISRAEL
(con'd)   †KOL ISRAEL, Tel Aviv

15665 USA
      †MONITOR RADIO INTL, South Carolina

      †MONITOR RADIO INTL, Via Saipan

15670 CHINA
      †CENTRAL PEOPLE'S BS, Kunming

15675 PAKISTAN
      †RADIO PAKISTAN, Islamabad
15685 USA
      †WWCR, Nashville, Tennessee

15695 USA
      WEWN, Birmingham, Alabama
      †WYFR-FAMILY RADIO, Okeechobee, Fl

15710 CHINA
      CENTRAL PEOPLE'S BS, Beijing

15725 USA
      KAIJ, Dallas, Texas
15745 USA
      †MONITOR RADIO INTL, Via Saipan

      †WVHA, Scotts Corners, Maine

15770 INDIA
      ALL INDIA RADIO, Aligarh
15880 CHINA
      †CENTRAL PEOPLE'S BS, Beijing

16000 AUSTRALIA
      VNG, Llandilo
16300 RUSSIA
      RADIO ROSSII
16330 RUSSIA
      †RADIO ROSSII, Moscow-Taldom
17387 INDIA
      †ALL INDIA RADIO, Aligarh

17485 CZECH REPUBLIC
      †RADIO PRAGUE, Litomyšl

      SLOVAKIA
      †R SLOVAKIA INTL, Rimavská Sobota
17500 TUNISIA
      †RTV TUNISIENNE, Sfax

SEASONAL S OR W   1-HR TIMESHIFT MIDYEAR ⟵ OR ⟶   JAMMING / OR ∧   EARLIEST HEARD ◁   LATEST HEARD ▷   NEW FOR 1997 †

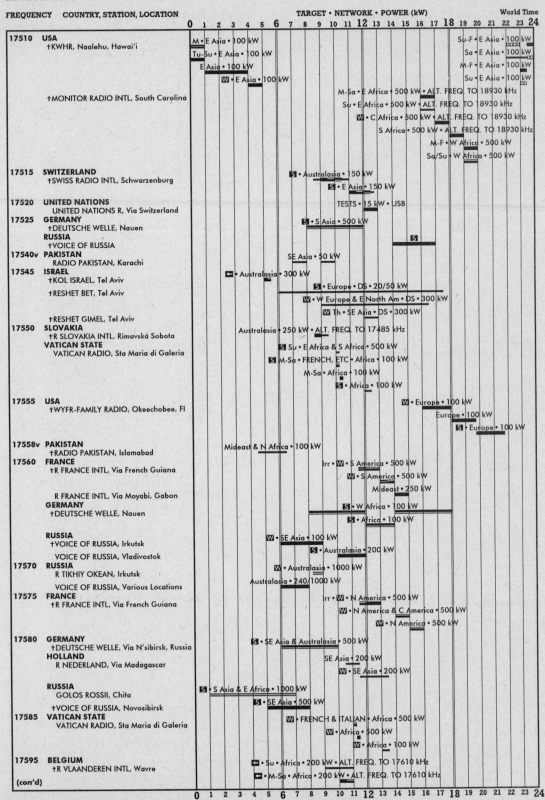

FREQUENCY   COUNTRY, STATION, LOCATION   TARGET • NETWORK • POWER (kW)   World Time

Frequency	Country, Station, Location	Target • Network • Power
17510	**USA** †KWHR, Naalehu, Hawai'i	M • E Asia • 100 kW; Tu-Su • E Asia • 100 kW; E Asia • 100 kW; W • E Asia • 100 kW; Su-F • E Asia • 100 kW; Sa • E Asia • 100 kW; M-F • E Asia • 100 kW; Su • E Asia • 100 kW
	†MONITOR RADIO INTL, South Carolina	M-Sa • E Africa • 500 kW • ALT. FREQ. TO 18930 kHz; Su • E Africa • 500 kW • ALT. FREQ. TO 18930 kHz; W • C Africa • 500 kW • ALT. FREQ. TO 18930 kHz; S Africa • 500 kW • ALT. FREQ. TO 18930 kHz; M-F • W Africa • 500 kW; Sa/Su • W Africa • 500 kW
17515	**SWITZERLAND** †SWISS RADIO INTL, Schwarzenburg	S • Australasia • 150 kW; S • E Asia • 150 kW
17520	**UNITED NATIONS** UNITED NATIONS R, Via Switzerland	TESTS • 15 kW • USB
17525	**GERMANY** †DEUTSCHE WELLE, Nauen	S • S Asia • 500 kW
	RUSSIA †VOICE OF RUSSIA	S
17540v	**PAKISTAN** RADIO PAKISTAN, Karachi	SE Asia • 50 kW
17545	**ISRAEL** †KOL ISRAEL, Tel Aviv	• Australasia • 300 kW
	†RESHET BET, Tel Aviv	S • Europe • DS • 20/50 kW; W • W Europe & E North Am • DS • 300 kW
	†RESHET GIMEL, Tel Aviv	W Th • SE Asia • DS • 300 kW
17550	**SLOVAKIA** †R SLOVAKIA INTL, Rimavská Sobota	Australasia • 250 kW • ALT. FREQ. TO 17485 kHz
	VATICAN STATE VATICAN RADIO, Sta Maria di Galeria	S Su • E Africa & S Africa • 500 kW; S M-Sa • FRENCH, ETC • Africa • 100 kW; M-Sa • Africa • 100 kW; S • Africa • 100 kW
17555	**USA** †WYFR-FAMILY RADIO, Okeechobee, Fl	W • Europe • 100 kW; Europe • 100 kW; S • Europe • 100 kW
17558v	**PAKISTAN** †RADIO PAKISTAN, Islamabad	Mideast & N Africa • 100 kW
17560	**FRANCE** †R FRANCE INTL, Via French Guiana	Irr • W • S America • 500 kW; W • S America • 500 kW; Mideast • 250 kW
	R FRANCE INTL, Via Moyabi, Gabon	
	GERMANY †DEUTSCHE WELLE, Nauen	S • W Africa • 100 kW; S • Africa • 100 kW
	RUSSIA †VOICE OF RUSSIA, Irkutsk	W • SE Asia • 100 kW
	VOICE OF RUSSIA, Vladivostok	S • Australasia • 200 kW
17570	**RUSSIA** R TIKHIY OKEAN, Irkutsk	W • Australasia • 1000 kW
	VOICE OF RUSSIA, Various Locations	Australasia • 240/1000 kW
17575	**FRANCE** †R FRANCE INTL, Via French Guiana	Irr • W • N America • 500 kW; W • N America & C America • 500 kW; W • N America • 500 kW
17580	**GERMANY** †DEUTSCHE WELLE, Via N'sibirsk, Russia	S • SE Asia & Australasia • 500 kW
	HOLLAND R NEDERLAND, Via Madagascar	SE Asia • 200 kW; W • SE Asia • 200 kW
	RUSSIA GOLOS ROSSII, Chita	S • S Asia & E Africa • 1000 kW
	†VOICE OF RUSSIA, Novosibirsk	S • SE Asia • 500 kW
17585	**VATICAN STATE** VATICAN RADIO, Sta Maria di Galeria	W • FRENCH & ITALIAN • Africa • 500 kW; W • Africa • 500 kW; W • Africa • 100 kW
17595	**BELGIUM** †R VLAANDEREN INTL, Wavre	Su • Africa • 200 kW • ALT. FREQ. TO 17610 kHz; M-Sa • Africa • 200 kW • ALT. FREQ. TO 17610 kHz

(con'd)

ENGLISH ▬   ARABIC ▧   CHINESE ▫▫▫   FRENCH ▭   GERMAN ▬   RUSSIAN ═   SPANISH ▬   OTHER ▬

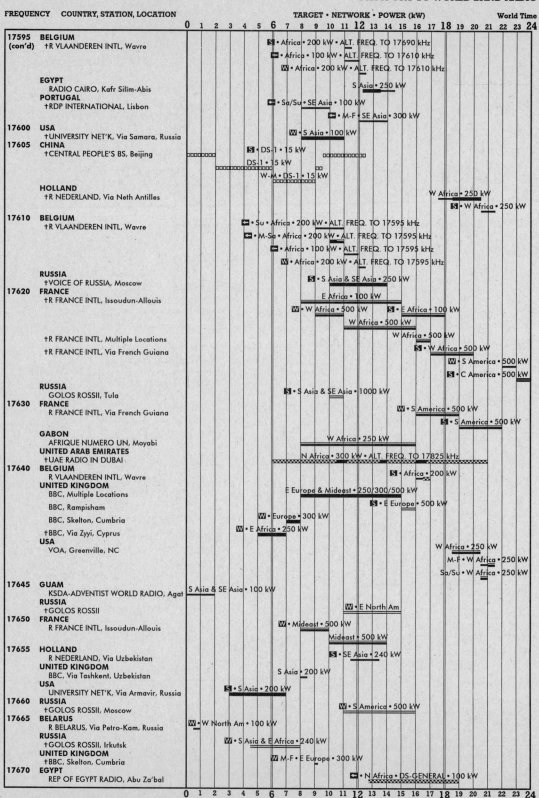

FREQUENCY　　COUNTRY, STATION, LOCATION

TARGET • NETWORK • POWER (kW)

World Time

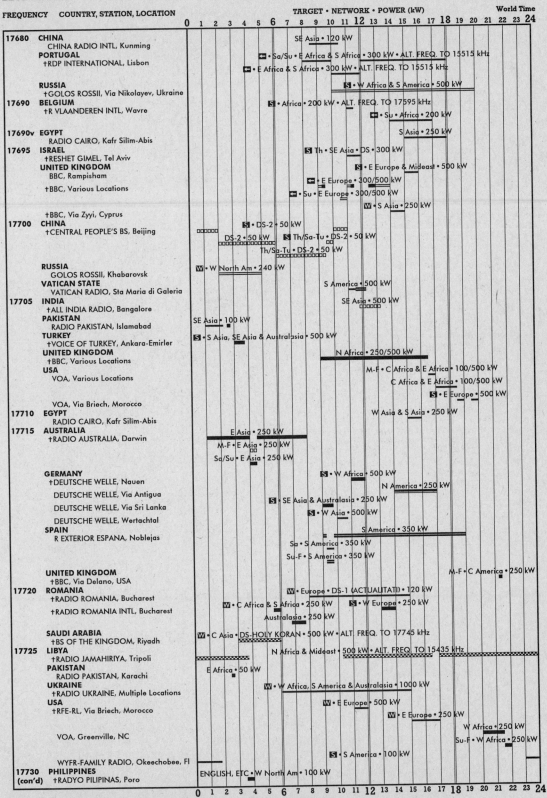

17680	CHINA
	CHINA RADIO INTL, Kunming — SE Asia • 120 kW
	PORTUGAL
	†RDP INTERNATIONAL, Lisbon — ▭ • Sa/Su • E Africa & S Africa • 300 kW • ALT. FREQ. TO 15515 kHz
	▭ • E Africa & S Africa • 300 kW • ALT. FREQ. TO 15515 kHz
	RUSSIA
	†GOLOS ROSSII, Via Nikolayev, Ukraine — Ⓢ • W Africa & S America • 500 kW
17690	BELGIUM
	†R VLAANDEREN INTL, Wavre — Ⓢ • Africa • 200 kW • ALT. FREQ. TO 17595 kHz
	▭ • Su • Africa • 200 kW
17690v	EGYPT
	RADIO CAIRO, Kafr Silīm-Abis — S Asia • 250 kW
17695	ISRAEL
	†RESHET GIMEL, Tel Aviv — Ⓢ Th • SE Asia • DS • 300 kW
	UNITED KINGDOM
	BBC, Rampisham — Ⓢ • E Europe & Mideast • 500 kW
	†BBC, Various Locations — ▭ • E Europe • 300/500 kW
	▭ • Su • E Europe • 300/500 kW
	†BBC, Via Zyyi, Cyprus — Ⓦ • S Asia • 250 kW
17700	CHINA
	†CENTRAL PEOPLE'S BS, Beijing — Ⓢ • DS-2 • 50 kW
	DS-2 • 50 kW Ⓢ Th/Sa-Tu • DS-2 • 50 kW
	Th/Sa-Tu • DS-2 • 50 kW
	RUSSIA
	GOLOS ROSSII, Khabarovsk — Ⓦ • W North Am • 240 kW
	VATICAN STATE
	VATICAN RADIO, Sta Maria di Galeria — S America • 500 kW
17705	INDIA
	†ALL INDIA RADIO, Bangalore — SE Asia • 500 kW
	PAKISTAN
	RADIO PAKISTAN, Islamabad — SE Asia • 100 kW
	TURKEY
	†VOICE OF TURKEY, Ankara-Emirler — Ⓢ • S Asia, SE Asia & Australasia • 500 kW
	UNITED KINGDOM
	†BBC, Various Locations — N Africa • 250/500 kW
	USA
	VOA, Various Locations — M-F • C Africa & E Africa • 100/500 kW
	C Africa & E Africa • 100/500 kW
	VOA, Via Briech, Morocco — Ⓢ • E Europe • 500 kW
17710	EGYPT
	RADIO CAIRO, Kafr Silīm-Abis — W Asia & S Asia • 250 kW
17715	AUSTRALIA
	†RADIO AUSTRALIA, Darwin — E Asia • 250 kW
	M-F • E Asia • 250 kW
	Sa/Su • E Asia • 250 kW
	GERMANY
	†DEUTSCHE WELLE, Nauen — Ⓢ • W Africa • 500 kW
	DEUTSCHE WELLE, Via Antigua — N America • 250 kW
	DEUTSCHE WELLE, Via Sri Lanka — Ⓢ • SE Asia & Australasia • 250 kW
	DEUTSCHE WELLE, Wertachtal — Ⓢ • W Asia • 500 kW
	SPAIN
	R EXTERIOR ESPANA, Noblejas — S America • 350 kW
	Sa • S America • 350 kW
	Su-F • S America • 350 kW
	UNITED KINGDOM
	†BBC, Via Delano, USA — M-F • C America • 250 kW
17720	ROMANIA
	†RADIO ROMANIA, Bucharest — Ⓦ • Europe • DS-1 (ACTUALITATI) • 120 kW
	†RADIO ROMANIA INTL, Bucharest — Ⓦ • C Africa & S Africa • 250 kW Ⓢ • W Europe • 250 kW
	Australasia • 250 kW
	SAUDI ARABIA
	†BS OF THE KINGDOM, Riyadh — Ⓦ • C Asia • DS-HOLY KORAN • 500 kW • ALT. FREQ. TO 17745 kHz
17725	LIBYA
	†RADIO JAMAHIRIYA, Tripoli — N Africa & Mideast • 500 kW • ALT. FREQ. TO 15435 kHz
	PAKISTAN
	RADIO PAKISTAN, Karachi — E Africa • 50 kW
	UKRAINE
	†RADIO UKRAINE, Multiple Locations — Ⓦ • W Africa, S America & Australasia • 1000 kW
	USA
	†RFE-RL, Via Briech, Morocco — Ⓦ • E Europe • 500 kW
	Ⓦ • E Europe • 250 kW
	VOA, Greenville, NC — W Africa • 250 kW
	Su-F • W Africa • 250 kW
	WYFR-FAMILY RADIO, Okeechobee, Fl — Ⓢ • S America • 100 kW
17730	PHILIPPINES
(con'd)	†RADYO PILIPINAS, Poro — ENGLISH, ETC • W North Am • 100 kW

ENGLISH ▬▬　　ARABIC ░░░　　CHINESE ⋯⋯　　FRENCH ▬▬　　GERMAN ▬▬　　RUSSIAN ═══　　SPANISH ▬▬　　OTHER ▬▬

FREQUENCY   COUNTRY, STATION, LOCATION

TARGET • NETWORK • POWER (kW)

World Time

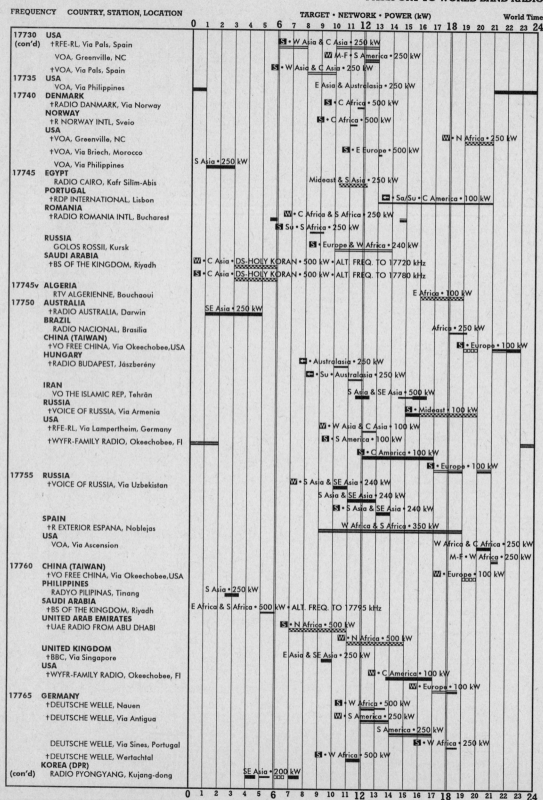

17730	USA	
(con'd)	†RFE-RL, Via Pals, Spain	S • W Asia & C Asia • 250 kW
	VOA, Greenville, NC	W • M-F • S America • 250 kW
17735	†VOA, Via Pals, Spain	S • W Asia & C Asia • 250 kW
17735	USA	
	VOA, Via Philippines	E Asia & Australasia • 250 kW
17740	DENMARK	
	†RADIO DANMARK, Via Norway	S • C Africa • 500 kW
	NORWAY	
	†R NORWAY INTL, Sveio	S • C Africa • 500 kW
	USA	
	†VOA, Greenville, NC	W • N Africa • 250 kW
	†VOA, Via Briech, Morocco	S • E Europe • 500 kW
	VOA, Via Philippines	S Asia • 250 kW
17745	EGYPT	
	RADIO CAIRO, Kafr Silim-Abis	Mideast & S Asia • 250 kW
	PORTUGAL	
	†RDP INTERNATIONAL, Lisbon	• Sa/Su • C America • 100 kW
	ROMANIA	
	†RADIO ROMANIA INTL, Bucharest	W • C Africa & S Africa • 250 kW
		S • Su • S Africa • 250 kW
	RUSSIA	
	GOLOS ROSSII, Kursk	S • Europe & W Africa • 240 kW
	SAUDI ARABIA	
	†BS OF THE KINGDOM, Riyadh	W • C Asia • DS-HOLY KORAN • 500 kW • ALT FREQ. TO 17720 kHz
		S • C Asia • DS-HOLY KORAN • 500 kW • ALT. FREQ. TO 17780 kHz
17745v	ALGERIA	
	RTV ALGERIENNE, Bouchaoui	E Africa • 100 kW
17750	AUSTRALIA	
	†RADIO AUSTRALIA, Darwin	SE Asia • 250 kW
	BRAZIL	
	RADIO NACIONAL, Brasilia	Africa • 250 kW
	CHINA (TAIWAN)	
	†VO FREE CHINA, Via Okeechobee,USA	S • Europe • 100 kW
	HUNGARY	
	†RADIO BUDAPEST, Jászberény	• Australasia • 250 kW
		• Su • Australasia • 250 kW
	IRAN	
	VO THE ISLAMIC REP, Tehrān	S Asia & SE Asia • 500 kW
	RUSSIA	
	†VOICE OF RUSSIA, Via Armenia	S • Mideast • 100 kW
	USA	
	†RFE-RL, Via Lampertheim, Germany	W • W Asia & C Asia • 100 kW
	†WYFR-FAMILY RADIO, Okeechobee, FI	S • S America • 100 kW
		S • C America • 100 kW
		S • Europe • 100 kW
17755	RUSSIA	
	†VOICE OF RUSSIA, Via Uzbekistan	W • S Asia & SE Asia • 240 kW
		S Asia & SE Asia • 240 kW
		S • S Asia & SE Asia • 240 kW
	SPAIN	
	†R EXTERIOR ESPANA, Noblejas	W Africa & S Africa • 350 kW
	USA	
	VOA, Via Ascension	W Africa & C Africa • 250 kW
		M-F • W Africa • 250 kW
17760	CHINA (TAIWAN)	
	†VO FREE CHINA, Via Okeechobee,USA	W • Europe • 100 kW
	PHILIPPINES	
	RADYO PILIPINAS, Tinang	S Asia • 250 kW
	SAUDI ARABIA	
	†BS OF THE KINGDOM, Riyadh	E Africa & S Africa • 500 kW • ALT. FREQ. TO 17795 kHz
	UNITED ARAB EMIRATES	
	†UAE RADIO FROM ABU DHABI	S • N Africa • 500 kW
		W • N Africa • 500 kW
	UNITED KINGDOM	
	†BBC, Via Singapore	E Asia & SE Asia • 250 kW
	USA	
	†WYFR-FAMILY RADIO, Okeechobee, FI	W • C America • 100 kW
		W • Europe • 100 kW
17765	GERMANY	
	†DEUTSCHE WELLE, Nauen	S • W Africa • 500 kW
	†DEUTSCHE WELLE, Via Antigua	W • S America • 250 kW
		S America • 250 kW
	DEUTSCHE WELLE, Via Sines, Portugal	S • W Africa • 250 kW
	†DEUTSCHE WELLE, Wertachtal	S • W Africa • 500 kW
	KOREA (DPR)	
(con'd)	RADIO PYONGYANG, Kujang-dong	SE Asia • 200 kW

SEASONAL S OR W   1-HR TIMESHIFT MIDYEAR ◄■ OR ■►   JAMMING / OR /\   EARLIEST HEARD ◄   LATEST HEARD ▷   NEW FOR 1997 †

FREQUENCY   COUNTRY, STATION, LOCATION   TARGET • NETWORK • POWER (kW)   World Time

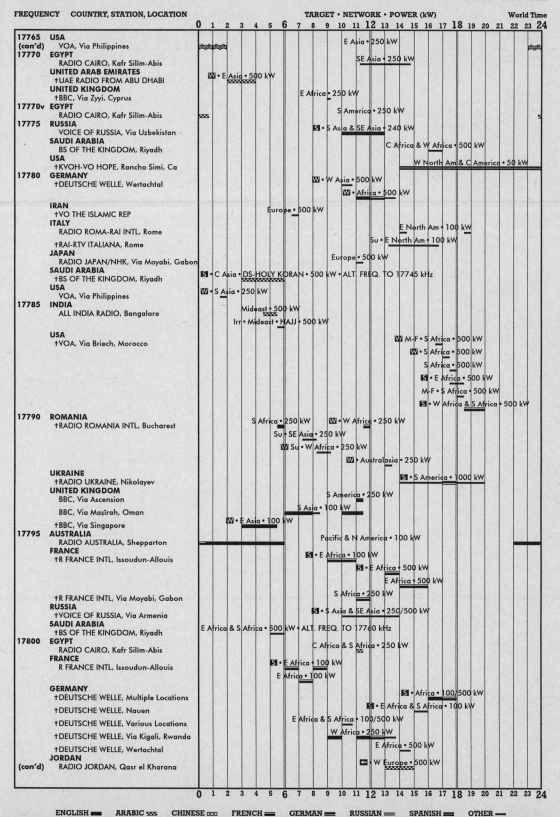

Frequency	Country, Station, Location	Target • Network • Power
17765 (con'd)	USA — VOA, Via Philippines	E Asia • 250 kW
17770	EGYPT — RADIO CAIRO, Kafr Silîm-Abis	SE Asia • 250 kW
	UNITED ARAB EMIRATES — †UAE RADIO FROM ABU DHABI	W • E Asia • 500 kW
	UNITED KINGDOM — †BBC, Via Zyyi, Cyprus	E Africa • 250 kW
17770v	EGYPT — RADIO CAIRO, Kafr Silîm-Abis	S America • 250 kW
17775	RUSSIA — VOICE OF RUSSIA, Via Uzbekistan	S • S Asia & SE Asia • 240 kW
	SAUDI ARABIA — BS OF THE KINGDOM, Riyadh	C Africa & W Africa • 500 kW
	USA — †KVOH-VO HOPE, Rancho Simi, Ca	W North Am & C America • 50 kW
17780	GERMANY — †DEUTSCHE WELLE, Wertachtal	W • W Asia • 500 kW / W • Africa • 500 kW
	IRAN — †VO THE ISLAMIC REP	Europe • 500 kW
	ITALY — RADIO ROMA-RAI INTL, Rome	E North Am • 100 kW / Su • E North Am • 100 kW
	†RAI-RTV ITALIANA, Rome	
	JAPAN — RADIO JAPAN/NHK, Via Moyabi, Gabon	Europe • 500 kW
	SAUDI ARABIA — †BS OF THE KINGDOM, Riyadh	S • C Asia • DS-HOLY KORAN • 500 kW • ALT. FREQ. TO 17745 kHz
	USA — VOA, Via Philippines	W • S Asia • 250 kW
17785	INDIA — ALL INDIA RADIO, Bangalore	Mideast • 500 kW / Irr • Mideast • HAJJ • 500 kW
	USA — †VOA, Via Briech, Morocco	W • M-F • S Africa • 500 kW / W • S Africa • 500 kW / S Africa • 500 kW / S • E Africa • 500 kW / M-F • S Africa • 500 kW / S • W Africa & S Africa • 500 kW
17790	ROMANIA — †RADIO ROMANIA INTL, Bucharest	S Africa • 250 kW / W • W Africa • 250 kW / Su • SE Asia • 250 kW / W Su • W Africa • 250 kW / W • Australasia • 250 kW
	UKRAINE — †RADIO UKRAINE, Nikolayev	S • S America • 1000 kW
	UNITED KINGDOM — BBC, Via Ascension	S America • 250 kW
	BBC, Via Maşîrah, Oman	S Asia • 100 kW
	†BBC, Via Singapore	W • E Asia • 100 kW
17795	AUSTRALIA — RADIO AUSTRALIA, Shepparton	Pacific & N America • 100 kW
	FRANCE — †R FRANCE INTL, Issoudun-Allouis	S • E Africa • 100 kW / S • E Africa • 500 kW / E Africa • 500 kW
	†R FRANCE INTL, Via Moyabi, Gabon	S Africa • 250 kW
	RUSSIA — †VOICE OF RUSSIA, Via Armenia	S • S Asia & SE Asia • 250/500 kW
	SAUDI ARABIA — †BS OF THE KINGDOM, Riyadh	E Africa & S Africa • 500 kW • ALT. FREQ. TO 17760 kHz
17800	EGYPT — RADIO CAIRO, Kafr Silîm-Abis	C Africa & S Africa • 250 kW
	FRANCE — R FRANCE INTL, Issoudun-Allouis	S • E Africa • 100 kW / E Africa • 100 kW
	GERMANY — †DEUTSCHE WELLE, Multiple Locations	S • Africa • 100/500 kW
	†DEUTSCHE WELLE, Nauen	S • E Africa & S Africa • 100 kW
	†DEUTSCHE WELLE, Various Locations	E Africa & S Africa • 100/500 kW
	†DEUTSCHE WELLE, Via Kigali, Rwanda	W Africa • 250 kW
	†DEUTSCHE WELLE, Wertachtal	E Africa • 500 kW
	JORDAN (con'd) — RADIO JORDAN, Qasr el Kharana	W Europe • 500 kW

ENGLISH ▬▬   ARABIC ✕✕✕   CHINESE □□□   FRENCH ▬▬   GERMAN ▬▬   RUSSIAN ▬▬   SPANISH ▬▬   OTHER ──

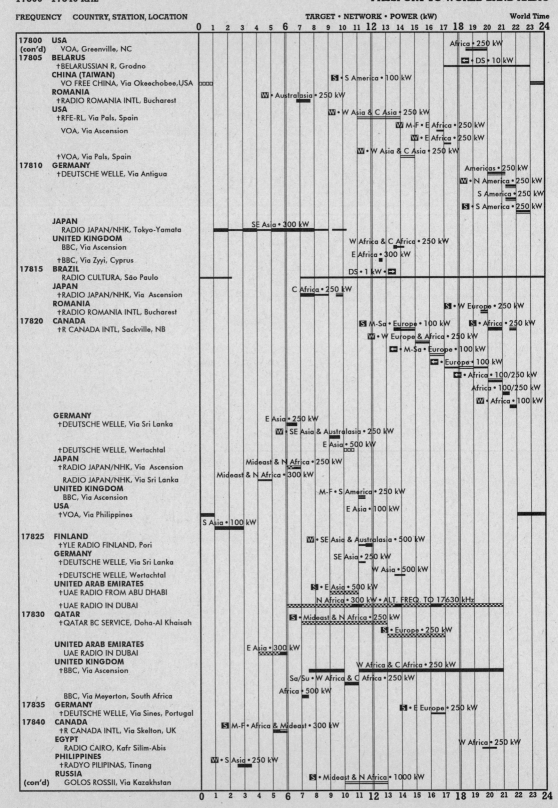

FREQUENCY   COUNTRY, STATION, LOCATION   TARGET • NETWORK • POWER (kW)   World Time

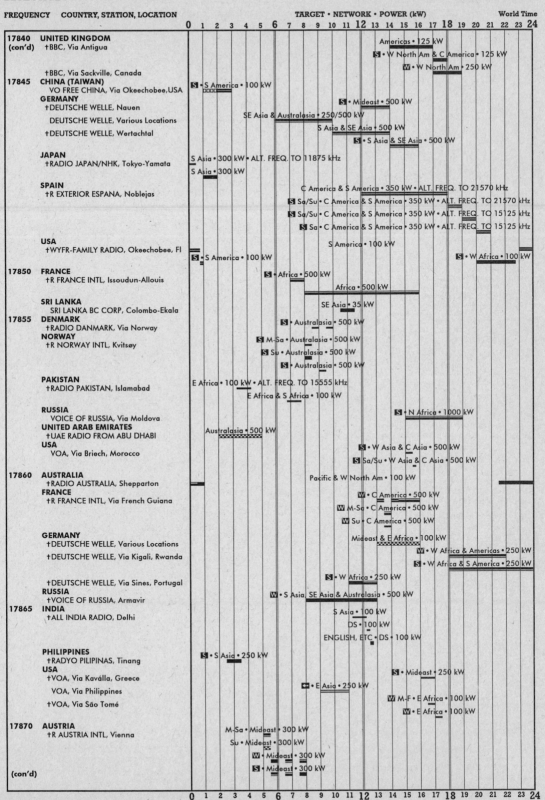

Frequency	Country, Station, Location
17840 (con'd)	**UNITED KINGDOM** †BBC, Via Antigua — Americas • 125 kW; S • W North Am & C America • 125 kW; W • W North Am • 250 kW
	†BBC, Via Sackville, Canada
17845	**CHINA (TAIWAN)** VO FREE CHINA, Via Okeechobee, USA — S • S America • 100 kW
	GERMANY †DEUTSCHE WELLE, Nauen — S • Mideast • 500 kW
	DEUTSCHE WELLE, Various Locations — SE Asia & Australasia • 250/500 kW
	†DEUTSCHE WELLE, Wertachtal — S Asia & SE Asia • 500 kW; S • S Asia & SE Asia • 500 kW
	JAPAN †RADIO JAPAN/NHK, Tokyo-Yamata — S Asia • 300 kW • ALT. FREQ. TO 11875 kHz; S Asia • 300 kW
	SPAIN †R EXTERIOR ESPANA, Noblejas — C America & S America • 350 kW • ALT. FREQ. TO 21570 kHz; S • Sa/Su • C America & S America • 350 kW • ALT. FREQ. TO 21570 kHz; S • Sa/Su • C America & S America • 350 kW • ALT. FREQ. TO 15125 kHz; S • Sa • C America & S America • 350 kW • ALT. FREQ. TO 15125 kHz
	USA †WYFR-FAMILY RADIO, Okeechobee, Fl — S America • 100 kW; S • S America • 100 kW; S • W Africa • 100 kW
17850	**FRANCE** †R FRANCE INTL, Issoudun-Allouis — S • Africa • 500 kW; Africa • 500 kW
	SRI LANKA SRI LANKA BC CORP, Colombo-Ekala — SE Asia • 35 kW
17855	**DENMARK** †RADIO DANMARK, Via Norway — S • Australasia • 500 kW
	NORWAY †R NORWAY INTL, Kvitsøy — S • M-Sa • Australasia • 500 kW; S • Su • Australasia • 500 kW; S • Australasia • 500 kW
	PAKISTAN †RADIO PAKISTAN, Islamabad — E Africa • 100 kW • ALT. FREQ. TO 15555 kHz; E Africa & S Africa • 100 kW
	RUSSIA VOICE OF RUSSIA, Via Moldova — S • N Africa • 1000 kW
	UNITED ARAB EMIRATES †UAE RADIO FROM ABU DHABI — Australasia • 500 kW
	USA VOA, Via Briech, Morocco — S • W Asia & C Asia • 500 kW; S • Sa/Su • W Asia & C Asia • 500 kW
17860	**AUSTRALIA** †RADIO AUSTRALIA, Shepparton — Pacific & W North Am • 100 kW
	FRANCE †R FRANCE INTL, Via French Guiana — W • C America • 500 kW; W • M-Sa • C America • 500 kW; W • Su • C America • 500 kW
	GERMANY †DEUTSCHE WELLE, Various Locations — Mideast & E Africa • 100 kW
	†DEUTSCHE WELLE, Via Kigali, Rwanda — W • W Africa & Americas • 250 kW; S • W Africa & S America • 250 kW
	†DEUTSCHE WELLE, Via Sines, Portugal — S • W Africa • 250 kW
	RUSSIA †VOICE OF RUSSIA, Armavir — W • S Asia, SE Asia & Australasia • 500 kW
17865	**INDIA** †ALL INDIA RADIO, Delhi — S Asia • 100 kW; DS • 100 kW; ENGLISH, ETC • DS • 100 kW
	PHILIPPINES †RADYO PILIPINAS, Tinang — S • S Asia • 250 kW
	USA †VOA, Via Kaválla, Greece — S • Mideast • 250 kW
	VOA, Via Philippines — C • E Asia • 250 kW
	†VOA, Via São Tomé — W • M-F • E Africa • 100 kW; W • E Africa • 100 kW
17870	**AUSTRIA** †R AUSTRIA INTL, Vienna — M-Sa • Mideast • 300 kW; Su • Mideast • 300 kW; W • Mideast • 300 kW; S • Mideast • 300 kW
(con'd)	

ENGLISH ▬   ARABIC ▨   CHINESE ▫▫▫   FRENCH ▭   GERMAN ▬▬   RUSSIAN ═   SPANISH ▭   OTHER ▭

FREQUENCY   COUNTRY, STATION, LOCATION   **TARGET • NETWORK • POWER (kW)**   **World Time**

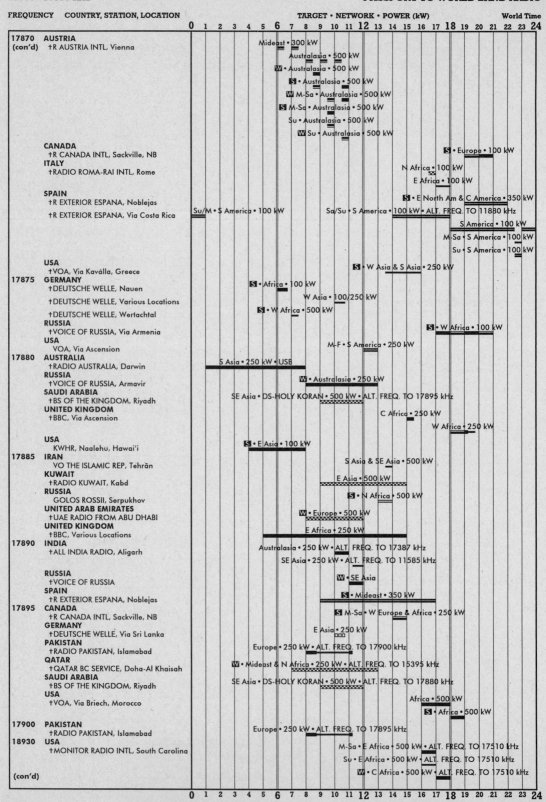

Frequency	Country, Station, Location	Target • Network • Power
17870 (con'd)	**AUSTRIA** †R AUSTRIA INTL, Vienna	Mideast • 300 kW
		Australasia • 500 kW
		W • Australasia • 500 kW
		S • Australasia • 500 kW
		W M-Sa • Australasia • 500 kW
		S M-Sa • Australasia • 500 kW
		Su • Australasia • 500 kW
		W Su • Australasia • 500 kW
	CANADA †R CANADA INTL, Sackville, NB	S • Europe • 100 kW
	ITALY †RADIO ROMA-RAI INTL, Rome	N Africa • 100 kW / E Africa • 100 kW
	SPAIN †R EXTERIOR ESPANA, Noblejas	S • E North Am & C America • 350 kW
	†R EXTERIOR ESPANA, Via Costa Rica	Su/M • S America • 100 kW / Sa/Su • S America • 100 kW • ALT. FREQ. TO 11880 kHz
		S America • 100 kW
		M-Sa • S America • 100 kW
		Su • S America • 100 kW
	USA †VOA, Via Kaválla, Greece	S • W Asia & S Asia • 250 kW
17875	**GERMANY** †DEUTSCHE WELLE, Nauen	S • Africa • 100 kW
	†DEUTSCHE WELLE, Various Locations	W Asia • 100/250 kW
	†DEUTSCHE WELLE, Wertachtal	S • W Africa • 500 kW
	RUSSIA †VOICE OF RUSSIA, Via Armenia	S • W Africa • 100 kW
	USA VOA, Via Ascension	M-F • S America • 250 kW
17880	**AUSTRALIA** †RADIO AUSTRALIA, Darwin	S Asia • 250 kW • USB
	RUSSIA †VOICE OF RUSSIA, Armavir	W • Australasia • 250 kW
	SAUDI ARABIA †BS OF THE KINGDOM, Riyadh	SE Asia • DS-HOLY KORAN • 500 kW • ALT. FREQ. TO 17895 kHz
	UNITED KINGDOM †BBC, Via Ascension	C Africa • 250 kW
		W Africa • 250 kW
	USA KWHR, Naalehu, Hawai'i	S • E Asia • 100 kW
17885	**IRAN** VO THE ISLAMIC REP, Tehrān	S Asia & SE Asia • 500 kW
	KUWAIT †RADIO KUWAIT, Kabd	E Asia • 500 kW
	RUSSIA GOLOS ROSSII, Serpukhov	S • N Africa • 500 kW
	UNITED ARAB EMIRATES †UAE RADIO FROM ABU DHABI	W • Europe • 500 kW
	UNITED KINGDOM †BBC, Various Locations	E Africa • 250 kW
17890	**INDIA** †ALL INDIA RADIO, Aligarh	Australasia • 250 kW • ALT. FREQ. TO 17387 kHz
		SE Asia • 250 kW • ALT. FREQ. TO 11585 kHz
	RUSSIA †VOICE OF RUSSIA	W • SE Asia
	SPAIN †R EXTERIOR ESPANA, Noblejas	S • Mideast • 350 kW
17895	**CANADA** †R CANADA INTL, Sackville, NB	S M-Sa • W Europe & Africa • 250 kW
	GERMANY †DEUTSCHE WELLE, Via Sri Lanka	E Asia • 250 kW
	PAKISTAN †RADIO PAKISTAN, Islamabad	Europe • 250 kW • ALT. FREQ. TO 17900 kHz
	QATAR †QATAR BC SERVICE, Doha-Al Khaisah	W • Mideast & N Africa • 250 kW • ALT. FREQ. TO 15395 kHz
	SAUDI ARABIA †BS OF THE KINGDOM, Riyadh	SE Asia • DS-HOLY KORAN • 500 kW • ALT. FREQ. TO 17880 kHz
	USA †VOA, Via Briech, Morocco	Africa • 500 kW
		S • Africa • 500 kW
17900	**PAKISTAN** †RADIO PAKISTAN, Islamabad	Europe • 250 kW • ALT. FREQ. TO 17895 kHz
18930	**USA** †MONITOR RADIO INTL, South Carolina	M-Sa • E Africa • 500 kW • ALT. FREQ. TO 17510 kHz
		Su • E Africa • 500 kW • ALT. FREQ. TO 17510 kHz
(con'd)		W • C Africa • 500 kW • ALT. FREQ. TO 17510 kHz

FREQUENCY   COUNTRY, STATION, LOCATION

TARGET • NETWORK • POWER (kW)   World Time

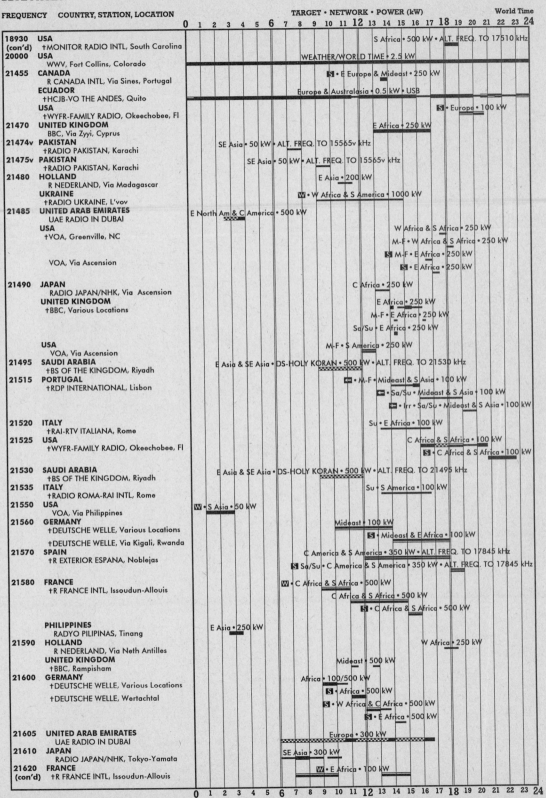

Frequency	Country, Station, Location	Details
18930 (con'd)	**USA** †MONITOR RADIO INTL, South Carolina	S Africa • 500 kW • ALT. FREQ. TO 17510 kHz
20000	**USA** WWV, Fort Collins, Colorado	WEATHER/WORLD TIME • 2.5 kW
21455	**CANADA** R CANADA INTL, Via Sines, Portugal	S • E Europe & Mideast • 250 kW
	ECUADOR †HCJB-VO THE ANDES, Quito	Europe & Australasia • 0.5 kW • USB
	USA †WYFR-FAMILY RADIO, Okeechobee, Fl	S • Europe • 100 kW
21470	**UNITED KINGDOM** BBC, Via Zyyi, Cyprus	E Africa • 250 kW
21474v	**PAKISTAN** †RADIO PAKISTAN, Karachi	SE Asia • 50 kW • ALT. FREQ. TO 15565v kHz
21475v	**PAKISTAN** †RADIO PAKISTAN, Karachi	SE Asia • 50 kW • ALT. FREQ. TO 15565v kHz
21480	**HOLLAND** R NEDERLAND, Via Madagascar	E Asia • 200 kW
	UKRAINE †RADIO UKRAINE, L'vov	W • W Africa & S America • 1000 kW
21485	**UNITED ARAB EMIRATES** UAE RADIO IN DUBAI	E North Am & C America • 500 kW
	USA †VOA, Greenville, NC	W Africa & S Africa • 250 kW
		M-F • W Africa & S Africa • 250 kW
	VOA, Via Ascension	S • M-F • E Africa • 250 kW
		S • E Africa • 250 kW
21490	**JAPAN** RADIO JAPAN/NHK, Via Ascension	C Africa • 250 kW
	UNITED KINGDOM †BBC, Various Locations	E Africa • 250 kW
		M-F • E Africa • 250 kW
		Sa/Su • E Africa • 250 kW
	USA VOA, Via Ascension	M-F • S America • 250 kW
21495	**SAUDI ARABIA** †BS OF THE KINGDOM, Riyadh	E Asia & SE Asia • DS-HOLY KORAN • 500 kW • ALT. FREQ. TO 21530 kHz
21515	**PORTUGAL** †RDP INTERNATIONAL, Lisbon	▣ • M-F • Mideast & S Asia • 100 kW
		▣ • Sa/Su • Mideast & S Asia • 100 kW
		▣ • Irr • Sa/Su • Mideast & S Asia • 100 kW
21520	**ITALY** †RAI-RTV ITALIANA, Rome	Su • E Africa • 100 kW
21525	**USA** †WYFR-FAMILY RADIO, Okeechobee, Fl	C Africa & S Africa • 100 kW
		S • C Africa & S Africa • 100 kW
21530	**SAUDI ARABIA** †BS OF THE KINGDOM, Riyadh	E Asia & SE Asia • DS-HOLY KORAN • 500 kW • ALT. FREQ. TO 21495 kHz
21535	**ITALY** †RADIO ROMA-RAI INTL, Rome	Su • S America • 100 kW
21550	**USA** VOA, Via Philippines	W • S Asia • 50 kW
21560	**GERMANY** †DEUTSCHE WELLE, Various Locations	Mideast • 100 kW
	†DEUTSCHE WELLE, Via Kigali, Rwanda	S • Mideast & E Africa • 100 kW
21570	**SPAIN** †R EXTERIOR ESPANA, Noblejas	C America & S America • 350 kW • ALT. FREQ. TO 17845 kHz
		S • Sa/Su • C America & S America • 350 kW • ALT. FREQ. TO 17845 kHz
21580	**FRANCE** †R FRANCE INTL, Issoudun-Allouis	W • C Africa & S Africa • 500 kW
		C Africa & S Africa • 500 kW
		S • C Africa & S Africa • 500 kW
	PHILIPPINES RADYO PILIPINAS, Tinang	E Asia • 250 kW
21590	**HOLLAND** R NEDERLAND, Via Neth Antilles	W Africa • 250 kW
	UNITED KINGDOM †BBC, Rampisham	Mideast • 500 kW
21600	**GERMANY** †DEUTSCHE WELLE, Various Locations	Africa • 100/500 kW
		S • Africa • 500 kW
	†DEUTSCHE WELLE, Wertachtal	S • W Africa & C Africa • 500 kW
		S • E Africa • 500 kW
21605	**UNITED ARAB EMIRATES** UAE RADIO IN DUBAI	Europe • 300 kW
21610	**JAPAN** RADIO JAPAN/NHK, Tokyo-Yamata	SE Asia • 300 kW
21620 (con'd)	**FRANCE** †R FRANCE INTL, Issoudun-Allouis	W • E Africa • 100 kW

0 1 2 3 4 5 6 7 8 9 10 11 12 13 14 15 16 17 18 19 20 21 22 23 24

ENGLISH ▬▬   ARABIC ⌇⌇⌇   CHINESE ▫▫▫   FRENCH ▬▬   GERMAN ▬▬   RUSSIAN ═══   SPANISH ▬▬   OTHER ▬▬

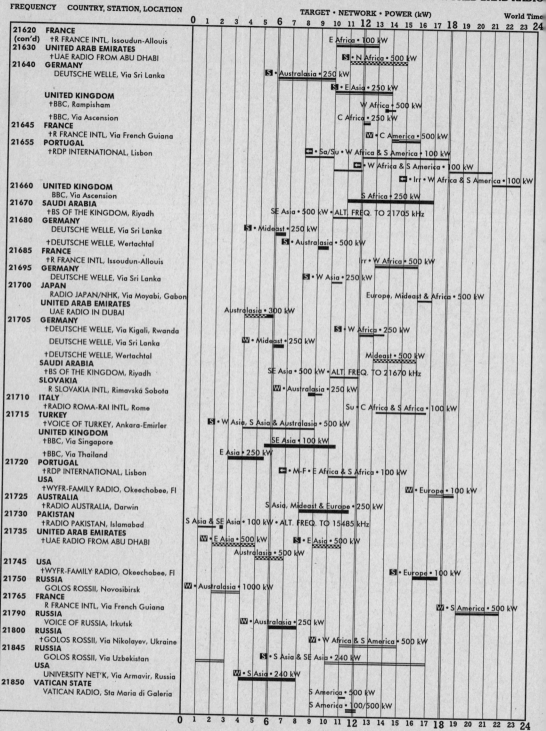

		TARGET • NETWORK • POWER (kW)
21620	**FRANCE**	
(con'd)	†R FRANCE INTL, Issoudun-Allouis	E Africa • 100 kW
21630	**UNITED ARAB EMIRATES**	
	†UAE RADIO FROM ABU DHABI	⑤ • N Africa • 500 kW
21640	**GERMANY**	
	DEUTSCHE WELLE, Via Sri Lanka	⑤ • Australasia • 250 kW
	UNITED KINGDOM	⑤ • E Asia • 250 kW
	†BBC, Rampisham	W Africa • 500 kW
	†BBC, Via Ascension	C Africa • 250 kW
21645	**FRANCE**	
	†R FRANCE INTL, Via French Guiana	W • C America • 500 kW
21655	**PORTUGAL**	
	†RDP INTERNATIONAL, Lisbon	⇔ • Sa/Su • W Africa & S America • 100 kW
		⇔ • W Africa & S America • 100 kW
		⇔ • Irr • W Africa & S America • 100 kW
21660	**UNITED KINGDOM**	
	BBC, Via Ascension	S Africa • 250 kW
21670	**SAUDI ARABIA**	
	†BS OF THE KINGDOM, Riyadh	SE Asia • 500 kW • ALT. FREQ. TO 21705 kHz
21680	**GERMANY**	
	DEUTSCHE WELLE, Via Sri Lanka	⑤ • Mideast • 250 kW
	†DEUTSCHE WELLE, Wertachtal	⑤ • Australasia • 500 kW
21685	**FRANCE**	
	†R FRANCE INTL, Issoudun-Allouis	Irr • W Africa • 500 kW
21695	**GERMANY**	
	DEUTSCHE WELLE, Via Sri Lanka	⑤ • W Asia • 250 kW
21700	**JAPAN**	
	RADIO JAPAN/NHK, Via Moyabi, Gabon	Europe, Mideast & Africa • 500 kW
	UNITED ARAB EMIRATES	
	UAE RADIO IN DUBAI	Australasia • 300 kW
21705	**GERMANY**	
	†DEUTSCHE WELLE, Via Kigali, Rwanda	⑤ • W Africa • 250 kW
	DEUTSCHE WELLE, Via Sri Lanka	W • Mideast • 250 kW
	†DEUTSCHE WELLE, Wertachtal	Mideast • 500 kW
	SAUDI ARABIA	
	†BS OF THE KINGDOM, Riyadh	SE Asia • 500 kW • ALT. FREQ. TO 21670 kHz
	SLOVAKIA	
	R SLOVAKIA INTL, Rimavská Sobota	W • Australasia • 250 kW
21710	**ITALY**	
	†RADIO ROMA-RAI INTL, Rome	Su • C Africa & S Africa • 100 kW
21715	**TURKEY**	
	†VOICE OF TURKEY, Ankara-Emirler	⑤ • W Asia, S Asia & Australasia • 500 kW
	UNITED KINGDOM	
	†BBC, Via Singapore	SE Asia • 100 kW
	†BBC, Via Thailand	E Asia • 250 kW
21720	**PORTUGAL**	
	†RDP INTERNATIONAL, Lisbon	⇔ • M-F • E Africa & S Africa • 100 kW
	USA	
	†WYFR-FAMILY RADIO, Okeechobee, Fl	W • Europe • 100 kW
21725	**AUSTRALIA**	
	†RADIO AUSTRALIA, Darwin	S Asia, Mideast & Europe • 250 kW
21730	**PAKISTAN**	
	†RADIO PAKISTAN, Islamabad	S Asia & SE Asia • 100 kW • ALT. FREQ. TO 15485 kHz
21735	**UNITED ARAB EMIRATES**	
	†UAE RADIO FROM ABU DHABI	W • E Asia • 500 kW ⑤ • E Asia • 500 kW
		Australasia • 500 kW
21745	**USA**	
	†WYFR-FAMILY RADIO, Okeechobee, Fl	⑤ • Europe • 100 kW
21750	**RUSSIA**	
	GOLOS ROSSII, Novosibirsk	W • Australasia • 1000 kW
21765	**FRANCE**	
	R FRANCE INTL, Via French Guiana	W • S America • 500 kW
21790	**RUSSIA**	
	VOICE OF RUSSIA, Irkutsk	W • Australasia • 250 kW
21800	**RUSSIA**	
	†GOLOS ROSSII, Via Nikolayev, Ukraine	W • W Africa & S America • 500 kW
21845	**RUSSIA**	
	GOLOS ROSSII, Via Uzbekistan	⑤ • S Asia & SE Asia • 240 kW
	USA	
	UNIVERSITY NET'K, Via Armavir, Russia	W • S Asia • 240 kW
21850	**VATICAN STATE**	
	VATICAN RADIO, Sta Maria di Galeria	S America • 500 kW
		S America • 100/500 kW

SEASONAL ⑤ OR W   1-HR TIMESHIFT MIDYEAR ⇔ OR ⇒   JAMMING / OR ∧   EARLIEST HEARD ◁   LATEST HEARD ▷   NEW FOR 1997 †